Argentina
Uruguay & Paraguay

Sandra Bao
Ben Greensfelder
Carolyn Hubbard
Alan Murphy
Danny Palmerlee

D1021030

LONELY PLANET PUBLICATIONS
Melbourne • Oakland • London • Paris

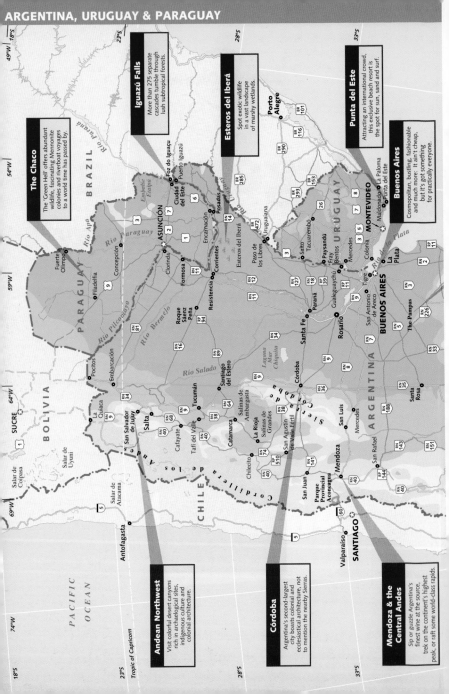

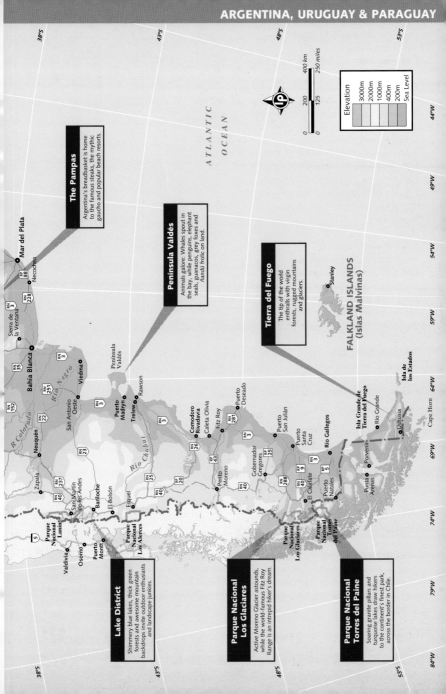

ARGENTINA, URUGUAY & PARAGUAY

Elevation
3000m
2000m
1000m
400m
200m
Sea Level

The Pampas
Argentina's breadbasket is home to the famous steaks, the mythic gaucho and popular beach resorts.

Peninsula Valdés
Animals galore: Whales spout in the bay, while penguins, elephant seals, guanacos, grey foxes and *ñandú* frolic on land.

Tierra del Fuego
The tip of the world enthralls with virgin forests, rugged mountains and glaciers.

FALKLAND ISLANDS (Islas Malvinas)

ATLANTIC OCEAN

Lake District
Shimmery blue lakes, thick green forests and awesome mountain backdrops invite outdoor enthusiasts and landscape junkies.

Parque Nacional Los Glaciares
Active Moreno Glacier astounds, while the world-famous Fitz Roy Range is an intrepid hiker's dream.

Parque Nacional Torres del Paine
Soaring granite pillars and turquoise lakes draw hikers to the continent's finest park, across the border in Chile.

Argentina, Uruguay & Paraguay
4th edition – April 2002
First published – August 1992

Published by
Lonely Planet Publications Pty Ltd ABN 36 005 607 983
90 Maribyrnong St, Footscray, Victoria 3011, Australia

Lonely Planet Offices
Australia Locked Bag 1, Footscray, Victoria 3011
USA 150 Linden St, Oakland, CA 94607
UK 10a Spring Place, London NW5 3BH
France 1 rue du Dahomey, 75011 Paris

Photographs
Many of the images in this guide are available for licensing from
Lonely Planet Images.
email: lpi@lonelyplanet.com.au
Web site: www.lonelyplanetimages.com

Front cover photograph
The landscape surrounding El Calafate on the way to
the Moreno Glacier, Patagonia (Sarah JH Hubbard)

Title page photographs
Argentina (Shannon Nace)
Uruguay (Wayne Walton)
Paraguay (Donald C Eastman)

ISBN 1 74059 027 9

text & maps © Lonely Planet Publications Pty Ltd 2002
photos © photographers as indicated 2002

Printed through Colorcraft Ltd, Hong Kong
Printed in China

Although the authors and Lonely Planet try to make the information as accurate as possible, we accept no responsibility for any loss, injury or inconvenience sustained by anyone using this book.

Contents

2   Contents

THE PAMPAS & THE ATLANTIC COAST   169

NORTHEAST ARGENTINA   213

CÓRDOBA & THE CENTRAL SIERRAS   283

MENDOZA & THE CENTRAL ANDES 310

THE ANDEAN NORTHWEST 351

THE LAKE DISTRICT 420

PATAGONIA 459

4　Contents

TIERRA DEL FUEGO　　　　　　　　　　　　　　　　　563

URUGUAY　　　　　　　　　　　　　　　　　　　　　　　588

PARAGUAY 660

LANGUAGE 719

GLOSSARY 725

THANKS 731

INDEX 733

CHAPTERS

BOLIVIA

BRAZIL

CHILE

PACIFIC OCEAN

Tropic of Capricorn

0   200   400 km
0   125   250 miles

ATLANTIC
OCEAN

FALKLAND ISLANDS
(Islas Malvinas)

OTHER MAPS
Argentina, Uruguay & Paraguay at front of book
Locator page 15
Argentina page 20
Provinces of Argentina page 21
Geographic Regions page 32

The Authors

Sandra Bao

Born to Chinese parents and raised in Buenos Aires, Sandra reluctantly came to the US when she was nine. Her introduction to America was Toledo, Ohio, in winter (it had been summer in Argentina) - however, she has fond memories of staying home from school when it was cancelled because of too much snow. She attended UC Santa Cruz, where she earned a BA in Psychology, which she finds useful except when seeking employment. Sandra has traveled extensively around the world and even taught Introductory English to a 90-student class at Cheju University in Korea. These days she spends her time rock climbing, trying to establish good taste in music, and hanging out in her cute Oakland pad with her husband, fellow LP writer Ben Greensfelder. Oh, yeah: she's also learning the bass with the hope that someday, perhaps after her stint as an LP author, she can become a full-blown rock star.

Ben Greensfelder

In 1954 Ben hitched from San Francisco to New York City, stowed away across the Atlantic on an ocean liner to Naples, and toured the Continent for two months. He returned to California and, six months later, was born, subsequently growing up in foggy Homestead Valley. Since then he's gone a bunch of other places and done a bunch of stuff (no felony convictions!). In addition to his research on Paraguay, Uruguay and Argentina, Ben served as the coordinating author of the 4th edition of LP's *Belize, Guatemala & Yucatán*, contributed a chapter to *Mexico*, and wrote a minute portion of the latest edition of the *Buenos Aires* city guide. He has been married to the incomparable Sandra Bao since 1993. The two have dreams of some day acquiring a Siamese cat.

Carolyn Hubbard

Raised in Canada, Australia and Washington State, Carolyn kept the adventure going throughout her adult life. She studied in Spain and Mexico before and during her university career, then lived and worked in New York City and Barcelona, punctuated by trips around Europe, Morocco and Southeast Asia. After landing back in the US, she moved to the Bay area and worked as a senior editor at Lonely Planet's US office. When memories of living beyond office walls grew too vague, she branched out to look for new challenges and adventures, one of which has been updating several chapters of this book.

Alan Murphy

After relinquishing his dream of cultivating a career in global espionage, Alan decided to tackle dodgy border crossings like everybody else – with a backpack and a fistful of cash. His subsequent adventures to the far corners of the planet convinced him to seek viable employment in a similar vein. Several years and a journalism degree later he landed at LP and, after a brief editing interlude, began updating guidebooks. Alan lives in Melbourne where tight deadlines and nights at the Retreat Hotel have become life when not researching. Alan has also worked on LP's *Southern Africa*, *South Africa*, *Africa*, *India*, *North India* and *Mexico*.

Danny Palmerlee

Born and raised in Gilroy, California, Danny began traveling at age 12, when he and a friend floated down Uvas Creek in an abandoned bathtub. Since then he has trekked through Montana and Wyoming, traveled extensively through Mexico, Central America, Ecuador, Europe and Morocco, and spent a debauched year running a hostel in Scotland. At some point he received a Sociology degree from UC Santa Cruz, though most of his travels were funded by a lucrative body jewelry business he co-owned with an entrepreneurial friend. Over the years, he has filled the gaps of freelance writing with woodworking, house painting and substitute teaching to keep himself joyfully broke.

FROM THE AUTHORS

Sandra Gracious thanks go to my *porteño* godparents, Elsa and Norberto Mallarini, for general support, adamant opinions and all those wonderful free dinners. Much appreciation also to Jorge Mallarini, for lending me his cool bike and generally keeping me entertained. Miguelangelo Tramontana clued me into the gay scene, while Sylvia Zapiola eagerly put in her two cents worth (and more) – thanks, guys. Lucas 'Diez Puntos' Markowiecki cheered me up by taking me out to some fabulous dinners and playing me *rock nacional*. Ariel Perduca gave good 'heavy-metal' insights on music, while José Serebrenik chipped in with porteño language quirks and other cultural pointers. Bill Ralston provided some needed expat conversations and local news, and I thank his students as well. Dennis Deminchuk is the most entertaining gay Canadian from Saskatoon I have ever met. Buenos Aires Freetime was my instant group of friends, and I also thank Roberto Salinas, Peter Johnson and Andrew Graham-Yooll. Lots of love to my parents, David and Fung Bao, and my brother, Daniel Bao, who have always been there for me. And I could not have done this without the love and support (and computer know-how) of my husband, Ben Greensfelder.

Ben In Buenos Aires, many thanks and much love to the familia Mallarini for taking such good care of me and Sandra; the same goes to

Fung and David Bao. In Montevideo, thanks go to José and Raquel at the Hotel Solís for their hospitality and advice. In Asunción, José Alberto Bareiro and Elva De La Torre provided loads of data on the city; thank you! A huge thanks to Penny Newbury for her enthusiastic and detailed descriptions of festivals and river trips in Paraguay. A shout out to Donna, Jessica and Tina (and thanks T for the cultural and linguistic insights), intrepid companions in Asunción and Ybycuí. An enormous ευχαριστώ to reader Aristea Parissi of Thessaloniki, whose book-length letter was humbling, informative and inspirational. Dawn, thanks for an unforgettable evening in Foz do Iguaçu; was it the turkey testicules? Finally, Sandra, *la coordinadora suprema*, thanks for letting me slide on my due dates, for always being ready to hit the road, and for the past 11 joyful years.

Carolyn Research trips wouldn't be half as enjoyable if it weren't for those people met on the way. To all of you (more than I can list) who made Patagonia and Tierra del Fuego all the more magical – thank you: Jorge Lutyk of *Turisteando por la Zona*; Francis Bassily in Ushuaia; Julio Giustozzi and Diego Marinelli for driving adventures; all the staff at the Secretaría de Turismo de Santa Cruz in Río Gallegos; Victoria Viel of Tepi Aike for family stories and hot soup; María Alicia Sacks at the tourist office in Puerto Madryn; Paul Walker of Puerto San Julián for sharing the history; Carlos, the computer healer, Gerson Reyes and Ivette Martínez in Punta Arenas; Hernan Jofre and Alfonso López in Puerto Natales; and Joanne Morrison of the Falkland Islands Tourist Board, who persevered graciously through a storm of emails. Much gratitude is extended to Wayne Bernhardson for his previous research and writing on Argentina.

Alan Firstly my gratitude to freelance writer Justine Vaisutis, whose creative linguistic skills and invaluable assistance with research was much appreciated. Also to the ever-efficient Jules at Flight Centre for coming up with the goods once again. Special thanks to Eduardo from the Catamarca tourist office for going well beyond the call of duty, and to his counterparts in Salta, La Rioja, Tucumán, Santiago del Estero and Jujuy. To the two *amigos* in the national parks office in Buenos Aires, thanks for your help and advice in fine detail. A warm thank you and cheerio to the folks at the Velvet Bar in Tucumán, for their cruisy vibes and good company. In Salta, thanks to the people at Hotel Italia for bending to our whim, minding our luggage and not selling it in our absence. Thanks also to those at Samiri Hostel for urging us to tackle one more early morning in order to enjoy the spectacular scenery en route to Cachi. A huge thanks to all the taxi drivers, waiters, bus drivers, hotel and shop staff, friendly faces at bus terminals and the people of Argentina in general, whose friendly understanding and helpful disposition made this such a memorable trip.

Danny First, I have to thank Julie Corson, who joined me on part of this dizzying journey and kept me smiling through the long hours that followed. A huge thanks goes to Peter Kruse for his wine knowledge, support and sick sense of humor. To Rolan and Han, thanks again for the rides. My deepest gratitude goes to my parents for their undying support and for allowing me to take over half the house while writing this one – cheers, you guys. In Buenos Aires, I owe many thanks to Diablo, Franco, Fernando, Mechi, Vicky, Venina, Diego, La Negra, Maxi, Santos and everyone else there who made me feel at home. Most of all, I have to thank Isabel García Calvo, whose friendship, help and hospitality (and introduction to *el truco*, Fernet and, I hate to admit it, River) brought so much life to my trip – see you on the bog, Isa. The folks in the tourist offices throughout Argentina were invariably helpful, but I'd like to extend a special thanks to Melina Paoloni in Bariloche, Viviana in Junín de los Andes, Gustavo in Córdoba, Petty in Esquel, Laura in Zapala, Carlos Villegas in General Alvear, Alejandra in Villa Gesell, and the entire staff at Mar del Plata's EMTUR office. I crossed paths with countless people who lent me a hand, gave me tips and made my travels memorable, including German Gruszczyk, Sandra Tárraga, Daniel Cadile and Roger Cangiani.

This Book

Sandra Bao coordinated this edition as well updating the frontmatter, Buenos Aires, Glossary and Language chapters and a portion of the Pampas & the Atlantic Coast chapter. Ben Greensfelder updated Uruguay and Paraguay and a significant part of Northeast Argentina. Carolyn Hubbard updated Patagonia, Tierra del Fuego and a bit of the Pampas. Alan Murphy updated the Andean Northwest. Danny Palmerlee updated Córdoba, Mendoza, Lake District as well as portions of the Pampas, Northeast Argentina and Patagonia.

Chris Moss contributed sections for History and Population & People in the Facts about Argentina chapter, as well as a sidebar on Argentine wine appearing in the Mendoza chapter. John Spriggs contributed sections for Literature in the Facts about Argentina chapter.

Wayne Bernhardson wrote the previous editions of this book. Much of his original text, especially in the History sections and boxed texts, remains.

FROM THE PUBLISHER

Time, time, time was not on our side. But sheer numbers helped beat the clock. China Williams, Christine Lee and Wendy Smith edited the book with help from Tom Valtin. Robert Reid served as the fearless senior editor while joining us in the trenches. Tom, Virginie Boone, Emily Wolman, China, Wendy, Robert and Christine proofed the book. David Zingarelli, Michael Johnson, Michele Posner, Maria Donohoe and Suki Gear also helped push this behemoth through. Ken DellaPenta indexed the book.

Sherry Veverka, with help from Annette Olson, headed the map-making process for this book. Through different stages, the following cartographers helped out: Anneka Imkamp, Bart Wright, Brad Lodge, Buck Cantwell, Carole Nuttall, David Ryder, Dion Good, Don Patterson, Gina Gillich, Graham Neale, Herman So, John Spelman, Kat Smith, Lee Espinole, Marjorie Hamm, Molly Green, Patrick Huerta, Patrick Phelan, Rachel Jereb, Rudie Watzig, Terence Philippe, Tessa Rottiers, Tim Lohnes and Tracey Croom.

Gerilyn Attebery and Ruth Askevold designed the book with guidance from Susan Rimerman. Beca Lafore designed the cover and Justin Marler drew the new illustrations. Other illustrations were provided by Mark Butler, Hugh D'Andrade, Hayden Foell, Lisa Summers and Jim Swanson.

Foreword

ABOUT LONELY PLANET GUIDEBOOKS

The story begins with a classic travel adventure: Tony and Maureen Wheeler's 1972 journey across Europe and Asia to Australia. Useful information about the overland trail did not exist at that time, so Tony and Maureen published the first Lonely Planet guidebook to meet a growing need.

From a kitchen table, then from a tiny office in Melbourne (Australia), Lonely Planet has become the largest independent travel publisher in the world, an international company with offices in Melbourne, Oakland (USA), London (UK) and Paris (France).

Today Lonely Planet guidebooks cover the globe. There is an ever-growing list of books, and there's information in a variety of forms and media. Some things haven't changed. The main aim is still to help make it possible for adventurous travelers to get out there – to explore and better understand the world.

At Lonely Planet we believe travelers can make a positive contribution to the countries they visit – if they respect their host communities and spend their money wisely. Since 1986 a percentage of the income from each book has been donated to aid projects and human-rights campaigns.

Updates Lonely Planet thoroughly updates each guidebook as often as possible. This usually means there are around two years between editions, although for more unusual or more stable destinations the gap can be longer. Check the imprint page (usually following the color map at the beginning of the book) for publication dates.

Between editions up-to-date information is available in two free newsletters – the paper *Planet Talk* and email *Comet* (to subscribe, contact any Lonely Planet office) – and on our Web site at www.lonelyplanet.com. The *Upgrades* section of the Web site covers a number of important and volatile destinations and is regularly updated by Lonely Planet authors. *Scoop* covers news and current affairs relevant to travelers. And, lastly, the *Thorn Tree* bulletin board and *Postcards* section of the site carry unverified, but fascinating, reports from travelers.

Correspondence The process of creating new editions begins with the letters, postcards and emails received from travelers. This correspondence often includes suggestions, criticisms and comments about the current editions. Interesting excerpts are immediately passed on via newsletters and the Web site, and everything goes to our authors to be verified when they're researching on the road. We're keen to get more feedback from organizations or individuals who represent communities visited by travelers.

Lonely Planet gathers information for everyone who's curious about the planet – and especially for those who explore it firsthand. Through guidebooks, phrasebooks, activity guides, maps, literature, newsletters, image library, TV series and Web site we act as an information exchange for a worldwide community of travelers.

Research Authors aim to gather sufficient practical information to enable travelers to make informed choices and to make the mechanics of a journey run smoothly. They also research historical and cultural background to help enrich the travel experience and allow travelers to understand and respond appropriately to cultural and environmental issues.

Authors don't stay in every hotel because that would mean spending a couple of months in each medium-size city and, no, they don't eat at every restaurant because that would mean stretching belts beyond capacity. They do visit hotels and restaurants to check standards and prices, but feedback based on readers' direct experiences can be very helpful.

Many of our authors work undercover; others aren't so secretive. None of them accept freebies in exchange for positive write-ups. And none of our guidebooks contain any advertising.

Production Authors submit their manuscripts and maps to offices in Australia, the USA, UK or France. Editors and cartographers – all experienced travelers themselves – then begin the process of assembling the pieces. When the book finally hits the shops, some things are already out of date, we start getting feedback from readers and the process begins again...

WARNING & REQUEST

Things change – prices go up, schedules change, good places go bad and bad places go bankrupt – nothing stays the same. So, if you find things better or worse, recently opened or long since closed, please tell us and help make the next edition even more accurate and useful. We genuinely value all the feedback we receive. A well-traveled team reads and acknowledges every letter, postcard and email and ensures that every morsel of information finds its way to the appropriate authors, editors and cartographers for verification.

Everyone who writes to us will find their name listed in the next edition of the appropriate guidebook. They will also receive the latest issue of *Planet Talk*, our quarterly printed newsletter, or *Comet*, our monthly email newsletter. Subscriptions to both newsletters are free. The very best contributions will be rewarded with a free guidebook.

We may edit, reproduce and incorporate your comments in all Lonely Planet products, such as guidebooks, Web sites and digital products, so let us know if you don't want your comments reproduced or your name acknowledged.

Send all correspondence to the Lonely Planet office closest to you:

Australia: Locked Bag 1, Footscray, Victoria 3011
USA: 150 Linden St, Oakland, CA 94607
UK: 10a Spring Place, London NW5 3BH
France: 1 rue du Dahomey, 75011 Paris

Or email us at: talk2us@lonelyplanet.com.au

For news, views and updates, see our Web site: www.lonelyplanet.com

HOW TO USE A LONELY PLANET GUIDEBOOK

The best way to use a Lonely Planet guidebook is any way you choose. At Lonely Planet, we believe the most memorable travel experiences are often those that are unexpected, and the finest discoveries are those you make yourself. Guidebooks are not intended to be used as if they provided a detailed set of infallible instructions!

Contents All Lonely Planet guidebooks follow roughly the same format. The Facts about the Destination chapters or sections give background information ranging from history to weather. Facts for the Visitor gives practical information on issues like visas and health. Getting There & Away gives a brief starting point for researching travel to and from the destination. Getting Around gives an overview of the transport options when you arrive.

The peculiar demands of each destination determine how subsequent chapters are broken up, but some things remain constant. We always start with background, then proceed to sights, places to stay, places to eat, entertainment, getting there and away, and getting around information – in that order.

Heading Hierarchy Lonely Planet headings are used in a strict hierarchical structure that can be visualized as a set of Russian dolls. Each heading (and its following text) is encompassed by any preceding heading that is higher on the hierarchical ladder.

Entry Points We do not assume guidebooks will be read from beginning to end, but that people will dip into them. The traditional entry points are the list of contents and the index. In addition, however, some books have a complete list of maps and an index map illustrating map coverage.

There may also be a color map that shows highlights. These highlights are dealt with in greater detail in the Facts for the Visitor chapter, along with planning questions and suggested itineraries. Each chapter covering a geographical region usually begins with a locator map and another list of highlights. Once you find something of interest in a list of highlights, turn to the index.

Maps Maps play a crucial role in Lonely Planet guidebooks and include a huge amount of information. A legend is printed on the back page. We seek to have complete consistency between maps and text and to have every important place in the text captured on a map. Map key numbers usually start in the top left corner.

Although inclusion in a guidebook usually implies a recommendation, we cannot list every good place. Exclusion does not necessarily imply criticism. In fact there are a number of reasons why we might exclude a place – sometimes it is simply inappropriate to encourage an influx of travelers.

Introduction

So you're going to the Southern Cone? Or perhaps only *thinking* about it? Well, think about it some more, and place these images of Argentina in your mind: the Western hemisphere's highest peaks, rising to almost 7000m and blanketed in virgin snow; the painted deserts of the northern Andes, high and dry with colonial cities and lanky cacti; legendary Iguazú Falls, a massive rush of water falling nearly 20 stories and extending as far as the eye can see; shimmering blue-green lakes stretching out between lush mountain forests in the Lake District; astounding southern glaciers actively calving huge slivers of ice; and the magnificent desolation of Patagonia, instilling a romantic tingle and wanderlust. Then there's Tierra del Fuego, the tip of the southern world, encompassing beautiful scenery and the southernmost city in

Argentina Update

Since the initial publication of this edition, Argentina's economic and political climate has changed dramatically. Years of economic stagnation reached crisis levels in December 2001 when, after several days of violent street protests left 27 dead, President Fernando de la Rúa resigned and a state of siege was declared. The value of the peso plummeted – and has stayed low to date – while unemployment and poverty levels rose. Argentina's economic woes have affected Uruguay's economy, which has particularly suffered from the decline in numbers of Argentine tourists.

Generally speaking, Argentina remains a safe destination for travelers. Social unrest has subsided, though travelers may wish to avoid large demonstrations, which can grow violent. Though petty crime has long been a concern in larger cities, Lonely Planet readers have not reported problems with crime in large numbers. Travelers should watch out for simple scams, such as vendors giving incorrect change or incorrect currency conversions.

On the flip side, tourism – both by international travelers and by Argentines who can no longer afford to travel abroad – is on the rise. Travelers may discover that two-tiered price structures – one price for Argentine nationals, and a second, higher price for foreigners – have been adopted in some industries, mostly for domestic flights. In general, however, the devalued peso means that Argentina is far less expensive for foreign travelers than it once was. Unless further economic shifts occur, travelers should expect that prices, especially for accommodation and in restaurants, are substantially lower than the prices quoted in this book. How much lower the prices are will fluctuate depending on the region, the season and current exchange rates.

the world, Ushuaia. Or how about a cruise to (relatively) nearby Antarctica?

Everywhere in Argentina, from the northern subtropical lowlands to the Patagonian shores, you will glimpse wildlife ranging from strange guanacos, rheas and capybaras to the more familiar flamingoes, whales and penguins.

Also, let's not forget the probable start of your adventure: The urban frenzy that is Buenos Aires. This sophisticated capital city circulates through bustling streets and grand avenues lined with historic edifices born of European architects. All around are beautiful *porteños* (inhabitants of Buenos Aires), elegantly coiffed and forever fashionable, passionately expressing their Spanish and Italian roots through energetic personalities and expansive body language. Old-time cafés, tango bars, fine restaurants (think succulent steaks!), late-night dancing and charming colonial neighborhoods complete this picture, and all this is just a start.

If you want to get away from the tourist beat, you can see backroads of grassland or lush forests and meet some of the friendliest folks in South America. Outside Argentina, you can even have some fun at the raucous summer beach resorts in Uruguay or explore the region's indigenous roots in Paraguay. These two under-appreciated countries are brimming with colonial architecture and Jesuit ruins, generations-old traditions, subtropical lowlands and an astounding range of wildlife – and you won't have to share it with many other tourists!

Argentina

Facts about Argentina

HISTORY

Despite its relative brevity, at least in a global sense, Argentine history is a complex and contentious topic. Many Argentine historians, and historians who write about Argentina, have explicit or implicit political perspectives that color both their choice of facts and their interpretation.

Native Peoples

Many history books portray Argentina as a homogeneous society founded on European immigration, but the country's pre-Columbian and colonial past add a complex origin to this common stereotype. When Europeans first arrived in the 16th century, South America's diverse economic and social systems ranged from densely settled civilizations in the central Andes and semisedentary agriculturalists of the tropical and temperate forests to nomadic hunters and gatherers of the Amazon and the Patagonian steppes. Modern anthropologists theorize that 20 major groups of indigenous people lived in the Argentine area.

On the eastern slopes of the central Andes, the Diaguita irrigated maize fields that supported permanent villages between present-day Salta and San Juan in northwest Argentina. Other groups, like the Comechingones near Córdoba, practiced a similar livelihood. To the east, in the forested Río Paraná delta across the Chaco scrubland, smaller Guaraní populations of shifting cultivators relied on maize, along with tuber crops like manioc (cassava) and sweet potatoes, though, highly mobile peoples hunted the guanaco (a wild relative of the llama) and the rhea (a large bird resembling an emu) with bow and arrow or *boleadoras* (heavily weighted thongs that could be thrown up to 100 yards to ensnare the hunted animal). In the far south, coastal groups like the Yahgans gathered shellfish and bird eggs.

Invasion & Colonization of the New World

The first Spaniards to the South American continent sought gold and silver above everything. The area now known as Argentina, Uruguay and Paraguay was first probed by Spanish navigator Juan Díaz de Solís in 1516 mainly to keep Portuguese competitors from gaining control of territories south of Brazil. Solís was also instructed to find a passage to the Pacific. Instead he sailed up what would later be named the Río de la Plata (River of Silver) to his unheroic death at the hands of Uruguayan tribes. Later Spanish explorations were launched from the Río de la Plata, and part of the territory was even named after the Latin word for silver *(argentum)*, but the mineral riches of the Inca Empire in Peru did not pan out in Argentina.

The precious metals they found in Peru were ruthlessly appropriated through outright robbery or through forcing the indigenous populations into virtual slavery. In the most densely populated parts of the Americas, some *encomenderos* (Spaniards who headed the system by which Spain procured the region's resources) became extraordinarily wealthy, but the system failed when the indigenous people could not withstand the onslaught of smallpox, influenza, typhus, and other Old World diseases brought in by the colonists. In some parts of the New World, introduced diseases reduced local populations by more than 95%.

In most of Argentina and the other modern Río de la Plata countries (Uruguay and Paraguay), the *encomienda* was less significant than in the Andes. The semisedentary and nomadic peoples of the riverine lowlands and the southern Pampas put up determined resistance. Around 1536, the Querandí routed Pedro de Mendoza's campers at Buenos Aires, and even into the late 19th century parts of the Pampas were not safe for colonizers. Abandoned Spanish livestock multiplied rapidly on the lush pastures of the Pampas and horses improved the natives' mobility and ability to strike. It wasn't until the Conquista del Desierto, the war of extermination against the Pampas people in the late 19th century, that Europeans finally usurped.

Since Querandí resistance discouraged early settlement of the lower Río de la Plata, settlers ended up in Paraguay's Asunción, founded in 1537 on the upper Río Paraná. The region's most significant early economic links were not directly with Spain, but with silver-rich Alto Perú (now Bolivia), where the bonanza mine at Potosí financed Spanish expansion; and with Lima, capital of the Viceroyalty of Peru. Although Spanish forces reestablished Buenos Aires by 1580, it remained a backwater in comparison to Andean settlements like Tucumán (founded 1571), Córdoba (1573), Salta (1582), La Rioja (1591) and Jujuy (1593). Spaniards from Chile settled the cities of Mendoza (1561), San Juan (1562) and San Luis (1596) in what became known as the Cuyo region. The Tucumán region provided mules, cloth and foodstuffs for Alto Perú; Cuyo produced wine and grain, while Buenos Aires languished.

The colonial-era decline of northwest Argentina's indigenous population produced a maldistribution of land that mirrored similar shifts in other Latin American countries. The appearance of *latifundios* (large landholdings) came about after the disappearance of encomiendas. Spanish immigrants and *criollos* (American-born Spaniards) began acquiring large tracts of the best land for agriculture and livestock; this new institution was the *hacienda*. As native populations gradually recovered or merged with the Spanish to form a mixed-race *(mestizo)* population, they found that the best lands had been monopolized and that their only economic alternative was the cultivation of *minifundios* (small plots) on inferior lands or dependent labor on the large estates.

While the hacienda was never as important in Argentina as it was in Peru or Mexico, the livestock *estancia* came to play a critical role in the development of Argentine society. When the Spaniards returned to the Río de la Plata estuary in the late 16th century, they found that the cattle and horses abandoned decades earlier had proliferated beyond belief. With commerce severely regulated under the Spanish, the inhabitants of colonial Buenos Aires looked to this livestock for their livelihood. The legendary gaucho of the Pampas emerged at this time; the South American counterpart to North America's cowboys, they hunted wild cattle and broke in wild horses.

Growth & Independence

Though isolated and legally prohibited from direct European commerce for nearly two centuries, the people of Buenos Aires pursued a flourishing contraband trade with Portuguese Brazil and non-peninsular European powers. Governed for too long at the tail end of an indirect supply line via the Caribbean, Panama and Peru, frustrated criollos sought to carry on direct trade with Spain. By naming Buenos Aires capital of the new Viceroyalty of the Río de la Plata in 1776, the Spanish crown explicitly acknowledged that the region had outgrown the mother country's political and economic domination.

Toward the end of the 18th century, criollos became increasingly dissatisfied and impatient with peninsular authority in all parts of the continent. The expulsion of British troops who briefly occupied Buenos Aires in 1806 and 1807 gave the people of the Río de la Plata new confidence in their ability to stand alone. They asserted this strength in the revolution of May 25, 1810.

Independence movements throughout South America united to expel Spain from the continent by the 1820s. Under the leadership of General José de San Martín and others, the United Provinces of the Río de la Plata (the direct forerunner of the Argentine Republic) declared formal independence at Tucumán in 1816. Ironically, British financial and logistical support made it possible for Argentina to break the Spanish yoke. In the process, Bolivia and Paraguay became independent countries rather than remaining part of the former Viceroyalty.

ARGENTINA

ARGENTINE NATIONAL & PROVINCIAL PARKS & RESERVES

1 Monumento Natural Laguna de los Pozuelos
2 PN Baritú
3 PN Calilegua
4 PN Los Cardones
5 PN Finca El Rey
6 RN Formosa
7 PN Río Pilcomayo
8 PN Iguazú
9 PN Chaco
10 RP Esteros del Iberá
11 PP Ischigualasto
12 PN Talampaya
13 PP Aconcagua
14 PP Volcán Tupungato
15 PN Sierra de las Quijadas
16 PN El Palmar
17 PN Diamante
18 PN Lihué Calel
19 PN Laguna Blanca
20 PN Lanín
21 PN Nahuel Huapi; PN Los Arrayanes
22 PN Lago Puelo
23 PN Los Alerces
24 RF Península Valdés
25 RP Punta Tombo
26 PN Perito Moreno
27 Monumento Natural Bosques Petrificados
28 PN Los Glaciares
29 PN Monte León
30 PN Tierra del Fuego

PROVINCES OF ARGENTINA

Tropic of Capricorn

BOLIVIA

CHILE

PARAGUAY

Jujuy

Salta

SAN SALVADOR
DE JUJUY

SALTA

Formosa

ASUNCIÓN

Tucumán

FORMOSA

Catamarca

Santiago
del
Estero

Chaco

RESISTENCIA

CORRIENTES

Misiones

POSADAS

CATAMARCA

SANTIAGO
DEL ESTERO

Corrientes

LA RIOJA

La Rioja

Santa
Fe

BRAZIL

30°S

San
Juan

CÓRDOBA

SANTA FE

SAN
JUAN

PARANÁ

MENDOZA

SAN
LUIS

CÓRDOBA

Entre
Ríos

SANTIAGO

URUGUAY

MONTEVIDEO

PACIFIC
OCEAN

Mendoza

San
Luis

BUENOS
AIRES

LA
PLATA

SANTA ROSA

Buenos
Aires

LaPampa

Neuquén

NEUQUÉN

Río Negro

40°S

VIEDMA

RAWSON

Chubut

ATLANTIC
OCEAN

Santa
Cruz

FALKLAND ISLANDS
(Islas Malvinas)

50°S

RÍO GALLEGOS

STANLEY

0   200   400 km
0   125   250 miles

Tierra
del Fuego

USHUAIA

⊙ Provincial Capital

80°W   70°W   60°W   50°W

ARGENTINA

Despite achieving independence, the provinces were united in name only. Lacking any effective central authority, the regional disparities obscured by Spanish rule became more obvious. This resulted in the rise of the *caudillos* (local strongmen), who commanded great personal loyalty and respect while resisting Buenos Aires as strongly as Buenos Aires had resisted Spain. Argentine educator and president Domingo F Sarmiento, though himself a product of the provinces, criticized the excesses of these caudillos in his classic *Life in the Argentine Republic in the Days of the Tyrants* (1845).

Who's Who – Past & Present

José de San Martín (1778-1850) Credited for breaking Spain's hold on Argentina in 1816, San Martín is probably Argentina's greatest national hero. He was a brilliant strategist who also helped liberate Chile and crush the Spanish stronghold in Lima, Peru. Despite his influence, San Martín was not a harsh leader, but rather a polite and sophisticated man from humble origins on the former Jesuit mission of Yapeyú on the Río Uruguay. The later internal power struggles of his country, which he could do nothing about, dampened his spirits. After all his accomplishments in Argentina, he ended up leaving for France to live out the rest of his life.

Domingo F Sarmiento (1811-88) Another educated and sophisticated man, Sarmiento was an enlightened writer who became the president of Argentina in 1868. He saw increasing European influence in his country as an advance over the 'barbaric' *caudillo* (provincial strongmen), whose conflicts were tearing the nation apart. Unlike San Martín, however, he managed to use his power of political office to unify Argentina into a more stable republic, razing the caudillos' power significantly. Sarmiento was also responsible for starting Argentina's golden age in 1880.

Eva 'Evita' Duarte (1919-52) The second wife of Juan Perón, Eva Duarte (more widely known as Evita) was revered by the lower classes she helped empower. A one-time radio and television actress, Evita used her charisma and influence to champion human social rights, to the horror of the established elite. The *descamisados* (shirtless ones), poor people she helped during her reign, were crushed by her early death of cancer at age 33. One visit to her grave in posh Recoleta cemetery (where some elite still resent her being buried) will give you an idea of the eternal devotion she inspires.

Juan Domingo Perón (1895-1974) President of Argentina from 1946-55, Perón was both admired and despised for *Peronism*, or his own brand of domestic policy and social justice. With Evita at his side, he set about reforming the domestic economy by nationalizing the country and giving laborers basic social benefits. Despite his seeming good will towards the people in general, his tactics included heavy-handed and fascist suppression of any opposition. Even the press and outspoken individuals like Jorge Luis Borges were attacked. After the death of Evita in 1952 his presidency unraveled, and in 1955 a coup sent him into exile. He returned to the presidency in 1973, but died in office less than a year later.

Che Guevara (1928-67) Che (which means 'hey, you'), the most legendary of all revolutionaries, was born Ernesto Guevara de la Serna in Rosario, Argentina. He originally trained to be a doctor, but emancipation of the poor seemed more his calling – a career he ended up pursuing with gusto. Che traveled to Mexico, where he met Fidel Castro and eventually helped him take Cuba in 1959. This success spurred him to try 'liberating' other Latin American countries, but his luck stopped in Bolivia, where he was captured and executed in the jungle. Now a martyr, his popularized and defiant image lives on.

Argentine politics was thus divided between the Federalists of the interior, who advocated provincial autonomy, and the Unitarists of Buenos Aires, who upheld central authority. The Federalists were mainly conservative provincial landowners and the rural working class (including a sub-stantial Afro-Argentine population that has almost completely disappeared) who re-sented Buenos Aires' centralized power. The Unitarists, led by intellectuals like Bernardino Rivadavia, were more cosmo-politan and looked to Europe for capital, immigrants and ideas. For nearly two

Who's Who – Past & Present

Jorge Luis Borges (1899-1986) A giant of literature, Borges is best known for the complex labyrinthine worlds and sophisticated mind teasers constructing his short stories. His family helped him to succeed: his dad encouraged Borges' creative writing, while his mother managed to chase away any possible distracting girlfriends. He was once a librarian, then a poultry inspector.

Borges went blind towards the end of his life, but kept publishing books. Despite his great and deserving accomplishments, he never won the Nobel Prize for literature.

Carlos Menem (1930-) As president of Argentina from 1989-99, Menem finally stabilized the country's economy and curbed runaway inflation. He may be best remembered, however, through the tabloid headlines. In 2001 he married a Chilean beauty queen half his age, and soon after was arrested for his possible involvement in an arms-trading scandal. His grown son died in a tragic heli-copter accident, and he harbors a bitter, estranged ex-wife and a daughter who won't talk to him. Menem actually seems to make more headlines than the current (and more boring) president, de la Rua, and Argentines may not have heard the last of him yet.

Mercedes Sosa (1935-) Hailing from Tucumán, jolly Sosa is probably South America's most famous folkloric singer. She's performed all over the world, enthralling millions of fans with her expressive contra alto voice and dedication to social equality. Known for her interpretations of zamba and chamamé music, Sosa also helped revive the political song movement in Latin America. For her efforts, she recently won the Latin Grammy Award for best folk artist.

Charly García (1951-) Possibly the most famous of Argentina's rock musicians, this rock pioneer originally wrote hippie-ish songs that provoked the military junta of 1976-83, inciting a court ap-pearance for subversive behavior. His wild antics have included jumping off a 9th-floor balcony into a swimming pool, but he's now a national icon, forever famous for his controversial interpre-tation of the Argentine national anthem.

Diego Maradona (1960-) The bad, bad boy of Argentine soccer, Diego played best and most famously for the Boca Juniors soccer team. Born poor but blessed with outstanding *fútbol* skills, he quickly rose to riches and stardom. The international spotlight shone on Diego in 1986, when he surreptitiously punched a ball into England's net to score the infamous 'hand of God' goal. Drugs and scandals followed him after that, eventually leading to his retirement in 1987, at the age of 37.

Carlos Gardel (1887-1935) Known as the songbird of Buenos Aires, Gardel's crooning voice made women swoon, hardened men cry and tango emerge from the bordellos of the capital city. This popular tango musician epitomized suave and gained fame in Argentina and other Latin American countries until his career was cut short by a fatal plane crash. See the boxed text 'Tango Anyone?' in the Buenos Aires chapter, for more.

decades, bloody and vindictive conflicts between the two factions left the country nearly exhausted.

The Reign of Rosas

Juan Manuel de Rosas came to prominence as a caudillo in Buenos Aires province and represented the interests of rural elites whose power depended on their estancias and *saladeros* (tanning and salting factories). But he also helped centralize political power in Buenos Aires and set other ominous precedents in Argentine political life, creating the *mazorca,* his ruthless political police force, and institutionalizing torture. In the words of Sarmiento:

The central consolidated despotic government of the landed proprietor, Don Juan Manuel Rosas... applied the knife of the Gaucho to the culture of Buenos Ayres, and destroyed the work of centuries – of civilization, law and liberty.

Rosas' dictatorial appetite required a large standing army, which consumed an increasing percentage of public expenditures. He also required all overseas trade to be funneled through the port of Buenos Aires rather than be shipped directly to or from the provinces.

Despite Federalist efforts, Buenos Aires continued to dominate the new country. After the Unitarists (and even some of Rosas' former allies) forced him from power in 1852, economic developments confirmed Buenos Aires' power in the coming decades. Rosas himself spent the last 25 years of his life in exile in Southampton, England.

Roots of Modern Argentina

And so a new era in Argentine development began. Sheep estancias, producing enormous quantities of wool in response to the nearly inexhaustible demands of English mills, supplanted the relatively stagnant cattle estancias. According to Argentine historian Hilda Sábato, the province of Buenos Aires was in the vanguard of this process, integrating Argentina into the global economy and consolidating the

country as a political entity. Steadily, European immigrants assumed important roles in crafts and commerce. In nearby areas of Buenos Aires province, small farms known as *chacras* supplied the city's food, but sheep displaced the semi-wild cattle of the surrounding estancias. In the periphery of the province, though, cattle estancias operated much as before.

The Constitution of 1853 (still in force today despite its frequent suspension) pointed to the triumph of Unitarism, even allowing the president to dissolve provincial administrations. The economic expression of Unitarism was Liberalism, an openness to foreign capital, which even now raises the hackles of many Argentine nationalists. As used in Argentina, the term Liberalism means something very different from what it means in Western Europe and North America.

According to historian David Rock, Liberalism had three main aspects: foreign investment, foreign trade and immigration. In the late 19th century, all three inundated the Humid Pampas, Mesopotamia and Córdoba, while lapping at the edges of some interior provinces. Basque and Irish refugees became the first shepherds, as both sheep numbers and wool exports increased nearly tenfold between 1850 and 1880. Some herders were independent family farmers on relatively small units, but the majority were sharecroppers, and the land itself remained in the hands of large landowners.

After 1880, Argentina became a major producer of cereal crops for export, as it still is today. The Humid Pampas was the focus of this development, whose origins lay in mid-century colonization projects focused on attracting European settlers. *Estancieros* rarely objected to occupation of lands that were nominally theirs, because new settlers provided a buffer between themselves and the still troublesome native peoples. Swiss, German, French and Italian farmers proved successful in provinces like Santa Fe and Entre Ríos.

Such developments did not eliminate *latifundios,* or large landholdings. Public lands were sold by the government at giveaway prices to pay its debts, encouraging speculators and reducing opportunities for poor immigrants whose only agricultural alternatives were sharecropping or seasonal labor. Many remained in Buenos Aires, steadily increasing the city's share of the country's population.

By reducing opportunities for family farming, land speculation and commodity exports also encouraged urban growth. The port city of Buenos Aires, which rapidly modernized in the 1880s, nearly doubled its population through immigration during that decade alone. Urban services such as transportation, power and water improved steadily. Because of the capital's increasing importance, it became an administratively distinct federal zone (the Capital Federal), effectively seceding from its namesake province.

British capital, amounting to one-third of Britain's total Latin American investment by 1890, dominated the Argentine economy. Most went to infrastructure improvements, such as railroads. By the turn of the 20th century, Argentina had a highly developed rail network, fanning out from Buenos Aires in all directions, but the economy remained vulnerable. But speculation led to a boom in land prices and paper money loans that depreciated in value, causing near collapse of the financial system.

From the mid-1890s until WWI, Argentina's economy recovered enough to take advantage of the opportunities presented by beef, mutton and wheat exports. Because of inequities in land distribution, though, this prosperity was not broad. Industry could not absorb all the immigration, and with the onset of the Great Depression, the military took power under conditions of indecisive and ineffectual civilian government, as well as considerable social unrest. An obscure but oddly visionary colonel, Juan Domingo Perón, was the first leader to try to come to grips with the country's economic crisis.

The Perón Decade

Lieutenant General Juan Perón (diehard supporters refuse to separate his name and rank) emerged in the 1940s to become Argentina's most revered, as well as most despised, political figure. He embodied the contradictions of the country itself: he rose to power through the elitist institution of the military, but enjoyed broad popularity among the public at large.

Perón was born in Lobos, Buenos Aires province, in 1895, and some years later his family relocated to Patagonia for an unsuccessful attempt at sheep farming. This is where he saw firsthand the most unsavory aspects of large, paternalistic sheep estancias, controlled almost exclusively by British interests.

Then as a young military officer, he witnessed the miserable physical and educational state of rural conscripts, the casualties of an inequitable social order. Sent to restore order in several labor disputes, he proved an attentive listener to working-class concerns, mediating labor settlements on the railways and sugar factories of the subtropical north.

Perón first came to national prominence after a military coup deposed President Ramón Castillo in 1943. Sensing an opportunity to assist the country's forgotten working class, Perón settled for a relatively minor post as head of the National Department of Labor. In this post, his success at organizing relief efforts after a major earthquake in the Andean city and province of San Juan earned praise throughout the country. In the process he also met Eva (Evita) Duarte, the actress who would

Eva Perón

become his second wife and make her own major contribution to Argentine history.

After being dislodged from his post and briefly incarcerated by jealous fellow officers, Perón ran for and won the presidency in 1946 (with the help of Evita) and again in 1952.

The working classes supported him for promoting domestic industrialization and economic independence from foreign interests. At the time, British capital built most of the railways that radiated from Buenos Aires, bringing agricultural commodities of the landowning elite to the capital city for shipment to European manufacturers. In return, inexpensive British products flooded domestic markets and retarded local industry. Perón also appealed to conservative nationalists, who distrusted the cosmopolitan landowning elite, and to intellectuals, who resented the role of foreign capital. The military looked to Perón, concerned that Argentina was overly dependent on foreign sources for raw materials and munitions as Europe was crumbling during WWII.

Beyond his politics was his charisma. During sojourns as Argentine military attaché in Fascist Italy and Nazi Germany, Perón grasped the importance of spectacle in public life and used his personal charisma to put it into practice. With the equally charismatic 'Evita' at his side, he would hold massive rallies from the balcony of the Casa Rosada. Giving voice to the disenfranchised masses, the Peróns enlisted them in their cause and alienated traditionally powerful sectors of Argentine society.

There was no disguising the Peróns' demagoguery and ambition. Evita once wrote that 'there are two things of which I am proud: my love for the people and my hatred for the oligarchy.' Despite huge congressional majorities, Perón's authoritarian tendencies led him to govern by decree rather than by consultation and consensus. His excessively personal approach created a political party, known formally as 'Justicialist' but popularly referred to as 'Peronist,' which has never completely transcended a stagnant re-

liance on its founder's charisma. Perón did not hesitate to use or condone intimidation and torture for political ends, although such activities never reached the level they would later during the state terrorism of the late 1970s.

Dynamic Evita, meanwhile, used their growing influence for her own sometimes vindictive goals, though she was mostly championed for her charitable work and women's rights campaigns. Still, many outspoken community figures, including Argentine literary great Jorge Luis Borges, suffered the Peróns' caprices.

Yet during the decade they lived and ruled together, the Peróns legitimized the trade-union movement and extended political rights and economic benefits to working-class people in matters of wages, pensions, job security and working conditions. They managed to secure voting rights for women by 1947. University education ceased to be the privilege of the elite, but instead became available to any capable individual. Many Argentines gained employment in the expanding state bureaucracy.

Despite their wide-ranging influence, the Peróns' tenure was no carnival. A virulent and often violent anti-clerical campaign divided the country toward the end of Perón's first presidency. Economic difficulties and rising inflation undermined his second presidency in 1952; Evita's death in the same year was another blow to the country. In late 1955, Perón fell victim to the so-called Revolución Libertadora, a coup that sent him into exile and initiated nearly three decades of catastrophic military rule, with only brief interludes of civilian government.

Perón's Exile & Return

After Perón left the country, Argentina's military government banned his Justicialist party. Perón himself wandered to Paraguay, Panama (where he met his third wife, Isabelita), Venezuela, the Dominican Republic and eventually to Spain, where he remained from 1961 to 1973.

During exile, Perón and his associates constantly plotted their return to Argentina.

Perón acquired a bizarre retinue of advisors, including his personal secretary, José López Rega, a spiritualist and extreme right-wing nationalist who acted like his Svengali or Rasputin. At Perón's Puerta de Hierro mansion in Madrid, where Evita's embalmed body lay after being rescued from an anonymous grave in Italy in 1971, López Rega reportedly conducted rituals over the casket to imbue Isabelita with Evita's charismatic qualities.

In the late 1960s, increasing economic problems and political instability, including strikes, political kidnappings and guerrilla warfare, marked Argentine political life. In the midst of these events, Perón's opportunity to return finally arrived in 1973, when the beleaguered military relaxed their objections to the Justicialist party and loyal Peronist Hector Cámpora was elected president. Cámpora himself was merely a stalking-horse for Perón and soon resigned, paving the way for new elections handily won by Perón.

After an 18-year exile, Perón once again symbolized Argentine unity, but there was no substance to his rule. His anticipated arrival at Buenos Aires' Ezeiza airport, attended by hundreds of thousands of people on a dark winter's night, resulted in violent clashes between supporters across the broad spectrum of Argentine politics. Chronically ill, Perón died in mid-1974, leaving a fragmented country. His ill-qualified wife Isabelita, elected as his running mate but under the spell of José López Rega, inherited the presidency.

The Dirty War & the Disappeared

In the late 1960s and early '70s, antigovernment feeling was rife and street protests often exploded into all-out riots, culminating in the so-called Cordobazo of May 1969, when university students and automobile plant workers fought pitched battles with the police for two days in the center of the city of Córdoba. Protesting government economic policies, including factory closures, taxes and dismissals, the workers were losing faith in the power of the traditional union, the Confederación General del Trabajo (CGT).

Armed guerrilla organizations like the Guevarist Ejército Revolucionario del Pueblo (ERP) and, working from bases in the eastern cities, the far larger and fervently nationalistic Peronist Montoneros emerged as radical opponents of the military, the oligarchies, US influence in Latin America and multinational companies. Perón's bumbling widow, Isabelita, along with her advisor, Rega, created the Triple A (Alianza Argentina Anticomunista), a death squad to take on the revolutionary groups. In 1974, this state-sponsored paramilitary force murdered prominent left-wing lawyers and intellectuals, sometimes at the rate of 50 a day. Violent confrontations between left and right were inevitable, and with increasing official corruption exacerbating Isabelita's incompetence, Argentina found itself plunged into chaos. The guerrilla organizations carried out bombings, kidnappings and robberies, often targeting the army. The economy was, as always when Argentina experienced civil disturbance, in tatters.

On March 24, 1976, a bloodless military coup, led by army general Jorge Rafael Videla, took control of the Argentine state apparatus and ushered in a period of terror and brutality. Aided by two other high-ranking officers, Emilio Massera from the navy and army sidekick General Roberto Viola, Videla was to attract more international attention to Argentina than ever in its history, though for the worst reasons.

Videla's sworn aim was to crush the guerrilla movements by any means necessary and thus restore social order – the Argentine press and public gave their support to the military junta. The Process of National Reorganization (known as El Proceso) was the euphemistic handle for the new government's dual policy of authoritarian rule and an economic agenda designed to encourage foreign investment. The minor successes of the latter were soon eclipsed by the horrors of state terrorism. Using CIA intelligence and 'interrogation' techniques, the security forces, often working undercover, were freed from the niceties of the constitution and went about the country arresting, torturing, raping and killing anyone on their hit list of suspected leftists. Liberals, intellectuals, journalists and trade union leaders were obvious targets, and while some armed revolutionaries were locked away, the randomness and violence of the police and army raids soon came to the notice of international media.

During the period between 1976 and 1983, often referred to as the Guerra Sucia or Dirty War, human rights groups estimate that some 30,000 people, mainly but not exclusively Argentine, were 'disappeared.' During these years, to disappear meant to be abducted, detained, tortured and probably killed with no hope of legal process. The armed forces and police ran numerous illegal detention centers, the most notorious of which was the Escuela de Mecánica de la Armada (Naval Mechanics School) in an exclusive northern suburb of Buenos Aires. For anyone crossing the street, even at midday, the presence of a black Ford Falcon without numbered plates and occupied by four men in sunglasses, induced outright terror. The dictatorship almost never acknowledged illegal detention of individuals, although it sometimes reported their deaths in battles or skirmishes with 'security forces.'

The details of the atrocities are documented in *Nunca Más,* a report compiled in 1983 by the Comisión Nacional sobre Desaparición de Personas (CONADEP), a committee chaired by leading author Ernesto Sábato prior to the 1985 trials of the military junta. Those who read the document soon realized they had been kept in the dark about the atrocities committed by the military government to counter 'subversion.' Ironically, the Dirty War ended only when the Argentine military attempted a real military objective.

Falklands/Malvinas War

Argentina's economy continued to decline during military rule. On the one hand, the government enacted strict economic measures, including a fixed exchange rate to eliminate speculation on the dollar, but it failed to reduce annual inflation below three digits. It did, however, aggravate unemployment and undermine local industry through cheap imports. Lip service to austerity brought in billions of dollars in loans, which were invested in grandiose public works projects like the toll road between downtown Buenos Aires and the airport at Ezeiza, while public officials pocketed much of the money and sent it overseas to Swiss bank accounts. Meanwhile, the military acquired the latest in European technology, including the deadly Exocet missile.

Under the weight of its import splurge and debt burden, the economy collapsed in chaos. Almost overnight, devaluation reduced the peso to a fraction of its former value, and inflation again reached astronomical levels. El Proceso was coming undone.

In late 1981, General Leopoldo Galtieri assumed the role of president. Rapid economic deterioration and popular discontent led to mass demonstrations at Casa Rosada and to desperate measures. To stay in power, Galtieri launched an invasion in April 1982 to dislodge the British from the Falkland Islands, which had been claimed by Argentina as the Islas Malvinas for nearly a century and a half.

Overnight, the nearly unopposed occupation of the Malvinas unleashed a wave of nationalist euphoria that subsided almost as fast as it had crested. Acting on faulty advice from civilian foreign minister Nicanor Costa Méndez, Galtieri underestimated the determined response of British Prime Minister Margaret Thatcher. Thatcher herself was having political difficulties and Britain was willing and able to absorb heavy naval losses to attain a remote goal. After only 74 days, Argentina's ill-trained, poorly motivated and mostly teenaged forces surrendered ignominiously, and the military meekly prepared to return government to civilian hands. In 1983, Argentines elected Raúl Alfonsín, of the Unión Cívica Radical (UCR, or Radical Civic Union), to the presidency. For more details on the war, see the boxed text 'When the Edge of the World Just Isn't Far Enough' in the Patagonia chapter.

Aftermath of the Dirty War

In his successful 1983 presidential campaign, Alfonsín pledged to prosecute military officers responsible for human-rights violations during the Dirty War. Evidence uncovered by the commission that produced *Nunca Más* contributed to the conviction of junta members including Videla, Viola and Admiral Emilio Massera for kidnapping, torture and homicide. Videla and Massera received life sentences, though in virtual luxury accommodations in a military prison.

When the government attempted to extend trials to junior officers, many of whom protested that they had been merely 'following orders,' these officers responded with uprisings in several different parts of the country. The timid administration succumbed to military demands and produced a Ley de la Obediencia Debida (Law of Due Obedience), allowing lower-ranking officers to use the defense that they were following orders, as well as a Punto Final (Stopping Point), beyond which no criminal or civil prosecutions could take place. These measures eliminated prosecutions of notorious individuals such as Navy Captain Alfredo Astiz (the Angel of Death), who was implicated in the disappearance of a Swedish-Argentine teenager and the highly publicized deaths of two French nuns who were thrown into the Río de la Plata from an airplane.

The Law of Due Obedience and the Stopping Point did not eliminate the Dirty War's divisive impact on Argentine politics; after 1987 the military reasserted its role in politics despite internal factionalism. In December 1990, prior to a visit by US president George Bush, a dissident junior officer movement known as the *carapintadas* (so-called after their custom of painting their faces with camouflage markings) occupied army headquarters across from the Casa Rosada and elsewhere in Buenos Aires. It hoped to encourage the military establishment to join in overthrowing then-President Carlos Menem, himself a prisoner during the Dirty War.

Ironically, Menem contributed to the controversy in an unexpected and unwarranted manner. Just after Christmas of that year, he pardoned Videla, Massera and their cohorts even though the Argentine public overwhelmingly opposed it. He also pardoned former Montonero guerrilla Mario Firmenich who, some speculated, still had access to substantial funds that might benefit Menem's Peronist party.

During the 1995 presidential campaign, Dirty War issues resurfaced spectacularly when journalist Horacio Verbitsky wrote *The Flight* (New York, New Press, 1996), a book based on interviews with former Navy Captain Adolfo Scilingo. Troubled but unrepentant, Scilingo acknowledged that he himself participated in regular weekly flights in which the navy threw political prisoners, alive but drugged, into the Atlantic. While such reports had long circulated, this was the first time any participant had openly admitted responsibility, and it ignited a clamor of protest for a more complete accounting of the disappeared – even though Alfonsín's law and Menem's pardons had eliminated any possibility of further prosecutions. Another revelation was that military chaplains had counseled and comforted the perpetrators of the killings.

Scilingo's 'confession' set off a chain of events that has yet to end. Army, air force and even religious heads apologized to the country for their conduct during the Dirty War. Navy officials, however, remained conspicuously silent and even spoke of promoting the disreputable Astiz, precipitating a minor diplomatic confrontation with France. Consequent objections forced Astiz's retirement from the navy. The former officer's statements in a magazine interview, where he declared himself 'the best-trained person in the country to kill a politician or journalist,' cost him both his retired military status and pension. He's now been sentenced to life imprisonment (in absentia) by a Paris court, and Italy is after him as well.

Demand for a complete list of the disappeared is still strong within Argentina. Human rights organizations like the Madres de la Plaza de Mayo and Las Abuelas de la Plaza de Mayo keep up their protests, campaigning for justice and, failing that, information about the Disappeared *(Desaparecidos)* and their children, believed to have been adopted by the military officers who might have played a role in their parents' deaths. The Abuelas and the HIJOS (Sons and Daughters) organizations are committed to naming all these illegally adopted children, now in their twenties. Meanwhile, the ringleaders get older and live in anonymity or the relative comfort of house arrest.

In 1998 a Buenos Aires judge ordered the incarceration of Videla during investigations as to his responsibility for the kidnapping of children born to political prisoners and given to military families for adoption – a crime not covered by the Punto Final and presidential pardons. At the same time, public outcry led to congressional repeal of the Punto Final and Obediencia Debida laws in 1998. This was not, however, retroactive, and most of the criminals of 1976-83 still walk the streets. Victims and human-rights activists in Buenos Aires have responded with the tactic of *escrache,* plastering the city with posters publicizing the faces and addresses of Dirty War criminals and demonstrating outside their residences.

Tucumán governor Antonio Domingo Bussi, a former general who led the army against the ERP insurrection and won the governorship by a small plurality in 1995, encountered a different problem when it was discovered he had hidden a large Swiss bank account allegedly created from Dirty War spoils. Though weakened politically and facing criminal charges, Bussi's Fuerza Republicana party held enough seats in the provincial legislature to prevent his impeachment in the short term.

Recent Developments

During Menem's tenure, which ran from 1989-1999, major issues had been new economic policies, corruption and the president's authoritarian tendencies. Menem did not refrain from ruling by decree, rather than consulting with Congress over legislation, and even interfering in the federal courts. His arrogance had him speaking of running again in 1999, even before winning a second term (he had already altered one constitutional amendment, and running a third consecutive term would have required a further amendment). He did not manage to further meddle with the constitution, although posters of 'Menem 2003' still decorate the streets of Buenos Aires.

Menem also aroused controversy in 1991 when he ordered Argentine warships to the Persian Gulf in support of the allied effort to liberate Kuwait (the ships gave logistical support, but did not participate in combat). Both right- and left-wing nationalists resented the president's apparent compliance toward the USA. More recently the military has undertaken other international missions, such as serving as peacekeepers in the former Yugoslavia. Kept busy with such tasks, the military has been remarkably quiet over the past few years; not many hope for a return of overt military domination of Argentina.

Former Buenos Aires Mayor Fernando de la Rúa won the election in 1999, partly because he steadfastly distanced himself from the flamboyance of the ex-president. He promised to reduce the burgeoning foreign debt and put an end to the corruption that had plagued the former administration. A valiant goal, but perhaps one unattainable for any Argentine government: a consequent vote-buying scandal that resulted in the passing of labor reforms originally put in place by Perón many decades earlier, demoralized the country and resulted in the resignation of de la Rúa's vice president, Carlos Alvarez. Increased taxes, reduced government spending and financial panic sparked nationwide strikes and riots on a regular basis. De la Rúa resigned in December 2001, and political uncertainty loomed on the nation's horizon.

GEOGRAPHY & CLIMATE

With a total land area of about 2.8 million sq km, excluding the South Atlantic islands and the Antarctic quadrant claimed as national territory, Argentina is the world's eighth-largest country, only slightly smaller than India. It stretches from La Quiaca on the Bolivian border to Ushuaia in Tierra del Fuego (a distance of nearly 3500km) and encompasses a wide variety of environments and terrain.

The Andes

The Andean chain runs the length of Argentina, from the Bolivian border in the north to the South Atlantic, where the chain disappears.

Rainfall can be erratic, although rain-fed agriculture is feasible from Tucumán northward. In most areas, perennial streams descending from the Andes provide irrigation water. In the extreme north lies the southern extension of the Bolivian altiplano, a thinly populated high plain between 3000m and 4000m in altitude and punctuated by even higher volcanic peaks. Although days can be surprisingly hot (sunburn is a serious hazard at high altitude), frosts occur almost nightly.

South of Tucumán, rainfall is inadequate for crops, but irrigation has brought prosperity to the wine-producing Cuyo region, consisting of the provinces of Mendoza, San Juan and San Luis.

On the region's far western edge is the massive Andean crest, featuring 6960m Aconcagua, South America's highest peak. Hot in summer, the area is pleasant the rest

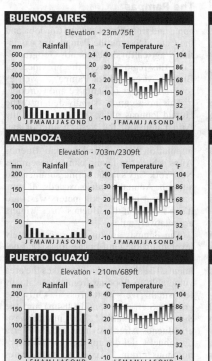

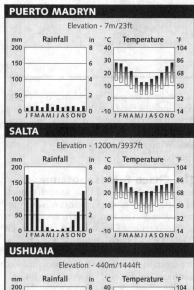

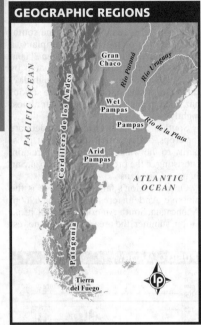

GEOGRAPHIC REGIONS

Gran Chaco

Río Paraná

Río Uruguay

PACIFIC OCEAN

Cordillera de los Andes

Wet Pampas

Pampas

Río de la Plata

Arid Pampas

ATLANTIC OCEAN

Patagonia

Tierra del Fuego

Corrientes, which make up most of the area known as Mesopotamia. Hot and humid Misiones, a politically important province surrounded on three sides by Brazil and Paraguay, contains part of the awesome Iguazú Falls, which descend from southern Brazil's Paraná Plateau.

Rainfall decreases from east to west; for example, Corrientes' annual average rainfall of about 1200mm contrasts with Santiago del Estero's 500mm, which is insufficient for rain-fed agriculture. Shallow summer flooding is common throughout Mesopotamia and the eastern Chaco, while only the immediate river floodplains become inundated in the west. The Chaco has a well-defined winter dry season, while Mesopotamia's rainfall is evenly distributed throughout the year.

The Pampas

Bordered by the Atlantic Ocean and Patagonia and stretching nearly to Córdoba and the Central Sierras, the Pampas are Argentina's agricultural heartland. Geographically, this region covers the provinces of Buenos Aires and La Pampa, as well as southern chunks of Santa Fe and Córdoba.

This area can be subdivided into the Humid Pampas, along the littoral, and the Arid Pampas of the western interior and the south. More than a third of the country's population lives in and around Buenos Aires, where the humid climate resembles New York City's in the spring, summer and autumn. Annual rainfall exceeds 900mm, but several hundred kilometers westward it's less than half that. Buenos Aires' winters are relatively mild.

The Pampas are an almost completely level plain of wind-borne loess (a fine-grained silt or clay) and river-deposited sediments. The absence of relief makes the area vulnerable to flooding from the relatively few small rivers that cross it. Only the granitic Sierra de Tandil (484m) and the Sierra de la Ventana (1273m), in southwestern Buenos Aires province, and the Sierra de Lihuel Calel disrupt the otherwise monotonous terrain. The coast of Buenos Aires province features attractive, sandy beaches

of the year despite cool winter nights. On occasion the *zonda,* a dry wind descending from the Andes, causes dramatic temperature increases (see the boxed text 'They Call the Wind El Zonda' in the Córdoba chapter).

The Chaco & Mesopotamia

East of the Andes and their foothills, much of northern Argentina consists of subtropical lowlands. The arid western area, known as the Argentine Chaco, is part of the much larger Gran Chaco region, which extends into Bolivia, Paraguay and Brazil. Summers are brutally hot here in the provinces of Santiago del Estero, Chaco, Formosa and northern Santa Fe and Córdoba. (See Northeast Argentina and Córdoba & the Central Sierras chapters for more information on these provinces.)

Between the Río Paraná and Río Uruguay, the climate is mild, and rainfall is heavy in the provinces of Entre Ríos and

at resorts like Mar del Plata and Necochea, which *porteños* (inhabitants of the capital) overrun in January and February.

Patagonia & the Lake District

Patagonia, of which the Lake District is a sub-region, is the region south of the Río Colorado, consisting of the provinces of Neuquén, Río Negro, Chubut and Santa Cruz. It's separated from Chilean Patagonia by the Andes.

The cordillera is high enough that Pacific storms drop most of their rain and snow on the Chilean side. In the extreme southern reaches of Patagonia, however, enough snow and ice still accumulate to form the largest Southern Hemisphere glaciers outside of Antarctica. Hiking, trekking, skiing and mountaineering are common recreational activities, depending on the season.

East of the Andean foothills, the cool, arid Patagonian steppes support huge flocks of sheep, whose wool is almost all exported to Europe. For such a southerly location, temperatures are relatively mild, even in winter, when more uniform atmospheric pressure moderates the strong gales that blow most of the year.

Except for urban clusters like Comodoro Rivadavia (center of the petroleum industry) and Río Gallegos (wool and meat packing), Patagonia is thinly populated. Tidal ranges along the Atlantic coast are too great for major port facilities. In the valley of the Río Negro and at the outlet of the Río Chubut, there's farming and cultivation of fruit orchards.

Tierra del Fuego

The world's southernmost permanently inhabited territory, Tierra del Fuego (Land of Fire) consists of one large island (Isla Grande), unequally divided between Chile and Argentina, and many smaller ones, some of which have been the source of longtime contention between the two countries. When Europeans first passed through the Strait of Magellan (which separates Isla Grande from the Patagonian mainland), the fires stemmed from the activities of the now endangered Yahgan people; nowadays, the fires result from the flaring of natural gas in the region's oil fields.

The northern half of Isla Grande, resembling the Patagonian steppes, is devoted to sheep grazing, while its southern half is mountainous and partly covered by forests and glaciers. As in Patagonia, winter conditions are rarely extreme, although trekking and outdoor camping are not advisable except for experienced mountaineers. For most visitors, though, the brief daylight hours during this season may be a greater deterrent than the weather.

ECOLOGY & ENVIRONMENT

Argentina's diverse environments have spawned environmental challenges ranging from pollution to deforestation to overgrazing. One highly visible example of an industrial problem includes the contamination of the Río Riachuelo in the Buenos Aires barrio of La Boca.

Thanks to diesel-spewing buses, countless private vehicles and fleets of taxis, the capital's dense traffic has the usual impact on air quality. The frequent rains, however, clear the air with some regularity.

Like other world megacities, Buenos Aires long ago outgrew local energy resources. Despite Argentina's self-sufficiency in petroleum and abundant (if sometimes remote) hydroelectric capacity, the Argentine government has promoted nuclear power since 1950. The 344-megawatt Atucha I reactor, near Buenos Aires, has supplied energy to the capital since 1974, but it operated only at half-capacity through the 1980s because cheaper hydroelectricity made nuclear power less competitive. There is another functioning reactor at Río Tercero, in Córdoba province.

Among the major contemporary issues has been the proposed placement of a nuclear waste dump in the Patagonian province of Chubut, a development that has induced many towns to declare themselves 'non-nuclear municipalities.'

FLORA & FAUNA

Because Argentina is so large and varied, it supports a wide range of flora and fauna.

The country's subtropical rainforests, palm savannas, high-altitude deserts, high-latitude steppes, humid temperate grasslands, alpine and sub-Antarctic forests and coastal areas all support distinctive biota that will be unfamiliar to most visitors, or at least to those from the Northern Hemisphere. To protect these environments, Argentina has created an extensive system of national parks. More detailed descriptions of both the parks and their characteristic species can be found in separate entries in the relevant geographical chapters.

In the high northern Andes, vegetation consists of sparse bunch grasses (ichu) and low, widely spaced shrubs, known collectively as tola. The most conspicuous animal is the domestic llama, but its wild cousins, the guanaco and vicuña, are also present, while migratory birds (including flamingos) inhabit the high saline lakes. In a few favored sites at lower elevations, most notably in Salta and Tucumán provinces, the summertime rains create geographical islands of dense subtropical forest, but wild animals outside of the occasional bird are much more difficult to spot.

In the Chaco, open savannas alternate with nearly impenetrable thorn forests, while Mesopotamian rainfall is sufficient to support swampy lowland forests as well as upland savanna. One of the best areas on the continent to enjoy wildlife is the swampy Esteros del Iberá, in Corrientes province, where animals such as swamp deer, capybara and caiman, along with many large migratory birds, are commonly seen. Misiones' native vegetation is mostly dense subtropical forest, though its upper elevations are studded with araucaria pines.

The once lush native grasses of the Argentine Pampas have suffered under grazing pressure from introduced European livestock and the proliferation of grain farms, so much so that very little native vegetation remains, except along watercourses like the Río Paraná. In less densely settled areas, including the arid Pampas of La Pampa province, guanacos, foxes and even pumas are not unusual sights. Many bodies of water, both permanent and seasonal, provide migratory bird habitats.

Most of Patagonia lies in the rain shadow of the Chilean Andes, so the vast steppes of southeastern Argentina resemble the sparse grasslands of the arid Andean highlands. Closer to the border there are pockets of dense Nothofagus (southern beech) and coniferous woodlands that owe their existence to the winter storms that sneak over the cordillera. Northern Tierra del Fuego is a grassy extension of the Patagonian steppe, but the heavy rainfall of the mountainous southern half supports verdant southern beech forests. As in the farther north, the guanaco is the most conspicuous mammal, but the flightless rhea, resembling the Old World ostrich, runs in flocks across the plains.

More notable in Patagonia and Tierra del Fuego is the wealth of coastal wildlife, ranging from penguins, cormorants and gulls to sea lions, fur seals, elephant seals and whales. Several coastal reserves, from Río Negro province south to Tierra del Fuego, are home to enormous concentrations of wildlife that are one of the region's greatest visitor attractions. Also see the wildlife special section in the Patagonia chapter.

NATIONAL & PROVINCIAL PARKS

Argentina's national parks lure visitors from around the world. One of Latin America's first national park systems, Argentina's dates from the turn of the 20th century, when explorer and surveyor Francisco P Moreno donated 7500 hectares near Bariloche to the state in return for guarantees that the parcel would be preserved for the enjoyment of all Argentines. This area is now part of Parque Nacional Nahuel Huapi in the Andean Lake District.

Since then, the country has established many other parks and reserves, mostly but not exclusively in the Andean region. There are also important provincial parks and reserves, such as Reserva Faunística Península Valdés, that do not fall within the national park system but deserve attention. In general, the national parks are more visitor-oriented than the provincial parks, but there are exceptions: Parque Nacional Perito Moreno has few visitor services, for example, while Península Valdés has many.

Note that some Argentine park personnel, including rangers, can be very cautious and patronizing with respect to activities beyond the most conventional and may sometimes exaggerate the difficulty of hikes and climbs.

Before seeing the national parks, visitors to Buenos Aires should stop at the national parks administration (Administración de Parques Nacionales; ☎ 4312-0783, Santa Fe 690) for maps and brochures, which are often in short supply in the parks themselves; there may be a charge for some of these. The following parks are listed generally north to south, west to east.

Monumento Natural Laguna de los Pozuelos – A large, high-altitude lake in Jujuy province supports abundant bird life, including three species of flamingos, on its 16,000 hectares.

Parque Nacional Baritú – On the Bolivian border in Salta province and accessible by road only through Bolivia, this park contains 72,000 hectares of nearly virgin subtropical montane forest.

Parque Nacional Calilegua – This scenic unit of 76,000 hectares protects a variety of ecosystems, from transitional lowland forest to subtropical montane forest to sub-Alpine grassland.

Parque Nacional Los Cardones – This scenic montane desert park (70,000 hectares) in the highlands west of Salta, protects the striking cardon cactus, which has been used for timber (among other things).

Parque Nacional Finca El Rey – In the eastern part of Salta province, this lush, mountainous park protects 44,000 hectares of subtropical and coniferous Andean forest.

Parque Nacional Río Pilcomayo – On the Paraguayan border is this park protecting 60,000 hectares of subtropical marshlands and palm savannas harboring birds, mammals and reptiles, such as caiman.

Parque Nacional Chaco – In Chaco province, this very accessible but little-visited park offers 15,000 hectares of dense, subtropical thorn forests, marshes and palm savannas, as well as colorful birds.

Parque Nacional Iguazú – On the border with Brazil and Paraguay is this very popular park containing awesome Iguazú Falls. Also preserved are 55,500 hectares of subtropical rain forest, with abundant birds, mammals and reptiles.

Parque Nacional Esteros del Iberá – In Corrientes province on the south side of the Esteros, this tranquil wetland reserve may be a better wildlife site than Brazil's famous Pantanal.

Parque Nacional El Palmar – This 8500-hectare park on the Río Uruguay protects the last extensive stands of *yatay* palm savanna, elsewhere destroyed or threatened by grazing. It's also good for bird watching.

Parque Nacional Talampaya – Among desert landscapes is this 270,000-hectare unit full of rich scenery and extraordinary geological, paleontological and archaeological resources.

Parque Provincial Ischigualasto – Also known as Valle de la Luna (Valley of the Moon), this park is a scenic paleontological preserve between sedimentary ranges of the Cerros Colorados and Cerro Los Rastros.

Parque Nacional Sierra de las Quijadas – In the northwestern corner of San Luis province, the polychrome desert canyons of this scenic 150,000-hectare unit have been the site of major dinosaur discoveries.

Parque Provincial Aconcagua – The highlight here is the Western Hemisphere's highest peak, 6960m Aconcagua, a major destination for mountaineers from around the world.

Parque Provincial Volcán Tupungato – The 6650m summit of Tupungato in Mendoza's second major provincial park is, according to most mountaineers, a more interesting and challenging objective than nearby Aconcagua.

Parque Nacional Lihué Calel – This picturesque 9900-hectare park has pinkish peaks and isolated valleys that support a surprising range of fauna and flora, as well as petroglyphs and some historical buildings.

Parque Nacional Laguna Blanca – Surrounded by ancient volcanoes and lava flows, this lake supports nesting colonies of black-necked swans, Andean flamingos and other distinctive birds.

Parque Nacional Lanín – The snow-covered, symmetrical cone of Volcán Lanín is the centerpiece of this large northern Patagonian park. Equally worthwhile are extensive forests of monkey puzzle trees (*Araucaria*) and southern beech.

Parque Nacional Nahuel Huapi – Lago Nahuel Huapi, an enormous trough carved by Pleistocene glaciers, filled by meltwater and surrounded by impressive peaks, is the focus of this scenic, 758,000-hectare park. Within the park's borders is the small Parque Nacional Los Arrayanes, which protects stands of the unique *arrayán* tree, a member of the myrtle family.

Parque Nacional Lago Puelo – High Andean peaks surround Lago Puelo, an aquamarine, low-altitude lake set along the Chilean border and draining into the Pacific near the town of El Bolsón.

Parque Nacional Los Alerces – This very attractive park protects 263,000 hectares of unique Valdivian forest, which includes impressive specimens of the *alerce* tree, resembling the California redwoods.

Reserva Faunística Península Valdés – A spectacular destination for wildlife enthusiasts. Marine mammals such as whales, sea lions and elephant seals are the main attraction, but there are also Magellanic penguins and the occasional killer whale.

Reserva Provincial Punta Tombo – This provincial reserve south of Trelew in Chubut province has an enormous nesting colony of burrowing Magellanic penguins and other seabirds.

Parque Nacional Perito Moreno – The 115,000 hectares of this park protect a series of awesome glacial lakes, alpine peaks and Andean-Patagonian forest. Wildlife includes herds of guanaco. For real solitude, this park and Monumento Natural Bosques Petrificados are the best bets in the Argentine system.

Monumento Natural Bosques Petrificados – This isolated 10,000-hectare park features immense specimens of petrified *Proaraucaria* trees from a bygone era, when the region contained a dense, humid forest.

Parque Nacional Monte León – In the province of Santa Cruz, a short distance south of the town of Piedrabuena, this newly designated unit is Argentina's first coastal national park outside Tierra del Fuego.

Parque Nacional Los Glaciares – One of Argentina's must-see attractions is the famous Moreno Glacier. The awesome pinnacles of the Fitz Roy Range invite an even longer stay. Southern beech forests cover substantial zones of the 600,000-hectare park.

Parque Nacional Tierra del Fuego – Argentina's first shoreline national park, this unit on the Beagle Channel west of Ushuaia stretches inland to envelop alpine glaciers and peaks within its 63,000 hectares. There are marine mammals, seabirds, shorebirds and extensive southern beech forests.

GOVERNMENT & POLITICS

After the end of military dictatorship in 1983, Argentina returned to the Constitution of 1853, which established a federal system similar to that of the USA. There are separate executive and bicameral legislative branches, an ostensibly independent judiciary and a theoretical balance of power among the three.

In 1994 a constitutional convention amended the document to permit the president's reelection while reducing the term to four years (from the previous six-year single term). It also eliminated the legal requirement that the president be a Roman Catholic, added an additional senator for each province and the city of Buenos Aires and lengthened the legislative year. The next presidential elections are due to take place in late 2003.

The president and the Congreso Nacional (comprising a 257-member Cámara de Diputados and a 72-member Senado) are popularly elected, as are provincial governors and legislatures. In practice, the president is far more powerful than his US counterpart and frequently governs by decree without consulting the Congreso; the president can also, and frequently does, intervene in provincial matters. When the constitutional convention established reelection of the president, it also created the office of Jefe de Gabinete, a sort of executive prime minister responsible to the Congreso.

Administratively, the country consists of a federal district (the city of Buenos Aires proper), plus 23 provinces, the territories of the South Atlantic islands (including the Falklands/Malvinas and South Georgia, under British administration) and the Argentine Antarctic (where territorial claims are on hold by international agreement).

Political Parties

Although personality is often more important than party, the spectrum of Argentine political parties is broad. At least 20 different parties are represented in the Congreso, but the most numerous are the Peronists (Justicialists) of the late Juan Perón, and the Unión Cívica Radical (UCR, misleadingly called the 'Radicals,' despite the fact that they usually represent middle-class interests) of former president Raúl Alfonsín. Though Argentines of all classes normally participate in political discussion, some observers have expressed concern about the apathy among younger voters, who have traditionally formed the activist sector of their parties.

Until the 1940s, when Perón revolutionized Argentine politics by overtly appealing to labor unions and other underrepresented sectors of society, the Radicals vied against parties tied to traditional conservative landowning interests for electoral supremacy. Within the Peronist party, there remain deeply divided factions, which, in the mid-1970s even conducted open warfare against each other. Former *Buenos Aires Herald* editor James Neilson has described the party as a 'promiscuous mixture of fascists, trotskyites, militarists, nationalists, Christian Democrats, socialists, feudalists, liberals, conservatives and infinitely flexible opportunists.'

Currently these divisions are less violent, but there is still friction. On one side are the official neoliberal adherents of former president Menem, who attempted to reduce the state's role in economic matters and limit the influence of militant labor. On the other are leftist and nationalist elements that see Menem's policies as capitulation to foreign institutions such as the World Bank and International Monetary Fund (IMF). Ultranationalist factions within the Justicialist party are not much happier despite their loathing of the left.

Other parties, much less numerous and influential, include the Partido Intransigente (PI, or Intransigent Party), the Democracia Cristiana (Christian Democrats) and the Movimiento para Integración y Desarollo (MID, or Movement for Integration and Development). Former economy minister Domingo Cavallo formed his own Partido Acción para la República (Action for the Republic) after a falling out with Menem. Recently formed parties include former Vice-President Carlos Alvarez' 1994 center-left coalition known as Frente del País Solidario (Frepaso). In 1997 it formed a subparty of the UCR known as Alianza (the Alliance), the party of Fernando de la Rúa, who resigned as president in December 2001.

Local parties and leaders dominate some provinces. In Neuquén, for instance, the Sapag family's Partido Popular Neuquino has been responsible for some of the country's most progressive social policies. In the province of Catamarca, the Saadi family is known for the most egregious corruption – even by Argentine standards – but their links to principals in a highly publicized murder case have dimmed their fortunes.

ECONOMY

Relating the tale of a relative who found an unusable 'treasure' of 10 billion old pesos in the mountains of Córdoba, one of the characters in Osvaldo Soriano's novel *Una Sombra Ya Pronto Serás* remarks that 'a country where finding a fortune is a waste of time isn't a serious country.'

Indeed, Argentina's inability to achieve its potential, despite abundant natural resources and a literate and sophisticated population, has mystified foreign observers for decades. With a per capita GDP of approximately US$8500 (a misleading figure because of the overvalued peso), Argentina is one of Latin America's wealthiest countries. It was also poised at the beginning of the early 20th century to be the economic peer of Australia and Canada. But instead of keeping pace with those countries, Argentina fell behind and its economy rollercoasters through a state of perpetual chaos. The country is currently burdened with a monstrous foreign debt (US$130 billion) unlikely to ever be repaid and high unemployment. The middle class is shrinking and the economy is suffering from a serious three-year slump: 2000 GDP real growth rate was .08%, down from 8% in 1997.

Since colonial times, the Argentine economy has relied on agricultural exports (hides, wool, beef and grains) gleaned from the fertile Pampas. But the richest agricultural lands of the Pampas remained under the control of relatively few individuals. With other rural people relegated to marginal lands or as dependent labor on large estates, Argentina reproduced the classic Latin American pattern of latifundio versus minifundio (large-versus-small land holdings).

Perón encouraged the development of an industrial base supported by state involvement to revive the Argentine economy. Over succeeding decades, however, the state's dominance in the economy outlived its usefulness. Many state enterprises became havens for corruption, including the proliferation of 'ñoquis,' or ghost employees, named after the traditional potato pasta served in Argentine households on the 29th day of each month – the implication is that they appear on the job just before the monthly paychecks are due. Such practices contributed to inflation rates often exceeding 50% per month.

The Peronist Menem administration (1989-99) was able to break the inflationary spiral by reducing public sector employment, selling off inefficient state enterprises and restricting labor union activities. The key measure, however, was economy minister Domingo Cavallo's convertibility law, which pegged the peso at parity with the US dollar; the government could print no more pesos than represented by hard currency reserves.

The selling off of state assets such as Aerolíneas Argentinas, the state petroleum enterprise YPF and the phone company ENTel was a one-time bonanza that reduced or eliminated short-term budget deficits. An unfortunate side effect of this privatization has been increasing unemployment. By late 1997, unemployment was at 13%, but even the government admitted that many of these new jobs were temporary, and sure enough in 2001 the percentage yo-yoed back up to almost 17%.

The crash of the Mexican peso in January 1995 put considerable pressure on the Argentine economy, as has the Asian meltdown of 1998. Add the devaluation of Brazil's currency, the real (which contrasted highly against the overvalued peso), and the rise of the powerful dollar and thus the peso with it, and Argentine exports have become too expensive and not competitive. Some economists believe that breaking the pesos' link to the dollar is what Argentina needs in the long run, despite the likely probability of immediate chaos, high inflation, political instability and loan defaults. Economic minister Domingo Cavallo promised that devaluation was out of the question, but shortly after his resignation in December 2001, Argentina devalued the peso.

The administration needs to maintain a governmental zero-deficit plan to follow guidelines and keep receiving a series of IMF loans, which the country desperately needs to balance its budget and get out of a severe three-year recession. This belt-tightening is hard to accept and the Argentine people are tired of cutting back again and again; many of the smartest are trying to leave the country to find decent work (lines are constant outside the Italian and Spanish embassies).

The largest sector of the economy is service (62%), followed by industry (32%), such as food processing, motor vehicles and consumer durables, and agriculture (6%).

Mercosur

The customs union of Brazil, Argentina, Uruguay and Paraguay, known as 'Mercosur,' is the world's third-largest such union and represents over 225 million people. By establishing a free-trade area, this trading bloc (with Bolivia and Chile as associate members) should theoretically facilitate commerce and reduce prices for imported goods among the member countries. The goal is to essentially have unfettered movement of products, labor, capital and services in the area. At present, however, the policy only requires them to impose a common external tariff on most imported goods, while internal customs barriers remain in place to protect local and national industries.

POPULATION & PEOPLE

Argentina's population of almost 37 million is unevenly distributed throughout the country. About a third reside in

Argentine Jokes

Argentines are some of the proudest folks in South America, and often get made fun of for it. Want to make fun of an Argentine? It's easy. And don't feel too bad about it – they make fun of themselves all the time. Here are some classic jokes:

• How does an Argentine commit suicide?

 He jumps off his ego.

• How do you recognize an Argentine spy?

 From the sign on his back that says, 'I am the greatest spy in the world.'

• A man meets an Argentine on the street and asks him for a light. The Argentine starts patting his pants, chest and seat pockets. 'Sorry,' he says, 'I can't find my lighter – but man, do I have a great body!'

• A psychologist calls his colleague at 2am in the morning. 'It's an emergency!' he says.

 'At two in the morning? It better be good,' says the colleague.

 'I have a unique client,' goes the first. 'It's an inferiority complex!'

 'An inferiority complex? But they're so common!' shouts the colleague.

 And the psychologist responds, 'Yes, but…an Argentine?'

Gran Buenos Aires (Greater Buenos Aires), which includes the Capital Federal and its suburbs in the Buenos Aires province. Other major population centers are Rosario, Córdoba, Tucumán, Mendoza and Bahía Blanca. South of Patagonia's Río Colorado the population is small and dispersed.

From the early 19th century, the Unitarist faction in Argentine politics had followed the dictum of Juan Bautista Alberdi, a native of Tucumán, who argued that 'to govern is to populate.' Unitarists saw Europe as a model for independent Argentina's aspirations and did everything possible to promote European immigration. Alberdi's ideas retain great appeal, surviving especially among geopoliticians who

fantasize about filling the country's vast empty spaces, Patagonia, and even Antarctica, with more Argentines.

Unlike the central Andean countries, which had large, urbanized indigenous populations when Europeans appeared on the scene, the Pampas core of present-day Argentina was sparsely populated by hunting and gathering peoples. Except in the northwest, where early colonization proceeded from Peru and Bolivia, European immigrants displaced relatively small numbers of native peoples. From the mid-19th century on, the trickle of Europeans became a flood, as Italians, Basques, Welsh, English, Ukrainians and immigrants of other nations inundated Buenos Aires. Italian surnames are even more common than Spanish ones, though Italian-Argentines do not constitute a cohesive, distinctive group in the way that Italian-Americans do in many cities in the USA.

Some groups have retained a distinctive cultural identity; these include the Anglo-Argentines throughout the country and the Welsh-Argentines in Chubut province (despite the near eclipse of Welsh as a living language). In some areas there are agricultural settlements with a definable ethnic heritage, for instance, the Germans of Eldorado in Misiones province, the Bulgarians and Yugoslavs of Roque Sáenz Peña in the Chaco and the Ukrainians of La Pampa.

Buenos Aires' Jewish community of almost a half-million people is one of the world's largest outside Israel. The community was the target of attacks in 1992 when the Israeli embassy was bombed, and in July 1994 when a bomb killed 87 people as it leveled the Jewish cultural center. On surrounding streets, one tree has been planted for each victim.

Middle Eastern immigrants, though not numerous, have attained great political influence. The most obvious case is former president Carlos Menem, of Syrian ancestry. The Saadis in Catamarca and the Sapags in Neuquén are other influential political families of Middle Eastern origin, while Colonel Mohammed Alí Seineldín (a fanatical Catholic despite his name) is an imprisoned leader of the army's fascist carapintada movement. Argentines refer indiscriminately to anyone of Middle Eastern ancestry (except Jews or Israelis) as *turco* (Turk), sometimes, though not always, with racist connotations.

Immigrants from Asia are a visible presence in many barrios of Buenos Aires and in the interior. For most Argentines, or visitors to Argentina, contact with these communities is most likely to be in a neighborhood kiosk or mini market, from behind a menu or while shopping for exotic foodstuffs, but their story is as complex as that of European immigrants.

The first Japanese arrived during the heyday of immigration in the late 19th century, establishing themselves as expert dry cleaners, a trade still associated with the community. Others gained recognition as horticulturalists and the Japanese Gardens in Palermo are a fitting memorial.

Since the 1980s, many Japanese in Argentina have repatriated to Japan. Today there are Spanish-speaking sumo wrestlers and even gaucho-style farmers in Japan.

There are estimated to be about 32,000 Koreans in Argentina. New immigrants succeeded in the textile industry and today the barrio of Once is busy with Korean knitting factories, many of which employ fellow immigrants from Bolivia and Peru.

There are around 29,000 Chinese, 60% from Taiwan and the rest from the People's Republic of China and Honk Kong. Living in enclaves, with the older members of the community still speaking Chinese, the population has a low profile in Buenos Aires. February's Chinese New Year celebrations are the only occasion when non-Chinese participate in community life, with the main party kicking off in the miniature China Town around Calle Arribeños beside the Belgrano railway station.

Many Chileans live in Argentine Patagonia, but their usual status as dependent laborers on sheep estancias marginalizes their position in Argentine society. Bolivian highlanders often serve as seasonal laborers *(peones golondrinas,* or swallows) in the sugar harvests of northwestern Argentina; some have moved to Buenos Aires, where they mainly work in construction. Numerous Peruvians, Paraguayans and Uruguayans also reside permanently in Argentina. Since the country's economic slowdown, many Argentines have begun to scapegoat undocumented foreign workers, even though those workers fill economic niches that few Argentines choose to fill themselves.

Estimates of the country's number of indigenous peoples range widely, but the Instituto Nacional de Estadística places a very conservative figure at around 100,000. The largest groups are the Quechua of the northwest and the Mapuche of northern Patagonia, but there are important populations of Guaraní, Tobas and others in the Chaco and in northeastern cities such as Resistencia and Santa Fe.

Argentina, like many South American countries, was involved in the African slave trade. Some worked in the mines of the Viceroyalty of the Río de la Plata, others as soldiers, peons and gauchos of the 19th century. Many scholars have argued that in 1810, blacks made up around 30% of the population of Buenos Aires and there are similar figures for the provincial towns of Tucumán, Córdoba and Mendoza. But by 1887, African-Argentines were just 2% of the population of Buenos Aires. Intermarriage, forced conscription in wars and disease had consumed the country's African population. There is however, a strong African influence in the tango and, especially, in *murga* dancing, which can be seen in the plazas in Buenos Aires. In Montevideo, the African *candombe* dance and music are very popular and a highlight of the city's street culture.

EDUCATION

Argentina's 95% literacy rate is one of Latin America's highest. From the ages of five to 12, education is free and compulsory, though attendance is low in some rural areas. Elite public secondary schools like the Colegio Nacional Buenos Aires, where the teachers are also university instructors, are unequaled by other public or private institutions, although some bilingual schools are very prestigious. Many government officials have graduate degrees from European or US universities. Economy Minister Domingo Cavallo, for instance, is a Harvard PhD.

Universities are traditionally free and open, but once students have chosen a specialization, their course of study is extremely rigid. Ready access to higher education has glutted Buenos Aires with large numbers of professionals, like doctors and lawyers, who are not easily absorbed into the city's economy, but are reluctant to relocate to the provinces. Private universities exist, but public universities in Buenos Aires, Córdoba and La Plata are more prominent.

In addition to university education, there is a tertiary system for the preparation of teachers, who do not need a university degree. Individuals who are not academically oriented can choose vocational training.

Argentina has had three Nobel Prize winners in science: Bernardo Houssay (Medicine, 1947), Luis Federico Leloir (Chemistry, 1970) and César Milstein (Biology, 1984). Two Argentines have won the prize in peace, Carlos Saavedra Lamas (1936) and Adolfo Perez Esquivel (1980). Traditionally, though, many academics have worked overseas because of Argentina's turbulent economy and political scene.

ARTS

Many Argentine intellectuals have been educated in European capitals, particularly Paris. In the 19th and early 20th centuries, Buenos Aires self-consciously emulated French trends in art, music and architecture, and now many Argentine artists have made their mark outside the country's borders.

Music & Dance

Music and dance are difficult to separate in Argentina. The palatial Teatro Colón, home of the Buenos Aires Opera, is one of the finest facilities of its kind in the world. Classical music and ballet, as well as modern dance, appear here and at similar (but much less grand) venues around Buenos Aires and the rest of Argentina.

Tango Probably the best-known manifestation of Argentine popular culture is the tango, both as music and dance, with important figures like the legendary Carlos Gardel, the late Julio Sosa and Astor Piazzolla, and contemporaries such as Susana Rinaldi, Adriana Varela, Eladia Blásquez and Osvaldo Pugliese. Tango is constantly on the radio, tops the bill at the capital's finest nightclubs and is often heard on the streets. Many foreigners go to Buenos Aires to study the famous dance, which is presently making a comeback. For more on the history of tango, see the boxed text 'Tango Anyone?'; for classes, *milongas* and shows, see the Buenos Aires chapter.

Folk The late Atahualpa Yupanqui was a giant of Argentine folk music, which takes much of its inspiration from the northwest Andean region and the countries to the north, especially Bolivia and Peru. Los Chalchaleros are a northern folk institution and they have recently celebrated their 50th anniversary.

Other contemporary performers include Mercedes Sosa of Tucumán (probably the best-known Argentine folk artist outside the South American continent), Suna Rocha (also an actress) of Córdoba, Antonio Tarragó Ross, Leon Gieco (modern enough to adopt and adapt a rap style at times) and the Conjunto Pro Música de Rosario.

Provincial folk music includes *cuarteto*, an evolving dance beat based in Córdoba and popular with all rungs of society despite working-class origins. It's marked by lovelorn lyrics and a constant, underlying 'tunga-tunga' rhythm traditionally shaped by the piano and string bass, with violin and accordion alongside. Carlos Jiménez is the best-known figure in this genre.

Chamamé comes from rural Corrientes, is related to the polka and has been adapted from European, African and Guaraní cultures. The accordion (or *bandoneón)*, guitar and double bass accompany a singer belting out compelling melodies, while dancers move to effervescent and playful melodies.

Zamba is a romantic, graceful dance where couples wave white handkerchiefs at each other in a teasing courtship ritual. The music is both melancholy and zesty, emphasized by almost galloping beats.

Jazz & Blues Internationally, Argentina's best-known jazz musician is probably Rosario-born saxophonist Gato Barbieri, though he rarely performs in the capital. Known best for his Hollywood soundtracks, porteño composer and pianist Lalo Schifrin moved to the US in the 1950s in order to play with jazz legends like Dizzy Gillespie and Eric Dolphy.

There are many jazz venues in Buenos Aires, mostly in the downtown area and San Telmo (see the Buenos Aires chapter).

Porteño blues band Memphis La Blusera, a credible live act, has worked with North American legend Taj Mahal. Las Blacanblus is a female vocal ensemble doing humorous, nearly a-cappella-style versions of blues standards.

Rock & Pop Rock musicians such as Charly García (formerly a member of the pioneering group Sui Generis) and Fito Púez (dismissed by some as excessively commercial) are national icons. García's version of the Argentine national anthem does what Jimi Hendrix did for 'The Star-Spangled Banner,' but it earned him a court appearance for allegedly lacking 'respect for national symbols.'

The band Les Luthiers satirizes the middle class and the military with irreverent songs played on unusual instruments, many of which the band built themselves. Another unusually colorful character is Sandro, a living Argentine clone of the King (Elvis, that is).

Popular Argentine groups playing *rock nacional* include the recently defunct Soda Stereo, hippyish Los Divididos (descendants of an earlier popular group known as Sumo), the unconventional Babasónicos, Patricio Rey y Sus Redonditos de Ricota and Los Ratones Paranóicos, who in 1995 opened for the Rolling Stones' spectacularly successful five-night stand in Buenos Aires. (The Ratones have definitely been influenced by the Stones, and one of their albums was produced by early Stones associate Andrew Loog Oldham.)

Los Fabulosos Cadillacs (winners of a Grammy in 1998 for best alternative Latin rock group) have popularized ska and reggae, as have groups like Los Auténticos Decadentes, Los Pericos and Los Cafres. Almafuerte, descended from the earlier Hermética, is Buenos Aires' leading (but surprisingly literate) heavy metal band; in the same genre are Rata Blanca and Riff. Actitud María Marta is a young but politically conscious rap group whose songs are about the children of the Disappeared and other controversial topics.

Singer Patricia Sosa's closest counterpart in the English-speaking world is Janis Joplin. The band Dos Minutos emulates punk-rock legend the Ramones, who are very popular in Argentina and have played the capital several times.

Literature

Argentina has a long and glorious literary history that dates back to the 19th century *gauchesca* poetry of Estanislao del Campo and José Hernández, author of the classic gaucho poem 'Martín Fierro.' Short story writers also figure in early Argentine literature, including Esteban Echeverría's 'The Slaughterhouse,' a protest against the Rosas dictatorship and considered the first Latin American short story.

Despite its rich history, Argentine writing only reached an international audience during the Latin American literary boom of the 1960s and '70s, when the stories of Jorge Luis Borges, Luisa Valenzuela, Julio Cortázar, Adolfo Bioy Casares and Silvina Ocampo, among many others, were widely translated for the first time.

The two writers most responsible for creating international interest in Argentine literature are Jorge Luis Borges (1899-1986) and Julio Cortázar (1914-1984). Their recognition as great Argentine writers is somewhat ironic, since neither considered themselves to be strictly part of an Argentine national literary tradition. Instead, both were more interested in universal themes and European culture, and European writers and philosophers heavily influenced their writing.

As a part-Jewish, part-English Argentine who was educated in Europe, Borges was influenced by everything from Jewish Cabalists to *The Arabian Nights* to HG Wells, Cervantes, Kafka and George Berkeley. Borges' dry ironic wit (he described the British-Argentine Falkland Islands war as 'two bald men fighting over a comb') suits his stories well. His tight, precise, paradoxical *ficciones* are part essay and part story, blurring the line between myth and truth and underscoring the idea that reality is only a matter of perception and that an infinite number of realities can exist simultaneously. His early stories like 'Death and the Compass' and 'Streetcorner Man' offer a metaphysical twist on Argentine themes, and his later works, such as 'The Lottery in Babylon,' 'The Circular Ruins' and 'Garden of the Forking Paths,' are works of fantasy. His short story collections published in English include *Labyrinths, The Aleph, A Universal History of Iniquity* and the recently compiled *Collected Fictions,* a complete collection of his stories.

Like Borges, Cortázar was a European-influenced Argentine. He was born in Belgium, discovered by Borges in the 1940s and died a French citizen in 1984. Despite being discovered and influenced by Borges, Cortázar's writing is quite different from Borges' 'coolly cerebral' ficciones. Cortázar's short stories and novels are more anthropological than Borges's stories. They often concern people living seemingly normal, almost mundane lives in a world where the surreal becomes commonplace, giving Cortázar the opportunity to address the idea of the absurd and

farce in modern life. Cortázar's most famous book is *Hopscotch,* a novel influenced by Borges' 'The Garden of the Forking Paths.' *Hopscotch* takes place simultaneously in Buenos Aires and Paris and requires the reader to first read the book straight through, then read it a second time, 'hopscotching' through the chapters in a prescribed but nonlinear pattern for a completely different take on the story. Cortázar short stories such as 'End of the Game' and 'Blow Up' (which Michelangelo Antonioni adapted to film in 1966) are compiled in the collection *End of the Game and Other Stories.*

Ernesto Sábato (1911-), a nuclear physicist turned writer, was greatly influenced by Borges and even cast him as a character in *On Heroes and Tombs.* This 1961 novel is a psychological exploration of people and places in Buenos Aires and has remained a cult favorite among Argentine youth. Other Sábato classics include *The Tunnel* (1950), an engrossing novella of a porteño painter so obsessed with his art that it distorts his relationship to everything and everyone else.

Since the 1970s a post-boom generation of Argentine writers has appeared on the scene. Moving away from the fantasy and complicated narrative style of the boom writers, post-boom writers are more reality-based, often reflecting the influence of popular culture and directly confronting the political realities of the authoritarian Argentina of the 1970s.

One of the most famous post-boom Argentine writers is Manuel Puig, who studied film in Italy and took up screenwriting before beginning his career as a short story writer and novelist. In the Argentine tradition, Puig did much of his writing in exile, fleeing Argentina during the Perón

Jorge Luis Borges

years and ultimately settling in Mexico. The influence of his life as a screenwriter comes through in Puig's stories, where he dispenses with narration and lets his characters tell their own stories. Puig's most famous story, 'Kiss of the Spider Woman' (which was made into a film in 1984), tells the story of two prisoners, a middle-aged gay man and a young revolutionary, who explore ideas of sexuality and suffering while acting out scenes from old movies. In addition, his novels *Betrayed by Rita Hayworth* and *Heartbreak Tango* have been translated into English.

Another popular post-boom writer is Luisa Valenzuela, who began her career as a journalist. Her novels, such as *Black Novel, The Lizard's Tail, Bedside Manners* and *Open Door,* often combine the humorous with the grotesque, in a real world setting.

The youngster of the post-boom generation is Rodrigo Fresan, whose novel *The History of Argentina* was a bestseller. His short stories appear in several anthologies of Argentine literature. Fresan's stories often deal with the uncertainty of life in modern Argentina.

Adolfo Bioy Casares' (1914-1999) hallucinatory novella *The Invention of Morel* (1985) deals with an inability or unwillingness to distinguish between fantasy and reality; it was a partial inspiration for the highly praised film *Man Facing Southeast.* His *Diary of the War of the Pig* (1972), set in Buenos Aires, is also available in translation.

The late Osvaldo Soriano (1943-1997), perhaps Argentina's most popular contemporary novelist, wrote *A Funny Dirty Little War,* later adapted into a film, and *Winter Quarters* (1989). In Soriano's *Shadows* (1993), the protagonist is lost in an Argentina where the names are the same, but all the familiar landmarks and points of reference have lost their meaning.

The most notorious Argentine fiction of recent years is Federico Andahazi's (1963-) sexually explicit but unquestionably literary *The Anatomist* (1998), which caused an uproar when the wealthy sponsor of a national literary prize tried to overturn the award her committee had given the author.

Horacio Quiroga's regionally based stories transcend both time and place without abandoning their setting. Some of his short fiction is available in English translation in *The Exiles and Other Stories.*

Doris Meyer's biography *Victoria Ocampo: Against the Wind and the Tide* (1990) is one of the few opportunities that English readers will have to read Ocampo's essays. Ocampo, like many female Argentine writers, have appeared less frequently in English translation than their male counterparts. Borges edited many issues of Ocampo's literary magazine *Sur,* which was a beacon for Spanish-language writers in the first half of the 20th century and also proved influential among writers in other languages, including members of England's Bloomsbury group.

Architecture

Argentina lacks the great pre-Columbian monuments of Peru and Bolivia, though a few significant archaeological sites dot the Andean Northwest. This region has notable if not abundant Spanish colonial architecture in cities such as Salta and Tucumán, and in villages in isolated areas like the Quebrada de Humahuaca. Other areas for colonial architecture, or at least atmosphere, include Córdoba and Carmen de Patagones. The city of Buenos Aires itself has scattered colonial examples, but is essentially a turn-of-the-century city whose architectural influences are predominantly French. Recent architecture tends to the pharaonic and impersonal, with a substantial number of modernistic buildings in the downtown area.

Architects in the Andean Lake District of northern Patagonia have adapted Middle European styles into appealing urban landscapes. Southern Patagonia, while not famous for its architecture, has an intriguing and unique Magellanic style of wooden houses with metal cladding, also present in southern Chile.

Catholicism, however, has provided Argentina with some of its finest monuments, from the modest but picturesque churches of the Andean Northwest to the

Jesuit missions of Mesopotamia, the colonial cathedral in Córdoba and the neo-Gothic basilicas of Luján and La Plata.

Painting

Like much of Argentine culture, the visual arts express a mixture of European derivations and criollo originality. The European influence has been so powerful that porteño art critic Jorge Glusberg argued that the 'colonial period' in Argentine art lasted into the mid-20th century, severed only by the outbreak of WWII. Nevertheless, there exists a thriving alternative and unconventional art scene, though many of the most innovative artists must go abroad – usually to Europe or North America – to make a living.

Early Argentine painting can pride itself on figures like self-taught Cándido López (1840-1902), a 19th-century military officer who lost his right hand in the war against Paraguay but rehabilitated himself well enough to paint more than 50 extraordinary oils on the conflict.

Many Argentine artists who studied in France or Italy produced work with demonstrably European themes, but some local manifestations of their work are memorable, such as the restored ceiling murals of Antonio Berni, Lino Spilimbergo and others in Buenos Aires' Galerías Pacífico shopping center. The late Benito Quinquela Martín, who put the working-class barrio of La Boca on the artistic map, painted brightly colored oils of life in the factories and on the waterfront.

Contemporary painting has eschewed the romantic without abandoning its regard for the countryside. Tucumán-born Víctor Hugo Quiroga's paintings, for instance, deal with provincial rather than porteño themes, but they successfully reflect the impact of modern global developments on criollo life. Porteño painter Guillermo Kuitca makes an imaginative use of cartographic images by integrating Germanic themes. Graciela Sacco is a multimedia artist who incorporates audio and video narratives into her arrangements of ready-made objects like plastic spoons and bar codes. And Xul

Solar, a multitalented phenomenon who was a good friend of Jorge Luis Borges, painted busy, Klee-inspired dreamscapes.

Contemporary Argentine art has gained recognition in international markets: Berni's 1954 painting *Juanito Laguna Bañándose entre Latas* (Juanito Laguna Washing Amongst the Trash), a protest against social and economic inequality, sold in New York for US$150,000 in 1997. Another Berni work, *Emigrantes,* sold for US$500,000 in 1996.

For a brief survey of modern Argentine art in English, look for Glusberg's *Art in Argentina* (Milan, Giancarlo Politi Editore, 1986). Readers who understand Spanish can try Rafael Squirru's *Arte Argentino Hoy* (Buenos Aires, Ediciones de Arte Gaglianone, 1983), a selection of work from 48 contemporary painters and sculptors illustrated in color.

Buenos Aires has a multitude of art galleries, most of which are very conventional but some of which deal with audacious modern art. For a brief listing, see the Shopping section in the Buenos Aires chapter.

Visitors should not overlook the often anonymous folk art in the streets – even political graffiti can be remarkably elaborate and eloquent. Of particular interest is *filete,* the ornamental line painting that once graced the capital's horsecarts, trucks and buses.

Sculpture

Given its French origins, official public art tends toward hero worship and the pompously monumental, expressed through prominent equestrian statues of military figures such as José de San Martín, Justo José Urquiza and Julio Argentino Roca. A welcome exception is the work of the late Rogelio Yrurtia, some of whose works deal sympathetically with the struggles and achievements of working people (such as his *Canto al Trabajo* in Plaza Eva Perón in San Telmo).

An even stronger counterpoint to Argentina's penchant for idols are modern works by individuals like sculptor Alberto Heredia, whose pieces ridicule the solemnity of official public art and have inspired political controversy. Heredia's powerful and controversial statue *El Caballero de la Máscara* depicts a 19th-century caudillo as a headless horseman; during the military dictatorship of 1976-83, the sculpture could not be exhibited under its original title *El Montonero,* which implied associations with guerrilla forces that had nothing to do with the artist's theme.

Another overtly political sculptor is Juan Carlos Distéfano, who used rich, textural surfaces of polyester, glass fiber and resins to achieve colorful surfaces on his sometimes disturbing themes. For comic relief, the surrealistic junk sculptures of Yoël Novoa appeal to audiences of almost any age or political persuasion.

If you're a sculpture buff and traveling around the northeastern reaches of the country, stop in Resistencia, which is well-known for its large number of public works.

Cinema

Despite the limited resources available to directors, Argentine cinema has achieved international stature, especially since the end of the military dictatorship of 1976-83. Many Argentine films, both before and after the Dirty War, are available on video.

María Luisa Bemberg, perhaps Argentina's best-known contemporary director, died in 1995. Her historically based films often illuminate the Argentine experience, particularly the relationship between women and the church. *Camila* recounts the tale of Catholic socialite Camila O'Gorman, who fell in love and ran away from Buenos Aires with a young Jesuit priest in 1847, before the repressive government of Rosas found and executed them both. (The film was nominated in 1984 for an Oscar in the best foreign language film category.)

Bemberg's English-language film *Miss Mary* (1986), starring Julie Christie, focuses on the experience of an English governess in Argentina. Her last directorial effort, *I Don't Want to Talk About It* (1992), is a bizarre love story starring Marcelo Mastroianni. Filmed in Colonia, Uruguay, across the river from Buenos Aires, it metaphorically explores issues of power and control in a provincial town.

Director Luis Puenzo's *The Official Story* (1985) deals with a controversial theme of the Dirty War – the adoption of the children of missing or murdered parents by those responsible for their disappearance or death. It stars Norma Leandro, a popular stage actress who has also worked in English-language films in the US. Some critics, however, rebuked Puenzo for apparently implying that Argentines were innocently ignorant of the flagrant atrocities of the time. The film won an Oscar for best foreign language film.

Eliseo Subiela's *Man Facing Southeast* (1986) takes part of its inspiration from Adolfo Bioy Casares' ingenious novella *The Invention of Morel*. Uruguayan poet Mario Benedetti has a cameo in Subiela's compelling *The Dark Side of the Heart* (1992), set in Buenos Aires and Montevideo. It's a daring love story with a surprise ending.

Héctor Babenco directed the English-language *Kiss of the Spider Woman* (1985), starring William Hurt and the late Raúl Julia. Based on Manuel Puig's novel, this tale portrays the intricate way in which the police and military abused political prisoners and exploited informers.

Director Fernando 'Pino' Solanas politicized the tango in *Tangos – The Exile of Gardel* (1985), dealing with the disrupted lives of a group of displaced Argentines during the Dirty War. The film's Parisian setting was ironically apropos for Francophile Argentina. (Solanas lived in exile in Paris following the military coup in 1976.) The late tango legend Astor Piazzola composed the soundtrack and appears in the film.

Marcelo Piñeyro's *Wild Horses* (1995) is, despite the director's denials, a road movie that starts with a curious Robin Hood-style bank robbery in Buenos Aires and ends with a chase in the province of Chubut.

Héctor Olivera's *The Night of the Pencils* (1986) retells the notorious case of half a dozen La Plata high school students abducted, tortured and killed by the military during the Dirty War. Olivera also adapted Osvaldo Soriano's satirical novels to the big screen in *A Funny Dirty Little War* (1983) and *Una Sombra Ya Pronto Serás* (1994). Despite its title, the former has almost nothing to do with the horrors of the military dictatorship, except perhaps indirectly.

Manuel Antín's *Don Segundo Sombra* (1969), based on Ricardo Güiraldes' gauchesco novel, is a coming-of-age on the Pampas film, set in the village of San Antonio de Areco. Antín's 1980 film *Long Ago and Far Away* mines similar material from William Henry Hudson's writings about his youth in Buenos Aires province.

Filmed around the scenic city of Tandil, in Buenos Aires province, Luis César D'Angiolillo's *Killing Grandpa* (1991) is a family drama with touches of humor and magical realism, starring veteran stage and screen actor Federico Luppi. Luppi appears in Adolfo Aristarain's *A Place in the World,* which was disqualified from the best foreign language film category at the 1992 Academy Awards since it was submitted by Uruguay, but produced mainly in Argentina; the film has drawn comparisons to the classic Hollywood Western *Shane.* Luppi also plays the lead in Mexican director's Guillermo del Toro's *Cronos* (1992), an offbeat science-fiction gangster film, and in US director John Sayles' Spanish-language *Men with Guns* (1997), an allegorical exploration of political violence in Latin America.

Although not a filmmaker himself, porteño composer Lalo Schifrin wrote much of the music for which Hollywood is best known, including themes and soundtracks for *Mission Impossible, Bullitt, Cool Hand Luke* and *Dirty Harry,* among many others.

Theater

Buenos Aires has a vigorous theater community, equivalent in its own way to New York, London or Paris, but even in the provinces, live theater is an important medium of expression. Legendary Argentine performers include Luis Sandrini and Lola Membrives, and famous European writers like Federico García Lorca and Jean Cocteau have explored the Buenos Aires theater scene. Probably Argentina's most famous contemporary playwright is Juan Carlos Gené, a former director of the Teatro General San Martín.

The theater season is liveliest from June through August, but there are always performances on the docket. Av Corrientes is the capital's Broadway or West End, but large and small theater companies (some quite unconventional) and venues dot the city. Many of the capital's most popular (and vulgar) shows move to the provincial beach resort of Mar del Plata for the summer.

Unlike stage actors in some countries, those in Argentina seem to move seamlessly among stage, film and television. Perhaps performers like Norma Leandro, Federico Luppi and China Zorrilla feel less self-conscious about moving among the various media, since the Argentine public is smaller and work opportunities fewer than in London, New York or Los Angeles. Some 150 Argentine plays have passed from the theater to film since the silent era.

SOCIETY & CONDUCT

Travelers of European ancestry stick out less in Argentina than in most other South American countries with large indigenous populations. Black and Asian travelers, however, will attract more attention, although this is less of an issue in Buenos Aires.

Argentines as a whole are gregarious and, once you make contact, much likelier to invite you to participate in their daily activities than, say, a Quechua llama herder in Bolivia. One of these activities, which you should give a shot, is the opportunity to drink *mate.* It's an acquired taste for sure, and an important ritual for many people from the Río de la Plata region, especially Uruguay. Another cultural tradition you won't want to miss is the *asado,* the famous Argentine barbecue. If you're not invited to one don't panic; just amble on into one of Argentina's many *parrillas* for a taste of the Pampas (see the boxed text 'Here's the Beef' in the Facts for the Visitor chapter).

Argentine Gestures

If you're at all a people watcher, you'll notice at least one thing about the people of Argentina: In conversations, these folks use their hands *a lot*. Gestures are a major way of communicating certain, uh, emotions. There are dozens of different gestures, so try to pick up on a few of them and figure out their meanings. Just remember that gestures may mean something innocuous in one culture while being very offensive in another. Also some gestures might not be widely understood in the north of the country.

Here are three common Argentine gestures that you may come across during your interactions with the locals:

1. Cup your hands as if you are holding two small melons. Then move your hands up and down as if you're weighing the melons. Meaning: *Pesado*, an emotionally heavy situation or difficult person, a 'pain.'
2. Brush the tips of the fingers of one hand outward, under the jaw and chin, with the palm of the hand toward the neck. This is often done once or twice. Meaning: I don't know; I don't care; who knows? This is a very insulting gesture in Italy, but in Argentina its meaning is more like the American shrug.
3. Bunch the fingertips of one hand together, pointing up. Move your hand up and down a few times. Meaning: What do you expect (exasperated)? What the hell do you mean? Can be used in an irritated manner or when joking with friends. Sometimes this gesture is combined with an index finger placed near the temple and twisted. Then it means, '*¿Estas loco?*' (Are you crazy?).

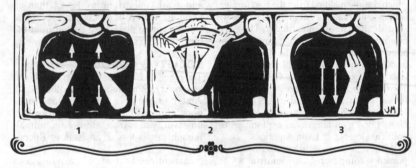

Argentines are more physically demonstrative than you might be used to, always exchanging kisses on the cheek in greeting – even among men. If you are introduced by a friend to someone you've never met, you'll be expected to kiss them on the cheek. In fact, if you hang out in Argentina long enough you may find yourself kissing complete strangers after a brief, serendipitous bonding experience. In formal situations, though, it is better to go with a handshake.

If you start chatting with the locals (many porteños can understand some English), be prepared to answer personal questions on marriage and children and more topical questions like life in your country of origin and how bad the economy is in Argentina. Sports, but especially soccer, is a good topic to get Argentines passionately riled up about; just ask them if they are for River (pronounced 'Reever') or for Boca, and why. (River Plate and Boca Juniors are arch enemies, and sometimes so are their fans.)

Dos & Don'ts

Remember to preface any request with the appropriate salutation – *buenos días* (good morning), *buenas tardes* (good afternoon) or *buenas noches* (good evening) – and use the formal *usted* unless you are certain that informality is appropriate.

When dealing with bureaucratic Argentine officialdom, try to be polite no matter how illogical or irritating the situation becomes. Showing respect goes a long way towards getting what you want; think of it as a game (and if you get angry you lose).

In Buenos Aires, porteños dress casually for most recreational activities, though informal dress is usually inappropriate for business, fancy restaurants, casinos and events like the symphony or opera. Be aware that some places that are informal by day may become very formal at night. If you come in winter, bring your fur coat; there's no danger of being splashed with red paint in Buenos Aires.

Some sensitive subjects you may want to avoid in conversation with Argentines (at least until you get to know them better) are the Dirty War and the Falklands (call them Las Islas Malvinas).

RELIGION

Roman Catholicism is the official state religion, though only a small percentage of Argentines attend mass regularly. Even so, you'll notice many signs of deep faith, such as Argentines crossing themselves when passing a church (while walking or riding by on a bus, for example). Up until fairly recently, the president of Argentina had to be Catholic.

Some popular beliefs have diverged from official Catholic doctrine, one of the best examples being the cult of the Difunta Correa. Based outside Buenos Aires in San Juan province, hundreds of thousands of professed Catholics make annual pilgrimages and offerings, despite the Church hierarchy's aggressive campaign against the Difunta Correa's veneration. (Luján is a more accepted religious destination and popular day trip from the capital, especially on weekends.)

Evangelical Protestantism is making inroads among traditionally Catholic believers – especially among the working class. Argentina has its share of Jehovah's Witnesses, Mormons and Hare Krishnas.

Spiritualism and veneration of the dead also have remarkable importance in Argentina. Novelist Tomás Eloy Martínez observed that Argentines honor national heroes like San Martín not on their birthday, but on the anniversary of their death. As the author's porteño godfather once said, 'When they're born, they're not famous!' Visitors to Buenos Aires' Recoleta and Chacarita cemeteries – vital sights for comprehending Argentine religious culture – will see steady processions of pilgrims going to the resting places of icons like Juan and Eva Perón, psychic Madre María and tango singer Carlos Gardel. Followers come to communicate and ask favors by laying their hands on the tombs and leaving arcane offerings (see the boxed text 'Life & Death in Recoleta & Chacarita' in the Buenos Aires chapter).

Like other Argentine institutions, the Catholic Church has many factions. During the late 1970s and early 1980s, the Church generally supported the de facto military government despite persecution, kidnapping, torture and murder of religious workers. These workers, adherents of the 'Liberation Theology' movement, often worked among the poor and dispossessed in both rural areas and the *villas miserias* (shantytowns) of Buenos Aires and other large cities. Such activism has resumed in today's more permissive political climate, but the Church hierarchy remains obstinate: The late Archbishop Antonio Quarracino of Buenos Aires, for example, defended former President Menem's pardon of the convicted murderers and torturers of the Proceso, and it appears that official chaplains acquiesced in Dirty War atrocities by counseling the perpetrators.

LANGUAGE

After flamboyance, the Italian-accented Argentine Spanish, called *castellano,* readily identifies an Argentine anywhere in the world. Though it's the official language and spoken throughout the country, some immigrant communities have retained their languages as a badge of identity. In central Patagonia, for instance, there are pockets of

Welsh speakers, but despite a recent revival the language is in danger of disappearing. Welsh cultural traditions remain strong in these regions, however, even catering to the tourist industry.

English is studied, spoken and understood by many Argentines (especially in the capital). Italian is the language of the largest immigrant group and also understood by some, as is French. German speakers are numerous enough to support a weekly porteño newspaper, *Argentinisches Tageblatt*.

Argentina has over a dozen native tongues, though some are spoken by very few individuals. In the Andean Northwest, Quechua speakers are numerous; most are also Spanish speakers. In the southern Andes, there are at least 40,000 Mapuche speakers. In northeastern Argentina, there are about 15,000 each of Guaraní and Toba speakers.

For useful words and phrases in Argentine Spanish, see the Language and Glossary chapters.

Facts for the Visitor

HIGHLIGHTS

Come to Argentina and take it all in: expansive scenery, exotic wildlife, exhilarating activities, rowdy (or relaxing) beaches and of course, cities thrumming with Latin American heartbeats with European accents. There's something for just about everyone, and something that will always surprise you, so pack your bags and get ready for some adventurous travel.

Cosmopolitan Buenos Aires Catch the hopping porteño scene in between the sultry tango and some truly comforting steaks. Goggle at beautiful old architecture and visit the unique neighborhoods that make this city a stunner. When you tire of the urban life, hop to the nearby waterways of the lush Río Paraná delta.

Madly Rushing Waters Turn an ear towards the thunderous roar at the spectacular Iguazú Falls, probably South America's most breathtaking sight. Surround yourself in toucan-filled jungles, and see the cascades flow with incredible beauty, stretching in tiered curtains of amazing power. You will be in awe.

Jesuit Ruins & Colonial Cities For glimpses into the past, visit the 17th-century Jesuit missions of Northeast Argentina, especially San Ignacio Miní. In the Andean Northwest, Salta is gracious and grand and retains exceptional examples of colonial architecture. Córdoba, in the Central Sierras, also boasts a well-preserved historic center of 17th-century Jesuit architecture and 19th-century neo-classical buildings.

Flat, Fertile & Feisty Pampas Grasp the mystique of the *gaucho* in his birthplace and stomping grounds: the Pampas. This prairie region is still full of tasty, grass-fed cows. Head around to the Atlantic shoreline with sunscreen in hand, and be prepared to summer it up at the boisterous beach resorts that attract fun-and-sun-seeking urbanites.

Wine & Altitude Sample the country's best grape products while wandering around pretty Mendoza. When you're on your feet again, seek out surrounding recreational activities like hiking, biking and whitewater rafting. Or, take a deep breath and climb the highest peak outside Asia – Cerro Aconcagua!

Nature, Nature, Nature Argentina's landscape is diverse, to say the least. In the Andean northwest scenic canyons, colorful mountains and cactus-dotted landscapes dominate. At a lower, more humid altitude, the swampy Argentine Mesopotamia in the northeast is largely undervisited but wildly beautiful.

Soaring volcanoes, shimmering lakes, sprawling forests and trout-rich rivers make the Lake District of the Andean slopes a recreational paradise.

Glimpse whales, elephant seals, rheas, guanacos and other critters in the deserts or along the shores of Península Valdés, a popular wildlife reserve on the Patagonian coast.

Power up the stupendous Fitz Roy Range in southern Patagonia – unique sights of jagged peaks and mushroom-caps of snow *if* you catch a clear day. Nearby in Parque Nacional Los Glaciares, the Moreno Glacier is an extremely dynamic hunk of ice with huge slivers sheering off and splashing into the water below, cracking thunderously along the way. You've never seen anything quite like it before, and so close up.

The Tip of the World Ushuaia, in Tierra del Fuego, is the city at the end of the road at the tip of the world. It is surrounded by some of the grandest scenery anywhere. What more is there to say?

SUGGESTED ITINERARIES

Argentina is such a huge country (the world's eighth largest) that your destinations and transport options will be determined by your available time and wallet thickness. Essentially, since most interesting places are so far apart, if you want to see more than just a few highlights in a few weeks, you should count on flying almost everywhere. There are relatively inexpensive flight coupons you can buy at travel agencies outside Argentina to make this more affordable; see the Getting Around chapter for more details.

Note very carefully that the itineraries listed below allow for the absolute minimum time you'll need to view the sights mentioned and don't take into account the very real possibilities of flight delays and other things that can go wrong. It's a good

What Sucks about Traveling in Argentina

OK. Argentina rocks, but the authors came across some things they could have lived without.

Restaurants
- ordering 'steak' on the menu and forgetting that 'steak' is a lonely chunk of meat; vegetables are a separate dish entirely
- ordering a plate of what you thought was cheap pasta, only to find out the sauce costs extra
- forgetting *again* about the extra US$2 or so per person charge for *cubierto*, the 'use' of utensils and bread

Bus Travel
- convincing entrepreneurial baggage handlers at bus stations that lifting your bag from the bus to the ground is worth much less than 5 pesos
- in Patagonia, on the RN3, having to take buses at ungodly hours of the morning so as to arrive in Buenos Aires at a civilized hour; and then having to endure loud rock music and videos en route
- needing to get out of this boring, depressing city *right now* but discovering at the bus station that you missed the only bus out that day by an hour
- having a sudden attack of the runs in the middle of a six-hour bus ride, and remembering that the snippy bus attendant *specifically* said to everyone that the toilet could only handle urine
- riding a bus through countryside you're dying to see only to have everyone close the curtains to block out the sun

Money
- not having enough small change to buy an *alfajor* (candy bar) or not finding anyone willing to give change for a one peso bill so you can take a bus
- not being able to get rid of your US$100 bill because it has been written on in ink, spelling unacceptability from almost any Argentine merchant

Hotels
- soaking the entire bathroom, including the only roll of toilet paper, because the showers aren't separated by a curtain from the rest of the bathroom
- thinking you found a bargain hotel, only to learn the price is by the hour

And Other Stuff
- driving three hours to a penguin colony outside Ushuaia only to find that the penguins have already left
- wishing someone would have warned you about the severity of hangovers produced by Fernet Branca, a potent Argentine favorite that's actually from Italy
- walking down the sidewalk and suddenly tromping on a nice, ripe pile of dog shit – one of many that dot practically every sidewalk

idea to be as flexible as possible, and willing to skip one destination so you can see another more in depth. You're on vacation, after all; relax and enjoy it!

One Week

Your introduction to Argentina will most likely be Buenos Aires, and that's great. You'll need at least three days to take in the city's major sites, after which you can book a flight to see Iguazú Falls for another two. Add two more days for a flight to the Moreno Glacier in Patagonia, and there goes your week. Poof.

Two Weeks

So you've seen the sights mentioned above. Now add Península Valdés for a couple days; the coastal wildlife will contrast nicely with the other spots. The Lake District is a key destination good for another two days at minimum. And while you're seeing the Moreno Glacier, be *sure* to visit Chile's spectacular Parque Nacional Torres del Paine, which is relatively close by. If you like to hike, you'll truly wish you had more than a couple days here.

We're still talking about flying exhaustively everywhere, you understand.

Three to Four Weeks

OK, now we're catching our breath. If you have this much time, you can add Ushuaia to the list above (if the thought of being at the end of the world appeals to you, and it should). Luckily, Argentina's southernmost city is picturesquely located and has some good surrounding sights, such as the hikes around glacier Martial and Parque Nacional Tierra del Fuego. Also consider seeing more of the Chilean Patagonia, or doing some world-class hiking in El Chaltén (near Mount Fitz Roy) or just spending more time in any previous place that sparked your fancy. Any of these options could easily fill up your three weeks.

Another idea would be to skip the tip of the southern cone and see a bit of the Argentine north, such as the wine city of Mendoza, where you can also partake in some outdoor pursuits. Add Córdoba, Argentina's second largest city, and perhaps another quick flight to Salta (a colonial treasure) and you've gotten a good taste of the country.

Two to Three Months

This much time will give you a better idea of Argentina as a whole. Do all of the above, perhaps with a couple bus rides thrown in for a sense of travel and scenery. (Patagonian scenery tends to be pretty bleak except for the Andes, so you don't need to bus around down there too much.) Stop in a town that appeals to you for a sense of the community. Go off the beaten track a bit; it's not too hard, and even around major destinations like Bariloche or Puerto Madryn you can find isolated pockets to explore. If you decide to spend more time in Buenos Aires, take some tango or Spanish lessons.

For a three-month stay, you can exhaust your 90-day visa and pretty much see the whole country in some depth. And you can do it on buses, which often (but surprisingly, not always) save you money. Your biggest concern at this point is not how much to see ('cause you'll see plenty) but how little to spend. Budget yourself carefully, because Argentina isn't cheap as long as the peso is still pegged to the US dollar.

PLANNING
When to Go

Argentina's seasons are reversed from the Northern Hemisphere's. For Buenos Aires, spring (September through November) and fall (March through May) are best temperature-wise. The December, January and February summer months are unpleasantly hot and humid, and during this time many porteños head for the coastal resorts; consequently, some museums and entertainment venues close down in the capital.

If you plan on seeing Patagonia, do go in summer (the weather's milder and more services are available). Up north, however, try to *avoid* summer (when you'll be baking in the desert or in tropical heat). If you like to ski, you'll want to hit the Andean resorts during winter, obviously.

Seasons South of the Equator

Aussies and Kiwis should know this already. To the 'top-side' readers, just think of it: You're on the 'bottom' side of the globe. There are handier things to figure out than if the water swirls down clockwise or counter-clockwise in the sink. (This you can test out when you're actually down there. We're not saying.) Most importantly, you should know the seasons in the Southern Hemisphere:

- Winter: June, July, August
- Spring: September, October, November
- Summer: December, January, February
- Fall: March, April, May

The most expensive times to travel are the Argentine vacation months of January, February and July; Easter week and holiday weekends are also choice travel dates for locals (try to book accommodations and transportation ahead of time).

Maps

Tourist offices throughout the country will give you free city maps that are good enough for the average traveler. (But the maps in this book are better, just so you realize.)

The Automóvil Club Argentino (ACA), at Av del Libertador 1850 in Buenos Aires, publishes regularly updated maps of cities and provinces. Members of foreign automobile clubs can purchase them at discount prices; bring your card and expect to pay around US$5 each. In most major cities, ACA has a service center that sells these maps, though not every center stocks them all.

If you're a member of the American Automobile Association (AAA), get the South American road map, which is good for initial planning, but not for on-the-road use. International Travel Maps (ITMB Publishing, 530 West Broadway, Vancouver BC, Canada V5Z 4A5, w www.itmb.com) has a *South America* map, also handy for reference. The Buenos Aires and Argentina maps are fairly good.

Geography nerds will adore the topographic maps available at the Instituto Geográfico Militar, open 8am to 1pm weekdays, at Cabildo 381 in Palermo (Subte: Ministro Carranza, or bus No 152). These maps are difficult to obtain outside the capital.

For easy-to-read convenience, get Lonely Planet's *Buenos Aires* city map, a laminated fold-out map that will have you negotiating the streets of the capital in no time. Major landmarks are listed.

What to Bring

There's nothing like being able to tote your necessities for a few weeks in a carry-on bag; inside, just two or three interchangeable outfits, one pair of shoes (you're wearing the other) and a few personal items.

If you forget something, you'll probably be able to buy it in Argentina. Most toiletries and over-the-counter medicines will be widely available, though name-brand products (especially foreign-made) are more expensive. Quality feminine hygiene and contact lens solutions are also available at reasonable prices. Every hotel, except for the cheapest dive, will offer clean sheets, towels and soap. You'll often have to provide these items for yourself at hostels, though most provide sheets. Expect those little shampoo and lotion bottles only at the most expensive hotels.

Bring good, comfortable walking shoes and perhaps a pair of sandals for hot weather. Zip-lock bags are handy to separate little stuff from big stuff, and wet stuff from dry stuff; always pack lotions and liquids in plastic bags, as they often leak (especially on airplane trips). A Swiss Army knife, packaged hand wipes and earplugs should be in every traveler's kit. Consider getting a thin cable and lock to secure your pack to a bus rack while you nap, or to the bed frame while you're outside your hotel room. Also bring a daypack for walking around town.

Extra passport-size photos are good in case you decide to travel to other countries and need to get a visa. Your hostel or student ID card can come in handy for certain discounts.

If you wear glasses or contacts, it's a good idea to have a copy of your prescription as well as an extra pair of glasses.

Seasons in the Southern Hemisphere are opposite the Northern Hemisphere, and Argentina is a mostly temperate country. In the subtropical north, especially in summer, carry breathable, quick-drying clothes. At higher elevations in the Andean Northwest and parts of Patagonia, warm and windproof clothing is necessary even in summer. In Buenos Aires, you'll want fairly stylish threads (unless you *want* to look like a grungy backpacker). Remember summers in the capital and up north are hot and humid.

Argentine outdoor equipment is not so easily available and generally inferior to that made in North America or Europe, so bring crucial camping supplies from home. Higher quality, brand-name outdoor products will be more expensive than at home.

One thing you'll have a hard time finding in Argentina is peanut butter.

Floss It

For the cost of a crummy cigar, you can buy a vacation-saving item. It's called dental floss, and its uses are innumerable. Got a fishhook but no line? Four words: green waxed dental floss. Forgot to pack a clothesline? You're in luck if you've packed dental floss. Tear in your jeans, rip in your pack? A little dental floss and a sewing needle, and life goes on.

Dental floss comes in 50m and 100m lengths and is sold in nifty little cases complete with built-in cutters. It's cheap, it's light, it's strong and it's outrageously useful. Some say dental floss can even remove decay-causing material from between teeth and upper gums. Now in cinnamon, mint and grape flavors. No kidding.

— Scott Doggett (from *Read this First: Central & South America*)

TOURIST OFFICES

Almost every city or town has a tourist office, usually on or near the main plaza or at the bus terminal. Each Argentine province also has its own representation in Buenos Aires; most, though not all of these are well-organized, often offering a computerized database of tourist information, and are well worth a visit before heading for the provinces. A few municipalities, mostly the Atlantic coastal resorts of Buenos Aires province, have separate offices in Buenos Aires.

For tourist offices in your own country, check with the nearest Argentine embassy or consulate (see Embassies & Consulates, later); many have a tourism representative in their delegation.

The offices listed below are provincial tourist offices (unless indicated otherwise) located in Buenos Aires.

Buenos Aires (☎ 4371-7045), Av Callao 235

Catamarca (☎ 4374-6891), Córdoba 2080

Chaco (☎ 4372-5209), Av Callao 322

Chubut (☎ 4382-2009), Sarmiento 1172

Córdoba (☎ 4372-2602), Av Callao 332

Corrientes (☎ 4394-2835), San Martín 333, 4th floor

Entre Ríos (☎ 4328-9327), Suipacha 844

Formosa (☎ 4383-0721), Hipólito Yrigoyen 1429

Jujuy (☎ 4393-6096), Av Santa Fe 967

La Pampa (☎ 4326-0511), Suipacha 346

La Rioja (☎ 4815-1929), Av Callao 745

Mar del Plata (municipal; ☎ 4384-5658), Av Corrientes 1660, Local 16

Mendoza (☎ 4371-0835), Av Callao 445

Misiones (☎ 4393-1211), Av Santa Fe 989

Neuquén (☎ 4326-6812), Perón 687

Pinamar (municipal; ☎ 4315-2680), Florida 930, 5th floor

Río Negro (☎ 4371-7273), Tucumán 1916

Salta (☎ 4326-2456), Diagonal Roque Sáenz Peña 933

San Clemente del Tuyú (municipal; ☎ 4381-0764), Bartolomé Mitre 1135

San Juan (☎ 4382-9241), Sarmiento 1251

San Luis (☎ 4822-0426), Azcuénaga 1087

Santa Cruz (☎ 4325-3098), Suipacha 1120

Santa Fe (☎ 4375-4572), Montevideo 373

ARGENTINA

Santiago del Estero (☎ 4326-9418), Florida 274

Tierra del Fuego (☎ 4322-7524), Av Sarmiento 745

Tucumán (☎ 4322-0010), Suipacha 140

Villa Carlos Paz (☎ 4322-0053), Florida 520, Local 38/39

Villa Gesell (municipal; ☎ 4374-5098), Bartolomé Mitre 1702

VISAS & DOCUMENTS
Passport

Argentina presently enjoys civilian government, and the police and military are relatively subdued, but the police can still demand identification at any moment. It's a good idea to carry a copy of your passport around town, especially if there is political unrest. In general, Argentines are very document-oriented, and a passport is necessary for cashing traveler's checks, checking into a hotel and many other routine activities.

Visas

Nationals of the USA, Canada, most Western European countries, Australia and New Zealand do not need visas to visit Argentina. In theory, upon arrival all non-visa visitors must obtain a free tourist card, good for 90 days and renewable for 90 more. In practice, immigration officials issue these only at major border crossings, such as airports and on the ferries and hydrofoils between Buenos Aires and Uruguay. Although you should not toss your card away, losing it is no major catastrophe; at most exit points, immigration officials will provide immediate replacement for free.

Dependent children traveling without *both* parents theoretically need a notarized document certifying that both parents agree to the child's travel. Parents may also wish to bring a copy of the custody form; however, there's a good chance they won't be asked for either document.

Very short visits to neighboring countries usually do not require visas. Despite what a travel agency might say, you probably don't need a Brazilian visa to cross from the Argentine town of Puerto Iguazú to Foz do Iguaçu and/or Ciudad del Este, Paraguay, if you return the same day, although you should bring your passport. The same is true at the Bolivian border town of Villazón, near La Quiaca, and the Paraguayan crossing at Encarnación, near Posadas. Remember though, that the information here can change quickly.

Visa Extensions For a 90-day extension in Buenos Aires, visit the Dirección Nacional de Migraciones (☎ 4317-0200), Antártida Argentina 1355. It's open 8am to 1pm weekdays. Set aside some time, money and patience, as this US$100 process can be bureaucratic and time-consuming; some opt to overstay their visa and pay a US$50 charge at the airport as they leave, though this may only work for a short overstay and is always risky. You should double-check this information with seasoned travelers or expats before attempting to do it.

Another option if you're staying more than three months is to cross into Colonia or Montevideo (both in Uruguay) for a day or two before your visa expires, then return with a new 90-day visa. During the off-season a ferry company may have a same-day roundtrip fare to Colonia for as little as US$30. However, this only works if you don't need a visa to enter Uruguay; Australians do.

Travel Insurance

In addition to health and accident insurance, a policy that protects baggage and valuables, like cameras and camcorders, is a good idea. Keep your insurance records separate from other possessions in case you have to make a claim. For information on health insurance, see Health later in this chapter.

Driver's License & Permits

Many motorists get an International or Inter-American Driving Permit to complement their national or state licenses. You may be able to rent a car with just your regular driver's license, however.

Drivers of Argentine vehicles must carry their title document (*tarjeta verde* or 'green card'); for foreign vehicles, customs permission is the acceptable substitute. Liability insurance is obligatory, and police often ask to see proof of insurance at checkpoints.

Hostel Cards

In Buenos Aires, the Red Argentina de Albergues Juveniles (RAAJ) is part of Argentina's energetic, nonprofit student-travel agency Asatej. It sells the Hostelling International card for US$20, which anyone of any age can obtain. RAAJ is much more professional than the moribund Asociación Argentina de Albergues de la Juventud, which sells a hostel card good only in Argentina and doesn't do much otherwise. (See Accommodations, later in this chapter, for contact information.)

Student & Youth Cards

The International Student Identity Card (ISIC), available from Asatej (see Useful Organizations later in this chapter), can help travelers obtain discounts on public transportation and museum admissions, but virtually any official-looking university identification may be an acceptable substitute.

Seniors Cards

Travelers over the age of 60 can sometimes obtain senior-citizen discounts on museum admissions and the like. Usually a passport with date of birth will be sufficient evidence of age.

Copies

All important documents (passport data page and visa page, credit cards, travel insurance policy, air/bus/train tickets, driving license etc) should be photocopied before you leave home. Leave one copy with someone at home and keep another with you, separate from the originals.

It's also a good idea to store details of your vital travel documents in Lonely Planet's free online Travel Vault in case you lose the photocopies or can't be bothered with them. Your password-protected Travel Vault is accessible online anywhere in the world; you can create it at **w** www.ekno.lonelyplanet.com.

EMBASSIES & CONSULATES
Argentine Embassies & Consulates

Argentina has diplomatic representation throughout Latin America, North America, Western Europe and Australia.

Australia
(☎ 02 6273 9111), Level 2/7 National Cct, Barton ACT 2600
(☎ 02 9251 3402), Level 13/1 Alfred St, Sydney NSW 2000

Bolivia
(☎ 02 353233), Calle Aspiazu 497, Casilla 64, La Paz

Brazil
(☎ 045 574 2969), Travessa Eduardo Bianchi 26, Foz do Iguaçu
(☎ 021 551 5498), Praia de Botafogo SL 201, Botafogo, Rio de Janeiro
(☎ 011 285 2274), Paulista 1106, 9th floor, São Paulo

Canada
(☎ 613-236-2351), 90 Sparks St, Suite 910, Ottawa, Ontario K1P 5B4
(☎ 514-842-6582), 2000 Peel St, Suite 710, Montreal, Quebec H3A 2W5

Chile
(☎ 02 222 8977), Vicuña Mackenna 41, Santiago
(☎ 65 253 996), Cauquenes 94, 2nd floor, Puerto Montt
(☎ 61 261 912), 21 de Mayo 1878, Punta Arenas

France
(☎ 01 45 53 33 00), 6 rue Cimarosa, 75116 Paris

Germany
(☎ 0228 228010), Adenauerallee 50-52, 53113 Bonn

New Zealand
(☎ 04 472 8330), Level 14/142 Lambton Quay, PO Box 5430 Wellington

Paraguay
(☎ 021 442151), Palma 319, 1st floor, Asunción
(☎ 071 201066), Carlos Antonio López 690, Encarnación

UK
(☎ 020 584 6494), 53 Hans Place, London SWI XOLA

Uruguay
(☎ 02-902-8623), WF Aldunate 1281, Montevideo
(☎ 052-22093), Av General Flores 215, Colonia
(☎ 0562-3225), 18 de Julio 1225, Fray Bentos
(☎ 072-22253), Leandro Gómez 1034, Paysandú
(☎ 042-441632), Calle 25 544, Punta del Este (open December 15-March 15 only)
(☎ 073-32931), General Artigas 1162, Salto

ARGENTINA

USA
(☎ 202-238-6460), 1718 Connecticut Ave NW, Washington, DC 20009

(☎ 212-603-0403), 12 W 56th St, New York, NY 10019

(☎ 213-954-9155), 5050 Wilshire Blvd, Suite 210, Los Angeles, CA 90036

(☎ 305-373-1889), 800 Brickell Ave, Penthouse 1, Miami, FL 33131

(☎ 312-819-2610), 205 N Michigan Ave, Suite 4209, Chicago, IL 60601

(☎ 713-871-8935), 3050 Post Oak Blvd, Suite 1625, Houston, TX 77056

Embassies & Consulates in Argentina

It's important to realize what your own embassy – the embassy of the country of which you are a citizen – can and can't do to help you if you get into trouble. Generally speaking, it won't be much help in emergencies if the trouble you're in is remotely your own fault. Remember that you are bound by the laws of the country you are in. Your embassy will not be sympathetic if you end up in jail after committing a crime locally, even if such actions are legal in your own country.

In genuine emergencies, you might get some assistance, but only if other channels have been exhausted. For example, if you need to get home urgently, a free ticket home is exceedingly unlikely – the embassy would expect you to have insurance. If you have all your money and documents stolen, it might assist with getting a new passport, but a loan for onward travel is out of the question.

Listed below are embassies and consulates in Buenos Aires (the map numbers refer to the maps in the Buenos Aires chapter). Some countries have both an embassy and a consulate here, but only the most central location is listed below). For diplomatic offices in other Argentine cities, see the related city section for contact information.

Australia
(☎ 4777-6580), Villanueva 1400, Belgrano

Belgium
(☎ 4331-0066, Map 3), Defensa 113, 8th floor, Montserrat

Bolivia
(☎ 4381-0539, Map 3), Av Belgrano 1670, 1st floor, Montserrat (also in La Quiaca, Mendoza, Salta, Jujuy, Tucumán)

Brazil
(☎ 4394-5264, Map 5), Carlos Pellegrini 1363, 5th floor, Retiro (also in Paso de Libres, Puerto Iguazú)

Canada
(☎ 4805-3032, Map 5), Tagle 2828, Palermo

Chile
(☎ 4394-6582, Map 3), San Martín 439, 9th floor, San Nicolás (also in Bahía Blanca, Bariloche, Comodoro Rivadavia, Esquel, Jujuy, Mendoza, Neuquén, Río Gallegos, Salta, Ushuaia)

Denmark
(☎ 4312-6901, Map 5), Leandro N Alem 1074, 9th floor, Retiro

France
(☎ 4312-2409, Map 5), Santa Fe 846, 4th floor, Retiro (also in Mendoza, Salta, Tucumán)

Germany
(☎ 4778-2500), Villanueva 1055, Palermo (also in Mendoza, Posadas, Salta, Tucumán)

Ireland
(☎ 4325-8588, Map 5), Suipacha 1380, 2nd floor, Retiro

Israel
(☎ 4338-2500, Map 3), Av de Mayo 701, 10th floor, Montserrat (also in Mendoza)

Italy
(☎ 4816-6132, Map 5), M T de Alvear 1125, Retiro (also in Mendoza, Neuquén, Salta, Jujuy, Tucumán)

Japan
(☎ 4318-8220, Map 3), Bouchard 547, 17th floor

Mexico
(☎ 4789-8819), Arcos 1650, Belgrano

Netherlands
(☎ 4334-4000, Map 3), Ave de Mayo 701, 19th floor, Montserrat

Norway
(☎ 4312-2204, Map 5), Esmeralda 909, 3rd floor, Retiro

Paraguay
(☎ 4814-4803, Map 3), Viamonte 1851, Balvanera (also in Clorinda, Corrientes, Posadas)

Peru
(☎ 4811-4619, Map 5), Av Córdoba 1345, 11th floor, Retiro

Spain
(☎ 4811-0078, Map 5), Guido 1760, Recoleta (also in Mendoza, Tucumán)

Sweden
(☎ 4342-1422, Map 3), Tacuarí 147, 6th floor, Montserrat

Switzerland
(☎ 4311-6491, Map 5), Santa Fe 846, 10th floor, Retiro

UK
(☎ 4803-7070, Map 5), Dr Luis Agote 2412, Palermo

Uruguay
(☎ 4807-3040, Map 5), Las Heras 1907, Recoleta (also in Colón, Concordia, Gualeguaychú)

USA
(☎ 4777-4533), Colombia 4300, Palermo

CUSTOMS

Argentine officials are generally courteous and reasonable toward tourists. If you cross the border frequently and carry an inordinate amount of electronic equipment, such as cameras or laptop computers, however, you should have a typed list of equipment and serial numbers (get it stamped by authorities while going into the country). A pile of the appropriate purchase receipts might also help.

Depending on where you have been, officials focus on different things. Travelers southbound from the central Andean countries may be searched for drugs, while those from bordering countries will have fruits and vegetables confiscated. Carrying firearms will pretty much get you into trouble no matter which country you're coming from.

MONEY

Argentine money tends to present real problems for visitors unaccustomed to hyperinflation. The institution of Domingo Cavallo's convertibility policy in 1991 (which paired the peso with the US dollar) brought temporary relief – and record lows in inflation. But things went haywire again in December 2001, when the government devalued the peso amidst an economic crisis that rocked the nation. Visitors to Argentina should keep a close watch on current economic events.

All prices in this book are given in US dollars (US$) unless otherwise indicated.

Currency

The present unit is the peso ($), which replaced the inflation-ravaged *austral* on January 1, 1992. The austral had replaced the *peso argentino* in 1985, which had replaced the *peso ley* in 1978, which had replaced the ordinary *peso* some years earlier. One new peso equals 10,000 australs, on par with the US dollar.

Paper money comes in denominations of two, five, 10, 20, 50 and 100 pesos. One peso equals 100 *centavos*; coins come in denominations of one (rare), five, 10, 25 and 50 centavos, and one peso.

At present, US dollars are accepted practically everywhere, but it's wise to carry some pesos; institutions like the post office and some bus companies, as well as a few nationalistic merchants, refuse to accept US currency.

Tattered Argentine banknotes seem to stay in circulation for decades, but few banks or businesses accept worn or defaced US bills. Make sure that yours are in seriously crispy, pristine shape. (In a pinch, American Express in Buenos Aires will probably change your older or written-on bills, and you don't have to be a member.) Counterfeiting, of both local and US bills, has become a problem in recent years, and merchants are very careful when accepting large denominations. You should be too; look for a clear watermark or running thread on the largest bills.

Keep a stash of change with you, both in small bills and coins; when you need that US$0.80 for the bus you'll find *kioskos* (small stores or newspaper stands) won't seem to have enough to give out.

Exchange Rates

At press time exchange rates were:

country	unit		peso
Australia	A$1	=	Arg $0.97
Bolivia	B$1	=	Arg $0.21
Brazil	R$1	=	Arg $0.80
Canada	C$1	=	Arg $1.17
Chile	Ch$1000	=	Arg $2.02
European Union	€1	=	Arg $1.63

country	unit		peso
Japan	¥100	=	Arg $1.42
New Zealand	NZ$1	=	Arg $0.81
Paraguay	₲1000	=	Arg $3.00
UK	UK£1	=	Arg $2.78
Uruguay	Ur$1	=	Arg $0.10
USA	US$1	=	Arg $1.85

Exchanging Money

US dollars are by far the preferred foreign currency, although Chilean and Uruguayan pesos can be readily exchanged at the borders. Only Buenos Aires will have a ready market for European currencies.

Cash & Traveler's Checks Cash dollars can be exchanged at banks, exchange houses (cambios) and hotels. There will probably be a small fee. Very high commissions are levied on traveler's checks, which are very difficult to cash anywhere and specifically *not* recommended. For American Express checks, try the American Express office in Buenos Aires (☎ 4312-1661), Arenales 707, which doesn't charge commission but will take out a few cents. Note that stores will *not* accept traveler's checks, and outside Buenos Aires it's even harder to change them.

Using cash (if you are confident in your ability to carry it safely) or an ATM card is the way to go in Argentina.

To exchange a large US bill, try going to a large supermarket and purchasing something. You'll receive change in pesos, and won't be charged the small fee that banks or cambios levy. The Subte (subway) in Buenos Aires is also good for this.

ATMs *Cajeros automáticos* (ATMs) are increasingly common in Argentina and can also be used for cash advances on major credit cards like MasterCard and Visa. Many but not all ATMs dispense US dollars as well as Argentine pesos, and you can get instructions in English.

Credit Cards The most widely accepted credit cards are Visa and MasterCard, though American Express and a few others are also valid in many establishments. Before you leave home, you'll want to warn your credit card company that it will be receiving whatever charges you'll be making from abroad. Because lost or stolen credit cards are vulnerable to abuse, credit card holders should consider enrolling in a protection plan to insure against serious financial loss.

Some businesses add a *recargo* (surcharge) of 5% to 10% towards credit-card purchases. Also, the actual amount you'll eventually pay depends upon the exchange rate not at the time of sale, but when the purchase is posted to an overseas account, sometimes weeks later.

If you use a credit card to pay for restaurant bills, be aware that tips can't usually be added to the bill. Some lower-end hotels and private tour companies will not accept credit cards. Holders of MasterCard and Visa can get cash advances at Argentine banks, and most ATMs will do the same.

International Transfers For travelers running out of money, American Express Money Gram is a quick and efficient (if costly) means of transferring funds from their home country to Argentina. American Express has a major office in Retiro and representatives throughout the country.

Costs

In the past, during periods of economic instability, Argentines would panic and buy US dollars, the exchange rate would collapse and the country would become absurdly cheap for any visitor with hard currency. At present the economy is relatively stable due to the stringent convertibility policy, making Buenos Aires nearly as expensive as European or North American cities.

Budget travel is still possible, however. Accommodations, food and transport will take the largest chunk of your change, but if you stay only at hostels, cook your own food (many hostels have kitchens) and take buses or the Subte (in Buenos Aires only),

Prices?

As this book was going to press, Argentina's government devalued the nation's wounded peso, ending a decade run of the peso's parity with the US dollar.

Be prepared to see in-country prices dramatically changed from those listed in this book. In the long run, however, Argentina may become a more affordable country for budget travelers.

you'll be able to get by on US$30 per day or less. Only compulsive shoestringers will make do on this budget; most folks will probably spend much more, especially if they want to eat some steaks and have some fun.

Tipping & Bargaining

In restaurants, it is customary to tip about 10% of the bill, but in times of economic distress Argentines frequently overlook the custom. In general, waiters are ill-paid, so if you can afford to eat out, you can afford to tip. Even a small *propina* will be appreciated, but note that restaurant tips can't be added to a credit card bill.

Taxi drivers don't expect tips, but it's customary to round up to the nearest peso if the difference isn't much. Cinema ushers receive a tip of 25 or 50 centavos.

Bargaining is not the way of life it is in Bolivia or Peru, but artisans' markets and downtown shops selling leather and other tourist goods may consider offers. (They do not inflate prices like in other South American countries.)

If you plan to stay several days at a hotel, try bargaining. Many upscale hotels will give discounts for payment in cash.

Taxes & Refunds

Under limited circumstances, foreign visitors may obtain refunds of the *impuesto de valor agregado* (IVA, or value-added tax) on purchases of Argentine products upon their departure from the country. A 'Tax Free' (in English) window decal identifies merchants participating in this program, but always verify their status before making your purchase. Tax refunds can be obtained for purchases of US$70 or more at one of these participating stores. To do so, present your passport to the merchant, who makes out an invoice for you. On leaving the country, keep the purchased items separate from the rest of your baggage; a customs official will check them.

With this invoice, you can obtain refunds in Buenos Aires at Ezeiza, Aeroparque Jorge Newbery and the Buquebus terminal at Darsena Norte.

POST & COMMUNICATIONS

Still more dependable than the post office are Argentine domestic couriers, such as Andreani and OCA, and international couriers, like DHL and Federal Express. The latter two have offices only in the largest cities, like Buenos Aires, while the former two usually serve as their connections to the interior of the country.

Post

Correo Argentino, the privatized postal service, has gotten more reliable over the years but mail still occasionally gets waylaid. Argentina's postal rates are among the world's most expensive. International letters and postcards to the Americas cost US$1.25 and to Europe and Australia US$1.50.

Certified and international express mail services are more expensive but a better value because of their dependability. Certified letters start at US$2.75 for up to 20g, while international express service begins at US$5.50 for up to 100g.

Airmail packages are expensive, while surface mail is much cheaper but less dependable. For essential overseas mail, send it *certificado* (registered). Mail may get 'lost' if it appears to contain money or anything else of value, though this is less common than it once was.

You can receive mail via poste restante or *lista de correos,* both equivalent to general delivery, at any Argentine post office. Instruct your correspondents to address letters clearly (capitalizing your last name) and to indicate a date until which the post office should hold them; otherwise, the mail will be returned or destroyed. Charges are US$1.50 per letter. To save money and hassle, have mail delivered to a friend or hotel.

If you're traveling around Argentina and want to lighten your load, consider going to a bus company and having them cargo your things back to Buenos Aires. Ask for *encomienda.* You can ship anything from the size of a shoebox to a bag weighing 30 or so kilos; items are held 20 to 30 days at Retiro bus station (or you can have someone pick them up). Cost depends on weight and distance, but is cheaper than Correo Argentino. From Buenos Aires you'd then just have to cart things to the airport; this can be a cheaper option than mailing straight overseas. Obviously, this option is only feasible if you have a ticket out of Buenos Aires.

Telephone & Fax

Argentina's country code is ☎ 54, and the Spanish term for area code is *característica.* For emergencies dial ☎ 107, police ☎ 101, fire ☎ 100. Directory Assistance is ☎ 110.

The easiest way to make a local phone call is to find a *locutorio* (small telephone office), which has private cabins where you make your calls and then pay all at once at the register. There's a locutorio practically on every other block, they cost about the same as street phones, are much quieter and you won't run out of coins. Most locutorios are supplied with phone books.

To use street phones, you'll pay with regular coins or *tarjetas telefónicas* (magnetic phone cards available at many kiosks). You'll only be able to speak for a limited

time before you get cut off, so carry enough credit.

Although Argentine telephone rates are fairly high, some rates have fallen. International collect calls or calls by credit card are not necessarily cheaper than calling from long-distance telephone offices. Long-distance offices are usually busy during evening and weekend discount hours, when overseas calls are cheaper. Prices for Europe are US$1 to US$3 per hour, depending on the time of day; calling to USA costs about the same, but Australia costs more.

Making international calls over the Internet, using the system *net2phone,* can be your cheapest option. Some of the larger Internet cafés in big cities are set up for this and can help you get started.

Lonely Planet's eKno global communication service provides low-cost international calls, free messaging services, email and other travel services. You can join online at ⓦ www.ekno.lonelyplanet.com, where you will find local-access numbers for a 24-hour customer-service center. Once you have joined, always check the eKno Web site for the latest access numbers for each country and updates on new features.

Faxes are widely used and available at most locutorios and Internet cafés. Costs are price of the call plus US$0.50 to US$1 per page.

International Direct Dialing From those parts of Argentina that have Discado Directo Internacional (DDI, or International Direct Dialing), it is now possible to get direct access to home-country operators for collect and credit-card calls from both private and public telephones; this is usually much cheaper than going through the Argentine carriers. Note that private locutorios will only rarely permit their facilities to be used for such calls, since they make no profit on them.

The following toll-free telephone numbers provide direct connections to home-country operators from Argentina.

Australia	☎ 0-800-555-6100
Canada	☎ 0-800-222-1004
France	☎ 0-800-555-3300
Germany	☎ 0-800-555-4900
Italy	☎ 0-800-555-3900
UK	☎ 0-800-555-4401 (British Telecom)
USA	☎ 0-800-222-1001 (AT&T)
	☎ 0-800-555-4288 (AT&T)
	☎ 0-800-555-1002 (MCI)
	☎ 0-800-555-1003 (Sprint)

Email & Internet Access

The Internet has struck it big in Argentina. There are lots Internet cafés around the country, and many locutorios also have Internet access. Rates in Buenos Aires are the cheapest of all (as low as US$2 per hour downtown), and connections are quick. Expect rates around the rest of Argentina to be about US$5 per hour. Some Spanish keyboards can be a little tricky, especially when trying to find the '@' symbol (or *'arroba'* in Spanish). You can ask the attendant *'¿Cómo se hace arroba?'* If that doesn't work try holding down the Alt key and typing 64 on the number pad with Num Lock on.

Consider using an Internet account to keep in touch with folks back home. As you're traveling, you can write missives every few days to let your friends and family know how your travels are progressing.

Traveling with a portable computer is a great way to stay in touch with life back home, but unless you know what you're doing, it's fraught with potential problems. If you plan to carry your notebook or palmtop computer with you, remember that the power-supply voltage in Argentina may vary from that at home. The best investment is a universal AC adapter for your appliance, which will enable you to plug it in anywhere without frying the innards of your equipment. You'll also need a plug adapter for each country you visit – often, it's easiest to buy these before you leave home.

Also, your PC-card modem may or may not work once you leave your home country, and you won't know for sure until you try. The safest option is to buy a reputable 'global' modem before you leave home, or

to buy a local PC-card modem if you're spending an extended time in Argentina. Keep in mind that the telephone socket in Argentina will probably be different from the one at home, so ensure that you have at least a US RJ-11 telephone adaptor that works with your modem. You can almost always find an adaptor that will convert from RJ-11 to the local variety. For more information on traveling with a portable computer, see **w** www.teleadapt.com or **w** www.warrior.com.

INTERNET RESOURCES

The World Wide Web is a rich resource for travelers. You can research your trip, hunt down bargain airfares, book hotels, check on weather conditions or chat with locals and other travelers about the best places to visit – or avoid!

Argentina, and Buenos Aires in particular, has spawned a growing mass of Internet resources. In this fast-moving field, change is the rule, and addresses and contents can change quickly. Remember that there is a great deal of inaccurate information on the Internet, and that some Web sites are updated very infrequently.

There's no better place to start your Web explorations than the Lonely Planet Web site (**w** www.lonelyplanet.com). Here, you'll find succinct summaries on traveling to most places on earth; postcards from other travelers; and the Thorn Tree bulletin board, where you can ask questions before you go or dispense advice when you get back. You can also find travel news and updates to many of our most popular guidebooks, while the subWWWay section links to the most useful travel resources elsewhere on the Web. It's all here and run by a great group of folks, to boot.

Here are some other useful addresses:

Centers for Disease Control w www.cdc.gov/ travel/temsam.htm – This is the CDC's health-information site for Argentina and surrounding regions.

US State Department w www.travel.state.gov/ argentina.html – Safety, health and traffic information on Argentina can be found on this site, which is mostly geared toward US citizens.

Latin American Network Information Center W www.lanic.utexas.edu/la/argentina – This site has a massive list of Argentine Web sites. If you can't find it here…well, never mind, 'cause you'll find it here.

Grippo W www.grippo.com.ar – Tons of Argentine businesses, including commercial enterprises, are listed on this site.

Expat Village.com W www.expatvillage.com – Folks moving to Buenos Aires should check out this Web site; it provides a variety of information, including a map of Evita's grave, trees of Buenos Aires and women's clubs.

Hostels.com W www.hostels.com/ar.html – This is a good place to find Hostelling International and non-HI affiliated hostels in Argentina.

Buenos Aires Herald W www.buenosairesherald.com – An international view of the country and world can be found at the Web site of this English-language newspaper.

Clarín.com W www.clarin.com.ar – A pretty complete version of Argentina's largest-circulation daily is offered online here.

La Nacion Line W www.lanacion.com.ar – This well-structured site offers content from one of Buenos Aires' oldest and most prestigious dailies.

Página/12 W www.pagina12.com – So-so and slow-slow is this Web site of the leftist daily known for the capital's best investigative journalism.

UkiNet W www.ukinet.com – Human-rights issues and historical articles from 1978-97 (in English) can be found at this Web site, run by a committed and talented group of independent journalists.

Fundacion Invertir Argentina W www.invertir.com/12busin.html – Predominately geared toward businesspeople visiting Buenos Aires, this Web site has some good stuff for tourists, too.

BOOKS

Buenos Aires is a major publishing center and has many excellent bookstores on or near Av Corrientes, though most have limited English-language books. For details, see the Buenos Aires chapter. For information on Argentine literature see the Facts about Argentina chapter.

Most books are published in different editions by different publishers in different countries. As a result, a book might be a hardcover rarity in one country while it's readily available in paperback in another. Fortunately, bookstores and libraries can

search by title or author, so your local bookstore or library is the best place to find out about the availability of the following recommended titles.

Lonely Planet

Other guidebooks can supplement and complement this one, especially if you are visiting additional South American countries. Lonely Planet's *Buenos Aires* city guide will give you much more detail on the rockin' Argentine capital, while *South America on a shoestring* will have you traveling in style throughout the continent. *Read This First: Central & South America* is a good starter for a first-time traveler. And you'll want the entertaining, practical and best-selling *Latin American Spanish phrasebook* so you can chat up the locals.

If you plan to do any trekking, or even some short walks, a good companion is Lonely Planet's *Trekking in the Patagonian Andes,* a detailed guide to walking in the Chilean and Argentine Patagonia, which includes contour maps.

Travel & Fiction

Argentina has inspired some excellent travel writing, most notably Bruce Chatwin's *In Patagonia* (1977), one of the most informed syntheses of life and landscape for any part of South America or the entire world. Avoid the patronizing *The Old Patagonian Express* (1980), whose best-selling author, Paul Theroux, unquestionably succeeds in his efforts to distance himself from the people and places he travels among.

American scientist George Gaylord Simpson's *Attending Marvels: A Patagonian Journal* (1934) starts, surprisingly but excitingly, with an account of the 1930 coup against President Hipólito Yrigoyen. AF Tschifferly's *Southern Cross to Pole Star* (1933, but frequently reprinted) recounts the Swiss author's ride from Buenos Aires to Washington DC, with two Argentine criollo horses, though only a small portion of the book deals with Argentina proper.

The late British naturalist Gerald Durrell wrote several frivolous but entertaining

A colorful café in the La Boca barrio of Buenos Aires

Ritzy Recoleta, Buenos Aires

Street musicians in La Boca, Buenos Aires

Office workers relax in the Plaza de Mayo, Buenos Aires.

A university student in Córdoba, Argentina

Schoolgirls studying in Salta, Argentina

accounts of his travels in Argentina, from Jujuy to Patagonia, in *The Drunken Forest* and *The Whispering Land*. Make a special effort to locate Lucas Bridges' *The Uttermost Part of the Earth* (1947), which describes his life among the indigenous peoples of Tierra del Fuego. Bridges' father was one of the earliest missionary settlers from the Falkland Islands and compiled an important dictionary of the Yahgan language.

Charles Darwin's *Voyage of the Beagle* (1838) is as vivid as yesterday; his account of the gauchos on the Pampas and in Patagonia evokes a way of life to which Argentines still pay symbolic homage, though it no longer really exists. Frequently reprinted, William Henry Hudson's *Idle Days in Patagonia* (1893) is a romantic account of the 19th-century naturalist's adventures in search of migratory birds. Also check out his *The Purple Land* (1885) and *Far Away and Long Ago* (1918).

Banned by the military dictatorship of El Proceso, Peruvian novelist Mario Vargas Llosa's *Aunt Julia and the Scriptwriter* offers amusing but ironic and unflattering observations of what other Latin Americans think of Argentines. Graham Greene's satirical novel *The Honorary Consul* recounts the kidnapping of an insignificant British diplomat by a small but committed revolutionary group in the slums of Corrientes.

A Secret for Julia, by Patricia Sagastizabal, won the 2000 Premio la Nacion (Argentina's equivalent to the Pulitzer) and has recently been translated into English. It's about a survivor of the Dirty War living in exile in London when years later one of her former torturers tracks her down.

History

General For the South American wars of independence, including Argentina's, a standard work is John Lynch's *The Spanish-American Revolutions 1808-1826* (1973). One of the best-known contemporary accounts of post-independence Argentina, often used as a university text, is Domingo Faustino Sarmiento's *Life in the Argentine Republic in the Days of the Tyrants*, an eloquent but often condescending critique of the Federalist caudillos and their followers. José Luis Romero analyzes the conflict between Unitarism and Federalism in *A History of Argentine Political Thought* (1968).

JH Parry's *The Discovery of South America* (1979) tells of the early European exploration in Argentina and elsewhere in South America. James Scobie's *Argentina: A City and a Nation* (1964) is a standard account of the country's development. The most up-to-date comprehensive history of the country, however, is David Rock's *Argentina 1516-1987: From Spanish Colonization to Alfonsín* (1987).

For an account of Britain's role in Argentina's 19th-century development, see HS Ferns' *Britain and Argentina in the Nineteenth Century* (1960). More recent is Alistair Henessy and John King's edited collection of essays, *The Land That England Lost: Argentina and Britain, A Special Relationship* (1992), which goes beyond the strictly political to deal with intriguing cultural topics like the English tango fad just prior to WWI.

Several historians have compared Argentina, Australia and Canada as exporters of primary products such as beef and wheat, and their subsequent economic development. Such comparisons include Tim Duncan and John Fogarty's *Australia and Argentina: On Parallel Paths* (1984), DC Platt and Guido di Tella's *Argentina, Australia and Canada: Studies in Comparative Development, 1970-1985* (1985) and Carl Solberg's *The Prairies and the Pampas: Agrarian Policy in Canada and Argentina, 1880-1930* (1987).

For an interpretation of the gaucho's role in Argentine history, see Richard W Slatta's *Gauchos and the Vanishing Frontier* (1983). More recently, Slatta has compared the gauchos with stockmen of other countries in the beautifully illustrated *Cowboys of the Americas* (1990). Nicholas Shumway's *The Invention of Argentina* (1991) offers a kind of intellectual history of the country.

For a much more contemporary, humorous account of Buenos Aires life in the early 1990s, pick up *Bad Times in Buenos Aires,* by Miranda France. Quirky and well-written, France delves deep into the dysfunctional porteño psyche and surfaces with vivid images and passionate characters, all the while creatively adding historical anecdotes and daily misadventures. It's not really a history book, but does detail a Buenos Aires that no longer exists today in quite the same fashion.

The Peróns A standard biography is Robert Alexander's *Juan Domingo Perón* (1979). Another important book is Frederick Turner and José Enrique Miguens' *Juan Perón and the Reshaping of Argentina* (1983). Also look at Joseph Page's *Perón: A Biography* (1983), and Robert Crassweller's *Perón and the Enigma of Argentina* (1987). A fascinating, fictionalized version of Perón's life, culminating in his return to Buenos Aires in 1973, is Tomás Eloy Martínez's *The Perón Novel* (1988).

Eva Perón speaks for herself, to some degree, in her ghostwritten biography *La Razón de Mi Vida* (My Mission in Life). VS Naipaul suggests that political violence and torture have long permeated Argentine society in his grim but eloquent essay *The Return of Eva Perón* (1980). Also try JM Taylor's *Eva Perón: The Myths of a Woman* (1979), or Martínez's novel *Santa Evita* (1996).

The Military & the Dirty War One good general overview of the military in Latin America is John J Johnson's *The Military and Society in Latin America* (1964). Robert Potash has published two complementary books on military interference in Argentine politics: *The Army and Politics in Argentina, 1928-1945: Yrigoyen to Perón* (1969), and *The Army and Politics in Argentina, 1945-1962: Perón to Frondizi* (1980).

The classic first-person account of state terrorism in the late 1970s is Jacobo Timmerman's *Prisoner Without a Name, Cell Without a Number* (1981). *Nunca Más,* the official report of the National Commission on the Disappeared, systematically details military abuses from 1976 to 1983. John Simpson and Jana Bennett's *The Disap-*

peared: Voices from a Secret War (1985) is a good general account. A highly regarded first novel on the Dirty War is US writer Lawrence Thornton's *Imagining Argentina* (1988).

Contemporary Argentine Politics For an analysis of the contradictions in Argentine society, read Gary Wynia's *Argentina in the Postwar Era: Politics and Economic Policy Making in a Divided Society*. A recent collection on the democratic transition is Monica Peralta-Ramos and Carlos Waisman's *From Military Rule to Liberal Democracy in Argentina*. David Erro's *Resolving the Argentine Paradox: Politics and Development, 1966-1992* provides a good analysis of contemporary Argentine politics and policies through the early Menem years, though it may be overly optimistic about current trends.

Che Guevara The 30th anniversary of Che's death, in 1997, produced a spate of biographies of varying quality, most of them both sympathetic to the guerilla leader but also critical of his shortcomings. Journalist Lee Anderson's *Che Guevara: A Revolutionary Life* has great material on Che's Argentine childhood and long-term goal of spreading the revolution to Argentina. Mexican academic Jorge Castañeda's *Compañero: The Life and Death of Che Guevara* is more analytical but still accessible. Castañeda's countryman, journalist-novelist Paco Ignacio Taibo, wrote *Guevara, also Known as Che,* which uses a hybrid style of biography and fiction, often in Che's own words.

Ernesto Guevara's *The Motorcycle Diaries: A Journey Around South America* (1995) is an early 1950s account of two Argentine medical students who rode a dilapidated motorcycle across northern Patagonia and into Chile before abandoning it to continue their trip by stowing away on a coastal freighter.

FILMS

For a brief introduction to the country, check out Lonely Planet's *Argentina* video.

Argentina has definitely been influenced by Hollywood, but it's also left a mark there. Carlos Gardel flashed his smile in several Spanish-language films, including *El Día Que Me Quieras,* and Hollywood used Argentina as a location in the movie *Taras Bulba* (1962), for instance, which was filmed partly around Salta.

Madonna's *Evita* (1996), directed by Alan Parker, caused controversy in the country as many resented the choice of cast. (Though in retrospect, there are similarities between Evita and Madonna: both can be described as promiscuous, savvy and powerful women over-glamorized by society and raised in less than well-to-do circumstances.)

Sex symbol Brad Pitt starred in *Seven Years in Tibet* (1997), which was filmed in the high Andes west of Mendoza. And, to see Buenos Aires blown to smithereens on the big screen, check out *Starship Troopers* (1997), a very violent but surprisingly good sci-fi flick.

An all-star cast of Richard Gere, Michael Caine and Bob Hoskins couldn't redeem John Mackenzie's *Beyond the Limit* (1983), an atrocious adaptation of Graham Greene's Corrientes-based novel *The Honorary Consul.* For a truly creepy English-language film with a Dirty War theme, see Martin Donovan's *Apartment Zero* (1989). It depicts many amusing aspects of porteño life as it follows an Anglo-Argentine film buff who takes a morbid interest in his mysterious North American housemate.

Sally Potter's *The Tango Lesson* (1997) is an autobiographical flick about a frustrated filmmaker who struggles with getting her movie made, travels to Buenos Aires and Paris, and ends up taking tango lessons from a sensual instructor (with whom she has an affair). Diego Curubeto's *Babilonia Gaucha* (in Spanish) is an entertaining exploration of the relationship between Hollywood and Argentina.

See Arts in the Facts about Argentina chapter for information on the local film industry and its personalities.

NEWSPAPERS & MAGAZINES

Argentina is South America's most literate country, supporting a wide spectrum of newspapers and magazines despite unceasing economic crisis. Freedom of the press has come a long way since the military dictatorship of 1976-83, but occasional censorship still occurs.

The English-language daily *Buenos Aires Herald* covers Argentina and the world from an international perspective, emphasizing commerce and finance. *Argentinisches Tageblatt* is a German-language weekly that appears Saturdays.

North American and European newspapers like the *New York Times, USA Today, Guardian* and *Le Monde* are available at kiosks on pedestrian Florida – at premium prices. Magazines like *Time, Newsweek* and the *Economist* are also fairly easy to obtain.

The capital has about 10 Spanish nationwide dailies, several of them now online (see Internet Resources earlier in this chapter), and some with unambiguous political leanings. The centrist tabloid *Clarín* has one of the largest circulation of any newspaper in the Spanish-speaking world, and publishes an excellent Sunday cultural section.

La Nación, founded in 1870 by former president Bartolomé Mitre, has moved from the right toward the center and has a circulation of about 80,000 daily. *La Prensa* is equally venerable, but much less influential.

The tabloid *Página/12* provides refreshing leftist perspectives and often breaks important stories that mainstream newspapers are slow to cover, but it has lost much of the innovative fervor that characterized its early years in the aftermath of the military dictatorship. Its circulation is about 20,000 daily.

Ambito Financiero, the morning voice of the capital's financial community, has an excellent entertainment and cultural section. *El Cronista* and *Buenos Aires Económico* are its rivals. All appear weekdays only.

The weekly magazine *Noticias* is the local equivalent to *Time* or *Newsweek,* while *Trespuntos* takes a more aggressive, investigative stance.

RADIO & TV

Dozens of FM stations offer music, news and information for everyone. FM 92.7 has 24-hour tango, FM 88 and 97.4 have classical music, FM 97.1 has BBC in English and FM 96.3 tunes into the Jewish community (in Spanish). There's even a radio station called Colifata run by mental patients, but it can only be heard within a mile or so of the Borda Hospital in Buenos Aires.

More popular stations include Radio Nacional (FM 96.5), with good news coverage, and Radio 10 (AM 1100), which is something like the National Enquirer of radio stations.

Legalization of privately owned television companies and the cable revolution have brought a wider variety of programming to the small screen. To be sure, there are countless game shows, dance parties and soap operas (novelas). The popular 'reality shows' have been a hit in Argentina as well. Even President Fernando de la Rúa has his own reality show. But there are also serious public-affairs programs on major stations at prime viewing times like Sunday evening. English-speakers can tune to CNN for news and ESPN for sports. Spanish and Chilean stations are also available.

PHOTOGRAPHY

Film in Argentina is comparable to that in Western countries, both in quality and price. A roll of 24-print roll of film will cost around US$5. Slide film ranges from US$6 to US$10 for 36 exposures.

Print developing is widely available in the country. For slide developing, you'll have fewer choices except in Buenos Aires. Developing and mounting 36 diapositivos (slides) will cost around US$15, but if you just have them developed they'll cost half as much, take less space in your luggage and be quicker to view. You can always have the best exposures mounted at home (or easily do it yourself to save money).

Slide film can also be purchased cheaply in Asunción, Paraguay, or in the free zones at Iquique and Punta Arenas, Chile. These are also good places to replace lost or stolen camera equipment, as prices are only

slightly higher than in North America, even if the selection is not so great.

TIME

Argentina is three hours behind GMT; the country does not observe daylight-savings time.

ELECTRICITY

Argentina's electric current operates on 220 volts, 50 cycles. There are two types of electric plugs: either two rounded prongs or three angled flat prongs. Adapters from one to the other are available.

WEIGHTS & MEASURES

Argentina, like practically every other country except the USA, uses the metric system. There's a conversion chart inside the back cover of this book.

LAUNDRY

Lavanderías, or laundromats, are common in Argentina. Most are closed on Sunday. Costs are about US$5 to US$6 per load to be washed, dried and folded; washing only costs less. Some inexpensive hotels and most youth hostels have places where you can wash your own clothes and hang them to dry. Mid- and top-range hotels offer laundry service at reasonable prices, but check charges in advance.

TOILETS

Public toilets in Argentina are better than in most of South America, but there are certainly exceptions. For the truly squeamish, the better restaurants and cafés are good alternatives. If you're looking for a bathroom while walking around, note that the large shopping malls often have public bathrooms available, but in a pinch you can always walk into a McDonald's. Always carry your own toilet paper, since it often runs out in public restrooms, and don't expect luxuries like soap, hot water and paper towels either.

Some visitors may find bidets a novelty; they are those strange shallow ceramic bowls with knobs and a drain, often accompanying toilets in hotel bathrooms.

They are meant for between-shower cleanings of nether regions. Turn knobs slowly or you may end up spraying yourself or the ceiling. Creative and adventurous uses of bidets by travelers have included clothes washing and foot bathing.

HEALTH

Although emergency medical care in Argentina's public hospitals is good and inexpensive, international travelers should take out comprehensive travel insurance before they leave home. If you're from a country with socialized medicine, you should find out what you'll need to do in order to be reimbursed for out-of-pocket money expenses.

In general, Argentina presents few serious health hazards. Before traveling, US residents can contact the international travel hotline (☎ 877-394-8747), a toll-free service at the Centers for Disease Control and Prevention (CDC) in Atlanta. Also useful is CDC's Web site at **w** www.cdc.gov/travel/. For the latest details while in Argentina, contact your country's consulate in Buenos Aires. The World Health Organization (**w** www.who.int/home-page/) also has travel health information.

Travel Health Guides

A number of books provide good information on travel health:

Healthy Travel Central & South America, by Isabelle Young (Lonely Planet, 2000) – The best all-around guide to carry; it's compact, detailed and well-organized.

Where There is No Doctor, by David Werner (Macmillan, 1994) – A very detailed guide intended for long-term workers, such as a Peace Corps volunteers, in underdeveloped areas.

Travel with Children, by Cathy Lanigan and Maureen Wheeler (Lonely Planet, 2001) – This recently updated book includes advice on travel health for younger children.

Predeparture Planning

Make sure you're healthy before you start traveling. If embarking on a long trip, make sure your teeth are in good shape, though Argentine dentists are excellent, especially those in Buenos Aires. If you wear glasses, take a spare pair and your prescription. You can get new eyeglasses made quickly and competently, depending on the prescription and frames; replacing contacts may prove a bit more time-consuming. If you require a particular medication, take an adequate supply and bring a prescription in case you lose your supply.

Immunizations Argentina requires no vaccinations for entry from any country, but if you are visiting neighboring tropical countries you should consider prophylaxis against typhoid, malaria and other diseases. The farther off the beaten track you go, the more necessary it is to take precautions.

It is important to understand the distinction between vaccines recommended for travel in certain areas and those required by law. Essentially the number of vaccines subject to international health regulations has been dramatically reduced over the last 10 years. Currently, yellow fever is the only vaccine subject to international health regulations. Vaccination as an entry requirement into a country is usually only enforced when coming from an infected area.

On the other hand, a number of vaccines are recommended for travel in certain areas. These may not be required by law but are suggested for your personal protection. All vaccinations should be recorded on an International Health Certificate, which is available from your physician or government health department.

Plan ahead for getting your vaccinations: Some of them require an initial shot followed later by a booster, while some vaccinations should not be given together. It is recommended you seek medical advice at least six weeks prior to travel. Note that smallpox has now been wiped out around the world, so immunization is no longer necessary.

Most travelers from Western countries will have been immunized against various diseases during childhood, but your doctor may still recommend booster shots against

Medical Kit Checklist

All standard medications are available in well-stocked pharmacies, and many common prescription drugs can be purchased legally over-the-counter in Argentina.

❑ **Antihistamine** – for sinus-related allergies (eg, hay fever), bites or stings and for preventing motion sickness

❑ **Antibiotics** – for travel off the beaten track, but requires a doctor's prescription; carry the prescription with you and follow prescribed administration

❑ **Antiseptic** (such as povidone-iodine) – for cuts and scrapes

❑ **Aspirin or paracetamol** (acetaminophen in the US) – for pain or fever

❑ **Bandages and Band-aids** – for wound treatment of minor injuries

❑ **Calamine lotion** – for easing irritation from bites or stings

❑ **Cold and flu tablets, throat lozenges and nasal decongestants**

❑ **Insect repellent, sunscreen lotion and water-purification tablets**

❑ **Lomotil or Imodium** – for diarrhea 'blocking'

❑ **Multivitamins** – for long trips when dietary vitamin intake may be inadequate

❑ **Prochlorperazine or metaclopramide** – for nausea and vomiting

❑ **Rehydration mixture** – for treating severe diarrhea and particularly important if traveling with children

❑ **Scissors, tweezers, thermometer** – note that airlines prohibit mercury thermometers

measles or polio, diseases still prevalent in many developing countries. The period of protection offered by vaccinations differs widely, and some are contraindicated if you are pregnant.

In some countries immunizations are available from airport or government health centers. Travel agents or airline offices will tell you where. Vaccinations include:

Tetanus & Diphtheria – Boosters are necessary every 10 years, and protection is highly recommended.

Polio – This is a serious, easily transmitted disease, still prevalent in many developing countries. Everyone should keep up to date with this vaccination. A booster every 10 years maintains immunity.

Hepatitis A – The most common travel-acquired illness can be prevented by vaccination. Protection can be provided in two ways: You can either have the hepatitis A vaccine, which gives good protection for at least a year (longer if you have a booster), or hepatitis A immunoglobulin, which protects you for a limited time (three to six months, depending on dose) and carries a theoretical possibility of blood-borne diseases like HIV, as it is a blood product (although this is a minuscule risk in most Western countries).

Hepatitis B – This disease is spread by blood or by sexual activity. Travelers who should consider a hepatitis B vaccination include those visiting countries where there are known to be many carriers, where blood transfusions may not be adequately screened or where sexual contact is a possibility. It involves three injections, the quickest course being over three weeks with a booster at 12 months. If you need both hepatitis A and B immunization, a combined vaccine may be available.

Health Insurance It's a good idea to get travel insurance to cover theft, loss and medical problems. There are a wide variety of policies, and a travel agent will have recommendations. International student travel policies handled by STA Travel, Council Travel or other student-travel organizations are usually good values. Some policies offer lower and higher medical expenses options, but the higher one is chiefly for countries like the USA, which has extremely expensive medical costs.

• Some policies specifically exclude 'dangerous activities' like scuba diving, motorcycling and even trekking. If these activities are on your agenda, avoid this sort of policy.

• You may prefer a policy that pays doctors or hospitals directly, rather than one that requires you to pay first and claim later. If you have to claim later, keep all documentation. Some policies ask you to call back (reverse charges) to a center in your home country for an immediate assessment of your problem.

• Check whether the policy covers ambulance fees or an emergency flight home. If you have to stretch out, you will need two seats, and somebody has to pay for it!

Basic Rules

Care in what you eat and drink is the most important health rule; stomach upsets are the most likely travel health problem (between 30% and 50% of travelers in a two-week stay experience this), but the majority of these upsets will be relatively minor. Don't become paranoid; after all, trying the local food is part of the experience of travel.

Food North Americans, Europeans and Australians who are not vegetarians will find Argentine food relatively bland and easy on the stomach. Salad greens and other fresh vegetables are safe to eat in virtually every part of the country.

Remember that if your food is poor or limited in availability, if you're traveling hard and fast and therefore missing meals, or if you simply lose your appetite, you can soon start to lose weight and compromise your immune system.

Water Buenos Aires' tap water is safe to drink; in restaurants, the term for this is *agua de canilla* or ask for *un jarro de agua* (a pitcher of water). In remote rural areas, where latrines may be close to wells, exercise caution. One geographical area of concern is the Impenetrable of the central Chaco, north of Roque Sáenz Peña, which has been the only region in the country to experience cholera outbreaks.

Bottled drinking water, both carbonated and noncarbonated, is widely available in Argentina.

If you prefer to purify water yourself, the simplest way is to boil it thoroughly – vigorous boiling for 10 minutes should be satisfactory even at high altitude (where water boils at a lower temperature, and germs are less likely to be killed).

Simple filtering will not remove all dangerous organisms, so if you cannot boil water it should be treated chemically. Chlorine tablets (Puritabs, Steritabs or other brand names) will kill many pathogens, but not some parasites such as *Giardia* and amoebic cysts. Iodine is very effective in purifying water and is available in tablet form (such as Potable Aqua), but follow the directions carefully – too much iodine can be harmful.

If you can't find tablets, tincture of iodine (2%) or iodine crystals can be used. Four drops of tincture of iodine per liter or quart of clear water is the recommended dosage; let the treated water stand for 20 to 30 minutes before drinking. Iodine crystals can also be used to purify water, but this is a more complicated process, as you must first prepare a saturated iodine solution (iodine loses its effectiveness if exposed to air or dampness, so keep it in a tightly sealed container). Flavored powder will help disguise the taste of treated water and is a good idea if you are traveling with children.

Everyday Health

Normal body temperature is 98.6°F or 37°C; more than 4°F (2°C) higher indicates a 'high' fever. The normal adult pulse rate is 60 to 80 per minute (children 80 to 100, babies 100 to 140). It is important to know how to take a temperature and a pulse rate.

Respiration (breathing) rate is also an indicator of illness. Count the number of breaths per minute: Between 12 and 20 is normal for adults and older children (up to 30 for younger children, 40 for babies). People with a high fever or serious respiratory illness (like pneumonia) breathe more quickly than normal. More than 40 shallow breaths a minute is usually an indication of pneumonia.

Medical Problems & Treatment

Potential medical problems can be broken down into several categories. First, there are the problems caused by extremes of temperature, altitude or motion. Then there are diseases and illnesses caused through poor environmental sanitation, animal or human contact and insect bites or stings. Simple cuts, bites and scratches can also cause problems.

Self-diagnosis and treatment can be risky, so wherever possible seek qualified help. Although we do give drug dosages in this section, they are for emergency use only. Medical advice should be sought where possible before administering any drugs. An embassy or consulate can usually recommend a good place to go for such advice.

Environmental Hazards

Altitude Sickness From Mendoza to Chile and northward to the Bolivian border, altitude sickness (apunamiento or soroche), also known as acute mountain sickness (AMS), represents a potential health hazard. In the thinner atmosphere above 3000m, or even lower in some cases, lack of oxygen causes many individuals to suffer headaches, nausea, shortness of breath, physical weakness and other symptoms that can lead to very serious consequences, especially if combined with heat exhaustion, sunburn or hypothermia.

There is no hard and fast rule as to how high is too high: AMS has been fatal at altitudes of 3000m, although it is much more common above 3450m. It is always wise to sleep at a lower altitude than the greatest height reached during the day. There are a number of other measures that can prevent or minimize AMS.

For mild cases, everyday painkillers such as aspirin or chachacoma, an herbal tea made from a common Andean shrub, will relieve symptoms until your body adapts. In the Andean Northwest, coca leaves are a common remedy, but authorities frown upon their usage, even by native peoples who sell them surreptitiously in the markets of Jujuy, Salta and other towns. If you experience AMS symptoms, avoid smoking, drinking alcohol, eating heavily or exercising strenuously. Most people recover within a few hours or days as their body produces more red blood cells to absorb oxygen, but if symptoms persist, it is imperative to descend to lower elevations. Following some simple guidelines will help:

- Ascend slowly – take frequent rest days, spending two to three nights for each climb of 1000m (3000ft). If you reach a high altitude by trekking, acclimatization takes place gradually, and you are less likely to be affected than if you fly direct.
- It is always wise to sleep at a lower altitude than the greatest height reached during the day, if possible. Also, once above 3000m, care should be taken not to increase the sleeping altitude by more than 300m per day.
- Drink extra fluids. Mountain air is dry and cold, and you lose moisture as you breathe.
- Eat light, high-carbohydrate meals for more energy. Snacks such as chocolate or dried fruit are easily available in Argentina.
- Avoid alcohol, which may increase the risk of dehydration.
- Avoid sedatives, which decrease respiration.

Fungal Infections Fungal infections, which occur with greater frequency in hot weather, are most likely to occur on the scalp, between the toes (athlete's foot) or fingers, in the groin and on the body (ringworm). You can get ringworm (which is a fungal infection, not a worm) from infected animals or other people. Athlete's foot can be picked up by walking on damp areas, such as shower floors.

To prevent fungal infections wear loose, comfortable clothes, avoid underwear made of artificial fibers, wash frequently and dry carefully. If you do get an infection, wash the infected area daily with a disinfectant or medicated soap and water, and rinse and dry well. Apply an antifungal powder, try to expose the infected area to air or sunlight as much as possible and wash all towels and underwear in hot water in addition to changing them often.

Heat Exhaustion & Sunburn Although Argentina is mostly a temperate country, its northern provinces lie within the Tropic of Capricorn, where the sun's direct rays can be devastating – sunburn is a particularly serious matter at high altitudes. In the western Chaco and other desert regions, where summer temperatures can exceed 40°C (100°F), dehydration is equally a problem. In far southern Patagonia and Tierra del Fuego, where the protective ozone layer has dissipated, sun protection is also a good idea despite the frequently overcast weather.

Use sunscreen and take extra care to cover areas not normally exposed to sun. Quality sunglasses and a Panama hat or baseball cap are excellent ideas. Aloe vera gel is good for mild sunburn. Protect your eyes with good-quality sunglasses, particularly if you will be near water, sand or snow.

Dehydration or salt deficiency can cause heat exhaustion. Take time to acclimatize to high temperatures and make sure that you get enough liquids. Salt tablets may also help, but adding extra salt to your food is better. Salt deficiency is characterized by fatigue, lethargy, headaches, giddiness and muscle cramps. Vomiting or diarrhea can also deplete your liquid and salt levels. Anhydrotic heat exhaustion, caused by the inability to sweat, is quite rare. Unlike the other forms of heat exhaustion, it is likely to strike people who have been in a hot climate for some time, rather than newcomers. Always carry a water bottle on long trips and take frequent drinks.

Heatstroke This serious, occasionally fatal, condition can occur if the body's heat-regulating mechanism breaks down and body temperature rises to dangerous levels. Long, continuous periods of exposure to high temperatures and insufficient fluids can leave you vulnerable to heatstroke. Avoid excessive alcohol intake or strenuous activity when you first arrive in a hot climate.

Symptoms include feeling unwell, not sweating very much (or at all) and a high body temperature (39°C to 41°C or 102°F to 106°F). Where sweating has ceased, the skin becomes flushed and red. Severe, throbbing headaches and lack of coordination also occur, and the sufferer may be confused or aggressive. Eventually the victim becomes delirious or convulses. Hospitalization is essential, but in the interim get victims out of the sun, remove their clothing, cover them with a wet sheet or towel and then fan continually. Give fluids if they are conscious.

Hypothermia At high altitudes in the mountains or high latitudes in Patagonia, cold and wet conditions can kill. Changeable weather at high altitudes can leave you vulnerable to exposure: After sunset, temperatures in the mountains or desert (even when simply taking a long bus trip) can drop from balmy to below freezing, while high winds and a sudden soaking can lower your body temperature too rapidly. If possible, avoid traveling alone; partners are more likely to avoid hypothermia successfully. If you must travel alone, especially when hiking, be sure someone knows your route and when you expect to return. In some areas, you should always be prepared for cold, wet or windy conditions even if you're just out walking or hitchhiking.

Hypothermia occurs when the body loses heat faster than it can produce heat and the core temperature of the body falls. It is surprisingly easy to progress from very cold to dangerously cold due to a combination of wind, wet clothing, fatigue and hunger, even if the air temperature is above freezing. It is best to dress in layers; silk, wool and some of the new artificial fibers are all good insulating materials. A hat is important, as a lot of heat is lost through the head. A strong, waterproof outer layer (and a 'space' blanket for emergencies) are essential. Always carry basic supplies, including food containing simple sugars to generate heat quickly, and fluid to drink.

Symptoms of hypothermia are exhaustion, numbness (particularly in the toes and fingers), shivering, slurred speech, irrational or violent behavior, lethargy, stumbling, dizzy spells, muscle cramps and violent bursts of energy. Irrationality may take the form of sufferers claiming they are warm and trying to take off their clothes.

To treat mild hypothermia, first get victims out of the wind and/or rain, remove their clothing if it's wet and replace it with dry, warm clothing. Give them hot liquids – not alcohol – and some high-calorie, easily digestible food. Do not rub victims; instead, allow them to slowly warm themselves. This should be enough to treat the early stages of hypothermia. Early recognition and treatment of mild hypothermia are the only ways to prevent severe hypothermia, which is a critical condition. In advanced stages it may be necessary to place victims in warm sleeping bags and get in with them.

Jet Lag Jet lag usually occurs when a person travels by air across more than three time zones (each time zone usually represents a one-hour time difference); however, some people experience it crossing only two zones. Many of the functions of the human body (such as temperature, pulse rate, and emptying of the bladder and bowels) are regulated by internal 24-hour cycles called circadian rhythms. When we travel long distances rapidly, our bodies take time to adjust to the 'new time' of our destination, and we may experience fatigue, disorientation, insomnia, anxiety, impaired concentration and loss of appetite. These effects will usually be gone within three days of arrival, but there are ways of minimizing the impact of jet lag:

• Rest for a couple of days prior to departure; try to avoid late nights and last-minute dashes for traveler's checks, passports and other important items.

• Try to select flight schedules that minimize sleep deprivation; arriving late in the day means you can go to sleep soon after you arrive. For very long flights, try to organize a stopover.

• Avoid excessive eating (which bloats the stomach) and alcohol (which causes dehydration) during the flight. Instead, drink plenty of noncarbonated, nonalcoholic drinks such as fruit juice or water.

• Avoid smoking, as this reduces the amount of oxygen in the airplane cabin even further and causes greater fatigue.

• Make yourself comfortable by wearing loose-fitting clothes and perhaps bringing an eye mask and earplugs to help you sleep.

Motion Sickness Eating lightly before and during a trip will reduce the chance of motion sickness. If you are prone to motion sickness, try to sit in a place that minimizes disturbance, for example, near the wing on aircraft or near the center on a bus. Fresh air usually helps; reading and cigarette smoke do not. Commercial motion-sickness preparations, which can cause drowsiness, have to be taken before the trip commences – once you already feel sick, it's too late. Ginger, a natural preventative, is available in capsule form.

Infectious Diseases

Cholera The cholera outbreak that swept Peru and some other South American countries in the early 1990s has so far not spread among the general population of Argentina, Uruguay and Paraguay, but it would be wise to take minimum precautions. Avoid raw seafood and do not consume ice in drinks in areas where drinking water may be suspect. Little frequented by foreigners, the Impenetrable of the mid-Chaco has been the site of Argentina's only cholera outbreaks.

The disease is characterized by a sudden onset of acute diarrhea with 'rice water' stools, vomiting, muscular cramps and extreme weakness. Seek medical help fast and treat for dehydration, which can be extreme.

If there is an appreciable delay in getting to the hospital, then begin taking tetracycline (one 250mg capsule four times daily for adults). Note that tectracycline is not recommended for children under nine years, nor for pregnant women.

A cholera vaccine exists, but is not very effective, and is not required as a condition of entry to any country in the world.

Diarrhea A change of water, food or climate can all cause the runs; diarrhea brought on by contaminated food or water is more serious. Despite all your precautions you may still have a mild bout of travelers' diarrhea, but a few rushed toilet trips with no other symptoms is not indicative of a serious problem. Moderate diarrhea, involving half a dozen loose movements in a day, is more of a nuisance.

Dehydration is the main danger with any diarrhea, particularly for children who can dehydrate quite quickly. Weak herbal tea with a little sugar, soda water or soft drinks allowed to go flat and diluted 50% with water are all good fluid replacements. With severe diarrhea a rehydrating solution is necessary to replace minerals and salts.

Commercially available oral rehydration salts (ORS) are very useful; add the contents of one packet to a liter of boiled or bottled water. In an emergency you can make up a solution of eight teaspoons of sugar to a liter of boiled water and provide salted crackers at the same time. Stick to a bland diet of bread, rice and bananas as you recover.

Lomotil or Imodium can bring relief from the symptoms, although they do not actually cure the problem. Only use these drugs if absolutely necessary – eg, if you *must* travel. Imodium is preferable for children. Do not use these drugs if the person has a high fever or is severely dehydrated. Antibiotics may be useful in treating diarrhea that is watery, with blood and mucous, and/or accompanied by a fever.

The recommended drugs (adults only) would be either norfloxacin, 400mg twice daily for three days, or ciprofloxacin, 500mg twice daily for three days.

The drug bismuth subsalicylate has also been used successfully. The dosage for adults is two tablets or 30ml, and for children it is one tablet or 10ml. This dose can be repeated every 30 minutes to one hour, with no more than eight doses in a 24-hour period.

The drug of choice for children would be co-trimoxazole (Bactrim, Septrin, Resprim) with dosage dependent on weight.

Dysentery This serious illness, caused by contaminated food or water, is characterized by severe diarrhea, often with blood or mucus in the stool. There are two kinds of dysentery: bacillary and amoebic. Bacillary dysentery is characterized by a high fever and rapid onset; headache, vomiting and stomach pains are also symptoms. It generally does not last longer than a week, but it is highly contagious. Amoebic dysentery is often more gradual in the onset of symptoms, with cramping abdominal pain and vomiting less likely; fever may not be present. It is not a self-limiting disease: It will persist until treated and can recur and cause long-term health problems.

A stool test is necessary to diagnose which kind of dysentery you might have, so you should seek medical help urgently. In case of an emergency, the drugs norfloxacin or ciprofloxacin can be used as presumptive treatment for bacillary dysentery, and metronidazole (Flagyl) can be used for amoebic dysentery.

For bacillary dysentery, norfloxacin 400mg twice daily for seven days, or ciprofloxacin 500mg twice daily for seven days, are the recommended dosages.

If you're unable to find either of these drugs, then a useful alternative is co-trimoxazole 160/800mg (Bactrim, Septrin, Resprim) twice daily for seven days. This is a sulpha drug and must not be used by people with a known sulpha allergy.

In the case of children, the drug co-trimoxazole is a reasonable first-line treatment. To deal with amoebic dysentery, the recommended adult dosage of metronidazole (Flagyl) is one 750mg to 800mg capsule three times daily for five days. Children ages 8 to 12 years should have half the adult dose; the dosage for younger children is one-third the adult dose.

An alternative to Flagyl is Tinidazole, known as Fasigyn, taken as a 2g daily dose for three days. Drinking alcohol must be avoided during treatment and for 48 hours afterward.

Giardiasis Commonly known as Giardia, and sometimes 'beaver fever,' this intestinal parasite is present in contaminated water. Giardia has even contaminated apparently pristine rushing streams in the backcountry.

Symptoms are stomach cramps, nausea, a bloated stomach, watery, foul-smelling diarrhea and frequent gas. Giardia can appear several weeks after exposure to the parasite; symptoms may disappear for a few days and then return, a pattern which may continue. Fasigyn or metronidazole (Flagyl) are the recommended drugs for treatment. Either can be used in a single treatment dose. Antibiotics are useless.

Hepatitis Hepatitis is a general term for inflammation of the liver. There are many causes of this condition: drugs, alcohol and infections are but a few. The discovery of new strains has led to a virtual alphabet soup, with hepatitis A, B, C, D, E and a rumored G. These letters identify specific agents that cause viral hepatitis. Viral hepatitis is an infection of the liver, which can lead to jaundice (yellow skin), fever, lethargy and digestive problems. It can have no symptoms at all, with the infected person not aware that he or she has the disease. Travelers shouldn't be too paranoid about this apparent proliferation of hepatitis strains; hep C, D, E and G are fairly rare (so far), and following the same precautions as for A and B should be all that's necessary to avoid them.

Viral hepatitis can be divided into two groups on the basis of how it is spread. The first route of transmission is via contaminated food and water, and the second route is via blood and bodily fluids.

Hepatitis A is a very common disease in most countries, especially those with poor standards of sanitation. Most people in developing countries are infected as children; they often don't develop symptoms, but do develop lifelong immunity. The disease poses a real threat to the traveler, as people are unlikely to have been exposed to hepatitis A in developed countries.

The symptoms are fever, chills, headache, fatigue, feelings of weakness and aches and pains, followed by loss of appetite, nausea, vomiting, abdominal pain, dark urine, light-colored feces and jaundiced skin; the whites of the eyes may also turn yellow. You should seek medical advice, but in general there is not much you can do apart from resting, drinking lots of fluids, eating lightly and avoiding fatty foods. People who have had hepatitis must forgo alcohol for six months after the illness, as hepatitis attacks the liver and it needs that amount of time to recover.

The routes of transmission are via contaminated water, shellfish contaminated by sewage or foodstuffs sold by food handlers with poor hygiene. Taking care with what you eat and drink can go a long way toward preventing this disease. If there is any risk of exposure, additional cover is highly recommended (see Immunizations earlier in this chapter).

Hepatitis B, which used to be called serum hepatitis, is spread through contact with infected blood, blood products or bodily fluids; for example, through sexual contact, unsterilized needles and blood transfusions. Other risk situations include having a shave or getting a tattoo in a local shop, or having your ears pierced. The symptoms of hep B are much the same as hep A except that they are more severe and may lead to irreparable liver damage or even liver cancer. Although there is no treatment for hepatitis B, a cheap and effective vaccine is available; see Immunizations earlier in this section.

Hepatitis C is similar to B but seems to lead to liver disease more rapidly. Often referred to as the 'Delta' virus, hepatitis D only occurs in chronic carriers of hepatitis B. Hepatitis E is a very recently discovered virus, of which little is yet known. It appears to be rather common in developing countries, generally causing mild hepatitis, although it can be very serious in pregnant women. Care with water supplies is the only current prevention, as there are no specific vaccines for this type of hepatitis. At present it doesn't appear to be too great a risk for travelers.

Hydatidosis Spread by contact with dogs that have eaten the entrails of infected sheep, this highly contagious disease is prevalent in areas like Argentine and Chilean Patagonia, where sheep numbers are very high, and dogs may come into contact with them. Though not cause for panic, it is a potentially serious matter; do not eat homemade sausages in this region, and avoid contact with sheepdogs in particular.

Sexually Transmitted Diseases Sexual contact with an infected partner spreads certain diseases. While abstinence is the only 100% effective preventative, using condoms also reduces your risk. Gonorrhea and syphilis are the most common of these diseases; sores, blisters or rashes around the genitals, discharges, or pain when urinating are common symptoms. Symptoms may be less marked or not observed at all in women. Syphilis symptoms eventually disappear completely, but the disease continues and can cause severe problems in later years. The treatment of gonorrhea and syphilis is by antibiotics.

There are numerous other sexually transmitted diseases, and effective treatment is available for most. However, there is no cure for herpes or, more importantly, AIDS (Acquired Immune Deficiency Syndrome). This life-threatening disease certainly exists in Argentina, Uruguay and Paraguay, though not on the scale that it does in Brazil or parts of the USA.

Two HIV/AIDS support lines in Buenos Aires are Fundación Buenos Aires SIDA (☎ 4304-5544), Carlos Calvo 1443 and Línea SIDA (☎ 4922-1617), Zuviría 64.

HIV (the Human Immunodeficiency Virus) may develop into AIDS. HIV is a major problem in many countries. Any exposure to blood, blood products or bodily fluids may put the individual at risk. Infection can come from having unprotected sex or sharing contaminated needles. Apart from abstinence, the most effective preventative is always to have safe sex using condoms. Without a blood test, it is impossible to detect the HIV-positive status of an otherwise healthy-looking person.

HIV/AIDS can also be spread through infected blood transfusions; many countries cannot afford to screen blood. It can also be spread by dirty needles – vaccinations, acupuncture, tattooing and ear or nose piercing can potentially be dangerous if the equipment is not clean. If you do need an injection, ask to see the syringe unwrapped in front of you, or better still, take a needle and syringe pack with you overseas; it is a cheap insurance package against the chance of HIV infection.

Fear of HIV infection should never preclude treatment for serious medical conditions. Although there may be a risk of infection, it is very small indeed. A good resource for help and information is the US Centers for Disease Control AIDS hotline (☎ 800-342-2437).

Insect-Borne Diseases

Chagas' Disease Darwin may have suffered from this parasitic disease, transmitted by a bug that lives in mud (adobe) huts and comes out to feed at night. The bite is often mistaken for that of a bedbug, but early symptoms of Chagas' disease include a hard, violet-colored swelling appearing in about a week at the site of the bite, followed by swelling of the lymph glands or by a fever. The long-term complications can be quite serious and can eventually lead to death years later. Most cases of Chagas' disease have appeared in Brazil, but travelers should avoid sleeping in or near mud huts. If you have no other choice, sleep under a mosquito net, use insecticides and insect repellents, and check for hidden insects.

Malaria There is a minor risk of malaria in rural areas of northern Argentina, bordering Bolivia in Salta and Jujuy provinces. Chloroquine is the recommended medication here.

Less Common Diseases

Rabies Dogs are noted carriers of rabies. Any bite, scratch or even lick from a warm-blooded, furry animal should be cleaned immediately and thoroughly. Scrub with soap and running water, and then clean with an alcohol solution. If there is any possibility that the animal is infected, medical help should be sought immediately. Even if the animal is not rabid, all bites should be treated seriously as they can become infected or can result in tetanus. A rabies vaccination is now available and should be considered if you are in a high-risk category – eg, if you intend to explore caves (bat bites can be dangerous) or work with animals.

Shellfish Poisoning In Argentine and Chilean Patagonia, most notably in Tierra del Fuego, collection of shellfish is not advisable and, in many cases, not permitted because of toxic 'red tide' conditions.

Tetanus Tetanus is difficult to treat but is preventable with immunization. Tetanus occurs when a wound becomes infected by a germ that lives in the feces of animals or people, so thoroughly clean all cuts, punctures or animal bites. Tetanus is also known as lockjaw, and the first symptom may be discomfort in swallowing, or stiffening of the jaw and neck; this is followed by painful convulsions of the jaw and the whole body.

Yellow Fever Yellow fever is a very low-risk matter in Argentina and Uruguay, which do not require vaccination certificates, and is only a slightly higher risk in Paraguay. Nevertheless, a certificate is a good idea for anyone visiting neighboring tropical countries.

Hantavirus Northern Patagonia, particularly the area around Bariloche and El Bolsón, has been the site of past outbreaks of a particularly lethal strain of hantavirus, spread through contact with rat urine or feces. The virus loses its potency on contact with sunlight or fresh air, so travelers should take caution to avoid places where rodents congregate, especially, but not only, abandoned buildings. While the odds of contracting hantavirus are statistically small, the consequences are potentially fatal.

Cuts, Bites & Stings

Skin punctures can easily become infected in hot climates and may be difficult to heal. Treat any cut with an antiseptic such as Betadine. When possible avoid bandages and Band-aids, which can keep wounds wet.

Bee and wasp stings are usually painful rather than dangerous. Calamine lotion will give relief, and ice packs will reduce the pain and swelling. Some spiders have dangerous bites, and scorpion stings are very painful, but neither is likely to be fatal. Bites are best avoided by not using bare hands to turn over rocks or large pieces of wood.

Snakebites do not cause instantaneous death, and antivenins are usually available. Seek medical help, if possible with the dead snake for identification, but don't attempt to catch the snake if there is even a remote possibility of being bitten again. In the case of a snakebite, avoid slashing and sucking

the wound, avoid tight tourniquets (a lightly constricting band above the bite can help), avoid ice, keep the affected area below the level of the heart and move it as little as possible. Do not ingest alcohol or any drugs. Stay calm and get to a medical facility as soon as possible.

In the case of spiders and scorpions, there are no special first-aid techniques. A black widow spider bite may be barely noticeable, but the venom can be dangerous, and if you're bitten you should seek medical attention immediately. Centipede, bee, wasp and ant bites and stings may be relieved by application of ice.

If you are hiking a long way from the nearest phone or other help, and you are bitten or stung, you should hike out and get help, particularly in the case of snake and spider bites. Reactions are often delayed for up to 12 hours, and you can hike out before then. It is recommended that you always hike with a companion.

Ticks are parasitic arachnids that may be present in brush, forest and grasslands, where hikers often get them on their legs or in their boots. The adults suck blood from hosts by burying their head into skin, but are often found unattached and can simply be brushed off. However, if one has attached itself to you, pulling it off and leaving its head in your skin increases the likelihood of infection or disease, as well as grossing you out.

To avoid ticks, use insect repellent. To remove an attached tick, use a pair of tweezers, grab it by the head and gently pull it straight out – do not twist it. (If no tweezers are available, use your fingers, but protect them from contamination with a piece of tissue or paper.) Disinfect the wound immediately. It was once recommended to touch the tick with a hot object like a match or a cigarette or to rub oil, alcohol or petroleum jelly on it. But these removal remedies are no longer recommended as they may cause the tick to regurgitate noxious substances or saliva into the wound. If you get sick in the next couple of weeks or notice a rash where you were bitten, consult a doctor.

Bedbugs live in various places, but particularly in dirty mattresses and bedding. Spots of blood on linen or on the wall around the bed can be read as a suggestion to find another hotel. Bedbugs leave itchy bites in neat rows. Calamine lotion helps to relieve itchiness.

All lice cause itching and discomfort. They make themselves at home in your hair (head lice), your clothing (body lice) or in your pubic hair (crabs). You catch lice through direct contact with infected people or by sharing combs, clothing and the like. A special powder or shampoo treatment will kill the lice, and infected clothing should then be washed in hot water.

Gynecological Problems & Pregnancy

Poor diet, lowered resistance due to the use of antibiotics for stomach upsets and even contraceptive pills can lead to vaginal infections when traveling in hot climates. Wearing skirts or loose-fitting trousers and cotton underwear helps prevent infections.

Yeast infections, characterized by a rash, itching and discharge, can be treated with a vinegar or even lemon-juice douche or with yogurt. Nystatin, miconazole or clotrimazole pessaries or vaginal cream are the usual treatments. Trichomonas is a more serious infection; symptoms are a discharge and a burning sensation when urinating. Sexual partners must also be treated, and if a vinegar-water douche is not effective, seek medical attention. Flagyl is the prescribed drug.

Most miscarriages occur during the first three months of pregnancy, so this is the riskiest time to travel. The last three months should also be spent within reasonable distance of good medical care, as serious problems can develop at this time. Pregnant women should avoid unnecessary medication, but vaccinations and malarial prophylactics should still be taken where possible. Additional care should be taken to prevent illness, and particular attention should be paid to diet and nutrition. Abortion is illegal, though not unheard of, in Argentina.

WOMEN TRAVELERS

Being a woman in Argentina is a challenge, especially if you are young, traveling alone and/or come with an inflexible liberal attitude. In some ways Argentina is a safer place for a woman than Europe, the USA and most other Latin American countries, but dealing with this machismo culture can be a real pain in the ass.

Some males brimming with testosterone feel the need to comment on a woman's attractiveness. This often happens when the woman is alone and walking by on the street; it occasionally happens to two or more women walking together, but never to a heterosexual couple. Verbal comments include crude language, hisses, whistles and *piropos*, which many Argentine males consider the art of complimenting a woman. Piropos are often vulgar, although some can be creative and even eloquent. (One cited in the *Buenos Aires Herald* was 'Oh God, the sky is parting and angels are falling.') Much as you may want to kick them where it counts, the best thing to do is completely ignore the comments. After all, many porteñas do enjoy getting these 'compliments,' and most men don't necessarily mean to be insulting; they're just doing what males in their culture were taught to do.

On the plus side of machismo, expect men to hold a door open for you and always let you enter first, including getting on buses; this gives you a better chance at grabbing an empty seat, so get in there quick.

GAY & LESBIAN TRAVELERS

Argentina is a strongly Catholic country, but there are enclaves of tolerance towards gays and lesbians in Buenos Aires. Argentine men are more physically demonstrative than their North American and European counterparts, so behaviors such as kissing on the cheek in greeting or a vigorous embrace is innocuous even to those who express unease with homosexuals. Lesbians walking hand-in-hand should attract little attention, since heterosexual Argentine women frequently do so, but this would be very conspicuous behavior for males. When in doubt, it's best to be discreet.

DISABLED TRAVELERS

Travelers with disabilities will find things somewhat difficult. The wheelchair-bound in particular will quickly realize that Buenos Aires' narrow, busy and uneven sidewalks are difficult to negotiate. Crossing streets is also a problem, since not every corner has ramps and Argentine drivers don't have much patience for slower pedestrians, handicapped or not. Nevertheless, Argentines with disabilities do get around, and in Buenos Aires there exist a few buses described as *piso bajo,* which lower to provide wheelchair lifts.

SENIOR TRAVELERS

Senior travelers should encounter no particular difficulties traveling in Argentina, where older citizens traditionally enjoy a great deal of respect; on crowded buses, for instance, most Argentines will readily offer their seat to an older person. Senior discounts on transportation and most other services are, however, virtually a thing of the past.

For travel packages with other seniors, check out W www.elderhostel.org and do a search for Argentina.

TRAVEL WITH CHILDREN

Argentina is extremely child-friendly in terms of safety, health, people's attitudes and family-oriented activities, although there are regional differences. The country's numerous plazas and public parks, many with playgrounds, are popular gathering spots for families.

Once children are old enough to cross the street safely and find their way back home, parents don't hesitate to send unaccompanied kids on errands and on visits to friends or neighbors. While most visiting parents are not likely to feel comfortable doing this, they can usually count on children being safe in public places.

Argentines are very helpful on public transport. Often someone will give up a seat for a parent and child, but if that does not occur, an older person may offer to put the child on his or her lap. This is also a country where people frequently touch each other, so your children may be patted on the head or gently caressed.

Basic restaurants provide a wide selection of food suitable for children (vegetables, pasta, meat, chicken, fish), but adult portions are normally so large that small children rarely need a separate order. Waiters are accustomed to providing extra plates and cutlery for children, though some places may add a small additional charge. Argentina's high-quality ice cream is a special treat.

Breast-feeding in public is not uncommon, though you'll want to be discreet and cover yourself. Poorly maintained public bathrooms may also be a concern for some parents. Always carry toilet paper and wet wipes. While a woman may take a young boy into the ladies' room, it would be socially unacceptable for a man to take a girl of any age into the mens' room.

USEFUL ORGANIZATIONS

These organizations are all located in Buenos Aires. Asatej (☎ 4312-0101 info, ☎ 4114-7500 sales, fax 4311-6158, W www.asatej.com), Florida 835, 3rd floor, is Argentina's nonprofit student-travel agency and can serve you 9am to 6pm weekdays. The organization encourages budget travel, and you don't have to be a student to take advantage of their services. Asatej is also affiliated with Hostelling International through the Red Argentina de Albergues Juveniles (see Accommodations later in this chapter for contact information).

The national parks administration (☎ 4312-0783), Santa Fe 690, provides information on national parks and stocks a small number of publications of interest to conservationists and wildlife enthusiasts. Another address of interest to conservationists is the pro-wildlife organization Fundación Vida Silvestre Argentina (☎/fax 4331-3631), Defensa 245. It opens 10am to 6pm weekdays, with a break for lunch.

Bird watchers can contact the Asociación Ornitológica del Plata (Aves Argentinas; ☎ 4312-8958, W www.avesargentinas.org.ar), 25 de Mayo 749. The association offers classes and trips around Buenos Aires and Argentina. Those interested in helping to save the environment can contact Greenpeace

(☎ 4962-2291, W www.greenpeace.org.ar), Mansilla 3046, a few blocks from the Agüero station on Línea D of the Subte.

If you're looking for a group of instant friends, contact Buenos Aires Freetime (e bafreetime@yahoo.com, W www.clubs .yahoo.com/clubs/buenosairesfreetime). The group's members change by the week, but most are Argentines with some expats sprinkled in, and most everyone speaks some English.

For information on ACA, Argentina's Automobile Association, see the Getting Around chapter.

DANGERS & ANNOYANCES

Argentina's flailing economy has prompted scattered riots (and President Fernando de la Rúa's resignation in December 2001) – it's wise to be aware of current political events. However, Argentina is generally safer than many other Latin American countries. You normally can comfortably walk around at all hours of the night in many (but not all) places. Check with locals to see where it's safe and where you need to be more careful. Especially in the cities, don't stagger around drunk, always be aware of your surroundings and look like you know where you're going with the attitude that you could kick anyone's ass who gives you grief.

Many Argentine drivers jump the gun when the traffic signal is about to change to green. They also drive very fast and change lanes unpredictably. Be wary of vehicles turning right; even though pedestrians at corners and crosswalks have legal right-of-way, very few drivers respect this and will hardly slow down when you are crossing. Be especially careful of buses, which can be reckless and because of their large size, particularly dangerous.

Purse-snatching and pickpocketing scenarios are more of a concern in the bigger cities, as in any country of the world. The usual street smarts will often keep you safe.

The state terrorism of the 1970s and 1980s has subsided, but deadly attempts on Jewish and Israeli centers in Buenos Aires in 1992 and 1994 raised questions about the government's commitment to public safety. In the months prior to the bombings, anti-Semitic incidents were increasingly common, and most landmarks of the Jewish community are now heavily fortified with concrete barriers, some of them thinly disguised as planters. Potential visitors concerned with domestic travel conditions in Argentina or any country should visit the Web site W www.le.ac.uk/dsp/ mfas.html, which is a list of different countries' ministries of foreign affairs.

The police and military may be of more concern than common criminals. Both military and police officials have been found responsible for extrajudicial killings of prisoners and conscripts, for which some officials have gone to prison, but foreign visitors are more likely to experience petty harassment. For motorists, so-called safety campaigns often result in citations for very minor equipment violations, which ostensibly carry very high fines (up to US$200 for an inadequate emergency brake). In most cases, corrupt officers will settle for less expensive *coimas* (bribes), but this requires considerable caution and tact on your part. For further information, see the Getting Around chapter.

Many Argentines are heavy smokers. Prepare yourself to be exposed to tobacco smoke in restaurants, bars, cafés, stores, offices and on the streets. A few restaurants have no-smoking areas. Local buses are relatively smoke-free, though the odd bus driver will actually light up while driving. On long-distance buses smoking is also prohibited, but some tobacco addict will occasionally try to get away with a puff. Don't try to smoke on the Subte, where it's prohibited; all domestic flights are smoke-free as well.

If you're bothered by second-hand smoke in an inappropriate setting, such as a taxi, plead an *alergia* (allergy) rather than getting indignant.

During holidays such as Christmas and New Year's, youths set off high-powered, poorly regulated and very dangerous firecrackers in the streets or even toss them from high-rise apartments. It may be better to stay inside at these times.

The declining economy may be responsible for a recent surge in muggings and thefts, some of which have occurred while the victims were riding in taxis. *Remises,* unmarked call taxis, are generally considered more secure than taxis hailed from the street, since established companies send them out. Most hotels and restaurants will gladly ring remises for you.

Almost all taxi drivers are honest people making a living, and here's some advice to keep them that way. Try not to give taxi drivers large bills; not only will they usually not 'have' change, but there have been cases where a driver will quickly and deftly replace a larger bill you give them with a smaller bill they claim you gave them. One solution is to verbalize how much you are giving them and ask if they have change for it *'¿Tienes cambio de un veinte?'* ('Do you have change for a twenty?'). Also, if you are obviously a tourist going to or from a touristy spot, don't ask how much a fare is somewhere as this makes for the temptation to quote you an inflated price rather than using the meter. It's also a good idea to lock the back doors after you get in.

BUSINESS HOURS

Traditionally, business hours in Argentina commence by 8am and break at midday for three or even four hours, during which people return home for lunch and a brief siesta. After the siesta, shops reopen until 8pm or 9pm. This schedule is still common in the provinces, but government offices and many businesses in Buenos Aires have adopted a more conventional 8am to 5pm schedule in the interests of 'greater efficiency.'

PUBLIC HOLIDAYS & SPECIAL EVENTS

Government offices and businesses are closed on the numerous public holidays. If the holiday falls on a mid-week day or weekend day, it's often bumped to the nearest Monday. Your public transport options are also more limited on holidays. Public holidays (when business and govern-

ment offices are closed) are preceded by an asterisk in the list below.

The following list of events does not include provincial holidays, which may vary considerably. For more specific events, check the listings of particular towns or cities.

*January 1 – Año Nuevo (New Year's Day) is usually heralded by raucous parties beginning the night before.

February/March (dates vary) – Carnaval, the pre-Lenten festival, is not as rockin' in Argentina as in Brazil, but the celebration is rowdy in the northeast, especially in the cities of Gualeguaychú and Corrientes.

February/March (dates vary) – Wine Harvest Festival kicks off with parades, folkloric events and a royal coronation – all in honor of Mendoza's intoxicating beverage.

*March/April (dates vary) – Viernes Santo (Good Friday) and Pascua (Easter) are usually spent with family and friends; many businesses close on Viernes Santo; Mar del Plata or Cordoba are popular destinations for Argentines who take a vacation during the holiday.

*April 2 – Día de las Malvinas commemorates the establishment of the Comandancia Política y Militar de las Malvinas in 1829, otherwise known as the day that Argentina claimed military rule over the Islas Malvinas (Falkland Islands). This power was exercised only once, during the Falklands war in 1982 (obviously the British had other ideas as to who had control).

*May 1 – Día del Trabajador (Labor Day) is usually spent laboring over the barbecue in many Argentine households.

May 8 – Día de Virgen of Luján is the day that large numbers of believers arrive in Luján to honor the Virgin Mary; other large pilgrimages to Luján take place in early October and on December 8 (see later).

*May 25 – Revolución de Mayo commemorates the 1810 revolution against Spain. The president recognizes this event by going to the cathedral and there's also a military parade. In many homes, people eat *pastelitos,* square, fried pastries similar to empanadas.

*June 20 – Día de la Bandera (Flag Day) is especially notable in Rosario, with ceremonies culminating at the city's flag monument, marking the anniversary of Belgrano's death.

*July 9 – Día de la Independencia is the day that Argentina officially declared its independence from Spain in 1816. On this day the president invites schoolchildren to have hot chocolate and churros with him; he also visits Tucumán (where independence was declared).

*August 17 – Día de San Martín marks the anniversary of José de San Martín's death (1778-1850). He is credited for breaking Spain's hold on Argentina in 1816.

*October 12 – Día de la Raza (Columbus Day)

November 10 – Día de la Tradición (Day of Traditional Culture) kicks off with a salute to the gaucho; this festival is especially significant in San Antonio de Areco, the most gaucho of towns.

*December 8 – Día de la Concepción Inmaculada is a religious holiday that celebrates the immaculate conception of the Virgin Mary, and pilgrimages are often made to holy sites on this day.

*December 25 – Navidad (Christmas Day)

ACTIVITIES

Argentina is full of places where you can find something exciting to do. Areas along the Andes, such as Mendoza and El Chaltén, attract rafters, climbers, skiers and trekkers. Certain sports, such as golfing and tennis, are traditionally for more elite sectors of Argentine society, although soccer *(fútbol)* is played by everyone. You'll see pick-up soccer games wherever you go, but unless you're *very* confident of your skills, you probably shouldn't join in. These people are serious about their national sport.

Skiing

Although surprisingly little-known to outsiders, Argentine skiing can be outstanding. Most locations offer super powder, good cover and plenty of sunny days, but prices are not cheap. Many resorts have large ski schools with instructors from all over the world, so even language is not a problem. At some of the older resorts equipment can be a little antiquated, but in general the quality of skiing more than compensates.

There are three main areas where skiers can indulge themselves: the southern Cuyo region, featuring Las Leñas and Los Molles near Malargüe; the Lakes District, including the Cerro Catedral complex near Bariloche and Chapelco near San Martín de los Andes; and the world's most southerly commercial skiing near Ushuaia in Tierra del Fuego. (These areas are covered in further detail later in this book.)

Cycling

Cycling has become a popular activity in this country, and many Argentines take long bike trips in summer. Both road and mountain bikes are common, but the latter are indispensable for riding on bad roads in remote areas. The best areas for relatively short, scenic spins are Mendoza and the Lake District, though desolate Patagonian gravel roads attract hardy mountain bikers willing to put up with the often insanely strong winds. Many towns and cities, especially those catering to the tourist trade, have places where you can rent bicycles, though these often aren't of great quality. For more information, see the Getting Around chapter.

Hiking & Mountaineering

Argentina's vast open spaces offer plenty of wilderness walks. The most popular areas are the southern Andean national parks along the Chilean border (from Lanín south to Los Glaciares), Tierra del Fuego and the high Andean reaches west of Mendoza. The northern Andes around the Valle de Humahuaca are also good, and the gentle Sierra de la Ventana and Sierras de Córdoba offer something off the beaten track.

See Lonely Planet's *Trekking in the Patagonian Andes* for more information on southern Andean walks.

Aconcagua, west of Mendoza, is a magnet for climbers, but there are plenty of other high peaks in the Andes – many of them more interesting than South America's highest point. The Fitz Roy Range, in southern Patagonia, is another popular area, as are the mountains of Parque Nacional Nahuel Huapi, around Bariloche.

Whitewater Rafting & Kayaking

This increasingly popular activity takes place on the rivers that descend from the Andean divide, from San Luis and Mendoza on south. The main possibilities are the Río

Mendoza and Río Diamante in the Mendoza region, the Río Hua Hum and Río Meliquina near San Martín de los Andes, and the Río Limay and Río Manso near Bariloche. Some of these, most notably the Limay, are gentle Class II floats, but most of the rest are Class III-plus whitewater.

LANGUAGE COURSES

Most opportunities for Spanish-language instruction are in Buenos Aires. Consult the classified section of the *Buenos Aires Herald* (especially on Sunday), which lists several institutes and private tutors, and even has opportunities for teaching English. For more information on recommended language institutes, see the Buenos Aires chapter.

Before signing up for a course, read the description carefully, note all fees and try to determine whether it suits your particular needs. Remember that small-group instruction or individual tutoring offer the best opportunities for improving language skills, but are obviously more expensive.

WORK

Many travelers come to Buenos Aires to teach English, and despite the economic downturn there's still work available for determined native English speakers (certified or not). Working at an institute, you can earn about US$12 to US$16 per hour for group classes, US$20 per hour and up for private classes. The city's high cost of living makes it hard to save money, though, especially if you want to have fun; and there are some slow periods, like the January and February summer vacation months. Check the classified section of the *Buenos Aires Herald* for leads, call up the institutes or visit expat bars and start networking. Residence and work permits are possible to obtain, but the effort is not worth it for some expats, and many work illegally.

ACCOMMODATIONS

The spectrum of accommodations in Argentina ranges from campgrounds to five-star luxury hotels. Where you stay will depend on your budget, standards and your location, as well as how thorough a search you care to make in an unfamiliar destination, but you should be able to find something reasonable. Expect the more tourist-oriented hotels to offer at least a smattering of staff able to speak English, though at more provincial accommodations you'll need to learn the basic 'How much do the rooms cost?' ('¿Cuánto cuestan las habitaciónes?') or 'Can I see a room?' ('¿Pudiera ver una habitación?') For all accommodations, expect price hikes during holiday periods such as Easter week or the month of July.

The price for budget accommodations can vary widely from city to city, but generally falls between US$10 per person (for a hostel bed) to about US$20 to US$35 for very simple double rooms, many with private bath. These may not include breakfast. Note that tourist offices are reluctant to recommend these places: This is partly because some of the cheapest places can be pretty squalid, but mostly because the staff think that foreign visitors should stay in the best and most expensive lodging. Mid-range hotels are around US$40 to US$60, and rooms pretty much always come with breakfast, private bath, TV and phone.

High-end hotels run US$70 and up, and often include amenities like a mini-fridge, cable TV, room service, a restaurant on the premises and a nice breakfast. These often do not include the whopping 21% IVA tax in their rates, so check beforehand. Some hotels in certain cities may cater to businesspeople, so you may be able to negotiate a special rate by flashing a business card (these same hotels also drop their rates on weekends).

In all price categories, hotel checkout times vary from around 10am to noon; while many places are flexible within reason, some will charge guests who overstay. Practically all of them provide temporary luggage storage for travelers with late afternoon or evening flights or bus trips.

For long-term rentals in the capital, see the Buenos Aires chapter. Note that you can extend a stay at practically any hotel in any city for a discounted price, and the longer you stay the deeper the discount. Make sure to negotiate this *before* you begin your stay.

Camping & Refugios

If traveling on a budget, especially coming overland from the central Andean countries, consider camping in Argentina. This way, you may be able to keep expenses for accommodations at roughly what you would pay for hotels in Bolivia or Peru. Nearly every Argentine city and many smaller towns have fairly centralized municipal (or recently privatized) campgrounds, where you can pitch a tent for about US$5 per night – sometimes more, sometimes less. Most Argentines arrive in their own automobiles, but backpackers are welcome.

These usually woodsy sites have excellent facilities – hot showers, toilets, laundry, a *fogón* (fire pit) for cooking, a restaurant or *confitería* (café), a grocery store, sometimes even a swimming pool. Personal possessions are generally secure, since attendants keep a watchful eye on the grounds, but don't leave cash or costly items like cameras lying around unnecessarily.

There are drawbacks, though. Argentines are renowned *trasnochadores* (night people). During summer vacation, it is not unusual for them to celebrate with an *asado* (barbecue) until almost daylight, so in extreme cases you may find sleep difficult unless you can isolate yourself on the margins of the campground – often the least-appealing areas. On the other hand, you may be invited to join in one of these gregarious groups. Otherwise, avoid the most popular tourist areas in the prime vacation months of January and February.

For comfort, invest in a good, dome-style tent with rainfly before coming to South America, where camping equipment is costlier and often inferior. A three-season sleeping bag should be adequate for almost any weather condition. A good petrol or kerosene-burning stove is also a good idea, since white gas *(bencina)* is expensive and available only at chemical supply shops or hardware stores. Firewood is a limited and often expensive resource. Bring mosquito repellent, since many campsites are near rivers or lakes.

There are, of course, opportunities for more rugged camping in the national parks and the backcountry. Parks have both organized sites resembling those in the cities and towns, and more isolated, rustic alternatives. Some parks have *refugios,* basic shelters for hikers in the high country.

Hostels

There are several youth hostels in Buenos Aires and throughout Argentina. Most are excellent places to stay, where you can meet and hang out with fellow travelers, both foreign and Argentine. All have common kitchens and living spaces, as well as shared baths; some have private rooms for couples. Remember that Argentines are late-nighters and can be noisy, so it's a good idea to bring earplugs along.

Most hostels don't insist on a youth hostel card, but they usually charge a couple dollars more for nonmembers. Since many hostels are open in summer only, especially in the provinces, it's a good idea to phone before heading on over.

Argentina's two competing hostel organizations, both based in Buenos Aires, are the Red Argentina de Alojamiento para Jóvenes (RAAJ; ☎ 4511-8712, fax 4312-0089; ⓦ www.hostels.org.ar), on the 3rd floor at Florida 835, and the Asociación Argentina de Albergues de la Juventud (AAAJ; ☎ 4476-1001), on the 2nd floor at Talcahuano 214. Both organizations overlap jurisdictions, but the former has a smaller and generally better list than the inferior AAAJ. A few hostel-style places belong to neither system, but some of these are nevertheless very good.

Hospedajes, Pénsiones & Residenciales

These offer cheap accommodations but the differences between them are sometimes ambiguous; all may even be called hotels. Rooms and furnishings are modest, usually including beds with clean sheets and blankets. Always ask to see a room. While some have private bathrooms, others come with shared facilities.

An *hospedaje* is usually a large family home with a few extra bedrooms (the bath is shared). Often they are not permanent businesses but temporary expedients in times of economic distress. Similarly, a *pensión* offers short-term accommodations in a family home but may also have permanent lodgers. Meals may be available.

Residenciales, which are permanent businesses, figure more commonly in tourist office lists. In general, they occupy buildings designed for short-stay accommodations, although some (known euphemistically as *albergues transitorios*) cater to clientele who intend only *very* short stays of two hours maximum. Prostitutes occasionally use them, but so do young Argentine couples with no other indoor alternative.

Hotels

Proper hotels vary from utilitarian one-star accommodations to five-star luxury, but do not assume a perfect correlation between these classifications and their standards. Many one-star places are a better value than three- and four-star lodgings. In general, hotels provide a room with attached private bath, often a telephone, and sometimes a television. Normally they have a confitería or restaurant and may include breakfast in the price. In the top categories you will have room and laundry service, a swimming pool and perhaps a gym, a bar, shopping galleries and other luxuries.

Rentals & Homestays

House and apartment rentals can save you money if you're staying in one place for an extended period. In resort locations, such as Mar del Plata or Bariloche, you can lodge several people for the price of one by seeking an apartment and cooking your own meals. Check tourist offices or newspapers for listings.

During the tourist season, mostly in the interior, families rent rooms to visitors. Often these are excellent bargains, permitting access to cooking and laundry facilities and hot showers, as well as encouraging contact with Argentines. Tourist offices in most smaller towns, but even in cities as large as Salta and Mendoza, maintain lists of such accommodations.

Estancias

An increasingly popular way of passing an Argentine vacation is to stay at an *estancia,* or ranch, both in the area around Buenos Aires and even in remote Patagonia. Some estancias that have only recently begun to take guests are barely prepared for a regular tourist influx and may even boot their own children out of bed to accommodate them. Many others, though, have been doing this for awhile and are set up fairly well (check tourist offices for listings). Expect costs per day at the more established tourist-oriented estancias to be over US$100, including room, board and some activities.

FOOD

Since Spanish livestock transformed the Pampas into enormous cattle ranches, the Argentine diet has relied on meat, but there is more regional variety to Argentine cuisine than most foreigners expect. You'll quickly recognize the Italian influence in ubiquitous offerings such as pizza, spaghetti, lasagna, cannelloni and ravioli. The Andean Northwest is notable for spicy dishes, more closely resembling the food of the central Andean highlands than the bland fare of the Pampas. From Mendoza north, Middle Eastern food is commonplace.

Argentine seafood, while less varied than Chilean, can be tasty, even though Argentines are not big fish eaters. In the Patagonian Lake District, game dishes like trout, boar and venison are regional specialties, while river fish in Mesopotamia and Misiones are outstanding. In the extreme south, where sheep graze the drier pastures, lamb often replaces beef in the typical asado.

Beef, though, is the focus of the Argentine diet; no meal is truly complete without it. Here, in fact, the Spanish word *carne* (meat) is synonymous with beef; lamb, venison and poultry are all something else (but sometimes these meats are called *carne blanca,* or white meat.) The most popular form is the *parrillada*, a mixed grill of steak and other cuts that no visiting carnivore should miss (see the special section 'Here's the Beef').

Since the early 1980s, health food and vegetarian fare have won a niche in the diets of some Argentines, but outside of Buenos Aires and a few other large cities vegetarian restaurants are less common. Even standard parrillas serve items acceptable to most vegetarians, such as green salads and pasta dishes like ravioli, cannelloni and *ñoquis* (just make sure it's not topped with a meat sauce). The words *sin carne* mean 'without meat.'

Vegans will have a harder time in this country, but there's always the supermarkets.

You'll find Chinese food in the capital but not often elsewhere; the quality is not outstanding but many offer *tenedor libre* (all you can eat, usually US$5 to US$10) for those on a budget. The penny-wise traveler can also check out any large supermarket's takeout counter or cafeteria, both of which have extensive selections of good, cheap food. High-cost and high-quality international cuisine is more available in larger cities.

Reservations aren't necessary at any eating establishments except the classiest restaurants. Be aware that many mid-range or top-end restaurants charge a US$1 to US$2 *cubierto* per person, which covers 'utensil rental' and bread but not the usual 10% service tip.

Here's a brief buffet of some common types of eateries in Argentina:

Cafés & Bars – If you're feeling peckish in the middle of the day, or just need a break from the sights, rest up at a local café. Everything from marriage proposals to business transactions to revolutions originates in Argentina's cafés, where many locals spend hours on end dawdling over a single cup of coffee. Simple food orders are usually available, and many also serve beer, wine and hard liquor, in case you can't wait for the sun to go down.

Argentina has a good number of bars and pubs – many of which also offer food. In stylish Buenos Aires, they are often well-decorated and play decent music. Argentines generally aren't heavy drinkers and the legal drinking age is 18.

Comedores, Confiterías & Restaurantes – For good-quality fast food, try bus or train terminal *comedores* (cafeterias), which usually have a limited menu of simple but filling fixed-price meals and short orders like *milanesas* (a thinly breaded and fried steak). *Confiterías* mostly serve sandwiches, salads, pastas and meats. There is, though, a great difference between the most humble and the most extravagant confiterías. Your basic *restaurante* offers much larger menus, including *parrillada* (grilled meats), seafood and short orders, all served by waitstaff; restaurantes can run from the homeliest hole-in-the-wall to the fanciest and most elegant eatery.

Fast food – Unsurprisingly, burger-oriented fast-food imports like McDonald's and Burger King are very trendy and popular in the big cities, and have already displaced their local counterparts such as *Pumper Nic*. All such fast-food joints are relatively expensive compared to standard restaurants serving much better food; do yourself a favor and avoid them (even parrillas can have better hamburgers, for a comparable price).

Parillas – If you like great steaks, you should definitely stop in at one of these; meat items ordered in non-parrilla places will often be inferior. The most prestigious, tourist-oriented parrillas in Buenos Aires are apparent: they'll have a stuffed bull in the entry or an asado pit in the window, or both. On the menu will be extensive grilled selections of beef, chicken, pork or lamb. Sides usually include french fries and salads, and the dessert list can be extensive as well. These places often have pasta dishes for unlucky vegetarians dragged along.

Breakfast

Argentines eat little or no breakfast. Most commonly they will have coffee, tea or *yerba mate* and *tostadas* (toast) with *manteca* (butter) or *mermelada* (jam). In cafés, *medialunas* (small croissants), either *de manteca* (sweet) or *de grasa* (plain), accompany *café con leche* (coffee with milk). Be sure to sample *facturas,* or sweet pastries, which are varied and excellent. Pastry shops are common and their windows will tempt you inside with displays of flaky concoctions stuffed with *dulce de leche* (a type of milky caramel) or *membrillo* (quince).

[continued on page 91]

HERE'S THE BEEF

You walk into a traditional *parrilla* (steak house), breezing past the stuffed bull and sizzling *asado* (barbecue grill) at the entrance, and sit down hungry, knife and fork in hand. You don't know a word of Spanish, you've never had to choose between more than two or three cuts of steak in your life and the menu has at least 10 different choices. Now, what do you do?

Don't fret. We'll give you a better idea of what will show up on your plate. There, of course, will always be variations from place to place, but no matter what you end up ordering it's unlikely to be unpalatable.

But first, you should have an idea of where Argentina's famous beef comes from. When the first Spaniards came over to Argentina from Europe, with the intention of colonizing the area, they brought some cows to keep them company. Because stubborn locals were unwilling to let themselves be dominated, the Spaniards' first efforts at establishing a colony proved unfruitful. They ended up abandoning the cattle in the Pampas and moving away, and here the herds found the bovine equivalent of heaven: plenty of lush, fertile grasses on which to feed, with few natural predators to limit their numbers. Things were great until the Europeans decided to start recolonizing the Pampas and capturing the cattle for their own use. (The gauchos, however, had been taking advantage of these free-roaming meals-on-the-hoof all along.)

Today, intermixing with other European bovine breeds has produced a pretty tasty introduction to the epitome of Argentina cuisine. Why is it so good? Any Argentine worth his or her salt will say it's because free-range Argentine cows eat nutritious Pampas grass, lacking in the massive quantities of corn, antibiotics and growth hormones that American or European stocks are given in feedlots. This makes for a leaner, more natural-tasting meat. (Though these days it's not entirely organic either: Efforts to reduce *aftosa*, or hoof and mouth disease, have resulted in Argentina's need to inoculate its herds.)

Because of their country's ability to produce enormous quantities of beef, Argentines

Left: an *asador* (parrilla chef) in traditional costume

Right: classic Argentine cuisine, grilled beef, spread-eagled over the open charcoal pit, at La Estancia restaurant in Buenos Aires

tend to eat a lot of the stuff. The average intake is around 60kg per person per year, or almost 133lbs, though in the past they ate even more. Most of this consuming takes place at the family asado, often held on Sundays in the backyards of houses all over the country. (If you are lucky enough to be invited to one, make *sure* you attend.) Here the art of grilling beef has been perfected. This usually involves cooking with coals and using only salt to prepare the meat. On the grill itself, which is often waist-high and made of bricks, slanted runners funnel the excess fat to the sides so as to avoid flare-ups, and an adjustable height system directs the perfect amount of heat to the meat. (In olden times on the Pampas, meat was crucified to stakes and placed in an open charcoal pit; some of these traditional pits can still be seen in some steak houses.)

Emerging from this family tradition, the commercial steak house offers a little bit of everything. The *parrillada,* or mixed grill, might have an assortment of *chorizo* (spicy sausage), *pollo* (chicken), *costillas* (ribs) and *carne* (beef). It can also come with more exotic items such as *chinchulines* (small intestines), *tripa gorda* (large intestine), *mojella* (thymus gland or sweetbreads), *ubre* (udder), *riñones* (kidneys) and *morcilla* (blood sausage). Try them all, though certain pieces take some getting used to. You can order a parillada for as many people as you want; they adjust their servings according to the party's size.

You could skip the mixed grill and dive right into the beef cuts. Here's a guide:

bife de chorizo	sirloin; a thick, juicy and popular cut
bife de costilla	T-bone; a cut close to the bone; also called *chuleta*
bife de lomo	tenderloin; a thinly cut, more tender piece
cuadril	rump steak; often a thin cut
ojo de bife	eye of round steak; a choice smaller morsel
tira de asado	a narrow strip of rib roast
vacío	flank steak; textured and chewy, but tasty

Other meat selections can include the following:

achuras	organ meats
cerdo	pork
chivito	goat
choripán	spicy sausage sandwich
cordero	lamb
lechón	suckling pig
matambre	a strip of meat rolled up with eggs and vegetables and served cold
ternera	veal

If you don't specify how you want your steak cooked, it will normally come *a punto* (medium). To get it pink on the inside ask for *jugoso* (rare), and if you want it well-done, say *bien hecho*. Be sure not to miss *chimichurri*, a tasty marinade often made of olive oil, garlic and parsley; it adds a spiciness to the steak. Occasionally you can also get *salsa criolla*, a condiment made of diced tomato, onion and parsley.

And after your delicious Argentine steak, consider passing by the *asadores* (barbecuers) to thank them for the tasty meal. At the larger, more touristy parrillas, you may even be able to get them to pose for a snapshot right next to the impressively large circular fire pits, complete with staked hunks of meat. It makes the perfect final memory of your Argentine culinary experience.

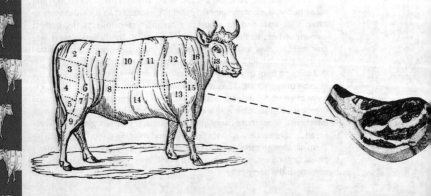

[continued from page 87]

Lunch & Dinner

Argentines compensate for skimpy breakfasts with large lunches, starting about noon or 1pm, and even larger dinners, hardly ever earlier than 9pm and often much later. In fact, it's not unusual to be eating in a popular restaurant packed with energetic diners at midnight, especially on a Saturday night. Lunch and dinner often consist of standard fare such as pizza, pasta or meat dishes.

Snacks

Eating late has some disadvantages; you get hungry early. Fortunately, there's the *merienda,* or teatime, in which to grab a snack and assuage those hunger pangs.

One of the world's finest snacks is the *empanada,* a tasty turnover stuffed with vegetables, hard-boiled egg, olives, beef, chicken, ham and cheese or other fillings. These are cheap (around US$1) and available almost everywhere; buy them by the dozen in a *rotisería* before a long bus or train trip. Empanadas *al horno* (baked) are lighter than empanadas *fritas* (fried).

Pizza, a common market and restaurant snack, is one of the least expensive items on the menu when purchased by the slice. In many local pizzerías it's cheaper to eat standing up at the counter than seated at a table. For the best pizza, avoid fancy pizza-cafés and go to real pizzerías.

Sandwiches de miga are wonderful dainty sandwiches made of a very thin-crusted white bread and filled with slices of ham and cheese. *Alfajores* are available at any kiosk and can be of a common packaged variety or *artesanal* (made by hand). Both varieties are great downed with tea; dulce de leche is sandwiched between two soft, thin shortbread cookies and the whole thing is bathed in a chocolate or meringue coating. Try Havana, Terrabusi or Jorgito brands.

Churros are also worth a taste. Look for the long, column-like fried things in a pastry shop. They're a bit like donuts and can come filled with dulce de leche or chocolate.

Desserts

Fresh fruit is the most common *postre* (dessert) in Argentine homes. In restaurants, *ensalada de fruta* (fruit salad), *flan* (egg custard) or *queso y dulce* (cheese with preserved fruit, also called *postre vigilante*) are frequent choices. The 'dulce' can consist of *batata* (sweet potato) or *membrillo*. Flan is topped with whipped cream or dulce de leche. Also give *budín de pan* a shot: it's a more solid version of flan.

Stemming from the Italian tradition, Argentine *helado* (ice cream) is world-class. Try a cone at one of Argentina's many ice creameries *(heladerías)*. Chains like Freddo (located throughout Buenos Aires) are great, but the best Argentine ice cream comes from smaller places that make their own batches; look for the words *elaboración propia* or *elaboración artesanal*. All types of heladerías, however, offer dozens of tempting flavors from the conventional vanilla to dulce de leche variations to exotic fruits and other unexpected mixtures (US$2 to US$4).

During winter, when Argentines rarely eat ice cream, the best heladerías often close. During the hot Buenos Aires summer, though, you might find yourself in line with many sweet-toothed porteños. *Granizado* means that the ice cream is usually sprinkled with chocolate flakes.

DRINKS

You'll be hard-pressed to find *mate* served anywhere, although it's the most famous and distinct Argentine drink (see the boxed text '*Mate* & its Ritual').

Soft Drinks

Soft drinks have always been a hit in Argentina, from the ubiquitous Coca-Cola and 7-Up to a wonderful *pomelo* (grapefruit) flavor called Paso de los Toros. Mineral water, both *con gas* (carbonated) and *sin gas* (plain) is widely available, but tap water is drinkable: ask for *un vaso de agua de canilla* (a glass of tap water) or *un jarro de agua* (a pitcher of tap water). If you're at a more local joint, try *un siphon de soda* (carbonated water in a spritzer bottle). It's cheap and good fun to squirt into your glass.

Fruit Juices & Licuados

Jugos are not so varied here as in tropical South America. For fresh-squeezed orange juice, ask for *jugo de naranja exprimido* – otherwise you may get canned or concentrated juice. Pomelo, *limón* (lemon) and *ananás* (pineapple) are also popular. *Jugo de manzana* (apple juice) is a specialty of the Río Negro region of Patagonia, but it's available everywhere.

Licuados are milk-blended fruit drinks, but they can also be made with water. Common flavors include banana, *durazno* (peach) and *pera* (pear).

Coffee, Tea & Hot Chocolate

Caffeine junkies will find some good, strong brew in Argentina's cafés. *Café chico* is a thick, dark coffee served in a very small cup. *Cortado* is a small coffee with a touch of milk, usually served in a glass – for a larger portion ask for *cortado doble*. Similar but containing more milk, café con leche is served for breakfast or teatime only; after a meal request a cortado. If you like milk, try a *lagrima*, which contains milk with a touch of coffee.

Tea sometimes comes with lemon slices, but if you drink it with milk, don't order *té con leche*, which means a tea bag immersed

Mate & Its Ritual

Nothing captures the essence of *argentinidad* (Argentinity) as well as the preparation and consumption of *mate* (pronounced **mah**-tay), perhaps the only cultural practice that truly transcends the barriers of ethnicity, class and occupation in Argentina. More than a simple drink like tea or coffee, *mate* is an elaborate ritual, shared among family, friends and coworkers. In many ways, sharing is the whole point.

Yerba mate is the dried, chopped leaf of *Ilex paraguayensis*, a relative of the common holly. Also known as Paraguayan tea, it became commercially important during the colonial era on the plantations of the Jesuit missions in the upper Río Paraná. Europeans quickly took to the beverage, crediting it with many admirable qualities. The Austrian Jesuit Martin Dobrizhoffer wrote that *mate* 'provokes a gentle perspiration, improves the appetite, speedily counteracts the languor arising from the burning climate and assuages both hunger and thirst.' After the Jesuits' expulsion in 1767, production declined, but since the early 20th century, production has increased dramatically.

Argentina is the world's largest producer and consumer of yerba *mate*. Argentines consume an average of 5kg per person per year, more than four times their average intake of coffee. It's also popular in parts of Chile, southern Brazil, Paraguay and, in particular, Uruguay, which consumes twice as much per capita as Argentina. Not surprisingly many *mate*-drinking Uruguayans will not go anywhere without a thermos under their arm and a *mate* gourd clasped in their hand.

Preparing *mate* is a ritual in itself. In the past, upper-class families even maintained a slave or servant whose sole responsibility was preparing and serving it. Nowadays, one person, the *cebador* (server), fills the *mate* gourd almost to the top with yerba, heating but not boiling the water in a *pava* (kettle) and pouring it into the vessel. Drinkers then sip the liquid through a *bombilla*, a silver straw with a bulbous filter at its lower end that prevents the yerba leaves from entering the tube.

Gourds can range from simple calabashes to carved wooden vessels to the ornate silver museum pieces of the 19th century. Bombillas also differ considerably, ranging in materials from inexpensive aluminum to silver and gold with intricate markings, and in design from long straight tubes to short, curved models.

in warm milk. Rather, ask the waiter for *un poquito de leche* (a little milk). Caffeine-free tea is hard to find. When you need a more substantial pick-me-up, try a *sub-marino,* a semisweet chocolate bar dissolved in steamed milk; it tastes similar to hot chocolate made with powder.

Everything comes with giant packs of sugar, and sugar-substitutes are readily available. Honey is called *miel.*

Alcoholic Drinks

Beer, wine, whiskey and gin should satisfy most travelers' alcoholic thirst, but don't overlook *ginebra bols* (which differs from gin) or *caña* (cane alcohol), both of which are national specialties.

Quilmes, brewed in the namesake Buenos Aires suburb but available everywhere, is a decent beer. Isenbeck is another popular national brand. In bars or cafés, ask for the excellent *chopp* (draft or lager). When ordering beer, you'll usually get a *picada* (snack plate of chips or peanuts).

Argentine wines receive less publicity abroad than Chilean ones, but *tintos* (reds) and *blancos* (whites) are both excellent and inexpensive, and some are becoming

---

Mate & Its Ritual

There is an informal etiquette for drinking *mate*. The cebador pours water slowly near the straw to produce a froth as he or she fills the gourd. The gourd then passes clockwise and this order, once established, continues. A good cebador will keep the *mate* going without changing the yerba for some time. Each participant drinks the gourd dry each time. A simple *gracias* will tell the server to pass you by.

There are marked regional differences in drinking *mate*. From the Pampas southwards, Argentines take it *amargo* (without sugar), while to the north they drink it *dulce* (sweet) with sugar and *yuyos* (aromatic herbs). Purists, who argue that sugar ruins the gourd, will keep separate gourds rather than alternate the two usages. In summer, Paraguayans drink *mate* ice-cold as *tereré*.

An invitation to *mate* is a cultural treat, although it's definitely an acquired taste and novices may find it bitter and very hot at first. On the second or third round, both the heat and bitterness will diminish. Don't hold the *mate* too long before passing it on. Drinking it is unlikely to affect either your health or finances, despite Dobrizhoffer's dubious warning.

Because drinking *mate* is a fairly complex process, it is rarely served in restaurants or cafés. As a foreigner, it is therefore easy to spend an entire holiday in Argentina without ever trying it. The simple solution is to do what traveling Argentines do: Buy a thermos (stores rarely lack a thermos shelf), a *mate*, a bombilla and a bag of herb. The entire set-up should cost you less than US$20, and browsing (and trying) the countless varieties of *mate* is a joy.

Before drinking from your gourd, you must first cure it by filling it with hot water and yerba and letting it soak for 24 hours. When it's ready, you have to fill your thermos; nearly all restaurants, cafés and hotels are accustomed to filling thermoses, sometimes charging about US$0.50. Simply whip out your thermos and ask: '*¿Podía calentar agua para mate?*' ('Would you mind heating water for *mate*?') At the sight of your thermos, most people will know what you need. Even gas stations are equipped with giant tanks of precisely heated water for drinkers on the road. Once you have your water, you're off to the park to join the rest of the locals drinking *mate* in the shade. By the end of the day, you should have several new Argentine friends helping to hone your new skills.

To learn more about *mate* check out **w** www.soygaucho.com/english/mate/index.html; for supplies, try **w** www.gauchogourmet.com.

world-class. (A bottle of good wine may be cheaper than a liter of Coca-Cola.) Especially at home, where jug wines are present at almost all meals, Argentines often dilute their wine with soda water to add some fizz and pace their drinking.

The major wine growing areas are near Mendoza, San Juan, La Rioja and Salta. Good brands include Lopez, Weinert, Orfila, Suter, San Felipe, Etchart, Navarro Correas and Nieto Senetiner. Try to avoid the cheapest wines such as Termidor and Santa Ana.

ENTERTAINMENT

Argentines are fond of music and dancing. Dance clubs both in Buenos Aires and the provinces open late and close even later; nobody goes before midnight, and things don't really start jumping until 2am. After sunrise, when the clubs close, partygoers head to a confitería or home for breakfast before collapsing in their beds.

Except in Buenos Aires, nightclubs tend to be disreputable places. Places listed in the *Buenos Aires Herald* as nightclubs are usually the more respectable ones; but in a Spanish context, the word 'nightclub' tends to imply a fairly seedy place with bar girls who are thinly disguised prostitutes.

Traditionally, Argentines jam the cinemas, although outside Buenos Aires the video revolution has meant the closure of many theaters that once counted on being the only show in town. Still, in the capital and larger cities, major theaters offer the latest films from Europe, the US and the rest of Latin America. Repertory houses, cultural centers and universities provide a chance to see classics or less-commercial films you may have missed.

In Buenos Aires, the main cinema districts are along Lavalle, Av Corrientes and Av Santa Fe, and the inner suburb of Belgrano. Prices have risen in recent years and now match those in North America or Europe, but most cinemas offer substantial discounts for first or midweek showings. On weekends, there are *transnoches* (late-night showings) around or after midnight.

Both in Buenos Aires and the provinces, live theater is well-attended and high quality, from the classics and serious drama to burlesque. Av Corrientes is Buenos Aires' Broadway or West End, but even in places like Villa Regina, a small town in Río Negro province, there are several active theater groups and venues for performances.

There are two main types of theater: a well-supported official theater and a more underground type that improvises and operates on a shoestring budget, often performing in public places like parks and plazas, or even in rented houses. Despite their limited budgets, these productions can be surprisingly professional.

SPECTATOR SPORTS

Spectator sports are limited primarily to soccer, horse racing, polo and boxing, though tennis, rugby, cricket, basketball and Formula One automobile racing have their adherents (visiting pedestrians and drivers may conclude that most Argentine drivers consider themselves Formula One competitors). Among the best-known Argentine athletes and sports figures are soccer legend Diego Maradona, tennis stars Guillermo Vilas and Gabriela Sabatini, the late boxers Oscar Bonavena and Carlos Monzón, and ex-Formula One standouts Carlos Reutemann and Juan Manuel Fangio.

Soccer (Fútbol)

By any standard, Argentine soccer is world-class. The national team won the World Cup in 1978. It also won in 1986, thanks to Diego Maradona, the bad, bad boy of soccer stardom. Buenos Aires has the highest density of first-division soccer teams in the world: Eight of the country's 20 are based in the capital, with another five in the extensive suburbs of Gran Buenos Aires. Most Argentines, however, tender a fierce allegiance to either River Plate or Boca Juniors.

Soccer is passionately watched and/or played by Argentines of all ages and classes. During a significant match-up, such as a *superclásico* between River and Boca, TVs all over the country are tuned into the game, all eyes riveted to the screen. Cafés, restaurants, shops and apartments harbor crowds that erupt in cheers when a goal is scored.

Fútbol Philosophy

'You can change your job, your house, your wife, even your sexual orientation…but you can *never* change your fútbol team.'

— Lucas Markowiecki, avid River Plate fan

After a triumphant victory, fans take to the streets, joyfully yelling to the world that their soccer team is the best in the universe. This is truly what Argentines love but it also brings heartbreak when their teams lose.

As in Europe, violence at games has become an unfortunate byproduct; *barras bravas* are the equivalent of British 'football hooligans.' But don't be overly paranoid; most games are secure and safe to attend. Stadiums in better neighborhoods, such as River Plate's, are calmer. If you do get a chance to see a game, take it: You'll witness Argentine passion at its finest. Be reasonable and don't wear any fancy jewelry, taking just enough money for the day. Also, wear neutral colors like black, white or tan. On the other hand, if you want to start some trouble at, say, a Boca-River match, start calling River fans *gallinas* (chickens) and *millionarios* (millionaires, disparagingly). Or, call Boca fans *bosteros* (cow patties) and *cerdos* (pigs). You may get some attention.

The season extends from March to December. In Buenos Aires, *entradas populares* (bleachers) cost around US$10, while *plateas* (fixed seats) cost US$20 and upward; prices ultimately depend on location and the significance of the match. For more information, contact the Asociación del Fútbol Argentino (☎ 4371-4276), at Viamonte 1366, Buenos Aires.

For an account of soccer's development and history in the Southern Cone, see British sociologist Tony Mason's brief and rather misleadingly titled *Soccer in South America*, which deals almost exclusively with Argentina, Uruguay and Brazil (1994). Uruguayan writer Eduardo Galeano has recently published *Soccer in Sun & Shadow* (1998), which contains many observations on Argentine soccer.

Polo

December's annual Campeonato Argentino Abierto de Polo (Argentine Open Polo Championship), held in the Buenos Aires barrio of Palermo, celebrated its centenary in 1993. Most polo events are open to the public free of charge; for current information, contact the Asociación Argentina de Polo (☎ 4343-0972), at Hipólito Yrigoyen 636 in Buenos Aires, which keeps a list of activities scheduled throughout the country.

For a selection of polo equipment, see the Buenos Aires chapter.

Rugby

Rugby, like soccer, traces its origins to the English, but is popular as an amateur participant sport. Even the asthmatic Ernesto 'Che' Guevara was an enthusiastic rugby player during his youth in Córdoba. The national team, the Pumas, plays the best international competitions.

SHOPPING

As Argentine food is famous for beef, so Argentine clothing is famous for leather. In Buenos Aires, many downtown shops cater to the tourist trade in leather jackets, handbags and shoes. Quality and prices can vary greatly, so shop around before buying. Shopkeepers are aggressive but sometimes open to bargaining.

Argentines are very fashion-conscious, with the latest styles displayed along Florida and Santa Fe in Buenos Aires and on main shopping streets in cities throughout the country. Bariloche is especially well-known for woolen goods. The best prices are available just before seasonal changes, as shops try to liquidate their inventory. Jewelry is another quality Argentine product, made frequently with 18-karat gold. In Buenos Aires, try the jewelry shops on Libertad, south of Corrientes.

Mate paraphernalia make good souvenirs. Gourds and bombillas range from simple and inexpensive aluminum, often sold in street kiosks, to elaborate and expensive gold and silver from jewelry stores or specialty shops. In the province of Salta, the distinctive *ponchos de Güemes* are a memorable choice.

In artisans' *ferias*, found throughout the country, the variety of handicrafts is extensive. There are good places in Buenos Aires (San Telmo's Plaza Dorrego, Recoleta's Plaza Francia and Belgrano's Plaza General Belgrano), Mendoza, Bariloche and El Bolsón. In the summer, the Atlantic Coast has many others.

Argentines are well-read and interested in both national and world literature, and Buenos Aires has a good selection of general- and special-interest bookstores. Since the end of the military dictatorship, the capital has re-established itself as a publishing center; April's Feria Internacional del Libro (book fair) is South America's largest, with over 600 exhibitors drawing more than a million visitors.

Foreign and foreign-language books tend to be very expensive, but there's a good selection (including this and other Lonely Planet guides) at Buenos Aires' better bookstores and, occasionally, those in the interior.

Many places add a surcharge to credit card purchases – ask before you pay.

SANDRA BAO

Let's tango, baby! Buenos Aires

MARY PEACHIN

Gaucho enjoying *mate* in Patagonia, Argentina

JOHN MAIER JR

Caution: The wines of Mendoza may cause blurry vision.

The old reflected in the new, Buenos Aires

Look, motorcycles! Buenos Aires street scene

Buenos Aires' Av 9 de Julio is 16 lanes of motoring mayhem.

Getting There & Away

AIR

Argentina has flights linked up with North America, the UK, Europe, Australia, New Zealand and South Africa; and from all South American countries except the Guianas. Alternatively, you can fly to a neighboring country, such as Chile or Brazil, and continue overland to Argentina.

Airports & Airlines

Nearly all international flights arrive at Buenos Aires' Aeropuerto Internacional Ministro Pistarini (commonly known as Ezeiza; ☎ 4480-0235), about a 45-minute bus ride out of town. Most domestic flights and some from Uruguay use Aeroparque Jorge Newbery (commonly known as Aeroparque; ☎ 4771-2071), a short distance from downtown Buenos Aires.

Airports in several provincial capitals and tourist destinations are earmarked as 'international': This usually means they receive flights from neighboring countries. Among these airports are Jujuy, Salta, Tucumán, Mendoza, Puerto Iguazú, Córdoba, Rosario, Bariloche, Río Gallegos and Ushuaia.

Major international airlines serving Argentina include Aeroflot, Air France, Alitalia, American Airlines, Aerolíneas Argentinas, Avianca, British Airways, Canadian Airlines International, Iberia, Japan Airlines, KLM, LanChile, Lloyd Aéreo Boliviano (LAB), Lufthansa Airlines, Malaysia Airlines, Pluna, Qantas Airways, South African Airways, Swissair, Transportes Aéreos Mercosur (TAM), TAP (Air Portugal), TransBrasil, United Airlines, Varig and VASP.

Due to increased security, especially in US airports, arrive several hours before departure and contact your airline for new restrictions regarding prohibited items in carry-on luggage.

Buying Tickets

From almost everywhere, South America is a relatively costly destination, but discount

Warning

The information in this chapter is particularly prone to change: Prices for international travel are volatile, routes are introduced and cancelled, airlines go out of business, schedules change, special deals come and go, and rules and visa requirements are amended. Airlines and governments seem to take a perverse pleasure in making price structures and regulations as complicated as possible – all done to get the most money out of you, of course. You should check directly with the airline or a travel agent to make sure you understand how a fare (and ticket you may buy) works. Realize that the travel industry is highly competitive, and there are many perks as well as pitfalls.

The upshot of this is that you should get opinions, quotes and advice from as many sources as possible before you part with your cash. The details given in the chapter should be regarded as pointers and are not a substitute for your own careful, up-to-date research. Good luck.

fares can reduce the bite considerably. To get the best air ticket prices, avoid general peak travel times such as July, early August and mid- to late December. It's best to consult individual airlines about these holidays because dates can vary. Exact fares may also be influenced by your country's peak traveling seasons (when demand for tickets goes up).

Buying a ticket for a given period of time, usually fewer than six months, often provides the best, most flexible deal. Start shopping early – some of the cheapest tickets must be purchased months in advance, and some popular flights sell out quickly.

Airlines are a good source of information for routes, schedules and standard fares, but they don't usually sell the cheapest tickets (except during fare wars, slow seasons and on the Internet). Buying from a travel agent will give you cheaper choices, and going to one that specializes in Latin American destinations will help even more. Whether you go directly through an airline or use an agent, always ask the representative to clarify the fare, the route, the duration of the journey and any restrictions on the ticket.

Among the best sources of information on cheap tickets are the travel pages of major newspapers such as the *New York Times*, *Los Angeles Times* and *San Francisco Examiner* for US departures, and Australia's *The Age* and *Sydney Morning Herald*. Similar listings are available in the travel sections of magazines such as the UK's *Time Out* and *TNT*. Ads in university newspapers and other local publications also offer cheap fares, but don't be surprised if they happen to be sold out when you contact the agents as these fares are usually for low-season on obscure airlines with many conditions attached.

You may decide to pay more than the rock-bottom fare by opting for the safety of a better known travel agent. Established firms like worldwide STA Travel, Council Travel in the USA, and Travel CUTS in Canada are valid alternatives, and they offer good prices to most destinations (see later for contact information).

One of the cheapest options for getting to Argentina is on a courier flight: You surrender some of your baggage allowance and accompany business equipment or documents in return for a significantly discounted fare. If the courier company is really desperate and needs someone to fly on very short notice, you may even score a free flight. The major drawbacks (in addition to being limited to carry-on baggage) are restricted travel dates, the often short travel periods allowed and the limited number of gateway airports in Europe (London) and North America (New York, Miami, Los Angeles, San Francisco, Chicago, Orlando and Washington, DC). Also, it's difficult to get more than one courier ticket for the same flight, so if you want to travel with someone, you'll both

have to juggle your schedules (possibly with different courier companies) or fly on different days.

Some of the best deals for travelers visiting many countries on different continents are Round-the-World (RTW) tickets. Itineraries from the USA, Europe or Australia that include five or six stopovers (including Buenos Aires) start from US$2000 or US$2500 and go up to US$4000 or more. Fares can vary widely; to get an idea, check out **W** www.airtreks.com and use their calculator to find approximate fares for whatever destinations you pick. Similar 'Circle Pacific' fares allow excursions between Australasia and South America. These types of tickets are certain to have restrictions, so check the fine print carefully.

Once you have your ticket, write down its number, together with the flight number and other details, and keep the information separate from the ticket itself. If the ticket is lost or stolen, this will help you get a replacement. It's also a good idea to make a copy of your air tickets (along with your passport information pages) and keep it at home with someone. And remember to buy travel insurance as early as possible.

Note: Use the fares quoted in this book as a guide only. They are approximate and based on rates advertised by travel agents and airlines at press time. Also, keep in mind that they do not include taxes, which can be significant. Quoted airfares do not necessarily constitute a recommendation for the carrier.

Buying Tickets Online The Internet is a great source for getting an idea of how much or how little fares can cost you. Most savvy airlines have Web sites that offer online ticket sales, sometimes discounted. The best sites will also give you schedules, departure and arrival hours, location of stopovers, types of airplane used and other useful information. You'll need a credit card to purchase tickets via the Internet.

Many travel companies sell tickets online only, and with a little digging these can turn out to be the cheapest ways to fly. Some of the biggest North American online

Air Travel Glossary

Alliances Many of the world's leading airlines are now intimately involved with each other, sharing everything from reservations systems and check-in to aircraft and frequent-flyer schemes. Opponents say that alliances restrict competition. Whatever the arguments, there is no doubt that big alliances are the way of the future.

Courier Fares Businesses often need to send urgent documents or freight securely and quickly. Courier companies hire people to accompany the package through customs and, in return, offer discounted tickets. However, you may have to surrender all your baggage allowance and take only carry-on luggage.

Full Fares Airlines traditionally offer 1st-class (coded F), business-class (coded J) and economy-class (coded Y) tickets. These days, there are so many promotional and discounted fares available that few passengers pay full fare.

Lost Tickets If you lose your airline ticket, an airline will usually treat it as a travelers check and, after inquiries, issue you with another one. Legally, however, an airline is entitled to treat it as cash, so if you lose it, then it could be gone forever. Take very good care of your tickets.

Onward Tickets An entry requirement for many countries is that you have a ticket out of the country. If you're unsure of your next move, the easiest solution is to buy the cheapest onward ticket to a neighboring country or a ticket (from a reliable airline) that can later be refunded if you do not use it.

Open-Jaw Tickets These are return tickets that can be used to fly out to one place but return from another. If available, this can save you time, money and from having to backtrack to your arrival point.

Overbooking Since every flight has some passengers who fail to show up, airlines often book more passengers than they have seats. Usually excess passengers make up for the no-shows, but occasionally somebody gets 'bumped' onto the next available flight. Who is it most likely to be? The passengers who check in late. If you do get 'bumped,' you are normally offered some form of compensation.

Reconfirmation Some airlines require you to reconfirm your flight at least 72 hours prior to departure. Check your travel documents to see if this is the case.

Restrictions Discounted tickets often have various restrictions on them – such as mandatory advance payment and penalties for alterations or cancellations. Others have restrictions on the minimum and maximum period you must be away.

Round-the-World Tickets RTW tickets give you a limited period (usually a year) in which to circumnavigate the globe. You can go anywhere the carrying airlines go, as long as you don't backtrack. The number of stopovers or total number of separate flights is decided before you set off. These can be great deals, so shop around.

Ticketless Travel Airlines are now using paperless tickets. On simple one-way or return trips, reservation details can be held on computer, and the passengers merely show identification to claim their seats.

Transferred Tickets Airline tickets cannot be transferred from one person to another. Travelers sometimes try to sell the return half of their tickets, but officials can ask you to prove that you are the person named on the ticket. On an international flight, the name on the ticket is compared with the name on the passport.

sellers are Travelocity (W www.travelocity
.com), Expedia (W www.expedia.com) and
Cheap Tickets (W www.cheaptickets.com).
In Europe, check out W www.etn.nl; in Australia, W www.travel.com.au. There are also
about ten thousand other, less-known
online companies that sell cheap tickets, so
poke around.

Travelers with Special Needs
If you have special needs of any sort – a
broken leg, dietary restrictions, need for a
wheelchair, responsibility for a baby, fear of
flying – you should let the airline know as
soon as possible so they can make arrangements accordingly. Remind them when you
reconfirm your booking (at least 72 hours
before departure) and again when you
check in at the airport. It may also be worth
calling several airlines before you make
your booking to find out how they would
handle your particular needs.

Airports and airlines can be surprisingly
helpful, but they do need advance warning.
Most international airports can provide
escorts from the check-in desk to the plane
where needed, and there should be ramps,
lifts, accessible toilets and reachable phones.
Aircraft toilets, on the other hand, are likely
to present a problem; travelers should
discuss this with the airline at an early stage
and, if necessary, with their doctor.

Guide dogs for the blind will often have
to travel in a specially pressurized baggage
compartment with other animals, away
from their owner, though smaller guide
dogs may be admitted to the cabin. Guide
dogs are not subject to quarantine as long as
they have proof of being vaccinated against
rabies.

Travelers with hearing difficulties can ask
that airport and in-flight announcements be
written down for them.

Children under two usually travel for 10%
of the standard fare (for free on some airlines) as long as they don't occupy a seat, but
they don't get a baggage allowance. 'Skycots'
should be provided by the airline if requested
in advance; these will take a child weighing up
to about 10kg (22 pounds). Children ages two
through 12 can usually occupy a seat for half

to two-thirds of full fare and do get a baggage
allowance. Strollers can often be taken on as
carry-on luggage.

Departure Tax
Departure taxes on international flights out
of Argentina are usually included in the price
of your ticket. Make sure you confirm this
with your travel agency or the airline office.
An airline ticket may sound cheap when you
pay for it, but if you have to add on taxes at
the airport it may not be such a good deal.

If your tax is not included, be prepared to
dish out at least US$30.50 for international
flights. Uruguay is an exception: To Montevideo, the tax is US$18.50, but it's a bit more
to Punta del Este.

The USA
The principal gateways are Miami, New
York and Los Angeles. Aerolíneas Argenti-
nas (☎ 800-333-0276) is Argentina's flag
carrier, but other airlines serving Buenos
Aires include American Airlines, British
Airways, Japan Airlines, Korean Air, Lan-
Chile, Lloyd Aéreo Boliviano (LAB),
United Airlines and Varig. Figure the very
lowest season roundtrip fares to be about
US$850 from the West Coast, US$650 from
New York or Miami, US$900 from Chicago
and US$1000 from Dallas. Add US$100 to
US$200 for high-season fares.

Travelers can check their local branch of
either Council Travel (☎ 800-226-8624,
W www.counciltravel.com) or the Student
Travel Network (STA; ☎ 800-777-0112,
W www.statravel.com), both of which offer
cheap flights, insurance and other travel
services. Another recommended agency is
eXito Latin America Travel (☎ 800-655-
4053, W www.exitotravel.com, 1212 Broadway, Oakland, CA 94612). They sell mainly
over the phone, but check their Web site beforehand to get an idea of prices.

For cheap courier flights, contact the Air
Courier Association (☎ 877-707-9658, W www
.cheaptrips.com, 350 Indiana St, Suite 300,
Golden, CO 80401). Other reliable courier
companies include Now Voyager (☎ 212-
431-1616, fax 212-334-5253, 74 Varick St,
Suite 307, New York, NY 10013) and Air

Facility (☎ 718-712-1769, 153 Rockaway Blvd, Jamaica, NY 11434). For up-to-date information on courier companies and fares, contact the International Association of Air Travel Couriers (☎ 561-582-8320, fax 561-582-1581, W www.iaatc.com, PO Box 1349, Lake Worth, FL 33460); its US$45 annual membership fee includes the bimonthly newsletter *Shoestring Traveler* (not related to Lonely Planet).

Canada & Mexico

Air Canada's Toronto-Buenos Aires route offers the only direct flights to Argentina (daily except Monday), but other airlines, such as American and Continental, make connections in New York, Miami and Los Angeles. Count on a low-season fare from Toronto to Buenos Aires to set you back around US$800, while a high season fare starts at US$1040.

Travel Cuts (☎ 800-667-2887, W www .travelcuts.com) is the Canadian student travel agency. Check their Web site for the location nearest to you.

Flights from Mexico City to Buenos Aires run about US$900 roundtrip. Asatej, the Argentine student travel agency (which also serves non-students), has several offices in Mexico. Check their Web site at www.asatej.org for the closest representative near you.

Australia & New Zealand

Aerolíneas Argentinas no longer has flights out of the Australia region, but maintains a Sydney office (☎ 02-9252-5150) at Level 4/189 Kent St. A roundtrip ticket from Australia to Buenos Aires averages around A$2000 in low season, A$2300 in high. (Low season in Australia is March to November, high season December to February.)

Qantas (☎ 13-1211 in Sydney, 09-357-8900 in Auckland) goes to Buenos Aires from Sydney three times a week, with some flights pausing in Auckland. Qantas also flies from Sydney to Tahiti twice a week to connect with LanChile's Tahiti-Easter Island-Santiago service, which has connections to Buenos Aires – a tempting flight if you want to see Easter Island or Tahiti. Air New Zealand does the same from Auck-

land. LanChile has a few offices in Australia, including Sydney (☎ 02-9244-2333), at 64 York St, and Melbourne (☎ 03-9920-3881), 310 King St.

Yet another way to get to Buenos Aires is to travel via the US (San Francisco, Los Angeles or Miami) with United Airlines (☎ 13-1777 in Sydney, 09-377-3886 in Auckland).

STA Travel (☎ 1-300-360 960 in Australia, W www.statravel.com) is a good place to find bargain airfares, and you don't have to be a student to use their services. Check their Web site for the location closest to you.

The UK

Direct services to Buenos Aires are available with Argentina's principal carrier Aerolíneas Argentinas (☎ 020-7494-1001 in London), as well as Aeroflot, Air France, Alitalia, British Airways, Iberia, KLM, Lufthansa, Pluna, Swissair, TAP (Air Portugal) and Trans Brasil. Varig has connections via Rio de Janeiro and São Paulo. A roundtrip ticket to Buenos Aires averages from UK£532 in low season to UK£724 in high season.

London's so-called 'bucket shops' can provide the best deals; check out newspapers or magazines such as the Saturday *Independent* or *Time Out* for suggestions. Since such shops come and go, it's worth inquiring about their affiliation with the Association of British Travel Agents (ABTA), which will guarantee a refund if the agent goes out of business. The following are reputable London bucket shops:

Campus Travel (☎ 0870-240-1010, W www.campus travel.co.uk), 52 Grosvenor Gardens, London SW1W 0AG

Journey Latin America (☎ 020-8747-3108, W www.journeylatinamerica.co.uk/), 12 & 13 Heathfield Terrace, Chiswick, London W4 4JE

South American Experience (☎ 020-7976-5511, W www.sax.mcmail.com/), 47 Causton St, London SW1P 4AT

STA Travel (☎ 020-7361-6262, W www.statravel .com), 86 Old Brompton Rd, London SW7 3LQ

Trailfinders (☎ 020-7938-3939, W www.trailfinder .com), 194 Kensington High St, London W8 7RG

Travelers interested in courier flights between London and Buenos Aires should contact British Airways Travel Shop (☎ 0870-606-1133, ⓦ www.baworldcargo.com/info; look under 'services'). You can also try the International Association of Air Travel couriers (see The USA, earlier, for contact information).

Continental Europe

The following travel agencies are good possibilities for bargain fares from Continental Europe.

France – Nouvelles Frontières (☎ 08-03-33-33-33, Minitel 3615 NF, ⓦ www.nouvelles-frontieres.com), 87, Boulevard de Grenelle 75738, Paris Cedex 15

Germany – STA Travel (☎ 030-311-0950, ⓦ www.statravel.com), Goethestrasse 73, Berlin (☎ 069-430191), Bergerstrasse 118, 60316, Frankfurt

Ireland – USIT Travel Office (☎ 01-602-1600, ⓦ www.usitnow.com), 19 Aston Quay, Dublin

Italy – CTS (☎ 06-462-0431), Via Genova 16, Rome

Netherlands – NBBS (☎ 020-624-0989), Rokin 38, Amsterdam
Malibu Travel (☎ 020-623-6814), Damrak 30, Amsterdam

Spain – TIVE (☎ 91-543-02-08), Fernando de Católico 86, Madrid

Switzerland – SSR Travel (☎ 01-261-29-55), Leonhardstrasse 10, 8001 Zurich

Asia & Africa

Carriers serving Buenos Aires directly from Asia, usually via North America, are Japan Airlines and Korean Air. Varig and VASP also have good connections via Rio de Janeiro or São Paulo.

Malaysia Airlines flies Wednesday and Sunday from Kuala Lumpur to Buenos Aires via Cape Town and Johannesburg. South African Airways flies several times a week from Johannesburg to Buenos Aires, with some flights connecting through São Paulo.

South America

Buenos Aires is fairly well connected to most other (usually capital) cities in Latin America. Here's a rough idea of some sample fares to Buenos Aires.

Destination	Costs
Asunción, Paraguay	US$295
Florianopolis, Brazil	US$230
La Paz, Bolivia	US$405
Lima, Peru	US$349
Montevideo, Uruguay	US$66
Puerto Alegre, Brazil	US$180
Punta del Este, Uruguay	US$90
Rio de Janeiro, Brazil	US$219
Santa Cruz, Bolivia	US$325
Santiago, Chile	US$179
São Paulo, Brazil	US$219

LAND

You'll have your choice of land crossings from neighboring Chile, Bolivia, Paraguay, Brazil and Uruguay; there are plenty of them. For more specific information, look up the border-crossing cities or towns later in this book.

Border Crossings

Chile Except in far southern Patagonia, every land crossing between Argentina and Chile involves crossing the Andes. Due to weather, some high-altitude passes close in winter. These closures can be unpredictable, so be aware that if you manage to cross on a clear day and a bad storm is riding your tail, you may be stuck a few days in the wrong country (providing you want to return, that is). There are so many actual crossings into Chile that below are listed just those that are most popular for foreign travelers:

Salta to San Pedro de Atacama – The altiplano scenery is stunningly beautiful up here. Keep in mind that it's a 12-hour bus ride, and that altitudes range from 1200m (Salta) to 2440m (San Pedro de Atacama) to around 4000m (in between).

Mendoza to Santiago – This is the most popular crossing between the two countries. The views are of giant mountains, and you may get a glimpse of the highest peak outside the Himalayas, 6960m Aconcagua.

Bariloche to Puerto Montt – There are lots of crossing choices in this area, but this famous route can be a destination in itself, with gorgeous lakes and scenic villages along the way. Expensive bus-boat combinations cost US$120 and take 12 hours (make advance bookings in summer). Still beautiful, regular bus services run around US$20 and take seven hours.

Los Antiguos to Chile Chico – Rather than taking the travelers' classic, famous and overpriced Navimag boat trip in Chile (the only public way to go to the Chilean Andes at this stretch other than flying), you can head along Ruta 40, Argentina's desolate version of the USA's Route 66. Either cross from Chile Chico to Los Antiguos, where you can head down to El Chaltén for world-class hiking, or go up the same way. This is best in summer, when there's actually transport available – it's a long, bumpy ride, but an adventure nonetheless.

El Calafate to Puerto Natales & Parque Nacional Torres del Paine – Probably the most beaten route down here, heading from the stupendous Moreno Glacier (near El Calafate) to the equally stupendous Parque Nacional Torres del Paine (near Puerto Natales). Several buses per day, more in summer, make this crossing.

Río Gallegos to Punta Arenas – Many daily buses run between these two cities, a six-hour trip. If you're relying on public transport, you'll have to go this way (rather than via the crossing at Primera Angostura, a shorter and more direct southerly route not available to these buses).

Ushuaia to Punta Arenas – There are daily buses in summer, but not so many in winter. It's a long trip (12 hours), which includes a 2½-hour ferry crossing at Porvenir, though some buses detour around the Primera Angostura ferry crossing.

Bolivia The following are options:

La Quiaca to Villazón – Many buses go from Jujuy and Salta to La Quiaca, where you must walk or take a taxi across the Bolivian border.

Aguas Blancas to Bermejo – From Orán, reached by bus from Salta or Jujuy, take a bus to Aguas Blancas and then Bermejo, where you can catch a bus to Tarija.

Pocitos to Yacuiba – Buses from Jujuy or Salta go to Tartagal and then on to the Bolivian border at Pocitos/Yacuiba, where there are trains to Santa Cruz.

Paraguay There are two direct border crossings between Argentina and Paraguay: Clorinda to Asunción, and Posadas to Encarnación. There's also a crossing that involves a brief detour through Brazil: Puerto Iguazú (Argentina) to Ciudad del Este (Paraguay) via Foz do Iguaçu (Brazil). All these crossings have frequent buses.

Brazil The most common crossing is from Puerto Iguazú to Foz do Iguaçu. Check both cities for more information on the peculiarities of this border crossing, especially if you're crossing the border into Brazil only to see the other side of Iguazú Falls.

There are also border crossings from Paso de los Libres (Argentina) to Uruguaiana (Brazil) and Santo Tomé (Argentina) to São Borja (Brazil).

Uruguay Border crossings from Argentine cities to Uruguayan cities include Gualeguaychú to Fray Bentos, Colón to Paysandú, and Concordia to Salto. All involve crossing bridges. Buses from Buenos Aires to Montevideo and other waterfront cities, however, are slower and less convenient than the ferries (or ferry-bus combinations) across the Río de la Plata (see the River section, later).

Bus

Travelers can bus to Argentina from most bordering countries. Buses are usually comfortable, modern and fairly clean. Crossing over does not involve too many hassles; just make sure that you have any proper visas beforehand.

Here are some sample fares to Buenos Aires from international destinations.

Destination	Duration in hours	Cost
Asunción, Paraguay	18	US$40
Foz do Iguaçu, Brazil	20	US$36
Montevideo, Uruguay	8	US$29
Punta del Este, Uruguay	9	US$35
Rio de Janeiro, Brazil	42	US$121
Santiago, Chile	20	US$60
São Paulo, Brazil	38	US$108

RIVER

From Buenos Aires, there are several ways to Uruguay that involve ferry or hydrofoil, and often require combinations with buses. For even more information, take a peek under the Getting There & Away sections in the Buenos Aires or corresponding Uruguayan city sections.

Buenos Aires to Montevideo – The most convenient river services to Montevideo are the comfortable, high-speed ferries that carry passengers from downtown Buenos Aires to the Uruguayan capital in only 2½ hours.

Buenos Aires to Colonia – There are daily ferries (2½ hours) and hydrofoils (45 minutes) to Colonia, with direct bus connections to Montevideo (3 hours more). Expect more launches during summer and holidays.

Buenos Aires to Piriápolis – In summer, a three-hour ferry ride connects the resort town of Piriápolis with the Argentine capital at least once a day. Glitzy Punta del Este is less than an hour from Piriápolis by bus.

Tigre to Carmelo – Regular passenger launches speed from the Buenos Aires suburb of Tigre to Carmelo (services also go to Montevideo and Colonia from Tigre). For information on getting to Tigre, see that section's Getting There & Away.

ORGANIZED TOURS

Myriad companies offer tours to Argentina, but most focus on Buenos Aires, Iguazú Falls, and Patagonia, including the Moreno Glacier and/or Península Valdés. Other parts of the country get less attention, so if you're interested in those areas, you may have to make arrangements in Buenos Aires.

North America

Well-established North American companies operating in Argentina include Wilderness Travel (☎ 510-558-2488, 800-368-2794, fax 510-558-2489, W www.wildernesstravel .com, 1102 9th St, Berkeley, CA 94710), which offers a 16-day Patagonian hiking adventure that will set you back US$4595 to US$5095, depending on group size; and Mountain Travel Sobek (☎ 510-527-8100, 888-627-6235, fax 510-525-7710, W www .mtsobek.com, 6420 Fairmount Ave, El Cerrito, CA 94530-3606), serving up 17- or 21-day easy, moderate or strenuous Patagonian hikes that range from US$3790 to US$4890.

Lost World Adventures (☎ 404-373-5820, 800-999-0558, fax 404-377-1902, W www .lostworldadventures.com, 112 Church St, Decatur, GA 30030) specializes in more exotic destinations in South America. Another possibility is Wildland Adventures (☎ 206-365-0686, 800-345-4453, fax 206-363-6615, W www.wildland.com, 3516 NE 155th St, Seattle, WA 98155-7412), which arranges 10-day itineraries through local guides and outfitters in Patagonia.

Focus Tours (☎ 505-466-4688, fax 505-466-4689, W www.focustours.com, 103 Moya Rd, Santa Fe, NM, 87505-8360) customizes good ecological tours especially for birders and naturalists. Groups of 6-8 people travel not only to popular destinations, but also to less-known corners of the country such as the Iberá wetlands, the Chaco region and Northeast Argentina.

Backroads (☎ 510-527-1555, 800-462-2848, fax 510-527-1444, W www.backroads .com, 801 Cedar St, Berkeley, CA 94710-1800) conducts an 11-day, US$3800 mountain-biking trip through the Chilean-Argentine Lake District, with stays in elegant hotels and cozy inns. Backroads also offers an equally luxurious nine-day Patagonian hiking trip for around US$5000.

Smithsonian Study Tours (☎ 202-357-4700, 877-338-8687, fax 202-633-9250, W www .smithsonianstudytours.org, 1100 Jefferson Dr SW, Washington DC, 20560-0702) whisks you off to Buenos Aires, Patagonia and Tierra del Fuego – much of the travel involving luxury cruises that run from US$5000 to US$20,000.

For travelers at least 55 years of age, Elderhostel (☎ 877-426-8056, fax 877-426-2166, W www.elderhostel.org, 11 Avenue de Lafayette, Boston, MA 02110-1746) operates tours to Buenos Aires and the north of Argentina, as well as Patagonia and the Lake District, starting around US$4200 including airfare. Outside the USA you can contact them at ☎ 1-978-323-4141, fax 1-617-426-0701.

Australia

In Australia, try World Expeditions (☎ 02-9264 3366, 1-300-720 000, fax 02-9261 1974, Ⓦ www.worldexpeditions.com.au, 441 Kent St, Sydney, NSW 2000). Tours on the South American continent include mostly Andean treks. Check their Web site for more national offices as well as some in New Zealand, the UK and the USA.

The UK

Journey Latin America (☎ 020-8747-3108, fax 020-8742-1312, Ⓦ www.journeylatin america.co.uk, 12 & 13 Heathfield Terrace, Chiswick, London W4 4JE) offers both basic tours with simple hotels and public transport, as well as more upscale packages. They also lead activity-based tours, such as mountain biking, horse riding and white-water rafting.

Explore Worldwide (☎ 0125-276-0000, fax 0125-276-0001, Ⓦ www.exploreworld wide.com, 1 Frederick St, Aldershot, Hants GU11 1LQ) will show you around Patagonia, including Península Valdés, Ushuaia, Parque Nacional Torres del Paine (Chile) and the Fitz Roy Range. If you don't live in England, check their Web site for a closer representative.

Getting Around

AIR

There are a few smaller domestic airlines that have popped up in the last decade or so, competing with giants Austral (who were going into bankruptcy proceedings at press time) and Aerolíneas Argentinas. Some specialize in flights to only certain parts of the country, but others have a more wide-ranging scope, and every so often may add new lines to different regions.

LAPA and Southern Winds (SW) compete with Aerolíneas and Austral on many routes, while Dinar flies mostly in the northwest. LAER goes mainly from Buenos Aires province to Argentina's northeast. LADE, the air force's passenger service, has some of the least expensive air tickets and makes Patagonian destinations its specialty. Note that in the summer and around holidays, all Patagonian flights may be heavily booked, and you should make reservations as far in advance as possible.

Flying with certain airlines on certain flights can be financially comparable or even cheaper than covering the same distance by bus, but demand is heavy and flights are often booked well in advance. Be aware that many major cities have connections only through Buenos Aires, though short-haul airlines such as SW link some provincial destinations without passing through the capital.

Air Passes

Check the rules carefully with all of the following air passes, as restrictions other than those listed below will apply. To take advantage of these passes, you must buy them outside either Argentina or South America, and you must have an international return ticket to Argentina.

If you're planning to travel around the country only by air, consider Aerolíneas Argentinas' 'Visit Argentina' pass, also valid on its domestic sister airline Austral. It's available for purchase only *outside* Argentina. Three flight coupons cost US$339 (US$299 if you buy your international ticket to Argentina with Aerolíneas) and each additional coupon (up to eight) costs US$105. They're good up to 60 days from date of purchase; one change of itinerary is free, but each additional change costs US$50. Two limiting factors are that each numbered flight uses up one coupon (so going from Puerto Iguazú to El Calafate uses up two coupons, since it passes through Buenos Aires), and you can't travel the same segment more than once in the same direction.

If you're planning to travel around Argentina, Brazil, Chile (except Easter Island), Paraguay and Uruguay, consider a 'Mercosur' pass, which can be a great deal. Costs for these travel coupons range from US$225 to US$870 and they're based on mileage traveled within seven to 30 days. Only two stopovers are allowed in each country (though the Iguazú Falls area can count as a third), and there's a maximum of eight flight coupons (plus Iguazú). Your points of origin and destination don't factor into these limitations, but you must have an international return ticket originating from outside South America. Changing your itinerary is allowed, though rerouting is not.

There's also a less common 'Visit South America' pass, run by the airlines of Oneworld Alliance (including American Airlines and LanChile; see **W** www .oneworldalliance.com). This pass encompasses Argentina, Bolivia, Brazil, Colombia, Chile (except Easter Island), Ecuador, Paraguay, Peru, Uruguay and Venezuela. You can travel up to 60 days (no minimum) as long as you don't fly any leg more than once in the same direction. There's a minimum of three flights (no maximum) and costs are based on mileage: Each travel leg ranges from US$80 to US$270. Rebooking and rerouting charges are US$40. This pass is also available only outside South America, in conjunction with an international ticket.

New Pricing Regulations for Domestic Flights

In September 2002, a new law was enacted: Travelers without Argentine passports may no longer purchase economy class tickets for domestic flights booked in-country. Locals can still fly economy class; all foreign travelers must now pay business-class or first-class fares.

Passports are checked by airline staff. If a discrepancy is discovered, the difference must be paid at the airport and the travel agency that booked the ticket will be fined.

Costs

One-way domestic airfares can vary widely, and like anywhere, ticket prices are not always dependent on distance alone.

To some popular tourist destinations such as Iguazú Falls, Bariloche, El Calafate or Península Valdés, packages that include airfare, hotel accommodations and airport transfers are often much better deals than just the price of the air ticket there (how good of a deal is dependent on high and low seasons, however).

Domestic departure taxes are usually included in the price of an air ticket. Make sure this is the case when you are buying your ticket, or be prepared to pay from US$5 to US$13 at the airport.

BUS

If you have the time to really travel in Argentina, you'll probably be taking long-distance buses. The bus network in this country goes almost everywhere, and this is the way most Argentines get from one place to the other. You'll also get to see lots of country scenery and backroad communities, and maybe even interact with the locals a bit.

Buses are fast and surprisingly comfortable. The more upscale bus lines, like Andesmar and TAC, have modern coaches with spacious and cushy seats, large windows, air-conditioning, toilets and sometimes even an attendant serving coffee and sweet snacks. Even less expensive lines have many of these features, though coaches may be older. Many seats in all these lines recline to making sleep easier, and overnight routes are a good option for saving time and money.

Note that most long-distance services make various stops along the way, to pick up and drop off passengers at intermediary towns. Stops are usually announced, but it's always a good idea to find out if this is where you want to get off.

If you lug a large pack, you'll often have to store it in the hold below. Security is good – an attendant will give you a tag to match the one put on your pack. Small tips are appreciated, but not always necessary. Have a small pack ready to take on your person; carry water, a healthy snack, toilet paper, reading material (ahem! this book), earplugs, camera, valuables and whatever else you can't live without for a few hours.

Most cities and towns have a central bus terminal where each company has its own ticket window. Some companies post fares and schedules prominently, and the ticket price and departure time is always on the ticket you buy. Expect (Argentine) fast-food stalls, *kioskos* and newspaper vendors inside or near almost every terminal. There aren't hotel touts or other traveler hassling-types at terminals in Argentina (except maybe for taxi drivers). And there's often a place to store your luggage; if you buy a ticket in advance from a certain company, they will often store your bags for free.

Usually you don't need to buy bus tickets ahead of time. Except holiday stretches such as late December, January and July, most buses aren't sold out. There are exceptions, however, and you don't want to find this out in some tiny town that only has one bus out that day – and it's full. As soon as you arrive somewhere that has limited services (like small towns), it's a good idea to find out which companies go to your next destination and when, and plan your trip out around that. Even in larger towns or cities it's a good idea to find out ahead of time when the bus leaves to your next destination.

Costs

Bus fares in Argentina are considerably costlier than in the Andean countries and somewhat more expensive than in Chile. A good rule of thumb is US$2 to US$3 per hour of journey, though Patagonia can be more expensive. Bus services are private rather than state-operated, and fares respond quickly to market conditions and inflation. Keep an eye out for the occasional promotional fare, especially where many bus companies compete for the same routes; your student ID card can occasionally turn up a discount. Expect to pay in cash; credit cards aren't accepted. Following are sample fares from Buenos Aires.

Destination	Duration in hours	Cost
Bahía Blanca	10	US$19
Bariloche	22	US$40
Comodoro Rivadavia	28	US$65
Córdoba	9½	US$16
La Quiaca	28	US$70
Mar del Plata	5½	US$20
Mendoza	16	US$35
Puerto Iguazú	16	US$45
Puerto Madryn	20	US$50
Resistencia	13	US$30
Rosario	4	US$21
Santa Fe	6	US$23
Santa Rosa	8	US$25

TRAIN

Despite major reductions in long-distance train service, rail lines continue to serve most of the Buenos Aires suburbs and some surrounding provinces. During holiday periods like Christmas or national holidays, buy tickets in advance. Train fares tend to be lower than comparable bus fares, but trains are slower and there are much fewer departure times and destinations. (See Getting There & Away in the Buenos Aires chapter for more information.)

Train buffs will want to take the narrow-gauge La Trochita (see that boxed text under Esquel in the Patagonia chapter), which runs from Esquel to El Maitén.

CAR & MOTORCYCLE

Because Argentina is so large, many parts are easily accessible only by motor vehicle despite the country's extensive public transport system. Especially in Patagonia, where distances are great and buses can be infrequent, you can't easily stop for something interesting at the side of the road and then continue on your merry way by public transport.

Unfortunately, operating a car is expensive. Although Argentina is self-sufficient in oil, the price of *nafta* (petrol) is about US$1.20 per liter (that's around US$4 per gallon to you Americans). However, in Patagonia (where much of Argentina's oil fields are) it's half that. Gas stations are fairly common, but outside the cities you should keep an eye on your gas gauge, and off the beaten track it's a good idea to carry extra fuel. Tolls are comparable to those in North America or Australia. In some areas, most notably Buenos Aires province, tolls on privatized highways are very high (as much as US$4 per 100km).

Formally, you must have an International or Inter-American Driving Permit to supplement your national or state driver's license. In practice, police rarely examine these documents closely and generally ignore the latter. They do not ignore automobile registration, insurance and tax documents, which must be up-to-date. Except in Buenos Aires, security problems are few, and you shouldn't be driving in Buenos Aires anyway.

Although motorbikes have become fashionable among some Argentines, they are very expensive, and there appears to be no

Know Your Signs

Certain warning signs on the road that are worth heeding include:

bache	pothole
cruce ferrocarril	railroad crossing
guardaganado	cattle guard
vado	dip

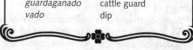

motorcycle rental agencies in Argentina. If you find one, however, please write in and tell us. Your fellow motorcyclists will appreciate it in the future.

Road Rules & Hazards

Anyone considering driving in Argentina should know that Argentine drivers are aggressive and commonly ignore speed limits, road signs and even traffic signals. Traffic accidents are the main cause of death for Argentines between the ages of five and 35. Don't drive unless you can be constantly vigilant and can adapt to the usually speedy flow of traffic.

Though most Argentine highways have a speed limit of 80km/h, and some have been raised to 100km/h or more, hardly anybody pays attention to these or any other regulations. During the Pampas harvest season, pay particular attention to slow-moving farm machinery, which, though not a hazard in its own right, brings out the worst in impatient Argentine motorists. Night driving is not recommended; in some regions animals hang out on the road, but more often, many drivers don't bother to use their headlights (perhaps they believe they're saving battery power).

Drivers must carry their *tarjeta verde,* or green card; for foreign vehicles, customs permission is the acceptable substitute. Also have on hand some emergency reflectors *(valizas),* and a one-kilo fire extinguisher. Headrests are required for the driver and each passenger, and motorcycle helmets are now obligatory, although this law is rarely enforced.

You won't often see police patrolling the highways, where high-speed, head-on crashes are common, but you will meet them at major intersections and roadside checkpoints where they conduct meticulous document and equipment checks. For instance, if the police ask to check your turn signals (which almost no Argentine bothers to use), brake lights, or hand brake, it may well be a warning of corruption in progress. Equipment violations can carry heavy fines, but such checks are more commonly pretexts for graft. The police may claim that

you must pay the fine at a local bank, which may not be open until the following day, or if it's on a weekend, until Monday. If you are uncertain about your rights, state in a very matter-of-fact manner your intention to contact your embassy or consulate, or feign such complete ignorance of Spanish that you're more trouble than the police think it's worth. Offer a *coima* (bribe) only if you are confident that it is 'appropriate' and unavoidable. Ask, *'¿Puedo pagar la multa ahora?'* ('Can I pay the fine right now?').

Rental

International rental agencies like Hertz, Avis and AI have offices in Buenos Aires and in other tourist areas throughout Argentina. To rent a car, you must be at least 21 years of age and have a valid driver's license; having an international driver's license wouldn't be a bad idea. You'll need to present a credit card and your passport, though.

Even at minor agencies, rental charges are now very high. The cheapest and smallest vehicles go for about US$42 per day with 50km included (you can sometimes negotiate a lower rate by paying in cash rather than by credit card). Rates are even higher in Patagonia: Expect to hand over US$100 per day in this region (though at least gas costs less). Although unlimited-mileage deals do exist, they are much more expensive. One potentially worthwhile tactic is to make a reservation with one of the major international agencies in your home country, which can sometimes guarantee lower rates.

If you opt for camping – feasible in or near most cities as well as the countryside – rather than staying in hotels, the money you save will offset a good part of the car rental cost.

Purchase

If you are spending several months in Argentina, purchasing a car is an alternative worth exploring, but it has both advantages and disadvantages. On one hand, it's more flexible than public transport and is likely to be cheaper than rentals, which can easily reach US$100 per day. If you resell the car at the end of your stay, it may turn out even more economical. On the other hand, any used car can be a risk, especially on Patagonia's rugged backroads.

If you purchase a car, you must deal with the exasperating Argentine bureaucracy. You must have the title *(tarjeta verde)*, and license tax payments must be up-to-date. As a foreigner, you may find it useful to carry a notarized document authorizing your use of the car, since the bureaucracy moves too slowly to change the title easily. In any event, Argentines rarely do so because of the expense involved – even vehicles 30 years old or more often bear the original purchaser's name.

As a foreigner you may own a vehicle in Argentina but, in theory at least, you may not take it out of the country even with a notarized authorization – although certain border crossings, such as Puerto Iguazú, appear to be more flexible. Contact your consulate for assistance and advice, but hardly anyone can prevail against a truly determined customs official.

Argentina's domestic automobile industry has left a reserve of serviceable used cars in the country. The most popular models are Peugeot 404s and Ford Falcons, for which parts are readily available, but do not expect to find a dependable used car for less than about US$3000. Prices will be higher for a *gasolero*, a vehicle that uses cheaper diesel fuel. There is probably a better stock of used cars, at more reasonable prices, in Chile.

Insurance

Liability insurance is obligatory in Argentina, and police may ask to see proof of insurance at checkpoints. Fortunately, coverage is reasonably priced. Insuring a US$18,000 car with basic liability insurance costs about US$45 per month, though with robbery and fire insurance the cost zooms to US$130. Cost is lower, of course, if you have an old rust bucket. If you plan on taking the car to neighboring countries, make sure it will remain covered (you'll have to pay extra). Among reputable insurers in Argentina

are Seguros Rivadavia, Mapfre and the Automóvil Club Argentino (ACA).

Automóvil Club Argentino

If you drive in Argentina, especially with your own car, it may be worthwhile to become a member of the Automóvil Club Argentino (ACA), which has offices, service stations and garages throughout the country, offering free road service and towing in and around major cities. ACA also recognizes members of its overseas affiliates, such as the American Automobile Association (AAA), as equivalent to its own members and grants them limited privileges, including discounts on maps, accommodations, camping and tours (bring your card). Membership costs about US$30 per month, which is more expensive than most of its overseas counterparts.

ACA's head office (☎ 4802-6061) is at Av del Libertador 1850, Palermo, in Buenos Aires. They have offices in every major city.

Shipping a Vehicle

Chile is probably the best country on the continent for shipping a vehicle from overseas, though the situation in Argentina is improving. Getting the vehicle out of customs typically involves routine paperwork. If the car is more than a few days in customs, however, storage charges can add up quickly. Do not leave anything whatsoever of value in the vehicle if at all possible. Theft of tools in particular is very common.

To find a reliable shipper, check the yellow pages of your local phone directory under 'Automobile Transporters.' Most transporters are accustomed to arranging shipments between North America and Europe, rather than from North America or Europe to South America, so it may take some of them time to work out details.

Motorcyclists have used Aerolíneas Argentinas air freight to ship their vehicles, but this is far more expensive than sea freight.

BICYCLE

If you dig cycling your way around a country, Argentina has some good potential.

It will also save you some dough: Partnered with camping, cycling can make your trip nearly as cheap as in the Andean countries. And of course you'll see more details and meet more curious locals.

Many Argentines use bikes for transportation, and cycling is becoming a popular recreational activity. Many towns have bike shops, but high-quality bikes are expensive and repair parts can be hard to come by.

Reasonable bicycle rentals (mostly mountain bikes) are available in Mendoza and Bariloche and other towns in the Lake District, where recreation is an important industry. Check and adjust your rental bike carefully before heading off on a long ride.

Racing bicycles are suitable for some paved roads, but these byways are often narrow; a *todo terreno* (mountain bike) is safer and more convenient, allowing you to use the unpaved shoulder and the very extensive network of graveled roads throughout the country. Argentine bicycles are improving in quality but are still not equal to their counterparts in Europe or the USA.

There are many good routes for bicycling, especially around the Patagonian Lake District and in the Andean Northwest; the highway from Tucumán to Tafí del Valle, the direct road from Salta to Jujuy, and the Quebrada de Cafayate would be exceptionally beautiful rides on generally good surfaces.

There are two major drawbacks to long-distance bicycling in Argentina. One is the wind, which in Patagonia can slow your progress to a crawl. The other is Argentine motorists: On many of the country's straight, narrow, two-lane highways, they can be a serious hazard to bicyclists. Make yourself as visible as possible, and wear a helmet. On gravel roads, be prepared for dust and rocks kicked up by passing vehicles. Of course you'll need to bring an adequate repair kit and extra parts (and the mental know-how to use them), some good directions (unpaved roads on maps can be unreliable) and enough food and water till the next town. In Patagonia, a windbreaker and warm clothing are essential. Don't expect too much traffic on some backroads, which may see one or two vehicles a day. Come prepared to fend completely for yourself.

Readers seeking more information on cycling in South America can find it in Walter Sienko's *Latin America by Bike*.

HITCHHIKING

Hitchhiking is never entirely safe in any country in the world, and it is not recommended. Travelers who decide to hitch should understand that they are taking a small but potentially serious risk. People who do choose to hitch will be safer if they travel in pairs and let someone know where they are planning to go.

Along with Chile, Argentina is probably the best country for hitching in all of South America. The major drawback is that Argentine vehicles are often stuffed full with families and children, but truckers will frequently pick up backpackers. At the *servicentros* at the outskirts of large Argentine cities, where truckers gas up their vehicles, it's often easy to solicit a ride.

Women can and do hitchhike alone, but should exercise caution and especially avoid getting into a car with more than one man. In Patagonia, where distances are great and vehicles few, hitchers should expect long waits and carry warm, windproof clothing. A water bottle is also a good idea, especially in the desert north. Also carry some healthy snack food.

There are a few routes along which hitching is undesirable. RN 40, from El Calafate to Perito Moreno and Río Mayo, is a challenge to your patience, and the lack of services along the way is a serious drawback. Up north, the scenic route from Tucumán to Cafayate is difficult past Tafí del Valle.

BOAT

Opportunities for boat or river travel in and around Argentina are very limited, though there are regular international services to/from Uruguay (see the Getting There & Away chapter). If you must be on the water, head to the Buenos Aires suburb of Tigre, where there are numerous boat excursions around the delta of the Río de la Plata.

LOCAL TRANSPORTATION
To/From the Airport

In some Argentine cities, airlines have a minibus operating in tandem with the flight schedule. Sometimes there is a city bus that stops at the airport. And there are *always* taxis.

In Buenos Aires, you have a few options getting to and from Aeroparque (the domestic airport) or Ezeiza. See the Buenos Aires chapter for details.

Bus

Local Argentine buses ('colectivos') are notorious for charging along the *avenidas*, spewing choking clouds of black smoke, all the while traveling at break-neck speeds. Riding on one is a good way to see the cities and get around, providing you can sort out the oft complex bus systems. Buses are clearly numbered and usually carry a placard indicating their final destination. Since many identically numbered buses serve slightly different routes (especially in bigger cities), pay attention to these placards. To ask 'Does this bus go to (the beach)?' say *'¿Va este colectivo a (la playa)?'*

Many folks, especially older people, have many routes memorized and will be glad to help you. They are a good source if your Spanish is at a level where you can understand their directions. Kiosk tenders can also be helpful. If you're going to be around in Buenos Aires awhile, invest in a bus booklet guide, available at most newsstands for US$5 to US$10 (look for rarer mini-versions). Many stops *(paradas)* in the capital have a sign listing the bus route. Be aware that the return route of any particular bus, due to all the one-way streets, will not follow the route you took to get there. For life-saving advice on riding Argentina's buses, see the boxed text 'Going Somewhere Fast?'

Subway

Buenos Aires is the only Argentine city with a subway system (known as Subte), and it's the quickest way of getting around the city center. For details, see the Buenos Aires chapter.

Going Somewhere Fast?

Here's some advice for riding the local buses (especially in Buenos Aires):

• Flag down your target bus by sticking your arm out and making eye contact with the driver. They will usually slow down, though at a busy stop shared by different lines your bus may zoom by while you're 'hiding' behind another bus taking on passengers.

• Have change ready before you board the bus. You'll either drop coins into a machine or run a magnetic card through one. Fares vary widely, but are usually under US$1. Always have change available: When you need it the most, you'll find it's hard to get!

• Seats toward the front are normally offered to older, visibly pregnant or kid-laden people. Go towards the back if you need to sit – unless you're an older, visibly pregnant or kid-laden person.

• The exit is always at the back; ring the buzzer for your stop. On crowded buses, watch your body and belongings as usual, and slap anybody whose hands start to wander.

• Hang on tight, and enjoy the ride!

Taxi & Remise

The people of Buenos Aires make frequent use of taxis, which are digitally metered and cheap. Outside Buenos Aires, meters are common but not universal, and it may be necessary to agree upon a fare in advance. Drivers are generally polite and honest, but there are exceptions; be sure the meter is set at zero. It is customary to round up the fare as a tip.

In areas like Patagonia, where public transportation can be scarce, it's possible to hire a cab with a driver for the day to visit places off the beaten track. If you bargain, this can actually be cheaper than a rental car, but negotiate the fee in advance.

Remises are radio taxis without meters that generally offer fixed fares within a given zone. They are an increasingly popular form of transportation and cost about as much as taxis. Though unlike taxis, they don't cruise the city in search of fares, but hotels and restaurants will phone them for you if you ask. (See Dangers & Annoyances in the Facts for the Visitor chapter for safety precautions when taking taxis.)

ORGANIZED TOURS

Movi Track (☎/fax 0387-431-6749, e movitrack@movitrack.com.ar), Buenos Aires 68, Oficina 1B, 4400 Salta, operates comfortable backroad excursions through northern Argentina and Chile in their custom-designed vehicle (available for charters as well). Owners Frank and Heike Neumann speak excellent English. Movi Track's Buenos Aires agent is Kraft Travel Service (☎/fax 4793-4062), E Lamarca 343, 1st floor, No 17, 1640 Martínez.

The Anglo-Argentine Estancia Huechahue, in Neuquén province, in a sheltered valley on the Río Aluminé, about 30km east of Junín de los Andes, offers all-inclusive riding and trekking holidays in pleasant surroundings both there and in Parque Nacional Lanín. Accommodations are very comfortable, amid apple orchards and tranquil forest plantations. For non-riding companions there are walking, bird watching, Indian history and the activities of a working estancia.

The basic daily price of US$245 per person includes transportation between Huechahue and San Martín de los Andes plus full board and beverages (the latter with minor exceptions). For more information, contact Jane Williams (e jane@satlink.com) and make reservations far in advance of the trip.

Buenos Aires

One of South America's most sophisticated and appealing cities is Buenos Aires, home to 3 million proud port city dwellers, or *porteños*. With extensive suburbs encompassing another 10 million people and a modern, bustling downtown adorned with numerous elegant older buildings, this cosmopolitan city surprises many travelers. It brims with refined and impeccably dressed inhabitants strutting about stylishly while chatting on cell phones or hanging out in moody cafés discussing world politics.

For the tourist, Buenos Aires delivers. Head south of the center to the weather-worn architecture and cobbled streets of San Telmo, birthplace of the tango. A bit farther south is La Boca, a rough-and-tumble port neighborhood of the most colorfully painted metal houses you can imagine. On the other side of town, to the north, lies chic Recoleta, trendy, park-filled Palermo and upscale, suburban Belgrano. All in all, you'll find plenty to keep you on your travelling toes in this exciting city.

HISTORY

In 1536, Pedro de Mendoza landed in present-day Buenos Aires and camped on a bluff above the Río de la Plata. Mendoza's oversized expedition, comprising 16 ships and nearly 1600 men, arrived too late in summer to plant crops, and the few Querandí hunter-gatherers reacted violently when the Spaniards forced them to seek food. Scant provisions and the unfriendly locals eventually forced some members of the expedition to sail up the Paraná, where they founded the city of Asunción among the more sedentary and obliging Guaraní peoples. Within five years, the Spaniards had completely abandoned Buenos Aires.

Thirty-four years later, in 1580, the Spaniards of Asunción, led by Juan de Garay, reestablished themselves on the west bank of the Río de la Plata. Even then, at

Highlights

- Cementerio de la Recoleta – Walking among the extravagant abodes of the wealthy and elite…and dead
- San Telmo – Falling for tango in its birthplace or shopping at the Sunday antique market
- Old-time cafés – Stepping backward in time and place
- Fútbol – Catching a game between the staunch rivals Boca Juniors and River Plate
- Teatro Colón – Watching a performance in Argentina's grandest theater
- Delta del Paraná – Skipping from the big city to this island wonderland

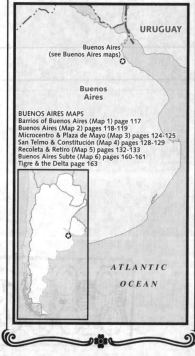

URUGUAY

Buenos Aires
(see Buenos Aires maps)

Buenos
Aires

BUENOS AIRES MAPS
Barrios of Buenos Aires (Map 1) page 117
Buenos Aires (Map 2) pages 118-119
Microcentro & Plaza de Mayo (Map 3) pages 124-125
San Telmo & Constitución (Map 4) pages 128-129
Recoleta & Retiro (Map 5) pages 132-133
Buenos Aires Subte (Map 6) pages 160-161
Tigre & the Delta page 163

ATLANTIC
OCEAN

the end of a tenuous supply line stretching from Madrid (via Panama and Lima, Peru), Buenos Aires was clearly subordinate to Asunción; the city survived but did not flourish. Garay himself died at the hands of the Querandí only three years later.

Over the next two centuries, Buenos Aires grew slowly but steadily on the basis of the enormous herds of feral cattle and horses that began to proliferate when the first Spaniards abandoned them on the lush pastures of the surrounding Pampas. As local frustration with Spain's mercantile restrictions grew, creative traders smuggled contraband from Portuguese and British vessels. In 1776 Buenos Aires became capital of the new Viceroyalty of the Río de la Plata, which included the famous silver district of Potosí (in present-day Bolivia). This new status as a capital signaled to the world that the adolescent city was outgrowing Spain's parental authority.

British invasions in 1806 and 1807 were a major turning point in late colonial times. Forces of *criollos* (American-born Spaniards) feigned cooperation with British forces occupying Buenos Aires, only to turn and repel them. Just three years later, on May 25, 1810, influential criollos confronted and deposed the viceroy, on the pretext that Spain's legitimate government had fallen.

Six years later, in Tucumán, the United Provinces of the River Plate declared independence, but they failed to resolve the growing conflict between two elite sectors: the landowners of the interior, concerned primarily with preserving their economic privileges, and the residents of Buenos Aires (not yet the capital), who maintained an outward orientation toward overseas commerce and European ideas. More than a decade of violence and uncertainty ensued before Federalist leader Juan Manuel de Rosas asserted his authority over Buenos Aires. His reign lasted 23 years, during which time the city's influence grew despite his opportunistic Federalist convictions. Rosas was overthrown in 1852, and ten years later Argentina had its first president: Bartolome Mitre. Soon after, the country's economy boomed on the richness of agriculture and the sheep industry.

In the 1880s, when Buenos Aires became the official federal capital, provincial authorities moved their offices to La Plata. Buenos Aires continued to thrive, however; agricultural exports flowed out, imports flowed in, and a new port was built. According to British diplomat James Bryce, who visited the capital at the turn of the 19th century, none of the leaders of Glasgow, Manchester or Chicago:

shewed greater enterprise and bolder conceptions than did the men of Buenos Ayres when on this exposed and shallow coast they made alongside their city a great ocean harbour.

These heady times were not overlooked by outsiders seeking a piece of the pie. European immigration boosted Argentina's population from 90,000 in 1854 to 177,000 in 1869 to 670,000 in 1895. By the early 1900s, Latin America's largest city had more than a million inhabitants, though unfortunately many of them were poor.

Rapid growth brought the usual problems, as families crowded into substandard housing, merchants and manufacturers kept wages low, and labor became increasingly militant. In 1919, under pressure from landowners and other elite sectors, President Hipólito Yrigoyen's Radical government ordered the army to suppress a metalworkers' strike in what became known as La Semana Trágica (the Tragic Week), setting an unfortunate precedent for the coming decades.

In the 1930s, ambitious municipal governments undertook a massive downtown modernization program, ramming broad avenues like Santa Fe, Córdoba, and Corrientes through the heart of the city and obliterating narrow colonial streets. Since WWII, Gran (Greater) Buenos Aires has sprawled to absorb many once-distant suburbs. Though smaller in population than Mexico City or São Paulo, Buenos Aires remains one of Latin America's dominant economic, political and cultural centers. But a city that once prided itself on its European sophistication and livability now shares the same problems as other Latin American megacities – air and noise pollution, decaying infrastructure, declining public services, unemployment and underemployment, and spreading shantytowns.

Not all signs are negative, though. Carlos Menem's economic reforms improved communications and other services through privatization, though at a very high cost. The administration also reduced a bloated public sector and devised an effective tax collection system to support public services, and as a result certain sectors of the economy, most notably finance and services, prospered for awhile.

Relatively recent constitutional reforms have given the city representative self-government for the first time, through an elected mayor and city council. The privatized subway system has expanded and improved service after decades of neglect. Certain neighborhoods have seen changes for the better; the once abandoned Puerto Madero complex on the waterfront has been remodeled into upscale lofts, offices, restaurants, a yacht harbor and open space. The country's continuing economic difficulties make the future unpredictable, but Buenos Aires remains a vibrant, cosmopolitan admixture of international capital and traditional barrio life.

ORIENTATION

Buenos Aires can be divided into two sections: the Capital Federal (population 3 million), which consists of 48 barrios (neighborhoods) and includes the compact downtown area, and Gran Buenos Aires (population 13 million), which includes both the Capital Federal and the surrounding metropolitan area. Travelers and tourists visiting the city pretty much keep to the Capital Federal, staying near downtown and easily accessing the most interesting barrios via an extensive public transportation system.

A few sub-neighborhoods complicate the city's layout, but most are marked on the maps. For example, Barrio Norte is the southern part of Recoleta, sizeable Palermo includes Palermo Viejo and Las Cañitas, La City is the compact downtown

financial district, and Once is the area around Estación Once.

The most important business and entertainment areas are strung along the wide avenues of Corrientes, Córdoba and Santa Fe, and on pedestrian Florida and Lavalle. One avenue you'll have no trouble recognizing is broad Av 9 de Julio; it's 16 lanes wide and runs all the way from San Telmo in the south to Retiro up north, with a sky-piercing white obelisk at its center.

Plaza de Mayo is a magnet for tourists and political activists alike. Situated at the eastern end of Av de Mayo, one of downtown's main east-west boulevards, the plaza is surrounded by a host of important buildings such as the Casa Rosada (Presidential Palace). A dozen blocks away, at the other end of Av de Mayo, is another significant edifice, El Palacio del Congreso (the Congress building). Buenos Aires' newest barrio, the dockside Puerto Madero, runs north to south along the Río de la Plata and is very pedestrian-friendly.

South of downtown is San Telmo, famous for cobblestone streets and tango shows, and La Boca, a blue-collar neighborhood known for its colorful metal houses. North of downtown is Recoleta (the most exclusive 'hood in town), Palermo (more middle-class and full of parks) and Belgrano (a more upscale residential area). And there you have it in a nutshell: Buenos Aires for the tourist.

INFORMATION
Tourist Offices

The national tourist office (☎ 4312-2232), Santa Fe 883, is open 9am to 5pm weekdays and dispenses information on all of Argentina; for detailed information on Buenos Aires, see the city's main tourist office at Balcarce 360 (☎ 4114-5794, ☎ 4114-5791 for free city tours). There are also tourist kiosks at Ezeiza International airport (☎ 4480-0224) and the mostly domestic Aeroparque Jorge Newbery (known simply as Aeroparque; ☎ 4773-9805). These last two do not provide flight information (call individual airlines instead).

Other city tourist offices include the centrally located kiosk at the intersection of

BARRIOS OF BUENOS AIRES (MAP 1)

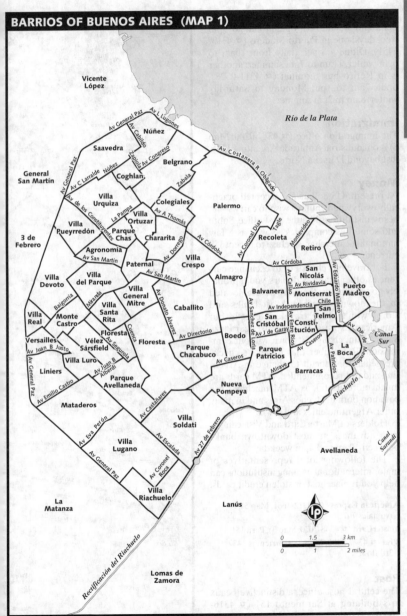

Vicente López

Núñez

Saavedra

Belgrano

Río de la Plata

General San Martín

Coghlan

Av Costanera R Obligado

3 de Febrero

Villa Urquiza

Colegiales

Palermo

Villa Pueyrredón

Villa Ortúzar

Parque Chas

Chacarita

Recoleta

Retiro

Agronomía

Villa Crespo

Puerto Madero

Villa Devoto

Paternal

Almagro

San Nicolás

Villa del Parque

Villa General Mitre

Balvanera

Montserrat

San Telmo

Villa Real

Villa Santa Rita

Caballito

San Cristóbal

Constitución

Monte Castro

Floresta

Boedo

Parque Patricios

La Boca

Versailles

Vélez Sársfield

Floresta

Canal Sur

Villa Luro

Parque Chacabuco

Barracas

Liniers

Parque Avellaneda

Nueva Pompeya

Riachuelo

Mataderos

Villa Soldati

Avellaneda

Canal Sarandí

Villa Lugano

Villa Riachuelo

Lanús

La Matanza

Rectificación del Riachuelo

Lomas de Zamora

0   1.5   3 km
0   1   2 miles

Av Florida and Diagonal Roque Sáenz Peña (no ☎; Map 3), open 10am to 5pm weekdays; one in Puerto Madero (☎ 4313-6451), Dique 4, open daily from 10am to 6pm winter, 11am to 7pm summer; another is in Retiro bus terminal (☎ 4311-0528), open 7am to 1pm Monday to Saturday winter, 8am to 2pm summer.

Immigration

The immigration office (☎ 4317-0200; Map 5) is on industrial Antártida Argentina 1335, just beyond Dársena Norte.

Money

At present, US dollars are accepted practically everywhere, but it's wise to carry some pesos; institutions like the post office, Subte and some bus companies, as well as a few nationalistic merchants, refuse to accept US currency.

For traveler's checks, or to exchange currencies other than US dollars, you'll probably go to cambios; there are several located in the downtown area. Most banks and stores won't touch traveler's checks, but American Express, Arenales 707 near Plaza San Martín, changes its own without commission. Remember that traveler's checks are generally difficult to change in Argentina and not recommended. ATM cards are much more useful, as ATM machines are common both in Buenos Aires and in many other Argentine cities and towns.

Holders of MasterCard and Visa can get cash advances at most downtown banks between 10am and 4pm weekdays.

The following local representatives of major international banking institutions can help you replace lost or stolen credit cards:

American Express (☎ 4312-1661; Map 5), Arenales 707

MasterCard (☎ 4348-7070; Map 3), Perú 151

Visa (☎ 4379-3400; Map 3), Corrientes 1437, 3rd floor

Post

The central post office, a distinctive beaux arts building at Sarmiento 151 (☎ 4316-3000), occupies an entire block. It's open

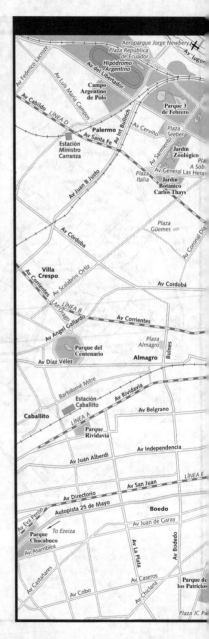

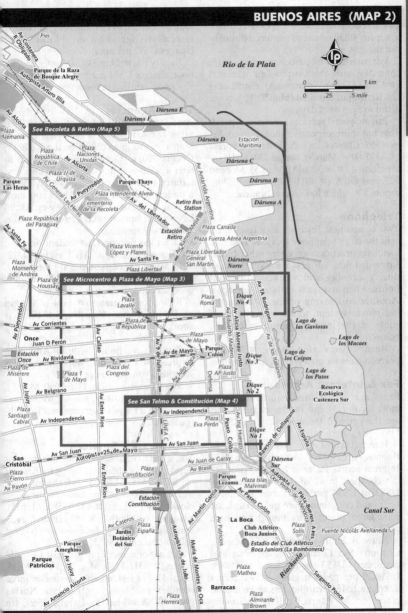

BUENOS AIRES (MAP 2)

Río de la Plata

0 .5 1 km
0 .25 .5 mile

Pier

Av Costanera R Obligado

Parque de la Raza de Bosque Alegre

Autopista Arturo Illia

Av Alcorta

Plaza Alemania

See Recoleta & Retiro (Map 5)

Dársena F

Dársena E

Dársena D

Estación Marítima

Plaza República de Chile

Plaza Naciones Unidas

Av Alcorta

Dársena C

Plaza JJ de Urquiza

Parque Thays

Av General Las Heras

Av Pueyrredón

Dársena B

Parque Las Heras

Plaza Intendente Alvear

Av del Libertador

Cementerio de la Recoleta

Av Santa Fe

Plaza República del Paraguay

Retiro Bus Station

Dársena A

Estación Retiro

Plaza Canadá

Av Ramón Mejía

Plaza Fuerza Aérea Argentina

Av Santa Fe

Plaza Vicente López y Planes

Plaza Monseñor de Andrea

Plaza Libertad

Plaza Libertador General San Martín

Dársena Norte

Plaza de Houssay

See Microcentro & Plaza de Mayo (Map 3)

Av Pueyrredón

Plaza Lavalle

Plaza Roma

Dique No 4

Av TA Rodríguez

Lago de las Gaviotas

Av Corrientes

Plaza de la República

Av Alicia Moreau Justo

Av Eduardo Madero

Once

Juan D Perón

Av Callao

Plaza de Mayo

Av 9 de Julio

Parque Colón

Dique No 3

Lago de los Coipos

Lago de los Macaes

Estación Once

Av Rividavia

Plaza 1 de Mayo

Plaza del Congreso

Av Julio Roca

Plaza AP Justo

Defensa

Av de los Italianos

Plaza de Miserere

Av Belgrano

Av Entre Ríos

Dique No 2

Lago de los Patos

Av Jujuy

Plaza Santiago Cabral

Av Independencia

See San Telmo & Constitución (Map 4)

Av Independencia

Plaza Eva Perón

Av Ing Huergo

Dique No 1

Av Paseo Colón

Ramson de Dellepiane

Reserva Ecológica Castenera Sur

LINEA C

Av San Juan

San Cristóbal

Av San Juan

Autopista 25 de Mayo

Plaza Constitución

Av Juan de Garay

Dársena Sur

Av España

Plaza Fierro

Av Entre Ríos

Av Brasil

Autopista La Plata Buenos Aires

Canal Sur

Av Pavón

Brasil

Parque Lezama

Plaza Islas Malvinas

Av Paseo Colón

Av Don Pedro de Mendoza

Estación Constitución

Av Caseros

Plaza España

Av Martín García

Av Patricios

La Boca

Club Atlético Boca Juniors

Plaza Solís

Puente Nicolás Avellaneda

Parque Ameghino

Jardín Botánico del Sur

Autopista 9 de Julio

María de Montes de Oca

Estadio del Club Atlético Boca Juniors (La Bombonera)

Riachuelo

Sargento Ponce

Parque Patricios

Av Jujuy

Av Amancio Alcorta

Plaza Matheu

Barracas

Plaza Herrera

Plaza Almirante Brown

8am to 8pm weekdays, 9am to 1pm Saturday and does not accept US dollars. There are many small branches scattered throughout the city.

For international parcels weighing more than 2kg, visit the Correo Internacional (☎ 4316-1777), on Antártida Argentina near the Retiro bus terminal (Map 5). Hours are 10am to 5pm weekdays.

Private postal services are more dependable but more expensive than Correo Argentino. Choices include Federal Express (☎ 4393-6054; Map 3), Maipú 753; DHL International (☎ 4630-1000; Map 3), Moreno 927; and OCA (☎ 4311-5305; Map 3), Viamonte 526, which has several branches.

Telephone

Two companies, Telecom and Telefónica, split the city's telephone services. There's a locutorio practically on every other block. Long-distance offices are usually busy during evening and weekend discount hours, when overseas calls are cheaper. Another cost-saving option is using the *net2phone* system, which is available at some of the larger Internet cafés (see below).

Buenos Aires' area code is ☎ 11. The porteño term for area code is *característica*.

Fax & Internet Access

Faxes are widely used and available at most locutorios and Internet cafés. Costs are the price of the call plus US$0.50 to US$1 per page.

Internet cafés are now common in Buenos Aires. Many locutorios also have Internet access. Rates in Buenos Aires are the cheapest in all of Argentina (around US$2 to US$4 per hour); competition is fierce and connections are quick. Here are some larger places to try, though you'll see cafés everywhere.

Network Internet (☎ 4893-2695; Map 5), Córdoba 543 Local 77, is spacious and clean, costs US$3 per hour and prints for US$0.20 per page. It gives 20% Internet discounts to ISIC cardholders and is a good place for the Internet calling *net2phone* service.

Towernet Cybercentro (☎ 4328-5744; Map 3), Lavalle 641, is another good one; it is central (right near Av Florida) and charges US$2 per hour.

Netcity (no ☎; Map 3), Corrientes 963, 1st floor, charges US$1 per half-hour and even has a non-smoking section.

Travel Agencies

Asatej (☎ 4312-0101 information, 4114-7500 sales, fax 4311-6158, ⓦ www.asatej.com; Map 5) has its main offices on the 3rd floor, Oficina 320, at Florida 835. Open 9am to 6pm weekdays, it has some of the cheapest airfares available, and you don't have to be a student to get them. You'll probably have to wait a long time in line, however. Asatej has several branch offices around Buenos Aires and Argentina.

Other less busy and less student-oriented travel agencies include AB Travel (☎ 4322-7372; Map 3), Galería Jardín at Florida 537, Local 332. In business for 25 years, it offers good service and English-speakers.

Kallpa tour operator (☎ 4394-1830; Map 3), Roque Saenz Peña 811, 5th floor, is another multilingual company offering travel services.

Don't leave home without American Express (☎ 4312-0900; Map 5), Arenales 707, but if you do, they're here.

Swan Turismo (☎/fax 4816-2080; Map 5), Cerrito 822, 9th floor, has a professional office with a range of services and English-speakers.

Photography Services

You won't have trouble finding quality print developing. For slide developing try Kinefot (☎ 4374-7445; Map 3), Talcahuano 244, which has two other locations on the same block, and Le Lab (☎ 4322-2585; Map 3), Viamonte 630, both near the center. Developing and mounting 36 *diapositivos* (slides) will cost around US$15.

For minor camera repairs, visit Gerardo Föhse (☎ 4311-1139; Map 5), Florida 835, Local 37. For fast, reliable service on more complex problems, contact José Norres (☎ 4373-0963; Map 3), Lavalle 1569, 4th floor, Oficina 403.

Libraries

The Biblioteca Nacional (National Library; ☎ 4806-97642; Map 5), Agüero 250, is open 8am to 9pm Monday through Saturday, 11am to 7pm Sunday.

The excellent Biblioteca Lincoln (☎ 4322-3855; Map 3), Maipú 686, carries several US newspapers like the *New York Times* and *Wall Street Journal*, as well as many English-language magazines. It's a nice, quiet place to read and rest.

Cultural Centers

One of Buenos Aires' best cultural resources is the high-rise Centro Cultural San Martín (☎ 4374-1251; Map 3), Sarmiento 1551. It has free or inexpensive galleries, film, music and lectures, as well as exhibitions of outdoor sculpture and occasional free concerts on summer evenings and weekends.

Centro Cultural Recoleta (☎ 4803-1041; Map 5), Junín 1930, also offers free or inexpensive events, including art exhibitions and outdoor films on summer evenings. Centro Cultural Borges (☎ 4319-5359; Map 3), Viamonte & San Martín, is one of the best, offering art exhibits, music, lectures and workshops. It's open 10am to 9pm Monday through Saturday, 12pm to 9pm Sunday. Admission is US$2 (seniors and students US$1), but it's free Monday.

A similar facility is the Complejo Cultural Ricardo Rojas (☎ 4954-5523; Map 3), Corrientes 2038, open 10am to 10pm Monday through Saturday; it also offers many interesting classes.

There are also several foreign cultural centers in town, such as the Instituto Cultural Argentino-Norteamericano (☎ 4322-3855; Map 3), Maipú 672; the Alianza Francesa (☎ 4322-0068; Map 3), Córdoba 946; Instituto Goethe (☎ 4311-8964; Map 3), Corrientes 319; and the British Arts Centre (☎ 4393-6941; Map 5), Suipacha 1333.

Medical Services

The capital's medical facilities include Palermo's Hospital Municipal Juan Fernández (☎ 4801-5555), Cerviño 3356, in addition to Hospital Alemán (☎ 4821-1700; Map 5),

Pueyrredón 1640. There's also the British Hospital (☎ 4304-1081), Perdriel 74, way over in Constitución.

Dangers & Annoyances

Buenos Aires is safer than many other big cities in the world. You can comfortably walk around at all hours of the night in many places (though not all). Take care very late at night around the Constitución area and on pedestrian Av Florida. Also watch yourself at night around some areas of San Telmo and especially La Boca (ask locals where it's unsafe to go). A recent crime wave, related to the current economic situation, has hit the city but is not specifically targeted at tourists.

Porteño drivers, like many Argentines, jump the gun when the traffic signal is about to change to green. They also drive very fast and change lanes unpredictably. Be wary of vehicles turning right; even though pedestrians at corners and crosswalks have legal right-of-way, very few drivers respect this and will hardly slow down when you are crossing. Be especially careful of buses, which can be reckless.

Lax pollution controls and a nation addicted to tobacco make for very bad air indeed, despite the city's name. Sensitive souls from countries where smoking is in decline should brace themselves for tobacco smoke everywhere.

Be aware of possible purse-snatchers and pickpockets (especially in crowded places like buses). Also don't be fooled by the diversion scam, which involves a stranger smearing something (mustard, ice-cream, or worse) on a hapless tourist who gets 'cleaned out' by an accomplice during the distraction.

Remember that if you're reasonably careful, the worst annoyance you'll experience is being short-changed, tripping on loose sidewalk tiles, stepping on the ubiquitous dog-shit pile or nearly getting flattened by a crazy bus driver. Watch your step.

See Dangers & Annoyances and Women Travelers in Facts for the Visitor for more tips on being city savvy.

MICROCENTRO & PLAZA DE MAYO (MAP 3)

The city's major public buildings reside in the downtown district known as Microcentro. Most of these buildings are centered around or near Plaza de Mayo at the confluence of Diagonal Roque Sáenz Peña and Av Julio Roca. The heart of Microcentro, Av Florida, has always been one of the capital's most fashionable shopping streets, and despite losing some status to Av Santa Fe and the ritzy neighborhood of Recoleta it remains a popular stroll. Today both Florida and perpendicular Lavalle are *peatonales* (pedestrian malls) that during the day are filled to capacity with bustling crowds of shoppers, tourists and businesspeople, along with some of the city's down-and-out.

Billed by countless porteños as 'the widest street in the world,' Av 9 de Julio is a pedestrian's worst nightmare. Its famous white Obelisco, at the intersection with Corrientes, juts skyward and is the locus for *fútbol* fans after key victories.

On the east side of the district is renovated Puerto Madero, a waterfront area that stretches south toward San Telmo. The project is an upscale recycling of formerly abandoned brick warehouses into upscale restaurants, offices and loft apartments, and it has become one of the trendiest places in the city.

Galerías Pacífico

Located right on the Florida pedestrian mall, this impressive Parisian-style shopping center (☎ 4319-5118, open 10am-9pm Mon-Sat, noon-9pm Sun) was built in 1889. Once home to railroad administrative offices, it later became state property after Juan Perón's nationalization program. In 1945, the completion of vaulted ceilings made space for a dozen panels painted by muralists Antonio Berni, Juan Carlos Castagnino and Lino Spilimbergo, among others. For years the building went semi-abandoned, but in 1992 Galerías Pacífico underwent its last renovation.

This beautiful structure, dotted with fairy lights at night, is now a central meeting place, sporting upscale stores and a large food court. Tourist-oriented tango shows and classes also take place here.

Museo Mitre

Bartolomé Mitre was a soldier, journalist and Argentina's first legitimate president under the Constitution of 1853. He spent much of his later 1862-68 term leading the country's armies against Paraguay. After leaving office, he founded the influential daily *La Nación*, still a porteño institution.

The Museo Mitre (☎ 4394-8240, San Martín 336; admission US$1; open 1pm-6pm weekdays, 2pm-6pm Sun) is a sprawling colonial edifice where Mitre lived with his family. It's a good reflection of 19th-century upper-class life and full of Mitre's personal effects, such as uniforms and antique furniture. A side exit once led directly to the newspaper's offices. Take a glance at the library, which holds more than 80,000 volumes.

Plaza de Mayo

Spreading out in front of the Casa Rosada, Plaza de Mayo is Buenos Aires' magnet for political activities, including vehement protests; every Thursday afternoon at 3:30pm, the Madres de la Plaza de Mayo still march around it in their unrelenting campaign for a full accounting of Dirty War atrocities.

Major buildings around the plaza include the Cabildo (town council, 1725-65), representing all that's left of the colonial arches that once surrounded the plaza, and the solemn Catedral Metropolitana. Within the cathedral is the tomb of repatriated General San Martín, who died in France. In the center of the plaza is the Pirámide de Mayo, a small obelisk built to mark the first anniversary of Buenos Aires' independence from Spain.

Museo del Cabildo Modern construction has twice truncated the mid-18th-century Cabildo (☎ 4334-1782, Bolívar 65; admission US$1; open 12:30pm-7pm Tues-Fri, 3pm-7pm Sun), but there remains a representative sample of the *recova* (colonnade) that once spanned the Plaza de Mayo. The two-story building itself is more intriguing than the scanty exhibits, which include mementos of the early 19th-century British invasions, some modern paintings in colonial and early independence-era styles, and religious art from missions of the Jesuits and other orders. Look for a small group of fascinating early photographs of the plaza. The attractive interior patio has a modest *confitería* serving sandwiches and the like. Guided tours take place at 4pm daily in Spanish.

Catedral Metropolitana Also on the Plaza de Mayo, the cathedral (built on the site of the original colonial church but not finished until 1827) is a religious landmark and an even more important national historical site. Carved above its triangular façade and neoclassical columns are bas-reliefs telling the story of Jacob and Joseph. Inside is the tomb of José de San Martín, Argentina's most revered hero. In the chaos following independence, San Martín chose exile in France, never returning alive to the shores of Argentina.

Casa Rosada At the east end of Plaza de Mayo is the unmistakable pink façade of the Casa Rosada (the presidential palace), which was begun during the presidency of Domingo F Sarmiento. The color of the building is thought to have come from Sarmiento's attempt at making peace during his 1868-1874 term (by blending the red of the Federalists with the white of the Unitarists). Others, however, think it comes from painting the palace with bovine blood, a historical practice.

The structure occupies a site where colonial riverbank fortifications once stood, but today, after repeated landfills, it stands more than a kilometer inland. From the building's balcony, Juan and Eva Perón, General Leopoldo Galtieri, Raúl Alfonsín and other politicians have convened throngs of impassioned Argentines when they needed to demonstrate public support. Pop-celebrity Madonna crooned from this very spot for her movie *Evita*. In 1955, naval aircraft strafed the Casa

Rosada and other nearby buildings in the Revolución Libertadora that toppled Juan Perón.

Off-limits during the military dictatorship of 1976-83, the Casa Rosada is now fairly accessible.

The attached **Museo de la Casa de Gobierno** (☎ 4344-3802, *Hipólito Yrigoyen 219; free; open 10am-6pm weekdays, 2pm-6pm Sun*) includes a chronology of Argentine presidents, but it stops at 1966 (perhaps because events since then are too painful). The interesting catacombs of the Fuerte Viejo, a colonial ruin dating from the 18th century, are visible from the pedestrian walkway on the west side of Parque Colón. Free guided tours of the museum take place at 11am and 4pm weekdays, 3pm and 4:30pm Sunday.

Free guided tours of the Casa Rosada and take place at 5pm weekdays (tours in English are only given at 5pm Friday). Make reservations at the museum or show up at least one hour in advance, and bring your passport.

Towering above the Casa Rosada, just south of Parque Colón, military engineers – inspired by the beaux arts Correo Central – built the army headquarters at the **Edificio Libertador**, the real center of Argentine political power for many decades. A twin building planned for the navy never got off the ground.

Manzana de las Luces

In colonial times, this block, bounded by Alsina, Bolívar, Moreno and Perú, was Buenos Aires' center of learning, and to some degree it still symbolizes high culture in the capital. The first to occupy the Manzana de las Luces were the Jesuits, and on the north side of the block remain two of the five original buildings of the Jesuit **Procuraduría**. Dating from 1730, these include defensive tunnels discovered in 1912. Since independence in 1810, this site has been occupied by the Universidad de Buenos Aires, whose entrance is at Perú 222. (Note the designation 'Universidad' on the façade, which extended across the entire block prior to an 1894 remodeling.)

ARGENTINA

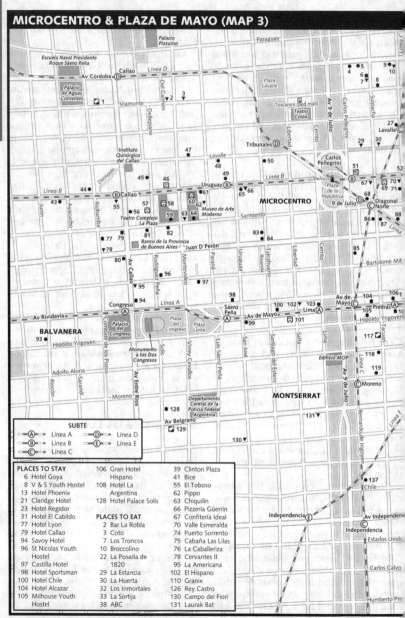

MICROCENTRO & PLAZA DE MAYO (MAP 3)

SUBTE

- Ⓐ Línea A
- Ⓑ Línea B
- Ⓒ Línea C
- Ⓓ Línea D
- Ⓔ Línea E

PLACES TO STAY

- 6 Hotel Goya
- 8 V & S Youth Hostel
- 13 Hotel Phoenix
- 21 Claridge Hotel
- 23 Hotel Regidor
- 31 Hotel El Cabildo
- 77 Hotel Lyon
- 79 Hotel Callao
- 94 Savoy Hotel
- 96 St Nicolas Youth Hostel
- 97 Castilla Hotel
- 98 Hotel Sportsman
- 100 Hotel Chile
- 104 Hotel Alcazar
- 105 Milhouse Youth Hostel
- 106 Gran Hotel Hispano
- 108 Hotel La Argentina
- 128 Hotel Palace Solis

PLACES TO EAT

- 2 Bar La Robla
- 3 Coto
- 7 Los Troncos
- 10 Broccolino
- 22 La Posada de 1820
- 29 La Estancia
- 30 La Huerta
- 32 Los Inmortales
- 33 La Sortija
- 38 ABC
- 39 Clinton Plaza
- 41 Bice
- 55 El Toboso
- 62 Pippo
- 63 Chiquilín
- 66 Pizzería Güerrín
- 67 Confitería Ideal
- 70 Valle Esmeralda
- 74 Puerto Sorrento
- 75 Cabaña Las Lilas
- 76 La Caballeriza
- 78 Cervantes II
- 95 La Americana
- 102 El Hispano
- 110 Granix
- 126 Rey Castro
- 130 Campo dei Fiori
- 131 Laurak Bat

MICROCENTRO & PLAZA DE MAYO (MAP 3)

Divino Buenos Ayres

Reserva Ecológica Castenera Sur

Edificio República

Av Córdoba
Viamonte
Tucumán
Plaza Roma
Luna Park
Post Office (Central)
Plazoleta del Tango
Sarmiento
Juan D Perón

LA CITY

Catedral Metropolitana
Casa Rosada
Palacio Municipal
Plaza de Mayo
Parque Colón
Puente de la Mujer

Edificio Libertador

Adolfo Alsina
Basílica de San Francisco
Moreno
Plaza AP Justo
Av Belgrano
Monumento a Roca

MONTSERRAT
México
Venezuela
Belgrano

Dique No 4
Dique No 3
Dique No 2

65 Cartelera Baires
68 Dinar Líneas Aéreas
69 Teatro Ópera
71 Buenos Aires Visión
72 El Ateneo
73 Museo Mitre
80 Tradfax (Spanish School)
81 Maluco Beleza (Disco)
82 Oxen
83 Kinefot
84 Asociación Argentina de Albergues de la Juventud (AAAJ)
85 Lloyd Aéreo Boliviano (LAB)
86 KLM
87 Flabella
88 Kallpa Tour Operator
89 Cubana de Aviación
90 Banco Central de la República Argentina
91 Archivo y Museo Histórico del Banco de la Provincia de Buenos Aires Dr Arturo Jaúretche
92 University of Buenos Aires
93 Aquilanti
99 Avila Bar
101 Teatro Avenida
103 Guayana
107 Café Tortoni; Academia Nacional del Tango
109 Israeli Consulate; Dutch Consulate
111 Municipal Tourist Kiosk
112 Pluna
113 Museo del Cabildo
114 Pirámide de Mayo
115 Museo de la Casa de Gobierno
116 Museo Fragata Sarmiento
117 Swedish Consulate
118 Palacio Alsina
119 DHL International
120 MasterCard
121 Legislatura de La Ciudad Autonoma de Buenos Aires
122 Belgian Embassy
123 La Puerto Rico
124 Museo de la Ciudad; Farmacia de la Estrella
125 El Querandí
127 Museo Nacional del Grabado (Casa de la Defensa)
132 Bolivian Consulate
133 Federación Argentino de Pato
133 Iglesia y Convento de Santo Domingo (Iglesia de Nuestra Señora del Rosario); Museo de la Basílica del Rosario
134 Instituto Nacional Belgraniano
135 La Ventana
136 La Trastienda
137 Del Sur (Spanish School)
138 Seddon Bar

0   150   300 m
0   150   300 yards

OTHER		
1 Paraguayan Consulate	20 Musimundo	47 José Norres (Camera Repair)
4 Varig	24 Delta; TransBrasil	48 Buenos Aires Tur
5 Alianza Francesa	26 Le Cigale	49 Visa
9 Japan Airlines	27 El Coleccionista	50 Librería Platero
11 Canadian Airlines	28 Mundo Latino	51 Netcity
12 Federal Express	34 Towernet Cybercentro	52 Laboclick
14 Galerías Pacífico; Patio de Comidas	35 Cacciola	53 Chilean Consulate
15 Centro Cultural Borges	36 Richmond	54 Instituto Goethe
16 Instituto Cultural Argentino-Norteamericano; Biblioteca Lincoln	37 AB Travel	56 ILEE (Spanish School)
	40 Japanese Embassy	57 Teatro El Vitral
	42 Tourist Information	58 Teatro La Plaza; Paseo La Plaza
17 Le Lab	43 Complejo Cultural Ricardo Rojas	59 Cartelera Vea Más
18 British Airways	44 El Beso	60 Teatro San Martín
19 OCA	45 Free Blues	61 El Gato Negro
	46 Teatro Presidente Alvear	64 Centro Cultural San Martín

Fronting Bolívar, the **Iglesia San Ignacio** with its rococo interior and late-baroque façade appeared in 1712 and is considered the city's oldest colonial church; after a demolition in 1904, there remains only a single original cloister. It shares a wall with the **Colegio Nacional de Buenos Aires** (1908), where generations of the Argentine elite have sent their children to receive secondary schooling.

Historical tours (☎ *4331-9534, Perú 272; tour price US$2, weekdays 3pm; Spanish only*) provide the only regular public access to the block's interior, where there's a small theater-in-the-round reconstruction of the city's first legislature, the neoclassical Sala de Representantes.

Palacio del Congreso

Costing more than twice its original budget to build, the Congreso set a precedent for contemporary Argentine public works projects. Modeled on the US Capitol in Washington, DC, and topped by an 85m green-hued copper dome, the palace was completed in 1906. It faces the Plaza del Congreso, where the **Monumento a los Dos Congresos** honors the congresses of 1810 in Buenos Aires and 1816 in Tucumán, both of which led to Argentine independence. The monument's enormous granite steps symbolize the high Andes, while the fountain at its base represents the Atlantic Ocean.

Free guided tours of the Senado (☎ 4959-3000) are available 11am weekdays (English, Spanish and French), and 11am (English) and 5pm (Spanish) Monday, Tuesday, Thursday and Friday; go to the entrance at Hipólito Irigoyen 1849. Tours of the Cámara de Diputados (lower house; ☎ 4370-7100) are available at 11am and 5pm Monday, Wednesday, Thursday and Friday (Spanish only); use the entrance at Rivadavia 1864.

Teatro Colón

Since it opened in 1908 with a presentation of *Aida,* this world-class facility for opera, ballet and classical music has impressed visitors. Even through times of economic hardship, the elaborate Colón (☎ *4378-7132 for tours,* ☎ *4378-7344 for shows, Libertad 621*) remains a high national priority, in part because it's the only facility of its kind in the country. There are no performances given from January to March.

Very worthwhile guided visits (which run all year) cost US$5 and take place hourly between 11am and 3pm weekdays, 9am and noon Saturday. Guides are available in Spanish, English, German, French, Portuguese and even Danish (only Spanish and English tours are always available). On these tours you can see the theater from basement workshops (that employ over 400 skilled carpenters, sculptors, wigmakers and costume designers) to rehearsal rooms and stage and seating areas. The enormous pillars, statues and other props are made of painted lightweight Styrofoam.

Occupying an entire city block, the imposing seven-story Colón seats 2500 spectators and has standing room for another thousand. The main entrance is on Libertad, opposite Plaza Lavalle; tours enter from the Viamonte side.

Other Museums & Historic Buildings

With the most stunning museum name on the continent, the **Archivo y Museo Histórico del Banco de la Provincia de Buenos Aires Dr Arturo Jáuretche** (☎ *4331-1775, Sarmiento 362; free; open 10am-6pm weekdays*) makes sense of Argentina's chaotic economic history from viceregal times to the present. There are also exhibits on paper money and counterfeiting, which have no doubt been scrupulously studied by Buenos Aires' current money forgers.

At the tiny **Museo Nacional del Teatro** (☎ *4815-8883, Interno 195, Córdoba 1199; free; open noon-7pm weekdays),* in the 1921 Teatro Cervantes, exhibits include a gaucho suit worn by tango singer Carlos Gardel for his Hollywood film *El Día Que Me Quieras.* Also on display is the *bandoneón* belonging to Paquita Bernardo (the first Argentine musician to play the accordion-like instrument).

The **Museo de la Ciudad** (☎ *4331-9855, Alsina 412, 1st floor; admission US$1, free Wed; open 11am-7pm weekdays, 3pm-7pm weekends)* has permanent and temporary exhibitions on porteño life and history. Housed in the same building, the **Farmacia de la Estrella** is a functioning homeopathic pharmacy with gorgeous woodwork and elaborate turn-of-the-19th-century ceiling murals depicting health-oriented themes.

The restored 19th-century Casa de la Defensa retains some elements of the historic structure in spite of an ill-advised 1970s remodeling. It houses the **Museo Nacional del Grabado** (☎ 4345-5300, Defensa 372; admission US$2; open 2pm-6pm Sun-Fri), a collection of mostly contemporary woodcuts and engravings. Admission usually includes a sample woodcut print.

Gutted by fire during the 1955 Revolución Libertadora against Perón, the 18th-century **Museo de la Basílica del Rosario** (☎ 4331-1668, Defensa & Belgrano; admission US$2, students US$1; open 9am-12:30pm & 1:30-3pm Thur, call for other days) contains relics of the British invasions and wars of independence. Alongside it, an eternal flame burns at the **Instituto Nacional Belgraniano**, which lionizes Argentina's second-greatest hero.

Puerto Madero's **Museo Fragata Sarmiento** (☎ 4334-9386; admission US$2; open 9am to 8pm daily) is on a ship in Dique No 3. On board are detailed records of its lengthy voyages, a gallery of its commanding officers, a poster for a 1945 film based on its history, and even the stuffed carcass of Lampazo, the ship's pet dog.

Near the foot of Corrientes, **Correo Central** (central post office; 1928) fills an entire city block. It took 20 years to complete this impressive and beautifully maintained beaux arts structure, originally modeled on New York City's main post office. The mansard (two-tier) roof was a later addition.

SAN TELMO (MAP 4)

South of the Plaza de Mayo, San Telmo is the birthplace of the tango, and an artist's quarter where bohemians find large spaces at low rents. It's also famous for the rugged street fighting that took place when British troops invaded the city in 1806, occupying it until the following year when covert resistance gave way to open counterattack. In the denouement, British forces advancing up narrow Calle Defensa were routed and driven back to their ships by an impromptu militia, supported by women and slaves pouring cauldrons of boiling oil and water from the rooftops and firing cannons from the balconies of the house at Defensa 372. Victory gave the porteños confidence in their ability to stand apart from Spain, though independence had to wait another decade.

After yellow fever hit the once-fashionable area in the late 19th century, the porteño elite evacuated to higher ground west and north of the present-day Microcentro. As immigrants poured into Argentina, many older houses became *conventillos* housing European families in cramped, divided quarters with inadequate sanitary facilities. These conditions still exist; look for crumbling older houses with clothes hanging out to dry on the balconies.

Plaza Dorrego

In the heart of San Telmo, Plaza Dorrego is the site of the Feria de San Telmo, a wonderful antiques market. Side streets are closed to traffic, and the plaza itself is filled with dozens of vendors selling old (and pricey) collectibles. Entertaining the crowds are street performers, including professional tango dancers. Nearby are many antiques stores, some ritzy and some rusty.

Museo Histórico Nacional

At Defensa and Brasil, Parque Lezama is the supposed site of Pedro de Mendoza's original foundation of the city in 1536, and appropriately home to the Museo Histórico Nacional (☎ 4307-1182, Defensa 1600; admission US$1; open 10:30am-5pm Tues-Fri, 1:30pm-5:30pm Sat). This national history museum offers a panoramic view of the Argentine experience, from its shaky beginnings and independence to the present. Paintings depict the Spanish domination of wealthy, civilized Peru, Columbus' triumphant return to Spain, and Mendoza's struggles on the shores of the Río de la Plata.

There are also portraits of major figures of the independence and republican periods, such as Simón Bolívar and his ally and rival Jose de San Martín, both in youth and in disillusioned old age. Juan Manuel de Rosas and his bitter but eloquent enemy Sarmiento are represented, as are portrayals of the British invasions of 1806 and 1807 and depictions of late-19th-century porteño life.

In the surrounding park, elderly locals gather to hang out and play chess. Across from the park is the striking turn-of-the-19th-century Russian Orthodox Church, **Iglesia Apostólica Ortodoxa Rusa**, the work of architect Alejandro Christopherson.

Museo Penitenciario Nacional

Half a block east from the plaza, the worthwhile Museo Penitenciario Nacional *(☎ 4362-0099, Humberto Primo 378; admission US$1; open 2pm-5pm Tue & Fri, 12pm-7pm weekends)* is attached to the Iglesia Nuestra Señora de Belén. This museum was originally a Jesuit convent, but later became a women's prison. The best items on display are a photograph of the famous anarchist Simón Radowitzky's release from prison in Ushuaia, in southern Argentina, and a wooden desk carved by inmates at Ushuaia for president Roberto M Ortiz. Next door, the Iglesia Nuestra Señora de Belén is an eccentrically styled building whose construction spanned from the 1730s to the early 1900s and involved at least five architects.

Other Museums
& Historic Buildings

Housed in a recycled tobacco warehouse, the **Museo de Arte Moderno** *(☎ 4361-1121, Av San Juan 350; admission US$1, free Wed; open 10am-8pm Tues-Fri, 11am-8pm weekends & holidays, closed Feb)* is a simple, roomy, brightly lit space exhibiting figurative works of Argentine artists as well as special rotating exhibitions and video events.

Well worth seeing is the private **Helft Collection** of modern Argentine art *(☎ 4307-9175)*; there are no regularly scheduled hours, but guided tours are available on request in Spanish, English, French, German, Italian and Hungarian; reservations are essential.

Over in Puerto Madero, the **Museo Corbeta Uruguay** *(☎ 4314-1090; admission*

PLACES TO STAY
1 Hotel Victoria
7 Buenos Ayres Hostel
9 Boquitas Pintadas
12 Hotel Bolívar
18 El Hostal de San Telmo
20 Residencial Carly
28 Hotel Residencial Bolívar

SUBTE
C — Línea C
E — Línea E

PLACES TO EAT
3 Abuela Pan
4 Sr Telmo
5 Ana y el Angel
13 DesNivel
14 Parrilla al Carbón
15 La Casa de Estéban de Luca
17 Las Marías
19 La Feria
24 Siga La Vaca
25 Estilo Campo

US$1; open 9am-9pm daily)* served as a coastal patrol vessel for nearly a century following its construction in 1874. The high point of its career was the rescue of shipwrecked Swedish Antarctic explorer Otto Nordenskjöld and his expedition in 1903.

LA BOCA

Literally Buenos Aires' most colorful barrio, La Boca was settled and built up by Italian immigrants along the Riachuelo, a small waterway lined with meatpacking plants and warehouses that separates Buenos Aires proper from the industrial

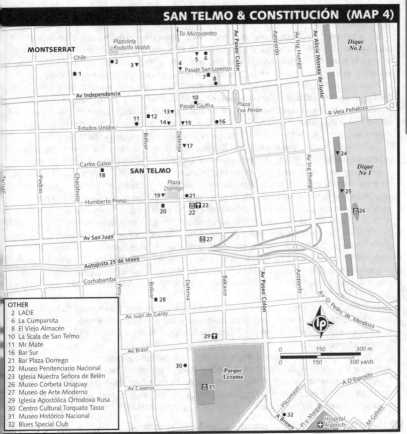

SAN TELMO & CONSTITUCIÓN (MAP 4)

OTHER
2 LADE
6 La Cumparsita
8 El Viejo Almacén
10 La Scala de San Telmo
11 Mr Mate
16 Bar Sur
21 Bar Plaza Dorrego
22 Museo Penitenciario Nacional
23 Iglesia Nuestra Señora de Belén
26 Museo Corbeta Uruguay
27 Museo de Arte Moderno
29 Iglesia Apostólica Ortodoxa Rusa
30 Centro Cultural Torquato Tasso
31 Museo Histórico Nacional
32 Blues Special Club

suburb of Avellaneda. Part of La Boca's color comes from the brightly painted houses of the Caminito, a favorite pedestrian walkway that was once a rail terminus and takes its name from a popular tango song. The rest comes from petroleum and industrial wastes tinting the waters of the Riachuelo, where rusting hulks and dredges lie offshore.

Areas like La Boca were once places where immigrants could find a foothold in the country, although conditions were less than idyllic. James Bryce, visiting at the turn of the 19th century, described them as:

a waste of scattered shanties…dirty and squalid, with corrugated iron roofs, their wooden boards gaping like rents in tattered clothes. These are inhabited by the newest and poorest of immigrants from southern Italy and southern Spain, a large and not very desirable element among whom anarchism is rife.

In fact, French Basques preceded the Italians in La Boca. Today the area is partly an artists' colony, the legacy of the late painter Benito Quinquela Martín, but it's still mostly a working-class neighborhood. The symbol of community solidarity is the Boca Juniors soccer team, once the club of disgraced, yet beloved, superstar Diego Maradona.

Life & Death in Recoleta & Chacarita

Death is the great equalizer, except in Buenos Aires. When the arteries harden after decades of drinking and dining at Recoleta's finest restaurants, the wealthy and powerful move ceremoniously across the street to the Cementerio de la Recoleta, joining their ancestors in a place they have visited religiously all their lives. Perhaps no other place says more about Argentine society.

According to Argentine novelist Tomás Eloy Martínez, Argentines are 'cadaver cultists' who honor their most revered national figures not on the date of their birth but on the date of their death. Nowhere is this obsession with mortality more evident than at Recoleta, where generations of the elite repose in the grandeur of ostentatious mausoleums. It is a common saying (and only a slight exaggeration) that 'It is cheaper to live extravagantly all your life than to be buried in Recoleta.'

Traditionally, money alone is not enough: you must have a surname like Anchorena, Alvear, Aramburu, Avellaneda, Mitre, Martínez de Hoz or Sarmiento. The remains of Evita Perón, secured in a subterranean vault, are an exception that infuriates the presumptive aristocracy. One reason for this is that the dead often play a peculiar, and more than just symbolic, role in Argentine politics. Evita came to rest in Recoleta only after her embalmed body's odyssey from South America to an obscure cemetery in Milan to her exiled husband's house in Madrid, finally returning to Buenos Aires in 1974. (Embalming is uncommon in Argentina.) The man responsible for her 'kidnapping' from Buenos Aires was General Pedro Aramburu, a bitter political enemy of the Peróns who reportedly sought the Vatican's help in sequestering the cadaver after Perón's overthrow in 1955.

Aramburu himself was held for 'ransom' by the left-wing Peronist Montoneros *after* his assassination in 1970. Only when the military government of General Alejandro Lanusse ensured Evita's return to Perón in Madrid did Aramburu's body reappear for entombment in Recoleta, now only a few short 'blocks' from Evita.

To locate Evita's grave, proceed to the first major intersection from the entrance. Turn left, continue until a mausoleum blocks your way, go around it and turn right at the wide 'street.' After a few blocks, look to your left and you'll probably see a few devoted fans at her site, along with bunches of flowers.

Juan Perón himself lies across town, in the much less exclusive graveyard of Chacarita, which opened in the 1870s to accommodate the yellow-fever victims of San Telmo and La Boca.

Although more democratic in conception, Chacarita's most elaborate tombs match Recoleta's finest. One of the most visited belongs to Carlos Gardel, the famous tango singer. Plaques from around the world cover the base of his life-size statue, many thanking him for favors granted. Like

There are some garish cantinas on Necochea, many of which housed brothels in the days before the tango was the respectable, middle-class phenomenon it is today. Only seasoned travelers highly confident in their street skills should walk along these side streets, however; camera-toting tourists should content themselves with fleeting views from the right side of buses No 29 or 152 out of town. La Boca can be very rough in spots, so it's best not to stray from the riverside walk or the tourist sections of Caminito, Del Valle Iberlucea and Magallanes streets, especially if you are alone (there's not much for the visitor to see outside these areas anyway).

To get to La Boca, take buses Nos 86, 29 or 152 from the Microcentro.

Museo de Bellas Artes de La Boca

Once the home and studio of Benito Quinquela Martín, La Boca's fine-arts museum (☎ 4301-1080, Pedro de Mendoza 1835; admission US$1 voluntary donation; open 10am-6pm Tue-Sun) exhibits his works and those of other early-20th-century Argentine artists.

Life & Death in Recoleta & Chacarita

Evita, Juan Perón and others, Gardel is a quasi-saint toward whom countless Argentines feel an almost religious devotion. The anniversary of Gardel's death (June 26, 1935), when pilgrims jam the cemetery's streets, is a major occasion.

One of the best places to witness this phenomenon is the Chacarita tomb of Madre María Salomé, a disciple of the famous healer Pancho Sierra. Every day, but especially on the second day of each month (she died on October 2, 1928), adherents of her cult leave floral tributes – white carnations are the favorite – and lay their hands on her sepulcher in spellbound supplication.

To visit Chacarita, which attracts fewer visitors than Recoleta, take Línea B of the Subte to the end of the line at Federico Lacroze and cross the street. Look for the family crypt of Juan Perón, a tomb marked as 'Tomás Perón' (Juan Perón's father), and do not miss the tombs of Gardel, Madre María, poet Alfonsina Storni, aviator Jorge Newbery, tango musician Aníbal 'Pichuco' Troilo and comedian Luis Sandrini. (Newbery, Gardel and Madre María are all on Diagonal 113, three blocks left of the main entrance.) Like Recoleta, Chacarita is open 7am to 6pm daily.

Around the corner from Chacarita are the Cementerio Alemán (German Cemetery) and the Cementerio Británico (British Cemetery), both far less extravagant than either Recoleta or Chacarita but with their own points of interest. The Cementerio Alemán contains a monument to Germany's WWII dead, though the symbolism is imperial rather than Hitlerian. The Británico is both more and less than its name suggests; there may be more Irish, Jewish, Armenian and Greek (among other immigrant groups) names on the tombs than there are truly British surnames. Perhaps the most notable headstone is that of Tierra del Fuego pioneer Lucas Bridges, author of the classic *The Uttermost Part of the Earth*, who died on board ship from Ushuaia, in southern Argentina, to Buenos Aires in 1950.

JOHN HAY

Cementerio de la Recoleta

Museo Histórico de Cera

Wax-figure reconstructions of historical figures and dioramas of scenes in Argentine history are the specialty of this rather tacky private institution (☎ 4301-1497, *Del Valle Iberlucea 1261; admission US$3; open 10am-6pm weekdays, 11am-8pm weekends*).

RECOLETA (MAP 5)

During the yellow-fever epidemic of the 1870s, many upper-class porteños relocated from San Telmo to Recoleta, now the city's ritziest neighborhood. You can best see the wealth of this sumptuous quarter in the old mansions located on Av Alvear.

Recoleta's many attractive public gardens and open spaces include Plaza Intendente Alvear, where the capital's largest crafts fair takes place on Sunday. One of the barrio's most characteristic and entertaining sights is its *paseaperros* – professional dog walkers who often stroll with a dozen or more canines on leash.

Cementerio de la Recoleta

Recoleta is best known for its astonishing necropolis where the deceased Argentine

ARGENTINA

RECOLETA & RETIRO (MAP 5)

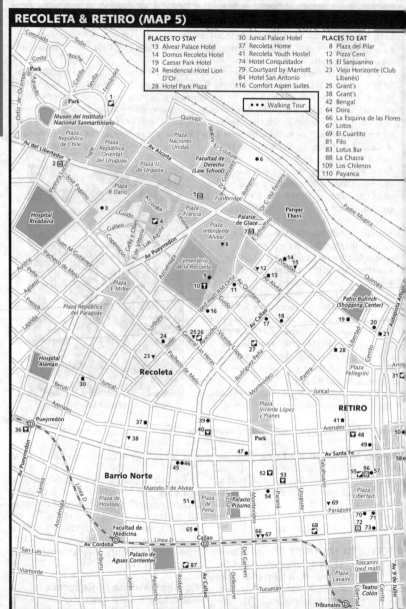

PLACES TO STAY
13 Alvear Palace Hotel
14 Domus Recoleta Hotel
19 Caesar Park Hotel
24 Residencial Hotel Lion D'Or
28 Hotel Park Plaza
30 Juncal Palace Hotel
37 Recoleta Home
41 Recoleta Youth Hostel
74 Hotel Conquistador
79 Courtyard by Marriott
84 Hotel San Antonio
116 Comfort Aspen Suites

PLACES TO EAT
8 Plaza del Pilar
12 Pizza Cero
15 El Sanjuanino
23 Viejo Horizonte (Club Libanés)
25 Grant's
38 Grant's
42 Bengal
64 Dora
66 La Esquina de las Flores
67 Lotos
69 El Cuartito
81 Filo
83 Lotus Bar
88 La Chacra
109 Los Chilenos
110 Payanca

• • • Walking Tour

RECOLETA & RETIRO (MAP 5)

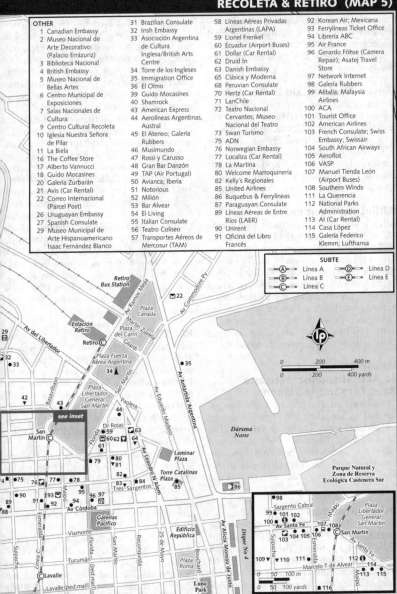

OTHER

1 Canadian Embassy
2 Museo Nacional de Arte Decorativo (Palacio Errázuriz)
3 Biblioteca Nacional
4 British Embassy
5 Museo Nacional de Bellas Artes
6 Centro Municipal de Exposiciones
7 Salas Nacionales de Cultura
9 Centro Cultural Recoleta
10 Iglesia Nuestra Señora de Pilar
11 La Biela
16 The Coffee Store
17 Alberto Vannucci
18 Guido Mocasines
20 Galería Zurbarán
21 Avis (Car Rental)
22 Correo Internacional (Parcel Post)
26 Uruguayan Embassy
27 Spanish Consulate
29 Museo Municipal de Arte Hispanoamericano Isaac Fernández Blanco

31 Brazilian Consulate
32 Irish Embassy
33 Asociación Argentina de Cultura Inglesa/British Arts Centre
34 Torre de los Ingleses
35 Immigration Office
36 El Olmo
39 Guido Mocasines
40 Shamrock
43 American Express
44 Aerolíneas Argentinas, Austral
45 El Ateneo; Galería Rubbers
46 Musimundo
47 Rossi y Carusso
48 Gran Bar Danzón
49 TAP (Air Portugal)
50 Avianca; Iberia
51 Notorious
52 Milión
53 Bar Alvear
54 El Living
55 Italian Consulate
56 Teatro Coliseo
57 Transportes Aéreos de Mercosur (TAM)

58 Líneas Aéreas Privadas Argentinas (LAPA)
59 Lionel Frenkel
60 Ecuador (Airport Buses)
61 Dollar (Car Rental)
62 Druid In
63 Danish Embassy
65 Clásica y Moderna
68 Peruvian Consulate
70 Hertz (Car Rental)
71 LanChile
72 Teatro Nacional Cervantes; Museo Nacional del Teatro
73 Swan Turismo
75 ADN
76 Norwegian Embassy
77 Localiza (Car Rental)
78 La Martina
80 Welcome Marroquinería
82 Kelly´s Regionales
85 United Airlines
86 Buquebus & Ferrylineas
87 Paraguayan Consulate
89 Líneas Aéreas de Entre Ríos (LAER)
90 Unirent
91 Oficina del Libro Francés

92 Korean Air; Mexicana
93 Ferrylineas Ticket Office
94 Librería ABC
95 Air France
96 Gerardo Föhse (Camera Repair); Asatej Travel Store
97 Network Internet
98 Galería Rubbers
99 Alitalia; Malaysia Airlines
100 ACA
101 Tourist Office
102 American Airlines
103 French Consulate; Swiss Embassy; Swissair
104 South African Airways
105 Aeroflot
106 VASP
107 Manuel Tienda León (Airport Buses)
108 Southern Winds
111 La Querencia
112 National Parks Administration
113 Al (Car Rental)
114 Casa López
115 Galería Federico Klemm; Lufthansa

SUBTE

━A━ Línea A   ━D━ Línea D
━B━ Línea B   ━E━ Línea E
━C━ Línea C

elite rest in ornate splendor. Alongside the cemetery, the **Iglesia de Nuestra Señora de Pilar**, a Baroque-style colonial church consecrated in 1732, is a national historical monument. See the boxed text 'Life & Death in Recoleta & Chacarita' for more historical information.

Museo Nacional de Bellas Artes

Unquestionably the country's most important art museum, Bellas Artes (☎ 4803-0802, Av del Libertador 1473; free; open 12:30pm-7:30pm Tues-Fri, 9:30am-7:30pm weekends & holidays) houses works by European masters like Renoir, Rodin, Monet, Toulouse-Lautrec and van Gogh, as well as 19th- and 20th-century Argentine artists.

Biblioteca Nacional

After a decade of construction problems and delays, the national library (☎ 4807-0885, Agüero 2502; open 9am-9pm weekdays, 12pm-8pm weekends) finally moved into this mushroom-shaped edifice in 1992. Prominent Argentine and Latin American literary figures such as Ernesto Sábato often lecture here. From up above you can see panoramic views of the capital. Spanish tours (☎ 4806-9764) are given at 3pm Monday to Saturday, except in summer.

Museo Municipal de Arte Hispanoamericano Isaac Fernández Blanco

Containing an exceptional collection of colonial art, including silverwork, paintings, costumes as well as antiques, this museum (☎ 4327-0272, Suipacha 1422; admission US$1, free Thur; open 2pm-7pm Tues-Sun, sometimes closed Jan) is set among attractive gardens at the colonial-style Palacio Noel.

Other Museums

Housed in the Palais de Glace, the **Salas Nacionales de Cultura** (☎ 4804-1163, Posadas 1725; open 2pm-8pm Tue-Fri, 3pm-8pm weekends) offers rotating cultural, artistic and historical exhibitions. This unusual circular building was once a skating rink. Admission varies depending on the program.

The **Museo Nacional de Arte Decorativo** (National Museum of Decorative Arts; ☎ 4802-6606, Av Libertador 1902; admission US$2-5; open 2pm-7pm daily) is located in the stunning beaux arts Palacio Errázuriz. Inside are period furniture, ceramics and paintings belonging to the original occupants of the mansion. There are also rotating exhibitions and the entry price is determined by what there is to see. Several different (Spanish) guided tours run on different days. Most are included in the price of admission. Give them a call for specific details.

Part of the original Franciscan convent alongside its namesake church and cemetery, the **Centro Cultural Recoleta** (☎ 4803-1041, Junín 1930; admission US$1; open 2pm-9pm Tues-Fri, 10am-9pm weekends & holidays) houses a variety of facilities including museums, galleries, exhibition halls and a cinema. Its Museo Participativo de Ciencias (☎ 4806-3456, admission US$5; open 9am-4pm weekdays, 3pm-7pm weekends & holidays) is a hands-on science museum. The Microcine offers films most days, and there are frequent free films outdoors in summer.

PALERMO

Ironically, the 19th-century dictator Juan Manuel de Rosas' most positive and enduring legacy is the wide-open spaces of Palermo, which straddle Av del Libertador northwest of Recoleta. Once the tyrant's private retreat, later a playground for Buenos Aires' elite, these parks have now become a major recreational resource for all classes of porteños.

On weekends, hundreds of recreation-seekers come to bike or stroll the parks' shady lanes and paddle canoes or pedal boats on its artificial lakes. Palermo also contains some good museums and the largest concentration of embassies in Buenos Aires.

At the junction of Serrano and Honduras, in an older area of Palermo called Palermo Viejo, is the newest center of porteño nightlife: the lively, often raucous Plaza Serrano (also known as Plaza Cortázar). The streets around this plaza are home to some of the most cutting-edge bars and restaurants in town – come here on a Friday or Saturday night and you'll see why.

Palermo is also home to the Rosedal (rose garden), Planetario Galileo Galilei, the Campo de Polo (polo grounds) and the Hipódromo Argentino (racetrack).

Jardín Japonés

These Japanese gardens (☎ 4804-4922, *Parque 3 de Febrero, Avs Casares & Berro; admission US$2/1 adult/child, free for retirees weekdays; open 10am-6pm daily)* are one of the capital's best-kept public spaces. Inside there's a Japanese restaurant, greenhouse, ponds filled with koi to feed, and of course beautiful gardens. On weekends there are art expositions and music.

Jardín Zoológico

Buenos Aires' zoo (☎ 4806-7411, *Las Heras & Sarmiento, admission US$5; open 10am-6pm Tues-Fri, 10am-7pm Sat-Sun)* is fairly decent, with South American animals well represented. Some of the buildings in here are impressive, especially the elephant house. Keep an eye on young children, especially near the alligator pit and big cat enclosures; the fences are easy to trespass. Roaming wild are waterfowl, patagonian hares, nutria and feral housecats.

Museo de Motivos Argentinos José Hernández

Brimming with the gaucho accoutrements that symbolize Argentina's folk culture, this museum (☎ 4802-7294, *Av del Libertador 2373; admission US$1; open 1am-7pm weekdays, 3pm-7pm weekends)* showcases items such as exquisite silverwork and vicuña ponchos from Catamarca. Also on display are revealing historical photographs of aristocratic families like the Martínez de Hoz in their tailored gaucho drag – the Argentine counterpart to US president George Bush and family posing as Texas buckaroos.

BELGRANO

Bustling Av Cabildo, the racing heart of Belgrano, is an overwhelming jumble of noise, neon, shops and restaurants. For a bit more peace and quiet, head to the blocks on either side of the avenue, where Belgrano becomes a barrio of middle- to upper-class apartments, leafy plazas and museums.

Once the site of the Congreso and executive offices, the **Museo Histórico Sarmiento** (☎ 4782-2354, *Juramento 2180; admission US$1; open 2pm-7pm Tues-Fri, 3pm-7pm Sun)* now contains memorabilia of Domingo F Sarmiento, one of Argentina's most famous statesmen and educators. The classically educated Sarmiento was an eloquent writer who analyzed 19th-century Argentina from a cosmopolitan, clearly Eurocentric point of view. There are free Spanish tours at 4pm Sunday. The closest Subte stop is Juramento station, two blocks away.

Nearby, the grand and spacious **Museo de Arte Español Enrique Larreta** (☎ 4784-4040, *Juramento 2291; admission US$1; open 2pm-8pm Mon & Wed-Fri, 3pm-8pm weekends)* contains the private art collection of the well-known novelist. There are also some magnificent gardens where open-air theater performances take place in summer and fall. Guided Spanish tours are given at 4pm and 6pm on Sunday.

A few blocks away, the **Museo Casa de Yrurtia** (☎ 4781-0385, *O'Higgins 2390; admission US$1; open 3pm-7pm Tues-Fri, 4pm-7pm weekends)* belonged to one of the country's greatest sculptors, Rogelio Yrurtia. The house is cluttered with his work and there's a small, attractive garden. Free guided tours take place at 4pm on the second and fourth Sunday of every month.

LANGUAGE COURSES

For general information and advice on language courses, see the Facts for the Visitor chapter.

The Instituto de Lengua Española para Extranjeros (ILEE; ☎/fax 4373-0223, **w** www.ilee.com.ar; Map 3), Callao 339, 3rd floor, has conversation-based courses at basic, intermediate and advanced levels. Private classes cost US$19 per hour, while group lessons are US$240 per week. The institute can help arrange accommodations in a private home for around US$500 per month for a single, US$375 per month (per

ARGENTINA

person) for a double, and it also puts together social and cultural activities.

Another good alternative is the CEDIC (☎/fax 4315-1156, **w** www.cedic.com.ar; Map 3), Reconquista 719, 11th floor. Two hours daily instruction for four weeks (or four hours daily instruction for two weeks) costs US$420 plus US$20 in course materials, while shorter courses cost US$10 per hour plus materials. Individual tutoring is US$20 hourly. Social activities are also organized.

Tradfax (☎/fax 4373-5581, **w** www.tradfax .com; Map 3), Callao 194, 2nd floor, offers 2½-hour daily classes in general Spanish for US$180 per week. Commercial Spanish classes cost about US$30 more per week, while private classes cost US$18 per hour. You can also learn Portuguese here, and the organization arranges lodging for about US$600 per month.

Del Sur (☎/fax 4334-0107, **w** www.delsur .com.ar; Map 3), Bernardo de Irigoyen 668, 1st floor, is another option. It is not as central as the others, but classes are friendly and informal. Group/private classes run US$270/380 and up for two weeks (10 hours per week).

The University of Buenos Aires (☎ 4343-1196, **w** www.cui.com.ar; Map 3), 25 de Mayo 221, offers long-term classes, which cost US$180 for approximately 48 hours of instruction. There are different programs from which to select and you can choose the intensity and number of hours a week you want to study. Note that facilities are in an old, decrepit building that's only slowly being remodeled.

The Centro Universitario de Idiomas (☎ 4823-6818), Córdoba 2636, west of center near the medical university, also has long-term Spanish courses. You can choose between three hours of instruction per week for four months, or six hours per week for two months. Each course costs US$200.

There are also many private tutors within the city, charging US$15 to US$18 per hour. Two good ones are Jose Serebrenik (☎/fax 4951-3393, **e** jserebrenik@miltimagen.com, **w** www.multicom.com.ar/ingles) and Dori Lieberman (☎/fax 4361-4843, e/mail dori@ sinectis.com.ar), both of whom speak English.

TANGO CLASSES & MILONGAS

Besides the clubs (some of which give classes) mentioned in the Entertainment section, there are many other alternatives for tango instruction. Practice sessions or more formal *milongas* (dances) are often held after night classes. It's advisable to call venues in advance, as class schedules listed here may have changed.

Also check free tango publications like *el tangauta* or *BA Tango*, which are full of offerings. For general information, contact the Academia Nacional del Tango (☎ 4345-6967; Map 3), Av de Mayo 831, above the Café Tortoni.

Upstairs at the Confitería Ideal (☎ 15-5006-4102; Map 3), Suipacha 384, there are milongas and classes (both US$5) practically every day and night except Saturday. Some are taught in English.

Viejo Correo (☎ 4958-0364), Díaz Velez 4820, offers classes at 8pm daily, with milongas afterwards (both US$5, some milongas free). The setting is a La Boca alleyway, with colored lights adding to the festive mood. It's a good place, but way west of center in Parque del Centenario.

Gricel (☎ 4957-7157), La Rioja 1180, is an established spot southwest of center in the neighborhood of San Cristóbal that offers tango classes (US$6) 8pm to 10pm daily; there are milongas on weekend nights.

At El Beso (☎ 4953-2794; Map 3), Riobamba 416, go up the stairs past the friendly young watchman (who loves to practice his English) for classes. Colored lights and artsy decor surround the dance floor. There are milongas long into the night on weekends (US$5).

In Palermo Viejo, classes given by El Viruta/La Estrella (☎ 4774-6357), Armenia 1366, are held in the large, modern building of the Asociación Cultural Armenia. Classes take place almost nightly except Monday and Thursday.

ORGANIZED TOURS

Many commercial agencies offer half-day and full-day city tours, but unless your time is very limited, it is best to try to get around on your own.

Buenos Aires Tur (☎ 4371-2304; Map 3), Lavalle 1444, and Buenos Aires Visión (☎ 4394-2986; Map 3), Esmeralda 356, 8th floor, both offer half-day bus tours (US$15) that visit locations in the Microcentro, San Telmo, La Boca, Recoleta and Palermo. Other tour options include visits to Tigre and the Delta via the Tren de la Costa (US$36) and a gaucho fiesta in Buenos Aires province (US$60). Tours are in English and Spanish; call them a day in advance. They also offer tango shows (US$40-45, more with dinner).

SPECIAL EVENTS

Buenos Aires has its own special brand of festivities, many oriented towards Argentina's traditional culture of horses, gauchos and tango. Since the dates of most of these events change every year, it's best to check with the national tourist office (☎ 4312-2232) or free publications like *Cuidad Abierta* (available at tourist offices and some museums and cultural centers).

Buenos Aires' official Carnaval is a very modest celebration by Brazilian standards, restricted to a small area near Plaza de Mayo. Expect to be sprayed with canned foam by complete strangers, and be sure to catch visiting troupe shows from Carnaval hotbeds like Corrientes and Gualeguaychú.

In late March, horse lovers flock to Palermo for the Exposición de Caballos Criollos, showcasing hardy Argentine-bred equines. It's run by the Asociación Criadores de Caballos Criollos (☎ 4961-2305), Larrea 670, 2nd floor, and is held at the Predio Ferial on Av Sarmiento (Subte: Plaza Italia).

Buenos Aires' annual book fair attracts more than a million book lovers during the first three weeks of April. It's held at the sprawling Centro Municipal de Exposiciones (☎ 4803-2414; Map 5), at Figueroa Alcorta and Pueyrredón.

The capital's major auto race officially takes place in early to mid-April at the Autódromo Municipal Oscar Gálvez (☎ 4605-3333), on the southern outskirts of the Capital Federal. Porteño motorists practice daily for this event on the streets of Buenos Aires, whether they're invited to participate in the race or not.

Mid-May's Feria de Galerías de Arte is a rapidly growing event featuring art from all around the world. The location can change from year to year, so check with the tourist office.

June 24 is the Día de la Muerte de Carlos Gardel, the anniversary of Gardel's death in a plane crash in Medellín, Colombia. Numerous tango events during the week bookend pilgrimages to the singer's tomb at Chacarita Cemetery.

Winter's biggest celebration is July's Exposición de Ganadería, Agricultura e Industria Internacional, the annual livestock and agricultural exhibition organized by the Asociación Criadores de Caballos Criollos (see above). Like the horsebreeders' fair, it takes place at the Predio Ferial.

In late November, runners can try their luck in the lemming-like Maratón Internacional de la Argentina, which draws up to 15,000 participants yearly. It takes place in Palermo; call the tourist office for details.

Día del Tango commemorates Gardel's December 11 birth date. There are many tango events around this time, and the singer's tomb at Chacarita draws crowds of pilgrims.

The spring polo season culminates in December's Campeonato Abierto Argentino de Polo (Argentine Open Polo Championship), taking place at Palermo's Campo Argentino de Polo (☎ 4774-4517), at Av del Libertador and Dorrego. For exact dates and details, contact the Asociación Argentina de Polo (☎ 4343-0972), Hipólito Yrigoyen 636. Around the same time, the gaucho sport of pato holds its Campeonato Argentino Abierto de Pato (Argentine Open Pato Championship); for details, contact the Federación Argentino de Pato (☎ 4331-0222; Map 3), Av Belgrano 530, 5th floor.

PLACES TO STAY

Buenos Aires offers a wide range of accommodations, from energetic youth hostels and simple but good family-oriented hotels to five-star luxury lodgings of jet-set stature.

Budget accommodations tend to be past their prime, though they're not necessarily bad. Many are in renovated older buildings, and prices range from US$10 per person for a hostel bed to about US$15 to US$35 for very simple double rooms. These generally don't include breakfast. Main areas for budget accommodations are around Constitución train station and Congreso, atmospheric San Telmo, and Microcentro (limited).

Mid-range hotels are either showing their age or have been cheaply remodeled; many are also in older renovated buildings with original features. Prices here hover around US$40 to US$80, and rooms pretty much always come with breakfast, private bath and TV. These hotels are scattered throughout the city, but many are concentrated in Congreso, Retiro and Microcentro.

High-end hotels run US$90 and up and include all the amenities. Many often do not include the whopping 21% IVA tax in their rates, so check. Nearly all of them have substantial discounts for cash payment and advance booking and purchase. Since many cater to businesspeople, you may be able to negotiate a special rate by flashing a business card (these same hotels also drop their rates on weekends). Most hotels in this upper range are located in Barrio Norte, Recoleta, Retiro and Microcentro.

Microcentro & Plaza de Mayo (Map 3)

Advantages of staying here are proximity to many of the city's top attractions, good restaurants and nightlife options, and easy access to a wide selection of public transport.

Budget Youth hostels and basic hotels are your best options in this price range. *Milhouse Youth Hostel* (☎ 4345-9604, W *www .milhousehostel.com, Hipólito Yrigoyen 959)* Dorm beds US$12-15 per person with breakfast, doubles US$40-44. Spanking new, this spacious colonial house boasts clean rooms, many surrounding an open patio. Balconied dorms facing the street can be grand, and common spaces are comfortable. There's also a kitchen and

rooftop terrace, though nearby discos can be noisy.

V & S Youth Hostel (☎ 4322-0994, W *.vsyhbue.com.ar, Viamonte 887)* Dorm beds US$16 per person with breakfast, singles/doubles US$40/45. Here's another wonderful and comfortable hostel. The location's great, the common room spacious and modern with large-screen TV, and the dorms spic-and-span and carpeted. The double with balcony is primo (book ahead). There's email access, a kitchen and patio with grill.

St Nicholas Youth Hostel (☎ 4373-8841, fax 4371-4364, e *stnicholashostal@hotmail .com, Bartolomé Mitre 1691)* Dorm beds US$12 per person with breakfast. Pretty new and nicely decorated, this spacious and tidy hostel's best feature is its rooftop terrace. There are some good common rooms too, but it can get noisy since there's a central open well.

Castilla Hotel (☎ 4383-4586, Bartolomé Mitre 1548) Rooms US$10 per person with private bath. This is a good budget find for women or well behaved heterosexual couples only – no solo male travelers otherwise. In an older, busily decorated open space (there's a great tiled floor), you get kitchen access, laundry facilities and a large terrace. Long term stays are available.

Hotel Sportsman (☎ 4381-8021, Rivadavia 1425) Singles/doubles US$18/27 with private bath, US$12/22 with shared. All rooms are different at this rustic, old-fashioned crash pad, so check out a couple of them before you decide. The leafy hallway-patios bring some light in to ease the rough edges a bit.

Hotel La Argentina (☎ 4342-0078, Av de Mayo 860) Singles/doubles US$20/30. Old, musty digs, with some rooms more charming than others; ask for a balcony. For this price, maybe you can tolerate the shaky elevator and peeling paint. The ancient floor tiles are atmospheric, at least.

Hotel Alcazar (☎ 4345-0926, Av de Mayo 935) Singles/doubles US$25/35, more with TV. Here's an older, nicer place with simple, clean and fairly good-sized rooms. It is nothing fancy, but a good deal and a good location.

Hotel Palace Solís (☎ *4371-6266, Solís 352*) Singles/doubles US$30/40. A little far from center, Solís offers good rooms surrounding a grand old sitting room. The building was originally built by Spaniards, and the hotel is presently run by some.

Mid-Range ***Hotel El Cabildo*** (☎/*fax 4322-6695, Lavalle 748*) Singles/doubles US$35/45. Decent rooms are basic, but clean and fairly spacious; it's still a good deal for the locale, right on pedestrian Lavalle. You can chat up the manager (in Spanish) about his siblings in San Francisco.

Hotel Chile (☎/*fax 4383-7877, Av de Mayo 1297*) Singles/doubles US$35/50. Try to snag one of the larger, nicer rooms at this art nouveau hotel (whose inside is modern). Corner rooms have better balconies, with views of the Congreso and Casa Rosada in the fall. Bring earplugs for the street noise.

Hotel Callao (☎/*fax 4374-3861, W www.hotelcallao.com.ar, Callao 292*) Singles/doubles US$40/50. The comfortably modern rooms here are immaculate and spacious, and many have balconies. Two are bigger and rounded, located in the turreted part of the building (but they don't cost more). With luck, the current remodel won't raise prices too much.

Gran Hotel Hispano (☎/*fax 4345-2020, W www.hhispano.com.ar, Av de Mayo 861*) Singles/doubles US$41/48 cash. Settle into a comfortable and nicely decorated room at this squeaky clean hotel with attractive open patio hall area; look at couple rooms because some are larger. There are nice common sitting spots, and generally it's a pretty good deal.

Hotel Goya (☎/*fax 4322-9311, e goyahotel@infovia.com.ar, Suipacha 748*) Singles/doubles US$45/55 classic, US$65/70 superior. Looking for an intimate, friendly, spotless, central, quiet, comfortable hotel at a good price? Try this place. The 'classic' rooms have showers that open to the sink area, while 'superior' rooms have enclosed showers. The US$100 presidential suite has a sofa and a tub with jets.

Hotel Lyon (☎ *4372-0100, fax 4814-4252, e hotel_lyon@ucsd.com, Riobamba 251*) Singles/doubles US$68/80. This hotel is perfect for the traveling family or a group that likes to stick together. Old apartments were converted to very spacious rooms with entry halls, large baths and even small snack rooms with fridges. Factor in the friendly staff and charming surroundings and you've got yourself a great deal.

Hotel Phoenix (☎ *4312-4845, fax 4311-2846, W www.hotelphoenix.com.ar, San Martín 780*) Singles/doubles US$69/85. This wonderful hotel is an architectural gem that once hosted the Prince of Wales. Old-fashioned but with modern conveniences, it sports a great elevator and charming labyrinth of open halls. The grand, high-ceilinged rooms are very spacious and decorated with antique furniture.

Top End ***Savoy Hotel*** (☎ *4370-8000, fax 4370-8080, W www.savoy-hotel.com.ar, Callao 181*) Doubles US$99. Every clean, modern room has an entryway sitting area, large bath and Internet connection. The hotel has an office for guests' use, and the nearby gym costs US$8 if you stay here. The occasional old touches are nice, too.

Claridge Hotel (☎ *4314-7700, fax 4314-8022, Tucumán 535*) Doubles US$155. Prices go up and down here, so call ahead. This venerable place is the best in the area, with very comfortable, clean and fruity-smelling rooms that are modern but still possess the old touch here and there. It's quiet and bright, and a good deal for this price range.

San Telmo & Constitución (Map 4)

San Telmo and Constitución are popular with budget travelers who don't particularly like hostels. Most of the hotel accommodations here are a bit older (and they show it), but the area has plenty of atmosphere such as wonderful cobbled streets, colonial buildings, good cheap eateries and great tango venues.

Budget ***El Hostal de San Telmo*** (☎ *4300-6899, fax 4300-9028, e elhostal@satlink.com,*

Carlos Calvo 614) Dorm beds US$10. Well-located is this labyrinthine hostel with small common spaces. Dorms are also rather cramped, with four to eight beds each, and the doubles are absolutely tiny. There's a patio, terrace with a grill, lockers, kitchen, laundry facilities, cable TV and Internet.

Residencial Carly (☎ *4361-7710, Humberto Primo 464)* Singles/doubles US$12/16 with private bath, less with shared. Next to lively Plaza Dorrego, these dilapidated digs have great patios, old atmosphere and high-ceilinged rooms, which are dim with saggy mattresses. There's also a kitchen on premises. It can get noisy with kids, but the location is great and it's cheap.

Hotel Victoria (☎/*fax 4361-2135, Chacabuco 726)* Singles/doubles US$15/25 with private bath, less with shared. Relaxing open patios spotlight this worn but friendly place, which has basic kitchen and laundry facilities. It's got personality, but some rooms can be a bit musty. It's popular with budget *tanguistas* (tango afficionados).

Hotel Bolívar (☎ *4361-5105, Bolívar 886)* Singles/doubles US$18/22-25 with private bath. Try to get one of the few rooms with sunny balconies here; others are also pretty simple line a patio.

Mid-Range *Boquitas Pintadas* (☎ *4381-6064,* W *www.boquitas-pintadas.com.ar, Estados Unidos 1393)* Doubles US$65-140. A few blocks west of San Telmo is this self-proclaimed 'pop' hotel, with six themed rooms sporting a different decor. Run by Germans, there are some nice terraces and a hot tub, quirky halls and a snazzy bar downstairs.

Recoleta & Retiro (Map 5)

For those with big bucks, Recoleta and Retiro offer the ritziest hotels, most upscale neighborhoods and best services, along with being well-located near downtown and some popular tourist sights.

Budget *Recoleta Youth Hostel* (☎ *4812-4419, fax 4815-6622,* e *recoletayouthhostel@ libertel.com.ar, Libertad 1218)* Dorm beds US$12, doubles US$30. A couple blocks

from the Recoleta border are these well-located cheap digs; Retiro bus terminal is a 15-minute walk. The hostel is in a charming old mansion with central patio, but staff here are lackadaisical and bathrooms can get grungy.

Hotel Lion D'Or (☎ *4803-8992, Pacheco de Melo 2019)* Singles/doubles range US$25/52 with private bath and depending on the room, US$18/33 with shared bath. Some rooms here are basic and depressing, some are absolutely grand. All are a bit rough around the edges, but in a charming older way, and the elevator is just great.

Mid-Range *Juncal Palace Hotel* (☎/*fax 4821-2770, Juncal 2282)* Singles/doubles US$35/45, more with TV. This intimate hotel is a great deal for Recoleta. There are only 26 rooms and it's booked every weekend, so call ahead.

Hotel San Antonio (☎ *4312-5381, fax 4314-9516, Paraguay 372)* Singles/doubles US$40/50. Small but friendly and comfortably old-fashioned, this 45-year-old hotel has cozy rooms sporting lots of wood details, though they're also a bit dark. The breakfast room is grand, and you're close to downtown.

Top End *Comfort Aspen Suites* (☎ *4313-9011, fax 4313-8059,* W *www.aspensuites .com.ar, Esmeralda 933)* Standards/suites US$100/120, possibly negotiable, weekends cheaper. Business folks like the modern, clean and very spacious rooms here, all with kitchenettes and TV (it's just like home). Inside rooms are quieter, and there's even a gym and sauna. For downtown, it's a great deal.

Hotel Conquistador (☎ *4328-3012, fax 4328-3252,* W *www.elconquistador.com.ar, Suipacha 948)* Doubles US$103, suites US$110. Halls and rooms aren't huge, but you can eat breakfast in a solarium, and a plush mezzanine bar overlooks the spacious lobby. There's an 'office center,' small gym and sauna.

Courtyard by Marriott (☎ *4318-3069, Florida 944)* Singles/doubles US$120, weekends US$95 two-night minimum. Right at the start of pedestrian Florida is this modern branch of the Marriott. It's just as clean as the nearby mother ship, the Marriott Plaza, but much less grand.

Domus Recoleta Hotel (☎ 4804-3471, fax 4806-3476, Posadas 1557) Singles/doubles US$120/140. Every room here is a suite, with sofa and desk included. It's pretty tranquil and a good deal for this area.

Hotel Park Plaza (☎ 4815-5028, fax 4815-4522, W www.parkplazahotels.com, Parera 183) Singles/doubles US$190, more in high season. Wear your ascot here; you'll fit right in. Elegance and tasteful decor predominate at this hotel on a fairly quiet street in upscale Recoleta. All rooms come with wet bar and mini-living spaces and are nicely lit and presented. Daily newspaper, spa and gym are included.

Caesar Park Hotel (☎ 4819-1100, fax 4819-1121, W www.caesar-park.com, Posadas 1232) Singles/doubles US$240/250, more in high season, doubles US$198 on weekends. Breeze into the marble lobby here to be surrounded by class and luxury and men in suits. Assume all the amenities in this price range.

Alvear Palace Hotel (☎ 4808-2100, fax 4804-0034, W www.alvearpalace.com, Alvear 1891) Doubles US$410, suites US$440 to US$3000. The Alvear is the most expensive hotel in Buenos Aires, though not the best bang for your buck; but that's not the point, is it? Expect every single amenity, including great service and true elegance.

Other Barrios

Che Lagarto (☎ 4304-7618, W www.che lagarto.com.ar, Combate de los Pozos 1151) Dorm beds US$10. This is your basic backpacker's hostel. It's not nearly as central, spacious or spiffy as some of the newer hostels, but it's been around awhile and it evokes a camaraderie-inducing atmosphere. It also offers tourist services and occasional social activities.

Hostel El Choique (☎ 4774-0277, Thames 2062) Dorm beds US$9, doubles US$30. This pleasant new hostel has around ten simple, smallish rooms (with lockers). Common areas within the maze-like halls

include a patio, study, and computer rooms, and cheap meals are available. Since this is the only inexpensive choice in Palermo Viejo, give them a call before you go. It also offers long-term accommodations (see below).

Como en Casa (☎ 4831-0517, fax 4831-2664, W www.comoencasa.com, Gurruchaga 2155) Singles/doubles US$30/55 with shared bath. This friendly and homey place in Palermo Viejo is attractively decorated and has simple, small rooms. There are plenty of good common spaces as well as kitchen access and a nice garden. See below for long-term accommodation rentals here.

Malabia House (☎ 4832-3345, W www .malabiahouse.com.ar, Malabia 1555) Singles US$60-80, doubles US$85-103 including taxes. Fifteen fine rooms along with gracious and charming common areas line this beautiful renovated house in Palermo Viejo. Candles, soft music and a comfortable homey feel make for a peaceful and even romantic stay.

Long-Term Accommodations

All places listed below are oriented toward monthly accommodations and thus have kitchen access, but any hostel or hotel listed above will significantly discount a long-term stay. Check the classifieds in the *Buenos Aires Herald* for apartment rentals.

Hotel Residencial Bolívar (☎ 4300-6507, Bolívar 1356; Map 4) Singles/doubles US$200/240 per month, more with private bath and balcony. It's an old, worn building, but with sunny and some breezy open areas. Rooms are very basic and suited for the truly serious budget traveler only.

Buenos Ayres Hostel (☎ 4361-0694, W www.buenosayreshostel.com, Pasaje San Lorenzo 320; Map 4) Shared rooms US$12/60/220 day/week/month. There are also two private rooms and small dorms available. Both foreigners and students stay here. The clean spaces are a bit labyrinthine but in a pleasant way. You also get coin laundry, patio, and living area with TV, all wrapped up in a small, personal spot that's close to the heart of San Telmo.

Recoleta Home (☎/*fax* 4824-8492, *Ayacucho 1232; Map 5*) US$350-420 per person per month for 2-4 person rooms with shared bath, US$20 per person per day. Here's a relatively new student residence in upscale Recoleta (travelers welcome). Included are daily maid service, Internet access, study room and TV room. Rooms are simple, spacious and bright.

Hostel El Choique (US$331 per month in 4-person dorms, including breakfast and one other meal) and *Como en Casa* (US$480-540 per month for a single) also offer long-term accommodations; see Other Barrios above, for reviews and contact information.

PLACES TO EAT

You'll eat well in Buenos Aires: food ranges from the cheap and simple to the costly and sophisticated. It's true that you'll have more options if you're a meat-eater, but if you prefer to contribute to the killing of innocent fruits and vegetables instead, there are plenty of meatless pastas, salads and other veggie concoctions to sample. There are even a few good vegetarian restaurants around town.

Basic fare in Buenos Aires is not the most innovative in the world. In run-of-the-mill restaurants, standard menu items include pasta dishes like ravioli and gnocchi, short orders like *milanesa* (a breaded cutlet), and the more economical cuts of beef, along with french fries, green salad, and dessert. For a little more money you can get the same sort of food prepared with better ingredients. Pizzerías are common and very popular, and many cafés serve food.

Recently there's been a trend towards exotic Asian cuisines such as Japanese, Vietnamese, Thai, and Indian, as well as their accompanying fusions. These new (and expensive) restaurants are concentrated in the gentrifying older neighborhoods of Palermo, northwest of Recoleta. One good place to catch up on the latest in food trends is Dereck Foster's Food & Wine section of the Sunday *Buenos Aires Herald*.

Microcentro & Plaza de Mayo (Map 3)

Budget *Coto* (*no* ☎, *Viamonte 1571*) Mains US$3. The express cafeteria upstairs at this supermarket will feed you for cheap, *if* you can stand the antiseptic and non-smoking environment.

Pizzería Güerrín (☎ 4371-8141, *Corrientes 1368*) Slices US$1.10. You can buy at the counter and eat standing up for the real cheap stuff, or take a seat and choose a greater variety of toppings for your pizza. There are lots of desserts too.

La Sortija (☎ 4328-0824, *Lavalle 663*) Mains US$2-6. Here's a cheap, local place, where you can fill up on a chunk of grilled meat, salad and drink for US$6 all told. The *vacio* (a chewy but tasty flank cut) is only US$2 per hefty half-portion.

Cervantes II (☎ 4372-5227, *Juan D Perón 1883*) Mains US$4-6. You can take out or eat in at this spacious, popular and cheap local parrilla. Get an *agua de siphon* (soda water) to go along with your US$4 *bife de chorizo* (sirloin steak), or savor some inexpensive *ravioles con tuco* (raviolis with sauce).

Patio de Comidas (*lower level, Galerías Pacífico*) Meals US$5-7. After shopping up a storm on pedestrian Florida, stop by this ritzy food court. It's great for a group of people who can't reach a consensus on what to eat.

Clinton Plaza (☎ 4314-6780, *Reconquista 545*) Mains US$5. Businesspeople jam this popular cafeteria-style lunch spot in the financial district. A steak and salad go for US$6.

Valle Esmeralda (☎ 4394-9266, *Esmeralda 370*) All-you-can-eat US$6; open lunch only. Here's a good vegetarian haven on busy Esmeralda; it has takeout too.

La Huerta (☎ 4327-2682, *Lavalle 895*) All-you-can-eat US$6. Popular with the business crowd, this veggie buffet on the 1st floor is pretty good and centrally located.

La Americana (☎ 4371-0202, *Callao 83*) There are some really good empanadas (US$0.90) at this traditional eatery, along with pizza slices (US$3). Eat cheaply at the stand-up counter or sit down and relax with a whole pizza pie (US$6-13). There are lots of interesting desserts, too, if you need an energy rush.

Pippo *(☎ 4374-6365, Paraná 356; ☎ 4375-5887, Montevideo 341)* Mains US$3.50-8,

weekday lunch special US$6 served until 6pm. Dishing up large servings of parrilla and pasta for small prices, it's no wonder Pippo's so popular with locals. There's a non-smoking section in back and service is efficient.

Lunfardo

Lunfardo came from immigrants of the late 1800s and was apparently used by some of the less desirable elements of society (such as thieves). Now it's used by everyone. Like any slang, it changes with the generations. Below are some of the spicier *lunfardo* terms that you may hear on the streets of Buenos Aires. Lunfardo is pretty much a porteño phenomenon. Interested in more details? Contact the Academia Porteña del Lunfardo (☎ 4383-2393), Estados Unidos 1379.

Useful Words

birra – beer

bondi – bus

boliche – disco or nightclub

boludo – jerk, asshole, idiot; often used among friends to mean 'hey stupid' or 'hey man,' but is an insult to strangers.

buena onda – good vibes

chamullar – to talk idly, to bullshit someone

carajo – asshole, prick, bloody hell

chabón/chabona – kid; often used affectionately

che – hey

fiaca – laziness

guita – money

laburar – to work; often associated with the usual negative connotations

mango – one peso

mina – woman

morfar – to eat or pig out

macanudo – great, fabulous

pibe/piba – cool young person

piola – cool, clever

pendejo – idiot

porro – marijuana, usually a joint

pucho – a cigarette or cigarette butt

quilombo – a mess or a house of prostitution

Useful Phrases

Es una masa.
something perfect, excellent or cool

diez puntos
ok, cool, great, fine (literally, 'ten points')

Le faltan un par de jugadores.
the equivalent of the expression 'He's not playing with a full deck' (literally, 'He's missing a pair of (fútbol) players')

Me mataste.
I don't know/I have no idea; used when responding to a question (literally, 'You've killed me.')

No le doy bola.
I don't give a shit.

Poner las pilas.
get energized (literally, 'Put the batteries in.')

¿Que haces fiera/Que haces titán?
What's up dude?

re interestante
very interesting; 're' (very) can be used with any adjective; try to roll that 'r.'

Soy Gardel con una guitarra eléctrica.
I am so stylin'/cool (literally, 'I am Gardel with an electric guitar.')

Che boludo, sos re boludo.
This is the most porteño phrase on earth. Ask a friendly local youth to explain it.

Mid-Range & Top End

Los Troncos (☎ 4322-1295, Suipacha 732) Mains US$4-12. The barbecue pit is in the window next to the stuffed cow. This is a great place for both meat eaters and vegetarians because there is so much on the menu. The chandeliers are rustic and the dark wood trim makes everything nice and atmospheric.

La Posada de 1820 (☎ 4314-4557, San Martín 606) Mains US$5-13.50. Choices include spinach crepes (US$4.50), tenderloin with mushrooms in mustard sauce (US$13.50), and a variety of meats and pasta. Short-order milanesas and a salad bar are also options in this are bustling restaurant with attentive service.

La Estancia (☎ 4326-0330, Lavalle 941) Mains US$5-15. Here's another good, congenial place for parrilla, with fun painted murals on the walls. It also serves special salads like Waldorf (celery, apples, bananas, nuts and mayonnaise – author's opinion, yuck!) and Rainbow (lots of colorful veggies) for US$12-15. The extensive wine list includes champagnes if you want to lighten up.

Broccolino (☎ 4393-0921, Esmeralda 776) Mains US$6-15. Come here if you enjoy choosing between 27 varieties of sauce for your rigatoni. Meats, salads and seafood are also on the menu, and there's apple strudel for dessert.

ABC (☎ 4393-3992, Lavalle 545) Mains US$6-15, daily specials US$9. This traditional German eatery has been around since 1929, tucked into a moody older space with dark wood panels. Suited waiters bring you specialties like sausages and sauerkraut, along with typical Argentine fare.

Los Inmortales (☎ 4322-5493, Lavalle 748) Pizzas US$6-17. Bite into great pizza while surrounded by photos of Gardel and his contemporaries. This place has plenty of

El Toboso (☎ 4374-8449, Corrientes 1838) Mains US$3.50-10, set menu US$5. Along with your basic parrilla, pastas and salads, you can order fish and omelettes. And if you haven't tried *lengua a la vinagreta* (marinated cow's tongue) by now, give it a shot for US$4. It's really not bad.

short-orders and sides, and is always popular. There are several branches around the city.

Granix (☎ 4343-4020, Florida 165, 1st floor of Galería Güemes) All-you-can-eat US$9; open weekdays for lunch only. This place is a bit hard to find; go up the stairs in the mall. It has a good food selection and is one of the swankier veggie places in Buenos Aires.

Rey Castro (☎ 4342-9998, Perú 342) Mains US$9-14. Rustic brick arches surround a spacious, smoky dining area. Music plays while trendy patrons sample Cuban seafood dishes; on weekends the music's live. Authentic cigars are for sale, and even Americans can buy them legally.

El Hispano (☎ 4382-7534, Salta 20) Mains US$6-14. Hanging hams lend congeniality to the traditional ambience at this Spanish seafood restaurant. Treats include grilled trout, mussels and fried calamari. Don't forget the chocolate mousse (US$4).

Bar La Robla (☎ 4811-4484, Viamonte 1615) Lunch specials US$3, mains US$7-10. Standard Argentine dishes and excellent seafood are cooked up here in a very pleasant and deli-like environment. It also offers a large cheese selection.

Chiquilín (☎ 4373-5163, Sarmiento 1599) Mains US$5-13. Typically packed at midnight on a Saturday night, this traditional parrilla efficiently serves good meat, pasta and seafood dishes in a ham-hanging, wine-bottle-lined place. There's even a nonsmoking section.

Campo dei Fiori (☎ 4381-1800, San José 491) Mains US$4-14. Choose a plate of ravioli, lasagna or ñoquis, but just remember the sauces are extra. Seafood and ubiquitous meats are also available, and the wine list goes on. The brick walls create a great atmosphere.

Laurak Bat (☎ 4381-0682, Belgrano 1144) Mains US$8-24. If you're itching for Basque seafood, you can visit this nice restaurant with relaxing music. It's not terribly central, but it does offer *pimentos de piquillo* (spicy, slow-roasted peppers from Spain) and mussels a la Provence.

San Telmo (Map 4)

DesNivel (☎ 4300-9081, Defensa 855) Mains US$3-5.50. This local joint is packed at lunch and serves *chorizo* (spicy sausage) and a wonderful *bife de lomo* (tenderloin steak). Add salad and double expresso, and you walk away happy and buzzing for US$10.

Sr Telmo (☎ 4363-0100, Defensa 756) Mains US$3-6. This is a good place to come if you're homesick for hamburgers, spinach pizza or frozen daiquiris. It has margaritas for US$5.50 and you'll sip them in fashionable surroundings.

Abuela Pan (☎ 4361-4936, Bolívar 707) Daily specials US$5-6. This is a tiny but peaceful spot near San Telmo serving healthy dishes and whole wheat bread.

Las Marías (☎ 4362-7563, Bolívar 949) Mains US$4-9, weekday lunch specials US$7. Bask in a tango-themed restaurant full of local color while selecting from the parrilla items or specialty pasta dishes like vegetable gnocchi and *sorrentinos* with four-cheese sauce.

Parrilla al Carbón (☎ 4300-7062, Estados Unidos 407) Mains US$4-7. Cheap meats, pastas and all the fixings await you at this small, casual joint that's great for a simple meal. It is popular with locals.

La Feria (☎ 4362-2354, Aieta 1095) Mains US$7-12. Movie stars peer down from their posters and the brick walls lend good atmosphere. Choose from melon with prosciutto, stuffed chicken with mashed apple or tenderloin in mushroom sauce. Don't forget dessert; the tiramisu's US$5.

La Casa de Estéban de Luca (☎ 4361-4338, Defensa 1000) Mains US$8-16, dinner special US$12. Fine food, tasteful decor and traditional atmosphere attract tourists and locals alike to this busy, historical eatery. Eats range from spinach crepes to grilled salmon or chicken with fried polenta.

Ana y el Angel (☎ 4361-8822, Chile 318) Mains US$14-23, set meals US$28-48. The walls here are ornamented to resemble the outsides of colorful, classy buildings. The international menu includes Patagonian lamb, filet mignon with arugula and bacon, and rabbit with white wine sauce.

Recoleta & Retiro (Map 5)

Budget *El Sanjuanino* (☎ 4805-2683, Posadas 1515) This small place looks like the inside of a wine barrel, with comforting deli-like decor. The spicy empanadas are US$1 each, and the tamales and *locro* (a spicy stew of maize, beans, beef, pork, and sausage) run US$5.

El Cuartito (☎ 4816-1758, Talcahuano 937) Pizza slices US$1-1.20. If you're in a hurry, this is a good place. Munch standing up at the counters; it's cheaper and faster that way and you can enjoy the old sports posters without turning around.

Lotos (☎ 4814-4552, Córdoba 1577) Mains US$2-3. This cafeteria-style place has hearty soups and extensive salad choices. Downstairs a health-food store sells fresh ginger, nori, herbal extracts and bakery goods.

La Esquina de las Flores (☎ 4813-3630, Córdoba 1587) Mains US$2.50-4.50. This clean and modern restaurant also has a small health-food store on the ground floor. Upstairs, choose from a changing menu of tasty and imaginative items.

Payanca (☎ 4893-2641, Suipacha 1015) Mains US$3-7. This is a good place for spicy northern Argentine cuisine such as locro. It's one of the best values in the barrio and has a congenial atmosphere.

Los Chilenos (☎ 4328-3123, Suipacha 1042) Mains US$4.50-13. This popular and casual downtown eatery is packed with businesspeople at lunchtime. One look at the extensive menu and you won't need to cross the Andes to get an idea of Chilean cuisine.

Grant's (☎ 4823-5894, Junín 1155; ☎ 4801-9099, Las Heras 1925) All-you-can-eat US$6-8 lunches, US$10-12 nights and weekends, drinks mandatory and extra. Here's one of the better buffets in town, with a fantastic assortment of foods to sample. You'll be rolling out of this joint no matter what, but try to choose carefully anyway, and eat slowly.

Pizza Cero (☎ 4804-2244, Schiaffino 2009) Pizzas US$8. Toppings include *palmitos* (hearts of palms), anchovies, pineapple and Roquefort cheese. With a leafy park across the street, you'll be sitting pretty at the sidewalk tables on warm summer evenings. This joint also does salads, fugazza (a cheeseless variety of pizza with sweet onions) and calzones.

Mid-Range & Top End *Viejo Horizonte* (☎ 4806-0553, Junín 1460) Mains US$6-15. Come to this Lebanese restaurant on a Friday night and a belly dancer will perform while you nibble on hummus, saffir salad and lamb with mint yogurt and garlic sauce.

Lotus Bar (☎ 4312-5706, Tres Sargentos 427) Mains US$7-16, 10% student discount. Listen to trendy music in modernistic surroundings while slurping your tom ka gai (chicken in coconut milk soup) or nibbling your partner's geng kiawan (pork and eggplant in green curry sauce).

Bengal (☎ 4394-8557, Arenales 837) Mains US$9-16. This small and very elegant Indian restaurant almost has the feel of being inside a plush tent. The chicken tandoori and lamb masala run US$14, while the dal makhi (a black lentil dish) is US$9.

Dora (☎ 4311-2891, Leandro N Alem 1016) Mains US$9-25. Prices for seafood and parrilla can be a bit steep at this popular lunchtime eatery, but the quality is good and the menu is extensive. Plant-lovers will enjoy the lush greenery.

La Chacra (☎ 4322-1409, Córdoba 941) Parrilla US$10. Resist the urge to ride the stuffed cow in the entryway and check out the *asado* (open barbeque grill) in the window instead. Inside, traditionally dressed waiters serve succulent grilled meats while deer and boar heads hang high on the walls and watch as you munch on their hoofed brethren.

Filo (☎ 4311-0312, San Martín 975) Mains US$10-15. Enjoy your pricey pizza, pasta and salads amidst movie posters, creative decor and lively music. Choose from the extensive drink selection to wash it all down.

There are many more restaurants in the nearby Plaza del Pilar, right next to the Centro Cultural Recoleta. The fun in this enclosed, upscale complex is looking around and finding the right place to stop for a meal.

Puerto Madero

You'll find restaurant after restaurant in this renovated waterfront area, popular for business power lunches. Most are fairly elegant and thus pricey; dress appropriately and be prepared to splurge. All these places line Av Alicia Moreau de Justo.

Bice (☎ 4315-6216, No 192; Map 3) Mains US$13-25. This is a great place to impress a hot date. Very expensive Italian pasta can be savored here; fettucine with shrimp sauce goes for US$22, and there's also high-priced seafood such as salmon and tuna, both for over US$20.

Puerto Sorrento (☎ 4319-8731, No 410; Map 3) Mains US$10-19. There are some surprises on this menu, like paella and tuna steak. Otherwise, choose from the many pasta dishes and pricier parrilla cuts.

Cabaña Las Lilas (☎ 4313-1336, No 516; Map 3) Mains US$12-20. The rustic decor and rattan furniture set the mood for fine beef, wine and service. If you're wallet matches its thickness, try the 800g, 3-inch-thick, US$32 baby beef steak.

La Caballeriza (☎ 4314-4444, No 580; Map 3) Mains US$8-14. Consider making reservations at this popular lunch spot, where you'll feel like you're dining in a renovated barn. The extensive menu features salads, sides, meats and dessert choices, and it even has English translations.

Siga la Vaca (☎ 4315-6801, No 1714; Map 4) All-you-can-eat US$12-15. If you like to see mountains of food, you'll find heaven here, so come hungry and don't expect anything too fancy. The weekday buffet lunches are cheaper than dinners.

Estilo Campo (☎ 4312-4546, No 1840; Map 4) Mains US$10-20. There's an impressive asado with an array of grilled meats, and you can even order rabbit and wild boar dishes (both US$16). This is a good place to bring your rich parents, especially if they foot the bill.

Palermo

La Cátedra (☎ 4777-4601, Cerviño 4699) Mains US$7-16.50. A few blocks northeast of the Palermo Subte stop, this elegant restaurant has atmospheric lighting and photos of horses on the walls. Order imaginative dishes like rabbit with forest mushrooms and polenta with lamb sauce, or go for homemade pastas and parrilla.

Garbis (☎ *4511-6600, Scalabrini Ortiz 3054)* Mains US$5.50-19, lunch special US$8. Seven blocks northeast of the Scalabrini Ortiz Subte stop, this popular Middle-Eastern restaurant serves shish kebabs, hummus, tabouli and mousakka, and a grand finale of baklava (US$4).

Katmandu (☎ *4963-1122, Córdoba 3547)* Mains US$10-14; open Mon-Sat dinner only. For an authentic taste of India, hike or bus on over (bus No 106 goes up Córdoba from the center). There are samosas (US$5) and hot curries on the menu, and the tandoori ghost is a delicious lamb marinated in milk and saffron.

Palermo Viejo This fashionable district has countless ethnic and recently opened restaurants, especially in and around the thriving nightlife area of Plaza Serrano.

Freud & Fahler (☎ *4833-2153, Gurruchaga 1750)* Mains US$11-16. The menu reads like poetry and philosophical discourse; order things like Season in Hell (brochette of organic chicken, US$13), Sailing to Argolidos, Seeking Love (lamb ribs with wine sauce, US$14), or Assassination on the Ides of March (mussels in Dijon sauce, US$14). The chef's a psychoanalyst.

Xalapa (☎ *4833-6102, El Salvador 4800)* Mains US$5-16. Brightly painted pastel walls and sidewalk seating comfort the hordes that come here to enjoy enchiladas, huevos rancheros, *carnitas* and *totopos* (deep fried tortillas). Frozen margaritas (US$6) comfort them even more.

Sudestada (☎ *4776-3777, Guatemala 5602)* Mains US$8-21. Come here if you like the spicy flavors; choose from curries, noodles and seafood plates representing most of the Southeast Asian nations. Drinks include Thai iced tea and coffee (US$1.50-2), lychee licuado (US$3) and whiskey sour with ginseng (US$6). Get *sago* (a tropical thickener) and fruit iced soup (US$6) for dessert.

Kayoko (☎ *4832-6158, Gurruchaga 1650)* Mains US$8.50-13; closed Sun. The wait-

resses with white-painted faces make service a bit shocking, but at least the wood deck out front is nice and personal. Rainbow sushi rolls come with colorful varieties of fish slices; other items available include tempura and yakitori.

Sarkis (☎ *4772-4911, Thames 1101)* Mains US$7-14. The menu's not extensive at this Middle Eastern restaurant, but the food is good. Order specialties like *kafta* (shish kebab) or falafel and top them off with baklava (US$3). The crowd's local and the atmosphere busy, clean and professional.

Las Cañitas A recently popular (but much smaller and more laid-back) restaurant scene has erupted in Palermo's northern area of Las Cañitas, bounded by Av Luis Maria Campos, Ortega y Gasset and Dorrego.

El Portugués (☎ *4771-8699, Baez 499)* Mains US$7-14, lunch specials US$5. This is one of the best (and least touristy) places for parrilla in Buenos Aires. Portions are huge; the half serving of bife de chorizo (US$7) can feed two or even three people. The ambience is modern and easygoing and the walls are decorated with braids of garlic. This place hops whenever it's open, even at midnight on weekends.

El Primo (☎ *4772-8441, Báez 302)* Mains US$7-12. Locals love this casual corner eatery decked out in chartreuse paint, high ceilings and colorful tablecloths. The lighting is nice too, but it's not a place for vegetarians.

Lotus Neo Thai (☎ *4771-4449, Ortega y Gasset 1782)* Mains US$9-17. It's not cheap, but the intimate decor includes exotic water lily lamps and elegant murals, and you can sit on pillows on the floor. The tom kai gai is US$11 and pad thai is US$12, plus there is a range of less common Southeast Asian dishes.

Club Zen (☎ *4772-8866, Huergo 366)* Mains US$10-16. The clean and modern atmosphere fits the expensive sushi rolls, with equally pricey nigiri, maki and sashimi right behind. Vegetable stir-fry complements the fusion menu. There are Japanese beers like Asahi and Kirin (US$4-9) and lots of sake.

Soul Café (☎ 4778-3115, *Báez 246*) Mains US$8-15. Enjoy sushi, grilled lamb or pasta with mussels in a red-tinted atmosphere. Drinks include the boogie shake (US$8) and a 'hot' margarita (laced with jalapeño; US$7).

Khalú (☎ 4777-4679, *Andrés Arguibel 2851*) Mains US$18-25. The lush garden entry, airy inside spaces and elegant decor accent this wonderfully romantic place. Changing menus are pure fusion: Asian, Caribbean and Colombian tastes all worked up by a French-trained chef.

ENTERTAINMENT

Buenos Aires has a wide range of entertainment options for every budget. There's live music, theater, tango (and other dances), sporting events, cutting-edge movies, jumpin' discos, smooth old-time cafés and rockin' bars. You can find something to do every day of the week and at practically every hour of the day.

Cartelera Vea Más (☎ 4372-7285, *Paseo La Plaza complex, Local 19; Map 3*) and *Cartelera Baires* (☎ 4372-5058, *Corrientes 1372; Map 3*) sell discount tickets to live shows and some movies. Most porteño newspapers have entertainment supplements on Friday. Free booklets *Buenos Aires Day & Night* and *Cuidad Abierta* list happenings around town.

For large-scale spectacles like the Beijing Circus, gypsy dancers or certain indoor sports like boxing, there's Luna Park (☎ 4324-1010, *Bouchard & Corrientes*). Admission prices vary from US$10 to US$60, depending on the show.

Cafés & Confiterías

Café society is a major force in the life of Argentines in general and porteños in particular; they spend hours solving their own problems, the country's and the rest of the world's problems – over a chessboard and a cheap *cortado* (coffee with milk).

Café Tortoni (☎ 4342-4328, *Av de Mayo 829; Map 3*) The epitome of Buenos Aires cafés, Tortonia was established over 100 years ago. Locals and tourists alike take in the grand old surroundings and order pricey

coffee and snacks while being served by traditionally dressed waiters.

La Puerto Rico (☎ 4331-2215, *Alsina 416; Map 3*) A block south of Plaza de Mayo, this contemporary of the Tortoni is much less atmospheric but equally historic. It serves great coffee and croissants. Check out the old photos on the walls.

El Gato Negro (☎ 4374-1730, *Corrientes 1669; Map 3*) Tea-lined wooden cabinets and spicy aromas welcome you to this little sipping paradise. Enjoy imported cups of coffee or tea along with breakfast and pastries.

Richmond (☎ 4322-1341, *Florida 468; Map 3*) If you're looking for a chess match or following the literary footsteps of Jorge Luis Borges, try this very traditional, pricey and richly lit place, which has been in the Microcentro since 1917.

Bar Plaza Dorrego (☎ 4361-0141, *Defensa 1098; Map 4*) You can't beat the atmosphere at this old joint; sip your café cortado by the sunny picture window and watch the world pass by. On Sunday, sidewalk tables are the star attraction.

Mr Mate (*mobile* ☎ 15-4088-4490, *Estados Unidos 523; Map 4*) Closed Mon. Savor different flavors of Argentina's national drink, as well as coffee, tea and snacks. This intimate spot also offers nightly tango, salsa and native dance classes along with shows.

Clásica y Moderna (☎ 4812-8707, *Callao 892; Map 5*) This established, brick-walled bookstore-café has live performances of folk, jazz, blues and tango. It's nicely lit and decorated and serves upscale meals.

La Biela (☎ 4804-0449, *Quintana 600; Map 5*) The porteño elite spend hours here, high on caffeine. Try the US$9.50 'special coffees' (most are laced with alcohol). It also serves Guinness for US$6.

The Coffee Store (☎ 4801-1473, *Junín 1771; Map 5*) Jonesin' for more than just your regular *café con leche*? Here's something different in Buenos Aires: flavored coffees. This café even has decaf! Snacks and desserts are also available.

Finis Terra (☎ 4831-0335, *Honduras 5190*) Closed Sun. Here's a casual yet unusual café-bar, located in Palermo Viejo. A few nights per week, storytellers will entertain while you sip your trendy drinks. Saturday is *cuentos eroticos*.

Bars

Seddon Bar (☎ 4342-3700, Defensa 695; Map 3) Antique train mirrors decorate this popular San Telmo nightspot, which has live jazz, blues, tango and even Beatles tunes on tap, along with US$3.50-5 beers and pricier munchies.

Le Cigale (☎ 4312-8275, 25 de Mayo 722; Map 3) A dark and moody atmosphere characterizes this sultry downtown watering hole. There's live music and cocktails like mai tais (US$8) and Latin lovers (US$6).

Shamrock (☎ 4812-3584, Rodríguez Peña 1220; Map 5) Rockin' during the late afternoon happy hour, this rollin' joint is decked out in dark wood and expats. Come throw a game of 501, or check out the DJ tunes and jam sessions on weekends.

Druid In (☎ 4312-3688, Reconquista 1040; Map 5) Just half a block from the too-popular Kilkenny is this much more intimate Irish bar. Live Celtic music plays at 11pm Friday, while Scottish bagpipes snazz things up good on Saturday.

Milión (☎ 4815-9925, Paraná 1048; Map 5) This richly elegant, dimly lit and very popular bar occupies three floors in a renovated old mansion. Pricey tapas accompany a wide range of drinks like white Russians, mint juleps and Long Island iced tea (all US$7).

Gran Bar Danzón (☎ 4811-1108, Libertad; Map 5) This is a nicely designed wine bar, popular with the young, fashionable crowd.

Van Koning (☎ 4772-9909, Báez 325) Dutch expats love this Las Cañitas pub, complete with dark wood beams, candles, blocky furniture and a seafaring theme. Choose from 40 brews; only Heineken and Quilmes are on draft.

The following bars are spread out in trendy Palermo Viejo. For the hippest scene in town, go to Plaza Serrano at 1am (or later) on a weekend night.

The Lock In (☎ 4832-6380, Honduras 5288) Here's a lowbrow yet cool and artsy

spot reminiscent of a Seattle watering hole. Rotating disco balls keep things dynamic, while the US$3-5 pints and various cocktails keep patrons happy.

Mundo Bizarro (☎ 4773-1967, Guatemala 4802) Red lights, black counters and a decidedly *lounge* feel give this joint a young and sexy touch. An American-food-themed menu is available.

El 5to Stone (☎ 4832-4961, Nicaragua & Thames) This self-proclaimed 'rocanrol' bar plays, as one might guess, lots of Rolling Stones tunes. Friday nights are jammed inside and out (the sidewalk seating's nice) with young, hip folks sporting black threads and coolly smoking cigarettes. It stays open until 6am on weekends.

Acabar (☎ 4772-0845, Honduras 5733) This place is unlike any spot you've ever been. People come to play board and puzzle games, and the countless rooms are decked out in arty colors. Sip your trendy drink among denim-clad youths, but don't expect peace amid the din of excited gaming voices.

Discos

Buenos Aires' *boliches*, or discos, can be exclusive and expensive; cover charges at the priciest joints are around US$15, not including drinks. Very few open before midnight and it's considered uncool to arrive before 2am. Dress well.

Divino Buenos Ayres (☎ 4316-8400, Grierson 225; Map 3). So what if it looks like a flattened Sydney Opera House? It's still got a dramatic setting, with a back deck that overlooks pretty Puerto Madero at night.

Mundo Latino (☎ 4328-6872, Esmeralda 565; Map 3) Admission US$10; open nightly except Sunday. Come here to mix mostly with other South American nationals. The modern dancing space pulses with salsa, merengue and pop tunes.

Maluco Beleza (☎ 4372-1737, Sarmiento 1728; Map 3) Admission US$10 Fri-Sat. Here's a popular Brazilian boliche set in an old mansion. There are lithe and barely clad professional dancers to stir the colorful crowd.

El Living (☎ 4811-4730, MT de Alvear 1540; Map 5) Open Thur-Sat. The bar shows trendy videos and is strewn with low tables and chain smokers, while the main dance hall is lined with cushy sofas for the wallflowers. Music includes soul, funk and US hits.

Puente Mitre Complex *(Casares & Sarmiento)* Admission US$5-10; open Thur-Sun. At least five different discos compete for clients here and it's a madhouse on weekends, teeming with youthful adrenaline. It's located in Palermo's 3 de Febrero park.

Buenos Aires News *(☎ 4778-1500, Av de la Infanta Isabel & Freyre)* Admission US$10/15 women/men. Stylish folks come here to look cutting-edge cool and dance till the morning light. It's also located in Palermo's 3 de Febrero park.

Pachá *(☎ 4788-4280, Costanera Norte & La Pampa)* Saturday nights are special here; famous guest DJs from countries like Israel and Germany spin tunes for the spiffy clientele. Bring a picture ID and hop Bus No 45 from if coming from the center.

Gay & Lesbian Venues

Buenos Aires' gay scene is alive and kicking, but you have to know where to look. Check current listings in *NX* magazine (US$7) or in the free booklet *La Otra Guía*.

The main cruising area is at Avs Santa Fe and Pueyrredón, where you can get discount coupons (which are also available at gay bars). Go to bars at midnight, don't bother to arrive at clubs before 2am, and be ready to party hard till the morning light. To wind down from a night of indulgence, head to the confitería ***El Olmo*** *(☎ 4821-5828, Santa Fe & Pueyrredón; Map 5)*.

The following are mainly bars although some offer shows.

Sitges *(☎ 4861-3763, Córdoba 4119)* Open Wed-Sun nights; 1 drink minimum. Packed on a Saturday night, this bar plays loud, beat-laden music in a simple brick space for a casual mixed clientele of amorous gays and lesbians.

Bach Bar *(no ☎, Cabrera 4390)* Open from 10pm Tues-Sun. This small and intimate venue is popular with lesbians. Weekend nights can get loud, with dancing amid the tables and artsy surroundings.

GSL *(Gasoil; ☎ 4864-4056, Bulnes 1250)* Admission US$10 including drink; open 12am Thur-Mon, weekend shows at 2am. Strippers, singers and *transformistas* entertain the gay and lesbian clientele among smoky colored lights.

Bar Alvear *(☎ 4816-9227, Alvear 1461; Map 5)* Blend in with the upper class at this bar with moving kaleidoscopic lights inside and fabulous window dressing outside.

The following are mainly dance clubs; most don't open until 1am.

Amerika *(☎ 4865-4416, Gascón 1040)* Admission US$8/10 Fri/Sat with coupon, US$15 without; open Fri & Sat. This dance club on the southern edge of Palermo Viejo fills its dance floor with techno, '90s hits and Latin; despite the free booze it's not insane (the floors get sticky, though). It's best on Saturday nights, and hets (also known as heterosexuals) are also welcome.

Glam *(☎ 4963-2521, Cabrera 3046)* No admission; 1 drink minimum. Techno music reverberates through the disco-ball room, brick hallways and bar patios. On the southern edge of Palermo Viejo, this club is jammed with mostly casually dressed, young gay men on Thursday and Saturday nights.

Palacio Alsina *(no ☎, Alsina 940; Map 3)* Admission US$8 with coupon, US$12 without; open Fri only. A fairy tale palace, with chandeliers, thick drapes and three balconied floors. Colored lights let you know you're not in Kansas anymore, as do the thick disco beats.

Oxen *(no ☎, Sarmiento 1662; Map 3)* Admission US$8-12, less with discount cards, includes drink. Step into this large, modern space and you'll feel like you're in a music video, with lights, action and good-looking guys checking each other out.

ADN *(no ☎, Suipacha 927; Map 5)* Admission free until 12:30am, then US$5-8 including drink; open Fri & Sat; lesbians only. Descend into a dark, womb-like space with video screens and all sorts of pop music.

Angel's *(no ☎, Viamonte 2168)* Admission US$6 with coupon, US$12 without; open Thur-Sat. Angel's is *the* place for transvestites, many in short skirts, high-heeled boots and platinum blonde wigs. On Saturday there's a male strip show.

Live Music Venues

Rock, Blues & Jazz *The Road* (☎ 4524-1234, Viceto Vega 5885) Admission US$3-5, includes drink; open Thur-Sun nights. Good old rock and roll plays here, along with blues. It's on the edge of Palermo Viejo, and a favorite with locals. Bring your earplugs because this place really jams.

El Samovar de Rasputín (☎ 4302-3190, Del Valle Iberlucea 1251) Admission US$5; open Fri & Sat nights. Blues biggie Taj Mahal has crooned here, though Argentine bands play most of the time. The decor is as eccentric as the owner Napo himself. Bus 29 gets you to La Boca from the center. Check out the photos of Napo with Keith Richards and Eric Clapton.

Blues Special Club (☎ 4854-2338, Almirante Brown 102; Map 4) Admission US$5-15. Fridays are good for jam sessions, while Saturday at midnight the shows really start rockin'. Famous blues folk like Dave Myers, Eddie King and Aron Burton have put in time here. Take Bus 29.

La Trastienda (☎ 4342-7650, Balcarce 460; Map 3) Admission US$5-8. Merengue and salsa, rock and blues, Latin pop and tango – it's all here in San Telmo, and coming at you live. Call for the changing schedule.

Notorious (☎ 4815-8473, Callao 966; Map 5) Admission US$8-10, student discount available. Up front you sit at modern glassy tables, listening to CDs before you buy them, while in back the café plays live jazz almost every night.

Gandalf (☎ 4824-4086, Guise 1924) Closed Mon. Drop in after midnight for their Friday and Saturday night jazz sessions. The atmosphere's pretty intimate, with blocky wooden tables and chairs surrounded by rustic brick walls.

Club de Vino (☎ 4833-0050, Cabrera 4737) Admission US$10-20. This place in Palermo Viejo has a good space for jazz and all things elegant; the schedule changes weekly so give them a buzz.

Flamenco & Folk For more information on flamenco venues and classes, check *Contratiempo* (☎ 4951-6608), a free monthly newsletter available at tourist offices, cultural centers and the Spanish embassy.

Avila Bar (☎ 4383-6974, Av de Mayo 1384; Map 3) Order dinner at this small Spanish restaurant and watch the free flamenco show, which starts at 11pm Thursday to Saturday.

La Panadería (☎ 4861-7233, Medrano 1502) This rustic restaurant has flamenco on Friday, but the surrounding area of archeological digs is worth seeing anytime.

La Peña del Colorado (☎ 4822-1038, Güemes 3657) Admission US$7/5 men/women after 11pm Thur-Sat; closed Mon. Pick up a provided guitar and strum it along with singing porteños. The rustic brick and stucco space reeks of local scents, and you can nibble some northern specialties too.

Tiempo de Gitanos (☎ 4776-6143, El Salvador 5575) Open Thur-Sun. This Palermo Viejo spot offers live jazz, blues, flamenco, candombe and folk music in an intimate and comfortable restaurant setting.

Guayana (☎ 4381-4350, Lima 27; Map 3) For great local working-class flavor, check out this nondescript confitería near 9 de Julio. There's live tango and folk music 12:30am to 5am on Friday and Saturday, and 10pm to 1am Sunday.

Mr Mate (☎ 15-4088-4490, Estados Unidos 523; Map 4) Friday and Saturday are folklore nights, and Mr Mate is a wonderfully friendly and cozy venue. (See also the review under Places to Eat.)

Tango Venues

Tango is experiencing a major boom at both the amateur and professional levels, and among all ages and classes. Free booklets *el tangauta* and *BA Tango* are both full of ads for shows and lessons. The following places mostly put on shows; see Tango classes, earlier in this chapter, for instruction and milongas (dance halls).

Feria de San Telmo (Plaza Dorrego; Map 4) Professional dancers entertain tourists on Sunday and only ask for your loose change.

[continued on page 155]

TANGO ANYONE?

The air hangs heavy, smoky and dark. Streams of diffused light illuminate a large, open space. A lone woman, dressed in a slit skirt and high heels, sits with knees crossed at one of the small tables surrounding a wooden dance floor. Her eyes dart from face to face, sweeping the crowd, looking for a subtle signal. Finally she picks out the *cabezazo*, a quick tilt of the head. She briefly considers the stranger's offer, decides, then nods with a slight smile. His smile is broader, and he gets up to approach her table. As he nears, she rises to meet him, and, joined together now, the new pair advances onto the dance floor, reaching it just as the sultry music begins to play. And they dance the tango.

The tango has a long and somewhat complex history. Its exact origins can't be pinpointed, but the dance is thought to have started in Buenos Aires during the 1880s. Legions of European immigrants, mostly lower-class men, arrived in the great village of Buenos Aires to seek their fortune in the new country. They settled on the capital's *arrabales* (fringes), but missing their motherlands and the women they left behind, they sought out bordellos to ease the loneliness. Here, the men mingled with prostitutes and – while waiting for them – invented a dance with one another. It was a strong blend of machismo, passion and longing, with an almost fighting edge to it: the dance was symbolic of a struggle for the possession of a woman – no surprise considering what they were waiting for.

Small musical ensembles were soon brought together in these bordellos to accompany early tangos, playing tunes influenced by Pampas *milonga* verse, Spanish and Italian melodies and African *candombe* drums. (The *bandoneón*, a type of small accordion, was brought to these sessions and has since become an inextricable part of the tango orchestra.) Here, the tango song was also born: it summarized the immigrants' new urban experience and was permeated with nostalgia for a disappearing way of life. Themes ranged from profound feelings about changing neighborhoods to the figure of the mother, male friendship and betrayal by women; not infrequently, raunchy lyrics were added.

So far the tango had been a form of male bonding, but when men started dancing with the prostitutes themselves rather than simply with each other, the dance became less melancholy and more sexually demonstrative. Unsurprisingly, this vulgarity was deeply frowned upon by Victorian porteño society, but it did manage to influence some brash young members of the upper classes. These rebel jet-setters took the new novelty to Paris and inflamed it into a craze – a dance that became an acceptable outlet of human desires expressed on the dance floors of elegant cabarets. The tango quickly spread through Europe and even reached the US during the early years of the 20th century; 1913 was considered by some to be 'the year of the tango.' When the evolved and popularized dance returned to Buenos Aires it came back refined and famous, and finally earned the respectability it deserved. The golden years of tango were just beginning.

Gardel & The Tango In June 1935, a Cuban woman committed suicide in Havana, while a woman in New York and another in Puerto Rico tried to poison themselves, all over a man none of them had ever met. The man, whose smiling photograph graced their rooms, had just died in a plane crash in Medellín, Colombia. On his body's long odyssey to its final resting place in Argentina, Latin Americans thronged to pay him tribute in Colombia, New York, Rio de Janeiro and Montevideo. Once in Buenos Aires, a horse-drawn carriage took him to the Cementerio de la Chacarita, where a special tomb had been erected. The man was tango singer Carlos Gardel, *El Zorzal Criollo*, the songbird of Buenos Aires.

Though born in France, Gardel was the epitome of the immigrant porteño. When he was three, his destitute, single mother brought him from Europe to Buenos Aires. In his youth, he worked at a variety of menial jobs but also managed to entertain neighbors with his rapturous singing. A performing career began after he befriended Uruguayan-born José Razzano, and they sang together in a popular duo until Razzano lost his voice. From 1917 onward, Gardel performed solo.

Carlos Gardel played a huge role in creating the tango *canción* (song), taking it out of Buenos Aires' brothels and tenements to Paris and New York. His croon-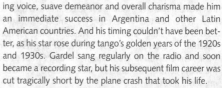ing voice, suave demeanor and overall charisma made him an immediate success in Argentina and other Latin American countries. And his timing couldn't have been better, as his star rose during tango's golden years of the 1920s and 1930s. Gardel sang regularly on the radio and soon became a recording star, but his subsequent film career was cut tragically short by the plane crash that took his life.

Each day a steady procession of pilgrims visits Carlos Gardel's plaque-covered sarcophagus in the Cementerio de la Chacarita, where a lit cigarette often smolders between the metal fingers of his life-size statue. On December 11, 1990, the centenary of his birth, his tomb was completely covered in floral tributes. The large, devoted community of his followers, known as *gardelianos*, cannot pass a day without listening to his songs or watching his films. Another measure of his ongoing influence is the common saying that 'Gardel sings better every day.' Elvis should be so lucky.

Carlos Gardel

Tango at a Milonga Today Tango is not an easy dance to describe, and it needs to be seen and experienced to fully appreciate it. Despite a long evolution from its bordello origins, it's still a sensual and erotic dance. The upper bodies are held upright and close, with faces almost touching. A man's hand is pressed against the woman's back, guiding her, while his other hand is clasped together in hers and extended outward. The lower body does most of the work for both partners. The woman's hips swivel and her legs alternate in short or wide sweeps and quick kicks, sometimes between the man's legs. All the while the man guides her and adds his own fancy pivoting moves. Abrupt pauses and changes of direction punctuate the dance. It's a serious business that takes tremendous concentration, and during the dance the pair will wear hard, purposeful expressions. Smiling and chatting are reserved for in between songs.

At a proper, established *milonga* (tango dance hall), choosing an adequate partner involves many levels of hidden codes, rules and signals that dancers must follow. After all, no serious *tanguista* (long-time tango dancer) wants to be caught dancing with someone stepping inexpertly on their toes (or expensive tango heels). In fact, some men will ask an unknown woman to dance only after the second song in a tango session, so as not to be stuck with her for the full four songs that make up a session. It's considered impolite to dance fewer than two songs with any partner, so if you are given a curt *'gracias'* after just one song, consider that partner unavailable for the rest of the night.

Your location and proximity to the dance floor can be critical. At some older milongas, the more established dancers have key tables reserved for them. Ideally, you want to have easy access to the floor and to other dancers' line of sight. You may notice couples sitting farther back in the shadows (they often dance just with each other), while singles place themselves right up front. And if a man comes into the room with a woman at his side, she is considered 'his' for the night. For couples to dance with partners besides one another, they either enter the room separately or else the man signals his intent by asking another woman to the floor. Then 'his' woman becomes open for asking.

The signal, or cabezazo, is one of the more interesting milonga traits. It involves a quick tilt of the head, eye contact and uplifted eyebrows. This can happen from all the way across the room. The woman to whom the cabezazo is directed either nods yes and smiles, or pretends not to have noticed it (a rejection, of course). If she says yes, the man gets up and escorts her to the floor. A hint: if you're at a milonga and don't want to dance, don't make too much eye contact with others in the crowd; you could be inadvertently breaking some hearts.

[continued from page 151]

Bar Sur (☎ 4362-6086, *Estados Unidos 299; Map 4*) Show & unlimited pizza US$15, drinks extra; show time 7pm-3am. This very intimate venue has about a dozen small tables surrounding a small dance floor.

Café Homero (☎ 4777-7015, *Cabrera 4946*) Admission US$7-20; open Fri-Sun nights. This cozy neighborhood *tanguería* in Palermo Viejo presents intimate tango shows and music.

Club del Vino (☎ 4833-0050, *Cabrera 4737*) Admission US$7-25; open Fri-Sat nights. Live blues, jazz and folk music all play at this club in Palermo Viejo, but Saturday nights are always tango. There's a fine restaurant, wine bar and small wine museum, and the theatrical space is nicely laid out and not too large.

La Cumparsita (☎ 4361-6880, *Chile 302; Map 4*) Show with 2 drinks & snack plate US$25; show time 10pm-4am. Small tango bands accompany the tango dancers here, with singers putting in their share.

Centro Cultural Torquato Tasso (☎ 4307-6506, *Defensa 1575; Map 4*) This colorful, spacious venue offers free or cheap tango shows at 11pm weekends, as well as free milongas (11pm Friday) with live orchestral accompaniment, which is a bit unique even here in Buenos Aires. Classes are available.

The following are the most expensive and touristy tango shows in BA, which is not to say they're bad. They just tend to be more sensationalized. Many have a dinner option; shows start around 10pm, but call ahead to confirm the exact time.

La Ventana (☎ 4331-0127, *Balcarce 431; Map 3*) Dinner & show US$70 & students US$50 with hotel pickup; US$45 for show only. Along with tango dances there are folkloric shows and altiplano music. The space is pretty modern and holds up to 240 people.

El Querandí (☎ 4345-1770, *Perú 302; Map 3*) Dinner & show US$60, show only US$45. This large corner venue, which is also a restaurant, offers tango and music on a high stage; dark wood details add atmosphere.

El Viejo Almacén (☎ 4307-7388, *Balcarce & Independencia; Map 4*) Show US$40, dinner US$20, includes wine and snacks. This is a long-running and highly regarded performance, with exceptionally professional singers, dancers and musicians.

Señor Tango (☎ 4303-0231, *Vieytes 1653*) Dinner & show US$55, show only US$40. This is one of the most extravagant shows in Buenos Aires; be prepared for mounted horses, a rising orchestra pit, rotating stages, dry ice and athletic dancing.

Classical Music, Opera & Theater

The regular season for classical music and opera runs from March through November, but is best June through August. Theater is good all year-round. Here's a sampling of some venues:

Teatro Colón (☎ 4378-7344, **W** *www.teatrocolon .org.ar, Libertad 621; Map 3*) This premier venue for the arts has hosted prominent figures like Enrico Caruso, Plácido Domingo and Luciano Pavarotti.

Teatro Avenida (☎ 4381-0662, *Av de Mayo 1222; Map 3*)

Teatro El Vitral (☎ 4371-0948, *Rodríguez Peña 344; Map 3*)

Teatro General San Martín (☎ 4371-0111, 0800-333-5254, *Corrientes 1530; Map 3*)

Teatro La Plaza (☎ 4370-5350, *Corrientes 1660; Map 3*)

Teatro Ópera (☎ 4326-1335, *Corrientes 860; Map 3*)

Teatro Presidente Alvear (☎ 4374-6076, *Corrientes 1659; Map 3*)

La Scala de San Telmo (☎ 4362-1187, *Pasaje Giuffra 371; Map 4*)

Teatro Coliseo (☎ 4816-6115, *Marcelo T del Alvear 1125; Map 5*)

Teatro Nacional Cervantes (☎ 4816-4224, *Libertad 815; Map 5*)

Cinemas

Buenos Aires is known for its cinemas, which play first-run films from around the world. The main cinema districts are along the Lavalle pedestrian mall west of Florida, and on Corrientes and Santa Fe; all are within easy walking distance from downtown. The larger shopping galleries also have cineplexes. There are half-price discounts on certain midweek days, and sometimes for the first afternoon showing.

Since Spanish translations of English-language film titles are often misleading, check the *Buenos Aires Herald* to be certain what's playing. Except for children's films and cartoon features, which are dubbed, foreign films almost always appear in the original language with Spanish subtitles.

SPECTATOR SPORTS

Spectator sports in Buenos Aires include soccer, horse racing, polo and the Argentine gaucho game of *pato*. Tennis, rugby, cricket and Formula One automobile racing also have a following.

Soccer

Argentine soccer is world-class: the national team won the World Cup in 1978 and 1986, and Buenos Aires has the highest density of first-division soccer teams in the world. For information on tickets and schedules, contact the clubs listed below. *Entradas populares* (standing-room admissions) cost about US$10, while *plateas* (fixed seats) cost US$20 and up. Tickets are usually bought at the stadium.

Argentinos Juniors (☎ 4551-6887), Punta Arenas 1271

Boca Juniors (☎ 4362-2260), Brandsen 805

Club Atlético Vélez Sarsfield (☎ 4641-5663), Juan B Justo 9200

Club Deportivo Español (☎ 4612-9648), Santiago de Compostela 3801

Club Ferrocarril Oeste (☎ 4431-9203), Avellaneda 1240

Club Huracán (☎ 4942-1965), Almancio Alcorta 2570

River Plate (☎ 4788-1200), Presidente Figueroa Alcorta 7597

San Lorenzo de Almagro (☎ 4922-7000). Fernández de la Cruz 2145

SHOPPING

Buenos Aires has some good buys. The main shopping zones are downtown along the Florida pedestrian mall and Av Santa Fe, although Recoleta is another worthwhile area

(but expensive). Ritzy shopping centers such as *Galerías Pacífico* (☎ 4311-6323, *Florida & Córdoba; Map 3), Patio Bullrich* (☎ 4815-3501, *Posadas & Libertad, Map 5), and Alto Palermo* (☎ 4821-6030, *Santa Fe & Coronel Diaz),* have begun to take business away from the traditional commercial centers.

The largest concentration of jewelry shops is on Libertad south of Corrientes. The barrio of Once, near the Once train station, is *the* place for cheap (though not the highest quality) clothing. Buenos Aires' best buys are antiques, leather goods, street-market crafts and souvenirs such as *mate* paraphernalia.

Soccer fans will find the best deals on shirts, flags and many other *fútbol* items either around the stadiums (especially on game days) or in and around the bus terminals (especially Retiro).

For antiques, go to San Telmo. Countless shops and galleries sell authentic stuff, though prices aren't cheap.

Below are a few recommended stores.

Leather Shoes & Products

Flabella (☎ 4322-6036, *Suipacha 263; Map 3)* for tango heels

Casa López (☎ 4311-3044, *Marcelo T de Alvear 640/658; Map 5)*

Guido Mocasines (☎ 4813-4095, *Rodríguez Peña 1290; Map 5); (☎ 4811-4567, Quintana 333; Map 5)*

Lionel Frenkel (☎ 4312-9806, *San Martín 1085; Map 5)*

Rossi y Carusso (☎ 4811-1965, *Santa Fe 1601; Map 5); (☎ 4319-5303, Galerías Pacificos; Map 3)*

Welcome Marroquinería (☎ 4312-8911, *Marcelo T de Alvear 500; Map 5)*

Crafts & Souvenirs

Kelly's Regionales (☎ 4311-5712, *Paraguay 431; Map 5)* for cowskin rugs, ponchos and tons of knick-knacks

La Querencia (☎ 4312-1879, *Esmeralda 1018; Map 5)* for cow udder bowls, horse gear and *mate* paraphernalia

Music

El Coleccionista (☎ 4322-0359, *Esmeralda 562; Map 3)* good selection and a knowledgeable staff

Free Blues (☎ 15-4057-4751, Rodríguez Peña 438; Map 3) for new and used CDs, cassettes and LPs

Musimundo (☎ 4322-9298, Florida 269; ☎ 4576-7977, Florida 665; Map 3); (☎ 4814-0393, Santa Fe 1844, Barrio Norte; Map 5) one of Buenos Aires' largest music retailers

Books

Aquilanti (☎ 4952-4546, Rincón 79; Map 3) for antique books

El Ateneo (☎ 4325-6801, Florida 340; Map 3); (☎ 4813-6052, Santa Fe 1860; Map 5) a wide selection of books in English and Spanish

Librería Platero (☎ 4382-2215, Talcahuano 485; Map 3) for hard-core bookworms only

Librería ABC (☎ 4314-8106, Córdoba 685; Map 5) a wide selection of books in English and German

Oficina del Libro Francés (☎ 4311-0363, Esmeralda 861; Map 5) for books in French only, mais oui

Librerías Turísticas (☎/fax 4963-2866, Paraguay 2457) for guidebooks and maps

Camping Supplies

Asatej Travel Store (☎ 4313-5445, Florida 835 first floor; Map 5) backpacks, sleeping bags and some clothing; ISIC cardholders receive 10-20% off purchases.

Fugate (☎ 4982-0203, Gascón 238) far from center, on Subte Línea A to Castro Barros

Polo Gear

Alberto Vannucci (☎ 4811-3112, Callao 1773; Map 5)

Jorge Cánaves (☎ 4785-3982, Libertador 6000, Belgrano)

La Martina (☎ 4576-7997, Paraguay 661; Map 5)

Art

Galería Ruth Benzacar (☎ 4313-8480, Florida 1000, 1st floor; Map 5)

Galería Federico Klemm (☎ 4312-2058, Marcelo T de Alvear 636, 1st floor; Map 5)

Galería Rubbers (☎ 4393-6010, Suipacha 1175; Map 5); (☎ 4816-1782, Santa Fe 1860, 2nd & 3rd floors; Map 5)

Galería Zurbarán (☎ 4815-1556, Cerrito 1522; Map 5)

Craft Fairs

Feria de San Telmo (Plaza Dorrego; Map 4) Sun only. This fair brims with antique stalls, tango shows and tourists taking it all in.

Recoleta fair (in front of Recoleta cemetery; Map 5) Open weekends. This popular event has hundreds of booths filled with leather goods, jewelry, hats, handmade crafts and some kitschy stuff. Bakers circulate pastry goods, and mimes perform (or just stand very still).

Feria Plaza Belgrano (Juramento & Cuba) Open 10am-8pm weekends & holidays. This Belgrano market is a popular place on a sunny weekend. You'll find good quality imaginative crafts here, as well as some tacky junk.

Feria de Mataderos (☎ 4687-5602, Av Lisandro de la Torre & Av de los Corrales) Open 11am-6pm Sun & holidays, April to December. In the southwestern barrio of Mataderos is this excellent, lively market with handmade goods, authentic parrilla and tasty sweets. It's frequented by gauchos, folk singers and costumed dancers. From downtown, take bus No 155 (also says 180) or 126.

GETTING THERE & AWAY
Air

Buenos Aires has two airports: Aeropuerto Internacional Ministro Pistarini (commonly known as Ezeiza) and Aeroparque Jorge Newbery (commonly known as Aeroparque).

International Many major international airlines have offices or representatives in Buenos Aires. Most of the following serve Ezeiza for long-distance international flights, but a few from neighboring countries use Aeroparque.

Aeroflot (☎ 4312-5573; Map 5), Santa Fe 822

Air France (☎ 4317-4700; Map 5), Paraguay 610, 14th floor

Alitalia (☎ 4310-9999; Map 5), Suipacha 1111, 28th floor

American Airlines (☎ 4318-1111; Map 5), Santa Fe 881

Avianca (☎ 4394-5990; Map 5), Carlos Pellegrini 1163, 4th floor

British Airways (☎ 4320-6600; Map 3), Viamonte 570

Canadian Airlines (☎ 4327-3640; Map 3), Córdoba 656

Cubana de Aviación (☎ 4326-5291; Map 3), Sarmiento 552, 11th floor

Delta (☎ 4312-1200; Map 3), Reconquista 737, 3rd floor (temporarily)

Iberia (☎ 4131-1000; Map 5), Carlos Pellegrini 1163, 1st floor

Japan Airlines (☎ 4393-1896; Map 3), Córdoba 836, 11th floor

KLM (☎ 4326-8422; Map 3), Suipacha 268, 9th floor

Korean Air (☎ 4311-9237; Map 5), Córdoba 755

LanChile (☎ 4378-2200; Map 5), Cerrito 866

Lloyd Aéreo Boliviano (LAB; ☎ 4323-1900; Map 3), Carlos Pellegrini 141

Lufthansa (☎ 4319-0600; Map 5), MT de Alvear 636

Malaysia Airlines (☎ 4314-1423; Map 5), Suipacha 1111, 14th floor

Mexicana (☎ 4312-6152; Map 5), Córdoba 755, 1st floor

Pluna (☎ 4342-4420; Map 3), Florida 1

Swissair (☎ 4319-0000; Map 5), Santa Fe 846

TAP (Air Portugal; ☎ 4811-0984; Map 5), Cerrito 1136

Trans Brasil (☎ 4312-0856; Map 3), Reconquista 737 4th floor

Transportes Aéreos de Mercosur (TAM; ☎ 4816-1000; Map 5), Cerrito 1026

United Airlines (☎ 4316-0777; Map 5), Eduardo Madero 900, 1st floor

Varig (☎ 4329-9211; Map 3), Córdoba 972, 4th floor

Vasp (☎ 4311-2699; Map 5), Santa Fe 784

Domestic Most domestic and some regional flights leave from Aeroparque Jorge Newbery, a short distance north of downtown, but a few use Ezeiza. To Uruguay, in particular, services from Aeroparque are cheaper and more convenient than the major international airlines at Ezeiza.

Aerolíneas Argentinas & Austral (☎ 0810-222-86527, Map 5), Leandro N Alem 1134

Dinar Líneas Aéreas (☎ 4327-8000; Map 3), Diagonal Roque Sáenz Peña 933

Líneas Aéreas del Estado (LADE; ☎ 4361-7071; Map 4), Perú 714

Líneas Aéreas de Entre Ríos (LAER; ☎ 4311-5237; Map 5), Suipacha 844

Líneas Aéreas Privadas Argentinas (LAPA; ☎ 4819-5272; Map 5), Carlos Pellegrini 1075

Southern Winds (☎ 4515-8600; Map 5), Santa Fe 784

Bus

Buenos Aires' massive and modern Retiro bus terminal is next to Retiro train station (Map 5). It's a quarter mile long and has slots for 75 buses. There are three floors: the bottom floor is for cargo shipments and luggage storage, the top for purchasing tickets and the middle for everything else. There are a couple of information booths (☎ 4310-0700) that provide general bus information and schedules; they'll also help you with the local bus system. Other services include a limited-hours tourist office at Local 83 (towards the middle of the station on the 2nd floor), telephone offices (some with Internet access), restaurants, cafés and dozens of small stores.

Bus companies are grouped by Argentina's geographical areas, so if you're going to Córdoba, all companies that serve that city will be close together. International companies are at the far northern end of the station.

You can buy a ticket to practically any destination in Argentina from Buenos Aires, and departures are fairly frequent to the most popular destinations. Reservations are not necessary except during peak summer and winter holiday seasons, but purchasing your ticket a day ahead of time is still not a bad idea.

Here are some destinations and fares:

Destinations	Duration in hours	Cost
Asunción (Par)	18	US$40
Bahía Blanca	10	US$19
Bariloche	22	US$40
Comodoro Rivadavia	28	US$65
Córdoba	9½	US$16
Foz do Iguaçu (Bra)	20	US$36
La Quiaca	28	US$70
Mar del Plata	5½	US$20
Mendoza	16	US$35
Montevideo (Uru)	8	US$29
Puerto Iguazú	16	US$45
Puerto Madryn	20	US$50
Punta del Este (Uru)	9	US$35
Resistencia	13	US$30
Rio de Janeiro (Bra)	42	US$121
Rosario	4	US$21
Santa Fé	6	US$23
Santa Rosa	8	US$25
Santiago (Chi)	20	US$60
São Paulo (Bra)	38	US$108

Be aware that these are just a sampling of prices available; your final ticket price will be determined by the particular bus company, time of travel (fares spike during high seasons like January, February, July and holiday weekends) and the general Argentine economy. Promotional prices are sometimes available, and you can try asking for a student discount at some companies (though this practice is becoming less common).

Train

Despite major reductions in long-distance train service, rail lines continue to serve most of the Buenos Aires suburbs and nearby provinces. Here are the following train stations (all served by Subte) and their destinations:

Estación Retiro (Map 5)
• Belgrano line (☎ 0800-777-3377) to the northern suburbs
• Mitre line (☎ 4317-4445) to Tigre, Rosario
• San Martín (☎ 4304-0023, 4311-8704) to the northern suburbs

Estación Constitución (Map 4)
• Roca line (☎ 4304-0028) to the southern suburbs, Rosario, La Plata, Bahía Blanca, Atlantic beach towns

Estación Once
• Sarmiento line (☎ 4861-0043) to the southwestern suburbs, Luján, Santa Rosa

Estación Lacroze
• Urquiza line (☎ 4553-9214) from the terminus of Subte Línea B (Map 3) to the northwestern suburbs

During holiday periods like Christmas or national holidays, buy tickets in advance. Remember that Atlantic beach destinations have many more trains in summer than at other times. Train fares tend to be lower than bus fares, but trains are slower and there are fewer departure times and destinations.

Car

You have to be very brave and patient to get behind the wheel in this country; quick reflexes wouldn't hurt either. For information on driving in Buenos Aires, see the Getting Around section, later. For information on driving in Argentina, see the Getting Around chapter.

Boat

Buenos Aires has daily ferry and hydrofoil services to Colonia, Uruguay (US$21-34), with bus connections to Montevideo (add US$8). There are also direct ferries to Montevideo (US$58), with bus connections to Punta del Este (add US$10). These sail from the Buquebus terminal or the Ferrylíneas terminal, both downtown near Av Antártida Argentina and Córdoba (Map 5). You can buy tickets right at the terminals, but Buquebus also has offices at the Patio Bullrich shopping center (Map 5) and in the main headquarters of ACA in Palermo on Av del Libertador 1850. Ferrylíneas has a ticketing office (☎ 4311-4700) at Maipú 866 (Map 5). There are many more services in the busy summer season.

Cacciola (☎ 4749-0329), Lavalle 520, Tigre, also has daily boat-bus combinations to Colonia (US$28) and Montevideo (US$38). You can even arrange to get picked up from downtown. Cacciola has an office (☎ 4394-5520) in Buenos Aires at Florida 520, 1st floor, Oficina 113 (Map 3).

Note that the prices quoted here are all one-way, and vary depending on the duration of the trip. Call the companies to verify details and times.

GETTING AROUND

Most of the tourist destinations are either walking distance from one another or within easy access by public transport.

To/From the Airports

Buenos Aires has two airports. Aeropuerto Internacional Ministro Pistarini (commonly known as Ezeiza) is about 35km south of downtown and serves mainly international destinations. Most domestic flights and some to Uruguay leave from Aeroparque Jorge Newbery (commonly known as Aeroparque), just a few kilometers north of downtown. Departure and arrival information for both airports, in English and Spanish, is available at ☎ 5480-6111.

Ezeiza The cheapest way to get to and from Ezeiza is the No 86 bus (US$1.35). If you're going to the airport be sure the bus says 'Ezeiza,' since not all No 86 buses go all the way to the airport. The bus starts in La Boca and goes along Av de Mayo past the Plaza del Congreso. Both buses leave Ezeiza from the Aerolíneas Argentinas terminal, a short walk from the international terminal where all carriers except Aerolíneas arrive. Because of heavy traffic, figure at least 1½ hours to Ezeiza.

Manuel Tienda León (☎ 4314-3636, Av Santa Fe 790; Map 5) runs a comfortable and efficient bus service to/from (US$14/11) Ezeiza. The drop-off and pick-up site in the city is from their office on Santa Fe 790. Regular services start at 4am from the city to airport and continue about every half-hour until 9:30pm. For an extra US$3 you can be dropped off at your hotel. Transfers from Ezeiza to Aeroparque costs US$11.

Competing with them is Ecuador (☎ 4312-8883, Florida 1045; Map 5), which charges slightly less to Ezeiza (from Ezeiza the price is the same). Buses depart hourly between 5:15am and 9:15pm. Both these bus services offer limited hotel pickup or drop off for a small extra charge, and travel time to the airport is about 40 minutes.

Depending on your point of departure, a taxi to Ezeiza from downtown will cost around US$25, including tolls. There's a monopoly syndicate at the airport itself (so outside taxis can't complete unless they are called in). You may be able to get a taxi ride into town for about US$35.

Aeroparque Jorge Newbery From just outside Aeroparque, on Av Costanera Rafael Obligado, city buses Nos 33 and 45 go close to downtown (don't cross the street; take them going south). To get to Aeroparque take buses Nos 33, 37 (make sure it says 'Ciudad Universitaria'), 45 or 160.

Manuel Tienda León and Ecuador (see above) both run buses to and from Aeroparque (US$5, 20 minutes) starting at 7:10am and continuing half-hourly to 9:40pm.

Taxis between the airport and downtown cost about US$8.

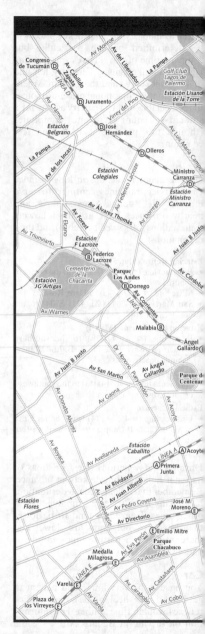

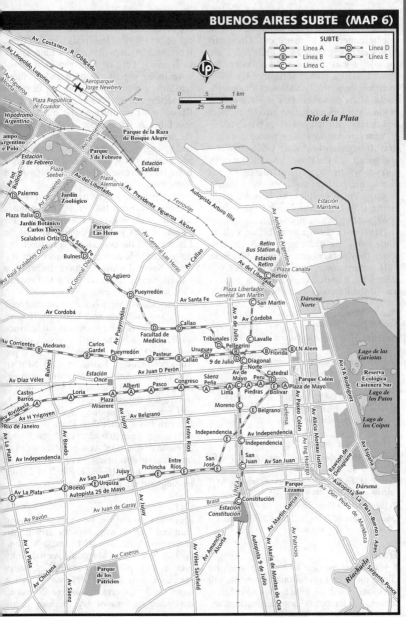

BUENOS AIRES SUBTE (MAP 6)

SUBTE
A Línea A
B Línea B
C Línea C
D Línea D
E Línea E

Bus

Buenos Aires' huge and complex bus system can be unnerving to figure out. Good bus guides, including *Guía Lumi* and *Guía T* are for sale at most kiosks and bookstores for about US$10; a pocket version of *Guía T* is sometimes available on the street for a couple bucks. Many porteños, such as older people or kiosk vendors, have memorized the system and can instantly tell you which bus to take.

Your fare will depend on where you want to go, though most rides are US$0.80. When you board, tell the driver your destination, and you will be charged accordingly. Or, act like a true porteño and just say *'ochenta'* (eighty). Put your coins (no bills accepted) in the ticket machine behind the driver; you'll receive any small change.

Have extra change available as well, as some coins are unceremoniously rejected (often they're fake but are great souvenirs).

Here are some bus routes to get you started. Each route has its own color, so after a while you'll recognize your bus more readily.

Plaza de Mayo to Ezeiza Airport: No 86 (Be sure placard says ' Ezeiza.')

Plaza San Martin to Aeroparque Jorge Newbery: No 45

La Boca, San Telmo, (near) Plaza de Mayo, Retiro, Recoleta, Palermo: No 152 north

La Boca, San Telmo, Plaza de Mayo, Obelisco, Teatro Colón, Palermo's parks: No 29 north

Barrio Norte, Teatro Colón, (near) Congreso, Constitución, La Boca: No 39 south

Palermo, Recoleta, Retiro, (near) Plaza de Mayo, San Telmo, La Boca: No 152 south

Palermo, Recoleta, Retiro, Constitución: No 59 south

Retiro via the length of Cerrito (essentially Av 9 de Julio) to Constitución: No 100 south

Retiro, Palermo Viejo: No 106 north

Once, Congreso, Plaza de Mayo, San Telmo, La Boca: No 64 east and south

Train

If you are an average tourist, you won't be taking the train to get around town; the rail lines are used to reach Buenos Aires' suburbs. For an idea of these destinations, see the Getting There & Away section, earlier.

Subte (Underground)

South America's oldest underground railway opened in 1913 and is still quick and efficient. It presently consists of five lines: Líneas A, B, C, D and E. Four of these run from downtown to the capital's western and northern outskirts, while Línea C runs north-south, connecting the two major train stations of Retiro and Constitución. The oldest Subte line, Línea A, offers a tarnished reminder of the city's elegant past, with its tiled stations and vintage wood trams. There are plans to add a new north-south line and extend Línea B beyond Lacroze. (See the Buenos Aires Subte map on the previous page.)

The private operator Metrovías has notably improved the Subte's cleanliness, security and emergency assistance. New Japanese cars have been introduced on Línea B, and the company has restored the magnificent tile artwork in many older stations. Several stations have impressive murals, mostly those on Línea D between Catedral and Palermo.

One-ride *cospeles* (tokens) or magnetic cards for the Subte cost US$0.70. To save time and hassle buy several rides, since queues can get backed up (especially during rush hour). Trains operate 5am to 10pm Monday through Saturday and 8am to 10pm Sunday. Service is frequent on weekdays, but on weekends you'll wait longer.

At a few stations, like Alberti on Línea A, you can only go in one direction (toward Primera Junta rather than Plaza de Mayo), so you may have to backtrack to reach your ultimate destination. At some stations, platforms are on opposite sides of the station, so verify which platform is needed *before* passing through the turnstiles.

Car

Motorists should be aware that between 7am and 7pm on weekdays the area in Microcentro bounded by Av Leandro N Alem, Av Córdoba, Av de Mayo and Av 9 de Julio is off limits to private motor vehicles, except for buses, taxis and delivery vans. Also, the lanes on Av Libertador change directions depending on time of day; there are more lanes going into the city in the morning and more going out of the city at night. Try not to run afoul of the local police; fines are stiff and bribing is rampant.

The following car-rental agencies are all in Retiro (Map 5):

AI (☎ 4311-1000), MT de Alvear 678
Avis (☎ 4326-5542), Cerrito 1527
Dollar (☎ 4315-8800), MT de Alvear 523
Hertz (☎ 4816-8001), Paraguay 1122
Localiza (☎ 4315-8384), Maipú 924

Taxi & Remise

Buenos Aires' numerous, reasonably priced taxis are conspicuous by their black-and-yellow paint jobs. Meters start at US$1.12 (as of June 2001), so make sure the meter is set to this amount when you start your ride. Drivers do not expect a big tip (even for longer trips to Ezeiza from downtown), but it's customary to let them keep small change.

Around Buenos Aires

There are several worthwhile attractions close to Buenos Aires. The riverside suburb of Tigre, a popular retreat, is the best base for exploring the waterways of the Delta del Paraná, including historic Isla Martín García. It's also the departure point for passenger ferries across the river to Uruguayan destinations, though Montevideo and Colonia can also be reached from the city center (see those sections in the Uruguay chapter for more information).

TIGRE & THE DELTA DEL PARANÁ

The delta's latte-colored waters surround this tranquil suburb, which comes alive on weekends as porteños retreat from the cement of Buenos Aires. Boats can take you farther into the narrow channels, where you can explore the local river life; there's also a tacky theme park that's good only for kids. The helpful tourist office (☎ 4512-4497), behind the McDonald's near Estación Fluvial, is open 9am to 5pm daily.

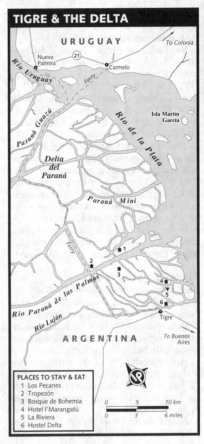

TIGRE & THE DELTA

PLACES TO STAY & EAT
1 Los Pecanes
2 Tropezón
3 Bosque de Bohemia
4 Hotel I'Marangatú
5 La Riviera
6 Hostel Delta

One of Tigre's best attractions is the **Puerto de Frutos** (☎ 4512-4493, Sarmiento 160; open 11am-7pm daily). A wide selection of fruit is sold here, along with many wicker products and other handmade objects. On weekends, a large craft fair adds to the din.

Museo Naval de la Nación (☎ 4749-0608, Paseo Victorica 602; admission US$2; open 8:30am-12:30pm Mon-Thur, 8am to 5:30pm Fri, 10am-6:30pm weekends) traces the history of the Argentine navy. **Museo de la Reconquista** (☎ 4512-4496, Padre Castañeda 470; free; open 10am-6pm Wed-Sun) was the house where Viceroy Liniers coordinated resistance to the early-19th-century British invasions; it also details the area's history.

For kayaking contact Nautical Escapes (☎ 4728-2865, e edward@nauticalescapes .com). Rentals cost US$15 for two hours, US$25 for half-day. Tours are available. For canoeing contact Selk'nam Canoas (☎ 4749-5202, e selknamcanoas@hotmail .com). Guided tours in wooden canoes cost US$10/15 for one/two hours.

The waterways of the delta region offer a glimpse into the way locals live along the peaceful canals without any transport other than boats. One popular destination is the Tres Bocas neighborhood, where you can take walks through a residential area; the narrow, sometimes muddy paths cross narrow channels via bridges. There are a couple of good lunch spots overlooking the water. The boat ride here takes 35 minutes.

Places to Stay & Eat

B&B Escauriza (☎ 4749-2499, fax 4749-3150, e alebyb@aol.com, Lavalle 557) Singles/ doubles US$50/70. Located in Tigre itself is this gorgeous and homey B&B. Six romantic bedrooms come with large balconies, and homemade meals are available.

Accommodations in the delta are few and far between, but this makes for a peaceful stay. All these places can provide meals, but boat transport is not typically included in the room price.

Hostel Delta (☎ 4728-0396) US$12 per person. This hostel offers nice park surroundings, a beach area and cheap canoe rentals. There's kitchen access and a great deck. To get here, take a taxi from Tigre (US$4) to the river crossing at Muelle Tecnao (US$1).

Hotel I'Marangatú (☎ 4728-0752) US$50 per person with half-board; 50-minute boat ride from Tigre. This spot is best for those seeking beach, pool and water sports.

Tropezón (☎ 4728-1012) US$65 per person with full board; 90-minute boat ride from Tigre. Get transported to the past at this atmospheric hotel boasting old delta architecture, a great terrace and good food. Rooms are traditionally styled, and there are peaceful walks.

Los Pecanes (☎ 4728-1932) Doubles US$72; 90-minute boat ride from Tigre. This homey and friendly place has many activities to keep you entertained, and the garden harbors some wonderfully relaxing hammocks. Homemade meals cost US$15.

Bosque de Bohemia (☎ 4728-0053) US$25 per person; 70-minute boat ride from Tigre. Come enjoy five clean rooms, grassy riverside lawns and good walks; there are also ping-pong tables and a volleyball court.

You'll find mainly traditional Argentine restaurants in town, the most atmospheric of which line Paseo Victoria, a pleasant riverside avenue right next to the Río Luján. Take a nice pre-supper walk to a nice spot to sit and watch the boats go humming by.

La Riviera (☎ 4728-0177) Mains US$4-14, set meals US$6-8. With relaxing sunny patios and river views, it's no wonder this restaurant is so popular. Good food like pasta, meats and fish completes the picture. It's a great place to stop for a drink and check out the local delta action.

Getting There & Away

To get to Tigre, you have several options. The fastest is taking the train line marked 'Tigre' from Retiro train station (frequent departures, 50 minutes, US$0.85); the final stop is almost at the tourist office. A more touristy alternative is to take the Mitre line from Retiro train station to its end at the Olivos station (US$0.85), where you board the pleasant Tren de la Costa (US$1.50-2), an upgraded train line that has stops at cafés and a fancy shopping center. The final station is a 10-minute walk away from the tourist office (near the Mercado de Frutos). You can also take buses from the Buenos Aires center to the Olivos station; these include Nos 59, 152, and 60. The No 60 goes all the way to Tigre itself and takes 1½ hours (US$1.35).

Getting Around

Three boating companies run frequent commuter launches from Tigre's Estación Fluvial (located near the tourist office) to various destinations in the delta for US$5 to US$12 roundtrip. These will drop you off or pick you up at any riverside dock; just flag them down as you would a bus.

A few companies offer guided tours of the delta region; these cost US$5 to US$10 and take one to two hours. You can also tour the delta using the commuter launches; this way you can stop off wherever you want, though you're at the mercy of the launches' timetables. Check them before you zoom off.

ISLA MARTÍN GARCÍA

While navigating the densely forested channels of the Río Tigre and Río Paraná en route to historic Isla Martín García, you can easily imagine what ideal hideaways these waterways were for colonial smugglers. Just off the Uruguayan coast, this 2km-square island is best known as an ex-prison camp. Four Argentine presidents have been detained here, and up until 1995 it was still used as a halfway house for prisoners near the end of their terms.

At present, the park-like island is a combination of historical monument, tranquil nature reserve and recreational retreat from bustling Buenos Aires. There's a grand total of six cars roaming the streets, and the only constant noise you'll hear is the hum of the huge generator (providing electricity to the 180 residents) and the cackling flocks of small green parrots that flit overhead. Bring mosquito repellant in summer.

History

Unlike the sedimentary islands of the flood-prone delta, Isla Martín García has a hard rock base and rises 27m above sea level; this high ground made it suitable as a viewpoint to guard the approach of the Río Uruguay and Río Paraná.

Many have contested possession of the strategic island in the past. Spain and Portugal scuffled during colonial times, and Irish Admiral Guillermo Brown gave the United Provinces of the River Plate their first major naval victory here in 1814 when a commando raid dislodged royalist troops (who consequently escaped across the river to Montevideo). Both England and France took advantage of Argentine conflicts with Brazil to occupy the island in the early 19th century, but for most of the 20th century the Argentine navy had control of Isla Martín García – though Uruguay has had recent claims as well. To pacify its neighbor, Argentina decided to de-militarize the island and now only supports a naval prefecture here.

Political prisoners confined on Isla Martín Garcia have included Presidents Hipólito Yrigoyen, Marcelo T de Alvear, Juan Perón and Arturo Frondizi.

Things to See & Do

Martín García's main points of interest are its **historic buildings**. The Ministro de Gobierno, uphill from the *muelle* (passenger pier), is also headquarters for the Oficina de Guardaparques (national park headquarters). Other interesting sites include the walled ruins of the former Cuartel (naval barracks); the Casa Intendencia, which housed Perón during his three-day stay on the isle; the Panadería Rocio, a still-operating bakery dating from 1913; the colorful and rococo Cine Teatro; the small Museo Histórico San Martín García; and the Casa de Ciencias Naturales. At the northwestern end of the island, the Puerto Viejo (old port) has fallen into disuse due to sediments that have clogged the anchorage.

The small and peaceful cemetery contains the headstones of many conscripts who died in an epidemic in the early 20th century. There's also a crematorium, accented by a tall circular chimney, which was used to dispose of diseased corpses during this epidemic; it now functions as a trash incinerator.

The densely forested northern part of the island offers quiet, pleasant **walks** if you don't mind fending off mosquitoes. South of the airstrip, the Zona Intangible is closed to hikers because of its botanical value and the hazard of fire; but look off toward the east and you'll see the Uruguayan coastline.

The restaurant Comedor El Solís has a **swimming pool** open in summer, so bring your swimsuit if you want a dip.

Organized Tours

Guided tours depart from Cacciola's terminal (☎ 4749-0329), Lavalle 520, in Tigre. Tickets are also available at the downtown Buenos Aires office (☎ 4393-6100; Map 3), Florida 520, 1st floor, Oficina 113. On Tuesday, Thursday, weekends and holidays, the enclosed and comfortable catamaran leaves Tigre at 8am, returning from Martín García at 4pm. The smooth voyage takes three hours each way and roundtrip fare is US$28; for US$35 you get a good carnivorous asado lunch too. Both prices include the tour.

Consider buying the lunch option during the winter, when many restaurants on the island may be closed. Drinks and small snacks are available on the boat at decent prices, but you may want to bring along cards or a book as the scenery along the way is less than spectacular. Make sure to reserve these tours at least a day in advance as they tend to fill up.

Places to Stay & Eat

Camping Albergues (☎ 4728-1808) Tent sites US$3.50 per person, dorm beds US$7.50/10 shared/private bath. The campground and hostel are pleasant enough and tranquil; it's a good idea to call for reservations, especially in summer and on weekends.

Hostería Martín García (☎ 4728-0119) Full-board US$85 per person with transportation to island, additional nights US$50. Consider staying the extra day only if you truly want to relax or read a thick book.

Comedor El Solís (☎ 4440-9404) All-you-can-eat US$10. The buffet includes tasty fish and dessert. This place may not always be open.

Fragata Hercules Set meal US$8-10. The food here (mostly grilled meat items) isn't bad, and it's a decent deal if you get it with the excursion.

Argentine tourists leave the island laden with *pan dulce* (a type of tasty fruitcake), usually after a visit to *Panadería Rocio*.

Touring the Delta via the Tren de la Costa

Inaugurated in 1891 as recreational transport, but closed for more than three decades prior to its resuscitation in 1995, the former Tren del Bajo connected the capital with its northern riverside suburbs. The new electric version is targeted at tourists (though locals also use it for transport) and runs from Olivos to Tigre, a 25-minute ride. There are 11 stops at recycled as well as brand new stations, many of which are accented with trendy cafés or shopping centers. It's a pleasant and quiet ride and the most tranquil way to get to Tigre. You'll glimpse the capital's lush suburbs, modest abodes and fancy mansions, a bit of the Río de la Plata's coastline, and as you get close to Tigre, some industrial hinterlands.

There are rental bikes (US$6 per hour) and in-line skates at Estación Barrancas. From here you can roll along a pleasant and fairly smooth pedestrian path that starts at Estación Libertador (you'd have to backtrack a couple of stations) and goes all the way to Estación San Isidro (one beyond Barrancas). On a bike, you can also explore the nearby coast and the historic town of San Isidro. On weekends and holidays, Estación Barrancas is the site for a small antiques market from 11am to 7pm.

If you'd rather explore on foot, get out at Estación San Isidro and walk around the fancy outdoor shopping mall there. Just up the hill from the mall is Plaza Mitre and San Isidro's cathedral. Strolling the historic streets behind the cathedral will turn up luxurious mansions and the occasional view over toward the coast.

The one-way fare is US$1.50 weekdays, US$2 weekends, and it allows you to make as many stops as you wish. Trains run approximately every 15 minutes. For more details, contact Tren de la Costa (☎ 4732-6000).

ARGENTINA

They're not cheap at US$5 and US$9, but it's one of those 'You're going to Isla Martín García? You *must* buy a fruitcake!' things.

Getting There & Away
Unless you want to charter a plane, you can only get to Isla Martín García by organized tour; see that section, earlier.

SAN ISIDRO
To the north of Buenos Aires is peaceful and residential San Isidro, a charming suburb lined with cobblestone streets and graceful buildings. Its historic heart is centered on Plaza Mitre and the beautiful neogothic **cathedral**. A stroll through the rambling neighborhood streets behind the cathedral will turn up some luxurious mansions (as well as more modest houses), and the occasional view toward the coast. Close by is the Tren de la Costa's San Isidro train station, with a fashionable outdoor shopping mall to explore.

The **Quinta Pueyrredón** (☎ 4512-3131, Rivera Indarte 48; free, open 2pm-6pm Tues, Thur & weekends, 3pm-7pm Tues, Thur & weekends Nov-Dec) is an ancient colonial mansion set on spacious garden grounds that open to wonderful views of the Río de la Plata. The building also houses a historical museum containing period items, including some relating to Argentine icon General Juan Martín de Pueyrredón, who owned the mansion in the early 1800s. From Plaza Mitre turn left at the cathedral and follow Av Libertador five blocks, turn left on Peña and go two blocks, then turn right onto Rivera Indarte.

Getting There & Around
If you're going to take a few peaceful hours to walk around San Isidro, the best way to get there is via the Tren de la Costa (US$1.50-2). From Retiro train station, take the Mitre line to its end at the Olivos station; cross Av Maipú and the Tren de la Costa is right there. You'll get off at the San Isidro station. From downtown Buenos Aires you can also catch Bus No 168, which drops you on Av Libertador, a couple blocks from Quinta Pueyrredón.

For ideas on exploring the area by bike or in-line skates, see the boxed text 'Touring the Delta via the Tren de la Costa.'

The Pampas & the Atlantic Coast

Argentina's celebrated Pampas, birthplace of the legendary gaucho, are mostly flat except for an extensive, resort-specked coastline (with some dunes) and several small but scenic mountain ranges. The variety of environments toward the west also lend a bit of texture to the country's agricultural heartland: rolling hills with native *caldén* forests, desert zones with saline lakes (which support flamingo and other birds) and extensive native grasslands. Geographically, this region covers the provinces of Buenos Aires and La Pampa, as well as southern chunks of Santa Fe and Córdoba.

Along the coast, resorts like Mar del Plata, Necochea and Pinamar teem with vacationing Argentines bronzing on the beaches during the southern continent's summer. Those in search of hilly terrain to climb and explore buzz inland towards Tandil or Sierra de la Ventana, while little-known Parque Nacional Lihué Calel more than justifies a detour from the standard routes to and from Patagonia. For travelers seeking cultural destinations, there is San Antonio de Areco, which wears the emblem of Argentina's gaucho culture, and colonial Luján, one of South America's most important religious centers. Large cities include bustling La Plata (capital of Buenos Aires province) and the Atlantic port of Bahía Blanca, which exudes a sophisticated, big-city feel.

History

The aboriginal inhabitants of the Pampas were Querandí hunter-gatherers, less numerous and more dispersed than the sedentary peoples of the Andean Northwest or even the semisedentary Guaraní of the upper Paraná basin. Subsisting mainly by hunting guanaco and rhea, the Querandí remained content until the Spanish began moving into the region.

The Querandí resisted the European invaders, besieging early settlements and preventing them from establishing any foothold in the area for more than half a

Highlights

- Atlantic resorts – Crowding the shores in summer for fun and sun

- San Antonio de Areco – Checking out the gaucho museum and shopping for high-quality artisan's goods

- Estancia life – Staying at a gaucho ranch and getting a feel for how the Pampas used to be – at least for rich landowners

- Luján – Making a pilgrimage or just picking up a tacky souvenir at this religious center

- La Plata – Exploring Argentina's best natural history museum, and goggling at the gigantic, stunning cathedral

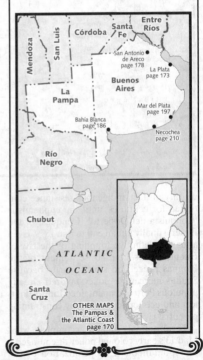

ARGENTINA

THE PAMPAS & THE ATLANTIC COAST

century. In fact, indigenous resistance continued for centuries, until the euphemistic 'Conquista del Desierto' (Conquest of the Desert) finally put an end to it in 1879. Even after the definitive founding of the city of Buenos Aires in 1580, settlement of the Pampas proceeded slowly, partly because Spain's mercantile policy favored already populous Peru and maintained Lima's political and economic primacy by constraining potential rivals.

Feral animals helped accomplish what Madrid's early colonial policy discouraged – the spontaneous Europeanization of the

Pampas. When the Spaniards abandoned their first settlement at Buenos Aires for the pleasures of Paraguay, they also left behind cattle and horses, which multiplied prodigiously on the succulent native grasses of the Pampas.

The wild cattle and horses became the backbone for two enduring and related legacies. The iconic gaucho persisted for many decades as a neo-hunter-gatherer and then as a symbol of an extreme but romantic Argentine nationalism known as *argentinidad*. Environmental impoverishment also became integral to Pampas culture, as grazing and opportunistic European weeds altered the native grasslands.

Upon Argentine independence in 1816, the country's doors opened wide to foreign commerce. The Pampas' meat-salting plants yielded only hides, tallow and salt beef – products with limited markets overseas. This trade, in turn, benefited the relatively few *estancieros* (ranchers) with the fortune to inherit or the foresight to grab large tracts of land. Some landowners did not survive the fall of *caudillo* (strongman) Juan Manuel de Rosas, whose policies had encouraged the alienation of public lands for grazing establishments, but others prospered as Buenos Aires experienced a late-19th-century wool boom from imported sheep.

Shortly after 1850, railroads, built largely with British capital, made it feasible to export wool and then beef, but the meat from rangy *criollo* (feral Pampas cattle) did not appeal to British tastes. Improved breeds required more succulent feed, such as alfalfa, but the estancieros could not produce this with the skeletal labor force available to them on their enormous holdings. Consequently, their traditional opposition to immigration declined as they sought to attract tenant farmers to their holdings.

Although estancieros had no intention of relinquishing their lands, the development of arable farmland was an indirect benefit of the intensification of raising stock. Growing alfalfa required preparatory cultivation, so landowners rented their properties to sharecroppers, who raised wheat for four or five years before moving elsewhere, and thus landowners benefited both from their share of the wheat crop and from their new alfalfa fields. Shortly after 1900, agricultural exports like maize, wheat and linseed exceeded the value of livestock products such as hides, wool and meat.

The Pampas are still famous for their beef, and estancias still dominate the economy, but smaller landholdings have increased in number, and Argentina has remained a major grain exporter. The province of Santa Fe, where rain-fed maize is the principal crop, has a more democratic land-ownership structure, but agriculture is now highly mechanized almost everywhere, and dependent on petroleum-based fertilizers and pesticides. In this sense, Argentina resembles other major grain-producing areas like Australia, Canada and the United States. Near Buenos Aires and other large cities, though, there is intensive cultivation of fruits and vegetables, as well as dairy farming.

Northern Pampas

Buenos Aires province is the country's largest, richest, most populous and most important province. Its wealth lies in the fruitful Pampas soil; high yields of hides, beef, wool and wheat for global markets have stamped Argentina on the world's economic map.

From the mid-19th century, the province and city of Buenos Aires were the undisputed political and economic center of the country. Buenos Aires' de facto secession as a federal zone subjugated the powerful province to national authority but didn't completely eliminate its influence. By the 1880s, after a brief but contentious civil war, the province responded by creating its own model city of La Plata.

Outside the Capital Federal a dense network of railroads and highways connects the agricultural towns of the Pampas, forming a symmetrical pattern on the provincial map. Most of these towns resemble each other as much as any part of the endlessly flat Pampas resembles another.

LA PLATA
☎ 0221 • pop 250,000
Almost a quarter-million people inhabit the bustling metropolis of La Plata. Despite being home to Argentina's best science museum, which has an almost Gothic feel and is appropriately located in a huge forested park; the most interesting thing about this university town may well be the history of its layout.

After Buenos Aires became Argentina's federal capital, Governor Dardo Rocha founded La Plata in 1882 to give the province its own new capital. After detailed study, Rocha chose engineer Pedro Benoit's elaborate city plan, which was based on balance and logic. The super-position of diagonals on a regular, 5km-square grid pattern created a distinctive star design that handily connected the major plazas. (Very pretty on paper, this blueprint now makes for confusion at many intersections, with up to eight streets going off in all directions.) To fill the blocks with buildings, an architectural competition was held; it brought together international designs that can still be seen in the city's many remaining European-flavored buildings. La Plata is probably the southern cone's first completely planned city.

Orientation

La Plata is 56km southeast of Buenos Aires via RP 14. Most of the bustle occurs around Plaza San Martín rather than Plaza Moreno, where most of the public buildings are located. It can be confusing to remain on the same street after crossing at an intersection with more than four corners; keep looking at street signs to make sure you haven't inadvertently veered off onto another street.

On each block, address numbers run in sequences of 50 rather than the customary 100.

Information

The city's tourist office (☎ 482-9656), Entidad Municipal de Turismo, will never earn the 'tourist office of the year award,' so don't expect anything too complex out of it. It's located just off Plaza San Martin and is more or less open from 10am to 6pm Monday through Friday.

Argentina's nonprofit student travel agency, Asatej (☎ 483-8673), has a local branch at Calle 5 No 990, at the corner of Calle 53.

In addition to serving as a telephone office, Locutorio San Martín, on Av 51 between Av 7 and Calle 8, is also a *cartelera*, offering discount tickets to local entertainment events.

ACA (☎ 482-9040) is at Calle 9 and Av 51.

The post office is at Calle 4 and Av 51; the postal code is 1900.

Instituto Cultural Británico-Argentino (☎ 489-9690), located off the Plaza Moreno

at Calle 12 No 869, hosts occasional cultural events and Friday night films.

Walking Tour

In the middle of **Plaza Moreno**, which occupies four square blocks, La Plata's **Piedra Fundacional** (Founding Stone) of 1882 marks the city's precise geographical center. Across from the plaza is the beautiful neo-Gothic **cathedral**, which was begun in 1885 but not inaugurated until 1932. Inspired by medieval antecedents in Cologne and Amiens, it has fine stained glass and polished granite floors. The tower, whose construction was suspended for many years, was finally completed recently.

On the opposite side of Plaza Moreno is the 1886 **Palacio Municipal**, designed in German Renaissance style by Hanoverian architect Hubert Stiers (for tours, contact the tourist office, above). Modern towers on either side of the palace house most of the provincial government offices. On the west side of the Plaza, the **Museo y Archivo Dardo Rocha** (☎ 427-5591; free; open 9am-6pm weekdays, 9am-1pm Jan-Feb) was the vacation house of the city's creator and contains many of his personal effects and a library.

Three blocks north, the **Teatro Argentino**, also known as the Centro de Artes y Espectáculos, looms in a strange architectural form that seems to serve best as a pigeon roost. It replaces an earlier, much more distinguished Italian building destroyed by fire. Opera, ballet and symphonies can be seen here (☎ 0800-666-5151 for information).

Three blocks farther northeast, opposite Plaza San Martín, is the ornate **Palacio de la Legislatura** (☎ 422-0081 for tours), also in German Renaissance style. Over to the west a couple blocks is the French Classic **Pasaje Dardo Rocha** (☎ 425-1990), once La Plata's main railroad station and now the city's major cultural center, containing three museums and a nice café. Detour a couple more blocks northwest to view the original buildings of the **Rectorado de la Universidad Nacional**. Built in 1905, this complex was once a bank, and now houses university

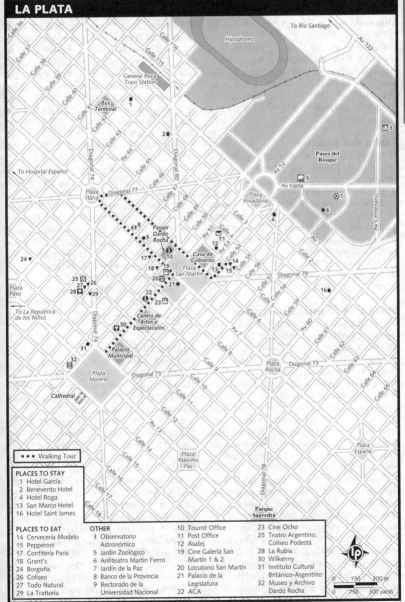

LA PLATA

To Río Santiago

Hipódromo

Calle 36
Calle 37
Calle 38
Calle 39
Calle 40
Calle 41
Calle 42
Calle 43

Calle 116
Calle 115

Av 122

General Roca
Train Station

Bus
Terminal

Diagonal 74
Av 44
Calle 444
Calle 45
Calle 46

Diagonal 80
Calle 47

Paseo del
Bosque

Av 52

To Hospital Español

Plaza
Italia
Diagonal 77

Calle 48
Calle 49

Plaza
Rivadavia

Av Iraola

Av Centenario

Pasaje
Dardo
Rocha

Calle 50

Av 51
Calle 4
Calle 3

Av 1

Casa de
Gobierno

Calle 53
Calle 54
Calle 55
Calle 56

Plaza
San Martín

Diagonal 79

24 ▼

Plaza
Paso

To La República
de los Niños

Calle 57
Calle 58
Calle 59

Av 60

Av 2

Diagonal 74

Centro de
Artes y
Espectáculos

Calle 5
Calle 6

Av 7

Plaza
Rocha
Diagonal 73

Av 61
Calle 62
Calle 63
Calle 64
Calle 65

Palacio
Municipal

Plaza
Moreno

Diagonal 73

Calle 8
Calle 9

Cathedral

Calle 10
Calle 11
Av 13
Calle 12

Diagonal 73

Plaza
España

Calle 15
Calle 16
Calle 17
Calle 18

Plaza
Máximo
Paz

Diagonal 78

Parque
Saavedra

••• Walking Tour

PLACES TO STAY
1 Hotel García
2 Benevento Hotel
4 Hotel Roga
13 San Marco Hotel
16 Hotel Saint James

PLACES TO EAT
14 Cervecería Modelo
15 Pepperoni
17 Confitería París
18 Grant's
24 Borgoña
26 Coliseo
27 Todo Natural
29 La Trattoría

OTHER
3 Observatorio
   Astronómico
5 Jardín Zoológico
6 Anfiteatro Martín Fierro
7 Jardín de la Paz
8 Banco de la Provincia
9 Rectorado de la
   Universidad Nacional

10 Tourist Office
11 Post Office
12 Asatej
19 Cine Galería San
   Martín 1 & 2
20 Locutorio San Martín
21 Palacio de la
   Legislatura
22 ACA

23 Cine Ocho
25 Teatro Argentino;
   Coliseo Podestá
28 La Rubia
30 Wilkenny
31 Instituto Cultural
   Británico-Argentino
32 Museo y Archivo
   Dardo Rocha

0   150   300 m
0   150   300 yards

administrative offices. If it's a weekend or holiday, have a look at the crafts fair, **Feria Artesanal**, on Plaza Italia, a few blocks farther west.

Return via Calle 6 to the Flemish Renaissance **Casa de Gobierno**, housing the provincial governor and his retinue, on the north side of Plaza San Martín. For a great rest, stroll up Calle 5 to the atmospheric landmark **Cervecería Modelo** for a cold beer or snack.

Paseo del Bosque

Plantations of eucalyptus, gingko, palm and subtropical hardwoods cover this 60-hectare park, expropriated from an estancia at the time of the city's founding. Its attractions include the **Anfiteatro Martín Fierro**, an open-air facility that hosts summer drama festivals; the **Museo de Ciencias Naturales** (see below); the **Observatorio Astronómico**; the symbolic United Nations of the Garden of Peace, **Jardín de la Paz**; a modest **Jardín Zoológico** and several university departments.

Museo de Ciencias Naturales

When Buenos Aires became the federal capital, provincial authorities built this notable museum (☎ 425-7744, Paseo del Bosque 1900; admission US$3; open 10am-6pm daily, closed Jan 1, May 1 & Dec 25) in the spacious park known as Paseo del Bosque. Housed in its grand old spaces are the paleontological, zoological, archaeological and anthropological collections of lifetime director Francisco P Moreno, the famous Patagonian explorer. There's a great ancient feel to this place; a charming mustiness takes you back in time.

Finished in 1889, the building consists of an attractive oval with four stories and mezzanines filled with showrooms, classrooms, workshops, laboratories and libraries. Its exterior mixes Corinthian columns, Ionic posterior walls and Hellenic windows, with Aztec and Inca-style embellishments. Since 1906, the university's school of natural sciences has functioned here. It's a very worthwhile stop and offers something for everyone.

Places to Stay

Hotels in La Plata aren't cheap, but at least it's an easy daytrip from Buenos Aires. Only higher-end hotels come with breakfast.

Hotel Saint James (☎ 421-8089, Calle 60 No 377) Singles/doubles US$20/30. The rooms are small, simple and dark, but they're the cheapest in town.

Hotel García (☎ 423-5369, Calle 2 No 525) Singles/doubles US$27/35. It's friendly and good enough for the price. Rooms face an outdoor hallway.

Hotel Roga (☎ 421-9553, Calle 54 No 334) Singles/doubles US$38/52. There's nothing wild or crazy here, just homey, modern rooms. Check out the fake 5-peso bill under the front counter glass.

Benevento Hotel (☎/fax 489-1078, Calle 2 No 645) Singles/doubles US$50/65. Here's a tastefully renovated old-style hotel with wood-floored rooms and nice décor. Singles are tiny, but doubles are fairly comfortable. All outside rooms have balconies.

San Marco Hotel (☎/fax 422-9322, Calle 54 No 523) Singles/doubles US$55/75. A nice lobby greets you at this friendly, quiet and tidy hotel within staggering distance of Cervecería Modelo.

Places to Eat

Borgoña (☎ 489-1018, Calles 11 & 44) Mains US$2-4. It's got a great old-time atmosphere, and colorful chairs add to the mix. Food's limited, though you can enjoy it outside at sidewalk tables.

Coliseo (☎ 422-8282, Calles 10 & 47) Sandwiches US$2.50-6. The food menu's limited to quick eats, but for tea and snacks this joint delivers. It's a good place to try a *licuado* (fruit-blended drink).

La Trattoria (☎ 422-6135, Calles 10 & 47) Mains US$3-11. It's large, modern, comfortable and sports two large-but-not-overbearing video screens. This is a popular place for pizza and sandwiches.

Confitería París (☎ 482-8840, corner of Av 7 & Calle 49) Mains US$4.50-6. This is great place to stop for coffee and pastries, and it's smoke-free. It's got lunch items and it's clean, modern and popular.

Pepperoni (☎ 423-4848, Calle 5 No 1117)
Pizzas US$4.50-10. Choose from a very wide
range of toppings for your pizza. The ambience is airy and light, and the surroundings
modern and pastel-colored.

Cervecería Modelo (☎ 421-1321, Calles 5
& 54) Mains US$4-13. Here's a wonderfully
traditional and comfortable spot to enjoy
drinks or a meal with the locals. There's even
a large TV screen for sports fans.

Grant's (☎ 483-0808, Calle 50 between 7 &
8) Buffet lunch US$6, more for dinner and
on Sat & Sun; mandatory drinks extra.
Here's a branch of this popular and extensive all-you-can-snarf. Come hungry.

Todo Natural (Calle 47 No 770) This
small natural-food store stocks dried fruit,
bulk grains and a few bakery products.

Entertainment

There are a few movie theatres, such as *Cine
Ocho* (☎ 482-5554, Calle 8 No 981) and
Cine San Martín (☎ 483-9947, Av 7 No 923).

La Rubia (☎ 422-5544, Calle 47 No 787) A
cool bar with a good feel and live music on
Fridays, it's a restaurant during the day, with
pizzas and short orders for US$3.50 to US$9.

Wilkenny (☎ 483-1772, Calles 11 & 50)
Come down to the closest thing to an Irish
pub in La Plata for some brews with locals
and a few foreigners.

Getting There & Away

The bus terminal (☎ 421-0992) is at Calles 4
and 42. Río de la Plata has buses every half
hour to and from Buenos Aires (US$4.50; 1
hour). In Buenos Aires, they leave from
outside Retiro train station on Av Zuviria;
the last bus back to Buenos Aires is at
10pm. Long-distance destinations from La
Plata include Mar del Plata (US$26; 5
hours) and Bahía Blance (US$32; 8 hours).

Trains run frequently between Buenos
Aires and La Plata (US$1.50; 1¼ hours),
whose turn-of-the-century Estación Ferrocarril General Roca (☎ 421-9377) features a
striking art nouveau dome and wrought-
iron awning. The last train returns around
11pm, but service starts up again between
3am and 4am.

AROUND LA PLATA

Evita Perón herself sponsored the scale-
model city called **La República de los Niños**
(☎ 484-0194, Camino General Belgrano Km
7 & Calle 501; adults US$1, children free;
open 10am-6pm daily), completed shortly
before her death in 1952, for the education
and enjoyment of children. From its Plaza
de la Amistad (Friendship Plaza), a steam
train circles this architectural hodgepodge
of medieval European and Islamic styles,
with motifs from Grimms' and Andersen's
fairy tales. Like most public works projects
of its era, it's showing its age, but is worth a
visit if you have crabby kids to appease;
otherwise it's sort of a bargain-basement
Disneyland.

República de los Niños is north of La
Plata in the suburb of Manuel Gonnet.
From Av 7 in La Plata, take bus No 518 or
273; note that not all No 273 buses go all the
way there.

LUJÁN
☎ 0232 • pop 95,000

The legend goes like this: In 1630, a wagon
pulled by oxen and containing a small
terra-cotta statue of the Virgin Mary suddenly got stuck on the road and would not
budge until the gauchos removed the
image. The wagon was heading from Per-
nambuco to a Portuguese farmer in Santiago del Estero, but the devoted owner
took this pause as a sign, cleared the site
and built a chapel where the Virgin had
chosen to stay, about 5km from present-day
Luján.

La Virgen de Luján soon became Argentina's patron saint, and she's since upgraded
her quarters to the French Gothic basilica,
one of the city's two main tourist attractions. The other is an exceptionally extensive colonial museum complex. A mostly
peaceful city located on the east bank of its
namesake river, Luján contains no intruding
high-rises, and the small commercial center
branches out from the basilica. It's essentially a religious tourist town, and the
number of stores and rolling carts selling
devotional souvenirs is astounding. There's

a leafy, elevated riverside area full of restaurants and more shops, and leisurely boat rides are available.

Every October since the Dirty War, a massive Peregrinación de la Juventud (youth pilgrimage) originates in Buenos Aires' Once Station. In the days of the military dictatorship, when any mass demonstration was forbidden, this 18-hour walk had tremendous symbolic importance, but since the restoration of democracy it has become more exclusively devotional. Other large gatherings take place April 21, when there's a celebration dedicated to the *caballo criollo* (the hardy national horse); May 8, the Virgin's day; the last Sunday in September, when gauchos come into town on horses (and there are horse piles everywhere); the third week of November, when antique carriages are paraded; and December 8 (Immaculate Conception Day), showcasing a nautical procession on the river.

Orientation & Information

Luján is around 65km west of Buenos Aires on RN 7. Most places of interest are near the basilica, though Plaza Colón, five blocks southeast via Calle San Martín, is another center of activity.

There's a tourist office (☎ 420044) at the bus terminal that's open 24 hours. The information kiosk (☎ 428680), at the corner of Lavalle and 9 de Julio, is open 10am to 6pm weekdays, 9am to 8pm Saturday and Sunday. The city's central tourist information office (☎ 433500), in a domed building at the west end of Lavalle, is open 7am to 1pm weekdays only.

The post office is at Mitre 575; Luján's postal code is 6700.

Basílica Nuestra Señora de Luján

Every year five million pilgrims from throughout Argentina visit Luján to honor the Virgin for her intercession in affairs of peace, health, forgiveness and consolation. The terminus of their journeys is this imposing basilica (☎ 435101 for hourly tours; US$3), whose hallowed halls are lined with confession boxes just before you reach the 'Virgencita,' who occupies a high chamber

behind the main altar. Devotees have lined the stairs with plaques acknowledging her favors. Under the basilica you can tour a crypt (US$2.50; every 30 minutes) that harbors virgin statues from all over the world. A joint tour of both these places costs US$4. The basilica is open 7:30am to 8pm daily; masses take place several times a day, mostly mornings and evenings.

Within the basilica, Irish visitors in particular will be interested to find Gaelic inscriptions, Irish surnames and a window dedicated to St Patrick.

Near the basilica, whose towers rise 106m above the Pampas, the slightly cheesy **Museo Devocióñal** (*San Martín & Padre Salvaire; admission US$1; open 1pm-6pm Tues-Fri, 10am-6pm weekends*) houses *ex-votos* (gifts) to the Virgin, including objects of silver, wood and wax, as well as musical instruments and icons from all over the world.

Complejo Museográfico Enrique Udaondo

This gorgeous colonial museum complex (☎ *420245, Lavalle & Padre Salvaire; admission US$1; open 12:15pm-5:30pm Wed-Fri, 10:15am-5:30pm weekends*) rambles with display rooms, pretty patios, gardens and tiled outdoor walkways. The Sala General Jose de San Martín showcases Argentina's battles for independence with historic etchings, presidential bios and period items. The Sala de Gaucho contains some beautiful *mate* ware, ponchos, horse gear, guitars and other gaucho paraphernalia, as well as a reconstruction of Ricardo Güialdes' (author of *Don Segundo Sombra*; 1886-1927) study. There's a Federal Era room, outlining Juan Manuel de Rosas' exploits (and some major anti-unitarian sentiment), the 'conquest' of the desert (essentially the conquest of Patagonia's indigenous people) and more period items including huge and nifty hair combs. Near the entry to the complex you'll also see a room portraying an old prison chamber, as the *cabildo* (town council) building used to be a prison.

The nearby **Museo de Transporte** (*same data as above*) has a remarkable collection of horse-pulled carriages from the late

1800s, including some truly fit for Cinderella. Also on display are a 'popemobile,' the first steam locomotive to serve the city from Buenos Aires and a monster of a hydroplane that was used to cross the Atlantic in 1926. The peaceful garden outside harbors some old wooden wagons and a brick windmill. The most offbeat exhibits, however, are the stuffed and scruffy remains of Gato and Mancha, the hardy Argentine criollo horses ridden by adventurer AF Tschiffely from Buenos Aires to Washington, DC. This trip took 2½ years, from 1925-28.

The complex also has a combined **library/archive** that's open 8am to 5:30pm weekdays.

Places to Stay

Many hotels include breakfast; note that weekend and holiday rates usually go up.

Camping El Triángulo (☎ 430116, RN 7 Km 69,500) One tent for 2-4 people US$15. About 10 blocks from the basilica, across the Río Luján, this campground is basic and imperfectly maintained, but it has plenty of shade and is OK for a night.

Hotel Carena (☎ 429884, Lavalle 114) Singles & doubles US$15/30. This is a basic, friendly place that's cheap and central; because of this it gets busy, so call ahead to reserve.

Hotel Royal (☎ 421295, 9 de Julio 696) Singles/doubles US$25/40. Opposite the bus terminal are some homey, worn and plain rooms with TV. At least it's friendly and there's a restaurant.

Hotel de la Paz (☎/fax 424034, 9 de Julio 1054) Singles/doubles US$35/40. The well-located and friendly Hotel de la Paz hints at old-time charm, though the rooms themselves are just OK. Still, it's not a bad deal in this price range.

Hotel Hoxón (☎/fax 429970, **w** www.hotel hoxon.com.ar, 9 de Julio 760) Singles/ doubles US$38-55; more with air con and fridge. Here's the best place to stay in town; rooms are modern, clean and very comfortable, and everything's fairly new. There's pool access, a gym and many other higher-class comforts.

Places to Eat

Carnivorous pilgrims won't go hungry in Luján; just don't expect much beyond traditional Argentine fare. The central parts of San Martín, 9 de Julio and the riverfront are all lined with restaurants ready to serve.

La Recova (☎ 422280, San Martín 1) Mains US$5-10. This large, friendly and popular *parrilla* (steakhouse) is on the riverfront, with some pleasant outdoor seating. On weekends the picture window grill is fired up for a full *asado* (barbecue) experience.

La Basílica (☎ 428376, San Martín 101) Mains US$5-12. Here's a good spot next to the basilica where you can settle in comfortably; the ambience is a bit old-fashioned and the menu covers the basics, including US$6 daily specials.

Berlín (San Martín 135) Mains US$5-12. The best part about this German-themed eatery is its sidewalk seating. Travelers missing the motherland can order up (Argentine versions of) German sausage with sauerkraut, and top them off with beer and strudel.

L'Eau Vive (☎ 421774, Constitución 2112) Set menu US$17; open noon-3pm & 8pm-10pm. Two kilometers from central Luján is this outstanding French restaurant run by Carmelite nuns from around the world. Hours are limited, but the service is friendly and attentive and the restaurant is entirely nonsmoking.

The Old Swan Pub (☎ 433346, San Martín 556) This atmospheric, old-time *confitería* (café) features tango on Thursday nights.

Getting There & Away

The bus terminal (☎ 420040) is at Av de Nuestra Señora de Luján and Almirante Brown, three blocks north of the basilica. Bright yellow Metrolíneas buses (Línea 52) arrive frequently from Buenos Aires' Plaza Miserere (next to Once train station; US$4.50; 2 hours). Transportes Atlántida (Línea 57) connects Luján with Buenos Aires' Plaza Italia (in Palermo; US$4.50; 2 hours). A few long-distance services are also available from Luján.

The train station (☎ 420439) is at Av España and Belgrano. There are daily trains to and from Once train station in Buenos Aires.

SAN ANTONIO DE ARECO
☎ 02326 • pop 16,000

Dating from the early-18th-century construction of a chapel in honor of San Antonio de Padua, this serene village is the symbolic center of Argentina's vestigial gaucho culture. It also hosts the country's biggest gaucho celebration, Día de la Tradición, in November. Nestled in the verdant Pampas of northern Buenos Aires province, Areco was the setting for Ricardo Güiraldes' famous coming-of-age-on-the-Pampas novel *Don Segundo Sombra* (1927). Güiraldes' nephew Adolfo played the role of Don Segundo in the 1969 film version, in which many locals served as extras.

Unlike many other Argentine towns, Areco's street life centers not around the plaza but on the main commercial street of Alsina, where there are many high-quality handicrafts for sale. The locals are friendly, with many men around town wearing traditional gaucho berets. It's the kind of town

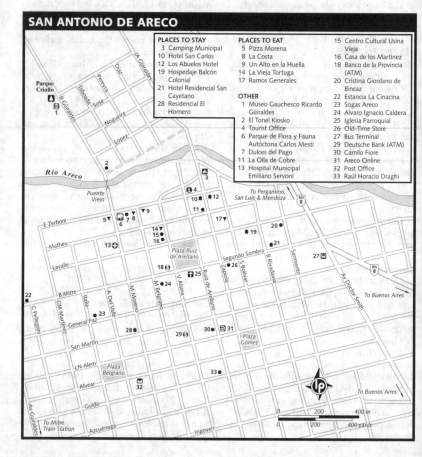

SAN ANTONIO DE ARECO

PLACES TO STAY
3 Camping Municipal
10 Hotel San Carlos
12 Los Abuelos Hotel
19 Hospedaje Balcón Colonial
21 Hotel Residencial San Cayetano
28 Residencial El Hornero

PLACES TO EAT
5 Pizza Morena
8 La Costa
9 Un Alto en la Huella
14 La Vieja Tortuga
17 Ramos Generales

OTHER
1 Museo Gauchesco Ricardo Güiraldes
2 El Tonel Kiosko
4 Tourist Office
6 Parque de Flora y Fauna Autóctona Carlos Mesti
7 Dulces del Pago
11 La Olla de Cobre
13 Hospital Municipal Emiliano Servoni
15 Centro Cultural Usina Vieja
16 Casa de los Martínez
18 Banco de la Provincia (ATM)
20 Cristina Giordano de Bincaz
22 Estancia La Cinacina
23 Sogas Areco
24 Alvaro Ignacio Caldera
25 Iglesia Parroquial
26 Old-Time Store
27 Bus Terminal
29 Deutsche Bank (ATM)
30 Camilo Fiore
31 Areco Online
32 Post Office
33 Raúl Horacio Draghi

where the post office closes for lunch, and nobody uses bicycle locks.

On the south bank of the Río Areco, 113km west of Buenos Aires, San Antonio de Areco is an exceptionally popular weekend destination for porteños. June 13 is the Día del Santo Patrono (Patron Saint's Day). Bring mosquito repellant in summer.

Orientation & Information

San Antonio is 113km west of Buenos Aires via RN 8. V Alsina is the main drag, though the town's numerous sites of interest and shops are scattered throughout the very walkable surrounding streets.

The tourist office (☎ 453165) is on E Zerboni and Ruiz de Arellano. It opens 8am to 2pm weekdays, 10am to 8:30pm Saturday and 10am to 5pm Sunday. If you can't wait to get back to Buenos Aires to check email, or visit Areco Online (☎ 455698, Ruiz de Arellano 285) for Internet access (US$2-3 per hour).

There are a few banks with ATMs around the Plaza Ruiz de Arellano. The postal service is at Alvear and Av Del Valle; the postal code is 2760.

Things to See & Do

Downtown The town's compact center lends itself to walking. At the beginning of the 18th century, **Plaza Ruiz de Arellano** was the site of the corrals belonging to the town's founding estanciero. At its center, the **Monumento a Vieytes** honors locally born Juan Hipólito Vieytes, a figure in the early independence movement. Around the plaza are several historic buildings, including the **Iglesia Parroquial** (Parish Church) and the **Casa de los Martínez** (site of the main house of the original Ruiz de Arellano estancia). The **Centro Cultural Usina Vieja**, half a block north of the plaza, is well worth a visit. At Segunda Sombra and Zapiola is a small, old-time store selling kiosk items. Stop in for an *alfajor*, check out the atmosphere and, if you're lucky, some local *paisanos* (country folk) will be hanging out.

The **Parque de Flora y Fauna Autóctona Carlos Mesti** (*no* ☎, *Zerboni & Moreno;*

admission US$2; open 9am-noon & 2pm-7pm daily) is Areco's modest zoo. Just to the north, conspicuously featured in the film version of *Don Segundo Sombra,* the **Puente Viejo** (old bridge; 1857) across the Río Areco follows the original cart road to northern Argentina. Once a toll crossing, it's now a pedestrian bridge leading to the **Parque Criollo y Museo Gauchesco Ricardo Güiraldes,** Areco's major attraction.

The elderly painter Osvaldo Gasparini and his son Luis operate the **Museo Gauchesco del Pintor Gasparini** (*☎ 453930, Alvear & Bolívar; free; open 8am-8pm Wed-Mon),* containing personal effects of Güiraldes as well as the owners' gauchesco artwork.

Ricardo Güiraldes and Segundo Ramírez, the real-life role model for the character Don Segundo Sombra, both lie in the **Cementerio Municipal** near RN 8 on Soldado Argentino, at the south end of town about 1½ km from the center.

Centro Cultural Usina Vieja Dating from 1901, the Centro Cultural Usina Vieja *(no* ☎, *Alsina 660; free; open 9am-3pm weekdays, 9am-5pm weekends)* is a museum in an old power plant that exhibits lithographs, sculpture, ancient radios, typewriters and microphones. There are some examples of Florencio Molina Campos' amusing caricatures of gaucho life, and even a small airplane. Works by local artists are also on display.

Parque Criollo y Museo Gauchesco Ricardo Güiraldes Inaugurated by the provincial government in 1938, a decade after Güiraldes' death, this museum *(☎ 454780, R Güiraldes & Sosa; admission US$2; open 11am-5pm Wed-Mon)* is a kind of Gaucholand of restored or fabricated buildings idealizing and fossilizing the history of the Pampas. Its contents are genuine, however, and the complex's 90 hectares also provide a good introduction to the gaucho as a modern cultural phenomenon.

The centerpiece of the complex is the **Casa del Museo,** a 20th-century reproduction of an 18th-century *casco* (ranch house). Inside are the desk and chair of Walter Owen, who translated the gauchesco classic

Martín Fierro into English; a wooden bed belonging to Juan Manuel de Rosas (perhaps the ultimate rural landowner); and lots of gorgeous horse gear and various works of gauchesque art. Two rooms are dedicated to Güiraldes himself, another to his wife Adelina del Carril de Güiraldes, and yet another to his painter-cousin Alberto.

Also on the premises is the **Pulpería La Blanqueada**, a mid-19th-century building with a credible re-creation of a rural tavern. Alongside the pulpería are **La Tahona**, an 1848 flour mill brought here from the town of Mercedes, and the **Galpón y Cuarto de Sogas**, where the estancia might have stored its carriages. Nearby is **La Ermita de San Antonio**, a colonial-style chapel with some colonial artifacts.

Estancia La Cinacina Right in town is Estancia La Cinacina (☎ *42045*, **W** *www .lacinacina.com.ar, B Mitre 9*), where US$30 buys an all-you-can-eat asado, entertainment in the form of folkloric music and dance, a tour of the estancia's museum and horseback riding. Call ahead for reservations and schedules.

Special Events

Lasting a week in November, the Fiesta de la Tradición (dating from 1906) celebrates San Antonio de Areco's gaucho past; by presidential decree, the town is the 'sede provincial de la tradición' (provincial site of tradition). The actual Día de la Tradición is November 10, but celebrations are moved to the following Sunday for convenience. Attractions include lectures, craft exhibits,

The Rise & Romance of the Gaucho

No one could have predicted the rise to respectability of that accidental icon, the Argentine gaucho. Dressed in baggy *bombacha* (baggy trousers), the modern gaucho, with a leather *rastra* round his waist and a sharp *facón* in his belt, is the idealized version of a complex historical figure. To many Argentines and foreigners, he is a latter-day version of the romantic characters portrayed in José Hernández' epic poem *Martín Fierro* and Ricardo Güiraldes' novel *Don Segundo Sombra*. Like his counterpart, the North American cowboy, he has received elaborate cinematic treatment. Ironically, only when he became a sanitized anachronism did he achieve celebrity.

Without the rich pastures of the Pampas and the cattle and horses that multiplied on them, the gaucho could never have flourished. In a sense, he replaced the Pampas Indian; usually a *mestizo*, he hunted burgeoning herds of cattle just as the Querandí Indians did the guanaco and rhea. As long as cattle were many, people few, and beef, hides and tallow of some commercial value, his subsistence and independence were assured. This achieved, he could amuse himself gambling and drinking in the saloon or *pulpería*.

Just as the gauchos had replaced the Pampas Indians, so large landowners squeezed out the gauchos. The primitive livestock economy gave way to *saladeros* (salting factories), which made use of a wider variety of products – processed hides, tallow and salted or jerked beef.

For their saladeros, landowners needed labor; the gaucho, with his horseback skills, was a desirable if unwilling source of manpower, and landowners used their influence to coerce him. Classifying the gaucho as a 'lawless' element, discriminatory laws soon prevented men without jobs from traveling freely over the Pampas. Punishment for 'vagrancy' was often military conscription. As sheep replaced cattle on the Pampas, land was fenced and marked, forcing the gaucho to the fringes or onto the estancias.

Unlike the frontier, the estancia was not a democracy, and the gaucho was no longer his own master. He became instead a hired hand for an institution whose physical aspects bespoke hierarchy. As European immigrants came to occupy many saladero jobs, which often were detested by real gauchos, friction arose between gaucho 'natives' and Italian 'gringos.' Despite resistance, the day of the free-roaming gaucho was over by the late 19th century.

guided tours of historic sites, displays of horsemanship, folk dancing and the like. If you're visiting Areco at this time, make reservations far in advance for the limited accommodations.

Places to Stay

Prices may rise 20% on weekends, when reservations are advisable and single rates are often not available. TV and private baths are included in all of these places. At peak times, the tourist office may be able to help with accommodations.

Camping Municipal (no ☎, *E Zerboni & Zapiola*) US$5 per site. It's spacious and shady here, and the river next door is peaceful when the rains aren't heavy.

Hospedaje Balcón Colonial (☎ 454854, *Lavalle 536*) Singles/doubles US$15/30.

Three great rooms await you at this new and charming place.

Hotel Residencial San Cayetano (☎ 452166, *Segundo Sombra & B Rivadavia*) Singles/doubles US$15/30 with breakfast. Decent rooms here are homey but by no means luxurious. It's a friendly place, though.

Hotel San Carlos (☎ 453106, *Zapiola & Zerboni*) Singles/doubles US$20/30; breakfast US$3; free bike use. The outdoor patio hallways are pleasant and carpeted rooms come small, but tidy.

Residencial El Hornero (☎ 452733, *M Moreno 250*) Singles/doubles US$20/35. Here's a little heaven for garden-lovers, with lush greenery surrounded by pleasant patio halls and sitting areas. Rooms are fine.

Los Abuelos Hotel (☎ 456390, *Zapiola & E Zerboni*) Singles/doubles US$20/40 with

The Rise & Romance of the Gaucho

Ironically, about this time Argentina discovered the gaucho's virtues in what has become known as *literatura gauchescha* (literature about the usually illiterate gauchos). *Martín Fierro* romanticized the life of the independent gaucho as he was disappearing, much as the open-range cowboy of the American West was romanticized.

Hernández deplored both opportunistic strongmen like Juan Manuel de Rosas, who claimed to speak for the gaucho, and 'civilizers' like Sarmiento, who had no scruples about discarding the people of the countryside. The gaucho's fierce independence, so often depicted as lawlessness, became admirable, and Hernández almost single-handedly rehabilitated the gaucho's image as Argentines sought an identity in a country rapidly being transformed by immigration and economic modernization. Having fought alongside the gaucho, Hernández eloquently championed him in the public forums of his country, noting the positive gaucho values that even Sarmiento admitted: courtesy, independence and generosity. By the time the gaucho's fate was decided, urban Argentines had elevated him to a mythical status, incorporating these values into their own ideology.

breakfast. This is your typical modern digs with a pool, though rooms are smallish and don't really grab you.

Places to Eat

San Antonio de Areco has fewer places to eat than you might expect, though the situation is improving.

Un Alto en la Huella (☎ 455595, M Belgrano & E Zerboni) Mains US$3.50-5. It's a basic parrilla with thatched roof and painted beams, all giving off a large yet cozy feel. If it's not too busy the old lady might mother you.

La Costa (☎ 452481, M Belgrano & E Zerboni) Mains US$3.50-12. Parrilla's on the menu, which comes in three languages. There's some nice outdoor seating.

Ramos Generales (☎ 456376, S Bolívar 66). Mains US$4-9. Decorated as an early-20th-century general store, this wonderfully cozy and quaint place cooks mostly basic Argentine dishes (though a few oddities like rabbit and duck are thrown in). There's a small store selling regional goods, too.

La Vieja Tortuga (☎ 456080, V Alsina 60) Mains US$4.50-8. There's live folkloric music Friday and Saturday at 10pm. Old silversmithing decor complements the brick walls, but the menu's no surprise.

Pizza Morena (☎ 456391, E Zerboni & M Moreno) Mains US$5-14; dinner only. Parrilla, pasta and seafood dishes serve tourists and locals alike, and you can sit outside on a warm day.

Shopping

Areco's artisans are known throughout the country, with many of their disciples practicing their trades in other cities and provinces. *Mate* paraphernalia, *rastras* (silver-studded belts) and *facones* (long-bladed knives), produced by skilled silversmiths, are among the most typical.

Raúl Horacio Draghi (☎ 454207, Guido 391) Internationally known Raúl Horacio Draghi works in leather as well as silver.

Alvaro Ignacio Caldera (☎ 455861, M Belgrano 213) Alvaro is a top silversmith who claims to have made a belt buckle for ex-president and tabloid fodder Carlos Menem. Custom-made items here take weeks to make and cost hundreds to thousands of pesos.

Sogas Areco (☎ 453797, General Paz near Italia) Check out this place for horse gear and gaucho clothing.

Cristina Giordano de Bincaz (☎ 452829, Sarmiento 112) There's a working loom here, plus some beautiful ponchos and *fajas* (intricate woven bands).

La Olla de Cobre (☎ 453105, Matheu near Zapiola) If you're looking for a gift of artisanal chocolates and tinned confections, come on over.

Dulces del Pago (☎ 454751, Zerboni 280) This store offers a good variety of fruit preserves, as well as homemade *dulce de leche*.

El Tonel Kiosko (no ☎, Güiraldes and Puente Viejo) For a funky time, check out the second-largest wine barrel in Argentina; it's at the kiosk just across the Puente Viejo. Take a gander at the goods inside, or sit down for coffee or *mate,* but don't expect a traditional café or many tables; it's a very eclectic place run by an odd couple.

Getting There & Away

Buses run frequently from Buenos Aires to Areco (US$8; 2 hours). General Belgrano, which leaves from the Don Seguno café (☎ 15-680868), and Chevallier, which leaves from its small station (☎ 453904), are located almost next to each other on Ruta 8. Both serve as the town's bus terminal. A few long-distance services are available; check at the terminal.

AROUND SAN ANTONIO DE ARECO

Surrounding San Antonio de Areco are a number of estancias that offer overnight accommodations starting at US$130 per person with all meals included. Director María Luisa Bemberg shot part of her historical drama *Camila* at **Estancia La Bamba** (☎ 02326-456-392), about 15km east of Areco.

Unquestionably the most historic of nearby estancias is the **Güiraldes family's Estancia La Porteña** (☎ 453770, 011-4822-1325 in Buenos Aires), which dates from

1850 and has a garden designed by the renowned French architect Charles Thays, responsible for Buenos Aires' major public parks. **Estancia El Ombú** (☎ 92080, 011-4710-2795 in Buenos Aires) belonged to General Pablo Ricchieri, who first inflicted universal military conscription on the country.

Areco's tourist office can give you more information on accommodations and tours, and in Buenos Aires the Secretaría de Turismo de la Nación (☎ 011-4312-2232), on Av Santa Fe 883, can print out a more complete list of Estancias around Buenos Aires.

Southern Pampas

The fertile flats of Argentina's pampas lands are only occasionally disrupted by the dimples of low mountain ranges. The easterly Sierras de Tandil are rounded hills whose peaks – none higher than 500m – take their names from the counties they cross: Olavarría, Azul, Tandil and Balcarce. Almost 300km away, the scenic Sierra de la Ventana, its jagged peaks rising to 1300m, attracts adventurous hikers and climbers. And over to the west one province are the modest granite boulders of Parque Nacional Lihué Calel.

Travelers looking for peaceful, laid-back towns will find Tandil and Sierra de la Ventana (both named for their nearby hills) excellent for relaxed exploration and activity. While the larger cities like Bahía Blanca and Santa Rosa aren't destinations in their own right, they do have some interesting surrounding highlights, and provide decent resting points while traveling to more popular destinations to the west and south of the country.

TANDIL
☎ 02293 • pop 130,000
Perhaps the most scenically diverse city in the Pampas, Tandil sits leisurely at the northern edge of the Sierras de Tandil, a 2.5-million-year-old mountain range worn down to gentle, grassy peaks and rocky outcroppings. It's a hub of rock climbing and mountain biking, and traditionally attracts masses of visitors at Easter to see Calvario,

a hill ostensibly resembling the site of Christ's crucifixion at Golgotha.

The city of Tandil arose from Fuerte Independencia, a military outpost established in 1823 by Martín Rodríguez. In the early 1870s, one of the most notorious incidents in provincial history began here when a group of renegade gauchos, followers of the eccentric healer Gerónimo de Solané (popularly known as Tata Dios), gathered at nearby Cerro La Movediza to distribute weapons before going on a murderous rampage against European settlers and recent immigrants.

Today Tandil is an important dairy zone, the heart of a rich cheese-producing region and home to esteemed schools of agronomy and lactose production. The hundreds of cheeses produced in the numerous *queserías* (cheese factories) around Tandil are sold in specialty stores throughout town. Downtown is relaxed, and there are numerous high-quality artisan shops along its cobblestone streets.

Orientation
Tandil is 384km south of Buenos Aires via RN 3 and RN 226, and 170km northwest of Mar del Plata via RN 226. The main commercial streets are Rodríguez and 9 de Julio, while the center of social activity is Plaza Independencia, a two-block area bounded by Rodríguez, Belgrano, Chacabuco and Pinto.

Information
The tourist office, Dirección de Turismo (☎ 432073), 9 de Julio 555, distributes a good city map and useful brochures. Check here or at the Plaza Hotel (see Places to Stay later) for local writer Elías El Hage's hilarious bilingual guide to Tandil; it's well worth the US$10.

ACA (☎ 425463) is at Rodríguez 399.

Banco Velox, on the corner of 9 de Julio and Pinto, and Bank Boston, Pinto 745, both have ATMs.

The post office is at 9 de Julio 455; Tandil's postal code is 7000. Cyber World (☎ 433975), at Rodríguez 827, charges US$2 per hour for Internet access; its hours are 10:30am until late.

Hospital Municipal Ramón Santamarina (☎ 422010) is at Paz 406.

Things to See & Do

Tandil's museums include the historic **Museo Tradiciónalista Fuerte Independencia** (no ☎, 4 de Abril 845; open 4pm-8pm Tues-Sun) and the **Museo de Bellas Artes** (☎ 432067, Chacabuco 353, open 5pm-8pm Tues-Sun).

Activities

The easy walk to **Parque Independencia** from the southwestern edge of downtown offers good views of the city, particularly at night. The **Dique del Fuerte**, only 12 blocks south of Plaza Independencia, is a huge reservoir where the Balneario Municipal operates three **swimming** pools. The Centro Nautico del Fuerte rents **canoes** and **kayaks** throughout the summer.

At the north edge of town, where Tata Dios gathered his supporters over a century ago, the **Piedra Movediza** (a 300-ton 'rocking stone') once teetered precariously atop **Cerro La Movediza** for many years before falling. The site still attracts visitors – go figure. Take bus No 503 (blue).

To go **horseback riding** in the Reserva Natural Sierra del Tigre, contact Gabriel Barletta (☎ 427725, mobile 1558-4833, Avellaneda 673; US$20-25). Licensed guide Christian Lopez runs the **Escuela de Escalada** (mobile ☎ 1562-7008, ⓔ mountain trekking@yahoo.com.ar) and offers rock climbing instruction and day trips. To explore the area by **mountain bike**, contact Carlos at Tandilia (☎ 425572, mobile 1563-2902, ⓦ www.centineo.com.ar; US$15 and up per person).

Places to Stay

Reservations are a must during summer, Easter week and on holiday weekends.

Camping Municipal Pinar de la Sierra (☎ 425370, Av San Gabriel & M de San Martín) US$8 per site for up to 4 people. Just beyond the Dique del Fuerte, this clean, shady facility has a grocery and hot showers. Some No 500 (yellow) buses go there – ask the driver.

Hotel Kaikú (☎ 423114, Mitre 902) Singles/doubles US$13/24, breakfast US$1. With a friendly staff, large bathrooms and a cheap restaurant attached, this modest and tidy hotel is good value.

Lo de Olga Gandolfi (☎ 440258, fax 422960, Chacabuco 977) US$18 per person with breakfast; reservations recommended. This beautifully renovated house has 11 spotless, uniquely decorated rooms. The owners put great care into the place and it feels like a home.

Hotel Austral (☎ 425606, 9 de Julio 725) Singles/doubles US$20/39. Carpeted rooms in this large, comfortable hotel all have TV and telephone.

Plaza Hotel (☎/fax 427160, General Pinto 438) Singles/doubles US$63/85 with breakfast. This modern hotel has splendid views from the upper rooms facing the plaza, and its confitería serves the best coffee in town.

Places to Eat

Grill Argentino (☎ 448666, Rodríguez 552) US$6-12. The meats and pastas are all good, but the large US$6 mozzarella pizza is especially alluring.

La Giralda (☎ 424830, Constitución y Rodríguez) All-you-can eat US$7. This parrilla is another Tandil institution. For a paltry price it's all the meat, empanadas and fries you can eat. The drink's extra.

El Viejo Trebol (☎ 442333, 14 de Julio & Mitre) US$8-15. Excellent all-you-can-eat parrillada, which often includes pork and venison, costs US$8.

Epoca de Quesos (☎ 448750, San Martín & 9 de Julio) US$8-15. In one of Tandil's oldest buildings, Epoca de Quesos sells over 130 different local cheeses and dozens of locally cured meats. You can taste and buy at the counter or sit in the cavernous back rooms and split a huge sampler plate over a beer.

Entertainment

For such a small town, Tandil has several good bars.

Bar Tolomé (☎ 422951, Mitre 602) Open 7:30am-late. Dead mid-week and lively on weekends, this relaxed bar serves pizzas and sandwiches when a beer's not enough.

Liver Pool (*9 de Julio & San Martín*) The British pub atmosphere and dedicated regulars make this spot a town favorite.

Gloria (*9 de Julio 975*) This two-floor disco plays pop hits and feels more like a big bar.

Shopping

La Yunta (☎ 437255, *Sarmiento 613*) La Yunta stocks an impressive selection of horse gear, leather goods and other gaucho souvenirs.

La Cuchillería (☎ 494937, *San Martín 786*) From 3-inch whittlers to 14-inch facónes, this high-end knife shop sells a wide array of quality handmade blades.

Talabartería Carlos A Berruti (☎ 425787, *Rodríguez 787*) Especially good for leather, this store also stocks an assortment of *mates,* knives, silverwork and ponchos.

Alquimía (☎ 425639, *9 de Julio 706*) Try this place for ceramics and woodcrafts made from the aromatic *palo santo,* a tree native to the Argentine Chaco.

Getting There & Away

Air LAER (☎ 429213), Hipólito Yrigoyen 714, flies six times weekly to Buenos Aires and to Necochea.

Bus Tandil's bus terminal (☎ 432092) is at Av Buzón 650 at Portugal. Several companies go to Buenos Aires daily. There are buses every two hours to Mar del Plata and frequent runs to other coastal destinations.

The following table shows approximate travel times at mid-season fares.

Destination	Duration in hours	Cost
Buenos Aires	5¼	US$19
Córdoba	13	US$48
General Alvear	12	US$40
Mar del Plata	3	US$9
Mendoza	15	US$56
Necochea	2¾	US$11
Rosario	9	US$41
San Juan	18	US$56
San Luis	12	US$45
Santiago del Estero	17	US$55
Tucumán	18	US$60

Getting Around

Tandil's excellent public transportation system reaches every important sight. Bus No 500 (yellow) goes to Dique del Fuerte and the municipal campground. No 501 (red) goes to the bus terminal, and No 503 (blue) goes to Cerro La Movediza, the university, and the bus terminal.

Localiza auto rentals (☎ 447099) is at Mitre 585. Prices start at around US$27 per day, plus US$0.23 per kilometer.

AROUND TANDIL

Estancia Acelain (☎ 420064, 441120, *RN 226 Km 205; open year-round*), the opulent Spanish-style mansion of Hispanophile writer Enrique Larreta (1875-1961), was built in 1924 with local stone and features furnishings and ornaments brought from the old country. Surrounded by dense woods, the estancia also features a natural lagoon with good mackerel fishing. The mansion is open to the public for day visits and overnight stays with full board (around US$125 per person).

Larreta, whose erudite historical novels made him famous, used Acelain as a country retreat from his Buenos Aires house in the barrio of Belgrano; the house is now a museum. The chapel has stained-glass windows imported from Germany.

Estancia Acelain is reached from RN 226 Km 205 between Tandil and Azul. The owners may provide transport to those who stay a few days.

BAHÍA BLANCA
☎ 0291 • pop 283,000

Grandiose buildings, an attractive plaza and boulevards lined with shade trees and palms give oft-overlooked Bahía Blanca the essence of a cosmopolitan city in miniature. With a few intriguing museums and a very convenient location, Bahía Blanca can be a worthwhile stop.

In an early effort to establish military control on the periphery of the Pampas, Colonel Ramón Estomba situated the pompously named Fortaleza Protectora Argentina at the natural harbor of Bahía Blanca in 1828. In 1884 the railway connected the area with Buenos Aires, but another 11 years passed before Bahía Blanca officially became a city. Only in recently has this port city flourished in commerce and industry, primarily through agriculture and petrochemicals.

Orientation & Information

Bahía Blanca is 654km southwest of Buenos Aires via RN 3, 530km east of Neuquén via RN 22, and 278km north of Viedma via RN 3.

The tourist office (☎ 459-4007), at Alsina 65, in the basement of the Munici-palidad, is open 8am to 7pm weekdays, 10am to 1pm Saturday. ACA (☎ 455-0076) is at Chiclana 305.

Bank hours are 8am to 1pm in summer, 10am to 3pm in winter. Change money and traveler's checks at Pullman Tour (☎ 455-4950) at San Martín 171. Banco de la Nación, at Estomba 52, may also change traveler's checks. The post office is at Moreno 34; the postal code is 8000.

Asatej (☎ 456-0666, ⓦ www.asatej.com – Spanish only), Zelerrayan 267, local 7, sells discount international flights, issues student ID cards and is the STA representative.

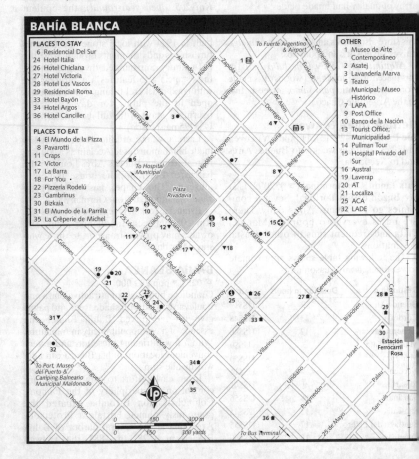

BAHÍA BLANCA

PLACES TO STAY
6 Residencial Del Sur
24 Hotel Italia
26 Hotel Chiclana
27 Hotel Victoria
28 Hotel Los Vascos
29 Residencial Roma
33 Hotel Bayón
34 Hotel Argos
36 Hotel Canciller

PLACES TO EAT
4 El Mundo de la Pizza
8 Pavarotti
11 Craps
12 Victor
14 La Barra
18 For You
22 Pizzería Rodelú
23 Gambrinus
30 Bizkaia
31 El Mundo de la Parrilla
35 La Crêperie de Michel

OTHER
1 Museo de Arte Contemporáneo
2 Asatej
3 Lavandería Marva
5 Teatro Municipal; Museo Histórico
7 LAPA
9 Post Office
10 Banco de la Nación
13 Tourist Office; Municipalidad
14 Pullman Tour
15 Hospital Privado del Sur
16 Austral
19 Laverap
20 AT
21 Localiza
25 ACA
32 LADE

Laverap is at Av Colón 197. Lavandería Marva is at Mitre 186. The Hospital Municipal (☎ 456-8484) is at Estomba 968, while the Hospital Privado del Sur (☎ 455-0270) is at Las Heras 164.

Things to See & Do

On the outskirts of town, in the former customs building hardly noticeable among the massive grain elevators and fortresslike power plant of Puerto Ingeniero White, the **Museo del Puerto** (☎ 457-3006, *Guillermo Torres 4131; admission by donation; 9am-noon weekdays, 3:30pm-7:30pm Sat & Sun; closed Jan*) is an iconoclastic tribute to immigrants and their heritage, and includes an archive with documents, photographs and recorded oral histories. The best time to visit is for a weekend afternoon tea, when local groups prepare regional delicacies, each week representing a different immigrant group. Live music often accompanies the refreshments. Bus Nos 500 & 504 from the plaza go to the museum.

The neoclassical Teatro Municipal, at Alsina and Dorrego, is the city's main performing arts center. In the same building is **Museo Histórico** (☎ 456-3117, *Dorrego 116; free; open 3pm-9pm Tues-Sat, 4pm-7pm Sun*). Also worth checking out is **Museo de Arte Contemporáneo** (☎ 459-4006, *Sarmiento 454; free; open 10am-1pm & 4pm-8pm Tues-Fri, 4pm-8pm Sat & Sun*), showcasing local and national artists.

On the weekends an artisans' market takes over Plaza Rivadavia, opposite the Municipalidad.

Places to Stay

Catering mainly to the business set, lodging in Bahía Blanca is generally overpriced for what's on offer; however, good deals can be found. The budget area is across from the train station. There is no lodging near the bus terminal.

Budget *Camping Balneario Municipal Maldonado* (☎ 455-1614, *Parque Marítimo Almirante Brown*) Sites US$5. Open year-round. This basic campground, 4km southwest of downtown, has saltwater swimming

pools. Hot water and electricity are available in summer only.

Hotel Los Vascos (☎ 452-9290, *Cerri 747*) Single US$8 with shared bath, single/double US$15/20 with private bath. Across from the train station, Los Vascos shows its age, but is well-kept by a gregarious owner. Rooms, some of which have small balconies, are accessed by an internal patio.

Residencial Roma (☎ 453-8500, *Cerri 759*) Single US$12 with shared bath, single/double US$20/30 with private bath. While the rooms are clean and quiet and the bathrooms plentiful, Roma, also across from the train station, has only green-lit hallways for personality.

Hotel Bayón (☎ 452-2504, *Chiclana 487*) Singles/doubles US$12/22 with shared bath, US$20/28 with private bath. Sputtering fluorescent lights, musty air and a cranky doorman don't do much for Bayón, but it is a pretty good value – except that there's no breakfast on offer.

Mid-Range & Top End *Residencial Del Sur* (☎ 452-2452, *Rodriguez 80*) Singles/doubles US$25/35 with private bath. Safe, secure but in the heart of the city, Del Sur comes recommended especially for women traveling alone. Breakfast is an additional US$3.

Hotel Canciller (☎ 453-8270, *Brown 667*) Singles/doubles US$27/37 with private bath. Owned by the same woman as Chiclana, you'll find the same style rooms, sans the charm of the building. Singles with shared bath also available for US$13.

Hotel Chiclana (☎ 453-0436, *Chiclana 370*) Singles/doubles US$29/39 with private bath, breakfast & TV. Once a mansion inhabited by the uppercrust and their servants, this hotel features excellent-value rooms, smartly decorated with pleasant lighting, good beds and an ample breakfast. Rooms in the old servants' quarters are particularly charming. An added bonus is the availability of US$10 rooms with shared bath. Best deal in town.

Hotel Victoria (☎ 452-0522, *General Paz 84*) Singles/doubles US$20/24 with shared bath, US$30/35 with private bath. Brimming with good-ol'-days charm, some rooms have balconies onto the street, while ones with shared bathrooms all give to a terrace walkway of burgundy walls, potted ferns and kaleidoscope tiling. This is a fun place to stay, especially if you hang out in the glow of the downstairs bar.

Hotel Italia (☎ 456-2700, fax 456-2700, *Brown 181*) Singles/doubles US$44/54. Well-lit large rooms have modern European features, but the best part is the over-sized beds.

Hotel Argos (☎ 455-0404, e reservas@ hotelargos.com, *España 149*) Singles/doubles US$85/105. Posh both outside and in, Argos offers top-of-the-line service in a sparkling hotel with plush, fully carpeted and very quiet rooms. Breakfast is buffet-style filling, the gym modern and the service professional without being pretentious.

Places to Eat
Budget *Pizzería Rodelú* (☎ 455-1332, *O'Higgins & Saavedra*) US$2-10. On a busy corner, Rodelú has pizza *a la piedra* (stone-cooked), varieties of those bland white-bread sandwiches and cheap breakfasts.

La Barra (☎ 451-7910, *Chiclana 155*) US$4-10. Casual and with good music, come here for pastas or sandwiches. Friday nights feature live music, sometimes open-mic.

Craps (☎ 451-8737, *López 10*) US$4-10. It's a shame about the name, but Craps is a great place to dine and get away from the bustle of the streets. The US$8 set-course lunch is the best deal, and cheap salads are large enough to share. There's also Internet access.

For You (☎ 453-9888, *Belgrano 69*) Tenedor libre US$6-8. You may be blinded by the lights, but you can eat all you want here. It's always busy and a good value.

Mid-Range *Bizkaia* (☎ 452-0191, *Soler 769*) US$6-10. Basque colors and cuisine dominate this small informal restaurant, favored by locals for fish and seafood. Expect a bit of a wait for the well-prepared dishes.

Víctor (☎ 452-3814, *Chiclana 83*) US$6-12. Choose from a variety of daily specials,

including *sorrentinos*, barbecued chicken or of course, parrilla. Service is attentive, but the atmosphere friendly and informal.

El Mundo de la Pizza (☎ 454-5054 *Dorrego 55*) US$7-10. This large diner with posters of silver-screen stars and old adverts is the venue for excellent pizzas and empanadas. It's considered the best pizzeria in town by many locals.

Pavarotti (☎ 450-0700, *Belgrano 272*, Three-course lunch US$8, US$14 with drinks. Outfitted like a wine cellar, with hams hooked on the ceiling, this cozy trattoria is a good value and has a superb wine list

El Mundo de la Parrilla (☎ 455-5101 *Colon 379*) Tenedor libre US$10-12; open 8pm-1am. For US$10 eat all the empanadas salad and meat you can manage in this lively, large and colorful spot. Wine is a bit expensive.

La Crêperie de Michel (☎ 451-0690 *España 214*) US$12; open 8pm-on Mon-Sun for lunch only Sat. An assortment of sweet and savory crepes all served in the epitome of quaint make this a great option for anyone ready for some French flare.

Gambrinus (☎ 452-2380, *Arribeños 164*, Prices US$15. If you're in the mood for some rude militant service and bratwurst, this cervecería is the place to be. It's been a local institution for more than a century and is a lively spot, but beware of the stuffed penguin.

Entertainment
For a night on the town, head to **Fuerte Ar gentino**, about nine blocks northeast from Plaza Rivadavia, where *boliches* and bars are clustered together in a convenient cul de-sac. There's a pleasant sculpture garden nearby to catch your breath.

Getting There & Away
Air Austral (☎ 456-0561), San Martín 298 and LAPA (☎ 454-6566, 456-4552) at Sole 68, fly daily to Buenos Aires (US$86 to US$124), the latter also serving Río Galle gos (US$97 to US$163) and Río Grande (US$125 to US$207). LADE (☎ 452-1063) Darregueira 21, has two flights weekly, one

puddle-jumper to Bariloche, the other to Trelew. Check for the latest schedules.

Bus A key transport hub for southern Buenos Aires province and points south, Bahía Blanca's bus terminal (☎ 481-9615), Brown 1700, is about 2km east of Plaza Rivadavia. All of the bus companies are represented and there's a decent snack bar. For transport to Sierra de la Ventana, La Estrella leaves daily except Saturday at 6am and 8:40pm; Expreso Cabildo leaves at 8:20pm weekdays and at 1:30pm Saturday; and Cerri Bus leaves at 7am, 1pm and 7pm.

Destination	Duration in hours	Cost
Bariloche	14	US$35-41
Buenos Aires	7-10	US$25-33
Comodoro Rivadavia	15	US$47
Córdoba	12½	US$48
La Plata	9	US$26-32
Mar del Plata	7	US$21
Mendoza	16	US$55
Neuquén	10	US$30
Río Gallegos	26	US$78
Sierra de la Ventana	2	US$5
Trelew	12	US$28-42

Train Trains leave from the once-grand but now rundown Estación Ferrocarril Roca (☎ 452-1168), Av Cerri 750, to Buenos Aires at 8:20pm Monday, Wednesday, Friday and Saturday via Lamadrid; and Tuesday, Thursday and Sunday via Pringles. Fares are US$15 *turista*, US$17 *primera*, US$23 *Pullman* and US$32 *coche cama*.

Getting Around
The airport (☎ 452-1665) is 15km east of town on the naval base, RN 3 Norte Km 674. Austral provides its own transport (US$3) to the airport.

Local buses cost US$0.70, but take only Tarjebus cards, available from kiosks. Bus Nos 505, 512, 514, 516 and 517 serve the terminal from downtown. Bus No 505 goes out Av Colón to Balneario Maldonado. For rental cars, try AT (☎ 454-3944), Colón 180, or Localiza (☎ 456-2526), Colón 194.

SIERRA DE LA VENTANA
☎ 0291 • pop 1450
Just 125km north of Bahía Blanca, this charming, slow-paced town is popular with Argentines but underappreciated by foreigners. A popular spot for those looking for time to just relax, the town has conventional facilities such as a casino, golf links and swimming pools, and it also offers a variety of hiking, climbing, riding, bicycling, kayaking and fishing opportunities.

To reach the town from Bahía Blanca, take RN 33 to Tornquist, then RP 76. Sierra de la Ventana is divided into two sectors by Río Sauce Grande: Villa Tivoli has all of the businesses and services, while Villa Arcadia is a more residential area and also the locale for many hotels.

Information
The tourist office (☎ 491-5303, e dirturismo @impsatl.com.ar), near the train station at Roca 17, distributes a useful packet of maps and flyers and can help find accommodations. It opens 7am to 1pm daily, 3pm to 9pm in summer, with abbreviated winter hours. Banco de la Provincia, at San Martín 260, has an ATM. The post office is at Av Roca and Alberdi; the postal code is 8168. Locutorio Televentana is at Av San Martín 291. Laverap is on Güemes near San Martín.

Places to Stay
Villa Tivoli *Camping El Paraíso* (☎ 491-5299, Los Paraísos & Diego Meyer) Adult/child US$5/3. This is a well-shaded, full facility campground on the river.

Camping La Carolina (no ☎, Circunvalación 58) US$3. Across the river and right by the train tracks, La Carolina caters to family camping.

Hospedaje La Perlita (☎ 491-5020, Calle E Morón) Singles US$12/10 with private/shared bath. Basic, clean rooms cluster around an overgrown garden at this very friendly and secure hostel, but there's no breakfast or kitchen use.

Hotel Atero (☎ 491-5002, fax 491-5344, Av San Martín & Güemes) Singles or doubles US$40. Right in the heart of town,

Atero is considered one of the best places to stay; rooms are large, cozily decorated and have modern bathrooms, and the management is conscientious and friendly. Breakfast is extra.

Villa Arcadia On the grounds near the hotel there's *Camping Pillahuinco (☎ 491-5151, Coronel Suarez & Punta Alta)* US$4. It's another good option and farther away from the bustle (and trains).

Ymcapolis (☎ 491-5004, fax 491-5061, Av Ymcapolis & Coronel Suarez) US$30-35 full pension only; US$4 per tent; open mid-Dec-Easter. Within this old, lofty 1908 building by the side of the river, this YMCA hostel caters mainly to student groups and families but keeps rooms set aside during summer high season. Check whether space is available before arriving.

Residencial Carlitos (☎ 491-5285, Coronel Suárez 80) US$21 per person with breakfast. Owner-run Carlitos offers foam mattresses, small bathrooms and a swimming pool, all in a large garden environment.

Hotel Pillahuincó (☎/fax 491-5151, Rayces 161) Singles/doubles US$53/76. Two mini-mansions are nestled together within sweeping luxurious gardens, complete with lawn chairs, birdbaths and peacocks, at this blast from a glorious past. Croquet, anyone?

Places to Eat

Sher (☎ 491-5055, Güemes s/n) US$6-12. Just off the main drag, you can find large portions of good pizza and pasta here, but drinks are expensive.

Sol y Luna (☎ 15-573-4565, Av San Martín 393) US$6-12. Pastas and pizzas are the way to go here, but don't overlook the soy burgers and other veggie specials, all served in an attractive dining room by the witty, friendly owners.

Golf Club (☎ 491-5113, Barrio Golf) US$6-15. Lots of light streams through this restaurant located on the side of the golf course. It's a good bet if you're looking for a slightly fancier night on the town.

Hotel Provincial (☎ 491-5024, Drago 130) US$6-15. Within this large hotel, the attractive bar/restaurant is a worthwhile spot

to enjoy a drink or snack while gazing over the rolling green hills.

Rali-Hue (☎ 491-5220, Av San Martín 307) US$9-15. At this excellent, informal parrilla, trays of meat are served crackling away and eaten with abandon on wooden plates.

Getting There & Away

Buses leave from Av San Martín, just next to the locutorio. Buy tickets in the small kiosk behind the ice cream shop. La Estrella goes to Buenos Aires (US$27.50; 8 hours) at 10:30pm daily except Saturday, to La Plata (US$28; 12 hours) at 8am daily and to Bahía Blanca (US$5; 2 hours) at 6:50am and 7pm daily. GeoTur (☎ 491-5355) runs door-to-door service between Sierra de la Ventana and Tornquist (US$3; 1 hour), stopping at Saldungaray and Villa Ventana (US$2) three times daily.

From the train station (☎ 491-5164) at Av San Martín & Roca, trains leave at 11pm Tuesday, Thursday and Sunday to Buenos Aires (US$16-18; 8-10 hours) and at 7am to Bahía Blanca (US$5; 2 hours).

AROUND SIERRA DE LA VENTANA

Lots of **trekking** and **climbing** options are on offer in this region. Well-recommended Geotur (☎ 491-5355, Av San Martín 193 in Sierra de la Ventana) organizes a wide range of such activities, including hikes of Cerro Tres Picos.

Villa Ventana

About 17km northwest of Sierra de la Ventana, Villa Ventana still retains, at least outside of peak season, the feel of a place yet undiscovered, which may make it more attractive than the more established Sierra de la Ventana. Dirt roads with names of birds cut through town in the pattern of an armadillo shell, each lane gorgeously shaded in a green circus of tall trees and curling ivy. Birdsongs and the clip-clop of horses' hooves may be the only sounds. However, as more people seeking serenity descend, the less serene it becomes: avoid weekends and Easter holidays.

Places to Stay & Eat If you're visiting during the peak season, book accommodations in advance; in the off-season, call to confirm what is open.

Camping Pablito (☎ 491-0019) US$3.50. About three blocks from the entrance to town, Pablito is a large, full-service (hot water, showers and firepots) campground open year-round.

Camping Municipal (☎ 491-0014, Tacuarita) US$4. Similar to Pablito when it comes to amenities, the municipal campground is farther away, which may offer some extra tranquility if it weren't for the owner's pack of dogs. Head through the village along Pillahuinco and turn left towards signs to the *dique* (dyke). The campground is on the other side of the river.

Residencial La Colina (☎ 491-0063, Pilahuinco & Carpintero) Doubles US$20. Warmly recommended, La Colina, to the east of the plaza and up a few blocks, has comfortable annex rooms with private bath. There's a small kitchen and it's run by a very congenial fellow who is knowledgeable about the area.

Hostería La Peninsula (☎ 491-0012, Golondrina & Cruz del Sur) Singles/doubles US$30/60 with half pension. Right at the entrance to town, this is the most ample lodging, managed by an elderly couple.

There are lots of cabins to rent; ask the tourist office for a list and help with vacancies. Recommended places include *La Ponderosa* (☎ 491-0078), *Rancho Villa* (☎ 491-0052) and *Pablito* (☎ 491-0019), all of which charge US$30-50 for a double, supply linens and have kitchens.

To grab a bite, try *Rancho Villa* (☎ 491-0052, Cruz del Sur & Zorzal) for burgers and fast food, *McRico* (no ☎, Cruz del Sur) for pizza or the more expensive *Las Golondrinas* (☎ 491-0047, Cruz del Sur & Hornero) for high-mountain cuisine. The latter is best just for drinks in a deluxe, relaxed environment.

Getting There & Away Shuttles connect Sierra de la Ventana with Villa Ventana (US$2; 20 minutes) at 6:40am, 10:40am and 7pm daily, leaving from the GeoTur office. To go to Sierra de la Ventana, take the GeoTur micro from the main plaza at 8am, 12:30pm and 7pm. Weekend times vary. A remise will cost about US$8-10. From Bahía Blanca, just ask to be dropped off at the entrance to town along RP 76.

Cerro Tres Picos

The 1239m Cerro Tres Picos, southwest of Villa Ventana but accessed from RP 76, is a worthwhile backpack trip. Since this is the private property of Estancia Funke, there is a US$5 admission charge. Contact Christian Klein (☎ 494-0058) for permission to hike and camp. Those making a day hike must begin by 9am; overnighters can start as late as 2pm.

Parque Provincial Ernesto Tornquist

Imposing wrought-iron gates mark the entrance to the scenic 6700-hectare Parque Provincial Ernesto Tornquist (☎ 491-0039; admission US$1; open 7:30am-6pm), 5km from Villa Ventana. The informative **Centro de Visitantes** has a well-organized display on local ecology enhanced by audiovisuals. The park's high point is the two-hour hike to 1136m **Cerro Ventana**, which offers dramatic views of surrounding hills and the distant Pampas. At the Cerro Ventana trailhead, rangers and volunteer guides collect the entry fee and guide groups along a short, well-marked and otherwise easy hike. Insistent hikers may be able to get permission to go solo by signing a waiver, although the guides are supposedly supplied for safety reasons. A later start is better to have the view to yourself instead of sharing it with dozens of porteños huffing and puffing their way to the crest of what is probably the country's most-climbed peak. In summer there are five-hour ranger-guided walks to the gorge at **Garganta del Diablo** (Devil's Throat).

Places to Stay *Campamento Base* (☎ 0291-491-0067, RP 76, Km 224) Campsites US$5 per person. This friendly campground at Cerro Ventana has shaded campsites with clean bathrooms and excellent hot showers.

Hotel El Mirador (☎ 0291-494-1338, RP 76, Km 226) Singles/doubles US$35/54 with breakfast, US$84 for 4-person cabin. Pleasant A-frame cabins and an ample hotel offer all the amenities of a three-star place, near Cerro Ventana.

SANTA ROSA
☎ 02954 • pop 82,000

About 600km from Buenos Aires is this tidy city founded in 1892. French, Spanish and Italian immigrants arrived with the expansion of the railroads at the turn of the 19th century, but one measure of Santa Rosa's continuing isolation and insignificance is that until 1951, the surrounding area remained a territory rather than a province.

Today Santa Rosa is not a tourist destination and won't knock your socks off as such, but at least it's not ugly and there's a nearby recreational lake west of center. Santa Rosa is also the base for exploring Parque Nacional Lihué Calel, an isolated but pretty park that's home to a surprising assortment of vegetation and wildlife.

Orientation
North of Av España, the city consists of a standard grid centered on the spotless but nearly shadeless Plaza San Martín, the site of a rather ugly modernistic cathedral. Most businesses are on the plaza and its surrounding streets, though a more recent focus of activity is the modern Centro Cívico, seven blocks east on Av Pedro Luro.

Information
The helpful tourist office (☎ 425060) is at Luro and San Martín, near the bus terminal. Hours are 7am to 8pm weekdays, 9am to 1pm and 4pm to 8pm weekends. There's also a tourist information center (☎ 422249) at the bus terminal, open 24 hours.

ACA (☎ 422435) is at Av San Martín 102, at the corner of Coronel Gil.

You'll find several ATMs in the center. The post office is at Hilario Lagos 258; Santa Rosa's postal code is 6300.

Things to See & Do
The **Museo de Ciencias Naturales y Antropológicas** (☎ 422693, Pellegrini 180; free; open 8am-5pm weekdays, 5pm-9pm weekends) contains natural science, archaeological, historical, artisanal, and fine-arts collections.

The **Museo de Artes** (☎ 427332, 9 de Julio & Villegas; free; open 8am-1pm & 4pm-7pm Tues-Fri, 4:30pm-9:30pm weekends) contains works by local and national artists.

The **Teatro Español** (☎ 455325, Hilario Lagos 54; free; open 10am-noon & 4pm-6:30pm weekdays, weekend hours vary) is Santa Rosa's major performing arts venue and dates from 1927.

Laguna Don Tomás, 1km west of center, is the place for locals to boat, swim, play sports or just stroll.

Places to Stay
Centro Recreativo Municipal Don Tomás (☎ 455358, west end of Av Uruguay) US$3 per person. From the bus terminal, take the local Transporte El Indio bus. Camping facilities are excellent and include picnic tables, parrillas, a swimming pool, hot showers, a fitness course for joggers and shade trees. Bring repellent for the ferocious mosquitoes.

Hostería Santa Rosa (☎ 423868, Hipólito Yrigoyen 696) Singles/doubles US$20/30. It's homey and friendly enough, and the rooms are fine. Near the bus terminal, this is a good deal.

Hostería Río Atuel (☎ 422597, Av Pedro Luro 356) Singles/doubles US$25/30. These worn digs are right across from the bus terminal. It fills up fast when the buses come in at night.

Hotel Calfucurá (☎ 423608, San Martín 695) Singles/doubles from US$59/65. Distinguished by the enormous mural of its namesake *cacique* (Indian chief), this high-rise is tops.

Places to Eat
La Recova (☎ 424444, Hipólito Yrigoyen & Avellaneda) Grab some sandwiches and coffee at this joint, located right on Plaza San Martín.

Restaurant San Martín (☎ 431099, Pellegrini 115) Don't expect anything fancy at this cheap but popular parrilla and pasta place.

La Tablita (☎ 15-664317, Urquiza 336) The US$10 parrillada here includes a wonderful buffet; come hungry.

Pizza Quattro (☎ 434457, *Sarmiento & Pellegrini*) Jonesin' for some pizza pie? Scratch that itch here.

Club Español (*no ☎, Hilario Lagos 237*) There's good Argentine and Spanish food here, as well as outstanding service – all at reasonable prices.

Getting There & Away
Austral (☎ 433076) is at Rivadavia 256. Southern Winds (☎ 02954-425952) lives at Swiss Travel agency, Pellegrini 219. Taxis to the airport, which is 3km from town, cost about US$3.

The bus terminal (☎ 422952, 422249) is at Luro 365. Destinations include Bahía Blanca (US$18; 5 hours), Buenos Aires (US$25; 8 hours), Puerto Madryn (US$37; 10 hours), Mendoza (US$41; 12 hours), Neuquén (US$24; 15 hours) and Bariloche (US$48; 21 hours).

The Ferrocarril Sarmiento (☎ 433451) is at Alsina and Pellegrini, but train services are much slower and less convenient than buses. There are trains to Buenos Aires several times per week. Fares hover around US$13 to US$20.

AROUND SANTA ROSA
Doctor Pedro Luro, an influential early resident, imported exotic game species such as Carpathian deer and European boar into the pastures and native caldén forests of **Reserva Provincial Parque Luro** (*admission US$1; open 9am-6pm, to 8pm in summer*), a 7500-hectare park that was formerly a hunting preserve. Luro also built an enormous French-style mansion (now a museum) to accommodate foreign hunters.

With the decline of sport hunting by the European aristocracy during and after WWI, followed by the Great Depression, Luro went bankrupt. His heirs had to sell the preserve, which fell into disrepair; animals escaped through holes in the fences, and some suffered depredation by poachers (which continues to this day). During and after WWII, Luro's successor Antonio Maura exploited the forests for firewood and charcoal, grazed cattle and sheep, and bred polo ponies.

Since its acquisition by the province in 1965, Parque Luro has served as a recreational and historical resource for the people of La Pampa, offering paths for **biking** and short **hiking** trails. Its **Centro de Interpretación** contains good material on local ecology and early forest exploitation, as well as on Luro and Maura.

Guided tours of the **Castillo Luro**, as the museum is known, give some insight into the personal indulgences that Argentine landowners could afford in the first half of the century, even for places where they spent only a month or two each year. Note, for instance, the walnut fireplace, an obsession that Luro was able to satisfy only by purchasing an entire Parisian restaurant.

Parque Luro is about 35km south of Santa Rosa via RN 35. Besides the museum, there are picnic areas, a small zoo, a restaurant and the **Sala de Caruajes**, a collection of turn-of-the-century carriages. There's daily bus service from Santa Rosa.

PARQUE NACIONAL LIHUÉ CALEL
Like the Sierras de Tandil and the Sierra de la Ventana in Buenos Aires province, Parque Nacional Lihué Calel (a Pehuenche phrase meaning Sierra de la Vida or Range of Life) is a series of small, isolated mountain ranges and valleys in the nearly featureless landscape of the Pampas. Located 226km southwest of Santa Rosa, its salmon-colored, exfoliating granite peaks do not exceed 600m but still manage to offer a variety of subtle environments that change with the seasons.

Though desert-like Lihué Calel receives only about 400mm of rainfall per year, water is an important factor in the landscape. Sudden storms can bring flash floods and create brief but impressive waterfalls over granite boulders near the visitor center. Even when the sky is cloudless, the subterranean streams in the valleys nourish the *monte*, a scrub forest with a surprising variety of plant species. Within the park's 10,000 hectares exist 345 species of plants, nearly half the total found in the entire province.

In this thinly populated area survives wildlife that is now extinct in the Humid Pampas farther east. Large felines including puma, yaguarundi and Geoffroy's cat have been glimpsed, but the most common predator is the Patagonian fox. Also in residence are other large mammals such as the guanaco (more common on the Patagonian steppe) and smaller species like the *mara* (Patagonian hare), *vizcacha* (a wild relative of the chinchilla) and armadillo.

The varied bird life includes the rhea-like *ñandú* and many birds of prey such as the *carancho* or crested caracara. Although you're not likely to encounter them unless you like to overturn rocks, be aware of the highly poisonous pit vipers commonly known as *yarará*.

Until General Roca's so-called Conquista del Desierto (Conquest of the Desert, 1879), Araucanian Indians successfully defended the area against European invasion. Archaeological evidence, including petroglyphs, recalls their presence and that of their ancestors. Lihué Calel was the last refuge of the Araucanian leader Namuncurá, who eluded Argentine forces for several years before finally surrendering.

More information is available at the tiny visitor's center (☎ 02952-436-595).

Things to See & Do

From the park campground, an excellent signed nature trail follows an intermittent stream through a dense thorn forest of *caldén*, a local species of a common worldwide genus, and other typical trees. This trail leads to a petroglyph site, unfortunately vandalized. The friendly and knowledgeable rangers accompany visitors if their schedule permits.

There's a marked trail to the 589m peak, which bears the charming name **Cerro de la Sociedad Científica Argentina**. Fortunately for the vertically challenged, this climb is fairly gradual. Watch for flowering cacti such as *Trichocereus candicans* between the boulders, but remember that the granite is very slippery when wet. From the summit, there are outstanding views of the entire sierra and its surrounding marshes and salt lakes,

such as Laguna Urre Lauquen to the southwest.

If you have a vehicle, visit **Viejo Casco**, the big house of former Estancia Santa María before the provincial government expropriated the land; it was later transferred to the national park system. It's possible to make a circuit via the **Valle de las Pinturas**, where there are some undamaged petroglyphs. Ask rangers for directions.

Places to Stay

Near the visitor center is a comfortable and free *campground* with shade trees, picnic tables, firepits, clean toilets, cold showers (great in the baking-hot summer) and electricity until 11pm (bring a flashlight). Nearby you're likely to see foxes, vizcachas and many, many birds. Stock up on food before arriving – the nearest decent supplies are at the town of Puelches, 35km south.

ACA Hostería (☎ 02952-436101) Singles/doubles US$20/30. If you don't want to camp, you have one choice: this unappealing place on the highway. Be wary of its restaurant.

Getting There & Away

From Santa Rosa, Tus goes to the park daily at 7am (US$11; 3¾ hours). Tersa takes you there at 9:30pm weekdays. These companies and schedules can easily change, so check what's available when you're there.

If you can afford it, driving is the best way to visit Parque Nacional Lihué Calel. To rent a car in Santa Rosa, there's Localiza (☎ 425773), Hipólito Yrigoyen 411.

The Atlantic Coast

For porteños and others from Buenos Aires province, summer means the beach, and the beach means the Atlantic coast in general, and Mar del Plata in particular. Every summer millions of Argentines take a holiday from their friends, families and co-workers, only to run into them on the beaches. Those who can't make it in person participate vicariously in the beach scene every afternoon via nationwide TV.

Beach blanket bedlam

Beach access is unrestricted, but *balnearios* (bathing resorts) are privately run, so access to toilets and showers is limited to those who rent tents. Legally, balnearios must have lifeguards, medical services, toilets and showers. Most also have confiterías and even shops.

Even by Argentine standards, prices are hard to pin down, since they rise every two weeks between December 15 and February 15, and then decline slowly until the end of March, when most hotels and residenciales close. Those that stay open year-round lower their prices considerably, though Semana Santa (Holy Week) is an excuse to raise them briefly.

North of Mar del Plata to Cabo San Antonio, gentle dunes rise behind the generally narrow beaches of the province. Southwest from Mar del Plata to Miramar, steep bluffs highlight the changing coastline, although access is still good for bathing. Beyond Miramar, toward Necochea, the broad sandy beaches delight bathers, fishing enthusiasts and windsurfers.

MAR DEL PLATA
☎ 0223 • pop 569,000
Argentines, especially porteños, love Mar del Plata. Between December and March they visit in droves, outnumbering locals three to one. During these summer months, high-rise timeshares and hotels swell with vacationers, restaurants beef up their staff,

the dozens of balnearios and public beaches fill with sunbathers and the dance clubs throb with revelers every night of the week.

The rest of the year the town is quiet. The port returns to normal as the crowds head home, the lines dissipate, balnearios drag in their umbrellas and prices drop. First impressions of the extremes to which this resort town has taken itself can be abhorrent. But, after spending a few days on its comically packed beaches, watching street performers on the beach-side Plaza Colón or exploring the wonders of the port, it's hard not to give in to the adoration the country feels for the place. If summer crowds aren't your bottle of lotion, visit in spring or autumn, when prices are lower and the area's natural attractions are easier to enjoy.

History
Europeans were slow to occupy this stretch of the coast, so Mar del Plata was a late bloomer. Not until 1747 did Jesuit missionaries try to evangelize the southern Pampas Indians – the only reminder of their efforts is the body of water known as Laguna de los Padres.

More than a century later, Portuguese investors established El Puerto de Laguna de los Padres, with a pier and a *saladero*. Beset by economic problems in the 1860s, they sold out to Patricio Peralta Ramos, who founded Mar del Plata proper in 1874. Peralta Ramos helped develop the area as a commercial and industrial center, and later as a beach resort. By the turn of the century, many upper-class porteño families owned summerhouses, some of which still grace Barrio Los Troncos.

Since the 1960s, multitudinous skyscrapers have risen out of control, leaving many beaches in the shade much of the day. As the 'Pearl of the Atlantic' has lost exclusivity, its architectural character and its calm, the Argentine elite have sought refuge in resorts such as nearby Pinamar or Punta del Este (Uruguay). Still, Mar del Plata remains the most successful Argentine beach town.

Orientation

Mar del Plata, 400km south of Buenos Aires via RN 2, sprawls along 8km of beaches, though most points of interest are in the downtown area, bounded by Av JB Justo (running roughly west from the port), Av Independencia (running roughly northeast-southwest) and the ocean. On street signs, the coastal road is called Av Peralta Ramos, but most people refer to it as Blvd Marítimo. Peatonal San Martín is the downtown pedestrian mall, and Rivadavia is pedestrianized through the summer.

Information

Mar del Plata's exceptionally helpful municipal tourist office (☎ 495-1777, e emtur@mardelplata.com.ar) is at Blvd Marítimo 2400, Local 60 in the old Rambla Hotel Provincial, opposite Plaza Colón. Since the city gets so crowded in summer, staff cope with tourists in assembly-line fashion, but they have maps, informative brochures, a monthly activities magazine and an efficient computerized information system. There is usually an English-speaker on duty. Hours are 8am to 10pm daily from mid-December to Semana Santa, 8am to 8pm the rest of the year. In summer, Emtur opens a branch at the bus terminal.

For basic information on other coastal resorts and the rest of Buenos Aires province, check next door at the provincial tourist office (☎ 495-5340). It opens 9am to 8pm weekdays, 9am to 1pm and 4pm to 8pm weekends.

ACA (☎ 491-2096) is at Av Colón 1450.

There are several money exchanges along San Martín and Rivadavia, including Jonestur, at San Martín 2574 and Av Luro 3191; and La Moneta, at Rivadavia 2623.

The post office is at Av Luro 2460; the postal code is 7600.

Acer, at Rivadavia 2724, offers reliable Internet service for US$3.50 an hour.

Oti International (☎ 494-5414), San Luis 1632, is the AmEx representative.

The Centro Cultural General Pueyrredón (☎ 499-7878), at Catamarca and 25 de Mayo, offers a variety of activities ranging from film screenings and theater to popular music, jazz, folklore, tango and the like.

The Sociedad de Cultura Inglesa (☎ 495-6513), San Luis 2498, has a library with newspapers, magazines and books in English, as well as occasional films and lectures.

There's a health clinic (☎ 493-2309) at Av Colón 3294, northwest of downtown. The hospital (☎ 477-0262) is at JB Justo 6700.

Walking Tour

A stroll past some of Mar del Plata's mansions leaves vivid impressions of the city's upper-class origins and relatively recent past, when it was still the playground of wealthy Argentines. Built in 1920, **Villa Normandy**, Viamonte 2213, is one of few examples of the French style that survived the renovation craze of the 1950s; it is now the Italian consulate. On the hilltop, the neo-Gothic **Stella Maris Church** (1910), at Brown 1054, features an impressive marble altar; its virgin is the patron saint of local fishermen. On the highest point of this hill, at Falucho 993, there are impressive views from the 88m **Torre Tanque** (1943; ☎ 451-1486; open 10am-1pm weekdays).

After descending Viamonte to Rodríguez Peña, walk toward the ocean to the **Chalet Los Troncos** (1938), Urquiza 3454, which lent its name to this distinguished neighborhood. The timber of the gate and fence are *quebracho* and *lapacho* hardwoods from Salta province. Lining Calles Urquiza, Quintana, Lavalle, Rodríguez Peña, Rivas and Almafuerte are examples of more recent but equally elite design. If you're up for a good stomp, try the longer route back to the center along Av Peralta Ramos, which offers expansive views from **Cabo Corrientes**.

Catedral de San Pedro

At San Martín and San Luis, this turn-of-the-century neo-Gothic building features gorgeous stained glass, an impressive central chandelier from France, English-tile floors and a ceiling of tiles from other European countries.

MAR DEL PLATA

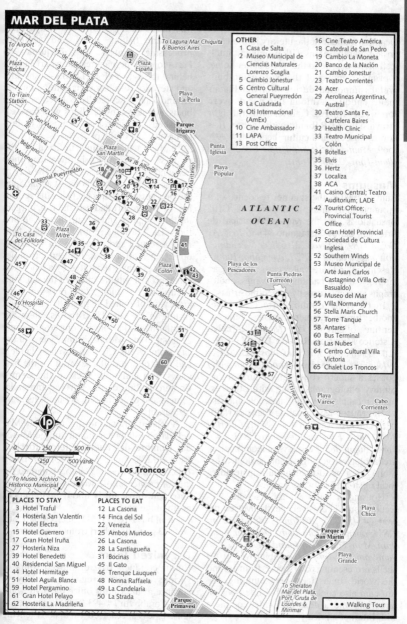

Los Troncos

ATLANTIC OCEAN

••• Walking Tour

Centro Cultural Villa Victoria

During the 1920s and 1930s, Victoria Ocampo, founder of the literary journal *Sur*, hosted literary salons with prominent intellectuals from around the world at her home, a prime example of the Norwegian-built prefabs imported during Mar del Plata's 'belle epoque.' Among her guests were Jorge Luis Borges, Gabriela Mistral, Igor Stravinsky and Rabindranath Tagore. It is now a museum and cultural center (☎ 492-0569, *Matheu 1851; admission US$2; open 10am-1pm & 5pm-11pm*).

Museums

Built in 1909 as the summer residence of a prominent Argentine family, the Villa Ortiz Basualdo is now the **Museo Municipal de Arte Juan Carlos Castagnino** (☎ 486-1636, *Av Colón 1189; bus Nos 221, 581 & 592; admission adult/student US$2/1; open 5pm-10pm*). Resembling a Loire Valley castle, its Belgian interior exhibits paintings, drawings, photographs and sculptures by Argentine artists.

In the Villa Emilio Mitre (1930), yet another former summer residence of the Argentine oligarchy, the **Museo Archivo Histórico Municipal Roberto T Barili** (☎ 495-1200, *Lamadrid 3870; bus Nos 523, 524 & 591; admission US$1; open noon-10pm daily*) houses a superb collection of turn-of-the-century photographs, along with other exhibits, recalling Mar del Plata's colorful past.

The **Museo Municipal de Ciencias Naturales Lorenzo Scaglia** (☎ 473-8791, *Libertad 3099, Plaza España; admission US$3; open 5pm-9:30pm daily*) displays paleontological, archaeological, geological and zoological exhibits. Its ground-floor aquarium features local fresh- and saltwater species.

Housing the most extensive seashell collection you'll likely ever see, the **Museo del Mar** (☎ 451-3553, *Colón 1114; admission US$3; open 9am-2am daily Dec-Mar, 8am-9pm Mon-Thur, 8am-midnight Fri & Sat, 9am-9pm Sun Apr-Nov*) exhibits over 30,000 shells, representing 6000 species from around the world. In a sleek new building, the museum also contains a small tide pool, an aquarium and a delightful café, complete with Internet service.

The Port

Mar del Plata is one of the country's most important fishing ports and seafood-processing centers. At **Baquina de Pescadores** – the picturesque wharf hidden behind the ugly YPF fuel tanks – fisherfolk and stevedores follow their routine on and around kaleidoscopically colored wooden boats, monitored by sea lions who have established a large colony – mostly male – along one side of the pier.

In the early morning, unfazed by the chilly sea breeze, the fishermen load their nets and crates before spending the day at sea, escorted by the sea lions. At about 5pm, the pier gets noisy and hectic as the returning fishermen sort and box the fish, bargain for the best price and tidy up their boats and tools. The sea lions return to seek or fight over a resting spot. Braving their horrendous stench affords excellent opportunities for photography – separated by a fence, you can approach within a meter of the sea lions.

Just past the colony is the port's fantastic graveyard of **ruined ships**, half-sunken and rusting in the sun. Here the **Escollera Sur** (southern jetty) begins its long stretch some 2km out to sea, with panoramic views of the city from its tip. Climb the yellow ladders and walk on top of the sea wall for the best views. You can walk back to the **Centro Comercial Puerto** (the port's commercial center) and close the day in one of its great restaurants.

A related attraction is the tribute to Mar del Plata's fishing community in the **Museo del Hombre del Puerto Cleto Ciocchini** (☎ 480-1228, *Padre Dutto 383; admission US$2; open 5pm-9pm Thur-Sat*), named for a local painter whose works are on display here. The museum is about eight blocks north of the port.

Local bus Nos 221, 511, 522, 551, 561, 562 and 593 go to the wharf from downtown.

Organized Tours

Emtur conducts free organized tours of various city sights; register one day in advance at the Emtur office on Blvd Marítimo. Combi-Tur (☎ 493-0732) has more extensive, less specialized excursions leaving daily at 3:30 pm from Plaza Colón, at Colón and Arenales.

The 30m *Crucero Anamora* (☎ 489-0310) offers one-hour harbor tours (US$10) several times daily from Dársena B at the port. Also departing from Dársena B, Turimar (☎ 489-7775) offers similar tours as well as six-hour fishing excursions (US$50) which leave weekends and holidays at 7am.

Special Events

Mar del Plata's elaborate tourist infrastructure guarantees a wide variety of special events throughout the year. On February 10 Mar del Plata celebrates Fundación de la Ciudad.

Started in 1950, though interrupted for decades by Argentina's political and economic woes, Mar del Plata's International Film Festival takes place in November. Participants come from a variety of countries from around the world.

Places to Stay

It's worth reiterating that prices climb considerably from month to month during summer and drop in the off-season, when many of Mar del Plata's 700 hotels and residenciales close their doors. Unless otherwise indicated, prices are from early high-season. The least expensive accommodations are near the bus terminal.

Budget South of town along RP 11 are several *campgrounds*, all very crowded in summer. Rates run about US$16 for up to four people. Rápido del Sud buses to Miramar stop at each one.

Among the choices are *Autocamping Del Faro* (☎ 467-1168, *Paseo Costanero Sur Pte Illia*), at Playa del Faro, which can be reached by bus Nos 221 & 511; *Camping Los Horneros* (☎ 469-9260, *Paseo Costanero Sur Presidente Illia 18*), 15km south of the Punta Mogotes lighthouse; and *Camping Las Brusquitas* (☎ 02291-493040, *Paseo Costanero Sur Presidente Illia 40*), 39km south of the lighthouse.

Hotel Pergamino (*Albergue Estudiantil;* ☎ 495-7927, fax 492-1548, Tucumán 2728) HI members US$12 per person with breakfast

in 4-bed rooms, non-members US$15 in private rooms. The place is very well-kept, though packed in summer when it's often worth sucking up the extra few pesos for a private room.

Hostería La Madrileña (☎ 451-2072, Sarmiento 2957) Singles/doubles US$12/20. Modest rooms with fans in this small family-run hotel are a good value.

Residencial San Miguel (☎ 495-7226, Tucumán 2383) US$13/15 per person without/with breakfast. Situated above a good, cheap salteña restaurant, this quirky place has spacious rooms with dilapidated baths.

Hotel Electra (☎ 495-4891, 3 de Febrero 2752) US$15 per person with breakfast. Though the price tag is more appealing than the rooms are, it's only a block off the beach and still a good value.

Hostería Niza (☎ 495-1695, e hotelniza@mail.com, Santiago del Estero 1843) Singles/doubles US$18/30 with private bath, US$12/25 off-season. This centrally located hostería, run by three delightful sisters, is an excellent value, though cold in the winter.

Mid-Range *Gran Hotel Pelayo* (☎/fax 451-2533, Sarmiento 2899) Singles/doubles US$20/30 with breakfast. This conventional hotel near the bus terminal has spotless rooms with good beds, a sunny breakfast room and a friendly owner.

Hostería San Valentín (☎/fax 495-4891, e valentin@lcnet.com.ar, Mitre 1168) Singles/doubles US$20/25 low-season with breakfast, TV & bath; 2 singles only. Reservations are recommended at this wonderfully cozy place that feels more like a home than a hostería.

Hotel Aguila Blanca (☎/fax 486-1285, Sarmiento 2455) US$30 per person with breakfast. Rooms with good baths are clean and comfortable, and the bar and lobby are pleasant for sitting around.

Hotel Traful (☎ 493-6650, fax 495-7084, Yrigoyen 1190) Singles/doubles US$35/75 with hearty breakfast. This nondescript three-star hotel near the ocean has modest rooms with air-conditioning, cable TV, telephones and mid-size baths.

Top End *Hotel Benedetti* (☎/fax 493-0031/32/33, Av Colón 2198) Doubles US$80. This comfortable hotel has good, plain rooms with TVs and substantial baths. The best part is the game room with pool, ping-pong and metagol.

Hotel Guerrero (☎ 491-8200, fax 495-8851, Av JB Alberdi 2258) Singles/doubles US$64/89 with breakfast. Small, cheerful rooms with en-suite fridges have a sort of Martha Stewart feel in this hotel just a block off the ocean.

Gran Hotel Iruña (☎ 491-1060, fax 491-1183, Av JB Alberdi 2270) Doubles US$104/119 without/with ocean view, breakfast included. Recently remodeled, this four-star hotel offers plush rooms with air-con and excellent baths, a game room and assistance with tours and excursions.

Hotel Hermitage (☎ 451-9081, fax 451-7235, e hermitage@lacapitalnet.com.ar, Blvd Marítimo 2657) Doubles without/with ocean views US$100/130, US$65 off-season, junior suite/suite US$150/350 all year. Built in 1942, this dignified Mar del Plata classic has a majestic lobby with sweeping ocean views, a casino and slightly worn but comfortably refined rooms.

Sheraton Mar del Plata (☎ 499-9000, fax 499-9009, Alem 4221) Doubles US$155-325 with ocean views, all with mini-bars, TV, breakfast, parking and use of pools and spa. Built on a golf course south of town, the Sheraton has stunning ocean views, an ultramodern feel and all the conveniences imaginable.

Places to Eat

Although Mar del Plata's numerous restaurants, pizzerias and snack bars usually hire extra help between December and March, they often struggle to keep up with impatient crowds, and there are always long lines. Around the bus terminal you can find very cheap *minutas* (sandwiches).

Budget *La Santiagueña* (☎ 478-6382, Belgrano 2486) Excellent empanadas (US$0.50-0.70), whopping bowls of *locro* (a thick maize and tripe soup, US$2.50) and hearty portions of *lentejas a la España* (lentil beef stew) are all as good as they are cheap.

La Casona (☎ 493-8943, Rivadavia 2598; ☎ 495-0208, San Martín 2501) US$5 and up; open 7am-midnight daily. The endless menu of pizzas, salads and sandwiches at both branches is dizzying and cheap.

Bocinas (Rivadavia 2262) US$3-7; open 8am-11pm Sun-Thur, 8am-late Fri & Sat. This place can't be topped when it comes to cheap thin-crust pizza; the US$3.25 mozzarella serves two and still tastes delicious.

Finca del Sol (☎ 495-6962, San Martín 2463) Vegetarian tenedor libre US$5 includes drink; open noon-3:30pm & 8pm-11pm Mon-Sat. Unfortunately, vegetarian in this case means bland, but, with a little imagination, you can assemble a fabulous salad.

Venezia (☎ 495-7205, Rivadavia 2301) This is arguably the best ice creamery downtown.

Mid-Range & Top-End *Ambos Mundos* (☎ 495-0450, Rivadavia 2644) US$5-12; open noon-4pm & 8pm-midnight daily. This local favorite serves abundant minutas and good *puchero de gallina* (chicken stew) at moderate prices.

La Strada (☎ 495-8992, Entre Ríos 2642) US$6-11; open 8pm-midnight Mon-Thur, noon-4pm & 8pm-midnight Sat-Sun. The best deal at this family-style parrilla is the US$5.50 parrillada, which includes salad and dessert. The drink is extra.

Il Gato (☎ 495-5309, Yrigoyen 2699) US$6-15. Parrilla, pasta and traditional Argentine dishes are all good at this relaxed, stylishly subdued eatery.

Nonna Raffaela (☎ 493-5861, Alberti 2583) Lunch specials US$3.50, dinner US$7-25; open noon-4pm & 8pm-1am daily. Reputedly the town's best pasta joint, Nonna Raffaela also serves excellent Italian-style seafood dishes, including lobster and octopus. Dinners get pricey.

La Candelaría (☎ 492-5533, Santa Fe 2633) US$8-18; open 8pm-midnight daily, additionally noon-4pm Sat-Sun. The friendly owners take excellent care of everything from decor to dinner at this cozy place with an imaginative menu.

Trenque Lauquen (☎ 493-7149, Bartolomé Mitre 2807) US$10-20. This is Mar del Plata's most highly esteemed parrilla and, though pricey, definitely serves the best meat in town.

Seafood at the restaurants in the Centro Comercial Puerto (the renovated old port) is invariably excellent, though costly. Try *La Caracola* (☎ 480-9113, Local 6) or the pricier, and reportedly superior, *El Viejo Pop* (☎ 480-0147).

Entertainment

Bars The area southwest of Plaza Mitre is particularly conducive to bar-hopping.

Botellas (☎ 491-3011, Córdoba 2355) Open 9pm-late daily & Sat afternoons. Due to a friendly staff and excellent atmosphere, it can be difficult to leave this eclectically decorated pub.

Antares (☎ 492-4455, Córdoba 3025) Open 8pm-late daily. The six homebrews on tap at Mar del Plata's only microbrewery include imperial stout, pale ale and barley wine – excellent cures for the Quilmes blues. Food is available.

La Cuadrada (☎ 495-4628, 9 de Julio 2737) Open noon-late daily. In an eccentrically remodeled colonial building, this café-cum-bar is truly a work of art worth stepping into. Check out the bizarre central fountain and the basement with furniture sculpted from the ground.

Las Nubes (☎ 486-2222, 28th floor Apart Hotel Torres de Manantiales, Alberdi 445) With panoramic views of Mar del Plata, this softly lit lounge makes for a gooey romantic rendezvous.

Dance Clubs After tanning on the beach all day, Argentines take their hot, bronzed bodies to the nightclubs and dance until the morning hours. The most popular clubs are along Av Constitución, about 3km from downtown. Bus No 551 from downtown runs along the entire avenue. Keep your eyes peeled during the day for discount flyers handed out along San Martín and Rivadavia.

Sobremonte (☎ 479-2600, Constitución 6690) Admission US$10-15. Open midnight-dawn daily Dec-Mar, Thur-Sat off-season. Ground-zero for the city's most fashionable summertime clubbers, Sobre-monte is three throbbing discos, a Mexican restaurant and a lounge all under one roof.

Chocolate (☎ 479-4848, Constitución 4451) Admission US$8-12. Open midnight-dawn daily Dec-Mar, Thur-Sat off-season. This is another long-time favorite, with two floors, a patio and a standard soundtrack covering everything from techno to *rock nacional*.

Azúcar (☎ 479-8531, Constitución 4478) Admission US$7-12. Azúcar attracts an older crowd into salsa and merengue and features stage dancers to keep you on your toes.

Live Music Mar del Plata has two *peñas* toward the north end of town, both featuring traditional and folk music.

Casa del Folklore (☎ 472-3955, San Juan 2543) Open 9pm Fri & Sat, nightly in summer. Music usually gets underway after 11pm at this lively peña northwest of downtown, where there's plenty of food, drink and dancing.

Casa de Salta (Av Libertad 3398) Open 11pm-1am Fri & Sat, nightly in summer. A dinner show (US$10-15) with stage performance. Get here early to get a table and you can sit until the music's over.

Elvis Café (☎ 492-4529, Almirante Brown 2639) This small venue features everything from Rolling Stones cover bands to live tango performances.

Theater When Buenos Aires shuts down in January, many shows come from the capital to Mar del Plata. Theaters mostly cater to vacationers by showing comedies that range from *café concert* (stand-up comedy) to vulgar but popular burlesque. As in Buenos Aires, there are *carteleras* that offer half-price tickets to movies and theater presentations. The local branch of Cartelera Baires is at Santa Fe 1844, Local 33.

Teatro Auditorium (☎ 493-6001, Blvd Marítimo 2280) Part of the casino complex, this place offers musical theater with quality actors from the capital.

Other venues include *Teatro Municipal Colón* (☎ 499-6210, Yrigoyen 1665), *Teatro Corrientes* (☎ 493-7918, Corrientes 1766) and *Teatro Santa Fe* (☎ 491-9728, Santa Fe 1854).

Casino *Casino Central* (☎ 495-7011, Av Marítimo 2300) Open 3pm-4am daily. Unlike its flashier counterparts in Las Vegas or Reno, this casino is an elegant venue at night, but less formal during the daytime.

Shopping

Feria de los Artesanos (Plaza San Martín) Every afternoon vendors set up their stalls on the plaza and sell everything from *mate* gourds and knives to sweaters and silverwork.

Mercado de Pulgas (Plaza Rocha) This relaxed flea market, selling everything and the kitchen sink, is at 20 de Septiembre between San Martín and Av Luro, seven blocks northwest of Plaza San Martín.

Mar del Plata is famous for sweaters and jackets. Shops along Av JB Justo, nicknamed 'Avenida del Pullover,' have competitive, near-wholesale prices. To get there, take bus No 561 or 562.

Getting There & Away

Air Aerolíneas Argentinas and Austral share offices (☎ 496-0101, fax 493-2432) at Moreno 2442 and have several daily flights to Buenos Aires (from US$59). LAPA (☎ 492-2112), at Córdoba 1621, flies to Buenos Aires (US$43-85) at least four times daily, and to Córdoba (US$89-159) Friday and Sunday.

Southern Winds (☎ 486-6666), at Güemes 2231, offers daily flights to Rosario (US$119-139) and Córdoba (US$119-139); on weekdays to Mendoza (US$129-169), Tucumán (US$159-179) and Salta (US$179-199); and Sunday to Neuquén (US$119-139) and Bariloche (US$189-209).

LADE (☎ 493-8220), Local 5 in the casino at Blvd Marítimo 2300, offers flights on Monday to Bahía Blanca (US$40), Viedma (US$57), Puerto Madryn (US$80) and Trelew (US$88); Tuesday to Buenos Aires (US$38 to US$49); Wednesday to Neuquén (US$76 to US$99) and Bariloche (US$100 to US$130); Thursday to Bahía Blanca, Viedma, Neuquén, San Martín de los Andes (US$95) and Bariloche; and Friday to Buenos Aires.

Bus Mar del Plata's busy bus terminal (☎ 451-5406) is very central at Alberti 1602. Dozens of companies serve most major destinations throughout the country. There are generally two departures per week to Patagonian destinations south of Bariloche. Rapido del Sud departs hourly for nearby coastal resorts.

The following are mid-season prices and may rise in the peak travel months of January and February.

Destination	Duration in hours	Cost
Bahía Blanca	7	US$31
Bariloche	19	US$75
Buenos Aires	5½	US$24-35
Comodoro Rivadavia	24	US$94
Córdoba	18	US$50
Jujuy	27	US$74
La Plata	5	US$27
Mendoza	18	US$60
Miramar	1	US$3
Necochea	2	US$8
Neuquén	12	US$35
Paraná	12½	US$60
Pinamar	2½	US$8.50
Posadas	19	US$60
Puerto Madryn	16½	US$72
Rosario	7½	US$20
Salta	26	US$74
San Juan	20	US$60
Santa Fe	12	US$58
Santiago del Estero	20	US$50
Trelew	18	US$72
Tucumán	24	US$57
Villa Gesell	1½	US$7

Train The train station (☎ 475-6076) is at Av Luro 4700 at Italia, about 20 blocks from the beach, and open 6am to midnight daily. Tickets can also be purchased at the Ferrobaires office (☎ 451-2501) in the bus terminal; hours are 8am to 9pm daily.

During summer, the tourist train El Marplatense travels seven times daily (eight on Sunday) to Buenos Aires. Reservations should be made far in advance, since it's usually booked solid through the season. One-way fares are turista US$16, primera

US$22, Pullman US$28 and the Sunday super Pullman US$40. There are daily departures through the slower seasons as well, when one-way fares are turista US$13, primera US$17, Pullman US$28 and super Pullman US$34.

Getting Around

Despite Mar del Plata's sprawl, frequent buses reach just about every place in town. For information on local destinations, the tourist office can help.

Aeropuerto Félix U Camet (☎ 479-0194, 479-2787) is at RN 2 Km 396, 10km north of the city. To get there by bus, take No 542 from the corner of Blvd Marítimo and Belgrano. Aerolíneas Argentinas (☎ 478-3314) has a minibus service for US$3.50. Otherwise, a taxi or *remise* costs about US$8 to US$10 per person.

Car rentals are available at Avis (☎ 470-2100, fax 470-2582) in the airport. Annie Millet Hertz (☎ 496-2772) is downtown at Córdoba 2149; Localiza (☎ 493-3461) is at Córdoba 2270.

AROUND MAR DEL PLATA
Mar Chiquita

Along RP 11, 34km north of Mar del Plata, the peaceful resort of Mar Chiquita is a paradise for swimming, fishing and windsurfing (there's a December windsurf regatta). Fed by creeks from the Sierras de Tandil and sheltered by a chain of sand dunes, its namesake estuary, Laguna Mar Chiquita, alternately drains into the ocean or absorbs seawater, depending on the tides. There are several campgrounds and hotels, including *Camping Playa Dorada* (☎ 493-9607).

From Mar del Plata's bus terminal and from the casino, Rápido del Sud goes eight times daily to Mar Chiquita. The cheaper Local bus No 221 (US$1.50) leaves hourly from stops along Blvd Marítimo. Ask the driver; some 221 buses stop short.

Museo del Automovilismo Juan Manuel Fangio

Named for Argentina's most famous race car driver, Museo del Automovilismo Juan Manuel Fangio (☎ 02266-425-540, Dardo

Rocha & Mitre, Balcarce; admission adult/child US$7/3; open 9am-7pm), one of the country's finest museums, preserves a multimillion-dollar collection of classic and racing cars in his birthplace of Balcarce, 60km northwest of Mar del Plata via RN 226. Occupying an early-20th-century building, the museum stresses the worldwide exploits of Fangio and his contemporaries, but also makes an effort to put automotive history into a global context.

Fangio, who died in 1995 at the age of 84, is the subject of Stirling Moss and Doug Nye's biographical tribute *Fangio: a Pirelli Album* (Motorbooks International). El Rápido runs frequent buses from Mar del Plata (US$4.25).

VILLA GESELL
☎ 02255 • pop 26,000

In the 1930s, merchant, inventor and nature-lover Carlos Gesell designed this resort of zigzag streets, planting acacias, poplars, oaks and pines to stabilize the shifting dunes. Though he envisioned a town merging with the forest he had created, it wasn't long before high-rise vacation shares began their malignant growth.

Still, Villa Gesell maintains a mellow, woodsy feel. It's known for its summer choral performances and rock and folk concerts, and its funky downtown lacks the slick elitism that graces its counterpart, Pinamar, just up the coast.

Orientation

Villa Gesell is 100km northeast of Mar del Plata via RP 11 and about 360km south of Buenos Aires via RP 11.

Avenida 3, Gesell's only paved road, parallels the beach and runs, from Av Buenos Aires north of town, south to the bus terminal and most of the campgrounds. Gesell's restaurant, shopping and entertainment center is along this thoroughfare between Paseos 102 and 110. Everything is within walking distance, including the beach, three-blocks to the south.

With few exceptions, streets are numbered rather than named. Avenidas (all 11 of them) run east-west, parallel to the beach.

Paseos, numbered 100 through 152, run north-south.

Information

The Secretaría de Turismo (☎ 458596, W www.gesell.com.ar), on Av Buenos Aires at Camino de los Pioneros (between RP 11 and Circunvalación), has a friendly staff and reliable maps. There's another, more convenient office in the municipality (☎ 462201), at Av 3 No 820, though it's only open in summer.

ACA (☎ 462273) is on Av 3 between Paseos 112 and 113.

The post office is on Av 3 between Paseos 105 and 106. The postal code is 7165.

The Hospital Municipal Arturo Illía (☎ 462618) is located at Calle 123 and Av 8.

Things to See & Do

The **Muelle de Pesca** (*Playa & Paseo 129*), Gesell's 15m fishing pier, offers year-round fishing for mackerel, rays, shark and other varieties.

Horseback riding is a popular activity at places like the **Escuela de Equitación San Jorge** (☎ *454464, Circunvalación & Paseo 102*), where you can rent horses independently or take guided excursions. Local golfers frequent the **Club de Golf** (☎ *458249, RP 11 & Av Buenos Aires*).

For bicycle rentals try **Casa Macca** (*branches:* ☎ *468013, Av Buenos Aires at Paseo 101;* ☎ *466030, Av 3 & Paseo 126; US$15 per day*) or **Rodados Lucky** (☎ *462965, Av 3 & Paseo 121*).

Organized Tours

Turismo Aventura Edy (☎ *463118, 466797, Av 3 & Paseo 111, Plaza Gesell; US$15 per person; daily Dec-Apr, Sat & Sun May-Nov*) runs trips to **Faro Querandí**, the local lighthouse, carrying up to 10 passengers in 4WD jeeps on a 30km trip over dunes, with stops along the way for photography, swimming and exploring. The lighthouse itself, one of the highest and most inaccessible in the country, soars impressively above the surrounding dense forest. Four-hour trips leave daily at 9am and 3pm.

Places to Stay

Listings below constitute only a fraction of Villa Gesell's 200-plus hotels, hosterías, hospedajes, aparthoteles and the like; only a handful are open all year.

Budget Gesell's dozen campgrounds usually charge US$5 to US$8 per person with a four-person minimum. Most close at the end of March, but three clustered at the south end of town on Av 3 are open all year. They are **Camping Casablanca** (☎ *470771*), **Camping Mar Dorado** (☎ *470963*) and **Camping Monte Bubi** (☎ *470732*).

Residencial Viya (☎ *462757,* e *residencial viya@gesell.com.ar, Av 5 No 582 between Paseos 105 & 106*) US$15 per person with breakfast; open year-round. Rooms are pleasant and open onto a small patio at this friendly, owner-operated residencial on a quiet street.

Hospedaje Villa Gesell (☎ *466368, Av 3 No 812*) US$15-18 per person; open year-round. The best part about this place is its centrality. The rooms are comfortable though windowless, and the doors all open onto an interior patio.

Hotel Aldea Marina (☎ *462835,* e *aldea marina@gesell.com.ar, Av 3 No 1481 between Paseos 114 & 115*) US$20 per person. The tidy Aldea Marina sits a fair distance from the shops and restaurants that line the avenue several blocks east.

Most of the rest of Gesell's cheaper lodging close their doors for fall and winter. When they open for summer, figure on spending between US$30 and US$40 for a double room with a private bath. Sprawling **Hospedaje Inti Huasi** (☎ *468365, Alameda 202 at Av Buenos Aires*); well-kept **Hospedaje Marino** (☎ *462436, Av 1 & Paseo 112*); and **Hospedaje Sarimar** (*no* ☎*, Av 3 between Paseos 117 and 118*) all offer comfortable accommodation.

Mid-Range *Hotel Teomar* (☎ *462310, fax 463140,* e *hotelteomar@gesell.com.ar, Av 4 & Paseo 104*) US$25-30 per person; open year-round. This nondescript but spotless hotel has comfortable rooms with excellent baths. Prices are lower if you skip the TV.

Hotel Bella Vista (☎/fax 462293, Av 4 & Paseo 114) US$30 per person with breakfast & TV; open year-round. One of the town's older hotels, the Bella Vista has an expansive back lawn, an inviting bar and clean, midsize rooms.

La Posada del Sol (☎ 462068, fax 465819, Av 4 No 642) Singles/doubles US$30/56 Dec 15-Mar, US$19/28 Nov-Dec 15; open Nov-Mar. If you want character in a hotel, this is the place; it has comfortable rooms, a lovely plant-filled comedor, a wandering garden and its own zoo, complete with flamingos.

Hotel Posada de la Villa (☎ 464855, Paseo 125 No 182 between Avs 1 & 2) Doubles/triples US$60/80 with breakfast, US$20 per person off-season; open year-round. This small hostería has charming rooms with TV and telephones, a pleasant breakfast room, a backyard and a wonderful staff.

Top End Most of Gesell's expensive hotels charge between US$80 and US$170 for a double in high season. Unfortunately, the majority close outside the summer months.

Hotel Terrazas Club (☎ 462181, fax 463214, Av 2 between Paseos 104 and 105) Open Dec-Mar. This luxury hotel has a good atmosphere, a swimming pool and most of the services you'd expect from a four-star establishment.

Hotel Gran International (☎ 468672, fax 466878, Av 1 No 303) Doubles US$70-100; open Oct-Apr. Only a block off the beach, this modern high-rise has oddly decorated, comfortable rooms, two small swimming pools and a sun deck.

Places to Eat

Villa Gesell has a wide variety of restaurants, mostly along Av 3, catering to all tastes and budgets.

La Jirafa Azul (☎ 462431, Av 3 No 186 between Av Buenos Aires and Paseo 102) US$4-10. The US$4.50 bowls of lentejas a la Española are delicious and filling. Daily specials are similarly priced, and the menu runs the gamut from pastas to sandwiches.

Cantina Arturito (☎ 465082, 463037, Av 3 No 2580 between Paseos 126 & 127) US$6-15. This owner-operated cantina serves large portions of exquisite risotto and homemade pasta, as well as shellfish and home-cured ham.

El Estribo (☎ 460234, Av 3 & Paseo 109) US$8-10. Ask anyone for the best parrilla in town and they'll send you to El Estribo. A bife de chorizo will set you back US$8.50 and the parrilla for two (with enough meat for three) costs US$19.

Cartegena de las Indias (☎ 462858, Av 3 No 215 at Paseo 102) US$15-30. Gesell's most upscale eatery will put a dent in your wallet, but the quality is excellent and the dishes imaginative.

Entertainment

For such a small town, Villa Gesell comes alive with music in the summer, when venues book everything from rock to choral music. Gesell is famous for its *Encuentros Corales,* an annual gathering of the country's best choirs.

Playa Hotel (☎ 458027, Alameda 205 and Calle 303, Barrio Norte) This European country-style hotel established Villa Gesell as a vacation resort, and every summer the Sociedad Camping Musical organizes chamber music concerts in its auditorium.

Anfiteatro del Pinar (☎ 467123, Av 10 & Paseo 102) Performances in Jan, Feb & Semana Santa. Gesell's Encuentros Corales take place annually in this lovely amphitheater.

Cine Teatro Atlas (☎ 462969, Paseo 108 between Avs 3 and 4) Such rock-and-roll greats as Charly García and Los Pericos have played this small theater which doubles as a cinema during off-season months. Call here or the tourist office for information.

Pueblo Límite (Av Buenos Aires, across from the tourist office) Admission US$5 off-season, US$8-10 in summer. A sort of small town mega-disco, this complex has two dance clubs, a Mexican restaurant, a bar and cheap food booths in the front. Eating at the comedores beforehand (summer only) gets you in for free.

Cheyenne (☎ *454024, Av Buenos Aires, across from the tourist office*) Admission free/US$7 without/with live music. Officially a bar for over-25s (though you only have to look it), Cheyenne has a small dance floor and a mellower vibe than the disco next door.

Shopping

Feria Artesanal, Regional y Artística This excellent arts and crafts fair, on Av 3 between Paseos 112 and 113, takes place every evening from mid-December through mid-March. The rest of the year it's a weekend-only event.

Getting There & Away

Aerolíneas Argentinas (☎ 458228, 458331), at Av Buenos Aires and Av 10 in town, may have daily flights between Buenos Aires and Villa Gesell (US$125 and up) during the summer. The most certain flights between Gesell and Buenos Aires (US$75-125) are with Southern Winds. Alemeda Turismo (☎ 468659), at Buenos Aires 752, represents all airlines in Villa Gesell.

The main bus terminal (☎ 477253) is at Av 3 and Paseo 140, on the south side of town. Most buses stop here first and then at the Parada Los Pinos Mini Terminal (☎ 458059), at the corner of Blvd Silvio Gesell and Av Buenos Aires, closer to the center of town. Get off here if you're walking.

Empresa Río de la Plata has several direct buses daily to Buenos Aires (US$24; 6 hours) in summer and offers combination tickets to Rosario, Córdoba and La Rioja. There are also daily runs to La Plata (US$20; 6½ hours) and Mar del Plata (US$7.60; 2 hours). Rápido del Sud leaves regularly to other coastal resorts.

PINAMAR
☎ 02254 • pop 25,000

Bathed by a tropical current from Brazil, Pinamar's waters are pleasantly warm, and its clean beaches slope gradually into a sea abundant with fish. Its extensive forests, sandy streets, luxury homes and hotels, chic shops and posh restaurants have made

Pinamar the 'in' place for wealthy Argentine families.

Pinamar was founded and designed in 1944 by architect Jorge Bunge, who figured out how to stabilize the shifting dunes by planting pines, acacias and pampas grass. It was *the* refuge for the country's upper echelons and remained so until relatively recently. Punta del Este, Uruguay, has lately gained popularity over Pinamar as a seaside getaway close to Buenos Aires. Pinamar's reputation was also tarnished in early 1997 by the murder of photojournalist José Luis Cabezas.

You don't see Pinamar's past, however, (or its hideous high-rises) when you're staring at the ocean or over the wheels of a dune buggy, and that's what families come here to do. The place seems to have more adventure sports and hip balnearios than any other resort along the coast. For nightlife, however, Pinamar is inferior to nearby Villa Gesell.

The adjacent resorts of Valería del Mar, Ostende and especially Cariló have a more exclusive, country-club atmosphere and merit a visit for those wishing to glean insights into upper-class Argentine life. You will probably be asked to leave your name at the security gates.

Orientation & Information

Pinamar sits 120km north of Mar del Plata via RP 11 and 320km southeast of Buenos Aires via RN 2. It was planned around an axis formed by Av Libertador, which runs parallel to the beach, and Av Bunge, which is perpendicular to the beach. On either side of Bunge, the streets form two large fans, making orientation tricky at first. The easiest way to keep track of your hotel is by picking and memorizing the nearest high-rise. The newer parts of town follow a conventional grid.

Most shops, restaurants and hotels are on or within a few blocks of Av Bunge, the main thoroughfare.

The busy municipal tourist office (☎ 491680), Av Bunge 654 at Libertador, has a good pocket-size map with useful descriptions of Pinamar, Valería, Ostende and

Cariló. ACA (☎ 482744) is at Del Cazón 1365.

The post office is at Jasón 524; the postal code is 7167. The main telephone office is at Jasón and Shaw.

The community hospital (☎ 491710) is at Shaw 250.

Activities
Through summer, Pinamar is a haven for every outdoor activity from windsurfing and waterskiing to horseback riding and hiking.

Several shops in town offer rental for **biking**, including Leo (☎ 488855, Bunge 1111; US$3-5/hour; open year-round) and Macca (☎ 494183, Bunge 1075; US$3-5/hour; open year-round).

The tourist office provides a list of folks who rent horses for **horseback riding** in the summer. Ismael (☎ 497700, Bunge & Av Intermedanos; US$10/hour) is the only one open year-round, but call ahead of time if it's a winter weekday.

Boards for **surfboarding** can be rented (US$5/hour) during summer from the pier, a few blocks south of Av Bunge. **Sky surfing** (that strange hybrid of surfing and paragliding) is the latest craze to hit Pinamar, and if you want to learn how to do it (or just watch someone else), go to Sport Beach, the last balneario located about 5km north of Av Bunge.

Here's a good one: **sand boarding**. To give it a shot, follow jeep tours to nearby dunes or contact Wenner Explorer (☎ 493531, Bunge & Av del Libertador; departures at 10am, 2:30pm & 5:30pm daily, year-round; US$15-25).

Fishing, especially for shark and bass, is popular year-round, both from the pier and by boat. Cantina Tulumei (see Places to Eat) offers four-hour fishing excursions (US$40) and will cook up the catch back at the cantina that evening.

Places to Stay
Pinamar lacks real budget accommodations – prices are notably higher than in Gesell – but there is a youth hostel in nearby Ostende. Reservations are a must in high-season. Prices below are for summer, but off-season rates are up to 40% lower.

Budget *Camping Saint Tropez (☎ 482498, Quintana & Nuestras Malvinas, Ostende)* US$15-20 in summer, US$10-15 off-season. Due to its choice beachfront location, this small site fills up quickly in summer.

Autocamping Moby Dick (☎ 486045, Av Víctor Hugo & Tuyú) US$15-20 in summer, US$10-15 off-season. Also in Ostende, Moby Dick has a dense tree canopy providing plenty of shade.

Albergue Bruno Valente (☎ 482908, Mitre & Nuestras Malvinas, Ostende) HI members $12/10 with/without breakfast, nonmembers US$14 with breakfast; open year-round. About eight blocks south of Pinamar's center, this large youth hostel gets packed in summer and cold and empty in winter. The kitchen is huge and the bathrooms are institutional. The building itself is a decaying historic hotel built in 1926.

Hospedaje Acacias (☎ 485175, Del Cangrejo 1358) Doubles US$30; open year-round. Cheerful, airy rooms open onto a small grassy area and the entire place has a welcoming feel.

Hospedaje Valle Fértil (☎ 484799, Del Cangrejo 1110) Doubles US$40; open Nov-Apr. This is a small, slightly disheveled place on a woodsy street surrounded by vacation blocks.

Hotel Africa (☎ 494443, Av Libertador 500) US$25 per person; open Sept-Apr. This hotel stands out not only for its yellow paint job, but for its tropical good-time feel – a rarity along this coast. It's a hip place with a gregarious owner, clean rooms, a small pool and a bar next door with live music in the summer.

Mid-Range *Hotel Berlín (☎ 482320, Rivadavia 326)* Singles/doubles US$35/60 & US$40/70; open year-round. You'll be hard pressed to find a friendlier place. The breakfast room is very relaxed and sunny, and rooms in both sectors are comfortable.

Hospedaje Rose Marie (☎ 482522, *Las Medusas 1381*) Doubles US$55. *Hotel Yacanto* (☎ 482367, *Rivadavia 509*) Doubles with TV US$63. These are two other good hotels, open December through March only.

Hotel Riviera (☎ 482334, *Del Tuyú 51*) Doubles about US$100; open Dec-Apr. Well-situated just off the beach, this large brick block looks better inside than it does outside. There's a pool, and rooms come with TV, telephone and refrigerators.

Top End *Hotel El Bufón del Rey* (☎ 482323, *Delfines 81*) About US$450/ week; open Dec-Apr. This charming hotel has an intriguing French sculpture of a jester with twins in his arms that allegedly helps infertile couples. The owners welcome visits from non-guests looking to improve fertility.

Hotel del Bosque (☎ 482480, *Av Bunge 1550*) Doubles US$148; open daily Oct-Apr & Fri-Sun in winter. Named for the four-acre eucalyptus grove it sits on, this four-star, ultramodern property is one of the finest in town. Its many amenities include paddle and tennis courts and a driving range. Unfortunately it's a long tramp to the beach.

Hotel Algeciras (☎ 485550, *Av Libertador 75*) Doubles US$188. This tasteful four-star hotel is an expansive brick chalet-style structure with a lovely pool, a jacuzzi, a sauna and luxurious rooms.

Places to Eat

From the local rotisseries to the most exclusive restaurants, Pinamar food is delicious but costly.

Freddo (*Av Bunge & Simbad El Marino*) Freddo scoops excellent ice cream, but it's closed in the dead of winter.

Empanadas de Tucumán (☎ 485916, *Constitución & Valle Fértil*) These may be the best empanadas (US$1 each) in town, and you won't find tamales (US$3.50 each) anywhere else.

Cantina Tulumei (☎ 488696, *Bunge 64*) Mains US$8. This is the place for reasonably priced, quality seafood, though the garlic shrimp and octopus plates get pricey.

El Vivero (☎ 495240, *Avs Bunge & Libertador*) Open Sept-Apr. This is an enormous and surprisingly high-quality vegetarian restaurant well worth a visit.

Con Estilo Criollo (☎ 490818, *Av Bunge & Marco Polo*) US$10-20. This esteemed parrilla serves superb pork and *chivito a la parrilla* (grilled kid).

Tante (☎ 494949, *De las Artes 35*) US$9-25; open noon-2am. Excellent German meals, including trout, venison and fondue can be had at this comfortable tea house. Delicious breads and cakes are served all day.

Getting There & Away

Pinamar shares Villa Gesell's airport. For tickets and information, contact Alemeda Turismo (☎ 481965), Av Bunge 799, the local airline representative. Also see Getting There & Away under Villa Gesell.

Pinamar's slick new bus terminal (☎ 403500) is at Jasón and Av Intermedanos. Rapido del Sud runs up and down the coast in both directions several times a day, stopping at all coastal destinations between Mar del Plata (US$8.40; 2½ hours) and San Clemente del Tuyú (US$5.80; 2 hours). There are also daily buses to Buenos Aires.

Trains run to Pinamar's Estación Divisadero (☎ 497973) in January and February only. Get tickets to Constitución (Buenos Aires) at the bus terminal.

SAN CLEMENTE DEL TUYÚ
☎ 02252 • pop 9800

While San Clemente del Tuyú is one of the closest beach resorts to the capital, it has maintained a very small-town feel that the resorts farther down the coast have lost to high-rises and posh houses. It's a laid-back family place with only a few choices for dinner and even fewer choices for nightlife. Most people favor the beaches to the south, but if you're simply after sun and sand, the place is perfect for a couple days.

It's only a few kilometers from Punta Rasa, the southern tip of Bahía Samborombón, and its location near Cabo San Antonio puts it on the flyway for migratory birds from as far away as Alaska and Canada.

Places to Stay & Eat
Campgrounds US$3 per person/tent. There are several at the entrance to town. San Clemente also has a number of reasonably priced, comfortable hotels with high-season prices around US$15 to US$22 per person.

Hotel Topo (☎ *421442, Av Costanera 1655*) US$15 per person with breakfast; open year-round. On the beach and three blocks from the center, this spotless family-run place, with small cheerful rooms, is an excellent deal.

Sol Mar Hotel (☎/fax *421438, Calle 50 & Av Costanera*) Singles/doubles US$60/70 Jan & Feb, US$35/60 Mar-Dec, cheaper without ocean views, breakfast included; open year-round, weekends-only in winter. Every room in this beachfront three-star hotel has a balcony, good beds, a TV and a telephone. Half and full pension are available.

Bon-Ami (☎ *430228, Calle 1 No 2451*) Mains US$3.50-10. Locals recommend this place for good parrilla and seafood.

Pizzería Tropicana (☎ *421176, Calle 1 & Calle 2*) US$4-8. Tropicana serves good pizza and tasty empanadas.

Getting There & Away
Frequent buses connect San Clemente with Buenos Aires from the bus terminal (☎ 421340) at Calle 10 and Av San Martín. There are also buses on down the coast toward Pinamar, Villa Gesell and Mar del Plata.

NECOCHEA
☎ 02262 • pop 84,765
Spread out around the mouth of the Río Quequén, Necochea is a family favorite. Despite being the second largest resort on the coast (complete with its mass of high-rises), it mysteriously maintains a beach-town feel. Its exceptionally wide beach continually encroaches on the abandoned, graffiti-covered structures that line the costanera, and the main drag is always sandy.

Though Necochea lacks the woodsy allure (as well as the elitism) of the smaller resorts of Pinamar and Villa Gesell, it has some of the best-value lodging on the coast.

Orientation
Necochea is 128km southwest of Mar del Plata via RP 88, the direct inland route. Car-clogged RN 11 is the coastal route from Cabo Corrientes in Mar del Plata. It takes you past dramatic headlands as far south as the family resort of Miramar, and then heads inland to RP 88.

The south-flowing Quequén Grande separates Neuquén, on its western bank, from the town of Quequén on the eastern side.

Though streets have both names and numbers, everyone uses the numbers. Even-numbered streets run parallel to the sea, and odd-numbered streets run perpendicular.

The focus of tourist activity is in 'La Villa,' the newer part of town between Av 10 and the beach. Calle 83 (Alfredo Butti) is its main commercial street. The area is dead in winter. Banks and other businesses that operate year-round are near Plaza Dardo Rocha in the old town, or Centro; most of the area's shops and restaurants line the streets just northwest of the Plaza.

Information
The municipal tourist office (☎ 430158, fax 425983, ⓦ www.necocheanet.com.ar), on the beach at Av 2 and Calle 79, is open 9am to 10pm daily. In winter it closes at 5pm. ACA (☎ 422106) is at Av 59 No 2073.

There are ATMs at Banco de Galicia, Calle 60 No 3164, and Banco de la Nación on the corner of Calle 6 and Calle 83.

The post office is at Av 58 and Calle 63; the postal code is 7630. For Internet service try Satelital at Calle 4 No 4063.

The municipal hospital (☎ 422405) is on Av 59, between Calles 100 and 104.

Things to See & Do
The dense pine woods of **Parque Provincial Miguel Lillo**, a large greenbelt along the beach, are widely used for bicycling, horseback riding, hiking and picnicking.

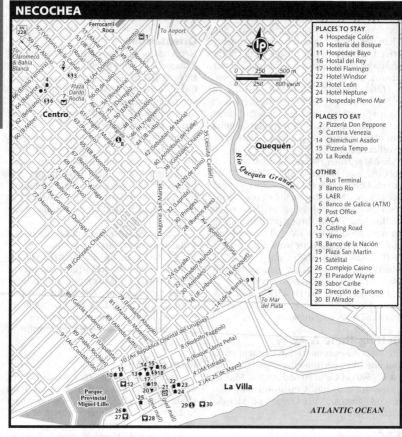

NECOCHEA

PLACES TO STAY
4 Hospedaje Colón
10 Hostería del Bosque
11 Hospedaje Bayo
16 Hostal del Rey
17 Hotel Flamingo
22 Hotel Windsor
23 Hotel León
24 Hotel Neptune
25 Hospedaje Pleno Mar

PLACES TO EAT
2 Pizzería Don Peppone
9 Cantina Venezia
14 Chimichurri Asador
15 Pizzería Tempo
20 La Rueda

OTHER
1 Bus Terminal
3 Banco Río
5 LAER
6 Banco de Galicia (ATM)
7 Post Office
8 ACA
12 Casting Road
13 Yamo
18 Banco de la Nación
19 Plaza San Martín
21 Satelital
26 Complejo Casino
27 El Parador Wayne
28 Sabor Caribe
29 Dirección de Turismo
30 El Mirador

The Río Quequén Grande, rich in
rainbow trout and mackerel, also allows for
adventurous canoeing, particularly around
the falls at Saltos del Quequén. At the
village of **Quequén** at the river's mouth,
several stranded shipwrecks offer good opportunities for exploration and photography
below sculpted cliffs. The **faro** (lighthouse) is
another local attraction.

Places to Stay
Budget Most accommodations are within
walking distance from the beach. The

months hotels stay open vary from year to
year depending on demand.

Camping Americano (☎ 435832, Av 2 &
Calle 101) US$5 per person. Pitch your tent
in Parque Lillo.

Hospedaje Bayo (☎ 423334, Calle 87 No
338) US$8-10 per person; open Sept-Apr.
Rooms in this popular little place are simple
and clean; most open onto a small interior
patio.

Hotel Neptune (☎ 422653, Calle 81 No 212)
US$10-12 per person with breakfast, US$7 in
winter; open year-round. Just off the beach,

this enticing little hotel is a steal; rooms are spotless, beds are solid and TVs come with the package.

Hospedaje Pleno Mar (☎ 422674, Calle 87 No 250) US$10-15 per person. In business for 40 years, this comfortable hotel still keeps high standards.

Hospedaje Colón (☎ 424825, Calle 62 No 3034) Singles/doubles US$13/25; open year-round. Though the beds sag and quarters are slightly cramped, each room comes with TV, telephone and winter-time heat.

Hostal del Rey (☎ 425170, Calle 81 No 335) Doubles US$22 with breakfast; open Sept-Apr. This cheerful hotel with large bathrooms is an excellent value.

Mid-Range *Hotel Windsor* (☎ 420695, Calle 4 No 3957) Doubles US$30 with breakfast; open year-round. The friendly owners here keep the place spotless and serve a strong cup of coffee in the small, well-lit breakfast area. Beds are firm and some bathrooms surprisingly large.

Hotel Flamingo (☎ 420049, Calle 83 No 333) Doubles around US$30. Rooms at this attractive hotel are airy and comfortable, especially if you get one in front with a balcony.

Top End *Hotel León* (☎ 424800, fax 431123, Av 79 No 229) Singles/doubles US$40/60 with breakfast; open year-round. This place shines just a little brighter than the standard mid-range Argentine hotel. It has a touch (no more) of elegance and the rooms are well-kept.

Hostería del Bosque (☎ 420002, e frigerio @infovia.com.ar, Calle 89 No 350) Doubles US$50-90; open year-round. This converted old house, across from the Parque Miguel Lillo, has excellent, beautifully furbished rooms and is one of the most inviting and unique hotels on the coast. The breakfast room opens onto a lovely garden and service is superb.

Places to Eat

Pizzería Don Peppone (☎ 426390, Av 59 No 2828) US$4-9. Head to this down-home family joint for good prices, fast service and excellent quality.

Pizzería Tempo (☎ 425100, Calle 83 No 310) US$4-8. The menu here goes far beyond pizzas and stays cheap. *Milanesas* and the like average US$4, and a US$10 pie serves three.

La Rueda (☎ 421215, Calle 4 No 4144) Four courses US$8. Popular even in the off-season, this place serves excellent, competitively priced parrillada, seafood and Italian cuisine.

Chimichurri Asador (☎ 420642, Calle 83 No 345) Full meal US$8. Well-liked for its delicious meats, this asador offers a special that includes asado, parrillada, empanadas, salad and dessert.

There are several seafood comedores down near the port on Av 59. One of the pricier ones, *Cantina Venezia*, is said to have the best seafood in town.

Entertainment

There are several dance clubs on the beach, impossible to miss on a weekend night.

El Mirador (☎ 15-505746, Av 2 & Calle 79, Playa) US$3-5; open Fri & Sat. Where Av 2 hits the beach, this tropically flavored club beats out the usual mix of *rock nacional*, house and international dance pop. Saturday has the older crowd.

Sabor Caribe (Av 2 & Calle 87, Playa) US$3-8; open Fri & Sat. For salsa, merengue and an overall good vibe try this disco at the end of Calle 87.

There are several small clubs off the beach that are Necochea staples. *Casting Road*, on Calle 87 between Calles 4 and 6, and *Yamo*, on Calle 85 between Calles 6 and 8, are both smaller bar-cum-dance clubs. *El Parador Wayne*, on Av 2 at Calle 89 near the casino, is another popular disco.

Complejo Casino (☎ 423335, Calle 89 & Calle 4) Free; open 9:30pm-3am daily in summer, 9:30pm-3am Fri-Sun in winter. It's always worth stopping by to feed the devil.

Getting There & Away

Aeropuerto Necochea (☎ 422473) is 12km north of town on RP 86. LAER (☎ 426184),

Calle 63 No 2825, has flights to Buenos Aires eight times weekly in summer (US$91).

The bus terminal (☎ 422470) is on Av 58 between Calle 47 and Av 45, near the river. Several companies run daily buses to Buenos Aires ($25; 7 hours). Empresa Córdoba Mar del Plata serves the interior, and there are often special services by other carriers in summer. El Rápido connects Necochea with

Mar del Plata (US$8; 2 hours), Bariloche, Tandil (US$11; 2¾ hours) and Santa Rosa. Rapido del Sud connects Necochea with other coastal destinations.

Trains run three times weekly from the Ferrocarril Roca station (☎ 450028) in neighboring Quequén to Constitución (Buenos Aires; US$16 turista, US$23 primera, US$29.40 Pullman; 9 hours).

Northeast Argentina

Northeast Argentina comprises the provinces of Santa Fe, Entre Ríos, Corrientes, Chaco, Formosa and Misiones. It covers a variety of landscapes, spanning from the fertile pampas of Santa Fe, to the palm savannas of the Gran Chaco, to the northeastern subtropical forests of Misiones. When fingers point to a map of Northeast Argentina, however, they usually land on Iguazú Falls in Misiones province, one of South America's most spectacular natural features, whose thundering falls measure more than 2km across. The province is also home to the region's second-most visited attraction, the magical 17th-century Jesuit ruins from which Misiones takes its name.

There are two main routes from Buenos Aires through Northeast Argentina: one on RN 9 and RN 11 along the Río Paraná, and another up RN 14 along the Río Uruguay. Santa Fe province borders the southern reaches of the Río Paraná and is the heartland of the Humid Pampas, an agricultural area of phenomenal fertility that offers little in terms of traditional sightseeing. The major exception is the port town of Rosario, on the upper Paraná river delta. The country's third-largest metropolis, Rosario is a cultured city with striking architecture and an attractive waterfront. The provincial capital is the city of Santa Fe, 150km north of Rosario on a tributary of the Paraná.

From Santa Fe, it's a quick ride through the Uranga Silvestre Begnis tunnel beneath the Río Paraná to the delightful city of Paraná, capital of Entre Ríos province. 'Entre Ríos' describes literally its location 'between rivers,' and those rivers are the province's principal attractions. With gallery forests providing shade along much of their banks, both rivers offer opportunities for camping and fishing, especially in winter, spring and autumn, when the weather is not oppressively hot. Across the province's rolling grasslands, on the Río Uruguay, Parque Nacional El Palmar protects some 8500 hectares of Entre Ríos' last stands of yatay palms.

Highlights

- Iguazú Falls – Taking in the spray and the deafening roar of one of the world's most majestic waterfalls

- San Ignacio Miní – Exploring the 17th-century settlements of the exquisitely crafted Jesuit ruins

- Reserva Provincial Esteros del Iberá – Hiking in the marshland wilderness, land of exotic wildlife and floating islands

- Corrientes province – Reveling with the crowd during Carnaval or dancing to *chamamé*

- Rosario – Sweating beneath the subtropical sun on the sandy beaches of the Upper Paraná River Delta

Corrientes province lies north of Entre Ríos. Fishing the Río Paraná is the area's traditional attraction, while the Parque Nacional Esteros del Iberá is another truly extraordinary draw. Both Corrientes city and province also hold the country's most notable Carnaval celebrations, and the capital has many historic buildings dating to colonial times.

The primary lures of Chaco and Formosa provinces are the wilderness marshlands of Parque Nacional Chaco and Parque Nacional Río Pilcomayo, both surprisingly undervisited considering their beauty.

History

Except for the western parts of the Santa Fe, Chaco and Formosa provinces, northeast Argentina is also referred to as the *Litoral,* meaning shore, because of the primacy of the Paraná and Uruguay rivers. Historically, the rivers' winding channels and sandbars made navigation difficult above present-day Rosario, while their breadth made cross-river communications equally awkward. The area between the two rivers, often referred to as Argentine Mesopotamia and comprising the provinces of Entre Ríos, Corrientes and Misiones, was effectively an island.

Mesopotamia differs greatly in history and geography from the Argentine heartland. The Guaraní peoples, indigenous to the area from northern Entre Ríos through Corrientes and into Paraguay and Brazil, were semi-sedentary agriculturalists, unlike the nomadic hunter-gatherers who populated the temperate Pampas. The Guaraní raised sweet potatoes, maize, manioc and beans, and river fish played an important role in their diet.

Rumors of wealthy Indian civilizations first drew Europeans to southern Mesopotamia, but Pedro de Mendoza's 1536 attempt to found Buenos Aires was thwarted by Querandí Indians. In 1537, Mendoza's lieutenant Juan de Ayolas established an upper Paraná beachhead at Asunción, where the Spaniards could obtain food and supplies from the friendlier Guaraní. Thus, settlement proceeded southward from

Asunción rather than northward from Buenos Aires. Corrientes was founded in 1588, Santa Fe about the same time.

After finding the nomadic Chaco Indians to be poor candidates for missionary instruction, Jesuit missionaries helped to colonize the upper regions of the Uruguay and Paraná rivers, concentrating the Guaraní in settlements that at least *approached* the Spanish ideal of 'reciprocal rights and responsibilities' in dealing with native populations. Starting around 1607, the Jesuits established 30 missions; the southernmost was established at Yapeyú, on the Río Uruguay in Corrientes province.

The missions competed with secular producers in the cultivation and sale of *yerba mate,* then the region's only important commodity. Perhaps as many as 100,000 Indians lived in the Jesuit settlements, which resembled other Spanish municipalities but operated with a political and economic autonomy that did not apply to other Iberian settlers. Portuguese slavers and secular Spaniards resented the missions' monopoly on the Indian labor and the communities' resulting wealth. In 1767, the Jesuits were expelled, and the mission communities disintegrated rapidly, with much of the area lapsing into virtual wilderness. Densely forested areas became a refuge for Indians unwilling to submit to the demands of secular Spaniards. (See the boxed text, 'The Jesuit Missions.')

Perhaps 15,000 Guaraní remain in the upper Paraná region, and their language survives in many place names and other words. One example is the common usage of the word *gurí,* meaning 'child.'

In Santa Fe province, many other indigenous groups, including the Toba and Mocoví, resisted and disrupted early Spanish settlements, keeping the province marginal in colonial times. The province grew dramatically after independence, benefiting from better overland communications to Buenos Aires and cities to the north and northwest, especially with the expansion of the railroads. About 4000 Mocoví Indians remain dispersed throughout the province.

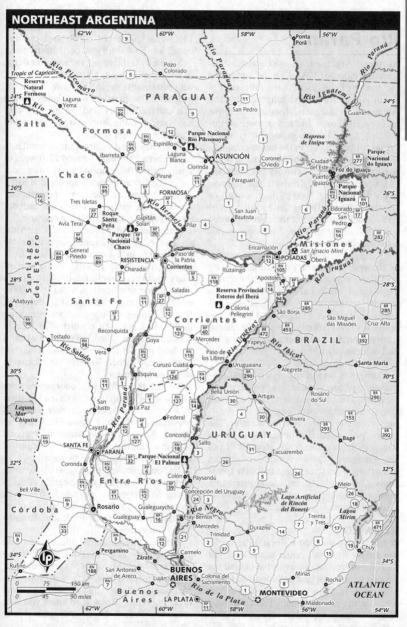

NORTHEAST ARGENTINA

Along the Río Paraná

Northeast Argentina's largest and most interesting cities sit baking in the sun along the banks of the Río Paraná. The river – South America's second longest, after the Amazon – is a central feature for those cities on its shores, and has become an important tourist attraction and primary means for cooling off in the summer. Sportfishing for *sábalo, surubí, dorado* and other river species attracts visitors from around the world, especially outside the oppressively hot summer. East of the river, in Corrientes province, the wetland wilderness of Esteros del Iberá, one of the country's most beautiful and least visited national parks, also draws many visitors.

Oceangoing vessels travel as far upriver as Rosario, the country's third-largest city and home to some impressive architecture, excellent nightlife and a long, pleasant *costanera* (waterfront). Though Rosario is Santa Fe province's largest and most economically powerful city, the title of administrative capital goes to Santa Fe, a somewhat dull modern city with some impressive colonial architecture.

Corrientes, one of the region's first permanent Spanish settlements and capital of its namesake province, is a laid-back and sweltering city with one of the best-preserved city centers in the country. The entire province of Corrientes shows a strong indigenous presence, especially from the Guaraní, whose vocabulary graces everything from street signs to local expressions. *Chamamé,* the nationally loved folk music of Corrientes, is heavily influenced by Guaraní language and music.

ROSARIO
☎ 0341 • pop 980,000 • elevation 25m

On arrival, Rosario's center seems loud, fast and claustrophobic. Slowly, from behind the broken neon signs and pollution-blackened high-rises, Rosario reveals itself as a fine 19th-century city, with many French Renaissance buildings, typical of turn-of-the-20th-century Argentine architecture. One of the joys in this city is rounding a monolithic 1960s-era apartment block and running smack into a two-story art deco masterpiece.

Situated on the upper Paraná river delta, Rosario has a long, accessible waterfront with restaurants, parks and *balnearios* (river beaches). The nearby river islands have a rich cultural history and are now popular hangouts for the hordes that brave the scorching summer sun.

Rosario's first European inhabitants settled here informally around 1720 without sanction from the Spanish Crown. After independence, Rosario quickly superseded Santa Fe as the province's economic powerhouse, though, to the irritation of *rosarinos,* the provincial capital retained political primacy.

The Central Argentine Land Company, an adjunct of the railroad, was responsible for bringing in agricultural colonists from Europe, for whom Rosario was a port of entry. Between 1869 and 1914, Rosario's population grew nearly tenfold to 223,000, easily overtaking the capital in numbers. Rosario's industrial importance through the first half of the 20th century – its role in agricultural exports and its economic ties to the beef market of the Chicago Mercantile Exchange – earned Rosario the nickname 'Chicago Argentino.'

Though the decline of economic and shipping activity through the 1960s led to a drop in the city's population and power, Rosario's importance as a port was rivaled only by Buenos Aires. Its title as Argentina's second city, however, was usurped by Córdoba – a status still hotly contested by rosarinos.

Nationalistic Argentines cherish Rosario, home of a monument to the nation's flag, as 'Cuna de la Bandera' (Cradle of the Flag), though the city is also the official birthplace of the legendary guerrilla leader Ernesto 'Che' Guevara.

Rosario has an active music scene and great restaurants, bars and nightclubs. It also has a brashness about it that you won't see in other major cities such as Córdoba or Mendoza. A slogan gracing many a tourist brochure reads, 'Rosario, to know you is to love you.' In fact, the city demands a little

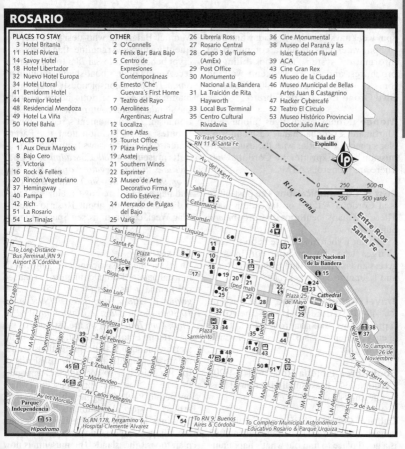

ROSARIO

PLACES TO STAY
3 Hotel Britania
11 Hotel Riviera
14 Savoy Hotel
18 Hotel Libertador
32 Nuevo Hotel Europa
34 Hotel Litoral
41 Benidorm Hotel
44 Romijor Hotel
48 Residencial Mendoza
49 Hotel La Viña
50 Hotel Bahía

PLACES TO EAT
1 Aux Deux Margots
8 Bajo Cero
9 Victoria
16 Rock & Fellers
20 Rincón Vegetariano
37 Hemingway
40 Pampa
42 Rich
51 La Rosario
54 Las Tinajas

OTHER
2 O'Connells
4 Fénix Bar; Bara Bajo
5 Centro de
   Expresiones
   Contemporáneas
6 Ernesto 'Che'
   Guevara's First Home
7 Teatro del Rayo
10 Aerolíneas
   Argentinas; Austral
12 Localiza
13 Cine Atlas
15 Tourist Office
17 Plaza Pringles
19 Asatej
21 Southern Winds
22 Exprinter
23 Museo de Arte
   Decorativo Firma y
   Odilio Estévez
24 Mercado de Pulgas
   del Bajo
25 Varig
26 Librería Ross
27 Rosario Central
28 Grupo 3 de Turismo
   (AmEx)
29 Post Office
30 Monumento
   Nacional a la Bandera
31 La Traición de Rita
   Hayworth
33 Local Bus Terminal
35 Centro Cultural
   Rivadavia
36 Cine Monumental
38 Museo del Paraná y las
   Islas; Estación Fluvial
39 ACA
43 Cine Gran Rex
45 Museo de la Ciudad
46 Museo Municipal de Bellas
   Artes Juan B Castagnino
47 Hacker Cybercafé
52 Teatro El Círculo
53 Museo Histórico Provincial
   Doctor Julio Marc

time, but exploration will surely be rewarded. Another slogan across some T-shirts puts things more precisely: *'Rosario, me mata'* (Rosario, you kill me).

Orientation

Rosario is 320km upstream from Buenos Aires on a bluff above the west bank of the main channel of the Río Paraná. RN 9, the main route to Córdoba, is also the major freeway connecting Rosario with Buenos Aires. Heading north to Santa Fe are RN 11 and its parallel freeway, A 008. Motorists can bypass the city on Av Circunvalación.

Rosario displays a very regular grid pattern except where the curvature of the bluffs above the river channel dictates otherwise. Traditionally, the focus of urban activities is Plaza 25 de Mayo, but the pedestrian streets of San Martín and Córdoba mark the commercial center. There are some 70 sq blocks of open space in Parque Independencia, southwest of downtown.

Information

Tourist Offices On the waterfront at Av Belgrano and Buenos Aires, the municipal tourist office (☎ 480-2230, fax 480-2237, e etur@rosario.gov.ar), is open 8am to 8pm weekdays Monday to Friday and 9am to 8pm weekends. It has a computerized information system and slick bilingual brochures, and offers weekend walking tours of the city. ACA (☎ 440-1278) is at Blvd Oroño 1302 at 3 de Febrero.

Money Money exchanges along San Martín and Córdoba change cash and traveler's checks, the latter with the usual commission. Try Exprinter at Córdoba 960. There are numerous ATMs.

Post & Communications The post office is at Córdoba 721; the postal code is 2000. There are many locutorios on Córdoba and San Martín.

Hacker Cybercafé, at 3 de Febrero 1280, charges US$2.50 per hour for Internet access and is open 9:30am to 3am weekdays and 1:30pm to 3am weekends.

Travel Agencies Grupo 3 de Turismo (☎ 449-1783), Córdoba 1147, is the AmEx representative. The nonprofit student travel agency Asatej (☎ 425-3798) is at Corrientes 653, 6th floor.

Bookstores Librería Ross (☎ 440-4820), Córdoba 1347, has a small selection of classics in English.

Cultural Centers The Centro Cultural Rivadavia (☎ 480-2401), Av San Martín 1080, is a good place to find out what's happening in town. It shows free or inexpensive films and hosts dance and theater events. Its galleries provide a showcase for the local arts community.

The Centro de Expresiones Contemporáneas (☎ 480-2243), Av Belgrano and Bajada Sargento Cabral, consists of recycled historical buildings now providing space for special exhibitions; there is sometimes an admission charge.

Medical Services Hospital Clemente Alvarez (☎ 480-2111) is at Rueda 1110, southwest of the city center.

Monumento Nacional a la Bandera

Manuel Belgrano, who designed the eloquently simple Argentine flag, rests in a crypt beneath a colossal 78m tower in architect Angel Guido's boat-shaped monument *Santa Fe 581,* a conspicuously overbearing manifestation of patriotic hubris even by the standards of a country known for its nationalism. The monument's redeeming attributes are its location near the Paraná waterfront and the views from its tower.

Its **museum** *(☎ 480-2238; admission US$1 includes tower elevator; open 2pm-7pm Mon, 9am-7pm Tues-Sun)* contains the original flag embroidered by Catalina de Vidal.

For information about Rosario's yearly Flag Week celebrations, see Special Events, later.

Museums

Thanks to the romantic and engaging murals of local painter Raúl Domínguez, the **Museo del Paraná y las Islas** *(☎ 440-0751, Av Belgrano & Rioja; admission US$1; open 10:30am-noon Tues, 2:30pm-4pm Wed & Thur, 4pm-7pm Sun),* on the 1st floor of the waterfront Estación Fluvial, is a far more worthwhile sight than the pretentious Monumento a la Bandera. Life on the islands of the Paraná River so enchanted Domínguez that he created this small museum (which opened in 1969), filling it with photographs, artifacts, historical documents and his own paintings. It's an interesting glimpse beyond the city grid, especially worth a visit if you plan to visit the islands. The museum is now run by Domínguez' wife Clemencia and their grandchildren, who will gladly answer any questions about the islands or the painter.

The **Museo Histórico Provincial Doctor Julio Marc** *(☎ 472-1457, Parque Independencia; free; open 9am-5pm Tues-Fri, 4pm-7pm Sat & Sun)* contains some pre-Columbian and colonial exhibits, but concentrates on post-Independence materials. There is also the municipal **Museo de la Ciudad** *(☎ 480-8665, Blvd Oroño 2300; free; open 9am-noon Tues-Fri, 3pm-7pm Sat & Sun).*

The **Museo Municipal de Bellas Artes Juan B Castagnino** *(☎ 480-2542, Av Pellegrini*

& Blvd Oroño; admission US$1; open noon-7pm Tues-Fri, 10am-7pm Sat & Sun) houses a permanent collection of European and Argentine fine art, with occasional contemporary exhibitions. There are wider-ranging collections at the **Museo de Arte Decorativo Firma y Odilio Estévez** *(☎ 480-2547, Santa Fe 748; free; open 4pm-8pm Wed-Sun)*.

La Costanera

One of Rosario's most attractive features is its waterfront. It stretches some 15km from its southern end at Parque Urquiza to the Embarcadero Costa Alta near the city's northern edge. The grassy, tree-filled **Costanera Sur**, just below downtown, stays busy year-round with family picnics, Sunday soccer matches, evening joggers and lip-hungry couples.

In summer, however, it's the **Costanera Norte** that attracts the crowds. The stretch along the busy Av E Carrasco, north of Av Puccio, has the most to offer. Here begins the **Rambla Cataluña**, a tree-lined riverfront with small sandy beaches, shoreline cafés, bars, volleyball nets and tanning bodies.

The widest beach is farther north at **Balneario La Florida** *(admission US$2; open end of Sept-May 1)*, with services including umbrellas, showers, clothing check and outdoor bars. The sidewalk stops at La Florida and picks up again at its northern edge at **Costa Alta** where there are more beaches and a pier with boats to the islands.

To Rambla Cataluña take bus No 103 or 107 from Plaza Sarmiento and get off (a good 20 minutes later) at Plaza Alberdi at Av Puccio. Walk downhill along Puccio to the river. The Rambla begins to the left.

River Islands

Rosario sits on the banks of the Río Paraná upper delta, an area characterized by largely uninhabited, subtropical islands and winding *riachos* (streams). **Isla Invernada** and **Isla Espinillo**, the two main islands visible from Rosario's shore (though part of neighboring Entre Ríos province), are accessible by boat year-round from Costa Alta (see the La Costanera section earlier) and from the Estación Fluvial (☎ 447-3838 or

448-1888), just southeast of the Monumento Nacional a la Bandera.

Boats from Costa Alta leave every 20 minutes (US$2 roundtrip), from 9am to 8pm in summer (less frequently in winter) to the various balnearios along the western shore of Isla Invernada. The balnearios are all pretty similar, with sandy beaches, gregarious summer crowds, cafés, ice cream stands, umbrella rentals, music, billboards and boats from the mainland. Bring plenty of sunblock.

From the Estación Fluvial there are regular boats to the southern balnearios of Costa Esperanza (which offers everything from quad-runners to boat trips), Vladimir and Oasis for US$3.50 roundtrip. You can also visit the island and settlement of **Charigüe**. Boats leave the Estación Fluvial at 9am, 12:30pm and 5pm on weekends only and cost US$5 roundtrip. The island has few restaurants, so pack a lunch.

The *Ciudad de Rosario I* (☎ 449-8688) offers two-hour cruises on the Paraná for US$5; it leaves from Estación Fluvial weekends and holidays at 4pm and 6:30pm.

Other Things to See & Do

Those interested in more distant environments can visit the planetarium at the **Complejo Municipal Astronómico Educativo Rosario** *(Municipal Observatory; ☎ 480-2554, Parque Urquiza; free)*, which has shows (US$2) from 5pm to 6pm Saturday and Sunday. From 9pm to 10pm, Friday through Sunday, visitors can view the austral skies through its 2250mm refractor telescope and 4500mm reflecting telescope. Parque Urquiza borders the river, about seven blocks southwest of the Estación Fluvial on Belgrano.

Though not on the formal tourist circuits, the apartment building at Entre Ríos 480, designed by famed architect Alejandro Bustillo, was where Ernesto Guevara Lynch and Celia de la Serna resided in 1928 after the birth of their son, Ernesto Guevara de la Serna, popularly known as 'Che.' According to biographer Jon Anderson, young Ernesto's birth certificate was falsified (he was born more than a month before the official date of June

14), but this was certainly **Che's first home**, however briefly.

Special Events

Every June, Rosario celebrates La Semana de la Bandera (Flag Week), climaxed by ceremonies on June 20, the anniversary of the death of Manuel Belgrano, the flag's designer. Additionally, the town has its own Semana de Rosario in the first week of October, as well as the national Encuentro de las Colectividades, a tribute to the country's immigrants, in November.

Places to Stay

Budget Open only from September to April, the island campground of *Bahía Caimán (mobile ☎ 155-421-755, Isla Invernada)* has sites for US$15. The *Egea* pushes off regularly from Costa Alta (see La Costanera section) to the island; the trip costs US$2 roundtrip. The campground itself, part of a balneario, has hot showers and electricity. Some supplies are available.

Unless otherwise specified all of the following rooms include private bathrooms.

Hotel Britania (☎ 440-6036, San Martín 364) Doubles US$12/15 without/with bath, singles US$10 without bath. Though the façade of this old hotel is more attractive than the interior, the place is very friendly, popular and by far the cheapest in town.

Hotel La Viña (☎ 421-4549, 3 de Febrero 1244) Singles/doubles US$15/25. This centrally located but faceless hotel is a good value for small rooms with TV and air-conditioning. However, some rooms with carpet have a very musty smell.

Hotel Bahía (☎ 421-7271, fax 449-1290, Maipú 1262) Singles/doubles US$20/30. This family-run place has small, clean, airless rooms with fan and winter heat.

Hotel Gran Confort (☎ 438-0486, Pasaje Quintanilla 657) Singles/doubles US$20/30 with breakfast, bath, air-con, TV & telephone. Easily the best deal near the long-distance bus terminal, this small place has spotless cozy rooms.

Residencial Mendoza (☎/fax 424-6544, Mendoza 1246) Singles/doubles US$25/30 with breakfast; TV, air-con & parking extra.

The rooms are clean and the beds are good; it's a no-frills place and best if you get a window.

Hotel Litoral (☎ 421-1426, Entre Ríos 1045) Singles/doubles US$26/38 with TV & fan. This modern-ish hotel, across from noisy Plaza Sarmiento, has attractive balconies in many of its rooms; otherwise they're small and dark.

Mid-Range Though exceptions certainly exist, Rosario's mid-range accommodations are generally run-of-the-mill.

Savoy Hotel (☎ 448-0075, 448-0071, San Lorenzo 1022) Singles/doubles US$33/50 with balcony & bath, US$30/45 interior with bath, US$15/23 with sink only, all with breakfast. Finally, a hotel with some character. This historic (and slightly decrepit) hotel has a grandiose marble staircase, a stately smoking room and clean rooms with period armoires. The balconied doubles without bath are a steal, and the communal bathrooms are fine.

Benidorm Hotel (☎ 421-9368, San Juan 1049) Singles/doubles US$35/50 with breakfast & parking. Most of the rooms at this friendly no-frills hotel have windows and firm beds.

Romijor Hotel (☎/fax 421-7276, Laprida 1050) Singles/doubles US$35/50 with TV. The rooms here are dark, but recently remodeled and therefore spotless and modern feeling.

Nuevo Hotel Europa (☎ 424-0382, e nuevohoteleuropeo@ciudad.com.ar, San Luis 1364) Singles/doubles US$40/50 with air-con & TV. Shabby on the outside, stylish on the inside, this hotel near Plaza Sarmiento is a good value.

Top End Rosario boasts numerous luxury hotels though two shine a bit brighter than the others.

Hotel Libertador (☎/fax 424-1005, w www.solans.com, Corrientes 752) Singles/doubles US$85/100 with breakfast. This modern four-star hotel has spacious rooms with plush beds and the usual modern amenities. Guests can also use the facilities at the Hotel Riviera.

Hotel Riviera (☎/fax 424-2058, W www solans.com, San Lorenzo 1060) Singles/doubles US$99/118 with breakfast. Hoteles Solans owns the four priciest hotels in town, and this is the best of them. Rooms are very comfortable, though typical of high-rise luxury hotels. A jacuzzi, a sauna, a gymnasium and a buffet breakfast are a few of the perks.

Places to Eat

Rincón Vegetariano (☎ 411-0833, Mitre 720) All-you-can-eat US$5/7 for one/two people, with juice. The salad bar at this vegetarian tenedor libre is delicious, but the hot dishes are mediocre.

Aux Deux Margots (no ☎, Entre Ríos at del Huerto) Mains US$3-8. This is a relaxing spot on the river for morning coffee, afternoon beer and a variety of sandwiches and light meals.

Victoria (☎ 425-7665, San Lorenzo & Roca) Mains US$4-10; open 7:30am-late Mon-Sat, 8pm-late Sun. This atmospheric café-cum-bar in an old brick building offers a US$6 lunch special and delicious salads. It's a great place for a beer, too.

Las Tinajas (☎ 481-7332, Pellegrini 1455) All-you-can-eat US$6 Mon-Fri lunch, US$9 Mon-Thur dinner, US$11 Fri-Sun dinner. This branch of the well-liked Las Tinajas chain puts even Las Vegas buffets to shame. More than 300 dishes, including seafood, fresh pastas, parrillada, salty Chinese food and loads of desserts.

Rock & Fellers (☎ 426-1252, Córdoba 2019) Lunch or dinner US$5-15; open 7am-late. Imagine a classy version of the Hard Rock Cafe in an ornate turn-of-the-20th-century building. Dishes include Turner Tenderloin, Lennon Chicken, sandwiches and ribs.

La Rosario (☎ 440-7985, Laprida 1220) Dinner US$9-15, US$3 extra with music. This small ultra-chic restaurant serves creative house specialties that are best enjoyed Thursday through Saturday nights when there's live music. Reservations are recommended.

Pampa (☎ 449-4303, Mendoza & Moreno) Dinner US$10-20. This stylish parrilla with a chic, nouveau-ranch feel serves some of the best grilled meats in town.

Rich (☎ 440-8657, San Juan 1031) Dinner US$12-25. Specializing in exquisite Italian-influenced cuisine in a beautiful old building, Rich is one of the finest and most atmospheric restaurants in town. Don't overlook the tasty rotisería alongside.

Hemingway (☎ 449-4626, Belgrano & Rioja, near Canal 5) Lunch or dinner US$12-20. Delicious seafood and river fish are served at this rather pricey spot on the river.

The spot for excellent ice cream is *Bajo Cero* (☎ 425-1538, Santa Fe & Roca). There are also several good, cheap cafés and riverside restaurants along the Rambla Cataluña.

Entertainment

Bars The Bara Bajo crowd (see Nightclubs, later) often starts out at the lively (and loud) *Fénix Bar* (no ☎, Tucumán 1002). Fénix is open 11:30pm until dawn Thursday through Saturday.

O'Connells (☎ 440-0512, Paraguay 212) Open 7pm-4am daily. Though Guinness and Kilkenny only come in the can, the place does have the Irish pub decor licked.

Nightclubs Clubs generally open their doors shortly after midnight, but the dance floors often remain deserted until after 2am, when the lines begin to form. There are several clubs northwest of downtown along Rivadavia. A cab from the center should cost around US$5. The two most popular clubs are listed below.

Bara Bajo (no ☎, San Martín 370) Admission US$6; open 2am-dawn Fri & Sat. This bar-like dance club plays house, techno and *rock nacional* and usually gets packed.

Satchmo (Rivadavia 2541) Admission US$7. No matter what they say, there's nothing New Orleans about this place. Recycled rock hits and the occasional dance tune attract an older, relatively conservative crowd.

Moebius (Rivadavia 2459) Admission US$6-8. The line at the door gets frighteningly large after about 2:30am but the thugs in front keep it orderly. Expect dance music.

During the summer, most of the nightclub action moves to the Costanera Norte mega-discos along Av Colombres and E Carrasco. The following are only a few of them.

Timotea (*Colombres 1340, south of Av Puccio*) Admission US$7-10; open year-round, Sat only in winter. *Marcha,* techno and the usual house rhythms keep a young crowd going wild into the wee hours.

Blue Velvet (*Colombres 1698, south of Av Puccio*), *Pancho Villa* (*Av Puccio 122, at Colombres*) and *El Faro*, north of Costa Alta, are similar mainstream discos that stay packed through the summer and busy on off-season weekends. They all charge around US$8 a head, which includes a free drink.

Theater The *Teatro El Círculo* (☎ 448-3784, 448-1089, Laprida 1235) is the city's main performing-arts venue.

Teatro del Rayo (☎ 424-6075, San Martín 473) Open 8:30pm Wed, Thur, Sat & Sun, 5pm Fri. This cozy theater and bar with wooden tables shows art films and cult classics on a small screen. It also has occasional theater performances.

La Traición de Rita Hayworth (*mobile ☎ 156-162-868, Dorrego 1170*) A small performing-arts venue, bar and café, this intimate place is well worth visiting. Reservations are recommended.

Spectator Sports
Rosario has two first-division soccer teams. **Newell's Old Boys** (☎ 421-1180) has offices and plays at Estadio Parque Independencia (☎ 424-4169). **Rosario Central** (☎ 421-0000, 421-4169) has offices at Mitre 857. Its stadium (☎ 438-9595) is at Blvd Avellaneda and Av Génova; tickets are also sold here. Always call to check on game times.

Shopping
Mercado de Pulgas del Bajo (*Av Belgrano & Buenos Aires*) This picturesque flea market, where dealers sell everything from silverwork to leather goods, takes place weekend and holiday afternoons.

Getting There & Away
Air Aerolíneas Argentinas (☎ 448-7492, 448-0185) and Austral (☎ 424-9332) share offices at Santa Fe 1412. Between them,

they fly more than three times a day to Buenos Aires (US$67).

Southern Winds (☎ 425-3808), Mitre 737, flies daily to Córdoba (US$59), continuing daily to Neuquén (US$139) and Tucumán (US$119), and most days to Salta (US$139). It also flies daily to Mar del Plata (US$119) and twice weekly to Bariloche (US$189).

Rosario's only international service is three times weekly to São Paulo and Belo Horizonte in Brazil with Varig (☎ 425-6262), Corrientes 729, 7th floor, office 710.

Bus Long-distance buses use the Estación Mariano Moreno (☎ 437-2384/5/6, W www.terminalrosario.com.ar), at Cafferata 702, near Santa Fe. From downtown Calle San Juan, take bus No 101.

Rosario is a major transport hub and there are direct daily services to nearly all major destinations, from Puerto Iguazú in the north to Comodoro Rivadavia down south.

There is international service to Asunción (US$48, 17 hours) and Ciudad del Este in Paraguay; Porto Alegre and Rio de Janeiro in Brazil; and Montevideo (US$40, 10 hours), Piriápolis and Punta del Este in Uruguay.

The following table shows mid-season fares, which may rise or fall depending on demand. All destinations are served daily and most several times a day. Travel times are approximate.

Destination	Duration in hours	Cost
Bariloche	24	US$75
Buenos Aires	4	US$21
Córdoba	6	US$22
Corrientes	12	US$29
Jujuy	16	US$40
La Plata	6	US$22
Mar del Plata	14	US$30
Mendoza	12	US$27
Neuquén	16	US$44
Paraná	2½	US$11
Resistencia	10	US$29
Salta	16	US$40
Santa Fe	2	US$10
Santiago del Estero	10	US$25
Tucumán	12	US$30

Train From Rosario's train station (☎ 439-2429), Av del Valle 2700, southbound services to Retiro, Buenos Aires (US$14) leave at 9am Monday through Saturday. Take bus No 120 from San Juan and Mitre to the station.

Getting Around

Aerolíneas Argentinas runs its own buses to Aeropuerto Fisherton (☎ 451-2997, 451-1226), 8km west of town. Public buses to Fisherton go only within about 1km of the airport. A taxi or remise costs about US$12.

From the local bus terminal on Plaza Sarmiento, the city's extensive system services virtually everywhere. To get to the city center from the long-distance terminal, take a bus marked 'Centro' or 'Plaza Sarmiento,' but buy a *tarjeta magnética* (magnetic bus card) from a terminal kiosk first; buses do not accept coins.

To rent a car, try Dollar Rent-a-Car ☎ 426-1700), at Paraguay 892, or Localiza, with offices at San Lorenzo 1286 (☎ 439-1336) and at Córdoba 4199 (☎ 435-1234).

SANTA FE

☎ 0242 • pop 450,000

Capital of the province of the same name, Santa Fe is a reserved city with a relatively long history. Its colonial and architectural heritage, however, is tucked into a nondescript urban setting, so it's easy to forget that Santa Fe is one of the country's oldest Spanish settlements – technically.

The original Santa Fe de la Veracruz, as Juan de Garay called it upon its foundation in 1573 while on expedition from Asunción, Paraguay, was nearly 80km northeast of present-day Santa Fe. By the mid-17th century, the location proved intolerable for the original Spanish settlers who, wearied of constant Indian raids, floods and isolation, packed the place up and moved it to its current location on a tributary of the Río Paraná. Although the city was rebuilt on the exact urban plan of abandoned Santa Fe La Vieja (Old Santa Fe), a neo-Parisian building boom in the 19th century and more recent construction have left only isolated colonial buildings. Those that remain, however, are well worth seeing.

Santa Fe also has some good nightlife. Most of it takes place in the Recoleta, an area a few blocks north of the *peatonal* (pedestrian mall), making the late-night wandering between drinking establishments very easy.

Orientation

Santa Fe's remaining colonial buildings are within a short walk of Plaza 25 de Mayo, the town's functional center. Avenida San Martín, north of the plaza, is the major commercial street; between Juan de Garay and Eva Perón, it's an attractive peatonal.

RN 11 links Santa Fe with Rosario (167km) and Buenos Aires (475km) to the south and with Resistencia (544km) and Asunción, Paraguay, to the north. Between Rosario and Santa Fe, the faster *autopista* (freeway) A 008 parallels the ordinary route. To the east, the Uranga Sylvestre Begnis tunnel (RN 168) beneath the Paraná connects Santa Fe with its twin city of Paraná (25km) in Entre Ríos province.

Information

Tourist Offices Located in the bus terminal at Belgrano 2910, Santa Fe's motivated, well-informed municipal tourist office (☎ 457-4123) has loads of brochures and detailed information in loose-leaf binders. It opens 7am to 1pm and 2pm to 8pm daily.

At the southern highway approach to town, another tourist office (☎ 457-1862) is open 7am to 1pm and 2pm to 8pm weekdays, 8am to 8pm Saturday. A tourist office at the Paseo del Restaurador (☎ 457-1881), north of downtown at Blvd Zavalla and JJ Paso, keeps the same hours.

ACA (☎ 455-3862) is at Av Rivadavia 3101, near Suipacha, with a second branch (☎ 455-4142) at Pellegrini and Av San Martín, north of La Recoleta.

Money Tourfe, San Martín 2500, collects 3% commission on traveler's checks. Several ATMs are along the San Martín peatonal.

Post & Communications The post office is at Av 27 de Febrero 2331, near Mendoza; the postal code is 3000. Telecom long-distance

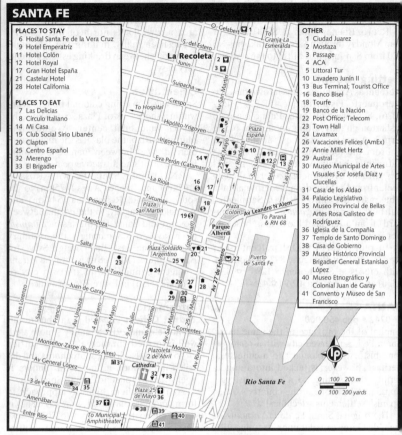

SANTA FE

PLACES TO STAY
6 Hostal Santa Fe de la Vera Cruz
9 Hotel Emperatriz
11 Hotel Colón
12 Hotel Royal
17 Gran Hotel España
21 Castelar Hotel
28 Hotel California

PLACES TO EAT
7 Las Delicias
8 Círculo Italiano
14 Mi Casa
18 Club Social Sirio Libanés
20 Clapton
22 Centro Español
32 Merengo
33 El Brigadier

OTHER
1 Ciudad Juarez
2 Mostaza
3 Passage
4 ACA
5 Littoral Tur
10 Lavadero Junín II
13 Bus Terminal; Tourist Office
16 Banco Bisel
18 Tourfe
19 Banco de la Nación
22 Post Office; Telecom
23 Town Hall
24 Lavamax
26 Vacaciones Felices (AmEx)
27 Annie Millet Hertz
29 Austral
30 Museo Municipal de Artes Visuales Sor Josefa Díaz y Clucellas
34 Casa de los Aldao
34 Palacio Legislativo
35 Museo Provincial de Bellas Artes Rosa Galisteo de Rodríguez
36 Iglesia de la Compañía
37 Templo de Santo Domingo
38 Casa de Gobierno
39 Museo Histórico Provincial Brigadier General Estanislao López
40 Museo Etnográfico y Colonial Juan de Garay
41 Convento y Museo de San Francisco

telephone services are upstairs at the bus terminal and at locutorios downtown.

Travel Agencies Vacaciones Felices (☎ 456-1608), Lisandro de la Torre 2632, Local 4, is the local AmEx representative.

Laundry Lavamax is on 9 de Julio between Salta and de la Torre. Lavadero Junín II is at Rivadavia 2834.

Medical Services Hospital Provincial José María Cullen (☎ 459-9719, 459-8337) is at Irigoyen Freyre, west of downtown.

Convento y Museo de San Francisco

Built in 1680, this convent and museum is Santa Fe's principal historical landmark (☎ 459-3303, Amenábar 2257; open 8am-noon & 4pm-7pm summer, closes 6:30pm winter). The walls, which are more than a meter thick, support a roof made from Paraguayan cedar and hardwood beams that are held together by fittings and wooden spikes rather than by nails. The handworked doors are original, and the baroque pulpit is laminated in gold. Like many other colonial churches, the building's floor plan duplicates the Holy Cross. Parts of the interior patio are open to the public, but the cloisters beyond are off-limits.

In addition to its architectural features, the church houses many works of colonial art. Note also the tomb of Padre Magallanes, a priest who was killed by a jaguar that, driven from the shores of the Paraná during the floods of 1825, took refuge in the church.

Adjacent to the church is a **historical museum** covering topics both sacred and secular from colonial and republican times.

Museums

In a moist but well-preserved late-17th-century building, the **Museo Histórico Provincial Brigadier General Estanislao López** (☎ 459-3760, San Martín 1490; open 8am-noon & 4pm-7pm Mon-Fri, 3pm-6pm Sat & Sun) contains permanent exhibits on the 19th-century civil wars, provincial governors (and caudillos), period furnishings and religious art, plus a room with temporary displays on more contemporary themes.

The most interesting single item in the **Museo Etnográfico y Colonial Juan de Garay** (☎ 459-5857, 25 de Mayo 1470; free, donation requested; open 8:30am-noon & 2:30pm-7pm Tues-Fri, 4pm-7pm Sat, Sun & holidays) is a scale model of the original settlement of Santa Fe La Vieja (Old Santa Fe). It has an excellent collection of Spanish colonial artifacts from excavations at the former settlement site, near present-day Cayastá, and displays of indigenous basketry, Spanish ceramics and coins.

The **Museo Provincial de Bellas Artes Rosa Galisteo de Rodríguez** (☎ 459-6142, 4 de Enero 1510; open 10am-noon Tues-Fri, 4pm-8pm Sat, Sun & holidays) is the provincial fine arts museum.

Granja La Esmeralda

On the northern outskirts of Santa Fe, this experimental farm (☎ 460-1042, 469-6001, Av Aristóbulo del Valle 8700; admission US$1.50; open 8am-7pm daily) also contains a worthwhile zoo that concentrates on provincial native fauna, including toucans, pumas, jaguars and a giant anteater, mostly in spacious enclosures. Bus No 10 bis, which crosses the San Martín peatonal, goes to the farm.

Other Things to See & Do

Santa Fe is one of Argentina's oldest cities, but the 20th century has changed its face considerably – in 1909, for example, the French Renaissance **Casa de Gobierno** (Government House) replaced the demolished colonial *cabildo* (town council) on Plaza 25 de Mayo. Four blocks west is the **Palacio Legislativo**, on 3 de Febrero, between 4 de Enero and Urquiza.

Many remaining colonial buildings are museums, although several revered churches still serve their original purpose. The exterior simplicity of the Jesuit **Iglesia de la Compañía**, on the east side of Plaza 25 de Mayo, masks an ornate interior. Dating from 1696, it's the province's best-preserved colonial church.

The **Templo de Santo Domingo**, at 3 de Febrero and 9 de Julio, dates from the mid-17th century but has undergone several modifications. Its interior is Ionian, while the exterior is a combination of Ionian and Roman styles.

The **Casa de los Aldao** (☎ 459-3222, Monseñor Zaspe 2845; free; open 8am-1pm Mon-Fri) is a restored two-story, early-18th-century house. Like others of its time, it has a tile roof, balconies and meter-thick walls.

Places to Stay

Hotel Royal (☎ 452-7359, Irigoyen Freyre 2256) Singles/doubles US$15/25 with bath, US$10/16 without. Cheap, claustrophobic and tolerable just about sums up this place; it'll do for a night.

Hotel Colón (☎ 452-1586, San Luis 2862) Singles/doubles US$10/15 with shared bath, US$20/35 with bath & breakfast, US$23/38 with bath, breakfast & TV. Though it's little more than five floors of characterless rooms, the place is cheap and clean.

Hotel California (☎ 452-3988, 25 de Mayo 2190) Singles/doubles US$17/25. This basic, undistinguished hotel is very friendly and has a dozen rooms with private bath.

Hotel Emperatriz (☎ 453-0061, *Irigoyen Freyre 2440*) Singles/doubles US$25/35 with breakfast, TV, air-con & heat. Easily the best value in town, this dignified family-run hotel occupies a beautifully remodeled private house. The rooms and baths are spotless and the owners' son José is very helpful.

Castelar Hotel (☎/fax 456-0999, *25 de Mayo 2349*) Singles/doubles US$42/57 with breakfast, TV, telephone & air-con. Considering its posh restaurant and the wood-paneled elegance of the lobby, the rooms here are surprisingly run-of-the-mill. The buffet breakfast, however, looks excellent.

Gran Hotel España (☎/fax 455-2264, e linverde@ssdfe.com.ar, *25 de Mayo 2647*) Singles/doubles US$53/69 with breakfast, TV & telephone. The rooms are rather plain for the price, but the place is unpretentious and the service friendly. Guests have access to the pool, the sauna and a small gym. The restaurant is worth a splurge even for nonguests.

Hostal Santa Fe de la Vera Cruz (☎/fax 455-1740, e hostal_santafe@ciudad.com.ar, *Av San Martín 2954*) Singles/doubles US$45/63 standard, US$72/89 superior, all with breakfast, air-con, parking, TV & telephone. Santa Fe's priciest hotel has comfortable well-kept rooms, 24-hour room service, a sauna, a decent bar and a good restaurant. The more expensive rooms are very plush.

Places to Eat

On Belgrano, across from the bus terminal, several very good, inexpensive places serve Argentine staples, such as empanadas, pizza and parrillada. Otherwise, around the peatonal is the best bet.

Clapton (☎ 453-2236, *San Martín 2300*) Lunch or dinner US$4-8. This modern café serves good pizzas, sandwiches and salads at relatively cheap prices.

Las Delicias (☎ 453-2126, *San Martín 2882*) Open 7am-1am Sun-Thur, 7am-3am Fri & Sat. This smart, old-fashioned café prepares sublime pastries and excellent chocolates for a faithful clientele. It's also good for imaginative sandwiches and cold beer.

Mi Casa (☎ 456-4712, *San Martín 2777*) All-you-can-eat meals US$5.50 Mon-Thur, US$6.80 Fri-Sun. The salad bar is excellent, the parrillada is mediocre and the Chinese dishes are salty – a good enough way to stuff yourself.

Club Social Sirio Libanés (*25 de Mayo & Eva Perón*) Lunch or dinner US$8-16. In a rather aristocratic dining room, attentive waiters serve well-prepared Middle-Eastern-style dishes; it's a unique place to eat.

Círculo Italiano (☎ 452-0628, *Hipólito Yrigoyen 2457*) Part of the Italian social club, Círculo Italiano prepares good, moderately priced lunch specials and tasty pastas.

El Brigadier (☎ 458-1607, *San Martín 1607*) This is a cheap parrilla in an old building with plenty of good river fish on the menu.

Centro Español (☎ 456-9968, *San Martín 2219*) Set in another of Santa Fe's social clubs, this is a classy Spanish restaurant with quality food.

El Quincho de Chiquito (☎ 460-2608, *Brown & Obispo Vieytes*) All-you-can-eat US$10-15; drinks extra. Tourists and locals both flock to this riverside eatery, some distance north of downtown. Because of its size, service is pretty impersonal, but it still serves outstanding grilled river fish, such as boga and sábalo, and exceptional hors d'oeuvres, such as fish empanadas. Take bus No 16 on Av Gálvez, which parallels Suipacha four blocks to the north.

Since 1851, little *Merengo* (☎ 459-3458, *General López 2634*) has been making some of the town's best *merengo alfajores*, Santa Fe's sugar-crusted version of the country's favorite snack.

Entertainment

Santa Fe's nightlife centers around the intersection of San Martín and Santiago del Estero, the heart of the area known as La Recoleta. Barhopping around here is easily done on foot and there are plenty of people out and about on weekend nights.

Mostaza (☎ 453-5333, *San Martín & Santiago del Estero*) A fun bar with an endless assortment of snacks and sandwiches,

Mostaza is a popular warm-up before the nightclubs.

Ciudad Juarez *(☎ 452-7383, 25 de Mayo 3424)* Another Recoleta stronghold, this Tex-Mex bar has a devoted crowd and loud music.

Passage *(☎ 453-3435, San Martín 3243)* Admission US$3. Passage is a good place to cut loose if only for its small size, central location and cheap cover.

Santa Fe's two main mega-discos are on the outskirts of town. A cab from the center of town to either club should cost US$4 to US$5.

La Divina *(Costanera Este)* This huge tent-like structure is the city's definitive summertime disco, playing everything from cumbia and *marcha español* to mainstream house and techno.

La Base *(Leandro Alem & Necochea)* Admission US$4-6. The newest and biggest of Santa Fe's *boliches*, this multiplex dance club attracts the crowds when La Divina shuts for the winter.

Teatro Municipal Primero de Mayo *(☎ 459-7777, Av San Martín 2020)* Designed in the French Renaissance style so common in turn-of-the-20th-century Argentina, this theater offers drama and dance performances.

Getting There & Away

Air Austral (☎ 459-8400), Lisandro de la Torre 2633, has 25 weekly flights to Buenos Aires (US$85). Littoral Tur (☎ 499-5414, 499-5512), San Martín 2984, is the representative of Líneas Aéreas de Entre Ríos (LAER), which flies daily except Sunday to Buenos Aires. Southern Winds (☎ 456-5256), San Jerónimo 2656, flies to Buenos Aires twice daily Monday through Friday and once a day on weekends.

Bus The bus terminal, Belgrano 2940, has a tourist office that posts all fares for destinations throughout the country, so you don't have to run from window to window for comparison.

Buses cross the river every 20 minutes to Paraná (US$2, 40 minutes). There are several daily departures to Rosario (US$12,

2½ hours), Córdoba (US$16, 5 hours) and Buenos Aires (US$20, 6 hours). Buses regularly head north to Corrientes (US$21, 10 hours), Resistencia (US$26), Formosa (US$30, 8 hours), Tucumán (US$35, 12 hours) and Puerto Iguazú (US$42, 13 hours). Several companies run daily to Mar del Plata (US$58, 12 hours) and west to Mendoza (US$37, 13 hours). Several carriers serve Bahía Blanca (US$65, 14 hours) and Patagonian destinations, including Neuquén (US$65, 16 hours) and Bariloche (US$95).

Penha, Norosur and Pluma all have international services to Porto Alegre and Florianópolis, Brazil. Godoy goes to Asunción, Paraguay (US$41, 13 hours); and Cora goes to Montevideo, Uruguay (US$45, 12 hours).

Getting Around

For US$0.75, city bus A (yellow) goes to Aeropuerto Sauce Viejo (☎ 457-0642), which is 7km south of town on RN 11. To rent a car, try the Annie Millet Hertz office (☎ 456-4480/81) at Lisandro de la Torre 2548.

AROUND SANTA FE
Alto Verde

Beyond Santa Fe, the Río Paraná has fostered a little-known but intriguing way of life among the people of 'suburban' villages, such as Alto Verde. When the river rises, these fisherfolk evacuate their houses for temporary refuge in the city, but when the floods recede they rebuild their houses on the same spot.

Shaded by enormous willows and other trees, Alto Verde is a picturesque fishing village on Isla Sirgadero. To reach the village, catch a launch from Puerto del Piojo, in the port complex at the east end of Calle Mendoza in Santa Fe, or take bus No 15 from Obispo Gelabert.

Cayastá

The Río San Javier has eroded away part of the Cayastá ruins, which is the original site of Santa Fe La Vieja, including half of the Plaza de Armas. However, excavations have revealed the sites of the cabildo and the Santo Domingo, San Francisco and Merced churches. Authorities have erected protective structures to guard the remains of these buildings. For educational purposes, they have also reconstructed a typical period house with furnishings. The site is open 8:30am to noon and 3:30pm to 7pm weekdays, 4pm to 7pm weekends and holidays from October through March. From April through September, it's open 8am to 1pm and 2pm to 6pm weekdays, 10am to 1pm and 3pm to 6pm weekends and holidays. You can usually talk your way onto the grounds even when it's closed.

Cayastá is 78km northeast of Santa Fe on RP 1. Paraná Medio bus company goes regularly from Santa Fe's bus terminal (US$4.50). Buy tickets at window number 14.

PARANÁ
☎ 0343 • pop 236,500

Though it's the capital of Entre Ríos province, Paraná retains a relaxed, small-town feel – much more so than Santa Fe just across the river. With low buildings and 19th-century architecture, its city center is compact and manageable, sloping gently down to the pleasant Parque Urquiza, which then drops its grassy shoulders to the costanera below.

The river is the city's main attraction. People come to fish, barbecue, drink *mate* and do their best to forget the oppressive summer heat. Much of the shore is a leisurely promenade with crumbling cement railings, drooping shade trees and broken steps down to the silted river.

Paraná's accommodation is comfortable, but its nightlife is slim. Beyond the few downtown sights, Paraná has little to offer aside from staring at the cathedral from a bench in the plaza or hanging out on the river with everyone else.

Orientation
Paraná sits on a high bluff on the east bank of the Río Paraná, 500km north of Buenos Aires via RN 9 and RN 11, which passes through Santa Fe; routes through southern Entre Ríos are shorter but slower because of substandard roads. The Uranga Silvestre Begnis tunnel, beneath the main channel of the Paraná, connects the city to Santa Fe.

The city plan is more irregular than most Argentine cities, with numerous diagonals, curving boulevards and complex intersections. Plaza 1 de Mayo is the town center; on Saturday mornings, virtually the entire town congregates for a *paseo* (outing) down the peatonal José de San Martín.

Except for San Martín, street names change on all sides of the plaza. At the north end of San Martín, Parque Urquiza extends more than a kilometer along the riverfront and the bluffs above it. Many other attractive parks and plazas are scattered throughout the city.

Information
The municipal tourist office (☎ 420-1674) is at San Martín 637, near the corner of La Paz; opening hours are from 8am to 8pm daily. There are also branches at the bus terminal (☎ 422-4282), at the park office (☎ 420-1837), on the riverfront between Bajada San Martín and Av Doctor Laurencena, and at the Oficina del Túnel, at the tunnel outlet, as you enter Paraná from Santa Fe. The provincial tourist office (☎ 422-3384) is at Laprida 5. ACA (☎ 431-1319) is at Buenos Aires 333.

Banco Francés, at San Martín 763, and Citibank, at the corner of 25 de Mayo and 9 de Julio, both have ATMs.

The post office is at 25 de Mayo and Monte Caseros; the postal code is 3100. Telecentro is a locutorio on San Martín between Uruguay and Pazos. Both La Red (☎ 423-709), Urquiza 790, and Conexion.com (☎ 431-5125), Rivadavia 665, offer reliable Internet access.

Lavadero Belgrano, at Belgrano 306 charges US$5.90 per load.

Hospital San Martín (☎ 423-4545, 421-8378) is at Presidente Perón 450, near Gualeguaychú.

Walking Tour
Walkers can see most of Paraná's key buildings in a short stroll starting at Plaza 1 de Mayo, where the post office occupies the former residence of General Urquiza. The

PARANÁ

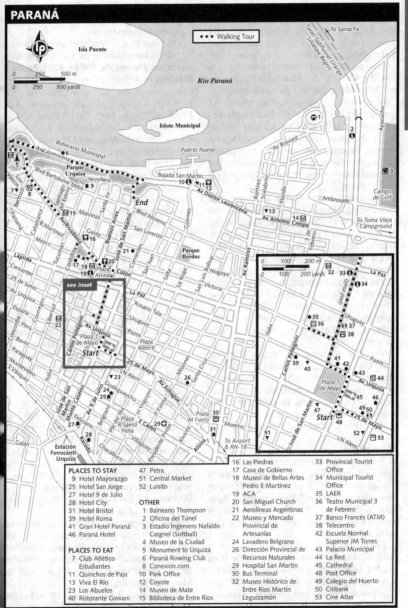

• • • Walking Tour

Isla Puente

Río Paraná

Islote Municipal

Balneario Municipal

Puerto Nuevo

End

Parque Urquiza

Parque Berduc

see inset

Plaza Alvear

Plaza 1 de Mayo

Start

Plaza Alberti

Plaza M Fierro

Plaza R Sáenz Peña

Estación Ferrocarril Urquiza

To Santa Fe

To Toma Vieja Campground

Campo de Golf

To Airport & RN-18

Túnel Subfluvial Uranga Silvestre Begins

PLACES TO STAY	OTHER	16 Las Piedras	33 Provincial Tourist
9 Hotel Mayorazgo	1 Balneario Thompson	17 Casa de Gobierno	Office
25 Hotel San Jorge	2 Oficina del Túnel	18 Museo de Bellas Artes	34 Municipal Tourist
27 Hotel 9 de Julio	3 Estadio Ingeniero Nafaldo	Pedro E Martínez	Office
28 Hotel City	Cargnel (Softball)	19 ACA	35 LAER
31 Hotel Bristol	4 Museo de la Ciudad	20 San Miguel Church	36 Teatro Municipal 3
39 Hotel Roma	5 Monument to Urquiza	21 Aerolíneas Argentinas	de Febrero
41 Gran Hotel Paraná	6 Paraná Rowing Club	22 Museo y Mercado	37 Banco Francés (ATM)
46 Paraná Hotel	8 Conexion.com	Provincial de	38 Telecentro
	10 Park Office	Artesanías	42 Escuela Normal
PLACES TO EAT	12 Coyote	24 Lavadero Belgrano	Superior JM Torres
7 Club Atlético	14 Museo de Mate	26 Dirección Provincial de	43 Palacio Municipal
Estudiantes	15 Biblioteca de Entre Ríos	Recursos Naturales	44 La Red
11 Quinchos de Paja		29 Hospital San Martín	45 Cathedral
13 Viva El Río		30 Bus Terminal	48 Post Office
23 Los Abuelos		32 Museo Histórico de	50 Colegio del Huerto
40 Ristorante Giovani		Entre Ríos Martín	50 Citibank
47 Petra		Leguizamón	53 Cine Atlas
51 Central Market			
52 Luisito			

cathedral has been on the plaza since 1730, though the current building, with its sky-blue tiled dome, dates from 1885. Its museum is open 5pm to 7pm daily. When Paraná was capital of the Argentine Confederation, the senate deliberated at what is now the **Colegio del Huerto**, at 9 de Julio and 25 de Mayo, behind the cathedral.

Just north of the cathedral, across Av Urquiza at Corrientes, is the **Palacio Municipal**, built in 1890. Directly across Corrientes, on the same intersection, is the **Escuela Normal Superior JM Torres**, the country's first teacher-training school, founded by the famous educator and president Domingo F Sarmiento.

Walk north on San Martín and hang a left onto 25 de Junio to see the **Teatro Municipal 3 de Febrero** (1908), at 25 de Junio 60. At the north end of the San Martín peatonal, several museums cluster around **Plaza Alvear** (see Museums, later). A block west, bounded by Córdoba, Laprida and Santa Fe, the **Centro Cívico** contains the provincial **Casa de Gobierno**, completed in 1890, and other government offices. Farther west, along the diagonal Av Rivadavia, is the **Biblioteca de Entre Ríos**, the provincial library.

You can continue to **Parque Urquiza**, walk the length of the park, and double back at the foot of San Martín to return to Plaza 1 de Mayo. The park has a number of significant monuments, including the **Monumento a Urquiza**, and also features the **Museo de la Ciudad** (see Museums, later).

Museums

Situated right on the waterfront Av Laurencena in Parque Urquiza, the **Museo de la Ciudad** (☎ 420-1838; admission US$1; open 8am-noon & 3:30pm-7:30pm Tues-Fri, 9am-noon & 3:30pm-7:30pm Sat, 3:30pm-7:30pm Sun) focuses on the city's urban past and surroundings.

Flaunting local pride, Plaza Alvear's modern **Museo Histórico de Entre Ríos Martín Leguizamón** (☎ 420-7869, Buenos Aires 286; admission US$1; open 7:30am-12:30pm & 3pm-7:30pm Tues-Fri, 9am-noon & 4pm-7pm Sat, 9am-noon Sun) contains

well-arranged displays of artifacts of 19th-century provincial life, along with outstanding portrait collections.

Oil paintings, illustrations and sculptures by provincial artists are the focus of the subterranean **Museo de Bellas Artes Pedro E Martínez** (☎ 420-7868, Buenos Aires 355; free; open 9am-noon & 4pm-9pm Tues-Fri, 10:30am-12:30pm & 5:30pm-8pm Sat, 10:30am-12:30pm Sun), just off Plaza Alvear.

Promoting handicrafts from throughout the province, the **Museo y Mercado Provincial de Artesanías** (☎ 422-4540, Av Urquiza 1239; free; open 8am-1pm & 4pm-7pm Mon-Fri, 8am-1pm Sat, 9am-noon Sun) is a combined crafts center and museum displaying a variety of media including wood, ceramics leather, metal, bone and iron.

The most unique museum in Paraná is Francisco Scutellá's **Museo de Mate** (☎ 422-0995, Antonio Crespo 159; admission US$1; open 7am-12:30pm & 4pm-8pm daily, closed Sat & Sun if sunny). Thousands of pieces of mate paraphernalia fill the shelves of this small museum, which boasts the tallest and the smallest mate gourds in the world. The ornate pieces made in Germany, England and Austria are testimony to the old countries' attempts to distinguish their drinking vessels (and identical habits) from indigenous and gaucho mate gourds; apparently they didn't take.

River Activities

From the northern edge of downtown, Parque Urquiza slopes steeply downward to the banks of the Río Paraná and the **Balneario Municipal**. During the summer months the waterfront fills with people strolling, fishing, swimming and practicing other languorous methods of staying cool. Beware of jejenes, annoying biting insects, along the river in summer.

River fishing is a popular local pastime, and tasty local game species like boga, sábalo, dorado and surubí reach considerable size. Contact the Dirección Provincial de Recursos Naturales (☎ 431-6773, 25 de Mayo 565) for licenses.

The Paraná Rowing Club (☎ 431-2048) conducts hour-long **river excursions** for

US$3; they leave at 3:30pm and 5pm Friday through Sunday from the Puerto Nuevo at Costanera and Vélez Sarsfield. Located on the riverfront, the rowing club has a café and you can use its facilities, including a private beach, a swimming pool and showers, for US$5 per day.

Paraná, unfortunately, plans to give its costanera – which is appealing in its weathered, crumbling state – a serious facelift. When (and if) it does, the waterfront may end up entirely different.

Special Events

Every January, Paraná hosts the Fiesta Provincial de Música y Artesanía Entrerriana, featuring regional folk music and crafts. In October, the Fiesta Provincial La Raya y La Hermandad acknowledges immigrants' contributions to provincial development.

Perhaps the most unusual event is February's recently revived Maratón Internacional Hernandárias-Paraná, an 88km swim that attracts contestants from around the world. It is part of the annual Fiesta del Río.

At Diamante, 44km south of Paraná, the January Fiesta Nacional de Jineteada y Folklore celebrates gaucho culture and music. Diamante is also the site of February's Fiesta Provincial del Pescador (Provincial Fisherman's Festival).

Places to Stay

Toma Vieja Campground (☎ 424-7721, *end of Av Blas Parera*) Sites US$8. On the scenic site of the old waterworks overlooking the river, Toma Vieja is Paranás only official (and only decent) campsite. Services include hot showers and electricity, and there's a store nearby. Bus No 5 leaves hourly from the terminal.

Hotel City (☎ 431-0086, fax 431-1701, *Blvd Racedo 231*) Singles/doubles US$19/34 with breakfast, bath, TV & parking. Directly opposite the train station, this simple hotel has a delightful patio garden and cool rooms with high ceilings. The price drops if you share a bath.

Hotel 9 de Julio (☎ 431-9857, fax 431-3047, *9 de Julio 674*) Singles/doubles US$23/34 with TV & breakfast. Some of the

colorful rooms here have surprisingly large bathrooms, the breakfast room is comfortable and the place is friendly.

Hotel Roma (☎ 431-2247, *Urquiza 1061*) Singles/doubles US$25/35 with TV & bath, air-con extra. Very centrally located, this cheerful, family-run place has clean, simple rooms. Get one with a balcony and you're set.

Hotel San Jorge (☎/fax 422-1685, 422-9910, *Belgrano 368*) Singles/doubles US$20/30 in front, US$28/38 in back with TV. Every room in this excellent, friendly place is spotless and newly remodeled. The back rooms are bigger and have TVs. Front rooms are fine but the two near the lobby are annoyingly noisy. There's a small kitchen, too.

Hotel Bristol (☎ 431-3961, *Alsina 221*) Singles/doubles US$25/35. This clean and attractive hotel is the best place near the bus terminal.

Paraná Hotel (☎ 423-1700, fax 422-3205, e *reservasparanahtl@hotelesparana.com.ar, 9 de Julio 60*) Singles/doubles US$39/56. This immaculate hotel, in a colonial building with small modern rooms, has a lovely patio, a game room and a friendly staff.

Gran Hotel Paraná (☎ 422-3900, fax 422-3979, *Urquiza 976*) Singles/doubles US$50-84/70-110. Smack on the Plaza 1 de Mayo, this chic, modern, four-star hotel has a game room, a gym, a terrace bar, 24-hour room service, a restaurant and a salon. Beds and baths are excellent.

Hotel Mayorazgo (☎ 423-0333, fax 423-0420, e *res_mayor@arnet.com.ar, Etchevehere & Miranda, Parque Urquiza*) Singles/doubles US$85/120 with buffet breakfast. Every room in this expansive five-star hotel faces the river; only those on the first floor, however, have huge balconies. A casino, a pool, a travel agency and tanning booths are a few of the amenities available.

Places to Eat

The *central market* at Pellegrini and Bavio is a great place to stock up on food.

Petra (☎ 423-0608, *25 de Mayo 32*) All-you-can-eat lunch/dinner US$4/5, drink not included. This is about the best deal north of Ushuaia – and the food is surprisingly good.

Los Abuelos (☎ 431-9662, 9 de Julio 279) Mains US$3.80-8. This is a warmly inviting family place, where a hearty plate of gnocchi al pesto or ravioli with cream sauce won't set you back much.

Club Atlético Estudiantes (☎ 422-2484, Los Vascos & Bertozzi) Inside the athletic club on the western end of Parque Urquiza, is one of the best seafood restaurants in town.

Viva El Río (☎ 431-9411, Antonio Crespo 71) Viva El Río is a reliable, popular seafood restaurant with good prices and a casual atmosphere.

Luisito (☎ 431-6912, 9 de Julio 140) This is one of the city's traditional favorites.

Quinchos de Paja (☎ 423-1845, Av Doctor Laurencena at Salta) Mains US$6-14. Locals and tourists alike flock to this seafood institution for delicious but, often pricey, river fish. To their dismay, it may close due to construction on the costanera.

Ristorante Giovani (☎ 423-0527, Av Urquiza 1045) Lunch or dinner US$7-18. Though the fish can be hit-or-miss, this highly esteemed, upscale parrilla serves excellent meats and delectable pastas.

Entertainment

Teatro 3 de Febrero (☎ 420-1657/58, 25 de Junio 60) This municipal theater puts on exhibitions of local art, inexpensive films and other activities.

Coyote (☎ 421-9286, Linieres 334) Open midnight-dawn Thur-Sat. This Tex-Mex-flavored dance club on the river plays the usual mix of mainstream *marcha,* house and salsa.

Las Piedras (☎ 422-9665, Rivadavia & Córdoba) Open 9am-1pm & 6pm-late daily. This bar-cum-sandwich shop has live music on Friday and Saturday nights, usually followed by dancing. It's a small, fun place.

If you have money to spare, you can gamble it at the *casino* in the Hotel Mayorazgo (see Places to Stay, earlier). It opens 9pm to 3am daily in winter; 9:30pm to 3:30am daily in summer.

Getting There & Away

Air Aerolíneas Argentinas (☎ 423-2425, 423-2601) has offices at Corrientes 563, but flights leave from Santa Fe's Aeropuerto Sauce Viejo. For details see Getting There & Away for Santa Fe.

Líneas Aéreas de Entre Ríos (LAER; ☎ 420-0810/11), with an office at Buenos Aires 120, flies from Paraná to Buenos Aires (US$65 and up) an average of four times daily. It operates its own minibus service to Aeropuerto Ciudad de Paraná, just outside the city limits.

Bus The bus terminal (☎ 422-1282) is on Av Ramírez between Posadas and Moreno, opposite Plaza Martín Fierro. Paraná is a center for provincial bus services, but Santa Fe is more convenient for long-distance trips. Buses leave every 20 minutes for Santa Fe (US$2, 40 minutes).

There are about 20 buses daily to Buenos Aires (US$23, 6½ hours) and numerous others to Rosario (US$12, 3 hours), Córdoba (US$16, 6 hours) and Mendoza (US$34, 15 hours). There are nightly departures to Corrientes (US$21, 8 hours) and Resistencia (US$20, 8½ hours), and daily departures to Puerto Iguazú (US$38, 15 hours). Buses regularly head north to Tucumán (US$35, 12 hours) and Salta (US$56, 17 hours). In summer there are daily departures to Mar del Plata (US$53, 13 hours).

International carriers go to Montevideo, Uruguay (US$41, 10 hours) four times weekly; and to Porto Alegre, Brazil (US$54, 12 hours).

Car Motorists should be aware of irritating document checks from the provincial police at each end of the Uranga Silvestre Begnis tunnel between Paraná and Santa Fe. The passenger vehicle toll is US$2.

LA PAZ
☎ 03437

On the east bank of the Paraná, about 160km northwest of Entre Ríos' provincial capital, La Paz is known for excellent fishing and good camping. In February it celebrates the **Fiesta Nacional de Pesca Variada de Río** (National River Fishing Festival).

The tourist office (☎ 422389) is at Echagüe 787. La Paz's postal code is 3190. For modest accommodations, try the basic, and rather cramped, *Residencial Las Dos M* (☎ 421303, *Urquiza 825),* where singles/doubles cost US$12/20. *Hotel Milton (*☎ *422232, Italia 1029)* offers more comfort for US$28/40.

CORRIENTES
☎ 03783 • pop 333,600

One of the oldest and most historical cities in Argentina, the capital of Corrientes province is also one of the most beautiful in the region. Its well-preserved Plaza 25 de Mayo is surrounded by a combination of Italianate and 19th-century French architec-

ture, and by older, slightly decrepit colonial buildings that betray the city's age and add to its charm. Much of its costanera is a wide, tree-lined walk, perfectly landscaped and full of people throughout the evening. Corrientes is a magnet for regional indigenous crafts, which artisans sell in the evening on the plaza JB Cabral and in the Museo de las Artesanías and its neighboring shops. Guaraní culture has a strong presence. On the downside, summers are brutally hot, and budget hotels tend to be dismal.

Corrientes sits just below the confluence of the Río Paraná and the Río Paraguay,

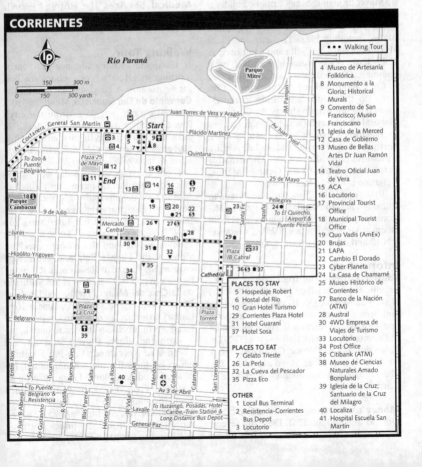

CORRIENTES

Río Paraná

Parque Mitre

••• Walking Tour

4 Museo de Artesanía Folklórica
8 Monumento a la Gloria; Historical Murals
9 Convento de San Francisco; Museo Franciscano
11 Iglesia de la Merced
12 Casa de Gobierno
13 Museo de Bellas Artes Dr Juan Ramón Vidal
14 Teatro Oficial Juan de Vera
15 ACA
16 Locutorio
17 Provincial Tourist Office
18 Municipal Tourist Office
19 Quo Vadis (AmEx)
20 Brujas
21 LAPA
22 Cambio El Dorado
23 Cyber Planeta
24 La Casa de Chamamé
25 Museo Histórico de Corrientes
27 Banco de la Nación (ATM)
28 Austral
30 4WD Empresa de Viajes de Turismo
33 Locutorio
34 Post Office
36 Citibank (ATM)
38 Museo de Ciencias Naturales Amado Bonpland
39 Iglesia de la Cruz; Santuario de la Cruz del Milagro
40 Localiza
41 Hospital Escuela San Martín

PLACES TO STAY
5 Hospedaje Robert
6 Hostal del Río
10 Gran Hotel Turismo
29 Corrientes Plaza Hotel
31 Hotel Guaraní
37 Hotel Sosa

PLACES TO EAT
7 Gelato Trieste
26 La Perla
32 La Cueva del Pescador
35 Pizza Eco

OTHER
1 Local Bus Terminal
2 Resistencia-Corrientes Bus Depot
3 Locutorio

Start

End

Plaza 25 de Mayo

Parque Cambacuá

Mercado Central

Plaza La Cruz

Plaza Torrent

Cathedral

Plaza JB Cabral

To Puente Belgrano & Resistencia

To Zoo & Puente Belgrano

To El Quincho, Airport & Puente Pexoa

To Ituzaingó, Posadas, Hotel Caribe, Train Station & Long Distance Bus Depot

0 150 300 m
0 150 300 yards

where it was founded by Spaniards moving south from Asunción in 1588. It was originally called Vera de los Siete Corrientes, after its founder Juan Torres de Vera y Aragón and the shifting *corrientes* (currents) of the Paraná. Corrientes suffered repeated Indian uprisings before establishing itself as the first Spanish settlement in the region. Also notable: Corrientes was the setting for Graham Greene's work of fiction *The Honorary Consul*.

Orientation

Corrientes' regular grid centers on Plaza 25 de Mayo, though the major public buildings are more spread out than in most Argentine cities. There are several other important plazas, including Plaza La Cruz and Plaza JB Cabral. Between Salta and San Lorenzo, Calle Junín is a peatonal along which most commercial activities are concentrated.

Calle Junín and most other areas of interest to the visitor are within a triangle formed by three main streets: Av Costanera General San Martín (which changes names to Plácido Martínez at its eastern end), north-south Av España, and Av 3 de Abril, a westward extension of Av Gobernador Ferré, which leads to the General Manuel Belgrano bridge to Resistencia.

To the east, RN 12 parallels the Paraná to Ituzaingó and to Posadas, the capital of Misiones province. Overland connections from Buenos Aires, which lies 1025km south via RN 12 and other roads, are good.

Information

Tourist Offices The friendly and helpful provincial tourist office (☎ 427200, 424565) is at 25 de Mayo 1330. It opens 7am to 1pm and 3pm to 9pm weekdays, 8am to noon and 4pm to 8pm weekends. There's a branch of the municipal tourist office (☎ 423779) at Pellegrini 542 in Parque Cambacuá. ACA (☎ 422844) is at 25 de Mayo and Mendoza. The Paraguayan consulate (☎ 426576) is at Córdoba 969.

Money You can change money at Cambio El Dorado, at 9 de Julio 1341. There are several banks with ATMs on and around 9 de Julio.

Post & Communications The post office is at the corner of San Juan and San Martín; the postal code is 3400. Locutorios are easy to find.

Cyber Planeta (mobile ☎ 15-684261) at San Lorenzo 735, and Brujas, at Mendoza 787, offer reliable Internet service.

Travel Agencies Quo Vadis (☎ 423096, fax 421958), Pellegrini 1140, is the AmEx representative. For less-conventional excursions, contact 4WD Empresa de Viajes de Turismo (☎/fax 433269), Junín 1062, Local 18.

Medical Services The Hospital Escuela San Martín (☎ 420697/98, 421371) is at Av 3 de Abril 1251.

Walking Tour

In Corrientes' stifling summer heat, early-morning or late-afternoon hours are best for sightseeing. A good starting point is the **Convento de San Francisco**, Mendoza 450, a colonial church that dates from the city's founding but was beautifully restored in 1939. The convent has its own museum, the **Museo Francisco** (☎ 422936; free; open 8am-noon & 5pm-9pm weekdays).

From the Convento, walk west along Plácido Martínez, detouring up Calle San Juan to view the innovative **historical murals** before strolling along the tree-lined Av Costanera, past the small but interesting **zoo** (☎ 427626, Av Costanera at Junín; free; open 10am-6pm). Beyond the zoo are excellent views of the **Puente Belgrano**, the bridge crossing the Paraná to Resistencia. Returning by Edison and Bolívar, stop at the **Santuario de la Cruz del Milagro** on the south side of Plaza La Cruz. The shrine contains a 16th-century cross that, according to legend, defied all efforts of rebellious Indians to burn it.

Continue along Bolívar and up San Lorenzo to the **cathedral** on Plaza Cabral, which contains the mausoleum and statue of local caudillo Colonel Genaro Berón de Astrada. From Plaza JB Cabral, return along the Junín peatonal to Salta and back toward the river, passing Plaza 25 de Mayo. An alternative route continues north on San Lorenzo to attractive **Parque Mitre**.

Monumento a la Gloria & Historical Murals

In recent years, the east side of San Juan, between Plácido Martínez and Quintana, has been transformed into a shady, beautifully landscaped park. A monument honors the Italian community, while a series of striking historical murals, extending more than 100m around the corner onto Quintana, chronicles the city's history since colonial times. It's a very attractive addition to a block that already features the colonial Convento de San Francisco.

Museums

The **Museo Histórico de Corrientes** (*9 de Julio 1044; free; open 8am-noon & 4pm-8pm weekdays*) exhibits weapons, antique furniture, coins and items dealing with religious and civil history. The museum also has a library.

The **Museo de Bellas Artes Doctor Juan Ramón Vidal** (*☎ 436722, San Juan 634; free; open 9am-noon & 6pm-9pm Tues-Sat*) emphasizes sculpture but has frequent special exhibitions.

Carnaval Correntino

Inspired by immigrants from the provincial town of Paso de los Libres on the Brazilian border, Corrientes' traditionally riotous **Carnaval** nearly disappeared until a recent revival, and it's once again an event worth attending. Celebrated Friday through Sunday the last three weekends in February and the first weekend of March, Carnaval attracts participants from neighboring provinces and countries to the parades along Av Ferré; crowds have reached 80,000.

Places to Stay

Corrientes' accommodations are relatively scarce and expensive. During Carnaval, however, the provincial tourist office maintains a list of *casas de familia* where lodging generally ranges from US$10 to US$20 per person. Most hotels offer substantial discounts for cash payment.

The nearest campground to Corrientes is *Molina Punta*, 5km from downtown,

reached by bus No 8 out Av Libertad (the eastward continuation of Pellegrini and Av Gobernador Ruiz); sites cost US$5 plus US$1 per vehicle.

Hospedaje Robert (*no ☎, La Rioja 415*) Singles/doubles US$15/25 with shared bath. This old wooden hotel is about as basic as they come, but it's in a good location near the river.

Hotel Sosa (*☎ 466747, Hipólito Yrigoyen 1676*) Singles/doubles US$25/35. Half a block from Plaza Cabral, this rundown but friendly hotel is proof that dismal rooms and saggy beds don't come cheap in Corrientes.

Gran Hotel Turismo (*☎ 433174, Entre Ríos 650*) Singles/doubles US$30/40. Built in 1948, this stately old hotel has an attractive restaurant, a large pool, a bar and an excellent riverside location. The rooms are slightly worn and the air-con a little noisy, but it's a uniquely inviting place.

Hotel Guaraní (*☎ 433800, fax 424620, e hguarani@espacio.com.ar, Mendoza 970*) Singles/doubles US$34/52 standard, US$54/67 superior, US$66/81 suites. Pay for the standard rooms and you still get a TV, the buffet breakfast and use of the pool, gym and sauna. Up your ante and you get a better paint job and softer carpet. It's a slick place with an upscale café.

Corrientes Plaza Hotel (*☎/fax 543783, e reserva@corrienteshotel.com.ar, Junín 1549*) Singles/doubles US$42/69 standard, US$67/85 superior, all with breakfast & parking. Excellent for its price range, this modern hotel on Plaza Cabral has spotless rooms, a lovely pool and a friendly staff.

Hostal del Río (*☎ 436100, fax 429726, e hostal_del_rio@infovia.com.ar, Plácido Martínez 1098*) Singles/doubles US$35/45 lower, US$50/60 upper, with breakfast & parking. The standard rooms in this riverfront high-rise are nondescript and comfortable; the upper rooms are excellent. All have air-con and most have views.

Places to Eat

The Junín peatonal has *cafés* and *confiterías* (pastry shops), but shuts down during the midday heat. The area in and around the *Mercado Central* on Junín between La Rioja and San Juan is prime hunting grounds for cheap eats.

La Perla (☎ 423008, 9 de Julio & Mendoza) Open 8am-1pm & 4pm-11pm Mon-Sat. An old-fashioned, Italian-style bakery and café that serves mind-altering pastries (US$2 and up) and excellent coffee; each cup comes with *chipasitos* (small cheese pastries). Everything is warm when the doors open at 4pm.

Pizza Eco (☎ 425900, Hipólito Yrigoyen 1108) Open 7am-1pm & 5pm-3am daily. Both the atmosphere and the pizza rate well at this friendly spot. Large pies average US$8, while a dozen empanadas cost US$6-8.

La Cueva del Pescador (☎ 422511, Hipólito Yrigoyen 1255) Prices are high but not outrageous at this very fine fish restaurant with good atmosphere.

Gelato Trieste (☎ 465333, San Juan & Quintana) The ice cream here is superb and the bougainvillea-covered *plazoleta* in front an inviting spot to eat it.

El Quincho and **Puente Pexoa** (see Entertainment, later) are cheap, down-home parrillas.

Entertainment

Teatro Oficial Juan de Vera (☎ 427743, San Juan 637) This theater honoring the city's colonial founder offers classical music concerts and other cultural events.

Corrientes is the heartland of the lively music and dance known as chamamé, and seeing a live performance is difficult outside the provinces of northeastern Argentina. Here, they're on every weekend. The two most popular places in Corrientes are:

El Quincho (no ☎, Av Pujol & JV Pampir, just northeast of the Pujol-Pellegrini roundabout) Music starts around 10pm Thur, 11pm Fri & Sat and 1pm Sunday. This down-home restaurant is an excellent spot for beef and chamamé. You can't beat US$5 for all-you-can-eat parrillada, so arrive hungry.

Puente Pexoa (☎ 451687, RN 12 at La Retonda Virgen de Itatí roundabout) Open 8:30pm, first band at 11:30pm Fri & Sat. This relaxed restaurant is ground-zero for

Chamamé

While the rest of the country is doing the tango, Northeast Argentina is dancing the *chamamé*. One of the country's most intoxicating musical forms, chamamé is rooted in the polka, which was brought to the littoral region by European immigrants in the early 19th century, and is heavily influenced by the music and language of the indigenous Guaraní. Its definitive sound is the accordion, which is traditionally accompanied by the guitar, the *guitarón*, the larger *bandoneón* accordion and the *contrabajo*, or double bass. Of course, a *conjunto* (band) is hardly complete without a singer or two.

Chamamé is as much a dance as it is a musical genre, and it's a lively one. It is a dance for a couple, except when the man takes his solo *zapateo*. Corrientes province is the heart of chamamé and is therefore the easiest place to find a live performance. Sitting in on an evening of music and dancing, or taking to the floor if you're brave, is one of the joys unique to the province.

chamamé, and it can get outrageously fun when the dancing starts. Men and women show up in full gaucho regalia, and up to four *conjuntos* (bands) may play each night. From downtown, take bus No 102 marked '17 de Agosto' 7km out of town to the Virgen de Itatí roundabout. It's just off the roundabout; the driver will point it out. A taxi back will cost US$8 to US$10.

Shopping

Museo de Artesanía Folklórica (Quintana 905) Open 8am-noon & 3pm-7pm Mon-Fri, 9am-noon & 4pm-7pm Sat. In a converted colonial house with an interior courtyard, this museum sells local crafts including palm and *espantillo* weavings, silver- and leatherwork and wood carvings. Fine antique crafts are on exhibit. Other rooms around the courtyard are occupied by working artisans who will sell to you directly.

La Casa de Chamamé (Pellegrini 1790) This CD shop specializes in Corrientes' roots music, and the friendly staff will let you listen before you buy.

Getting There & Away

Air Austral (☎ 423918), Junín 1301, flies to Buenos Aires twice daily (only once on Sunday), and to Posadas (US$62) on Sunday. There are also flights to Buenos Aires from nearby Resistencia, with both Austral and Aerolíneas Argentinas. LAPA (☎ 431625/28), 9 de Julio 1261, flies 10 times weekly to Buenos Aires (US$59-79).

Bus Resistencia, northwest of Corrientes in El Chaco province, has better long-distance bus connections, especially to the west and northwest (see Resistencia, later in this chapter). Buses to Resistencia (US$2, 40 minutes) leave regularly throughout the day from the local bus terminal on Av Costanera General San Martín at La Rioja. Buses to provincial destinations like Goya and Esquina also leave from here.

Corrientes' long-distance bus terminal (☎ 442149) is on Av Maipú between Manatiales and Nicaragua.

At least four buses daily head to Buenos Aires (US$35-50, 12 hours), some via Paraná, Santa Fe and Rosario, and others via Entre Ríos. There are regular runs to Posadas (US$18, 4½ hours), capital of Misiones province, where there are connections to the former Jesuit missions and to Puerto Iguazú (US$35, 10 hours). Transportes El Zonda crosses the Chaco to Tucumán, and Puerto Tirol serves the western bank of the Paraná, with routes running from Formosa south to Buenos Aires.

Tata/El Rápido goes to Paso de los Libres, on the Brazilian border (6 hours), via the interior city of Mercedes, which is the place to access the Esteros del Iberá preserve. Empresa Tala goes to Uruguaiana, Brazil and Asunción, Paraguay. Co-Bra offers direct service to Brazil.

Getting Around

Local bus No 8 goes to the airport (☎ 431628), about 10km east of town on RN 12. Austral runs a minibus to Resistencia to coincide with flight schedules.

Bus No 6 runs between the local bus terminal on the Costanera and the long-distance terminal on Av Maipú. Bus No 103 connects the long-distance terminal with downtown.

For car rental, try Localiza (☎ 426270) at Av 3 de Abril 1047.

PASO DE LA PATRIA
☎ 03783

Superb sportfishing has made this flood-prone resort of unpaved streets, 30km northeast of Corrientes at the confluence of the Paraguay and Paraná rivers, an international destination for knowledgeable and avid anglers. High season is July to September; early October to early March is the closed season.

The tourist office (☎ 494007) is at 25 de Mayo 518. Paso de la Patria's postal code is 3904.

There is frequent bus service to and from Corrientes.

Fiesta Internacional del Dorado

The highlight of this annual festival, which is held in mid-August, is a four-day competition for the largest specimens of the carnivorous dorado, known as the 'tiger of the Paraná ' for its fighting nature. The dorado weighs up to 25kg, and the minimum allowable catch size is 75cm. Entry costs around US$60 per person. In addition to the dorado, other local sport species include the surubí (weighing up to 70kg), the tasty boga, sábalo, pejerrey, pacú, patí, manduví, mangrullo, chafalote and armado. Methods include trolling, spinning and fly casting. Night fishing is possible.

Places to Stay

Several campgrounds charge about US$5 to US$6 per tent per day, plus US$3 per vehicle, with all facilities. Many *correntinos* have weekend houses here and often rent them to visitors. Prices for a two-bedroom house start at around US$60 per day for up to six people. For more information, contact the tourist office.

One alternative for local accommodations is *Le Apart Hotel* (☎ 494174, 25 de

Mayo 1201), which charges US$120 per day with breakfast for up to four people.

MERCEDES
☎ 03773 • pop 20,750

Though Mercedes is a long way off the Río Paraná, it's most easily reached from Corrientes. It's an enticingly laid-back place with an attractive downtown almost devoid of modern buildings. There's nothing to do here but sit and watch the day unfold along its cobblestoned streets.

Most visitors to Mercedes are en route to the spectacular wetlands of the Esteros del Iberá. Mercedes' other satellite attraction is the utterly surreal roadside shrine to the Gaucho Antonio Gil, an enormously popular religious phenomenon (see the boxed text, 'Gaucho Antonio Gil'), 9km west of town.

The post office is at the corner of Rivadavia and Martínez; the postal code is 3470.

Places to Stay
At the Antonio Gil shrine, you'll find inexpensive *camping* in an otherwise desolate area.

Hotel Ita Pucú (☎ 421015, *Batalla de Salta 645)* Singles/doubles US$15/25 with air-con. With a sort of spaghetti western feel, this friendly low-roofed hotel has plenty of character and decent rooms that open onto a grassy garden. Breakfast is extra.

Petit Hotel Sol (☎ 420283, *San Martín 519)* Singles/doubles US$20/30; breakfast US$3; air-con US$8 extra. The 10 rooms in this converted, late-19th-century house open onto a plant-filled tile patio. The front rooms are bigger than the new, more comfortable rooms in the back. All are spotless.

Places to Eat
Poravory (☎ 422508, *Belgrano & Pujol)* Breakfast US$2-4. One block off the plaza toward the terminal, this country kitchen-style café serves good breakfasts with fresh juices and mediocre coffee.

La Casa de Chirola (☎ 422308, *Sarmiento & Pujol)* Lunch or dinner US$4-7. Good for lunch or dinner, this family-run place on the Plaza 25 de Mayo serves good pastas, sandwiches and weekend parrillada.

Shopping
Chac Cueros (☎ 420341, *San Martín 853)* This small shop specializes in high-quality leather goods made from the ultra-soft, naturally dimpled hides of *carpincho* (those odd, overgrown, guinea-pig-like animals). Purses, jackets, moccasins, boots and belts are all available in the light-brown leather displayed in store windows throughout Argentina.

Getting There & Away
The bus terminal is at San Martín and Alfredo Perreyra.

Gaucho Antonio Gil

Second only to the Difunta Correa (see the Mendoza chapter) as an object of popular devotion in Argentina, the Gaucho Antonio Gil was a Robin Hood–type figure whose shrine just outside Mercedes, in Corrientes province, attracts tens of thousands of pilgrims every year. Unlike the Difunta Correa, who probably never existed, Antonio Gil was an actual historical figure, a 19th-century conscript who deserted the army of Colonel Juan de la Cruz Salazar and spent several years on the run, supported by the poor of the Corrientes countryside. Even as a judicial pardon awaited him in the town of Goya, Gil was finally captured and reportedly hanged from the espinillo tree that still stands near his crypt. His legend soon spread beyond the province and Northeast Argentina.

Antonio Gil's last resting place is now the site of numerous chapels and storehouses holding thousands of votive offerings (T-shirts, bicycles, pistols, knives, license plates, photographs, cigarettes, hair clippings, entire racks of wedding gowns) brought by those who believe in the Gaucho's miracles. Though less common than those of the Difunta Correa, Gaucho Gil roadside sites are especially conspicuous for their dozens of bright red flags flying in the breeze. January 8, the date of Gil's death, attracts the most pilgrims to the Mercedes site.

Itatí buses to Colonia Pellegrini (US$8, 2 hours), in the Esteros del Iberá, leave at 5am and 2pm Monday, 2pm Tuesday through Friday and 10am Saturday.

There are daily departures to Buenos Aires (US$25, 9 hours), La Plata (US$30, 12 hours), Resistencia (US$10, 4 hours) and Corrientes (US$9, 3½ hours).

RESERVA PROVINCIAL ESTEROS DEL IBERÁ

Esteros del Iberá, a wetlands wilderness covering 13,000 sq km in the north-central part of the province (14% of its entire territory), is a wildlife cornucopia comparable with – if not superior to – Brazil's Pantanal. Aquatic plants and grasses, including 'floating islands,' dominate the marsh vegetation, while trees are relatively few. The most notable wildlife species are reptiles such as the caiman, mammals such as the maned wolf, howler monkey, neotropical otter, capybara, pampas and swamp deer and more than 350 bird species. Much (but not all) of the wildlife is nocturnal.

For independent travelers, the settlement of Colonia Pellegrini, 120km northwest of Mercedes on Laguna Iberá, is the easiest place to organize trips into the marshes. Though some groceries are available in Pellegrini itself, the best place to purchase most supplies is the town of Mercedes, 107km southwest of Colonia Pellegrini. The park is most enjoyable in winter and spring when the heat is far less oppressive.

Organized Tours

Since the logistics of visiting the Esteros are awkward, organized tours can be a good alternative. Day-trip launch tours, which cost about US$20 per hour for up to five people, are a bargain for what they offer.

Estancia Capi-Vari (☎/fax 03773-420180), Beltrán 190 in Mercedes, arranges stays on an estancia at the southwestern corner of the reserve. Both Posada Aguapé and Hostería Ñandé Retá also offer excursions into the wetlands (see Places to Stay, later).

Places to Stay

Camping is possible at Colonia Pellegrini for about US$2 per person.

Hostería Ñandé Retá (☎ 03773-421741, ☎/fax 03773-420155 in Mercedes, mobile ☎ 03773-15-629536) US$42 per person with full board. This peaceful, rustic and comfortable hostería is a bargain. They also arrange transport from Mercedes and offer tours of the wetlands.

Posada Aguapé (☎ 03773-499412 in Corrientes, ☎ 011-4742-3015 in Buenos Aires, ℮ aguape@interserver.com.ar, ⓦ www .iberaesteros.com.ar; by mail, contact María Paz Galmarini, Coronel Obarrio 1038, 1642 San Isidro, Provincia de Buenos Aires) Singles/doubles US$60/80 with breakfast, US$110/190 with full board, canoe and kayak use and one motor boat excursion. This luxurious colonial-style posada is in a beautiful setting above the lake and has a swimming pool and bar. Numerous excursions, including an excellent bird-watching tour, can be arranged on site. Spanish, English, French, German and Italian are all spoken.

Getting There & Away

Colonia Pellegrini, 107km northeast of Mercedes via RP 40, is the best center for visiting the Esteros. There is frequent public transportation between Paso de los Libres and Corrientes to Mercedes, where Itatí buses to Colonia Pellegrini (US$8, 2 hours) leave at 5am and 2pm Monday, 2pm Tuesday through Friday and 10am Saturday. They return to Mercedes at 6am Monday through Saturday, and also at 1pm Saturday.

Along the Río Uruguay

Lively Carnaval celebrations, a 19th-century palace, hot-spring spas and a national park preserving palm groves teeming with wildlife are among the attractions along the Uruguay. As with the Paraná, aquatic recreation, especially sportfishing, draws many visitors to the region. The river also constitutes Argentina's northern border with Uruguay and, farther north, Brazil. Four bridges and a dam provide easy access to these neighbors, whose influences have blended with those of indigenous and immigrant groups to produce interesting and sometimes surprising results.

The Uruguay and Paraná converge just north of Buenos Aires to flow into the Río de la Plata. In Gualeguaychú, the first major town along the Uruguay, you begin to see shops and stands selling *feijoada* (Brazil's national dish) and *chipa* (manioc-flour rolls, a Guaraní staple omnipresent in Paraguay). RN 14 runs north from Gualeguaychú roughly paralleling the Uruguay as far as Santo Tomé in Corrientes province, the last town covered in this section. It passes densely forested riverside areas and runs through grasslands where cattle graze alongside rheas.

GUALEGUAYCHÚ
☎ 03446 • pop 68,000
Gualeguaychú is the first substantial town encountered by travelers arriving in Entre Ríos from Buenos Aires. While not a major destination for most foreigners, it has considerable historical interest, offers good river recreation, holds one of Argentina's best carnivals and leads to the most southerly bridge crossing into Uruguay.

Orientation
Some 220km north of Buenos Aires and 13km east of RN 14, Gualeguaychú sits on the east bank of its namesake river, a tributary of the Uruguay. Plaza San Martín, occupying four square blocks, is the center of its very regular grid pattern. RN 136 bypasses the city center en route to the Puente Internacional General Libertador San Martín, a toll bridge leading to the Uruguayan city of Fray Bentos.

Information
The tourist office (☎ 423688) is on Tiscornia near its intersection with the Av Costanera, south of Plaza Colón. It opens daily 8am to 10pm in summer, 8am to 8pm in winter and has good brochures and maps and a list of accommodations. A branch at the bus terminal was not yet open at the time of research. ACA (☎ 426088) is at Urquiza and Chacabuco. The Uruguayan consulate (☎ 426168) is at Rivadavia 510.

There are several banks, mostly with ATMs, along Av 25 de Mayo. The post office is at Urquiza and Ángel Elías; the postal code is 2820. Both the Telecentro at the bus terminal and at 25 de Mayo 562 offer Internet access.

Hospital Centenario (☎ 427831) is at 25 de Mayo and Pasteur, at the western approach to town.

Things to See & Do
A handful of colonial buildings remain in Gualeguaychú, in addition to more recent ones important in Argentine political and literary history. The **Museo Haedo** *(San José 105; open 9am-11:45pm Wed-Sat, 6pm-8:45pm Fri & Sat)*, just off Plaza San Martín, is the municipal museum, occupying the oldest house in town (1800).

In the mid-19th century, the colonial **Casa de Andrade**, at Andrade and Borques, belonged to *entrerriano* poet, journalist, diplomat and politician Olegario Andrade. **Casa de Fray Mocho**, at Fray Mocho 135, was the birthplace of José S Álvarez, founder of the influential satirical magazine *Caras y Caretas* at the turn of the 20th century; Fray Mocho was his pen name. Dating from the early 20th century, the unusual **Casa de la Cultura** *(☎ 427989, Calle 25 de Mayo, near Montevideo)* has occasional public exhibitions, and is the place to contact for entrance to the houses listed above.

The **Teatro Gualeguaychú** *(☎ 431757, Urquiza 705; open 7am-9pm Mon-Fri)* was inaugurated in 1914 with a performance of *Aïda*, and still hosts symphony, ballet and theater. Check at the Casa de la Cultura for tours.

At the former train station, at the south end of Maipú, the **Museo Ferroviario** *(Maestra Piccini & Maipú)* is an open-air exhibit of steam locomotives, dining cars and other hardware from provincial rail history. Alongside the museum, on Blvd Irazusta, the new **Corsódromo** is the main site for Gualeguaychú's lively Carnaval (see Special Events, later).

Parque Unzué is a spacious greenbelt across the river, and it is good for swimming,

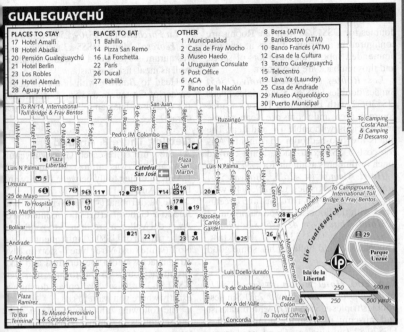

GUALEGUAYCHÚ

PLACES TO STAY	PLACES TO EAT	OTHER	
17 Hotel Amalfi	11 Bahillo	1 Municipalidad	8 Bersa (ATM)
18 Hotel Abadía	14 Pizza San Remo	2 Casa de Fray Mocho	9 BankBoston (ATM)
20 Pensión Gualeguaychú	16 La Forchetta	3 Museo Haedo	10 Banco Francés (ATM)
21 Hotel Berlín	22 París	4 Uruguayan Consulate	12 Casa de la Cultura
23 Los Robles	26 Ducal	5 Post Office	13 Teatro Gualeyguaychú
24 Hotel Alemán	27 Bahillo	6 ACA	15 Telecentro
28 Aguay Hotel		7 Banco de la Nación	19 Lava Ya (Laundry)
			25 Casa de Andrade
			29 Museo Arqueológico
			30 Puerto Municipal

picnicking, camping, fishing and relaxing. It also contains the city's **Museo Arqueológico** (☎ *428820, Parque Unzué; open 6pm-9pm Mon-Sat*).

A stroll along the costanera yields views across the river to the park and various inlets and landscapes. Guided tours of the river are offered on the launch *Ciudad de Gualeguaychú* (☎ *423248*). Call or contact the tourist office on the costanera. Tours cost US$3 to US$5 and leave from the Puerto Municipal.

Special Events

Gualeguaychú's summer Carnaval has a national and even international reputation, so if you can't go to Rio or Bahía, make a stop here any weekend from mid-January to late February. Admission to the Corsódromo costs about US$15, plus another US$2 to US$3 to guarantee a seat.

Every October for more than 30 years, on the Día de la Raza weekend, high-school students have built and paraded floats through the city during the Fiesta Provincial de Carrozas Estudiantiles. Other local celebrations include numerous *jineteadas* (rodeos) throughout the year.

Places to Stay

Budget *Camping Costa Azul* (☎ *423984, Av Costanera s/n*) Sites US$12 for up to four people. This campground, 200m north of the bridge to Parque Unzué, has good facilities, but take plenty of mosquito repellent in summer.

Camping El Descanso (mobile ☎ *15-637892, Av Costanera s/n*) Sites US$12 for up to four people. Similar to the Costa Azul, this campground is another 200m up the costanera.

Pensión Gualeguaychú (☎ *424132, 25 de Mayo 456*) US$10 per person with shared bath. This clean and friendly place, with many rooms and an inner courtyard, is one of the cheapest in town.

Mid-Range The laid-back *Hotel Amalfi* (☎ 425677, 25 de Mayo 579) has singles/doubles for US$15/25 with fan. Rooms are configured in a variety of ways at this recommended spot; some have lots of space, and those in back are very quiet.

Los Robles (☎ 426469, Bolívar 565) Singles/doubles US$18/25 and triples/quads US$30/32 with breakfast. There's a nice common area, and rooms are clean, simple and spacious, with cable TV and heat. The quads are two-bedroom apartments. Air-con costs US$5 extra, and a home-cooked lunch or dinner is available for US$7.

Hotel Alemán (☎ 426153, Bolívar 535) Singles/doubles/triples US$20/30/40 with breakfast. These clean rooms are decent-sized, with tile floors and good bathrooms.

Hotel Abadía (☎ 427675, San Martín 588) Doubles US$33 with breakfast. This pleasant old building has some good rooms.

Top End *Hotel Berlín* (☎/fax 425111, e hotelberlin.com.ar, Bolívar 733) Singles/doubles/triples US$45/60/72 with breakfast and air-con; in summer doubles/triples US$70/82 (no singles). Good-sized, comfortable rooms have central heat and cable TV. Attached parking is included in rates.

Aguay Hotel (☎ 422099, e hotelaguay@ciudad.com.ar, Av Costanera 130) Singles/doubles/triples US$60/82/95 with buffet breakfast. All rooms in this modern hotel have balconies (most with great views overlooking the river), excellent baths, air-con and heat. There's also a small gym, a rooftop pool and spa and a garage – a very good value.

Places to Eat

Pizza San Remo (☎ 426891, 25 de Mayo 634) Mains US$2.50-7. Choose from a good variety of calzones, pizzas, fugazza and more, all served amid a delightful combination of old and new decor.

París (☎ 422158, Pellegrini 62) Mains US$3-9. This spacious restaurant serves parrillada, fish, etc. Check out the carpeted columns and the good wine list.

Ducal (☎ 427602, San Lorenzo & Andrade) Mains US$4-9. Ducal looks right

across the costanera to the river and serves good fish, pasta and meat.

La Forchetta (☎ 433109, 25 de Mayo & 3 de Febrero) Mains US$5-13. This upscale restaurant serves good specialty salads as well as meat, fish and pasta.

Head to *Bahillo*, with branches at the corner of Costanera and San Lorenzo, and the corner of Díaz and 25 de Mayo, for ice cream.

Getting There & Around

At the time of research Gualeguaychú's new airport was almost finished, with LAER planning to fly between the city and Buenos Aires.

The bus terminal (☎ 440688) is at Bulevar Jurado & General Artigas (a continuation of Av A del Valle), more than 3km southwest of the plaza. For US$0.80, infrequent buses – No 2 (white) and No 3 (blue) – stop on Blvd Artigas across from the terminal and take circuitous routes to the town center. For US$2.50-3 a remise will drop you downtown exactly where you want to go.

The following table shows winter fares and schedules; in summer transport is more frequent and sometimes more expensive. All destinations are served daily and most several times a day. Travel times are approximate.

Destination	Duration in hours	Cost
Buenos Aires	3½	US$15
Colón	1½	US$7
Concepción	1¼	US$4.50
Concordia	3	US$14
Corrientes	6½	US$20
Fray Bentos (Uru)	1	US$5.50
Mercedes (Uru)	1½	US$7.50
Paraná	4½	US$14
Paso de los Libres	7	US$20
Resistencia	10	US$30
Rosario	7½	US$28
Santa Fe	5½	US$17

Three times weekly, El Litoral offers service to Córdoba (US$40, 11 hours) by way of Santa Fe. Three Expreso Singer buses pass

Gualeguaychú on the highway en route to Puerto Iguazú (15 hours) between 3pm and 8:15pm.

CONCEPCIÓN
☎ 03442 • pop 57,000

Concepción del Uruguay is a crossroads town. Its tourist services make it a suitable stopover for travelers on long trips north, and it has some interesting architecture in its own right. Concepción is on the Río Uruguay east of the junction of RN 14 from Buenos Aires and RP 39 to Paraná, and midway between Gualeguaychú and Parque Nacional El Palmar.

Concepción has some great architecture, particularly around the plaza. Don't miss the *casino*, *police headquarters* or the *basilica*. The basilica's left wing holds Urquiza's remains in a replica of Napoleon's mausoleum.

The region's primary attraction, however, is Palácio San José, which was General Urquiza's enormous residence, 30km west of town. Here, Urquiza was assassinated by the forces of his rival, Ricardo López Jordán. (See the section on Palácio San José, later in this chapter.)

Orientation
The bus terminal is between Rocamora and Galarza. Calle 9 de Julio is one block south of Galarza, and all three streets lead east to the river. On the way, Rocamora passes one block north of the central Plaza General Francisco Ramírez, Galarza runs along the north edge and 9 de Julio hits the middle.

Information
The main tourist office (☎ 440812), open 8am to 8pm daily, is at Elías 50 (at Galarza) on the edge of town, eight blocks west of the terminal. A more conveniently located office (☎ 425820), is eight blocks east of the terminal at 9 de Julio 844, but it opens only from 7am to 1pm daily. An ATM that accepts most cards is in the bus terminal.

Places to Stay & Eat
Balneario Municipal Itapé (☎ 427852, Av 3 de Febrero s/n) Sites US$5 for two people.

This basic campground is 15 blocks south of the plaza. It closes in winter.

Banco Pelay (☎ 427130, e bancopelay@ cedelu.com, Isla de las Garzas) Sites US$5 for two people. This enormous full-service campground, also closed in winter, is about 5km north of downtown. The island on the Río Uruguay it occupies has sandy beaches.

Residencial Centro (☎ 427429, Mariano Moreno 130) Singles/doubles/triples/quads US$18/29/39/45. Clean, tranquil and friendly, with grapevines shading a central patio, the Centro is less than two blocks south of the main plaza.

Hotel General Francisco Ramírez (☎ 428109, fax 428710, Blvd Los Constituyentes 52/100) Singles/doubles/triples US$22/45/55 with breakfast. At the bus terminal, but nicer than that sounds, the Ramírez has smallish but bright, clean and comfortable rooms with good views. Get one as high up as possible, and facing away from the buses.

Grand Hotel (☎/fax 425586, Eva Perón at Rocamora) Singles/doubles/triples US$32/48/65 to US$45/60/75, all with breakfast, air-con & parking. The standards are better decorated than the superior rooms at this two-star hotel that was built in the 1930s. One block west and one block north of the plaza, the Grand has a gym and a good old feel to it. Rates rise in summer.

In addition to the restaurant at the Hotel General Ramírez, there are several restaurants on the streets just north of the plaza, including *La Delfina* (☎ 433240, Eva Perón 125), a US$7 tenedor-libre parrilla.

Getting There & Around
The bus terminal (☎ 422352) is at General Galarza and Chiloteguy, 10 blocks west of the plaza. Bus No 1 (US$0.70) runs between it and the plaza, and other colectivos serve the campgrounds for the same price. A remise to the plaza costs US$1.

Several buses leave daily from the terminal to Buenos Aires (US$17, 4½ hours), Gualeguaychú (US$4.50, 1¼ hours), Colón (US$1.50, 45 minutes), Concordia (US$4, 2½ hours) and Paraná (US$8, 5 hours).

At least two buses serve Paso de los Libres (US$22, 8 hours) and Corrientes (US$28, 14 hours), and three Expreso Singer buses stop in Concepción en route to Puerto Iguazú (13 hours) between 5pm and 9pm.

Paccot goes to Paysandú, Uruguay (US$4.25, 1½ hours) three times daily Monday to Saturday and once (at 8pm) on Sunday.

PALACIO SAN JOSÉ

Topped by twin towers and surrounded by elegant gardens, Justo José Urquiza's ostentatious pink palace (☎ 03442-432620, RN 39 Km 30; admission adult/child US$2/1; open 9am-1pm & 2pm-5:30pm weekdays, 8:30am-8pm weekends) is about 33km west of Concepción via RP 39. It was built in part to show up Urquiza's arch-rival Rosas in Buenos Aires, and in part to demonstrate the power and wealth of Entre Ríos. Local caudillo Urquiza, commanding an army of provincial loyalists, Unitarists, Brazilians and Uruguayans, was largely responsible for Rosas' downfall in 1852 and the eventual adoption of Argentina's modern constitution.

Allies like Sarmiento and Mitre supped at Urquiza's 8.5m dining-room table and slept in the palatial bedrooms. Urquiza's wife, 25 years his junior, turned the bedroom where López Jordán murdered her husband into a permanent shrine.

Buses from Concepción to Basavilbaso run at 7:30am, 11:30am and noon and will drop you at the turnoff to the palace (US$2.25, 30 minutes). From here, it's a half-hour walk to the grounds. Enough people visit the site that you should be able to ask for a lift back to town. Taos Tour (☎ 428710, Leguizamón 64) in Concepción offers transport from town and guided tours of the palace for US$10 per person (plus admission) in groups of five. They'll take smaller groups for slightly higher prices.

COLÓN

☎ 03447 • pop 17,000

Colón has an attractive waterfront lined with many impressive older buildings, and a new geothermal spa. One of three main Entre Ríos border crossings, it sits on the west bank of the Río Uruguay, connected to the Uruguayan city of Paysandú by the Puente Internacional General Artigas.

In mid-February, the city hosts the **Fiesta Nacional de la Artesanía**, a crafts fair held in Parque Quirós that features live folkloric entertainment by nationally known artists.

The **Termas de Colón** (mobile ☎ 1564-4556, Lavalle & Sabatier; admission adults/children age 3-11 US$3/1 adults/children age 3-11; open 6pm-9pm Tues-Fri, 9am-9pm Sat & Sun), at the north edge of town, is a thermal spa with 10 pools, both indoor and outdoor, ranging from 33°C to 40°C. The source is a 1500m-deep well drilled to tap the region's abundant geothermal aquifers.

Some 4km northwest of Colón is the **Molino Forclaz**, the area's first flour mill. It's also worth visiting the nearby village of **Colonia San José**, 8km west, where in 1857 European pioneers established the country's second agricultural colony. An interesting regional **museum** (mobile ☎ 1564-4091; admission US$1; open 10am-noon & 4pm-6pm Tues-Sun) displays period tools and memorabilia.

Open 6am to 8pm Monday to Friday, 8am to 8pm Saturday and Sunday, the tourist office (☎ 421996) occupies the former Aduana (Customs Building), built by Urquiza at Gouchon and Av Costanera. The Uruguayan consulate (☎ 421999), at San Martín 417, is open from 8am to 2pm weekdays. The post office is at Artigas and 12 de Abril; Colón's postal code is 3280.

Places to Stay

Camping Municipal Norte (☎ 421917, Alejo Peyret & Paysandú) Sites US$8 for two people. Closed in winter except for long weekends, this campground is almost at the water's edge, and stretches north from the foot of Paysandú almost to the termas complex. There is also more camping for the same price near the river on the south side of town.

Hospedaje Bolívar (☎ 422721, Bolívar 577) US$10 per person. Phone ahead, as this inexpensive hospedaje is often full.

Hotel Holimasú (☎ 421305, fax 421305, Belgrano 28) Singles/doubles US$22/38. This hotel on Plaza San Martín has large, quiet, clean and comfortable (though dark) rooms with fan and heat. Air-con is US$0.50 an hour extra.

Places to Eat

Nuevo Mundo (☎ 424502, General Paz 28) All-you-can-eat US$6 Mon-Thur, US$7 Fri-Sun. This Chinese *tenedor libre* has simple but elegant decor. You can eat in or take out for lunch or dinner.

La Cosquilla del Ángel (☎ 423711, Alejo Peyret 180) Mains US$6-14. A block from the water, this is a class joint in every respect except for the names of the dishes. Don't let the sobriquet 'Mr Ed' keep you from ordering the delightful salad of mixed greens topped with walnuts and surrounded by *aceto verde,* a purée of greens and vinegar. Preparation, presentation and service are all top-notch, with a very good and reasonably priced wine list, as well.

Getting There & Around

Colón's bus terminal (☎ 421716) is at Rocamora and 9 de Julio, seven blocks inland (roughly west) of the river and eight blocks north of the main shopping and entertainment street, 12 de Abril. The many north-south buses that stop here also pass the entrance to Parque Nacional El Palmar.

Paccot and Copay go to Paysandú, Uruguay (US$3.25, 45 minutes) five times daily Monday to Saturday, and once (at 8:30pm) on Sunday.

PARQUE NACIONAL EL PALMAR

On the west bank of the Río Uruguay, midway between Colón and Concordia, 8500-hectare Parque Nacional El Palmar (☎ 03447-493031, RN 14 Km 199; admission adults/children US$5/2.50) preserves the last extensive stands of yatay palm on the Argentine littoral. In the 19th century, the native yatay covered large parts of Entre Ríos, Uruguay and southern Brazil, but the intensification of agriculture, ranching and forestry throughout the region destroyed much of the palm savannas and inhibited the species' reproduction.

Most of the remaining palms in El Palmar are relics, some more than two centuries old, but under protection from grazing and fire they have once again begun to reproduce. Reaching a maximum height of about 18m, with a trunk diameter of 40cm, the larger specimens clustered throughout the park accentuate a striking and soothing subtropical landscape that lends itself to photography. The grasslands and the gallery forests along the river and creeks shelter much wildlife, including birds, mammals and reptiles.

Most activities are oriented toward the park's natural attractions. Park admission is collected at the entrance on RN 14 between 7am and 7pm, but the gate is open 24 hours.

Information

All the park's main facilities are 12km down the dirt road leading from the entrance. The visitor center (open 8am to 6pm daily) has displays on natural history, including a small herpetarium (reptile house), and offers video shows throughout the day. The park administration was once the *casco* (main house) of the estancia. Guided bicycle tours of the park leave from a concession near the center.

Wildlife Viewing

To view wildlife, go for walks along the watercourses or through the palm savannas, preferably in early morning or just before sunset. The most conspicuous bird is the *ñandú* or rhea, but there are also numerous parakeets, cormorants, egrets, herons, storks, caracaras, woodpeckers and kingfishers. Among the mammals, the *carpincho* or capybara, a semi-aquatic rodent weighing up to 60kg, and the vizcacha, a relative of the chinchilla, are common sights, but there are also foxes, raccoons and wild boar.

Vizcachas inhabit the campground; their nocturnal squeaks and reflective eyes sometimes disturb campers, but they are harmless (as are the enormous toads that invade the showers and toilets at night). The same is not true of the *yarará,* a deadly pit viper that inhabits the savannas. Bites are rare, but watch your step and wear high boots and long trousers when hiking.

Río Uruguay

There is excellent access to the river for swimming and boating from the campground (which is across the parking lot from the visitor center), as well as a series of short hiking trails that make up El Paseo de la Glorieta.

Arroyo Los Loros & Arroyo El Palmar

Arroyo Los Loros, a short distance north of the campground by gravel road, is a good place to observe wildlife. Five kilometers south of the visitor center is Arroyo El Palmar, a pleasant stream with a beautiful swimming hole, accessible by a good gravel road. It's a fine place to see birds and, crossing the ruined bridge, visitors can walk for several kilometers along a palm-lined road now being reclaimed by savanna grasses.

Places to Stay & Eat

Los Loros (☎ 03447-493031) Sites US$4-6 per tent, plus US$4-6 per person. This campground across the parking lot from the visitor center is the only place to stay in the park. It has shady level sites, hot showers, electricity and a small store. Rates vary with the season; 'family plans,' for two adults and one to three children, can bring them down.

The nearest hotels are in the cities of Concordia, about 65km north of the park entrance on RN 14, and Colón, roughly the same distance south.

La Cosquilla (☎ 03447-493031) Mains US$4-17. Run by the owner of La Cosquilla del Ángel in Colón (see Places to Eat in the Colón section of this chapter), this restaurant next to the visitor center has the same menu, plus tasty sandwiches starting at US$1.80. Fancy a bottle of Veuve Clicquot after a long day's hike?

Getting There & Away

El Palmar is 360km northwest of Buenos Aires on RN 14, a major national highway, so there are frequent north-south bus services. Any bus running between Buenos Aires and Concordia, or between Concordia and Gualeguaychú, Concepción or Colón, will drop you at the park entrance. There is no public transport to the visitor center and camping area, but hitching should not be difficult in summer. A remise between Colón or Concordia and the visitor center should cost about US$35. Some drivers will throw in a brief car tour of the park at the same price. Try René at Remís Colón (☎ 03447-422221), in Colón at Alem 13. A remise to town from the park entrance can run as low as US$15.

CONCORDIA

☎ 0345 • pop 150,000

Visitors come to this attractive agricultural and livestock center on the Río Uruguay mostly for its riverside beaches and fishing, but the city holds some other attractions. It also offers a border crossing via the Salto Grande hydroelectric project, to the Uruguayan city of Salto.

Concordia, 431km north of Buenos Aires and 65km north of Parque Nacional El Palmar via RN 14, has been hit hard by the country's recent financial crisis. The flour mill has closed, and the citrus industry (a mainstay of the local economy) is suffering, leading to at least temporary cancellation of the annual citrus festival. Political differences between the province's governor and the head of the municipality have led to the governor's withholding of funds, which has in turn led to angry political protests in the city.

Information

The municipal tourist office (☎ 421-2137), next to the cathedral, is open 7am to 8pm daily. ACA (☎ 421-6544) is at Pellegrini and Corrientes. The Uruguayan consulate (421-0380) is at Pellegrini 709.

There are several banks with ATMs in the vicinity of Plaza 25 de Mayo. The post office is on Hipólito Yrigoyen between 1 de Mayo and Buenos Aires; the postal code is 3200. For phone calls and Internet access, Telecentro Colón and Cibercentro Colón are side by side on Pellegrini at Plaza 25 de Mayo.

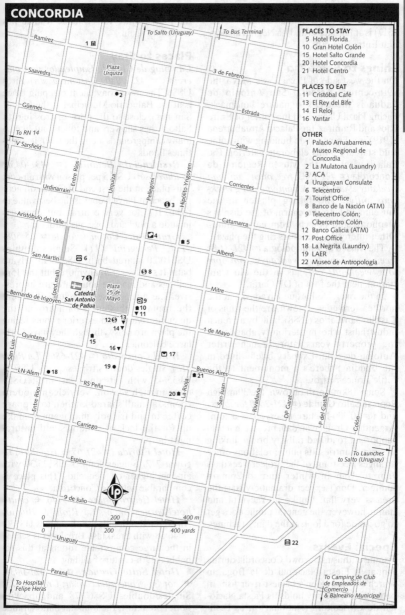

CONCORDIA

PLACES TO STAY
5 Hotel Florida
10 Gran Hotel Colón
15 Hotel Salto Grande
20 Hotel Concordia
21 Hotel Centro

PLACES TO EAT
11 Cristóbal Café
13 El Rey del Bife
14 El Reloj
16 Yantar

OTHER
1 Palacio Arruabarrena;
   Museo Regional de
   Concordia
2 La Mulatona (Laundry)
3 ACA
4 Uruguayan Consulate
6 Telecentro
7 Tourist Office
8 Banco de la Nación (ATM)
9 Telecentro Colón;
   Cibercentro Colón
12 Banco Galicia (ATM)
17 Post Office
18 La Negrita (Laundry)
19 LAER
22 Museo de Antropología

Ramírez

To Salto (Uruguay)

To Bus Terminal

Saavedra

Plaza
Urquiza

3 de Febrero

Güemes

Estrada

To RN 14

V Sarsfield

Salta

Entre Ríos

Urquiza

Pellegrini

Hipólito Yrigoyen

Corrientes

Urdinarrain

Aristóbulo del Valle

Catamarca

San Martín

Alberdi

Bernardo de Irigoyen

Mitre

Catedral
San Antonio
de Padua

Plaza
25 de
Mayo

1 de Mayo

Quintana

San Luis

Buenos Aires

LN Alem

RS Peña

Rivadavia

San Juan

DP Garat

L P del Castillo

Colón

Carriego

To Launches
to Salto (Uruguay)

Espino

9 de Julio

0   200   400 m
0   200   400 yards

Uruguay

Paraná

To Hospital
Felipe Heras

To Camping de Club
de Empleados de
Comercio
& Balneario Municipal

Hospital Felipe Heras (☎ 421-2580) is at Entre Ríos 135. La Mulatona laundry (☎ 421-1517) is at Estrada 43 and La Negrita laundry is at Entre Ríos 505.

Things to See & Do

On the west side of Plaza 25 de Mayo, the 19th-century **Catedral San Antonio de Padua** is the city's signature landmark. Facing Plaza Urquiza, at the corner of Entre Ríos and Ramírez, the **Palacio Arruabarrena** (1919) is a French-style building with some wild statuary on its elaborate exterior. The Palacio contains the **Museo Regional de Concordia** (☎ 421-1883; free; open 7am-7pm weekdays, 9am-1pm & 5pm-9pm long weekends only). The falling plaster in the museum adds to the charm of the displays of photos and objects from earlier times. Other interesting buildings ring the plaza.

The **Museo de Antropología** (☎ 421-3149; free; open 7am-4pm weekdays, 3pm-6pm long weekends only) is in the old train station, near the foot of DP Garat.

In the riverside Parque Rivadavia, at the northeastern edge of town, are the ruins of **Castillo San Carlos** (1888), built by a French industrialist who mysteriously abandoned the property years later. French writer Antoine de Saint-Exupéry briefly lived in the building; there's a monument to the Little Prince nearby.

Some 18km north of town, the 39m-high **Represa Salto Grande** (☎ 421-2600 for tours) and its 80,000-hectare reservoir is a joint Argentine-Uruguayan dam project that also supports a road and railway bridge linking the two countries. Its public-relations office arranges free tours of the project weekdays 7am to 1pm in winter and to 2pm in summer. Don't expect dramatic vistas; the area is very flat. Unlike at Yacyretá and Itaipú, however, the general public does get to go inside for a look at the dam's turbines.

Special Events

Fishing enthusiasts crowd Concordia during January's Fiesta Nacional de la Boga, in search of the region's tastiest river fish. In better times, the city holds its Fiesta Nacional de Citricultura (National Citrus Festival) the first week in December. Check with the tourist office to see if the festival has started up again.

Places to Stay

Camping de Club de Empleados de Comercio (☎ 422-0080, Costanera s/n) Sites US$8. The most convenient camping place is at the Balneario Municipal at the foot of San Juan, close to the port for crossings to Salto. It has showers and toilets, but like so many campgrounds along the river, it sometimes floods.

Residencial Betania (☎ 431-0456, Coldaroli s/n) US$15 per person with air-con. This place, at the east end of Coldaroli near the beach at Playa Nebel, is the best value in town. It's not very central, but comforts include a pool and spacious gardens.

Gran Hotel Colón (mobile ☎ 15-508-3121, Pellegrini 611) Singles/doubles US$10/20 shared bath, US$20/30 private bath. It's not so *gran* anymore, but the 15m ceilings and massive courtyard are impressive. The manager seems reluctant to rent the rooms with shared bath around the quiet courtyard, and exterior rooms facing the plaza are noisy (though they have fairly large balconies).

Hotel Concordia (☎ 421-6869, La Rioja 518) Singles/doubles/triples/quads US$24/30/35/45 with air-con, heat, fans; US$5 more in high season. Very clean modern rooms, a small shared kitchen to prepare coffee in and friendly management make up for the lack of windows and natural light here.

Hotel Florida (☎ 421-6536, Hipólito Yrigoyen 717) Singles/doubles US$25/30 with air-con, higher on weekends. This place is comparable with the Concordia.

Hotel Centro (☎/fax 421-7746, e centro hotel@arnet.com.ar, La Rioja & Buenos Aires) Singles/doubles/triples/quads US$30/38/46/58 with breakfast. Breakfast is served in the large comfortable rooms at this rehabbed 19th-century building.

Hotel Salto Grande (☎/fax 421-0034, e hotelsg@concordia.com.ar; Urquiza 575, Singles/doubles US$67/78 and up, with buffet breakfast. The four-star Salto Grande has a restaurant, a pool and good views from the upper floors.

Places to Eat

Cristóbal Café (☎ 421-5736, Pellegrini & 1 de Mayo) Mains US$2-4. The TVs give it a sort of sports-bar atmosphere – and it *does* have a full bar – but it's all nicely done, as are the pizzas, meat and chicken served here.

El Reloj (Pellegrini 580) Mains US$2.50-5. This spacious brick-walled pizzeria has good ambience.

Yantar (☎ 421-0414, Pellegrini 570) Mains US$3-8. Pasta is the draw at this modest parrilla that also serves empanadas, local river fish and US$5 *menúes* (daily set meals). The *ravioles de verdura* (vegetable ravioli) are great, and *con salsa bolognesa* (with meat sauce) is a good way to get them.

El Rey del Bife (☎ 421-2644, Pellegrini 590) Mains US$3-11. Despite its name, 'The King of Beef,' this popular place has the town's best selection of local fish – surubí, boga and dorado – and seafood. They sometimes have *vizcacha en escabeche* (vizcacha in marinade).

De la Plaza (☎ 421-2899, 1 de Mayo 59) Mains US$5-10. Menúes are available for US$10 every night but Saturday at this subtly decorated parrilla.

Getting There & Away

LAER (☎ 421-1007), Pellegrini 538, has seven flights a week to Buenos Aires (US$57-76) and six to Paso de los Libres (US$30). A separate US$3.50 departure tax is collected at the airport.

The bus terminal (☎ 421-7235) is 13 blocks north of Plaza 25 de Mayo, at Justo and Hipólito Yrigoyen.

Two Flecha Bus and two Chadre buses go to Salto, Uruguay (US$3, 1¼ hour), between 11:30am and 6:30pm Monday to Saturday.

Long-distance bus services between Buenos Aires and the provinces of Corrientes and Misiones resemble those passing through Gualeguaychú, Concepción and Colón. Three Expreso Singer buses stop en route to Puerto Iguazú (12 hours) between 5:30pm and 10:45pm. Many buses serve Buenos Aires (US$25, 6¼ hours), and Flecha Bus has direct service to La Plata.

From the port beyond the east end of Carriego, launches cross the river to Salto (US$4, 15 minutes) four times a day in winter, five in summer, between 9am and 6pm Monday to Saturday. At the time of research, Sunday service had been cancelled, but it may resume.

Getting Around

The airport (☎ 425-1987) is 14km north of town. A US$3 LAER shuttle meets passengers at the terminal. It can also pick you up at your hotel on the way out if you arrange it with the office. Remises charge about US$9 for the trip.

Micro No 2 (US$0.70) takes Yrigoyen south from the terminal to the center. On its northward run No 2 stops at the entrance to Parque Rivadavia; catch it on Pellegrini in front of Banco de la Nación.

PASO DE LOS LIBRES
☎ 03772 • pop 39,000

About 700km north of Buenos Aires and 370km south of Posadas on RN 14, Paso de los Libres is a stopover and border-crossing town. It offers Corrientes province's easiest access to Brazil to the much larger city of Uruguaiana on the opposite bank of the river. There's not much reason to linger here.

Orientation & Information

On the west bank of the Uruguay, Paso de los Libres has a standard rectangular grid, centered on Plaza Independencia. The principal commercial street is Av Colón, one block west. The international bridge to Uruguaiana is about 10 blocks southwest.

There's no tourist office, but try the ACA office near the border complex before the bridge. The Brazilian consulate (☎ 425411) is on Plaza Independencia at Mitre 842.

Telecentro Mercosur is at Colón 975. Libres Cambio is at Av Colón 901. Hospital San José (☎ 421404) is on Calle T Alisio, on the east side of Plaza España.

Places to Stay & Eat

Hotel Capri (☎ 421260, M Llanes s/n) Singles/doubles US$15/25 with breakfast. Across the dirt lot from the bus terminal, the Capri is the place to be if you need a lie-down and an early breakfast between bus treks.

Hotel Iberá (☎ *421848, Coronel López 1091*) Singles/doubles US$20/30 with air-con. This comfortable hotel has rooms with bath and very welcome air-con.

Hotel Alejandro Primero (☎ *424101, fax 424103, Pago Largo 1156*) Singles/doubles/triples/quads US$45/59/69/79 with air-con. The best hotel in town has a restaurant and huge rooms, with good views of the river and Uruguaiana from the upper floors. Cash customers receive a substantial discount, making it an even better value.

In addition to the Alejandro's restaurant, there are a couple of restaurants around Plaza Independencia, as well as food stalls outside the bus terminal.

Getting There & Away
LAER (☎ 422282), in the Hotel Alejandro Primero (see Places to Stay, earlier), flies to Concordia (US$30) and Buenos Aires (US$79-104) eight times weekly. There's a larger airport on the Brazilian side.

The bus terminal (☎ 425600) is at Av San Martín and Santiago del Estero. Crucero del Norte passes through Paso de los Libres daily en route between Buenos Aires (US$35, 9½ hours) and Posadas (US$14, 6 hours). Flecha Bus has a Saturday bus that serves Colón, Concepción and Gualeguaychú on the way to Buenos Aires. More buses bypass the town but can drop you off at the Esso station on RN 14, from which a taxi can take you the 16km downtown.

Tata/El Rápido serves Corrientes (US$10, 6 hours), via the interior city of Mercedes, from which it is possible to visit the Esteros del Iberá. There are also daily buses to Paraná and Santa Fe, and service to Rosario Friday to Wednesday. Also Friday to Wednesday, Paso de los Libres is a stopover between Córdoba and Puerto Iguazú.

Vans to Uruguaiana, Brazil (US$1), leave frequently from 7am onwards, stopping on Av San Martín at Av Colón and across from the bus terminal, among other places.

Getting Around
A remise from the airport to town runs around US$8. The area between the bus terminal and downtown is dodgy; walk through it at your own risk. Minibuses between the terminal and downtown (a minimum of 13 blocks) cost US$0.50 to US$0.70 depending on the distance. Taxi rates are posted outside the terminal.

YAPEYÚ
☎ 03772 • pop 1200
This placid village on the west bank of the Río Uruguay, 55km north of Paso de los Libres and 6km southeast of RN 14, was founded in 1626 as the southernmost of the Jesuit missions. With dirt streets and a slow pace, Yapeyú is a good place to relax and spend a lazy day or three. You're more likely to smell baking bread here than the various noxious fumes common in many Argentine population centers, but the nocturnal tranquility is sometimes shattered by dogs barking throughout the town.

Under the Jesuits the reducción had a population of more than 8000 Guaraní Indians tending as many as 80,000 cattle. After the order was expelled in 1767, the Indians dispersed and the mission fell into ruins. Many houses in the area are built of red sandstone blocks salvaged from mission buildings. Another historical note: José de San Martín, Argentina's greatest national hero, was born here in 1778, in a modest dwelling whose ruins still exist in a protected site.

Things to See & Do
Everything in town is within easy walking distance of the central Plaza San Martín. On its south side is the **Museo de Cultura Jesuítica** (no ☎; free; open 8am-noon & 2:30pm-6:30pm daily), with a carved image of the Vírgen Morena (the Virgin Mary in indigenous form) and several small stylized Guaraní dwellings set among the foundations of mission buildings. The photographic displays are a good introduction to the mission zone. A sundial and a few other mission relics are also on display.

At the plaza's east side, a 20th-century structure encloses what remains of the **Casa** de San Martín, the Liberator's modest birthplace, its interior covered with tributary plaques. Horses sometimes graze on the grounds at night.

On the west side of the plaza, the Gothic-spired parish **church** dates from 1899, but contains some important images from the Jesuit period.

The **Museo Sanmartiniano** *(Av del Libertador s/n; free)* contains a number of artifacts and documents from San Martín and his family. It's in the Granaderos regiment at the south end of Av del Libertador.

Places to Stay & Eat

Yapeyú has limited accommodations.

Camping Paraíso (Maipo s/n) US$5 per tent; open summer and long weekends only. This campground near the river has hot showers, but insects can be abundant and the most low-lying areas can flood in heavy rain – choose your site carefully.

Hotel San Martín (☎ 493120, fax 493998, Sargento Cabral 712) Singles/doubles $13/20 with fan. This cheerful hotel is on the plaza. Rooms have TVs and face an inner courtyard; there's not much natural light if you want privacy.

El Parador Yapeyú (☎ 493056, Paso de los Andes & San Martín) Singles/doubles US$30/40 with air-con. Bungalows at the river's edge enjoy a pool and comedor, and laundry service is available.

Restaurant El Paraíso (☎ 493053, Gregoria Matorras s/n) US$2-4; open 7am-midnight daily. The menu is simple but there are views of the river here, two doors south of the Casa de San Martín. Out front is a large, 300-year-old *palo borracho* tree, in which, they say, a young San Martín used to play. With a grand bulbous, thorny trunk, this is a particularly fine example of this species, which is seen throughout Central and South America.

Getting There & Away

The small bus terminal is at Av del Libertador and Sargento Cabral, two blocks west of the plaza. Crucero del Norte stops twice a day en route between Paso de los Libres (US$4, 1 hour) and Posadas (US$13, 5 hours). Tata serves Buenos Aires. More buses stop on the highway at town's edge.

Buses sometimes arrive early, and you may have to stand for a few hours once you board.

SANTO TOMÉ

☎ 03756 • pop 21,000

Santo Tomé is 140km north of Yapeyú via RN 14. It's possible to cross to the Brazilian town of São Borja, which also has Jesuit ruins, via a bridge across the Río Uruguay.

The *Hotel ACA (☎ 420162, fax 420506, Belgrano 958)* offers good singles/doubles/triples for US$36/45/57, and there are several *campgrounds* along Av San Martín.

Crucero del Norte and Singer run four to five buses daily to Posadas (US$9, 2½ hours) and Paso de los Libres (US$10, 3½ hours). The latter also exchanges pesos for Brazilian reais.

Posadas & the Jesuit Missions

The ruins of 17th-century Jesuit *reducciones* (see boxed text, 'The Jesuit Missions') are the major attraction in this region, which also offers a fleeting glimpse of a major hydroelectric project. Posadas, the capital of Misiones Province, is also a gateway to Iguazú Falls, as well as to Brazil and Paraguay, and is also a possible base for exploration of the missions, including those across the Paraná in Paraguay.

The landscape here is an attraction as well. Approaching Posadas from the south you will see a change to gently rolling low hills, stands of bamboo and papaya and manioc plantations. The highway passes tea and *mate* plantations growing from the region's trademark red soil.

Misiones' Sierra Central separates the watersheds of the Paraná and Uruguay. The range reaches as high as 800m, though it rarely exceeds 500m. The natural vegetation is mostly subtropical forest, as well as some large remaining stands of native araucaria, which resemble pine trees. The province is the country's largest producer of *yerba mate*, the staple drink of Argentines and of many Uruguayans, Paraguayans and Brazilians. In recent years plantation forestry has become an important industry, with northern-hemisphere pines and Australian eucalyptus replacing the native araucarias.

POSADAS
☎ 03752 • pop 250,000

Posadas is a modern riverside city with an abundance of shade trees, a brief stopover en route to Paraguay or Iguazú for most travelers. It's within striking distance of several

Jesuit missions, including San Ignacio Mini about 50km east, and, across the river on the Paraguayan side, Trinidad and Jesús. The city has lost some of its low-lying areas to flooding from the Yacyretá hydroelectric project, another possible side trip.

Posadas was originally part of Corrientes province, but in the 1880s became the capital of the newly created territory of Misiones. It served as the gateway to the pioneering agricultural communities of interior Misiones and in 1912 was linked with Buenos Aires by the Urquiza railway. Today, Posadas is the province's commercial center.

The Jesuit Missions

Beginning in 1607 in the upper Paraná region of Paraguay and Argentina, in isolated areas largely overlooked by secular Spaniards, the Jesuits brought about a major political, economic and cultural transformation among the native Guaraní. The remarkable success of the order aroused envy and intrigue against them, and eventually brought them down.

Sixteen of the 30 missions that were in operation in the 18th century were in present-day Argentina, mostly in Misiones with a few in Corrientes, while the remainder were equally distributed between modern Paraguay and Brazil. Their organizational principle was *reducción* or *congregación*, the common Spanish practice of concentrating the Indians, breaking their nomadic habits and reorganizing their political structure.

The first challenge to the Jesuits came from the Portuguese slave raiders of São Paulo. Only two decades after their establishment, 11 of the first 13 missions were destroyed and their native inhabitants abducted. The Jesuits responded by moving operations westward and raising an army to repel any further incursions. The evacuation of the missions was an epic event – the Jesuits and Indians rafted down the Paraná to the precipitous Guairá Falls (now inundated by the Brazilian-Paraguayan Itaipú dam), descended to their base and built new rafts to continue the journey. Thousands of Indians perished, but the Jesuits successfully re-established themselves at new sites.

Slavers were not the only menace. Some local *caciques* (chiefs) resented the Jesuit conversion of their peoples, and the physical concentration of the Indians accelerated the spread of smallpox and other European diseases to which the Indians had little natural immunity. Between 1717 and 1719 alone, an epidemic killed off nearly a sixth of the mission population. In succeeding decades, discontent among secular Spaniards (*comuneros*) in Corrientes led to further devastating invasions. Eventually, these disturbances and exaggerated rumors of Jesuit intrigue resulted in the order's expulsion in 1767. The Jesuits resisted but by 1768 were forced to abandon the missions completely. Much of the native population fled to avoid mistreatment at the hands of the comuneros, and most of the abandoned settlements either became overgrown by jungle or were dismantled for use in other construction.

The mission economy was largely agricultural and diversified. The Indians raised their own subsistence crops (maize, sweet potatoes and cassava) but also labored on communal fields. *Yerba mate* was the most important plantation crop, but cotton, citrus and tobacco were also significant. Within the settlement itself, intensive vegetable gardening took place. Outside the settlement,

Orientation

Posadas is on the south bank of the upper Río Paraná, 1310km north of Buenos Aires by RN 14, 310km east of Corrientes via RN 12 and 300km southwest of Puerto Iguazú, also via RN 12. A handsome, modern international bridge links Posadas with the Paraguayan city of Encarnación.

Plaza 9 de Julio is the center of Posadas' standard grid and of the city center. Av Mitre is the southern boundary of the center and leads east to the international bridge.

Theoretically, all downtown streets have been renumbered, but new and old systems continue to exist side by side, creating great confusion for nonresidents, since many locals use the old system. In this text the newer, four-digit street numbers are given as much as possible; some places, such as the Paraguayan consulate, still cling to their old three-digit addresses.

Information

The well-organized, well-informed provincial tourist office (☎ 447540/5, toll-free 800-555-0297 from within the province, e turismo@misiones.gov.ar) is at Colón 1985 between Córdoba and La Rioja. Offering numerous

The Jesuit Missions

native herders tended the mission's numerous livestock. When the Jesuits were expelled, San Ignacio Miní had a population of 3200 souls, close to 32,000 head of cattle and more than 64,000 sheep and goats.

Life on the reducción was probably less idyllic than portrayed in the film *The Mission*, but the labor was certainly less odious than elsewhere. The Jesuits closely regulated many aspects of everyday life, such as education and dress, but their exuberant approach to work made mission residence sufficiently attractive that many Indians chose it over the grim certainties of the encomienda. With the aid of skilled German priests, the Guaraní learned crafts and trades, such as weaving, baking, carpentry, cabinetmaking and the design of musical instruments. Unfortunately, these skills were useless to them in the post-mission world.

Today **San Ignacio Miní** (near Posadas) is the best-restored and most well-preserved of the missions, retaining a significant portion of the carved stone decoration on its enormous main church. Many of the surrounding workshops and residences have been restored, giving a good idea of the former layout, though all buildings, including the temple, are roofless.

Between San Ignacio and Posadas are two more large ruins, **Santa Ana** and **Loreto**. They are mostly covered by vegetation, but Santa Ana's main temple has been cleared and its walls shored up by interior scaffolding. A very spooky 20th-century cemetery adds to the interest here, and the site is easily reached. Loreto is farther off the highway and in a much earlier stage of restoration; if you're short on time, this is the one to skip. It's possible to stay overnight at good, cheap accommodations at the site's entrance, however.

Across the Paraná in Paraguay lie **Trinidad** and **Jesús** (see the Paraguay chapter for more on visiting those missions), ranking just behind San Ignacio Miní in the quantity and size of standing structures. Adding to the appeal are their unique settings. Unlike the Argentine missions' forested and mostly flat locations, both of the Paraguayan sites are on grassy promontories affording good distant views, especially from the upper walls of the main temple at Jesús.

Very little remains of most other former reducciones. In some, such as **San Ignacio Guazú** and **Santa María**, both in southern Paraguay, a former chapel or other section of the mission houses wonderful collections of wooden carvings and other artifacts from Jesuit times. In others, such as **Yapeyú** in Argentina's Corrientes province, modest museums stand on the site of the reducciones and local churches hold whatever precious icons remain from the bygone era.

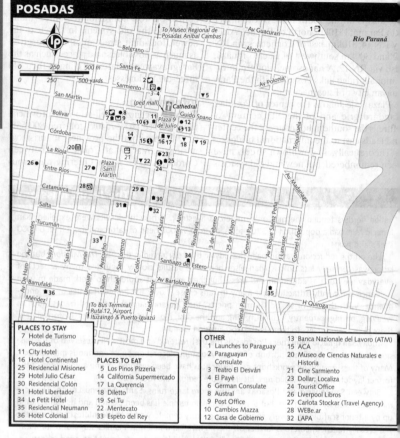

POSADAS

To Museo Regional de
Posadas Aníbal Cambas

Río Paraná

Av Guacurari
Alvear
Belgrano
Santa Fe
Sarmiento
San Martín
(ped mall)
Bolívar
Córdoba
La Rioja
Entre Ríos
Catamarca
Salta
Tucumán
Av Corrientes
Jujuy
San Luis
Junín
Ayacucho
San Lorenzo
Colón
Uruguay
Israel
Líbano
Rademacher
Rivadavia
Barrufaldi
Méndez
To Bus Terminal,
Ruta 12, Airport,
Ituzaingó & Puerto Iguazú
Santiago del Estero
Av Bartolomé Mitre
Av Azara
Buenos Aires
Rivadavia
3 de Febrero
25 de Mayo
General Paz
Av Roque Sáenz Peña
J Lamusse
Coronel López
Triquinuela
Av Madariaga
H Quiroga
Plaza 9
de Julio
Guido Spano
Cathedral
Plaza
San Martín
Av Polonia

PLACES TO STAY
7   Hotel de Turismo
    Posadas
11 City Hotel
16 Hotel Continental
25 Residencial Misiones
29 Hotel Julio César
30 Residencial Colón
31 Hotel Libertador
34 Le Petit Hotel
35 Residencial Neumann
36 Hotel Colonial

PLACES TO EAT
5   Los Pinos Pizzería
14 California Supermercado
17 La Querencia
18 Diletto
19 Sei Tu
22 Mentecato
33 Espeto del Rey

OTHER
1   Launches to Paraguay
2   Paraguayan
    Consulate
3   Teatro El Desván
4   El Payé
6   German Consulate
8   Austral
9   Post Office
10 Cambios Mazza
12 Casa de Gobierno
13 Banca Nazionale del Lavoro (ATM)
15 ACA
20 Museo de Ciencias Naturales e
    Historia
21 Cine Sarmiento
23 Dollar; Localiza
24 Tourist Office
26 Liverpool Libros
27 Carlota Stockar (Travel Agency)
28 WEBe.ar
32 LAPA

maps and brochures, it's open 7am to 8pm weekdays, 8am to noon and 4:30 to 8pm weekends and holidays.

ACA (☎ 436955) is at Córdoba and Colón. You can find the Paraguayan consulate (☎ 423858) at San Lorenzo 179, while the German consulate (☎ 435508; open 8am to noon weekdays) is at Junín 1811 on the 1st floor.

Cambios Mazza, on Bolívar between San Lorenzo and Colón, changes traveler's checks for a 1% commission plus US$0.25 per check. Banca Nazionale del Lavoro has an ATM on Bolívar, at the southeastern corner of Plaza 9 de Julio, and there are several others downtown.

The post office is at Bolívar and Ayacucho; the postal code is 3300. Many of the numerous locutorios in town offer expensive and mediocre Internet access. WEBe.ar, at Junín 2168, has good connections, air-conditions o' ergonomic stations and only charges US$2 an hour.

Carlota Stockar, at Junín 2054, is a full-service travel agency with a student division. Liverpool Libros, on Av Corrientes at the foot of Entre Ríos, has English-language books. Hospital General R Madariaga

447775) is about 1km south of downtown, at Av López Torres 1177.

Things to See & Do

The impressive 19th-century façade of the **Casa de Gobierno** stretches along almost the entire east side of Plaza 9 de Julio.

The natural-history section of the **Museo de Ciencias Naturales e Historia** (☎ 423893, San Luis 384; free; open 7am-noon & 2pm-8pm weekdays, 9am-noon weekends) focuses on fauna and the geology and mineralogy of the province. The museum also has an excellent serpentarium (with demonstrations of venom extraction), an aviary and an aquarium. Its historical section stresses prehistory, the Jesuit missions and modern colonization.

At the north end of Alberdi in Parque República de Paraguay, the **Museo Regional de Posadas Aníbal Cambas** (no ☎, Alberdi 600; free; open 7:30am-noon & 3pm-5:30pm Tues-Fri, 9am-noon & 2pm-6pm Sat, 4pm-7pm Sun & holidays) has an interesting collection of stuffed natural-history specimens, ethnographic artifacts and historical relics.

Special Events

Posadas celebrates Carnaval (in February or March, depending on the year) with great gusto, and seems to try to outdo other Mesopotamian cities in the skimpiness of dancers' costumes.

Places to Stay

Budget Posadas offers a small selection of cheap accommodations, but you'll find better values across the river in Encarnación, Paraguay.

Residencial Neumann (☎ 424675, Roque Sáenz Peña 665) Doubles US$20 (no singles). This place, between Mitre and Santiago del Estero, has cave-like rooms and a pool table and bar upstairs.

Residencial Misiones (☎ 430133, Av Azara 1960) Singles/doubles US$15/30. It's casual, clean and quiet here, and a well-equipped kitchen and clothes-washing facilities are at guests' disposal. Rooms vary in quality, so choose carefully.

Mid-Range *Residencial Colón* (☎ 425085, Colón 2169) Singles/doubles US$20/30 with breakfast. The simple, clean rooms here have small windows and little sound insulation from neighboring rooms. It will do in a pinch, but spend a little more elsewhere and you can do much better.

City Hotel (☎/fax 433901, e hotelcity@ arnet.com.ar, Colón 280) Singles/doubles US$23/35 with breakfast and air-con. This hotel faces Plaza 9 de Julio. Rooms have TV and comfortable beds. Bunk on the 8th or 9th floor for good views of the river or plaza. Any higher and the noise from the elevators is disturbing.

Hotel de Turismo Posadas (☎ 437401, Bolívar 171) Singles/doubles US$25/38 with breakfast and air-con. The rooms at this very friendly high-rise have a nautical theme and the bathroom doors resemble hatches. Rooms have TV and balconies; upper floors have good river views.

Hotel Colonial (☎/fax 436149, Barrufaldi 2419) Singles/doubles/triples US$25/40/50 with breakfast and air-con. It's not central, but it's well-maintained and on a quiet street. Reservations are advisable.

Le Petit Hotel (☎ 436031, e lepetit@ hotmail.com, Santiago del Estero 1635) Singles/doubles US$28/38 and triples/quads US$50/65 with breakfast and air-con. The nicest place in town in this price range; cool, quiet and very welcoming green rooms have cable TV, phones and fans. Offstreet parking is available, and reservations are recommended.

Top End All hotels in this category have air-con and cable TV, and serve a buffet breakfast.

Hotel Libertador (☎ 436901, fax 439448, San Lorenzo 2208) Singles/doubles US$45/55. Though rooms are good-sized and comfortable, even with a 10% cash discount the Libertador is a bit overpriced.

Hotel Continental (☎ 440990, e hotel@ hoteleramisiones.com.ar, Bolívar 314) Singles/doubles/triples US$55/78/100. On Plaza 9 de Julio, this is the best value in the category. There's a garage, and the spacious rooms have minibars, big TVs and excellent views of the plaza and river.

Hotel Julio César (☎ 420599, e *reservas @juliocesarhotel.com.ar*, w *www.julio cesar.com.ar, Entre Ríos 1951)* Singles/ doubles US$72/88. The city's only four-star facility has large, modern comfortable rooms with satellite TV and minibar, and a pool, gym, restaurant and parking. Cash customers get a 5% discount.

Places to Eat

Mentecato (☎ 428380, *San Lorenzo 1971)* Mains US$3-7. Mentecato serves good breakfast, lunch and minutas amid stylish decor that blends the trendy and the old-fashioned.

Espeto del Rey (no ☎, Tucumán & Ayacucho) All-you-can-eat US$7. It's a sign of hard economic times that the del Rey has become a tenedor libre. Mandioca salad is part of the spread.

Los Pinos Pizzeria (☎ 427252, *Buenos Aires & Sarmiento)* Mains US$3-12. The place to go for pizza, draft beer or empanadas. The lovely old building began as a pharmacy.

La Querencia (☎ 437117, *Bolívar 322)* Mains US$3.50-14. This is Posadas' spiffiest parrilla, on the south side of Plaza 9 de Julio.

Diletto (☎ 449784, *Bolívar 1729)* Mains US$4.50-15. Probably the fanciest restaurant in town, Diletto is a good place to try the region's enormous frogs: Their *ranas a la provenzal* is the whole body, not just the legs. The extensive fish menu includes trout.

Sei Tu (Bolívar & Buenos Aires) Ice cream!

California Supermercado, on Córdoba between Ayacucho and San Lorenzo, is very well-stocked and reasonably priced, and has a good selection of cheap prepared food such as sandwiches and milanesas.

Entertainment

Teatro El Desván, a theater company on Sarmiento between Colón and San Lorenzo, offers works by major Spanish-language playwrights such as Federico García Lorca, and also has a children's theater.

Shopping

El Payé (no ☎, Colón 1574) Though it has a good selection of *mate* paraphernalia (gourds and bombillas), basketry, wood carvings and ceramics, El Payé is struggling to stay open.

Getting There & Away

Air Buenos Aires (US$108-204) is served at least daily by Austral (☎ 435031), at Ayacucho 264 near San Martín, and LAPA (☎ 426700, toll-free 0800-444-9949), at Cata marca and Colón.

Bus The bus terminal (☎ 425800) is at Quaranta (Ruta 12) and Av Santa Catalina, reachable from downtown by bus Nos 8, 15, 21 and 24 (US$0.70). If you're coming from the south, don't get off at the first terminal (at the 'cruce'); be sure you're as far into town as possible.

The following table shows winter fares; summer service will be more frequent and sometimes more expensive. All of the following destinations are served daily and most several times a day. Travel times are approximate.

Destination	Duration in hours	Cost
Asunción (Par)	6	US$13
Buenos Aires	14	US$30-45
Córdoba	18	US$43
Corrientes	4	US$16
Paso de los Libres	6	US$14
Ituzaingó	1	US$5.50
Porto Alegre (Bra)	12	US$48
Puerto Iguazú	5½	US$20
Resistencia	5	US$20
Rosario	16	US$39
San Ignacio	1	US$3.50
São Paulo (Bra)	24	US$62
Tucumán	18	US$43
Yapeyú	5	US$13

Horianski and Águila Dorada buses to San Ignacio Miní (US$3.50, 1 hour) begin at 5:15am and continue roughly half-hourly.

Buses to Encarnación, Paraguay, leave every 20 minutes from outside the terminal, stopping at the corner of Mitre and Junín and passing through downtown via Ayacucho, San Martín and Av Roque Sáenz Peña

With border formalities, the trip can take more than an hour, but is often quicker; fares are US$1.50 *común*, US$2 *servicio diferencial* (with air-con).

To get your Argentine exit stamp, you'll need to get off the bus on the Posadas side of the bridge and cross the road to the immigration counter. Locals usually stay on the bus; hold on to your ticket to catch the next one when you're done. On the Paraguayan side, everyone gets off for passport checks but buses don't wait.

Although US$1.25 launches cross the Paraná to Encarnación from the dock at the east end of Av Guacurarí, they are pretty much for locals only. Foreigners' passports are not stamped at the docks; you must make the long trek to the foot of the bridge for this, and getting caught without a stamp in Paraguay can result in a US$75 fine.

Getting Around

Austral runs its own minibus to the airport, 12km southwest of town via RN 12. The No 8 bus (US$0.70) also goes there from San Lorenzo between La Rioja and Entre Ríos, as does the No 24 from Junín south of Córdoba. A remise costs about US$10.

Localiza (☎ 432322), at Colón 1935 between Bolívar and Córdoba, is a very straightforward and honest rental agency. Dollar (☎ 435484) is almost next door. A toll of US$3.30 is charged on RN 12 shortly out of town on the way north to the missions, and again on the way back.

AROUND POSADAS
Yacyretá Dam

This gigantic hydroelectric project is in Corrientes province near the town of Ituzaingó, 1½ hours west of Posadas by bus. Completed in 1997, it formed a monstrous reservoir of 1800 sq km, inundated low-lying areas of Posadas and Encarnación, and forced the relocation of nearly 40,000 people. Multibillion-dollar cost overruns on the corruption-riddled project added greatly to Argentina's foreign debt.

The Argentine-Paraguayan Entidad Binacional Yacyretá (☎ 03786-420059, interno 13333) gives free tours of the project. They

leave from the public-relations office at 9am, 11am, 3:15pm and 4:30pm Monday to Saturday and holidays, and at 9am and 11am on Sunday. Guides are well-rehearsed, but the bus rarely slows and never stops for photographs.

A museum displays artifacts unearthed in the process of construction and a scale model of the project, and you can also see the city built to house the dam workers.

Visitors opting to stay overnight in Ituzaingó might try **Hotel Géminis** *(☎ 03786-420324, Corrientes 943)*, where double rooms run US$28 with breakfast. Águila Dorada (among others) links Ituzaingó with Posadas (US$5.50, 1 hour) and Corrientes.

Santa Ana & Loreto

These are two of the former Jesuit reducciones that gave Misiones province its name. They are both off of RN 12 heading east and north toward San Ignacio (the site of a third and better-restored mission) and Puerto Iguazú.

At Santa Ana *(admission US$1; open 7am-6pm daily)*, which was founded 43km northeast of Posadas in 1633, dense forest has been partially removed to reveal a settlement that once housed 2000 Guaraní neophytes. About the only thing uncovered and still standing are the walls of the main church, which have been propped up with interior scaffolding. A few photogenic strangler figs grow atop the walls, lending a dramatic effect to what must have been a magnificent building in its time, though none of its decorative embellishments remain.

To the right side of the church is the cemetery, used by villagers into the latter half of the 20th century but now neglected. Here are overgrown graves and crypts with doors agape, revealing coffins fallen from their shelves and burst open; if this place doesn't give you the willies, you haven't watched enough horror movies. Some of the markers toward the back bear Japanese writing.

Loreto *(admission US$1; open 7am-6:30pm daily)*, founded in 1632, has even fewer visible remains than Santa Ana, and may not be worth the effort to visit via public transport. The old stone latrine and a chapel are partially restored. A wander along the path through the forest reveals many low stretches of wall and big moss-covered building stones, while plaques quoting descriptions of the buildings by early Jesuit fathers contribute to the atmosphere.

Both sites have very modest museums at their entrances, as well as cafés serving light meals. Loreto even has *accommodations* (US$20 for a three-bed room with kitchen facilities) open to tourists.

Getting There & Away Buses heading north from Posadas stop at the turnoffs on RN 12 for both sites. Santa Ana's is at Km 43, from where it's a 1km walk to the ruins. Loreto's is at Km 48, with a 3km walk.

SAN IGNACIO
☎ 03752 • pop 5000

The village of San Ignacio contains the ruins of San Ignacio Miní, the most impressive remnants of all the former reducciones in the region, including those in Paraguay. The site can be seen on a day trip from Posadas, but lodging in town allows more time to explore it and other sights. Everything in town is within walking distance.

San Ignacio is 56km northeast of Posadas via RN 12. From the highway junction, the broad Av Sarmiento leads about 1km to Calle Rivadavia, which leads six blocks north to the ruins.

San Ignacio Miní

These mission ruins *(entrance: Calle Alberdi s/n; admission US$1.50; open 7am-7pm daily)* are impressive for the quantity of carved ornamentation still visible and for the amount of restoration done. No roofs remain, but many of the living quarters and workshops have been re-erected.

First founded in 1611 in the state of Paraná, Brazil, but abandoned after repeated attacks by Brazilian slavers, San Ignacio was established at its present site in 1696 and functioned until the Jesuits finally gave in to the order of expulsion in 1768. The ruins, rediscovered in 1897 and restored

between 1940 and 1948, belong to a style known as 'Guaraní baroque.' At its peak, in 1733, the reducción had a Guaraní population of nearly 4000.

The entrance is on the north side on Calle Alberdi, where visitors pass through the interpretive center, which features some very good historical displays (and some slightly hokey ones) including a model of the mission, before emerging onto the grounds. Every night there is a *Luz y Sonido* (light and sound show) at the ruins; it costs US$2.50.

San Ignacio Miní's centerpiece is the enormous red sandstone church. At 74m long and 24m wide with walls 2m thick at the base, it is the focal point of the settlement. Scaffolding keeps some of the walls from collapsing, but the weathered wood blends well with the surroundings. For photography, focus on the details, especially the elaborately carved doorways.

Just west of the cabildo (on the church's west side) is a row of columns. A strangler fig has grown around one of them, leaving the column barely visible; it is billed as the 'tree with the heart of stone.'

Just before the exit is another museum containing some excellent carved paving stones and another model.

Casa de Horacio Quiroga

Uruguayan-born of Argentine parents, Quiroga was a poet and novelist who also dabbled in other activities, including snapping some of the earliest photographs of the rediscovered ruins at San Ignacio Miní and farming cotton (unsuccessfully) in the Chaco. He lived in San Ignacio from 1910 to 1917, when his first wife committed suicide (as did Quiroga himself, terminally ill, 20 years later). For more on Quiroga, including literary suggestions, see the Literature section of the Facts About Argentina chapter.

Quiroga's house *(☎ 470124, Av Quiroga s/n; admission US$2; open 8am-7pm daily winter, 8am-8pm daily summer)* is at the south end of town, offering grand views of the Río Paraná. A small museum contains photos and some of the writer's possessions and first editions.

Quiroga's permanent **Casa de Piedra** is one of those simple but lovely houses that artists seem to inhabit, and holds various memorabilia, including butterfly specimens, an enormous snakeskin and the writer's rusted motorcycle (without sidecar). A replica of his initial wooden house, built for Nemesio Juárez's 1996 biographical film *Historias de Amor, de Locura y de Muerte* (Stories of Love, Madness and Death), stands nearby.

Places to Stay

Hospedaje Salpeterer (☎ 470362, Centenario s/n) Rooms US$8 per person with kitchen facilities, US$10 with private bath; US$3 per person to pitch tent. This place, which is also known as Hospedaje Alemán, is a short walk from the bus terminal.

Hospedaje El Descanso (☎ 470207, Pellegrini 270) Singles/doubles US$8/20. About 10 blocks south and east of the bus terminal, El Descanso has spotless rooms and friendly German-speaking management.

Hotel San Ignacio (☎ 470422, fax 470422, Sarmiento & San Martín) Singles/doubles/ triples US$15/25/30 low season, US$20/ 30/39 high season (July), all with air-con & heat. The SI is recommended for its facilities, which include a locutorio, a bar with pool tables and cabañas housing up to four people (in addition to the regular rooms).

Places to Eat

There are several places to eat near the exit to the ruins on Rivadavia, including *Coco* (☎ 470331, Medina 501), which serves home-style dinners from US$4. *La Carpa Azul* (☎ 470117, Rivadavia 1295) is more an assembly-line comedor, but its swimming pool can provide relief from the heat.

Don Valentín (mobile ☎ 156-47961, Alberdi 444), just across from the entrance to the ruins, is good if somewhat pricey, with mains for US$3 to US$7 and menúes for US$5 to US$10.

Getting There & Away

The bus terminal is at the west end of Av Sarmiento, the main road into town. Services are frequent between Posadas (US$3.50, 1 hour)

and Puerto Iguazú (US$17, 4 hours) with several companies, but buses along RN 12 also stop readily en route in either direction.

Iguazú Falls

Located at the extreme northeastern tip of Argentina, the Cataratas del Iguazú (Iguazú Falls) are among the most awe-inspiring sights on the planet. These waterfalls are of such magnitude and sheer power that they make others seem puny by comparison. They lie split between Brazil and Argentina within 2100 sq km of national park, much of it rain forest teeming with unique flora and fauna – there are thousands of species of insects, hundreds of species of birds and many mammals and reptiles.

The falls are easily reached from either side of the Argentine-Brazilian border, as well as from nearby Paraguay. A good selection of inexpensive food and lodging can be found in both Puerto Iguazú, Argentina, and Foz do Iguaçu, Brazil. These cities have their own entries later in this section.

History & Geology

Álvar Núñez Cabeza de Vaca and his expedition were the first Europeans to view the falls, in 1542. According to Guaraní tradition, the falls originated when an Indian warrior named Caroba incurred the wrath of a forest god by escaping downriver in a canoe with a young girl named Naipur, with whom the god had become infatuated. Enraged, the god caused the riverbed to collapse in front of the lovers, producing a line of precipitous falls over which Naipur fell and, at their base, turned into a rock. Caroba survived as a tree overlooking his fallen lover.

The geological origins of the falls are more prosaic. In southern Brazil, the Río Iguazú passes over a basaltic plateau that ends abruptly just east of the confluence with the Paraná. Where the lava flow stopped, thousands of cubic meters of water per second now plunge down as much as 80m into sedimentary terrain below. Before reaching the falls, the river divides into many channels

IGUAZÚ FALLS & AROUND

with hidden reefs, rocks and islands separating the many visually distinctive cascades that together form the famous *cataratas*. In total, the falls are more than 2km across.

Seeing the Falls

Opinion is divided as to which side – the Brazilian or the Argentine – offers the best views of the falls. Try to see both, and if at all possible, visit on clear days. The difference between a clear and an overcast day at the falls is vast, only in part because of the rainbows and butterflies that emerge when the sun is shining. Ideally you should allow for a multiple-day stay to have a better shot at optimal conditions.

While the Argentine side – with its variety of trails and two free boat rides – offers many more opportunities to see individual falls close up, the Brazilian side yields the more panoramic views, allowing visitors to get a better idea of the immensity of the entire falls. And the Brazilian side has one extreme close-up from a catwalk at the bottom of the falls that is not to be missed. One intriguing option is the free full-moon tours of the Argentine side of the falls; see Parque Nacional Iguazú for details.

You can base yourself on either side and easily see everything there is to see.

THE NATIONAL PARKS
Flora & Fauna

Brazil's Parque Nacional do Iguaçu is the larger of the two, at 1500 sq km, but Argentina's 550-sq-km Parque Nacional Iguazú is far more pristine. High temperatures, rainfall and humidity encourage a diverse habitat, and the parks' subtropical rain forest contains more than 2000 identified plant species, countless insects, 400 species of birds and many mammals and reptiles.

Resembling the tropical Amazonian rain forest to the north, the forests of the falls region consist of multiple levels, the highest a closed canopy more than 30m tall. Beneath the canopy are several additional levels of trees, plus a dense ground-level growth of shrubs and herbaceous plants. One of the most interesting species is the *guapoy* or strangler fig, an epiphyte that uses a large tree for support until it finally asphyxiates its host. This species covers the ruins of many abandoned Jesuit mission buildings elsewhere in the province.

Other epiphytes exploit their hosts without harming them. Orchids use the limbs of large trees like the lapacho or *palo rosa* for support only, absorbing essential nutrients from rainfall or the atmosphere. At lower levels in the forest, you will find wild specimens of *yerba mate,* which Argentines and other residents of the Río de la Plata region use for tea.

Mammals and other wildlife are not easily seen in the parks, because many are either nocturnal or avoid humans – which is not difficult in the dense undergrowth. This is the case, for instance, with large cats such as the puma and jaguar. The largest mammal is the tapir, which is a distant relative of the horse, but the most commonly seen is the coati, a relative of the raccoon. It is not unusual to see iguanas, and do watch out for snakes.

Birds deserve special mention. Many birds that you might see in zoos or pet shops are found in the wild here, including toucans, parrots, parakeets and other colorful species.

The best time to see them is early morning along watercourses or in the forest, although the trees around the visitor center do not lack flocks.

Dangers & Annoyances

The Río Iguazú's currents are strong and swift; more than one tourist has been swept downriver and drowned in the area of Isla San Martín. It should go without saying that no one should get too close to the falls proper.

Park wildlife is potentially dangerous – in 1997, a jaguar killed the infant son of a park ranger. While this is not cause for hysteria, visitors should respect the big cats. In the unlikely event that you encounter one, don't panic. Speak calmly but loudly, do not run or turn your back on the animal, and do everything possible to appear bigger than you are, by waving your arms or clothing for example.

A much more likely encounter (almost a certain one on the Argentine side's Paseo Inferior) is with the bands of begging coatis that have become accustomed to human presence. Though these clownish omnivores with their prehensile-looking noses seem tame, they can become aggressive if fed (or teased with food), and they will bite. You've heard the spiel: They're wild animals, and feeding them harms them and can be dangerous for you as well. Be content with taking photos, and hold on to your lens cap.

Humans may abscond with your personal belongings, so watch your things while hiking. Though not epidemic, it happens.

You are likely to get soaked from the spray at the falls. Keeping your cash, documents and camera in plastic bags is not a bad idea.

Parque Nacional Iguazú

At the time of research, the park (☎ 03757-420180, 03757-420722; admission US$9; open 9am-6pm daily) was getting a new visitor center with lockers and other amenities, including a small train to take visitors from the park entrance to the falls. When the national budget allows, the center hands out informational brochures with maps. The old center's small but worthwhile museum will probably move. A gift shop, restaurants and snack bars are among the many other facilities at the park.

On the three nights around the full moon, rangers lead free tours of the falls; you don't even have to pay admission to the park. Weather permitting, these leave at 8:30pm and 10:30pm. El Práctico buses charging the usual US$2 leave the Puerto Iguazú terminal at 8pm and 10pm on these nights.

The Falls The tower near the old visitor center offers a good overall view, but walking around is the best way to see the falls. Plan your hikes before or after the midmorning influx of tour buses. At midday, you can take a break from the heat at the restaurant and confitería here.

Signs point the way to the two circuits, the Paseo Superior and Paseo Inferior, that provide most of the viewing opportunities via a series of trails, bridges and *pasarelas* (catwalks). The Paseo Superior is entirely level and gives good views of the tops of several cascades and across to more. The Paseo Inferior descends to the river, passing delightfully close to more falls on the way. This is prime coati country, but remember, no matter how cute they look, don't feed them. At the bottom of the path a free launch makes the short crossing to Isla Grande San Martín, an island with a trail of its own that gives the closest look at several falls, including Salto San Martín, a huge, furious cauldron of water whose violence is second only to the Garganta del Diablo. It's possible to picnic and swim in the lee side of the island, but don't venture too far off the beach.

Back on the mainland, take a bus or taxi south (upstream) to Puerto Canoas (buses cost US$0.50 for the 4km ride and don't run when the road is wet) to see the star of the aquatic show, the mind-bending Garganta del Diablo (Devil's Throat). An old pasarela here is being rebuilt; until the work is completed, a free launch ferries visitors to the intact section of the catwalk directly overlooking the cataract.

Of all the sights on earth, the Garganta del Diablo must come closest to the experience of sailing off the edge of a flat earth imagined by early European sailors. On three sides, the deafening cascade plunges to a murky destination; the vapors soaking the viewer blur the base of the falls and rise in a smokelike plume that can often be seen from several kilometers away.

Activities Relatively few visitors venture beyond the immediate area of the falls to appreciate the park's forest scenery and wildlife. Because the forest is so dense, there are few trails, but walks along the road beyond Puerto Canoas will usually reward you with wildlife sightings.

About 400m east and south of the big Sheraton hotel, along the road, is the entrance to the **Sendero Macuco** interpretive nature trail, which leads through dense forest to a nearly hidden waterfall, **Salto Arrechea**. The first 3km of the trail, to the top of the fall, is almost completely level, but a steep lateral drops to the base of the falls and beyond to the Río Iguazú, about 650m in all. This part of the trail is muddy and slippery – watch your step and figure about an hour each way from the trailhead. Early morning is the best time for the trip, with better opportunities to see wildlife, which may include bands of *caí* monkeys. Take mosquito repellent.

To get elsewhere in the forest, hitch or hire a car to go out RN 101 toward the village of Bernardo de Irigoyen. Few visitors explore this part of the park, but it is still nearly pristine forest.

Iguazú Jungle Explorer (☎ 03757-421600), also east of the Sheraton, offers various excursions: by speedy inflatable boats to the bottom of several of the waterfalls (including the Garganta del Diablo, of course); by large 4WD flatbed trucks along the Sendero Yacaratiá; rafting down the upper Iguazú; various combinations of these and other trips as well.

Places to Stay Aside from the pricey Sheraton hotel (see Places to Stay in the Puerto Iguazú section, later), the only lodging option within the park is *Camping Ñandú*, a free rudimentary (and sometimes flooded) campground with pit toilets but no water, a short distance south of Puerto Canoas. Contact the park administration (☎ 03757-420722) to register for a stay here.

Getting There & Away The park is 20km northeast of Puerto Iguazú by paved highway. From Puerto Iguazú's terminal, buses leave hourly for the park (US$2, 30 minutes) between 7:45am and 6:45pm, with return trips between 8:45am and 7:45pm – catch an early one to avoid the heat and the tour buses that swarm around the falls about 11am, when noisy Brazilian helicopters also begin their flights. The buses make flag stops at points along the highway. A cab from town to the park entrance is about US$15.

If you're based in Foz do Iguaçu, inexpensive tours to the Argentine park give you more time to spend at the falls, without the hassle of waiting for bus connections (see Organized Tours in the Foz do Iguaçu section, later). The Foz do Iguaçu Getting Around section has bus details for service to Puerto Iguazú.

Parque Nacional do Iguaçu (Brazil)

The Brazilian park *(admission US$4, payable in Brazilian currency only; open 8am-6pm Tues-Sun in summer, 8am-5pm in winter, 1pm-5pm Mon year-round)* sports an enormous new visitor center with very little in it other than a ticket booth, exchange window and ATM, big lockers (US$1.25 for 24 hours), fabulous bathrooms and a gift shop. The parking lot adjacent to the center charges US$3.25 per car.

When buying tickets visitors are asked their nationality (which is then printed on the ticket!). Double-decker buses leave about every 15 minutes from the back of the visitor center for the pleasant, forested ride into the falls part of the park. Keep your eyes peeled for animals. Recorded messages in different languages warn and inform you about various things, including the three stops the bus makes.

The first stop is the **Macuco Safari**, where for US$33 you can ride through the jungle in a trailer pulled by a jeep. The second stop is lovely Hotel Tropical das Cataratas (see Places to Stay in the Foz do Iguaçu section, later), the best place to get off. From here you walk 1.5km down a paved **trail** with brilliant views of the falls on the Argentine side, the jungle and the river below. The views build up to the grand finale at the end of the trail: a concrete catwalk jutting out into the river at the foot of the falls, getting you within shouting distance of the Garganta del Diablo and nearly spitting distance of the Brazilian falls. But don't spit, the constant wind created by the dropping water will just blow it back in your face. You'll get wet here one way or the other. On a clear day in the afternoon you should be able to see a circular rainbow in the spray.

Also at the end of the trail is an elevator (US$1) up to a viewing platform at the top of the falls at Porto Canoas, the last stop of the double-decker buses. By 2005 the Brazilian government plans to complete an enormous five-story viewing platform replete with bigger elevator and a cable car. How this will affect current facilities in the interim is unclear.

Porto Canoas has a gift shop, a *fast-food restaurant* and an excellent *buffet restaurant* with hot and cold dishes and an outstanding salad bar featuring arugula, watercress and much more for US$12. Whether you opt to eat or just down a cold one, you should sit out on the deck for a million-dollar view of the river and the top of the falls before catching the bus back.

Though Argentina has banned helicopter flights over its side of the falls because they disturb wildlife, including nesting birds, Brazilian helicopters still make the flights on their side. A 10-minute ride costs US$60 per person.

Getting There & Away On weekdays 'Parque Nacional' buses run from Foz do Iguaçu's urban bus terminal to the park entrance (US$0.50, 40 minutes) between 6am and midnight (every 20 minutes until 8pm and every 30 minutes thereafter), making stops along Av Juscelino Kubitschek and Av das Cataratas. On weekends and holidays, buses run roughly every 40 minutes

between 8am and 6pm. Don't forget the park's curtailed Monday hours.

A taxi from downtown Foz to the park entrance costs around US$16.

To access the Brazilian park from Puerto Iguazú (see Getting Around Puerto Iguazú) you can take a bus all the way to Foz do Iguaçu's terminal and catch the 'Parque Nacional' bus. To save time and avoid backtracking, get off instead at Av das Cataratas, just beyond immigration on the Brazilian side of the bridge, and flag down the Parque Nacional bus there. If you're only planning to spend a day visiting the park, border formalities are usually minimal, but it's wise to check ahead of time. (See Entering Brazil in the Foz do Iguaçu section, later.)

PUERTO IGUAZÚ
☎ 03757 • pop 27,000

At the confluence of the Río Paraná and the Río Iguazú, woodsy Puerto Iguazú hosts most visitors to the Argentine side of the falls. It is far less hazardous than Foz do Iguaçu (Brazil) and Ciudad del Este (Paraguay), and prices for food and accommodations are surprisingly reasonable. By staying here and making day trips to the Brazilian side, travelers can avoid purchasing a Brazilian visa.

Orientation
Some 300km northeast of Posadas via paved RN 12 (which passes through a corner of the national park), Puerto Iguazú has an irregular city plan, but is small enough that you will find your way around easily. The main drag is the diagonal Av Victoria Aguirre, but most services are just north of this in a rabbit warren of streets that cross each other at odd angles.

The Hito Argentino, a small obelisk at the confluence of the Paraná and Iguazú (at the west end of Av Tres Fronteras), marks the beginning of Argentine territory. From here you can see Brazil and Paraguay, both of which have similar markers on their sides of the confluence.

Information
The tourist office (☎ 420800, toll-free 0800-555-0297), Av Victoria Aguirre 311, is open

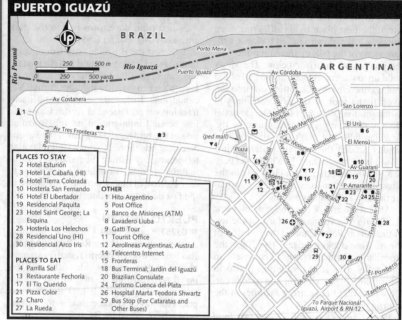

PUERTO IGUAZÚ

BRAZIL

Río Paraná

Río Iguazú

Porto Meira

Puerto Iguazú

ARGENTINA

Av Costanera

Av Córdoba

San Lorenzo

El Urú

El Mensú

Av Tres Fronteras

(ped mall)

Plaza

Av Guaraní

P. Amarante

To Parque Nacional
Iguazú, Airport & RN 12

PLACES TO STAY
2 Hotel Esturión
3 Hotel La Cabaña (HI)
6 Hotel Tierra Colorada
10 Hostería San Fernando
16 Hotel El Libertador
19 Residencial Paquita
23 Hotel Saint George; La
   Esquina
25 Hostería Los Helechos
28 Residencial Uno (HI)
30 Residencial Arco Iris

PLACES TO EAT
4 Parrilla Sol
13 Restaurante Fechoría
17 El Tío Querido
21 Pizza Color
22 Charo
27 La Rueda

OTHER
1 Hito Argentino
5 Post Office
7 Banco de Misiones (ATM)
8 Lavadero Liuba
9 Gatti Tour
11 Tourist Office
12 Aerolíneas Argentinas, Austral
14 Telecentro Internet
15 Fronteras
18 Bus Terminal; Jardín del Iguazú
20 Brazilian Consulate
24 Turismo Cuenca del Plata
26 Hospital Marta Teodora Shwartz
29 Bus Stop (For Cataratas and
   Other Buses)

8am to noon and 2pm to 8pm weekdays, 8am
to noon and 4pm to 8pm weekends. Depending on staffing, service ranges from
indifferent to very friendly and informative. ACA (☎ 420165) is on the highway
to the park, at Km 4. The Brazilian
consulate (☎ 421348) is at Esquiú and Av
Guaraní.

Banco de Misiones has an ATM at Av
Victoria Aguirre 330. The post office is at Av
San Martín 780; the postal code is 3370.
Telecentro Internet is at Av Aguirre and Av
Brasil.

Lavadero Liuba is at Bompland and Av
Misiones, while Hospital Marta Teodora
Shwartz (☎ 420288) is at Av Victoria Aguirre
and Ushuaia.

Motorists should be aware that car theft
is quite common in the triple-border area,
though carjacking is unusual on the Argentine side of the border. It's a good idea to
engage antitheft devices in the car and
secure parking at night.

Organized Tours

Many local operators offer day tours to the
Brazilian side of the falls. For about US$30,
these include a meal and a trip to Itaipú
dam and Ciudad del Este in Paraguay. One
reader recommendation is Turismo Cuenca
del Plata (☎ 421062), on Paulino Amarante
near Hostería Los Helechos. Readers have
also recommended tours arranged by the
tourist office.

Places to Stay

Note that prices may be higher during
Semana Santa, during the July holiday
season and sometimes in January if demand
is heavy. The 'tropical breakfast' offered by
some hotels is a buffet with fresh fruit in the
lineup.

Budget *Camping El Pindo* (☎ 421797, RN
12 Km 3) Sites are US$3 per person plus
US$3 per tent; dorm rooms US$5 per person
plus US$1 sheet rental. The campground is

at the edge of town, very convenient to the *rotonda* (traffic circle) bus stop. It has a pool, clean bathrooms and hot water after 6pm.

Residencial Uno *(☎/fax 420529, Fray Luis Beltrán 116)* Beds US$5 per person. This is one of Puerto Iguazú's two HI-affiliated hostels. Of the pair, it has the better hostel atmosphere.

Residencial Arco Iris *(☎ 422124, Curupy 45)* Singles/doubles US$8/15. This family-style residencial is clean, roomy, quiet and very popular with travelers. Rates are slightly higher in season.

Hostería San Fernando *(☎ 421429, Av Córdoba 693)* Singles/doubles US$11/18 with breakfast and fan. This place, opposite the bus terminal, has agreeable rooms and is popular with tour groups.

Hotel Tierra Colorada *(☎/fax 420649, El Urú 265)* Singles/doubles/triples US$12/18/24 (US$5 higher in July). Though rooms are slightly humid, they're clean and have tile floors. The hotel has a pool and friendly management. Air-con costs US$3-5 extra.

Hotel La Cabaña *(☎ 420564, Av Tres Fronteras 434)* Singles/doubles US$12/24 with HI card, US$15/25 without, all with breakfast. This HI affiliate is more like a motel than a hostel, offering more privacy but less contact with other travelers. It has a pool and is near the river and trails. Management is friendly, while rooms are musty and worn but adequate.

Residencial Paquita *(☎/fax 420434, Av Córdoba 158)* Singles/doubles/triples/quads US$15/25/30/35; US$3 extra for air-con. A helpful old dear runs this recommended place near the bus terminal. It has big, clean, bright, comfy and quiet rooms with TV and good baths, plus off-street parking.

Hostería Los Helechos *(☎/fax 420338, Paulino Amarante 76)* Singles/doubles US$20/30 low season; doubles US$35 high season (no singles); US$5 extra for air-con & TV. A very good value in low season, Los Helechos has tile floors, a restaurant and pool. Some rooms face the park like grounds.

Mid-Range *Hotel El Libertador (☎ 420570, fax 420984, e consultas@ellibertadoriguazu .com.ar, Bompland 475)* Singles/doubles/

triples US$30/40/50 in low season, doubles/triples US$45/55 in high season (no singles), all with breakfast and air-con. The Libertador occupies a big and modern but aging 1950s-tropical-style building with central air-con and a pool. Some rooms have balconies.

Hotel Saint George *(☎ 420633, fax 420651, e hotelsaintgeorge@fnn.net, Av Córdoba 148)* Singles/doubles US$30/35 low season, US$60/80 high season. This perennial favorite has a pool, restaurant and unremarkable rooms that aren't worth the high season price.

Top End All rooms in this category have air-con and television. Some can be booked at very good rates as part of a package from Buenos Aires; airfare and transfers plus a room for two or three nights can amount to not much more than airfare alone.

Hotel Esturión *(☎/fax 420100, e hotel esturion@iguazunet.com, Av Tres Fronteras 650)* Doubles US$110 with tropical breakfast. Some rooms at this sprawling complex overlook the river confluence. A pool and tennis courts are among the amenities here.

Hotel Cataratas *(☎ 421100, fax 421090, e hotelcataratas@iguazu.net, w www.hotel cataratas.com.ar, Ruta 12 Km 4)* Singles/doubles US$120/140 & up with breakfast. Not to be confused with the grand old Cataratas on the Brazilian side, this almost-new hotel has large, very comfortable rooms with all the amenities, plus a pool, tennis court, gym, sauna and more on green landscaped grounds outside of town. Avoid the mediocre restaurant, however.

Sheraton Internacional Iguazú *(☎ 491800, toll-free 0800-888-9180, fax 420311, Parque Nacional Iguazú)* Doubles US$206/255 with jungle/falls view. As seen from outside, this resort near the park's visitor center couldn't be situated much worse or be much uglier, but inside it's first rate. All rooms have balconies and tile floors, and facilities include restaurants, tennis courts, a gym and a pool.

Places to Eat
For the cheapest eats, stroll around the triangle formed by Av Brasil, Perito Moreno

and Ingeniero Eppens. One reader recommends the Saturday fruit market at Córdoba and Félix de Azara.

Parrilla Sol (☎ *422179, Av Tres Fronteras 162)* Mains US$3-8. Just west of the main plaza, Sol serves the usual variety of dishes in an indoor/outdoor setting.

Jardín del Iguazú (☎ *420850)* Mains US$3-8. This recommended parrilla is at the bus terminal.

Fechoría Restaurante (☎ *420182, Eppens 294)* Mains US$3-9. This is a good breakfast choice, serving omelets and the like.

Pizza Color (☎ *420206, Córdoba 135)* Mains US$3-11. Pizza is served in casual patio surroundings at this popular place.

Charo (☎ *421529, Córdoba 106)* Mains US$3-14. Come for parrilla and pizza, plus cheap pasta and a US$6 menúe that is served all day.

La Rueda (☎ *422531, Córdoba 28)* Mains US$3.75-15. La Rueda serves good pasta, parrilla and grilled surubí in a pleasing ambience created in part by murals and an impressive bamboo ceiling.

El Tío Querido (☎ *420027, Bompland s/n)* This is another good parrilla/pizzeria, with US$6 menúes, alongside the Hotel El Libertador.

Entertainment
Puerto Iguazú is surprisingly weak on nightlife, but ***Fronteras*** (no ☎, *Aguirre near Brazil)* occasionally has live music in its patio.

Getting There & Away
Aerolíneas Argentinas (☎ 420168), Victoria Aguirre 295, flies four to five times daily to Buenos Aires for US$144 to US$252.

The bus terminal (☎ 420854) is at Córdoba and Misiones. Agencia Noelia (☎ 422722) in Local 2 sells tickets for most lines. Numerous buses serve Posadas (US$19, 6 hours) passing San Ignacio (US$16, 5 hours) on the way.

Service to Corrientes (US$25, 9½ hours) often continues to Resistencia (US$26, 10 hours). Expreso Singer serves Córdoba (US$48, 23 hours). Singer and others serve Buenos Aires (US$35-40, 20 hours), La Plata (US$39, 22 hours), Santa Fe (US$42, 13 hours) and Paraná (US$38. 15 hours).

There are international services, as well as Brazilian domestic services, across the border in Foz do Iguaçu.

Getting Around
Gatti Tour (☎ 03757-420954) at Misiones 38. charges US$5 to the airport and makes hotel pickups; phone for reservations. Remises run about US$18.

Frequent buses with three different lines cross to Foz do Iguaçu, Brazil (US$1.50) and to Ciudad del Este, Paraguay (US$2) from Platform 1 at the bus terminal. All of these buses will stop near the rotonda at the edge of town.

Groups of three or more hoping to see both sides of the falls as well as Ciudad del Este and the Itaipú hydroelectric project may find a shared cab or remise a good idea: figure up to US$80 for a full day of sightseeing. The tourist office on Av Aguirre may be able to arrange such trips for less. Strictly as transport to Foz do Iguaçu, a taxi costs around US$35.

For information on immigration procedures, see Entering Brazil in the Foz do Iguaçu Information section.

FOZ DO IGUAÇU (BRAZIL)
☎ 045 (country code 55) • pop 270,000
Foz do Iguaçu makes a good base from which to see both sides of the falls. With the devaluation of the *real*, food and lodging here have become a bargain for foreign travelers, especially those with dollars. Good nightlife and an interesting variety of food to choose from up the ante. On the downside, Foz's high-rise buildings and relatively sparse greenery make its streets hotter than those of woodsy Puerto Iguazú, Argentina, and there is more street crime here. Another factor to consider is the cost of a Brazilian visa (recommended for anything more than a day trip for those who require visas); if you're not pushing on into Brazil, you may want to avoid that expense. See Entering Brazil, later in this section, for more details.

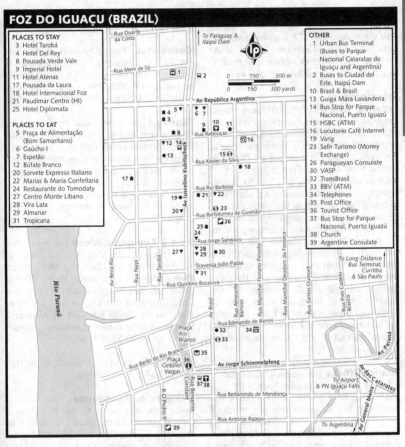

FOZ DO IGUAÇU (BRAZIL)

PLACES TO STAY
3 Hotel Tarobá
4 Hotel Del Rey
8 Pousada Verde Vale
11 Imperial Hotel
11 Hotel Atenas
17 Pousada da Laura
18 Hotel Internacional Foz
21 Paudimar Centro (HI)
25 Hotel Diplomata

PLACES TO EAT
5 Praça de Alimentação
  (Bom Samaritano)
6 Gaúcho I
7 Espetão
12 Búfalo Branco
20 Sorvete Expresso Italiano
22 Marias & Maria Confeitaria
24 Restaurante do Tomodaty
27 Centro Monte Líbano
28 Vira Lata
29 Almanar
31 Tropicana

OTHER
1 Urban Bus Terminal
  (Buses to Parque
  Nacional Cataratas do
  Iguaçu and Argentina)
2 Buses to Ciudad del
  Este, Itaipú Dam
10 Brasil & Brasil
13 Guiga Mara Lavanderia
14 Bus Stop for Parque
  Nacional, Puerto Iguazú
15 HSBC (ATM)
16 Locutorio Café Internet
19 Varig
23 Safir Turismo (Money
  Exchange)
26 Paraguayan Consulate
30 VASP
32 TransBrasil
33 BBV (ATM)
34 Telephones
35 Post Office
36 Tourist Office
37 Bus Stop for Parque
  Nacional, Puerto Iguazú
38 Church
39 Argentine Consulate

With the 1970 construction of the Itaipú hydroelectric project, the city's population exploded from a modest 34,000, and commercial opportunities across the river in Ciudad del Este attracted many other new ethnic communities. Today, Foz is home to several thousand Muslims, many of them of Lebanese origin, and smaller communities of Japanese and Koreans, as well.

Orientation

Foz do Iguaçu is at the confluence of the Iguaçu and Paraná Rivers, 630km south of Curitiba by BR 277. The Ponte Presidente Tancredo Neves is a bridge that links the city to Puerto Iguazú, Argentina, across the Rio Iguaçu, while the Ponte da Amizade connects it to Ciudad del Este, Paraguay, across the Paraná. It sprawls to the north beyond the latter's extents and to the south and east nearly to the river separating it from the former. Fifteen kilometers upstream is Itaipú, the largest operating hydroelectric project in the world.

Foz do Iguaçu has a compact center with a fairly regular grid. Av das Cataratas, at the southwest edge of town, becomes Rodovia das Cataratas and leads 20km to the world-famous falls via BR 469, passing the turnoff for the Argentine border on the way. Westbound BR 277 leads to Ciudad del Este. The main downtown street is Av Juscelino Kubitschek, often referred to simply as 'JK' (pronounced zho-ta **ka**).

Information

Entering Brazil For day-trippers border formalities are minimal; you need your passport, but neither Argentine nor Brazilian authorities should stamp it. From time to time, however, readers have reported that Australian, New Zealand, French, British or US citizens needed a visa to cross to Foz do Iguaçu, so check in advance. It doesn't hurt to travel light, ie, with as little gear as possible, to establish your temporary status.

If you're spending the night or continuing on into Brazil, let the bus driver know you need to clear immigration, and try to get a ticket from the conductor if the bus won't wait. Both Argentine and Brazilian formalities are usually handled on the Brazilian side of the bridge on the way out. Those just passing through Foz on the way to Ciudad del Este in Paraguay must get an Argentine exit stamp but not a Brazilian entrance stamp.

Tourist Offices The municipality's tourist office is at Praça Getúlio Vargas (☎ 523-8581; open 8am to 8pm daily), and it has booths at the long-distance bus terminal (☎ 522-2590; open 6:30am to 6:30pm daily) and airport (open 9am until the last plane daily). All have maps, lists of hotels (one-star and above only) and tourist newspapers with English-language descriptions of attractions. Most of the staffers speak English, and some also speak Italian, Spanish or German. Quality of information can range from awful to good.

Teletur (☎ toll-free 0800-451516) maintains an information service with English-speaking operators from 7am to 11pm daily. The Paudimar youth hostel also has a booth in the *rodoviária* (long-distance bus terminal) dispensing useful information.

The bimonthly publication *Folha da Amizade*, available at many hotels, contains some useful information, mostly in Portuguese but also in English and Spanish.

Consulates The Argentine consulate (☎ 574-2969), Travessa Eduardo Bianchi 26, is open 9:30am to 2pm weekdays. Paraguay's consulate (☎ 523-2898), Bartolomeu de Gusmão 738, is open 8am to 8pm weekdays.

Money Most hotels and restaurants in town accept dollars, Paraguayan guaraníes and Argentine pesos. Calculate rates as it's often cheaper to pay in reais. Safir Tursimo, on Av Brasil at Bartolomeu de Gusmão, changes both cash and traveler's checks, the latter with a 6% commission. BBV has an ATM on Av Brasil at the east end of Rio Branco.

Post & Communications The post office is on Praça Getúlio Vargas, at the corner of Av Juscelino Kubitschek and Rio Branco. Phone calls can be made from various offices around town, including Locutorio Café Internet (also known as Café Pizza Net), on Rebouças just east of Almirante Barroso, which also offers decent Internet access for US$2.50 an hour.

Laundry Guiga Mara Lavanderia, at Rua Tarobá 834, washes clothes.

Dangers & Annoyances Don't try to make your way down to the Rio Paraná; there is no path on the steep hillside and the shantytown on the city's eastern edge is not a salubrious neighborhood. Beware of taxi drivers and of touts wearing official-looking badges, caps, T-shirts or vests who try to direct new arrivals to accommodations. They will tell you the hotel you want no longer exists or is located in a dangerous part of town, then try to extract commissions from you and/or the place they steer you to.

Usina Hidrelétrica Itaipu

Free guided tours of the Brazilian side of the Itaipu hydroelectric project take place at 8am, 9am, 10am, 2pm, 3pm and 4pm Monday to Saturday; for details on the project, see the Ciudad del Este section in the Paraguay chapter. The Centro de Recepção de Visitantes (☎ 520-6398) is 10km north of Foz at Av Tancredo Neves 6702. The project maintains a Web page at w www.itaipu.gov.br.

Across Av Juscelino Kubitschek from Foz's downtown local bus terminal, No 110 and 120 buses (US$0.50) run north every 10 minutes from 5:30am until 11pm. Their last stop is at the Ecomuseu (☎ 520-5817), at Av Tancredo Neves 6001, about 600m from the visitor center; it opens 2pm to 5pm on Monday, and 9am to 11am and 2pm to 5pm Tuesday through Saturday.

Organized Tours

Both branches of the Paudimar hostel as well as the Hotel del Rey (see Places to Stay) offer economical all-day trips to the Argentine side of the falls. These trips cost US$10 per person, plus park admission, as compared to US$7 in bus fare for doing it on your own. The hostels offer excursions to such places as Salto Monday and the Monumento Natural Moisés Bertoni (see Around Ciudad del Este in the Paraguay chapter), both of which can be visited by land or by boat. Paudimar also provides transportation (US$10) to and from the free full-moon falls tours on the Argentine side.

Places to Stay

Budget With the devaluation of the *real*, lodging in Foz has become a much better value.

Paudimar Campestre (☎/fax 572-2430, e paudimarcampestre@paudimar.com.br, w www.paudimar.com.br, Rodovia das Cataratas Km 12.5) Sites US$3.50 per person; dorm beds US$7.50/9 with/without HI card. This hostel also has air-con cabañas for US$10/12.50 per person and offers kitchen facilities, Internet access, a pool and very good tourist information and services, including cheap tours to the Argentine side of the falls. If you're arriving late at the rodoviária, airport or Argentine border, they will pay half of your taxi fare to the hostel.

Paudimar (☎/fax 574-5503, e paudimar centro@paudimar.com, Rui Barbosa 634)

Beds US$5/6 per person with/without HI card. Breakfast is included at the downtown branch of the hostel, which has four- and six-bed dorms plus a few doubles (some with air-con), all at the same rates and with their own baths. All the amenities of the Campestre are here too, except the cabañas and pool.

Hotel Atenas (☎ 574-2563, Almirante Barroso 2215) Singles/doubles/triples US$5/6/7.50 with private bath, US$2.50/5/7.50 with shared bath. Though it's on a corner frequented by prostitutes at night, it's not a particularly dangerous neighborhood, the rooms are decent and the rates here are among the cheapest in town.

Pousada Verde Vale (☎ 574-2925, Rebouças 547) Singles/doubles US$5/7.50 with private bath. The rooms with shared bath are not recommended here; the walls are paper-thin and there may be some short-stay traffic. The private bath situation is perfectly adequate, if damp, and there's a fan.

Mid-Range A longtime favorite, homey and friendly *Pousada da Laura (☎/fax 572-3378, Naipi 671)* has singles/doubles US$10/12 with breakfast and fan. The well-traveled owner's dollarization of prices has bumped this place out of the budget range, however.

Hotel Tarobá (☎ 523-9722, fax 547-2402, e taroba@foznet.com.br, Rua Tarobá 1048) Singles/doubles/triples US$9/13/18 with buffet breakfast & air-con. These fairly comfy rooms have TVs, phones and parquet or tile floors, and there's a pool.

Imperial Hotel (☎ 523-1299, Av Brasil 168) Singles/doubles/triples US$10/15/23 with air-con. This place is clean and friendly, with big doubles and good baths.

Hotel Del Rey (☎/fax 523-2027, e hoteldelrey@hotmail.com, w www.hotel delreyfoz.com.br, Rua Tarobá 1020) Singles/doubles/triples US$12/15/23 with air-con & buffet breakfast. Cable TV, minibars, a small pool, friendly service, a great breakfast and very quiet back rooms combine to make this one of the best values in town.

Hotel Diplomata (☎/fax 523-1615, e hoteldiplomata@ieg.com.br, Av Brasil

678) Singles/doubles/triples US$15/25/35 with breakfast & air-con. Tile-floored rooms with fridges are nothing special, but the pool has an agreeable courtyard restaurant serving lunch and dinner.

Top End True five-star luxury awaits you at this modern, sparkling, high-rise *Hotel Internacional Foz* (☎ 521-4100, fax 521-4101, e reservas@fnn.net, w www.internacional-foz.com.br, Almirante Barosso & Xavier da Silva). Singles/doubles go for US$85/95 and include a buffet breakfast. Large rooms have all the amenities, including free high-speed Internet connections. The upper floors have bird's-eye views, and one of the restaurants has the loftiest view of all. Non-smoking rooms are available, and there's a pool, gym, sauna and more.

Hotel Tropical das Cataratas (☎ 521-7000, fax 574-1688, e ggrctr@tropicalhotel.com.br, Parque Nacional do Iguaçú) Singles US$168-234, doubles US$192-538. A grand old hotel right in the park and near the falls, the Cataratas has elegant common areas, a pool, tennis courts, a restaurant and more. The rooms themselves are not so luxe, but the setting and overall ambience may make it all worth it.

Places to Eat

As in Uruguay and Argentina, many establishments in Foz have gone all-you-can-eat to attract bargain-conscious clientele in these tough economic times.

Marias & Maria Confitaría (☎ 574-5472, Av Brasil 505) is a reader-recommended place that sells tasty baked goods, sandwiches and hot chocolate.

Vira Lata (☎ 574-2909, Jorge Sanways & Av Juscelino Kubitschek) All-you-can-eat US$1.50. It may not be the best food, but at these prices who can complain?

Tropicana (☎ 574-1701, Av Juscelino Kubitschek 228) Mains US$2.50-3.75. Tropicana is an inexpensive *churrascaria* (the Brazilian equivalent of the parrilla) and pizzeria.

Gaúcho I (no ☎, Av República Argentina 822) All-you-can-eat US$2.75. This churrascaria is next door to Espetão, and has similar food and ambience.

Espetão (☎ 523-8732, Av República Argentina 824) All-you-can-eat US$3. This is a modest churrascaria, with a modest salad bar and good meat in a semi-open-air setting.

Bom Samaritano (☎ 523-2311, República Argentina & Av Juscelino Kubitschek) All-you-can-eat US$3. This friendly restaurant is the centerpiece of the Praça de Alimentação (food court) it's located in, and has meat, pasta, salads and such traditional Brazilian dishes as *feijoada* (meat stew with rice and beans).

Restaurante do Tomodaty (☎ 572-2691, Av Juscelino Kubitschek 428) Mains US$1.75-6.25. Inexpensive Japanese food is the specialty here, including sushi and sashimi (no, it's not river fish; it comes by refrigerated truck) and noodles.

Búfalo Branco (☎ 523-9744, Tarobá & Rebouças) All-you-can-eat US$9. At this upscale churrascaria, jacketed waiters bring an endless procession of meat to your table. The salad bar is top-notch and the desserts are tasty. Don't leave without trying the 'spit sausage' and the turkey testicles. If you don't want the full spread you may be able to negotiate a price.

Tasty *shwarmas* (rotisserie lamb in pita bread) go for US$0.75 at *Centro Monte Líbano* (Av Juscelino Kubitschek 185), a Lebanese market. Consider following your shwarma up with baklava and other gooey sweets from *Almanar* (Av Juscelino Kubitschek s/n), a Middle Eastern bakery just south of Rua Sanways.

Many flavors of soft-serve ice cream are sold at *Sorvete Expresso Italiano* (Av Juscelino Kubitschek 421).

Entertainment

Brasil & Brasil (☎ 523-1013, Av Brasil & Rebouças) Frequent live music is the draw at this popular open-air bar, where you can dance from 8pm or 9pm to the wee hours. Drinks are cheap but be sure to keep track or pay as you go. B-girls operate here also, so if a pretty local miss starts to chat you up, it's best to determine exactly what's what before jumping into action.

Shopping

The *Feira Iguaçu* is a line of stalls selling handicrafts and other items. It extends along Rebouças for about half a block either side of Av Brasil.

Getting There & Away

Most flights are domestic services to Rio de Janeiro (US$136), São Paulo (US$75) in addition to intermediate points with VASP (☎ 523-2212), Av Brasil 845, and Varig (☎ 523-2111), Av Juscelino Kubitschek 463.

Long-distance bus services from Foz do Iguaçu include 10 daily to Curitiba (US$20, 9½ hours) via BR 277, six to São Paulo (US$31, 17 hours) and two to Rio (US$40, 21 hours).

Getting Around

To get to/from the airport, catch the 'Parque Nacional' bus from the urban bus terminal or one of the stops along Av Juscelino Kubitschek; the trip takes 30 minutes and costs US$0.50. A taxi costs about US$12.

All long-distance buses arrive and depart from the rodoviária (☎ 522-2950), 6km northeast of downtown on Av Costa e Silva. To get downtown, walk downhill to the bus stop and catch any 'Centro' bus. They start at 5:30am and run roughly every 15 minutes until 1am.

Buses to Puerto Iguazú (US$1.50 to US$2) start from the terminal at 8am and run roughly every 15 minutes daily (every half hour on Sunday and holidays) until 8pm; they make a few stops along Av Juscelino Kubitschek. Buses for Ciudad del Este, Paraguay (US$0.80), begin running at 7am and leave every 10 minutes (every half hour on Sunday and holidays); catch them on JK across from the urban bus terminal. The bridge can back up badly as early as 7:30am due to Paraguayan customs checks, so if you need to be somewhere, catch the first bus or allow yourself extra time. Avoid sitting opposite the rear doors, as ne'er-do-wells along the bridge make a sport of tossing things through the doors at passengers.

The Gran Chaco

The Gran Chaco is a vast alluvial lowland, stretching north from the northern edges of Santa Fe and Córdoba provinces, across the entire provinces of Chaco and Formosa, and into western Paraguay, eastern Bolivia and along the southwestern edge of Brazil. It reaches west through most of Santiago del Estero province, drying up as it goes, and skirts the southeastern edge of Salta province. The western side, known as the Dry Chaco, or *Chaco Seco,* has been deemed the *Impenetrable,* due to its severe lack of water across an endless plain of nearly impassible thorn scrub.

The Wet Chaco *(Chaco Húmedo),* to the east, offers more to see, especially – almost solely – to nature enthusiasts and bird-lovers. The gallery forests, marshes and palm savannas of Parque Nacional Chaco, as well as the subtropical marshlands of Parque Nacional Río Pilcomayo, on the Paraguayan border, offer excellent birding opportunities and the rare chance of spotting such mammals as howler monkeys or giant anteaters. These areas are best visited in the cooler, drier months of April through November.

Resistencia, capital of Chaco province, is really the only city that stands out up here, and it does so primarily because of a unique artistic tradition and cultural commitment that has led to hundreds of public sculptures throughout the city.

It's going to be a beautiful day in the Gran Chaco.

Crossing the Chaco to Salta along the northern RN 81 from Formosa is brutal and can take nearly two days; RN 16 from Resistencia is much faster.

History

In colonial times, Europeans avoided the hot, desolate Chaco, whose few hunter-gatherer peoples resisted colonization and were not numerous enough to justify their pacification for encomiendas. Today, about 20,000 Guaycurú (Toba, Mocoví) and Mataco peoples remain in both the region's interior and urban areas.

The earliest Spanish settlement was probably Concepción del Bermejo (75km north of present-day Roque Sáenz Peña), which was founded in 1585 but abandoned in 1632 due to Indian resistance; its remains were rediscovered only recently. After the mid-18th century, Jesuit missionaries had some success among the Abipone people, but the religious order's expulsion from the Americas in 1767 again delayed European settlement.

Permanent settlement came much later. Oppressive summer heat, Indian resistance and poisonous snakes discouraged exploration of the dense thorn forests until the mid-19th century, when woodcutters from Corrientes entered the region's forests to exploit the valuable hardwood *quebracho* tree, whose name literally means 'axe breaker.' This eventually opened the region to agricultural expansion, which has primarily taken the form of cotton and cattle production.

Colonization proceeded from the province and city of Corrientes but was not really permanent until 1872. Resistencia, founded in 1750 as the Jesuit reducción of San Fernando del Río Negro, was the jumping-off point for woodcutters. The two railroads built across the Chaco have made it easier to get logs to Resistencia and Formosa, where there is sufficient water to process the tannins from the quebracho, which is then used for tanning leather.

Most of the region's agricultural development took place after 1930, when cotton production increased rapidly. New settlers of mostly Central European origin – Austrians, Bulgarians, Czechs, Russians, Yugoslavs and some Spaniards – came via the Humid Pampas. The region is currently suffering accelerated forest clearance for rain-fed agriculture, as cotton and oil crops, especially sunflowers, become more important. Petroleum exploration is also proceeding in the area north of Castelli, along the border between the two provinces.

RESISTENCIA

☎ 03722 • pop 300,000

Provincial capital and gateway to the Chaco, Resistencia requires a bit of endurance, especially in summer when its brutally hot and humid streets seem to choke beneath the sun. That said, the town is a sort of cultural oasis, rightfully deemed the 'city of sculptures' for the hundreds of sculptures that grace public spaces throughout the city.

Resistencia has some interesting cultural centers and museums, including the unusual Fogón de los Arrieros – an eclectic museum, cultural center and bar all in one – whose founder, Aldo Boglietti, later initiated Resistencia's growth into Northeast Argentina's 'open-air museum.' The city has little in the way of notable architecture and even less when it comes to hotels, but its interesting artistic tradition makes it a worthwhile stopover.

First settled in 1750, Resistencia grew rapidly with the development of the tannin industry and subsequent agricultural progress. It acquired its name after successful resistance (*resistencia*) against numerous indigenous attacks throughout the 19th century.

Orientation

Plaza 25 de Mayo is the focus of the city center. Occupying four square blocks, the plaza is one of South America's largest public squares. It has eight fountains and numerous sculptures, and is planted with quebracho, *ceibo, lapacho* and other native trees.

Street names change at the plaza. Av Sarmiento is the main access route from RN 16, which leads east to Corrientes, and west to

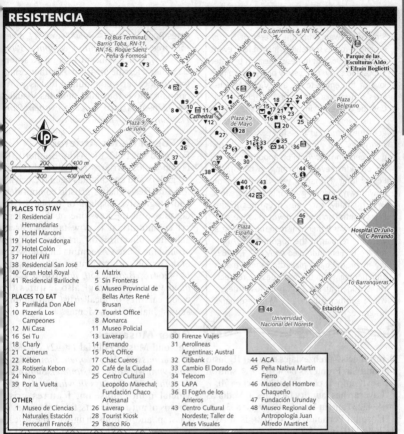

RESISTENCIA

PLACES TO STAY
2 Residencial Hernandarias
9 Hotel Marconi
19 Hotel Covadonga
27 Hotel Colón
37 Hotel Alfil
38 Residencial San José
40 Gran Hotel Royal
41 Residencial Bariloche

PLACES TO EAT
3 Parrillada Don Abel
10 Pizzería Los Campeones
12 Mi Casa
16 Sei Tu
18 Charly
21 Camerun
22 Kebon
23 Rotisería Kebon
24 Nino
39 Por la Vuelta

OTHER
1 Museo de Ciencias Naturales Estación Ferrocarril Francés
4 Matrix
5 Sin Fronteras
6 Museo Provincial de Bellas Artes René Brusan
7 Tourist Office
8 Monarca
11 Museo Policial
13 Laverap
14 Fernando
15 Post Office
17 Chac Cueros
20 Café de la Ciudad
25 Centro Cultural Leopoldo Marechal; Fundación Chaco Artesanal
26 Laverap
28 Tourist Kiosk
29 Banco Río
30 Firenze Viajes
31 Aerolíneas Argentinas; Austral
32 Citibank
33 Cambio El Dorado
34 Telecom
35 LAPA
36 El Fogón de los Arrieros
43 Centro Cultural Nordeste; Taller de Artes Visuales
44 ACA
45 Peña Nativa Martín Fierro
46 Museo del Hombre Chaqueño
47 Fundación Urunday
48 Museo Regional de Antropología Juan Alfredo Martinet

Roque Sáenz Peña and across the Chaco to Salta and Santiago del Estero. Av 25 de Mayo leads northwest from the plaza to RN 11, which also goes north to Formosa and the Paraguayan border at Clorinda.

Information

The Resistencia provincial tourist office, (☎ 423547, e direccion.turismo@ecom chaco.com.ar) is at Santa Fe 178. It opens 7:30am to 1pm and 3pm to 7:30pm weekdays. There's also a tourist kiosk (☎ 458289) at Roca on Plaza 25 de Mayo, open 8am to 9pm weekdays and 9am to midnight weekends.

ACA (☎ 470507) is at Av 9 de Julio and Av Italia, three blocks from Plaza 25 de Mayo.

Cambio El Dorado, Jose María Paz 36, changes traveler's checks at reasonable rates. There are several ATMs in and around Plaza 25 de Mayo.

The post office faces Plaza 25 de Mayo at Sarmiento and Yrigoyen; the postal code is 3500. Locutorios are easy to find; try the Telecom on the corner of 9 de Julio and Pellegrini. For cheap Internet access, try Matrix (☎ 449666), at Roca 401.

Among the best established travel agencies are Firenze Viajes (☎ 433333, fax 433933,

A Town's Best Friend

Stray dogs wandering the streets of South American towns sometimes inspire fear, even outright panic. Not in Resistencia. In the late 1950s and early '60s a stray dog inspired the love of the entire town, and Víctor Marchese's statue on Calle Mitre, in front of the Casa de Gobierno, immortalizes him.

His name was Fernando. As the story goes, he wandered the streets and slept in doorways and finally befriended a bank manager, who allowed Fernando to join him for breakfast every morning in his office. Before long, Fernando was the delight of downtown, inspiring people's daydreams with his daily, carefree adventures in the Plaza Central. In a town devoted to the arts, Fernando was Bohemianism in fur, and was a welcome regular at the Fogón de los Arrieros. When Fernando died on May 19, 1963, the municipal band played a funeral march and people shut their shades in respect. He is buried at the Fogón de los Arrieros, where another sculpture by Marchese marks his grave.

e resistencia@firenzeviajes.com), at JB Justo 148, and Sin Fronteras (☎ 431055, e sinfronterasevt@infovia.com.ar), at Necochea 70.

Laverap has laundry facilities at Vedia 23 (☎ 424223) and at Vedia 319 (☎ 445833).

Hospital Perrando (☎ 425050) is at Av 9 de Julio 1101, near Mena.

Sculptures

There's insufficient space to provide details for the more than 300 sculptures in city parks and on sidewalks, but the tourist office, when it has funds, distributes a list with their locations, offering a purposeful introduction to the city. (Do walk around early in the morning, before the suffocating summer heat.) The best starting point is the **Parque de las Esculturas Aldo y Efraín Boglietti**, at Avs Laprida and Sarmiento, alongside the old French railroad station (which houses the Museo de Ciencias Naturales; for more information see Other Museums, later).

If you prefer your sculptures under a roo check out the **Museo Provincial de Bella Artes René Brusan** (☎ 448000 ex 2511, Mitr 150; free; open 8am-noon & 6pm-8:30pr Tues-Fri), which concentrates on Resisten cia's characteristic art form. Another cente for the local arts community that is wort popping into is the **Taller de Artes Visuale** (☎ 422695, Arturo Illia 353; open 9am 11:30am & 4pm-7pm weekdays).

El Fogón de los Arrieros

Founded in 1942 by Aldo Boglietti, E Fogón de los Arrieros is a cultural cente art gallery and bar that has been the drivin force of Resistencia's artistic commitmen and progressive displays of public art fo decades. Still the keystone of the region' art community, it is now famous for it eclectic collection of art objects fron around the Chaco, Argentina and the worl of the region's arts community. The museun (☎ 426418, Brown 350; admission US$2 open 9am-11pm daily) also features th wood carvings of local artist and cultura activist Juan de Dios Mena.

Other Museums

The odd **Museo Policial** (☎ 421551, Roc 233; admission US$1; open 8am-noon & 5pm-9pm weekdays in summer, 8am-noon & 4pm-8pm weekdays in winter), the pro vincial police museum, features grisl photos of auto accidents, tales of crimes o passion, and tedious drug-war rhetoric. I redeems itself with absorbing accounts o cuatrerismo (cattle rustling, still wide spread in the province) and social ban ditry, including the remarkable tale of two 1960s outlaws who, after killing a police man, lived for five years on the run, helped by the poor rural people of the province Police officers accompany visitors o guided tours.

Archaeology, rather than the muc broader field of anthropology, is the focu of the **Museo Regional de Antropologia Juan Alfredo Martinet** (☎ 422257, Av La Heras 727; free; open 8am-noon & 4pm 8pm weekdays) at the Universidad Nacio nal del Noreste.

The **Museo de Ciencias Naturales** (☎ 423864, Pellegrini 802, Parque de las Esculturas; free; open 8am-noon & 4pm-8pm weekdays) is worth a glimpse if only for its location in the old Estación Ferrocarril Francés (French railroad station) in the Parque de las Esculturas (note the 1882 Hardy locomotive outside). It has a good collection of stuffed birds of the region.

The **Museo del Hombre Chaqueño** (☎ 426112, Arturo Illia 655; free; open 8am-noon & 4pm-8pm weekdays, 5pm-9pm Sat), the Museum of Chaco Man, focuses on the colonization of the Chaco and has exhibits and information on the Guaraní, Mocoví, Komlek and Mataco provincial indigenous cultures.

Special Events

During the third week of July, Resistencia's Plaza 25 de Mayo hosts the Concurso Nacional e Internacional de Escultura y Madera, a competition in which the participants have seven days to carve a trunk of urunday (a native tree) into a work of art. (Local sculptors are nothing if not adaptable: In 1998, contestants from this sweltering city won a prize for the best ice sculpture in the 1998 Winter Olympics at Sapporo, Japan.) For more information, contact the Fundación Urunday (☎ 436694), Av San Martín 465.

In August, the Exposición de Ganadería showcases the region's best livestock.

Places to Stay

Budget Resistencia's choices for budget accommodations are slim.

Camping Parque 2 de Febrero (☎ 458323, Av Avalos 1100) Sites US$4 plus US$1 per person This well-staffed campground has good facilities, including shade, but can get crowded and noisy in high season – not least because of the dance clubs across the road.

Residencial San José (☎ 426062, Frondizi 306) Singles/doubles US$15/25 with bath. Though the rooms are somewhat musty, this ramshackle place is clean and friendly. The showers have electric showerheads, and the price is the lowest in town.

Residencial Bariloche (☎ 421412, Obligado 239) Singles/doubles US$20/30 with bath. Dimly lit rooms open onto a covered central patio that, unfortunately, can get pretty noisy. It's basic, clean and reliable.

Hotel Alfil (☎ 420882, Santa María de Oro 495) Singles/doubles US$22/27 with bath, breakfast & parking. Hotel Alfil is small, simple and friendly, and its tile-floored rooms, with decent baths, are a good value. Breakfast is not served on Sunday.

Residencial Hernandarias (☎ 427088, fax 434425, Av Hernandarias 215) Singles/doubles US$25/37. In a rather dismal location on a busy street, this residencial has clean, tiled rooms with air-con, TV and above-average beds. Most rooms have windows.

Mid-Range One of the best values in town, the spotless and friendly *Hotel Marconi* (☎ 421978, e hotelmarconi@ciudad.com.ar, Perón 352) has only two drawbacks: bad coffee and the deafeningly noisy disco across the street. Singles/doubles cost US$29/39 with breakfast, air-con, TV and telephone. An interior room on weekends is a must.

Gran Hotel Royal (☎ 443666, fax 424586, e hotelroyal@infovia.com.ar, José M Paz 297) Singles/doubles US$38/48 with breakfast, TV, air-con & parking. The centrally located Gran Hotel Royal has spotless, carpeted rooms and, compared to others of this quality in town, a surprisingly low price tag.

Hotel Colón (☎/fax 422861, e hotel colon@lared.com.ar, Santa María de Oro 143) Singles/doubles US$39/59 with air-con & TV. Since 1927 this superbly located hotel has been renting small, well-kept rooms, some with excellent bathrooms and bathtubs.

Top End Resistencia's favorite luxury hotel is the *Hotel Covadonga* (☎ 444444, fax 443444, e hotelcovadonga@ infovia.com.ar, Güemes 200). Singles/doubles go for US$69/78 with breakfast air-con, TV and telephone. The excellent rooms have plush beds and spacious baths. Facilities include a pool, a sauna, a small gym and a bar.

ARGENTINA

Places to Eat

Eating well in Resistencia is easily done, and there's no need to break the bank to do it (though opportunities exist). Restaurants with wholesome affordable food are plentiful.

Try *Camerun* (☎ 446783, *Güemes 272*) for take-out empanadas at US$3 per fried dozen and US$3.50 per baked dozen; it's about as cheap as they come anywhere. Pizzas are US$3-7 and they'll deliver free of charge.

Pizzería Los Campeones (☎ 424285, *Perón 300*) Pizzas US$5-10. This down-home pizzería also serves unbeatable slices at US$1 a pop.

Nino (☎ 449977, *Don Bosco 133*) Breakfast US$2-4, lunch or dinner US$4-9. This cool, relaxed café serves burgers, sandwiches and a wide selection of salads.

Mi Casa (☎ 447898, *Vedia 169*) All-you-can-eat US$5-7; open noon-3:30pm & 8pm-midnight daily. Get here early if you want the freshest food. The salads are good and the hot plates typical of tenedor libres.

Kebon (☎ 422385, *Güemes & Don Bosco*) Some argue this is the best restaurant in town. For budget-watchers, its rotisería of the same name next door is a bargain for take-away and delivery food.

Parrillada Don Abel (☎ 449252, *Cangallo & Perón*) Lunch or dinner US$8-17. This parrilla is inside a homey *quincho* (thatched roof building) and serves substantial portions of pasta and grilled surubí in addition to the usual grilled beef. The two-person parrillada costs US$10.

Por la Vuelta (☎ 440985, *Obligado 33*) Lunch or dinner US$8-18. Also known as Restaurant Nalhia, this social club restaurant is recommended for international cuisine – it's also a good place to watch Resistencia socialites work their manners.

Charly (☎ 439304, *restaurant: Güemes 213; rotisserie: Brown 71*) Lunch or dinner US$10-20. Charly does good international of local river fish. You'll save money taking out from the restaurant's rotisserie around the corner.

One reader has pointed out *Sei Tu* (☎ 437444, *Yrigoyen 99*) for excellent ice cream.

Entertainment

Peña Nativa Martín Fierro (☎ 423167, *Av 9 de Julio 695*) Try this place on Friday or Saturday nights after 10pm for live folk music and tango. It also has a parrilla restaurant.

El Fogón de los Arrieros (☎ 426418, *Brown 350*). Stopping into El Fogón's friendly bar – a local institution for decades – is almost mandatory. The attached cultural center presents occasional live music and small-scale theatrical events. Call for information. (See also El Fogón de los Arrieros, earlier.)

Centro Cultural Leopoldo Marechal (☎ 422649, *Pellegrini 272*) Open 9am-noon & 7pm-9pm weekdays. This cultural center has regular art exhibitions and performances.

Café de la Ciudad (☎ 420214, *Pellegrini 109*) Open 7am-2am Sun-Thur, 1pm-dawn Fri & Sat. With an eclectic pub-like atmosphere, this bar-café gets lively on weekend nights. It's also good for morning coffee and afternoon sandwiches (US$2-7).

Monarca (mobile ☎ 15-668088, *Perón 393*) Admission US$3 with drink. The kids go Friday and the older crowd Saturday. The street out front gets nearly as lively as the dance floor and the music requires plenty of drinks.

Shopping

Chac Cueros (☎/fax 433-604, *Güemes 163*) Chac Cueros specializes in high-quality leather goods made from the hide of *carpinchos*, the animals valued for the suede produced from their tan, naturally dimpled skin.

Fundación Chaco Artesanal (☎ 459372, *Pellegrini 272*) Open 8am-1pm & 5pm-8pm Mon-Sat, 8am-1pm Sun. This association, in the Centro Cultural Leopoldo Marechal, sells an outstanding selection of indigenous crafts.

Getting There & Away

Air Aerolíneas Argentinas (☎ 445553) and Austral (☎ 446800) share offices at Frondiz 99. Austral flies twice daily to Buenos Aires (US$161) except Sunday, when it only flies once. LAPA (☎ 430201), Pellegrini 100, flies daily to Buenos Aires (US$59-129). Southern Winds (☎ 443300) is at Güemes 251.

Bus Resistencia is an important hub of bus travel for destinations in all directions. Godoy Resistencia buses make the rounds between Corrientes and Resistencia (US$2, 40 minutes) at frequent intervals throughout the day.

There are frequent, daily services to the destinations listed below. The fares listed here are midseason rates and may rise or fall throughout the year.

Destination	Duration in hours	Cost
Buenos Aires	13	US$25
Córdoba	12	US$30
Formosa	2	US$8
Gualeguaychú	10	US$30
Laguna Blanca	5½	US$17
La Plata	15½	US$30
Mendoza	24	US$57
Mercedes	4	US$12
Naick-Neck	5	US$15
Paraná	8½	US$20
Posadas	5½	US$18
Puerto Iguazú	9½	US$26
Roque Sáenz Peña	2	US$10
Rosario	9½	US$30
Salta	12	US$36
San Luis	20	US$60
Santa Fe	7	US$19
Tucumán	12	US$30

Godoy SRL, El Tala and Empresa Yacyretá have early morning buses to Asunción, Paraguay (US$17, 5 hours).

Getting Around

Aeropuerto San Martín is 6km south of town on RN 11; take bus No 3 (black letters) from the post office on Plaza 25 de Mayo.

The bus terminal (☎ 461098) is at Av MacLean and Islas Malvinas. Take bus No 3 (a minibus) or No 10 from the Casa de Gobierno (near the post office) on Plaza 25 de Mayo.

City buses cost US$0.70; pay on board.

PARQUE NACIONAL CHACO

Preserving several diverse ecosystems that reflect subtle differences in relief, soils and rainfall, this very accessible but little-known park (☎ 03725-496166; park entrance US$5; open year-round) protects 15,000 hectares of the humid eastern Chaco. It is 115km northwest of Resistencia via RN 16 and RP 9.

Ecologically, Parque Nacional Chaco falls within the 'estuarine and gallery forest' subregion of the Gran Chaco, but the park encompasses a variety of marshes, open grasslands, palm savannas, scrub forest and denser gallery forests. The most widespread ecosystem is the *monte fuerte*, where mature specimens of quebracho, algarrobo and lapacho reach above 20m, while lower stories of immature trees and shrubs provide a variety of habitats at distinct elevations.

Scrub forests form a transitional environment to seasonally inundated savanna grasslands, punctuated by *caranday* and *pindó* palms. More open grasslands have traditionally been maintained by human activities, including grazing and associated fires, but these are disappearing. Marshes and gallery forests cover the smallest areas, but they are biologically the most productive. The meandering Río Negro has left several shallow oxbow lakes where dense aquatic vegetation flourishes.

Mammals are few and rarely seen, but birds are abundant, including the rhea, jabirú stork, roseate spoonbill, cormorants, common caracaras and other less conspicuous species. The most abundant insect species is the mosquito, so plan your trip during the relatively dry, cool winter (when you'll also avoid the blistering summer heat) and bring insect repellent.

Park service personnel are extremely hospitable and will accompany visitors if their duties permit.

Activities

Hiking and bird watching are the principal activities, best done in early morning or around sunset. Some inundated areas are accessible only while horseback riding; inquire about horses and guides in Capitán Solari, 6km east of the park.

Places to Stay & Eat

In Capitán Solari, the municipalidad provides information on *casas de familia* in town. Several families open their doors, at fair prices, to travelers.

Camping is the only alternative at the park itself. Fortunately, there are numerous shaded sites with clean showers (cold water only) and toilets, despite many ants and other harmless *bichos* (critters). A tent or other shelter is essential. There are fire pits, picnic tables, plenty of wood lying around for fuel, and no fees, but beware of Panchi, the rangers' pet monkey, who will steal anything not tied down.

Weekends can be crowded with visitors from Resistencia, but at other times you may have the park to yourself. Sometimes on weekends a concessionaire from Resistencia sells meals, but it's better to bring everything you need from Resistencia or Capitán Solari.

Getting There & Away

Capitán Solari is 2½ hours from Resistencia by bus (US$4.50). La Estrella has four buses daily, at 6:30am, 12:30pm, 5:30pm and 8pm; return buses from Capitán Solari to Resistencia leave at 5:30am, 11:30am and 5pm.

From Capitán Solari, you will have to walk the 5km or catch a lift to the park entrance. Transport is easy to find by asking around in town, or ask at the municipalidad for Sr Mendoza who will drive you there for around US$2. The road may be impassable for motor vehicles in wet weather. If possible, avoid walking in the midday heat.

ROQUE SÁENZ PEÑA
☎ 03732 • pop 75,000

Properly speaking, this city, 168km west of Resistencia, goes by the cumbersome name of Presidencia Roque Sáenz Peña, after the Argentine leader responsible for the adoption of electoral reform and universal male suffrage in 1912.

Primarily a service center for cotton and sunflower growers, Roque Sáenz Peña became a visitor attraction for its thermal baths, fortuitously discovered by drillers seeking potable water in 1937. Unfortunately, those baths are now dry, and the city currently lacks the funds to re-tap them. This brutally hot city, which has one of the

country's better zoos, is the gateway to the 'Impenetrable' of the central Chaco.

Chaco province grows nearly two-thirds of the country's total cotton crop, so in May, Roque Sáenz Peña hosts the Fiesta Nacional del Algodón (National Cotton Festival).

Orientation & Information

Roque Sáenz Peña straddles RN 16, which connects Resistencia with Salta. Its regular grid plan centers on willow-shaded Plaza San Martín; Av San Martín is the principal commercial street.

The municipal tourist office (no ☎) is in the thermal bath complex at Brown 541. It opens 8am to noon and 5pm to 8pm weekdays; and 8am to noon on Saturday. ACA (☎ 420471) is at Rivadavia and 25 de Mayo.

For currency exchange try Banco de la Nación at Av San Martín 301; it has an ATM.

The post office is at Belgrano 602, at Mitre; the postal code is 3700. There's a Telefónica locutorio at Av San Martín 692.

Hospital 4 de Junio (☎ 421404) is at Las Malvinas 1350.

Parque Zoológico y Complejo Ecológico

At the junction of RN 16 and Ruta 95, 3km east of downtown, this spacious and nationally renowned zoo and botanical garden emphasizes regionally important birds and mammals rather than ecological exotics. Featured species are tapir and jaguar.

The zoo (☎ 422145; admission US$1 per adult plus US$1 per vehicle, kids free; open 7am-7pm daily) has two large artificial lakes frequented by migratory waterfowl. Bus No 2 goes from downtown to the zoo, which is within reasonable walking distance if it's not too hot.

Places to Stay

Camping El Descanso Sites US$6. Along the eastern approach to town just north of RN 16, this campground has good, shady facilities, but can be noisy on weekends. Take bus No 1 from downtown.

Hotel Asturias (☎ 420210, Belgrano 402 at Calles 9 & 10) Singles/doubles US$15/25, US$20/$30 with air-con, US$10/20 with shared bath. This well-kept, old hotel still has some integrity from days past, though you'd never know it from the outside (there's not even a sign). The older rooms have more character.

Orel Hotel (☎ 424139, e ifmalina@ yahoo.com.ar, Saavedra & San Martín) Singles/doubles US$23/36 with bath & cable TV. The rooms here are simple, clean and colorful. The owner may offer excursions to the Teuco and Bermejito Rivers region north of Sáenz Peña.

Hotel Gualok (☎ 420521, Av San Martín 1198) Singles/doubles US$54/76. Part of the thermal-baths complex, this four-star hotel with a restaurant, shows some serious wear.

Places to Eat
In addition to the hotel restaurants, there are numerous restaurants and confiterías along Av San Martín.

Old family-run *El Nuevo Colono* (☎ 422338, San Martín 755) serves filling sandwiches and pastas for US$3.50 and under; it's likely the best deal in town. At the corner of Calles 14 and 23, *Sky Blue* (Mitre & Mariano Moreno) is an outdoor *chopería* that is good for evening pizza and beer. It opens at 8pm and stays open late.

Getting There & Away
The bus terminal (☎ 420280) is about seven blocks east of downtown, on Petris (Calle 19) between Avellaneda and López y Planes; take bus No 1 from Av Mitre.

There are daily departures to Buenos Aires (US$35-53, 17 hours), Córdoba (US$38, 15 hours), Formosa (US$20, 6 hours), Posadas (US$16, 7 hours), Resistencia (US$10, 2 hours), Rosario (US$20, 11 hours), Salta (US$35, 9 hours), Santa Fe (US$20, 9½ hours) and Tucumán (US$20, 10 hours).

Many trans-Chaco services from Resistencia pick up passengers here as well.

FORMOSA
☎ 03717 • pop 203,000
Aching beneath the sun on a horseshoe bend of the Río Paraguay, Formosa is primarily a stop on the way to Paraguay or the nearby Parque Nacional Río Pilcomayo. This far north, with its Paraguayan street market, cheap liquados and evening platoons of adolescent motor-scooter racers, Argentina begins to paint a different picture. It's a good place to get a feel for the country across the river, and a much better place to stay than Clorinda, where you cross the border.

Orientation
Formosa is 169km north of Resistencia and 113km south of Clorinda (on the border with Paraguay) via RN 11. It is also possible, though still not easy, to cross the northern Chaco via RN 81 and continue to Bolivia.

Av Doctor Luis Gutñiski, as RN 11 is called as it passes through town, heads eastward to Plaza San Martín, a four-block public park beyond which Av 25 de Mayo, the heart of the city, continues to the shores of the Río Paraguay.

From the north side of Plaza San Martín, Av Independencia is RN 11, heading north. Av Circunvalación allows motorists to avoid the downtown area.

Unlike in many Argentine towns, street names do not change on either side of the plaza but rather along either side of Av Gonzales Lelong, seven blocks north of the plaza.

Information
The provincial tourist office (☎ 420442) is at Uriburu 820 near Fontana. It's open 7am to 1pm and 4pm to 8pm weekdays.

Banco de Galicia has an ATM at Av 25 de Mayo 160. The post office is on Plaza San Martín at Av 9 de Julio 930; Formosa's postal code is 3600. There's a Telecom locutorio on 25 de Mayo between Moreno and Rivadavia. One travel agency, Turismo de Castro (☎ 434777), is at 25 de Mayo 275. The Hospital Central (☎ 426194) is at Salta 545.

Museo Histórico
In the Casa Fotheringham, a pioneer residence that was the province's first Casa de Gobierno, the municipal historical museum (no ☎, Belgrano & Av 25 de Mayo; free; open 8am-noon & 4pm-7pm weekdays, 8am-noon

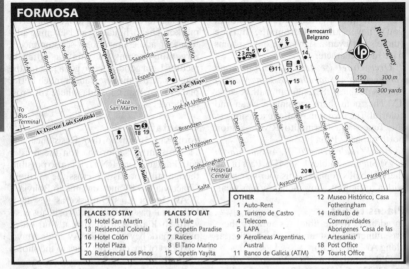

FORMOSA

PLACES TO STAY
10 Hotel San Martín
13 Residencial Colonial
16 Hotel Colón
17 Hotel Plaza
20 Residencial Los Pinos

PLACES TO EAT
2 Il Viale
6 Copetín Paradise
7 Raíces
8 El Tano Marino
15 Copetín Yayita

OTHER
1 Auto-Rent
3 Turismo de Castro
4 Telecom
5 LAPA
9 Aerolíneas Argentinas,
   Austral
11 Banco de Galicia (ATM)
12 Museo Histórico, Casa
    Fotheringham
14 Instituto de
    Communidades
    Aborígenes 'Casa de las
    Artesanías'
18 Post Office
19 Tourist Office

Sat) focuses on the foundation and development of Formosa. The province was part of the Paraguayan Chaco until the 19th-century War of the Triple Alliance, and the museum houses uniforms, weapons and relics from the period. There are a few old indigenous weavings as well.

Special Events

Formosa's annual Fiesta del Río, lasting a week in mid-November, features an impressive nocturnal religious procession in which 150 boats from Corrientes sail up the Río Paraguay.

In February, Formosa celebrates Carnaval on weekends, while Día de la Fundación de Formosa celebrates the city's founding on April 8. The Fiesta de la Virgen de la Catedral honors the Virgen del Carmen, Formosa's patron saint, on July 16.

Places to Stay

Camping Banco Provincial *(☎ 429877, RN 11 at El Cruce)* Sites US$5 per person. About 4km south of Formosa on RN 11, this decent campground has well-kept facilities, including a swimming pool and tennis courts.

In town, ACA *(Av Gutñiski 3025)* will sometimes permit people to park or pitch a tent overnight on its spacious grounds.

Residencial Los Pinos *(☎ 436948, Ayacucho 1399)* Singles/doubles US$10/27 with bath, doubles with air-con. In a quiet area on the corner of Ayacucho and Belgrano, this friendly place has basic rooms, a small patio and a basin for washing clothes; it's simple and pleasant.

Residencial Colonial *(☎ 426346, San Martín 879)* Singles/doubles US$20/25 with bath. This dilapidated hotel with a plain, colonial feel has dreary rooms with fans.

Hotel San Martín *(☎ 426769, Av 25 de Mayo 380)* Singles/doubles US$20/30 with bath & air-con. Though some rooms desperately need a paint job, the hotel is one of the best values in town. Showers have electric showerheads.

Hotel Colón *(☎ 426547, fax 420719, Belgrano 1068)* Singles/doubles US$25/36 with breakfast, US$32/44 with air-con, TV & breakfast. Rooms in the newer sector start at US$38/55 with air-con & TV. Down near the river, Hotel Colón offers good, clean accommodation and professional service.

Hotel Plaza (☎ 426767, e plazahotel@ciudad.com.ar, Uriburu 920) Singles/doubles US$40/55 with TV, air-con, bath & breakfast, singles without air-con US$32. If you don't mind the overpowering smell of industrial room-freshener you'll do fine at this clean, run-of-the-mill hotel.

Places to Eat

Raíces (☎ 427058, Av 25 de Mayo 65) Mains US$6-11. This refined, locally esteemed restaurant has more than 13 surubí dishes on the menu as well as plenty of tasty meat, chicken and pasta dishes.

El Tano Marino (☎ 420628, Av 25 de Mayo 55) Mains US$6-11. El Tano Marino is similar in price and quality to Raíces, next door.

Copetín Paradise (☎ 429045, Rivadavia 724) Lunch or dinner US$3-6. This popular hole-in-the-wall serves excellent empanadas at US$3 to US$4 per dozen and decent pasta dishes for US$3. Sandwiches are also cheap, and licuados go for US$1.50.

Copetín Yayita (☎ 431322, Belgrano 926) Mains US$2.50-5. Gnocchi, ravioli, lomitos and burgers all cost less than US$3 at this funky copetín. Licuados are cheap, and the *sopa de bagre* (catfish soup) is very popular.

Il Viale (☎ 430974, Av 25 de Mayo 287) Mains US$4-7. In addition to coffee, this confitería serves good, though pricey, sandwiches and burgers.

Shopping

Instituto de Communidades Aborigenes 'Casa de las Artesanias' (no ☎, San Martín 82) Open 8am-12:30pm & 4pm-8pm Mon-Sat. In a historic building near the river, this artisan cooperative sells string bags, *palo santo* wood carvings, weavings and other items. The goods range from shoddy to beautiful. All proceeds go to the indigenous communities – the Mataco, Toba and Pilaga – who make the crafts.

Getting There & Away

Air Austral (☎ 429392, 429314), Av 25 de Mayo 603, flies daily to Buenos Aires. LAPA (☎ 435979), Av 25 de Mayo 215, flies daily except Sunday to Corrientes (US$13 to US$23), a flight that continues to Buenos Aires (US$59-149).

Bus Formosa's modern bus terminal (☎ 451766) is on Av Gutñiski and Antártida Argentina, 15 blocks west of Plaza San Martín.

Godoy Cruz leaves daily at 8:45am and 7:30pm to Clorinda (US$5, 1¾ hours) on the Paraguayan border, and continues to Laguna Blanca (US$8, 3 hours) and Naick-Neck, both at Parque Nacional Río Pilcomayo. Navarro makes the same runs at different times. Buses also leave daily to Asunción, Paraguay (US$9, 3 hours).

There are daily departures to Buenos Aires (US$35, 16 hours), Córdoba (US$42, 15 hours), Rosario (US$30, 12 hours), Santa Fe (US$34, 11 hours), Salta (US$52, 15 hours), Tucumán (US$40, 14 hours) and La Plata (US$40, 17½ hours).

Getting Around

Aeropuerto El Pucú is only 4km south of town along RN 11, so cabs are an inexpensive option.

Bus Nos 4, 9 and 11 all run between Plaza San Martín and the bus terminal.

For car rental, try Auto-Rent (☎ 431721), at España 557, or MAS Autos (☎ 436010) at 25 de Mayo and Julio Roca.

CLORINDA
☎ 03718 • pop 45,000

Notorious for fierce customs checks, squalid Clorinda is the border crossing to Asunción, Paraguay, via the Puente Internacional San Ignacio de Loyola. The Paraguayan consulate (☎ 03718-421988) is at José F Cancio 1393.

Godoy Cruz buses cross the border at regular intervals from Clorinda's bus terminal at San Martín and Paraguay, where Navarro buses to Parque Nacional Río Pilcomayo also depart. There's a Paraguayan consulate (☎ 421988) at José F Cancio 1393. The postal code is 3610.

Formosa is a more agreeable place to stay, but if you're stuck, there's inexpensive lodging for about US$13/20 a single/double at *Residencial Ortega* (☎ 421593, Libertad

1213), and at the clean *Hotel San Martín* (☎ *421211, 12 de Octubre 1150).*

PARQUE NACIONAL RÍO PILCOMAYO

West of Clorinda, the wildlife-rich marshlands of 60,000-hectare Parque Nacional Río Pilcomayo resembling Parque Nacional Chaco in its ecology and environments, hug the Paraguayan border. Its outstanding feature is shallow, shimmering **Laguna Blanca**, where, at sunset, *yacarés* (alligators) lurk on the lake surface. Other wildlife (except for birds) is likelier to be heard than seen among the dense aquatic vegetation.

From the park's campground, a wooden *pasarela* (walkway) leads to the lakeshore, where there is a platform overlook about 5m high, plus three lake-level platforms for swimming and sunbathing (the water is barely a meter deep). It's especially tranquil and appealing late in the day, after picnickers and day trippers have returned to Clorinda and Formosa, but carry plenty of mosquito repellent.

Places to Stay & Eat

The free *camping* facilities are seldom used except on weekends; automobiles cannot enter the campground proper but must park nearby. There are showers in the bathrooms, but the water is saline and most people prefer the lake, which offers relief from the heat. Just outside the park entrance, a small shop sells basic food and cold drinks, including beer.

Hotel Guaraní (☎ *03718-470024, San Martín & Sargento Cabral)* Singles/doubles US$14/20. In the town of Laguna Blanca, 11km beyond the turnoff, this hotel is basic and tolerable for a night or two.

Getting There & Away

Godoy Cruz and Navarro run buses from Formosa and Clorinda along RN 86 to Naick-Neck and Laguna Blanca. The three-hour trip from Formosa costs US$8. The ranger station and information center is in Laguna Blanca on the RN 86. You will have to hike, hitch or take a remise to get the 5km from the turnoff on RN 86 to the park entrance.

Córdoba & the Central Sierras

The Pampas stretch eastward from Buenos Aires some 700km before the relentlessly flat plains are finally broken by the Sierras de Córdoba, separating them from the Andes to the west. Excluding Patagonia, Córdoba province lies in the virtual center of the country. The geologically complex Sierras consist of three longitudinal ranges and reach as high as 2800m. Stretching 500km from north to south, they give birth to several east-flowing rivers, prosaically named Primero (First), Segundo (Second), Tercero (Third) and Cuarto (Fourth).

The region's major attraction is the beautifully preserved colonial architecture of the capital city of Córdoba, but its scenic mountain hinterland offers literally hundreds of small towns and even tinier villages. Resorts like Villa General Belgrano and Mina Clavero were once refuges for the rich, but now attract thousands who come to hike, fish, swim, ride horses, paraglide and party. The attractive Jesuit estancias (especially in the towns of Jesús María and Alta Gracia) scattered throughout the Sierras have always been an attraction, but have lately received special attention since UNESCO declared five of them World Heritage Sites in 2000. The Sierras also have reservoirs, artificial sandy beaches and gaudy casinos.

The capital is a convenient base for exploring the surrounding mountains, and public transport to the most popular mountain towns and resorts is well-established. The Sierras' southernmost resort town is Merlo, in the northeast corner of neighboring San Luis Province. From there it's only a short distance to the namesake capital of San Luis (covered in this chapter), a convenient stopover before turning west to Mendoza.

History

Before the arrival of the Spaniards, indigenous sedentary Comechingones occupied the area around Córdoba. Like their counterparts farther north, they were maize

Highlights

- Córdoba – Admiring 17th-century architecture or dancing till dawn in the country's second-largest city
- Jesuit Ruins – Exploring the 17th-century ruins of Alta Gracia and Jesús María
- Mountain Streams – Taking a dip in the swimming holes outside Cosquín and Mina Clavero
- Mountain Towns – Riding horseback through La Falda or La Cumbre
- Punilla Valley – Getting a bird's-eye view from the world-famous paragliding launch at Cuchi Corral, near La Cumbre

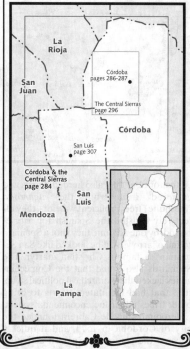

283

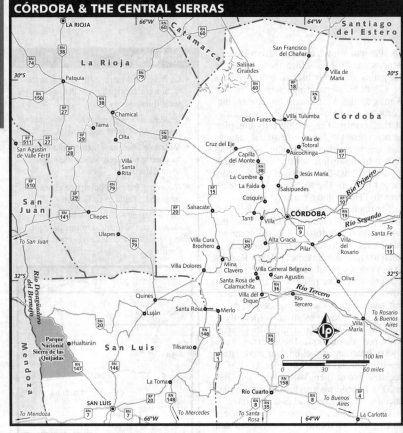

CÓRDOBA & THE CENTRAL SIERRAS

cultivators, but they also herded llamas and gathered fruit from the *algarrobo* (mesquite) tree. Proficient warriors, they effectively resisted the Spanish for a brief period; by one account, they shot a Spaniard so full of arrows that he 'looked like San Sebastián,' a famous Christian martyr. The Spaniards also found that the Comechingones lacked the hierarchical political structure that had facilitated efforts to bring other tribes under the encomienda system.

Jerónimo Luis de Cabrera founded the city of Córdoba in 1573, and it quickly became the center for Spanish activities, with a strong missionary presence. It was a center for education, fine arts and architecture, and Buenos Aires depended on the city's connections to the north. With the creation of the Viceroyalty of the Río de la Plata, followed by Argentine independence, Córdoba underwent the same reorientation as the rest of the country, becoming subject to the economic whims of the port capital. Nevertheless, the city later benefited from increased foreign trade, doubling its population between 1840 and 1860.

Both the influx of European immigrants into the country and the expansion of the ailway in the late 19th century dramatically timulated the growth of the province. Still, ecause of the phenomenal growth in Buenos Aires and the Pampas, Córdoba experienced a relative decline.

By the middle of the 20th century, the ocal establishment's political conservatism roused so much dissatisfaction among the opulace, especially in the university, that it pawned an aggressive reform movement, vhich had a lasting impact both locally and ationally. In the late 1960s, university students and auto workers forged a coalition hat nearly unseated the de facto military overnment of General Juan Carlos Onganía in an uprising known as the *cordobazo*.

Today, after the chaos of the 1970s and early 1980s, the region's economy has again leclined as a result of the automobile industry's obsolete equipment and the general stagnation of the Argentine economy.

Córdoba

☎ 0351 • pop 1,300,000 • elevation 400m
Córdoba, capital of the provincial heart of Argentina, is a clean, cosmopolitan city with a rich and tangible history. It proudly lays claim to being the country's second city, a title contested by Rosario but indisputable if judged in terms of sheer size. And although this is the country's second-largest city, its well-preserved historic center and bordering neighborhoods are easily explored by foot. The 17th-century Jesuit architecture of the Manzana Jesuítica, the 19th-century neoclassical buildings of the Nueva Córdoba area and the hip restaurants of Barrio Güemes are all within walking distance of each other. The city is also an excellent base for exploring the surrounding mountains.

Other Argentines say that if asked directions, a *cordobés* (person from Córdoba) will steer you incorrectly, not for the Latin American dictate that bad directions beat no directions, but for fun. Cordobeses are more likely to walk you across town to make sure you get there, however, than to steer you wrong, and they are distinctly friendly and open, but there is definitely a unique twist to their collective sense of humor.

ORIENTATION
Córdoba is 710km northwest of Buenos Aires and 330km south of Santiago del Estero via RN 9. Plaza San Martín is its urban nucleus; most colonial attractions lie within a quadrant demarcated by Av Olmos to the north, Av Maipú to the east, Blvd Illia to the south and Av General Paz to the west. The commercial center is just northwest of the plaza, where the main pedestrian malls, 25 de Mayo and Rivera Indarte, intersect each other. Obispo Trejo, just west of the plaza, has the finest concentration of colonial buildings.

Just south of downtown, Parque Sarmiento offers relief from the bustling, densely built downtown, but the largest open space is Parque General San Martín, on the banks of the Suquía on the northwestern outskirts of town.

East-west streets change names at San Martín/Independencia and north-south streets change at Deán Funes/Rosario de Santa Fe.

INFORMATION
Tourist Offices
The provincial and municipal tourist boards together maintain their main information office (☎ 428-5856) in the historic Casa Cabildo, at Independencia 30. Hours are 8am to 9pm weekdays, 9am to noon and 5pm to 8pm weekends.

There is an additional municipal tourist office (☎ 428-5843, 428-5600) below the Casa del Obispo Mercadillo at Calle Rosario de Santa Fe 39, on the north side of the plaza, open weekday business hours only. The provincial tourist board has a branch (☎ 433-1544) at Tucumán 360, hours are 8am to 2pm weekdays; and another (☎ 433-1980) at the bus terminal, hours are 7:30am to 8:30pm weekdays, 8am to 8pm weekends. An additional office (☎ 434-8390) is at Aeropuerto Pajas Blancas, and is open 8am to 8pm weekdays.

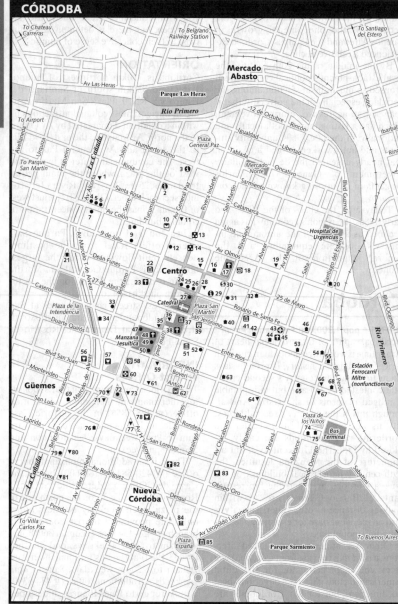

CÓRDOBA

ACA (☎ 421-4636) is at Av General Paz and Humberto Primo, eight blocks north of Plaza San Martín.

Money

For changing cash or traveler's checks, try Barujel at the corner of Rivadavia and 25 de Mayo. There are many ATMs downtown and at the bus station.

Post & Communications

The post office is at Av General Paz 201; central Córdoba's postal code is 5000. For 24-hour Internet access, try Internet 24 at Duarte Quirós 49; rates are US$1 per hour until 4pm, and US$1.50 per hour from 4pm through the night. Radiocentro.bar (☎ 428-0166), a cozier cybercafé and bar at Rivadavia 150, charges US$2 per hour for Internet access.

Travel Agencies

The American Express representative is Grupo 3 de Turismo (☎ 428-3000), Rivadavia 26/28, Oficina 4. The nonprofit student travel agency Asatej (☎ 423-7421) shares an office with Alessandria Viajes at Belgrano 194.

Medical Services

The emergency hospital (☎ 421-0243) is at Catamarca and Blvd Guzmán.

CENTRO

Downtown Córdoba is a treasure of colonial buildings and other historical monuments.

Cathedral

Begun in 1577, the construction of Córdoba's cathedral dragged on for over two centuries under several architects, including Jesuits and Franciscans, and though impressive, lacks any sense of architectural unity. Crowned by a Romanesque dome, it overlooks Plaza San Martín, at Independencia and 27 de Abril.

Interred within the cathedral are several notable figures in Argentine and regional history, including Gregorio Funes (a cleric and an important politician in the early independence period); General José María Paz (a military strategist and politician who fought as a young man in the wars of independence, and later against Rosas and other Federalist caudillos); and Fray Mamerto Esquiú (a Catamarca-born Franciscan priest who strongly influenced Argentina's constitution of 1853).

Manzana Jesuítica

Córdoba's Jesuit Block, like that of Buenos Aires, is also known as the Manzana de las Luces or 'Block of Enlightenment,' and was initially associated with the influential Jesuit order.

Designed by the Flemish Padre Philippe Lemaire, the **Iglesia Compañía de Jesús**, at Obispo Trejo and Caseros, dates from 1645 but was not completed until 1671, with the successful execution of Lemaire's plan for a cedar roof in the form of an inverted ship's hull. Lemaire was once, unsurprisingly, a boat builder. It has a modest exterior and an ornate but tasteful interior, with a baroque altarpiece carved of Paraguayan cedar from Misiones Province. The **Capilla Doméstica** *(Domestic Chapel; free; guided tours 10am Tues, 5pm Thur, 10am & 5pm weekends),* completed in 1644, sits directly behind the church on Caseros. Its ornate ceiling was made with cowhide stretched over a skeleton of thick taguaro cane and painted with pigments composed partially of boiled bones.

In 1613, Fray Fernando de Trejo y Sanabria founded the Seminario Convictorio de San Javier, which, after being elevated to university status in 1622, became the **Universidad Nacional de Córdoba**. At Obispo Trejo 242, the university is the oldest in the country and contains, among other national treasures, part of the Jesuits' Grand Library.

Next door, at Obispo Trejo 294, the **Colegio Nacional de Monserrat** dates from 1782, though the college itself was founded in 1687 and transferred after the Jesuit expulsion. Though the interior cloisters are original, the exterior was considerably modified in 1927 by restoring architect Jaime Roca, who gave the building its present baroque flare.

In 2000, UNESCO declared the Manzana Jesuítica a World Heritage Site,

along with five Jesuit estancias throughout the province.

Museo Histórico Provincial Marqués de Sobremonte

This claims to be one of the country's most important historical museums *(☎ 433-1661 Rosario de Santa Fe 218; admission US$1 open 9am-1pm & 3pm-7pm Tues-Sat, 10am 1pm Sun, morning only Mon-Sat summer)* It is housed in an 18th-century house that once belonged to Rafael Núñez, the colonial governor of Córdoba and later Viceroyal of the Río de la Plata. It has 26 rooms and five interior patios, but its most notable feature is a wrought-iron balcony supported by carved wooden brackets. Exhibits include collections of religious paintings, indigenous and gaucho weapons, musical instruments, leather and wooden trunks, furniture and other miscellany.

Cripta Jesuítica

The Jesuits, at the beginning of the 18th century, built the Cripta Jesuítica *(no ☎ Rivera Indarte & Av Colón; free; open 9am 8pm weekdays, 9am-1pm & 3pm-7pm weekends).* It was originally designed as a novitiate and later converted to a crypt and crematorium. Abandoned after the Jesuit expulsion, it was demolished and buried around 1829 when the city, while expanding Av Colón, knocked the roof into the subterranean naves and built over the entire structure. It remained all but forgotten until Telecom, while laying underground telephone cable in 1989, accidentally ran into it The city, with a new outlook on such national treasures, exquisitely restored the crypt and uses it regularly for musical and theatrical performances and conferences Entrances, which one might mistake for subway stairs, lie on either side of Av Colón in the middle of the Rivera Indarte pedestrian mall.

Museo Municipal de Bellas Artes Dr Genaro Pérez

This museum is prized for its collection of cordobés paintings from the 19th and 20th centuries. Works, including those by Emilio

Caraffa, Lucio Fontana, Lino Spilimbergo, Antonio Berni and Antonio Seguí, chronologically display the history of the cordobés school of painting, at the front of which stands the museum's namesake, Genaro Pérez. The Palacio Garzón, an unusual turn-of-the-century building named for its original owner, houses the museum (☎ 433-1512, Av General Paz 33; free; open 9:30am-1:30pm & 4:30pm-8:30pm Tues-Fri, 10am-8pm weekends).

Plaza San Martín & Around

The plaza dates to 1577 and, besides being the official city center, is still kilometer-zero for the oldest provincial roads. The plaza's western side is dominated by the white arcade of the restored Cabildo, completed in 1785 and containing three interior patios, as well as basement cells. All are open to the public as part of the Museo de la Ciudad (☎ 433-1543, Independencia 30; free; open 4pm-9pm Mon, 9am-1pm Tues-Sun), which also exhibits relics from the city's past and a few contemporary art pieces.

The slightly hidden Casa del Obispo Mercadillo, at Rosario de Santa Fe 39 on the plaza's northern side, is worth a look for its impressive colonial wrought-iron balcony.

Occupying nearly half a city block, at the corner of Caseros and Independencia, the Iglesia de Santa Teresa y Convento de Carmelitas Descalzas de San José was completed in 1628 and has functioned ever since as a closed-order convent for Carmelite nuns. Only the church itself is open to visitors. Once part of the convent, the Museo de Arte Religioso Juan de Tejeda (☎ 423-0175, Independencia 122; admission US$1; open 9:30am-12:30pm Wed-Sat), next door, exhibits religious artifacts, as well as paintings by cordobés masters including Emilio Caraffa, Genaro Pérez and Antonio Seguí.

The Hospital San Roque, at the corner of Santa Fe and Salta, dates from 1763, though most of the building is newer. Alongside it, the Iglesia San Roque (1764) retains more of its historical integrity. Later ecclesiastical landmarks include the Basílica Nuestra Señora de la Merced, completed in 1826, on Rivadavia between Av Olmos and 25 de Mayo, and the Basílica de Santo Domingo (1857-61), at the corner of Av General Paz and Deán Funes. The latter houses the Virgen del Rosario y del Milagro, the patron saint of Córdoba.

There are guided tours of the provincial legislature (Rivera Indarte & Deán Funes; free; tours 11am weekdays), which was completed in 1885.

NUEVA CÓRDOBA

Before the northwestern neighborhoods of Chateau Carreras and Cerro de las Rosas lured the city's elite to their peaceful hillsides, Nueva Córdoba was the neighborhood of the cordobés aristocracy. The area, loosely bound by Av Vélez Sársfield, Blvd Illia and Parque Sarmiento, was, until very recently, characterized primarily by its turn-of-the-century, neoclassical architecture. A recent building craze, due primarily to the area's burgeoning popularity among students, gave the area its new architectural characteristic – brick high-rise apartment towers. Still, a stroll past the stately old residences that line the wide Av Yrigoyen reveals the area's aristocratic past.

Nueva Córdoba's landmark building, the private Palacio Ferrerya, stands nearly hidden behind a hedge-covered fence just before Plaza España at the southern end of Yrigoyen. It was built in 1900 and designed by Ernest Sanson in the Louis XVI style. On the way down Yrigoyen, swing a left on Obispo Oro to see the neo-Gothic Parroquia Sagrado Corazón de Jesús (de los Capuchinos) at Buenos Aires. It was built between 1928 and 1934. Among the numerous sculptures that cover the churches façade are those of Atlases symbolically struggling to bare the spiritual weight of the religious figures above them (and sins and guilt of the rest of us).

One of the city's best modern art museums is the neoclassical Museo Provincial de Bellas Artes Emilio Caraffa (☎ 433-3414, Yrigoyen 651, Plaza España; admission US$2; open 11am-7pm Tues-Sun). It stands ostentatiously on the western side of Plaza España. Architect Juan Kronfuss designed the building as a museum and it was inaugurated in 1916.

South of the museum the city unfolds into its largest open-space area, the **Parque Sarmiento**, designed by Charles Thays, the architect who designed Mendoza's Parque General San Martín.

GÜEMES

Once a strictly working-class neighborhood, Güemes is now known for the eclectic **antique stores** and **artisan shops** that line the main drag of Belgrano, between Rodriguez and Laprida, and its weekend **feria artesanal** (*Rodriguez & Belgrano; open 4pm-10pm weekends*) with antique vendors, arts and crafts and a healthy dose of Córdobas' hippies. Güemes also has numerous excellent restaurants. A good way back to the city center is along **La Cañada**, an acacia-lined stone canal that runs dry in the summer and flows plentifully in fall and winter. Inspired by a severe flood in 1939, it was completed in 1943 to keep winter run-off at bay.

SPECIAL EVENTS

During the first three weeks of April, the city puts on a large crafts market (locally called 'FICA') at the city fairgrounds, on the town's north side near Chateau Carrera stadium. Bus No 31 from Plaza San Martín goes there.

Córdoba celebrates the founding of the city on July 6. Mid-September's Feria del Libro is a regional book fair, smaller than Buenos Aires' but still significant enough to draw literary figures of the stature of Eduardo Galeano; Córdoba is a notable regional publishing center.

PLACES TO STAY
Budget

As usual, most economy lodging is near the bus terminal and the train station. The nearest *campground (no ☎)* is in Parque General San Martín, 13km from downtown. City bus No 31 from Plaza San Martín goes as far as the Complejo Ferial (fair complex), leaving about 1km left to hitch or walk. The campground itself is spacious, but there's only limited shade. Showers and toilets could be cleaner and

the water supply is unreliable, but it's passable. Sites cost around US$4.

Residencial Thanoa (☎ 421-7279, San Jerónimo 479) Singles/doubles US$10/15 with shared bath. Spacious, slightly dilapidated rooms have double doors opening onto an interior patio. It's very basic but cheerful and cheap.

Hospedaje Suzy (no ☎, Entre Ríos 528) Singles/doubles US$15/24 with shared bath. This no-frills, single-story, owner-operated hotel has a pleasant, safe feel and clean rooms.

Residencial Victoria (☎ 421-0189, 25 de Mayo 240) Singles/doubles US$15/30 with bath, US$10 per person with shared bath. This sprawling hotel in a turn-of-the-century building has an anonymous feel, drab rooms and several beat-up communal kitchens; the owners are slowly remodeling.

Hotel Florida (☎ 422-6373, Rosario de Santa Fe 459) Singles/doubles US$20/30 with bath, US$25/35 with air-conditioning & TV. These ample rooms have interior windows and are all good values.

Hotel Roma Termini (☎ 421-9398, Entre Ríos 687) Singles/doubles US$20/28 with bath, TV & telephone. Though it's a dull area, the price is good for this well-kept place with substantial baths.

Gran Hotel Bristol (☎ 423-9950, fax 423-2216, Pasaje Tómas Oliver 64) Singles/doubles US$20/30 with bath & TV. This nondescript high-rise is fine if you get a balcony, otherwise the mustiness can make the rooms a bit claustrophobic.

Mid-Range

Prices for all mid-range hotels include private bathrooms.

Hotel Garden (☎ 421-4729, 25 de Mayo 35) Singles/doubles US$20/40 with TV. This attractive, spotless hotel has an excellent location, a friendly staff, firm beds, good showers and two interior patios.

Hotel Gran Rex (☎ 423-8659, fax 423-8961, Vélez Sársfield 601) Singles/doubles US$27/42 with TV & breakfast. The Gran Rex is a large, old, impersonal place with clean, worn rooms.

Hotel Viña de Italia (☎ 422-6589, e vitalia@infovia.com.ar, San Jerónimo

611) Singles/doubles US$30/45 with breakfast & parking. There's a bit of elegance left in this hotel, and the mid-size rooms all include TV, telephone, air-con and heat.

Hotel Heydi (☎ *421-8906,* e *hotel heydi@arnet.com.ar, Illia 615)* Singles/ doubles US$35/49. This is the best of the bunch near the bus terminal – a modern place with a friendly staff and lots of extended-stay students.

Hotel Riviera (☎ *422-3969, Balcarce 74)* Singles/doubles around US$35/50. With tile floors, firm beds and large baths, this Spartan hotel near the bus terminal is almost uncomfortably clean.

Hotel Dallas (☎ *421-6091, San Jerónimo 339)* Singles/doubles US$42/53. This unique, spotless hotel has a pseudo-Victorian common-room, complete with fireplace, and dark, comfortable rooms with good baths.

Hotel Sussex (☎ *422-9070/75,* e *hotel sussex@onenet.com.ar, San Jerónimo 125)* Singles/doubles US$45/60 with breakfast, TV & telephone. In a beautiful building only a block off the main plaza, the Sussex is one of Córdoba's oldest hotels, though its remodeled rooms have a worn '70s feel. The 11th-floor restaurant has stunning views.

Hotel Waldorf (☎/fax *422-8051,* e *conser jeria@hotelwaldorfcba.com, Av Olmos 531)* Singles/doubles US$45/50 with breakfast, parking, TV & telephone. In a lifeless location, the Waldorf has decent, carpeted rooms, large bathrooms in addition to a 2pm checkout.

Top End

Córdoba's top-end hotels cater to the city's itinerant business crowd, and most offer substantial weekend discounts. All prices include breakfast and en-suite bathroom, TV, telephone and air-con.

Hotel Mediterráneo (☎ *424-0086, fax 424-0111,* e *hotelmed@satlink.com, Av Marcelo de Alvear 10)* Singles/doubles US$54/75. The Mediterráneo has a first-floor pool and sundeck and generic rooms with good beds.

Hotel Felipe II (☎ *421-4752,* e *hotelfel@ satlink.com.ar, San Jerónimo 279)* Singles/ doubles US$62/80. The downstairs decor is

chic, the café and bar are crowded, and the rooms are appealing.

Hotel de la Cañada (☎ *421-4649,* e *hdelac@agora.com.ar, Av Alvear 580)* Singles/doubles US$71/94. This stylish wood and brick construction near the Cañada is one of the city's swankiest hotels. Rooms are immaculate and perks include a swimming pool, sauna, gym, terrace bar and an army of uppity staff members.

Hotel NH Panorama (☎ *420-4000, fax 410-3900,* e *info@nh-panorama.com.ar, Marcelo T de Alvear 251)* Doubles US$100. This immaculate hotel on the Cañada has a swimming pool, sauna, an attentive staff and an ultra-modern feel.

Ducal Suites (☎ *426-8888, fax 426-8840, Corrientes 207)* Singles/doubles US$110/ 130. This is another modern beauty, where guests have access to a pool, gym, sauna and jacuzzis; the spacious rooms have kitchenettes, but no utensils.

PLACES TO EAT
Budget

Mercado Norte (Rivadavia & Oncativo) has excellent inexpensive eats, such as pizza, empanadas and lager beer. Many other cheap eateries line Blvd Perón, near the train and bus terminals, and along side streets such as San Jerónimo, numerous video bars serve meals – the evening's shows are posted outside.

Patio Olmos Food Courts (Illia & Vélez Sársfield) Mains US$3.50-7. Several readers have pointed out these fast-food counters in the Patio Olmos Shopping Center for everything from sandwiches and salads to Chinese and Mexican food.

For cheap Middle Eastern food try *La Zete* (☎ *421-6352, Corrientes & Salguero).* Near the bus terminal, both **Formula 500** (☎ *421-9952, Entre Ríos 601)* and *Mc Rico's* (☎ *428-1684),* across the street, serve cheap *lomitos* (steak sandwiches), pastas and the like. The best hot churros in town are pumped out at the *churro stand* on San Martín just north of the plaza.

5 Esquinas Empanadas (*Garzón 491)* This hole-in-the-wall whips out excellent, fresh-baked empanadas to go at only US$0.50 a pop.

Verde Que te Quiero Verde (☎ 421-8820, 9 de Julio 36) Mains US$3-7; open lunch only. Lunch specials are cheap at this excellent vegetarian restaurant, but you'll double your tab buying servings by the kilo at the irresistible buffet counter.

Sol & Luna (☎ 425-1189, General Paz 278) Mains US$3 & up. One reader recommends this vegetarian restaurant for an excellent buffet of pizzas, grains, salads and desserts.

La Perla (☎ 421-4112, Olmos 265) Mains US$4-12; open noon-3:30pm & 8pm-12:30am daily. This popular, down-home eatery, with a hilariously attentive staff, has huge lunch specials and filling Italian- and Spanish-influenced mains.

Rock & Fellers (☎ 424-3960, Yrigoyen 320) Mains US$6; open 7am-4am weekdays, 9am-4am weekends. Burgers, Tex-Mex dishes and sandwiches make the top 10 at this rock-and-roll diner and bar.

Mandarina (☎ 426-4909, Obispo Trejo 171) Mains US$6-15. Chinese cuisine, pizzas and pastas are cooked with flare at this cozy hideaway, and the mixed drinks are enormous.

Mid-Range & Top End

La Nieta 'e La Pancha (☎ 469-0229, Belgrano 783) Mains US$10-18; open 8pm-1am Tues-Sun. A wonderful staff prepares and serves delectable regional specialties, including an excellent *cabrito adobado* (marinated kid). It's also one of the few places that serves *mate*.

Las Tinajas (☎ 411-4150, San Juan 32) Lunch US$6 weekdays, US$10 weekends, dinner US$10 nightly. The country's largest *tenedor libre* (all-you-can-eat) serves a mind-boggling array of international cuisine.

El Ruedo (☎ 422-4453, Obispo Trejo 84) The food is unremarkable but the outdoor tables on the *peatonal* (pedestrian mall) are great for people-watching in a beautiful spot.

Alcorta (☎ 424-7452, Alcorta 330) Mains US$11-20; open lunch & dinner. This up-market parrilla, esteemed for its grilled meats, also serves delicious pasta and fish.

El Arrabal (☎ 460-2990, Belgrano 899) Mains US$12-25. Imaginative regional and house specialties include pork medallions in an herbed wine sauce. Pastas start around US$6, and the parrillada is delicious. The real reason to come, however, is for the live music – tango every night after 11pm. Make a reservation.

Las Rías de Galicia (☎ 428-1333, Montevideo 271) Mains US$10-18. It's hard to top the seafood, especially the shellfish, at this stylish place. It also offers a three-course *menú ejecutivo* (fixed lunch) for US$7.50 with drink.

ENTERTAINMENT

The city offers two-hour tango lessons (weather permitting) on the outdoor **Patio del Tango** in the Patio Mayor of the historic Cabildo, Friday evenings at 9:30pm. Contact the municipal tourist office (☎ 428-5856) in the Cabildo for information.

La Voz del Interior, Córdoba's main newspaper, has a reasonably comprehensive entertainment section with show times and the like.

Dance Clubs

Clubbing in Córdoba usually means one of two neighborhoods: Chateau Carreras or Mercado Abasto. The largest, trendiest and many claim best, *boliches* (nightclubs) are around the intersection of Av Cárcano and del Diamante in Chateau Carreras. To get there, take Bus No 31 from the Plaza San Martín; a cab is the easiest way back. The Mercado Abasto (also called as the *zona roja* or red-light district), has an edgier feel, is closer to downtown and has numerous extremely popular (though perhaps less fashion-minded) discos. Cab drivers know the clubs.

Carreras (mobile ☎ 15-676-2767, Cárcano & del Diamante, Chateau Carreras) This is the city's premier disco, the place to be seen, the club of clubs, the only place the fashion-set would ever be caught.

Hangar 18 (no ☎, Blvd Las Heras 118, Mercado Abasto) Córdoba's definitive gay disco attracts a diverse crowd and excellent DJs. On a good night the whole place can lose its collective head.

El Mariscal (☎ 15-563-7333, 15-509-9654, Bajada Alvear 69, Mercado Abasto) This is a smaller club where house and techno are the standards. As usual, when the DJs are good, it's good.

Capitán Blue (no ☎, Carlos Tillard 115, Mercado Abasto) This popular after-hours club doesn't get moving until around 5am, peaking well after dawn.

La Belle (no ☎, Bajada Alvear & Vias Ferrocarril, Mercado Abasto) The prime night here is Thursday night, when the place gets absurdly packed with beer-swilling boogiers, shaking to everything from Creedence to The Cure.

Other top clubs in Chateau Carreras include **Villa Pancho**, **Rosa Mora** and, for trance, *El Rey (☎ 484-3135, del Diamante s/n)*, all in the Cárcano-del Diamante area.

Downtown, try the amiable and smaller *Costa Cañada (no ☎, de Alvear 386)*.

Bars

Córdoba's drink of choice is Fernet (a strong, medicinal tasting, herbed liquor from Italy), almost always mixed with Coke. If you don't mind a rough morning, start in on the *Fernet con Coke* – it gets addictive.

María María (no ☎, San Juan 230) Across from Patio Olmos, this dark, cozy bar often gets excellent bands playing a variety of styles. It's a comfortable place good for dancing or sitting around.

Dublin (☎ 460-1651, Chacabuco 605) Open 11pm-4am weekdays, 8pm-late weekends. Though the *craic* is a little less than Irish, the tables and booths are comfy, the food is good and the Guinness is, well, US$4.80 a can.

El Infierno (☎ 15-542-3601, Independencia & Montevideo) Open 11pm-late Wed-Sat. A variety of music and a boisterous crowd make for a fun, noisy bar with dim parlor ambience.

Both **Rock & Fellers** and **Mandarina** (see Places to Eat) are good, mellow places to knock a few back over a conversation that doesn't require straining your vocal chords.

Theater

Teatro del Libertador General San Martín (☎ 433-2319, ⓦ www.teatrolibertador.com.ar, Vélez Sársfield 365) Box office open 9am-9pm. It's well worth going to a performance here, if only to see the opulence of the country's most historic theater. Also known as the Teatro Nuevo or the Teatro Rivera Indarte (its original name) the theater was completed in 1891, designed by the Italian engineer Francisco Tamburini. The floor was designed to be mechanically raised and leveled to the stage, so seats could be removed, allowing for grand parties among the aristocracy of the early 1900s. Be discreet if you bring your camera.

Teatro Real (☎ 433-1670, San Jerónimo 66) This is Córdoba's main performance hall after the Teatro San Martín. Programs are available at the box office.

SPECTATOR SPORTS

Córdoba's first-division soccer teams are Belgrano (referred to as 'La B') and Talleres de Córdoba (unsurprisingly, 'La T'). Both have their own stadiums but play most of their games at the Estadio Olímpico de Córdoba (☎ 481-2829, Parque Chateau Carreras), built for the 1978 World Cup. Take Bus No 31 to get there. Belgrano's stadium and offices (☎ 480-0852) are at Arturo Orgaz 510. The Talleres stadium is at General Ricchieri 1595, while its offices (☎ 423-3576) are downtown at Rosario de Santa Fe 11.

SHOPPING

Antique stores line Calle Belgrano in Barrio Güemes, where there is also a fun weekend arts and crafts fair (see Barrio Güemes, earlier). Otherwise try the following stores downtown.

Regionales La Fama (☎ 422-8354, fax 425-8385, 9 de Julio 336) Open 9am-6pm weekdays, 9am-1pm Sat. This store deals in high-quality artisan knives, leather goods, alpaca woolens and other regional crafts.

La Emilia (☎ 423-8402, Deán Funes 18) Though this shop has its share of shoddy souvenirs, there's still plenty of good regional crafts to choose from.

ARGENTINA

GETTING THERE & AWAY
Air
Aerolíneas Argentinas and Austral share offices (☎/fax 482-1025) at Av Colón 520. Aerolíneas has more than 40 flights weekly to Buenos Aires (US$47 to US$148), as well as a daily flight to Mendoza (US$64 to US$69). Austral has 60 a week to Buenos Aires and over 20 to Mendoza.

LAPA (☎ 426-3336), Av Colón 534, flies four times daily to Buenos Aires (from US$86). Dinar (☎ 426-2020), Av Colón 533, flies twice daily weekdays and once Saturday to Buenos Aires; the morning flight connects to Comodoro Rivadavia.

Southern Winds (☎ 446-7866), Av Colón 544, flies several times a day to Buenos Aires, Mendoza, Rosario, Salta and Tucumán; and at least once daily to Santa Fe, Resistencia, San Juan, Neuquén Río Gallegos, Comodoro Rivadavia and Ushuaia. It flies four times a week to Bariloche, and to El Calafate on weekends.

Bus
The Córdoba bus terminal (NETOC; ☎ 423-4199, 423-0532) is at Blvd Perón 300. Facilities include a pharmacy, travel agency, post office, day-care center, photo lab, banks and ATMs, public telephones, shops, restaurants and other utterly unexpected services, such as hot showers. Almost an afterthought, dozens of bus companies serve local, provincial, national and international destinations.

Sierras del Córdoba, Sierras de Calamuchita and Transportes La Cumbre all serve Córdoba's mountain hinterlands, including Villa General Belgrano (US$6; 2 hours), Mina Clavero (US$10.65; 3 hours) and Villa de las Rosas (US$11; 4 hours). Other nearby mountain destinations are easier and more quickly reached from the Mercado Sur minibus terminal (see Minibus, later).

Buses to Patagonia are invariably *coche cama* (sleepers), usually with breakfast and dinner.

There are often several and sometimes more than a dozen daily departures to the destinations listed below. Check the terminal tourist office (☎ 433-1980) for the best deals, cheapest fares and highest services. The following prices are mid-low season and will fluctuate between companies and with the country's travel demands.

Destination	Duration in hours	Cost
Bahía Blanca	12	US$48
Bariloche	22	US$70
Buenos Aires	10	US$16-60
Catamarca	6	US$13
Comodoro Rivadavia	25	US$80
Corrientes	12	US$39
Esquel	25	US$84
Formosa	15	US$42
Jujuy	12	US$25
La Plata	11	US$27
Mar del Plata	16	US$55
Merlo	5½	US$12
Montevideo	15	US$47
Neuquén	16	US$48
Paraná	6	US$16
Puerto Iguazú	20	US$48
Puerto Madryn	18	US$71
Resistencia	12	US$38
Río Gallegos	36	US$105
Roque Sáenz Peña	14	US$45
Rosario	6	US$25
Salta	12	US$35
San Juan	7	US$20
San Luis	6	US$14
San Martín de los Andes	22	US$70
Santa Fe	5	US$15
Santiago del Estero	5	US$17
Tandil	15	US$45
Trelew	20	US$63
Tucumán	8	US$17

Among others, Expreso Uspallata, TAC and Tas Choapa sell connecting tickets to Chilean destinations including Santiago and Val Paraiso (both US$35; 16 hours), though most involve changing buses in Mendoza.

La Veloz del Norte goes to Orán (US$38; 15 hours), on the Bolivian border, while Panamericano, Atahualpa and El Tucumano go to Tucumán and Salta, continuing to Bolivian border crossings at La Quiaca and

Pocitos. Expreso Encon goes to Paso de los Libres, on the Brazilian border, via Av Colón and Concordia. Cora serves Montevideo four times weekly with connections to Brazil; Penha also has Brazilian services. There are at least two weekly services to Asunción, Paraguay (US$57; 15 hours).

Minibus

Frequent minibuses go to Villa Carlos Paz (US$2.25; 45 minutes), Cosquín (US$3.50; 1¼ hours), La Falda (US$4.75; 2 hours), La Cumbre (US$6; 2½ hours), Capilla del Monte (US$7; 3 hours), Jesús María (US$2.60; 1 hour) and Alta Gracia (US$2.10; 1 hour) and leave from the Mercado Sur Minibus Terminal on Blvd Illia, between Buenos Aires and Ituzaingo.

Train

When it is functioning (at the time of writing it was not), the tourist-oriented Tren de las Sierras (☎ 482-2252) leaves the Mitre train station on weekends for Cosquín (2 hours), La Falda, Huerta Grande (2½ hours), La Cumbre and Capilla del Monte (3¾ hours). Contact the Casa Cabildo tourist office (see Tourist Offices, earlier) for ever-changing information.

GETTING AROUND

Pajas Blancas Airport (☎ 484-8390) is 15km north of town via Av Monseñor Pablo Cabrera. From the main bus terminal, the Empresa Ciudad de Córdoba bus marked 'Salsipuedes' goes to the airport.

For US$3.50, Rubin Turismo (☎ 422-5857), at San Martín 5, office 2, offers hourly shuttle service to the airport.

At the time of writing, city buses required *cospeles* (tokens), available for US$0.70 from kiosks. However, the city was considering revamping its entire system of local bus transport. If it does, fare collection, as well as bus numbers, will more than likely change. The city bus numbers and information in this chapter refer to the original system. Check with the tourist office for updated information.

A car is very useful for visiting some of the nearby Jesuit estancias that cannot be reached by bus. The only convenient rental car agency is AI (☎ 422-4867, **e** rentacar@ powernet.com.ar), in the Hotel Dorá, at Entre Ríos 70, or at the airport (☎ 481-7157). Prices start around US$42 per day and US$0.23 per kilometer over 50km.

The Central Sierras

The Central Sierras tend to take a back seat, at least in the eyes of foreigners, to the dramatic scenery of the nearby Andes, but the area's small resort towns and outdoor opportunities are boundless. The beautifully situated towns of La Falda, La Cumbre and Capilla del Monte lie north of the capital along the RN 38 in the Punilla Valley and are great spots to simply kick back, hike or swim, especially in spring and fall when the crowds thin out. Southwest of the capital are the towns of Alta Gracia, with its Jesuit ruins, and Villa General Belgrano, an odd Germanesque resort. RN 20 is the southwestern route through the spectacular Altas Cumbres, crossing the southern mountains to the river-crossed town of Mina Clavero and down the western slopes of the Sierra de Comechingones to the mountain resort of Merlo, on the eastern edge of San Luis Province.

The provincial tourist office in Córdoba provides thorough maps and slick brochures of the entire region. The towns covered in this section are easily accessible by public transport (see Getting There & Away in the Córdoba section, earlier), but many tiny, remote towns and Jesuit estancias can only be reached with your own wheels. The Sierras' dense network of roads, many well-paved but others only gravel, make them good candidates for bicycle touring; Argentine drivers here seem a bit less ruthless than elsewhere in the country. A mountain bike is still the best choice.

Outside the busy summer season, prices for accommodations can be much lower (sometimes by at least half) and bargaining is possible, but many places close by the end of March. Unless noted otherwise, prices listed throughout this section are for high season.

THE CENTRAL SIERRAS

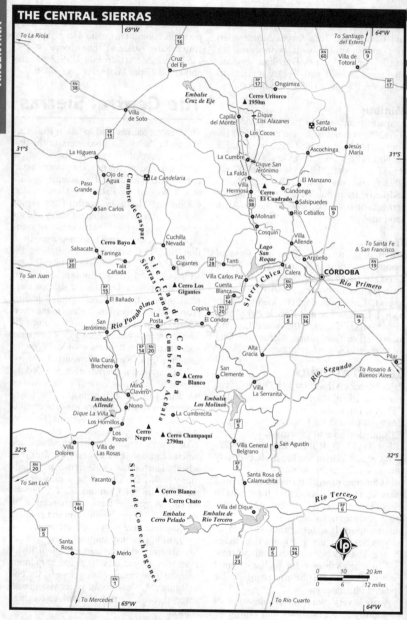

VILLA CARLOS PAZ
☎ 03541 • pop 46,400 • elevation 600m

Only 36km west of Córdoba, on the shores of so-called Lago San Roque (in reality, a large reservoir), Villa Carlos Paz is a minor-league, freshwater Mar del Plata with more than 12,000 hotel spaces. In summer, thousands of tourists crowd its lakeshores, pack its dance floors and descend upon its disproportionate number of kitschy attractions, including a monstrous cuckoo clock, a chairlift and an action-packed Wild West gunfighter village.

The well-organized tourist office (☎ 436430, W www.carlospazturismo.com.ar), in the middle of the San Martín-Yrigoyen intersection, is open 7am to 11pm in summer, 7am to 9pm the rest of the year; there's a branch office (☎ 421624) at the bus terminal at San Martín 400. Both distribute useful maps and guides to local services.

The post office is at Av San Martín 190; the postal code is 5152. There are several locutorios along Av San Martín; ATMs are numerous.

Things to See & Do
Almost every Argentine household seems to have photos of family members riding the **Aerosilla Carlos Paz** (☎ 422254; admission US$10; open year-round), a chairlift that has carried tens of thousands to the 953m summit of Cerro de la Cruz since 1955. People mysteriously flock, cameras ready, to the giant **cuckoo clock** in the middle of the Av Uruguay-Sarmiento roundabout and wait for the bird to pop out on the hour.

Places to Stay
ACA Campground (☎ 422132, Av San Martín & Nahuel Huapi) Of the town's two campgrounds, this one on the lakeshore is the best. To get there take Bus No 1 from Av San Martín.

Carlos Paz admittedly has some excellent hotels, but they're packed through the summer; the tourist office offers a complete list.

Hostel Acapulco (☎ 421929, e chrisproch @hotmail.com, La Paz 75) Rooms US$10 per person with kitchen privileges, pool, sundeck and laundry facilities. Though slightly run-down, these mini-apartments, sleeping two to six people, are an excellent deal.

Hotel Ritz (☎ 422126, e hotelritz@ arnet.com.ar, Uruguay 38) Singles/doubles US$16/25 with breakfast, TV & telephone. This is a cheerful place on an ugly street with a kitschy interior and friendly owners.

Hostería Alpenrose (☎/fax 430095, Hipólito Yrigoyen 615) Low season singles/doubles US$25/36 with breakfast, TV & telephone. This beautiful brick hotel with copious windows has a pool, a yard and excellent rooms.

Places to Eat
Dozens of restaurants line 9 de Julio just north of the river.

Guacamole Ranch (☎ 432613, 9 de Julio 50) Mains US$3.50-5. The lineup at this Mexican restaurant includes burritos, nachos, tacos and a good guacamole-chicken sandwich.

La Playa del Ciervo (☎ 15-530850) Open 10:30am-7:30pm weekdays, 10:30am-1am weekends. Try this outdoor café, at the end of Irigoyen on the lake, for an afternoon beer or evening coffee.

Entertainment
People drive hours to Carlos Paz just to go to *Keops* (☎ 422647, Roque Sáenz Peña & Séneca), one of the province's most legendary dance clubs. For *quarteto, cumbia,* salsa and *rock nacional,* try *Coyote* (☎ 434666, Av Illia s/n), on the river mouth just below the Uruguay bridge.

Getting There & Away
Buses head to Córdoba (US$3; 45 minutes) every 15 minutes from the bus terminal at San Martín 400. There are regular departures to Alta Gracia (US$2.25; 1 hour), Cosquín (US$2.10; 30 minutes), La Falda (US$3.40; 45 minutes) and La Cumbre (US$4.30; 1¾ hours).

Some long-distance companies from Buenos Aires (from US$20) start and end their Córdoba routes here. There are daily services to La Plata (US$30; 12 hours), Paraná (US$20; 7 hours), Mendoza (US$20; 10 hours), Rosario (US$24; 7 hours), San Juan (US$20; 7 hours) and Santa Fe (US$18; 6 hours).

COSQUÍN

☎ 03541 • pop 18,000 • elevation 720m

Cosquín, 26km north of Carlos Paz on the RN 38, is known for its Festival Nacional del Folklore, a nine-day national folk music festival, held the last week of January since 1961. The town gets packed for the festival, stays busy all summer and goes pleasantly dead the rest of the year. The surrounding countryside and numerous *balnearios* (river beaches) make the town one of the more appealing destinations near the provincial capital, only 63km away via RN 38.

The municipal tourist office (☎ 453701), San Martín 560, is open 8am to 9pm weekdays, 9am to 6pm weekends, and has a good map of the town. Cosquín's postal code is 5166.

Things to See & Do

The most popular **swimming hole**, with an 8m diving platform, is La Toma, at the end of Pan de Azúcar off San Martín on the Río Cosquín. East of town, 1260m **Cerro Pan de Azúcar** offers good views of the Sierras and, on a clear day, the city of Córdoba. Hitch or walk (buses are few) 5km to a saddle where a steep 25-minute climb to the summit will save you US$7 for the *aerosilla* (chairlift). Otherwise, a taxi there runs about US$13 roundtrip, and the driver will wait while you ride.

Places to Stay & Eat

The nearest campground is *Camping Festival* (☎ 480577), at Santa María de la Punilla, about 4km south of Cosquín.

Hotel Ideal (☎ 453043, Perón 1159) Singles/doubles US$15/25 with bath, TV & fan. Near the bus terminal, this pleasant, owner-operated hotel is wonderfully friendly and reasonably comfortable.

Petit Hotel (☎ 451311, A Sabattini 739) Singles/doubles US$27/37. This friendly,

quiet hotel has an attractive patio with a parrilla for asados.

Hotel del Valle (☎ 452802, San Martín 330) Singles/doubles US$40/50. This is a friendly place near the river.

Paraíso de las Sierras (☎/fax 452190, ℮ paraiso@argosmail.com.ar, San Martín 729) Singles/doubles US$65/75. The well-landscaped back patio, complete with pool and bar, makes this modern place very inviting.

Pizzería Raffaelo (no ☎, San Martín 730) Mains US$5-10. This place is known for its pizzas, but don't shy away from the pastas and empanadas.

Parrilla Saint Jean (☎ 451059, San Martín 200) Mains US$7-20. Locals insist this is the best parrilla in town.

Getting There & Away

There are numerous daily departures north to La Falda (US$1.60; 45 minutes), La Cumbre (US$2.50; 1¼ hours) and Capilla del Monte; and south every 20 minutes to Carlos Paz (US$2.10; 30 minutes) and Córdoba (US$3.50; 1¼ hours). There are direct services to Mendoza (US$23; 14 hours) daily at 11:20pm.

LA FALDA

☎ 03548 • pop 14,617 • elevation 934m

Twenty kilometers north of Cosquín on RN 38, woodsy La Falda sits at the base of the precipitous Sierras Chicas in the center of the Punilla Valley. It prides itself on being the home of the historic (and now defunct) Hotel Eden, built in 1897, where the guest list included the names of Albert Einstein, the Duke of Savoy and several Argentine presidents. Most visitors, however, come simply to escape the bustle of the city, to wander La Falda's hilly streets and explore its surrounding countryside on horseback or by foot.

The tourist office (☎ 423007, ℮ turismo lafalda@ punillanet.com.ar), Av España 50, is open 7am to 9pm daily. The post office is at Av Argentina 199; La Falda's postal code is 5172.

Things to See & Do

One of La Falda's two noteworthy museums is **Museo de Trenes en Miniatura**

Miniature Train Museum; ☎ *423041, Las Murallas 200; admission US$6; open 9:30am-8:30pm summer, 10am-12:30pm & 3pm-7pm Sat, Sun & holidays rest of year).* Ceramics from the region are exhibited at the **Museo Arqueológico Ambato** *(no ☎, Cuesta del Lago 1469, Hotel Eden; admission US$2; open 9:30am-1pm & 3pm-9pm daily).* While there you can take a guided tour of the once extravagant, now decaying **Hotel Eden** *(no ☎; admission US$3; tours 9:30am-1pm & 3pm-7pm daily).*

A favorite **hiking** trail takes about two hours to the nearby summit of 1350m Cerro La Banderita. Pick up a town map to orient yourself and head east to the last intersection on Av Eden and east again on Cuesta del Lago, one block to the north; this turns into Austria, which heads into the hills and eventually toward the summit.

For those interested in **horseback riding**, Sura Elly (☎ 422335) rents horses, normally without guides.

Organized Tours

Turismo Extreme (☎ 425157, e turismo extreme@yahoo.com.ar) offers 4x4 excursions into the surrounding mountains; prices start at US$25. Javier Heredia (☎ 15-635960) is a local nature guide.

Places to Stay & Eat

Camping Balneario Siete Cascadas *(☎ 421207)* Sites US$4 per person. On the Dique La Falda (La Falda reservoir), west of town, this is the closest camping.

Hotel San Remo *(☎ 424875, Av Argentina 105)* Rooms US$12 per person with breakfast. The grassy backyard and pool make this hotel particularly attractive.

Hostería Marina *(☎ 422640, Güemes 134)* Rooms US$12 per person with breakfast. This simple little place has a sunny front patio, a small pool and friendly owners.

Residencial Old Garden *(☎ 422842, Capital Federal 28)* Rooms US$18/36 with breakfast. The live-in owners take excellent care of their guests in this cozy, converted old house with a garden and pool.

La Parrilla de Raúl *(☎ 421128, Av Edén 1000)* Mains US$7-15. This is one of the best parrillas on Av Eden.

Pizza & Pasta Libre *(☎ 425513, Av Eden 500)* For US$3 you can eat all the pizza and pasta you want; it fills the belly.

Getting There & Away

The bus terminal sits on the RN 38, just north of Av Eden. There are regular buses and minibuses south to Cosquín (US$1.60; 45 minutes), Carlos Paz (US$3.40; 1¼ hours), Córdoba (US$4.75; 2 hours) and Mina Clavero (US$13; 4½ hours); and north to La Cumbre (30 minutes) and Capilla del Monte (1 hour). There are regular long-distance runs to Buenos Aires (from US$22; 12 hours), La Rioja (US$15; 6 hours), Mar del Plata (US$46; 18 hours), Santa Fe (US$23; 8 hours), Paraná (US$24; 9 hours) and Rosario (US$29; 7½ hours). Mendoza, San Juan and Resistencia are also frequently served.

If you have a car (or a reliable thumb) the narrow, zigzag Camino El Cuadrado road is a dramatic route over the 1500m Cerro El Cuadrado to Salsipuedes, Río Ceballos and back to Córdoba.

LA CUMBRE

☎ 03548 • pop 7100 • elevation 1141m

Some 18km north of La Falda, La Cumbre sits high in the Punilla Valley on the western shoulders of the Sierras Chicas. La Cumbre means 'the peak' and it took its name in 1892 as the last and highest stop on the old railway line from Córdoba. It's now a painfully relaxing town with an artistic bent and an agreeable mountain climate. La Cumbre is an excellent base for fishing, hiking and horseback riding, but has become famous – world famous – for one pursuit: flying. The launch at nearby Cuchi Corral, 480m above the Punilla Valley floor, was home to the 1999 Paragliding World Cup and draws paragliders and hang gliders from all over for its supreme conditions.

The friendly tourist office (☎ 451154, w www.alacumbre.com) is in the old train station at Av Caraffa 300 near San Martín, not far from the bus terminal. It has a crude but helpful map of the town and surroundings. La Cumbre's postal code is 5178. Banco de la Provincia de Córdoba, at the corner of Lopez y Planes and 25 de Mayo, has an ATM.

Things to See & Do

Trails around town are shown on the map provided by the tourist office. The closest **swimming hole**, El Chorrito, is on the San Jerónimo River a short hike upstream from town. There are excellent views from the **Cristo Redentor**, a 7m statue of Christ on a 300m hilltop east of town; from the Plaza 25 de Mayo, cross the river and walk east on Córdoba toward the mountains, the trail begins after a quick jog to the left after crossing Cabrera. From the Cristo Redentor, a 4km unmarked trail heads southeast to the **San Jerónimo Dam**. At the dam, ask Carlos the caretaker for permission to hike further upstream on the trail, which winds about 15km up to a **rehabilitation center** *(admission US$2; open 9am-8pm)* for black howler monkeys from Formosa Province. The dam can also be reached by road, heading east from the golf course at the southern end of Belgrano.

For **horseback riding** contact Chachito Silva (☎ 451703, Pje Beiró s/n), or Relinchos (☎ 492142, Cruz Grande). Interested in **cycling**? Palmira Bicycles (☎ 452249, Rivadavia 377; US$3/hour, US$10/day) has a few bikes for rent.

If you're taken by a strong urge to go **flying**, be it by paraglider, hang glider or ultralight, contact the Aerodromo La Cumbre (☎ 452544, Camino a los Troncos s/n); the Escuela de Parapentes (☎ 15-631095) at Cuchi Corral; or Extreme (☎ 491677). If you simply want to jump out of a plane, contact Skydive La Cumbre (☎ 451624).

For **guided hikes**, try the Escuela de Montaña G Mallory (☎ 492271).

Places to Stay & Eat

Camping El Cristo (☎ 451893, Monseñor P Cabrera s/n) Site US$5. Below the Cristo Redentor east of town, La Cumbre's exceptional campgrounds are only a short tramp from the center.

Residencial Peti (☎ 452173, General Paz & Rivadavia) Rooms US$12-15 per person with breakfast & bath. Near the bus terminal, the Peti has small, plain rooms and a rooftop terrace.

Hostería Casa Blanca (☎ 451735, Tucumán 60) Rooms US$25 high-season per person with breakfast, US$10-12 low-season per person. This converted old house has spacious rooms, good en-suite bathrooms and a comfortable breakfast room.

Casa Caraffa (no ☎, Caraffa & Rivadavia) Mains US$6-18. Known as 'La Parrilla de Billy' after its attentive owner, this excellent restaurant, across from the tourist office, serves superb meats and delicious pastas.

La Casaona del Toboso (☎ 451436, Belgrano 349) This is another local favorite where you're guaranteed to eat well.

Getting There & Away

Minibuses depart regularly from La Cumbre's convenient bus terminal, at General Paz near Caraffa, and head north to Capilla del Monte or south to La Falda, Cosquín, Villa Carlos Paz and Córdoba (US$6; 2½ hours). There is service to Buenos Aires, but other long-distance buses generally leave from Córdoba.

AROUND LA CUMBRE

Capilla Del Monte is an attractive town (elevation 979m) 18km north of La Cumbre on the RN 38. It not only attracts paragliders and outdoor enthusiasts to its surrounding countryside, but reputedly receives frequent visits from UFOs *(Ovnis)* as well, most frequently to the nearby 1979m-Cerro Uritorco. It has plenty of *restaurants* and *lodging*, and the tourist office (☎ 0548-481341) is at Rivadavia 540. There is frequent bus service south to Córdoba (US$7; 3 hours), stopping at all towns on the RN 38, and long-distance service to Buenos Aires.

JESÚS MARÍA

Forty-eight kilometers north of Córdoba via the RN 9, Jesús María (population 27,000) is home to one of the finest Jesuit estancias.

The Jesuits, after losing their operating capital to pirates off the Brazilian coast, sold wine from Jesús María to support their university in colonial Córdoba; the estancia dates back to 1618. Jesús María is also home to the annual Fiesta Nacional de Doma y Folklore, a celebration of gaucho horsemanship and customs.

Set on superbly landscaped grounds, the church and convent now constitute the **Museo Jesuítico Nacional de Jesús María** (☎ 03525-420126; admission US$1; open 8am-7pm weekdays, 10am-noon & 3pm-7pm weekends summer, 9am-6pm weekdays, 10am-noon & 2pm-6pm weekends winter). The museum has good archaeological pieces from the indigenous Comechingones, informative maps of the missionary trajectory and well-restored (though dubiously authentic) rooms.

Frequent buses leave Córdoba's main bus terminal daily for Jesús María (US$2.60; 1 hour), which has limited accommodations and one notable restaurant, *El Faro*.

ALTA GRACIA
☎ 03547 • pop 39,000 • elevation 550m
Only 35km southwest of Córdoba, the colonial mountain town of Alta Gracia is steeped in history – past illustrious residents range from Jesuit pioneers to Viceroy Santiago Liniers, Spanish composer and civil war refugee Manuel de Falla and revolutionary Che Guevara (who spent his adolescence here). In the first half of the 20th century, the town (whose architecture closely resembles parts of Mar del Plata) was a summer retreat for the Argentine oligarchy, though it's not the social center it once was.

Alta Gracia's main attraction (though the new Che museum may soon gain ground) is its expansive Jesuit estancia, one of the finest in the province. Alta Gracia is an easy day trip from the capital.

Information
The tourist office (☎ 423455) occupies an office in the Reloj Público, the clock tower at the corner of Av del Tajamar and Calle del Molino; hours are 7am to 8pm daily in winter, 7am to 9pm in summer, and until midnight Friday and Saturday in January.

The post office is at the corner of Av Belgrano and Olmos; the postal code is 5186.

Things to See & Do
From 1643 to 1762, Jesuit fathers built the **Iglesia Parroquial Nuestra Señora de la Merced** on the west side of the central Plaza Manuel Solares; directly south of the church, the colonial Jesuit workshops of **El Obraje** (1643) are now a public school.

Liniers, one of the last officials to occupy the post of Viceroy of the River Plate, was a hero for resisting the British invasion of Buenos Aires in 1806, but was executed for his loyalty to Spain and opposition to Argentine independence. Buried in his native France, he once resided in what is now the **Museo Histórico Nacional del Virrey Liniers** (☎ 421303; admission US$2, free Wed; open 9am-1pm & 3pm-7pm Tues-Fri; 9:30am-12:30pm & 3:30pm-6pm Sat, Sun & holidays), alongside the church. Admission includes an informative guided tour.

Directly north of the museum, across Av Belgrano, the **Tajamar** (1659) is one of the city's several 17th-century dams, which together made up the complex system of field irrigation created by the Jesuits. Some blocks west, on Av Vélez Sársfield, is the crumbling **Sierras Hotel**, which, during Alta Gracia's social heyday, was the meeting place for the elite (including Che's relatives). Though the interior is nearly gutted, the exterior is almost intact and there are ostensible plans to refurbish this historic landmark.

In the 1930s, the youthful Ernesto Guevara's family moved here because a doctor recommended the dry climate for his asthma (see boxed text 'The Legend of Che Guevara'). Though Che lived in several houses, the family's primary residence was Villa Beatriz, which stayed a private residence until being purchased recently by the city and converted into the **Museo Casa de Ernesto Che Guevara** (no ☎, Avellaneda 501). Its cozy interior is now adorned with a photographic display of Che's life; the museum was inaugurated on June 14, 2001, what would have been Che's 73rd birthday.

ARGENTINA

The Legend of Che Guevara

One of Cuba's greatest revolutionary heroes, in some ways even eclipsing Fidel Castro himself, was an Argentine. Ernesto Guevara, known by the common Argentine interjection 'che,' was born in the city of Rosario in 1928 and spent his first years in Buenos Aires. In 1932, after Guevara's doctor recommended a drier climate for his severe asthma, Guevara's parents moved to the mountain resort of Alta Gracia, where the young Guevara would spend his adolescence. He later studied medicine in the capital, and, in 1952, spent six months riding a motorcycle around South America, a journey that would steer Guevara's sights beyond middle-class Argentina to the plight of South America's poor. Che later traveled to Central America but was forced to flee Guatemala during the CIA-sponsored ousting of President Jacobo Arbenz; he fatefully landed in Mexico, where he met Fidel Castro and other exiles, who together would sail to Cuba on a rickety old yacht and begin the revolution that overthrew Cuban dictator Fulgencio Batista in 1959.

Ernesto 'Che' Guevara

If you feel like putting ass to saddle, contact Señor Walter Segado (☎ 421504), at Agrupación Gaucho, who offers guided **horseback rides** to visitors in the surrounding mountains.

Places to Stay & Eat

Hostería Asturias (☎ 423668, Vélez Sársfield 127) Singles/doubles US$15/20 with private bath. This hotel is in a fine old railroad building and fills up quickly.

Hostal Hispania (☎/fax 426555, Vélez Sársfield 57) Singles/doubles US$30/50 with breakfast. The rooms are incredibly spacious in this beautiful turn-of-the-century building – an excellent choice.

Trattoria Oro (☎ 422933, España 18) This trattoria, opposite Plaza Manuel Solar, has a varied menu and excellent service.

Getting There & Away

Minibuses to Córdoba (US$2.10; 1 hour) leave regularly from the main plaza at Belgrano near Calle del Molino. Córdoba-bound buses also leave from the new bus terminal at Tacuarí and Perón near the river. Buses to Villa General Belgrano stop every hour on the RP 5 in front of the Bar Don Mario, about 20 blocks out Av San Martín from the center.

VILLA GENERAL BELGRANO
☎ 03546 • pop 6000 • elevation 820m

Surrounded by evergreens high in the Calamuchita Valley, Villa General Belgrano is Córdoba's cultural and gastronomical anomaly. The relaxed resort town deems itself the 'Pueblos de las Culturas' (Village of the Cultures) and flaunts its Teutonic origins as a settlement of unrepatriated survivors from the German battleship *Graf Spee*, which sunk near Montevideo during WWII.

Since 1964 the town has even celebrated its own Oktoberfest (elevated in 1972 to status of National Beer Festival) during the first two weekends in October. Aside from its scenery, Villa General Belgrano is your one chance to fill up on scrumptious pastries, chocolate, *torta selva negra* (black forest cake), goulash and, at the local microbrewery, delicious German style-lagers.

Three small rivers, El Sauce, Los Molles and La Toma, burble through the town,

The Legend of Che Guevara

Unable to resign himself to the bureaucratic task of building Cuban socialism, Guevara tried, unsuccessfully, to spread revolution in the Congo, Argentina and finally Bolivia, where he died in 1967. Today, Che is known less for his eloquent writings and speeches than for his striking black-and-white portrait as the beret-wearing rebel taken by photojournalist Alberto Diaz Gutierrez (professionally known as Alberto Korda) in 1960; the image graces everything from T-shirts and baseball caps to watch ads and CD covers. Although these commercialized versions of Che are hardly a poke to the belly of global capitalism, they have managed to irritate some; Alberto Korda sued Smirnoff in 2000 for using his famous photograph to sell vodka, and a 1998 Taco Bell ad, in which a talking, beret-wearing Chihuahua barks 'Viva Gorditas' to a cheering crowd, sparked furor in Miami's Cuban-American community.

The 30th anniversary of Che's death, in 1997, produced some unlikely tributes to Che – two decades earlier, no one could have guessed that the Argentine government, then under the thumb of a right-wing military dictatorship, would one day issue a postage stamp honoring Che's Argentine roots.

The municipality of Alta Gracia recently purchased Che's adolescent home in town and turned it into the **Museo Casa de Ernesto Che Guevara** (see Alta Gracia for details); it was inaugurated on June 14, 2001, what would have been Che's 73rd birthday. And if you're in Buenos Aires, take a peek inside **Primer Museo Histórico Dr Ernesto Che Guevara** (☎ 4903-3285, Nicasio Oroño 458; free; open 5pm-10pm weekends only), a funky garage-sale-like assortment of Che memorabilia.

which is located 85km southwest of the capital via RP 5.

The tourist office (☎ 461215, **w** www.elsitiodelavilla.com/municipio), on Plaza José Hernández, is open 8am to 9pm daily. The postal code is 5194. To go **horseback riding**, contact Sr Martinez (☎ 461488), who sets up behind the bus terminal in summer and charges around US$8 an hour. To go **mountain biking**, go to La Biela (☎ 461618, San Martín 342) or Fly Machine (☎ 462425, Roca 257) to rent bikes.

Places to Stay & Eat

In the December-March high season, hotel prices rise and rooms book quickly.

Camping San José (☎ 462496) Sites US$6 per person; open Dec-April & during Oktoberfest. You will find here a lovely wooded, full-service campground just east of town on the RP 5.

Albergue El Rincón (☎ 461323, **e** rincon@calamuchitanet.com.ar) Dorm bed US$8, room US$12 per person with private bath, tent site US$4; breakfast US$2.50, lunch & dinner US$7. This beautiful Dutch-owned hostel, surrounded by

forest, has excellent dorm rooms (US$2 one-time sheet fee), an outdoor kitchen and parrilla and its own biodynamic farm. It's a good 600m walk from behind the bus terminal; follow the signs.

Bremen Hotel (☎ 461133, fax 461258, **e** info@hotelbremen.com, RP 5 Km 741) Singles/doubles US$65/98. From its relaxing tea room to the spacious bedrooms, this old hotel is truly exquisite.

Hotel Prater (☎ 461167, **e** prater@tecomnet.com.ar, El Quebracho 4) Rooms US$29/20 per person high/low season. This is one of the better values in town.

There are numerous restaurants along the main strip of Roca and San Martín.

Cervecería Viejo Munich (☎ 463122, San Martín 362) Mains US$3-15. The town's microbrewery serves delicious goulash, spaetzle and, of course, excellent beer.

Getting There & Away

The bus station is on Vélez Sársfield, uphill from San Martín, the main thoroughfare. Buses leave every hour for Córdoba (US$6; 2 hours), and daily to Buenos Aires (US$35; 11 hours).

MINA CLAVERO
☎ 03544 • pop 6500 • 915m

This popular resort gets busy in the summer but turns wonderfully quiet in the spring and fall. The limpid streams, rocky waterfalls, numerous swimming holes and idyllic mountain landscapes provide a relaxing escape for refugees from the faster-paced life of Córdoba and Buenos Aires. Hiking the rocky banks of the Río Mina Clavero only requires a short walk out of town.

Orientation & Information

Mina Clavero is 170km southwest of Córdoba via RN 20, the splendid Nuevo Camino de las Altas Cumbres (Highway of the High Peaks). It sits at the confluence of Río de Los Sauces and Río Panaholma, in the Valle de Traslasierra. The streams converge and become the Río Mina Clavero, which divides the town.

From the bus terminal, walk down to the Río Mina Clavero, hang a right on the shoreline path, and you'll soon hit San Martín, the main drag. Most hotels lie to the right.

The tourist office (☎ 470171), Av San Martín 1464, is open 8am to 10pm daily, with the standard brochures and a decent map of town.

Banco de la Nación, Av San Martín 898, and Banco de la Provincia, Av San Martín 1982, change US cash and have ATMs.

The post office is at Av San Martín and Pampa de Achala; the postal code is 5889. The Hospital Vecinal (☎ 470285) is at Fleming 1332.

Things to See & Do

Mina Clavero's balnearios get mobbed in the summer, but are peaceful, often empty, the rest of the year. The magnificent, boulder-strewn gorges of the Río Mina Clavero are easily explored; simply walk east on Urquiza from San Martín and follow the signs about 1km uphill to **Nido de Agila**, the best swimming hole around, and carry on from there. **Los Cajones** (or La Juntura) is another popular swimming hole in the middle of town, below Av 26 de Enero where the rivers meet. Head west along the Río Los Sauces and you'll hit **Los Elefantes**, a balneario named for its elephant-like rock formations.

Places to Stay

Many accommodations close around the end of March, when the town almost rolls up the sidewalks. Unless otherwise indicated, rates are for high-season doubles, and low-season prices may be much lower (when single rates are easy to get).

Autocamping Río Abajo (☎ 471-0730) Sites US$4 per person; open year-round. This campground, 3km south of town toward Nono, has shady riverside grounds, impeccable bathrooms, hot showers and laundry facilities.

Hostería Champaquí (☎ 470393, e *champaqui1@yahoo.com, Intendente Oviedo 1439*) Singles/doubles US$12/25 with breakfast. Though the rooms are small, the rooftop terrace, garden, laundry facilities and *metagol* (foosball) make this an excellent value.

La Flor Serrana (☎ 471481, *San Martín 1619*) Doubles US$24 with breakfast. Exceptionally friendly owners Robert and Andrea run a simple, spotless hotel and serve a superb breakfast.

Hotel Coronado (☎ 472388, *San Martín 1495*) Doubles US$30 with breakfast. Rooms are nondescript but cozy and there's a good café downstairs.

Hotel Palace (☎ 470390, *Mitre 847*) Doubles US$50. The highlight of this 40-room hotel is the huge backyard that slopes to the riverside.

Places to Eat

Lo de Jorge (☎ 470343, *Poeta Lugones 1417*) Mains US$7-16. This upscale *quincho* (steak restaurant) serves good abundant parrillada at reasonable prices.

Rincón Suizo (☎ 470447, *Champaqui 1200*) US$3-8. This comfy teahouse on the river prides itself on its homemade ice creams and torta selva negra, but a café con leche alone runs US$3.

Parrilla de Carmen (☎ 470621, *San Martín 1335*) Mains US$3-7. Step in here for US$3.50 bowls of *locro* (a hearty maize and tripe soup), huge lomitos, cheap lunch specials and good atmosphere.

Getting There & Away
The bus terminal is at Mitre 1191, across the Río Mina Clavero from the town center. There are several daily buses to Córdoba (US$10.65; 3 hours) and Villa Dolores (US$3.20; 1 hour), and at least three a day to Merlo (US$8; 2½ hours). TAC has daily service to San Luis, Mendoza and Buenos Aires (US$35; 15 hours) in summer, but less frequently in winter, when you may have to go to Villa Dolores.

AROUND MINA CLAVERO
Museo Rocsen
Operated by Juan Santiago Bouchon, an anthropologist, curator and passionate collector who first came to Argentina in 1950 as cultural attaché in the French embassy, this eclectic museum (☎ 03544-498218; admission US$4; open 9am-sunset) reveals just how strange the world really is. It contains over 11,000 pieces including antique motorcycles, mounted butterflies, Esso gas pumps, human skulls, Buddha statues, film projectors, Catholic altars, 19th-century instruments of torture, a shrunken head and a 1200-year-old Peruvian mummy. It's truly a one-of-a-kind museum, and requires plenty of time to explore.

The museum is 5km outside the pastoral village of Nono, a onetime indigenous settlement 9km south of Mina Clavero. There are regular minibuses from Mina Clavero to Nono's main plaza, from where you'll have to take a taxi (US$4 one-way) or walk.

Cerro Champaquí
The easiest starting point to the summit of 2790m Cerro Champaquí, the province's highest peak, is the charming village of Villa de Las Rosas, 31km south of Mina Clavero. The tourist office (☎ 03544-494407), on the plaza, is open 9am to 1pm and 3pm to 7pm daily, and can provide a list of mountain guides.

Otherwise, especially off-season, consult the tourist office in Mina Clavero.

For camping try **Camping Guasmara**, which charges US$10 per site. The basic **Hostería Las Rejas** (☎ 03544-494433), a block off the plaza, charges US$17 per

person and will do the trick for a night. **Estación Azul**, on the plaza, is a decent, if not the only, restaurant.

MERLO
☎ 02656 • pop 15,000 • elevation 890m
The climate continues to dry up as the RN 20 slowly winds its way down into neighboring San Luis Province. As it does it passes the RP 5, which continues directly south to the town of Villa Merlo, a growing resort known for its gentle microclimate (the local tourist industry buzzword) in a relatively dry area. On the western slope of the Sierras de Comechingones, the town struggles to retain a colonial atmosphere downtown, though most people come for the pricey hotels that dot the hillsides above.

Downtown's activity centers around Plaza Sobremonte, but most tourist services are two blocks south, along Av del Sol, which climbs steeply eastward into the quiet foothills of El Rincón. It's a long, hot tramp from downtown into the hills and, without a car or stamina and walking shoes, visitors will be riding the plastic seats of the shuttles that run about hourly between the two areas.

Merlo is 109km southwest of Mina Clavero, but actually tucked into the northeast corner of San Luis Province, 180km from the capital via RN 20 to La Toma and RN 148 to Santa Rosa del Conlara. From there, RP 5 leads directly east to Merlo.

Information
The municipal tourist office (☎ 476078), Coronel Mercau 605, has maps and information on hotels and campgrounds, but little on activities. The provincial tourist office (☎ 476079), at the traffic circle junction of RP 5 and RP 1, is open 8am to 8pm daily (to 10pm in summer).

The post office is at Coronel Mercau 579; the postal code is 5881.

Places to Stay
Merlo's abundant accommodations tend to be crowded in summer, around Semana Santa and during winter holidays in July.

Camping Don Juan (☎ 475942) Sites US$5. This shady and tidy site in El Rincón, about 2km from the town center via Av del Sol, has superb views of the Sierras. Empresa la Costa buses go there hourly.

Yana-Munay (☎ 475055, Av de los Césares 3261) Rooms US$15 per person with breakfast. This outstanding tea house in El Rincón has a couple of rooftop bedrooms with expansive views toward the west; each includes a private bath and a superb breakfast. Its hillside gardens are an exquisite spot for tea even if you don't plan to stay the night (see Places to Eat).

Residencial Amancay (☎ 475311, Av del Sol 500) Doubles US$25. This low-key motel has clean rooms with comfy beds and large baths; it's plain but a good value.

Hostería Argentina (☎/fax 475825, Av Los Almendros 102) Doubles US$42 with breakfast. One of the best places downtown, this small hotel has a lovely breakfast room, a small garden and plenty of plants.

Hotel Parque (☎ 475110, Av del Sol 821) Doubles US$44-49 with breakfast, US$55-60 with full board. Nine units of rooms are spread out over expansive grounds; there's pitch-and-put golf, a tennis court and a pool.

Hostería de los Césares (☎ 475543, Av de los Césares 1545) Doubles US$60 with breakfast & dinner. This handsome hotel has sweeping views from its terrace, a large garden with a pool and excellent, newly remodeled rooms.

Places to Eat

Most hotels, especially top-end ones, have restaurants that are open to the general public.

Yana-Munay (☎ 475055, Av de los Césares 3261) Open 4pm to one hour after sunset. For afternoon tea (the closer to sunset, the better), don't miss the hillside gardens at this top-notch tea house in El Rincón.

El Establo (☎ 475352, Av del Sol 450) Mains US$6-12. One of the town's best, this classy parrilla grills a superb bife de chorizo, an even better bife de lomo and delicious mollejas (sweetbreads).

La Posta (☎ 475867, Poeta Agüero 200) Mains US$6-11. Merlo's other esteemed pa-

rrilla serves more regional specialties, including a delicious chivito con chanfaina (kid with a thick meat stew).

Getting There & Away

The new bus terminal is on the RN 1 at Calle de las Ovejas, about eight blocks south of the center. Buses go daily to Mina Clavero (US$8; 3 hours), Villa Carlos Paz (US$11; 5 hours), Córdoba (US$12; 5½ hours), San Luis (US$9.50; 3 hours), Mendoza (US$25; 6½ hours), Buenos Aires (US$45; 12 hours) and Rosario.

SAN LUIS

☎ 02652 • pop 57,846 • elevation 700m

San Luis is the capital of its namesake province, popularly known as La Puerta de Cuyo, or The Door to Cuyo; Cuyo describes the combined provinces of Mendoza, San Juan and San Luis, though within Cuyo's regional identity, residents of San Luis province resolutely assert their singularity as puntanos. San Luis' hill country, which draws many Argentine visitors but very few foreigners, is a western extension of the Sierras de Córdoba.

The capital is a convenient stopover if you're heading west to Mendoza from Merlo, or east toward Buenos Aires, and is also the closest major town to the Parque Nacional Sierra de las Quijadas, a nature reserve and dinosaur site comparable to San Juan's Parque Provincial Ischigualasto. When it comes to city sights, restaurants and accommodations, however, San Luis (founded in 1594) pales in comparison to the nearby capitals of Mendoza and San Juan, though on Sundays it shows a soft side.

Orientation

On the north bank of the Río Chorrillos, San Luis is 260km from Mendoza via RN 7, 456km from Córdoba via RN 148 and 850km from Buenos Aires via either RN 7 or RN 8.

The commercial center is along the parallel streets of San Martín and Rivadavia between Plaza Pringles in the north and Plaza Independencia in the south.

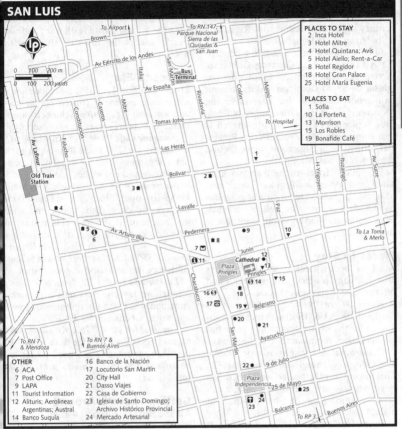

SAN LUIS

0   100   200 m
0   100   200 yards

PLACES TO STAY
2   Inca Hotel
3   Hotel Mitre
4   Hotel Quintana; Avis
5   Hotel Aiello; Rent-a-Car
8   Hotel Regidor
18 Hotel Gran Palace
25 Hotel María Eugenia

PLACES TO EAT
1   Sofia
10 La Porteña
13 Morrison
15 Los Robles
19 Bonafide Café

OTHER
6   ACA
7   Post Office
9   LAPA
11 Tourist Information
12 Alituris; Aerolíneas
    Argentinas; Austral
14 Banco Suquía
16 Banco de la Nación
17 Locutorio San Martín
20 City Hall
21 Dasso Viajes
22 Casa de Gobierno
23 Iglesia de Santo Domingo;
    Archivo Histórico Provincial
24 Mercado Artesanal

To Airport
To RN 147;
Parque Nacional
Sierra de las
Quijadas &
San Juan
Brown
Av Ejército de los Andes
Bus
Terminal
Av España
Tomas Jofré
Las Heras
Bolívar
Lavalle
Pedernera
Junín
Cathedral
Plaza
Pringles
Pringles
Belgrano
Ayacucho
9 de Julio
Plaza
Independencia
25 de Mayo
Balcarce
To Hospital
To La Toma
& Merlo
To RN 7
& Mendoza
To RN 7 &
Buenos Aires
To RP 3
Old Train
Station

Information

The tourist office (☎ 423957, 0800-666-6176), open 8am to 10pm weekdays and 8am to 8pm weekends, is at the triangular intersection formed by Junín, San Martín and Av Arturo Illia. Depending on funds, the provincial government sometimes publishes a tourist guide, in both Spanish and readable English, with a small but good atlas of the province. ACA (☎ 423188) is at Av Illia 401.

Local travel agencies include Alituris (☎ 423034), Av Colón 733, and Dasso Viajes (☎ 421017) at Rivadavia 540. Alituris also changes dollars and Chilean pesos 8am to noon weekdays, 8:30am to 12:30pm Saturday. Several banks, mostly around Plaza Pringles, have ATMs.

The post office is at Arturo Illia and San Martín; the postal code is 5700. Locutorio San Martín is at San Martín 633.

The regional hospital (☎ 422627) is at Av República Oriental del Uruguay 150 (the eastward extension of Bolívar).

Things to See & Do

Local materials, including provincial woods such as algarrobo for windows and frames, and white marble for steps and columns, complement the French tiles of the 19th-century **Iglesia Catedral**, on Rivadavia across from Plaza Pringles.

On the north side of Plaza Independencia is the provincial **Casa de Gobierno**. Across the plaza, on the south side, the **Iglesia de Santo Domingo** and its convent date from the 1930s, but reproduce the Moorish style of the 17th-century building they replaced. Part of the old church is visible inside the **Archivo Histórico Provincial**, with striking algarrobo doors, around the corner on San Martín.

Dominican friars at the **mercado artesanal** (no ☎; open 7am-1pm weekdays), next to Iglesia de Santo Domingo, sell gorgeous handmade wool rugs as well as ceramics, onyx crafts and weavings from elsewhere in the province.

Places to Stay

San Luis' better hotels cater to a business crowd, filling up quickly on weekdays and offering discounts on weekends.

Hotel Mitre (☎ 424599, Mitre 1043) Singles/doubles US$15/30 with breakfast. Attended by the owner, this simple place has cramped, dark rooms and a small back patio.

Residencial María Eugenia (☎ 430361, 25 de Mayo 741) Singles/doubles US$17/29. This recently refurbished residence has large, clean rooms with shared bath; it can be noisy during the day, but it's quiet at night. Upstairs rooms are better.

Inca Hotel (☎/fax 424923, Bolívar 943) Singles/doubles US$25/35 with TV. This is the best of the lot, but book ahead.

Hotel Gran Palace (☎ 422059, Rivadavia 657) Singles/doubles US$30/42 with TV & breakfast. This large block-like hotel has pleasant rooms with large baths.

Hotel Regidor (☎ 423303, fax 424756, San Martín 848) Singles/doubles US$35/50 with TV. Rooms here are plain but comfortable; it's a good value.

Hotel Aiello (☎ 425609, fax 425694, Av Illia 431) Singles/doubles US$45/58 with breakfast & TV. Big with the business crowd, this comfortable hotel has a good bar-café and a small back patio.

Hotel Quintana (☎ 438400, Av Illia 546) Singles/doubles from US$68/78. The Quintana has a good onsite restaurant and confitería and is the town's only four-star hotel.

Places to Eat

Traditional San Luis dishes include locro empanadas de horno (baked empanadas) and cazuela de gallina (chicken soup) restaurants, however, are in short supply.

Bonafide Café (☎ 442945, Rivadavia 615) Breakfast US$2-4; open 8am-10pm Mon-Sat. For espresso and the usual pastries, it's tough to beat the Bonafide.

Morrison (☎ 440818, Pringles 830) Mains US$5-10; open 7am-2am daily. Pizzas, burgers and decent hot sandwiches make up the menu at this pub-cum-restaurant with a rock-and-roll edge.

Sofía (☎ 427960, Av Colón & Bolívar) Mains US$5-14. Sofía serves a bit of Spanish cuisine, pastas and good seafood dishes.

La Porteña (☎ 431722, Junín 696) This is a longtime favorite serving cheap pizzas, empanadas at US$5 per dozen, good pastas and a quarter chicken for US$2.50.

Los Robles (☎ 436767, Av Colón 684) Mains US$8-18. One of the town's best, this upscale restaurant serves good pastas and parrillada and tasty chivito a la parrilla (grilled kid).

Getting There & Around

Air The San Luis airport (☎ 423047, 422427) is only 3km outside the center; taxis cost around US$3.

Aerolíneas Argentinas/Austral (☎ 432111), Av Colón 733, flies twice daily to Buenos Aires except weekends, when there's one flight daily. It also flies daily except Sunday to San Juan.

LAPA (☎ 431753), at Pedernera 863, flies nonstop to Buenos Aires (US$109) once daily Monday and Wednesday, and twice daily Tuesday, Thursday and Friday. The morning flights stop in Villa Mercedes.

Bus & Car The San Luis bus terminal (☎ 424021) is on España between San Martín and Rivadavia.

There are hourly buses to Mendoza (US$13; 3½ hours) and several daily buses to San Juan (US$14; 4 hours), Córdoba (US$20; 6½ hours), Rosario (US$25; 10 hours), Santa Fe (US$30; 10 hours) and Paraná.

There's at least one bus a day to Resistencia (US$60; 20 hours), and several to Mar del Plata.

Transportes Ticsa heads south to Bariloche (via the Río Negro valley and Neuquén) four times weekly.

Expreso Jocolí covers provincial destinations including Villa Mercedes, Merlo, San Martín, Unión, Trapiche, Florida and Pozo de los Funes. Empresa Dasso also travels to small provincial towns.

Avis (☎ 429548) has an office at Hotel Quintana, Av Illia 546; Rent-a-Car (☎ 425609) is in the Hotel Aeillo.

PARQUE NACIONAL SIERRA DE LAS QUIJADAS

Resembling San Juan's Parque Provincial Ischigualasto, this rarely visited national park sets aside 150,000 hectares of red sandstone canyons and dry lake beds among the Sierra de las Quijadas, whose peaks reach 1200m at Cerro Portillo. The Universidad Nacional de San Luis and New York's Museum of Natural History are collaborating on paleontological excavations here and have discovered dinosaur tracks and fossils from the Lower Cretaceous, about 120 million years ago.

Despite the shortage of visitors, access to the park is excellent – buses from San Luis to San Juan will drop visitors just beyond the village of Hualtarán, about 110km northwest of San Luis via RN 147 (the highway to San Juan). At this point, a 6km dirt road leads west to a viewpoint overlooking the **Potrero de la Aguada**, a scenic depression beneath the peaks of the Sierra that collects the runoff from much of the park and is a prime wildlife area. It's sometimes possible to catch a lift from the junction, where the park rangers have a house, to the overlook.

Hiking possibilities are excellent, but the complex canyons require a tremendous sense of direction or, preferably, a local guide. Even experienced hikers should beware summer rains and flash floods, which make the canyons extremely dangerous.

Guides can be hired at the park entrance. One well-liked and very knowledgeable local guide is David Rivarola (☎ 15-543629, e rivarola@unsl.edu.ar; US$60 for 1-5 people when you provide a car, US$35 per person when he provides the car). Rivarola works with the Department of Geology at the Universidad Nacional de San Luis and offers informed eight-hour tours through the park. Those who know Spanish can acquire his thorough, self-published guidebook *El Parque Nacional Sierra de las Quijadas y sus Recursos Naturales*, for about US$4, either at the park store or at the provincial tourist office in San Luis.

There's a shady *campground*, free of charge, near the overlook, and a small store with groceries and drinks, including very welcome ice-cold beer. Park entrance is free.

Mendoza & the Central Andes

Mendocinos, inhabitants of Mendoza province, call their home La Tierra de Sol y Buen Vino, the Land of Sun and Good Wine. Driving through Mendoza and parts of San Juan province, with vineyards often stretching endlessly in both directions, one might never guess that the region is actually a desert. The provinces lie in the rain shadow of the massive Andean crest, and aside from Mendoza's summertime hail storms (see the boxed text 'One Hail of a Summer') the region gets almost no precipitation. Enough snowfall accumulates on the eastern slopes of the Andes, however, to sustain rivers that irrigate the extensive lowland vineyards, nourishing one of the regions major attractions – wineries and wine. Visitors are also drawn year round to the dramatic barrier of the Andes, which towers over the western flanks of Mendoza and San Juan provinces. Contained in this stretch of mountains is the fabled Cerro Aconcagua, at 6962m the highest peak in the Americas. The Andes offer excellent hiking, trekking and climbing in summer and – in the case of Las Leñas – world-class skiing in winter. Whitewater rafting on the lower stretches of the Río Mendoza and Río Diamante has also become a major attraction. The region offers several provincial nature parks and reserves as well as remote thermal baths.

Many travelers visit Mendoza en route between Santiago, Chile, and Buenos Aires, but one should not overlook its northern neighbor San Juan and its less-visited but equally impressive outdoor attractions such as Parque Provincial Ischigualasto (Valle de La Luna).

History

The provinces of Mendoza, San Juan and, to some extent, neighboring San Luis (see the Cordoba & the Sierras chapter) are traditionally known as the Cuyo, a term which derives from the indigenous Huarpe word *cuyum,* meaning 'sandy earth.' The Huarpes

Highlights

- Wine – Sampling Malbec wine in the bodegas near Mendoza
- Las Leñas – Snowboarding and skiing on these world-class slopes
- Thermal Baths – Sliding into an Andean sulfuric bath amidst the ruins of Puente del Inca
- Rafting – Getting soaked on the rapids of the Mendoza and Diamante Rivers
- Parque Provincial Ischigualasto – Watching the canyons glow red with the sunset in the Valley of the Moon
- Climbing – Ascending 6960m Cerro Aconcagua, the Americas' highest peak

OTHER MAPS
Mendoza & the Central Andes
page 311
Parque Provincial Aconcagua
page 330

MENDOZA & THE CENTRAL ANDES

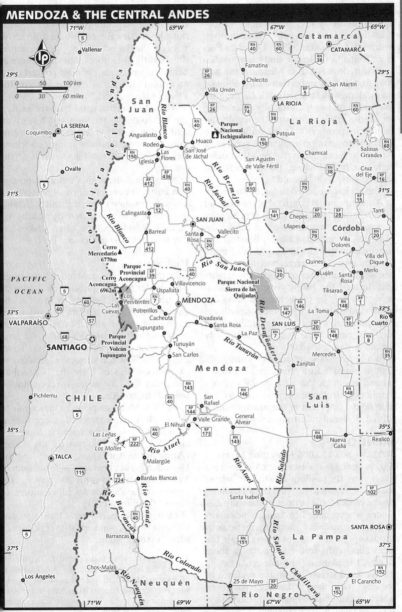

were the original practitioners of irrigated agriculture in the region, and their population was large enough to encourage Spaniards to cross the 3850m Uspallata Pass from Santiago, Chile, to found *encomiendas*.

Irrigated vineyards in Mendoza and San Juan first became important during colonial times, along with fattened cattle for the Santiago market, but the difficulty of crossing the Andes in winter isolated the region and limited its prosperity. Local vintners were still able to develop commerce across the Andes to Santiago, but Argentine independence in 1810 closed these outlets, and the economy soon faltered.

The region remained isolated from much of Argentina until the arrival of the railroad in 1884, which increased regional prosperity by supporting the expansion of cultivation of grapes, olives and alfalfa for livestock. As provincial authorities like Governor Emilio Civit promoted modernization of the irrigation system, an influx of Italian immigrants transformed the countryside, and federal economic policies protected a growing domestic industry which still relies heavily on wine production (see boxed text 'Finer and Finer Argentine Wine') and olives, primarily for the domestic market.

While minerals are relatively insignificant within Mendoza province, it has major oil and gas fields that provide 25% of Argentina's petroleum; coupled with hydroelectric development in the nearby Andes, this has fostered industrial development.

MENDOZA

☎ 0261 • pop 130,000 • elevation 747m

Except during long siesta hours, Mendoza is a lively city. Its bustling downtown, where locals congregate to read the latest headlines on the chalkboards in front of the daily *Los Andes,* is surrounded by tranquil neighborhoods, where, every morning, meticulous shopkeepers and housekeepers swab the sidewalks with kerosene to keep them shining. The *acequias* (irrigation canals) along its tree-lined streets are visible evidence of the city's indigenous and colonial past, even where modern quake-proof construction has replaced fallen historic buildings.

Mendoza has fewer pedestrian malls than other Argentine cities, but its wide downtown sidewalks contribute to an active street life, and a virtual canopy of trees, predominantly sycamores, alleviate summer heat. On weekends open-air concerts and an artisans' market often take place on the Plaza Independencia.

The city makes a good base for exploring the Andes to the west and has excellent restaurants, relaxing cafés, interesting museums, countless shopping opportunities and some of the finest plazas in the country.

Mendoza is the region's most important administrative and commercial center, with a significant state university and a growing industrial base supported by nearby oil fields. Earthquakes have often shaken the city, most recently in October 1997.

History

Like the rest of Cuyo, Mendoza was originally under Chilean jurisdiction. Pedro de Castillo founded the city in 1561 at the eastern end of the Uspallata Pass from Santiago and named it after the Chilean Governor García Hurtado de Mendoza. Not until the creation of the Viceroyalty of the River Plate in 1777, which subjected Mendoza to the Intendencia of Córdoba (Córdoban rule), did the city undergo reorientation toward Buenos Aires.

In 1814, Mendoza played a major role in the South American wars of independence, as General José de San Martín chose the city to train his Ejército de los Andes (Army of the Andes) prior to crossing the Uspallata Pass to liberate Chile. In honor of San Martín and his army, the pass is now known as the Paso de los Libertadores, or Pass of the Liberators.

Only a few years later, Darwin passed through and found post-independence Mendoza depressing:

To my mind the town had a stupid, forlorn aspect. Neither the boasted alameda, nor the scenery, is at all comparable with that of Santiago; but to those who, coming from Buenos Aires, have just crossed the unvaried Pampas, the gardens and orchards must appear delightful.

Arrival of the railroad, along with the modernization of provincial irrigation works, returned Mendoza to prosperity, and today 80% of the country's wine comes from bodegas in and around the city. Construction of oil-fired and hydroelectric power plants has encouraged the development of petrochemicals and light industry, diversifying the city's economic base and related services, and promoting population growth.

Orientation

Mendoza is 1040km west of Buenos Aires via RN 7 and 340km northwest of Santiago de Chile via the Los Libertadores border complex, whose trans-Andean tunnel has supplanted the higher Uspallata route.

Strictly speaking, the provincial capital proper is a relatively small area with a population of only about 130,000, but the inclusion of the departments of Las Heras, Guaymallén and Godoy Cruz, along with nearby Maipú and Luján de Cuyo, swells the population of Gran Mendoza (Greater Mendoza) to nearly 900,000.

The city's five central plazas are arranged like the five-roll on a die, with Plaza Independencia in the middle and four smaller plazas lying two blocks from each of its corners. Beautifully tiled Plaza España deserves special mention.

Avenida San Martín is the main thoroughfare, crossing the city from north to south, and Avenida Las Heras is the principal commercial street.

A good place to orient yourself is the Terraza Mirador, the rooftop terrace at City Hall (9 de Julio 500), which offers panoramic views of the city and surroundings. It's open to the public 8am to 8pm daily.

Information

Tourist Offices The head municipal tourist office (☎ 449-5185, fax 449-5186), inside City Hall, is open 8:30am to 1:30pm weekdays. For most purposes, though, the municipal tourist office (☎ 420-1333) on the broad Garibaldi sidewalk near Av San Martín is the most convenient information source. Open 9am to 9pm daily, it has good maps and detailed handouts, and there's usually an English speaker on hand. The best available map, sold here for US$7, is Guía Roja's *Todo Mendoza – Planos Gran Mendoza y Provincia*. Another municipal tourist office (☎ 429-6298) is at Las Heras and Mitre. There's also an office (☎ 431-3001), open 7am to 11pm, in the bus terminal.

The provincial tourist office (☎ 420-2800), Av San Martín 1143, is open weekdays 8am to 10pm. They have good maps, but no other brochures.

ACA (☎ 420-2900) is at Av San Martín and Amigorena.

For information on the southern portion of Mendoza province, contact the Casa de San Rafael (☎ 420-1475), Av Alem 308, and/or the Casa de Malargüe (☎ 425-9564), España 1075.

Immigration & Consulates The immigration office (☎ 424-3512) is at San Martín 1859 in Godoy Cruz, south of the city center. Mendoza has consulates for the following countries:

Bolivia (☎ 429-2458), Garibaldi 380

Chile (☎ 425-4844), Paso de los Andes 1147

France (☎ 423-1542), Av Houssay 790

Germany (☎ 429-6539), Montevideo 127, 1st floor, No 6

Israel (☎ 428-2140), Lamadrid 738

Italy (☎ 423-1640), Necochea 712

Spain (☎ 420-2252), Agustín Alvarez 455

Money Cambio Santiago, Av San Martín 1199, is one of the few places open on Saturday (until 8pm); it takes a 2% commission on traveler's checks. Cambio Exprinter, another exchange house, is at Av San Martín 1198.

Two downtown banks are also architectural landmarks: the massive Banco Mendoza, at the corner of Gutiérrez and San Martín, and Banco de la Nación, at Necochea and 9 de Julio. There are many ATMs downtown.

Post & Communications The post office is on San Martín at Colón; central Mendoza's postal code is 5500. There are many *locutorios*,

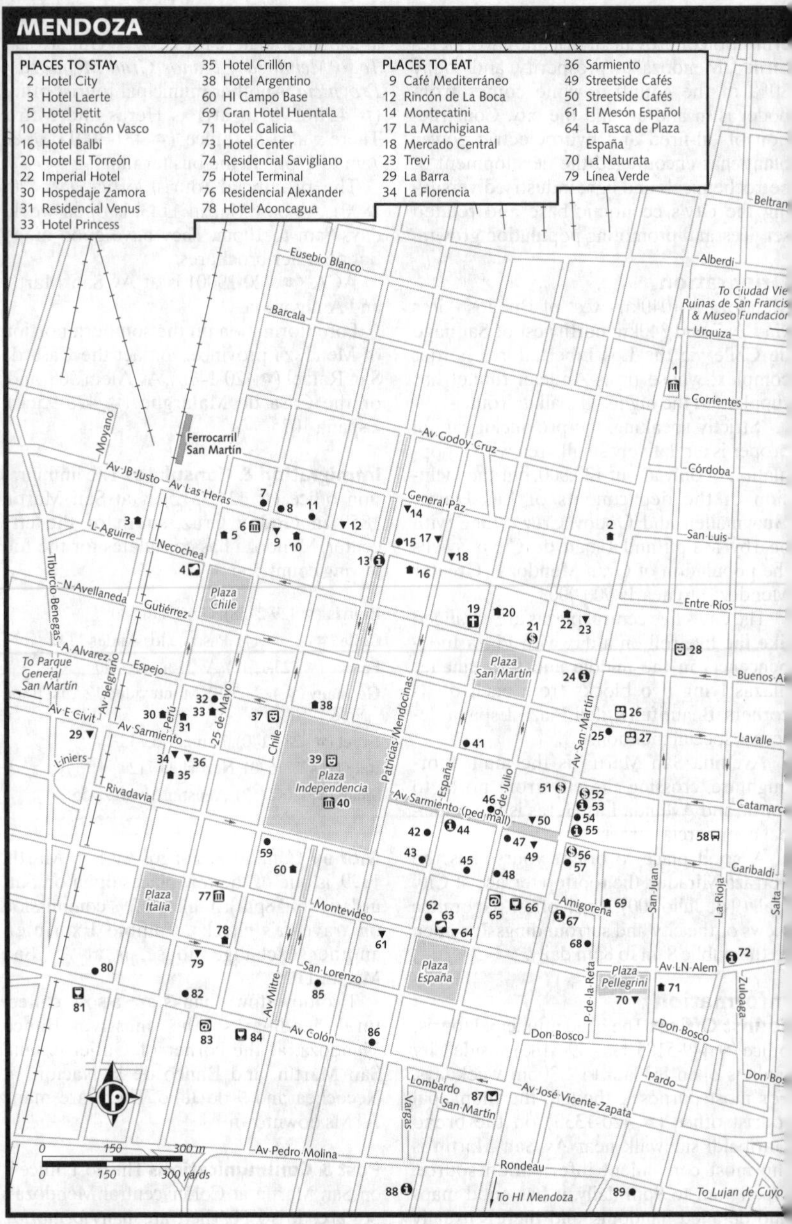

MENDOZA
PLACES TO STAY
2 Hotel City
3 Hotel Laerte
5 Hotel Petit
10 Hotel Rincón Vasco
16 Hotel Balbi
20 Hotel El Torreón
22 Imperial Hotel
30 Hospedaje Zamora
31 Residencial Venus
33 Hotel Princess
35 Hotel Crillón
38 Hotel Argentino
60 HI Campo Base
69 Gran Hotel Huentala
71 Hotel Galicia
73 Hotel Center
74 Residencial Savigliano
75 Hotel Terminal
76 Residencial Alexander
78 Hotel Aconcagua
PLACES TO EAT
9 Café Mediterráneo
12 Rincón de La Boca
14 Montecatini
17 La Marchigiana
18 Mercado Central
23 Trevi
29 La Barra
34 La Florencia
36 Sarmiento
49 Streetside Cafés
50 Streetside Cafés
61 El Mesón Español
64 La Tasca de Plaza España
70 La Naturata
79 Línea Verde
Eusebio Blanco
Barcala
Beltran
Alberdi
To Ciudad Vieja, Ruinas de San Francisco & Museo Fundacional
Urquiza
Corrientes
Av Godoy Cruz
Córdoba
Ferrocarril San Martín
Moyano
Av JB Justo
Av Las Heras
General Paz
L Aguirre
Necochea
San Luis
Tiburcio Benegas
N Avellaneda
Gutiérrez
Plaza Chile
Entre Ríos
A Alvarez
Espejo
To Parque General San Martín
Av Belgrano
Plaza San Martín
Buenos Aires
Av E Civit
Perú
25 de Mayo
Chile
Patricias Mendocinas
Av San Martín
Av Sarmiento
Lavalle
Liniers
Plaza Independencia
España
9 de Julio
Rivadavia
Av Sarmiento (ped mall)
Catamarca
Garibaldi
Plaza Italia
Montevideo
Amigorena
San Juan
La Rioja
Salta
San Lorenzo
Plaza España
Av LN Alem
Plaza Pellegrini
P de la Reta
Zuloaga
Av Mitre
Av Colón
Don Bosco
Pardo
Lombardo
San Martín
Av José Vicente Zapata
Vargas
Av Pedro Molina
Rondeau
To HI Mendoza
To Lujan de Cuyo
0 150 300 m
0 150 300 yards

OTHER	
1 Museo Histórico General San Martín	48 Aymará Turismo
4 Italian Consulate	51 Cambio Exprinter
6 Museo Popular Callejero	52 Cambio Santiago
7 Turismo Jocolí	53 Provincial Tourist Office
8 Esquí Mendoza Competición	54 Mercado Artesanal
11 Turismo Mendoza	55 Municipal Tourist Office
13 Municipal Tourist Office	56 Telefónica
15 Las Viñas	57 Yenny
19 Iglesia; Convento y Basílica de San Francisco	58 Bus to Maipú
21 Banco de la Nación	59 Instituto Cultural Argentino Norteamericano
24 Asatej	62 Southern Winds
25 Betancourt Rafting	63 German Consulate
26 Cine Opera	65 Web House
27 Cine Emperador (Universidad Nacional del Cuyo)	66 La Reserva
28 Teatro Mendoza	67 ACA
32 Instituto Dante Alighieri	68 Dollar Rent-a-Car; Aruba Car Rental
37 Teatro Independencia	72 Casa de San Rafael
39 Teatro Quintanilla	77 Museo del Pasado Cuyano
40 Museo Municipal de Arte Moderno	80 Extreme
41 Andesmar	81 Pop Bar
42 Isc Viajes (AmEx)	82 Laverap
43 LAPA	83 Club Web
44 Casa de Malargüe	84 Tenorio
45 Lan Chile	85 La Lavandería
46 Dinar	86 Thrifty Car Rental
47 Aerolíneas Argentinas; Austral	87 Post Office
	88 Terraza Mirador; Municipal Tourist Office; City Hall
	89 Iaim Instituto Cultural

such as Telefónica, at the corner of Sarmiento and San Martín, where you can order a drink while you make your call.

For Internet access, try Web House, Rivadavia 56, open 8:30am to 4am; or Club Web, Colón 474, open 8:30am to 2:30am.

Travel Agencies The student travel agency Asatej (☎/fax 429-0087/29, ⊜ tstudent@satlink.com) is at San Martín 1366, Local 16. The AmEx representative is Isc Viajes (☎ 425-9259), Av España 1016.

Bookstores Yenny (☎ 423-5317), at San Martín 1087 has a small section of classics and trashy best-sellers in English.

Cultural Centers The Instituto Cultural Argentino Norteamericano (☎ 423-6367) is at Chile 987. The Alianza Francesa (☎ 423-4614) is at Chile 1754, and the Instituto Dante Alighieri (☎ 425-7613) at Espejo 638.

Laundry Laverap (☎ 423-9706) is at Colón 547, and La Lavandería (☎ 429-4782) at San Lorenzo 352.

Medical Services Mendoza's hospital (☎ 420-0600, 420-0063) is at José F Moreno and Alem. If you need an ambulance, call the Servicio Coordinado de Emergencia (☎ 428-0000).

Museo Fundacional

One might call Mendoza's sparkling Museo Fundacional (☎ 425-6927, Alberdi & Videla Castillo, Ciudad Vieja; admission adult/student US$1.50/1; open 8am-8pm Mon-Sat, 3pm-10pm Sun) empty, but it would be more accurate to call it spacious. The high-ceilinged structure on Plaza Pedro del Castillo protects excavations of the colonial Cabildo (town council), destroyed by an earthquake in 1861, and the slaughterhouse that was subsequently built on the Cabildo's foundations. At that time, the city's geographical focus shifted west and south to its present location.

The museum starts at the beginning – the Big Bang – and works through all of human evolution as if the city of Mendoza were the

Map labels:

To Ciudad Vieja, Museo Fundacional & Ruinas de San Francisco

Parque Bernardo O'Higgins

Plaza Sarmiento

To Airport

Plaza Almirante Brown

spital tral

Bus Terminal

Av Acceso Este

Ituzaingó · JF Moreno · Montecaseros · PB Palacios · Av R Videla · Albania · Alberdi · JF Moreno · Pedro Palacios · cente López · Güemes · Alberdi

climax of the process. Nevertheless, for all the subtle pretensions, it's one of few Argentine museums that acknowledge the indigenous Huarpes' role in the region's development and its contemporary *mestizo* culture. There are several good dioramas of the city at various stages of its development, a decent selection of historical photographs (most of them lamentably small) and ancient and modern artifacts.

Museo Popular Callejero

This innovative sidewalk museum along Av Las Heras between 25 de Mayo and Perú consists of a series of encased dioramas depicting changes in one of Mendoza's major avenues since its 1830 creation in a dry watercourse. Because it's on the street it's open to viewing 24 hours a day and always free.

Museo Histórico General San Martín

José de San Martín's name graces parks, squares and streets everywhere in Argentina, but the Libertador is especially dear to Mendoza, where he resided with his family and recruited and trained his army to cross into Chile. This museum (☎ 425-7947, Remedios Escalada de San Martín 1843; admission US$1; open 9am-1pm Mon-Fri) is in his honor.

Other Museums

Paintings and sculptures by Argentine artists, particularly Mendocinos, add flavor to the **Emiliano Guiñazú Fine Arts Museum** (Casa de Fader; ☎ 496-0224, San Martín 3651; bus No 200 from downtown; admission US$1; open 8:30am-1pm & 2pm-7:30pm Tues-Fri, 3pm-7pm Sat & Sun) in a distinguished historical residence in the suburb of Luján de Cuyo.

The historical **Museo del Pasado Cuyano** (☎ 423-6031, Montevideo 544; admission US$1; open 9:30-12:30 Mon-Fri summer only) has period furniture and other relics from the city's and region's past.

The **Museo Municipal de Arte Moderno** (☎ 425-7279, Plaza Independencia; admission US$ 1; open 9am-1pm & 4pm-9pm Mon-Sat), underground at Plaza Indepen-

dencia, is a relatively small but well-organized facility with rotating modern and contemporary art exhibits.

Iglesia, Convento & Basílica de San Francisco

Many mendocinos consider the image at this church (no ☎, Necochea 201; admission US$1; open 9am-1pm Mon-Sat) of the Virgin of Cuyo, patron of San Martín's Ejército de los Andes (Army of the Andes), miraculous because it survived Mendoza's devastating 1968 earthquake. In the Virgin's semicircular chamber, visitors leave tributes to her and to San Martín. A mausoleum within the building holds the remains of San Martín's daughter, son-in-law and granddaughter, which were repatriated from France in 1951.

Ruinas de San Francisco

Occupying an entire block in the Ciudad Vieja (Old Town) at the corner of Ituzaingó and Fray Luis Beltrán, these ruins belonged to a Jesuit-built church/school that dates from 1638. After the Jesuits were expelled in 1767, the Franciscans, whose own church was demolished in the 1782 earthquake, took over the buildings. The Old Town is about seven blocks northeast of downtown; it's easiest to walk north on San Martín and hang a right on Alberdi to Ituzaingó; otherwise, head north on Ituzaingó.

Parque General San Martín

Originally forged for the Turkish Sultan Hamid II, the impressive gates to this 420-hectare park west of downtown came from England. Designed by architect Charles Thays (who designed Parque Sarmiento in Córdoba) in 1897 and donated to the provincial government by two-time governor and later senator Emilio Civit, the park itself has 50,000 trees of about 700 different species and is popular for weekend family outings and other activities. The famous **Cerro de la Gloria** features a monument to San Martín's Ejército de los Andes for their liberation of Argentina, Chile and Peru from the Spaniards. On clear days, views of the valley make the climb especially rewarding.

Within the park, several museums focus on archaeology, mineralogy and natural history, including the **Museo de Ciencias Naturales y Antropológicas Juan Cornelio Moyano** (☎ 428-7666; admission US$2; open 8am-1pm, 2pm-7:30pm Mon-Fri, 3pm-7pm Sat & Sun), the **Museo Domingo Faustino Sarmiento** (☎ 428-1133; free; open 8am-5pm Mon-Fri), and the **Museo Arqueológico de la Universidad Nacional de Cuyo** (☎ 449-4093; admission US$1; open 8am-1pm, 3pm-7:30pm Mon-Fri).

Bus No 110 ('Favorita') from around Plaza Independencia or Plaza España goes to the park, continuing to the **Jardín Zoológico** (zoo; ☎ 428-1700; admission US$3; open 9am-6pm daily), occupying an impressive hillside setting. From the park entrance, open-air buses called bateas carry visitors to the summit of Cerro de la Gloria.

Activities

Mendoza and its Andean hinterland constitute one of Argentina's major outdoor recreation areas, with numerous agencies organizing expeditions for climbers and trekkers, rafting trips on the Río Mendoza and other rivers, mule trips and cycling trips. Among these agencies are the following:

Andesport (climbing, trekking, mule trips)
(☎ 424-1003)
Rufino Ortega 390

Aymará Turismo (mule trips, trekking, rafting)
(☎ 420-2064)
9 de Julio 1023

Betancourt Rafting (rafting, mountain biking, parasailing)
(☎ 429-9965, w www.betancourt.com.ar)
Lavalle 35, Local 8

Campo Base Adventures & Expeditions (climbing, trekking, horseback, city bikes)
(☎ 429-0707, w www.cerroaconcagua.com)
Mitre 946

Piuquén Viajes (mule trips, trekking across the Andes)
(☎ 425-3983, 430-8029)
Alvarez 332

Rumbo al Horizonte (climbing, skiing, expeditions, adventure courses)
(☎ 452-0641)
Caseros 1053, Godoy Cruz

Travesía (rafting, trekking)
(☎ 428-2677, mobile ☎ 15-558-9533)
Reconquista 1080, Godoy Cruz

Climbing & Mountaineering For the latest information, contact the Club Andinista Mendoza (☎ 431-9870, Fray Luis Beltrán 357, Guaymallén). Experienced local guides include Fernando Grajales (☎/fax 429-3830, e expediciones@grajales.net, José Fedérico Moreno 898); and Rudy Parra at Aconcagua Trek (☎/fax 431-7003, e rudy@lanet.com.ar, Güiraldes 246, Dorrego).

For climbing and hiking equipment, both rental and purchase, try Orviz (☎ 425-1281, Av JB Justo 550).

Skiing & Snowboarding For purchase and rental of ski and snowboard equipment, try Esquí Mendoza Competición (☎ 429-7944, Las Heras 583); Extreme (☎ 429-0733, Colón 733) or Rezagos de Ejército (☎ 423-3791, Mitre 2002). All charge around US$15 per day for a skis-boots-poles package and US$25 per day for a snowboard with boots. Most rent gloves, jackets and tire chains as well.

White-Water Rafting The major rivers are the Mendoza and the Diamante, near San Rafael. Most of the outfits mentioned above offer trips ranging from half-day excursions (from US$30) to overnight (from US$190) and three-day expeditions (from US$350). Río Extremo Rafting and Argentina Rafting Expediciones are two well-regarded rafting outfits based in Portrerillos (see that section for details).

Language Courses

IAIM Instituto Intercultural (☎ 429-0269, fax 424-8840, e info@intercultural.com.ar, Rondeau 277) offers Spanish-language instruction for foreigners.

Organized Tours

Get a route map of the city's Bus Turístico (Tourist Bus; ☎ 420-1333, municipal tourist office), whose well-versed guides, some of them English-speaking, offer the best possible orientation to the city for US$7. Good for 24 hours, the ticket allows you to board and re-board at any of several fixed stops throughout the city. The circuit begins at the corner of Garibaldi and Av San Martín, near the municipal tourist office, and goes as far as the summit of Cerro de la Gloria. Hours are 10am to 8pm daily from January 1 to Semana Santa (March or April).

Several conventional travel agencies organize trips in and around town, including Turismo Mendoza (☎/fax 429-2013), at Las Heras 543; Turismo Sepean (☎ 420-4162), at Primitivo de la Reta 1088; and Turismo Jocolí (☎ 423-0466, e turismojocoli@super net.com.ar), at Av Las Heras 601. Among the possibilities are half-day tours of the city (US$12); tours of the wineries and Dique Cipoletti (US$13); or full-day tours to Villavicencio (US$17), or the high cordillera around Potrerillos, Vallecitos and Uspallata (US$28). More distant excursions, to the Difunta Correa shrine in San Juan (US$29) and the Cañon del Atuel (US$39), as well as winter ski trips, are also possible.

Special Events

Mendoza's biggest annual event, the Fiesta Nacional de la Vendimia (Wine Harvest Festival), lasts about a week, from late February to early March. It features a parade on Av San Martín with floats from each department of the province, numerous concerts and folkloric events, and it all culminates in the coronation of the festival's queen in the Parque General San Martín amphitheater.

In February, the provincial equivalent of the Tour de France occurs, called the Vuelta Ciclística de Mendoza. In July and August, the Festival de la Nieve (Snow Festival) features ski competitions.

Places to Stay

Budget Mendoza has abundant accommodations in all categories. The tourist booth at the bus terminal may help find good rooms at bargain prices, while the downtown office at San Martín and Garibaldi also keeps a list of *casas de familia* (homestays) offering accommodations from about US$10 to US$15 single.

For March's Fiesta de la Vendimia, reservations are advisable.

Churrasqueras del Parque (☎ 428-0511, *Parque General San Martín*) US$2.50 per person, per tent, & per vehicle; bus No 50, or 110 from downtown. This convenient campground has good facilities, but its popular restaurant can make things noisy late at night, especially on weekends.

Parque Suizo (☎ 444-1991, 428-3915) US$12 per site up to 3 persons; bus No 11, *interno* (route placard) 115, from Av Sarmiento. This large, woodsy campground, 9km from downtown on Av Champagnat in El Challao, has good facilities, a grocery and a swimming pool.

HI Campo Base (☎ 429-0707, w www .campo-base.com.ar, Mitre 946) Dorm bed US$8, breakfast US$1.50, three doubles available. This lively hostel just off the main plaza is popular with climbers, and is a great place to meet people embarking on or returning from expeditions. Both owners are also guides. Perks include bike rentals, kitchen, communal *asados,* organized tours and lots of talk. Some rooms have cozy bunks and lockers, others are basic.

HI Mendoza (☎/fax 424-0018, w www .hostelmendoza.net, España 343) US$1 with breakfast, US$10 HI members. This friendly, comfortable hostel is less than central but offers meals, email access, entertainment and organized tours.

Mendoza's cheapest hotel accommodations are (no surprise) near the bus terminal, on Güemes and nearby streets. The best of the dives, which isn't saying much, are *Hotel Terminal* (☎ 431-3893, Alberdi 261), at US$10 per person with bath; and the musty-smelling *Residencial Alexander (no ☎ Güemes 294)* for US$10 per person with shared bath.

Residencial Savigliano (☎ 423-7746, Pedro Palacios 944) Singles US$15/20 with shared/private bath, doubles US$20/25, dorm beds US$10. Across Av Videla from the bus terminal (take the pedestrian underpass), this clean residencial is a welcome step up from the others. Rates include breakfast, reasonable privacy, comfortable atmosphere and access to cable TV.

Hotel Center (☎ 423-7234, Alem 547) Singles/doubles US$20/30 with bath. Worn out and characterless, this one only toys with the idea of value.

Hotel Galicia (☎ 420-2619, San Juan 881) Singles/doubles US$15/30 with bath. This simple, old place has dark but clean rooms, laundry facilities and a friendly staff.

Mid-Range Rooms at most mid-range hotels include private bathrooms.

Imperial Hotel (☎ 423-4671, Las Heras 88) Doubles US$25 with bath & breakfast. The Imperial is a no-frills, good-value place with clean, carpeted rooms.

Residencial Venus (☎/fax 425-4147, Perú 1155) Singles/doubles US$20/30 with bath & TV, breakfast extra. One of the best values in town, this residencial has a relaxing patio and spotless rooms. You couldn't swing a cat in the back rooms, but the front rooms are enormous.

Hospedaje Zamora (☎ 425-7537, Perú 1156) Singles/doubles US$20/30 with bath, breakfast extra. This popular place has a bit more colonial charm than the Venus across the street (same owners), but rooms are about the same quality.

Hotel City (☎ 425-1343, General Paz 95) Singles/doubles US$24/39. The price here includes TV, bath and air-con, but rooms have little character.

Hotel Laerte (☎ 423-0875, Leonidas Aguirre 19) Singles/doubles US$25/45 with breakfast & air-con. Though rather plain, this hotel is a good value.

Hotel Petit (☎ 423-2099, fax 425-0682, Perú 1459) Singles/doubles US$25/40 high-season, with breakfast. The Petit has clean, small rooms with substantial baths.

Hotel Rincón Vasco (☎ 423-3033, Las Heras 590) Singles/doubles US$26/37 with breakfast. In an excellent location on the restaurant-strewn Av Las Heras, this slightly worn hotel is a good value, especially if you get a balcony (and don't mind the street noise).

Hotel Argentino (☎ 425-4000, Espejo 455) Singles/doubles US$39/55 with breakfast, parking & air-con. One of few lodgings on the Plaza Independencia, this quality hotel has comfy rooms, a back patio and a restaurant.

Top End Rooms at most top end hotels include private bathrooms.

Hotel El Torreón (☎ 423-3900, España 1433) Singles/doubles US$50/60 with continental breakfast, TV, air-con, telephone & parking; German and English spoken. The staff here is attentive, and the rooms are mid-sized and clean.

Hotel Crillón (☎ 429-8494, fax 423-8963, Perú 1065) Singles/doubles US$60/75. This is a modern, unpretentious place with carpeted rooms, solid beds and plenty of good restaurants nearby.

Hotel Princess (☎ 423-5669, 25 de Mayo 1168) Singles/doubles US$70/90 with breakfast, TV & telephone. The Princess has sharply decorated rooms, a small interior patio and an appealing location near the Plaza Indepencia.

Hotel Balbi (☎ 423-3500, fax 438-0626, Las Heras 340) Singles/doubles US$85/105, with breakfast, TV, air-con & telephone. This four-star hotel has a swimming pool, posh rooms and a professional staff.

Hotel Aconcagua (☎ 420-4455, San Lorenzo 545) Singles/doubles US$83/125. Hotel Aconcagua has it all, with manicurists and hairstylists on premises, a sauna and pool and some multilingual staff. When it's busy, however, expect glacially slow checkouts.

Gran Hotel Huentala (☎ 420-0802, fax 420-0664, Primitivo de la Reta 1007) Singles/doubles US$94/142 with breakfast & parking. Rooms are worn but spacious, with comfy chairs and good bathrooms. Value is questionable, even with the sauna and small rooftop pool.

Places to Eat

Probably the best budget choice is the *Mercado Central*, at Av Las Heras and Patricias Mendocinas, where a variety of stalls offer inexpensive pizza, *empanadas*, sandwiches and groceries in general; its exceptional value and great atmosphere make it one of Mendoza's highlights.

Sarmiento (☎ 438-0824, Sarmiento 658) All-you-can-eat US$7 Mon-Fri, US$9 Sat &

Sun. Sarmiento does the standard *parrilla* and pasta menu well; it's a good value during the week.

La Naturata (☎ 15-508-7424, *Vicente López 177*) Buffet US$6, mains US$7, salads US$3. The vegetarian buffet here is small and the food simple, but it's tasty and wholesome.

Rincón de La Boca (☎ 425-6848, *Las Heras 479*) Pizzas US$6-12. Many argue this is the best pizza in town (it's the crust), and the outdoor seating, friendly service, low prices and *chopps* (draft beer) make it hard to beat. The branch in the Mercado Central sells slices.

La Florencia (☎ 429-1564, *Sarmiento & Perú*) Salads US$4-6, mains US$8-12. Like Sarmiento next door, La Floriencia's outdoor seating and reliable menu of pasta and parrilla make it a good choice on a warm night.

Montecatini (☎ 425-2111, *General Paz 370*) Mains US$7-18. High-quality pastas are served in an upscale atmosphere, with prices to match.

Trevi (☎ 423-3195, *Las Heras 68*) Mains US$8-15. Trevi has outstanding lasagna, though you'll have to put up with the flood-lit dining room to enjoy it.

La Marchigiana (☎ 423-0751, *Patricias Mendocinas 1550*) Mains US$8-12. Mendoza's finest Italian restaurant is well worth the splurge; it draws celebrities, but the gracious hostess welcomes everyone.

La Barra (☎ 15-654-1950, *Belgrano 1086*) Meats US$10-13. This is a relaxed parrilla with a wood-cabin feel and above-average grills.

El Mesón Español (☎ 429-6175, *Montevideo 244*) Mains US$9, full meal US$12-18. For typical Spanish food and atmosphere plus customary weekend flamenco, this is the spot.

La Tasca de Plaza España (☎ 423-3466, *Montevideo 117*) Full meal US$10-16. With excellent Mediterranean and Spanish tapas (mostly seafood), great wines, intimate atmosphere, good art and friendly service, La Tasca is one of the best restaurants in town.

Línea Verde (☎ 423-9806, *San Lorenzo 550*) This is a reliable vegetarian option that also has a takeaway *rotisería*.

Also try *Café Mediterráneo* (☎ 425-9429, *Las Heras 596*) for interesting, moderately priced lunch specials. *Las Vía* (☎ 425-0053, *Catamarca 76*) is another vegetarian option.

There are several *streetside cafés and restaurants* with outdoor seating along the Sarmiento peatonal between 9 de Julio and San Martín; they're good for coffee and breakfast, decent for lunch or dinner, and great for people-watching.

Entertainment

Check the tourist offices or museums for a copy of *La Guía*, a monthly publication with comprehensive listings of dance, musical and theatrical performances, art exhibitions and cultural events. *Los Andes*, the daily rag, also has a good entertainment section.

Bars Bars in Mendoza generally don't require cover charges.

La Reserva (☎ 420-3531, *Rivadavia 32*) This small, predominantly gay bar gets a mixed crowd and some great entertainment, including flamenco, drag shows, electronica DJ's and theater, always followed by dancing until the wee hours; the fun kicks in after midnight.

Pop Bar (*Colón 740*) Of several popular bars along Colón, this spot, with its neo minimalist pop-art bent, is the most hopping of the bunch.

Tenorio (☎ 420-2986, *Colón 462*) Open 8am-late Mon-Sat, 6pm-late Sun. This is a relaxed place to disappear over a beer; it's also a good choice for enjoying an afternoon book.

Dance Clubs Finding a dance floor generally means abandoning downtown for one of two areas: Tthe northwest suburb of El Challao, or Chacras de Coria, along the RP 82 in the southern outskirts. The former is reached by bus No 115 from Sarmiento the latter by bus No 206 from Rioja. In both cases simply asking the driver for *los boliches* (the nightclubs) is usually enough to find the right stop.

Homero (*Av Champagnat s/n, El Challao*) Admission US$3-8; open Fri &

at. This is one of the biggest and most popular nightclubs in El Challao, usually with excellent DJ's. It's the first club in a line of several.

Aloha (Ruta 82 s/n, Chacras de Coria) Admission US$3-8; open Fri-Sun. This club draws an older crowd and can really get moving.

Other discos that draw crowds to Chacras de Coria, all located fairly close to one another, are *Runner, Olimpo, Sketch* and *Cimento*. Admission fees are similar to those at Homero and Aloha.

Theater The main theaters in town are *Teatro Quintanilla (☎ 423-2310),* in the Plaza Independencia alongside the Museo de Arte Moderno; the nearby *Teatro Independencia (☎ 438-0644),* at the corner of Espejo and Chile; and *Teatro Mendoza (☎ 429-7279, San Juan 1427),* where performances are hosted by the Universidad Nacional del Cuyo.

Shopping

Plaza de las Artes (Plaza Independencia) This outdoor crafts market takes place on Friday, Saturday and Sunday, lasting until well after dark.

Mercado Artesanal (☎ 420-4239, downtairs, Av San Martín 1143) Open 8am-4pm Mon-Fri. This cooperative offers provincial handicrafts, including vertical-loom weavings (Huarpe-style) from the northwest of the province; horizontal looms (Araucanianstyle) from the south; woven baskets from Lagunas del Rosario; and lots of braided, untanned-leather horse gear. Prices are reasonable and the knowledgeable staff is eager to talk about the crafts and the artisans, who receive the proceeds directly.

Las Viñas (☎ 425-1520, Las Heras 399) One of many places to shop along this stretch of Las Heras, Las Viñas has a wide selection of Argentine crafts.

Getting There & Away

Air Aerolíneas Argentinas (☎ 420-4185) and Austral share offices at Sarmiento 82; Aerolíneas flies three times daily to Buenos Aires' Aeroparque Jorge Newbury (US$57

to US$196) except on Saturday (two flights) and daily to the capital's Ezeiza via Córdoba. Austral has 24 flights weekly to Aeroparque.

LanChile (☎ 425-7900), Rivadavia 135, flies twice daily to Santiago de Chile, the only international flights from Mendoza.

LAPA (☎ 423-1000), España 1002, flies 20 times weekly to Aeroparque (from US$132). Dinar (☎ 420-4520), Sarmiento 119, flies twice weekdays and once Saturday to Aeroparque.

Andesmar (☎ 438-0654), Espejo 189, flies two times daily except on Saturday to Córdoba (from US$64) and to Tucumán (from US$162), weekdays to Rosario (from US$139), and at least daily (except Saturday) to Salta (from US$151).

Southern Winds (☎ 429-7077) España 943, flies at least twice daily to Córdoba (US$63 to US$131) and Rosario (US$139 to US$195); and twice daily (except Sundays when there is only one flight) to Tucumán (US$150 to US$260), Salta (US$161 to US$218), Neuquén (US$120 to US$176), Rio Gallegos (US$233 to US$290), and Comodoro Rivadavia (US$200 to US$257). It flies once daily to Resistencia (US$161 to US$218); once daily Monday through Saturday to Ushuaia (US$233 to US$274); and once daily on Tuesday, Thursday and Saturday to Bariloche (US$161 to US$229).

Bus Mendoza is a major transport hub from which you can get just about anywhere in the country. There are daily departures from Mendoza's bus terminal (☎ 431-5000, 431-3001), Av Gobernador Videla and Av Acceso Este, in Guaymallén, to the destinations in the following table, and sometimes upwards of 10 to 20 per day to major cities such as Buenos Aires, Córdoba, La Rioja, Catamarca, Salta and Tucumán. Prices reflect midseason fares and will fluctuate depending on travel demand and the level of service you chose.

Domestic Several companies send buses daily to Uspallata (US$9, 2 hours) and Los

Penitentes (US$12, 4 hours) for Parque Provincial Aconcagua. Buses to Chile also pass the park, but are often full with through passengers.

Services are numerous to San Juan (US$10, 2½ hours) San Luis (US$14, 3½ hours) and the San Luis mountain resort of Merlo. Less frequent daily buses run to Barreal (4 hours), Calingasta, San Agustín del Valle Fértil (6 hours) and San José de Jáchal, all in northern San Juan Province. There are also daily departures south to San Rafael (US$10, 3½ hours), General Alvear and Malargüe (US$20, 7 hours).

In ski season, several companies go directly to Las Leñas (US$15, 6½ hours), including Turismo Mendoza, Autotransportes Mendoza, Expreso Uspallata and Turismo Luján, but the only daily services are with TAC (changing buses in San Rafael) and Mendoza Viajes, which leaves from Sarmiento and 9 de Julio rather than the terminal.

A number of companies offer morning service to the Difunta Correa Shrine (US$15 roundtrip) in San Juan province Friday through Monday; it's two hours each way and the bus waits two hours before returning. Weekday trips are possible with Transportes La Cumbre.

Additional domestic destinations are covered in the table below.

Destination	Duration in hours	Cost
Bahía Blanca	16	US$55
Bariloche	20	US$63
Buenos Aires	13-17	US$35-55
Catamarca	10	US$30
Chilecito	10½	US$26
Córdoba	11	US$25
Jujuy	20	US$50
Mar del Plata	19	US$60
Neuquén	12	US$40
Puerto Madryn	23	US$73
Rosario	12	US$30
Salta	18	US$49
San Martín de los Andes	19½	US$67
Santa Fe	14	US$33
Santa Rosa, La Pampa	14	US$39
Tucumán	14	US$39
Zapala	9½	US$48

International Numerous companies cross the Andes every day via RN 7, the Paso de Los Libertadores, to Santiago de Chile (US$20, 6½ hours), Viña del Mar and Valparaíso (US$20, 8 hours). The pass sometimes closes in winter due to bad weather; one reader reported waiting two weeks before it reopened. While closures are usually shorter, be prepared to wait if weather gets extreme.

Several carriers have connections to Lima, Perú (US$110, 60-72 hours), via Santiago, including El Rápido, Tas Choapa and Ormeño. There are at least two weekly departures to Montevideo, Uruguay (from US$50, 22 hours), some with onward connections to Punta del Este and Brazil.

Getting Around

To/From the Airport Plumerillo International Airport (☎ 488-0944, 488-2603) is 6km north of downtown on RN 40. Bus No 68 ('Aeropuerto') from Calle Salta goes straight to the terminal.

Bus Mendoza's bus terminal (☎ 431-5000, 431-3001) is at Av Gobernador Videla and Av Acceso Este, in Guaymallén (which is really just across the street from downtown). After arriving, walk under the Videla underpass (it's lined with merchandise stalls) and you'll be heading toward the center, about 15 minutes away. Otherwise the 'Villa Nueva' trolley (actually a bus) connects the terminal with downtown at Lavalle, between Av San Martín and San Juan.

Stores of every description fill the station, along with cafés, food stalls, a helpful tourist office and hot showers for US$2.

Mendoza is more spread out than most Argentine cities, so you'll need to tighten your shoelaces or learn about the bus system to get around. Local buses cost US$0.55 – more for longer distances such as a the trip to the airport – and require a magnetic Mendobus card, which can be purchased at most kiosks in denominations of US$2 and US$5. Most bus lines (lineas) also have internal route numbers (internos) posted in the window; for example, linea 200 light post interno 204 or 206; watch for both numbers. Internos usually indicate more precisely where the bus will take you. The 'Villa Nueva' trolley runs between downtown (at Lavalle between San Martín and San Juan) and the bus terminal.

Car Rental cars can be tricky to get at the airport, but easier downtown. Dollar Rent-a-Car (☎ 429-9939, e dollar@mendoza.com.ar) is at Primitivo de la Reta 936, Local 6; Aruba Car Rental (☎ 423-4071) is next door at Local 5; Thrifty (☎ 423-5640) is at Colón 241.

AROUND MENDOZA

There are varied sights and recreational opportunities in and near Mendoza. Almost all of them are possible day trips, but some more distant ones would be more suitable for at least an overnight stay.

Vineries

Thanks to a complex and very old system of river-fed aqueducts, land that was once a desert now supports nearly 80% of the country's wine production. Mendoza province is wine country, and most of the wineries near the capital offer tours and tastings. Countless tourist agencies offer day tours to vineries, hitting several in a precisely planned day, but it's easy enough to visit them on your own if you wish. All winery tours and tastings are free, though some push hard for sales at the end. Malbec is the definitive Argentine wine.

If you're short on time, Bodega Santa Ana (in the suburb of Guaymallén) and Bodega Escorihuela (in the suburb of Godoy Cruz) are both within the city limits and can be visited in a few hours; the beautiful Escorihuela should be seen no matter how much time you have.

With a full day, it's easy to hop buses and hit several of the area's most appealing vineries – not to mention wine museums – in the outskirts of neighboring Maipú, only 16km away. Mendoza's tourist office on Garibaldi at San Martín provides a basic but helpful map of the area and its wineries. Buses to Maipú leave from La Rioja, between Garibaldi and Catamarca in downtown Mendoza. In Maipú, they chug up and down the main rural roads outside of town, following no apparent schedule, and can be flagged down just about anywhere – bus drivers will usually tell you the bus number you need for your destination if you happen to stop the wrong one.

Another option is the area of Luján de Cuyo, 19km south of Mendoza, which has three important wineries offering tours and tastings; buses to these wineries leave from Mendoza's bus terminal. If you're busing it for the day, the simplest thing is to chose between Maipú and Luján del Cuyo instead of trying to hit both towns in a single day (though it can be done). If you want to cut the slog and hit as many bodegas as possible, however, renting a car is advisable – and after a few tasting room visits, you'll have as much confidence behind the wheel as an aspiring Argentine rally driver (not that this practice is encouraged).

Bodega Escorihuela (☎ 0261-424-2744, e escorihuelaadm@ simza.com.ar, Belgrano & Pte Alvear, Godoy Cruz; bus 'T' from Sarmiento at San Martín; tours 9:30am, 10:30am, 11:30am, 12:30pm, 2:30pm & 3:30pm daily). Founded in 1884, Bodega Escorihuela is one of the country's oldest and most prestigious wineries, known in particular for its Malbec and Syrah wines. It has an art gallery, a restaurant and a famous barrel from Nancy, France, with an impressive sculpture of Dionysus.

Bodega Santa Ana (☎ 0261-421-1000, Roca & Urquiza, Villa Nueva, Guaymallén; bus No 200 'Buena Nueva via Godoy Cruz' from La Rioja; open 8:30am-5pm Mon-Fri). If you're been pinching pennies, you'll surely come across Santa Ana among the inexpensive wines on restaurant menus. It does, however, boast some excellent wines which you can taste following, broke or not, after the friendly tour.

Bodega La Rural (Museo del Vino) (☎ 0261-497-2013, Montecaseros 2625, Coquimbito, Maipú; bus No 173; open 9:30am-5:30pm Mon-Fri, tours every half-hour; 10am-1pm Sat & Sun, tours every hour). Maker of the esteemed San Felipe, Rutini and Felipe Rutini wines, Bodega La Rural

Finer & Finer Argentine Wine

Wine making goes back over 500 years in Argentina, to when the first Spanish colonists planted grapes in several regions of the interior. The Jesuits planted their own vineyards in the north, developing the *criolla* grape. It wasn't until the immigration boom of the 19th century that French, Italian and Spanish settlers began to take enology seriously, bringing in their countries' best grapes to grow vines in western Argentina, where the rain shadow of the Andes provided an ideal setting for industrial viticulture. The opening of the railway line between Buenos Aires and Mendoza in 1884 meant the wine could travel to the wealthy capital and compete with the imported bottles kept in patricians' cellars.

But for all the French mansions in Buenos Aires, the wines never rivaled European ones. Up until a mere decade ago, the most famous thing about *vino argentino* was that it never left the country. The second most famous thing was that – according to critics and merchants – this was just as well, since the vast majority of wines produced by Argentine *bodegas* were too low-grade for export. As a result, the natives were welcome – and encouraged – to drink every last drop.

This they certainly did. Though Argentina has been the world's fifth-largest wine producer for some time, the domestic market traditionally drank almost every drop of the stuff. In the 1960s, annual consumption stood as high as 25 liters per capita, compared with around 10 liters at present. That said, any good *asado* is still incomplete without a bottle of *vino fino* (a decent varietal or a blend), or, at the low end, a *vino comun* (table wine) in a flagon with a blast of soda to smooth its rough edges. Recently, as beer has gained in popularity in Argentina, the big vineyards have had to market themselves internationally, necessitating better wine-making technology and a better product. On the whole, the response from international wine competitions, critics and consumers has been favorable, and Argentine wines are now a common sight worldwide.

Still, there are compelling reasons to indulge in a drop or three of Argentine wine while in-country and check out the local wine scene. One, you get to visit Argentina's wine mecca, Mendoza, with its hundreds of charming vineyards producing almost three quarters of the country's total wine crop. Here irrigation techniques first introduced by the native Huarpe Indians are still used to water the desertlike landscape. The upscale ambitions of big, high-tech vineyards like Etchart, Norton, Catena and La Agricola are gradually rubbing off on smaller producers, and all are keen to show of their wares. Whether you are visiting a major establishment or a small operation, if you're lucky the owners – and many wineries are still family-owned and run – will be around to show you their grand old oak barrels and latest international-standard metallic vats.

Another reason for wine-inspired travel is that while only a few dozen big-brand labels are exported, the choice of labels within Argentina is vast, and some exceptional wines are available only

should be top on your list if only for its outstanding wine museum, the biggest in South America. Tours are offered in English, the guides are very friendly, and there's no hard sell in the tasting room.

Bodega Viña El Cerno (☎ *0261-481-156 Moreno 631, Coquimbito, Maipú; bus N 170; tours 9am-5pm Mon-Fri, or with reserva tions Sat & Sun*). Built in 1864, this romant cally small winery, surrounded by vineyard

Finer & Finer Argentine Wine

at their source or in the big city bistros. The vineyards often do wine tasting at the end of brief tours, and chances are they'll spoil you. Finally, and crucially, wine – like other legal vices – is pretty cheap in Argentina, even when the quaffing is of a high quality.

Argentine wines are made from grapes of European origin, and the familiar Cabernet, Chardonnay and Syrah varieties abound. The hot climate in Mendoza favors reds, and Argentine Malbecs, rightly famed in international wine circles, can be outstanding. For fans of white, Torrontés, a Spanish grape unpopular outside Argentina, produces some of the best bottles. For a few pesos, wines produced by Graffigna, Santa Julia and San Telmo are ultra-reliable; for a bottle from the south, Río Negro's Patagonia is very good. If you want to splurge, try Catena or Weinert wines, and the local bubbly from Moet & Chandon is a relatively economical way to look rich.

Corkage can double the prices in bars and restaurants so check the menu offerings.

— Chris Moss

A scientist tests a recent vintage to see if it's ready for the market. Mendoza has over 2000 wineries (bodegas) and produces 80% of Argentina's wines.

was abandoned for years until it was restored and reopened six years ago. About five people work the place, including its two owners. Depending on your guide, tours can range from relaxed and personal to speedy and cold (often depending on the guide's assessment of visitors' spending potential). Either way, though, it's well worth a visit.

Bodega Giol (☎ 0261-497-6777, Ozamis 1040, Maipú; bus No 174; tours 9am-7pm

Mon-Sat, 11am-2pm Sun). Giol is known for its turn-of-the-century brick facade and the magnificent barrel won by the winery in France in 1910. Next door is the **Museo Nacional de Vino y Vendimia** *(no ☎, Ozamis 914; admission US$1; open 10am-7pm Mon-Sat, 10am-1pm Sun).*

Bodega Lagarde *(☎ 0261-498-0011, San Martín 1745, Luján de Cuyo; bus No 204 from bus terminal; tours 10am, 11am, noon, 2:30pm, 3:30pm & 4:30pm Mon-Fri, or with reservations Sat & Sun).* A big producer of Malbec and Cabernet, this expansive winery is also worth a visit.

Bodegas Chandon *(☎ 0261-490-9900, RN 40, Km 29, Luján de Cuyo; bus No 380 from bus terminal; open 9:30am-12:30pm & 2pm-3:30pm Mon-Fri most of the year until 5pm Mon-Fri & 9:30-12:30 Sun in Feb, Mar & July).* This modern winery is popular with tour groups and known for its sparkling wines. Tours are available in English.

Calvario de la Carrodilla

A national monument since 1975, this church *(bus Nos 10 & 200; free; open 10am-noon & 5pm-8pm Mon-Fri)* in Carrodilla, Godoy Cruz, houses an image of the Virgin of Carrodilla, the patron of vineyards, brought from Spain in 1778. A center of pilgrimage for Mendocinos and other Argentines, it also has samples of indigenous colonial sculpture.

Cacheuta

About 40km west of Mendoza in the department of Luján de Cuyo, Cacheuta (altitude 1237m) is renowned for its medicinal thermal waters and agreeable microclimate. There is lodging at **Hotel Termas Cacheuta** *(☎ 02624-482082, RP 82, Km 38; ☎ 0261-431-6085, fax 0261-431-6089 in Mendoza),* singles/doubles US$115/192 with full board. The rooms are pleasant but unexceptional for the price, which includes a swimming pool, hot tubs, massage, mountain bikes in addition to recreation programs. The local mailing address is Rodríguez Peña 1412, Godoy Cruz, Mendoza. Nonguests may use the baths for US$10 per person.

Campers can pitch a tent at **Campin̄** **Termas de Cacheuta** *(☎ 482082, RN 7, Km 39)* for US$4 per person. For eats, **Mis Montañas** is a well-regarded restaurant.

Potrerillos

Passing through a typical pre-cordilleran landscape along the Río Blanco, the main source of drinking water for the capital, westbound RN 7 leads to the Andean resort of Potrerillos (altitude 1351m), 45km from Mendoza. Bird watching is excellent in summer, but the area is also becoming a mecca for white-water rafting.

Rafting and kayaking on the Río Mendoza and the Diamante (near San Rafael) is arranged by Argentina Rafting Expediciones *(☎ 02624-482037, fax 02624-482036, mobile ☎ 155-691700, ☒ argentina rafting.com; river trips US$20-120),* opposite the ACA campground. River trips range from a 5km, one-hour Class II to a 50km, five-hour Class III-IV descent over two days. This company also arranges trekking and mountain bike expeditions.

Descents of the Río Mendoza are also conducted by Río Extremo Rafting *(☎/fax 02624-482007, mobile ☎ 02611-5563-0986, 02611-5563-6558, ☒ rioextremo@trivu.com, Av Los Cóndores s/n, or Güemes 785, Dpto 9, Godoy Cruz, Mendoza; US$25-299).*

Camping del ACA, on RN 7 at Km 50, costs US$10 per site for members, US$12 for nonmembers. There are two hotels in town: the modest **Hotel de Turismo** and the luxurious **Gran Hotel Potrerillos** *(☎ 0261 423-3000)* charging US$78/84 with breakfast, US$96/120 half-board, and US$114/150 with full board. **Armando** is a reliable restaurant in town.

Termas Villavicencio

If you've ordered *agua mineral* from any restaurant or café, odds are you've ended up at one point or another with a bottle of Villavicencio on your table. These springs are the source, and their spectacular mountain setting once hosted the prestigious thermal baths resort of the *Gran Hotel de Villavicencio.* Popular with the Argentine elite during the middle of the 20th century,

ιe resort has been closed for more than a
εcade due to legal entanglements. It was
εheduled to reopen in 1995 but there has
εen no discernible movement, and at this
riting the resort remains closed.

Panoramic views from the *caracoles*
ιwinding roads) leading to Villavicencio (al-
τude 1800m) make the journey an attrac-
on in itself. There is free camping alongside
Iostería Villavicencio, which serves simple
ιeals. Expreso Jocolí, in Mendoza, runs
uses from the terminal to Villavicencio
ξ1km northwest of Mendoza on RP 52) on
Vednesday, Saturday and Sunday.

ΙSPALLATA

ϖ 02624 • pop 3000 • elevation 1751m
ιhe polychrome mountains surrounding
ιis crossroads village, 105km west of
ιendoza via RN 7, so resemble highland
ɛntral Asia that director Jean-Jacques
΄nnaud used it as the location for the epic
ım *Seven Years in Tibet*, starring Brad Pitt.
΅or travelers, it's an excellent base for ex-
loring the scenic sierras, though it's a
retty desolate place.

The tourist office (no ϖ) is in one of the
ttle shops behind the YPF gas station and
εeps irregular hours. There's a post office
postal code 5545) and a branch of Banco
ε Mendoza, but no ATM.

hings to See & Do

Λ good rock-climbing area known as **Cerro
Λontura** is along RN 7 en route to Parque
΄rovincial Aconcagua and the Paso de los
ιibertadores to Chile, but farther up ·the
ılley the rock is too friable for safe climbing.

A kilometer north of the highway junc-
on in Uspallata, a signed lateral leads to
ιins and a free museum at the **Bóvedas
Λistóricas Uspallata**, a smelting site since
ιre-Columbian times. On view are diora-
ιas of battles that took place on General
ιregorio de Las Heras' campaign across
ιe Andes in support of San Martín.

Mendoza-bound motorists should con-
ιder taking the **Caracoles de Villavicencio**,
good gravel road even more scenic than
ιaved RN 7. A road sign at Uspallata re-
ιtricts the descent *(bajada)* to 2pm-8pm and

the ascent *(subida)* to 7am-noon, but at this
writing the road appears to be open to two-
way traffic at all hours.

Places to Stay & Eat

Camping Municipal (ϖ 420009) US$5 per
site. Uspallata's poplar-shaded campground
is 500m north of the Villavicencio junction
on RP 52. The north end of the facilities, near
the wood-fire-stoked hot showers, is much
quieter and a better place to pitch a tent.

Hotel Viena (ϖ 420046, Av Las Heras
240) US$15 per person. This warmly recom-
mended hotel, east of the highway junction,
has simple, comfortable rooms with bath.

Hostería Los Cóndores (ϖ 420002, fax
420303, e hostcondores@lanet.com.ar, Las
Heras s/n) Singles/doubles US$30/50. Closer
to the junction, this hotel has spacious, carpeted rooms with huge baths and an onsite
restaurant.

Hotel Valle Andino (ϖ 420033,
e weekend@infovia.com.ar, RN 7 s/n)
US$42/51/60 per person with breakfast/half-
board/full board. This hotel, at the southern
approach to town on RN 7, is upscale but
still not outrageously expensive. It has an
indoor pool, tennis courts, a game room, a
reading room and a TV lounge.

Hotel Uspallata (ϖ/fax 420003/66/67,
e cds-uspa@alsitio.net, RN 7 Km 1149)
Singles/doubles US$52/74 with breakfast,
US$62/94 half board, US$72/114 full board.
Though it looks a bit shopworn since its Peronist glory days, this resort hotel, about
1km west of the junction, offers spacious
grounds, tennis courts, a huge swimming
pool, a bar, a bowling alley, pool tables and
a restaurant.

Parrilla San Cayetano (ϖ 420149)
Behind the YPF station, this parrilla is a
convenient stop offering decent food for
travelers en route to and from Chile.

Café Tibet (mobile ϖ 0261-15-656-7224)
This place, near the junction in Uspallata's
only strip mall, capitalizes on town's cinematic notoriety and serves decent food.

Getting There & Away

Expreso Uspallata runs five buses every
weekday, four on weekends, from Mendoza

ARGENTINA

to Uspallata (US$8, 2½ hours); the 6am, 7am and 10:15am buses continue to the settlement of Las Cuevas, near the Chilean border, and stop en-route at Los Penitentes, Puente del Inca and the turnoff to Laguna Los Horcones for Parque Provincial Aconcagua. Buses back to Mendoza from Uspallata (five per day) leave from the Expreso Uspallata office in the little strip mall near the junction. Two of these buses begin their route in Las Cuevas, leaving that settlement at 11:30 am and 4:30pm, passing Los Horcones, Puente del Inca and Los Penitentes before stopping in Uspallata.

Buses between Mendoza and Santiago will carry passengers to points near and across the border, but are often full.

SKI RESORTS

While the soil lies barren and the poplars stand leafless, the snow brings visitors to the province from Argentina and overseas.

The two ski areas nearest to Mendoza are covered here; for the fashionable Las Leñas and Los Molles resorts, see the relevant information under Malargüe.

Vallecitos

Just 80km southwest of Mendoza, ranging between 2900 and 3200m in the Cordón del Plata, Vallecitos (☎ 0261-431-2713 in Mendoza; resort open July-early Oct), is the area's smallest and least expensive ski resort. Owned by the Ski Club Mendoza, the resort is 88 hectares of treeless slopes with six downhill runs.

Most skiers stay in Mendoza since the resort is so close, but affordable *Hostería La Canaleta* (☎ 0261-431-2779) has four-bunk rooms with private baths, as well as a restaurant and a snack bar. The cheapest accommodations are at *Refugio San Antonio* (no ☎), with private rooms, shared baths and a restaurant; and the comfier *Hostería Cerro Nevado* (no ☎).

Los Penitentes

Both the scenery and the snowcover are excellent at Los Penitentes (☎ 02624-420229, **w** www.lospenitentes.com), 165km west of Mendoza via RN 7, which offers downhill

and cross-country skiing at an altitude o 2580m. Lifts and accommodations ar modern, and the vertical drop on some of it 21 runs is more than 700m. Services includ a ski school, equipment rentals (skis US$2 per day, snowboards US$30) and severa restaurants and cafeterias. For transporta tion details, see the Uspallata Getting Ther & Away section. Places to stay include:

Hostel Los Penitentes (☎ 0261-429-070 in Mendoza, **e** info@campo-base.com.ar US$10 per person. This cozy converte cabin, owned by Mendoza's HI Camp Base, accommodates 20 in close quarter and has a kitchen, wood-burning stove an a shared bath – good fun with the righ crowd.

Hostería Los Penitentes (contact Lo Penitentes office ☎ 0261-427-1641, Paso d los Andes 1615, Departamento C, Godo Cruz) Doubles with private bath aroun US$400 per week during ski season, plus restaurant and bar.

Hostería Ayelén (☎ 0261-427-1123, fa. 427-1283, **e** hotelayelen@ciudad.com.ar postal address: Juan B Justo 1490, 554 Godoy Cruz, Mendoza) Singles/double US$53/70 summer, US$88/114 in ski season 6-8 person rooms at US$22 per person wit breakfast. This four-star resort hotel offer comfortable accommodations.

PUENTE DEL INCA

One of Argentina's most striking natura wonders, this stone bridge over the Río d las Cuevas glows a dazzling orange from th sediment deposited by the warm sulfuri waters that flow from the rocks beside it The brick ruins of an old spa, built as part o a resort and later destroyed by flood, si beneath the bridge, slowly yielding thei form to the sulfuric buildup from th thermal water that trickles over, around an through it; it makes for an unforgettable dip

Puente del Inca, 2720m above sea leve and 177km from Mendoza, sits betwee Parque Provincial Aconcagua and Parqu Provincial Volcán Tupungato. It enjoys spectacular setting, and whether or not yo climb, it's a good base for exploring th area. Trekkers and climbers can head north o the base of Aconcagua, south to the pinacles of **Los Penitentes** (so-named because ney resemble a line of monks), or even arther south to 6650m **Tupungato** (see 'arque Provincial Tupungato later in this hapter).

In summer, *camping* is possible at the earby mini ski resort of *Los Puquios* (☎ *02624-420190*). There are two accommolations options at Puente del Inca.

Refugio La Vieja Estación (☎ *0261-429-707 in Mendoza,* e *info@campo-base com.ar,* w *cerroaconcagua.com*) US$10 per lorm bed. This rustic hostel, In Puente del nca's old wooden train station built in the ate 1800's, is popular with climbers during eak-season but can be wonderfully quiet ther times of the year. It's only a stone's hrow from the thermal waters.

Hostería Puente del Inca (☎ *02624-20222, 0261-438-0480 in Mendoza, RN 7* *Km 175)* Singles/doubles US$40/50 with breakfast. Multi-bed rooms are much heaper and also include breakfast. It has a *estaurant* and may help arrange trekking and mules.

The nearby military outpost sells basic ood supplies, but you're best off bringing our own. For transportation details, see the Jspallata Getting There & Away section.

PARQUE PROVINCIAL ACONCAGUA

North of RN 7, nearly hugging the Chilean border, Parque Provincial Aconcagua projects 71,000 hectares of the wild high ountry surrounding the Western Hemiphere's highest summit, 6960m Cerro Aconcagua. Passing motorists (and those vho can time their buses correctly) can stop o enjoy the view of the peak from **Laguna Los Horcones**, a 2km walk from the parking ot just north of the highway.

There's a ranger available 8am to 9pm veekdays, 8am to 8pm Saturday. There are also rangers at the junction to Plaza Francia, about 5km north of Los Horcones; at Plaza de Mulas on the main route o the peak; at Refugio Las Leñas, on the Polish Glacier Route up the Río de las Vacas to the east; and at Plaza Argentina,

the last major camping area along the Polish Glacier Route.

Only highly experienced climbers should consider climbing Aconcagua without the relative safety of an organized tour; very often, skilled climbers themselves hire guides who know the mountain's Jeckle-and-Hyde weather changes.

Cerro Aconcagua

Often called the 'roof of the Americas,' the volcanic andesite summit of Aconcagua covers a base of uplifted marine sediments. The origin of the name is unclear; one possibility is the Quechua term *Ackon-Cahuac*, meaning 'stone sentinel,' while another is the Mapuche phrase *Acon-Hue,* signifying 'that which comes from the other side.'

Italian-Swiss climber Mathias Zurbriggen made the first recorded ascent in 1897. Since then, the peak has become a favorite destination for climbers from around the world, even though it is technically less challenging than other nearby peaks, most notably Tupungato to the south. In 1985, the Club Andinista Mendoza's discovery of an Inca mummy at 5300m on the mountain's southwest face proved that the high peaks were a pre-Columbian funerary site.

Reaching the summit requires a commitment of at least 13 to 15 days, including acclimatization time; some climbers prefer the longer but more scenic, less crowded, and more technical Polish route. Potential climbers should acquire RJ Seeker's climbing guide *Aconcagua* (Seattle, The Mountaineers, 1994). There's less detailed information in the 3rd edition of Bradt Publications' *Backpacking in Chile & Argentina.* The Internet information page (w www.aconcagua.com.ar) is also helpful.

Nonclimbers can trek to *base camps* and *refugios* beneath the permanent snow line; note that tour operators and climbing guides set up seasonal tents at the best campsites en route to and at the base camps, so independent climbers and trekkers usually get the leftover spots. On the Northwest Route there is also a rather luxurious and expensive Hotel Plaza de Mulas *(radio* ☎ *0261-425-7065).*

PARQUE PROVINCIAL ACONCAGUA

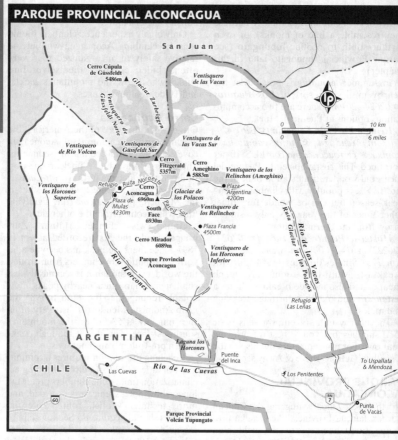

If you don't plan on climbing and would simply like to get a look at the mountain, the short hike up to Laguna Los Horcones offers excellent views of the peak and its spectacular surroundings.

Permits From December to March, permits are obligatory for both trekking and climbing in Parque Provincial Aconcagua; park rangers at Laguna Horcones will not permit visitors to proceed up the Quebrada de los Horcones without one. Fees vary according to the complex park-use seasons. Permits cost US$40 for trekkers (seven days), and US$160

for climbers (20 days) during high-season from December 15 through January 31 US$30 for trekkers and US$120 for climber during mid-season, from December 1 to De cember 14 and February 1 through February 20; and US$30 (trekking) and US$80 (climb ing) in low season, from November 1 through November 30 and February 21 through March 15. A shorter, three-day trekking permit is available for US$20 (al seasons) to Plaza Francia only, but its lack o flexibility makes it a poorer deal than the permit for the longer period. Argentine na tionals pay half price at all times.

Permits are available only in Mendoza and are sold at one of two locations, depending on where park management decides to sell them. At the time of writing, park permits were being sold at the provincial tourist office (☎ 0261-420-2800, San Martín 1143, see Tourist Offices in the Mendoza section, earlier). Check here first. If not they will probably be available at the Dirección de Recursos Naturales Renovables (☎ 0261-425-2090, Av Boulogne Sur Mer s/n; open 8am-8pm Mon-Fri, 8am-noon Sat & Sun) in the Parque San Martín in Mendoza.

Routes There are three main routes up Cerro Aconcagua. The most popular one, approached by a 40km trail from Los Horcones, is the **Ruta Noroeste** (Northwest Route) from Plaza de Mulas, 4230m above sea level. The **Pared Sur** (South Face), approached from the base camp at Plaza Francia via a 36km trail from Los Horcones, is a demanding technical climb.

From Punta de Vacas, 15km southeast of Puente del Inca, the longer but more scenic **Ruta Glaciar de los Polacos** (Polish Glacier Route) first ascends the Río de las Vacas to the base camp at Plaza Argentina, a distance of 76km. Wiktor Ostrowski and others pioneered this route in 1934. Climbers on this route must carry ropes, screws and ice axes, in addition to the usual tent, warm sleeping bag and clothing, and plastic boots. This route is more expensive because it requires the use of mules for a longer period.

Mules The cost of renting cargo mules, which can carry about 60kg each, has gone through the roof – the standard fee among outfitters is US$120 for the first mule from Puente del Inca to Plaza de Mulas, though two mules cost only US$160. A party of three should pay about US$240 to get their gear to the Polish Glacier Route base camp and back.

For mules, contact Rudy Parra at Aconcagua Trek (see below); or Fernando Grajales (see below) who operates from Hostería Puente del Inca from December through February. One party recommends Carlos Cuesta, who lives next to the cemetery at Puente del Inca. If you're going up on an organized tour, the mule situation is, of course, covered.

Organized Tours Many of the adventure-travel agencies in and around Mendoza arrange excursions into the high mountains; see the Mendoza Activities section for contact information. It is also possible to arrange trips with overseas operators; for details, see Organized Tours in the Getting There & Away chapter.

The most established operators in the area are Fernando Grajales (☎/fax 0261-429-3830, e expediciones@grajales.net), José Fedérico Moreno 898, 5500 in Mendoza, and Rudy Parra's Aconcagua Trek (☎/fax 0261-431-7003, e rudy@lanet.com.ar), Güiraldes 246, 5519 Dorrego, Mendoza. Also try Campo Base Adventures & Expeditions (see the Mendoza Activities section).

Several guides from the Asociación de Guías de Montaña lead two-week trips to Aconcagua, among them Alejandro Randis (☎ 0261-496-3461), Daniel Pizarro (☎ 0261-423-0698) and Gabriel Cabrera of Rumbo al Horizonte (☎ 0261-452-0641). The trips leave from Mendoza by bus to Puente del Inca, then follow the Ruta Noroeste, partly on mule.

Getting There & Away

The two park entrances – Punta de Vacas and Laguna Los Horcones – are directly off RN 7 and well signed. The Los Horcones turnoff is only 4km past Puente del Inca. If you have a car, you're fine. If you're part of an organized tour, transportation will be provided. If you're on your own, take a 6am, 7am or 10:15am Expreso Uspallata bus (see the Uspallata Getting There & Away section) from Mendoza. Buses bound for Chile will stop at Puente del Inca, but these often fill up with passengers going all the way through.

From Los Horcones, you can walk back along the RN 7 to Puente del Inca or time your buses and catch a Mendoza-bound bus back down.

LAS CUEVAS & CRISTO REDENTOR

Pounded by chilly but exhilarating winds, nearly 4000m above sea level on the Argentine-Chilean border, the rugged high Andes make a fitting backdrop for Cristo Redentor, the famous monument erected after a territorial dispute between the two countries was settled in 1902. The view is a must-see either with a tour or by private car (a tunnel has replaced the hairpin road to the top as the border crossing into Chile), but the first autumn snowfall closes the route.

Travellers can stay nearby in the tiny town of **Las Cuevas**, 10km before the border and 15km from Puente del Inca. Try the affordable and aptly named *Hostería Las Cuevas (no ☎)*.

Parque Provincial Volcán Tupungato

Tupungato (6650m) is an impressive volcano, partly covered by snowfields and glaciers, and serious climbers consider the mountain a far more challenging, interesting and technical climb than Aconcagua. The main approach is from the town of Tunuyán, 82km south of Mendoza via RN 40, where the tourist office (☎ 02622-488097, 422193), at República de Siria and Alem, can provide information. Many of the same outfitters who arrange Aconcagua treks can also deal with Tupungato.

SAN RAFAEL

☎ 02627 • pop 98,000 • elevation 690m

The streets of downtown San Rafael are lined with sycamores. The open irrigation channels that water them trace the city's clean, tiled sidewalks – and everywhere, there are bicycles.

There is nothing to do in town (part of its allure) except wander its shady streets and plazas or while the day away in a café. There are, however, several esteemed wineries around town that are well worth a visit. San Rafael, beneath the distant backdrop of scenic peaks, has lately become a popular base for exploring (or driving through) the nearby Cañon de Atuel, and for scenic rafting on the Río Atuel.

Founded as a military outpost, San Rafael is now a modern commercial-industrial center, busy but with a small-town feel. Its *acequias* (irrigation canals) are a reminder that this is a desert, and that the town's trees, along with some 60,000 hectares of outlying vineyards, are all irrigated by the nearby Atuel and Diamante rivers.

Orientation

San Rafael is 230km southeast of the city of Mendoza via RN 40 and RN 143, and 189km northeast of Malargüe via RN 40. The main thoroughfare is RN 143, known as Av Hipólito Yrigoyen west of Av El Libertador/Av San Martín, the city's main north-south axis. East of Libertador/San Martín, RN 143 is known as Av Bartolomé Mitre. Most areas of interest to visitors are northwest of the Yrigoyen-San Martín intersection.

Information

The municipal tourist office (☎ 424217, toll-free ☎ 0800-222-2555), Av Hipólito Yrigoyen 745, has helpful staff and useful brochures and maps. It's open 8am to 8:30pm daily (to 10pm in summer).

Cambio Santiago, at Almafuerte 64, charges 2½% on traveler's checks. Several banks along Yrigoyen have ATMs, including Banco de Galicia at Yrigoyen 28.

The post office is at San Lorenzo and Barcala; the postal code is 5600.

There are numerous agencies offering standard local excursions to Valle Grande and nearby wineries. Try Leufú (☎/fax 428164), Cabildo 1483, which does rafting, mountain biking and other activities.

San Rafael's Hospital (☎ 424490) is at Emilio Civit 151, at the corner of Corrientes.

Wineries

San Rafael has several wineries offering free tours and tasting. Four are within walking or cycling distance of town, west on RN 143, which has a welcome bike path along its side. Of these, the modern and highly regarded **Bianchi Champañera** *(☎ 455353, Ruta 143 y Calle El Salto; open 9am-12:30 & 3pm-6pm)*, is the farthest west.

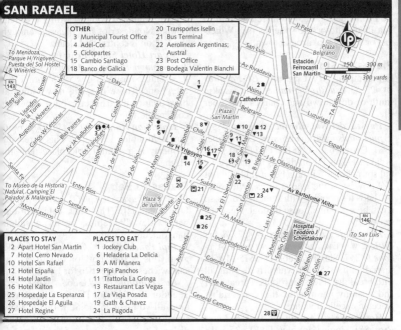

SAN RAFAEL

OTHER
3 Municipal Tourist Office
4 Adel-Cor
5 Ciclopartes
15 Cambio Santiago
18 Banco de Galicia
20 Transportes Iselín
21 Bus Terminal
22 Aerolineas Argentinas;
Austral
23 Post Office
28 Bodega Valentín Bianchi

PLACES TO STAY
2 Apart Hotel San Martín
7 Hotel Cerro Nevado
10 Hotel San Rafael
12 Hotel España
14 Hotel Jardín
16 Hotel Kalton
25 Hospedaje La Esperanza
26 Hospedaje El Aguila
27 Hotel Regine

PLACES TO EAT
1 Jockey Club
6 Heladería La Delicia
8 A Mi Manera
9 Pipi Panchos
11 Trattoría La Gringa
13 Restaurant Las Vegas
17 La Vieja Posada
19 Gath & Chavez
24 La Pagoda

out still only 6km away. Tours are friendly, offering a glimpse into the making of sparkling wine (champagne), and English is spoken.

Only about 4km out, **Bodega & Champañera Salafia** (☎ 430095, Yrigoyen 3800; open 8am-3:30pm) makes sparkling wine and excellent Malbec and Cabernet. It's a worthwhile visit, especially for the tasting. **Suter** (☎ 421076, Yrigoyen 2850; open 8:30am-4:30pm Mon-Thur, 8:30am-3:30pm Fri, 9am-4:30pm Sat) is a rather unromantic, modern affair, but a mandatory stop for the whopping 30% discount and free half-bottle. **Jean Rivier** (☎ 432675, Yrigoyen 2385; open 8am-11am & 3pm-6pm Mon-Sat) is the closest to town. Run by the sons of its Swiss founder, this traditional winery is prized for its Chenin Blanc and Tocais as well as its blended reds.

In town, **Bodega Valentín Bianchi** (☎ 422046, Torres 500; open 9am-5pm Mon-Fri) is the original winery founded by award-winning winemaker Don Valentín in 1928. The production of sparkling wine was moved out to the Bianchi Champañera, and this attractive bodega now concentrates solely on its fine Chardonnays, Malbecs and Cabernets and table wines.

Other Things to See & Do
Worthwhile sights are **Parque Hipólito Yrigoyen**, at the west end of town, the **Catedral**, at Belgrano and Pellegrini on the north side of Plaza San Martín, and the **Museo de Historia Natural** (☎ 422121 interno 290, Isla Río Diamante; admission US$1; open 7am-1pm & 2pm-8pm daily), 6km south of downtown on Isla Río Diamante, an island in the middle of the river.

San Rafael is flat (which explains the bikes) and when in Rome...get a bike. Choices are slim, but first try **Ciclopartes** (☎ 430260, Chile 445; US$15 per day; open 8am-1pm & 4pm-8:30pm Mon-Sat). Otherwise try **Adel-Cor** (☎ 420102, Yrigoyen &

Los Frances; US$12 per day; same hours). You can ride the bike path (really!) out to Isla Diamante or the wineries (see Wineries) or simply tool around town.

Places to Stay

For camping, try **Camping El Parador** (☎ 427983, *Isla Río Diamante),* which is 6km south of downtown and charges US$5 per site.

Puesta del Sol Hostel (☎/fax 434881, e *puestadelsol@infovia.com.ar, Deán Funes 998)* Dorm bed US$10, US$12.50 with breakfast. This HI affiliate is an impressive but sprawling affair on a beautiful lot about 1½km west of the tourist office. With over 240 beds it's popular with student groups, so it can be a real madhouse (though quiet off-season).

Hospedaje La Esperanza (☎ 427978, fax 430160, w *www.laesperanza-sr.com.ar, Avellaneda 263)* Singles/doubles US$15/24 with shared bath, US$20/30 with private bath, all with breakfast. Pleasant rooms, a great staff and a sunny patio make this comfortable place an excellent value.

Hospedaje El Aguila (☎ 430886, *Entre Ríos 88)* Singles/doubles US$15/25 with bath & TV. This subdued but friendly hotel has spotless rooms and decent beds.

Prices for the following hotels all include breakfast and private bathrooms.

Hotel Cerro Nevado (☎ 423993, fax 428209, Yrigoyen 376) Singles/doubles US$25/34 with TV & telephone. This is a central place with clean carpeted rooms.

Hotel España (☎ 424055, Av San Martín 270) Singles/doubles US$18/32 & US$24/42. The cheaper rooms in the appealing colonial sector open onto a small patio, while the pricier modern rooms are spacious and quiet.

Hotel Regine (☎ 421470, Independencia 623) Singles/doubles US$31/59. This is a large, attractive place in a quiet area with a swimming pool and a grassy yard.

Hotel Jardín (☎/fax 434621, Yrigoyen 283) Singles/doubles US$33/53 with TV & telephone. An immaculate new place, the Jardín has good service, firm beds and spacious rooms.

Hotel Kalton (☎ 430047, Yrigoyen 120) Singles/doubles US$44/64 with TV & telephone. Nondescript but pleasant enough the Kalton is central and clean.

Apart Hotel San Martín (☎/fax 433363 e *hotelsanmartin@infovia.com.ar, San Martín 435)* Singles/doubles US$55/75 with TV & telephone. These dazzling new rooms al have their own kitchenettes but a somewhat cold, modern feel.

Hotel San Rafael (☎/fax 430127, Day 30, Singles/doubles US$63/88. This three-star property is a comfortable place near the plaza.

Places to Eat

Gath & Chavez (☎ 434960, San Martín 98) Open 8am-late. This slick café-cum-bar, with sidewalk tables, is an excellent hangout, day or night.

Pipi Panchos (no ☎) On Chile near Pellegrini, this is the spot for *lomitos* (steak sandwiches); you get two for US$2.50.

La Pagoda (☎ 433868, Mitre 216) Tenedor libre US$6. This is a small, reliable all-you-can-eat joint with the usual smattering of salad, chicken and Chinese dishes.

La Vieja Posada (☎ 15-585107, Pellegrini 15) US$5-9. If you want to fill the belly cheaply, do it at a wholesome, family place like this.

Restaurant Las Vegas (☎ 421390, San Martín 226) Three set courses US$7.50. This is a decent parrilla.

Tratoría La Gringa (☎ 436500, Chile 26) Full meals US$7-13. This modern, well-liked pasta house has a long menu of pizzas and pastas at reasonable prices.

A Mi Manera (☎ 422907, Salas 199) This elaborate eatery has good atmosphere and decent meats and pastas, though it's slightly pricey.

Jockey Club (☎ 422336, Belgrano 330) Tenedor libre US$10 to US$12. One of the town's finer restaurants offers all-you-can-eat with good meats and pastas but an unimpressive salad bar.

Heladería La Delicia (☎ 421103, Buenos Aires 49) Open noon-11pm daily. Good ice cream, great patio.

One Hail of a Summer

As if Mendoza province's desert climate wasn't challenge enough for the region's grape growers, the meteorological powers-that-be had to throw in summer hailstorms to boot. Southern Mendoza is one of the most hail-prone regions on the planet, and when the stones fall here, they're not just pea-size annoyances. *Tormentas Granizadas* (hailstorms) in Mendoza sometimes produce stones the size of golf balls; in the most severe cases, stones have reached nearly 500 grams in weight, about the size of a North American baseball. Falling balls of ice are hard enough on an automobile – not to mention a head – but they can destroy an entire season's grape harvest in less than 30 minutes. For a province that produces some 70% of the country's wine, this is not to be taken lightly.

The most straightforward and obvious precaution taken by vineyard owners can be witnessed everywhere; just watch for the black, plastic protective mesh stretched over most of the region's vines. Stories also abound of large-scale landowners shooting explosives into those towering tell-tale cumulous clouds forming over their vineyards. At some point, however, someone decided that a small falling rocket can be as dangerous as a hailstone if you're standing in the wrong place. The province now spends millions of dollars annually contracting companies like Weather Modification Inc of Fargo North Dakota, which uses jet aircraft and a bit of Russian rocket technology to launch what are essentially 'ice bombs' into the storm system. Once fired, the flarelike device essentially 'seeds' a storm cloud with ice crystals, creating a higher density of small hailstones rather than fewer big ones. But even with storm-altering technology, Mendoza loses about 10-15% of its grape harvest annually to hail.

Automobiles, on the other hand, receive token protection with *refugios granizeros* (hailstorm shelters), erected every now and again along the roads of southern Mendoza. The most humorous of these shelters are the ones without covers (according to locals, some folks feel they can put the strong plastic coverings to better use elsewhere). With the province playing Zeus, however, the odds of taking a hailstone to the head are slim indeed.

Getting There & Around

Aerolíneas Argentinas /Austral (☎ 420878), Mitre 102, flies daily to Buenos Aires (from US$132).

San Rafael's bus terminal is on Coronel Suárez between Avellaneda and Alma-fuerte. Most services from Mendoza to Buenos Aires province and points south pass through here. A number of carriers offer direct nightly service to Buenos Aires (US$35-46, 13 hours).

There are numerous daily departures to Mendoza (US$10, 3 hours), Malargüe (US$9, 2½ hours), and General Alvear (US$5.50, 1½ hours); and at least three daily to Las Leñas (US$4.50, 3 hours) and El Nihuil (US$4.50, 1½ hours). Buses head daily to San Luis (US$16, 4 hours) and San Juan (US$18, 6 hours).

Other carriers go to Mar del Plata (US$54, 16 hours) and Neuquén (US$24, 8 hours), with transfers to coastal Patagonian destinations and Bariloche. There are also daily departures to Córdoba (US$38, 12 hours), Rosario (US$38, 12 hours) and Santa Fe.

Transportes Iselín (☎ 435998), Suarez 255, goes to to Valle Grande/Cañon del Atuel (see around San Rafael for details). Buses leave from the front of the office.

The best (and one of the only) deals on rental cars is with Renta Autos (☎/fax 424623, 15-661449, rentaautos@infovia.com .ar), which operates by phone and delivers the car.

AROUND SAN RAFAEL

South of San Rafael along the Río Atuel, RP 173 passes through a multicolored ravine that locals compare to Arizona's Grand Canyon of the Colorado, though much of **Cañon del Atuel** has been submerged by four hydroelectric dams, the last one completed in 1998. Nevertheless, there is whitewater rafting on its upper reaches, and Portal del Atuel (☎ 02627-423583), the tourist complex at Km 35 at Valle Grande, does short but scenic floats down the river as well as other excursions, including horseback riding and a relaxing catamaran tour on the reservoir.

El Nihuil, 79km from San Rafael, is one of the province's main watersports centers. Its 9600-hectare reservoir, **Dique El Nihuil**, has a constant breeze that makes it suitable for windsurfing and sailing; other activities include swimming, canoeing and fishing.

Camping Club de Pescadores (☎ 426087) offers tent sites for US$10 and 4-person bungalows for US$80. This campground also has a restaurant and store.

El Nihuil proper has several *restaurants* and a gas station.

Numerous San Rafael tour companies run day trips out here to Valle Grande starting at US$20. For bus service to Valle Grande, Transportes Iselín leaves from in front of its office in San Rafael (see the San Rafael Getting There & Around section) at 7:30am, 12:40pm and 6:30pm Monday through Friday, and at 9am and 12:40pm on Saturday and Sunday (US$3.50, 1 hour).

GENERAL ALVEAR
☎ 02625 • pop 45,000 • elevation 466m

The southern gateway to Mendoza Province, General Alvear lacks the shady tree-lined streets that are so appealing in San Rafael farther north.

Southern Mendoza is a major cattle-breeding region. Each year around the second week of May, over 5000 *terneros* (calves) are sold in General Alvear to buyers from the pampas during the town's Fiesta National de La Ganadería de Zonas Áridas (National Festival of Arid-Region Cattle Breeders). Attended by over 80,000 people, the festival is similar to the North American rodeo, but with gaucho horsemanship shows, live music, crafts and supposedly the world's biggest asado.

General Alvear is 90km east of San Rafael via RN 143. The tourist office (☎ 424594, [e] mga-des@slatinos.com.ar) is at the corner of Av Alvear Este and Buenos Aires.

Places to Stay & Eat
There are a couple decent hotels in town, including the following.

Hotel Alhambra (☎ 422327, Sarmiento 55) Singles/doubles US$15/20 with private bath, fan & TV. If you don't mind cramped rooms this is a fine little place near the main plaza, and there's a small back yard.

Grosso Hotel (☎ 420392, Av Alvear Oeste & Lange) Singles/doubles US$15/25 with bath & air-con. This newly renovated place, with clean rooms and a downstairs café, is a good value.

El Parador (☎ 422187, Av Alvear Este 162) US$7 is a fair price for this popular tenedor libre, which includes parrillada.

Shopping
If you want to stock up on wine, do it at the down-home **Vineria La Casa de Baco** (*open 8am-2pm & 4:30-8:30 Mon-Sat, 8am-2pm Sun*) on Libertador Norte near Roque Sáenz Peña; the prices are great.

Getting There & Away
Buses running between San Rafael and Mendoza regularly stop in General Alvear.

MALARGÜE
☎ 02627 • pop 24,000 • elevation 1400m

In the dry pre-cordillera of the Andes, 189km southwest of San Rafael via paved RP 144 and RN 40, Malargüe draws visitors not so much for the town – it's not a particularly attractive place – but for outdoor pursuits in the spectacular dry mountains around it. For skiers, it's a cheaper budget alternative to the luxury hotels of nearby Las Leñas ski resort; the closer and cheaper resort of Los Molles recently initiated a deep discount on lift tickets for anyone staying in Malargüe. Two fauna reserves, Payén and Laguna Llancanelo, are close by, and caving is possible at Caverna de las Brujas and Pozo de las Animas.

Orientation & Information

Malargüe is 189km southwest of San Rafael via paved RP 144 and RN 40, which becomes Av San Martín through town. The helpful tourist office (☎ 471659, 470148, 0800-666-8569) has facilities at the northern end of town, directly on the highway.

The post office is at Adolfo Puebla and Saturnino Torres; Malargüe's postal code is 5613. Banco de la Nación, at the corner of San Martín and Inalicán, has an ATM.

Things to See & Do

At the northern approach to town, Malargüe's **Parque de Ayer** is a shady, professionally landscaped park that also serves as something of an open-air museum for objects that won't fit into the regional museum. Just south of the park, the **Molino de Rufino Ortega** is a former flour mill built by the town's founder.

Organized Tours

Several companies offer excellent 4WD and horseback excursions, and if you don't have a car these are generally the best way to get into the surrounding mountains. Possible day trips include Caverna de las Brujas, the Aguas Termales Los Molles and the marvelous Laguna Llancancelo, a high mountain lake visited by over 100 species of birds, including flamingos. Day trips start at around US$20 per person. The owner of **Karen Travel** (☎/fax 470342, San Martín 1056) speaks English and offers some enticing (and reportedly very well run) trips. Other reputable outfits include **Cari-Lauquen** (☎ 470025, fax 471958, e carilauq @slatinos.com.ar), and **Huarpes del Sol** (☎ 15-584842, Illesca 220).

Places to Stay & Eat

Malargüe has abundant, reasonably priced accommodations, though prices rise during ski season. Los Molles ski resort recently began offering a 50% discount on lift tickets to anyone staying here.

The closest place to camp is at *Camping Municipal Malargüe* (☎ 470691, Alfonso Capdevila s/n), Sites US$5 ; at the north end of town; open year-round.

Hostería La Posta (☎ 15-660633, San Martín 646) Dorm bed & breakfast US$15 high season, US$10 low. The communal bathrooms are a bit shabby, and the rooms are only decent, but it's cheap.

Hotel de Turismo (☎ 471042, Av San Martín 224) Singles/doubles US$33/47 with private bath, breakfast, TV & telephone. Rooms here are plain but comfortable and spacious; the upstairs rooms are the best.

Hotel Bambi (☎/fax 471237, Av San Martín 410) Singles/doubles US$40/60 high season with private bath & breakfast. This friendly place has clean rooms with basic baths.

Hotel Portal del Valle (☎ 471294, RN 40 s/n) US$50 per person with half-board. This well-regarded hotel at the north end of town is the finest in Malargüe.

La Posta (☎ 471306, Av Roca 374) This is the best restaurant in town, serving local specialities such as *chivito* (barbecued goat) and trout, and great US$4 lunch specials.

Getting There & Around

There are flights to and from Buenos Aires in ski season only, leaving from the Malargüe airport (☎ 470098) at the south end of town. The Aerolíneas/Austral representative is Karen Travel (☎ 470342), Av San Martín 1056.

The bus terminal is at the corner of Av General Roca and Aldao. To Mendoza (US$20, 6 hours), there are several direct buses daily, plus others requiring a change in San Rafael (US$9, 2½ hours).

There is daily service in summer from Malargüe across the 2500m Paso Pehuenche and down the spectacular canyon of the Río Maule to Talca, Chile.

For transportation to Los Molles and Las Leñas ski resorts, contact any of the travel agencies listed under Organized Tours, earlier. They offer roundtrip shuttle service, including ski rentals, from US$15 to $US20 per person. Karen Travel offers particularly good deals.

Autotransportes Malargüe leaves from Plaza San Martín, at Torres, to Las Leñas (US$10); contact the tourist office for departure times.

AROUND MALARGÜE
Caverna de Las Brujas
Malargüe travel agencies arrange excursions (US$20 per person plus US$10 entrance fee with an obligatory guide) to this magical limestone cave on Cerro Moncol, 72km south of Malargüe and 8km north of Bardas Blancas along RN 40. Its name means 'cave of the witches' and locals say it was once a place of ritual and witchcraft.

Los Molles
Los Molles is a small, quiet ski resort along RP 222 in the transverse valley of the Río Salado, 55km northwest of Malargüe. Single 1100m lifts carry skiers up the relatively gentle slopes, covering 90 hectares, while the thermal baths (US$6) provide a local attraction.

On the road to more exclusive Las Leñas, Los Molles' accommodations include the comfortable A-frame *Hotel Lahuen-Co* (☎ *02627-499700*), charging US$30 per person with half-board. Prices also include two dips in the nearby thermal baths.

There are also a couple small *guesthouses*. It is cheaper to stay here or in Malargüe and ski at Las Leñas, but both places lack the larger resort's nightlife.

LAS LEÑAS
Designed primarily to attract wealthy foreigners, Las Leñas is Argentina's most self-consciously prestigious ski resort, but despite the glitter it's not totally out of the question for budget travelers. Since its opening in 1983, it has attracted an international clientele who spend their days on the slopes and nights partying until the sun comes up.

Open mid-June to late September, with international competitions every year, Las Leñas is 445km south of Mendoza, 200km southwest of San Rafael and only 70km from Malargüe, all via RN 40 and RP 222.

Its 33 runs cover 3300 hectares; the area has a base altitude of 2200m, but the slopes reach 3430m for a maximum drop of 1230m. One of the runs has lights and music twice a week, and there is a ski school with classes at several levels, taught in Spanish, English, French, German, Italian and Portuguese.

Outside the ski season, Las Leñas is also attempting to attract summer visitors who enjoy weeklong packages offering activities such as windsurfing, mountain biking, horseback riding and hiking.

Lift Tickets & Rentals
Prices for lift tickets vary considerably throughout the ski season. Children's tickets are discounted about 30%. One-day tickets range from US$27 in low season to US$42 in high season (half-day US$18 to US$32). There are corresponding rates for three-day, four-day, one-week, two-week and season passes.

Lifts run 9am to 5pm daily. Rental equipment is readily available and will set you back about US$20 per day for skis and US$30 per day for snowboards.

Places to Stay & Eat
Las Leñas has a small village with three luxury hotels and a group of apart-hotels, all under the same management. They are generally booked as part of a weeklong package, which includes lodging, unlimited skiing and two meals per day. All booking is done centrally in Buenos Aires (☎ *011-4393-8031, fax 011-4394-1905,* e *maxisol@ infovia.com.ar, Juncal 858, 1st floor)* or through Badino Turismo (☎ *011-4326-1351, fax 4393-2568, Paraguay 930, Buenos Aires)*. Reservations can also be made online at www.laslenas.com.

The most extravagant of Las Leña's lodging is the five-star, 99-room *Hotel Piscis*. This prestigious hotel has wood-burning stoves, a gymnasium, sauna facilities, an indoor swimming pool, the elegant Las Cuatro Estaciones restaurant, a bar, a casino and shops. Depending on the time of the season, weekly adult package rates range from US$912 to US$2435 per person, double occupancy.

Hotel Aries is a four-star hotel with a sauna, gym facilities, a restaurant and luxuriously comfortable rooms. Its rates range from US$750 to US$1490. The 47-room *Hotel Escorpio* is nominally three stars, but still top-notch, with an excellent restaurant. Package rates here range from US$730 to US$1820 in high season.

Apart Hotel Gemenis and *Apart Hotel Delphos* offer similar packages without meals but do have well-equipped kitchenettes, and guests can use the facilities at Hotel Piscis. Weekly rates range from US$360 to US$1365 per person.

There are also small *apartments* with two to six beds and shared bathrooms, equipped for travelers to cook for themselves. Budget travelers can stay more economically at Los Molles, 20km down the road, or at Malargüe, 70km away.

Restaurants in the village run the comestible gamut, from cafés, sandwich shops and pizzerías to upscale hotel dining rooms. The finest restaurant of all is *Las Cuatro Estaciones*, in the Hotel Piscis.

Getting There & Away
In season, there are charter flights from Buenos Aires to Malargüe for about US$320 roundtrip, including transfers to and from Las Leñas. Airport transfers alone cost US$25 roundtrip to Malargüe, US$90 to San Rafael.

There is scheduled bus service in season from Mendoza, San Rafael and Malargüe with several companies; for details, see the respective cities' Getting There & Away sections.

SAN JUAN
☎ 0264 • pop 118,486 • elevation 650m
Capital of its namesake province, San Juan lies 165km north of Mendoza, and despite its administrative status, modern construction and wide, tree-lined avenues, the city retains the rhythm and cordiality of a small town. With an annual average of nine hours of sun daily, the city is nicknamed Residencia del Sol (Residence of the Sun). As in Mendoza, the streets are empty during siesta hours, between noon and 4pm.

Founded as San Juan de la Frontera in 1562 by Juan Jufré de Loaysa y Montesso, the desert city struggled in its early years, and from colonial times to the present, San Juan has lagged behind larger and more influential Mendoza. Though surrounding vineyards and orchards have grown and improved, it has failed to attract supporting industries and lies off the region's principal transit routes.

A massive 1944 earthquake destroyed the city center, and Juan Perón's subsequent relief efforts are what first made him a national figure. Completely rebuilt since then, the downtown sparkles from the efforts of full-time custodians who sweep the sidewalks and water and patrol the parks and plazas, shooing people off the manicured lawns. As in Mendoza, people swab the sidewalks with kerosene to keep them shining.

Orientation
San Juan is 170km north of Mendoza via RN 40, which passes through San Juan from north to south, and 1140km from Buenos Aires. Like most Argentine cities, San Juan's grid pattern makes orientation very easy; the addition of cardinal points to street addresses helps even more. East-west Av San Martín and north-south Calle Mendoza divide the city into quadrants. The functional center of town is south of Av San Martín.

Information
The provincial tourist office (☎ 422-2431), Sarmiento 24 Sur, has a good map of the city and its surroundings plus useful information and brochures on the rest of the province, particularly Parque Provincial Ischigualasto (Valle de la Luna). Hours are 7am to 9pm weekdays, 9am to 9pm weekends; 8am-4pm daily in winter. The satellite office at the bus terminal is open 7am to 8pm weekdays, 9am to 1pm weekends.

ACA (☎ 422-3781) is at 9 de Julio 802.

Cambio Santiago is at General Acha 52 Sur, and there are several downtown ATMs.

The post office is at Av Ignacio de la Roza 259 Este; the postal code is 5400. There are many locutorios. Cybercafé San Juan, at José Ignacio de la Roza 192 Oeste, charges US$2.50 per hour for Internet service and keeps the doors open between 9am and 2am.

They Call the Wind El Zonda

While traveling through San Juan, especially in fall and winter, you may become acquainted – through hearsay if not through experience – with one of the region's meteorological marvels: *el zonda*. Much like the Chinook of the Rockies or the foehn of the European Alps, the zonda is a dry, warm wind that can raise a cold day's temperatures from freezing to nearly 20°C (68°F). The zonda originates with storms in the Pacific that blow eastward, hit the Andes, dump their moisture and come whipping down the eastern slopes, picking up heat as they go. The wind, which varies from mild to howling, can last several days; *sanjuaninos* (people from San Juan) can step outside and tell you when it will end – and that it will be cold when it does. It's a regular occurrence, giving the region – and the sanjuaninos – a severe seasonal schizophrenia, especially in winter.

Several agencies organize trips to the interior or to other provinces. Saitur Saul Saidel (☎ 422-2700, e saitur@saulsaidel.com, José Ignacio de la Roza 112 Este) offers city tours and day trips, usually contracted through Raúl Romarión (☎ 155-669816), to Valle de La Luna (Ischigualasto) and Valle de Zonda. Also try Mario Agüero Turismo (☎ 422-3652), at General Acha 17 Norte.

Laverap laundry is at Rivadavia 498 Oeste.

The Hospital Rawson (☎ 422-2272) is at General Paz and Estados Unidos.

Museums

The **Casa de Sarmiento** (☎ 422-4603, Sarmiento 21 Sur; admission US$1; open 9am–7pm winter; 9am–1pm & 3pm–8pm summer except Mon & Sat, when it's open mornings only) is named for Domingo Faustino Sarmiento, whose prolific writing as a politician, diplomat, educator and journalist made him a public figure both within and beyond Argentina. Exiled in Chile during the reign of Rosas, he wrote the polemic *Life in the Argentine Republic in the Days of the Tyrants*, still available in English and used in many Latin American history courses. In office from 1868 to 1874, he was the first Argentine president from the interior provinces.

Sarmiento's *Recuerdos de Provincia* recounted his childhood in this house, and his memories of his mother, Doña Paula Albarracín, who paid for part of the house's construction by weaving cloth in a loom under the fig tree that still stands in the front patio. It is now a museum with plenty of related memorabilia, paintings and occasional theatrical reenactments by costumed actors.

Named after the local 19th-century painter, the **Museo de Bellas Artes Franklin Rawson** (☎ 422-9638, General Paz 737 Este; free; open 9am–12:30pm Mon-Fri) provides a good overview of Argentine painting, sculpture, drawing and engraving from artists including Prilidiano Pueyrredón, Raymond Monvoisin (a Frenchman who lived in Argentina), Ernesto de la Cárcova and Rawson himself.

Located in the same building, the **Museo Histórico Provincial Agustín Gnecco** (☎ 422-9638; free; open 9am–12:30pm Mon-Fri) has a notable collection of historical material related to San Juan's colonial life and political development.

The most interesting specimen at the **Museo de Ciencias Naturales** (*Museum of Natural Sciences;* ☎ 421-6774; free; open 8am–1pm & 3pm–8pm Mon-Fri, 9am–noon Sat) is the skeleton of the dinosaur *Herrerasaurus* from Ischigualasto, though there are plenty of provincial minerals, fossils and other exhibits to mull over. The museum is next to the old train station on Av España at Maipú.

Convento de Santo Domingo

Constructed after the earthquake, the present Dominican convent, at Av San Martín and Entre Ríos, lacks the grandeur of the 17th-century original, which was the order's richest convent in the territory. The only part of the old building to survive the quake was the cell occupied by San Martín. During several brief visits in 1815, he held

SAN JUAN

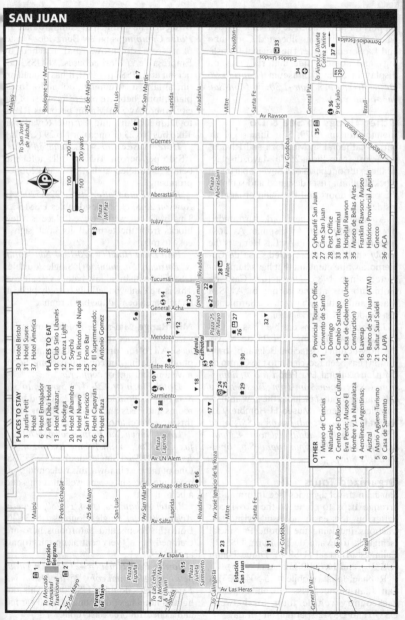

PLACES TO STAY
3 Jardín Petit Hotel
6 Hotel Embajador
7 Petit Dibú Hotel
13 Hotel Alkazar; La Bodega
20 Hotel Alhambra
23 Hotel Nuevo San Francisco
26 Hotel Capayán
29 Hotel Plaza
30 Hotel Bristol
31 Hotel Susex
37 Hotel América

PLACES TO EAT
10 Club Sirio Libanés
12 Cereza Light
17 Soychú
18 Un Rincón de Napoli
25 Fono Bar
32 El Supermercado; Antonio Gomez

OTHER
1 Museo de Ciencias Naturales
2 Centro de Difusión Cultural Eva Perón; Museo El Hombre y La Naturaleza
4 Aerolíneas Argentinas; Austral
5 Mario Agüero Turismo
8 Casa de Sarmiento
9 Provincial Tourist Office
11 Convento de Santo Domingo
14 Cambio Santiago
15 Casa de Gobierno (Under Construction)
16 Laverap
19 Banco de San Juan (ATM)
21 Saitur Saul Saidel
22 LAPA
24 Cybercafé San Juan
27 Cine San Juan
28 Post Office
33 Bus Terminal
34 Hospital Rawson
35 Museo de Bellas Artes Franklin Rawson; Museo Histórico Provincial Agustín Gnecco
36 ACA

meetings to solicit political and financial support for his Ejército de los Andes, one of whose local divisions liberated Coquimbo and La Serena, Chile. The original furnishings and some other materials are on display in a small museum *(Laprida 96 Oeste; free; open 9am-1:30pm Mon-Sat, 9am-noon Sun)*.

Other Things to See & Do

Inaugurated in 1979, San Juan's grimly barren **cathedral**, at Mendoza and Rivadavia across from Plaza 25 de Mayo, displays all the exterior charm of a Soviet apartment block. Italian artists designed and sculpted the bronze doors and the main ornaments inside.

Another dubious landmark, surrounded by Av San Martín, Av España, Av Jose Ignacio de la Roza and Av Las Heras, is the **empty shell of the projected Casa de Gobierno**, a white elephant that has sat uncompleted since 1985. The actual Casa de Gobierno sits at the corner of Av San Martín and Paula Albarracín de Sarmiento, just inside Av Circunvalación.

Just north of the ostensible Casa de Gobierno, at Av España and 25 de Mayo, the now-defunct Estación Belgrano (train station) has been recycled into the **Centro de Difusión Cultural Eva Perón** *(no ☎; admission US$1; open 9am-1pm Tues-Sun)*, a cultural center that includes the new anthropological museum, **Museo El Hombre y La Naturaleza** *(no ☎; admission US$1; open 9:30am-noon daily, additional hours 4:30pm-8:30pm Mon-Fri, 6pm-10pm Sat, 6pm-midnight Sun)*.

Organized Tours

San Juan travel agencies (see Information) arrange trips to some of the province's better but less easily accessible visitor attractions, including the Parque Provincial Ischigualasto (Valle de La Luna, US$52), Calingasta/Barreal (US$50), Dique Ullum (US$16), and Jáchal/Pismanta (US$45).

Raphael Joliat (mobile ☎ 15-504-3933), a San Juan-based Swiss citizen, conducts backcountry vehicle tours for between US$70 and US$120 per person per day.

Places to Stay

Budget The municipal campground, *El Pinar Camping* is on Av Benavídez Oeste, 6km from downtown and reached by Empresa de la Marina buses. At US$3 per person and US$2 per tent, it has a small artificial lake, a swimming pool and a forest plantation. There are other sites west of the city, where Av San Martín becomes RP 14 to Dique Ullum and Parque Rivadavia. Take bus No 23 (Zonda) or No 29 (Ullum).

Hotel Susex (no ☎, España 348 Sur) US$15 per person. This no-frills hotel was being remodeled at last visit and looked promising.

Hotel Embajador (☎ 422-5520, Av Rawson 25 Sur) Singles/doubles US$15/25. This basic but well-received place is a few blocks from the terminal; its small sign is easy to miss.

Petit Dibú Hotel (☎ 420-1034, San Martín & Patricias Sanjuaninas) Singles/doubles US$25/30 with breakfast, bath, TV & air-con. This is a clean, wonderfully friendly place in an ugly area behind the bus terminal.

Mid-Range Mid-range hotels show more variation in price than in standards or services. All offer private bathrooms, telephones, heating, air-con and parking. Some have a restaurant or *confitería*.

Hotel Plaza (☎ 422-5179, Sarmiento 344 Sur) Singles/doubles US$25/35. Good bathrooms and beds and spacious rooms make this large hotel another good value.

Hotel Nuevo San Francisco (☎ 427-2821, fax 422-3760, ⓔ nhsf@sinectis.com.ar, Av España 284 Sur) Singles/doubles US$25/35. One of the best in town, this welcoming, immaculate hotel has some well-lit rooms and a helpful staff.

Hotel Alhambra (☎ 421-4780, General Acha 180 Sur) Singles/doubles US$30/40. Both the rooms and bathrooms here are cramped, but it's very central; upstairs rooms are best.

Jardín Petit Hotel (☎ 421-1825, ⓔ jardin petithotel@hotmail.com, 25 de Mayo 345 Este) Singles/doubles US$30/40. This delightful hotel has tidy rooms, a small garden and a cheerful breakfast room.

Hotel América (☎ 421-4514, fax 427-2692, e hotelam@impsat1.com.ar, 9 de Julio 1052 Este) Singles/doubles US$30/40 & US$39/49, all with half-board. This is an excellent value in a drab location; it conveniently offers excursions through an on-site tour operator. It's a popular place with a good restaurant.

Hotel Bristol (☎ 421-4629, fax 421-4778, Entre Ríos 368 Sur) Singles/doubles US$32/45. This no-frills hotel has small but comfortable rooms.

Top End Most top end hotels cater to business travelers. *Hotel Capayán* (☎/fax 421-4222, e hcapayan@infovia.com.ar, Mitre 31 Este) Singles/doubles US$47/60. Popular with the business crowd, this stylish hotel has a bar and lounge and an excellent location on the central plaza.

Hotel Alkazar (☎ 421-4965, fax 421-4977 Laprida 82 Este) Singles/doubles US$98/120 with breakfast. Services at this five-star hotel include a spa, sauna and on-site masseuses; rooms are luxurious.

Places to Eat

A wide range of cuisines are available in this provincial hub.

Cereza Light (☎ 420-0320, Mendoza & Laprida) US$2-4. Delicious juices and imaginative *liquados* (fruit shakes) can be had at this corner café.

Fono Bar (☎ 421-7217, Mitre & Sarmiento) US$2-5; open 6am-1am daily. Drink espresso, munch ham-and-cheese *media lunas*, smoke cigarettes, sip *Fernet con Coke*, make a phone call or just watch the news in this tiny café.

Club Sirio Libanés (☎ 422-3841, Entre Ríos 33 Sur) Full meal US$9-16. This classy establishment serves dishes with a Middle Eastern flare. The *pollo deshuesado en salsa de ajillo* (boned chicken in garlic sauce) is especially good.

La Bodega (☎ 421-4965, Laprida 82 Este) This sumptuous, expensive French restaurant is in the Hotel Alkazar.

Wiesbaden (☎ 426-1869, Av Circunvalación near Av San Martín) Wiesbaden, near the outskirts of town, serves good German food.

La Nonna María (☎ 426-2277, Av San Martín & Perito Moreno) Mains US$8. Superb home-cooked pastas can be found at this attractive town favorite.

Antonio Gomez (☎ 422-9406, General Acha 447, Local 1) Open 7am-4pm Mon-Sat. In the busy *supermercado* (the old indoor market), this restaurant serves delectable hot churros for breakfast and inexpensive paella and shellfish for lunch.

Soychú (☎ 422-1939, Ignacio de la Roza 223 Oeste) Tenedor libre US$6. This vegetarian restaurant serves a highly recommended all-you-can-eat lunch.

Un Rincón de Napoli (☎ 422-7221, Rivadavia 175 Oeste) US$4-8; open noon-late. Pizzas, pastas and cold beer are the order of the day here; food to go is also available.

Las Leñas (☎ 423-2100, Av San Martín 1670 Oeste) US$7-18. This oversized *quincho* (thatched-roof construction) gets festive on weekends and serves excellent meat and monstrous portions of pasta.

Shopping

Inaugurated in 1985 to promote local handicrafts, the *Mercado Artesanal Tradicional* (Traditional Artisans Market; 25 de Mayo & Urquiza; open 8am-8pm Sat, Sun & holidays) is in the Parque de Mayo, beneath the Auditorio Juan Victoria. The brightly colored *mantas* (shawls) of Jáchal and the warm ponchos are particularly attractive.

Getting There & Away

Air Aerolíneas Argentinas/Austral (☎ 421-4158), Av San Martín 215 Oeste, flies twice daily to Buenos Aires (US$132) except Sunday (once only) and daily except Saturday to San Luis. LAPA (☎ 421-6039), Av José de la Roza, flies once daily to Buenos Aires (US$149).

Southern Winds (☎ 420-2000, 420-2100), Mitre 118 Oeste, flies once daily to Córdoba, once daily, except Saturday, to Neuquen, Rosario and Salta, and once a day Monday through Friday to Mendoza and Tucumán.

Bus The bus terminal (☎ 422-1604) is at Estados Unidos 492 Sur. International services to Santiago (US$20, 10 hours), Viña del Mar and Valparaíso, Chile, are provided by several companies, all requiring a change of buses in Mendoza.

Except in summer, when there may be direct buses, service to Patagonian destinations south of Neuquén requires changing buses in Mendoza, though through-tickets can be purchased in San Juan.

Various companies serve the following destinations at least once a day and go to major destinations like Buenos Aires, Córdoba, Mendoza and San Luis several times daily. Buses to Mar del Plata (US$60, 20 hours) leave once every Monday, Wednesday, Friday and Sunday.

Destination	Duration in hours	Cost
Bahía Blanca	19	US$55
Buenos Aires	14	US$55
Catamarca	8	US$18
Córdoba	8	US$30
Jujuy	18	US$35
La Rioja	6	US$14
Mendoza	2½	US$9
Mina Clavero	6	US$23
Neuquén	15½	US$45
Paraná	15	US$42
Rosario	14	US$50
Salta	17	US$35
San Agustín de Valle Fértil	4½	US$12
San José de Jáchal	3	US$8
San Luis	4	US$14
Santa Fe	14	US$40
Tucumán	13	US$28

If you're heading to Córdoba, 20 de Junio takes the scenic Altas Cumbres route, stopping in Merlo and Mina Clavero.

Border Crossings The scenic Agua Negra pass from San Juan to La Serena, Chile (via RN150), is open to automobiles only. Buses still do not take this route, but go via Mendoza instead.

Getting Around

Aeropuerto Las Chacritas (☎ 425-4133) is 13km southeast of town on RN 20. A taxi or *remise* costs US$10 to US$14. For car rental, try Localiza (☎ 421-9494), at Av Rioja 1187 Sur.

AROUND SAN JUAN
Wineries

For samples of the region's famed *blanco sanjuanino* (San Juan white wine) and champagne, visit **Antigua Bodega Chirino** (☎ 421-4327, Salta 782 Norte; open 8:30am-12:30pm daily, 4:30pm-8:30pm Mon-Sat).

One of South America's most curious wineries, **Cavas de Zonda** (☎ 494-5144, Zonda; open 9am-noon, 4pm-6pm daily) lies west of San Juan via the RP 12 near the town of Zonda, in a cave. This champagne maker boasts having the only wine cellar in South America whose 'roof is a mountain,' and, true or not, its temperatures are perfect for cellaring its excellent sparkling wines. And hey…it's a darn good marketing tool. Bus No 23 leaves the terminal from platform 20 six times daily.

Ten kilometers south of San Juan on the RN 40, **Anahata** (☎ 422-5807, Huerta Orgánica Anahata, Calle 11 s/n, 300m east of RN 40) makes some of the country's only organic champagne. Bus No 24 leaves the terminal seven times daily and will stop at the winery entrance.

Dique Ullum

Only 18km west of San Juan, this 3200-hectare reservoir is a center for nautical sports – swimming, fishing, kayaking, waterskiing and windsurfing (though no rental equipment is available). Bus No 23 from Av Salta or No 29 from the terminal via Av Córdoba both go hourly to the dam outlet.

There's a good hike from the outlet to the summit of 1800m **Cerro Tres Marías** in the Serranía de Marquesado, on the south side of the reservoir. Get off the bus from San Juan at El Castillito/El Paredón del Dique restaurant and climb the Stations-of-the-Cross Trail, then continue 1¼½ hours southwest over the dry hills to the summit. Take plenty of water, since it's very hot and exposed; early morning and late afternoon are the best times to enjoy the panoramic views.

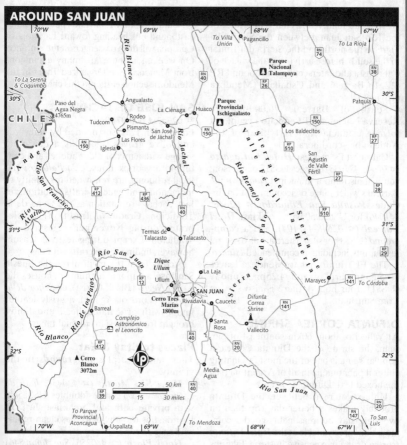

AROUND SAN JUAN

Museo Arqueológico La Laja

Focusing on regional prehistory, this museum *(no ☎; admission US$2; open 9am-5pm daily)* is part of the provincial university. It has seven display rooms, organized chronologically from the Fortuna culture of 6500 BC to the Incas and their trans-Andean contemporaries, with mummies, basketry, tools of many different materials, sculptures, petroglyphs and the remains of cultivated plants.

The Moorish-style building was once a hotel that featured thermal baths, which are still in use – after your visit, enjoy a

hot soak for US$2. The museum grounds include reproductions of natural environments, farming systems, petroglyphs and house types, all built to scale.

Alongside the museum are the welcome **hot sulfuric baths** of Termales la Laja *(admission US$2; open 9am-9pm daily)*.

To reach the museum, 25km north of San Juan in the village of La Laja, take any bus No 20 ('Albardón') from Av Córdoba or the bus terminal in San Juan. Those leaving the terminal at 8:40am, 10:45am, 12:25pm, 1:15pm and 3:45pm go all the way there.

Reserva Nacional El Leoncito

West of San Juan, RP 12 climbs the valley of the Río San Juan, between the Sierra del Tigre to the north and the Sierra del Tontal to the south, before arriving at the village of Calingasta and intersecting southbound RP 412, to Barreal and Uspallata (Mendoza province).

South of Barreal, 76,000-hectare Reserva Nacional El Leoncito occupies a former estancia that is typical of the Andean pre-cordillera.

Calingasta's modest *Hotel Calingasta* (☎ *02648-421033*) charges US$15 per person; you will also find a municipal *campground*. Barreal's wider range of accommodations includes *Posada San Eduardo* (☎ *02648-441046*) for US$35/50 with breakfast, *Hotel Barreal* (☎ *02648-441104*), and a *campground* (US$8 per site). There are also several restaurants, including recommended *Isidoro*.

The El Triunfo bus to Mendoza leaves at 5:55am Friday and 4:25pm Sunday (US$11, four hours); there is also service from San Juan.

DIFUNTA CORREA SHRINE

At Vallecito, about 60km southeast of San Juan, the shrine of the Difunta Correa, a popular saint, is one of the most fascinating cultural phenomena in all of Argentina (see the boxed text 'Difunta Correa').

Unless you're a believer, the Difunta probably makes a better day trip than an overnight stay, but reasonably good accommodations are available at the *Hotel Difunta Correa* or the inexpensive hostería. Pilgrims *camp* almost anywhere they feel like.

Food options include good street food, two *quinchos* (thatched-roof, open-sided buildings) with *minutas* (short order food), and *Comedor Don Roque* (RN 20 at village entrance), which has terrific soup and empanadas on Sunday.

Getting There & Away

Empresa Vallecito goes daily from San Juan to the shrine (US$7.70 roundtrip; 1¼ hour each way) at 8:30am and 4:30pm, Monday through Saturday, and waits about an hour and 15 minutes before returning. On Sunday there are roundtrip buses at 8am, 10:30am, 11:45am, 3:30pm, 4:15pm and 7pm. Any other eastbound bus heading toward La Rioja or Córdoba will drop passengers at the entrance. On weekends, there are many excursions from Mendoza (see Organized Tours in the Mendoza section earlier in this chapter).

SAN JOSÉ DE JÁCHAL
☎ 02647 • pop 9700

Founded in 1751, surrounded by vineyards and olive groves, Jáchal is a charming village with a mix of older adobes and contemporary brick houses. *Jachalleros,* the local residents, are renowned for fidelity to indigenous and gaucho crafts traditions; in fact, Jáchal's reputation as the Cuna de la Tradición (Cradle of Tradition) is celebrated during November's Fiesta de la Tradición. Except during festival season, however, finding these crafts isn't easy.

Across from the main plaza, the **Iglesia San José**, a national monument, houses the *Cristo Negro* (Black Christ), or *Señor de la Agonía* (Lord of Agony), a grisly leather image with articulated head and limbs, brought from Potosí in colonial times.

Places to Stay & Eat

There are several *campgrounds* in the vicinity.

Hotel San Martín (☎ *420431, Juan de Etchegaray 387*) Singles/doubles US$25/40 with private bath and breakfast. Just off Florida, this friendly place has clean rooms with saggy beds.

Hotel Plaza (☎ *420256, San Juan 546*) Singles/doubles US$18/28 shared bath, US$26/40 private bath. Actually on the 200 block of San Juan, this pleasant hotel has an airy lobby and midsize rooms.

El Chatito Flores (no ☎, San Juan 751) US$5 will get you a good roast half-chicken with fries and a beer, but there's chivito and asado too.

Getting There & Away

The bus terminal is at the corner of San Juan and Obispo Zapata. There are several daily buses to San Juan (US$8, 3 hours) and Mendoza (US$16).

Difunta Correa

Legend has it that during the civil wars of the 1840s, Deolinda Correa followed the movements of her sickly conscript husband's battalion on foot through the deserts of San Juan, carrying food, water and their baby son in her arms. When her meager supplies ran out, thirst, hunger and exhaustion killed her, but when passing muleteers found them, the infant was still nursing at the dead woman's breast. (There are many versions of this story, but the main points are the same, despite uncertainty that Deolinda Correa ever actually existed.) Commemorating this apparent miracle, her shrine at Vallecito is widely believed to be the site of her death.

Difunta literally means 'defunct,' and Correa is her surname. Technically she is not a saint but rather a 'soul,' a dead person who performs miracles and intercedes for people; the child's survival was the first of a series of miracles attributed to her. Since the 1940s, her shrine, originally a simple hilltop cross, has grown into a small village with its own gas station, school, post office, police station and church. At 17 chapels or exhibit rooms, devotees leave gifts in exchange for supernatural favors. In addition, there are two hotels, several restaurants, a commercial gallery with souvenir shops, and offices for the nonprofit organization that administers the site.

A visit to the shrine is an unusual and worthwhile experience even for nonbelievers. The religious imagery and material manifestations resemble no other Christian shrine in Latin America – many people build and leave elaborate models of homes and cars obtained through her intercession. Pilgrims, locals and even merchants are all eager to talk about the Difunta. It is perhaps the strongest popular belief system in a country that harbors a variety of unusual religious practices independent of Roman Catholicism – the official state religion – even if they are clearly related to it. Believers tell of miraculous cures, assistance during difficult childbirth, economic windfalls and protection of travelers.

Interestingly, truckers are especially devoted. From La Quiaca, on the Bolivian border, to Ushuaia in Tierra del Fuego, you will see roadside shrines with images of the Difunta Correa, wax candles, small bank notes, and the unmistakable bottles of water left to quench her thirst. At some sites there appear to be enough parts lying around to build a car from scratch, but do not mistake wheels, brake shoes and crankshafts for piles of trash, and refrain from taking anything away unless you really need it, since it is said that the Difunta also has a vengeful streak.

Despite lack of government support and the Catholic Church's open antagonism, the shrine of Difunta Correa has grown as belief in her miraculous powers has become more widespread. People visit the shrine all year round, but at Easter, May 1, and Christmas, up to 200,000 pilgrims descend on Vallecito. Weekends are busier and more interesting than weekdays.

AROUND SAN JOSÉ DE JÁCHAL

A day trip on RN 40 north of San Juan allows visitors to pass through a beautiful landscape that is rich with folkloric traditions and rarely seen by foreigners. East of Jáchal, the road climbs the precipitous **Cuesta de Huaco**, with a view of Los Cauquenes dam, before arriving at the village of **Huaco**, whose 200-year-old Viejo Molino (Old Mill) justifies the trip. It is the birthplace of poet Don Buenaventura Luna, who put the Jachallero culture in the map. There is no public transport from San Juan out this route.

Backtracking to RN 150, you cross the **Cuesta del Viento** and pass through the tunnels of Rodeo to the west of Jáchal to the department of Iglesia, home of the pre-cordillera thermal baths of **Pismanta**. Part of the Hotel Termas de Pismanta complex, the 42°C waters are recommended for rheumatic ailments, circulation and general cleansing and relaxation. Non-guests pay US$4 to use the facilities. Iglesia SRL minibuses leave the San Juan bus terminal four times a week, and take RP 436 to Jáchal, stopping at Iglesia and Pismanta.

There are two places to stay at Pismanta, absolutely nothing to do other than soak in the tubs or stare across the desolate landscape, and nowhere to eat outside the hotels.

Hotel Termas de Pismanta (☎ 02647-497002) US$50 or US$65 per person full board. In the middle of nowhere, this comfortable hotel shows the wear of its 50-odd years; in fact, the whole place feels caught in a time warp. In addition to several private baths, it has an outdoor swimming pool, continually filled by the warm thermal waters.

Hospedaje La Olla (☎ 02647-497003) US$25 full board. This is a basic place with lots of character (and plenty of animal skins around).

RN 150 continues westwards to La Serena and Coquimbo, both in Chile, via the 4765m **Paso de Agua Negra**. South of Pismanta, RP 436 returns to RN 40 and San Juan.

SAN AGUSTÍN DE VALLE FÉRTIL

☎ 02646 • pop 3000

If you're hankering for the hair-raising bus rides so generously offered in other South American countries, you can at least get a taste of them on the hairpin, cliffside turns on the way up to San Agustín. The town itself is a convenient base for exploring nearby Ischigualasto Provincial Park, and accommodations, lately on the upswing with the park's growing popularity, are cheap and basic.

Founded in 1788, San Agustín de Valle Fértil is a cheerful village where people sit on the sidewalks on summer evenings greeting passersby. On weekends they drag out the parrillas to sell grilled chicken or beef. There are as many bicycles as automobiles, and even the usually aggressive Argentine motorist appears to appreciate the relaxed pace.

Thanks to its temperate climate and high rainfall, San Agustín's colorful hills, rivers, exuberant flora, and varied fauna contrast dramatically with the desert landscapes of the rest of the province. The main economic activities are farming and animal husbandry and mining. San Agustín celebrates the anniversary of its founding on April 4.

Orientation & Information

San Agustín lies among the Sierra Pampeanas – gentle sedimentary mountains cut by impressive canyons, 247km northeast of San Juan via RN 141 and RP 510, which continues to Ischigualasto and La Rioja. San Agustín is small enough that locals pay little attention to street names, so ask directions.

Open 7am to 1pm and 5pm to 10pm weekdays, 8am to 1pm only Saturday, the municipal tourist office, on General Acha directly across from the plaza, is exceptionally helpful with general information, and they can also help arrange car or mule excursions into the mountain canyons and backcountry. The private Cámara de Turismo maintains an office at the bus terminal.

The post office is at Laprida and Mendoza, and there's a locutorio on Rivadavia, on the way to the reservoir.

Things to See & Do

Spending a day by the Río Seco is pleasant and relaxing, whether you are fishing, sunbathing or walking. About 300m across the river are the petroglyphs of **Piedra Pintada**, and about 500m farther north are the **Morteros Indígenas** (Indian Mortars).

The village of **La Majadita**, 7km from San Agustín by mule, cart or foot, is only reachable during the winter dry season, since the road crosses the river several times. You can find *lodging* at a local rancho, where you can eat kid goat and goat cheese, and have fresh milk in the morning.

Places to Stay & Eat

Camping Municipal (no ☎) US$8 per site. It's not a bargain, but it has a good shady location near the river.

Camping Valle Fértil (☎ 420015, Rivadavia s/n) US$10 per site. This shady ground, under a monotone cover of eucalyptus trees, has better facilities than Camping Municipal. Given its popularity among sanjuaninos, it gets very crowded during long weekends and holidays. It's on the way down to the river.

Pensión Doña Zoila (☎ 420147, Mendoza s/n) Singles/doubles US$8/12. The rooms are boxlike and as basic as they come, but Doña Zoila takes excellent care of her guests. It's half a block off the plaza.

Hospedaje Los Olivos (☎ 420115, Santa Fe s/n) US$10 per person with private bath. Character far exceeds comfort at this basic, friendly place.

Hospedaje San Agustín (☎ 420004, Rivadavia s/n) US$10 per person. This basic *hospedaje* has rooms with private baths and hot water, plus a restaurant/confitería.

Hostería & Cabañas Valle Fértil (☎ 420015) Singles/doubles in hostería US$45/60 with breakfast, US$56/82 half-board, US$67/104 full board, 4-person cabañas US$80. This place has the wraps on lodging in town with a well-sited hostería above the reservoir and fully equipped cabañas nearby. The hostería also has a good *restaurant*, serving food from 6am to 11pm daily. Both are reached from Rivadavia on the way to the river.

Most lodgings offer food at additional costs. Otherwise, try *Rancho Criollo*, a parrilla on Tucumán whose sign reads 'Parrilla Astiqueño'; two names, same place.

Getting There & Away

The bus terminal is on Mitre between Entre Ríos and Mendoza. There are daily buses to and from San Juan (US$12, 4½ hours). Monday and Friday buses to La Rioja (US$7) can drop off passengers at the Ischigualasto turnoff.

Ask at the tourist office to arrange a private car to Parque Provincial Ischigualasto for about US$80; otherwise taxis cost about US$200.

PARQUE PROVINCIAL ISCHIGUALASTO

Over time the persistent action of water has exposed a wealth of fossils (some 180 million years old from the Triassic period) in Parque Provincial Ischigualasto (Valle de la Luna). Named for an early Paleo-Indian culture, the park is in some ways comparable to North American national parks like Bryce Canyon or Zion. The park's museum displays a variety of fossils, including the carnivorous dinosaur *Herrerasaurus* (not unlike *Tyrannosaurus rex)*, the *Eoraptor lunensis* (the oldest-known predatory dinosaur) and good dioramas of the park's paleo-environments.

Colloquially known as one of South America's many Valles de la Luna (Valleys of the Moon), 63,000-hectare Ischigualasto is a desert valley between two sedimentary mountain ranges, the Cerros Colorados in the east and Cerro Los Rastros in the west. Over millennia, at every meander in the canyon, the waters of the nearly dry Río Ischigualasto have carved distinctive shapes in the malleable red sandstone, monochrome clay and volcanic ash. Predictably, some of these forms have acquired popular names, including Cancha de Bochas (The Ball Court), El Submarino (The Submarine) and El Gusano (The Worm) among others. The desert flora of algarrobo trees, shrubs and cacti complement the eerie landforms.

From the visitor center, isolated 1748m **Cerro Morado** is a three- to four-hour walk, gaining nearly 800m in elevation and yielding outstanding views of the surrounding area. Take plenty of drinking water and high-energy snacks.

Organized Tours

If you have no private vehicle, an organized tour is the only feasible way to visit the park. These are easily organized in San Agustín, where you will surely be greeted by offers upon arrival. Otherwise ask the tourist office there about hiring a car and driver. The private Cámara de Turismo at the bus station in San Agustín also offers tours. Alternatively, contact Noli Sánchez or Jorge Gargiulo (☎ 02646-491100) at the park, or Triassic Tour (☎ 0264-423-0358), Hipólito Yrigoyen 294 Sur in San Juan. Tour rates are about US$25 per person for a minimum of four people in a 10- passenger minibus, or US$70 per person with a three-person minimum requirement. Day trips are also possible through any of the travel agencies in San Juan; they generally depart San Juan at 5am and return well after dark.

Places to Stay & Eat

Camping is permitted at the visitor center, which also has a confitería with simple meals (breakfast and lunch) and cold drinks; dried fruits and bottled olives from the province are also available. There are toilets and showers, but because water must be trucked in, don't count on them. There is no shade.

Getting There & Away

Ischigualasto is about 80km north of San Agustín via RP 510 and a paved lateral to the northwest. Given its size and isolation, the only practical way to visit the park is by private vehicle or organized tour. If you drive out on your own, after you arrive at the visitor center and pay the US$5 entrance fee, one of the rangers will accompany your vehicle on a two-hour, 45km circuit through the park. Note that the park roads are unpaved and some can be impassable after a rain, necessitating an abbreviated trip.

The Empresa Vallecito bus from San Juan to La Rioja stops at the Los Baldecitos checkpoint on RP 510, but improved RN 150 from Jáchal is shorter and may supersede the former route.

The Andean Northwest

Argentina's most 'traditional' region, the Noroeste Andino (Andean Northwest) consists of the provinces of Jujuy, Salta, Tucumán, La Rioja, Catamarca and Santiago del Estero; all of which had thriving cities when Buenos Aires was still an insignificant hinterland. Today, these cities vary from the brash and energetic Tucumán to the gracious tourist headquarters of Salta.

The region's tangible pre-Columbian and colonial past make the trip south from Peru and Bolivia to the Argentine heartland a journey through time as well as space. Even now, the northern provinces resemble the Andean countries much more than they do the cultural core of the Argentine Pampas. Substantial Quechua communities exist as far south as Santiago del Estero.

If you find wine and cobblestone streets appealing then you're in the right part of the world, but it is perhaps the startling landscapes throughout the region (particularly in Salta and Jujuy) that will, more than anything else, sear itself in your mind.

History

In pre-Columbian times, the Noroeste was the most densely populated part of what is now Argentina, with perhaps two-thirds of the population. Several indigenous groups, most notably the Diaguita, practiced irrigated maize agriculture in the valleys of the eastern Andean foothills. Other groups included the Lules, southwest of present-day Salta; the Tonocote, around Santiago del Estero; and the Omaguaca of Jujuy.

Decades before the European invasion, the Incas began to expand their influence among the Diaguita and other southern Andean peoples. The area remained peripheral to but oriented toward the agricultural Andean civilizations rather than toward the foragers of the Pampas; when Spaniards replaced the Inca at the apex of political authority, the Europeans benefited from and reinforced this orientation.

Highlights

- Quebrada de Humahuaca – Soaking up the traditional Andean atmosphere in this astonishingly stunning valley
- Tren a las Nubes – Traversing the clouds on Argentina's most famous train ride
- Quebrada de Cafayate – Snaking through canyons and enjoying a drop in the region's wineries
- Tucumán – Mixing it up with the locals in dining and drinking establishments
- Tafí del Valle – Hiking the beautiful surroundings of this stunning hill station
- Belén – Shopping for fine woven goods in the country's self-styled poncho capital

ARGENTINA

THE ANDEAN NORTHWEST

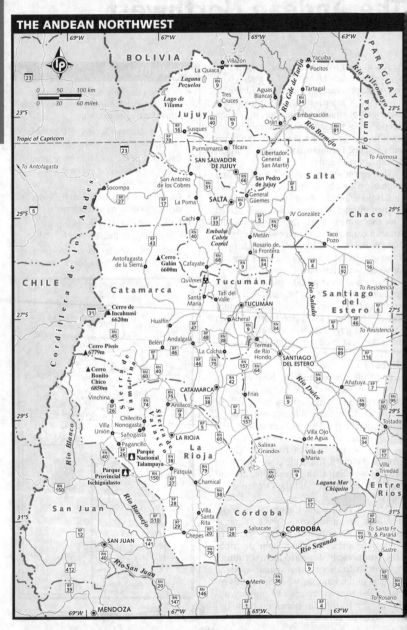

ARGENTINA

The first Spaniard to visit the region was Diego de Almagro, whose expedition from Cuzco to Santiago de Chile traced the eastern side of the Andes before crossing the heights of the Puna de Atacama. The Spaniards hoped that the indigenous populations would be large enough for substantial encomiendas, but the area never matched Peru's wealth of labor and tribute.

In colonial times, Tucumán was an economic satellite of the bonanza silver mine at Potosí, in present-day Bolivia. In part, the Spaniards had no alternative to this northward orientation, since the crown's mercantile policy decreed that commerce between Spain and the colonies had to be routed through Lima, by sea to Panama, across the isthmus to the Caribbean and then across the Atlantic.

Only after the creation of the Viceroyalty of the Río de la Plata in 1776 did this orientation change, as Buenos Aires slowly emerged from Lima's shadow. The opening of the Atlantic to legal shipping toward the end of the colonial period, followed by political independence, relegated Jujuy and Salta to economic marginality, but the adoption of sugar cane reversed Tucumán's economic orientation and increased its importance in the new country.

Jujuy & Salta Provinces

One of Argentina's smallest and poorest provinces, Jujuy is nevertheless rich in archaeological and cultural resources. Bounded by Bolivia to the north, Chile to the west and Salta province to the south and east, Jujuy is a southern extension of the high Andean steppe (altiplano), where soaring volcanic peaks tower over saline lakes (salares) above 4000m in the thinly populated west. To the east, a lower range of foothills gives way to deeply dissected river valleys like the Quebrada de Humahuaca, whose Río Grande has exposed some spectacular desert landforms, before

I'm Not Paying US$...for That!

Budget travelers approaching Jujuy from Bolivia are likely to find Argentine prices an unpleasant shock. Before panicking and dashing back across the border, look at alternatives for cheaper lodging, food and transportation suggested in this chapter and elsewhere in the book.

Generally, the Northwest is not a particularly expensive region compared to the rest of Argentina. You can usually find a bed for around US$10 (sometimes less), and regional and local dishes keep food prices down (tasty empanadas are about US$0.30 each). Although buses are generally expensive, popular runs, such as Jujuy to Salta (US$5), tend to be affordable.

opening onto subtropical lowlands toward the Gran Chaco. Jujuy has several wildlife and fauna reserves, though access is generally not easy.

In the Noroeste, Salta is the province with everything. Argentina's best-preserved colonial city, the provincial capital, is the center for excursions to the montane subtropical forests of Parque Nacional El Rey, the polychrome desert canyons of El Toro and Cafayate, along with their vineyards, and the sterile but scenic salt lakes and volcanoes of the high puna. Hundreds of archaeological sites and colonial buildings testify to Salta's importance in both pre-Columbian and colonial times, even though it declined with Argentine independence. Today tourism serves an increasingly important role in Salta's fortunes.

SAN SALVADOR DE JUJUY
☎ 0388 • pop 231,800 • elevation 1240m
Jujuy is a tranquil town with a frontier atmosphere. Situated at the southern end of the Quebrada de Humahuaca, the climate is perpetually springlike, due mainly to the city's distinction as being the highest provincial capital in the country.

Jujuy really lacks the energy of a big city and a couple of days exploring its museums

JUJUY & SALTA PROVINCES

and churches will probably be enough for most travelers. The lack of diversions usually propels people north, deeper into the astounding Quebrada de Humahuaca, or south to Salta within a few days.

You are likely to see more Quechua in this city than any other in the northwest, lending a particularly Andean feel to the place.

The Spaniards founded San Salvador de Jujuy in 1592 as the most northerly of their colonial cities in present-day Argentina. Now commonly known as simply Jujuy, the town's proper name distinguished it as a

Spanish settlement and also avoided confusion with nearby San Pedro de Jujuy.

On August 23, 1812, during the wars of independence, General Belgrano ordered the evacuation of Jujuy. Its citizens complied and the city was razed to prevent advancing royalist forces, loyal to the Spanish crown, from capturing the strategic site. The province of Jujuy bore the brunt of conflict during these wars, with Spain launching repeated invasions down the Quebrada de Humahuaca, from Bolivia; the city of Jujuy was sacked by royalists twice in latter years

Orientation

Jujuy sits above the floodplain of the Río Grande at its confluence with the smaller Río Xibi Xibi. Jujuy consists of two main parts: the old city, with a fairly regular grid pattern between the Río Grande and the Río Xibi Xibi, and a newer area south of the Xibi Xibi that sprawls up the nearby hills. Shantytowns crowd the floodplain of the Río Grande beneath the San Martín bridge.

Information

The provincial tourist office (☎ 422-1325, e setjujuy@uol.com.ar), at Urquiza 354, is in the old train station. The staff are some of the best that a traveler might come across in northwest Argentina; they are unusually well organized and keen to offer assistance. Opening hours are 7am to 9pm weekdays and 9am to 9pm on weekends.

There is also a branch of the provincial tourist office at the bus terminal; it is open 7:30am to 8:30pm weekdays and 8am to 8pm on weekends. ACA (☎ 422568) is at Senador Pérez and Alvear.

The following countries have consulates in the city: Bolivia (☎ 424-0501), Independencia 1098, open 9am to 1pm weekdays; Chile (☎ 426-1905), Pacarú 50, Los Perales; call for appointment; and Italy (☎ 422-3199), Av Fascio 660.

Graffiti Turismo, on the corner of Belgrano and Otero, changes cash, but commissions can be substantial. Try Banco Francés for cashing traveler's checks.

The postal code is 4600. There's a locutorio at the corner of Belgrano and Lavalle that has Internet access for US$3 an hour.

For excursions, try Tea Turismo (☎ 423-6270, fax 422-2357, e teajujuy@imagine.com.ar) at San Martín 128.

A good bookstore, Rayuela Libros (☎ 423-0658), is at Belgrano 638.

Cathedral

Dating from 1763, on the west side of Plaza Belgrano, Jujuy's cathedral replaced a 17th-century predecessor destroyed by Calchaquí Indians. Its outstanding feature, salvaged from the original church, is the gold-laminated Spanish baroque pulpit, probably built by local artisans under the direction of a European master. You can visit the cathedral between 8am and 12:30pm or 5pm to 8:30pm daily. On the plaza, directly across the street, a lively artisans market sells excellent pottery.

Cabildo (Museo Policial)

On the north side of Plaza Belgrano, is this colonial building and police museum (☎ 423-7715; free; open 8am-1pm & 3pm-9pm daily). The building and its attractive colonnade deserve more attention than the museum housed within, which pays indiscriminate homage to authority, and glories in grisly photographs of crimes and accidents. Strangely, there are plans to turn it into a cultural center.

Museo Histórico Provincial

During Argentina's civil wars, a bullet pierced through the imposing wooden door of this colonial house, killing General Juan Lavalle, a hero of the wars of independence. The story of Lavalle and other provincial events unfolds in this museum (☎ 422-1355, Lavalle 256; admission US$1; open 8am-12:30pm & 4pm-8pm weekdays, 9am-1pm & 4pm-8pm weekends). There is also a collection of religious and colonial art, exhibits on the independence era, the evacuation of Jujuy, provincial governors and 19th-century fashion.

Iglesia y Convento San Francisco

While the Franciscan order has been in Jujuy since 1599, the current church and convent, the third at the corner of Belgrano and Lavalle, dates only from 1912. Nevertheless, its Museo Histórico Franciscano Jujuy (open 8am-noon & 5pm-8:30pm daily) retains diverse relics from the early Franciscan presence, as well as a strong selection of colonial art from the Cuzco school. (Cuzco school is a world-renowned style of painting that came about in the 17th-century. Indigenous Peruvians were taught to paint by Spanish conquerors in the style of the great Spanish and Flemish masterpieces. It all started in the city of Cuzco, in Peru, and still exists today.)

ARGENTINA

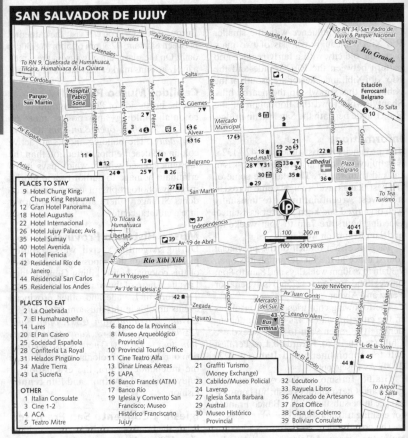

SAN SALVADOR DE JUJUY

PLACES TO STAY
9   Hotel Chung King;
     Chung King Restaurant
12 Gran Hotel Panorama
18 Hotel Augustus
22 Hotel Internacional
26 Hotel Jujuy Palace; Avis
35 Hotel Sumay
40 Hotel Avenida
41 Hotel Fenicia
42 Residencial Río de
     Janeiro
44 Residencial San Carlos
45 Residencial los Andes

PLACES TO EAT
2   La Quebrada
7   El Humahuaqueño
14 Lares
20 El Pan Casero
25 Sociedad Española
28 Confitería La Royal
31 Helados Pingüino
34 Madre Tierra
43 La Sucreña

OTHER
1   Italian Consulate
3   Cine 1-2
5   ACA
7   Teatro Mitre

6   Banco de la Provincia
8   Museo Arqueológico
     Provincial
10 Provincial Tourist Office
11 Cine Teatro Alfa
13 Dinar Líneas Aéreas
15 LAPA
16 Banco Francés (ATM)
17 Banco Río
19 Iglesia y Convento San
     Francisco; Museo
     Histórico Franciscano
     Jujuy

21 Graffiti Turismo
     (Money Exchange)
23 Cabildo/Museo Policial
24 Laverap
27 Iglesia Santa Barbara
29 Austral
30 Museo Histórico
     Provincial

32 Locutorio
33 Rayuela Libros
36 Mercado de Artesanos
37 Post Office
38 Casa de Gobierno
39 Bolivian Consulate

Other Museums & Churches

Paintings from the Cuzco school decorate the walls of **Iglesia Santa Bárbara**, a colonial church at the intersection of Lamadrid and San Martín. At the time of research the church was closed for repairs, but if you're keen for a look inside, wander around the corner to Santa Bárbara school and ask the nuns for the key to the place.

Take a look at the region's cultural evolution at the **Museo Arqueológico Provincial** (☎ 422-1315, Lavalle 434; free; open 7:30am-1pm & 2pm-9pm Sun-Fri, 7:30am-1pm Sat).

Mercado del Sur

Jujuy's lively southern market, opposite the bus terminal at Av Dorrego and Leandro Alem, is a genuine trading post where Quechua men and women swig *mazamorra* (a pasty maize soup served cold) and surreptitiously peddle coca leaves (unofficially tolerated for native people, despite Argentine drug laws).

Special Events

In August, Jujuy's biggest event, the week-long Semana de Jujuy, commemorates Belgrano's evacuation of the city during the vars of independence. The next largest gathering is the religious pilgrimage known as the Peregrinaje a la Virgen del Río Blanco y Paypaya on October 7.

The March harvest festival is the Festival de la Humita y El Folclor, while May's Fiesta de la Minería honors the mining industry. September's Fiesta Nacional de los Estudiantes is a student festival featuring elaborate floats.

Places to Stay

Budget Jujuy's budget accommodations are mostly near the old train and bus terminals.

Camping del Círculo de Suboficiales (☎ 422-7900, Av Bolivia) Sites US$5 for vehicles, tent & up to 4 persons. Jujuy's campground is 3km west of Parque San Martín. This former municipal site needs upgraded toilets and showers, although the shade cover has improved. To get here, take bus No , 9, 14 or 19 from downtown. If you don't like the look of the facilities, try *Camping El Refugio* (☎ 490-9344, RN 9), just past Círculo de Suboficiales.

Residencial Río de Janeiro (☎ 422-3700, José de la Iglesia 1356) Doubles US$13/14 with shared/private bath. This friendly place, west of the bus terminal, is among the cheapest in Jujuy. The private and shared bathrooms all have good hot showers.

Hotel Chung King (☎ 422-8142, Alvear 627) Singles/doubles US$8/12 with shared bath, US$12/20 with private bath. Probably the best budget option near the city center, it's a poky little place and some rooms are better than others, so have a look at a few.

Residencial los Andes (☎ 422-4315, República de Siria 456) Singles/doubles US$12/15 with shared bath, US$18/22 with private bath. This residencial, a few blocks east of the bus terminal, is a better value than some mid-range hotels. Some rooms even come with a TV, and the rooms upstairs have much better light.

Residencial San Carlos (☎ 422-2286, República de Siria 459) Singles/doubles US$12/17 with shared bath, US$20/25 with private bath. San Carlos has spotless rooms and is more like a small hotel. It is across the street from the previous listing and it's

pretty difficult to choose between the two. Let's not split hairs – try tossing a coin.

Mid-Range Well positioned between the city and the bus terminal, *Hotel Avenida* (☎ 423-6136, Av 19 de Abril 469) offers singles/doubles for US$17/34. The rooms are small, dark and looking a bit tired these days. Nevertheless there is a shortage of decent hotels in this range and this one is tidy enough.

Hotel Sumay (☎/fax 423-5065, Otero 232) Singles/doubles US$36/48 with breakfast. Rooms here have TV, air-con and telephones. It's a notch up in luxury, is fairly central and has a cozy little bar-confitería. Staff can also help organize excursions.

Hotel Fenicia (☎ 423-1800, fax 423-3129, Av 19 de Abril 427) Singles/doubles US$30/50. This hotel overlooks the Xibi Xibi, and its rooms have great balconies.

Hotel Augustus (☎ 423-0203, fax 423-0209, Belgrano 715) Singles/doubles US$48/68 to US$60/77. This central option is very comfortable, has bright rooms (some bigger than others) and some very good views of the city.

Top End Closer to the center, *Hotel Internacional* (☎ 423-1599, fax 423-0533, Belgrano 501) is a high-rise property with all the trimmings. Singles/doubles will set you back US$60/80.

Gran Hotel Panorama (☎/fax 423-2533, Belgrano 1295) Singles/doubles US$60/80 with breakfast. The Panorama is a four-star property with plain but spacious rooms that could be better presented. However this is partly redeemed by the huge windows giving great views of the city skyline.

Hotel Jujuy Palace (☎ 423-0433, e jpalace @imagine.com.ar, Belgrano 1060) Singles/doubles US$60/80. This stylish hotel is a class act and if you're looking for the top of the line in Jujuy – here it is. The large rooms are spotlessly clean, tastefully decorated and have terrific views.

Places to Eat

Upstairs at the *Mercado Municipal*, at Alvear and Balcarce, several eateries serve inexpensive regional specialties, which are generally spicier than elsewhere in Argentina; try *chicharrón con mote* (stir-fried pork with boiled maize). Another local favorite is the modest-looking but interesting **La Sucreña**, at Leandro Alem and Av Dorrego, which serves a spicy *sopa de maní* (peanut soup).

El Pan Casero (*Belgrano 619*) This is a natural-foods bakery specializing in whole meal products.

A couple of places with regional sweets on offer for US$0.20 to US$5 are **El Humahuaqueño** (*Güemes 920*) and **La Quebrada** (*Senador Pérez 476*).

Confitería La Royal (☎ 422-6202, *Belgrano 766*) Breakfast US$4. Slap-bang in the middle of town, La Royal is a good spot for people-watching, a steaming mug of coffee and a read of the morning newspaper.

Chung King (☎ 422-8142, *Alvear 627*) Mains $3-12. This misleadingly named place is actually three. There is a pizzeria, a restaurant with an extensive Argentine menu and fine service, and a peña with regional artists providing entertainment while you have dinner. They are all grouped together – it seems the owners must have been buying up real estate for years along this street!

Sociedad Española (☎ 423-5065, *Belgrano 1102*) Mains US$5. This traditional Spanish restaurant serves fine food, including paella, in a pleasant atmosphere.

Lares (*Belgrano 1055*) Mains US$3-5. A bar-restaurant with a sophisticated but relaxed ambience, Lares has a great upstairs bar area, serves some interesting food, such as crepes, and is worth the walk three blocks west of the center.

Madre Tierra (☎ 422-9578, *Otero 294*) 4-course lunch US$7; open noon-2pm Mon-Sat. Madre Tierra is an Argentine standout. The vegetarian food here is excellent and the salads, crepes and soups can be washed down with either carrot or apple juice. It's an earthy place where the simple, wholesome, home-cooked food makes a welcome change to the standard Argentine fare.

On and near the Belgrano pedestrian mall are numerous confiterías and excellent ice creameries, most notably **Helados Pingüino**. On a hot Sunday afternoon, there is a constant stream of people outside the place feverishly licking their delicious *helados*, which quickly turn to puddles for those who are slow of tongue.

Entertainment
Lares (see Places to Eat) is a good spot for a quiet drink in the evenings. There is comfortable seating and the bar area is very relaxed and friendly.

Teatro Mitre (☎ 422782, *Alvear 1009*) Built in 1901, this theater sponsors plays and similar cultural events.

Spectator Sports
Jujuy's first-division soccer team, **Gimnasia y Esgrima** (☎ 422-8011), has offices at Güemes 1031 but plays at the stadium at Av El Éxodo 78.

Getting There & Away
Air Austral (☎ 422-7198), San Martín 735, only flies from Salta. LAPA (☎ 423-8444), Belgrano 1053, flies daily to Buenos Aires (US$98 to US$298) and daily to Salta (though this short hop doesn't make much sense).

Lloyd Aéreo Boliviano operates out of Salta and Tucumán. Dinar Líneas Aéreas (☎ 423-7100), Senador Pérez 308, Local 3, flies every day (US$153 to US$292) to Buenos Aires.

Bus The bus terminal (☎ 422-1375), at Av Dorrego and Iguazú, has provincial and long-distance services, but Salta has more alternatives.

International Chile-bound bus companies running services from Salta include Geminus and Tur Bus, but neither have an office in Jujuy. Both will stop here however, before crossing the Paso de Jama, if requested; to organize this, contact ☎ 426-3764 or mobile ☎ 1550-02013.

There are frequent services south to Salta and north to destinations in the Quebrada de Humahuaca as far as the Bolivian border at La Quiaca. For Parque Nacional Calilegua, there are services every half hour throughout the day to San Pedro and Libertador San Martín.

The following table lists some sample fares:

Destination	Duration in hours	Cost
Buenos Aires	23	US$40-65
Catamarca	10	US$25
Córdoba	20½	US$30
Humahuaca	2½	US$6.50
La Quiaca	4	US$15
La Rioja	8	US$25
Libertador San Martín	2	US$6
Mendoza	14	US$35
Pocitos	6	US$11
Purmamarca	1¼	US$3.50
Resistencia	18	US$44
Salta	2	US$5
San Juan	10	US$30
San Pedro	1	US$3.50
Tilcara	1¾	US$5
Tucumán	5	US$18
Uquía	2½	US$6
Yuto	3	US$7.50

Getting Around

Tea Turismo runs minibuses to Aeropuerto Internacional Dr Horacio Guzmán (☎ 491-1103), 32km southeast of town, for US$5 (LAPA flights). Dinar Líneas Aéreas provides its own airport transfers.

If you're after a rental car, Avis (☎ 423-0433) is at Hotel Jujuy Palace, which is located at Belgrano 1060.

LA QUIACA & VILLAZÓN (BOLIVIA)

☎ 0388 • pop 12,400 • elevation 3442m

Near Abra Pampa, a forlornly windy town 90km north of Humahuaca, RN 9 becomes a dusty graveled road (gradually being paved) that climbs abruptly to the high altiplano typical of southern Bolivia. Except in the summer rainy season, nightly frosts make agriculture precarious, so people concentrate subsistence efforts on livestock (such as llamas, sheep, goats and a few cows) that can survive on the sparse *ichu* grass. Off the main highway, look for flocks of the endangered vicuña, a wild relative of the llama and alpaca.

At the end of the highway are the border crossing towns of La Quiaca and its Bolivian twin Villazón. La Quiaca has become a ghost town. With the closure of the railroad and the fact that most locals do their shopping in Villazón for lower prices, it's one of few Argentine towns that lacks a lively street life, especially at night. But then only a travel writer would visit a border town – everyone else is just passing through.

Orientation

La Quiaca consists of two discrete sections, separated by the tracks of the defunct train station; most services are west of the tracks. At the north end of town, a bridge across the Río Villazón (also called Río La Quiaca) links La Quiaca with Villazón. To get to Argentine and Bolivian customs you have to walk or take a taxi colectivo to the bridge, on the east side of the tracks, then cross on foot.

Information

For maps or motorist services, visit the ACA station at RN 9 and Sánchez de Bustamente.

The Bolivian Consulate, at Av Sarmiento 529 next to Hotel Crystal, charges a hefty US$20 for a 30-day visa and is open from 9:30am to 1pm weekdays. If you do need a visa, make sure you get it here before attempting the border crossing. The border is open 24 hours. (For more on border crossings, see Visa & Documents in the Facts for the Visitor chapter.)

Banco de la Nación, at RN 9 and Pellegrini, will not cash traveler's checks, so you may have to cross to Villazón to change at Universo Tours. If you need an ATM, try Banco Jujuy at Árabe Siria 445.

The postal code is 4650. The post office is at San Juan and Sarmiento. The locutorio is at Av España and 25 de Mayo; note that phone calls are expensive here (double Salta prices), and no collect calls of any sort are possible.

On the Bolivian side of the border, the Argentine consulate is on a street facing the railway line, one block west of Av República Argentina. It's open 9 am to 1 pm weekdays.

You need to be more on your guard in Villazón than in other parts of Bolivia. Like

ARGENTINA

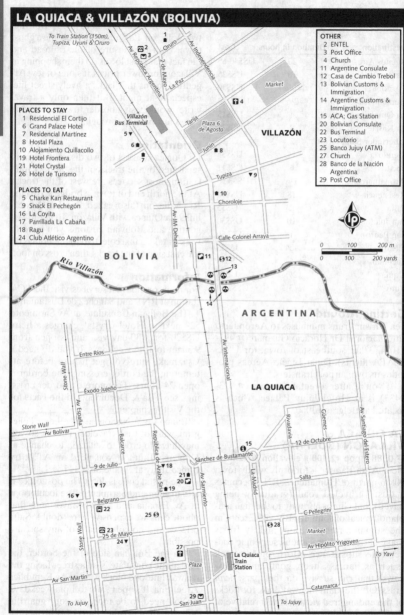

LA QUIACA & VILLAZÓN (BOLIVIA)

To Train Station (150m),
Tupiza, Uyuni & Oruro

Villazón
Bus Terminal

VILLAZÓN

Plaza 6
de Agosto

Market

Río Villazón

BOLIVIA

ARGENTINA

LA QUIACA

La Quiaca
Train
Station

Plaza

Market

To Yavi

To Jujuy

To Jujuy

PLACES TO STAY
1 Residencial El Cortijo
6 Grand Palace Hotel
7 Residencial Martínez
8 Hostal Plaza
10 Alojamiento Quillacollo
19 Hotel Frontera
21 Hotel Crystal
26 Hotel de Turismo

PLACES TO EAT
5 Charke Kan Restaurant
9 Snack El Pechegón
16 La Coyita
17 Parrillada La Cabaña
18 Ragu
24 Club Atlético Argentino

OTHER
2 ENTEL
3 Post Office
4 Church
11 Argentine Consulate
12 Casa de Cambio Trebol
13 Bolivian Customs &
     Immigration
14 Argentine Customs &
     Immigration
15 ACA; Gas Station
20 Bolivian Consulate
22 Bus Terminal
23 Locutorio
25 Banco Jujuy (ATM)
27 Church
28 Banco de la Nación
     Argentina
29 Post Office

0   100   200 m
0   100   200 yards

many frontier towns, fake police scams, baggage theft, pickpocketing and counterfeit US banknotes are big business here.

From October to April, there's a one-hour time difference between Bolivia and Argentina (noon in Villazón is 1pm in La Quiaca). From May to September, the Argentine province of Jujuy, where La Quiaca is located, operates on Bolivian time (only more efficiently).

Places to Stay
Hotel Frontera (☎ 422269, Belgrano & Árabe Siria) Rooms US$8 per person with shared bath. Accommodations are cheaper on the Bolivian side, but you could try this very basic and unimpressive hotel with its simple, clean rooms.

Hotel Crystal (☎ 452255, Sarmiento 543) Singles/doubles US$10/16 with shared bath, US$18/30 with private bath. This hotel with small, dark rooms is a pretty good option in this price range. It can get cold at night though and the hot water system is dodgy.

Hotel de Turismo (☎ 422243, San Martín & Árabe Siria) Singles/doubles US$35/50 with private bath & breakfast. A modern, spacious place that is by far the best accommodations in town, hence the price; the competition is not exactly banging down their front door. Rooms have heating, TV and telephones and there is an Internet terminal in the foyer.

Accommodations in Villazón are cheaper but not always better than in La Quiaca. **Residencial Martínez** (☎ 0596-3353), opposite the bus terminal, is an OK place to crash. Singles/doubles with shared bath cost US$3.90/7.85. Across the street and similarly priced, the **Grand Palace Hotel** (☎ 0596-5544) is really the bland palace, but has clean rooms (some windowless). The cafeteria does good breakfast.

A travelers' favorite is **Residencial El Cortijo** (☎ 0596-2093), two blocks north of the bus terminal. Rooms with shared bath cost US$4.70 per person, US$7.85 with private bath. The good, new **Hostal Plaza** (☎ 0596-3535), on the plaza, charges US$7.85/12.50 for singles/doubles with bath. There are also singles with shared bath, which are cheaper.

Places to Eat
Parrillada La Cabaña (Av España 550) 4-course set lunch US$2. This diner, between 9 de Julio and Belgrano, serves regional specialties and is very popular with locals. The set lunch is an absolute bargain.

La Coyita (Av España & Belgrano) Mains US$2-6. This is a parrilla just across the road from the bus terminal. It has a large menu including tasties such as pizza, milanesa (breaded steak) and pastas.

Ragu (9 de Julio & Árabe Siria) Mains US$2-5. Ragu is a bar serving simple meals (such as chicken, milanesa and lomito) and is endowed with a terrific potbellied stove for those frosty nights. Check out the stylish cash register.

Club Atlético Argentino (Balcarce & 25 de Mayo) Mains US$2-8. This club, serving standard Argentine fare, is also worth a look. Have a back-up plan though, as their opening hours can be a little erratic.

Food choices are limited on the Bolivian side. Try the **Charke Kan Restaurant**, opposite the bus terminal, which is good but rather grimy.

Getting There & Away
From the bus terminal at Belgrano and Av España several companies have frequent connections to Jujuy (US$16, 6 hours) and less frequently to Salta (US$22, 8 hours) and intermediate points. There is no transport to Bolivia leaving from here.

There are plenty of touts at the bus terminal all vying for your business. They'll tell you anything, including 'all buses are direct to Salta and take just six hours!' Be firm and find out the real deal from the bus company ticket offices.

In Villazón, all northbound buses depart from around the central terminal. Buses leave for Tupiza at 7 am, 3 and 5 pm daily (US$2.35, 3 hours). Some continue or make connections to Potosí (US$4, 9-13 hours) with further connections to Sucre, Oruro, Cochabamba and La Paz. There are departures along the amazing route to Tarija continuing to Bermejo and Yacuiba at 11 am and 8:30 pm daily (US$3.15, 8 hours).

AROUND LA QUIACA
Yavi
While there's not much to do in La Quiaca, the colonial village of Yavi (☎ 03887), 16km east via paved RP 5, more than justifies a detour; if waiting for a southbound bus, check your bags and spend a morning or afternoon in the milder climate of the sheltered valley of the Río Yavi.

The altar, paintings, and woodcarvings of its patron and several other saints has brought much renown to Yavi's **Iglesia de San Francisco** *(open 9am-noon & 3pm-6pm Tues-Fri, 9am-noon Sat)*. This church is in remarkable condition for a late-17th-century building. It's presumably open the hours listed above, but you may still have to track down the caretaker to get in; alternatively ask at the nearby museum. Two blocks south of the church are the ruins of the **molino**, a small flour mill.

Across the street from the church, in less than splendid condition, the **Casa del Marqués Campero** belonged to a Spanish noble whose marriage to the holder of the original *encomienda* created a family that dominated the regional economy in the 18th century. Now a museum *(free; open 9am-noon daily)*, it contains nothing of the Marqués' possessions, which are scattered around Jujuy, Hornillos and Salta, but the eclectic contents (like an old Victrola) lend it a certain charm and there's an interesting antiquarian library. A small mercado artesanal is also here and you can purchase locally made woolen goods.

Near Yavi there are several short hikes in the Cerros Colorados, including one to rock paintings and petroglyphs at **Las Cuevas** and another to springs at **Agua de Castilla**. Alejandro Toro (☎ 490523), who works in the park alongside the Casa del Marqués Campero, is a knowledgeable local guide.

Hostal de Yavi (☎ 490523, e elportillo @cootepal.com.ar, Güemes 222) Rooms half-board US$35 per person with bath. This place is not cheap but it's a great place to stay if you are overnighting. Yavi has very clean facilities in a cozy building. The friendly staff can organize guides and excursions in the local area.

Flota La Quinqueña provides regular public transport from La Quiaca to Yavi (US$15), but shared cabs (US$15 round-trip, including waiting time) are another alternative. Every half hour or so, there's a pickup truck (US$1) that runs from La Quiaca's Mercado Municipal on Av Hipólito Yrigoyen.

Monumento Natural Laguna de los Pozuelos
Three species of flamingos plus coots, geese, ducks and many other birds breed along the barren shores of this 16,000-hectare lake, at an altitude of nearly 4000m. You may also see the endangered vicuña. The lake has been declared a RAMSAR site (an international conservation designation for wetland habitats and associated wildlife) because of its importance to waterbirds. There are archaeological sites here as well.

Because the park is so isolated, a car is the best transportation option, but carry extra fuel; there is no gasoline available beyond Abra Pampa, midway between Humahuaca and La Quiaca. Make sure you also take plenty of drinking water. Be aware that heavy summer rains can make the unpaved routes off the main highway impassable.

From Abra Pampa it is possible to take a local bus on a roundtrip through the park (there are two services a week) or there are mid-morning buses to Rinconada, west of the lake, where there are simple accommodations. Empresa Mendoza goes daily (US$7) and on request, the bus will drop you off at the Río Cincel ranger station, where it's a 7km walk over level puna to the lake.

Camping is possible on very exposed sites, with basic infrastructure, at the ranger station. For the latest information, ask at the tourist office in Jujuy or at the Centro Cultural in Abra Pampa.

QUEBRADA DE HUMAHUACA
The long, narrow Quebrada de Humahuaca, north of Jujuy, is an artist's palette of color splashed on barren hillsides dwarfing the hamlets where Quechua peasants scratch a living from irrigated agriculture and scrawny livestock.

Because the Spaniards colonized this area from Peru in the late 16th century, it has many cultural features that recall the Andean countries, particularly the numerous historic adobe churches. Earthquakes leveled many of the originals, which were often rebuilt in the 17th and 18th centuries with thick walls, simple bell towers and striking doors and paneling hewn from the wood of the unusual cardón cactus. Whether you come south from La Quiaca or head north from Jujuy, there's something interesting every few miles on this colonial post route between Potosí and Buenos Aires.

The valley's main settlement is the village of Humahuaca, 130km from Jujuy, but there are so many worthwhile sights that the convenience of a car would be a big plus if you have a group to share expenses. Otherwise, buses are frequent enough that you should be able to do the canyon on a 'whistle-stop' basis, flagging down a bus when you need one. It is best to visit the Quebrada in the morning, when there's little wind and before the afternoon heat. Northbound travelers recommend the right side of the bus for better views (southbound, the left side).

HUMAHUACA
☎ 03887 • pop 6200 • elevation 3000m
Picturesque Humahuaca, the largest settlement between Jujuy and the Bolivian border, is a village of narrow, cobbled streets and adobe houses, with a large Quechua population. It's one of the most popular destinations for budget travelers exploring the Quebrada. Locals will occasionally target tourists aggressively, offering unsolicited guide services, although this is only likely to be visible during high season.

Orientation & Information
Straddling the Río Grande east of RN 9, Humahuaca is very compact so everything is within easy walking distance. The town center is between the highway and the river, but there are important archaeological sites across the bridge.

The tourist office, in the Cabildo at Tucumán and Jujuy, is only open from 7am to about 12:30pm on weekdays.

Banco de Jujuy at Jujuy 337 has an ATM that accepts credit cards.

The postal code is 4630. The post office is on Buenos Aires, across from the plaza and there's a locutorio at Jujuy 399, behind the Municipalidad.

Hospital Belgrano, Santa Fe 34, is open 8am to 1pm and 2pm to 6pm daily, but there's always someone on duty for any emergency that might arise.

Things to See & Do
Built in 1641, Humahuaca's Iglesia de la Candelaria faces the plaza on Calle Buenos Aires. It contains an image of the town's patron saint as well as 18th-century oils by Marcos Sapaca, a painter of the Cuzco school.

Across from the church, municipal offices occupy the Cabildo, famous for its clock tower, where a life-size figure of San Francisco Solano emerges daily at noon to deliver a benediction. Tourists and locals alike gather in the plaza to watch the spectacle, but be sure to arrive early because the clock is erratic and the figure appears only briefly.

From the plaza, a staircase climbs to the Monumento a la Independencia, a chauvinistic travesty that is not the best work of Tilcara sculptor Ernesto Soto Avendaño. The Indian statue is a textbook example of indigenismo, a twisted nationalist tendency in Latin American art and literature that romantically extols the virtues of native cultures overwhelmed by European expansion.

Local writer and Quechua activist Sixto Vázquez Zuleta, who prefers his Quechua name of Toqo, runs the private and expensive Museo Folklórico Regional (Buenos Aires 447; admission US$5; open 8am-8pm daily), which is open for guided tours only, with a minimum group of three or four. Toqo speaks little English but passable German. The museum is alongside the youth hostel.

Special Events
Besides the Carnaval Norteño, celebrated throughout the Quebrada in February, Humahuaca observes February 2 as the day of its patron saint, the Virgen de Candelaria.

Places to Stay

El Portillo (☎ *421288,* e *elportillo @cootepal.com.ar, Tucumán 69*) Dorms beds/doubles US$6/16. Without a doubt this clean, basic place is the best budget option in town. The friendly owner is knowledgeable about the area, can organize excursions and is probably the best source of tourist information in town. El Portillo is very central; it is just around the corner from the plaza.

Albergue Juvenil (☎ *421064, Buenos Aires 435*) Dorm beds US$4/6 for members/nonmembers. This Hostelling International place offers hot showers and kitchen facilities, but standards have fallen and it's fairly disorganized.

Posada del Sol (☎ *490508*) Dorm beds US$7 per person. Just 400m across the bridge, Posada del Sol is run by the owners of its namesake café, half a block east of the plaza. It's a little ramshackle and improvised, but has personality, hot showers, homemade bread and free tea and coffee.

Residencial Humahuaca (☎ *421141, Córdoba 401*) Singles/doubles US$10/18 with shared bath, US$20/25 with private bath. This simple, inexpensive hotel is near Corrientes, half a block from the bus terminal. It was getting a makeover at the time of research and the signs were very promising.

Hotel de Turismo (☎ *421154, Buenos Aires 630*) Singles/doubles US$27/45 with bath and breakfast. This two-star property is the town's top-end lodging, despite its drabness. The hallways are reminiscent of a prison, but the spacious rooms are surprisingly good with private balconies and pleasant views.

Places to Eat

El Fortín (☎ *421126, Buenos Aires 200*) Starters US$0.50-3, mains US$3-8. El Fortín is worth a look, and is particularly good for groups. Specialties of the region are served, so you'll be able to tuck into a steaming bowl of *locro* (a spicy stew of maize, beans, beef, pork, and sausage).

Restaurant Pinocho (*Buenos Aires 452*) Mains US$2-4. Directly across from the youth hostel, this small, friendly, handy eatery does filling milanesas, tasty empanadas and a variety of other good meals.

La Cacharpaya (☎ *421016, Jujuy 317*) Mains US$2-6. For regional dishes including tamales, empanadas and chicken, try thi spot on Jujuy, between Santiago del Estere and Tucumán.

There's an acceptable *confitería* at the bus terminal, but on Belgrano very close to the bus terminal, is *El Rancho Confitería*, a better alternative for coffee and a light meal.

Peña de Fortunato (*San Luis & Jujuy*) Regional cuisine and live folk music are dished up here.

Shopping

Visit the *handicrafts market*, near the train station, for woolen goods, souvenirs and the atmosphere. The quality is excellent, bu northbound travelers will probably find similar items at lower prices in Bolivia.

Getting There & Away

The bus terminal is at Belgrano and Entre Ríos, about three blocks south of the plaza. There are numerous southbound buses to Salta and Jujuy, and northbound buses to La Quiaca (US$11, 2½ hours).

Transportes Mendoza (☎ 421016), at Belgrano and Salta, offers service to the Andean village of Iruya (US$8/13 one-way/roundtrip, 3 hours) daily except Thursday, at 10:15am and return from Iruya at 3pm; buses may not leave at all in summer when it rains. Tickets are available from the bus terminal.

AROUND HUMAHUACA
Coctaca

Covering about 40 hectares, Coctaca contains northwestern Argentina's most extensive pre-Columbian ruins. Although they have not yet been excavated, many of the ruins appear to have been broad agricultural terraces on an alluvial fan, though there are also obvious outlines of clusters of buildings. The nearby school trains guides to the site. Even if you aren't an archaeology buff, the ruins are still interesting.

After rains, the road may be impassable. It's possible to hike 10km to the ruins, but leave before the heat of the day and take water. After crossing the bridge across the Río Grande in Humahuaca, follow the dirt road north and bear left until you see the village of Coctaca.

Uquía

The 17th-century **Iglesia de San Francisco de Paula** in this roadside village displays a restored collection of paintings from the Cuzco school, featuring the famous *Ángeles arcabuceros*, which are angels armed with Spanish colonial weapons. The church is normally closed except during mass. Intending visitors should ask at the house of Adriana Valdivieso, two blocks south of the plaza; she keeps the 17th-century key and will accompany visitors to the church.

Hostal de Uquía (☎ 03887-490523) This is a new place in Uquía but the clock beat the book's researchers, who didn't get a chance to check it out. There are, however, rooms with private bath and an attached restaurant. Tourist information is also available here.

Iruya

The beautiful village of Iruya is a speck of white in a valley with startling splashes of colored rocks, in the northwest of Salta province. The cobbled streets, well-preserved church and white-washed buildings give Iruya an ageless feel and it's a great spot to kick back from the road for a couple of days. There are also excellent walks in the surrounding countryside.

Buses leave most days from Humahuaca. If you're driving, there is 50km of dirt track to negotiate off RN 9, between Humahuaca and Abra Pampa.

TILCARA
☎ 0388 • pop 3300 • elevation 2461m
Tilcara's most conspicuous feature is a classic Andean *pucará*, a pre-Columbian fortification, that commands unobstructed views of the Quebrada de Humahuaca. The town's several museums and other interesting characteristics, including its reputation

as an artists colony, make it a highly desirable stopover. Many *jujeños* (inhabitants of Jujuy) have weekend houses here, where hiking in the surrounding hills is a popular diversion.

When arriving in Tilcara your first impression may be that you're finally leaving behind the urban glitz and getting off the beaten track into Quechua territory. But be warned: You may have to go a little farther. Plaza Prado in the center of town is covered with souvenir stalls and there's parking around the plaza, reserved for tourists!

Orientation & Information
Tilcara, on the east bank of the Río Grande, is connected by a bridge to RN 9, which leads south to Jujuy and north to Humahuaca and La Quiaca. Its central grid is irregular beyond the village nucleus, focused on Plaza Prado. As in many small Argentine villages, people pay scant attention to street names and numbers.

The eager provincial tourist office (☎ 495-5002) has a makeshift office on Belgrano, next to Hotel de Turismo. It has plenty of information about accommodations.

The post office is at Plaza Prado, on the corner of Belgrano and Rivadavia. There is a locutorio at the corner of Bolívar and Lavalle, on the north side of Plaza Prado.

El Pucará
Rising above the sediments of the Río Grande valley, an isolated hill provides the site for this reconstructed pre-Columbian fortification (☎ 495-5073; admission US$2; open 9am-6pm daily), 1km south of the village center. It was discovered in 1903 and reconstructed in the 1950s. It was built from stone by indigenous people and is one of the biggest in the region. It's basically a fortified town with restored houses and on old church. Very little is known about the site but it is quite large and there are terrific views.

There are even better views from the hill on the road leading to the fort; from the south end of the bridge across the Río Huasamayo, it's an easy 15-minute climb to the top.

Museo Arqueológico Dr Eduardo Casanova

The Universidad de Buenos Aires runs this outstanding, well-displayed collection of regional artifacts (☎ 495-5006, Belgrano 445; admission US$2, free Tues; open 9am-noon & 2pm-6pm weekdays). There are some artifacts from the site of the Pucará and exhibits give an insight into the life of people living around that time. The museum is located in a striking colonial house on the south side of Plaza Prado. Admission is also good for El Pucará (see above).

Museo Ernesto Soto Avendaño

Ernesto Soto Avendaño, a sculptor from Olavarría (Buenos Aires province) who spent most of his life in Tilcara, was the perpetrator of Humahuaca's appalling monument to the heroes of Argentine independence. This collection of his better work is alongside the Museo Arqueológico, but was closed for renovations at the time of research.

Museo José Antonio Terry

Also located in a colonial building on the east side of Plaza Prado is this art museum (☎ 495-5005, Rivadavia 459; admission US$2, free Thur; open 9am-7pm Tues-Sat, 9am-6pm Sun). It features the work of a Buenos Airesborn painter whose themes were largely rural and indigenous; his oils depict native weavers, market and street scenes and portraits.

Museo Irureta de Bellas Artes

Half a block west of Plaza Prado is Tilcara's modern-art museum (☎ 495-5124, Bolívar & Belgrano; free; open 10am-1pm & 3pm-6pm Tues-Sun). It displays an appealing collection of paintings, drawings, engravings and sculptures by a variety of contemporary Argentine artists. Hugo Irureta founded the place and has a collection on display along with many others including Libero Badii and Ricardo Carpani.

Special Events

Tilcara celebrates several festivals throughout the year, the most notable of which is January's Enero Tilcareño, with sports, music and cultural activities. February's Carnaval is equally important in other Quebrada villages, as is April's Semana Santa (Holy Week). August's indigenous Pachamama (Mother Earth) festival is also worthwhile.

Places to Stay & Eat

Autocamping El Jardín (☎ 495-5128, Belgrano) Sites US$3/2 per adult/child. This campground, at the west end of Belgrano near the river, is a congenial place with hot showers and attractive vegetable and flower gardens.

Hostel Malka (☎ 495-5197, fax 495-5200, e malka@hostels.org.ar, San Martín) Dorms beds/doubles US$10/35; breakfast and dinner are extra. Relocated porteños Juan and Teresa Brambati offer guests excellent Hostelling International accommodations at this secluded, hilltop hostel, four blocks from Plaza Prado at the east end of San Martín. Juan also arranges horseback riding, trekking and vehicle tours in the area, including Iruya (US$150 per vehicle or per tour).

Hospedaje El Pucará (☎ 495-5050, Ernesto Padilla) Singles US$10-15, doubles US$15-20 with shared or private bath, camping US$2 per person. One block west and two blocks south of the plaza, this hospedaje has very clean rooms in small, squat flatlets set in an attractive garden.

Hotel El Antigal (☎/fax 495-5020, Rivadavia) Singles/doubles US$15/25 with bath; breakfast US$3 per person. Half a block from the plaza, Antigal is rather like an English cottage inside. Rooms are out the back, set around a central, sunny courtyard and have those comforts you may not want to leave home without such as cable TV. Its restaurant is worth trying for the locro (US$3).

Hotel de Turismo (☎/fax 495-5002, e tilca hot@imagine.com.ar, Belgrano 590) Singles/doubles US$38/45 with bath. The swimming pool at this utilitarian two-star place is usually empty. Some rooms have good views.

There is a small **kiosk** in front of the bus terminal selling sandwiches, lomitos and milanesas for under US$5.

El Cafecito (*Belgrano & Rivadavia*), opposite the post office, seems appropriate to a more urbane setting, but it's an agreeable spot for coffee and croissants.

Pacha Mama (☎ *495-5293, Belgrano 590*) Meat dishes US$4-6, pasta US$4-5. A large eatery with a good bar, PM has a decent menu, although it's a bit expensive. Get here early if you like your *medialunas* (croissants) and forget the toasties – they're *tiny*.

La Peñalta is a folkloric peña with live music on the north side of Plaza Prado.

Getting There & Away
The bus terminal is about 500m west of the town center. All the bus companies have kiosks at the bus terminal. There are 26 buses daily to Jujuy (US$5, 2 hours), six of which continue to Salta. The 24 daily northbound services to Humahuaca (US$2, 45 minutes) and La Quiaca also stop in Tilcara, and there are several buses daily to Purmamarca.

AROUND TILCARA
From an overlook on RN 9, only a few kilometers south of Tilcara, the astounding hillside cemetery of **Maimará**, a picturesque valley settlement beneath the hill known as La Paleta del Pintor (the Painter's Palette) is a can't-miss photo opportunity. The town also has a worthwhile anthropological and historical museum.

Part of a chain that ran from Lima to Buenos Aires during viceregal times, **La Posta de Hornillos** (*free; open 9am-6pm Wed-Mon*) is a beautifully restored way station 11km north of the Purmamarca turnoff. It was the scene of several important battles during the wars of independence. The informal but informative guided tours make this an obligatory stop on the way through the Quebrada.

For information about Parque Nacional Calilegua, see National Parks of Jujuy & Salta Provinces, later in this chapter.

PURMAMARCA
☎ 0388
Beneath the polychrome Cerro de los Siete Colores (Hill of Seven Colors), a few kilometers west of RN 9 via RP 52, this tiny

village's outstanding asset is its 17th-century Iglesia Santa Rosa de Lima.

There are simple accommodations in town including *Hostería La Posta* (☎ *490-8029*), which has triple rooms (with bath) only, and a decent restaurant; and *Residencial Aramayo* (☎ *490-8028*), opposite the police station, charging about US$12/20 for clean singles/doubles with bath.

There are many buses to Jujuy (US$3.50, 1 hour) and others to Tilcara and Humahuaca. Tilcara is about 30km away.

SALTA
☎ 0387 • pop 486,500 • elevation 1200m
Salta is gracious, grand and imposing and would perhaps be subdued, except for the constant ebb and flow of travelers passing through on their way to/from Bolivia. They give the city an injection of life and energy that makes Salta the best place in northwest Argentina to hang out for a few days. There is a huge range of places to stay, from a growing number of backpacker hostels through to five-star luxury, with just about everything else in between. The bar-cum-café-cum-pub scene seems to change frequently but chances are you will find somewhere to tap into the local nightlife. Plaza 9 de Julio reflects the city's tag as Argentina's best-preserved colonial city. It's one of the main reasons Salta is such a joy to just wander around. If you need to arrange anything through a travel agent this is a good place to do it, as the town is crawling with them.

History
Founded in 1582 by Hernando de Lerma, Salta lies in a basin surrounded by verdant peaks. This valley's perpetual spring attracted the Spaniards, who could pasture animals in the surrounding countryside and produce crops that could not grow in the frigid Bolivian highlands, where the mining industry created enormous demand for hides, mules and food. When extension of the Belgrano railroad made it feasible to market sugar to the immigrant cities of the Pampas, the city recovered slightly from its 19th-century decline.

Orientation

From the central Plaza 9 de Julio, Salta's conventional grid extends in all directions until it ascends the eastern overlooks of Cerro 20 de Febrero and Cerro San Bernardo, whose streets hug their contours. Although Salta has sprawled considerably, most points of interest are within a few blocks of Plaza 9 de Julio. North-south streets change their names on either side of the plaza, but the names of east-west streets are continuous.

Information

Tourist Offices The provincial tourist office (☎ 431-0950, e tursalta@salnet.com.ar), Buenos Aires 93, is open 8am to 9pm weekdays and 9am to 8pm weekends. It has some English-speaking staff, brochures and maps, and is helpful in locating accommodations in private houses.

The municipal tourist office (☎ 437-3341), at the corner of Av San Martín and Buenos Aires, is open 7am to 8pm weekdays, 9am to 8pm on weekends. In high season it maintains a smaller office at the bus terminal, which closes from 1pm to 4pm.

The national park administration (☎ 431-0255), Santa Fe 23, has information on the province's several national parks. It is open weekday mornings only.

ACA (☎ 431-0551) is at Rivadavia and Mitre.

Immigration & Consulates Migraciones (☎ 422-0438) is at Maipú 35, 11 blocks west of Plaza 9 de Julio.

The following were correct at the time of research, however these offices do tend to move about, so ask at the provincial tourist office if you are having trouble locating a consulate.

Bolivia (☎ 421-1040), Mariano Boedo 34; open 9am to 2pm weekdays

Chile (☎ 431-1857), Santiago del Estero 965; open 8am to 1pm weekdays

France (☎ 431-4726), Santa Fe 156; open 8:30pm to 9:30pm, Monday and Wednesday

Germany (☎ 421-6525), Urquiza 409; open 9am to 11am on Monday, Wednesday and Friday

Italy (☎ 431-4455), Santiago del Estero 497

PLACES TO STAY
6 Residencial Balcarce
10 Samiri Youth Hostel
14 Hotel Provincial
20 Residencial San Jorge
21 Casa del Peregrino
24 Hostal Travellers
28 Hotel Petit
29 Mária de Toffoli Rooms
30 Cumbre Hotel
39 Victoria Plaza Hotel
40 Hotel Colonial
45 Residencial España
50 Hotel Regidor
56 Hotel Salta
63 Residencial Florida
64 Hotel Italia
66 Residencial Elena
68 Hotel Las Tinajas

PLACES TO EAT
7 Heladería Fili
11 Heladería Rosmari
17 Trattoria Mamma Mia
18 Viejo Jack
31 Il Gelato
34 Cafe Van Gogh
37 New Time Cafe; Casa de Gobierno
42 El Solar del Convento
60 El Palacio de la Pizza
70 Álvarez

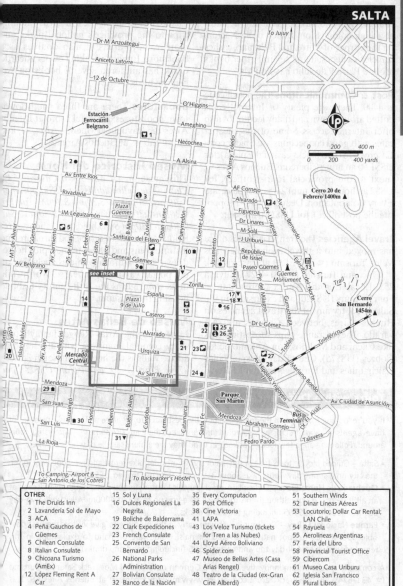

Cerro 20 de
Febrero 1400m ▲

Cerro
San Bernardo
1454m ▲

0   200   400 m
0   200   400 yards

see inset

Parque
San Martín

Bus
Terminal

To Jujuy

To Camping, Airport &
San Antonio de los Cobres

To Backpacker's Hostel

OTHER

1 The Druids Inn	15 Sol y Luna	35 Every Computacion	51 Southern Winds
2 Lavandería Sol de Mayo	16 Dulces Regionales La Negrita	36 Post Office	52 Dinar Lineas Aéreas
3 ACA	19 Boliche de Balderrama	38 Cine Victoria	53 Locutorio; Dollar Car Rental; LAN Chile
4 Peña Gauchos de Güemes	22 Clark Expediciones	41 LAPA	54 Rayuela
5 Chilean Consulate	23 French Consulate	43 Los Veloz Turismo (tickets for Tren a las Nubes)	55 Aerolíneas Argentinas
8 Italian Consulate	26 National Parks Administration	44 Lloyd Aéreo Boliviano	58 Feria del Libro
9 Chicoana Turismo (AmEx)	26 National Parks Administration	46 Spider.com	58 Provincial Tourist Office
12 López Fleming Rent A Car	27 Bolivian Consulate	47 Museo de Bellas Artes (Casa Arias Rengel)	59 Cibercom
13 Museo Antropológico Juan M Leguizamón	32 Banco de la Nación (ATM)	48 Teatro de la Ciudad (ex-Gran Cine Alberdi)	61 Museo Casa Uriburu
	33 Cambio Dinar	49 Cabildo/Museo Histórico del Norte	62 Iglesia San Francisco
			65 Plural Libros
			67 German Consulate
			69 Municipal Tourist Office

Money Cambio Dinar, at Mitre 101, changes cash and traveler's checks, the latter at a high commission. Banco de la Nación, on the corner of Mitre and Belgrano, cashes traveler's checks; it and several other banks around Plaza 9 de Julio have ATMs.

Post & Communications The postal code is 4400. There are plenty of Internet cafés dotted around town and many locutorios also offer Internet access. Some of the cheaper cafés with good connections are Spider.com, Caseros 316 (two blocks east of the plaza), for US$1.50 an hour; Cibercom, Buenos Aires 97 (next to the provincial tourist office), for US$2 an hour, open until 2am most days; and Every Computacion, Deán Funes 141 (opposite the post office), for US$1.80 an hour.

Travel Agencies The Tren a las Nubes office has moved into a travel agency called Los Veloz Turismo (☎ 431-1010) at Caseros 404.

Chicoana Turismo (☎ 431-4027), Zuviría 255, Local 1, is the AmEx representative. For city tours (US$20) and excursions in the Salta area, try any of the travel agencies on Buenos Aires, between Caseros and Alvarado. They arrange trips to destinations like Cachi and Molinos, San Antonio de los Cobres (US$75), Cuesta del Obispo, Valles Calchaquíes and Parque Nacional El Rey.

Clark Expediciones (☎/fax 421-5390), Caseros 121, specializes in bird-watching trips to the province's national parks and more remote areas. It also doubles as a bookstore; English-speaking owner Ricardo Clark has authored several books on Argentine birds.

Bookstores There are three good downtown bookstores: Feria del Libro at Buenos Aires 83; Rayuela at Buenos Aires 94; and Plural Libros at Buenos Aires 220.

Museo Histórico del Norte

This museum (☎ 421-5340, Caseros 549, Plaza 9 de Julio; admission US$1.50; open 9:30am-1:30pm & 3:30pm-8:30pm Tue-Fri, 9:30am-1:30pm & 4:30pm-8:30pm Sat, 9:30am-1:30pm Sun) holds collections of religious and modern art, period furniture and historic coins and paper money, plus horse-drawn and ox-drawn vehicles, including an old postal wagon and a hearse. Worthwhile in its own right is the 18th-century Cabildo housing the museum.

Museo de Bellas Artes

Lodged in the Arias Rengel family's two-story colonial mansion, with its 2m-thick adobe walls, is the fine-arts museum (☎ 421-4714, Florida 20; admission US$1; open

---

Tours with a Difference

If you're looking for a tour in the region, Salta is the best place to organize it. There is a plethora of travel agents in town offering fairly standard itineraries, but there are also some very interesting tours around. Following are a few ideas, but keep in mind they are a mere sample of what's on offer:

- **Salta** – Guided bicycle tours take in the major sights, includes bike rental and is a good way to see the city on a sunny day. Tours take about 3½ hours and cost around US$22.

- **Quebrada de Humahuaca** – Difficult-to-reach Iruya is located among some magical landscape at an altitude of 2700m, although this route will take you up to about 4000m. A leisurely two-day bus trip, it costs US$165 (including food and drinks).

- **Parque Nacional El Rey** – This tour leaves very early in the morning to give visitors the best possible opportunity to spot native birds and animals. Guides are on hand to explain life in this remote forest. It's a full-day trip and costs US$85 (including food and drinks).

A company specializing in innovative tours is a German outfit called Movitrack Safaris & Turismo (☎ 431-6749, e movitrack@arnet.com.ar, w www.movitrack.com.ar) at Buenos Aires 68. It is worth checking out, but spend a bit of time comparing deals before booking.

*am-1pm & 4pm-8:30pm Tues-Sat, 9am-1pm
Sun).* It displays both modern painting and
sculpture. The interior patio features a
wooden staircase that leads to a hanging
balcony.

Museo Casa Uriburu

The family of José Evaristo Uriburu, who
was twice President of the Republic (both
times briefly), lived in this 18th-century
house. A well-preserved collection of period
furniture is displayed at the museum
*(☎ 421-5340, Caseros 417; admission US$1;
open 9:30am-1:30pm & 3:30pm-8:30pm Tue-
Fri, 9:30am-1:30pm & 4:30pm-8:30pm Sat,
9:30am-1:30pm Sun).*

Cathedral

Salta's 19th-century cathedral *(España &
Mitre; open 7am-noon & 4pm-8pm daily)*
harbors the ashes of General Martín Miguel
de Güemes, a native *salteño* and independence hero, as well as those of other important historical figures; even today, the
gauchos of Salta province proudly flaunt
their red-striped *ponchos de Güemes.*

Iglesia San Francisco

Testing the boundary between the ornate
and the gaudy, this brightly painted church
*(Caseros & Córdoba; open 8am-noon &
4pm-11pm daily)* is an unmistakable Salta
landmark, thanks especially to its conspicuous bell tower.

Convento de San Bernardo

Only Carmelite nuns may enter this 16th-
century convent, but visitors can approach
the blindingly whitewashed adobe building
(consider sunglasses) to admire the carved,
18th-century algarrobo door. At Caseros
and Santa Fe, the building was originally a
hermitage, later a hospital and, later still, a
convent proper.

Cerro San Bernardo

For outstanding views of Salta and its surroundings, take the **teleférico** *(gondola;
☎ 431-0641; adults/kids US$6/4 roundtrip)*
from Parque San Martín to the top and
back. A trail that takes you up the hill

begins at the Güemes monument at the top
of Paseo Güemes.

On the lower slopes of Cerro San
Bernardo is the **Museo Antropológico Juan
M Leguizamón** *(☎ 422-2960, Ejército del
Norte & Polo Sur; admission US$1; open
1pm-6pm Mon, 8am-6pm Tues-Fri, 9am-
1pm Sat, 10am-1pm Sun).* It has good repre-
sentations of local ceramics, especially from
the Tastil ruins (the region's largest pre-Inca
town), but has also been guilty of some out-
dated and even bizarre material on the peo-
pling of the Americas – including one panel
suggesting that humans might have reached
the Americas originally via Antarctica.

Places to Stay

Budget One of Argentina's best campgrounds, *Camping Municipal Carlos
Xamena (☎ 423-1341, República del Libouo)*
has 500 tent sites and one of the world's
largest swimming pools (it takes a week to
fill in the spring). Sites costs US$2/1 per
adult/child, plus US$2 per car and US$3 per
tent. From downtown, take southbound bus
No 13 ('Balneario'), which also connects
with the train station. The major drawback is
that in summer, when *salteños* flock here to
catch some rays, they play unpleasantly loud
music for the swimmers and sunbathers.
Mercifully, they switch off the sound system
by early evening. You can purchase food and
drinks at the nearby supermarket.

*Backpacker's Hostel (☎/fax 423-5910,
e hostelsalta@backpackerssalta.com, Buenos
Aires 930)* Dorm beds $8/9 members/non-
members with kitchen facilities. This hostel,
10 blocks south of Plaza 9 de Julio and 13
blocks from the bus terminal, is the
Hostelling International affiliate. Despite
the hostel's cramped conditions, the enthusiastic Argentine-Israeli management has
made it very popular. They offer Internet
access to guests, run a book exchange and
can arrange tours. It's a good place to organize a group to rent a car to explore the high
country. The hostel also has free transfers
from the bus terminal. Bus No 12 from the
terminal stops nearby.

*Samiri Youth Hostel (☎ 431-4579, e samiri
salta@hotmail.com, Vincente López 353)*

Dorm beds/doubles US$8/20. Samiri comes highly recommended. A small hostel, more like a budget guesthouse, the facilities are immaculate and the staff are friendly. The real bonus here though is the great courtyard with vines growing up the whitewashed walls giving the whole place a Mediterranean feel. The front door on Vincente López looks like an entrance to a castle.

Hostal Travellers (☎ 421-4772, e *traveller salta@hotmail.com, San Martín & Santa Fe)* Dorm beds/doubles US$8/18. Only three blocks from the bus terminal, this grungy hostel is central and has kitchen and laundry facilities. The dorms are pretty good but the doubles aren't that crash hot.

Casa del Peregrino (☎ 432-0423, Alvarado 351)* Dorm beds US$8 in 6-bed rooms with shared bath, US$10 in 4-bed rooms with private bath. This spotlessly clean place is recommended as a great budget alternative. It's very friendly and well kept but perhaps not the place for party animals.

The provincial tourist office maintains a list of private houses that are an excellent alternative to bottom-end hotels.

María de Toffoli (☎ 431-8948, Mendoza 915)* Rooms US$10 per person. This place, one of the most popular and central, is run by one of three sisters. The other two let rooms in their own houses next door (☎ 421-2233, Mendoza 917)* and (☎ 421-7383, Mendoza 919)*. All have pleasant patios, kitchen facilities and spotless bathrooms.

Residencial Balcarce (☎ 431-8135, e *hotelbalcarce@hotmail.com, Balcarce 460)* Singles/doubles US$12/18 with shared bath, US$20/25 with private bath. Near the train station, Balcarce has small cramped rooms in need of a facelift. However it's cheap and the rooms are located in a beautiful old building with a grand central courtyard.

Residencial San Jorge (☎/fax 421-0443, e *hotelsanjorge@arnet.com.ar, Esteco 244)* Dorm beds US$9 per person with shared bath, singles/doubles US$20/25 with private bath. This establishment is two blocks south and six blocks west of Plaza 9 de Julio. San Jorge is an excellent option if you want to

pay backpacker prices without the hostel environment. Rooms are in a large attractive corner house. Take bus No 3 or 10 from the bus terminal.

Hotel Italia (☎ 421-4050, Alberdi 231)* Singles/doubles US$19/27. The friendly owners of this excellent hotel will probably give you a discount if you're Italian. Its central location is a huge asset, ensuring the plain but spacious, sunny rooms overlooking the pedestrian mall along Alberdi are a great value.

Residencial Elena (☎ 421-1529, Buenos Aires 256)* Singles/doubles US$20/24. This attractive option is in a neocolonial building with an interior patio. Calling itself a residencial is being coy – it's a mansion! The only blemish is that the bathrooms could be cleaner.

Residencial España (☎ 432-0898, España 319)* Singles/doubles US$20/25. Nice and central but with dark rooms, the jury is still out on this one. It is very friendly however and there are good-size bathrooms and common sitting areas; it would probably seem a little more cheery with a good crowd.

Residencial Florida (☎ 421-2133, Urquiza 718)* Singles/doubles/triples US$20/27/39. This residencial is central but architecturally undistinguished. The light, airy rooms are fairly sterile but those with balconies offer great views.

Mid-Range With singles/doubles for US$22/30, *Hotel Las Tinajas* (☎ 431-8197, Lerma 288)* is one of the cheaper mid-range options, though the rooms here are nothing to jump on the phone and tell the folks at home about. However it is small, central and friendly, and the rooms are clean as a whistle, if a little cramped.

Hotel Petit (☎/fax 421-3012, e *petit_hotel @ciudad.com.ar, Hipólito Yrigoyen 225)* Singles/doubles US$20/30. The Spanish-villastyle rooms at the foot of Cerro San Bernardo are excellent and well worth the tariff with great mountain views. If you want luxuries such as TV and breakfast, you'll pay a little more. Don't forget to duck outside the rooms to avoid people whizzing by on the teleférico above.

Hotel Colonial (☎ 431-0805, fax 431-4249, e hotelcolonial@salnet.com.ar, Zuviría 6) Singles/doubles US$30/50. This grand old place was getting a well-deserved paint job when it was researched. Rooms facing the street have balconies, and are OK, but you're really paying for the location.

Hotel Regidor (☎/fax 431-1305, Buenos Aires 8) Singles/doubles US$40/60. This downtown hotel is near Plaza 9 de Julio. The passageways inside make you feel like you're staying in an old European castle. It's cheaper if you pay cash.

Cumbre Hotel (☎/fax 431-7770, e cumbre @salnet.com.ar, Ituzaingó 585) Singles/doubles US$45/70, with breakfast. This is a good choice, and the spacious, modern rooms come with all the trimmings. Big discounts are offered if paying cash.

Top End The *Victoria Plaza Hotel* (☎ 431-8500, fax 431-0634, e vplaza@arnet.com.ar, Zuviría 16) offers standard singles/doubles for US$65/82, and VIP singles/doubles for US$75/92. Rates for suites are even higher. What is impressive about this hotel is the carpet in the elevators – lovely! But it's the couches in the rooms that really give a sense of lavishness.

Hotel Salta (☎ 431-0740, e hotelsalta@ arnet.com,ar, Buenos Aires 1) Singles/doubles US$75/100. This is an attractive, centrally located property, but several readers have found it to be less than an outstanding value. In its defense, some of the small rooms have magnificent views; if you're paying these rates make sure you get a view.

Hotel Provincial (☎ 432-2003, e reservas@ hotelprovincial.com.ar, Caseros 786) Rooms US$88. Another luxury option with all the trimmings, Hotel Provincial is for the discerning businessperson.

Places to Eat

Mercado Central (Florida & San Martín) This large, lively market is one of the cheapest places in town. You can supplement inexpensive pizza, empanadas and *humitas* (stuffed corn dough, resembling Mexican tamales) with fresh fruit and vegetables.

Even if you're not a budget traveler, it's a good idea to pay the market a visit.

Café Van Gogh (☎ 431-4659, España & Zuviría) Breakfast US$2.50, snacks US$2-4. This trendy place for breakfast seems perpetually busy, giving it a good buzz. Importantly, the steaming coffee is the real deal.

New Time Café (Mitre & Caseros) Breakfast US$2.50-5.50, snacks US$3-5. Opposite the mall (Alberdi), this popular spot is the best people-watching eatery on the plaza. The mouth-watering medialunas here are in a class of their own.

Álvarez (☎ 421-4523, Buenos Aires 302) Empanadas US$0.50, mains under US$5. Álvarez has large portions of palatable, cheap food. The menu is mixed, the service is great and a soccer game is usually on the TV.

Viejo Jack (☎ 422-3911, Av Virrey Toledo 145) and *Viejo Jack II* (☎ 439-2802, Av Reyes Católicos 1465) Starters US$3-4, parrillada US$4-9. These are separate branches of a popular, no-nonsense parrilla that has drawn enthusiastic readers' reviews.

Trattoria Mamma Mia (☎ 422-5061, Pasaje Zorrilla 1) Starters US$1-2, pastas US$5-6. For delectable, varied pasta at reasonable prices, check out this trattoria; dessert prices are also good, and there's no-smoking seating, making it popular for families.

El Solar del Convento (☎ 439-3666, Caseros 444) Starters US$4-7, fish dishes US$8-10. If you want to treat yourself without blowing the budget, try this place. The menu is reasonably extensive with an interesting selection of parrilladas. The service is attentive and it's the little things, such as a champagne aperitif when you take your seat, that makes you feel spoiled. It also has a very good selection of regional wines.

El Palacio de la Pizza (☎ 421-4989, Caseros 437) Pizza US$5.50-10, chicken dishes US$3-5. An old, reliable choice for pizza close to the center, this place has huge open windows making dining very pleasant on a sunny day.

Salta has several fine ice creameries, including *Heladería Rosmari* (Pueyrredón 202), *Heladería Fili* (Avs Belgrano & Sarmiento) and *Il Gelato* (Buenos Aires 606). Ice creams range from US$1 to US$3.

Entertainment

A lot of cafés around the plaza, such as *Van Gogh* and *New Time* have live music late at night on weekends.

Sol y Luna (☎ 422-4695, *España 211*) This groovy, small bar is good for a drink and has live music, usually starting at about 11pm on weekends (free entry). If there's no live music, then the background vibe will be mellow homegrown grooves.

The Druids Inn (☎ 431-6877, *Mitre 918*) A small theme bar with bold furniture and bright walls, it doesn't exactly transport you back to medieval Ireland, but there is a happy hour at midnight on Friday and Saturday. Importantly, Guinness (in cans) is available.

La Casona del Molino (☎ 434-2835, *Luis Burela 1*) Mains US$7-17. For impromptu entertainment, don't miss this former mansion, about 20 blocks west of Plaza 9 de Julio. A real Salta experience, it also serves great empanadas and humitas in several spacious rooms, each with different performers (though the distinction between audience and performer is dubious in this participatory milieu).

Boliche de Balderrama (☎ 421-1542, *San Martín 1126*) This former bohemian haunt is now a popular peña and a good place to catch regional folk music. It's a big, solid place and the walls are adorned with photos and paintings of Argentine artists as well as a distasteful display of animal skins. A cover charge for the music is sometimes added to your dinner bill.

If you feel like something a bit more racy, *Skombroso* nightclub is just a couple of doors down.

Peña Gauchos de Güemes (☎ 421-0820, *Av Uruguay 750*) Entry US$6 per person. Another traditional place, this one is more expensive and less spontaneous than La Casona del Molino.

Teatro de la Ciudad (☎ 437-3350, *Alberdi 62*) Formerly the Gran Cine Alberdi, this venue now features live theater and music performances.

Shopping

Mercado Artesanal (☎ 439-2808, *west end of Av San Martín*) Open 8am-8:30pm. For souvenirs, this provincially sponsored market is the most noteworthy place. Articles for sale include native handicrafts like hammocks, string bags, ceramics, basketry, leather work and the region's distinctive ponchos. To get here, take bus Nos 2, 3 or 7 from downtown.

Horacio Bertero's shop In the Cabildo, opposite Hotel Salta, Horacio Bertero is a protégé of silversmith Raúl Horacio Draghi, San Antonio de Areco's best-known artisan.

Dulces Regionales La Negrita (☎ 421-1833, *España 79*) For those with a sweet tooth, this outlet sells outstanding local sweets.

Getting There & Away

Air Aerolíneas Argentinas (☎ 431-0866), Caseros 475, flies three times daily (except Sunday, with only two flights) to Buenos Aires (US$155 to US$378).

Dinar Líneas Aéreas (☎ 431-0500), at Buenos Aires 46, will soon move their office to Mitre 101. They fly nonstop twice a day to Buenos Aires (US$154 to US$166), and every Saturday to Buenos Aires via Tucumán (US$42).

LAPA (☎ 431-7080), Caseros 492, flies twice daily to Buenos Aires (US$155 to US$279), and daily to Jujuy.

Lloyd Aéreo Boliviano (☎ 431-0320), Deán Funes 29, flies Monday, Tuesday, Thursday, Saturday and Sunday to Santa Cruz, Bolivia (US$182 to US$261), with onward connections. LANChile (☎ 431-8982), Buenos Aires 88, Local 31, has seasonal flights across the Andes.

Southern Winds (☎ 421-0808), Buenos Aires 22, flies twice a day weekday and once a day on weekends, to Córdoba (US$105 to US$162); daily to Rosario (US$162 to US$218) and Mendoza (US$162 to US$218); daily to Neuquén (US$184 to US$241); Tuesday, Wednesday and Thursday to Tucumán (US$41); Wednesday and Saturday to Bariloche (US$195 to US$252); and Tuesday to Buenos Aires (US$185 to US$333).

Bus Salta's bus terminal (☎ 431-5227), on Av Hipólito Yrigoyen southeast of downtown, has frequent services to all parts of the country. Most companies are located in the

erminal, but a few have offices nearby or
elsewhere in town. There are plans for a
fancy new terminal to be built on the same
site, replacing the current aging facility; but
when this is due to take place is anyone's
guess.

Géminis (☎ 431-7979) go to destinations
in neighboring Chile and it has an office at
the terminal. Tur Bus (☎ 431-9719) also
makes the trip across the Andes to various
Chilean towns and has an office at Syria 638.

El Quebradeño (☎ 431-4068) goes daily
to San Antonio de los Cobres and Empresa
Marcos Rueda (☎ 421-4447) serves the altiplano village of Cachi, departing daily at
7am except Tuesday, Thursday and Saturday, when it also has a second service departing in the afternoon at 1pm.

The following are sample fares to destinations in Argentina and neighboring
countries.

Destination	Duration in hours	Cost
Angastaco	6	US$17.50
Antofagasta (Chi)	15	US$42
Arica (Chi)	24	US$47
Asunción (Par)	16	US$60
Buenos Aires	22	US$40-66
Cachi	4¼	US$14
Cafayate	3½	US$12
Calama (Chi)	13	US$38
Catamarca	6	US$23
Córdoba	14	US$20-39
Iquique (Chi)	23	US$47
Jujuy	2	US$5
La Quiaca	7	US$18
La Rioja	14	US$30
Mar del Plata	23	US$88
Mendoza	18	US$50-60
Molinos	6½	US$20
Resistencia	13	US$46
Rosario	18	US$54
San Antonio de los Cobres	5	US$11
San Juan	16	US$45-54
San Pedro de Atacama (Chi)	12	US$35
Santiago (Chi)	24	US$68-88
Santiago del Estero	7	US$18
Tucumán	4½	US$12

Train The Ferrocarril Belgrano (☎ 421-
3161), Ameghino 690, no longer offers
regular passenger services. One of Salta's
popular attractions, though, is the scenic ride
to and beyond the mining town of San
Antonio de los Cobres on the famous Tren a
las Nubes (see San Antonio de los Cobres or
Tren a las Nubes, later, for details).

The local freight, leaving Wednesday at
about 9:20am (the ticket office opens at
8am; reservations can not be made) and returning Friday at 7pm, is a cheaper alternative for getting to San Antonio de los
Cobres. These times vary according to
loading schedules, which may lengthen the
duration of the trip. It also goes farther, on a
29-hour marathon ride to the Chilean
border at Socompa (US$10 to San Antonio,
US$30 to Socompa). From San Antonio de
los Cobres you can catch a return El Quebradeño bus to Salta (departing at 9am;
$11), or get a taxi for about US$60 (but
you'll need four people).

Getting Around

Aeropuerto Internacional El Aybal (☎ 437-
5113) is 9km southwest of town on RP 51;
buses to and from the airport cost US$3.

Local bus No 5 connects the train station
and downtown with the bus terminal on Av
Hipólito Yrigoyen, which is southeast of
downtown. Bus No 13 connects the station
with the municipal campground.

Renting a car is a good way to see Salta's
countryside, but it's far from cheap; figure a
minimum of US$27 per day plus US$0.27
per kilometer, plus US$17 for insurance.
Three-day deals with 800km included are
available for about US$280 plus insurance.
Among the agencies are López Fleming
(☎ 421-4143) at Av Güemes 92 and Dollar
(☎ 432-1616, ⓔ dollarsalta@arnet.com.ar) at
Buenos Aires 88. There are other car-rental
agencies next to Dollar if you want to
compare prices.

SAN ANTONIO DE LOS COBRES
☎ 0387 • pop 3500 • elevation 3750m

San Antonio de los Cobres is a largely
Quechua town, but the posters and political
graffiti scribbled on its adobe walls serve as

reminders that it's still part of Argentina. For truly intrepid travelers, it offers one of the most interesting border crossings in all of Argentina, paralleling the routes of the muleteers across the Puna de Atacama to the Pacific coast of Chile via the famous Tren a las Nubes.

In colonial times, transportation from northwestern Argentina depended on pack trains, most of which passed through the Quebrada de Humahuaca on the way to Potosí, but an alternative route crossed the rugged elevations of the Puna de Atacama to the Pacific and then continued to Lima. A member of Diego de Almagro's party, the first Spaniards to cross the puna, left an indelible account of the dismal 800km crossing, which took 20 days in the best of times:

Many men and many horses froze to death, for neither their clothes nor their armor could protect them from the freezing wind.... Many of those who had died remained, frozen solid, still on foot and propped against the rocks, and the horses they had been leading also frozen, not decomposed, but as fresh as if they had just died; and later expeditions...short of food, came upon these horses and were glad to eat them.

Places to Stay & Eat

Until recent times, San Antonio had only the most basic accommodations and food, and still, for the most part, what you see is what you get.

Hospedaje Belgrano (☎ 490-9025, *Belgrano*) Rooms US$10 per person with breakfast. This friendly hospedaje offers basic lodging.

Hospedaje Los Andes (no ☎, *Belgrano*) Rooms US$10 per person with shared bath. A similar standard to Hospedaje Belgrano, rooms are plain but adequate. Plenty of blankets are provided (nights are always cold at this elevation). There's a restaurant and limited food and drink are also available in the few shops.

Hostería de las Nubes (☎ 490-9059, *Caseros 441*) Singles/doubles US$35/50 with breakfast. This hotel goes a long way to filling the accommodations gap with 12 rooms with private baths, double-glazed windows, and a total of 30 beds. It also has a

restaurant, central heating and a TV lounge. Rates can rise by 20% in the July to August peak season.

Getting There & Away

There are daily buses from Salta to San Antonio de los Cobres (US$11, 5 hours) with El Quebradeño. See below for details on the scenic Tren a las Nubes trip from Salta to San Antonio de los Cobres and beyond.

Do not waste time trying to hitch across the Andes because there are almost no vehicles; even the summer (December–February) buses operated by Géminis from Salta now go via the Paso de Jama.

TREN A LAS NUBES & THE CHILEAN CROSSING

From Salta, the Tren a las Nubes (Train to the Clouds) leaves the Lerma Valley to ascend the multicolored Quebrada del Toro, continuing past the important ruins of Tastil, as it parallels RN 51. To reach the heights of the puna on the Chilean border 571km west (though the Tren a las Nubes travels less than half this distance), the track makes countless switchbacks and even spirals, passes through 21 tunnels more than 3000m in total length, and crosses 31 iron bridges and 13 viaducts. The trip's highlight, a stunning viaduct 64m high and 224m long, weighing 1600 tons, and spanning an enormous desert canyon at La Polvorilla, is a magnificent engineering achievement unjustified on any reasonable economic grounds. At Abra Chorillos, an altitude of 4575m makes this the fourth-highest operating line in the world.

From March to November, Tren a las Nubes Turismo (☎ 0387-431-1010, W www .trenubes.com.ar, Caseros & Deán Funes, Salta) operates the Tren a las Nubes service as far as La Polvorilla; most trips depart on Saturdays only, although they are more frequent during the July-August holidays. Departures vary depending on interest in the service, but to give you a rough idea per month: March has two; April, five; May, three; June, three; July, 14; August, seven; September, six; October, five; and November,

Who's on the Train?

British capital and engineers built most of Argentina's railways, but the line from Salta to the Chilean border, used by the Tren a las Nubes, is one of the few exceptions. New York-born Richard Maury, who also worked in Cuba, came to Argentina in 1906 at the age of 24. He modified an earlier design for the awesome La Polvorilla viaduct and, with a crew of 1300 laborers, built a two-section steel bridge over the Río Toro. The project was first proposed in 1905, but work didn't begin until 1921 and wasn't completed until 1948.

Workers on the Huaytiquina line came from around the world. Legend says that one of the immigrant applicants was a taciturn Yugoslav exile, who started at Campo Quijano and worked his way up the Quebrada de Toro before returning to Buenos Aires and, later, to Europe. In World War II, Josip Broz led a guerrilla struggle against the Nazis and, after the war, became president of his country. Most know him as Marshal Tito.

Readers interested in more detail should consult Federico Kirbus' *El Fascinante Tren a las Nubes*, available in both Buenos Aires and Salta.

tour. The train leaves at 7:05am and returns to Salta at 10:15pm. The fare is US$105 for the 438km roundtrip, which reaches a maximum altitude of 4200m. Meals are additional, ranging from a US$11 fixed-price lunch in the dining car to sandwiches and hamburgers for US$2 to US$5.

Freight trains from Salta, which you may be able to catch in Rosario de Lerma or San Antonio de los Cobres, are a cheaper alternative to the Tren a las Nubes; for more details, see the Getting There & Away entry for the city of Salta. Freights are the only possibility from December to February. The route travels through the gigantic salt lakes of the puna to the Chilean border station at Socompa. From Socompa it is feasible to catch the Chilean freight to the Atacama Desert station of Baquedano on the Carretera Panamericana, about 100km from the port of Antofagasta. On the Chilean side, this is a rugged, uncomfortable trip, not for the squeamish.

At Socompa, 3900m above sea level, passengers must clear Argentine and Chilean immigration and customs before seeking permission to ride the infrequent westbound freights; it is not unusual to wait several days for a train. The Chilean station agent will radio for permission to carry passengers in the train's caboose; while permission is fairly routine, it is not guaranteed. Purchase some Chilean pesos before leaving Salta, since the agent may offer *very* unfavorable exchange rates for US dollars.

From Socompa, the train descends with impressive views of Volcán Socompa (6051m) to the east and Llullaillaco (6739m) to the south, through vast monochrome deserts that few visitors to the continent ever see. At the abandoned mining station of Augusta Victoria, the crew may ask you to disembark while the train backtracks to another isolated mining outpost, but it will return. You may, however, wish to try hitching to Antofagasta. In this isolated area, mining trucks serve as informal public transport and almost certainly will stop. Otherwise, sleep in the abandoned station, which is far more comfortable than the caboose, until the train returns.

VALLES CALCHAQUÍES

Definitely one of Argentina's most appealing off-the-beaten-track areas, the Valles Calchaquíes combine striking natural landscapes with unique cultural and historical resources. The vernacular architecture merits special attention – even modest adobe houses might have neoclassical columns and/or Moorish arches. The town of Cachi is the most accessible and pleasant to wander around; also the bus trip there is well worth it.

In these valleys, north and south of Cafayate and one of the main routes across the Andes to Chile and Peru, Calchaquí Indians put up some of the stiffest resistance to Spanish rule. In the 17th century, plagued with labor shortages, the Spaniards twice tried to impose forced labor obligations on the Calchaquíes, but found themselves having to maintain armed forces to prevent the Indians from sowing crops and attacking pack trains.

Military domination did not solve Spanish labor problems, since their only solution was to relocate the Indians as far away as Buenos Aires, whose suburb of Quilmes bears the name of one group of these displaced people. The last descendants of the 270 families transported to the vice-regal capital had died or had dispersed by the time of Argentine independence.

When their resistance failed, the Calchaquíes lost the productive land that had sustained them for centuries and would have done so much longer. Those riches found their way into the hands of Spaniards who formed large rural estates, the haciendas of the Andes.

Cachi

☎ 03868 • pop 1800 • elevation 2280m

With its scenic surroundings, cobbled streets, 18th-century church and archaeological museum, Cachi is probably the single most appealing stopover among the valley's more accessible settlements.

On the west side of Plaza 9 de Julio, the **Mercado Artesanal** (☎ 491053, **w** www.salnet.com.ar/cachi/; open 9am-2pm & 3pm-8pm weekdays, 10am-3pm & 5pm-8pm Sat, 10am-3pm Sun) is both a crafts market and the de facto tourist office.

On the east side of the plaza, the simple but attractive **Iglesia San José** (1796) features a three-bell tower, graceful arches, and a tightly fitted ceiling of cardón wood. The confessional and other features are also made of cardon.

Directly south of the church, Cachi's **Museo Arqueológico Pío Pablo Díaz** (admission US$1; open 8:30am-6:30pm weekdays, 10am-2pm Sat) presents a professionally

arranged account of the surrounding area's cultural evolution. Except for the improbable suggestion that the first South American ceramics arrived by sea from Japan 5400 years ago, the museum is a welcome contrast to many provincial institutions that make little effort to interpret their materials in a regional context.

Places to Stay & Eat On a hilltop about 1km southwest of the plaza, *Camping Municipal* has shaded sites surrounded by hedges for US$5; sites without hedges are slightly cheaper. On the same site as the campground, the *Albergue Municipal* charges US$3/5 for a bed in 10- to 15-bed dorms without/with bedding.

Hotel Nevado de Cachi (☎ 491004) Rooms US$10 per person. A modest, good value, central hotel, it's just off the plaza next to bus stop.

Hospedaje El Cortijo de María Luisa (☎ 491034) Rooms US$15 per person. This charming, recycled colonial-style building is truly one of the best in the country. It's a cozy little nook-and-cranny place. You get your own small sitting room, use of the kitchen and there's a good chance you'll have the whole place to yourself.

Hostería Cachi (☎ 491105) Singles/doubles US$28/43 members, US$37/57 non-members. This is an ACA property opposite the previous listing; it was closed for a major overhaul during research but those in the know said it would be reopening soon.

On the north side of the plaza, *Confitería Cachi* is a good place for a coffee after your bus ride into town. It also does a range of excellent meals including milanesas and set lunches.

Getting There & Away You can reach Cachi by the Marcos Rueda bus from Salta There is one bus a day to Salta (US$14/25 one-way/roundtrip, 4¼ hours) at 7:15am except Tuesday, Wednesday and Saturday when there is also a second bus in the afternoon at 1pm.

From Cachi, buses continue to La Poma, an old hacienda town that, for all practical purposes, is the end of the line. The road

Mountains & Kids

The bus ride from Salta to Cachi is one of the most spectacular you are ever likely to undertake. The bus grinds its way up narrow, winding roads that twist and curl around the imposing Cuesta de Obispo, giving passengers sweeping views of valley floors and peaks that seem to mirror endlessly into the distance. It's tempting to stick your nose out the window as you career up and down the winding roads. Certainly locals know the real value of the scenery – they hold wailing kids up to the windows and the result is nearly always silence. Now, that's impressive!

Just before Cachi, as you enter Parque Nacional Los Cardones, the landscape levels out to plains of cardones standing sentry in terrain reminiscent of a lunar landscape.

Cachi may be time-consuming to reach by public transport but it's definitely worth the detour. The journey is the best part of the trip.

---

beyond, to San Antonio de los Cobres, is impassable except for vehicles with 4WD; it's much easier to approach San Antonio from Salta via the Quebrada del Toro.

Molinos & Around
☎ 03868 • pop 500 • elevation 2000m

Dating from 17th-century encomiendas, Molinos takes its name from the still-operative grain mill on the Río Calchaquí; the town's restored 18th-century **Iglesia de San Pedro de Nolasco**, in the Cuzco style, features twin bell towers and a traditional tiled roof. Like Angastaco, Molinos was a way station on the trans-Andean route to Chile and Peru. Well into the 20th century, pack trains passed here with skins, wool, blankets and wood for sale in Salta and subsequent shipment to Buenos Aires.

About 1.5km west of Molinos is the **Criadero Coquera**, where INTA, Argentina's agricultural extension service, raises vicuñas; alongside it is the **Casa de Entre Ríos**, part of the former Estancia Luracatao, where there's a very fine artisans market with spectacular alpaca ponchos de Güemes for sale.

Hostal Provincial de Molinos (☎ 494002) Singles/doubles US$65/85 with breakfast. Across from the church, this 18th-century property is also known as the Casa de Isasmendi, after encomendero Nicolás Severo de Isasmendi (1753-1857). Isasmendi, Salta's last colonial governor, was born, lived and died in this sprawling residence in a town that was a stronghold of

royalist resistance. Restored in 1988, it features a small but worthwhile archaeology museum and a small artisans shop. The patio, shaded by a spreading pepper tree, is also worth a stop.

Travelers lacking the funds to stay at the Hostal Provincial de Molinos can try *Camping Municipal* at US$3 per person. The tidy campground has access to the showers and toilets at the adjacent *Albergue Municipal* where beds are US$10 per person in an impeccable facility with half a dozen rooms, each outfitted with two single beds.

Daily, except Tuesday and Thursday, at 6:45am a Marcos Rueda bus goes to Salta (US$20, 7 hours) via RN 40 through Cachi and RP 33 through Parque Nacional Los Cardones.

Angastaco
☎ 03868 • pop 650 • elevation 1900m

From Cafayate, paved RN 40 continues north to San Carlos, beyond which it becomes a bumpy, dusty gravel surface passing among wildly tilted sedimentary beds even more interesting than the Quebrada de Cafayate. Angastaco, 74km north of Cafayate and 51km beyond San Carlos, resembles other oasis settlements placed at regular intervals in the Valles Calchaquíes, with vineyards, fields of peppers and ruins of an ancient pucará. You'll also find an **archaeological museum**.

With rooms for US$7 per person, *Pensión Cardón* is cheap, clean and a good value for the price. Breakfast is also available. At *Hostería Angastaco* (☎ 491123, mobile 1563-9016), singles/doubles go for US$25/35 with breakfast. There's a swimming pool here. Dinners cost about US$5, and the manager's daughter also organizes horseback rides for about US$10 per hour.

Marcos Rueda has a bus to Molinos, Cachi and Salta (US$18, 6 hours). There's also a daily bus to Cafayate.

QUEBRADA DE CAFAYATE

Salta's Lerma valley receives abundant rainfall from summer storms that drop their load on the slopes surrounding the city, but higher ranges to the south and west inhibit the penetration of subtropical storms. In several areas, the rivers that descend from the Andes have carved deep *quebradas* (canyons) through these arid zones, exposing the multicolored sedimentary strata under the surface soils.

Many of these layers have eroded to strange, sometimes unearthly formations, which southbound travelers from Salta can appreciate from paved RN 68, but which are even more intriguing when explored up close. For its extraordinary scenery, the canyon deserves national or provincial park status.

Properly speaking, the Quebrada de Cafayate is the Quebrada del Río de las Conchas, after the river that eroded the canyon. Beyond the tiny village of Alemania, about 100km south of Salta, the scenery changes suddenly and dramatically from verdant hillsides to barren, reddish sandstones. To the east, the Sierra de Carahuasi is the backdrop for distinctive landforms bearing evocative names like Garganta del Diablo (Devil's Throat), El Anfiteatro (The Amphitheater), El Sapo (The Toad), El Fraile (The Friar; a nearby farm sells empanadas and cold drinks), El Obelisco (The Obelisk), and Los Castillos (The Castles). Just north of Cafayate, Los Médanos is an extensive dune field.

Getting There & Away

There are several ways to explore or at least see the canyon. The ideal option is renting a car (which is possible in Salta but not in Cafayate) or renting a bicycle (which is possible in Cafayate); you could also take the bus, hitch or walk. Tours from Salta are brief and regimented.

Here is the lowdown for those without a private vehicle: You can disembark from any El Indio bus (with your rental bike or by foot), tour around for awhile and then flag another bus later on. Be aware of the schedules between Salta and Cafayate, as you probably don't want to get stuck in the canyon after dark (although if you have a tent, there are worse places to camp). Also carry food and plenty of water in this hot, dry environment. Alternatively you could hitch between the most interesting sites, but you may want to catch one of the buses if it gets late.

A good place to start your exploration is the impressive box canyon of Garganta del Diablo. Remember that the most interesting portion is much too far to walk in a single day, so see as much as you can before continuing to Cafayate; you can always double back the next day.

CAFAYATE

☎ 03868 • pop 9200 • elevation 1700m

The most important town in extreme southwestern Salta province, Cafayate is a popular tourist destination, but rarely overrun with visitors except on weekends. It is small and slow-paced and a great base to explore the surrounding countryside of the Quebrada de Cafayate. Everything is within walking distance – including the wineries, where you can taste a local drop or two – but why not do as the locals do and get around on a bicycle.

Cafayate also has many young artists and craftspeople, and you can check out local handicrafts at the mercado artesanal, on Güemes across from the tourist office; it's open from 9am to 10pm daily.

Orientation & Information

Cafayate sits at 1660m at the foot of the Calchaquí Valley, near the junction between RN 40, which goes northwest to Molinos and Cachi, and RN 68, which goes to Salta through the Quebrada de Cafayate. Through town, RN 40 is Av Güemes. As in many provincial towns, few people bother with street names.

The tourist information kiosk (mobile ☎ 1563-9708), at the northeast corner of Plaza San Martín, is open 8am to 8pm on weekdays, and 8am to 1pm and 3pm to 9pm on weekends.

It's better to change money elsewhere, but try Banco de la Nación on the plaza, or the larger shops or hotels.

The postal code is 4427. The post office is at Güemes and Córdoba. A locutorio is at the corner of Güemes and Belgrano, and at the corner of Güemes and Alvarado.

If you need to get wired, La Satamanca Cyber Café on Güemes, between Belgrano and Hurtado, can help for US$5 an hour.

Museo Arqueológico

In this private museum (☎ 421054, Colón & Calchaquí; tours US$1), the late Rodolfo Bravo, a dedicated aficionado of and expert on the region, left an astounding personal collection of Calchaquí ceramics, as well as colonial and more recent artifacts, such as elaborate horse gear and wine casks. While there's not much explanation, the material itself is worth seeing. Drop in at any reasonable hour, as his widow and son still give tours.

Wineries

The Museo de Vitivinicultura (Güemes; admission US$1; open 10am-1pm & 5pm-8pm weekdays) near Colón, details the history of local wine production.

Three nearby wineries offer tours and tastings; these are free but it's good taste to buy a bottle of wine after the tastings. The 1000-hectare Bodega Etchart (☎ 421529, RN 40; open 7:30am-noon & 3pm-6:30pm weekdays, 8am-noon Sat) is at the southern approach to town.

At the north end of town, the smaller 100-hectare Bodega La Banda (Vasija Secreta; ☎ 421850, RN 40; open 9am-1pm & 3pm-7pm daily) offers cheerful tours, which are recommended and can be done in

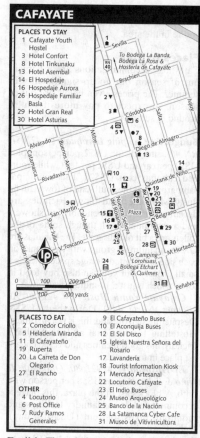

CAFAYATE

PLACES TO STAY
1 Cafayate Youth Hostel
3 Hotel Confort
8 Hotel Tinkunaku
13 Hotel Asembal
14 El Hospedaje
16 Hospedaje Aurora
26 Hospedaje Familiar Basla
29 Hotel Gran Real
30 Hotel Asturias

PLACES TO EAT
2 Comedor Criollo
5 Heladería Miranda
11 El Cafayateño
19 Ruperta
20 La Carreta de Don Olegario
27 El Rancho

OTHER
4 Locutorio
6 Post Office
7 Rudy Ramos Generales
9 El Cafayateño Buses
10 El Aconquija Buses
12 El Sol Disco
15 Iglesia Nuestra Señora del Rosario
17 Lavandería
18 Tourist Information Kiosk
21 Mercado Artesanal
22 Locutorio Cafayate
23 El Indio Buses
24 Museo Arqueológico
25 Banco de la Nación
28 La Satamanca Cyber Cafe
31 Museo de Vitivinicultura

English. The whole place is classified as a national museum.

Bodega La Rosa (RN 40; open 8am-5pm Mon-Thur, 8am-4pm Fri, 9am-1pm weekends), belonging to Michel Torino, is near the RP 68 junction to the Quebrada de Cafayate, north of town. The imposing Casa de Alto, an Italian-style villa at the junction, is no longer part of the Torino properties and is not open to the public.

Special Events

La Semana de Cafayate, at the end of February or beginning of March, is a three-day folklore festival. The annual Fiesta de la Virgen, in early October, is worthwhile if you're in the area.

Places to Stay

Cafayate's accommodations are a bargain out of season but go up significantly in summer. The prices given below are out of season, so expect to pay more if you're around in summer.

Budget At *Camping Lorohuasi* (☎ 421051, *RN 40*), sites go for US$2 per person, plus US$2 per car and US$2 per tent, while four-bed cabañas cost US$20. This municipal campground at the south end of town can be dusty when the wind blows. Facilities are decent and include dependably hot showers and a swimming pool, though some of the toilets are a bit of a disgrace. The cabañas are OK for an intimate group, with two bunks on each side and limited storage space. There's a small grocery, but you can also buy food in town, which is just a 10-minute walk away.

Cafayate Youth Hostel (☎ 421440, *Av Güemes Norte 441*) Dorm beds US$5. Despite the sign outside, this is not an official Hostelling International affiliate. Still, it's friendly, has good facilities and is the cheapest place in town.

El Hospedaje (☎ 421680, *Quintana de Niño & Salta*) Rooms US$8 per person with bath. A block east of the plaza, this place is recommended. It has laundry facilities and mountain bikes for rent (US$10 a day). Rooms are simple, clean and a good size. Readers have sent great feedback about this place.

Hospedaje Familiar Basla (☎ 421098, *Nuestra Señora del Rosario 153*) Rooms US$8 per person. This hospedaje has clean multibed rooms that sleep six. It's a sunny little place that is good if it isn't crowded.

Hospedaje Aurora (☎ 421342, *Nuestra Señora del Rosario 73*) Rooms US$10 per person with bath. This little gem is very central, right next to Iglesia Nuestra Señora del Rosario. The rooms sleep four, the bathrooms are good-sized, and you can use the owner's kitchen.

Mid-Range & Top End Singles/doubles ar US$15/20 with breakfast at *Hotel Confo (☎ 421091, Av Güemes Norte 232)* With th luxury of an adjoining craft shop, this hotel tastefully furnished and has lots of creepin vines, giving it a cool, relaxed ambience. T top it off the rooms are spotless.

Hotel Tinkunaku (☎ 421148, *Diego d Almagro 12*) Singles/doubles US$12/20 wit breakfast. In a quiet location, the rooms her are clean and spacious but a bit dark. I you're driving, there is parking for your ca

Hotel Asembal (☎ 421065, *Güemes Almagro*) Singles/doubles US$12/24. Thi very friendly hotel is a bit classier than other in the area with a large central fireplace i the restaurant.

Hotel Gran Real (☎ 421231, fax 42101 Güemes 128) Singles/doubles US$25/3 with breakfast. The dingy downstairs conf tería at this hotel does not enhance it appeal. The rooms however are anothe story with little balconies that have grea views of the mountains.

Hotel Asturias (☎ 421328, fax 42104 Güemes 154) Singles/doubles US$30/40. Th place has little character but again the ba conies are easily the best features of th rooms. You pay a bit more if you want a T in your room.

Hostería de Cafayate (☎ 421296, RN 4 Singles/doubles US$30/43 with breakfast fo members, US$35/50 nonmembers. This hos tería, north of town, is a bargain for AC members. Prices quoted here are for hig season; in the low season they are muc cheaper.

Places to Eat

El Cafayateño (*Quintana de Niño Nuestra Señora del Rosario*) Mains US$2- A good spot for breakfast in the sun or light meal, this café is a popular little plac

Ruperta (☎ 421838, *Güemes & Quintan de Niño*) Pastas US$1-2.50, meat dishe US$3-4. Ruperta is a little confused; doesn't quite know whether to be a resta rant or a fast-food joint. It's a big barn of place, good for a cheap meal, but the food nothing special.

A Drop of Vino? Why Not!

Cafayate's warm, dry and sunny climate is ideal for the cultivation of wine grapes and several major Argentine vintners have vineyards around town. A local specialty is the fruity, dry *torrontés* white, an excellent lunch wine; some variations are so dry they almost evaporate off your tongue! Invariably, buying a bottle of wine is much cheaper at one of the wineries than in the café-restaurants in town. You'll probably pay around US$5 for a bottle of brut, which is recommended, and of course you get to taste before buying. The reds on offer are certainly not bad either; don't hesitate to give a cabernet a go.

La Carreta de Don Olegario (☎ 421004, Güemes 2) Starters US$2-5, mains US$3-8. There's an appealing menu here with many regional dishes (such as locro), but not everything is always available.

Comedor Criollo (☎ 421140, Güemes Norte 254) Parrillada for 2 US$10. This cheap eatery, between Alvarado and Brachieri, serves large portions of unexceptional Argentine food with the occasional regional specialty.

El Rancho (☎ 421256, Güemes & Belgrano) Mains US$4-10. Also serving regional specialties, El Rancho is a bit more intimate, despite the name, with a large fireplace surrounded by tables, perfect for warming the tush on chilly winter nights.

Heladería Miranda (*Güemes between Córdoba & Diego de Almagro*) Ice creams US$1-3. This heladería has imaginative wine-flavored ice creams – torrontés and cabernet.

Getting There & Away

El Indio, on Belgrano between Güemes and Salta, has four buses daily to Salta (US$12, 4 hours), except Sunday when there are three. There are also four daily to San Carlos (US$1.20, 40 minutes), up the Valle Calchaquí, except on Sunday when there are three, and one to Angastaco (US$6,

2 hours). El Cafayateño, at the corner of San Martín and Buenos Aires, goes twice daily to Salta except Sunday (once).

From Mitre 77, El Aconquija's three times daily buses to Tucumán (US$21.60, 5½ hours) pass through Tafí del Valle; one goes via Santa María (US$6, 2 hours).

Getting Around

For US$10, Rudy Ramos Generales, Av Güemes Norte 175, rents mountain bikes from 8:30am to 3pm, time enough to take an early Salta bus to El Anfiteatro and ride back to town through the Quebrada de Cafayate.

AROUND CAFAYATE
Quilmes

Dating from about AD 1000, Quilmes (*admission US$2; open 8am-6pm daily*) was a complex urban settlement that occupied about 30 hectares and housed as many as 5000 people. The Quilmes Indians survived contact with the Incas, which occurred from about AD 1480 onwards, but could not outlast the siege of the Spaniards who, in 1667, deported the last 2000 inhabitants to Buenos Aires.

Quilmes' thick walls underscore its defensive purpose, but clearly this was more than just a pucará. Dense construction sprawls both north and south from the central nucleus, where the outlines of buildings, in a variety of shapes, are obvious even to the casual observer. For revealing views of the extent of the ruins, climb the trails up either flank of the nucleus, which offer vistas of the valley once only glimpsed by the city's defenders. Give yourself at least half a day, preferably more, to explore the nucleus and the surrounding area.

There is a small museum at the entrance, whose admission charge also entitles you to explore the ruins (which feature hired tourist llamas). The museum shop features a good selection of artisanal goods at relatively small markups.

Places to Stay & Eat It is possible to *camp* on-site, but shade is limited.

Hotel Ruinas de Quilmes (☎ 03892-421075) Singles/doubles US$60/80 with breakfast. This hotel blends so well into its surrounding that it's surprisingly inconspicuous from outside, but its high ceilings and skylights manage to convey the expansiveness of the desert.

The museum now has a *confitería* for basic meals.

Getting There & Away Buses from Cafayate to Santa María or Tafí del Valle will drop passengers at the junction, but from there you'll have to walk or hitch (there is little traffic) 5km to the ruins. It will probably be easier to get a lift back to the highway, since you can approach any vehicle visiting the ruins.

If you want to visit Quilmes another option is to hire a taxi in Cafayate. You should be able to bargain a driver down to about US$35 for the roundtrip. This is an excellent value if there are three or four of you.

Santa María
☎ 03838 • pop 11,000

The northernmost settlement along RN 40 in Catamarca province, the crossroads town of Santa María de Yokavil lies in the midst of a richly endowed archaeological zone and is home to the **Museo Arqueológico Provincial Eric Boman** *(open 8:30am-1pm & 5pm-9pm Mon-Sat)*. This museum is named for the French archaeologist who did extensive pioneering research here in the early 20th century. This tidy oasis is just 35km south of Quilmes, and 80km northwest of Tafí del Valle in Tucumán province, and it is a good stopover or base for visits to Quilmes.

Places to stay in town include *Residencial Inti Huaico* *(Belgrano 146)*, which has been recommended. *Hotel Perez* (☎ 420257, *San Martín 94)* has passable singles/doubles for US$10/20 with bath; cheaper singles with shared bath are also available. *Hotel Provincial de Turismo* (☎/fax 420240, *San Martín & Primera de Mayo)* is a comfortable place with a swimming pool and heating. Singles/doubles cost US$20/30 with breakfast; rooms with TV cost slightly more.

Some but not all buses en route between Tucumán, Tafí del Valle and Cafayate stop here.

NATIONAL PARKS OF JUJUY & SALTA PROVINCES

Jujuy and Salta provinces have four important national parks, but only Los Cardones and Calilegua are easily accessible. El Rey is increasingly accessible thanks to road improvements, while Baritú must be approached through Bolivia. If you're in Buenos Aires, it's a good idea to contact the very helpful national parks administration (☎ 4311-0303), Av Santa Fe 690, for information; the office is open from 10am to 5pm on weekdays. Alternatively you could drop into the office in Salta at Santa Fe 23.

Parque Nacional Calilegua

On the eastern borders of Jujuy province, the high and arid altiplano gives way to the dense subtropical cloud forest of the Serranía de Calilegua, whose preservation is the goal of this accessible, 75,000-hectare park. At the park's highest elevations, about 3600m, verdant Cerro Hermoso reaches above the forest and offers boundless views of the Gran Chaco to the east. Bird life is abundant and colorful, but the tracks of rare mammals, such as puma and jaguar, are easier to see than the animals themselves.

In 2000, both the Argentine branch of Greenpeace and the local Aymará (Kolla) organization Tinkunaku lost their battle to halt construction of a gas pipeline that will run through Calilegua and nearby Baritú, and across the Andes to Antofagasta in Chile. There is concern that this pipeline will threaten regional ecosystems in the national parks.

Information Park headquarters (☎ 03886-422046) is in the village of Calilegua just off RN 34, north of Libertador General San Martín. Donated by the Ledesma sugar mill, the building includes a visitor center with exhibits on the region's national parks and monuments, including Calilegua, Baritú, El Rey, and Laguna de los Pozuelos. The staff can also provide the latest information on

sert landscape of San Juan province, Argentina

eading for the hills in San Juan province, Argentina

JUDY BELLAH

The spectacular cascades of Iguazú Falls straddle the border between Argentina and Brazil.

JASON EDWARDS

Oh mama mara, mama mara let me go!

ALFREDO MAIQUEZ

Aspen trees reaching yellow fingers to the sky.

road conditions, since many areas are inaccessible during the summer rainy season.

At the park entrance (free; open 9am-6pm daily), just north of Libertador General San Martín on RP 83 heading toward Valle Grande, there is an Intendencia (☎ 03886-422046, **e** pncalilegua@cooperlib.com.ar) where you may be able to pick up maps and any last-minute information you're after.

Flora & Fauna Receiving 2000mm of precipitation a year, but with a defined winter dry season, Calilegua comprises a variety of ecosystems correlated with altitude. The transitional *selva*, from 350m and 500m above sea level, consists of tree species common in the Gran Chaco, such as lapacho and *palo amarillo*, which drop their leaves in winter. Between 550m and 1600m, the cloud forest forms a dense canopy of trees more than 30m tall, punctuated by ferns, epiphytes and lianas, covered by a thick fog in summer and autumn. Above 1200m, the montane forest is composed of pines (a general term for almost any conifer, such as cedar), aliso and *queñoa*. Above 2600m this grades into moist puna grasslands, which become drier as one proceeds west toward the Quebrada de Humahuaca.

The 230 bird species include the condor, brown eagle, torrent duck and the colorful toucan. Important mammals, rarely seen in the dense forest, include tapir, puma, jaguar, collared peccary and otter.

Things to See & Do Nature-oriented activities will be the focus of any visit to Calilegua. The best places to view birds and mammals are near the stream courses in the early morning or very late afternoon, just before dark. From the ranger station at Mesada de las Colmenas, follow the steep, rugged and badly overgrown trail down to a beautiful creek usually marked with numerous animal tracks, including those of large cats. The descent takes perhaps an hour, the ascent twice that.

There are seven different trails in the park ranging from a few hundred meters to a couple of kilometers. Generally the trails are poorly marked and range in difficulty –

you should ask the rangers for advice. Local guides are available at about US$3 per hour; recommendations have been given for Patricia (☎ 03886-421501) in Libertador General San Martín.

There are excellent views from 3600m Cerro Hermoso, although there are no detailed maps; ask rangers for directions. Ordinary vehicles cannot go far past the Mesada de las Colmenas, but the road itself offers outstanding views of Cerro Hermoso and the nearly impenetrable forests of its steep ravines.

From Valle Grande, beyond the park boundaries to the west, it's possible to hike to Humahuaca along the Sierra de Zenta or to Tilcara, but the treks take at least a week. It's also possible to do the hike in the other direction; see Juan Brambati at Tilcara's Hostel Malka for summer departures.

Places to Stay & Eat Camping is the only alternative in the park itself. The developed *camping site* (US$2 per person), at Aguas Negras on a short lateral road near the ranger station at the entrance, has balky bathrooms and water shortages. Beware of mosquitoes, which are a lesser problem at higher elevations. Although there are no other developed campsites, you can camp on a level area at the ranger station at Mesada de las Colmenas, which has great open views to the east.

There are several places to stay in nearby Libertador General San Martín including *Hotel Los Lapachos* (☎ 03886-425798, *Entre Ríos 400*), where clean rooms are US$35/45 for singles/doubles with breakfast.

Hotel Posada del Sol (☎ 03886-424900, **e** posadadelsol@cooprlib.com.ar, Los Ceibos & Pucará) Singles/doubles US$40/60 with breakfast. This swish hotel offers up well-appointed rooms around an attractive courtyard and swimming pool. The hotel can arrange excursions and also includes the *Restaurant del Valle*.

Getting There & Away La Veloz del Norte buses between Salta and Orán stop at the excellent and reasonable restaurant belonging to the Club Social San Lorenzo, next door to the park headquarters. There are many buses to Ledesma, only a couple kilometers south of Calilegua.

There are local buses every day from Libertador General San Martín to Valle Grande (2 hours) that go through the park; buses generally leave early in the morning and return late in the evening. Inquire at the park headquarters' visitor center for the most current information.

If you're in a group, a taxi is a good option. It costs US$0.50 per person from Libertador General San Martín to Parque Nacional Calilegua (four people to a taxi). You should arrange the price before you get in the taxi.

Otherwise, it should be possible to hitch to the park and Valle Grande with the logging trucks that pass through the park on RP 83. Start from the bridge at the north end of the town of Libertador General San Martín, where there is a good dirt road through mostly shady terrain to Aguas Negras, 8km west.

Parque Nacional Los Cardones

Occupying some 65,000 hectares on both sides of the winding highway from Salta to Cachi across the Cuesta del Obispo, Parque Nacional Los Cardones takes its name from the candelabra cactus known as the cardón, the park's most striking plant species. Only 100km from Salta, the park finally obtained official national park status in 1997.

In the absence of forests in the Andean foothills and the puna, the cardón has long been an important source of timber for rafters, doors, window frames, and similar uses. As such, it is commonly found in native construction and in the region's colonial churches. According to Argentine writer Federico Kirbus, clusters of cardones can be indicators of archaeological sites; the indigenous people of the puna ate its sweet black seed, which, after passing through the intestinal tract, readily sprouted around their latrines.

Los Cardones is free to enter and still has no visitor services, but there is a ranger in Payogasta, 11km north of Cachi. Make sure you take plenty of water and protection from the sun. Buses between Salta and Cachi will

drop you off or pick you up, but verify times. Other than the national park office you could try the provincial tourist office in Salta for information. Salta's Backpacker's Hostel (see Salta Places to Stay, earlier), sometimes arranges trips to the park.

Parque Nacional Baritú

Hugging the Bolivian border in Salta province, Baritú is the northernmost of the three Argentine parks conserving subtropical montane forest. Like Parque Nacional Calilegua and El Rey, it protects diverse flora and harbors a large number of endangered or threatened mammals, including black howler and capuchin monkeys, the southern river otter, Geoffroy's cat, the jaguar and the Brazilian tapir. The park's emblem is the *ardilla roja* (yungas forest squirrel), which inhabits the moist montane forest above 1300m. Admission to the park is free and information can be obtained from the visitor center at Parque Nacional Calilegua (☎ 03886-422046).

It was here, in 1963, that Che Guevara's psychopathic disciple Jorge Ricardo Masetti tried to start the Argentine revolution by infiltrating from Bolivia. At present, the only road access to Baritú is through Bolivia, where southbound travelers from Tarija may inquire about entry via a lateral of the highway that goes to the border station at Bermejo/Aguas Blancas. There are currently no facilities for visitors.

The national parks administration recently accepted the offer of an extra 8000 hectares of land north of the current Baritú border, from Techint and Gasoducto Norandino, the companies responsible for the gas pipeline through Calilegua and Baritú parks (see Parque Nacional Calilegua earlier). If the property titles are successfully transferred, the land will be incorporated into the park as part of a negotiated settlement.

Parque Nacional Finca El Rey

Confined to a narrow strip no wider than about 50km, Argentina's subtropical humid forests extend from the Bolivian frontier south of Tarija almost to the border between

Tucumán and Catamarca provinces. Parque Nacional Finca El Rey, comprising 44,000 hectares almost directly east of Salta, is the southernmost Argentine park protecting this unusual habitat, the most biologically diverse in the country. The park takes its name from the estancia that formerly occupied the area and whose expropriation led to the park's creation.

The park's emblem is the giant toucan, appropriate because of the abundant bird life, but the mosquito might be just as appropriate (check yourself for ticks, for that matter). Most of the same mammals found in Baritú and Calilegua are also present here. The staff maintain a vehicular nature trail along the Río Popayán and there's a foot trail (actually an abandoned road) to moss-covered **Pozo Verde**, a 2½-hour climb to an area teeming with bird life. There are several shorter trails.

Entry to the park is free and the best time to visit is between April and October.

There is free *camping* at the park's headquarters, in a grassy area with water and pit toilets, but no other infrastructure; there is also a campground at Popayán. The park's comfortable *hostería* was closed at the time of research, but contact the national park office in Salta for up-to-date information.

As the crow flies, El Rey is only about 100km from Salta, but via paved RN 9, paved but rutted RP 5, and RP 20 it's more than 200km from the provincial capital. There is public transport as far as the junction of RN 9 and RP 5, but even if you can hitch to the second junction, there's little traffic for the last 46km before the park headquarters. The latter road is much improved, but even 4WD vehicles are no sure bet in heavy summer rains.

Tucumán & Around

Tucumán is Argentina's smallest province, but its size belies its importance. From colonial times, when it was an important way station en route to Potosí, through the early independence period and into the present, Tucumán has played a critical role in the country's political and economic history. In contemporary Argentina, Tucumán means sugar, and while this monoculture has enabled the province to develop secondary industry, it has also created tremendous inequities in wealth and land distribution, as well as ecological problems.

TUCUMÁN
☎ 0381 • pop 532,000 • elevation 420m
Tucumán (formally known as San Miguel de Tucumán), unlike its provincial cousins to the south, is a brash, energetic, seductive city that has a real buzz on the streets, particularly in the evening. The impression of this sophisticated city is that it is on the brink of urban greatness. We're not talking Buenos Aires here, but Tucumán is the cradle of Argentine independence and the city proudly wears that label. It has flourished in the past, and given an economic boost, it will probably do so again in the future. Tucumán has a character all of its own with its colonial and 19th-century historical sites, lots of cultural attractions, some swinging nightspots and the din of the city's many hip café-bars.

History
Founded in 1565, Tucumán and its hinterland were oriented toward Salta and Bolivia for most of the colonial period. Only during and after Argentine independence did Tucumán distinguish itself from the rest of the region. In the culmination of the ferment of the early 19th century, Tucumán hosted the congress that declared Argentine independence in 1816. Dominated by Unitarist merchants, lawyers, soldiers and clergy, the congress accomplished little else; despite a virtual boycott by Federalist factions, it failed to agree on a constitution that would have institutionalized a constitutional monarchy in hopes of attracting European support.

Unlike other colonial cities of the Noroeste, Tucumán successfully reoriented its economy after independence. Modern Tucumán dates from the late 19th century and owes its importance to location; at the southern end of the frost-free zone of sugarcane production, it was just close enough to Buenos Aires to take advantage of access to

ARGENTINA

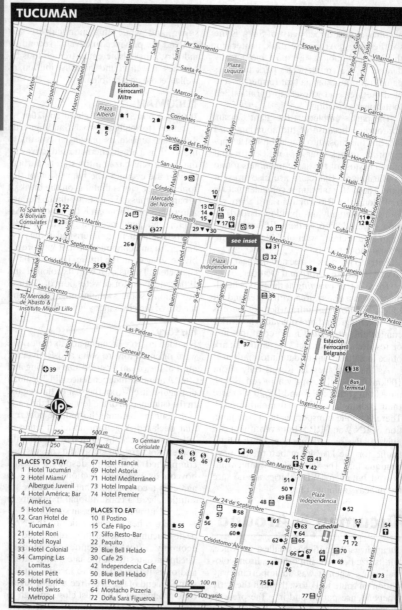

TUCUMÁN

the federal capital's growing market. By 1874, a railroad connected Tucumán with Córdoba, permitting easy transport of sugar, and local and British capital contributed to the industry's growth.

Orientation

Tucumán's geographical focus is the rectangular Plaza Independencia, site of major public buildings like the Casa de Gobierno; street names change north and south of Av 24 de Setiembre, west of Av Alem/Mitre and east of Av Avellaneda/Sáenz Peña.

Information

Tourist Offices Tucumán's provincial tourist office (☎ 430-3644) is at 24 de Setiembre 484, on Plaza Independencia. It's open from 8am to 10pm daily and is helpful, but provincial financial troubles have left it short on brochures and tourist literature. There is also an information office at the bus terminal.

ACA (☎ 431-1522) is at Crisóstomo Álvarez 901.

Consulates Many foreign countries (mostly European) have consulates in Tucumán.

Bolivia (☎ 425-2224), Av Aconquila 1117

France (☎ 421-8202), Crisóstomo Álvarez 471; open at 6:30pm Monday and Friday only, appointment necessary

Germany (☎ 424-2730), 9 de Julio 1042; open 4pm to 8pm Monday and Wednesday

Italy (☎ 422-3830, fax 431-0423), 5th floor, San Martín 623; open 9:30am to 5pm Tuesday

Spain (☎ 435-3042), Mate de Luna 4107; open 9am to noon Monday, Tuesday, Thursday and Friday

Money There are several exchange houses on San Martín between Maipú and Junín. Maguitur, San Martín 765, cashes traveler's checks for a 1.25% commission with a US$5 minimum exchange. It is open 8:30am to 2pm and 4pm to 6:30pm on weekdays and 10am to noon on Saturday. Many downtown banks have ATMs.

Post & Communications The postal code is 4000. There are plenty of Internet cafés

OTHER

3 Nonino
6 Locutorio
7 Lavandería Marva
8 Casa del Obispo Colombres
9 Tucumán Cybercenter
11 RentaCar
13 Post Office
14 El Ateneo
16 Centro Cultural Eugenio
   Flavio Virela (Universidad
   Nacional de Tucumán);
   Museo Arqueológico
18 Sir Harris
19 Web City
20 Cine Atlas
24 Cine Candilejas I/II
25 Citibank
26 Dinar; Líneas Aéreas
27 Maguitur
28 Duport Turismo
31 Círculo Bar; Velvet Discos;
   Círculo de la Prensa
32 Teatro Orestes Caviglia
35 ACA
36 Museo Iramain
37 Móvil Renta
38 Shopping del Jardín
39 Hospital Padilla
40 Italian Consulate
41 Iglesia San Francisco

43 Locutorio
44 Banco Galicia
45 Banco France's
46 Banco de Boston
47 Banco de la Nación
48 Museo Folklórico Manuel
   Belgrano
49 Casa Padilla
51 Casa de Gobierno
52 Centro Cultural Dr
   Alberto Rougués
54 Iglesia La Merced
56 Patsa Turismo (AmEx)
57 Cine Majestic
59 LAN Chile
60 LAPA
62 Southern Winds
63 Provincial Tourist Office
65 Museo de Bellas Artes
   Timoteo Navarro
66 French Consulate
68 Bar Gaston
70 Museo Histórico de la
   Provincia
75 Basílica Santo Domingo
76 Aerolíneas Argentinas
77 Casa de la Independencia

dotted around town all varying in connection speed and price. Two of the cheapest (US$2 per hour) with good connections are Tucumán Cybercenter, San Juan 612, open 9am to 11pm Monday to Saturday and 6pm to 11pm Sunday; and Web City, Mendoza 383, open daily.

Travel Agencies Patsa Turismo (☎ 421-6806), Chacabuco 38, is the AmEx representative, but it does not exchange currency. Duport Turismo (☎ 422-0000, e duporttur@tucbbs.com.ar), Mendoza 720, Local 3, offers city tours (US$20) and excursions to Tafí del Valle (US$40); for another US$15, the Tafí trip can include the ruins at Quilmes.

Bookstores El Ateneo at 25 de Mayo 182 is a good example of Tucumán's sophistication. It's a combination of a bookstore and a café – you won't find many cities up this way hosting such a creation. El Ateneo has books in English and Spanish and plenty of maps of the region.

Cultural Centers To learn what's happening in town, visit the Universidad Nacional de Tucumán's Centro Cultural Eugenio Flavio Virela (☎ 421-6024), 25 de Mayo 265, which has art exhibitions, an auditorium, and a small café, a respite from the noisy downtown streets. There are also crafts for sale.

The Centro Cultural Dr Alberto Rougués (☎ 422-7976), Laprida 31, has rotating exhibits of provincial painters. It's open 8am to 1pm and 5pm to 9pm weekdays, 10am to 12:30pm and 6:30pm to 8:30pm on Saturday. Entry is US$1.

Casa Padilla

Alongside the Casa de Gobierno, this partly restored mid-19th-century house first belonged to provincial governor José Frías (1792-1874), then to his mayor son-in-law Ángel Padilla and to the latter's son. A display of European art and period furniture make up that collection and the house's museum (*25 de Mayo 36; admission US$1; open 9:30am-12:30pm & 4:30pm-7:30pm weekdays, 9am-noon Sat*).

Casa de la Independencia (Casa Historical)

Unitarist lawyers and clerics (Federalists boycotted the meeting) declared Argentina's independence from Spain on July 9, 1816, in this dazzlingly whitewashed late-colonial house (*☎ 431-0826, Congreso 151; admission US$2; open 9am-1pm & 4pm-6pm weekdays, 9am-1pm weekends*). Portraits of the signatories line the walls of the room where the declaration was signed.

The interior patio is a pleasant refuge from Tucumán's commercial bustle. The house is 1½ blocks south of Plaza Independencia. There's a light-and-sound show nightly except Thursday at 8:30pm; entry is US$4/2 for adults/children.

Museo Folklórico Manuel Belgrano

Occupying a colonial house that once belonged to the family of Bishop José Eusebio Colombres, a major figure in the independence movement who also fostered local sugar cultivation, is this pleasant and interesting museum (*☎ 421-8250, 24 de Setiembre 565*). At the time of research, the museum was temporarily closed for renovation, but it features a good collection of Río de la Plata horse gear, indigenous musical instruments and weavings, Toba wood carvings, Quilmes pottery and samples of *randa* (an intricate lace resembling Paraguayan *ñandutí*) from the village of Monteros, 53km south of Tucumán. Some items are for sale in the museum shop.

Casa del Obispo Colombres

In the center of Parque 9 de Julio (formerly Bishop Colombres' El Bajo plantation), this 18th-century house (*free; open 8am-7pm daily*) contains the first ox-powered *trapiche* (sugar mill) of Tucumán's post-independence industry. Guided tours, in Spanish, explain the operation of the mill, some of whose equipment is still in working order.

Instituto Miguel Lillo

Life-size replicas of dinosaurs and other fossils from San Juan's Parque Provincial

Ischigualasto populate the garden of this natural history museum (☎ 423-4127, Miguel Lillo 251; free; open 9am-noon & 3pm-6pm weekdays).

Other Public Buildings & Museums

Tucumán is a historic city with a wealth of museums and other public buildings. The most imposing downtown landmark is the turn-of-the-20th-century **Casa de Gobierno**, which replaced the colonial Cabildo on Plaza Independencia. The 1860 **Basílica Santo Domingo** (9 de Julio; open 9am-1pm & 4pm-8pm daily), Crisóstomo Álvarez and San Lorenzo, and the **Cathedral** (24 de Setiembre & Congreso; open 7:30am-1pm & 4:30pm-10pm Mon-Sat, 8am-1pm & 5pm-10pm Sun), which dates from 1845, are major ecclesiastical holdings.

The **Museo Iramain** (☎ 421-1874, Entre Ríos 27; free; open 9am-1pm & 6:30pm-9:30pm weekdays) has collections of Argentine paintings and sculpture. Dating from 1905, the **Museo de Bellas Artes Timoteo Navarro** (☎ 422-7300, 9 de Julio 56; free; open 8am-noon & 4pm-8pm weekdays) has changing exhibits, including some very imaginative sculpture.

Other noteworthy museums include the **Museo Histórico de la Provincia** (☎ 431-1039, Congreso 56; admission US$1; open 9:30am-12:30pm & 4pm-7pm weekdays, 9am-noon Sat), President Nicolás Avellaneda's birthplace; and the **Museo Arqueológico** (☎ 422-1692, 25 de Mayo 265; admission US$1.50/1 with/without guide; open 8am-noon & 4pm-8pm weekdays) in the Universidad Nacional de Tucumán, which displays collections on northwestern Argentine prehistory.

Activities & Guided Tours

The staff at the provincial tourist office have information on a variety of outdoor activities. Trekking and hiking are popular in the Sierra de Aconquija; one popular excursion is the four-day hike to Tafí del Valle. Readers have enthusiastically recommended Héctor Heredia (☎ 422-6205, fax 430-2222, Balcarce 1067) as a mountain guide for the Sierra, Tafí del Valle and surrounding areas. Héctor (also known as 'El Oso' or 'the Bear') can arrange extended treks in the provinces of Tucumán and Catamarca, and gives a good explanation of what to expect in advance.

Special Events

Celebrations of Día de la Independencia (Argentina's Independence Day) on July 9 are especially vigorous in Tucumán, the cradle of the country's independence. *Tucumanos* also celebrate the Batalla de Tucumán (Battle of Tucumán) on September 24.

Places to Stay

The cheapest places to stay are near the old bus terminal but are pretty shabby. The area around Plaza Alberdi and the Ferrocarril Mitre has experienced something of a revival in recent years, with upgraded but still reasonably priced accommodations and restaurants.

Budget Camping is possible at *Las Lomitas* in Parque 9 de Julio, about 10 blocks from the new bus terminal via Av Benjamín Aráoz. The unfenced site is less secure than most Argentine campgrounds; although theft is unlikely, inform the attendant when you leave. If tent camping, choose your site carefully; lower-lying parts flood when it rains heavily. Campsites are about US$4.

Alternatively, *Camping de la Policía* is about five blocks south of the bus terminal and costs US$3 per person. To find out more about this place inquire at the provincial tourist office.

Hotel Tucumán (☎ 422-1809, Catamarca 573) Singles/doubles US$12/15 with shared bath, US$15/25 with private bath. This hotel has basic, tidy rooms with *tiny* bathrooms. There is also a pleasant sunny central courtyard area.

Hotel Royal (☎ 421-8697, San Martín 1198) Singles/doubles US$10/20. Five blocks to the west of the center, this hotel has an industrial decor that interior designers would kill for. The old-fashioned, high-ceiling rooms are well kept.

Hotel Petit (☎ 421-3902, Crisóstomo Álvarez 765) Singles/doubles US$10/15 with shared bath, US$18/24 with private bath. Friendly Petit is easily the best central budget choice in town. It's housed in gracious old premises that are anything but petite.

Hotel Viena (☎ 431-0313, Santiago del Estero 1054) Rooms US$10 per person. This residencial, opposite the Mitre station, is probably the best budget option in this area. The upstairs rooms are bright with new furniture and the bathrooms are very clean.

Hotel Florida (☎ 422-6674, 24 de Setiembre 610) Singles/doubles US$15/25 with fan & bath. Just off Plaza Independencia, this is a small, quiet, very central hotel; upstairs rooms have better light. You are really paying for the excellent location.

Albergue Juvenil (☎ 431-0265, fax 422-2405, Junín 580) Singles/doubles US$20/30 with breakfast. Tucumán's AAAJ-affiliated hostel occupies part of the mid-range Hotel Miami. The Hostelling International card is obligatory. It's hardly a bargain at these rates, so although it may be a good spot to meet other travelers, you'd probably be better off in another budget option.

Hotel Roni (☎ 421-1434, San Martín 1177) Singles/doubles US$22/25. The Roni wins an award for one of the weirdest entrances to any Argentine hotel – a bridge leads from the hallway into the lobby. Rooms are dark and gothic and not a bad value for two people, but overpriced for singles.

Mid-Range Singles/doubles go for US$28/38 with breakfast at modern, boxy **Hotel Astoria** (☎/fax 421-3101, Congreso 88), just off Plaza Independencia. The old rooms are comfortable and have views of the city. The street itself is very noisy.

Hotel Impala (☎ 431-0371, Crisóstomo Álvarez 277) Singles/doubles US$20/30 with bath. This downtown option is clean and a great value. It's even cheaper if you stay more than one night. Rooms come with a TV and are fairly small, but the bathrooms are spotless.

Hotel Francia (☎/fax 431-0781, e hotel francia@arnet.com.ar, Crisóstomo Álvarez 467) Singles/doubles/triples US$26/36/45. The Francia is near the Impala. Rooms are elegantly furnished and the bathrooms are larger than average. Room service is available and there are also more luxurious (and more expensive) rooms.

Hotel América (☎/fax 430-0810, e hotel america@noanet.com.ar, Santiago del Estero 1064) Singles/doubles US$25/35. This spiffy place is also a good value. It has a quirky design that gives it style. The wallpaper might make you cringe but you'll love the medieval light shades.

Hotel Miami (☎ 431-0265, fax 422-2405, e miamihotel@infovia.com.ar, Junín 580) Singles/doubles US$29/39. The Miami has old, clean rooms and it's very friendly.

Hotel Colonial (☎/fax 431-1523, San Martín 35) Singles/doubles US$35/45. This place comes recommended; though there's nothing remotely colonial about this very modern building. The rooms have an art deco touch.

Top End Modern but attractive **Hotel Mediterráneo** (☎ 431-0025, toll-free fax 0800-777-3682, e info@hotelmediterraneo.com.ar, 24 de Setiembre 364) is situated opposite Plaza Independencia. Singles/doubles cost US$35/45 and have cable TV and room service; English and French are spoken. The large spotless rooms are probably the best value in this range; the triples are particularly good.

Hotel Premier (☎/fax 431-0381, e info@ redcarlosv.com, Crisóstomo Álvarez 510) Singles/doubles US$60/70. With plain, simple rooms, you are paying for prestige and location in this grand, musty old hotel.

Hotel Swiss Metropol (☎ 431-1180, e metropol@arnet.com.ar, 24 de Setiembre 524) Singles/doubles US$82/104. This is another centrally located high-rise with a sparkling foyer and eager service.

Gran Hotel de Tucumán (☎ 450-2250, e ghotel@arnet.com.ar, Av Los Próceres 380) Singles/doubles US$120/140. If you can't do without life's luxuries, or you're just on for a real treat, then this is the place for you. Fronting Parque 9 de Julio, this five-star property is the city's best and most expensive.

Places to Eat

Independencia Café (☎ 430-3588, 25 de Mayo & San Martín) Breakfast US$1.70, lunch US$3-4. Try this busy little place, with its rushed service, for a breakfast of coffee, soda water and two medialunas (and orange juice for a small extra charge).

Café 25 (☎ 422-8688, 25 de Mayo 198) Sandwiches US$2-4, lomitos US$3, cakes US$3.50. At the all-pine Café 25 on the trendy corner of 25 de Mayo and Mendoza, you can mix with the beautiful people, have coffee and cake and watch the outside world bustle by. The fresh juices served here are simply luscious.

Café Filipo (☎ 421-9687, 25 de Mayo & Mendoza) Sandwiches US$2-4. Good for snacks and delicious coffee, this is the most traditional of the eateries in this busy area.

Doña Sara Figueroa (☎ 422-6533, 24 de Setiembre 358) Mains US$5. Basic dining with regional specialties is what's on offer here. Middle Eastern food is sometimes on the menu also.

Silfo Resto-Bar (☎ 422-2393, 25 de Mayo 205) Salads US$3-6, pizzas US$5-8. The food in this lively restaurant is refreshingly imaginative. Had enough meat dishes in Argentina? Then try the fresh, crisp salads here.

El Portal (☎ 422-6024, 24 de Setiembre) Mains US$3-10. Half a block east of Plaza Independencia, try the chicken empanadas, humitas and other tasty regional specialties at this modest-looking eatery, one of several small stands at the same address.

Il Postino (☎ 421-0440, 25 de Mayo & Córdoba) Tapas $4-7, mains $6-12. Pizza and pasta are served with panache in this old atmospheric warehouse eatery. Get here early on weekends, as it's very popular. Possibly the best pizzas you might have in this part of Argentina.

Mostacho Pizzeria (☎ 430-4162, 9 de Julio 26) Large pizzas US$7-12. While some of the more traditional pizzerias have gone down the gurgler in Tucumán, this fine eatery has popped up. It's very cheap and has lots of promotions, such as two pieces of pizza and a drink for US$1.50. It also does inexpensive pasta dishes.

Keep an eye out for outlets of **Blue Bell Helado** around town. The delicious cake-like blocks of ice cream are simply too tempting for most mortals. There is one on 9 de Julio opposite Plaza Independencia.

Entertainment

Círculo Bar (Mendoza 240) Open 11:30am-3pm & 6pm-late daily. Easily the funkiest bar in town, this new place is small and has cool music, hip furniture and a student atmosphere. It gets going late and there is live music on Tuesday and Sunday, a free movie on Wednesday and every other night there's a DJ pumping out a mixed bag of tunes. Discos come and go, but this is the best place to ask about what's hot around town. If you get peckish, snacks, mainly pasta, are available for US$2.50 to US$5. At the same place is Velvet Discos, which sells CDs, and **Círculo de la Prensa**, which is good for live performance.

Bar América (☎/fax 430-0810, Santiago del Estero 1064) Opposite Plaza Alberdi, this large bar sometimes has live music and is a good spot for a crowd.

Sir Harris (Laprida 206) On the corner of Laprida and Mendoza, this British-style pub pulls a classy crowd and pours a decent Guinness (even if it is out of a can). There is a small pub menu and the service is very good.

Bar Gastón (Congreso & Crisóstomo Álvarez) This is a cute little bar with brick and cushion booths in a quiet spot away from the trendy café-bars in the north of the city. Gastón has a homely feel and is good for a quiet drink from the large cocktail menu; if you like a dram you're in luck as they have a selection of national whiskies.

Nonino (☎ 421-6098, Junín 545) This cultural center presents live folkloric music, including tango, and theater.

Getting There & Away

Air Aerolíneas Argentinas (☎ 431-1030), 9 de Julio 112, flies daily to Salta (US$42 to US$55) and Buenos Aires (US$132). LAPA

(☎ 430-2330), Buenos Aires 95, flies twice daily to Buenos Aires (US$132) except Saturday and Sunday (once only).

Dinar Líneas Aéreas (☎ 430-0652), at Junín 58, flies three times a day to Buenos Aires (from US$109) and once a week to Salta on Saturday (US$39).

Southern Winds (☎ 0810-777-7979, **e** swtuc@infovia.com.ar), 9 de Julio 77, has flights three times a day to Córdoba (US$64 to US$132) except Sunday (twice daily); they also fly daily to Mendoza (US$151 to US$208); daily to Rosario (US$151 to US$208); Monday, Wednesday and Friday, in summer only, to Mar del Plata (US$150); daily to Neuquén (US$173 to US$230); Tuesday, Thursday, Saturday and Sunday to Bariloche (US$175 to US$242); and daily to Buenos Aires (US$170 to US$300).

LANChile (☎ 422-4899), Buenos Aires 39, Local 7, has seasonal flights over the Andes to destinations in Chile. Lloyd Aéreo Boliviano (☎ 422-3030), San Martín 667, flies to Santa Cruz in Bolivia, with onward connections.

Bus At Brígido Terán 350, Tucumán's sparkling bus terminal (☎ 422-2221) is a major public-works project with 60 platforms, a post office, telephone services, a supermarket, bars and restaurants. In the complex, Shopping del Jardín's information booth (☎ 430-6400, 430-2060) is open 6:30am to 11:30pm daily and provides information on the station and the shopping center only.

The following table lists sample destinations and fares from Tucumán.

Destination	Duration in hours	Cost
Amaichá del Valle	4	US$14
Buenos Aires	16	US$38-46
Belén	8	US$16
Cafayate	5½	US$22
Catamarca	4	US$12
Córdoba	8	US$22
Jujuy	4	US$15
La Rioja	6	US$17
Mar del Plata	5	US$25
Mendoza	13	US$37
Neuquén	18	US$75
Pocitos	8	US$25
Posadas	14	US$35
Resistencia	2	US$26
Río Gallegos	40	US$150
Salta	30 minutes	US$15
San Juan	12	US$32-38
San Martín	22	US$101
Santiago (Chi)	23	US$45-59
Santiago del Estero	2	US$8
Tafí del Valle	3	US$8
Termas de Río Hondo	1	US$5
Trelew	21	US$102

Getting Around

Aeropuerto Internacional Benjamín Matienzo (☎ 426-4906) is 8km east of downtown via Av Gobernador del Campo, the northern boundary of Parque 9 de Julio. Empresa 120 Alderete runs airport minibuses (US$1) that leave from the bus terminal every 20 minutes during the day.

For getting around the city, keep in mind that buses do not accept cash, so you must buy *cospeles* (US$0.60) at downtown kiosks; they are less readily available elsewhere in the city.

If you want to rent a car, try Móvil Renta (☎ 431-0550) at San Lorenzo 370 or RentaCar (☎ 421-1372) at Av Soldati/Los Próceres 380.

AROUND TUCUMÁN

Until 1767, the ruins of **San José de Lules**, 20km south of Tucumán, was a Jesuit reducción among the region's Lule Indians. After the Jesuits' expulsion, the Dominicans assumed control of the complex, whose present ruins date from the 1880s and once served as a school. The small museum has replicas of colonial documents and a plethora of busts of various Argentine independence heroes. There are numerous ghost stories about the place, and legends of buried Jesuit treasure.

To get to Lules, a pleasant site for an afternoon outing, take the Trébol, Provincial or El Centauro bus from downtown Tucumán.

TAFÍ DEL VALLE
☎ 03867 • pop 6000 • elevation 2100m

About 100km from Tucumán the narrow gorge of the Río de los Sosas, with its dense, verdant subtropical forest on all sides, opens onto a misty valley beneath the snowy peaks of the Sierra del Aconquija. The precipitous mountain road (RN 38 to RP 307) from Tucumán to Tafí del Valle is a spectacular trip and well worth staying awake for on the bus.

When summer heat drives *tucumanos* out of the provincial capital, they seek refuge in the cool heights around the hill station of Tafí del Valle, whose population can swell to 15,000 or more. The town makes a pleasant stopover with some good hiking opportunities, although it's probably best avoided at the height of summer.

Orientation & Information
Av Miguel Critto is the main street running east to west. If you turn left out of the bus terminal, onto Av Miguel Critto, walk about 200m and turn left again, you will be heading into the center of town. Juan de Perón runs south off Critto just before the plaza, most places to eat are along here, as well as souvenir shops and a couple of places to stay. Most public services are on or near the Centro Cívico, which features an unusual semicircular plaza.

Tafís helpful Casa del Turista (☎ 421084) on Av Miguel Critto, near the plaza, is open from 8am to 10pm daily in summer and from 8am to 6pm daily in winter.

Banco de la Provincia, in the Centro Cívico, changes US dollars cash. Long-distance telephones are also here.

Capilla La Banda
This 18th-century Jesuit chapel (☎ 421685, Av José Friás Silva; admission US$1; open 8am-10pm daily in summer, 8am-6pm daily in winter), acquired by the Frías Silva family of Tucumán on the Jesuits' expulsion and then expanded in the 1830s, was restored to its original configuration in the 1970s. Note the escape tunnel in the chapel. The small archaeological collection consists mostly of funerary urns, but also religious art of the Cuzco school, ecclesiastical vestments and period furniture that once belonged to the Frías Silvas. (This collection may be moved to a nearby museum; inquire at the Casa del Turista.) Guided tours are available.

The chapel is a short distance south of downtown. Cross the bridge over the Río Tafí del Valle then follow the road around to the right onto José Silva. Turn left onto the third dirt road along the left-hand side of José Silva. The chapel is a little way along.

Hiking
Several nearby peaks and destinations make hiking in the mountains around Tafí del Valle an attractive prospect; try 3000m **Cerro El Matadero**, a four- to five-hour climb; 3800m **Cerro Pabellón** (six hours); and 4600m **Cerro El Negrito**, reached from the statue of Cristo Redentor on RN 307 to Acheral. The village of La Ciénaga is about seven hours away. The trails are badly marked, and no trail maps are available. You can hire a guide for about US$5 an hour. Ask for more information at Casa del Turista.

Places to Stay
Autocamping del Sauce (☎ 421084, Av Palenques) Campsites/bunks US$2.50/5 per person. Tafís campground, to the west of the town center, is acceptable at this price, but toilets and showers are very run-down, although the grounds are well kept. Shade is limited (a lesser problem in overcast Tafí than elsewhere in the country). Bunks in small cabañas are available, but these would be very claustrophobic at their maximum capacity of four persons.

Hospedaje del Valle (☎ 421641, Av Juan de Perón) Rooms US$10 per person. Undoubtedly the best budget option in town, this central hospedaje is close to the corner of Av Miguel Critto. Rooms are sparkling clean and have private baths.

Hostería de Atep (☎ 421061, Menhires 78) Dorm beds US$12/25 bed only/full board. This is a union-run establishment that is a little reminiscent of a high-school camp. It's about 300m east of the plaza, accessible off Av Miguel Critto.

Hostería Huayra Puca (Menhires 71) Singles/doubles/triples US$29/44/56. This is a smaller more intimate place with very comfy rooms; it's just south of Atep.

Hostería Los Cuartos (☎ 421444, ⓔ losval @infovia.com.ar, Av Juan Calchaquí) Singles/doubles US$20/35. This is probably the best value around this price and very handy for the bus terminal. The modern rooms here are very tidy with new furniture, TV, telephone and central heating. Common areas have huge fireplaces. You pay a little extra for a room with views of the reservoir and surrounding mountains. To get here turn right out of the bus terminal onto Miguel Critto, then take the first left 100m down and left again onto Juan Calchaquí. The hotel is 50m down on the left-hand side.

Hostería del ACA (☎/fax 421027, Gobernador Campero & San Martín) Singles/ doubles US$30/45. This well-kept hotel theoretically accepts members only, but in practice they're much less discriminating. It's set on a large property and has some great views.

Hostería Lunahuana (☎/fax 421330, ⓔ info@lunahuana.com.ar, Av Miguel Critto 540) Singles/doubles US$70/90 with half-board. If you've got the pesos you'll enjoy this top of the line place. Rooms have a separate upstairs sitting area.

Places to Eat

Bar El Paraíso (☎ 1558-75179, Juan de Perón 176) Sandwiches US$1.50-3, mains US$4-6. This bar is where locals congregate to dine cheaply and watch Seagal or Stallone videos. There is a pleasant patio overlooking Juan de Perón.

La Estancia (Av Miguel Critto) Parrillada US$4. This is a basic place across from Hostería Lunahuana, and it is good for a quick bite while you're waiting for your next bus.

Pub El Ciervo (☎ 421518, Juan de Perón) Mains US$4-9.50. Alongside the YPF gas station, Pub El Ciervo has moderately priced *minutas* (quick meals), including humitas and juicy tender steaks. It's a reliable little eatery with a menu in English and a large fireplace.

El Rancho de Félix (Juan de Perón) Mains US$4-10; open 11:30am-3:30pm & 8pm-midnight daily. El Rancho, which serves regional food, is probably the best choice in town. It's down the south end of Juan de Perón just before the bridge over Río Tafí del Valle.

El Portal de Tafí (Juan de Perón 200) Starters US$3-5, mains US$7-8. Repulsively kitschy decor – especially the animal skins stretched across the walls – is the order of the day here. But there's a good and varied menu of sandwiches, meat and pasta.

There's a cozy *bar* at the bus terminal, good for whiling away a few hours before your next bus.

Getting There & Away

Tafí's brand spanking new bus terminal is on Miguel Critto, near the corner of Av Juan Calchaquí, about 600m east of the town center. Empresa Aconquija has eight buses a day to Tucumán (US$8, 2½ hours). Buses heading the other way, direct to Cafayate, leave twice a day (US$14, 4 hours). Buses to Amaichá del Valle and Quilmes are US$6 and US$10, respectively.

Beyond Tafí, the paved road zigzags over the 3050m pass known as Abra del Infiernillo (Little Hell Pass), an alternative route to Cafayate and Salta, passing the impressive Diaguita ruins at Quilmes.

Getting Around

Hourly in summer, every three hours in winter, local Aconquija buses do most of the circuit around Cerro El Pelado, in the middle of the valley. One goes on the north side, another on the south side, so it's possible to make a circuit of the valley by walking the link between them.

TERMAS DE RÍO HONDO

☎ 03858 • pop 27,000 • elevation 270m

Termas de Río Hondo's primary attraction is its thermal springs and even the most basic accommodations have hot mineral baths. Very much a destination for Argentine tourists, Río Hondo is not as interesting for international visitors; unless you are partial to expensive taxis, rows of tacky souvenir shops and unkempt parks. It's an easy place for a fool to be parted with his/her money.

That being said, at least out of season you'll be comfortable at bargain-basement prices, as competition between hotels is hot, making it a decent spot to overnight. The restaurant scene is also pretty good and if you're partial to sweet substances the many shops selling excellent chocolates around town won't disappoint.

The town has two unusual features: its triangular Plaza San Martín and one of the country's few public monuments to Juan and Evita Perón.

Outside town, the 30,000-hectare Dique Frontal is a reservoir used for water sports such as swimming, boating, fishing and windsurfing.

Information

The helpful municipal tourist office (☎ 421721), Caseros 132, between Rivadavia and Sarmiento, is open 7am to 1pm and 3pm to 9pm daily (shorter hours in summer). *El Frontal de Río Hondo*, the town's weekly newspaper, publishes a 24-page supplement (US$2) of information about thermal baths.

Only Banco de la Nación, on Caseros, does foreign exchange, but don't expect to change traveler's checks.

The postal code is 4220. The post office is on Av Alberdi between 9 de Julio and Maipú. There are several locutorios, including one on Rivadavia, which should have Internet access by the time you read this.

The Hospital Rural (☎ 421578) is at Antonio Taboada and Buenos Aires, west of downtown.

Places to Stay

Along the river, several campgrounds near downtown charge around US$4 for a campsite: *Camping Mirador* (☎ 421392), *Camping del Río* (☎ 421985) and *Camping La Olla* (☎ 423157).

Camping del ACA (☎ 421648) Sites US$4. Several kilometers outside town, on the road to the Dique Frontal, is this friendly, shady and spotless campground, but the noise from the *cucuyos* (insects in the trees) can be deafening in summer.

Most of Río Hondo's hotels close in summer, but a few remain open. Prices nearly double during the July-August high season; unless otherwise indicated, those below are low season.

Hotel La Ponderosa (mobile ☎ 1559-52299, España 129) Rooms US$6 per person. Easily this is the budget bargain in Río Hondo, with the convenience of being next to the bus terminal thrown in. The brand-spanking new rooms have comfy beds and large bathrooms. You don't need to be Catholic to stay here, but the religious paraphernalia doesn't leave you guessing the owner's faith.

Residencial Anush (mobile ☎ 1567-83061, Libertad 37) Rooms US$8 per person. This is one of the best values in town. The simple, but comfortable rooms come with a kitchenette, so you can self-cater.

Hotel Termal Los Felipe (☎ 421484, San Francisco Solano 230) Singles/doubles US$22/30. A large place with a great outdoor area around a swimming pool, Felipe is comfortable, modern and smells of fresh paint, although the rooms are perhaps a tad overpriced. Out of season, try bargaining.

Casino Center Hotel (☎/fax 421346, ⓔ hoteltermalcasino center@hotmail.com, Caseros 126) Singles/doubles US$30/40. Friendly and exhibiting a warm '70s decor, this hotel is very handy if you want to have a flutter at the casino across the road.

Hotel Los Pinos (☎ 421043, ⓔ info @lospinoshotel.com.ar, Maipú 201) Doubles US$68/89 for colonial/Americano rooms. This is a four-star property in a fabulous building with everything you need to help relax including a pool, solarium, tennis courts and an old-style cinema that shows films twice daily.

Places to Eat

A short stroll around town will reveal a plethora of eateries; here are a few favorites.

ARGENTINA

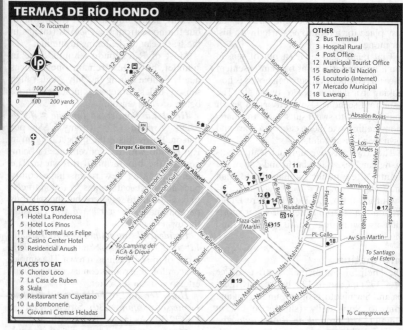

TERMAS DE RÍO HONDO

OTHER
2 Bus Terminal
3 Hospital Rural
4 Post Office
12 Municipal Tourist Office
15 Banco de la Nación
16 Locutorio (Internet)
17 Mercado Municipal
18 Laverap

PLACES TO STAY
1 Hotel La Ponderosa
5 Hotel Los Pinos
11 Hotel Termal Los Felipe
13 Casino Center Hotel
19 Residencial Anush

PLACES TO EAT
6 Chorizo Loco
7 La Casa de Ruben
8 Skala
9 Restaurant San Cayetano
10 La Bombonerie
14 Giovanni Cremas Heladas

Skala *(Sarmiento & Caseros)* Sandwiches $3-4, pizzas $7. A restaurant-cum-café-cum-bar, Skala has modern decor and is good for breakfast in the morning (coffee and medialunas US$2) or cocktails in the evening.

La Casa de Ruben (☎ 421265, *Sarmiento 69*) Starters US$3.50, mains US$6-8. Possessing a good enough reputation among locals that it doesn't need to pitch for business in the low season, La Casa is worth trying.

Chorizo Loco (☎ 422303, *Alberdi & Sarmiento*) Mains $4-10. This place (translated as 'crazy sausage') specializes in grilled meats.

Restaurant San Cayetano (☎ 421872, *Caseros 204*) Salads $2-4, pastas $3-6. To escape the tourist hype try this plain, old-fashioned restaurant, which has a mixed menu, a good wine list and attentive service.

Giovanni Cremas Heladas has a couple of outlets around town, including one on Rivadavia. Head here to sample Río Hondo's best ice cream. For those with an even sweeter tooth, head for **La Bombonerie**; if you get out of this place without a bag of chocolates, then you did better than most.

Getting There & Away

The bus terminal (☎ 421513) is on Las Heras between España and 12 de Octubre, half a dozen blocks west of the plaza and two blocks north of Av Alberdi. The following is a list of sample destinations and fares.

Destination	Duration in hours	Cost
Buenos Aires	15	US$40
Córdoba	7	US$16
Entre Ríos	9	US$32
Jujuy	5	US$20
La Plata	16½	US$43
La Rioja	6	US$20
Mar del Plata	21	US$60
Mendoza	10	US$35
Paraná	9	US$32
Rosario	10	US$32

Salta	5	US$19
San Juan	9	US$30
Santa Fe	11	US$40
Santiago del Estero	1	US$3
Tucumán	1	US$4.50

Getting Around

Empresa 4 de Junio (☎ 421826) goes to the Dique Frontal for US$0.60. Catch it downtown along RN 9 or Av Juan de Perón.

SANTIAGO DEL ESTERO

☎ 0385 • pop 230,050 • elevation 200m

In many respects Santiago del Estero is a stopover place, receiving visitors traveling between Buenos Aires and Salta looking to break their journey. The city itself, however, is pleasant with some good cafés and interesting colonial buildings and museums. It holds an important place in Argentine history as the 'Madre de Ciudades' (Mother of Cities). Founded in 1553, it was Spain's first urban settlement in what is now Argentina, and for centuries it was an important stopover between the Pampas and the mines of Bolivia.

If you're looking to just relax for a few days or take a longer break, Catamarca is probably a bit more attractive, while nearby Tucumán is far more exciting.

Orientation

Reflecting its early settlement, Santiago's urban plan is more irregular than most Argentine cities. The town center is Plaza Libertad, from which Av Libertad, trending southwest to northeast, bisects the city. North and south of the plaza, Av Independencia and the pedestrian mall Av Tucumán become important commercial areas, but Av Belgrano, which crosses Av Libertad and roughly parallels Tucumán/Independencia, is the main thoroughfare. Belgrano divides itself into Norte (North) and Sur (South) on either side of Av Rivadavia. Street names change on either side of Avs Libertad and Belgrano.

Information

The helpful provincial tourist office (☎ 421-4243, toll-free 0800-450016) is at Av Libertad 417, opposite Plaza Libertad. Besides providing visitor information, it displays work by local artists. Opening hours are 7:30am to 1pm and 3pm to 9pm weekdays, 9am to noon Saturdays, most of the year; in the May to October peak season, Saturday hours are 9am to noon and 5pm to 8pm.

ACA (☎ 421-2270) is at Av Sáenz Peña and Belgrano.

The best place to try changing traveler's checks (and cash) is Banco Galicia on Avellaneda, opposite Plaza Libertad. Several downtown banks have ATMs.

The postal code is 4200. Cybernauta on Independencia, close to the corner of Mitre, has 24-hour Internet connections for US$2.50 an hour. If you're near the Plaza Libertad, drop into Tequila (see Places to Eat), which has some Internet terminals upstairs.

Intijet (☎ 422-7534), at 24 de Setiembre 249, should be able to help with travel arrangements in the province.

Museo Wagner de Ciencias Antropológicas y Naturales

Chronologically arranged and splendidly displayed, this natural history and archaeological collection focuses on fossils, funerary urns (owls and snakes are recurring motifs) and Chaco ethnography. A friendly staff offers free guided tours of the museum (☎ 421-1380, Avellaneda 355; free; open 7:30am-1:30pm & 2pm-8pm weekdays, 10am-noon weekends).

Museo Histórico Provincial Dr Oreste di Lullo

Exhibits at the late-colonial house of Pedro Díaz Gallo, with its beautiful patios and colonnades, emphasize postcolonial history, displaying religious and civil art, materials on elite local families, and coins and paper money (☎ 421-2893, Urquiza 354; free; open 7:30am-1:30pm & 2pm-8pm weekdays, 10am-noon weekends).

Parque Aguirre

Named for the city's founder and only 10 blocks from Plaza Libertad, this enormous park has a small zoo, camping areas, a swimming pool (when the erratic Río Dulce

ARGENTINA

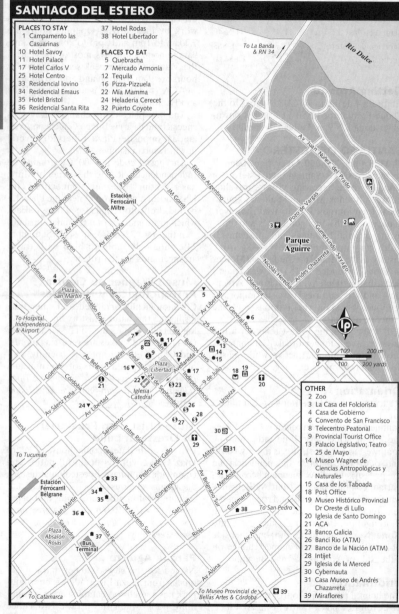

SANTIAGO DEL ESTERO

PLACES TO STAY
1 Campamento las Casuarinas
10 Hotel Savoy
11 Hotel Palace
17 Hotel Carlos V
25 Hotel Centro
33 Residencial Iovino
34 Residencial Emaus
35 Hotel Bristol
36 Residencial Santa Rita
37 Hotel Rodas
38 Hotel Libertador

PLACES TO EAT
5 Quebracha
7 Mercado Armonía
12 Tequila
16 Pizza-Pizzuela
22 Mía Mamma
24 Heladeria Cerecet
32 Puerto Coyote

OTHER
2 Zoo
3 La Casa del Folclorista
4 Casa de Gobierno
6 Convento de San Francisco
8 Telecentro Peatonal
9 Provincial Tourist Office
13 Palacio Legislativo; Teatro 25 de Mayo
14 Museo Wagner de Ciencias Antropológicas y Naturales
15 Casa de los Taboada
18 Post Office
19 Museo Histórico Provincial Dr Oreste di Lullo
20 Iglesia de Santo Domingo
21 ACA
23 Banco Galicia
26 Banci Rio (ATM)
27 Banco de la Nación (ATM)
28 Intijet
29 Iglesia de la Merced
30 Cybernauta
31 Casa Museo de Andrés Chazarreta
39 Miraflores

provides sufficient water) and – be alert! – a drivers' training center operated by ACA.

Other Museums & Historic Buildings

Santiago has many interesting colonial buildings and museums, as well as several more recent ones. Check out the **Convento de San Francisco** *(open 8am-noon & 6:30pm-late daily)*, on Avellaneda between Av General Roca and Olaechea, where San Francisco Solano, a Franciscan monk who worked with the area's indigenous population, resided in a 16th-century cell.

The **Iglesia de Santo Domingo** *(25 de Mayo & Urquiza; open 8am-noon & 6:30pm-late daily)*, the **Casa de los Taboada** *(Buenos Aires 136)* and the **Museo Provincial de Bellas Artes** *(☎ 421-1839, Belgrano Sur 1560; free; open 8am-noon & 2pm-8pm weekdays, 9am-noon weekends)* also deserve a look. There's also the folkloric **Casa Museo de Andrés Chazarreta** *(☎ 421-1905, Mitre 127; free; open by appointment)*.

Monuments of more contemporary significance are the neocolonial **Casa de Gobierno** (which opened in 1953, on the 400th anniversary of the founding of the city), west of downtown on Plaza San Martín; and the **Palacio Legislativo** at the corner of Avellaneda and 25 de Mayo.

Special Events

Santiago's chaotic Carnaval, in February, resembles celebrations in the Quebrada de Humahuaca. During the entire last week of July, *santiaguinos* celebrate the founding of the city.

Places to Stay

Budget Except around the bus terminal, there's not much really cheap lodging.

Campamento las Casuarinas Sites US$6. This municipal campground is normally a pleasant, shady, secure area in Parque Aguirre, less than a kilometer from Plaza Libertad, but it can be oppressively crowded and deafeningly noisy on weekends.

Residencial Santa Rita *(☎ 422-0625, Santa Fe 273)* Singles/doubles US$10/20 with shared bath, US$15/25 with private bath. Probably one of the best in this range and

close to the bus terminal, the small, clean rooms are a good value.

Residencial Iovino *(☎/fax 421-3311, Moreno Sur 602)* Singles/doubles US$10/15 with shared bath, US$13/25 with private bath. A rabbit warren inside, Iovino is a large dark place that's a bit ragged, but one of the cheapest in the area; rooms are reasonably tidy.

Residencial Emaus *(☎ 421-5893, Moreno Sur 675)* Singles/doubles US$15/25 with breakfast. This tiny residencial has only five rooms with TV and bath, but it's friendly and spotlessly clean.

Mid-Range Right next door to the bus terminal, *Hotel Rodas* *(☎ 421-4229, Pedro León Gallo 430)* is a very handy place for late-night arrivals. Large and clean singles/doubles cost US$22/28. The small café downstairs is convenient, though the coffee leaves something to be desired.

Hotel Bristol *(☎ 421-8387, Moreno Sur 677)* Singles/doubles US$25/40 for old rooms, US$30/45 for new rooms. Modern but rather sterile, the Bristol is a solid place with a swimming pool. It also provides transport to the airport.

Hotel Palace *(☎ 421-2700, ⓔ palace hotel@ssdnet.com.ar, Tucumán 19)* Singles/doubles US$25/40. This central place has rooms overlooking Plaza Libertad and is reasonably tidy.

Hotel Savoy *(☎ 421-1234, fax 421-1235, Tucumán 39)* Singles/doubles US$27/48 with breakfast. Grand but bland, the Savoy has some character, but it has small rooms and very cramped bathrooms.

Top End Located in the heart of the city's financial district, *Hotel Centro* *(☎/fax 422-4350, ⓔ ly@teletel.com.ar, 9 de Julio 131)* is a very comfortable businessperson's refuge. Singles/doubles cost US$38/50.

Hotel Libertador *(☎/fax 421-9252, ⓔ hot_lib@arnet.com.ar, Catamarca 47)* Singles/doubles US$39/50. A bit out of the center, in a quiet street, this place has all the trimmings but a rather apathetic management.

Hotel Carlos V *(☎ 424-0303, fax 422-5100, ⓔ hotelcarlosv@arnet.com.ar, Independencia 110)* Singles/doubles US$55/75, suites

US$110/200. If you like your creature comforts and having doors opened for you at every turn, Carlos V, the city's top hotel, is for you.

Places to Eat

There are a lot of cheap *eateries* on Pl Gallo, just opposite the bus terminal, offering filling meals for US$2-3. *Mercado Armonía* on Tucumán, between Pellegrini and Salta, is Santiago's market and is cheap but less appealing than some Argentine markets.

Mía Mamma (☎ 421-9715, 24 de Setiembre 15) Starters US$3-4, pastas US$3-6. A moderately priced, friendly eatery that has a very extensive menu of delicious Italian dishes and parrillada (US$12 for two people), plus a good and inexpensive salad bar.

Pizza-Pizzuela (☎ 424-1392, Absalón Rojas 78) Pizzas US$7-10, pastas under US$5. This central pizzeria serves up no-fuss food that is quick and hot. If you're not that hungry, it does mini-pizzas (*pizzetas*) for about US$3.

Puerto Coyote (☎ 424-1172, 24 de Setiembre & Mendoza) Pizzas US$11, calzones US$14; open 8pm-12:30pm. This place has a great outdoor eating area in a quiet part of town. Meals are very filling.

Tequila (☎ 422-0745, Independencia 46) Sandwiches US$2-4, Mains US$2.50-9. There are several good restaurants and popular confiterías around Plaza Libertad, such as this one, which has an excellent outdoor upstairs terrace overlooking the plaza. It's a good spot for breakfast.

Quebracha (☎ 422-4972, Pelligrini & Av General Roca) Starters US$3-7, pastas US$5, parrillada US$7-10. The mouthwatering food at this sophisticated, but affordable parrilla is complemented by the extensive wine list.

Heladería Cerecet, on the corner of Av Libertad and Córdoba, has some of the best ice cream in town served in drab, no-nonsense surroundings. A double cone costs US$1.

Entertainment

La Casa del Folclorista (Pozo de Vargas, Parque Aguirre) Entry US$2. To the east of town, this is a big barn of a place that has live folk bands some evenings.

Miraflores (☎ 422-3703, Av Belgrano Sur 1370) A pub and parrilla hosting live rock bands, Miraflores really takes off on weekends.

There are three discos inconveniently located to the east of the town center on the *autopista* in La Banda. They are *Bay Say*, *El Portón* and *Mirage*. They're open from about 10:30pm on weekends and entry costs between US$10 and US$15.

Teatro 25 de Mayo (☎ 421-4141) Within the same building as the Palacio Legislativo is Teatro 25 de Mayo, Santiago's prime theater venue.

Getting There & Away

Air Dinar Líneas Aéreas flies daily to Buenos Aires (US$121) at 5:30pm. Tickets can be booked at most travel agencies throughout the city.

Argentines scream for frosted treats.

Bus Santiago's aging bus terminal (☎ 421-3746) is at Pedro León Gallo and Saavedra, eight blocks southwest of Plaza Libertad. Below are sample destinations and fares to all parts of the country.

Destination	Duration in hours	Cost
Bahía Blanca	20	US$66
Bariloche	31	US$102
Buenos Aires	13	US$40
Catamarca	4½	US$15
Córdoba	6	US$16
Corrientes	9	US$22
Jujuy	7	US$22
La Rioja	12	US$25
Mar del Plata	19	US$61
Mendoza	17	US$45
Neuquén	22	US$73
Paraná	9½	US$28
Pocitos	13	US$32
Resistencia	8	US$21
Río Gallegos	44	US$130
Roque Sáenz Peña	6	US$16
Rosario	9	US$28
Salta	6	US$22
San Juan	16	US$40
Santa Fe	7½	US$26
Santa Rosa	15	US$45
Termas de Río Hondo	1	US$3
Tucumán	2	US$5

Getting Around

Bus No 19 goes to Aeropuerto Mal Paso (☎ 434-0337), 6km southwest of downtown on Av Madre de Ciudades. A taxi from the city center costs US$5.

Central Santiago del Estero is compact and walking suffices for almost everything except connections to the train station and the airport. If you're weary, a taxi just about anywhere around town is US$1.

Catamarca & La Rioja

Among modern Argentina's provinces, remote La Rioja and Catamarca are poor relations, but they are rich in scenery, folklore and tradition. Both were home to several important pre-Columbian cultures, mostly maize cultivators, who developed unique pottery techniques and styles, and the region has many important archaeological sites.

Offering great beauty to visitors with a vehicle and time to explore, these provinces require a little patience and a desire to get off the beaten track; those who do make the effort will be rewarded with wonderful scenery, friendly locals and open spaces all to themselves.

CATAMARCA

☎ 03833 • pop 142,000 • elevation 530m
Catamarca has more of an upbeat feel in recent times, even though economically it has remained a provincial backwater (although major devotional holidays attract large numbers of visitors). The city is a relaxing, endearing place, good for taking a break from the road for a couple of days. There are a number of trendy eateries and bars around the central Plaza 25 de Mayo, giving this area and the Rivadavia pedestrian mall a good buzz in the evenings. The modernization of the bus terminal is complete and provides some good options for travelers waiting for their next bus. In fact it's a major draw at night (see the boxed text 'A Destination All Its Own,' later in this section). Catamarca's magnificent cathedral, opposite Plaza 25 de Mayo, is also well worth a visit after dark.

Orientation

Nearly everything is within walking distance in the city center, an area 12 blocks square circumscribed by four wide avenues: Av Belgrano to the north, Av Alem to the east, Güemes to the south, and Virgen del Valle to the west. The focus of downtown is the beautifully designed Plaza 25 de Mayo (the work of Carlos Thays, who also designed Parque San Martín in Mendoza and Tucumán's Parque 9 de Julio), a shady refuge from the summer heat. South of the plaza, Rivadavia is a permanent pedestrian mall between San Martín and Mota Botello.

Information

The municipal tourist office (☎ 437413), Sarmiento 450, is in the Museo Arqueológico; it's open 7am to 8pm weekdays and 9am to 8pm weekends. It has a decent downtown map, a good services brochure and friendly, competent staff. A tourist desk can also be found at the bus terminal on weekday mornings.

Open daily 8am to 8pm, the provincial tourist office (☎ 437594, e turismo catamarca@cedeconet.com.ar) is in the Manzana del Turismo (Tourism Block) at the corner of Av Virgen del Valle and General Roca; the entrance is on General Roca. There is also a temporary tourist information office more centrally located on Av República, opposite Plaza 25 de Mayo (opening hours are the same as the main office).

ACA (☎ 424513) is at República 102.

The postal code is 4700. There's a locutorio on Rivadavia with Internet facilities, connections cost US$3 an hour. The cheapest option to get wired is at a kiosk on Esquiú, which charges US$1 an hour.

Yokavil Turismo (☎ 430066), in the Galería Paseo del Centro at Rivadavia 916,

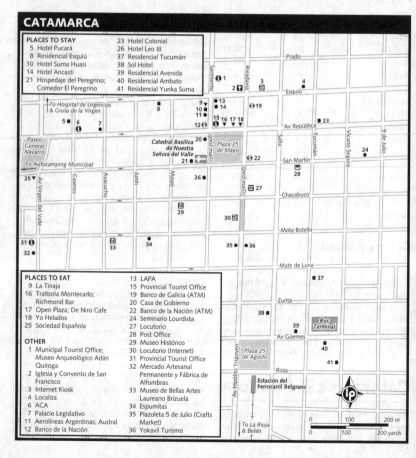

CATAMARCA

PLACES TO STAY
5 Hotel Pucará
8 Residencial Esquiú
10 Hotel Suma Huasi
14 Hotel Ancasti
21 Hospedaje del Peregrino;
   Comedor El Peregrino
23 Hotel Colonial
26 Hotel Leo III
37 Residencial Tucumán
38 Sol Hotel
39 Residencial Avenida
40 Residencial Ambato
41 Residencial Yunka Suma

PLACES TO EAT
9 La Tinaja
16 Trattoria Montecarlo;
   Richmond Bar
17 Open Plaza; De Niro Cafe
18 Yo Helados
25 Sociedad Española

OTHER
1 Municipal Tourist Office;
   Museo Arqueológico Adán
   Quiroga
2 Iglesia y Convento de San
   Francisco
3 Internet Kiosk
4 Localiza
7 Palacio Legislativo
11 Aerolíneas Argentinas; Austral
12 Banco de la Nación
13 LAPA
15 Provincial Tourist Office
19 Banco de Galicia (ATM)
20 Casa de Gobierno
22 Banco de la Nación (ATM)
24 Seminario Lourdista
27 Locutorio
28 Post Office
29 Museo Histórico
30 Locutorio (Internet)
31 Provincial Tourist Office
32 Mercado Artesanal
   Permanente y Fábrica de
   Alfombras
33 Museo de Bellas Artes
   Laureano Brizuela
34 Espumitas
35 Plazoleta 5 de Julio (Crafts
   Market)
36 Yokavil Turismo

arranges tours to area attractions, including Gruta de la Virgen del Valle (US$18).

Catedral Basílica de Nuestra Señora del Valle

Opposite Plaza 25 de Mayo, and dating from 1859, the cathedral shelters the Virgen del Valle, which is the patron of Catamarca and one of northern Argentina's most venerated images since the 17th century. Her diamond-studded crown can be seen in early April and on December 8, when multitudes of pilgrims converge on Catamarca to pay her homage. (She is also, in a curious juxtaposition of the sacred and profane, the *Patrona Nacional de Turismo*.)

The cathedral also contains an elaborately carved altar to St Joseph, an ornate baroque pulpit and an exhibition of paintings of the Virgin.

Museo Arqueológico Adán Quiroga

Mundane presentation and interpretive shortcomings keep the three distinct collections at this museum *(☎ 437413, Sarmiento 450; admission US$1; open 7am-1pm & 2pm-8pm weekdays, 9am-noon & 3pm-8pm weekends)* from forming a coherent whole despite its impressive artifacts, and the most worthwhile items may be the contemporary paintings in the foyer. The first display hall contains assorted tools, ceramics, funerary pots and mummies from 3000 BC to the 18th century, but the tedious descriptive chronologies of items in traditional glass cabinets detracts from their quality. The colonial-history room mixes disparate objects like rifles and musical instruments with fossils. The third room, also historical, presents ecclesiastical material and the personal effects of Fray Mamerto Esquiú. Guides for large groups are available on request.

Museo Histórico

Occupying only a single room in a neoclassical building with Corinthian columns, the city's historical museum *(☎ 437562, Chacabuco 425; free; open 8am-noon & 3pm-7pm weekdays)* limits itself to nicely arranged portraits of provincial governors, supplemented by their personal artifacts. There is, however, almost no interpretation. Official hours are not always adhered to and you usually have to ask someone to open it up.

Museo de Bellas Artes Laureano Brizuela

Named for a prominent *catamarqueño* painter, the fine-arts museum *(☎ 437563, Mota Botello 239; free; open 8am-noon & 3pm-8pm weekdays)* exhibits his own works along with those of Varela Lezama, Roberto Gray, Antonio Berni, Benito Quinquela Martín, Vicente Forte and others.

Other Historic Buildings

Catamarca's provincial **Casa de Gobierno** (1859) is on the west side of Plaza 25 de Mayo, while the more recent, utilitarian **Palacio Legislativo** is on República between Caseros and Ayacucho.

The imposing neocolonial **Iglesia y Convento de San Francisco** (1892), at Esquiú and Rivadavia, holds the cell of Fray Mamerto Esquiú, a 19th-century priest celebrated for speeches in defense of the Constitution of 1853. A crystal box holding the priest's heart reposes in a locked room after being stolen and left on the roof some years ago.

Now occupied by a private school but dating from 1890, the former **Seminario Lourdista** (Lourdist Seminary) is a prominent landmark in the city, thanks to its conspicuous twin bell towers. It's on San Martín between Vicario Segura and 9 de Julio.

At the south end of Rivadavia, opposite Plaza 25 de Agosto, the **Estación del Ferrocarril Belgrano** is a striking landmark even though the trains no longer run.

Special Events

Fiesta de Nuestra Señora del Valle takes place for two weeks after Easter. In an impressive manifestation of popular religion, hordes of pilgrims come from the interior and from other Andean provinces to honor the Virgen del Valle.

Fiesta Nacional del Poncho is held in the last fortnight of July. A crafts and industrial fair accompanies this festival of folkloric music and dance celebrating the importance of the poncho in the province.

During Día de la Virgen, pilgrims from throughout the country overrun Catamarca to pay homage to the Virgen del Valle on December 8, the city's patron saint's day.

Places to Stay

Budget Five kilometers west of town, in the Sierra de Ambato foothills, *Autocamping Municipal (RP 4)* is a pleasant spot by the Río El Tala. Sites costs US$5/2/1 per tent/vehicle/person. It has two shortcomings: As the city's major recreation site, with two swimming pools, it gets loud and crowded on weekends and holidays (forget about sleeping) and it also has fierce mosquitoes. Bathrooms and showers are clean and there is electricity. To get here, take bus No 101 from Convento de San Francisco, on Esquiú, or from the bus terminal on Vicario Segura. The *confitería* has a friendly staff and basic food, but it's cheaper to buy your own provisions in town.

The tourist office keeps a list of private residences offering inexpensive lodging; other than that, residenciales are probably your best bet.

Hospedaje del Peregrino (☎ 431203, Sarmiento 653) Dorm beds US$5/7 without/with bedding rental. The cheapest option in town is to share the pilgrims' dormitory accommodations here.

Residencial Yunka Suma (☎ 423034, Vicario Segura 1255) Singles/doubles US$12/20 with private bath. This drab residencial is pretty basic but the rooms are clean and you'll probably get a better price if you stay more than one night.

Residencial Avenida (☎ 422139, Av Güemes 754) Singles/doubles US$12/20 with shared bath, US$16/24 with private bath. A frayed but friendly place near the bus terminal, Avenida is often full so you may need to book ahead. It has a relaxing, central courtyard area.

Residencial Esquiú (☎ 422284, Esquiú 365) Singles/doubles US$16/26. This attractive residencial is secure and a good value, and it's also a block northwest of the center.

Residencial Ambato (☎ 422142, Av Güemes 841) Singles/doubles US$18/25 with bath. This place has small clean rooms with ceiling fans and is very close to the bus terminal. Guests can use the kitchen.

Mid-Range At *Sol Hotel (☎ 430803, e solhotel@hotmail.com, Salta 1142)* singles/doubles with shared bath and kitchenette go for US$20/30, with private bath you'll pay US$28/38. Architecturally dreary but otherwise congenial, this hotel is a good value at these rates. There are great views of town from the rooftop patio.

Residencial Tucumán (☎ 422209, Tucumán 1040) Singles/doubles US$22/29 with bath, plus US$4 for air-con. This well-run, immaculately presented residencial has spotless rooms, is an excellent value, and is about a one-minute walk from the bus terminal.

Hotel Colonial (☎/fax 423502, República 802) Singles/doubles US$25/33. This is a pleasant old-style place with friendly staff.

Hotel Suma Huasi (☎ 425199, Sarmiento 541) Singles/doubles US$37/46. This very central hotel offers discounts to ACA members.

Top End Singles/doubles cost US$40/60 with breakfast at *Hotel Ancasti (☎ 435951, e hotelancasti@cedeconet.com.ar, Sarmiento 520)*. It's a pretty classy hotel and worth the extra cash in this range. The elevator looks a lot like the TARDIS in the TV show *Dr Who*.

Hotel Pucará (☎ 430698, 430688, Caseros 501) Singles/doubles US$39/49 with breakfast. A mix of class and tack, cool Pucará has decent rooms at reasonable prices.

Hotel Leo III (☎ 432080, Sarmiento 727) Singles/doubles US$56/70. This downtown property is top of the line and is in a great location. The magnificent views from the small balconies in the rooms are almost solely worth the extra money.

Places to Eat

The least-expensive eateries cater to the town's religious pilgrims.

Open Plaza (☎ 404718, República 580) Mains US$2-6. Electric neon red and blue lighting gives this funky place a nightclub feel, which is probably where most of its patrons are from in the wee hours. The food is simple and filling and they also have a good range of cocktails.

Comedor El Peregrino (☎ *431203*) Mains US$4-6. In the gallery behind the cathedral, this place has empanadas and pasta, or more expensive dishes with meat.

La Tinaja (☎ *435853, Sarmiento 533*) Mains US$5. La Tinaja has low prices and sometimes live music. It's handy if you're staying in the center.

Trattoria Montecarlo (☎ *433584, República 550*) Starters US$2.50-4, mains US$6-12. This trattoria specializes in pasta and also does chicken dishes. It's simple, wholesome food.

De Niro Café (*República 590*) Mains US$6-12. Next to Open Plaza, this place has a larger menu, including pizzas and meat dishes, and is a good spot for coffee in the mornings.

Sociedad Española (☎ *431896, Av Virgen del Valle 725*) Seafood US$10-15; open for lunch & dinner daily. Traditional Spanish dishes, including seafood, are served here. It's a grand old place, worth the trek for some fine dining.

Yo Helados (*República & Rivadavia*) Ice cream US$1-3. This chain store serves good ice cream.

The bus terminal has an upstairs ***food hall*** serving burgers, pizzas and other fast food, good for a meal while waiting for your next bus. There are also a couple of cafés here.

Entertainment

Richmond Bar (☎ *423823, República 534*) A good place for a quiet drink in the evening is this mirrored-ceiling bar; or if you like your entertainment livelier, things heat up on a Saturday night when there is tango from 11pm.

Shopping

Mercado Artesanal Permanente y Fábrica de Alfombras (*Virgen del Valle 945*) Open 8am-12:30pm & 4pm-8:30pm weekdays, 9am-noon & 4:30pm-8pm Sat, 9am-noon Sun. For Catamarca's characteristic hand-

tied rugs, visit this market, next to the provincial tourist office. Besides rugs, the market sells ponchos, blankets, jewelry, red onyx sculptures, musical instruments, hand-spun sheep and llama wool, and basketry.

There's also a small, informal ***crafts market*** in the evening on Plazoleta 5 de Julio, on Rivadavia.

Catamarca is the place to buy walnuts, including rich but tasty *nueces confitadas* (sugared walnuts), olives, raisins and wines. Regional specialty shops are concentrated on Sarmiento, between Plaza 25 de Mayo and the Convento de San Francisco.

Getting There & Away

Air Aerolíneas Argentinas (☎ 424460), Sarmiento 589, flies daily except Sunday to Buenos Aires (US$80 to US$200). Austral, at the same office, flies daily except Saturday to Santiago del Estero (US$50) and Buenos Aires. LAPA (☎ 434772), Sarmiento 506, flies Monday, Friday, and Sunday to La Rioja and Buenos Aires.

A Destination All Its Own

Looking for a spot of excitement when the sun goes down in Catamarca? If the plaza's drinking holes are looking a little sparse, it may be because patrons are living it up at the town's epicenter of entertainment: the bus terminal. A much-needed facelift recently turned the depressed terminal into a sparkling case in point of the city's desire to cater for bus-weary travelers.

Depending on your impression, 'genius' or 'confused' might be terms you'd use to describe those who conspired to include cafés, restaurants, a cinema complex and, last but not least, a theme park (rides and all) with a title that encompasses the true culture and tradition of the Andes – Aussie Park!

If you find yourself with a frustrating layover, the abundance of distractions will quickly turn you into the designer's biggest fan.

– Justine Vaisutis

Bus The long-overdue facelift of Catamarca's privatized bus terminal (☎ 423415), Av Güemes 850, is now complete and is a vast improvement.

Following are sample destinations and fares around the country.

Destination	Duration in hours	Cost
Andalgalá	5	US$10
Aimogasta	3	US$9
Belén	4	US$13
Buenos Aires	16	US$50
Comodoro Rivadavia	20	US$103
Córdoba	5	US$15
Fiambalá	5½	US$15
Jujuy	11	US$23
Londres	3½	US$13
Mendoza	10	US$28
Paraná	18	US$50
Pocitos	15	US$30
Posadas	18	US$50
Resistencia	24	US$72
Rosario	11	US$40
Salta	10	US$21
San Juan	8	US$22
Santa Rosa	16	US$44
Santiago del Estero	4	US$15
Tinogasta	5	US$13
Tucumán	3½	US$10

Getting Around
For US$5, Aerolíneas Servicios Diferenciales minibus goes to Aeropuerto Felipe Varela (☎ 430080, 435582), on RP 33, 22km east of town. For car rental, go to Localiza (☎ 435838), Esquiú 786.

AROUND CATAMARCA
According to local legend, in 1619 or 1620 the image of the Virgen del Valle appeared in **Gruta de la Virgen del Valle**, 7km north of downtown on RP 32. The present image is a replica of that in Catamarca's cathedral, and a protective structure shelters the grotto itself. Empresa Cotca's bus No 104 goes to the Gruta every 40 minutes.

The Sierra de Famatina, the province's highest mountain range, is visible from the road to picturesque **Villa Las Pirquitas**, near the dam of the same name, 29km north of Catamarca via RN 75. The foothills en route shelter small villages with hospitable people and interesting vernacular architecture.

Camping is possible in the basic balneario, where the shallows are too muddy for swimming.

Hostería Municipal (☎ 492030) Singles/doubles US$20/35 with meals. This very attractive hotel offers a great value.

From Catamarca's bus terminal, Empresa Cotca's bus No 101 leaves hourly for the village.

ANDALGALÁ
At the north end of the Sierra de Manchao, 200km from Catamarca via RN 75 and RP 46, Andalgalá is a possible stopover on the scenic route from Catamarca to Belén via the Cuesta de Chilca; RP 46 continues west to the equally scenic Cuesta de Belén. Gutiérrez buses from Catamarca to Belén take this very spectacular route.

Hotel Provincial de Turismo (☎ 03835-423024, Sarmiento 444) offers good clean accommodations in the town. Singles/doubles with private bath and breakfast will set you back US$18/36. There's a reasonable self-serve *restaurant* on the north side of the plaza.

BELÉN
☎ 03835 • pop 8300 • elevation 1250m
Have you ever thought, 'Geez, a poncho is a cool thing!' Then you're in the right place. The self-appointed poncho capital of the country, Belén is one of the best places for woven goods, particularly ponchos, in Argentina. There are many *teleras* (textile workshops) dotted around town turning out their wares, made from llama, sheep and vicuña wool.

Belén is also the major settlement in the area and offers the best facilities for some kilometers, including decent accommodations and a couple of good restaurants.

Before the arrival of the Spaniards in the mid-16th century, the area around Belén was Calchaquí territory on the periphery of the Inca empire. After the Incas fell, it became the encomienda of Pedro Ramírez Velasco, founder of La Rioja, but its history s intricately intertwined with nearby Londres, a Spanish settlement shifted several times because of floods and Calchaquí resistance (see Around Belén). More than a century passed before, in 1681, the priest José Bartolomé Olmos de Aguilera divided a land grant among veterans of the Calchaquí wars on the condition that they support evangelization in the area.

Orientation & Information
In the western highlands of Catamarca, Belén is 89km west of Andalgalá and 289km from the provincial capital, and 180km southwest of Santa María. The municipal tourist office is at the foot of Cerro de la Virgen, on the western edge of town. The postal code is 4750.

Things to See & Do
The neoclassical brick **Iglesia Nuestra Señora de Belén**, dates from 1907 and faces Plaza Olmos y Aguilera and is well shaded by pines and colossal pepper trees. The provincial **Museo Cóndor Huasi** *(Lavalle & Rivadavia; admission US$1; open 8am-noon & 5pm-8pm weekdays)* displays an impressive assortment of Diaguita artifacts.

On December 20, the town officially celebrates its founding (Día de la Fundación) but festivities begin at least a week earlier with a dance at the foot of the Cerro de la Virgen, three blocks west of the plaza. A steep 1900m trail leads to a 15m statue of the Virgin, side-by-side with a 4.5m image of the Christ child.

Places to Stay & Eat
Hotel Turismo *(☎/fax 461501, Belgrano & Cubas)* Singles/doubles US$21/27 with breakfast. Camping for US$10 per tent is possible on the shady, well-kept grounds of this hotel, but the toilets for campers are not for the squeamish and there are no showers. The hotel proper is very reasonably priced.

Hotel Samay *(☎ 461320, Urquiza 349)* Singles/doubles US$35/45. Rooms here come with TV and are clean and comfortable, but by no means lavish.

Hotel Gómez *(☎ 461388, Calchaquí 141)* Singles/doubles US$16/23. This is a basic

place to fall back on if the previous two listings are full.

On summer nights, restaurants near Plaza Olmos y Aguilera set up tables right on the plaza itself.

Half a block south of the plaza, there's an anonymous **bakery** *(Lavalle 329)* producing exquisitely lemony *empanadas árabes*.

El Único *(General Roca & Sarmiento)* Mains US$2-10. This is a decent parrilla with an attractive *quincho*. The locro is worth trying here.

Fénix *(Sarmiento & Rivadavia)* Mains US$4-6. Opposite the bus terminal, Fénix serves palatable Middle Eastern food.

Bar Sarmiento *(Lavalle)* This bar, at the plaza's southwest corner, is cheap and popular throughout the day.

There are several good *ice creameries* around the plaza.

Shopping
Try **El Kollita**, in the 200 block of Belgrano, for woven goods, including ponchos. **Regionales Los Antonitos** *(☎ 461940, Lavalle 418)* is another good option for woven ware.

Getting There & Away
Belén's bus terminal, at the corner of Sarmiento and Rivadavia, one block south and one block west of the plaza, has both provincial and limited long-distance services. Destinations include Andalgalá, Catamarca (US$13, 4 hours), Chumbichá, Córdoba (US$23, 14 hours), La Rioja, Salta (US$19, 12½ hours), Santa María (US$9, 5 hours), Tinogasta and Tucumán (US$16, 8 hours).

AROUND BELÉN
Only 15km southwest of Belén, sleepy **Londres** (population 1800) is the province's oldest Spanish settlement, dating from 1558, though it moved several times before returning here in 1612; the inhabitants fled again during the Calchaquí uprising of 1632. The Festival Provincial de la Nuez (Provincial Walnut Festival) takes place here the first fortnight of February, but more interesting are the nearby Inca ruins at Shinkal. From Belén, seven local buses daily go to Londres.

About 60km north of Belén via RN 40, the village of **Hualfín** features a colonial chapel beneath a small promontory whose 142-step staircase leads to a *mirador* with panoramic views of cultivated fields and the distant desert. Buses between Belén and Santa María stop here.

Rooms are US$10 per person at *Hostería Hualfín*. This crumbling but atmospheric hotel, in what was once an imposing late-colonial house, also serves meals. Around town, look for locally grown paprika often sprinkled on creamy slices of goat cheese.

ANILLACO
☎ 03827 • pop 900 • elevation 1300m

About 130km north of La Rioja via RN 75, Anillaco has drawn unwelcome attention as, literally, a monument to corruption. Former president Carlos Menem's bucolic birthplace features an international airport and an 18-hole professional golf course whose financing has been the subject of constant speculation in the Argentine press. Several TV journalists who exposed the scandal in a program entitled 'Menem's Disneyland' were fired by a station owner who declared 'I see nothing wrong with the country giving the president the gift of an airstrip.' Since the recent investigation into the arms scandal that Menem is allegedly involved in (which has also led to an investigation into whether he profited from illicit dealings during his presidency), it seems increasingly likely that extravagances such as these may be the subject of scrutiny by investigators.

Something may be putrid here, but the scenery is worth a look and the highland climate is a refreshing change from sultry La Rioja.

Hostería Anillaco (☎/fax 494064, Coronel Barros) has singles/doubles with breakfast US$20/40 for ACA members, US$30/48 with breakfast for nonmembers. This place is comfortable enough, although it is a much better value for members. You'll pay more if you want a TV and telephone in your room. *Hostería Los Amigos (☎ 494107)* is another alternative, offering singles/doubles for US$26/40.

For transport from La Rioja, try Inter Rioja, Av Rivadavia 519.

LA RIOJA
☎ 03822 • pop 147,800 • elevation 500m

When arriving in La Rioja, the visitor is struck by the breathtaking backdrop of the Sierra de Velasco, which gives the city a rather wild feel. The presence of the mobile-phone clique, however, soon dispels this myth. A short walk around the shady Plaza 25 de Mayo soon gives an indication of life in laid-back La Rioja. With several grand ecclesiastical buildings and a couple of interesting museums, the city is well worth a short stopover.

Juan Ramírez de Velasco founded Todos los Santos de la Nueva Rioja in 1591. Dominican, Jesuit and Franciscan missionaries helped 'pacify' the Diaguita Indians and paved the way for Spanish colonization of what Vásquez de Espinosa called 'a bit of Paradise.'

The city's appearance reflects the conflict and accommodation between colonizer and colonized: the architecture combines European designs with native techniques and local materials. Many early buildings were destroyed in the 1894 earthquake, but the city has been entirely rebuilt.

Orientation & Information

At the base of the picturesque Sierra de Velasco, La Rioja is relatively small, with all points of interest and most hotels within easy walking distance of each other.

North-south streets change their names at Rivadavia, but east-west streets are continuous.

The friendly, eager municipal tourist office (☎ 427103, fax 426648), Av Perón 715, distributes a good city map and brochures of other provincial destinations. Hotel information includes only officially registered hotels, excluding many cheaper possibilities. Opening hours are 8am to 1pm and 4pm to 9pm weekdays, 8am to noon on weekends.

The provincial tourist office (☎ 428839, e turismolarioja@hotmail.com), at Av Perón and Urquiza, is also helpful. It's open 8am to 1pm and 4pm to 9pm weekdays; on

LA RIOJA

PLACES TO STAY
2   Residencial Florida
12 Residencial Don José
18 Hotel Savoy
24 Hotel Plaza
31 Pensión 9 de Julio
33 Apart Hotel Prisma
40 Hotel El Gran
    Embajador
41 Hotel Imperial
42 Residencial Anita
43 Hospedaje Sumaj Kanki
49 Hotel de Turismo
50 King's Hotel; King's
    Rent A Car

PLACES TO EAT
1   Macoco
9   Café del Paseo
19 Hawai
21 Confitería Restaurant
29 La Vieja Casona
48 El Milagro

OTHER
3   Museo Inca Huasi
4   Convento de San Francisco
5   Mamá Espuma (Laundry)
6   Museo Folklórico
7   Escuela Normal de Maestros
8   Banco de la Nación

10 Locutorio
11 Convento de Santo
    Domingo
13 Mercado Artesanal de La
    Rioja
14 Andesmar
15 Aerolíneas Argentinas
16 Cine Sussex
17 Casa de Gobierno
20 Cafe de la Plaza
22 Banco de Galicia (ATM)
23 Inter Rioja
25 LAPA
26 Furlan Viajes
27 Western Union office

28 Museo Histórico de La Rioja
30 Casa de Joaquín V González
32 Nuevo Banco de La Rioja
34 Iglesia de la Merced
35 Maxi Bus & Esso Service
    Station
36 Municipal Tourist Office
    (Dimutur)
37 Post Office
38 ACA
39 Palacio Legislativo
44 Provincial Tourist Office
45 Laundry
46 Inter Rioja (Tickets)
47 Locutorio Avenida

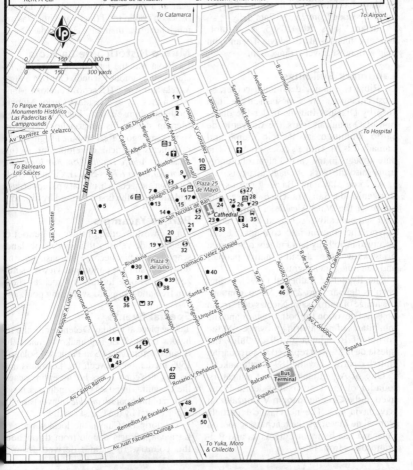

weekends, there's usually a *guardia* (watchman) on hand.

ACA (☎ 425381) is at Vélez Sársfield and Copiapó.

La Rioja has no money-exchange offices, and bank hours are limited, but some travel agencies may change money. Banco de Galicia changes US dollars and does credit card advances. There are also several banks with ATMs.

The postal code is 5300. The locutorio office at 529 Pelagio Luna, opposite Plaza 25 de Mayo, has Internet facilities for US$4 per hour; it is open from 7am to 2am daily.

Furlan Viajes (☎ 420895, e furlanlr @arnet.com.ar) is at Rivadavia 479 and can help with most travel arrangements.

Landmark Buildings

La Rioja is a major devotional center, so most landmarks are ecclesiastical. Built in 1623 by Diaguita Indians under the direction of Dominican friars, the **Convento de Santo Domingo**, at Pelagio Luna and Lamadrid, is Argentina's oldest convent. The date appears in the carved algarrobo doorframe, also the work of Diaguita artists.

At 25 de Mayo and Bazán y Bustos, the **Convento de San Francisco** houses the image of the Niño Alcalde, a Christ child icon symbolically recognized as the city's mayor. The convent also contains the cell occupied in 1592 by San Francisco Solano, a priest known for educating native peoples and defending their rights.

The Byzantine **Cathedral** (1899), at San Nicolás de Bari and 25 de Mayo, contains the image of patron saint Nicolás de Bari, an object of devotion for both *riojanos* and the inhabitants of neighboring provinces. At the corner of Rivadavia and 9 de Julio, the **Iglesia de la Merced** replaced a Mercedarian church destroyed by the 1894 earthquake.

One of Argentina's greatest educators, founder of the Universidad de La Plata, lived in the **Casa de Joaquín V González**, at Rivadavia 952. The neoclassical **Escuela Normal de Maestros**, the teachers' school on Pelagio Luna between Catamarca and Belgrano, dates from 1884.

Museo Folklórico

While this museum (☎ 428500, *Pelagio Luna 811; admission US$1.50; open 9am-noon & 4pm-8pm Tues-Fri, 9am-noon Sun*) credibly re-creates an authentic 19th-century house, with all the furnishings and objects necessary for everyday life, its thematic exhibits are even better. One hall displays ceramic reproductions representing mythological beings from local folklore, but it also contains particularly good Tinkunako materials (see Special Events later in this section), horse gear, an artisans workshop and even diet statistics on criollo food (locro and humitas are much healthier than fatty empanadas).

Museo Histórico de La Rioja

La Rioja was the land of the caudillos, including the famous Facundo Quiroga, Felipe Varela and Ángel (Chacho) Peñaloza. Many Argentines say ex-President Carlos Menem modeled himself on Facundo, though Menem shaved his muttonchop sideburns some years ago. Offering some insight into the province's political development is this museum (*Adolfo Dávila 79; admission US$1; open 8am-noon Tues-Sat*). Exhibits include Quiroga's stagecoach, military paraphernalia and the die of the first coin used by his army.

Parque Yacampis

On the western edge of town at the foot of the Sierra de Velasco, this once neatly landscaped park has become increasingly run-down, but still has panoramic views, a small zoo where some local fauna such as rheas run free and a popular swimming pool.

Special Events

Taking place at midday December 31, the religious ritual of El Tinkunako reenacts the original ceremony of San Francisco Solano's 1593 mediation between the Diaguitas and the Spanish conquerors. For accepting peace, the Diaguitas imposed two conditions: resignation of the Spanish *alcalde* (mayor) and his replacement by the Christ child.

Folkloric La Chaya, the local variant of Carnaval, attracts people from throughout the country. Its name, derived from a

Quechua word meaning 'to get someone wet,' should give you an idea of what to expect.

Festival del Viñador, honoring local vintners, takes place at the beginning of the Villa Unión's March grape harvest. During the festival there is music, dancing and tasting of regional wines, most notably the artisanal *vino patero*, made by traditional foot stomping of the grapes. Villa Unión is west of La Rioja and approximately 260km by road.

Places to Stay

Budget Parque Yacampis, at Av Ramírez de Velasco, 3km out of town, has a free and shady but deteriorating *campground* whose swimming pool (not free) is its only redeeming feature.

Several campgrounds occupy sites along RN 75 (formerly RP 1) west of town, including *Country Las Vegas* at 8km and *Sociedad Siriolibanesa* at 11km. Rates are around US$5 per tent; from Av Perón, bus No 1 goes only as far as the Las Vegas (US$0.75) before turning around.

La Rioja lacks a large tourist infrastructure, especially in budget hotels, but the tourist office maintains a list of private homes offering accommodations for about US$12 per person.

Hospedaje Sumaj Kanky (☎ 422299, *Av Castro Barros & Coronel Lagos*) Rooms US$10 per person with shared bath. This place provides modest but clean accommodations, although it can get noisy.

Residencial Don José (*Av Perón 419*) Rooms US$25 with bath. A more central option, Don José is an excellent value. Small, clean rooms sleep up to three people. Avoid rooms fronting the road, as they can be noisy. Check out is 24 hours.

Residencial Florida (☎ 426563, *8 de Diciembre 524*) Singles/doubles US$15/25. The Florida is popular and has small but comfy rooms. Singles have shared baths, doubles have private baths.

Mid-Range Very central and in a grand old building, *Pensión 9 de Julio* (☎ 426955, *Copiapó & Dalmacio Vélez Sársfield*) has cute little singles/doubles with TV for US$20/30. It's a very good value. There's a shady outdoor patio area overlooking plaza.

Residencial Anita (☎ 424836, *Lagos 476*) Singles/doubles US$25/35. This family-oriented residencial is one of the best in town and worth every cent. Rooms are more like a hotel and it's spotless. It feels like you're staying at a favorite aunt's place.

Hotel Savoy (☎ 426894, *Av Roque A Luna 14*) Singles/doubles US$25/35 with shared bath, US$35/45 with private bath. On the river, the rates at Savoy include breakfast. The more expensive rooms are much better and have TV, air-con and telephone; there's a bar and a confitería for breakfast.

Motel Yacampis (☎ 425216, *Av Ramirez de Velazco*) Singles/doubles US$26/39 members, US$39/55 nonmembers. In rundown Parque Yacampis, 3km northwest of downtown, this ACA property is a good value for members, but not such a bargain for nonmembers.

Hotel Imperial (☎ 422478, *Mariano Moreno 345*) Singles/doubles US$35/45. The Imperial is a big, open, spooky kind of place with a half-finished foyer in a quiet street near Anita. Rooms have TV, air-con and a telephone.

Hotel de Turismo (☎ 422005, *Av Perón & Quiroga*) Singles/doubles US$50/70 with breakfast. This hotel is a bit more luxurious than others in this category, with a swimming pool and solarium. It's friendly and the room rates depend on how busy they are.

Top End La Rioja's more expensive hotels are in hot competition and when things are quiet, you'll get some good deals. Discounts are generally available if you pay cash and aren't afraid to bargain.

Hotel El Gran Embajador (☎/fax 438580, *San Martín 250*) Singles/doubles US$35/45 with breakfast. This sunny little place is very tidy; the rooms upstairs are larger and sunnier and some have balconies.

King's Hotel (☎ 422122, *Av Quiroga 1070*) Singles/doubles/triples US$80/110/140. King's often hosts conferences, so it's good to book in advance. It's possibly the snobbiest place in town, but if that gets you hot under the collar you can take a dip in their swimming pool.

Apart Hotel Prisma (☎ 421567, *Rivadavia & Buenos Aires*) Singles/doubles US$35/50. This hotel is very central and the rooms have a small kitchen, television and telephone.

Hotel Plaza (☎ 425215, fax 422127, 9 de Julio & San Nicolás de Bari) Singles/doubles US$71/82 with breakfast. The Plaza has room service, a swimming pool and a bar. The rooftop terrace has good views.

Places to Eat

Regional dishes to look for include locro, juicy and spicy empanadas differing from the drier ones of the Pampas, *chivito asado* (barbecued goat), humita, *quesillo* (a cheese specialty) and olives. Don't miss the local bread, baked in *hornos de barro* (adobe ovens). There is also a good selection of dried fruits, preserves and jams from apples, figs, peaches and pears. Don't hesitate to order house wines, which are invariably excellent.

Café del Paseo (☎ 422069, *Pelagio Luna & 25 de Mayo*) Sandwiches US$3-5, pizzas US$3.50. An appealing Spanish-mission-style confitería, this place has a great outdoor area that's terrific for a spot of people-watching. Del Paseo is where the new meets the old: the mobile-phone clique mingles with families and tables of older men chewing the fat over another slow-paced La Rioja day.

Confitería Restaurant (☎ 435894, *Rivadavia & San Martín*) Snacks US$3-5, mains US$10-20. A spunky spot, it's good for a coffee and a read of the newspaper. Kevin Costner coolly looking down from his prime spot on a central pillar seems a little incongruous.

Hawai (*Rivadavia & Yrigoyen*) Breakfast under US$5, sandwiches under US$4. Overlooking Plaza 9 de Julio, this old-fashioned eatery serves good honest food at cheap prices. The outdoor tables are great for watching the world go by. The banana milkshakes are very refreshing on a hot day.

El Milagro (☎ 430939, *Av Perón 1200*) Mains from US$6; open from 9pm. This

is another good option for Argentine specialties.

Macoco (8 de Diciembre & Joaquín González) Pizzas US$5, chicken & chips US$6; open 11am-3pm & 8pm-late daily. Very handy if you're staying at the Residencial Florida, this restaurant's pizzas here are just like the ones Papa used to make…well, almost.

La Vieja Casona (☎ 425996, *Rivadavia 427*) Starters US$4-8, mains US$10-30. Places serving regional specialties, as well as standard Argentine dishes like parrillada, include this one. It's a large, open, slate-floor restaurant with wonderful smells wafting from the busy kitchen.

Entertainment

Café de la Plaza (☎ 421866, *Rivadavia & Yrigoyen*) The place to look beautiful in town (although we got in OK), it pulls a surprisingly mixed crowd, making it a good place for a drink. The ambient trance in the background may just get your toes tapping.

If you're up for a late night, there are a number of discos where you can show the locals your latest moves. They all cost around US$5/3 for guys/girls, although there are often promotions where women get in for free – very chauvinistic. All open about 1am or 2am on weekends and pound away until the early morning. These include **Moro** (*Av Laprida & Buenos Aires*), **Millennium**, opposite the Colegio Nacional on San Martín, and **Yuka** (☎ 1567-6226, *Av Félix de la Colina*), which also has a restaurant where you can chow down on lomitos and pizzas.

Coliseo La Quebrada (Av San Francisco) Performers of the stature of Leon Gieco perform at this venue, 5.5km west of downtown; other events include theatrical performances.

Shopping

La Rioja has unique weavings that combine indigenous techniques and skill with Spanish designs and color combinations. The typical *mantas* (bedspreads) feature floral patterns over a solid background. Spanish influence is also visible in silverwork, including tableware.

ornaments, religious objects and horse gear. La Rioja's pottery is entirely indigenous; artists utilize local clay to make distinctive pots, plates and flowerpots.

Mercado Artesanal de La Rioja (Pelagio Luna 792) Open 8am-noon & 4pm-8pm Tues-Fri, 9am-noon weekends. La Rioja crafts are exhibited and sold here, as are other popular artworks at prices lower than most souvenir shops.

Riojano wine has a national reputation; Saúl Menem, father of the ex-president, founded one of the major bodegas.

Getting There & Away

Air Aerolíneas Argentinas (☎ 426307), Belgrano 63, flies twice each weekday and once daily on weekends to Buenos Aires (US$121 to US$227). LAPA (☎ 435281), 9 de Julio 86, flies daily except Saturday to Buenos Aires (US$133); Tuesday and Thursday flights stop in Catamarca (US$26).

Bus La Rioja's bus terminal (☎ 425453) is at Artigas and España, though plans to build a new terminal have been mooted. A few companies, serving regional destinations, have separate downtown terminals.

Inter Rioja (☎ 421577), Rivadavia 519, goes north to Anillaco and intermediate points via RN 1. La Riojana (☎ 435279), Buenos Aires 132, goes to Chilecito. Maxi Bus (☎ 435979), Rivadavia and Adolfo Dávila, runs the cheapest minibus service to Chilecito four times daily for US$10 roundtrip. Carhuva (☎ 436380), Dorrego 96, goes to Villa Unión, Vinchina and Villa Castelli, in the province's western cordillera.

Destination	Duration in hours	Cost
Buenos Aires	22	US$56
Catamarca	2	US$8
Chilecito	3	US$5
Córdoba	6	US$18
Jujuy	11	US$28
Mendoza	8	US$22
Pagancillo	3½	US$9
Pocitos	14	US$30
Salta	11	US$30
San Juan	6	US$15
San Luis	12	US$37
Santiago del Estero	7	US$28
Tucumán	6	US$14
Villa Unión	4	US$10

Getting Around

From Plaza 9 de Julio, bus No 3 goes to Aeropuerto Vicente Almonacid (☎ 425483), 7km east of town on RP 5. An airport cab costs around US$6.50. A taxi from the bus terminal to the city center costs about US$2.

King's Rent A Car (☎ 422122) is in the King's Hotel, at Av Quiroga and Copiapó.

AROUND LA RIOJA

According to legend, San Francisco Solano converted many Diaguita Indians at the site of **Monumento Histórico Las Padercitas**, a Franciscan-built colonial adobe chapel now sheltered by a stone temple, 7km west of town on RN 75. On the second Sunday of August, pilgrims convene to pay homage to the saint. Buses No 1 and 3 go to the site.

Beyond Las Padercitas, RN 75 climbs and winds past attractive summer homes, bright red sandstone cliffs, lush vegetation, and dark purple peaks whose cacti remind you that the area is semidesert.

Balneario Los Sauces, 15km from La Rioja at the dam, is a pleasant place for a leisurely picnic or outing.

From Balneario Los Sauces you can hike or drive up the dirt road to 1680m **Cerro de la Cruz**, which affords panoramic views of the Yacampis Valley and the village of Sanagasta. The top also has a ramp for hang gliding, a popular local activity. Sanagasta-bound buses can drop you off here.

CHILECITO

☎ 03825 • pop 26,000

The snow-capped peaks that surround Chilecito provide a marked contrast to this hot barren little town, the province's second-largest city. In a scenic valley at the foot of the massive Nevado de Famatina (and Cerro Velazco), it's a quiet place, easy to get around on foot and is worth a day at the most. Wine-tasting is a good way to while away a few hours waiting for your next bus. If you want to taste some of the region's specialties, including wines, walnuts and olives, drop into the municipal tourist office (Digetur) shop.

Information

The provincial tourist office (☎ 422688), on Castro y Bazán between La Plata and Joaquín V González, has enthusiastic staff and good material; it's open 7am to 1pm and 3pm to 9pm weekdays, 8am to 9pm weekends. The municipal tourist office (Digetur) has a small shop with limited tourist information, opposite Plazoleta Santa Rita, on Mitre between Castro Barros and Zelada y Dávila. Digetur also has an office at the bus terminal.

Banco de la Nación and Nuevo Banco de La Rioja (ATM) are on opposite corners of Plaza Sarmiento. Banco Macro has an ATM on Castro Barros between 25 de Mayo and 9 de Julio.

The postal code is 5360. The post office is at Joaquín V González and Pelagio Luna.

The locutorio is on Joaquín V González near Castro y Bazán.

Museo Molino de San Francisco

Chilecito founder Don Domingo de Castro y Bazán owned this colonial flour mill, whose museum (*J Ocampo 63; free; open 8am-noon & 3pm-7pm Tues-Sun*) houses an eclectic assemblage of archaeological tools, antique arms, early colonial documents, minerals, traditional wood and leather crafts, plus weavings and paintings. The building itself merits a visit, but the artifacts are a big plus.

Samay Huasi

Joaquín V González, founder of the prestigious Universidad Nacional de La Plata, used this building, 3km from Chilecito past La Puntilla, as his country retreat. Now belonging to the university, the building houses a natural sciences, archaeology and mineralogy museum (*admission US$1; open 8am-1pm & 1:30pm-7:30pm weekdays,*

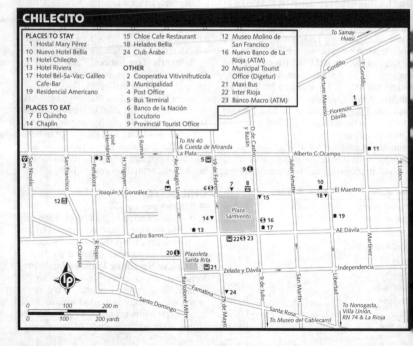

CHILECITO

PLACES TO STAY
1 Hostal Mary Pérez
10 Nuevo Hotel Bellia
11 Hotel Chilecito
13 Hotel Riviera
17 Hotel Bel-Sa-Vac; Galileo Cafe-Bar
19 Residencial Americano

PLACES TO EAT
7 El Quincho
14 Chaplin

15 Chloe Cafe Restaurant
18 Helados Bellia
24 Club Árabe

OTHER
2 Cooperativa Vitivinifrutícola
3 Municipalidad
4 Post Office
5 Bus Terminal
6 Banco de la Nación
8 Locutorio
9 Provincial Tourist Office

12 Museo Molino de San Francisco
16 Nuevo Banco de La Rioja (ATM)
20 Municipal Tourist Office (Digetur)
21 Maxi Bus
22 Inter Rioja
23 Banco Macro (ATM)

JANICE SHELDON

rugged peaks of Parque Nacional Nahuel Huapi, Argentina

ROBERTO SONCIN GEROMETTA

ow going along the Siete Lagos route in the Lake District of Argentina.

SARAH JH HUBBARD

The visual and audible splendor of the Moreno Glacier advancing in Patagonia.

JANE SWEENEY

Magellanic penguin – 'Is this my best side?'

JASON EDWARDS

Elephant seal – a face only a mother could love

8am-noon & 2pm-6:30pm weekends) and a valuable collection of paintings by Argentine artists.

Cooperativa Vitivinifrutícola (Winery)

La Rioja is one of the best areas to taste the fruity white torrontés, though it's far from the only wine the province has to offer. One block north and five blocks west of Plaza Sarmiento is the province's largest winery (☎ 423150, *La Plata 646*). It's open to visitors for tours and tastings. Tours take place at 7:30am, 9:30am and 12:30pm weekdays; there's an excellent selection of wine, as well as dried fruit, for sale.

Museo del Cablecarril

From the southern approach to Chilecito, about 2km southwest of Plaza Sarmiento, Estación No 1 del Cablecarril was the initial stop on the nine-station trip to La Mejicana. More than 260 towers sustained the 36km cable to its ultimate destination, 3510m higher than the town itself.

The cable-car line was constructed in 1903; the on-site museum *(free, but a tip is appropriate; open 7am-1pm & 2pm-8pm weekdays)* preserves the still-functional (though rarely used) wagons that, until 1935, carried men and supplies to the mine, in a little less than four hours. A 39-step spiral staircase climbs to the platform, where ore carts and even passenger carts now wait silently in line. Alongside the platform is a wooden crane, built of Sitka spruce in 1913.

Well-versed municipal guides lead tours, in Spanish only, from the museum proper in the former mine offices, where there are mining artifacts, minerals and communications equipment, including an early mobile phone.

Places to Stay

The tourist office keeps a list of private homes, which are the cheapest accommodations in town for about US$10 per person.

Nuevo Hotel Bellia (☎ 422181, *Maestro 198*) Singles/doubles US$15/25 with bath. The squat, clean rooms with fan here are a

good value. There's also a large grassy area, excellent for working on the tan.

Residencial Americano (☎ 422804, *Libertad 68*) Singles/doubles US$15/30 with bath. You might like this sunny, bright place. Some rooms have terrific views of the Nevado de Famatina and the staff are very friendly. Breakfast is only US$1.

Hostal Mary Pérez (☎ 423156, **e** *hostal_mp@hotmail.com, Florencio Dávila 280*) Singles/doubles US$20/40 with private bath & breakfast. A neat little residencial in the northeast of town, it's more like a family-run hotel. Rooms come with TV and telephone.

Hotel Chilecito (☎ 1566-6358, *Timoteo Gordillo 101*) Singles/doubles US$20/32 with bath members, US$30/48 nonmembers. For members and affiliates at least, ACA's utilitarian Hotel Chilecito is the best value, although it's no bargain for nonmembers. It also has a good restaurant and pleasant common areas.

Two central hotels worth a look are *Hotel Riviera* (*Castro Barros 158*) where singles/doubles are about US$24/35 and *Hotel Bel-Sa-Vac* (☎ 422533, *9 de Julio & Dávila*), which is a bit poky but the rooms are tidy enough. It's a bit more expensive at US$32/46.

Places to Eat

El Quincho (*Joaquín V González 50*) Mains under $4. This simple, cheap eatery serves parrillada among other Argentine food, and the outdoor tables overlook the plaza. A big spread for two people is about US$10.

Galileo Café-Bar (*Dávila & 9 de Julio*) Lunches US$2-3.50. This trendy spot is about as close as Chilecito comes to sophistication. A good place for coffee (US$2) and watching the passing traffic from the outdoor tables.

Chaplin (*25 de Mayo 54*) Mains US$3-6. There's good, inexpensive pasta here.

Club Árabe (*25 de Mayo & Santa Rosa*) Mains US$5-6. The hospitable owners of this place offer great food despite a limited menu; in summer, ask for grapes fresh off the vine.

Chloe Café Restaurant (☎ 422723, *Maestro & 9 de Julio*) Mains US$5-10. The best restaurant in town, chic Chloe has local specialties such as chicken in white wine sauce. There is also a good selection of local wines.

Helados Bellia (El Maestro & Libertad) is good for fine ice cream.

Getting There & Away

The bus terminal is at La Plata and 19 de Febrero. Some bus companies running minibuses in the area have separate offices around the plaza. La Riojana on El Maestro and Inter Rioja on Castro Barros, opposite Plaza Sarmiento, go to La Rioja regularly every day. Maxi Bus at Zelada y Dávila also goes to La Rioja about four times daily for US$10 roundtrip.

Transporte Ariel (☎ 422161) has minibuses that leave from the bus terminal for Nonogasta (US$1) and Sañogasta (US$1.50).

There are regular services from the terminal to Buenos Aires (US$66, 25 hours), Córdoba (US$24, 6 hours), Rosario, Villa Unión, San Juan (US$22, 7 hours), Patquía, Mendoza (US$26, 9 hours) and La Rioja (US$5, 3 hours).

AROUND CHILECITO

Only the roaring water of the *acequias* (irrigation ditches) disrupts the peaceful, unpaved streets of **Nonogasta**, birthplace of educator Joaquín V González. In a prosperous agricultural valley 16km south of Chilecito, this small town features charming adobe architecture (including González's house and a 17th-century church), polite and friendly people, and good wines from Bodegas Nicarí. Transporte Ariel makes the run between Chilecito and Nonogasta regularly.

With 800 turns, **Cuesta de Miranda**, a mountainous stretch of RN 40 through the Sierra de Sañogasta, about 56km west of Chilecito, is one of the most spectacular in Argentina's northern Andes and one of the province's major scenic attractions. Although not paved, the surface is smooth and wide enough for vehicle safety; still, sounding the horn before the innumerable blind turns is a good idea. At the highest point, 2020m above sea level, there is a vista from which the Río

Miranda looks like a frozen silver ribbon below.

PARQUE NACIONAL TALAMPAYA

Riojanos like to compare Talampaya, a 215,000-hectare national park southwest of Chilecito, to the USA's Grand Canyon. A better comparison would be southern Utah's arid canyon country, since only a trickle of permanent surface water winds through what, in the Quechua language, translates as the 'Dry River of the Tala.' This is a fitting description for this desert of scorching days, chilly nights, infrequent but torrential summer rains and gusty spring winds.

Talampaya's upgrade in recent years from provincial to national park status means it should attract more attention, visits are likely to increase and visitor services to improve, but for the moment both are limited.

Visitors may not use their own vehicles on park roads; only contracted guides with pickup trucks offer tours of sandy canyons where aboriginal petroglyphs and mortars adorn streambed sites. Nesting condors scatter from cliffside nests as vehicles invade their otherwise undisturbed habitat. On the usual two-hour tour from the park's headquarters, vehicles pass the dunes of **El Playón**, leading to the **Puerta de Talampaya** (Gate of Talampaya) entrance to the canyon. During a brief stop, passengers walk a sandy trail to the petroglyphs and mortars.

Back on the road, the vehicles enter the red sandstone canyon, whose eastern wall reveals a conspicuous fault. The next major stops are the **Chimenea del Eco**, an extraordinary echo chamber where your voice seems to come back louder than your original call, and a nature trail to the **Bosquecillo** (Little Forest), a representative sample of native vegetation. On the return the major point is **El Cañón de los Farallones** (Canyon of Cliffs) where, besides condors and turkey vultures, you may see eagles and other birds of prey 150m above the canyon floor.

Longer four-hour excursions are possible to Los Pizarrones and other sites like Los Cajones, Ciudad Perdida and Los Chañares.

Two-hour excursions in the park cost US$40 for up to eight persons; proceeds go directly to guides. Three-hour trips cost US$90 for up to eight persons and six-hour trips are US$130. These trips can be organized inside the park. If you can, sit in front with the guide one way, and in the back of the truck the other way.

Orientation & Information

Talampaya is 141km southwest of Chilecito via a combination of RN 40's scenic Cuesta de Miranda route, RP 18 and RP 26. Via RP 26, it is 55km south of Villa Unión and 58km north of Los Baldecitos, the turnoff to San Juan's Parque Provincial Ischigualasto.

From the junction with RP 26, a paved eastbound lateral leads 14km to the Puerta de Talampaya entrance, where there's a *confitería* (☎ *03825-470397*), serving simple meals and cold drinks; it is also a visitor center; a ranger is usually on duty to collect the US$3 admission. There are some good dinosaur illustrations depicting the early Triassic, 250 million years ago.

There is also a park office (☎ 03825-470356) in Villa Unión.

Places to Stay

There are no accommodations in the park itself, though it's possible to *camp* informally at the confitería, which has toilets but no showers.

Pagancillo, just 29km north of the park, is probably the best place for basic accommodations in the area. If you stay here it may be possible to get a lift into the park with the ranger. There are five *casas de familia* in Pagancillo; these accommodations cost about US$10/15 for singles/doubles.

Hospedaje Pagancillo (☎ *03825-470397, mobile 1567-1160)* US$12 per person; dinner US$7. Readers have reported good things about this place. It has just three rooms that can take up to 10 people but there are plans for an extension. The facilities are very clean and it's a family-run place.

Getting There & Away

Travelers without their own cars can take the Transportes Rápido bus from La Rioja to Pagancillo, 29km from Talampaya, where most of the park personnel reside; from there the rangers will help you get to the park, where it is necessary to pay for the excursions.

The Lake District

The Lake District is one of Argentina's most beloved travel destinations, visited each year by thousands who come to ski, hike, climb, camp, fish, swim and otherwise enjoy the spectacular mountain scenery and hundreds of chilly, glacially formed lakes that give the region its name. An ideal way to explore this area, where national parks are the main attraction, is with a backpack, tent and campstove, allowing you to ditch the crowds and have the trees – not to mention a lake – to yourself. That said, there are numerous interesting towns and tranquil mountain resorts that will entice even the most nature-loving anti-urbanites back to civilization. The Lake District is also known for its scenic passes and lake crossings to Chile, which shares the Andean peaks and Valdivian forests with its Argentine companion.

Neuquén, the capital of the province of the same name, is geographically distinct from the rest of the Lake District, but it serves as one of the area's major transport hubs. From Neuquén it's a short ride east, past Zapala and Parque Provincial Laguna Blanca, to the unpretentious town of Junín de los Andes. From there RN 234 bends southwest and the dry, often desolate scenery finally gives way to dense forest near the fashionable resort town of San Martín de los Andes, a good base for exploring Parque Nacional Lanín. South of San Martín, RN 234 is known as the Siete Lagos route, because it winds around, climbs into and drops through breathtaking scenery to the lakeside resort of Villa La Angostura.

Bariloche is the region's urban nucleus, and its unrivaled setting on the southeastern shore of Lago Nahuel Huapi, the largest lake in the region, brings a mixed bag of high-rise hotels, summer crowds, excellent restaurants and affordable accommodations. It makes a good base for exploring Parque Nacional Nahuel Huapi or for hitting the slopes of nearby Gran Catedral in winter. Bariloche is the chief transport hub for destinations in southern Patagonia

Highlights

- Siete Lagos Route – Enjoying the views on spectacular, lake-spotted RN 234
- Parque Nacional Lanín – Waking up lakeside and watching your breath on the brisk morning air
- Snow time – Carving up the slopes of Gran Catedral or Cerro Chapelco in July
- Bariloche – Hiking, biking or horse-trekking with shimmering lakes in the distance
- Parque Nacional Nahuel Huapi – Kissing the world goodbye and hitting the early-autumn backcountry
- El Bolsón – Sleeping in nearby mountain *refugios* and returning to town for strawberry waffles at the crafts fair

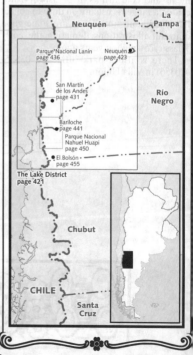

420

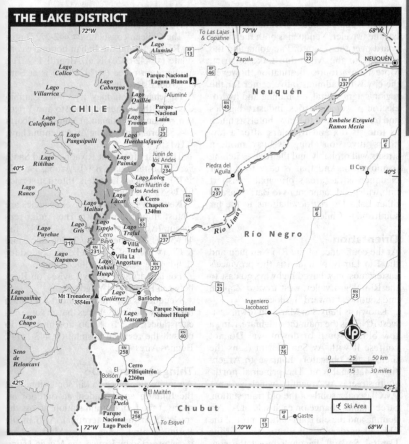

and Chile, and a short ride from the laid-back town of El Bolsón.

The original inhabitants of the region were the Puelches and Pehuenches, hunter-gatherers named for their dependence on the pehuén, a conifer whose pine nuts formed the basis of their diet. These names were given to them by the Mapuche, who migrated into the region from the west as the Spanish pushed south and east from Chile during the 16th and 17th centuries. The Mapuches soon dominated the region, learning to tame and ride the feral horses that had multiplied on the Pampas, and

using their new mobility to make life hard for anyone who invaded their territory.

Only in the late 19th century, during the Conquista del Desierto (Conquest of the Desert), when Argentina waged its war of extermination against the indigenous peoples of the Pampas, was the state able to establish a permanent presence. The Mapuches now live mostly in small settlements or reservations throughout the region. Mapudungun, the language of the Mapuches, is perhaps their most obvious presence; Mapuche vocabulary peppers the Spanish of rural Lake District areas, and Mapuche names are everywhere.

NEUQUÉN

☎ 0299 • pop 235,000 • elevation 265m

For the traveler, Neuquén is both the diving board over the ocean of Patagonia and the gateway to the Argentine Lake District. More than a tourist destination, however, the city is the administrative center for the region's agricultural, oil, mining and hydroelectric power industries. Industry bigwigs and businessfolk fill the city's hotels as much as tourists do, and travelers, after a few hours' diversion along its busy, modern streets, will probably find themselves itching to move on. And that is easy to do, for Neuquén is the area's principal transport hub, with good connections to Bariloche and other Lake District destinations, to the far south and to Chile.

Orientation

At the confluence of the Río Neuquén and the Río Limay, Neuquén is the province's easternmost city. Paved highways go east to the Río Negro valley, west toward Zapala, and southwest toward Bariloche.

Known as Félix San Martín in town, east-west RN 22 is the main thoroughfare, lying a few blocks south of downtown. Do not confuse it with Av San Martín (sans the 'Félix'), the obligatory homage to Argentina's national icon. The principal north-south street is Av Argentina, which becomes Av Olascoaga south of the old train station. Street names change on each side of Av Argentina and the old train station; most of the old rail yard now constitutes the Parque Central. Several diagonals bisect the conventional grid.

Information

The provincial tourist office (☎ 442-4089, W www.neuquentur.com.ar) is at Félix San Martín 182; it's open 7am to 9pm weekdays, 8am to 8pm weekends. Neuquén province generally provides free, up-to-date maps and brochures that contain truly useful material rather than the standard glossy photos. The municipal tourist office (no ☎) maintains a kiosk on the median strip of Av Argentina between Rodríguez and Alberdi.

ACA (☎ 442-2325) is on the diagonal 25 de Mayo at Rivadavia.

The Chilean consulate (☎ 442-2727) is at La Rioja 241, and the Italian honorary consulate (☎ 442-0020) is at Alberdi 139. The immigration office (☎ 442-2061) is at Santiago del Estero 466.

For changing money, try either Cambio Olano, at the corner of JB Justo and Yrigoyen, or Cambio Pullman, at Ministro Alcorta 144. Several banks along Av Argentina have ATMs.

The post office is at Rivadavia and Santa Fe; the postal code is 8300. Arrobas (☎ 443-5678), Gonzales 17, offers Internet service for US$3.50 an hour.

Neuquén's dozens of travel agencies are almost all near downtown. The AmEx representative is Zanellato (☎ 442-3741, fax 443-3337), Av Independencia 366. Sebastian & Co. (☎ 442-3592), Santa Fe 64, is good for standard services and airline tickets.

For laundry service, try Lavisec, on Roca between Brown and Yrigoyen.

Neuquén is known throughout Argentina for quality medical services that, in some circumstances, are free. Do not hesitate to consult the regional hospital (☎ 443-1474), Buenos Aires 421.

Things to See & Do

An interesting place to kill some time is at the **Juntarte en el Andén**, an outdoor art space at the former train station, across the tracks from the bus terminal. Also in the Parque Central, facing Av San Martín where it's intersected by Brown, the **Museo Municipal Dr Gregorio Álvarez** (☎ 442-5430; admission US$1; open 8:30am-7pm Mon-Fri, 6pm-9pm Sat & Sun) was once the repair shed for locomotives on the British-built Ferrocarril del Sud. Erected in 1902, the building now holds permanent exhibits on northern Patagonian dinosaurs, as well as on regional prehistory and ethnography.

Special Events

January's annual Regata del Río Negro is an internationally recognized kayak race that starts in Neuquén and ends a week

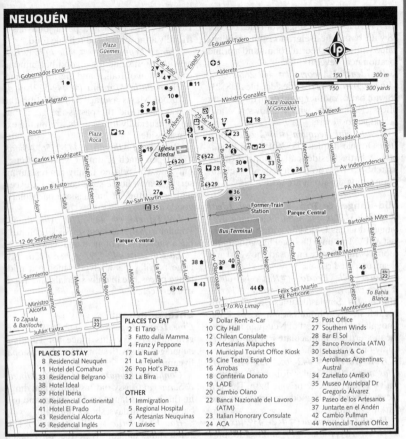

NEUQUÉN

PLACES TO EAT	9 Dollar Rent-a-Car	25 Post Office
2 El Tano	10 City Hall	27 Southern Winds
3 Fatto dalla Mamma	12 Chilean Consulate	28 Bar El Sol
4 Franz y Peppone	13 Artesanías Mapuches	29 Banco Provincia (ATM)
17 La Rural	14 Municipal Tourist Office Kiosk	30 Sebastian & Co
21 La Tejuela	15 Cine Teatro Español	31 Aerolineas Argentinas;
26 Pop Hot's Pizza	16 Arrobas	Austral
32 La Birra	18 Confitería Donato	34 Zanellato (AmEx)
	19 LADE	35 Museo Municipal Dr
PLACES TO STAY	20 Cambio Olano	Gregorio Álvarez
8 Residencial Neuquén	22 Banca Nazionale del Lavoro	36 Paseo de los Artesanos
11 Hotel del Comahue	(ATM)	37 Juntarte en el Andén
33 Residencial Belgrano	23 Italian Honorary Consulate	42 Cambio Pullman
38 Hotel Ideal	24 ACA	44 Provincial Tourist Office
39 Hotel Iberia		
40 Residencial Continental	OTHER	
41 Hotel El Prado	1 Immigration	
43 Residencial Alcorta	5 Regional Hospital	
45 Residencial Inglés	6 Artesanías Neuquinas	
	7 Lavisec	

later in Viedma, at the Atlantic mouth of the Río Negro.

Places to Stay

Neuquén's hotels are numerous but less than a good value at the lower end of the spectrum; even mid-range hotels rarely include breakfast.

Budget Part of the Balneario Municipal along the Río Limay, at the south end of town, *Camping Municipal* (☎ 448-5228) offers spots for US$4 per tent, plus US$1 per person. It's closed April 1 to mid-September. To get here, take bus No 103 from downtown to Obreros Argentinos and Copahue.

Residencial Inglés (☎ 442-2252, Félix San Martín 534) Singles/doubles US$15/25 with private bath. This is a plain, friendly place, and, though the price is right, the location is dismal.

Residencial Continental (☎ 448-3812, Perito Moreno 90) Singles/doubles US$15/25, US$20/30 with bath. The Continental is a good deal near the bus terminal, with dark but clean rooms.

Residencial Belgrano (☎ 448-0612, 442-4311, Rivadavia 283) Singles/doubles US$18/28 with bath. The Belgrano is an excellent value with small, cheerful rooms and a prime location near several cafés.

Residencial Alcorta (☎ 442-2652/5359, Ministro Alcorta 84) Singles/doubles US$21/28 with bath. Another good deal, the Alcorta offers clean rooms with windows; TV and breakfast cost extra.

Residencial Neuquén (☎ 442-2403, Roca 109) Doubles/triples US$25/45 with breakfast & bath. Residencial Neuquén offers matchbox-size rooms, but they're clean; those facing the street are noisy.

Mid-Range & Top End *Hotel Ideal* (☎ 442-2431, fax 448-4598, Olascoaga 243) Singles/doubles US$34/54 with bath, breakfast & TV. This no-frills hotel has good bathrooms (with the rare enclosed showers) and clean, carpeted rooms.

Hotel El Prado (☎/fax 448-6000, e hotelelprado@infovia.com.ar, Perito Moreno 484) Singles/doubles US$40/60 with breakfast, TV, phone, sauna & parking. Though not the priciest of Neuquén's hotels, the modern and immaculate El Prado is certainly one of its finest.

Hotel Iberia (☎ 442-3653, fax 443-6401, Olascoaga 294) Singles/doubles US$49/66 with TV, telephone & private bath. This is a pleasant hotel with good service, a bar and parking facilities.

Hotel del Comahue (☎ 442-2439, fax 447-3331, Av Argentina 377) Singles/doubles US$114/121. This five-star, full-service hotel charges an extra US$5 for spa-use and US$11 for parking – there goes the 10% discount for cash payment.

Places to Eat
The many confiterías along Av Argentina are all pleasant spots for breakfast and morning coffee.

El Tano (☎ 447-1147, 9 de Julio 70) This place serves tasty pizzas for US$7.

Pop Hot's Pizza (☎ 448-8888, Yrigoyen 90) Prices US$5-8. Pop's has good music and ambience and whips out a quality pizza to boot.

La Birra (☎ 443-4344, Santa Fe 19) Mains US$6-10. This pizza and pasta joint has a friendly atmosphere and reliable food.

Franz y Peppone (no ☎, 9 de Julio & Belgrano) Try this one for a good but unusual combination of Italian and German cuisine.

Fatto dalla Mamma (☎ 442-5291, 9 de Julio 56) Mains average US$10. Both the house decor and the pastas are great, but prices, especially for desserts, are on the expensive side.

Restaurant Alberdi (☎ 442-2556, Alberdi 176) Open lunch & dinner Mon-Sat, lunch only Sun. This relaxed, family-run restaurant serves hearty, home-style cooking at excellent prices; the set lunches are particularly good values.

La Tejuela (☎ 443-7114, Alberdi 59) Popular with the business set, slick La Tejuela has a varied menu of meat and seafood.

La Rural (☎ 442-4297, Alberdi 126) This large parrilla has a diverse menu at midrange prices, cheap daily specials and attentive service.

Entertainment
Cine Teatro Español (☎ 442-2048, Av Argentina 271) Try this place for English-language flicks with subtitles and occasional live music.

Confitería Donato (☎ 442-6950, Alberdi & Santa Fe) Classy, old-fashioned and dimly lit, this bar has tango on Thursdays and live bands on Saturdays; shows start late.

Bar El Sol (no ☎, Rivadavia 71) This comfortable hangout is perfect for relaxed late-night boozing.

Shopping
Paseo de los Artesanos (no ☎, Av Independencia Neuquén, Parque Central) Open 10am-9pm Wed-Sun. Neuquén's largest selection of regional handicrafts is at this outlet, near Buenos Aires, north of the old train station.

Artesanías Neuquinas (☎ 442-3806, Roca 155) is a provincially sponsored store that offers a wide variety of high-quality Mapuche and other crafts. Also try *Artesanías Mapuches* (☎ 443-2155, Roca 62) for good local crafts.

Getting There & Away

Air Aerolíneas Argentina/Austral (☎ 444-0736), Santa Fe 52, flies to Buenos Aires (US$130) twice daily and to Córdoba (US$209) once daily. LAPA (☎ 447-2385), M Mango 385, or at the airport (☎ 444-0662), flies weekdays to Bariloche (US$41 to US$76) and three times each weekday, twice Saturday and once Sunday to Buenos Aires (US$59 to US$149).

LADE (☎ 443-1153), Brown 163, flies Monday and Friday to Viedma (US$44); Wednesday and Friday to Mar del Plata (US$88) and Buenos Aires (US$95); Wednesday, Thursday and Friday to Bariloche (US$47); Thursday to Zapala (US$20), El Bolsón (US$43), El Maitén (US$43), Esquel (US$52), Comodoro Rivadavia (US$72 to US$120) and San Martín de los Andes (US$31); and Friday to Bahía Blanca (US$41).

Southern Winds (☎ 442-0124, 444-1284), Av San Martín 107, flies three times daily to Córdoba (US$94) and twice daily to Rosario (US$152), Mendoza (US$133), Tucumán (US$186) and Salta (US$186); flights to Tucumán require a four-hour layover in Córdoba. The company also flies once daily to Comodoro Rivadavia (US$145), Río Gallegos (US$190) and Ushuaia (US$204).

Bus Neuquén's bus terminal (☎ 442-4903), on the south side of Parque Central at Bartolomé Mitre 147, is a major hub for provincial, national and international bus services.

Several carriers offer service to Chile: Narbus and Igi-Llaima go to Temuco (US$40, 14 hours) via Zapala and the Pino Hachado pass, nightly (except Wednesday) at midnight. Igi-Llaima/El Petróleo combine service to Temuco (US$45, 15 hours) over Paso Tromen via Junín de los Andes nightly at 11pm. Andesmar goes three times a week to Osorno (US$43, 12 hours) and Puerto Montt (US$48, 13 hours) via Paso Cardenal A Samoré.

Neuquén is a jumping-off point for deep-south Patagonian destinations. Northern destinations such as Catamarca, San Juan, Tucumán, Salta and Jujuy require a bus change in Mendoza, though the entire ticket can be purchased in Neuquén.

The following table lists daily departures to nearly all long-distance destinations; provincial destinations are served numerous times daily.

Destination	Duration in hours	Cost
Aluminé	6	US$20
Bahía Blanca	7	US$20
Bariloche	6	US$16
Buenos Aires	17	US$30
Comodoro Rivadavia	15	US$65
Córdoba	15	US$53
El Bolsón	10	US$42
Esquel	11	US$40
Junín de los Andes	6	US$25
Mar del Plata	14	US$30
Mendoza	11	US$35
Puerto Madryn	10	US$40
Río Gallegos	28	US$115
Rosario	14	US$70
San Martín de los Andes	7	US$27
San Rafael	8	US$24
Santa Rosa	8	US$22
Trelew	11	US$42
Villa La Angostura	8	US$27
Zapala	3	US$10

Getting Around

Turismo Lanín connects the main bus terminal with Neuquén's airport (☎ 443-1444), west of town on RN 22.

Neuquén is a good province to explore by automobile, but foreigners should be aware that RN 22, both east along the Río Negro valley and west toward Zapala, is a rough road with heavy truck traffic and some of Argentina's most hell-bent drivers. On that note, try Dollar Rent-a-Car (☎ 442-0587), Belgrano 18, one of few choices downtown.

ZAPALA

☎ 02942 • pop 35,000 • elevation 1200m

Windy, dusty and economically depressed, Zapala is little more than an ordinary desert mining town. The main excuse – and an excellent one at that – for rolling into Zapala is to visit the nearby Parque Nacional Laguna Blanca. But beyond its friendly inhabitants, the town itself won't hold the average traveler for long.

Zapala's main street is Av San Martín, which is an exit off the roundabout junction of RN 22 (which heads east to Neuquén and north to Las Lajas) and RN 40 (heading southwest to Junín de los Andes and north to Chos Malal).

Information

The helpful tourist office (☎ 421132) is in a kiosk on the grassy median of Av San Martín at Almirante Brown; hours are 8am to 8pm daily year-round.

For information on Parque Nacional Laguna Blanca, visit the national park office (☎ 431982, e lagunablanca@zapala.com.ar) at Ceballos 446.

There's no money-exchange office, but Banco de la Provincia del Neuquén, Cháneton 460, has an ATM.

The post office is at Av San Martín and Cháneton; the postal code is 8340. There's a Telecenter locutorio at Etcheluz 527.

The regional hospital (☎ 431555) at Luis Monti 155, can attend to your various medical needs.

Museo Olsacher

In spacious quarters near the bus terminal, this agreeably surprising mineralogical museum (no ☎, Etcheluz & Ejército Argentino; free; open 7am-2pm & 6pm-9pm weekdays, 5pm-9pm weekends) contains more than 3500 exhibits – including numerous fossils – from 80 countries.

Places to Stay

Zapala's limited but decent accommodations are fairly costly except for the free Camping Municipal (☎ 422095), on Calle Sapag south of the railroad tracks, which has hot showers but funky toilets.

Residencial Coliqueo (☎ 421308, Etcheluz 159) Singles/doubles US$20/30; breakfast US$2.50. Above a two-table pool hall, these spacious, plain rooms all have TVs and bathtubs.

Hotel Pehuén (☎/fax 423135, Etcheluz & Elena de la Vega) Singles/doubles US$21/34 with bath, TV & phone. Near the bus terminal, this is a friendly little place with a decent restaurant below.

Hotel Hue Melén (☎ 422344, fax 422407, Almirante Brown 929) Singles/doubles US$38/64 with breakfast & bath. This three-star has-been offers stark but spacious rooms and a 10% discount for cash payment. It has one of Zapala's 'finer' dining establishments.

Places to Eat

El Chancho Rengo (☎ 422795, Av San Martín & Etcheluz) It's likely half the town saunters in here for an espresso each day. Outdoor tables and good coffee and sandwiches make it great for a light bite.

La Zingarella (☎ 422218, Houssay 654) Head up San Martín to the roundabout, hang a right on Houssay (as RN 22 is called in town) and you'll hit this local favorite for family cookin'; it's on the left-hand side, between Paraguay and Chile.

Shopping

Artesanía Andina (☎ 421552, Houssay 1150) This is one of the only shops in town for regional crafts. It's two blocks past La Zingarella restaurant.

Getting There & Away

Air LADE (☎ 430134), Uriburu 397, flies Wednesday to Neuquén (US$20) and Thursday to Bariloche (US$26), El Maitén (US$35), Esquel (US$44), and Comodoro Rivadavia (US$78). Cabs to Zapala's airport (☎ 431496), southwest of town at the junction of RN 40 and RP 46, cost about US$6.

Bus The bus terminal (mobile ☎ 15-661540) is at Etcheluz and Uriburu. Westbound buses from Neuquén en route to Junín de los Andes, San Martín de los Andes and Temuco, Chile, pass through Zapala. There is Monday, Wednesday and Friday service to Temuco, Chile (US$43, 10 hours) via Paso Tromen.

Most services to Buenos Aires (US$55, 16 hours) require changing buses in Neuquén (US$10, 3 hours), the nearest major transport hub. There are several daily buses to San Martín de los Andes (US$20, 3½ hours) and to the ski resort of Copahue, on the Chilean border.

Ticsa serves San Juan and San Luis three times weekly, while TAC connects the cities of Mendoza (US$45, 14½ hours) and San Rafael with Bariloche (US$20) via Zapala on Monday, Wednesday and Friday in each direction.

Albus goes to Laguna Blanca (US$5) and Aluminé (US$10) Monday, Wednesday and Friday at 9:20pm, while Aluminé Viajes goes to Laguna Blanca (US$3.50) and Aluminé at 7:30pm.

AROUND ZAPALA
Parque Nacional Laguna Blanca
At 1275m above sea level and surrounded by striking volcanic deserts, Laguna Blanca is only 10m deep, an interior drainage lake that formed when lava flows dammed two small streams. Only 30km southwest of Zapala, the lake is too alkaline for fish but hosts many bird species, including coots, ducks, grebes, upland geese, gulls and even a few flamingos. The 11,250-hectare park primarily protects the habitat of the black-necked swan, a permanent resident. Its breeding colonies, on a peninsula in the lake, have been fenced off to prevent disturbance by livestock.

Starting 10km south of Zapala, paved and well-marked RP 46 leads directly through the park toward the Andean town of Aluminé; for transport details, see Zapala. If these schedules do not serve you, a cab or remise is not unreasonable, and there's sufficient traffic to make hitching feasible.

There is a small improved *campground* with windbreaks, but bring all your own food; though there's a visitor center, there's no place to eat.

Primeros Pinos
This ski resort near Las Lajas, 55km northwest of Zapala via RN 22, has a 700m vertical drop. For information, contact the tourist office (☎ 421132) in Zapala (see previous section).

Plaza Huincul
About an hour east of Zapala, not quite halfway to Neuquén on RP 22, the settlement of Plaza Huincul is one of Argentina's major petroleum centers, but for visitors it's more significant for the important **Museo Municipal Carmen Funes** (☎ 02942-465486, *Córdoba 55; admission US$2; open 8am-8pm weekdays, 4pm-8pm weekends*), a dinosaur museum and research center that is home to remains of the herbivore *Argentino saurus huinculensis*. One of the largest known dinosaurs, it measured an incredible 40m long and 18m high. While perhaps not worth a major detour in its own right, it certainly justifies a stop for travelers en route to or from Zapala and San Martín de los Andes. There's a free municipal *campground* in nearby Cutral-Có. All buses between Neuquén and Zapala stop here.

ALUMINÉ
☎ 02942 • pop 2500
Situated 103km north of Junín de los Andes via RP 23, the fishing resort of Aluminé offers access to the northern sector of Parque Nacional Lanín. The Río Aluminé, which parallels RP 23 for most of its length, is one of the country's most highly regarded trout streams.

For information, consult the department of tourism (☎ 496154) or its information center (☎ 496001) at RP 23 and San Juan Bosco. In early April, Aluminé celebrates the Fiesta del Pehuén in honor of the unique trees that cover the slopes of the Andes. There are several hosterías in town, including the simple *Nid Car* (☎ 496131, C Joubert & Benigar), which charges US$18/30 single/double. Several nearby Mapuche reservations sell traditional weavings. For bus services, see Zapala.

JUNÍN DE LOS ANDES
☎ 02972 • pop 10,000 • elevation 800m
The barren mountains surrounding Junín de los Andes are strikingly different than those of the similarly named San Martín de los Andes, only 41km south. By the traditional definition of 'beautiful mountain resort,' Junín is admittedly less attractive than it's prestigious, leafy neighbor – but for that, it's also less expensive and can serve as a better base for exploring Parque Nacional Lanín. Attracting fly-fishing enthusiasts from just

about everywhere, Junín deems itself the trout capital of Neuquén Province and, to drive the point home, uses trout-shaped street signs.

With several Mapuche settlements, the area's indigenous culture weighs in as heavily as resort culture and the city has two fine Mapuche museums. A six-hectare sculpture park depicts the history of the Conquista del Desierto; Junín was founded in 1883 as an army outpost during this war against the native inhabitants (see Invasion & Colonization of the New World, in the History section of the Facts about Argentina chapter).

Orientation

Junín de los Andes is just south of the confluence of the Río Curruhue and the larger Río Chimehuín, which forms the city's eastern limit. Paved RN 234 (known as Blvd Juan Manuel de Rosas in town) is the main thoroughfare, leading south to San Martín de los Andes and 116km northwest to Zapala via RN 40. North of town, graveled RP 23 heads to the fishing resort of Aluminé, while several secondary roads branch westward to Parque Nacional Lanín.

The city center is between the highway and the river. Do not confuse Av San Martín, which runs on the west side of Plaza San Martín, with Félix San Martín, two blocks farther west.

Information

The enthusiastically helpful tourist office (☎ 491160, e turismo@jandes.com.ar) is at Padre Milanesio 596 at Coronel Suárez, facing Plaza San Martín. Hours are 8am to 10pm daily. In addition to fishing permits, the office provides a complete list of Junín's licensed fishing guides.

For information on nearby Parque Nacional Lanín (see that section, later in this chapter), visit the park office, next to the tourist office but facing Coronel Suárez; it's open 9am to 8:30pm weekdays and 2:30pm to 8:30pm weekends. The Club Andino Junín de los Andes (☎ 491637, Padre Milanesio 568, Local 12), in the Paseo Artesanal, provides information on climbing Volcán

Tromen and other excursions within the national park.

Banco de la Provincia de Neuquén is on Av San Martín between Suárez and Lamadrid, opposite the plaza. The post office is at Suárez and Don Bosco; the postal code is 8371.

It's easiest to make local or long-distance calls from the locutorio at Padre Milanesio 540, opposite the plaza. Laverap Pehuén is at Ponte 340. The local hospital (☎ 491162) is at Ponte and Padre Milanesio.

Things to See & Do

Junín's surroundings are more appealing than the town itself, but the Salesian-organized Museo Mapuche (no ☎, Ginés Ponte 540; free) is worth a look for its ethnographic and historical materials. The Museo Moisés Roca Jalil (no ☎, Coronel Suárez & San Martín; free; open 10am-noon Mon, Wed & Fri) is a private collection with more than 400 Mapuche weavings and archeological pieces.

West of town, near the end of Av Antártida Argentina, a wide dirt path called the Vía Cristi winds its way up the small Cerro de La Cruz (to get there, follow the cross). Sixteen 'stations' are situated along the path, each with impressive sculptures, bas-reliefs and mosaics vividly depicting the Conquest of the Desert, Mapuche legends, Christian themes and indigenous history. The Vía is a great source of local pride, designed by architect and sculptor Alejandro Santana and brought to life by him and a dedicated crew of local artists and tradespeople. Though the whole installation is not scheduled for completion until 2003 (primarily to finish work on the 45m, half-buried sculpture of Christ), much of the artwork is already finished and offers a fine reward for the walk up; it's especially appealing in the morning when the sun is gentle. Santana also remodeled Junín's delightful church with Mapuche weavings and symbology.

The area around Junín is prime trout-fishing country, and many North American and European fly-casters annually hit the nearby streams. The Río Aluminé, north of Junín, is an especially choice area, but fishing is possible even within city limits. Catch-and-release is often obligatory. For detailed information and equipment, visit the Fly Shop (☎ 491548, Illeras 378), west of the RN 234 (Blvd Juan Manuel de Rosas) at the northwest edge of town. Neuquén fishing licenses cost US$100 for the season, US$60 for a month, or US$30 for a week; trolling licenses cost an extra US$60 for the season.

Special Events

Every year, Junín celebrates its own lively Carnaval del Pehuén with parades, costumes, live music and the usual water balloons. No one will mistake it for Rio de Janeiro or Bahia, but if you're in the area it can be entertaining.

In January, the Feria y Exposición Ganadera displays the best of local cattle, horses, sheep, poultry and rabbits. There are also exhibitions of horsemanship, as well as local crafts exhibits, but this is the estanciero's show – the peons and the people get their chance at mid-February's Festival del Puestero, where the name of the game is music, food and fun, rather than livestock trading.

In early August, the Mapuche celebrate their crafts skills in the Semana de Artesanía Aborígen.

Places to Stay

Camping La Isla (☎ 491461) Sites US$6 per person. This municipal campground sits on the pleasant banks of the Río Chimehuín, three blocks east of the plaza. It has the standard facilities; showers are available 8am to 10am and 8pm to 10pm for US$1.

Hostería Chimehuín (☎ 491132, fax 491319, e hosteriachimehuin@jandes.com.ar, Coronel Suárez & 25 de Mayo) US$15-20 per person with breakfast & bath. On lush grounds near the river, this lovely hostería offers rooms in its old main lodge or in a modern sector outside; all are subtle, comfortable and exceptional values – perfect for a short fishing holiday. The breakfast is excellent, the service is tops and the atmosphere is welcoming. Half-board (breakfast and dinner) is available.

Posada Pehuén (☎ 491569, Coronel Suárez 560) Singles/doubles US$20/30 with private bath (low season), US$25 per person with half-board (high season). Attentive owners Eduardo and Rosi run this cozy little place in their attractive home and will help arrange all types of excursions. It's located between the plaza and the river.

Hostería del Montañés (☎ 491155, San Martín 555) Singles/doubles US$20/35. This hotel is run-of-the-mill, but fine.

Residencial El Cedro (☎ 492044, Lamadrid 409) Singles/doubles US$20/40 with breakfast & bath. Just off the plaza, this small, colorful place has plenty of indoor plants and decent rooms.

Places to Eat

Junín has fairly mediocre restaurants, though local specialties like trout, wild boar or venison may be available.

With entrées running US$6 to US$12, *Ruca Hueney* (☎ 491113, Padre Milanesio 641) is reliable and has the most extensive menu in town. Junín's main pizzeria, *Roble Bar* (☎ 491124, Ponte 331), offers baked empanadas and sandwiches as well. *Rotisería Tandil* (no ☎, Coronel Suárez 431), just east of the plaza, has excellent take-out empanadas.

Getting There & Away

Air Junín and San Martín de los Andes share Chapelco airport, which lies midway between the two towns. For more information, see Getting There & Away in the San Martín de los Andes section, later.

Bus The bus terminal (☎ 492038) is at Olavarría and Félix San Martín. Centenario uses the Zapala route to Neuquén (US$25, 6 hours), as does El Petróleo; both continue to Bahía Blanca and Buenos Aires (US$60, 22 hours). El Petróleo goes Tuesday to Aluminé (US$13, 3 hours) and to San Martín de los Andes (US$3.50, 1 hour), while Centenario goes to San Martín three times daily except Sunday, when it goes twice.

Ko-Ko has service to Bariloche (US$16, 4 hours) via both the paved Rinconada route and the dusty but far more scenic Siete Lagos alternative.

TAC and Andesmar head north to Mendoza. On Monday and Thursday, TUS goes to Córdoba (US$80, 21 hours) via Santa Rosa, La Pampa, while Chevallier provides services to Buenos Aires (US$60, 22 hours).

Empresa San Martín links Junín with neighboring San Martín de los Andes (US$4, 1 hour) and crosses the Andes to Temuco, Chile, via Paso Tromen. Other carriers serving Chile include Igi-Llaima and JAC.

SAN MARTÍN DE LOS ANDES
☎ 02972 • pop 26,000 • elevation 645m

Situated on a small bay on the eastern end of Lago Lácar, San Martín de los Andes is a fashionable and relatively costly mountain resort, drawing visitors (hordes of them in summer) to its quiet tree-lined streets and attractive lakeside beaches. The town is also the northern jumping-off point for the scenically neck-straining Siete Lagos route, which runs south to Villa La Angostura and Bariloche.

Thanks partly to a height limit on new construction, San Martín de los Andes retains some of the charm and architectural unity that once attracted people to Bariloche, though the burgeoning hotels, restaurants and time-shares have taken their toll. San Martín's principal outlying attractions are the Cerro Chapelco ski resort and Parque Nacional Lanín, though nearby Junín de los Andes is a potentially cheaper base for exploring the latter.

Orientation
Nestled in striking mountain scenery, San Martín straddles RN 234, which passes through town southbound to Villa La Angostura, and Lago Nahuel Huapi. Northbound RN 234 heads to Zapala via Junín de los Andes.

Almost everything in San Martín de los Andes is within walking distance of the *centro cívico* (civic center), and the shady lakefront park and pier are a delightful place to spend an afternoon. Av San Martín is the main commercial street, running north from the lakefront toward the highway to Junín.

Information
Tourist Offices Across from Plaza San Martín, on the corner of San Martín and Rosas, the well-organized tourist office (☎/fax 425500, e munitur@smandes.com.ar) provides surprisingly candid information on hotels and restaurants, plus excellent brochures and maps. It's open 8am to 10pm daily, and also sells fishing licenses.

Open 7am to 1pm weekdays, the Intendencia del Parque Nacional Lanín (☎ 427233, Emilio Frey 749) provides limited maps and brochures. Nieves de Chapelco (☎ 429845, 427845), on San Martín at Elordi, across from Plaza San Martín, provides information and sells lift tickets for the Cerro Chapelco ski resort.

Money On weekdays try Banco de la Nación, Av San Martín 687, which has an ATM. The only official cambio is Andina Internacional, at Capitán Drury 876.

Post & Communications The post office is at Roca and Coronel Pérez; the postal code is 8370. Cooperativa Telefónica is at Capitán Drury 761. Abolengo (see Places to Eat) offers Internet access at a budget-busting US$6 per hour.

Travel Agencies Grupo 3 de Turismo (☎ 428453), San Martín 1141, Local 1, is the AmEx representative. The agencies listed in the Activities section, as well as many others along Av San Martín, Belgrano and Elordi, offer standard services as well as excursions.

Laundry Laverap (☎ 428820) is at Capitán Drury 880 and Villegas 972.

Medical Services Ramón Carrillo Hospital (☎ 427211) is at Coronel Rohde and Av San Martín.

Museo Primeros Pobladores
Regional archaeological and ethnographic items such as arrowheads, spear points, pottery and musical instruments are the focus of this museum (*no ☎; admission US$1; open 2pm-7pm weekdays*), two doors north of the tourist office, on Rosas near Roca.

SAN MARTÍN DE LOS ANDES

PLACES TO STAY
1 Puma Youth Hostel (HI)
2 Hostería La Cheminee
5 Hostería Las Lucarnas
27 Hostería Tisú
29 Rosa de los Viajes
34 Hotel Caupolicán
40 Residencial Italia
45 Residencial Los Pinos
46 Residencial Casa Alta
47 Hostería La Mása
48 Hostería del Chapelco
49 Hostería La Raclette
50 Hostería Las Lengas

PLACES TO EAT
12 Abolengo
19 Rotisería Viviana
22 Piscis
23 Heladería Andina
25 Café de la Plaza
26 Mendieta
28 Paprika
38 Heladería Charlot
41 Trattoria Mi Viejo Pepe
42 Pura Vida
44 Las Catalinas

OTHER
3 LADE
4 Post Office
6 La Colina
7 Intendencia del Parque Nacional Lanín
8 Museo Primeros Pobladores
9 Cooperativa Telefónica
10 Artesanías Neuquinas
11 Tourist Office
13 Southern Winds
14 Tiempo Patagónico; Cerro Torre
15 Hansen
16 Avis
17 Nieves de Chapelco
18 Ramón Carrillo Hospital
20 Bumps
21 Ici Viajes
24 Banco de la Nación (ATM)
30 Kosem
31 Andina Internacional (Money Exchange)
32 Laverap
33 Pucará
35 Laverap
36 La Oveja Negra
37 HG Rodados
39 Grupo 3 de Turismo (AmEx)
43 El Claro Turismo
51 Casino

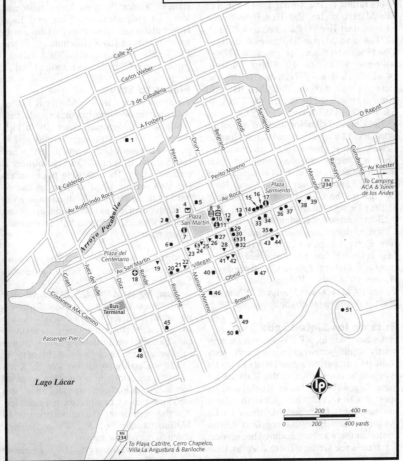

Activities

Mountain biking is an excellent way to explore the surrounding area. You can rent bikes for about US$15 per day at HG Rodados (☎ 427345, Av San Martín 1061), opposite Plaza Sarmiento. Try peddling about 4km south on RN 234 to Playa Catritre, where there is a long, rocky (and often busy) beach; it's a good alternative to taking the bus, though the shoreline is better for tanning and swimming than for riding.

For **rafting** on the Río Meliquina, south of San Martín, or the Río Hua Hum to the west, contact Tiempo Patagónico (☎ 427113, 427114, San Martín 950), which charges US$45 with transfers; Ici Viajes (☎ 427800, Villegas 590) and El Claro Turismo (☎ 428876, Villegas 977) charge roughly the same. A full day on the Class III Río Aluminé is offered by Pucará (☎ 427218, Av San Martín 943); the cost is US$50.

Trekking and **climbing** are also important activities in Parque Nacional Lanín. Horacio Peloso, who is known by his nickname 'El Oso,' is a highly regarded mountain guide who arranges trips and rents equipment for climbing Lanín; contact him at Cerro Torre (☎ 429162, San Martín 960). Otherwise contact Tiempo Patagónico or Pucará.

Skiing and **snowboarding** at nearby Cerro Chapelco draws enthusiastic winter crowds (see Cerro Chapelco in the Around San Martín section, later). In town, rental equipment is available for about US$20 per day at Bumps (☎ 428491, Villegas 570) and La Colina (☎ 427414, San Martín 532). You can also rent equipment on the mountain.

Ruta de los Siete Lagos

From San Martín, RP 234 follows an eminently scenic but rough, narrow and dusty route past numerous alpine lakes to Villa La Angostura. It's known as the Ruta de los Siete Lagos (Seven Lakes Route) and its spectacular scenery has made the drive famous. Tours from San Martín, Villa La Angostura and Bariloche regularly do this route, but there's also scheduled bus service; for details, see Getting There & Away, later in this section.

Special Events

San Martín celebrates its founding on February 4 with speeches, parades and other festivities; the parade itself is an entertainingly incongruous mix of military folks, firefighters, gauchos, polo players and foxhunters.

Organized Tours

San Martín's several travel agencies offer full-day tours to a number of outlying sights, including Lahuén Co thermal baths(US$35), northwest of San Martín on RP 62 near the Chilean border; the Siete Lagos route and Villa La Angostura (US$30); and Lago Huechulafquen, Lago Paimún (the northwestern arm of Lago Huechulafquen) and Parque Nacional Lanín (US$30). A half-day trip to Cerro Chapelco costs around US$14.

Places to Stay

As a tourist center, San Martín is loaded with accommodations, but they're relatively costly in all categories, especially in high summer (January through March) and in peak ski season (July and August) when reservations are a must. Quality, however, is generally high. The following prices reflect the high season, when single rates can be hard to find; often a 10% discount is given for cash payment. In low season, prices can drop by 40%. All rooms include private bath unless noted.

Budget If you're not camping, it's slim pickin's when it comes to cheap lodging in San Martín.

Camping ACA (☎ 427332, Av Koessler 2640) Sites US$5 per person, 2-person minimum fee. Even when crowded, it's easy to find a quiet (though perhaps less aesthetically pleasing) site at this spacious, attractive campground on the eastern outskirts of town.

Playa Catritre (☎ 426986, RN 234 Km 5 sur) is a pleasant site about 4km south of San Martín in Parque Nacional Lanín. Sites US$5 per person, two-person minimum fee. Another option at the same price is *El Molino (☎ 426350, RN 234 Km 5 norte)*, about 5km north of town.

Puma Youth Hostel (☎ 422443, e puma@ smandes.com.ar, A Fosbery 535) Dorm beds

US$13 per person, with one-time US$2 sheet-rental fee. This is a pleasant, well-kept HI-affiliated hostel with a helpful young owner and small dorm rooms, each with a bathroom. One double room is available for US$33.

Residencial Los Pinos (☎ 427207, *Almirante Brown 420*) Rooms US$20 per person with breakfast. An excellent value in a quiet area, this friendly residencial has cheerful rooms and a sunny breakfast room.

Residencial Italia (☎ 427590, *Coronel Pérez 977*) Doubles US$40. The friendly owner lives downstairs and rents out a few clean, quiet rooms above. She has one four-person apartment with a kitchen for US$100 per night.

Hostería Tisú (☎ 427231, *Av San Martín 771*) Singles/doubles US$25/40. This standard hostería offers large but sparse rooms; mattresses are a bit thin.

Mid-Range At **Rosa de los Viajes** (☎/*fax 427320, Av San Martín 821*), the rooms are a bit sparse, but the hotel is central and comfortable, and the staff is welcoming. Singles/doubles run around US$30/45.

Hostería Las Lucarnas (☎ 427085, *fax 427985, Coronel Pérez 632*) Singles/doubles US$35/60 with breakfast, parking & Internet access. This tasteful stone and wood structure has simple, cozy rooms; try for a spot upstairs.

Residencial Casa Alta (☎ 427456, e *casaalta@smandes.com.ar, Obeid 659*) Singles/doubles US$40/50 with breakfast. This homey, family-operated place offers three cozy rooms, wisely booked in advanced. Besides Spanish, owner Pepe Guitiérrez speaks German, French, Portuguese, English and *lunfardo* (street slang of Buenos Aires). Guests have access to email and Pepe's personal library.

Top End An upscale resort town, San Martín has loads of tasteful top-end accommodations.

Hostería La Raclette (☎ 427664, *fax 427921*, e *laraclette@smandes.com.ar, Coronel Pérez 1172*) Singles/doubles US$50/65 with breakfast. An excellent value, this immaculate stucco and wood chalet boasts unique, cozy rooms with appealing decor.

Hostería del Chapelco (☎ 427610, *fax 427097*, e *hcchapelco@smandes.com.ar, Brown 297*) Doubles/triples US$55/80, 4-person cabañas US$120. The building is attractive, the rooms are nondescript, and its lakeside location can't be beat.

Hostería Las Lengas (☎ 427659, *fax 427938*, e *laslengas@smandes.com.ar, Coronel Pérez 1175*) Singles/doubles US$90/130 with breakfast. Though the place is slightly overpriced, there's a sauna and swimming pool. Rooms are spacious and the beds excellent.

Hotel Caupolicán (☎ 427658, *fax 427090, Av San Martín 969*) Singles/doubles US$95/130 with breakfast, TV & en-suite fridge. This relaxing hotel has a game room, a bar and excellent rooms with plush beds.

Hostería La Masía (☎/*fax 427688*, e *lamasia@smandes.com.ar, Obeid 811*) Singles US$80-110, doubles US$98-120. With a beautiful bar, cozy downstairs reading nooks, a paddle ball court and mid-size rooms with luxurious baths, this is one of San Martín's best.

Hostería La Cheminee (☎/*fax 542972, 427617, Av Roca & M Moreno*) Doubles US$175. The whopping price tag includes the communal jacuzzi, sauna and swimming pool and over-cheery rooms in a handsome hostería.

Places to Eat

Café de la Plaza (☎ 428488, *San Martín & Coronel Pérez*) Breakfast US$3-6. Though not inexpensive, this pleasant sidewalk café is a good breakfast choice.

Rotisería Viviana (☎ 428917, *San Martín 489*) Lunch or dinner US$4-8. This is an outstanding choice for take-out food, particularly the superb, but cheap, baked empanadas.

Abolengo (☎ 427732, *San Martín 806*) For coffee, chocolate and croissants, try this little café.

Piscis (☎ 427601, *Villegas 598*) This town has many parrillas, including this traditional favorite, which usually gets mobbed in the evening.

Mendieta (☎ 429301, San Martín 713) Long lines form outside Mendieta, a more upscale parrilla named for the dog of the famous cartoon gaucho, Inodoro (that is, 'Toilet') Pereyra.

Las Catalinas (☎ 427203, Villegas & Elordi) All-you-can-eat US$8.50. The food is only decent, but there's a good salad bar – and you can stuff yourself.

Pura Vida (☎ 429302, Villegas 745) This restaurant has a small, mostly vegetarian menu, plus some chicken and fish items; service is first-rate and the food is delicious.

Trattoria Mi Viejo Pepe (☎ 427415, Villegas 725) This Italian restaurant is an expensive but delicious option.

Paprika (☎ 427056, Villegas 744) With pricey Central European food, Paprika is a welcome break from the usual menu.

You can top off your feed with delectable ice cream at either *Heladería Andina (☎ 427071, San Martín 595)* or *Heladería Charlot (☎ 428561, San Martín 1017)*.

Shopping

Many local shops sell regional products and handicrafts. *Artesanías Neuquinas (☎ 428396, Rosas 790)* offers local indigenous weavings and crafts. *La Oveja Negra (☎ 427248, Av San Martín 1045)* is a good shop for Mapuche textiles. Also specializing in artisanal textiles, *Kosem (no ☎, Capitán Drury 846)* is worth popping into.

Getting There & Away

Air Tiempo Patagónico and Pucará (see Activities, earlier) represent Aerolíneas Argentinas/Austral, which flies daily except Wednesday to Buenos Aires (US$163).

LADE (☎ 427672, General Roca 636) flies Wednesday to Zapala (US$20) and Neuquén (US$31); Thursday to Bariloche (US$22); and Friday to Neuquén (US$31), Viedma (US$69), Bahía Blanca (US$78), Mar del Plata (US$105) and Buenos Aires (US$112).

Bus The bus terminal (☎ 427044) is at Villegas and Juez del Valle.

On Tuesday, Thursday and Saturday at 6am, Igi-Llaima takes RP 60 over Paso Tromen (also known as Mumuil Malal) to Temuco, Chile (US$25, 6 hours), passing the majestic Volcán Lanín en route; sit on the left for views. Empresa San Martín goes on Tuesday, Thursday and Saturday at the same hour. There is no Sunday service.

El Petróleo takes RP 48 over Paso Hua Hum to Chile daily at 12:30pm. The bus terminates at Puerto Pirehueico (US$8.50, 2 hours) on its namesake lake; from there a ferry (payable *only* in Chilean pesos) crosses the lake to Puerto Fuy, from where there are onward buses toward Valdivia.

From San Martín, there is direct service in summer via RN 231 over Paso Cardenal A Samoré (Puyehue) to Osorno (US$25) and Puerto Montt.

If you're heading to Villa Traful or Bariloche, Transportes Ko-Ko regularly takes the scenic Siete Lagos route (RN 234) instead of the longer but smoother Rinconada route. To Aluminé (US$14, 3 hours) El Petróleo leaves on Tuesday only, at 8am.

There are frequent daily departures to the destinations listed in the following table.

Destination	Duration in hours	Cost
Bahía Blanca	15	US$49
Bariloche	4	US$15
Buenos Aires	23	US$60
Córdoba	22	US$79
Junín de los Andes	1	US$4
Mendoza	13	US$71
Neuquén	6½	US$27
Viedma	18	US$53
Villa La Angostura	2½	US$13
Villa Traful	2½	US$12
Zapala	4	US$20

Boat Plumas Verdes (☎ 428427, 427380) sails from the Muelle de Pasajeros (passenger pier) on the Av Costanera to Paso Hua Hum on the Chilean border daily at 10am. This departure time sometimes changes; call the ferry company or check with the tourist office. The fare is US$30 plus a US$1 national park fee.

Getting Around

Chapelco airport (☎ 428388) is midway between San Martín and Junín, on RN 234. Al Sur (☎ 422903) runs shuttles between San Martín and the airport; call for hotel pickup.

Transport options slim down during low season. In summer, Transportes Airen goes twice daily to Puerto Canoas on Lago Huechulafquen (US$9) and will stop at campgrounds en route. Albus goes to the beach at Playa Catritre (US$1.50) several times daily, while Transportes Ko-Ko runs four buses daily to Lago Lolog (US$2) in summer only.

Car rental agencies include Hansen (☎ 427997), San Martín 532; Avis (☎ 427704), at Av San Martín 998; and El Claro (☎ 428876), at Villegas 977.

AROUND SAN MARTÍN DE LOS ANDES
Cerro Chapelco

Only 20km southeast of San Martín, Cerro Chapelco (☎ 02972-427157) is one of Argentina's principal winter-sports centers, with runs for beginners and experts, and a maximum elevation of 1920m. Ski season runs mid-June to mid-October, with the Fiesta Nacional del Montañés, the annual ski festival, held the first half of August.

Lift-ticket prices vary, depending on when you go; half-day passes run from US$18 to US$33 for adults, US$13 to US$26 for children. Full-day passes range from US$22 to US$37 for adults and US$18 to US$30 for children.

Weeklong, 15-day and seasonal passes are also available.

The resort has a downtown information center (see Tourist Offices in the San Martín section, earlier) that also sells lift tickets. Rental equipment is available on site as well as in town (see Activities in the San Martín section, earlier).

Transportes Ko-Ko runs two buses each day (three in summer) to the park from San Martín's bus terminal. Travel agencies in San Martín also offer packages with shuttle service.

PARQUE NACIONAL LANÍN

Dominating the view in all directions along the Chilean border, the snowcapped cone of 3776m Volcán Lanín is the centerpiece of Parque Nacional Lanín, which extends 150km from Parque Nacional Nahuel Huapi in the south to Lago Ñorquinco in the north.

Protecting 379,000 hectares of native Patagonian forest, the Lanín park is home to many of the same species that characterize more southerly Patagonian forests, such as the southern beeches *lenga*, *ñire* and *coihue*. More botanically unique to the area, however, are the extensive stands of the broadleaf deciduous southern beech *raulí* and the curious pehuén, or monkey puzzle tree *(Araucaria araucana)*, a pine-like conifer whose nuts have long been a dietary staple for the Pehuenches and Mapuches. Note that only indigenous people may gather *piñones* (pine nuts) from the pehuenes.

The *pehvén*, or monkey puzzle tree

In addition to the views of Volcán Lanín and the unusual forests, the park also has recreational attractions in the numerous finger-shaped lakes carved by Pleistocene glaciers. Excellent campsites are abundant, though some of the less developed but more accessible places are unfortunately dirty and polluted.

The towns of San Martín de los Andes, Junín de los Andes and Aluminé are the best starting points for exploring Lanín, its glacial lakes and the backcountry.

Information

The Intendencia del Parque Nacional Lanín in San Martín de los Andes (see that town's Information section) produces brochures on camping, hiking and climbing in various parts of the park. These brochures are also distributed in the area's tourist offices. Scattered throughout the park proper are several ranger stations, but they usually lack printed materials.

Lago Lácar

From San Martín, at the east end of the lake, there is bus service on RP 48, which runs along Lago Lácar to the Chilean border at Paso Hua Hum. You can also take a boat excursion from San Martín to Hua Hum, where there are numerous hiking trails, and free and organized campsites.

Lago Lolog

Fifteen kilometers north of San Martín de los Andes, this largely undeveloped area has fishing and good camping at **Camping Puerto Arturo** (US$2 per person) and **Camping Lolog** (US$2 per person). Transportes Ko-Ko runs four buses daily, in summer only, to Lago Lolog from San Martín; the bus costs US$2.

Lago Huechulafquen

The park's largest lake is also one of its most central and accessible areas. Despite limited public transport, it can be reached from San Martín and Junín de los Andes. RP 61 climbs from a junction just north of Junín, west to Huechulafquen and the smaller Lago Paimún, offering outstanding

PARQUE NACIONAL LANÍN

views of Volcán Lanín and access to trailheads of several excellent hikes. Source of the Río Chimehuín, Huechulafquen offers superb fishing at its outlet.

From the ranger station at Puerto Canoa, a good trail climbs to a viewpoint on Lanín's shoulder, where it's possible to hike across to Paso Tromen or continue climbing to either of two refugios: The **RIM refugio** belongs to the army's Regimiento de Infantería de Montaña, while the **CAJA refugio** belongs to the Club Andino Junín de los Andes (see Junín de los Andes' Information section, earlier). Both are fairly rustic but well kept, and either can be a staging point for attempting the summit (see Lago Tromen, later, for more detail, including information about permits and equipment). The initial segment follows an abandoned road, but after about 40 minutes it becomes a pleasant woodsy trail along the **Arroyo Rucu Leufu**, an attractive mountain stream; yellow paint blazes mark the route where it is not obvious. Halfway to the refugio is an extensive **pehuén forest**, the southernmost in the park, which makes the walk worthwhile if you lack time for the entire route. The route to RIM's refugio, about 2450m above sea level, takes about seven hours one-way, while the trail to CAJA's refugio takes a bit longer.

Another good backcountry hike circles **Lago Paimún**. This requires about two days from Puerto Canoa; you return to the north side of the lake by crossing a cable platform strung across the narrows between Huechulafquen and Paimún. A shorter alternative hike goes from the campground at Piedra Mala to **Cascada El Saltillo**, a nearby forest waterfall. If your car lacks 4WD, leave it at the logjam 'bridge' that crosses the creek and walk to Piedra Mala – the road, passable by any ordinary vehicle to this point, quickly worsens. Horses are available for rent at Piedra Mala.

Along the highway are many campsites, some free and others inexpensive. Travelers camping in the free sites in the narrow area between the lakes and the highway must dig a latrine and remove their own trash. If you camp at the organized sites (which, though not luxurious, are maintained), you'll support Mapuche concessionaires who at least derive some income from lands that were theirs before the state usurped them a century ago.

Fees at *Camping Raquithue* are US$3 per person, while those at *Camping Piedra Mala* are US$4.50 per person; *Bahía Cañicul* charges US$6.50 with electricity, US$5.50 without. Limited supplies are available, but Junín de los Andes has a better selection at lower prices.

Noncampers with money can stay at *Hostería Refugio Pescador* (☎ 02972-491132) at Puerto Canoa, or the three-star *Hostería Paimún* (☎ 02972-491211); both cater to fishing parties and charge around US$90 per person with full board.

Lago Tromen

This northern approach to Volcán Lanín, which straddles the Argentine-Chilean border, is also the shortest and usually the earliest in the season to open for hikers and climbers. En route from Junín, note the unique volcanic landforms. Before climbing Lanín, ask permission at the Intendencia del Parque Nacional Lanín in San Martín or, if necessary, of the Gendarmería (border guards) in Junín. It's obligatory to show equipment, including plastic tools, crampons, ice axe and clothing – including sunglasses, sunscreen, gloves, hats and padded jackets.

From the trailhead at the Argentine border station, it's five to seven hours to the *CAJA refugio* (capacity 14 persons), at 2600m on the Camino de Mulas route; above that point, snow equipment is necessary. There's a shorter but steeper route along the ridge known as the Espina del Pescado, where it's possible to stay at the *RIM refugio* (capacity 20 persons), at 2450m. Trekkers can cross the Sierra Mamuil Malal to Lago Huechulafquen via Arroyo Rucu Leufu.

Hostería San Huberto (☎ 02972-491238, 428437), on the north side of RP 60, on private land with prime trout streams, offers accommodations with full board for a paltry US$400 per double.

Lago Quillén

Situated in the park's densest pehuén forests, this isolated lake is accessible by dirt road from Rahué, 17km south of Aluminé, and has many good *campsites*. Other nearby lakes include Lago Rucachoroi, directly west of Aluminé, and Lago Ñorquinco on the park's northern border. There are Mapuche reservations at Rucachoroi and Quillén.

Getting There & Away

Although the park is close to San Martín and Junín, public transport is minimal; see the entries on those towns for details. With some patience, hitching is feasible in high season. Buses over the Hua Hum and

Tromen passes from San Martín and Junín to Chile will carry passengers to intermediate destinations, but they are often full. Pickup trucks from Junín carry six or seven backpackers to Puerto Canoas for about US$5 per person.

VILLA TRAFUL
☎ 02944

A pinprick on the south shore of Lago Traful, Villa Traful offers excellent opportunities for camping, hiking and fishing in a relatively undeveloped area of Parque Nacional Nahuel Huapi. It's a tranquil resort village, 80km north of Bariloche via RP 65.

Other than camping, the cheapest lodging is *Hostería Villa Traful* (☎ 479005), at a modest US$20 per person with breakfast. Popular with fly-casters, the most extravagant is *Rincón del Pescador* (☎/fax 479028), which charges US$80 per night; their trout dinners are worth a try.

Albus has daily services to San Martín de los Andes and Bariloche.

VILLA LA ANGOSTURA
☎ 02944 • pop 6000 • elevation 850m

On the northwestern shore of Lago Nahuel Huapi, Villa La Angostura is a tranquil resort of attractive cabins and small hosterías tucked sporadically into the lakeside evergreens – well, most of it is anyway. The village consists of two distinct areas: El Cruce, which is the commercial center along the highway, and La Villa, nestled against the lakeshore, 3km to the south. Though La Villa is more residential, it still has hotels, shops, services and, unlike El Cruce, lake access. Despite rapid growth, this densely forested resort does not dominate its surroundings, so that, except along the highway, visitors are hardly aware of being in a town.

Villa La Angostura's most accessible natural asset is Parque Nacional Los Arrayanes, a small peninsula dangling some 12km into the lake from La Villa's edge. Nearby Cerro Bayo is a small but popular winter-sports center.

Orientation

Villa La Angostura is near the junction of RN 231 from Bariloche, which crosses the Andes to Puyehue and Osorno, Chile, and RN 234, which leads northward to San Martín de los Andes (100km). The junction gives the commercial strip of town its name El Cruce (The Crossroads).

Through town, RN 231 is known as Av Los Arrayanes and Av Siete (7) Lagos. La Villa is a 3km walk toward the lake on Blvd Nahuel Huapi.

La Villa and around are easily seen on foot, but if you're venturing further out, taxis and remises are the only means of getting to the trailheads. They leave from the local terminal on Av Siete Lagos, just north of Los Arrayanes.

Information

The helpful tourist office (☎ 494124, e turismo@angosturatur.com), at Av Siete Lagos 93 in El Cruce, has a good selection of maps and brochures. It's open 8:30am to 9pm daily. The local park administration office (☎ 494152) is on Nahuel Huapi, in La Villa.

Banco de la Provincia, on Av Los Arrayanes between Las Mutisias and Los Notros, has an ATM. The post office is in El Cruce; the postal code is 8407. There's a locutorio in the Galería Inacayal on Av Los Arrayanes in El Cruce.

Parque Nacional Los Arrayanes

This inconspicuous, overlooked park, encompassing the entire Quetrihué peninsula, protects remaining stands of the cinnamon-barked arrayán, a member of the myrtle family. In Mapudungun, language of the Mapuche, the peninsula's name means 'place of the arrayanes.'

Tiny Rivers

Argentina can't lay claim to the longest river in the world (the Nile is a long way away), but that won't stop it from claiming the shortest: The Río Correntoso, which flows between Lago Correntoso and Lago Nahuel Huapi, is a wee 250m long. Go fish.

Park headquarters are at the southern end of the peninsula, near the largest concentration of arrayanes, an area known as **El Bosque**. It's a three-hour, 12km hike from La Villa to the tip of the peninsula, on an excellent **interpretive nature trail**; brochures are available in the tourist office at El Cruce. You can also hike out and get the ferry back from the point, or vice versa (check with the tourist office for ever-changing ferry times). Regulations require hikers to leave the park by 4pm, so you should start early in the morning. There are two small lakes along the trail.

From the park's northern entrance at La Villa, a very steep 20-minute hike leads to two **panoramic overlooks** of Lago Nahuel Huapi.

Cerro Belvedere

A 4km **hiking trail** starts from Av Siete Lagos, northwest of the tourist office, and leads to an **overlook** with good views of Lago Correntoso, Nahuel Huapi and the surrounding mountains. It then continues another 3km to the 1992m summit. After visiting the overlook, retrace your steps to a nearby junction that leads to **Cascada Inayacal**, a 50m waterfall.

Centro de Ski Cerro Bayo

From June to September, lifts carry skiers from the 1050m base up to 1700m at this relatively inexpensive winter resort (☎ 494189; half-day pass US$16-22 adult, , US$10-18 child; full-day pass US$18-26 adult, US$12-20 child), 9km southeast of El Cruce via RP 66. All facilities, including rental equipment, are available on site. Rates depend on whether you come during peak, mid- or low season.

Activities & Organized Tours

Renting a mountain bike is a great way to explore the surrounding area. For **biking** try renting from Ian (mobile ☎ 15-557294, Blvd Nahuel Huapi 2150 in La Villa; Topa Topa 102 in El Cruce). The cost is US$8 for a half-day, US$12 for a full day.

Las Taguas (☎ 494494, e angostura@ lastaguas.com, Arrayanes 141, near Blvd Nahuel Huapi) offers numerous excursions, including **rafting** on the Río Manso and the Río Aluminé, **guided treks** (US$30 per day with food), and excellent **horseback rides** (US$15) in the surrounding mountains. Angostura Turismo (☎ 494405), also on Av Arrayanes, offers similar excursions.

Places to Stay

Except for camping and Angostura's one hostel, accommodations tend to be pricey; in summer, single rooms are almost impossible to find – expect to pay for two people. The following prices are for high season.

Camping Unquehué (☎ 494922, Av Siete Lagos s/n) Sites US$5 per person. This campground lies a convenient 500m beyond the tourist office. The hot showers are dependable, but the toilets are sometimes dirty.

Camping Cullumche (☎ 494160, Blvd Quetrihué s/n) Sites US$5 per person. Well-signed from Blvd Nahuel Huapi, this secluded but large lakeside campground is owned by the University of Cuyo. It can get very busy in summer, but when it's quiet, it's lovely.

Also try *Camping Correntoso* (☎ 494829) on Lago Correntoso north of town; rates are US$6 per person. There are also *free sites* along Lago Nahuel Huapi.

Albergue El Hongo (☎ 495043, Calle Pehuenches 872) Dorm beds US$10 with one-time US$5 sheet- & towel-rental fee. This small, clean hostel with communal kitchen is up in the trees in Barrio Norte, removed – for better or worse – from both the lake and town. Walk out Av Siete Lagos and hang a right just before the YPF gas station; walk to the end, turn left on Pehuenches, and look for the sign on the right.

Residencial Don Pedro (☎ 494269, Belvedere & Los Maquis, El Cruce) Doubles US$40. Though it's away from the lake, it's convenient; the rooms walk the line between cozy and cramped.

Residencial Río Bonito (☎ 494110, Topa Topa 260) Singles/doubles US$40/49. Two blocks from the bus terminal in El Cruce, this is a friendly no-frills place, but it's relatively cheap.

Hotel Angostura (☎ 494224, 494280, Blvd Nahuel Huapi s/n) Doubles US$80. Built in the 1930s, this lovely hotel overlooks the lake and has an excellent restaurant. Service is tops.

Hostería Las Balsas (☎ *494308)* Rooms US$110 per person with breakfast. Set on a small bay south of El Cruce, this is a large and luxurious three-star property.

Places to Eat

There are several restaurants and confiterías in El Cruce along Los Arrayanes and its cross streets.

Try *La Buena Vida* (☎ *495200, Av Arrayanes 167)* for breakfast and early-morning churros, or reasonably priced burgers and pastas. *Parrilla Las Varas* (☎ *494405, Av Arrayanes 235)* is a local favorite for grilled meats.

Rincón Suizo (☎ *494248, Av Los Arrayanes 44)* Near Av Siete Lagos, this quaint little eatery serves good fondue and other Swiss specialties, and has outdoor seating.

Boliche de Alberto (☎ *495337, Av Siete Lagos 727)* Mains US$6-12. Bariloche's famed parrilla has a location in Angostura, and it's well worth the splurge. It's near Camping Unquehué.

Getting There & Away

Villa La Angostura's bus terminal is at the junction of Av Siete Lagos and Av Arrayanes in El Cruce. Transportes Ko-Ko and others stop in El Cruce on runs between Bariloche and San Martín de los Andes.

For Chile, Río de La Plata goes daily to Osorno (US$15, 3 hours) and on to Puerto Montt (US$18, 4 hours). Other companies stop in El Cruce en route from Bariloche, but they are often full.

There are numerous daily departures to Bariloche (US$6, 2 hours) and two daily departures with TEC to Neuquén (US$28, 9 hours). Albus goes five times daily to San Martín de los Andes (US$13, 3 hours) by the scenic Siete Lagos route.

Daily ferries run to the tip of nearby Quetrihué peninsula, Parque Nacional Los Arrayanes; they leave from the dock next to Hotel Angostura in La Villa (see Places to Stay).

Getting Around

Transportes 15 de Mayo runs hourly buses from the terminal to La Villa, up Av Siete Lagos to Lago Correntoso, and south down Av Arrayanes to Puerto Manzano on Lago Nahuel Huapi. From July through September, and December through March, 15 de Mayo runs six or seven daily buses to the ski resort at Cerro Bayo.

BARILOCHE

☎ 02944 • pop 80,000 • elevation 770m

Once a tranquil and prestigious resort for the Argentine elite, Bariloche (formerly San Carlos de Bariloche) has become, for better or worse, the Lake District's principal destination. It offers unrivaled resources for independent trekkers and climbers preparing to take to the backcountry of Parque Nacional Nahuel Huapi, as well as countless travel operators for those seeking climbing guides, fishing guides, horse rentals, rafting companies and rental equipment. The urban center of the Argentine Lake District, the city is also an important transportation hub for those heading into southern Patagonia or east to Chile.

Bariloche's proximity to the region's best ski resort makes it ground-zero for the country's snow-heads, and, for Argentine secondary students, it's *the* destination for the graduation bash. It is also perhaps the chocolate capital of Argentina, and the only thing that approaches the amount of storefront window space dedicated to fresh chocolate is the infinite number of peculiar gnomes of all sizes and demeanors sold in nearly every shop downtown.

Officially founded in 1902, the city really began to attract visitors after the southern branch of the Ferrocarril Roca train line arrived in 1934 and architect Ezequiel Bustillo adapted Central European styles into a tasteful urban plan. Bariloche is now known for its alpine architecture, which is given a Patagonian twist through the use of local hardwoods and unique stone construction, as seen in the buildings of Bustillo's civic center.

The flip side of Bariloche's gain in popularity is uncontrolled growth: In the last two

ARGENTINA

BARILOCHE

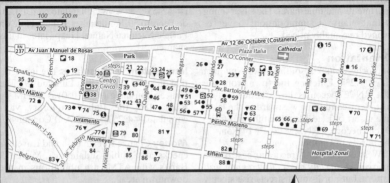

Lago Nahuel Huapi

PLACES TO STAY
4 Hotel Panamericano
5 Hostería La Sureña
6 Casa de Familia Pirker
7 Casa de Familia Arko
8 Residencial Güemes
9 Hostería El Radal
11 Albergue Patagonia Andina; Aguas Blancas
16 Hostería El Ñire
27 Hotel Pucón
32 Hostería Sur
34 Hospedaje Tito
36 Hotel Aconcagua
45 Hotel Internacional
66 Hotel 7 de Febrero
67 Hotel Los Andes
69 Hotel Panorámico
72 Hotel Edelweiss
82 Albergue Ruca Hueney
86 Hostería El Ciervo Rojo
88 La Bolsa de Deporte

PLACES TO EAT
10 El Vegetariano
21 La Andinita
23 El Viejo Munich
25 Don Pancho
28 Pilgrim
30 Ahumadero Familia Weiss
39 Cocodrilos
42 Helados Jauja
43 La Alpina
51 De la Granja
57 La Vizcacha
61 Cerros Nevados
62 Simoca
64 La Quesería
70 El Mundo de la Pizza
71 Restaurant Cachari
74 Rock Chicken; Amúncar
76 La Esquina de las Flores
78 Días de Zapata
83 El Boliche de Alberto
83 La Colina
84 Almacén Naturista Maná
85 La Andina
87 Boliche de Alberto Pastas

OTHER
1 Grisú
2 Roket
3 Cerebro
12 Club de Caza y Pesca
13 Bikeway
14 Pub Moritz
15 Río Negro Provincial Tourist Office
17 ACA
18 Chilean Consulate
19 Immigration
20 Museo de la Patagonia
22 Bariloche Rafting
24 El Refugio; Budget
26 By Pass
29 Fenoglio
31 Italian Honorary Vice Consulate
33 Dirty Bikes
35 Al
37 Post Office
38 Municipal Tourist Office
40 Cambio Sudamérica
41 Baruzzi Deportes
44 Expediciones Náuticas
46 Aerolíneas Argentinas; Via Bariloche Airport Shuttle; LADE; TAN; Southern Winds
47 Salón Cultural de Usos Múltiples (SCUM)
48 Paseo de los Artesanos
49 Del Turista
50 Karnak Expediciones
52 Cyber Mac Café
53 Cumbres Patagonia
54 Martín Pescador
55 Laverap
56 Catedral Turismo
58 Tom Wesley Viajes de Aventura
59 Hiver Turismo (AmEx)
60 Local Bus Stop
63 LAPA
65 Bariloche Bikes
68 Pub 1970
73 Avis
75 Intendencia del Parque Nacional Nahuel Huapi
77 Club Andino Bariloche
79 Museo Arquitectónico
80 Laverap

decades, the town has suffered as its quaint neighborhoods have given way to high-rise apartments and timeshares. The silver lining is that many accommodations have remained reasonably priced.

Orientation

Bariloche is 460km southwest of Neuquén via RN 237. Entering the town from the east, RN 237 becomes the Av 12 de Octubre costanera, continuing westward to the lakeside resort of Llao Llao. Southbound Calle Onelli becomes RN 258 to El Bolsón, on the border of Chubut province.

West of the Río Ñireco and east of the civic center, the city has a fairly regular grid pattern, but north-south streets rise steeply from the lakeshore – some so steeply that they become staircases. The principal commercial area is along Av Bartolomé Mitre. Do not confuse similarly named VA O'Connor (also known as Vicealmirante O'Connor or Eduardo O'Connor) with John O'Connor, which cross each other near the lakefront. Similarly, Perito Moreno and Ruiz Moreno intersect near Diagonal Capraro, at the east end of the downtown area.

Information

Tourist Offices The municipal tourist office (☎ 423022, 423122, e securismo@bariloche .com.ar), in the centro cívico, is open 8am to 9pm daily. It has many giveaways, including useful maps and the blatantly commercial but still useful *Guía Busch*, updated annually and loaded with basic tourist information about Bariloche and its surroundings. The office also maintains a kiosk at the Paseo de los Artesanos, at Perito Moreno and Villegas; the kiosk is open 9:30am to 1pm and 5pm to 8:30pm daily.

The Río Negro provincial tourist office (☎ 423188/89, e securrn@bariloche.com .ar), at the corner of Av 12 de Octubre and Emilio Frey, has information on the province, including an excellent provincial map and useful brochures in English and Spanish.

For motorists, ACA (☎ 423001) is at 12 de Octubre 785.

For park information, contact the Intendencia del Parque Nacional Nahuel Huapi

(☎ 423111), San Martín 24. Another excellent source is the Club Andino Bariloche (☎ 424531, w www.clubandino.com.ar), 20 de Febrero 30. For details, see the section on Parque Nacional Nahuel Huapi, later in this chapter.

Immigration & Consulates The immigration office (☎ 423043) is at Libertad 191. The Chilean consulate (☎ 423050) is at HM de Rosas 180; the Italian honorary vice-consulate (☎ 422603) is at VA O'Connor 467.

Money Change foreign cash and traveler's checks at Cambio Sudamérica, Mitre 63. Banks with ATMs are ubiquitous in the downtown area.

Post & Communications The post office is alongside the municipal tourist office, at the civic center; the postal code is 8400. Just outside the tourist office are direct lines to the USA (ATT, MCI, Sprint), Japan, Spain, France, Italy, Chile and Brazil for collect and credit card calls.

For Internet service, try El Refugio, at Mitre 106, 2nd floor; or Cyber Mac Café, at Rolando 217, which also serves coffee and snacks.

Travel Agencies Bariloche may sink beneath lake level under the weight of its travel agencies, most of which are along Av Bartolomé Mitre and immediate cross streets. The AmEx representative is Hiver Turismo (☎ 423792), Mitre 387.

Cultural Centers There are occasional exhibitions at the Salón Cultural de Usos Múltiples (☎ 422775 interno 23), Perito Moreno and Villegas, which is also known as SCUM, an acronymn that hits very close to home for one Lonely Planet author.

Laundry Among others try Laverap, on Rolando between Mitre and Perito Moreno, or on Quaglia between Perito Moreno and Elflein.

Medical Services The hospital (☎ 426100) is at Perito Moreno 601.

Civic Center

Hotels and time-shares have eliminated much of Bariloche's alpine charm, but architect Ezequiel Bustillo's log-and-stone buildings, housing the post office, tourist office, municipality and museum, still deserve a visit – if you can evade the plaza photographers soliciting your portrait with their St Bernards and Siberian huskies.

Museo de la Patagonia

Lifelike stuffed animals, professionally presented archaeological and ethnographic materials, and critically enlightening historical evaluations on such topics as Mapuche resistance to the Conquista del Desierto and Bariloche's urban development, make this diverse museum (☎ 422309, admission US$2.50; open 10am-12:30pm & 2pm-7pm Tues-Fri, 10am-1pm Mon & Sat) in the civic center one of the country's best. It has a specialized library, and there is a bookstore in the lobby.

Activities

Bariloche and the Nahuel Huapi region are one of Argentina's major outdoor recreation areas, and numerous operators offer a variety of outdoor activities, particularly horseback riding, mountain biking and white-water rafting. Among these operators, some of which are accessible by post office box (casilla), phone and fax only, are the following:

Adventure World (☎ 460164, fax 422637), Casilla (PO Box) 234, or at Cerro Catedral – mountain biking, rafting, riding

Aguas Blancas (☎ 432799), Morales 564, in Albergue Patagonia Andina – rafting

Amúncar (☎ 431627, fax 423187, e cecilia@bariloche.com.ar), Av San Martín 82, 1st floor – rafting, trekking

Bariloche Rafting (☎/fax 424854, 435708), Mitre 86, Local 5 – rafting

Cabalgatas Carol Jones (☎ 426508, e caroljones@infovia.com.ar), Casilla (PO Box) 1436 – riding

Cumbres Patagonia (☎ 423283, fax 431835, e cumbres@bariloche.com.ar), Villegas 222, and in Hotel Llao Llao (☎ 448350 interno 550) – fishing, rafting, riding

Expediciones Náuticas (☎/fax 431777), Mitre 125, 1st floor, Oficina 126 – rafting

Karnak Expediciones (☎/fax 425290), Mitre 265, Local 18 – rafting, riding, trekking

La Bolsa del Deporte (see Places to Stay, later) – mountain biking, trekking

Tom Wesley Viajes de Aventura (☎/fax 435040), Mitre 385 or Av Bustillo Km 15.5 – riding, mountain biking

Mountain Biking Bicycles are ideal for the Circuito Chico (though this 60km loop demands endurance) and other trips near Bariloche; most roads are paved, the gravel roads are good, and Argentine drivers are less ruthless, slowing and even stopping for the scenery. Mountain-bike rental, usually including gloves and helmet, costs about US$15 per day at a number of places. Try Bariloche Bikes (☎ 424657, Moreno 520), Bikeway (☎ 424202, VA O'Connor 867) or Dirty Bikes (☎ 425616, VA O'Connor 681).

Fishing Fishing for both native and exotic species draws visitors from around the world to Argentina's accessible Andean-Patagonian parks, from Lago Puelo and Los Alerces in the south to Lanín in the north. The most popular introduced species are European brown trout, rainbow trout, brook trout and landlocked Atlantic salmon, which reach impressive sizes. Native species, which should be thrown back, are generally smaller; these include *perca* (perch), *puyen*, Patagonian *pejerrey*, and the rare *peladilla*.

On larger lakes, such as Nahuel Huapi, trolling is the preferred method, while fly-fishing is the rule on most rivers. Night fishing is prohibited. The season runs mid-November to mid-April. For more information, contact the Club de Caza y Pesca (Hunting and Fishing Club; ☎ 422785, Costanera 12 de Octubre & Onelli). For rental equipment, try Baruzzi Deportes (☎ 424922, 428374, Urquiza 250) or Martín Pescador (☎ 422275, Rolando 257).

Seasonal licenses, available from the national parks office at the civic center, or from larger sporting-goods stores in town, cost US$100 for non-Argentines. Monthly licenses cost US$60, weekly licenses US$30 and daily licenses US$10. There are US$40 surcharges for 'preferential' areas and trolling.

Horseback Riding Horseback excursions start at around US$20 for two hours or US$40 per half day. There are longer excursions around the lower Río Manso (US$75 full day) or into Chile (US$500 several days).

Mountaineering & Trekking The national park office distributes a brochure with a simple map, adequate for initial planning, that rates hikes as easy, medium or difficult and suggests possible loops. Many of these hikes are detailed in the 2nd edition of Lonely Planet's *Trekking in the Patagonian Andes*, by Clem Lindenmayer.

The Club Andino Bariloche (see Tourist Offices, earlier in this section) provides information and issues obligatory permits for trekking in Parque Nacional Nahuel Huapi. For US$3, their *Mapa General de la Guía de Sendas y Picadas* is cartographically mediocre, but has good trail descriptions. They sell three additional trekking maps, all of which include mountain bike trails.

Another good source of information and advice, especially for climbing the more difficult peaks, is the Asociación Argentina de Guías de Montaña (Argentine Association of Mountain Guides; ☎ 422567, Neumeyer 60), behind the Club Andino Bariloche. Both organizations also lead excursions in the area.

Skiing The runs around Bariloche were once South America's trendiest, but other areas in Argentina (especially Las Leñas, near Mendoza) and Chile (Portillo and Valle Nevado) have pretty much superseded the Nahuel Huapi area, which is more popular with Argentines than foreigners. Gran Catedral, the largest and most popular area, brings together two formerly separate areas, Cerro Catedral and Lado Bueno; skiers can buy one

Bring boots made for walkin', amiga.

ticket valid for lifts in both areas. There is also the smaller Piedras Blancas area on Cerro Otto; for details, see the Parque Nacional Nahuel Huapi section later in this chapter.

If you need lessons, contact the ski schools at Cerro Catedral (☎ 423776), or the Club Andino Bariloche (see Tourist Offices). For rental equipment, try Baruzzi Deportes or Martín Pescador (see Fishing, earlier). Equipment is also available on site at Piedras Blancas and Gran Catedral.

In addition to downhill skiing, there are also cross-country opportunities.

Water Sports Rafting and kayaking on the Río Limay (an easy Class II float, US$35) and the Río Manso (a Class III white-water descent with some Class IV segments, US$65) have become increasingly popular in recent years. The latter are generally 20km day trips, including transfers, a hearty lunch and neoprene wet suits, helmets and other equipment.

Sailing, windsurfing and canoeing have all become popular on Lago Nahuel Huapi and other nearby lakes and streams. For equipment rentals, contact Martín Pescador or Barruzi Deportes (see Fishing, earlier).

Paragliding The mountains around Bariloche make for spectacular paragliding. If you wish to take to the sky, it will cost you between US$70 and US$100 for a tandem flight with, among others, Luis Rosenkjer (☎ 427588, mobile 15-568388) or Parapente Bariloche (☎ 15-552403 cellular, Cerro Otto base).

Organized Tours
Parque Nacional Nahuel Huapi offers infinite outdoor possibilities. This section suggests some organized excursions, but consult the Parque Nacional Nahuel Huapi section for more detailed information. Catedral Turismo (☎/fax 427143/44, 425444,

Perito Moreno 238) covers the destinations mentioned here, but so do many other travel agencies. If you belong to ACA (see Tourist Offices) or any of their overseas affiliates, the nice people at the office can arrange these excursions at discounts of at east 10%.

Trips to Isla Huemul, in Lago Nahuel Huapi, leave from Puerto San Carlos, just below the civic center.

Half-day trips from Bariloche include Cerro Otto, Cerro Catedral (US$13 without chairlift access), the Circuito Chico west of own (US$13) and Cerro López (US$29).

Full-day trips include the delightful town of El Bolsón (US$29); Isla Victoria and Parque Nacional Los Arrayanes (US$30; for details, see Villa La Angostura, earlier in this chapter); San Martín de los Andes via Siete Lagos (US$34); and Cerro Tronador and Cascada Los Alerces via Lago Mascardi (US$29).

Albergue Alaska (see Places to Stay) offers a series of well-received camping tours; they range from the four-day Safari Siete Lagos (US$170 plus US$30 for the food kitty) and the identically priced four-day Safari Los Alerces, to the 11-day Safari Patagónico (US$440 plus US$80 for food) and the 18-day Safari del Fin del Mundo (US$1300 plus US$160 for food), which goes all the way to Tierra del Fuego.

Special Events

For ten days in August, Bariloche holds its Fiesta Nacional de la Nieve (National Snow Festival). In January and February, the Festival de Música de Verano (Summer Music Festival) puts on several different events, including the Festival de Música de Cámara (Chamber Music Festival), the Festival de Bronces (Brass Festival), and the Festival de Música Antigua (Ancient Music Festival). May 3 is the Fiesta Nacional de la Rosa Mosqueta, celebrating the fruit of the wild shrub used in many regional delicacies.

Places to Stay

From camping and private houses to five-star hotels, Bariloche's abundant accommodations make it possible to find good values even in

high season, when reservations are a good idea. The municipal tourist office maintains a computer database with current prices, including listings for places outside town.

Budget The most popular destination in the Lake District, Bariloche is loaded with good budget accommodations.

La Selva Negra (☎ 441013, Av Bustillo Km 2.9) Sites US$7. La Selva Negra, 3km west of town on the road to Llao Llao, is the nearest organized camping area. It has good facilities, and you can step outside your tent to pick apples in the fall.

Other sites between Bariloche and Llao Llao include *Camping Yeti* (☎ 442073, Km 5.6) and *Camping Petunia* (☎ 461969, Km 13.5); both cost US$6 per site.

Albergue Alaska (☎/fax 461564, e alaska@bariloche.com.ar, w www.visit bariloche.com/alaska; Lilinquen 328) Dorm beds US$8/10 low/high season. Bariloche's official HI facility is 7.5km west of town just off Av Bustillo; bus Nos 10, 20 & 21 drop passengers nearby. It has 44 beds, including three double rooms. Rates include kitchen privileges and laundry facilities; prices are slightly higher for nonmembers. Breakfast costs US$2 more. It also rents mountain bikes, and arranges tours and ski transfers.

Albergue Ruca Hueney (☎ 433986, 437026, rucahueney@bariloche.com.ar, Elflein 396) Dorm beds US$8-11, one double with private bath US$25. Run by its extremely helpful young owner, this small hostel has immaculate rooms, a good kitchen, a fireplace and Internet access. There's heaps of travel information around, and smoking is prohibited indoors.

La Bolsa de Deporte (☎/fax 423529, e bolsadep@bariloche.com.ar, Elflein 385) Dorm beds US$8-12. Perks here include kitchen privileges, a small climbing wall, ping-pong and lockers. Some rooms are cramped but the building itself is a work of art. Climbing information circulates freely.

Albergue Patagonia Andina (☎ 421861, e patagoniaandina@bariloche.com.ar, Morales 564) Dorm beds US$8-10 per person. This excellently located hostel is in an older house. Some rooms are small, but the common spaces are good. Rafting and trekking excursions can be arranged on site.

Casa de Familia Pirker (☎ 424873, 24 de Septiembre 230) Rooms US$10 per person, 1-bedroom apartment US$20. This place is quiet, friendly and comfortable, and the rooms are appealing.

Casa de Familia Arko (☎ 423109, Güemes 691) Rooms US$10 per person. Loving owner Señora Arko speaks German, English, French and Spanish and rents out rooms in two pleasant cottages behind her house. For US$5 you can pitch a tent in the backyard.

Hotel Los Andes (☎ 422222, Perito Moreno 594) Rooms US$12 per person, US$14 with bath. Only the rooms with shared bath have views. Beds are saggy and quarters a bit dismal.

Hospedaje Tito (☎ 424039, VA O'Connor 745) Rooms US$15 per person with bath. Unimpressive except for the price, this friendly place is often full.

Hotel 7 de Febrero (☎ 422244, Perito Moreno 534) Rooms US$15 per person. Though conventional, this modest hotel is an excellent value if you get an upper room with a view, and the staff is great.

Residencial Güemes (☎ 424785, Güemes 715) Doubles US$30 with bath. In the quiet neighborhood of Barrio Belgrano, this nondescript place is a good deal.

Mid-Range Prices for the following hotels all include private bathrooms.

Hostería El Ñire (☎ 423041, e elnire@bariloche.com.ar, John O'Connor 94) Singles/doubles US$25/35. A block from the cathedral, this inviting hostería has small rooms and friendly owners who speak English, French and German.

Hotel Panorámico (☎ 423468, Perito Moreno 646) Singles/doubles US$25/36. Open high-season only, this hotel is appealing for its views and moderate price.

Hotel Pucón (☎ 426164, Rolando 118) Singles/doubles US$25/40. The monstrous Hotel Pucón is very central, and rooms on the upper levels have views of the lakes.

Hostería El Radal (☎ 422551, 24 de Septiembre 46) Rooms US$25 per person with breakfast. A lush backyard and a lovely

common room make this family-run establishment particularly attractive.

Hotel Internacional (☎ 425938, Mitre 171) Singles/doubles US$30/40. The rooms here are crisp and clean, if not conventional; shoot for an upper level facing the lake for views.

Hostería Sur (☎ 422677, Beschtedt 101) Singles/doubles US$30/45 with breakfast. This hostería has very large beds in some very small rooms. The breakfast is generous.

Hostería La Sureña (☎ 422013, fax 424875, San Martín 432) Singles/doubles US$42/56 with breakfast. The small rooms are less appealing than the building's attractive chalet style suggests, but the owners are very friendly.

Hostería El Ciervo Rojo (☎ 43524f e ciervorojo@ciudad.com.ar, Elflein 115) Singles/doubles US$40/60 with breakfast. Book in advance if you'd like to shack up at this pleasant, attractively restored hostería. Upstairs rooms are superior to those downstairs. Dinner costs only US$5 extra.

Top End The **Hotel Aconcagua** (☎ 424718 San Martín 289) is a modern three-star hotel with spacious rooms and attractive bathrooms. However, at US$70/80 for singles/doubles, it is a bit overpriced.

Hotel Edelweiss (☎ 426165, e reservada @edelweiss.com.ar, San Martín 202) Doubles US$187. Even with a fourth-floor swimming pool, sauna, buffet breakfast, lake views and in-house masseurs, the price is still a kick in the pants.

Hotel Panamericano (☎/fax 425846/50 San Martín 536) Singles/doubles US$220 235. The Panamericano boasts a tenth-floor swimming pool with an attached health spa. This is Bariloche's most luxurious, complete with casino.

Places to Eat

Bariloche has some of Argentina's best food and it would take several wallet-breaking, belt-bursting and intestinally challenging weeks to sample all of the worthwhile restaurants. Regional specialties, including *jabalí* (wild boar), *ciervo* (venison) and *trucha* (trout), are especially worth watching out for. Note that most formal restaurants collect a *cubierto* (cover charge) for bread and cutlery.

Ahumadero Familia Weiss (☎ 435789, *Palacios & VA O'Connor*) Mains US$7-14. Specializing in smoked game and fish (as well as architectural extremism), Familia Weiss is a local favorite with live music on weekend nights.

La Vizcacha (☎ 422109, *Rolando 279*) This excellent parrilla offers pleasant atmosphere and outstanding service. Besides the usual beef, its standard parrillada for two includes chicken breast garnished with red peppers, deer pâté and Roquefort cheese spreads. With a liter of house wine the bill comes to about US$25 for two.

La Andina (☎ 423017, *Elflein 95*) This modest eatery serves cheap pastas and pizzas, savory empanadas and a decent US$5 plate of the day.

El Boliche de Alberto (☎ 431433, *Villegas 347*) It's worth dining at this esteemed parrilla simply to see the astonished look on tourists faces when a slab of beef the size of a football lands on the table; it's the US$10 *bife de chorizo* (the US$6 portion is plenty). Service is abrupt, but the meat is an experience. With wine and side dishes, the bill hits about US$20 a head.

Boliche de Alberto Pastas (☎ 431084, *Elflein 163*) Alberto does pastas almost as good as he does beef, and he follows suit with huge portions.

De la Granja (☎ 435939, *Villegas 216*) Mains US$9.50. Parrillada from US$6.50. This recommended eatery features farm-fresh ingredients at moderate prices.

La Esquina de las Flores (no ☎, *20 de Febrero 313*) The landmark Buenos Aires vegetarian restaurant and natural-foods market has a local branch.

El Vegetariano (☎ 421820, *20 de Febrero 730*) This cozy vegetarian restaurant serves sublime three-course set lunches and dinners, including tea, for US$10.

La Alpina (☎ 425693, *Perito Moreno 98*) Mains US$10-15. Open 10am-midnight. La Alpina has drawn praise for quality food; it's very cozy and good for coffee, tea, sweets and, surprisingly, *mate*, which is seldom found on restaurant menus.

El Viejo Munich (☎ 422336, *Mitre 102*) Befitting its name, El Viejo Munich has excellent draft beer, served with complimentary peanuts. The food is up to par as well.

Pilgrim (☎ 421686, *Palacios 167*) In atmosphere, Pilgrim approaches its self-proclaimed title of 'Celtic pub.' It serves Irish main dishes, Spanish tapas and a smattering of regional dishes. The local microbrews and imported ales are particularly appealing.

Días de Zapata (☎ 423128, *Morales 362*) Mains average US$10. The owners are from Mexico's Distrito Federal, so it's not surprising they turn out superb Mexican food, including three varieties of knock-out fajitas.

Cerros Nevados (☎ 436918, *Perito Moreno 388*) All-you-can-eat lunch/dinner US$8/10. This popular tenedor libre has a huge buffet and plenty of salad fixings.

Simoca (☎ 426467, *Palacios 264*) If you can't make it north for a bowl of *locro* (a hearty maize and tripe stew) you can get a delicious serving here for US$6 – cheap empanadas, tamales and pastas too.

Restaurant Cachari (no ☎, *Perito Moreno 802*) Set lunch US$4. The Italian-style food at this small family joint may not be gourmet, but it's wholesome, filling and cheap.

Helados Jauja (no ☎, *Perito Moreno 14*) This is easily some of Bariloche's best ice cream.

There are countless affordable pizzerías in Bariloche. Among them are **Cocodrilos** (☎ 426640, *Mitre 5*), **La Andinita** (☎ 422257, *Mitre 56*) and **El Mundo de la Pizza** (☎ 423461, *Mitre 759*). For moderately priced grilled meats and chicken, try **Rock Chicken** (☎ 424684, *Av San Martín 82*), and for cheap hot dogs and sandwiches try **Don Pancho** (no ☎, *Mitre 150*).

To stock up on your own supplies try **La Colina** (☎ 422925, *20 de Febrero 471*) for fresh fruits and vegetables; **La Quesería** (☎ 422398, *Palacios 294*) for cheese, olives and salami; and **Almacén Naturista Maná** (☎ 426021, *Neumeyer 40*) for health food and whole-grain breads.

Entertainment
Several over-the-top dance clubs along Av Juan Manuel de Rosas attract a younger

crowd and tend to be expensive, often charging up to US$25, though they generously throw in a drink. Among them are *Cerebro* (☎ 424965, Rosas 406), *Roket* (☎ 431940, Rosas 424) and *Grisú* (☎ 422269, Rosas 574). With a pseudo Egyptian interior, *By Pass* (☎ 420549, Rolando 155) is the latest disco craze.

Both *Pilgrim* and *El Viejo Munich* (see Places to Eat) are good for a relaxing beer or two and stay open fairly late. *Pub Moritz* (Mitre 1530) attracts folks around 25 to 30 years old, as does the fun *Pub 1970*, on Mitre between Emilio Frey and John O'Connor.

Shopping

Bariloche is renowned for its sweets and confections, and dozens of stores downtown, from national chains to mom-and-pop shops, sell chocolates of every style imaginable. The pair listed here are Bariloche institutions, fun for the eyes as well as the mouth.

Del Turista (no ☎, Mitre 239) This is a virtual supermarket of chocolate and a good place for a cheap stand-up cappuccino or hot chocolate, as well as dessert.

Fenoglio (☎ 423119, Mitre & Rolando) This is another big one with excellent chocolates.

Hand-made cutlery, especially knives with finely woven leather handles, are another good thing to buy in Bariloche. They're far from cheap, but you'll pay twice as much for them up north.

Paseo de los Artesanos (no ☎, Villegas & Perito Moreno) Open 10am-9pm daily. Local craftspeople display their wares of wool, wood, leather, silver and other media here.

Getting There & Away

Air Aerolíneas Argentinas/Austral, LADE and Southern Winds all have offices in the Via Firenze center at Quaglia 238/242, downtown.

Aerolíneas Argentinas (☎ 422425) flies to Buenos Aires (US$199) twice daily Monday through Wednesday and three times daily the rest of the week. LAPA (☎ 437685, Palacios 266) flies twice daily to Aeroparque (US$199).

LADE (☎ 423562) flies Monday to Neuquén (US$47) and Viedma (US$72); Wednesday to San Martín de los Andes

(US$20), Zapala (US$26) and Neuquén (US$33 to US$42), as well as to Mar del Plata (US$100 to US$130) and Buenos Aires (US$110); Thursday to El Bolsón (US$20) El Maitén (US$20) and Esquel (US$20) Friday to Esquel, Puerto Madryn (US$53) Trelew (US$53 to US$74) and Comodoro Rivadavia (US$60 to US$80), and to San Martín de los Andes, Neuquén, Viedma Bahía Blanca (US$81) and Buenos Aires.

October through April, Southern Winds (☎ 423704) flies to El Calafate (US$131) at 9am on Wednesday and at 11am Sunday, this flight continues to Ushuaia (US$130) – it's cheaper to fly to Ushuaia because of lower airport taxes. The company operates the same flight on Sunday only, May through September. On Tuesday, Thursday, Saturday and Sunday, Southern Winds also flies to Córdoba (US$144), Mendoza (US$150), Salta (US$184), Tucumán (US$172) and Rosario (US$144).

Bus Bariloche's bus terminal (☎ 426999) and train station are located across the Río Ñireco on RN 237. Shop around for the best deals, since fares vary and there are frequent promotions. During high season, it's wise to buy tickets at least a day in advance.

The principal route to Chile is over the Cardenal A Samoré (Puyehue) pass to Osorno (US$18) and Puerto Montt (US$19, 6 to 8 hours), which has onward connections to northern and southern Chilean destinations. Several companies, including Río de la Plata, Bus Norte, Tas-Choapa and Andesmar, make the run.

Buses heading north to San Juan (US$63 to US$72), La Rioja (US$74), Catamarca (US$86), Tucumán (US$89), Jujuy (US$106) and Salta (US$105) often involve a transfer and sometimes a long layover in Mendoza. Buses to northeastern destinations in Corrientes, Chaco and Misiones provinces usually connect through Buenos Aires, though you could also head to Rosario where there are frequent services northeast.

To San Martín de los Andes and Junín de los Andes, both Albus and Transportes Ko-Ko sometimes take the scenic (though often chokingly dusty) Siete Lagos route (RN 234), rather than the longer, paved La Rinconada (RN 40) route.

There are daily departures to the destinations in the following table. Regional destinations are served several times a day.

Destination	Duration in hours	Cost
Bahía Blanca	14	US$50
Buenos Aires	23	US$80
Comodoro Rivadavia	14	US$55
Córdoba	22	US$75
El Bolsón	2	US$8
El Maitén	3½	US$14
Esquel	4½	US$15
Junín de los Andes	4	US$16
Mendoza	19	US$57
Neuquén	6	US$20
Puerto Madryn	14	US$50
Río Gallegos	28	US$90
Rosario	23	US$76
San Martín de los Andes	4½	US$18
San Rafael	17	US$45
Santa Rosa	11	US$45
Trewlew	13	US$46
Viedma	16	US$45
Villa La Angostura	2	US$6

Train The train station is across the Río Ñireco on RN 237 next to the bus station. Departures for Viedma (16 hours) are Thursday and Sunday at 6pm; fares are US$20 turista, US$28 primera, US$46 Pullman. Departure times change frequently so it's best to check with the tourist office beforehand.

Boat Catedral Turismo (☎/fax 427143/44, 425444, ⓦ www.catedralturismo.com), Perito Moreno 238, is the representative for the Cruce de Lagos, the scenic bus and boat combination over the Andes to Puerto Montt, Chile (US$120, 12 hours). From Bariloche the journey begins with a 9am shuttle from Catedral's office to Puerto Pañuelo. The passenger ferry from Puerto Pañuelo leaves immediately after the shuttle arrives, so if you want to check out Llao Llao, you're better off getting there ahead of time on your own; tickets can be purchased at the dock. Service is daily in the summer and weekdays the rest of the year.

It is possible to do the trip in segments, or purchase the whole ticket and stretch out the trip over various days. Prices are: Bariloche to Puerto Pañuelo (US$5), Puerto Pañuelo to Puerto Blest (US$14), Puerto Blest to Puerto Frías (US$7), Puerto Frías to Peulla, Chile (US$60), Peulla to Petrohué (US$27), and Petrohué to Puerto Montt (US$7).

Fruits and vegetables are not allowed into Chile. Bicycles are allowed on the boats, but not on the buses, so cyclists will have to ride the stretches between Bariloche and Pañuelo (25km), Puerto Blest and Puerto Alegre (15km), Puerto Frías and Peulla (27km), and Petrohué and Puerto Montt (76km); the tourist office may have information about alternative transport between Petrohué and Puerto Montt for cyclists hoping to avoid the ride.

Though the trip rarely sells out, it's best to book it at least a day in advance.

Getting Around
To/From the Airport Bariloche's airport (☎ 422767) is 15km east of town via RN 237 and RP 80. Via Bariloche (☎ 429012) shuttles connects the airport with town (US$3, 15 minutes). Buses leave every hour to the airport, starting at 9:30am, from in front of the airline offices at Quaglia 242. A taxi or remise costs about US$10.

Bus At the main local bus stop, on Perito Moreno between Rolando and Palacios, Codao del Sur and Ómnibus 3 de Mayo run hourly buses during summer to Cerro Catedral for US$3 one-way. Codao uses Av de los Pioneros, while 3 de Mayo takes Av Bustillo. In summer 3 de Mayo goes four times daily to Lago Mascardi.

From 6am to midnight, municipal bus No 20 leaves the main bus stop every 20 minutes for the attractive lakeside settlements of Llao Llao and Puerto Pañuelo (US$2, 40 minutes). Buses No 10 and 11 also go to Colonia Suiza (US$2) 14 times daily. During summer, three of these, at 8:05am, noon and 5:40pm, continue to Puerto Pañuelo, allowing you to do the Circuito Chico (see Parque Nacional Nahuel Huapi, below) using inexpensive public transport. Departure times from Puerto Pañuelo back to Bariloche via Colonia Suiza are 9:40am, 1:40pm and 6:40pm. You can also walk any section and flag down buses en route.

Ómnibus 3 de Mayo buses No 50 and 51 go to Lago Gutiérrez (US$2) every 30 minutes, while in summer the company's 'Línea Mascardi' goes to Villa Mascardi (US$3.50) and Los Rápidos (US$5) three times daily. Their 'Línea El Manso' goes twice Friday and once Sunday to Río Villegas and El Manso (US$8), on the southwestern border of Parque Nacional Nahuel Huapi.

Buses No 70, 71 and 83 stop at the main bus stop, connecting downtown with the bus terminal (US$1).

Car Bariloche is loaded with the standard car-rental agencies. Try AI (☎ 422582, fax 427494), San Martín 235; Amúncar (☎ 431627, fax 423187), San Martín 82, 1st floor; Avis (☎ 431648, fax 431649), San Martín 130; and Budget (☎ 422482, fax 426700), Mitre 106, 1st floor.

PARQUE NACIONAL NAHUEL HUAPI
☎ 02944

One of Argentina's most visited national parks, Nahuel Huapi occupies 750,000 hectares in mountainous southwestern Neuquén and western Río Negro provinces. The park's centerpiece is Lago Nahuel Huapi, a glacial remnant over 100km long that covers more than 500 sq km. The lake is the source of the Río Limay, a major tributary of the Río Negro. To the west a ridge of high peaks separates Argentina from Chile; the tallest is 3554m Tronador, an extinct volcano that still lives up to its name (meaning 'Thunderer') when blocks of ice tumble from its glaciers. During the summer months, wildflowers blanket the alpine meadows.

Nahuel Huapi was created to preserve local flora and fauna, including its Andean-Patagonian forests and rare animals. Tree species are much the same as those found in Parque Nacional Los Alerces (see that section, later in this chapter), while the important animal species include the *huemul*, or Andean deer, and the miniature deer known as *pudú*. Most visitors are unlikely to see either of these, but several species of introduced deer are common, as are native birds. Native and introduced fish species offer excellent sport.

In 1904, Francisco Pascasio Moreno bequeathed the lands that make up Parque Nacional Nahuel Huapi to the Argentine state, stipulating that they 'be conserved as a natural public park' and emphasizing his

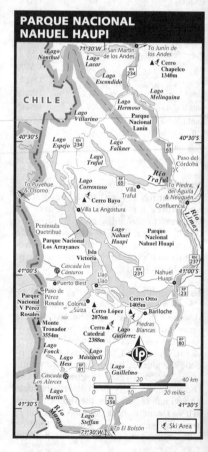

desire that 'the current features of their perimeter not be altered, and that there be no additional constructions other than those that facilitate the comforts of the cultured visitor.' At present, though, Argentina's oldest national park is reminiscent of Yosemite in the United States, attracting so many people that the very values Moreno expressed are at risk.

The US-based National Outdoor Leadership School (NOLS; ☎ 307-332-5300 in USA, ☒ www.nols.edu), 288 W Main St, Lander, WY 82520, runs a Semester in Patagonia program that lasts 75 days (university credit possible), taking place partly in Parque Nacional Nahuel Huapi. Most of the program takes place in Chile, however, where NOLS's base is the town of Coyhaique.

A good source of information about the park is the national park office in Bariloche (see Tourist Offices in the Bariloche section, earlier).

Books

For trekking maps and information about hiking in the region, see Lonely Planet's *Trekking in the Patagonian Andes*, by Clem Lindenmayer or, if you read Spanish, the locally published *Las Montañas de Bariloche*, by Toncek Arko and Raúl Izaguirre. Claudio Chehébar and Eduardo Ramilo's *Fauna del Parque Nacional Nahuel Huapi* (produced by the Administración de Parques Nacionales and Asociación Amigos del Museo de la Patagonia Francisco P Moreno) is a Spanish-language guide to the park's animal life.

Circuito Chico

One of the area's most popular and scenic excursions, the Circuito Chico begins on Av Bustillo, on Bariloche's outskirts, and continues on to the tranquil resort of **Llao Llao**, named for the 'Indian bread' fungus from the coihue tree. At **Cerro Campanario**, Av Bustillo Km 17, the Aerosilla Campanario (☎ 427274) lifts passengers to a panoramic view of Lago Nahuel Huapi for US$10.

Llao Llao's **Puerto Pañuelo** is the point of departure for the boat and bus excursion across the Andes to Chile, as well as to Parque Nacional Los Arrayanes on Penín-

sula Quetrihué, though you can visit Los Arrayanes more easily and cheaply from Villa La Angostura (see that section, earlier in this chapter).

Even if you don't plan to spend a night or two in the state-built **Hotel Llao Llao** (☎ 448530, fax 445781), Argentina's most famous hotel, take a stroll around the grounds. The hotel charges US$320 per double, or, with lake views, US$423, US$535 or US$622 depending on the room. 'Studios' cost US$498 per night, and a cabaña will set you back a mere US$650.

From Llao Llao you can double back to **Colonia Suiza**, named for its early Swiss colonists. A modest *confitería* has excellent pastries, and there are several *campgrounds*.

The road passes the trailhead to 2076m **Cerro López**, a three-hour climb, before returning to Bariloche.

At the top of Cerro López it's possible to spend the night at Club Andino Bariloche's **Refugio López** (☎ 423750 in Bariloche for reservations) where meals are also available (for more information see Places to Stay, later).

Although travel agencies offer the Circuito Chico as a tour (US$13 through most agencies in Bariloche), it's easily done on public transportation or, if you're up for a 60km peddle, by bicycle (see Getting Around and Activities in the Bariloche section).

Isla Victoria

In Lago Nahuel Huapi, Isla Victoria is a large island on which the Argentine park service trains park rangers, attracting students from throughout Latin America. Boats to Isla Victoria leave from Llao Llao's Puerto Pañuelo (US$22), or from Bariloche's Puerto San Carlos (US$30); neither include the US$3 park-entrance fee.

Cerro Otto

Cerro Otto (altitude 1405m) is an 8km hike on a gravel road west from Bariloche. There's enough traffic that hitching is feasible, and it's also a steep and tiring but rewarding bicycle route. The Teleférico Cerro Otto (☎ 441035), at Km 5 on Av de Los Pioneros, carries adult passengers to the summit for US$15, children for US$5; a free bus leaves from the corner of Mitre and Villegas or Perito Moreno and Independencia to the base of the mountain. Bring food and drink – prices at the summit confitería are truly extortionate.

Piedras Blancas (☎ *425720 interno 1708, Km 6 on the Cerro Otto road*) is the nearest ski area to Bariloche, and a popular area for summertime hiking.

There's a trail from Piedras Blancas to Club Andino's *Refugio Berghof* (☎ *424531, mobile 1560-3201*), at an elevation of 1240m; make reservations, since there are only 20 beds. Meals are available here. For more information, see Places to Stay, below. The refugio also contains the **Museo de Montaña Otto Meiling** (*guided visit US$1.50*), named for a pioneering climber.

Cerro Catedral

This 2388m peak, 20km southwest of Bariloche, contains the area's most important ski center, the **Centro de Deportes Invernales Antonio M Lynch**. Several chairlifts and the Aerosilla Cerro Bellavista (US$16) carry passengers up to 2000m, where there is a *restaurant/confitería* offering excellent panoramas.

There is a good mix of easy, intermediate and advanced skiing runs, with steep advanced runs at the top and some tree runs near the base. Lift lines can develop at this very popular resort, but the capacity is substantial enough that waits are not excessive.

Rates for lift passes vary from low to mid-to high season, starting at US$22 and going up to US$40 per day for adults, US$18 to US$32 for children. One-week passes entail substantial savings at US$110 to US$200 for adults, US$90 to US$160 for children. Basic rental equipment is cheap, but quality gear is more expensive.

Gran Catedral also has several ski schools at Villa Catedral, at the base of the lifts, including Robles Catedral (☎ 460050), Ski Club (☎ 460012) and Ski Total (☎ 460094).

The Aerosilla Cerro Bellavista also takes passengers up the mountain during summer, from 10am to 5pm daily except Monday. Several trekking trails begin near the top of the lift: One relatively easy four-hour walk goes to Club Andino's *Refugio Emilio Frey* (☎ *424831*), where 40 beds and simple meals are available. This refugio itself is exposed, but there are sheltered tent sites in what is also Argentina's prime **rock-climbing** area. For more information see Places to Stay, below.

Hostería del Cerro (☎ *460026*), at the base of the lifts, charges US$123/176 for singles/doubles in high season. Alternatively you can stay in Bariloche; public transport from there is excellent, consisting of hourly buses from downtown with Micro Ómnibus 3 de Mayo (see Getting Around in the Bariloche section, earlier).

Monte Tronador

Traveling via Lago Mascardi, it's a full-day trip up a dusty, single-lane dirt road to Pampa Linda to visit the Ventisquero Negro (Black Glacier) and the base of Tronador (3554m). Traffic goes up in the morning (until 2pm) and down in the afternoon (after 4pm). For US$12 one-way, US$20 return, the Club Andino Bariloche organizes summer transport to Pampa Linda daily at 9am, returning at 5pm, with Transporte RM (☎ 423918).

The area around Tronador resembles, in some ways, California's Yosemite Valley – you have to set your sights above the hotels, confiterías and parking lots to focus on the dozens of waterfalls that plunge over the flanks of the extinct volcanoes.

From Pampa Linda, hikers can approach the snowline Club Andino *Refugio Otto Meiling* (☎ *461861*) on foot and continue to Laguna Frías via the Paso de las Nubes; it's a five- to seven-hour walk to an elevation of 2000m. It's also possible to complete the trip in the opposite direction by taking Cerro Catedral's ferry from Puerto Pañuelo to Puerto Blest, and then hiking up the Río Frías to Paso de las Nubes before descending to Pampa Linda via the Río Alerce.

Climbers intending to scale Tronador should anticipate a three- to four-day technical climb requiring experience on rock, snow and ice. Hostería Pampa Linda (see below) arranges horseback riding in the area.

Places to Stay

In addition to those campgrounds in the immediate Bariloche area, there are sites at Lago Gutiérrez, Lago Mascardi, Lago Guillelmo, Lago Los Moscos, Lago Roca and Pampa Linda. Refugios charge US$6 per night, US$1.50 for day use, and US$3 extra for kitchen privileges.

Within the park are a number of hotels tending to the luxurious, though the moderately priced *Hostería Pampa Linda* (☎ 423757, 422181) charges US$25/40 for singles/doubles with breakfast off-season, US$45/60 in peak season from January through March. Meals are also reasonable; full board costs an additional US$24 per person. At *Hotel Tronador* (☎ 468127, fax 441062), at the northwest end of Lago Mascardi on the Pampa Linda road, doubles cost US$90 per person with half-board.

EL BOLSÓN

☎ 02944 • pop 20,000 • elevation 300m

The 42nd parallel defines the border between Río Negro and Chubut provinces and lends its name, Grado 42, to the mountains and fertile valley that surround El Bolsón, a laid-back little town synonymous with the ponytailed back-to-nature folks who began to flock here in the 1970s. Since then, El Bolsón became the first town in Argentina to declare itself a 'non-nuclear zone' and an 'ecological municipality.' The town welcomes backpackers, who often find it a relief from Bariloche's commercialism and find themselves stuffing their bellies with natural and vegetarian foods and the excellent beer, sweets, jams and honey made from the local harvest.

Rows of poplars lend a Mediterranean appearance to the local *chacras* (farms), most of which are devoted to hops (El Bolsón produces nearly three-quarters of the country's hops), soft fruits like strawberries and raspberries, and orchard crops like cherries and apples. The local economy relies on tourism, agriculture and forestry. Motorists should note that El Bolsón is the northernmost spot to purchase gasoline at Patagonian discount prices.

Orientation

Near the southwestern border of Río Negro province, El Bolsón lies in a basin surrounded by high mountains, dominated by the longitudinal ridges of Cerro Piltriquitrón to the east and the Cordón Nevado along the Chilean border to the west. On the east bank of the Río Quemquemtreu, it is roughly midway between Bariloche and Esquel, each about 130km via RN 258 from Bolsón. South of Bolsón, in Chubut Province, the road is either paved or being paved, while the stretch of road 90km north of Bolsón toward Bariloche is paved.

From the south, RN 258 enters town as the diagonal Av Belgrano and becomes north-south Av San Martín through town. The principal landmark is the ovoid Plaza Pagano, which has a small artificial (and often dry) lake. Most services are nearby.

Information

The tourist office (☎/fax 492604) is at Av San Martín and Roca, at the north end of Plaza Pagano. It has a good town map and brochures, plus thorough information on accommodations, food, tours and services. Maps of the surrounding area are crude at best. In summer, it's open 8am to 10pm weekdays, 9am to 10pm Saturday, and 10am to 10pm Sunday; the rest of the year, hours are 9am to 6pm. Visitors interested in the surrounding mountains – one of the best reasons for coming to Bolsón – can contact the Club Andino Piltriquitrón (☎ 492600, open January and February only), on Sarmiento between Roca and Feliciano. For

Feelin' Groovy

Strolling the streets of El Bolsón, you may find yourself feeling unusually centered, relaxed, calmed or downright better than usual. Look no further for explanation than Cerro Piltiquitrón, the jagged mountain east of town – it is said to be one of the earth's 'energy centers.' But keep your head together, for legend also has it that the area is frequently visited by OVNIs, Spanish for UFOs.

motorists, ACA (☎ 492260) is at Avs Belgrano and San Martín.

Banco de la Nación, at Av San Martín and Pellegrini, has an ATM.

The post office is at Av San Martín 2806; the postal code is 8430. For phone service, try Cooperativa Telefónica at Juez Fernández 429, at the south end of Plaza Pagano.

Radio Alas, at FM 89.1, is El Bolsón's community-based, free-form radio station, offering an outstanding mix of folk, blues, jazz and other programs.

Travel agencies include Patagonia Adventure (☎ 492513), at Pablo Hube 418, and Grado 42 (☎ 493124), Belgrano 406, which offers extensive trekking, mountain biking and other tours.

For laundry, try La Burbuja, at the corner of San Martín and Paso.

The hospital (☎ 492240) is on Perito Moreno, behind Plaza Pagano.

Feria Artesanal

Tuesday, Thursday and Saturday, local craftspeople sell their wares along the south end of Plaza Pagano from 10:30am to 3pm. The market boasts over 320 registered (and countless unregistered) artists, who make and sell everything from sculpted wooden cutting boards and hand-crafted *mate* gourds to jewelry, flutes and marionettes. With numerous food vendors, it's also an excellent (and affordable) opportunity to sample local delicacies.

Special Events

Local beer gets headlines during the Festival Nacional del Lúpulo (National Hops Festival), which takes place during four days in mid-February.

Places to Stay

Budget Budget travelers are more than welcome in El Bolsón, where reasonable prices are the rule rather than the exception. The tourist office maintains a list of private houses that offer lodging.

Camping Refugio Patagónico (mobile ☎ 15-635463, Islas Malvinas s/n) Sites US$4 per person, tents only. On the southeast end of Islas Malvinas, this pleasant campground

is only a skip from town. Shade is minimal but the apple trees and a nearby mountair make it a lovely spot. Showers are included

Camping La Chacra (☎ 492111) US$5 per person. Off Av Belgrano on the easterr edge of town, this campground is grassy anc partially shaded.

Albergue El Pueblito (☎ 493560, e pueblito@hostels.org.ar) Dorm beds US$8/9 HI members/nonmembers. Hourly local buses from town. This HI affiliate, abou 4km north of town in Barrio Luján, is a good place to meet Argentine backpackers. It's a friendly facility with beds for 40 people and places to camp as well.

Residencial Salinas (☎ 492396, Roca 641) Rooms US$10 per person with shared bath. Residencial Salinas is small, basic, friendly and very central. The upstairs room is cozy (but cold in winter). There's a communal stove and wash basin, and a small backyard.

Hospedaje Unelén (☎ 492729, Azcuénaga 134) Rooms US$10/12 per person with shared/private bath. This is a friendly no-frills place with a communal kitchen.

Hostería Steiner (☎ 492224, Av San Martín 670) Rooms US$15 per person with bath. On the southern outskirts of town, Hostería Steiner has been the home of its friendly Austrian owner since 1933. It sits on a beautiful, tree-filled lot with an expansive lawn and plenty of flowers. The newer rooms are motel-style with views of the garden, while those in the main building are more traditional. Breakfast and dinner are available.

Residencial Las Margaritas (☎ 493620, Güemes 480) Singles/doubles US$15/30 with breakfast & bath. Las Margaritas is pretty run-of-the-mill, but it's clean.

Mid-Range Even El Bolsón's mid-range accommodations are generally good values.

Residencial Valle Nuevo (☎ 492087, 25 de Mayo 2329) Doubles US$26. The rooms here do the trick, and some have kitchens.

La Posada de Hamelin (☎ 492030, e gcapece@elbolson.com, Granollers 2179) Singles/doubles US$25/35; breakfast US$3.50. Open Nov-Apr. This handsome hostería has only four rooms, each of them

EL BOLSÓN

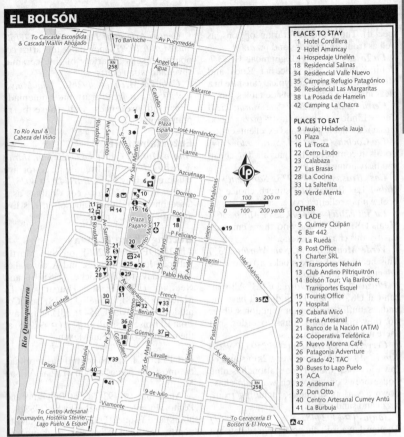

PLACES TO STAY
1 Hotel Cordillera
2 Hotel Amancay
4 Hospedaje Unelén
18 Residencial Salinas
34 Residencial Valle Nuevo
35 Camping Refugio Patagónico
36 Residencial Las Margaritas
38 La Posada de Hamelin
42 Camping La Chacra

PLACES TO EAT
9 Jauja; Heladería Jauja
10 Plaza
16 La Tosca
22 Cerro Lindo
23 Calabaza
27 Las Brasas
28 La Cocina
33 La Salteñita
39 Verde Menta

OTHER
3 LADE
5 Quimey Quipán
6 Bar 442
7 La Rueda
8 Post Office
11 Charter SRL
12 Transportes Nehuén
13 Club Andino Piltriquitrón
14 Bolsón Tour; Vía Bariloche; Transportes Esquel
15 Tourist Office
17 Hospital
19 Cabaña Micó
20 Feria Artesanal
21 Banco de la Nación (ATM)
24 Cooperativa Telefónica
25 Nuevo Morena Café
26 Patagonia Adventure
29 Grado 42; TAC
30 Buses to Lago Puelo
31 ACA
32 Andesmar
37 Don Otto
40 Centro Artesanal Cumey Antú
41 La Burbuja

delightfully cozy and with a private bath. Reserve ahead of time if you hope to stay.

Hotel Amancay (π/fax 492222, e amancay@red42.com.ar, Av San Martín 3217) Singles/doubles US$30/45 with private bath & breakfast. This is a clean, comfy, conventional hotel; it almost feels classy for El Bolsón.

Hotel Cordillera (π/fax 492235, e cordillerahotel@elbolson.com, Av San Martín 3210) Singles/doubles US$40/54. This three-star property is the biggest in town, with spacious rooms and good views from the upper floor.

Places to Eat

El Bolsón's restaurants lack Bariloche's variety, but the food is a consistently good value and often outstanding, thanks largely to fresh, local ingredients and careful preparation.

The *Feria Artesanal* (see listing, earlier) is by far the best, most economical place to eat. Goodies here include fresh fruit; Belgian waffles with berries and cream; huge empanadas for US$0.50, sandwiches, frittatas, *milanesa de soja* (soy patties), locally brewed beer and regional desserts.

Calabaza (π 492910, San Martín 2518) Breakfast at Calabaza, which starts around

US$2.50, is particularly delicious, though they do a good US$3.50 *plato del día* (daily special). There are vegetarian options, as well as trout, empanadas and pizza.

La Tosca (☎ 493669) Light meals US$3-7. Behind the tourist office at Roca and Moreno, La Tosca offers typical café fare in a pleasant atmosphere – outside tables, too.

Cerro Lindo (☎ 492899, *San Martín 2524*) Cerro Lindo has large, tasty pizzas, good music, reasonable prices and excellent service.

La Cocina (☎ 491453, *Sarmiento 2434*) Locals recommend this parrilla for cheap and tasty home cooking.

Las Brasas (☎ 492923, *Sarmiento & Hube*) Las Brasas is a superb choice for beef, with excellent service.

La Salteñita (☎ 493749, *25 de Mayo 2367*) Meals US$2-5. For spicy northern empanadas, try this cheap rotisserie.

Verde Menta (no ☎, *San Martín 2137*) This health-food store stocks a reasonable selection of whole foods.

Plaza (☎ 492136, *Dorrego 423*) All-you-can-eat US$7. While Plaza doesn't have the endless buffet that bigger tenedores libres do, they make many items to order, and there are good salad fixings.

Cervecería El Bolsón (☎ 492595, *RN 258 Km 123.9*) The local brewery, 2km south of town just past the service station, has nine house brews on tap, which will help chase down a variety of meals, including trout, pizza and sandwiches.

Jauja (☎ 492448, *San Martín 2867*) Though Jauja isn't cheap, its ingredients are first-rate, the preparation is excellent, the decor appealing, and the service agreeable. Its extensive menu includes pasta with tasty sauces, pizza, fish, vegetarian plates, homemade bread and locally brewed beer. Save room to gorge yourself on the astoundingly good homemade ice cream next door at *Heladería Jauja*, one of Argentina's very best.

Shopping
Besides the twice-weekly *Feria Artesanal*, there are several other outlets for local arts and crafts.

Centro Artesanal Cumey Antú (no ☎, *Av San Martín 2020*) Open 9am-1pm. This outlet sells high-quality Mapuche clothing and weavings.

Centro Artesanal Peumayén (☎ 491150, *San Martín 1059*) Open daily, this artist co-operative sells a variety of fine ceramic, silver and wood crafts.

Cabaña Micó (☎ 492691, *Isla Malvinas 2753*) For fresh fruit and homemade jams and preserves, visit these berry plantations.

Entertainment
Nuevo Morena Café (☎ 492725, *San Martín & Pablo Hube*) is a friendly place for live music, especially blues. *Bar 442* (☎ 492313, *Perito Moreno & Dorrego*) doubles as a disco on Friday nights and often has live music on Saturday nights.

Getting There & Away
Air LADE (☎ 492206), on San Martín between José Hernández and Azcona, flies Wednesday to Bariloche (US$20) and Neuquén (US$43); and Thursday to El Maitén (US$18), Esquel (US$18) and Comodoro Rivadavia (US$49). All flights leave from El Bolsón's small airport (☎ 492066) at the north end of Av San Martín.

Bus El Bolsón has no central bus terminal, but most companies are on or near Av San Martín.

Andesmar (☎ 492178), at Belgrano and Perito Moreno, goes to Bariloche (US$10, 2 hours) and Esquel (US$16, 3 hours), and to points north, usually with a change in Neuquén (US$42, 10 hours). Charter SRL (☎ 492333), at the corner of Sarmiento and Roca, also goes to Bariloche.

Via Bariloche is represented by Bolsón Tour (☎ 491676, *Roca 357*) and goes several times a day to Bariloche and Esquel and at least once a day to Buenos Aires. Transportes Esquel, at the same address, goes to Esquel on Tuesday and Friday at 8:30am.

TAC, represented by Grado 42 (☎ 493124, *Belgrano 406*), goes to Bariloche and Neuquén; the company sells tickets to Mendoza, Córdoba and other northern destinations, though you'll have to change buses in Neuquén.

Don Otto (☎ 493910), at the corner of Belgrano and Güemes, goes to Bariloche and Comodoro Rivadavia, with connections in Esquel for Trelew and Puerto Madryn.

Transportes Nehuén (☎ 491831), on Sarmiento near Roca, goes to El Maitén, Bariloche, Los Alerces and local destinations.

Getting Around

Bus Local bus service to nearby sights is extensive during the busy summer months, but sporadic in fall and winter. The tourist office provides up-to-date information.

Transportes Nehuén (☎ 491831), on Sarmiento near Roca, has summer buses to many local destinations.

La Golondrina (☎ 492557) goes to Cascada Mallín Ahogado, leaving from the south end of Plaza Pagano, while buses to Río Azul depart Bolsón Tour (☎ 492161), at Roca 359.

Quimey Quipán (☎ 499172), Perito Moreno 2960, sends roundtrip buses to Lago Puelo (US$3, 30 minutes) at 7am, 9:30am, 12:15pm, 3:30pm, 6pm and 9pm. The buses depart from the corner of San Martín and Sarmiento.

Taxi Taxis or remises are a reasonable mode of transport to nearby trailheads and campgrounds. Companies include Radio Taxi Glaciar (☎ 492892), Patagonia (☎ 493907) and Suremiss (☎ 492895).

AROUND EL BOLSÓN

The outskirts of El Bolsón offer numerous ridges, waterfalls and forests for hikers to explore. If you give yourself plenty of time, and pack food and water, some of the following places can be reached by foot from town, though buses and remises to trailheads are reasonable. **Mountain biking** is an excellent way to get out on your own; for rentals try La Rueda (☎ 492465, Sarmiento 2972), in El Bolsón. Rentals cost US$7/10 per half-day/day.

Cabeza del Indio

On a ridge-top 8km west of town, this metamorphic rock resembles a toothless hippie as much as it does a stereotypical profile of a 'noble savage,' from which the name 'Indian Head' was derived. The 7km trail up to the rock is reached by walking west on Azcuénaga from town. Part of it traverses a narrow ledge that offers the best views of the formation itself, but by climbing from an earlier junction you can obtain better views of the Río Azul and, in the distance to the south, Parque Nacional Lago Puelo.

Cascada Mallín Ahogado

This small waterfall, on the Arroyo del Medio, is 10km north of town, west of RN 258. Beyond the falls, a gravel road leads to Club Andino Piltriquitrón's *Refugio Perito Moreno (☎ 493912)*; it costs US$5-10 a night, and meals are an additional US$8. The refugio has capacity for 80 people.

From the refugio, it's 2½ hours to the 2206m summit of **Cerro Perito Moreno**. In winter, there's skiing at the Centro de Deportes Invernales Perito Moreno, where the base elevation is 1000m. The T-bar lifts reach 1450m.

Cascada Escondida

Downstream from the Cascada Mallín Ahogado, this waterfall is 8km from El Bolsón. There is a footpath beyond the bridge across the river at the west end of Av Pueyrredón.

Cerro Piltriquitrón

Dominating the landscape east of Bolsón, the 2260m summit of this granitic ridge yields panoramic views westward across the valley of the Río Azul to the Andean crest along the Chilean border. After driving or walking to the 1000m level (the 11km trip from El Bolsón costs about US$15 by taxi), another hour's steep, dusty walk leads through the impressive **Bosque Tallado (Sculpture Forest)** to the Club Andino's *Refugio Piltriquitrón (☎ 492024)*. Beds here are an outstanding value at US$6 per person, but bring your own sleeping bag. Moderately priced meals are available.

From the refugio a steep footpath climbs along the rusted tow bar, then levels off and circles east around the peak before climbing again precipitously up loose scree to the summit, marked by a brightly painted cement block. On a clear day, the tiring two-hour climb (conspicuously marked by paint blazes) rewards the hiker with views south beyond Lago Puelo, northwest to Cerro Tronador and, beyond the border, the snow-topped cone of Volcán Osorno in Chile. Water is abundant along most of the summit route, but hikers should carry a canteen and bring lunch to enjoy at the top.

Cerro Lindo

Southwest of Bolsón, a trail from Camping Río Azul goes to *Refugio Cerro Lindo* (☎ 492763), where you can get a bed for US$10; meals are extra. It's about four hours to the refugio, from which the trail continues to the 2150m summit.

El Hoyo

Just across the provincial border in Chubut, this town's microclimate makes it the local 'fresh fruit capital.' Nearby Lago Epuyén has good camping and hiking. For transport details, see El Bolsón's Getting There & Away section.

Parque Nacional Lago Puelo

In Chubut province, only 15km south of El Bolsón, this windy, azure lake is suitable for swimming, fishing, boating, hiking and camping. There are regular buses from El Bolsón in summer, but there's reduced service on Sunday and off-season, when you may have to hitch.

There are both free and fee campsites at the park entrance, including *Camping Lago Puelo* (☎ 499186), which charges US$5 per person.

The Argentine navy maintains a trailer close to the dock, where the launches *Juana de Arco* (☎ 493415) and *Popeye 2000* take passengers across the lake to Argentina's Pacific Ocean outlet at the Chilean border (US$10, 3 hours). From there it's possible to continue by foot or horseback to the Chilean town of Puelo on the Seno de Reloncaví,

with connections to Puerto Montt. This walk takes roughly three days; for details on guided trips, contact Grado 42 in El Bolsón (see that section's Information section).

For US$30, the launches also take passengers to El Turbio, at the south end of the lake, where there's a *campground*.

EL MAITÉN

☎ 02945 • pop 3000

In open range country on the upper reaches of the Río Chubut, about 70km southeast of El Bolsón, this small, dusty town is the end of the line for La Trochita, the old narrow-gauge steam train running between Esquel and El Maitén. It's also home to the work-shops for La Trochita and a graveyard of antique steam locomotives and other rail-road hardware – a train aficionado's dream and an exceptional subject for photography.

Every February, the Fiesta Provincial del Trencito commemorates the railroad that put El Maitén on the map and keeps it there; it now doubles as the Fiesta Nacional del Tren a Vapor (National Steam Train Festi-val). Drawing people from all over the prov-ince and the country, it features riding and horse-taming competitions, live music and superb produce and pastries, including homemade jams and jellies.

The *Camping Municipal*, directly on the river, charges US$2 per person, but gets crowded and noisy during the festival. *Hostería La Vasconia*, on the plaza across from the train station, charges about US$15 per person.

Getting There & Away

Transportes Jacobsen buses connect El Maitén with Esquel at 8am Monday, Tuesday, Friday and Saturday. There's also regular minibus service to and from El Bolsón with Transportes Nehuén.

La Trochita (☎ 495190) goes to Esquel (US$25, about 6½ hours) at 2pm Wednes-day; it departs Esquel for El Maitén at 11am Thursday.

Patagonia

Exploring southern Patagonia in 1878, Lady Florence Dixie wrote 'Without doubt there are wild countries more favoured by Nature in many ways. But nowhere else are you so completely alone. Nowhere else is there an area of 10,000 square miles which you may gallop over, and where…you are safe from the persecutions of fevers, friends… telegrams, letters and every other nuisance you are elsewhere liable to be exposed to.'

Although its name evokes images of jagged mountains, crashing glaciers and roaring rivers, Patagonia's most present characteristic is its endless expanse of nothingness, both an attraction and a lesson in boredom for the overland traveler. The RN 40, which parallels the Andes, is the great adventure, passing by some of the best archaeological gems in the region, the most inaccessible parts of the country and the awesome jagged peaks of the Fitz Roy Range. The RN 3 along the eastern seaboard is a yawn of a long haul through the region's most historic and industrial area, accessing marine reserve Península Valdés, the Welsh settlements, petrified forests and historic oceanfront towns. A few roads connect the two highways, creating a graph of quirky towns, estancias and isolated outposts that just might be the most Patagonia of all. Ask locals what's best about Patagonia and most speak of the sky: Sunrises and sunsets cast endless streaks of amber and red, and night skies drip with stars.

This chapter covers the region from its political beginnings at Río Negro, skipping to the area south of Río Chubut and covering the vast region through the provinces of Chubut and Santa Cruz to the Strait of Magellan. Chilean Patagonia's main cities of Puerto Natales and Punta Arenas are included, as is Torres del Paine.

History

The origin of Patagonia's name is obscure, but one theory asserts that it derives from the region's native inhabitants, encountered

Highlights

- Peninsula Valdés – Watching southern right whales majestically breach and calves play at Puerto Pirámides

- RN 40 – Bumping down the fabled road or stopping in rickety bars to catch a drink or two

- Parque Nacional Los Glaciares – Hiking with the Fitz Roy range looming beside you

- Glaciar Perito Moreno – Creaking, crashing icebergs calving off this, one of the few advancing glaciers in the world

- Estancias – Participating at a sheep ranch or just watching others do the work or feasting on lambchops while soaking up stories of the land

Neuquén • La Pampa

Patagonia page 461   Carmen de Patagones & Viedma page 463

Río Negro

Parque Nacional Los Alerces page 518   Reserva Faunística Península Valdés page 475   Puerto Madryn page 468

Esquel page 511   Trelew page 478

Chubut

Comodoro Rivadavia page 491   ATLANTIC OCEAN

CHILE   Santa Cruz   Puerto Deseado page 495

The Fitz Roy Area page 526

Around El Calafate & PN Los Glaciares page 536

El Calafate page 533

Río Gallegos page 503

Parque Nacional Torres del Paine page 559   Puerto Natales page 554

Punta Arenas pages 540–541

PACIFIC OCEAN

by Magellan's crew as they wintered in 1520 at Bahía San Julián, in the present-day province of Santa Cruz. According to this explanation, the Tehuelche Indians, tall of stature and wearing moccasins that made their feet appear exceptionally large, may have led Magellan to apply the name after the Spanish word *pata*, meaning paw or foot. On encountering the Tehuelche, Antonio Pigafetta, an Italian nobleman on Magellan's crew, remarked that one of them:

> was so tall we reached only to his waist, and he was well proportioned.... He was dressed in the skins of animals skillfully sewn together.... His feet were shod with the same kind of skins, which covered his feet in the manner of shoes.... The captain-general (Magellan) called these people Patagoni.

Another theory speculates that Magellan may have adopted the term 'Patagón,' the name of a fictional monster from a Spanish romance of the period, and applied it to the Tehuelche. In another parallel to the romance, Magellan abducted two locals to take them to Spain, but one escaped and the other died en route.

The Tehuelche were divided into geographic groups: the Günün-A-Künna, living in the region from Neuquén to Río Chubut, and the Aonikenk, south to the Strait of Magellan. Aonikenk subsisted mainly on guanaco and ñandú, moving around depending on the hunt. Each place chosen to set up camp was called *aike,* a term used in many places around Patagonia. In present-day Chilean Patagonia, Alacaluf and Aonikenk avoided contact with Europeans until the late 1800s.

Starting in the early 16th century, the gold-hungry Spanish spread tales of Trapalanda, an austral El Dorado somewhere in the southern Andes, but no early expedition had ever found it or even ventured very deep into the region. Instead the Spanish established strategic ocean-fronting outposts and a whaling station at Puerto Deseado.

Even after independence opened South America to visitors from countries other than Spain, Patagonia was among the last thoroughly explored areas, and the arid, windy *meseta* (tableland) failed to attract

Europeans until the big wool boom in the mid-1800s. When purebred sheep brought over from the Falkland Islands as an experiment prospered on the supposedly worthless land in southern Santa Cruz province, 'white gold' fever took over. By the early 18th century nearly two million animals, used for wool and meat, grazed the area. Pioneers from Scotland and the Falklands soon came to take advantage of the new economy. As more land was opened to sheep grazing, the Tehuelche were further threatened. In efforts to free up the land of the indigenous people, in 1879 General Julio Argentino Roca carried out a ruthless war of extermination against the region's first inhabitants, known as the Conquista del Desierto (Conquest of the Desert). This 'war' doubled the area under state control and opened up Patagonia to settlement. Eager to occupy the area before the Chileans could, the Argentine government made enormous land grants that became the large sheep *estancias* (ranches) that still occupy much of the area today.

Responding to the brutality towards the indigenous and hoping to 'save' as many as they could, Salesian order missionaries began to penetrate the region. In a sad 'help strikes again' scenario, it is possible that offering refuge to the indigenous further helped the military's and landowners' efforts of their extermination.

Today the area is only thinly populated. In the province of Santa Cruz, about 160,000 people live in the almost 244,000 hectares sq. In other words, there is less than one person per sq km – one of the lowest population densities in the world.

Geography & Climate

All of Argentine Patagonia lies in the rain shadow of the Chilean Andes, which block most Pacific storms. After the storms drop their snow and rain on the seaward slopes of the Andes in Chile, the powerful dry westerlies blow almost incessantly across the semi-arid to arid Patagonian plains. Because of oceanic influence where the South American continent tapers toward the south, the region's climate is generally temperate, but winter temperatures can drop well below

freezing. The Campo de Hielo Sur (Southern Continental Ice Field), extending from Chile into parts of Argentina, is the site of the two countries' last remaining border dispute.

The Río Santa Cruz, born in the Fitz Roy Range and the glacial troughs of Lago Viedma and Lago Argentino, slices through the steppe to form a deep, broad, and scenic canyon, eventually reaching the sea at Puerto Santa Cruz.

Economy

The region's most traditional economic feature, the sprawling sheep estancia, has taken a mighty blow in the last decade; the 1991 eruption of Volcán Hudson on the Chilean side of Lago Buenos Aires covered vast areas in volcanic ash, causing the death of much livestock for lack of forage. A severe winter in 1995 further deepened the plight. Plunging wool prices since then have caused many estancias to close and others to re-identify themselves as tourist destinations. Some, in response, have sold out to corporate investors like Benetton, while others have passed into the hands of high-profile figures, often US movie stars, for their personal pleasure.

Eclipsing wool as the main economic contribution is the large supply of fossil fuel tapped throughout the region. Oil fields near Comodoro Rivadavia in Chubut help make Argentina self-sufficient in petroleum, and the country even exports some to neighboring countries.

Coastal Patagonia (Along RN 3)

Argentina's coastal RN 3 cuts through some of the most dreary landscape in Patagonia, from Carmen de Patagones to Río Gallegos. Stretches from one town to the next can be long and boring, but highlights there are, especially for wildlife and history buffs. Península Valdés, accessed from Puerto Madryn, is world-renowned for its sheltered bays where Atlantic right whales come from June to September. Reserva Provincial Punta Tombo and Cabo Dos Bahías have some of the largest colonies of Magellanic penguins, which flock to the shores from December to March. Río Deseado is habitat to an exceptional variety of seabirds.

The region's history of settlement is apparent at the Welsh settlements of Trelew and Gaiman, while Puerto San Julián is the bay at which Magellan first encountered the Tehuelche that inspired the name Patagonia. For those with their own transportation, petrified forests near Colonia Sarmiento and south of Caleta Olivia are worthwhile stops, as are estancias around Río Gallegos. Those cruising up or down this eastern seaboard by bus should note that schedules are based on Buenos Aires, departing and arriving in some towns in the dead of night.

CARMEN DE PATAGONES
☎ 02920 • pop 17,300

The historic gateway to Patagonia, Carmen de Patagones is the southernmost city in Buenos Aires province, sitting 950km south of Buenos Aires via RN 3. Well-preserved buildings and steep cobble streets speak to its historic founding in 1779, when Francisco de Viedma founded both the town of Viedma and a fort along this northern shore of the river. The first colonists to arrive hailed from the first the Spanish county of Maragatería in León (townspeople were called *maragatos*, a moniker that survives today) and built their first dwellings in the side of the hills. Carmen de Patagones claim to fame came in 1827, when their smaller and less-equipped forces repelled superior invaders during the war with Brazil.

Information

The city's municipal tourist office (☎ 461777 interno 253, e dirturpatagones@infovia .com.ar, Bynon 186) is open 7am to 9pm weekdays and, in summer only, 10am to 1pm and 4pm to 9pm weekends.

Banco de la Nación, at Paraguay 2, and Banco de Buenos Aires have ATMs. The post office is at Paraguay 38; the postal code is 8504. Locutorio 1 is at Olivera 9, Locutorio 2 at Rivadavia 379.

ARGENTINA

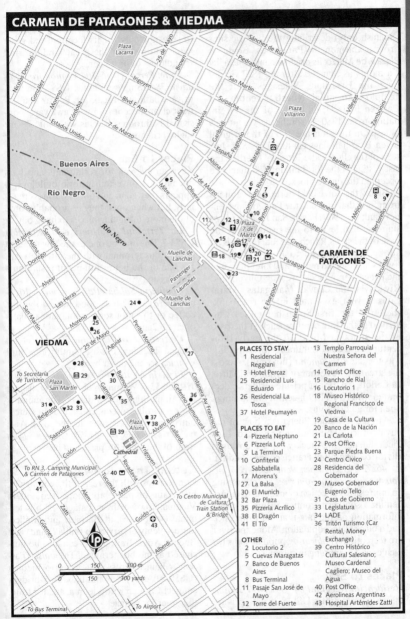

CARMEN DE PATAGONES & VIEDMA

PLACES TO STAY
1 Residencial Reggiani
3 Hotel Percaz
25 Residencial Luis Eduardo
26 Residencial La Tosca
37 Hotel Peumayén

PLACES TO EAT
4 Pizzería Neptuno
6 Pizzería Loft
9 La Terminal
10 Confitería Sabbatella
17 Morena's
27 La Balsa
30 El Munich
32 Bar Plaza
35 Pizzería Acrílico
38 El Dragón
41 El Tío

OTHER
2 Locutorio 2
5 Cuevas Maragatas
7 Banco de Buenos Aires
8 Bus Terminal
11 Pasaje San José de Mayo
12 Torre del Fuerte
13 Templo Parroquial Nuestra Señora del Carmen
14 Tourist Office
15 Rancho de Rial
16 Locutorio 1
18 Museo Histórico Regional Francisco de Viedma
19 Casa de la Cultura
20 Banco de la Nación
21 La Carlota
22 Post Office
23 Parque Piedra Buena
24 Centro Civico
28 Residencia del Gobernador
29 Museo Gobernador Eugenio Tello
31 Casa de Gobierno
33 Legislatura
34 LADE
36 Tritón Turismo (Car Rental, Money Exchange)
39 Centro Histórico Cultural Salesiano; Museo Cardenal Cagliero; Museo del Agua
40 Post Office
42 Aerolineas Argentinas
43 Hospital Artémides Zatti

Things to See & Do

The tourist office distributes brochures (Spanish only) describing the historic sites around Carmen de Patagones. Begin at **Plaza 7 de Marzo**; its original name, Plaza del Carmen, was changed after the 1827 victory over the Brazilians. Salesians built the **Templo Parroquial Nuestra Señora del Carmen** in 1883; its image of the Virgin, dating from 1780, is southern Argentina's oldest. On the altar are two of the original seven Brazilian flags captured in 1827. Just west of the church, the **Torre del Fuerte** is the last vestige of the fort built in 1780 that once occupied the entire block.

Below the Torre del Fuerte, twin cannons from forts that guarded the Patagonian frontier flank the 1960s **Pasaje San José de Mayo** staircase that leads to the riverside. At the base of the steps, **Rancho de Rial** (1820) is an adobe that belonged to Juan J Rial, the town's first elected mayor and later justice of the peace. Three blocks west on Olivera and Rivadavia, the **Cuevas Maragatas** (Maragatas Caves), excavated in the riverbank, sheltered the first Spanish families who arrived in the 18th century. Back at the base of the stairs, at Mitre 27, the early-19th-century **Casa de la Cultura**, restored in 1981, was the site of a *tahona* (flourmill). Across the street, at the corner of Bynon and Mitre, **La Carlota** is a former private residence decorated with typical 19th-century furnishings, open for guided tours.

At **Parque Piedra Buena** is a bust of the naval officer and Patagonian hero Luis Piedrabuena. One block west is the **Museo Histórico Regional Francisco de Viedma**, (☎ 462729; US$1; open 9am-noon & 7pm-9pm weekdays, 7pm-9pm weekends), housing an impressive collection of artifacts from Argentina's southern frontier, including some information on the fact that the town once had a black slave population. Along the river are recreational *balnearios*, popular spots for picnics and swimming in summer.

Places to Stay

Residencial Reggiani (☎ 15-608619, Bynon 422) Singles/doubles US$18/28 with private bath and breakfast. In a comfortable, rambling family house, Reggiani is a great place to stay, not only for its location and good value, but also for the great kindness and friendliness of its owner.

Hotel Percaz (☎ 464104, Comodoro Rivadavia 384) Singles/doubles US$23/36 with private bath and breakfast. Percaz is a no-frills, clean, decent spot with awkwardly designed bathrooms. Rooms with out TV are slightly cheaper.

Places to Eat

Keep an eye out for restaurants and bars opening in converted historic buildings; it appears they go in and out of business regularly, but when open they're probably some of the more intriguing places to hang out.

La Terminal (Barbieri & Bertorello) US$3-7. This may be one of the few times to go to a bus terminal with the intent to eat. It's one of the better full-menu restaurants and fills up.

Confitería Sabbatella (Comodoro Rivadavia 218) US$2-6. A good place to go for coffee or to shoot some pool, Sabbatella is open till 2am.

Pizzería Loft (Alsina 70) US$4-10. Closed Tuesday. Pizzas, hamburgers and *minutas* are the order here.

Pizzería Neptuno (Comodoro Rivadavia 310) US$3-8. Within an old building, fishing nets drape high above diners. The menu is basic – tortillas, pizzas, chicken dishes, etc – but reported to be consistently good. Also try out ***Morena's*** (☎ 461378, Olivera 11) in front of the plaza for pizza and beers.

Getting There & Away

Connections with the rest of the country by bus, train, or plane are more frequent in Viedma; however from Patagones' bus terminal (☎ 462666), at Barbieri and Méjico, there's plenty of service to Bahía Blanca and Buenos Aires. Train tickets can also be purchased at the bus terminal. The *balsa* (passenger launch) crosses the river to Viedma (US$0.50) every few minutes. Two bridges connect Carmen with Viedma, one for train, the other for vehicles.

VIEDMA
☎ 02920 • pop 79,000

Río Negro's provincial capital, Viedma, 960km from Buenos Aires and 275km south of Bahía Blanca, plays second fiddle to majestic Carmen de Patagones, but it is a compact practical base, with more traveler services and bus connections. In 1779, with his men dying of fever and lack of water at Península Valdés, Francisco de Viedma put ashore to found the city that would later take his name. In 1879 it became the residence of the governor of Patagonia and the political and administrative locus of the country's enormous southern territory. A century later, in the 1980s, the Alfonsín administration proposed moving the federal capital here from Buenos Aires.

Information
The tourist office (☎ 427171) is in the Centro Municipal de Cultura, on Av Viedma between 7 de Marzo and Urquiza. It's open all year: from 9am to 9pm daily in summer, with shorter hours the rest of the year. There's also an office at the bus terminal with lodging and transport information, open daily.

The provincial Secretaría de Turismo (☎ 422150, fax 421249), Caseros 1425, has brochures and information for the whole province. ACA (☎ 422441) is at Blvd Heroes de Malvinas 962. Tritón Turismo (☎ 430129), Namuncurá 78, changes money and rents cars.

The post office is at Rivadavia 151; the postal code is 8500. Internet access is available at bargain prices at the Centro de Cultura from 9am to 12:30pm weekdays only; closed in January. Hospital Artémides Zatti (☎ 422333) is at Rivadavia 351.

Things to See & Do
Tehuelche tools, artifacts, and human remains, as well as exhibits on European settlement, are on display at the Museo Gobernador Eugenio Tello (no ☎, San Martín 263; open 9am-noon weekdays), which also functions as a research center in architecture, archaeology, physical and cultural anthropology and geography.

The Centro Histórico Cultural Salesiano (Colón & Rivadavia) in the former Vicariato de la Patagonia, a massive 1890 brick structure, houses the Museo Cardenal Cagliero (☎ 424190, Rivadavia 34; open 7am-2pm weekdays), which tells the story of the Salesian order, plus the Museo del Agua, del Suelo y del Riego (☎ 431569, Colón 498; open 9am-11am weekdays), where you can learn more than you'll probably ever need to know about the region's water systems.

The tourist office can arrange city walking tours and tours to nearby attractions for US$40-80, depending on group size and time. Tritón Turismo does the same. River cruises may be available; ask individual launch operators at the pier.

Special Events
The Regata del Río Negro, in the second half of January, includes a weeklong kayak race that begins in Neuquén and ends in Viedma, a distance of about 500km.

Places to Stay
Camping Municipal (☎ 421341) US$4 per person plus one-time US$4 fee per tent. This friendly riverside campground about 10 blocks west of RN 3 is easily reached by Comarca bus from downtown. The partially shaded grounds are tidy, though some plots are poorly marked. Beware mosquitoes in summer.

Residencial La Tosca (☎ 428508, Alsina 349) Singles/doubles US$20/35 to US$25/40. By far the best choice in town, all rooms have private baths, breakfast is included and the pleasant staff is very helpful. The next-door gym hosts basketball matches, so some evenings can be a bit noisy.

Residencial Luis Eduardo (☎ 420669, Sarmiento 366) Singles/doubles US$25/35. Rooms at Luis Eduardo come with satin bedcovers, gaudy tiles and small bathrooms, although some have bathtubs.

Hotel Peumayén (☎ 425234, Buenos Aires 334) Singles/doubles US$33/55 weekdays, US$23/38 weekends. This is where the business and banking set stay when in town. Peumayén offers professional service, but the higher weekday rate can be a turnoff. Try for a room overlooking the plaza, or for one on the 4th floor.

Places to Eat

Pizzería Acrílico (☎ 421530, Saavedra 326) US$4-10. Locals mob this pizzeria in the evening; it has flashy decor, good pizza and mid-range prices, although pasta dishes are bit steep.

El Munich (☎ 421108, Buenos Aires 161) US$5. The best meal here is a heaping bowl of fresh homemade pastas, especially gnocchi. A plateful, jug of house wine and dessert will put you back less than US$7.

El Tío (Av Zatti & Colón) US$4-13. Closed Monday. A fun old restaurant charmed with tradition, El Tío serves up all the usual fare.

La Balsa (☎ 431974, Av Villarino) US$7-12. With views over the river and attentive service, La Balsa is a top pick for a more formal meal.

El Dragón (Buenos Aires 366) US$5-7. The good buffet spread keeps this place busy with locals during lunch and dinner. The vegetables are fresh and the Chinese dishes palatable; drinks aren't cheap, though.

Bar Plaza (Belgrano & Tucumán) Bustling with the government pros whining about the economy over a Marlboro and coffee, Bar Plaza is a good place to get a feel for the heart of Viedma.

Getting There & Away

Air Aerolíneas Argentinas (☎ 423033), Mitre 402, flies on weekdays to Buenos Aires (US$109 to US$167). LADE (☎ 424420), Saavedra 403, flies in and out of Viedma en route to most nearby cities. Sample prices are Puerto Madryn (US$28), Mar del Plata (US$57), Bariloche (US$72) and Buenos Aires (US$80). Check the airlines for latest schedules and itineraries.

Bus Viedma's bus terminal (☎ 426850) is 13 blocks south of downtown, at Guido 1580 and Av General Perón. Companies include El Cóndor (☎ 423714), Fredes Turismo (☎ 430578), Ceferino (☎ 426691), 3 de Mayo

(☎ 425839), Las Grutas (☎ 425952), in addition to Tus-Andesmar (425952), Transporte Mansilla (☎ 421385), Transportadora Patagónica (425952) and Transporte El Valle (☎ 427501). To Puerto Madryn, Don Otto and El Cóndor offer the best service. To Bariloche, 3 de Mayo goes via Ruta 23, while El Valle takes Ruta 22 then Ruta 6, making lots of stops along the way.

To get to Balneario El Cóndor (US$2) and La Lobería (US$4), Ceferino leaves from Plaza Alsina six times daily in summer, three times daily the rest of the year.

Destination	Duration in hours	Cost
Bahía Blanca	4	US$13
Bariloche	14	US$40-52
Buenos Aires	13	US$35-55
Comodoro Rivadavia	10	US$37
Esquel	10	US$32
La Plata	12	US$34
Las Grutas	2½	US$10
Neuquén	8	US$20-30
Puerto Madryn	5	US$16-20
Trelew	5½	US$22

Train From Estación Viedma, on the southeast outskirts of town, Sefepa (☎ 422130) runs westbound trains to Bariloche (16½ hours) and all towns en route at 6pm Wednesday and Sunday in summer, and Monday and Friday at 6pm the rest of the year. Fares are US$20 primera, US$46 Pullman, US$66 bed; children aged five to 12 pay half.

Getting Around

Aeropuerto Gobernador Castello (☎ 422001) is 15km southwest of town on RP 51. There's no airport bus service; a cab or *remise* costs about US$7. From the pier at the foot of 25 de Mayo, a *balsa* (passenger launch) connects Viedma to Carmen de Patagones (US$0.50) 6:30am to 10pm weekdays, 7am to 9pm Saturday, and 9am to 9pm Sunday. Tritón Turismo (☎ 430129, Namuncurá 78) rents cars.

COASTAL RÍO NEGRO

Río Negro's 400km of coastline teems with activity in the summer, but closes down the rest of the year. Coined as La Ruta de los Acantilados (Route of the Cliffs), this stretch of coastline's beauty resides in the majestic cliffs, some 20m high and accumulated between 3 and 13 million years ago. As the ocean batters the cliff faces, a treasury of fossils, mainly mollusks and bivalves, has been found. At **Balneario El Cóndor**, a resort 32km from Viedma, a large breeding colony of burrowing parrots makes its home in the cliff faces, but the main draw is the century-old lighthouse, Patagonia's oldest. Lodging includes *Camping Ina Lauquen* (☎ 430249) for US$2.50 per person, but expect motorhomes, and *Hospedaje Río de los Sauces* (☎ 497193) for US$20 per person.

Sixty kilometers from Viedma via RP 1, on the north coast of Golfo San Matías, the **Reserva Faunística de Punta Bermeja (La Lobería)** offers good lookouts to view a permanent colony of about 2000 southern sea lions. Peak numbers can be seen during the spring mating season, when fights between males are common as they come ashore to establish harems of up to 10 females each. From December onward, the females give birth. The observation balcony, directly above the mating beaches, is safe and unobtrusive. Barren and windy *Camping La Lobería* charges US$2 per person and per tent.

At the northwestern edge of the Golfo San Matías, 179km west of Viedma along RN 3, the crowded resort of **Las Grutas** owes its name (The Grottos) to the caves that the sea has eroded in the cliffs. Because of an exceptional tidal range, the beaches can expand for hundreds of meters or shrink to just a few. The tourist office (☎ 02934-497470) at Galería Antares, Primera Bajada, has information on accommodations. Buses leave hourly to San Antonio Oeste, 15km away, with more lodging and services.

Sierra Grande, 125km south of Las Grutas, has two things going for it: gasoline at *precios patagónicos* – less than half the price in Las Grutas/San Antonio Oeste – and tours of abandoned coalmines. Given that, it's easy to fill up the tank or grab a quick snack (all northbound buses stop here) and carry on.

PUERTO MADRYN
☎ 02965 • pop 60,000

Nestled in a protected cove on the Golfo Nuevo, Puerto Madryn is most known as a jumping-off point to the wildlife sanctuary of Península Valdés, but has its own allure as an active beach town. Porteños come here to escape city chaos, while tourists from all corners come to catch glimpses of the town's biggest attraction: the visiting right whales. Madryn's campus of the Universidad de la Patagonia is known for its marine biology department, while ecological centers in town promote education and conservation. On the flip side, Madryn is now the country's second-largest fishing port and is home to Aluar, Argentina's first aluminum plant, built in 1974.

Founded by Welsh settlers in 1886, the town takes its name from Love Parry, Baron of Madryn. A couple of statues along the *costanera* (beach road) pay tribute to the Welsh: one to the role women have played, and the other, at the far south end of town, to the Tehuelche, to whom the Welsh were much indebted for their survival.

Orientation

Puerto Madryn is just east of RN 3, 1371km south of Buenos Aires, 439km north of Comodoro Rivadavia, and 65km north of Trelew. The hub of activity spreads along the beach sidewalk and the two main parallel avenues – Roca and 25 de Mayo – which, along with Yrigoyen (leads to the bus terminal) and Gales (leads to RN 3) constitute the center of town. Blvd Brown is the main drag alongside the beaches to the south.

Information

The tourist office (☎ 453504, 452148, e muni cipio_madryn@cpsarg.com) at Av Roca 223, near the corner of 28 de Julio, is open 7am to 10pm daily from mid-December to mid-March, but the rest of the year hours are 7am to 1pm and 3pm to 9pm weekdays, 8am to noon and 4:30pm to 8:30pm weekends. The staff is helpful and efficient, and there's usually an English speaker on duty. Useful and entertaining tips from travelers can be found in the *libro de reclamos*. During the

PUERTO MADRYN

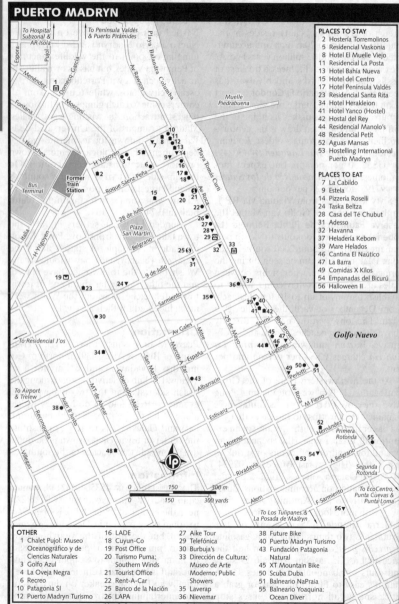

PLACES TO STAY
2 Hostería Torremolinos
5 Residencial Vaskonia
8 Hotel El Muelle Viejo
11 Residencial La Posta
13 Hotel Bahía Nueva
15 Hotel del Centro
17 Hotel Península Valdés
23 Residencial Santa Rita
34 Hotel Herakleion
41 Hotel Yanco (Hostel)
42 Hostal del Rey
44 Residencial Manolo's
48 Residencial Petit
52 Aguas Mansas
53 Hostelling International
   Puerto Madryn

PLACES TO EAT
7 La Cabildo
9 Estela
14 Pizzería Roselli
24 Taska Beltza
28 Casa del Té Chubut
31 Adesso
32 Havanna
37 Heladería Kebom
39 Mare Helados
46 Cantina El Naútico
47 La Barra
49 Comidas X Kilos
54 Empanadas del Bicurú
56 Halloween II

Golfo Nuevo

To Residencial J'os

To Airport
& Trelew

To Los Tulipanes &
La Posada de Madryn

To EcoCentro,
Punta Cuevas &
Punta Loma

Primera
Rotonda

Segunda
Rotonda

0	150	300 m
0	150	300 yards

OTHER
1 Chalet Pujol: Museo
   Oceanográfico y de
   Ciencias Naturales
3 Golfo Azul
4 La Oveja Negra
6 Recreo
10 Patagonia SI
12 Puerto Madryn Turismo
16 LADE
18 Cuyun-Co
19 Post Office
20 Turismo Puma;
   Southern Winds
21 Tourist Office
22 Rent-A-Car
25 Banco de la Nación
26 LAPA
27 Aike Tour
29 Telefónica
30 Burbuja's
33 Dirección de Cultura;
   Museo de Arte
   Moderno; Public
   Showers
35 Laverap
36 Nievemar
38 Future Bike
40 Puerto Madryn Turismo
43 Fundación Patagonia
   Natural
45 XT Mountain Bike
50 Scuba Duba
51 Balneario NaPraia
55 Balneario Yoaquina:
   Ocean Diver

summer, the office organizes a variety of events, which may include videos and lectures or historic walking tours.

The tourist offices sells a pass called 'Pase Azul' (US$18), which includes entrance to Península Valdés, EcoCentro, Museo Paleontológico Feruglio (in Trelew) and to one of the following: Punta Tombo, Cabo Dos Bahías or Monumento Natural Bosques Petrificados.

Banco de la Nación, 9 de Julio 117, changes traveler's checks. Some travel agencies accept traveler's checks as payment for excursions.

The post office is at Belgrano and Gobernador Maíz; the postal code is 9120. Call centers abound, including a large Telefónica at the corner of Av Roca and 9 de Julio.

Recreo, at the corner of 25 de Mayo and RS Peña, has a worthwhile selection of regional books and a small sampling of English-language travel guides.

Laundry service can be found at Laverap (☎ 472593, 25 de Mayo 529) and Burbuja's (Maíz 438). Showers are available for US$1 in the *baños públicos* (public baths), downstairs at the Dirección de Cultura, Av Roca 444.

Puerto Madryn's Hospital Subzonal AR Isola (☎ 451240) is at Pujol 247.

Museo Oceanográfico y de Ciencias Naturales

Where else can one feel up strands of seaweed or ogle at a preserved octopus all within the grandeur of a catalog-ordered 1917 Victorian? At this museum in the Chalet Pujol (☎ 451139, Domecq García & Menéndez; admission US$2; open 9am-noon & 4pm-8:30pm weekdays, 4pm-9pm weekends) a caracole staircase leads into small rooms of marine and land mammal exhibits, plus collections of Welsh wares. Most of it looks geared to a school science class and the explanations are in Spanish, but it's visually informative and creatively presented. Twist up to the cupola for panoramic views of the port.

EcoCentro

A true celebration of the area's marine treasures, EcoCentro (☎ 457470, Julio Verne 3784; adult/child, student, retired US$7/5; open 9am-noon & 3pm-8pm Tues-Sun Oct 1-Dec 14; 3pm-8pm Tues-Sun Mar 15-Sept 30; 6pm-10pm Tues-Sun Dec 15-Mar 14) is not to be missed. Any trip to Valdés will be enhanced by a few hours at this masterpiece of interactive displays that gracefully combine years of scientific research with artistic sensitivity. Exhibits discuss the unique marine ecosystem, the breeding habits of the right whales, dolphin sounds, stories of southern elephant seal harems, a tidepool full of activity, and much more. The center conducts ongoing research and organizes educational projects with local schools. An English-language guidebook of the exhibits is available at the front desk.

Equally impressive is the building itself, from which whales may be spotted. A three-story tower acts as a library, with the top story, all glass and comfy couches, a great place to read, write, or think about the fragile ocean community. Shuttles run three times daily from the tourist office on Av Roca to the center, located just beyond the Indio Tehuelche statue.

Fundación Patagonia Natural

A well-run nongovernmental organization (☎ 474363, Marcos A Zar 760, the foundation monitors environmental issues in Patagonia, mainly in the coastal areas. In a small converted house and yard, volunteers diligently nurse back to health injured birds and the occasional marine mammal. Some, like the one-winged brown eagle, are now permanent residents.

Activities

Diving Night dives are offered at Golfo Azul (☎ 471649, e golfoazul@pinosub.com, Yrigoyen & Mitre) which also offers a three-day, two-night diving trip aboard a catamaran for US$450, all-inclusive. Scuba Duba (☎ 452699, Brown 893) is another quality operator. Most of the balnearios also offer diving, including Ocean Diver (☎ 472569, Balneario Yoaquina). Dives range from US$50 to US$80; bring a certification card.

Windsurfing & Kayaking In summer only, Balneario NaPraia (☎ 473715, Blvd Brown

& Perlotti), rents regular and wide boards for US$15/10, offers a course of six classes for US$90 and kayaks for US$7/5 hour/half-hour. South of Muelle Piedrabuena, Playa Tomás Curti is a popular windsurfing area.

Biking Try XT Mountain Bike (☎ 472232, Av Roca 742) for guided tours (US$16 to US$35) and mountain bike rental by the hour, half-day or full day. Future Bike (☎ 15-665108, Juan B Justo 683) rents for US$10 per day. Balneario NaPraia charges US$6/15 per hour/day.

Organized Tours

Tours to Península Valdés vary from US$25 to US$30, and the quality can vary as well, depending on the vehicle used and flexibility of the tour. Distances are long, meaning that most of the day is spent en route. Talk to other travelers and visit a handful of operators before choosing. Book tours at least a day in advance.

Aike Tour (☎ 450720, e aiketour@infovia.com.ar, Av Roca 353) also offers Valdés jaunts in four-wheel drive. Readers recommend Cuyun-Co (☎ 451845, e cuyunco@satlink.com.ar, Roca 165) for flexible and personal tours. Also worth checking out, Turismo Puma (☎ 471482, 28 de Julio 46) has been recommended for small groups, nature walks and excursions incorporating whale watching. Mar y Valle (☎ 472872, Av Roca 297, local 4) and Nievemar (☎ 455544, Roca 549, local 3) charge slightly less for the basic tour.

Tours to Punta Tombo from Puerto Madryn tend to be cheaper than those offered in Trelew, but require additional dull driving time and less time with the penguins.

Places to Stay

Check the tourist office for a lodgings board that maintains a list of apartments for rent on a daily, weekly, or monthly basis. Prices usually range from US$10 to US$15 per day per person. Budget to mid-range places do not generally include breakfast in their prices.

Budget City bus No 2 from downtown will take you to within 500m of the southern campgrounds.

Camping ACA (☎ 452952, Camino al Indio, 3.5km from center) Members/non-members US$13/16 per day up to 4 people with car, trailer & tent; closed winter. Large trees offer shelter from the incessant wind at this 800-site facility toward Punta Cuevas.

Camping Municipal Sud (☎ 455640, Camino al Indio, 3km from center) US$14 per day up to 4 people, tent and car; open year-round. Less sheltered and large, this one's a bit daunting, but the sites are well designed and clean. Bike rental costs US$7 to US$12.

El Golfito (☎ 454544, e cnas_pto-madryn@arnet.com.ar, Camino a Punta Loma, 4km from center) US$3.50 per person, including tent, car & showers; hostel bed US$6.50, bring your own bedding; open year-round. Partially forested and with direct beach access, this Club Náutico Atlántico Sud property is probably the best bet, especially with the option of a real bed in the 85-bed hostel.

Hostelling International Puerto Madryn (☎/fax 474426, e madrynhi@hostels.org.ar, 25 de Mayo 1136) US$10/12 members/non-members; closed after Easter. In a quiet neighborhood and on spacious grounds, this hostel has large rooms. Some travelers have found the staff disagreeable and suggest not planning tours through the hostel.

Hotel Yanco (☎ 471581, Av Roca 626) Beds US$12. This is one of those hotels that let in the backpacker crowd even though it cramps their style. Lower-end but very decent hotel rooms are opened to share with whomever else shows up. Only those with Hostelling International card in hand are allowed. There's a casino downstairs, so earplugs are advisable.

Residencial Santa Rita (☎ 471050, e santaritapm@infovia.com.ar, Gobernador Maíz 370) Singles/doubles US$15/25 with kitchen access. Santa Rita promotes a fun, community feel.

Residencial Vaskonia (☎ 472581, 25 de Mayo 43) Singles/doubles US$15/24.

Adequate rooms are a bit dark and musty, but the beds comfortable – that is, if you can sleep through all the thumping of the surrounding discos: join the party or unpack the plugs. There's no breakfast service or kitchen access.

Hotel del Centro (*☎/fax 473742, 28 de Julio 149*) Singles/doubles US$15/25, with shared bath US$10. Travelers give this place mixed reviews: Could be due to the owner's gruff apathy, flat foam beds, the 'do not walk hallways topless or barefoot' rule, or its dank darkness. To its advantage are a grape arbor and *parrilla* pit, a kitchen, old rooms with elaborate tile and stamped tin ceilings, and its dead-center-of-town location.

Residencial Petit (*☎ 451460, MT de Alvear 845*) Singles/doubles US$18/32. Motel-style in design, this is a good place if you're driving and need to check on the car from the window throughout the night.

Residencial J'os (*☎ 471433. Bolívar 75*) Singles/doubles US$20/30, rooms with shared bath US$10. Basic rooms are spotless, but a bit dark, and the in-room bathrooms are small, but the place has a pleasant, peaceful calm about it and very amiable owners.

Mid-Range The best mid-range option in a great location, is *Residencial La Posta* (*☎ 472422, fax 454027,* e *laposta01@ infovia.com.ar, Av Roca 33*) with singles/ doubles for US$30/40. Attended by a caring family, rooms are clean, spacious and quiet. The wildlife display in the outside hallway is the work of one of the owners.

Hotel Herakleion (*☎/fax 452222, Gobernador Maíz 545*) Singles/doubles US$25/35. No hidden treasures here, just plain simple rooms, sparkling clean with renovated bathrooms and all facing a well-groomed yard perfect for a toss of Frisbee or nap in the sun. Family-owned and -run means attentive service and curious glances from the kids.

Residencial Manolo's (*☎ 472390, Av Roca 763*) Singles/doubles US$30/35. Set back from the busy road, this place has a family atmosphere and good rooms with good-size private bathrooms. There's also a six-person apartment for US$70 per day.

Hotel El Muelle Viejo (*☎ 471284, Yrigoyen 38*) Singles/doubles US$30/50. Crisp white linen curtains and bedspreads accent pale wood furniture and plump beds, and bathrooms have bathtubs. The older area of the hotel doesn't have quite the same feel, but prices are cheaper. Breakfast is US$3 extra. In high season, they don't offer single rooms.

La Posada de Madryn (*☎ 474087, Abraham Mathews 2951*) Singles/doubles US$50/70. Located at the southern limit where town turns to pampa, the Posada is inconvenient to town and beaches, but offers tranquility and rolling green lawns. Be aware, however, that student groups take over from July to December.

Hostal del Rey (*☎ 471156, Blvd Brown 681*) Singles/doubles US$40/50. It's right on the beach, but tends to be rather dull in both structure and service. The rooms are good quality, but you get the cramped all-in-one bathrooms.

Hosteria Torremolinos (*☎/fax 453215, Zar 64,* e *torremolinos@arnet.com.ar*) Singles/doubles US$40/55. Intimate Torremolinos is a good option for couples: well-furnished impeccable rooms featuring queen-size beds and bathtubs. Pale wood and cream interiors keep the place feeling cool, and Internet access is free.

Top End Singles/doubles will set you back US$45/50 at *Aguas Mansas* (*☎ 473103, 456626, José Hernández 51*). Closer to the beach than other top-dime spots, here you'll find a smart, well-run small place that is a cool getaway from the nearby beach scene.

Los Tulipanes (*☎/fax 471840, Lewis Jones 150*). Doubles US$80. Well-designed rooms with kitchenettes look over a small garden and puddle of a pool. Very attractively appointed, Los Tulipanes offers all of the perks of a four-star hotel, with a pleasant degree of friendliness.

Hotel Bahía Nueva (*☎/fax 451677, 450045, e/mail hotel@bahianueva.com.ar, Av Roca 67*) Singles/doubles US$77/97. Bahía Nueva does a stellar job of mixing casual comfort with top-end services. All of the rooms are well groomed, but only a few have decent views of the water. No worries, the hotel makes sure guests have plenty to do both in and out of the hotel with a living room/library full of regional interest books, a bar with billiards and a TV (mostly to view movies and documentaries) and plenty of information on tours. Breakfast receives extra marks for the buffet and fresh regional pastries.

Hotel Península Valdés (☎ 471292, fax 452584, e info@hotel-peninsula-valdes.com, Av Roca 155) Singles/doubles US$100/110 to US$110/125. The Valdés delivers with excellent service and rooms with fabulous views (ask for an ocean view, above the treeline). All of the rooms have air-con/heat, piped-in music and cable TV. Luxury continues with a spa, massage and beauty parlor.

Places to Eat

Comidas X Kilos (☎ 453270, Av Roca 870) US$6. Although it doesn't offer the spread of most *tenedores libres,* readers praise the prices.

Estela (☎ 451573, Roque Sáenz Peña 27) Parrilla US$10, pastas US$8; closed Mon. Estela offers some of the best parrilla in town, tasty pasta dishes and a good dose of hearty conversation.

Taska Beltza (☎ 15-668085, 9 de Julio 345) US$6-12. Closed Mon. Chef 'Negro' spins delicately prepared, generous dishes in this old Basque Center. From robust pasta to tender steamed fish, each meal is expertly seasoned and made with the utmost attention. Homemade banana ice cream served with dark chocolate sauce and *dulce de leche* is one way to get to heaven.

Cantina El Náutico (☎ 471404, Av Roca 790) US$8-10. Photos of Argentine celebrities attest to the popularity of this touristy seafood house. An array of fish or seafood is on offer; check what's in season and then sauce it up with a lemony creamy *salsa Maitre D'Hotel.* While meals are moderately priced, drinks are expensive.

Adesso (☎ 453070, 25 de Mayo & 9 de Julio) US$5-10. This is an outstanding pizza and pasta restaurant with pleasant, unpretentious decor.

La Barra (☎ 454279, Blvd Brown 779) US$4-11. Stone-baked, thin-crust pizzas and heaping bowls of salads keep this large and boisterous place packed day and night.

Halloween II (☎ 450909, Av Roca 1355) US$4-10. We're wondering about the name too, but not enough to stop enjoying some of the best take-away pizza in the 'hood.

Pizzería Roselli (☎ 472451, Av Roca & Roque Sáenz Peña) US$4-9. Under renovations while researching, local institution Roselli should be open for what many consider the best pizzas in town (and the competition is stiff here).

Empanadas del Bicurú (☎ 471046, Av Roca 1143) US$1-3. Order a pizza or a stack of empanadas and head to the beach. *La Cabildo* (☎ 471284, H Yrigoyen 36) offers a similar operation on the other side of town.

Yoaquina (☎ 456058, Brown between 1st & 2nd rotunda) US$7-9. Dark wood and pompous waitstaff clashes with the beachside scene, but when it's hot outside, the cool inside makes a good place for a coffee or drink (eat elsewhere).

NaPraia (☎ 473715, Brown 860) US$4-7 breakfast, US$6.50 lunch. A more informal choice for beachside eating, this one offers power breakfasts and crunchy salads.

Casa del Té Chubut (☎ 451311, Av Roca 369) US$10. Just like Gaiman, but with a beach view, this local institution is known for *alfajores* and tasty *torta galesa* (Welsh black cake).

Havanna (☎ 473373, Roca 401) US$1.50-4. Sugarbomb alfajores and specialty coffees just may wind you up enough to flip like a dolphin. It's open Sunday mornings, too.

Mares Helados (Av Roca 600) US$1.50-4.50. Got a hankering for tiramisu or dulce de leche *granatizado*? Leave room for a dish of Mares. Or try the equally good and almost more popular *Heladería Kebom* (Av Roca 540).

Entertainment

Bars and dance clubs come and go with the marine life, so ask what's hip for the moment.

La Oveja Negra (Yrigoyen 144) Burlap sacks and live music are the fare at this bar.

Getting There & Away

Air Though Puerto Madryn has had its own convenient Aeródromo El Tehuelche since 1989, nearly all commercial flights still arrive at Trelew, 65km south (see the Trelew Getting There & Away section). The local airport tax is US$2.

Dinar (☎ 454950) has direct service from Puerto Madryn to Buenos Aires (US$120) and to Comodoro Rivadavia; both leave daily at noon. Southern Winds (28 de Julio 46) also flies to/from Buenos Aires, as does LAPA's new airline ARG, with service on Thursday and Sunday. ARG also connects to El Calafate.

LADE (☎ 451256, Av Roca 119) flies its puddle jumper on Monday to (in order of landings): Esquel (US$41), Bariloche (US$50), Neuquén (US$55-80), Viedma (US$125) and Mar del Plata. On Tuesday it goes to Viedma (US$32), Bahía Blanca (US$50), Mar del Plata (US$80) and Buenos Aires (US$90); on Friday to Trelew and Comodoro Rivadavia (US$39).

LAPA (☎ 451048, Roca 303, local 2) has bus shuttle service to the airport at Trelew.

Bus Puerto Madryn's bus terminal is located behind the historic Estación del Ferrocarril Patagónico (1889), on Doctor Avila between Independencia and Necochea. Bus companies include Línea 28 de Julio (☎ 472056), TAC (☎ 451537), Don Otto (☎ 451675), Que Bus (☎ 455805), Andesmar and El Cóndor (☎ 473764), Mar y Valle (☎ 472056) and TUS/TUP (☎ 451962).

Destination	Duration in hours	Cost
Bariloche	14	US$50
Buenos Aires	20	US$35-50
Córdoba	18	US$42-67
Comodoro Rivadavia	6	US$17
Esquel	8	US$28
Mendoza	23	US$68-72
Neuquén	12	US$27-32
Puerto Pirámides	1½	US$6.50
Río Gallegos	16	US$42-52
Trelew	1	US$4

Getting Around

To/From the Airport Aeródromo El Tehuelche (☎ 451909) is 5km west of town, at the junction with RN 3.

Southbound Línea 28 de Julio buses from Puerto Madryn to Trelew, which run hourly Monday through Saturday between 6:15am and 10:30pm, will stop at Trelew's airport on request. Aerolíneas Argentinas also runs a bus from Trelew's airport to Puerto Madryn (US$10). LAPA has its own airport shuttle, leaving two hours before flight time from its downtown offices.

Car If you're renting a car to visit the sites of Península Valdés, keep in mind a roundtrip is a little over 300km. A group of three or four persons sharing expenses can make a rental car or remise a relatively reasonable and more flexible alternative to bus tours.

Rent-A-Car (☎ 15-515054, Av Roca 277) has vehicles for US$80 to US$90 for 400km, including insurance. Patagonia SI (☎ 455106, Av Roca 27) charges US$75 to US$105 with free mileage. Puerto Madryn Turismo, with branches at Roca 624 (☎ 452355) and Roca 41 (☎ 456453), charges US$45 for 50km, US$65 for 150km and US$90 for 300km, not including insurance. All of the above rates reflect cash payment. All northbound motorists should note that the last place for cheap gas is 139km north in Sierra Grande.

AROUND PUERTO MADRYN

Home to a sea lion rookery, the **Reserva Faunística Punta Loma** *(admission US$5)*, is 17km southwest of Puerto Madryn via a good but winding gravel road. The overlook is about 15m from the animals. Many travel agencies organize tours; otherwise, hire a car or taxi.

Some 20km north of Puerto Madryn is **Playa Flecha**, which is a recommended whale-watching spot in season.

RESERVA FAUNÍSTICA PENÍNSULA VALDÉS

One of South America's finest wildlife reserves, the Península Valdés is home to sea lions, elephant seals, guanacos, rheas,

Magellanic penguins and many other seabirds. But the biggest attraction – literally and figuratively – is the southern right whale, known in Spanish as the *ballena franca*, which comes to breed between June and mid-December. The breeding zones along the Golfo Nuevo, Golfo San José, and the coastline near Caleta Valdés from Punta Norte to Punte Hércules are a designated Monumento Natural Ballena Franca Austral; whales are most likely to be spotted in the warmer, more enclosed waters of these areas. Península Valdés became a UNESCO World Heritage Site in 1999. (For information on the region's fauna, see the special section 'Patagonia Wildlife,' later in this chapter.)

Sheep estancias occupy most of the peninsula's interior, which includes one of the world's lowest continental depressions,

CHRIS BARTON

Sheep pen and windmill on an estancia in Península Valdés

the salt flats of Salina Grande and Salina Chica, 42m below sea level. At the turn of the century, Puerto Pirámides, the peninsula's only village, was the shipping port for the salt extracted from Salina Grande.

About 18km north of Puerto Madryn, paved RP 2 branches off RN 3 across the Istmo Carlos Ameghino to the entrance of the Península Valdés reserve *(admission US$7; valid for two days)* where the **Centro de Interpretación** *(open 8am-8pm Mon-Sun)* focuses on natural history, displays a full right whale skeleton, and has material on the peninsula's colonization, from the area's first Spanish settlement at Fuerte San José to later mineral exploration. While there, be sure to climb up the observation tower to catch the stunning panoramic view.

Isla de los Pájaros

In Golfo San José, 800m north of the isthmus, this bird sanctuary is off-limits to humans, but visible through a powerful telescope; it contains a replica of a chapel built at Fuerte San José. See the boxed text 'Please…Draw Me A Sheep' to find out how this small island figures in Antoine de St-Exupéry's *The Little Prince*.

Punta Delgada

In the peninsula's southeast corner, about 70km from Puerto Pirámides, sea lions and, in spring, a large colony of elephant seals are visible from the cliffs, but the sites farther north offer better views. The lighthouse is now a luxury hotel and decent restaurant, at which tour groups sometimes take lunch.

Caleta Valdés

In spring, elephant seals haul themselves onto the long gravel spit at this sheltered bay on the eastern shore. In September, females give birth to pups, while males fight it out to impress the females, all of which makes for a circus of activity and fantastic photo ops – just don't get too close. Guanaco sometimes stroll along the beach. Between Caleta Valdés and Punta Norte is a substantial colony of burrowing Magellanic penguins.

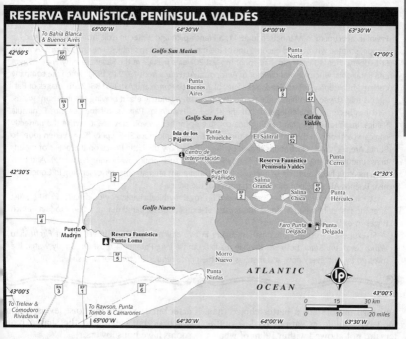

RESERVA FAUNÍSTICA PENÍNSULA VALDÉS

Punta Norte

Rarely visited by tour groups (mainly for reasons of time and distance), Punta Norte has an enormous mixed colony of sea lions and elephant seals. But the real thrill is the orcas; from mid-February through mid-April they come here to feast on the unsuspecting colonies of sea lions. Chances are you won't see a high-tide attack in all its gory glory, but the grace of the orcas is reason enough to journey here. There's a snack bar and small but good museum focusing on marine mammals, with details on the area's sealing history and on the Tehuelche.

Puerto Pirámides

What was once a sleepy salt-exporting port is now an unpretentious, relaxed village and the preferred base for whale-watching trips and exploring the peninsula. It's the only place with a variety of lodging and food.

In summer, weekends can get ridiculously crowded, but off-season and weekdays Pirámides regains its serenity. Av de las Ballenas is the main street in town, with most of the lodging options. There's no bank, so change money in Puerto Madryn or Trelew. Most tourist activities are clustered around the half-moon sandy beach. For visitors without cars, there's a sea lion colony only 4km from town, with good views across the Golfo Nuevo toward Puerto Madryn.

Activities

Whale-watching excursions cost around US$20 and can be arranged in Puerto Pirámides. Hidrosport (☎ 495065), Aquatours (☎ 495015) and Peke Sosa (☎ 495010), all near the beach, offer similar trips. When deciding which to use, ask other travelers and check what kind of boat will be used: Smaller, Zodiac-style inflatable rafts with

Please...Draw Me a Sheep

From an apartment in Manhattan in 1941, a French pilot and writer, in exile from the battlefields in Europe, scripted what would become one of the most read children's fables, *The Little Prince*. Antoine St-Exupéry, then 40 years old, had spent the last 20 years flying – in the Sahara, the Pyrenees, Egypt and Patagonia, where he was director of Aeropostal Argentina from 1929 to 1931, when the company declared bankruptcy. Intertwined in the lines of *The Little Prince* and Asteroid B612 are images of Patagonia that stayed with him while flying over the barren landscape and braving the incessant winds.

It has become popular legend that the shape of Isla de los Pájaros, off the coast of Península Valdés, inspired the elephant-eating boa constrictor (or hat, as you may see it), while the perfectly conical volcanoes on the asteroid owe their shape to the volcanoes St-Exupéry flew over en route to Punta Arenas, Chile. Illustrations drawn by the author show the Little Prince on the peaks of mountains, unquestionably those in the Fitz Roy Range (one such peak now bearing his name). And possibly, meeting two young daughters of a French immigrant after an emergency landing in Concordia, near Buenos Aires, helped mold the character of the prince.

St-Exupéry never witnessed the influence his royal mythical character would have; in 1944, just after the first publication of *The Little Prince*, St-Exupéry disappeared during a flight to join French forces-in-exile stationed in Algiers.

St-Exupéry's years in Patagonia also figure in two critically acclaimed novels, *Night Flight*, and *Wind, Sand and Stars*, both worthwhile reads on those long Patagonia trips. Or, simply watch the miles go by, and every now and then, as the little prince requested, try to draw a sheep.

outboard motors are a better choice than the larger bulldozer variety. By law, outfitters are not allowed within 100m of whales without cutting the motor, nor allowed to pursue them.

Personalized **trekking** expeditions within the peninsula can be organized with some of Pirámides' locals: ask for Juan Pablo at Mammadeus (see Places to Eat), or for Eduardo Villella at El Refugio de Luna (see Places to Stay).

Places to Stay

Camping Municipal (☎ 495084) US$4 per person. Sites at this campground, though not well marked, are sheltered from the wind. It has clean toilets, showers – timed but hot – for US$1, and a store. In summer, the place gets very crowded and finding a corner may be difficult. Whatever you do, avoid camping on the beach: High tide is high and will wash sleeping logs away.

Hospedaje El Español (☎ 495025, *Av de las Ballenas s/n*) US$8 per person. Shack up in one of the oldest buildings in town, where old tin roofs and walls provide lots of char-

acter but don't help the noise levels. Rooms are basic but clean, and the shared bathrooms have hot showers.

Casa Pyrámides (☎ 495046, *Av de las Ballenas s/n*) US$8-10. Another historic tin house, this one, run by 'Tía Alicia' is a tad more familiar, and the rooms have windows.

Estancia del Sol (*El Libanés*, ☎ 495007, *Av de las Ballenas s/n*) Singles/doubles US$23/46. The earnest owners of Sol do their best to make for a pleasant stay in the modest rooms, but the barking dogs don't help. It's popular with families and students, and has a decent confitería attached. Breakfast is included.

Refugio de Luna (☎ 495083, e refugio deluna@infovia.com.ar, *Av de las Ballenas s/n*) Doubles US$80. Much more a private home than a refugio, Sylvina and Eduardo Villella welcome folks to share in their family's routine. The attractive, but crunched, guest cabin is perched above the house with excellent views, while the main house is warmly welcoming and spacious. Sylvia leads morning yoga sessions and Eduardo organizes hikes around the peninsula. Breakfast is included.

Paradise Resort (☎ 495030, fax 495003, e *paradise@satlink.com, Av de las Ballenas s/n)* Singles/doubles US$85-95. Paradise offers top-notch, very attractive and cool brick-wall rooms, some with stellar views. More informal cabins and bungalows are good options for families and groups. Future plans for the Paradise may include a sauna and other 'spa resort' attractions. Reserve in advance for possible discounts. Breakfast is included.

Places to Eat
Mammadeus (☎ 495050) US$5-15. Fresh shellfish is the fare, and the hearty fish stew is a taste bonanza. Good tunes keep the place mellow and the staff keeps it friendly. On summer nights Mammadeus goes disco.

El Monasterio (☎ 495031, Av de las Ballenas s/n) US$8-10. Walk into this pink tin hut, pick up a magazine and share a feast of shellfish expertly prepared with garlic, white wine and butter. Wash it all down with a cheap chilled wine. Pastas and pizzas are equally recommended.

Pub Paradise (☎ 495030, Av de las Ballenas s/n) US$4-12. Synonymous with Pirámides, Paradise is the town's hangout and popular stop for tour groups. Enjoy the buzz of activity with a cold beer, sandwich or pizza while watching the sunset spin the bluffs gold.

Estancia del Sol (☎ 495007, Av de las Ballenas s/n) US$3 breakfast, US$6.50 fixed-price lunch, US$7-10 dinner. Homemade scones in the morning and decent meals at midday make this a decent alternative.

For groceries, head to *La Araña Bionica (Av de las Ballenas s/n)*, which hopefully you won't find in your food.

Getting There & Around
Twice daily in summer the Mar y Valle bus goes from Puerto Madryn to Puerto Pirámides (US$7, 1½ hours), with limited service in the off season. Bus tours from Puerto Madryn may allow passengers to get off at Puerto Pirámides, if it's the last stop on the tour, but discount fare doesn't apply.

If you're driving, take it slow. The road to the peninsula is all potholes and detours, and a favorite snooze spot for estancia sheep. Roads on the peninsula are gravel and washboard, plus have spots of sand to send wheels spinning. If you're in a rental car, make sure you get all the details on the insurance policy. Hitchhiking to and in the peninsula is nearly impossible and bike travel long and unnervingly windy.

TRELEW
☎ 02965 • pop 90,000
Walk along Trelew's downtown streets and you're likely to hear elders exchanging news in Welsh or see a tutor conducting classes to keep the antique language alive. Historic buildings maintain a sense of heritage, and are reminders of illustrious times and types. Founded in 1886 as a railway junction to unite the Río Chubut valley with the beaches of the Golfo Nuevo, Trelew owes its name to the Welsh contraction of *tre* (town) and *lew* (after Lewis Jones, who promoted railway expansion).

During the following 30 years, the railway reached Gaiman, the Welsh built their Salón San David, and Spanish and Italian immigrants began to settle in the area. In 1956, the federal government promoted Patagonian industrial development and Trelew's population and skyline skyrocketed.

Close to the Welsh villages of Gaiman and Dolavon, as well as Punta Tombo (relatively speaking), Trelew is an attractive base for exploring the area.

Orientation
Trelew is 65km south of Puerto Madryn via RN 3. The center of town surrounds Plaza Independencia, with most services on Calles 25 de Mayo and San Martín, and along Av Fontana, two blocks east. East-west streets change their names on either side of Av Fontana. Between the main north-south streets are semi-pedestrian passageways.

Information
The competent and well-stocked tourist office (☎ 426819, fax 420139, Mitre 837) is open 8:30am to 9pm daily, closing at 8pm on

ARGENTINA

TRELEW

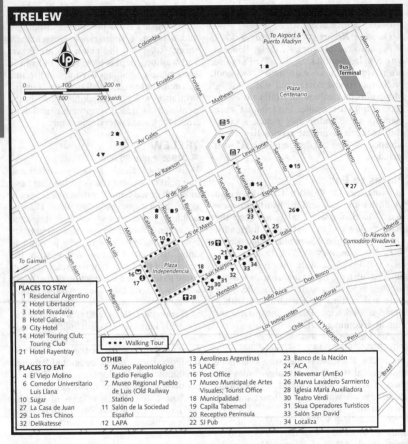

PLACES TO STAY
1 Residencial Argentino
2 Hotel Libertador
3 Hotel Rivadavia
8 Hotel Galicia
9 City Hotel
14 Hotel Touring Club;
　Touring Club
21 Hotel Rayentray

PLACES TO EAT
4 El Viejo Molino
6 Comedor Universitario
　Luis Llana
10 Sugar
27 La Casa de Juan
29 Los Tres Chinos
32 Delikatesse

OTHER
5 Museo Paleontológico
　Egidio Feruglio
7 Museo Regional Pueblo
　de Luis (Old Railway
　Station)
11 Salón de la Sociedad
　Español
12 LAPA

13 Aerolíneas Argentinas
15 LADE
16 Post Office
17 Museo Municipal de Artes
　Visuales; Tourist Office
18 Municipalidad
19 Capilla Tabernacl
20 Receptivo Peninsula
22 SJ Pub

23 Banco de la Nación
24 ACA
25 Nievemar (AmEx)
26 Marva Lavadero Sarmiento
28 Iglesia María Auxiliadora
30 Teatro Verdi
31 Skua Operadores Turísticos
33 Salón San David
34 Localiza

● ● ● Walking Tour

weekends in low season. There's also an airport information booth (☎ 420060) open for incoming flights. The tourist offices sell a pass called 'Pase Azul' (US$18), which includes entrance to the Museo Paleontológico Feruglio and a number of regional attractions. ACA (☎ 435197) is at Av Fontana and Italia.

Scores of banks, open 8am to 1pm, can be found in the downtown area, most of them with ATMs. The post office is at Calle 25 de Mayo and Mitre; the postal code is 9100. Get laundry done at Marva Lavadero Sarmiento, Sarmiento 363.

Walking Tour

The tourist office distributes an informative brochure, in Spanish and English, describing most but not all of the city's historic buildings. A good starting point is the **Museo Regional Pueblo de Luis** at the former railway station (1889), at the north end of Av Fontana. Half a block south, on Fontana, the **Touring Club** began in 1906 as Hotel Martino before expanding to become, at least briefly, Patagonia's best hotel. While its glory days are past, it's still an interesting edifice and a popular gathering place.

Banco de la Nación started operations in 1899 after being relocated from Rawson following floods on the Río Chubut, but the present building at Fontana and 25 de Mayo dates from 1922; note the clock tower. One block south and one block west, at San Martín 92, the Salón San David *(open 4pm to 8pm weekdays)* is a Welsh community center built in 1913 that often hosts the Eisteddfod (see Special Events). Half a block north on Belgrano, the Capilla Tabernacl (1889), Trelew's oldest building, still has Welsh-language services. Italian immigrants inaugurated the Teatro Verdi, on San Martín between Belgrano and Rivadavia, as a skating rink in 1914.

At the southeast corner of Plaza Independencia, the Municipalidad (1931) houses city offices; the plaza's most interesting feature is its Victorian gingerbread kiosco, dating from 1910. On the west side of the plaza, on Calle Mitre, the Museo Municipal de Artes Visuales and the tourist office (1903) are housed in Trelew's first school, which also housed the Distrito Militar. On the north side, at 25 de Mayo 237, Spanish immigrants built the Salón de la Sociedad Española (1920), which hosted local theater productions.

Museo Regional Pueblo de Luis

In the former railway station, this museum *(☎ 424062; Av Fontana & 9 de Julio; adult/child US$2/1; open 7am-1pm & 3pm-9pm weekdays Dec-Feb; 7am-1pm & 2pm-8pm weekdays Mar-Nov)* displays historical photographs, clothing and period furnishings, but lacks explanations. The train stopped running in 1961, but the antique steam engine and other machinery outside are worth a stop.

Museo Paleontológico Egidio Feruglio

The pride of Trelew, this well-organized and attractive museum *(☎ 420012, Av Fontana & Rawson; adult/student, retiree, child US$6/4; open 10am-8pm Mon-Sun Dec-Mar, 10am-5pm weekdays April-Nov)* covers natural history through well-thought-out displays of dinosaur skeletons and fossils of plant and marine life. Nature sounds and a (mediocre) video accent the informative plaques; however, if you can't read the Spanish explanations, the experience falls short. The collection includes local dinosaurs, such as the *Tehuelchesaurus*, *Patagosaurus* and *Titanosaurus*. Feruglio was an Italian paleontologist who came to Argentina in 1925 as a petroleum geologist for YPF.

Make reservations here for group tours to Parque Paleontológico Bryn Gwyn, near Gaiman.

Organized Tours

Local travel agencies run excursions to Reserva Provincial Punta Tombo (US$30 plus US$7 admission), some passing by Puerto Rawson on the way back to see *toninas overas* (Commerson's dolphins) when conditions are agreeable. The actual time at Punta Tombo is only about 1½ hours. Other tours take in Dique Ameghino (US$30), a canyon near Dolavon. Day trips to Península Valdés are on offer, but going to Puerto Madryn first is a much better option: There are more choices, prices are better and the trip won't have as many hours of driving time. Note that distances to these sites are very long and more time is spent in transit than at the attractions; take along snacks and water. Local agencies worth checking out are Nievemar (☎ 434114, Italia 20), which accepts traveler's checks as payment, Skua Operadores Turísticos (☎ 432277, San Martín 150) and Receptivo Península (☎ 434702, San Martín 125).

Special Events

The Eisteddfod de Chubut, a Welsh literary and musical festival, has been held here since 1875 and continues, in late October, every year. On July 28, the *Gwyl y Glaniad* celebrates the landing of the first Welsh by taking tea in one of the many chapels. On October 20, the Aniversario de la Ciudad commemorates the city's founding in 1886.

Places to Stay

Camping Club Huracán *(☎ 434380, 4km south on RN 25)* US$3 per person. Open Oct-Mar. The campground has hot showers and electricity, but very limited public transport. The same applies to *Camping Patagonia* (☎ 428968, *RN 7 to Rawson*), with sites for US$3.

Residencial Argentino (☎ 436134, *Moreno 93*) Singles/doubles US$12/20. An impersonal stone maze of a place near the bus terminal, Argentino offers decent clean and comfortable rooms with landscape murals everywhere. Breakfast is an additional US$2.

Hotel Rivadavia (☎ 434472, fax 423491, *Rivadavia 55*) Singles/doubles US$20/40. Up on a hill, owner-run Rivadavia offers right-size firm mattresses, but the cramped bathroom setup means showers get seats wet. Breakfast served in the TV-oriented lobby.

Welsh in Patagonia

Welsh nationalists, frustrated with English domination, sought a land where they could exercise sufficient political autonomy to retain their language, religion and cultural identity. Deciding on desolate Patagonia, they appealed to the government of Argentina, which, after initial misgivings due partly to the British presence in the Falkland Islands, offered them a land grant in the lower part of the Río Chubut valley in 1863.

Disillusion and misfortune plagued the 153 first arrivals from the brig *Mimosa* in the winter of 1865. The Patagonian desert bore no resemblance to their verdant homeland, and several children died in a storm that turned a two-day coastal voyage into a 17-day ordeal. Only a handful of the immigrants were farmers in well-watered Wales, yet their livelihood was to be agriculture in arid Chubut. After near starvation in the early years, the colonists engineered suitable irrigation systems with the help from Tehuelche living in the area, and increased their harvests, permitting the gradual absorption of more Welsh immigrants.

Eventually, the Welsh occupied the entire lower Chubut valley and founded the towns of Rawson, Trelew, Puerto Madryn and Gaiman.

Hotel Touring Club (☎ 433998, fax 425790, *Av Fontana 240*) Singles/doubles US$25/35. In the quest for historic allure, this place is a jackpot and an excellent value. Rooms are adequate, with quaint old touches and modern conveniences and the common quarters are gloriously old-fashioned.

Hotel Galicia (☎ 433802, fax 434302, *9 de Julio 214*) Singles/doubles US$30/40 with breakfast. The best mid-range option, Galicia has cozy rooms with luxury style, good bathrooms and friendly staff. Cheaper singles are available for US$20, but they're cramped, thin-walled and lack ventilation.

City Hotel (☎/fax 433951, *Rivadavia 254*) Singles/doubles US$30/40 with breakfast. Friendly and in the heart of it all, City Hotel is a great choice. The indoor patio rooms are quieter and all of the rooms sport good mattresses.

Hotel Libertador (☎/fax 420220, *Rivadavia 31*) Singles/doubles US$58/78, with 10% cash discount. Comfortable rooms are all softly decorated with indirect light and flowing curtains, while the bathrooms have large bathtubs. This is the best top-end option in town. Breakfast is buffet-style and the parking is free.

Hotel Rayentray (☎ 434702, fax 434704, *San Martín 101*) Singles/doubles US$60/70. The four stars mean attentive service, but the mirror and faux-leather decor of the rooms may not appeal. The top floor spa has a pool, gym, sauna and beauty parlor, but could be much improved.

Places to Eat

Comedor Universitario Luis Yllana (*9 de Julio & Fontana*) US$2. Line up with university students for the cheapest meal in town. Lunch is served 12:30pm to 2pm, dinner 7pm to 9pm. You'll get what's on the menu (ranges from lentils to hamburgers to polenta) plus a small dessert and juice.

Sugar (☎ 435978, *25 de Mayo 247*) US$5-12. A popular place for snacks and drinks across from the plaza, Sugar offers quality meals, including an assortment of salads and daily menus, along with pleasant service.

Los Tres Chinos (☎ 437280, *San Martín 188*) US$6. Eat all you want, including

parrilla and some so-so Chinese dishes. As in all of these style places, drinks are overpriced.

La Casa de Juan (☎ 421534, Moreno 360) US$4-12. Considered the best pizzeria around town, Juan also offers an assortment of pastas, all served in a cozy dining area.

Delikatesse (☎ 430716, Belgrano & San Martín) US$8-12. Brightly lit and much frequented, this pizzeria offers typical meals and bland but large pasta dishes, all topped off with oft-times pretentious service.

El Viejo Molino (☎/fax 428019, Gales 250) US$6-15. In a 1910 flourmill, the Molino is a smart, attractive place, popular on weekend nights. Enjoy a parrilla – of beef, chicken or even veggies, or a variety of pastas or fish. A good wine list adds to the pleasure.

Libertador (☎ 420220) US$9-13. Fresh meat and ingredients plus homemade pastas and a traditional menu make this hotel's restaurant worth the walk.

Entertainment

Touring Club (☎ 433997, Av Fontana 240) Open 24 hours. The lore of the place will inspire anyone to hunch over the marbletop tables, order a drink from the bar and start writing in that journal or start up a heated conversation. The humming fluorescent bulbs, shuffling waiters, historic photos and marbled mirrors all add to the enchantment.

SJ Pub (☎ 423474, San Martín 57) In the front is a nondescript pleasant ice-cream parlor, but the back is a great dark-wood bar featuring cans of draft Guinness and Kilkenny and friendly bar staff.

Getting There & Away

Air Aerolíneas Argentinas (☎ 420210, 25 de Mayo 33) flies twice daily on weekdays and once daily on weekends to Buenos Aires (US$148 to US$242). LAPA (☎ 423440, Belgrano 285) flies twice daily to Buenos Aires (US$142 to US$243).

LADE (☎ 435740, Sarmiento 282) flies to Bariloche (US$62) on Monday via Puerto Madryn (US$20) and Esquel (US$47) and on Friday via Neuquén (US$58) and Viedma (US$38). On Tuesday it flies to Mar del Plata (US$88) via Puerto Madryn, Viedma and Bahía Blanca (US$59). Airport tax is US$6.

Bus Trelew's bus terminal (☎ 420121) is at Urquiza and Lewis Jones, six blocks northeast of downtown. Empresa 28 de Julio (☎ 432429) goes to Gaiman (US$1.70) 20 times a day between 7:20am and 10:45pm (weekend service reduced), most continuing to Dolavon (US$3.20). Pick up a schedule at the stand in the terminal. Buses to Rawson (US$1.40) leave every 15 minutes.

Empresa 28 de Julio and Empresa Mar y Valle (☎ 432429) have hourly buses to Puerto Madryn (US$4 to US$5, 1 hour). Mar y Valle goes to Puerto Pirámides (US$12.50, 3 hours) Thursday and Sunday morning, with additional service in summer, and to Esquel (US$28) once daily. El Ñandú (☎ 427499) goes to Camarones (US$16, 3 hours) four times a week and to Dique Ameghino (US$7, US$11 roundtrip) once a week.

Long-distance bus companies include Empresa Mar y Valle (☎ 432429), El Cóndor (☎ 431675), Que Bus (☎ 422760), Andesmar (☎ 433535), TAC (☎ 431452), Empresa TUS (☎ 421343), El Pingüino (☎ 427400) and Don Otto (☎ 429496).

There are several departures daily for Buenos Aires, with Don Otto offering the most comfortable and direct service. Only Don Otto goes to Mar del Plata, while TAC goes to La Plata. TAC and Andesmar service the most towns. For Comodoro Rivadavia there are a few daily departures with TAC, El Pingüino, Don Otto or Andesmar, all of which also continue on to Puerto San Julian and Río Gallegos.

Destination	Duration in hours	Cost
Bahía Blanca	12	US$31
Bariloche	13	US$40-56
Buenos Aires	21	US$40-65
Caleta Olivia	6	US$19
Córdoba	19	US$44-68
Comodoro Rivadavia	5	US$16
La Plata	19	US$55
Mar del Plata	17	US$74
Mendoza	24	US$74
Neuquén	10	US$24-34
Río Gallegos	17	US$48
Viedma/Carmen de Patagones	7	US$21

ARGENTINA

Getting Around

Trelew's modern airport (☎ 433443) is on RN 3, 5km north of town. Taxis to downtown costs US$8, to Puerto Madryn US$45 and to Gaiman US$16.

Included among car rental agencies are Avis (☎ 434634) at Paraguay 105, and Localiza (☎ 435344) at San Martín 88, both of which have representatives at the airport.

GAIMAN
☎ 02965 • pop 5400

Teahouses, dinosaur fossils, Welsh-speaking *abuelos* (grandparents), seaweed and stockings factories, and a park of recycled soda cans: Gaiman is, to say the least, random.

Tehuelche once wintered in this river valley, thus the name Gaiman, meaning Stony Point or Arrow Point. Welsh constructed their first house here in 1874 and continued to settle the area, peacefully coexisting with the Tehuelche. Later immigrant groups of criollos, Germans and Anglos joined the Welsh and continued cultivation of fruit, vegetables and fodder in the lower Río Chubut valley. Today, historic houses are testament to the Welsh history, while teahouses try to hold on to the afternoon tradition, increasingly diluted by overbaked tourism. About 30% of the residents claim Welsh ancestry. Gaiman is 17km west of Trelew via RN 25. The town's touristy center is little more than a criss-cross of streets snuggled between Río Chubut and dry barren hills. Av Eugenio Tello is the main road, connecting the main entrance to town to Plaza Roca. Most of the sites and teahouses are within four blocks of the plaza. The area across the river is the more industrial and residential zone.

The Casa de Informes (☎ 491152), Rivadavia & Belgrano, is open 9am to 6pm weekdays, and 2pm to 6pm weekends. The post office is at the corner of Juan Evans and Hipólito Yrigoyen, just north of the bridge over the river. The area code is the same as Trelew's.

Things to See & Do

Around town are some architecturally distinctive churches and chapels. **Primera Casa** *(Eugenio Tello & Juan C Evans; admission US$1; open 9am-1pm & 2pm-8pm weekdays, 2pm-8pm weekends)* is the first house, built in 1874 by David Roberts. Dating from 1906, the **Colegio Camwy** *(Michael Jones & Rivadavia)* is considered the first secondary school in Patagonia.

The **Museo Antropológico** *(Bouchard & Michael Jones; admission US$1; open 9am-1pm & 2pm-8pm weekdays, 2pm-8pm weekends)* is a humble homage to the indigenous groups' cultures and history. Nearby is the 300m **Túnel del Ferrocarril**, a brick tunnel through which the first trains to Dolavon passed in 1914. Where train tracks used to be is now a road leading to the highway and a favored spot for smitten teens.

The old railway station houses the **Museo Histórico Regional Gales** *(☎ 491007, Sarmiento & 28 de Julio; admission US$1; open 10am-11:30am & 4pm-8pm Tues-Fri, 4pm-8pm weekends)*, a fine small museum with an intriguing collection of pioneer photographs and household items.

At the entrance to town is **Parque El Desafío** *(☎ 491340, Av Alte Brown; adult/child US$5/3, ticket good for another visit; open till 6pm Mon-Sun)*, the masterpiece park of junk created by eccentric octogenarian Joaquín Alonso. Soda-can flowers, bottle-bottom bulbs and walkways of cable and piping lead to installments of whimsy, the explanations wittingly mocking of today's values. El Desafío gained Guinness World Record status in 1998 as the largest 'recycled' park. Right on the riverbank, parts of it are sometimes flooded, but that doesn't stop Alonso from continuing. More impressive than the park itself is Alonso, whose wisdom and humor are found on the plaques that pepper the park. As one proclaims, '*Si quieres vivir mejor, mezcla a tu sensatez unos gramos de locura*' ('If you want to live better, mix up your sensibility with a few grams of craziness').

Places to Stay

Camping 'Nain' *(☎ 15-665589, Chacra 227, Bryn Gwyn)* US$2.50 per person. Not very central, but the campground has all the regular amenities). Or try *Camping Dan y*

Coed (☎ 491280) for US$2.50 per person, with hot showers.

Hostería Gwesty Tywi (☎/fax 491292, M Jones 342, e gwestywi@infovia.com.ar) US$25/44. Run by a friendly Argentine-Welsh couple, this B&B is an immaculate and comfortable home away from home, popular with visitors from Wales and documentary groups.

Plas y Coed (☎ 491133, e normastella_r@ yahoo.com.ar, M Jones 123) Singles/doubles US$25/40. Next to the teahouse, the hospedaje also has a pleasant living area and library.

Places to Eat
Tarten afal, tarten gwstard, cacen ffrwythau, cpwnj jam and *bara brith* and a bottomless pot of tea – mouth watering yet? For those splurging on afternoon tea, keep into consideration that busloads of tourists may descend upon you, tainting the experience: look for places without the buses in front, or wait until they depart. The teahouses open after 3pm.

Plas y Coed (☎ 491133, M Jones 123) US$10. The first teahouse in town, this one is smaller and not as 'cute' as the others, but you can choose your goodies, and the owner, Marta Rees, will make sure you leave with a belly full.

Ty Cymraeg (☎ 491010, A Matthews 74) US$12. Some consider Cymraeg to have the most authentic style of tea service, in the most authentic of houses.

Ty Draw Ir Avon (☎ 15-689462, Juan Evans 195) US$10. Open from 2pm. On the other side of the river, tea here comes without the twee and doily service, but the delightful couple who run it are Welsh descendents, speak the language and serve up a hearty plate of cakes, all prepared with fresh ingredients from their own farm. Open from 2pm, you can also buy cakes by the kilo.

Ty Nain (☎ 491126, Hipólito Yrigoyen 283) US$10. Open weekends in low season. For pure aesthetic, Ty Nain wins. Ivy-covered whitewashed walls lead to a cozy room accented with authentic Welsh artifacts. Check out the small museum when teatime is finished.

Gustos (☎ 491828, E Tello 156) serves pizza and basic meals, as does confitería **Tabern Las** (☎ 15-665097, E Tello & 9 de Julio).

Shopping
Look for local crafts at **Paseo Artesanal Crefft Werin** (Av Tello & Miguel Jones), just opposite Plaza Roca.

Getting There & Away
Stopping directly in front of Plaza Roca, Empresa 28 de Julio has 20 buses daily to and from Trelew, also serving Dolavon, but weekend services are fewer. The return fare to Gaiman is US$2.80. Remise service in Gaiman is cheaper than in Trelew; the trip to Trelew costs US$7.

AROUND GAIMAN
In the badlands along the Río Chubut, 8km south of Gaiman via RP 5, **Parque Paleontológico Bryn Gwyn** (admission adult/retiree & child US$4/3; open 11am-7pm Mon-Sun) is open to visitors for three-hour guided tours along a well-designed nature trail that is almost literally a walk through time: The Río Chubut has exposed a wealth of fossils from as far back as the Tertiary, about 40 million years ago. While the oldest sediments here are too recent for dinosaurs, there are remains of terrestrial mammals in the volcanic Sarmiento formation, deposited prior to the building of the Andes, and later marine mammals and fish of the Puerto Madryn and Gaiman formations, when subtropical seas covered the low-lying area. Some of the fossils are in situ, while others have been excavated and mounted in glass display cases. Guided tours can be arranged through the affiliated Museo Paleontológico Egidio Feruglio in Trelew (see that entry in the Trelew section for contact information).

DOLAVON
Dolavon, Welsh for 'river meadow,' has so far avoided the tourism mess of its neighbor and remains about as authentic a historic Welsh agricultural town as can be.

continued on page 487

PATAGONIA WILDLIFE

A whole cast of wild characters hangs out along the rugged coast of Patagonia. Jackass penguins, killer whales and elephant seals – to name just a few – are some of the big-name stars that draw wildlife spectators to these lonely shores. Read on for a profile of some of the region's top celebrities.

Magellanic Penguin

When: October to March, peak season December through February

Where: Península Valdés, Punta Tombo, Cabo Dos Bahías, Seno Otway (Chile)

What: *Sphenicus magellanicus*; in Spanish *pingüino magellánico*

Also known as the jackass penguin for its characteristic braying sound, the Magellanic penguin is black to brown in shading and has two black-and-white bars going across the upper chest. They average 1½ feet in height and weigh about 7lbs. Winters are spent at sea, but males arrive on land in late August, followed by territorial fights in September as nests and burrows are prepared. In October, females lay their eggs. Come mid-November, when eggs are hatched, the males and females take turns caring for and feeding the chicks with regurgitated squid and small fish. In December, it's a madhouse of hungry demanding chicks, adults coming in and out of the sea with food, and predatory birds trying to pick out the weaklings. Come January, chicks start to molt and take their first steps into the sea, and by February, it's a traffic jam at the beach as chicks take to the sea. By March, juveniles start their migration north, followed in April by the adults.

Penguins are awkward on land, but in the water they are graceful and swift, with speeds of up to 8km/h. They are also naturally curious, though if approached too quickly they scamper into their burrows or toboggan back into the water. They will bite if you get too close. The least disruptive way to observe them is to sit near the burrows and wait for them to come to you.

Over a million pairs of these penguins exist, but their populations are mostly threatened by human activity and oil spills.

Southern Right Whale

When: June to mid-December, peak season September and October

Where: Golfo Nuevo and the Golfo San José, Península Valdés

What: *Eubalaena australis*; in Spanish *ballena franca austral*

Averaging nearly 12m in length and weighing more than 30 tons, southern right whales enter the shallow waters of Península Valdés in the spring to breed and bear young. Females, which are larger than males, will copulate a year after giving birth, and may pick out the best male partner by fending off the pack of males trailing her for hours to see which one can sustain. For the past 30 years, researchers have been able to track individual whales by noting the pattern of callosities, made white against the black skin by clusters of parasites, found on the whale's head and body. Right whales don't have teeth, but trap plankton and krill with fringed plates (baleens) that hang from the upper jaw. The slow-moving right whale was a favorite target of whalers because, unlike other species, it remained floating on the surface after being killed; after more than half a century of legal protection, South Atlantic right whale populations are slowly recovering.

Killer Whale

When: June to mid-December, peak season September and October
Where: Península Valdés
What: *Ornicus orca*; in Spanish *orca*

These large dolphins, black with white underbellies, live in pods consisting of one male, a cluster of females and the young. Upon maturity, the males leave the pod to create their own. Males, which can reach more than 9m in length and weigh as much as 6000kg, live an average of 30 years, while the females, substantially smaller at 7m and about 4000km, live about 50 years, calving approximately every 10 years. The ominous dorsal fin can reach nearly 2m high. They prey on fish, penguins, dolphins and seals, and will hunt in groups to prey upon larger whales. At Punta Norte near Península Valdés they hunt sea lions and elephant seals by almost beaching themselves and waiting for the waters to wash a few unfortunates their way. In the 1970s, groups concerned with the livelihood of the sea lions requested the whales be shot, to either kill or scare them away, before they decimated the sea lion colonies. Fortunately, this reaction was short lived and made clear the inevitability of the food chain.

Southern Sea Lion

When: year-round
Where: widely distributed along Patagonia coasts
What: *Otaria flavescens*; in Spanish *lobo marino*

Aggressive (don't approach them too closely for photo ops) southern sea lions feed largely on squid and the occasional penguin. The bull has a thick neck and large head with longer hair around the neck, creating the appearance of a lion's mane. An adult male can weigh about 300kg and measure 2m, while the females weigh around 200kg. Bulls fight to control their harems and breed with up to 10 females in a season. Females give birth once each season, with less than a week before being ready for mating again. Unlike the elephant seal, pups nurse only from their mothers.

Southern Elephant Seal

When: year-round; births and mating between September and November

Where: widely distributed along Patagonia coasts; Península Valdés, Punta Norte and Caleta Valdés

What: *Mirounga leonina*; in Spanish *elefante marino*

Elephant seals take their common name from the male's enormous proboscis, which does indeed resemble an elephant's trunk. Males reach nearly 7m in length and can weigh over 3500kg, but the females are substantially smaller. They spend most of the year at sea, and have been observed to dive to a depth of 1500m and stay submerged for over an hour in search of squid and other marine life. (The average dive depth and duration are 1000m and 23 minutes.)

Península Valdés has the only breeding colony of southern elephant seals on the South American continent. The bull elephant comes ashore in late winter or early spring, breeding after the already pregnant females arrive and give birth. Dominant males known as 'beachmasters' control harems of up to 100 females but must constantly fight off challenges from bachelor males. Females give birth to a pup once a year, each pregnancy lasting 11 months of that year. For 19 days after the birth the female nurses the pup, during which time she will lose close to 40% of her body weight, while the pup's increases by 300%. Pups will sometimes nurse from other females. After the 19 days, the mother becomes available for breeding again.

Commerson's Dolphin

When: December to March

Where: Puerto San Julián, Playa Unión, Puerto Deseado

What: *Cephalorhynchus commersonii*; in Spanish *tonina overa*

Outgoing and acrobatic, the Commerson's dolphin is a favorite along shallow areas of coastal Patagonia. Adults are quite small, about 1.5m in length, and brilliantly patterned in black and white with a rounded dorsal fin. Young mammals are gray, brown and black; the brown slowly disappears and the gray fades to striking white. In small groups, they play around the sides of boats, breaching frequently and sometimes bowriding. They eat shrimp, squid and bottom-dwelling fish. In Argentina, they are illegally captured to use as crab bait.

ontinued from page 483

/ooden waterwheels line the canal, framed
y swaying poplars. The historic center is full
f brick buildings, including the 1930 **Molino**
arinero *(☎ 432277, Maipú 61; admission*
'S$2; open upon calling owner Romano Gi-
latini) with still-functioning machinery.
rom the late 1800s, flour was highly ac-
aimed and a main industry in the valley,
alted in the 1940s when the government
arted subsidizing wheat farming in the
orth.

A visit can be a rewarding, but slow one,
ood to simply soak up a bygone time and
rink a slow brew in one of the historic
orner bars.

Camping Municipal, near the northern
ntrance, is dusty and the baths might be
ocked, but it's free. Otherwise, the YPF
tation on the outskirts of town has lodging
or US$10 a person in some cabins out back;
nquire at the station's kiosk.

Línea 28 de Julio runs buses daily between
relew and Dolavon, via Gaiman, most of
/hich use the highway; the others take much
onger on the surface roads. Dolavon is 18km
/est of Gaiman by paved RN 25.

AROUND DOLAVON

ixty kilometers from Dolavon at Km 112
n RN 25 (before the gas station and turnoff
o Dique Ameghino), look for signs to
osque Petrificado Florentino Ameghino.
Jnder development at the time of writing,
his park, 4km from the road, has at least 10
arefully exposed trunks of *lauráceas* from
he Paleocene era, some 58 million years
go. Many of the well-preserved trunks are
ver 30m long, some over 1m wide.

Continue another 22km to **Dique Amegh-**
no, a canyon of red rock and kaolin quar-
ies. The dam-controlled river is active with
irdlife. The dam itself is none too thrilling,
vhile the company town, Villa Verde, is an
rganized graph shaded by sky-high poplars.
On summer weekends the place gets packed
/ith not-so-local locals seeking cool shade.

Camping Valle Verde *(☎ 15-512517, 1km*
rom Villa Verde on Ruta 31) US$4 per site.
JS$12 tenedor libre lunch. In an exceptional

setting between red rock and river, sites are
boxy and squashed together, but there's
plenty of room on the premises, amidst clusters of fruit trees. The generous family that
runs the camping has details on *agroturismo*
tours in the area.

Camping Municipal *(☎ 490329)* US$3
per person, US$2 showers. Spreading out
endlessly along the riverbank, sites near the
end of the road are the better option. All the
necessary comforts are provided.

Los Siete Robles *(☎ 421746, Villa Verde)*
US$10 per bed, US$50 8-person cabins; open
summer only. Pleasant management runs this
attractive place. Fixed-price lunches of US$10
are also a good value, or try **Parrilla Don**
Segundo, with meals for US$3 to US$10.

PLAYA UNIÓN
☎ 02965

Near Trelew, Rawson has the status of
Chubut's provincial capital, but Playa
Unión's got the capital attraction: *toninas*
overas (Commerson's dolphins; see the
special section on Patagonian wildlife). The
area's main play station, Playa Unión is a
long stretch of white sand beach with
blocks of summer homes, all ending at
Puerto Rawson and the mouth of the Río
Chubut. Surfing, as the tourist leaflet says,
'on thick, hollow, trouble-crested waves,'
and windsurfing are prime activities from
February to late April, but you'll need your
own boards.

Tourist information is available at Rawson
& Juan Manuel del Rosas (☎ 496588), and in
Rawson at Moreno 650 (☎ 481990, interno
124), both open 7am to 8pm daily.

Leaving from Puerto Rawson, tonina
tours cost around US$20, last about 1½
hours and run only in season, from April to
December. For reservations, call either
Toninas Adventure *(☎ 15-666542)* or
Capitán Tonina *(☎ 498041)*.

Lodging is better in Trelew, except for
those who prefer to camp. **Camping Mutual**
Gaiman *(☎ 496157, Nahuelpan & Ramón*
Lista) US$3. Although a few blocks from
the beach, this is the closest to beach
camping you'll get. While on the beach, take
advantage of the fresh seafood brought in

every afternoon to the port: Try either *Cantina El Marinero* (☎ 496030) or *Cantina Marcelino* (☎ 496031).

Getting There & Away

Empresas Rawson and 28 de Julio buses depart from Trelew to Rawson several times daily Monday to Friday and every 20 to 30 minutes on weekends. Get off either at the tourist office on the plaza or the bus station and hop on an Empresa Bahía bus marked 'Playa Union.' Buses go all the way to Puerto Rawson before turning around.

RESERVA PROVINCIAL PUNTA TOMBO

Continental South America's largest penguin nesting ground, Punta Tombo *(admission US$7; open dawn-dusk, Aug-late Mar or early Apr)* has a colony of over a half-million Magellanic penguins, and attracts many seabirds and shorebirds, most notably king and rock cormorants, giant petrels, kelp gulls, flightless steamer ducks and black oystercatchers.

Trelew-based agencies run tours (US$30, not including entrance fee), but may cancel if bad weather makes the dirt roads impassable. If possible, come in the early morning to beat the crowds. Most of the nesting area is fenced off: Respect the limits and remember that penguins can inflict serious bites. Punta Tombo is 110km south of Trelew via gravel but in good condition RP 1, and a short southeast lateral.

Motorists can proceed south to Camarones (see below) via scenic but desolate Cabo Raso.

CAMARONES & CABO DOS BAHÍAS
☎ 02965 • pop 1200

Small Camarones is a quiet getaway and the closest town to the Cabo Dos Bahías nature reserve. Spanish explorer Don Simón de Alcazaba y Sotomayor sailed into the bay around 1545, naming it part of his attempted Provincia de Nueva León. When the wool industry took off, Camarones became the area's main port for building supplies, wool and sheepskins. But when Comodoro got its massive port, Camarones was all but deserted. The wool from here is of very high quality, a fact that didn't go unnoticed by justice of the peace Don Mario Tomás Perón, who operated the area's largest estancia, Porvenir, on which son Juan would romp about.

Isolated **Cabo Dos Bahías** *(US$5)* attracts far fewer visitors than Punta Tombo, making it a worthwhile alternative. You'll be rewarded with a colony of over 30,000 nesting penguins in spring and summer, some of the largest concentrations of guanacos and rheas on the coast, plus a variety of seabirds, sea lions, fur seals and foxes.

From RN 3, about 180km south of Trelew, paved RP 30 leads 72km to town. Another 30km southeast is Cabo Dos Bahías. The annual Fiesta Nacional del Salmón (National Salmon Festival) takes place in early February.

The tourist office (☎ 0297-4963104), in the municipal building, has a few leaflets about the area.

Places to Stay & Eat

Camping Camarones (San Martín) US$3 per person, US$2 per vehicle; open year-round. Near the historic post office and right at the waterfront port, the somewhat shaded campground is central, but rather small. Bathrooms have hot showers and there's electricity. At Cabo Dos Bahías pitch a tent at *Club Naútico* or on any of the beaches en route.

Bahía del Ensueño (☎ 0297-4963077, Belgrano & 9 de Julio) Cabins US$80 for 5 persons, residencial US$10/15 shared/private bath. Cramped A-frame cabins offer a bit more privacy, while other rooms are adequate and have kitchen privileges. Otherwise, *Residencial Mar Azul*, run by the same owner, charges US$10 for rooms with shared bath. For information and keys to both places, go to Farmacia Las Brisas at San Martín & Sarmiento.

Hotel Kau-I-keukenk (☎ 0297-4963004, Sarmiento & Roca) Singles/doubles US$15/20 with shared bath, US$20/30 with private bath; *menú del día* US$15. Rooms in the newer wing have heat, views and better bathrooms. Lunch is all-you-can-eat seafood appetizers, fish entrees and parrilla. The breakfast, at US$4, isn't as good a value.

Getting There & Away

Ñandú buses to Camarones (US$16) leave Trelew at 8am Monday and Friday, 6pm Tuesday and Wednesday. For transport to Cabo Dos Bahías, talk with Don Roberto of Kau-I-keunkenk (US$25 per person) or Tour Veno-An, part of Bahía del Sueño (around US$50 per trip).

COMODORO RIVADAVIA

☎ 0297 • pop 160,000

Surrounded by low hills of wind-energy farms, oil pipelines and drilling dogs, Comodoro (as it is commonly known) has little in its favor. But, as a gateway to other nearby attractions and the eastern end of the highway that leads to Coyhaique, Chile, it offers some decent traveler services, most centered on and around the principal commercial streets Av San Martín and Rivadavia. If you do hang around, the state-of-the-art petroleum museum or a walk up 212m Cerro Chenque, smack dab in the middle of the city, make good excursions.

Founded in 1901, Comodoro was once a transport hub for agricultural and cattle products from nearby Sarmiento. But the town struck it rich in 1907 when workers drilling for water found petroleum instead. Near the country's first major oil find, Comodoro became a state pet, gaining a large port, airport and paved roads, and is now a powerhouse in the Argentine oil industry. Foreign companies played a significant role in early development, but the state soon dominated the sector through YPF, which is now owned by a foreign company. Like many other towns along this stretch, the current recession has taken its toll.

Information

The tourist office (☎ 446-2376, Rivadavia 430) is open 8am to 8pm Monday to Saturday. It also has a space at the bus terminal, open the same hours. ACA (☎ 446-4036) has maps and road information at Dorrego and Alvear.

Most of Comodoro's numerous banks and ATMs are along Av San Martín. Travel agencies along Av San Martín may also change cash, but not traveler's checks. The post office is at Av San Martín and Moreno; the postal code is 9000. Call centers abound around downtown. Centro Internet Comodoro, at San Martín 536, stays open late. Laverap is at Rivadavia 287. The Hospital Regional (☎ 446-2542) is at Hipólito Yrigoyen 950.

Museo Regional Patagónico

Decaying natural history specimens at this museum (☎ 477-1017, Av Rivadavia & Chacabuco; free; open 9am-7pm weekdays) nearly overshadow the small yet entertaining archaeological and historical items, including some good pottery and spear points and materials on early South African Boer immigrants.

Museo Nacional del Petróleo

Built by the former state oil agency YPF but now managed by the Universidad Nacional de Patagonia, the petroleum museum (☎ 455-9558, San Lorenzo 250; admission US$3.50; open 9am-5pm Tues-Fri, 3pm-6pm weekends; guided tours 10:30am, 3pm & 4pm Tues-Fri, 3pm & 4pm weekends) boasts vivid exhibits on the region's natural and cultural history, early and modern oil technology, and social and historical aspects of petroleum development. Historical photographs merit special mention, but there are also fascinating, detailed models of tankers, refineries, and the entire zone of exploitation. The museum is in the suburb of General Mosconi (named for YPF's first administrator), a few kilometers north of downtown. Take bus No 7 Laprida or No 8 Palazzo bus from downtown, or a remise for US$3.

Organized Tours

Many agencies arrange trips to Bosque Petrificado Sarmiento (US$65, minimum three passengers; see that entry later in this chapter) and Cueva de las Manos (US$100, minimum three passengers). The local operators are Total Travel (☎/fax 444-5465, Sarmiento 649), also specializing in ski trips, and Turismo Aonik'enk (☎/fax 446-6768, e aonikenk@satlink.com, Urquiza 573).

Mónica Jury and Pedro Mangini (☎ 446-5337, e ruta-40@satlink.com) organize well-informed personalized 4x4 trips around Patagonia, mainly on RN 40, plus they offer excursions to the Bosque Petrificado Sarmiento (US$50). They speak English, German and Italian.

Places to Stay

Catering mainly to business travelers and long-term laborers, lodging here fits two categories: the ritzy and the rundown (and often full). However, there are a few decent spots.

Camping Municipal (☎ 4452918, Rada Tilly) US$2.50/1.50 per adult/child, US$3 per tent. About 15km south of Comodoro, this campground in the windy beach resort of Rada Tilly has evenly distributed sites with windbreaking shrubs. Frequent buses leave from Comodoro's bus station.

Amutui Mi Quimei Hue (☎ 454-8876, RN 3 Km 12) US$2 per person, US$5 night fee. A bit harder to get to (ask bus driver to drop you off), this site southwest of the city is open all year, has hot water showers and a small farm.

Hotel del Valle (☎ 444-1300, A del Valle 1476) Shared/private bath US$10/20. Even though the rooms lack ventilation, this is one of the best deals in town, with large clean baths, sofas galore and a gregarious owner.

Hotel Español (☎ 446-0116, 9 de Julio 950) US$15/18 shared/private bath. Catering mainly to groups of male workers, Español offers stuffy dark rooms with all-in-one bathrooms.

Hospedaje Cari-Hue (☎ 447-2946, Belgrano 563) Singles/doubles US$15/25 with private bath. It's a rather quirky place with gnomes in the hallway and an owner bordering on the eccentric. But it's central, albeit noisy.

Hostería Rúa Marina (☎ 446-8777, Belgrano 738) Singles/doubles US$20/30 with private bath. Some rooms don't have windows, but have ceiling fans. It's the friendly and welcoming staff, plus a small gym and excellent location that make Rúa Marina a favorite.

Austral Hotel (☎/fax 447-2200, Moren 725) Singles/doubles US$78/96 to US$11. 131. Business hotel extraordinaire, thi labyrinthine place offers boxy 'inexpensive rooms hidden in the back and pricey bus ness suites. Attentive staff, Internet acces and a sweeping breakfast buffet add to th sparkle.

Comodoro Hotel (☎ 447-2300, 9 de Juli 770) Singles/doubles US$59/74 standard US$65/80 superior. Drab standard room have plump beds and bidet showers, whil the superior ones are much more attractive remodeled with larger bathrooms. Interne access and buffet breakfast come included.

Places to Eat

Rotisería Andafama (☎ 446-3882, Rivadavi & Alvear) US$1-3. A ways from downtown but locals swear the best empanada (takeout only) are here.

La Fonte D'Oro (☎ 446-0804, San Martí 494) US$2-6. Simple sandwiches and piles o pastries, plus costly coffee, keep this a popula hangout to watch a match, read a paper o catch up on the gossip, and it's open 24 hours

La Cantina (☎ 446-0023, Belgrano 845 US$3-12. Check the windows for daily spe cials when the already cheap pastas an pizzas are even more of a bargain. Pizzas drip with cheese and the pastas come with ampl sauce, although neither wins culinary kudos

Los Tres Chinos (☎ 444-1168, Rivadavi 341) US$7. The best deal in town and always crowded, Los Tres Chinos has a spread o over 40 different items plus parrilla. Drinks are expensive.

La Barca (☎ 447-3710, Belgrano 935, US$4-12. Order from the menu or heap or portions from the buffet. Seafood is the specialty.

Pizzería Giulietta (☎ 461201, Belgrano 851) US$5-12. Of the offerings along this stretch, this one has the best pizza.

La Tradición (☎ 446-5800, Mitre 675) US$6-14. A popular and top-quality parrilla. La Tradición offers a variety of excellently prepared dishes: Try the tenderloin prepared with ham, cheese and bacon with a stack of fries, or chicken in a red-wine sauce. Leave room for the desserts.

COMODORO RIVADAVIA

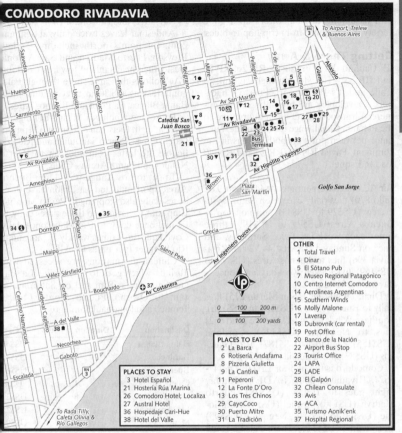

To Airport, Trelew & Buenos Aires

Catedral San Juan Bosco

Bus Terminal

Plaza San Martín

Golfo San Jorge

To Rada Tilly, Caleta Olivia & Río Gallegos

0   100   200 m
0   100   200 yards

PLACES TO STAY
3 Hotel Español
21 Hostería Rúa Marina
26 Comodoro Hotel; Localiza
27 Austral Hotel
36 Hospedaje Cari-Hue
38 Hotel del Valle

PLACES TO EAT
2 La Barca
6 Rotisería Andafama
8 Pizzería Giulietta
9 La Cantina
11 Peperoni
12 La Fonte D'Oro
13 Los Tres Chinos
29 CayoCoco
30 Puerto Mitre
31 La Tradición

OTHER
1 Total Travel
4 Dinar
5 El Sótano Pub
7 Museo Regional Patagónico
10 Centro Internet Comodoro
14 Aerolíneas Argentinas
15 Southern Winds
16 Molly Malone
17 Laverap
18 Dubrovnik (car rental)
19 Post Office
20 Banco de la Nación
22 Airport Bus Stop
23 Tourist Office
24 LAPA
25 LADE
28 El Galpón
32 Chilean Consulate
33 Avis
34 ACA
35 Turismo Aonik'enk
37 Hospital Regional

Puerto Mitre (☎ 447-6175, Mitre & Ameghino) US$10-15. Clever decorations and stylish service are hardly noticed once the cheesy pizza with fresh toppings and the right-priced beers come around.

CayoCoco (☎ 447-3033, Rivadavia 102) US$11-16. Kitty-corner to the gigantic Anónima supermarket, CayoCoco wood-fires up an imaginative assortment of pizzas and calzones.

Peperoni (☎ 446-9683, Rivadavia 481) US$11-20. Well regarded for consistently good pastas, such as the seafood *sorrentinos* and delicately prepared fish entrees. The salads (US$6 to US$8.50) alone could be a meal.

Entertainment

Molly Malone (☎ 447-8330, San Martín & 9 de Julio) US$1.50-4. Run by the 'Golden Oldies' rugby veterans, this small brick-and-tin corner café is a pleasant stop for a coffee or Quilmes in the afternoon.

El Galpón (no ☎, Rivadavia 120) US$2.50-5 beer, US$9-12 appetizer plates. Four types of brews to choose from, each one is a quencher and the right way to wash down a German-style plate of meat cuts and cheeses.

El Sótano Pub *(San Martín 239)* Hidden in a basement, this bar offers up a good variety of live music from trip-hop to blues.

Getting There & Away

'El Camino del Corredor' – RN 26, RP 20 and RP 55 – is a straight highway link to Chile and it's Pacific port, Puerto Chacabuco. Developers are promoting this commercial transport route as an alternative to the Panama Canal, since it's the shortest distance between ports on both oceans in the continent. Paved RN 26, RP 20 and RN 40 lead to Esquel.

Air Aerolíneas Argentinas (☎ 444-0050, 9 de Julio 870) flies daily except on Saturday to Trelew (US$29 to US$43), and nonstop to Buenos Aires (US$77 to US$199) three times each weekday, twice Saturday, and once on Sunday. LAPA (☎ 447-2400, Rivadavia 396) flies to Buenos Aires (US$79 to US$169) twice each weekday and once a day on weekends.

Dinar (☎ 444-1111, San Martín 215) flies daily to Buenos Aires (US$109 to US$170). Southern Winds (☎ 447-1111, 9 de Julio 852) flies to Neuquén (US$131), Córdoba (US$155), Mendoza (US$187), Río Gallegos (US$87) and Ushuaia (US$120).

Comodoro is the hub for LADE (☎ 447-6624, Rivadavia 360). LADE's Monday flight goes to Trelew (US$28), Puerto Madryn (US$40), Esquel (US$43), Bariloche (US$60 to US$80), Neuquén (US$93) and Viedma (US$116). There's also a route to Perito Moreno (US$29), El Calafate (US$61) and Río Gallegos (US$72). On Thursday the route is Puerto Deseado (US$25), San Julián (US$39), Gobernador Gregores (US$39), Santa Cruz (US$47), Río Gallegos (US$66) and, sometimes, Ushuaia (US$107).

Schedules and routes change frequently, so inquire at the office. Airport tax is US$6.

Bus Comodoro's bus terminal (☎ 446-7305) is at Ameghino & 25 de Mayo. All bus lines plying RN 3 stop here. Companies include Andesmar (☎ 446-8894), El Pingüino (☎ 447-9104), TAC (☎ 444-3376), Sportsman

(☎ 444-2988), La Unión (☎ 446-2822), Etap (☎ 447-4841) and El Condor (☎ 447-2485).

Andesmar leaves twice daily, at 5am and 2pm, for points north including Trelew, Rawson, Puerto Madryn and San Antonio Oeste, then heads inland towards Córdoba. TAC follows the same route through Patagonia, leaving at 8:30am, but continues on to Bahía Blanca, La Plata and Buenos Aires.

For southern points, TAC and El Pingüino leave at night (between 8:40pm and 11pm) to Caleta Olivia, Puerto San Julián and Río Gallegos; the latter continues on to Puerto Natales and Punta Arenas, Chile.

To get to Los Antiguos on Lago Buenos Aires, Sportsman and La Unión have three buses daily, also stopping in Perito Moreno. Etap runs to Sarmiento three times daily, to Esquel once daily, to Río Mayo once daily, Coyhaique three times weekly at 1am and to Río Senguer four times weekly.

Chilean destinations are accessed with Turibus, which goes to Coyhaique Tuesday and Saturday at 8am and on Saturdays at 8am to Osorno, Puerto Montt, Castro, Temuco and long-haul Santiago.

Destination	Duration in hours	Cost
Bahía Blanca	15	US$50
Bariloche	14	US$45
Buenos Aires	24	US$60
Caleta Olivia	1	US$4
Esquel	8	US$29
Los Antiguos	6	US$25
Mendoza	31	US$99
Puerto Deseado	4	US$17
Puerto Madryn	7	US$20
Río Gallegos	11	US$30
Trelew	6	US$16
Viedma	10	US$35

Getting Around

Aeropuerto General Mosconi (☎ 447-3355 interno 163) is north of the city, but the No 8 Patagonia Argentina (Directo Palazzo) bus goes there directly from the downtown bus terminal.

Expreso Rada Tilly (☎ 445-1363) links Comodoro to the nearby beach resort about every half-hour weekdays, less frequently on weekends. The last bus leaves Como-doro's terminal at 11:30pm weekdays, 12:30am Saturday nights/Sunday mornings, and 11:20pm Sunday evenings.

Rental cars are available at Localiza (☎ 446-0334) in Hotel Comodoro and Austral, or at Avis (☎ 447-6382, 9 de Julio 687). Dubrovnik (☎ 444-1844, Moreno 858) rents 4x4 vehicles.

SARMIENTO
☎ 0297 • pop 7200

After 148km of drudgery desert and oil der-ricks along RN 26 and RP 20, from Como-doro, tree-green Sarmiento, with Lago Musters and Lago Colué Huapi nearby, is an inviting stop, and the gateway to the petri-fied forests, 30km south. Considered the southernmost irrigated town, it's been an agricultural center since its founding in 1897. Unfortunately, the industry has come at a cost: Colué Huapi is a puddle of its former self, a cause of concern for area ecologists.

There's a tourist office (☎ 489-8220, e turismo@coopsar.com.ar) at Av Reg In-fanteria 25.

In town, the surprisingly good **Museo Re-gional Desiderio Torres** *(free; open 10:30am-1pm & 5pm-8pm Mon-Sat, 10:30am to 4:30pm Sun)* has archeological and paleon-tology displays, plus indigenous artifacts, with an emphasis on weavings. Just before the entrance to town, at Lote 58, is **Granja San José** *(☎ 489-3733)*, a hydroponics farm that sells exquisite fruit jams.

Room and board is available at recom-mended *La Chacra Labrador (☎ 489-3329, e agna@coopsar.com.ar)*, where the atten-tive owners also organize excursions to nearby attractions. Etap buses run to Sar-miento (US$10).

BOSQUE PETRIFICADO SARMIENTO

These petrified forests *(admission US$5; open dawn-dusk)*, outside of Sarmiento, are much more easily accessed than the Monu-mento Natural Bosques Petrificados farther south. A trail leads through a beautifully quiet and ghostly area that has the appear-ance of a lumber mill gone mad; 'wood'

chips cover the ground and huge petrified logs are scattered about. Unlike the petrified forest in Santa Cruz, the trunks here are not of original fallen trees, but were brought from the mountainous regions by strong river currents about 65 million years ago. The most impressive area of the park has a handful of large trunks set against the red and orange striated bluffs.

Tour buses usually leave by 5pm. Try, if you can, to stay through sunset, when the striped bluffs of Cerro Abigarrado and the multi-hued hills turn brilliantly vivid. As you leave the park, the rangers will, if suspicious, ask you to empty your pockets and packs to expose any stolen pieces. A 'box of shame' shows what some have tried to sneak out. It's possible to arrange a car and driver (about US$40) in Sarmiento. See Comodoro Rivadavia's Organized Tours section.

CALETA OLIVIA
☎ 0297 • pop 42,000

On coastal RN 3, oil- and fish-processing port Caleta Olivia has little to recommend it, but is a convenient place to change buses to more inspiring locales, such as the petri-fied forests, Los Antiguos or Puerto Deseado. In 1901, the port was created as part of a plan to run telegraph along the coast, and was named after the only woman on board that first ship.

Discovery of oil turned the face of indus-try from wool and sheep transport to petro-leum hub, as evidenced by the Casperlike 10m-high **Monumento al Obrero Petrolero** dominating the downtown traffic circle. Col-loquially called 'El Gorosito,' the muscular oil worker looks north, symbolizing the link between this area's industry and how it ben-efits the northern reaches of the country.

Orientation & Information

Entering Caleta Olivia from the north, RN 3 becomes part of Av Jorge Newbery, then Av San Martín (the main thoroughfare), contin-uing after the traffic circle along southeast diagonal Av Eva Perón. The southwest diag-onal, Av Independencia, becomes RP 12. Most streets run diagonal to San Martín, except in the northeast quadrant. The pebbly beach and port are four blocks east of the traffic circle.

The enthusiastic tourist office (☎ 485-0988), at Av San Martín & Güemes, near the monument, is open 7am to 10pm in summer, 8am to 5pm the rest of the year. The post office is on 25 de Mayo at Hipólito Yrigoyen. Banks don't change traveler's checks but have ATMs.

Places to Stay

For what accommodations offer, prices are steep, and breakfast an additional cost.

Camping Municipal (☎ 485-0999 interno 476, Brown & Guttero) 1/2 backpackers US$3/4.50, with car US$5/6. In an exposed lot near the pebbly beach, the campground is open year-round, has 24-hour security, hot showers and barbecue pits.

Posada Don David (☎ 857-7661, Hipólito Yrigoyen 2385) Singles/doubles US$10/15. Basic rooms line up along a tight corridor and the shared baths need a major rehab, but overall, Don David is pleasant, clean and well run.

Residencial Las Vegas (☎ 485-1177, Hipólito Yrigoyen 2094) US$15 with private bath. With a kind owner and some quiet back rooms, this is one of the better places, although the rooms lack ventilation.

Hotel Capri (☎ 485-1132, José Hernández 1145) Singles/doubles US$20/30. For over 40 years, the fun-loving couple here has offered decent rooms, all off a central hallway. The rooms upstairs are better.

Hotel Robert (☎ 485-1452, fax 485-2924, Av San Martín 2151) Singles/doubles US$41/62 to US$52/77. Overpriced sterile rooms and tasteless meals taint Robert's two- to three-star status. Still, it's the executive's choice and the best hotel in town.

Places to Eat

Posada Don David (☎ 857-7661, Hipólito Yrigoyen 2385) US$2-6. Start with a crisp salad before plunging into a bowl of home-made pasta or parrilla in this recommended casual eatery, frequented by locals.

Café Lo de Andres (☎ 485-3870, Independencia 1157) US$2-5; open 24 hours. There are plenty of cafés along this stretch, but this one stands out for its breakfasts and list of highballs.

El Puerto (☎ 485-1313, Av Independencia 1060) US$7-16. Linen-fresh and formal, El Puerto's meals are a bit too costly, but if you feel the need for a business-style lunch, this is the best choice in town.

Getting There & Away

The bus terminal is about 3km from downtown at Humberto Bequin and Tierra del Fuego. A remise to the town center is US$3. The main north-south carriers leave for Comodoro Rivadavia (US$5; 1 hour) hourly from 7am to 11pm, with less service on Sunday, and to Río Gallegos (US$25; 8 hours) about four times daily between 8:30pm and 2am, passing by Puerto San Julián. Sportsman buses run to Puerto Deseado (US$13; 4 hours) at 7:40am and 8:45pm, and La Unión buses at 1:30pm and 7:30pm.

For Perito Moreno (US$17, 4 hours) and Los Antiguos (US$20, 5 hours), on Lago Buenos Aires, two buses leave daily at 7am and one at 5:50pm.

PUERTO DESEADO
☎ 0297 • pop 11,000

Some 120km from the RN 3 junction, RN 281 weaves through valleys of warbled pink rock, ending in the attractive and serene deep-sea fishing town of Puerto Deseado. The slow pace and the historic buildings, plus the submerged estuary of Ría Deseado, brimming with seabirds and marine wildlife, make Puerto Deseado a worthwhile detour.

After a destructive storm in 1520, Hernando de Magallanes stayed in the sheltered waters of the estuary to repair the fleet, first naming the area 'Río de los Trabajos.' In 1586 English privateer Cavendish explored every nook and cranny of the estuary and named it after his ship *Desire*, the name that stuck. Fleets from around the world descended on the port for whaling and seal hunting, compelling the Spanish crown to send a squadron of colonists, under the command of Antonio de Viedma. A blustery winter didn't bode well for them, however, and more than 30 died of scurvy. Those who survived moved inland to form the new colony of Floridablanca, which lasted only three years. In 1834, Darwin explored the estuary, as did Perito Moreno in 1876; both wrote elaborately about the area in their respective travelogues.

Orientation & Information

Puerto Deseado is 125km from the RN 3 junction of Fitz Roy via RN 281. The main center of activity is the axis formed by Avs José de San Martín and Almirante Brown.

Deseado's 'Ría Deseada' tourist office (☎ 15-6234351, San Martín 1525) is open 8am to 3pm weekdays, or go to the the Vagón Histórico, at San Martín and Almirante Brown, open 10am to 9pm daily from December through Easter. Banks along San Martín have ATMs. The post office is at San Martín 1075; the postal code is 9050. Ecowash laundry service is at Piedra Buena 859.

Things to See & Do

Puerto Deseado's historical monuments testify to the town's better days as the port terminus of the Ferrocarril Patagónico, a cargo and passenger route that hauled wool and lead from Chilean mines from Pico

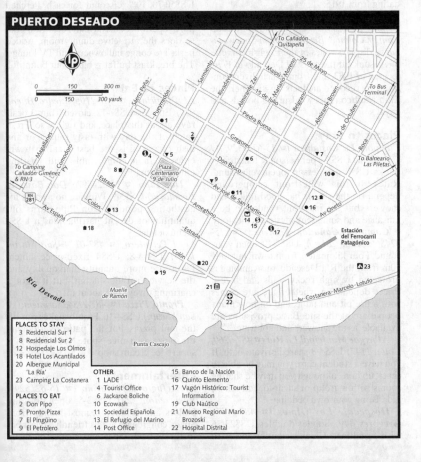

PUERTO DESEADO

0   150   300 m
0   150   300 yards

To Cañadón Quitapeña

To Bus Terminal

To Balneario Las Piletas

To Camping Cañadón Giménez & RN 3

Plaza Centenario 9 de Julio

Estación del Ferrocarril Patagónico

Ría Deseada

Muelle de Ramón

Punta Cascajo

Av Costanera - Marcelo Lotufo

PLACES TO STAY
3 Residencial Sur 1
8 Residencial Sur 2
12 Hospedaje Los Olmos
18 Hotel Los Acantilados
20 Albergue Municipal 'La Ría'
23 Camping La Costanera

PLACES TO EAT
2 Don Pipo
5 Pronto Pizza
7 El Pingüino
9 El Petrolero

OTHER
1 LADE
4 Tourist Office
6 Jackaroe Boliche
10 Ecowash
11 Sociedad Española
13 El Refugio del Marino
14 Post Office

15 Banco de la Nación
16 Quinto Elemento
17 Vagón Histórico: Tourist Information
19 Club Naútico
21 Museo Regional Mario Brozoski
22 Hospital Distrital

Truncado and Las Heras, 280km northwest. The imposing English-designed **Estación del Ferrocarril Patagónico**, near Av Oneto, was the coastal terminus for the line, built of local stone by Yugoslav stonecutters. In the center of town, the 1898 **Vagón Histórico** *(Av San Martín & Almirante Brown)* is locally known as the car from which rebel leader Facón Grande prepared the 'Patagonia Rebellion.' (In 1979, the car was going to be sold for scrap, but the townspeople blocked the roads to keep the car in its rightful spot.) A few blocks west is the attractive **Sociedad Española** *(San Martín 1176)*, dating from 1915.

The simple **Museo Regional Mario Brozoski** *(☎ 487-0673,* e *brozoski@pdeseado .com.ar, Colón & Belgrano, 10am-5pm weekdays)*, displays relics of the English corvette *Swift*, sunk off the coast of Deseado in 1776, located in 1982, and from which divers continue to recover artifacts. In summer, the **Club Naútico** rents windsurfing boards and kayaks.

Places to Stay

Camping La Costanera (☎ 15-6249329, Av Costanera) US$3-4 per person & tent, trailer bunks US$7 per person; open year-round. Rates at this waterfront campground depend on the site. It has good toilets and showers, but the incessant winds can be a nuisance and some tent sites are a bit stony.

Camping Cañadón Giménez (☎ 15-6248602, Ruta 281 s/n) US$5-10; open year-round. Four kilometers from town, but only 50m from the Ría Deseado, this camping is protected by high rocky walls and forest. Prices depend on whether the site comes with a fire pit and table, and on how many people are at the site. Basic provisions are available, as are showers and hot water.

Albergue Municipal La Ría (☎ 487-0260, Colón 1147) US$5/8 shared/private bath. If you have a student card, you may be able to shack up here, although you may be sharing rooms with a group of sugar-loaded school kids. Bring your own bedding.

Hospedaje Los Olmos (☎ 487-0077, Gregores 849) Singles/doubles US$23/36 with breakfast. Clean, friendly and with

parking, this is the best budget choice in the town.

Residencial Sur 1 (☎ 487-0522, Ameghino 1640) Singles/doubles US$24/40. Large and well run, Sur is often busy with traveling workers – fishing crews, mainly. Rooms are basic, bathrooms sparkling clean and the breakfast included. When this one fills up, guests go to *Residencial Sur 2 (Pueyrredón 367)*, which is smaller but has the same level of quality.

Hotel Los Acantilados (☎/fax 487-2167, e *acantour@pdeseado.com.ar Pueyrredón & España)* Singles/doubles US$30/42 to US$50/70, 10% discount for cash. Perched upon a pink-stone bluff overlooking the port, superior rooms have the best views, but so does the attractive dining room. Added perks are congenial owners, and TV lounge. The breakfast buffet is bland but bountiful.

Places to Eat

El Pingüino (☎ 487-2105, Piedra Buena 950) Entrees US$7-12; closed Thur. Locals rave about this place, and rightly so. Fresh catch of the day with tasty sauces, or any dish of pasta, is the best meal in town, enjoyed in a comfortable and bustling dining room.

Don Pipo (☎ 15-6248976, Don Bosco & Rivadavia) US$3-9. Winning no awards for aesthetics, popular Don Pipo turns out quantities of decent parrilla, plus a US$8 menú del día.

El Petrolero (☎ 487-0114, San Martín 1294) US$4-8; US$4 fixed-price lunch. Pastas are more quantity than quality, and the service rather solemn, but it's got a charming divey style about it.

Pronto Pizza (☎ 487-2134, Sarmiento & San Martín) US$4-10. Pronto makes run-of-the-mill pizzas, but the patio overlooking the plaza is a nice spot. Next door is a superb ice cream shop.

Entertainment

El Refugio del Marino (☎ 15-6215290, Pueyrredón 224) US$2-5; open to 2am. Sailors and fishermen, most hailing from Spain, congregate at this friendly, stylish bar to throw back tapas and glasses of cheap *tinto* (red wine). Come in the evening to listen to the boys swap stories. Late-night dancing spots are *Jackaroe Boliche (Moreno 663)* and *Quinto Elemento (Don Bosco & 12 de Octubre)*.

Getting There & Away

LADE (☎ 487-1204, Don Bosco 1580) flies Thursdays to San Julián, Santa Cruz and Río Gallegos. The bus terminal is at Sargento Cabral 1302, at the northeast corner of town, about eight blocks from San Martín & Oneto. There are five departures daily Monday to Saturday and three on Sunday to Caleta Olivia (US$15, 3 hours). Three buses continue to Comodoro Rivadavia (US$19, 4½ hours). Leaving on the 1pm bus allows for the quickest connection to Perito Moreno and Los Antiguos. One bus leaves nightly for Río Gallegos, via bleak and desolate Fitz Roy (US$32; 10 hours).

RESERVA NATURAL RÍA DESEADO

Considered one of the more important marine preserves in the world, Ría Deseado is the unique result of a river abandoning its bed, allowing the South Atlantic waters to invade 40km inland and create a perfect shelter for marine life. Several islands and other sites are nesting habitat for seabirds, including Magellanic penguins, petrels, oystercatchers, herons, terns and five species of cormorants. Isla Chaffers is the main spot for the penguins, while Banco Cormorán offers protection to rock cormorants and the strikingly beautiful gray cormorant. Isla de los Pingüinos has nesting rockhoppers and breeding elephant seals. Commerson's dolphins, sea lions, guanacos and ñandús can also be seen while touring the estuary.

Darwin Expediciones-Gipsy Tours (☎ 15-624755, España 2601) run circuits that take in viewing of Commerson's dolphins, Isla Chaffers, Banco Cormorán, and a walk to a penguin colony of Isla de los Pájaros (US$25, 2½ hours). Another tour takes in all of the above plus another 15km of the estuary (US$40, 5 hours). There's a four- to five-person minimum and tours leave depending on tides, usually early morning and

mid-afternoon. Also try Los Vikingos (☎ 487-0020, mobile 15-6245141, Estrada 1275), which also has bilingual guides and organizes overland trips. Trips to Isla de los Pingüinos are possible with both outfitters but cost up to US$160, with a four-person minimum. The best time to visit is from December to April.

MONUMENTO NATURAL BOSQUES PETRIFICADOS

During Jurassic times, 150 million years ago, this area enjoyed a humid, temperate climate with flourishing forests, but intense volcanic activity buried them in ash. Erosion later exposed the mineralized *Proaraucaria* trees (ancestors of the modern *araucaria*, unique to the Southern Hemisphere), up to 3m in diameter and 35m in length. Today, the 15,000-hectare **Petrified Forest Natural Monument** has a short interpretive trail, leading from park headquarters, to the largest concentration of petrified trees. Until its legal protection in 1954, the area was consistently plundered for some of its finest specimens; do not perpetuate this unsavory tradition by taking even the tiniest souvenir.

Other parts of the scenic desert park also merit exploration, but consult with park rangers before continuing far on the road toward the peak of Madre e Hija. There is no water at the site, so bring your own.

The park is 157km south of Caleta Olivia, accessed from an excellent gravel road leading 50km west from RN 3. There is no public transportation directly to the park. Buses from Caleta Olivia can drop you at the junction, but you may wait several hours for a lift into the park. Los Vikingos (☎ 0297-487-0020, 15-6245141, Estrada 1275, Puerto Deseado) runs tours from Puerto Deseado for US$45, or try Transporte Fede (☎ 0297-15-6244878, Gobernador Gregores 1142, Puerto Deseado). In summer, you could try hitching (don't attempt in winter, when the area is bitterly cold) but be prepared for the chance you don't get a ride.

There is *camping*, as well as provisions, at **La Paloma**, midway between RN 3 and park headquarters. Camping in the park is strictly prohibited.

PUERTO SAN JULIÁN

☎ 02962 • pop 7000

One of the more historically intriguing towns along the coast, Puerto San Julián, 341km south of Caleta Olivia, can claim to be the place where the name 'Patagonia' came to be, and where the likes of Magellan, Viedma, Drake and Darwin all stopped. Today, it's a sleepy place of wide boulevards and square development, with little outward recognition of its rich history, except for its excellent museum. This is a decent stop along the coastal route, and *the* place to see Commerson's dolphins.

In the winter of 1520, Magellan's crew wintered in the sheltered harbor of San Julián, where their encounter with the Tehuelche led to the naming of Patagonia (see the boxed text 'Don't Rock the Boat, or History Repeats Itself'). In 1780 Antonio de Viedma established the Floridablanca colony that lasted only a few years. Only the wool boom of the late 19th century brought permanent settlement, thanks to pioneering Scots. From the turn of the century until the decline of wool prices in the past 20 years, the British-owned San Julián Sheep Farming Company was the area's most powerful economic force. Nowadays, seafood processing and, to a lesser degree, gold and silver mining are important industries.

Information

From mid-December to March, there's an information stand at the EG3 station, north of the highway junction; it's open 10am to 10pm daily. The Dirección de Turismo (☎ 454396, e centur@uvc.com.ar, Av Hernando de Magallanes), about 20m from Hostería Municipal, keeps long hours, from 7am to 1am weekdays, 10am to 1am weekends, allowing late-night travelers to get lodging information, if needed.

Nearly all public services are near the east end of Av San Martín, close to the tip of the peninsula. Banco de la Nación occupies an attractive Victorian building at Mitre and Belgrano. The post office is at Av San Martín and Belgrano. Locutorios are at San Martín and Saavedra and at Mitre and Moreno.

Things to See & Do

Much recommended **Museo Regional y de Arte Marino** (*Vieytes & Rivadavia; free; open 9am-1pm & 4pm-9pm weekdays, 10am-1pm & 4pm-9pm weekends*), in a classic Magellanic house, features archaeological artifacts and historical materials, as well as contemporary fine art. Well-informed guides, some of whom speak English, put the many objects in intriguing historical context. Included is rock art from different epochs, roof tiles created by settlers by molding the clay with their thighs, a chunk of rock with a well-preserved dinosaur foot (it was first used as construction material along the main boulevard, but quickly given museum status), a wheel from one of Saint-Exupéry's planes, and images of the first settlers.

At the **Centro Artesanal** and **Escuela Taller de Cerámica** (*Moreno & Mitre*) local artisans work on weavings, knitted wear and ceramics made of local clay. The adjacent store sells a humble assortment of the artwork.

The ruins of **Floridablanca**, 10km west of town, cannot be accessed now that Benetton owns the land, but there's nothing to see anyway since what is of interest is buried underground. Equally not to bother with are the ruins of the Swift **Frigorífico** (mutton freezer), which operated between 1912 and 1967. However, the road that meanders north, passing the freezer and going by the tomb of *Beagle* lieutenant Sholl, continues to starkly beautiful beaches, such as Cabo Curioso and Playa de los Caracoles, where large amounts of fossilized shells have been found. You'll need your own wheels, or a remise will cost upwards of US$30 to zip around the main sites.

Boat trips around Bahía San Julián going to the rookeries of penguins and imperial cormorants at Banco Cormorán and Banco Justicia are run by **Expediciones Pinocho** (*☎ 452856, Mitre & 9 de Julio*), located next to the restaurant Muelle Viejo, for US$20 per person, maximum eight persons. The trips last 1½ hours and there's a good chance you'll see the Commerson's dolphin (best months from December to March).

Don't Rock the Boat, or History Repeats Itself

To the east of Europe were spices and riches but the voyage was difficult; many ambitious sailors dreamed of reaching these exotic lands from the west. Confident he could find the route through the New World, but rebuffed by his own king, Portuguese explorer Ferdinand Magellan convinced the teenage Spanish king Charles I in 1518 to fund an expedition. With the rather generous funds granted to him, Magellan bought the *Naos, Santiago, Concepción, Victoria, Trinidad* and *San Antonio.* The Spanish captains of the ships were none too thrilled to have a foreigner, let alone Portuguese, boss them around, but in September 1519, Magellan and a crew of 270 men, including the young Italian, Pigafetta, headed out to sea.

Uncommunicative and unwilling to explain the voyage's plans, Magellan soon frustrated his crew. Within a few months, Juan de Cartagena, appointed by his father, Bishop Fonseca to keep an eye on Magellan, unsuccessfully attempted mutiny and was imprisoned.

Along the South American coast, Magellan pushed his fleet farther south, and farther into blustery autumnal winds and storms in search of the 'secret' passage. At the end of March, 1520, six months after setting sail and still with no sign of the passage, Magellan ordered the fleet to winter at the protected bay at San Julián. The captains urged him to turn back to Spain, but Magellan held fast to his goal. Amid the tension, on Easter Sunday, Magellan invited the captains to participate in mass on land, followed by dinner on his ship, but some refused the offer. The following day, Juan de Cartagena rallied two other captains, Gaspar de Quesada and Luis de Mendoza, to sneak three boats out of the bay and head back to Spain. Magellan quickly took control of Mendoza's boat, during which Mendoza was stabbed to death, and blockaded the ships.

In front of the officers and crew, Mendoza's body was drawn, quartered and hung on gibbets posted at four positions – north, south, east and west – on the bay (a method used to evoke in the crew the fear of eternal damnation). On April 7, Quesada was decapitated by his own servant, whom Magellan had forced into the deed under the threat of death, and also quartered and hung on the gallows.

Cartagena, on the other hand, was kept prisoner onboard throughout the winter, during which time the crew spotted and met the giant Tehuelche, inspiring the term 'Patagonia.' When the fleet was ready to set sail again, after four months at San Julián, Cartagena was left on land, marooned with a priest and the barest of provisions.

...and Chapter Two....

Fifty-eight years later, in September 1577, English pirate Francis Drake set sail from Plymouth, England, on the *Pelican* along with four other ships. The nature of his trip, though touted as an expedition to find 'Terra Australis' or a passage to the West, was really a chance to plunder the Spanish and Portuguese vessels returning heavy with gold from the New World. Just as Cartagena was commissioned in Magellan's fleet to keep an eye on the leader and incite trouble should the expedition go astray, so was Drake's close friend Doughty persuaded by the Lord Treasurer of England to keep Drake from changing the expedition. No sooner had they set sail than Doughty began persuading the crew to mutiny. In June 1578, they encountered the quiet bay at San Julián, where Drake also decided to winter. While on land, some of the crew discovered the remains of the gallows erected by Magellan, along with human bones below a fir pole, most likely the bones of the two marooned.

Believing that any more incitement on Doughty's part would jeopardize the expedition, Drake had him arrested and charged with mutiny. The next day, Doughty was beheaded on the same 'Island of Justice' used by Magellan to execute and quarter his mutineers. Drake grabbed Doughty's head, shook it and yelled to the men 'This is the last of the traitors!' Two months later, in August 1578, the fleet set sail, continuing on to complete the second circumnavigation of the globe.

In summer, the **Club Náutico** (☎ *453009, Mitre & 9 de Julio*) may rent kayaks or have opportunities for small-boat sailing.

Places to Stay & Eat

Autocamping Municipal (☎ *452860, Vélez Sarsfield*) US$3 per person, plus US$5 per car, US$2.50 per motorcycle. On the waterfront at the north end of Vélez Sarsfield, this campground has hot showers, a laundry, and tall hedges for windbreaks. If you only want to hang out for the day, you can use showers for US$1.50. Other camping options include *Cabo Curioso* (20km north of town) and *Playa La Mina* farther north, which has a sea lion rookery, both remote and free. Some readers caution about the rats in the area but note the setting is superb.

Hospedaje Sarasa (☎ *452315, Piedrabuena 811*) US$15 per person, with shared bath. Three-rooms tiny, Sarasa is inevitably familiar and cozy.

Posada Kau Yenu (☎ *452431, Av San Martín between Piedrabuena & Sarmiento*) Singles/doubles/triples US$25/35/55. Kau Yenu means 'friendly home' and helpful owner Don Ernesto fills the place with affection and good spirits. Cozy and small, service is personal and the breakfast breads homemade.

Hotel Álamo (☎ *454092; ask for the hotel*) Singles/doubles US$26/36 with private bath. Next to the EG3 gas station and the RN 3 junction, Alamo is a small, adequate place with a good restaurant.

Residencial Sada (☎ *452013, Av San Martín 1112*) Singles/doubles US$35/48 private bath. With large bathrooms and warm and clean rooms, Sada is a good bet. Breakfast is included.

Hotel Municipal de Turismo (☎ *452300, 25 de Mayo 917*) Singles/doubles US$35/55. The zigzag corridor design means all rooms have bay views. It's welcoming and professionally run, and the rooms are quiet, clean, have TV and shipshape bathrooms. Rates don't include breakfast, and the adjacent confitería's a tad too pricey.

El Muelle Viejo (☎ *453009, 9 de Julio & Mitre*) Pastas US$5-13. This place is part of the Club Náutico, so you can gaze over the bay while enjoying well-prepared fresh catch, breadsticks and Roquefort butter, and attentive service.

La Rural (☎ *454149, Ameghino 811*) Near the museum, La Rural is a good spot for minutas or parrilla.

Entertainment

Casa Lara (*San Martín & Ameghino*) US$3-7. Charm at its finest, this is *the* place in town to mingle over a drink or quick meal in the late evening hours, all the while surrounded by nostalgia and nostalgic locals, gingham and lace, in a building dating from 1901.

Getting There & Away

Air LADE (☎ 452137, Berutti 985) drops by Thursday on its route to Gobernador Gregores (US$20) and Río Gallegos (US$28), and Friday to Puerto Deseado (US$22) and Comodoro Rivadavia (US$39).

Bus The bus terminal (☎ 452082) is on San Martín between Sargento Cabral and Pellegrini. Most north- and southbound buses service San Julián, including Andesmar, TAC, and El Pingüino, but most arrive and depart at insane hours (between 1am and 3am.) Check out Don Otto, which has service at 6:30am, and Andesmar, with early morning and late evening departures. TAC has the most comfortable buses. If you're thinking of getting off at Fitz Roy to continue on to Puerto Deseado, think again: Buses arrive at a demonic hour and there's nowhere to stay.

Transporte Cerro San Lorenzo (☎ 452403, Berutti 970) goes to Gobernador Gregores on Tuesday and Saturday at 7am and Thursday and Sunday at 1pm (US$17). The service may continue on to Laguna Posadas, near the Chilean border.

Fares in either direction, to Caleta Olivia and Comodoro Rivadavia or Río Gallegos, cost between US$13 and US$18, but Pingüino costs less. Door-to-door service options are Sur Servicio (☎ 454144) to Comodoro Rivadavia and Gold Tour (☎ 452265) to Río Gallegos (US$20 or more).

ESTANCIA LA MARÍA

Some 150km from San Julián amidst the Patagonia steppe, Estancia La María has some 87 caves with excellently preserved rock paintings that date back 13,000 years. Three different cultures, all before the Tehuelche, adorned these geologic corners in what is today probably the most important discovery of *arte rupestre* (cave paintings) in Patagonia. The only way to see these treasures, however, is by guided tour with the estancia owners.

This is also a great choice for those looking for a night on an estancia. La María is accessed via RP 25 and RP 77. Contact the owner, Fernando Behm (☎ 02962-452269, fax 452328, Saavedra 1168, Puerto San Julián) for reservations and transportation options. Prices run US$25 for a double with private bath, US$15 with shared bath, US$4 for camping, US$5 for breakfast and US$12 for lunch or dinner. It's open from October through April.

COMANDANTE LUIS PIEDRABUENA
☎ 02962

Between Puerto San Julián and this desolate town is the **Gran Bajo de San Julián**, with the lowest point (105m below sea level), some say, on the continent. But you might not see it, as many buses ply this route at night. Those needing a transport break will find lodging and food but little else in this RN 3 pit stop 127km south of San Julián and 235km north of Río Gallegos.

In 1859, one of Argentina's more popular explorers, Luis Piedrabuena, proud and anxious to help the country claim land, built a house and planted trees on the strategic island of Pavón in the Río Santa Cruz. Julia Dufour, his wife, was the first female settler in Patagonia.

Tourist information (☎ 498301) is available at the bus terminal. There is no ATM.

Places to Stay & Eat

Camping Municipal Isla Pavón (☎ 497187, 02966-15623453) US$7 per site. Under the trees on the historic island, sites are shady and clean but crowded on seasonal week-

ends. Hot water, 24-hour electricity and US$2 showers are available.

Hotel accommodations include *Hotel Internacional* (☎ 497197, Gregorio Ibáñez 99) for US$13/22 with shared bath, *El Álamo* (☎ 497249, Lavalle 8) for US$25/35 with private bath, both with confiterías, or *Hotel Huayén* (☎ 497265, Belgrano 321) for US$23/28 with private bath.

Getting There & Away

The bus terminal is at Ibáñez and Menéndez, but passing buses will also pick up passengers along RN 3. All of the main north-south carriers stop here throughout the week, many arriving and leaving late at night.

It may be possible to hitch to El Calafate, 45km south of Piedrabuena, along RP 9, a decent gravel road that passes numerous estancias. The route has panoramic views of the canyon of the Río Santa Cruz, but hitching is generally difficult because of heavy competition. If you're trying, head to the junction near ACA.

PARQUE NACIONAL MONTE LEÓN

Monte León's sandy beaches and striking headlands are home to Magellanic penguins, sea lions and unusual geographic features like La Olla (a huge cave-like structure eroded by the ocean). Perhaps its most interesting attraction is Isla Monte León, a high offshore stack once exploited by guano collectors – the cable tram that carried the guano over to the mainland wouldn't need much work to be operable again.

Now being recolonized by king cormorants, Dominican gulls, skuas and other birds, Isla Monte León is accessible at low tide, when it's also possible to walk in La Olla, but the tidal range is great and the water returns fast.

There is no public transport to Monte León, which is 58km south of Piedrabuena via paved RN 3 and graveled RP 63, rough in spots but passable for any vehicle in good weather. There is *camping*, with limited services, but no other accommodations.

RÍO GALLEGOS
☎ 02966 • pop 90,000

Most travelers transfer in and out of this southern tip town, heading to El Calafate, Punta Arenas or Tierra del Fuego. But this wind-pummeled provincial capital, also the largest town south of Comodoro Rivadavia, has a surprising assortment of museums and restored historic buildings that make for an interesting stay. Unfortunately, since the town caters mainly to the business set, lodging and restaurants are pricey but fail to deliver quality.

As the wool industry boomed in the early 1900s, Río Gallegos attracted Chileans and Brits, most from the Malvinas/Falklands, seeking more land and fortune. Less than 20% of the original population was native Argentine. Butch Cassidy, the Sundance Kid and their posse arrived in town in February 1905 under the premise of wanting to purchase some land to raise livestock, but robbed the bank instead of some US$100,000 in cash and silver.

When coal was discovered in Río Turbio, 230km west near the Chilean border, the narrow-gauge railway transported the deposits to the port. Gallegos' main industry is now centered around the nearby oilfields, while coal deposits have been retransported to oceangoing vessels at Punta Loyola. Home to a large military base, Río Gallegos played an active role during the Falklands War, the memory of which is still very sensitive to the locals. Around town are memorials and small galleries of memoirs from the battles.

Information
Tourist Offices The energetic provincial tourist office (☎ 422702, Av Roca 863), next door to the post office, is open 9am to 10pm weekdays and also weekends in summer. It has maps and a helpful list of accommodations, transport and excursions.

The municipal tourist offices are located in the Casa Abuela Paredes (☎ 436917, Abuela Paredes & Gobernador Lista), open 9am to 8pm weekdays, and at the bus terminal (☎ 442159), open 7am to 9pm weekdays, 10am to 1pm and 4pm to 8pm weekends. ACA (☎ 420477) is at Orkeke 10, near the river.

Immigration & Consulates Immigration (☎ 420205), Urquiza 144, is open from 8am to 8pm weekdays. The Chilean consulate (☎ 422364) at Mariano Moreno 148 is open 8am to 1pm.

Money Cambio El Pingüino (Zapiola 469) changes US cash, traveler's checks (for a modest commission) and Chilean pesos. Thaler Agencia de Cambio is at Errazuriz 46, local 11. Most banks are on or near Av Roca and have ATMs.

Post & Communications The post office is at Av Julio Roca 893; the postal code is 9400. There are numerous locutorios, including Telefax at Av Roca 1328. About the swankiest place in Patagonia to read email is CyberCafé, at Roca 923.

Travel Agencies Escalatur (☎ 434021, fax 422466) at Roca 998 runs trips to El Calafate and Cabo Vírgenes (US$60), as does Tur Aike (☎ 422436) at Zapiola 63.

Laundry Aike Lavar (☎ 420759) is at Corrientes 277.

Medical Services The Hospital Regional (☎ 420025) is at José Ingenieros 98.

Museums
At the Complejo Cultural Provincial, the **Museo Regional Padre Manuel Jesús Molina** (☎ 423290, Ramón y Cajal 51; free; open 10am-8pm weekdays, 11am-7pm weekends) has temporary exhibitions of modern art plus a fairly good permanent display on geology, dinosaurs, Tehuelche ethnology (with excellent photographs), and local history. Of course, there's also the version of the omnipresent milodón (see the Cueva del Milodón section later in this chapter for a description). More colorful still is the science room with fun interactive exhibits.

Opposite Plaza San Martín, the first art museum in the province, **Museo de Arte Eduardo Minnicelli** (Maipú 13; free; open 10am-7pm weekdays, 3pm-7pm weekends) houses paintings by Santa Cruz artists, but

RÍO GALLEGOS

PLACES TO STAY
3 El Viejo Miramar
6 Hotel Sehuen
7 Hotel Oviedo
8 La Posada
12 Hotel Nevada
13 Hotel Comercio
21 Hotel Cabo Vírgenes
22 Hotel Croacia
23 Hotel París
30 Hotel Costa Río
38 Hotel Santa Cruz
39 Hotel Colonial

PLACES TO EAT
15 Panadería Zapiola
16 El Dragón
17 La Parrilla Díaz
18 Bartolo
20 Restaurant Natural
28 J@va Cybercafe
36 El Horreo

OTHER
1 Casa Abuela Paredes:
   Municipal Tourist Office
2 Museo de los Pioneros
4 Funda Cruz
5 ACA
9 Aike Lavar
10 Telefax
11 Cambio El Pengüino
14 LAPA
19 Localiza
24 Cine Carrera; Paseo
   Carrera
25 LADE
26 Club Británico
27 Escalatur
29 Southern Winds
31 Tur Aike
32 Aerolíneas Argentinas
33 Post Office
34 Deco Bar
35 Provincial Tourist Office
37 Banco de la Nación
40 Immigration
41 Chilean Consulate
42 Iglesia Catedral Nuestra
   Señora del Lubán
43 Museo de Arte Eduardo
   Minnicelli
44 Thaler Agencia de
   Cambio
45 Rincón Gaucho
46 Complejo Cultural
   Regional: Museo
   Regional Padre Manuel
   Jesús Molina; Prepap
47 Hospital Regional
48 Riestra Rent A Car

Río Gallegos

Plaza
San Martín

To Bus Terminal
& El Calafate

To Tierra
del Fuego

RN 3

0   200   400 m
0   200   400 yards

once housed the staff of a landmark local school. Built from Chilean wood by local indigenous people, the green and white **Iglesia Catedral Nuestra Señora del Lubán** *(San Martín 753; free; open 10am-5pm weekdays, 2pm-6pm weekends)* dates from 1900; guided tours are available.

In 1888, Dr Arthur Fenton catalog-ordered a prefabricated metal-clad house from England, a style now associated with southern Patagonia; it now houses the **Museo de los Pioneros** *(☎ 437763, Sebastián Elcano & Alberdi; free; open 10am-8pm daily)* with exceptional displays on early immigrant life. Catalina Ness de Parisi, the last Tehuelche descendent, lived here until her death, when her family donated the house to the government. **Funda Cruz** *(Gobernador Lista 60)* is an attractive wooden house, also brought prefabricated from England. Once a customs office, it was abandoned in 1947 and now hosts cultural activities as well as a *salón de té*.

Down the street, **Casa Abuela Paredes** *(Abuela Paredes & Gobernador Lista)* was a popular gathering place for shipping officials; it now houses weaving workshops. On Alberdi between Muratore and Comodoro Rivadavia is a string of historic houses, most of them government offices. At the time of writing, an **open-air museum** was being created at the site of the old terminus for the narrow-gauge railway from Río Turbio, at Gobernador Lista and Mendoza.

Places to Stay

Budget On RN 3 west of the bus terminal, the gas station YPF has a large parking lot where passing truckers stop to snooze; there are a few sites to pitch tents in a pinch.

Polideportivo Atsa (☎ 442310, Asturias & Yugoslavia) US$3 per person, US$3 per vehicle; singles/doubles US$20/30. A better camping option is at this sports complex, about 400m southwest of the bus terminal, where there are also rooms. Showers cost US$2.

Hospedaje Mary (☎ 423789, Valentín Alsina 71) US$10 per person with breakfast.

Outside of town, near the cemetery, Mary's offers kitchen access (taxi US$3 from bus station).

Hotel Colonial (☎ 422329, Bernardino Rivadavia & Urquiza) US$12-15 per person. Family-oriented, this home-turned-hotel provides comfortable rooms, helpful management, strongbox and a US$3 breakfast. It's about the best budget choice near the center.

Hospedaja Elcira (☎ 429856, Zuccarino 431) US$15 shared rooms. You'll feel right at home at this discreet place near Calle Estrada, just a 20-minute walk from the bus station (taxi US$2). The bathrooms are large and the rooms clean. The congenial owner may offer kitchen privileges. They also run tours to penguin colonies and El Calafate.

Hotel Cabo Vírgenes (☎ 422141, Comodoro Rivadavia 252) Singles/doubles US$25/35. Close to the estuary, this is an acceptable option offering professional service, but doesn't take credit cards.

Hotel Nevada (☎ 425990, fax 435790, Zapiola 480) Singles/doubles US$22/38. The jungle of plants in the lobby lends a slightly disagreeable mustiness to the place, but the rooms are adequate. Shared baths are very cramped and few. If you're staying, consider the pricier rooms. Service tends to be a bit lax.

La Posada (☎ 436445, Ameghino 331) Singles or doubles US$35. One of the more attractive places in town, the Posada fills up fast with out-of-towners waiting for medical appointments. The rooms are cool, carpeted and clean and all surround a sunny internal garden. Meals (breakfast US$2.50) are served in the ranch-style dining area.

Mid-Range Singles/doubles typically go for US$28/40 at *Hotel Oviedo (☎ 420118, Libertad 746)*. Walk the squeaky halls to your red-satin bed in this lackluster lodging. All the rooms have private baths, with small showers equipped with bidets. Parking is available.

Hotel París (☎/fax 422432, Av Roca 1040) Singles/doubles US$29/42 private bath, US$20/29 shared bath. Those seeking the obscure will appreciate historic París, once called Gran Hotel and featured in the film *La Patagonia Rebelde*. Some rooms have been restored, but retain the original charm, while others maintain walls stained in stories, and bedsprings and floorboards that squeak and creak all night. Breakfast is extra for those in rooms with shared bath.

Hotel Croacia (☎/fax 422997, Urquiza 431) Singles/doubles US$33/44. Once a reunion center for the local Yugoslav community, 20-room Croacia is run by a conscientious couple that provides top-quality service. Rooms are quiet with good-size bathrooms. An abundant breakfast is an extra US$3.

Hotel Sehuen (☎ 425683, Rawson 160) Singles/doubles US$38/42-48. Bright and airy, Sehuen is another favorite for the business set, but is a good value for the average traveler. Prices vary depending on the size of the room, all of which are kept spotlessly clean.

El Viejo Miramar (☎ 430401, Roca 1630) Singles/doubles US$40/50. Right next to the Esso station, this is an attractive, personable place with comfortable, somewhat dark rooms. The owner opens his kitchen to heat up water and provides parking.

Top End A favorite for the business crowd three-star *Hotel Comercio (☎ 422458, fax 422172, Av Roca 1302)* has modern renovated singles/doubles with large bathrooms for US$54/76. There are plush sofas in the lobby and a breezy bar. Rooms fronting the street can be noisy.

Hotel Santa Cruz (☎ 420601, fax 420603, Av Roca 701) Singles/doubles US$44/60. Also carrying the triple stars, Santa Cruz has inviting rooms with good firm beds, but the bathrooms one might call tiny. Opt for rooms along the internal patio. US$10 gets you time in the sauna.

Hotel Costa Río (☎/fax 423412, Av San Martín 673) Singles/doubles US$90/124. The newest and costliest hotel in town, Costa Río's rooms are mini apartments, some with kitchenettes, others with full kitchens and all grandly spacious and quiet. Discounts are given for cash payment and to ACA members.

Places to Eat
J@vaCyberCafé (☎ 422775, Roca 923) US$3-6. After checking email, enjoy breakfast, sandwiches or a beer while flipping through an English magazine.

La Parrilla Díaz (☎ 420203, Av Roca 1143) Salads US$4-9, mains US$7-14. Attentive service and an extensive menu, including a good array of salads and pastas, keep Díaz the most popular diner in town.

El Horreo (☎ 420060, Av Roca 862) US$9-14. In the historic Sociedad Española building, this is *the* formal dining option in town, with an emphasis on Spanish cuisine and a pleasant upstairs bar.

Bartolo (☎ 427297, Sarmiento 124) Parrilla for two US$26, pizzas US$6.50-15. Stone-oven pizzas with fresh toppings and parrilla are the highlights here, but the create-your-own salads are equally good.

Paseo Carrera (☎ 427289, Roca 1012) US$7. In the cinema lobby, this popular, informal bar serves homemade pastas, pizzas and daily specials, plus good coffee.

Restaurant Natural (☎ 437311, Avellaneda 25) Lunch US$2.50-5, dinner US$7-10. As part of the town's tennis club, meals here emphasize natural, well-prepared foods, which can be enjoyed while watching games in the indoor court.

El Dragón (☎ 429811, 9 de Julio 39) US$9-10 tenedor libre. Under extreme lights and with Chinese pop music wailing, the buffet has plenty to choose from, including parrilla.

Panadería Zapiola (Rawson & Zapiola) US$1-3. Come here for an excellent selection of empanadas and pastries to pack away.

Entertainment
Club Británico (☎ 425223, Roca 935) Mainly a formal restaurant, this is a great retreat for those feeling wispy for a scotch whiskey in a Brit-style gentleman's bar (but don't expect the Brits).

Deco Bar (no ☎, Alcorta 57) Open Thurs-Sun from 10pm. Creative lighting and occasional live music make Deco a worth-it nightspot.

Shopping

Rincón Gaucho (☎ 420669, Av Roca 619) Anything needed to be a well-outfitted gaucho is here. The owner enthusiastically points out the purposes and customs of every hat as well. One of those authentic criollo felt hats costs US$58, while a basic gaucho one runs US$25.

Prepap (*Ramón y Cajal 51*) Open 9am-8pm. Part of the Complejo Cultural is this high-quality artisan center, which sells attractive knit sweaters and woven shawls.

Getting There & Away

Air Aerolíneas Argentinas (☎ 422020, Av San Martín 545) flies daily to Buenos Aires (US$107 to US$217) via Ushuaia (US$56), and in summer via Trelew; and twice daily except Sunday (once only) nonstop to Buenos Aires.

Southern Winds (☎ 437171, Av San Martín 661) has flights to El Calafate Saturdays, to Ushuaia Monday through Saturday. It flies to Comodoro, Neuquén and Córdoba weekdays and Sundays, and also Monday to Saturday, continuing on to Rosario, Tucumán and Salta.

LAPA (☎ 428382, Estrada 71) flies daily to Río Grande (US$27 to US$47); Tuesday, Thursday and Saturday to Ushuaia (US$35 to US$61); daily to Bahía Blanca (US$97 to US$163), Trelew (US$62 to US$108) and Buenos Aires (US$109 to US$217).

LADE planes (☎ 422316, Fagnano 53) flies Tuesday to Río Grande (US$26) and Ushuaia (US$36), and direct to Ushuaia on Thursday. Wednesday and Friday flights go to El Calafate (US$25), Gobernador Gregores (US$32), Perito Moreno (US$58) and Comodoro Rivadavia (US$66).

Bus Río Gallegos is a major hub for bus travel. The bus terminal (☎ 442159) is at the corner of RN 3 and Av Eva Perón. Bus companies include El Pingüino (☎ 422338, 442169), Interlagos (☎ 442080), Taqsa (☎ 423130, 442194), Bus Sur (☎ 442687), Andesmar (☎ 442195), Sportman (☎ 442595) and TAC (☎ 442042). Buses to Chile include Ghisoni (☎ 442687), Magallanes Tour

(☎ 442765) and Pacheco (☎ 442765). Puerto Natales-bound travelers can also take buses to Río Turbio, from where numerous buses cross the border.

At the airport, Taqsa (☎ 442000) leaves directly to El Calafate, Puerto Natales (via Río Turbio) and El Chaltén for slightly more than the bus terminal fares. Escalatur (☎ 434021, Alberdi 2) runs door-to-door service to San Julián at 5pm weekdays.

Destination	Duration in hours	Cost
Bariloche	16	US$71-119
Buenos Aires	40	US$70-100
Caleta Olivia	8	US$27
Córdoba	38	US$85
Comodoro Rivadavia	9	US$22-31
El Calafate	4½	US$20
El Chaltén	9	US$50
Los Antiguos	12	US$55
Mendoza	39	US$139
Puerto Madryn	15	US$43-52
Puerto Natales (Chi)	6	US$18
Punta Arenas (Chi)	5	US$20
Río Turbio	5	US$15-20
San Julián	4½	US$18
Trelew	14	US$45

Getting Around

Cabs from the airport to downtown cost US$6 to US$8. To save money, share a cab with other arrivals. Cabs charge also US$6 to get to the bus terminal, or take local bus Nos 1 or 12 (the placard must say 'terminal') from Av Roca (US$1.20).

Car rental is expensive (up to US$100 per day) due to the gravel and potholed conditions of the roads to most places of interest. Agencies include Localiza (☎ 424417, Sarmiento 237) and Riestra Rent A Car (☎ 421321, Av San Martín 1504). Rental deals are much better in Punta Arenas, Chile.

ESTANCIAS AROUND RÍO GALLEGOS

The estancias that opened up to travelers afford the visitor an attractive travel alternative and an education into the ways of a

Patagonia lifestyle. These are not hotels, but families that have renovated a few rooms of the former family housing into comfortable lodgings. Meals are usually taken with the owners, and conversations and participation in the daily life of the estancia are encouraged. Making reservations early is a must, as they can fill up fast. Most are open only in the high season. For estancias in Santa Cruz province, you can find out more information on the Web site **w** www.estanciasdesantacruz.com.

The estancia's nucleus usually consisted of a settlement cluster, including the owner's or manager's *casco* (the main house), family housing for foremen and other married employees, and a bunkhouse for single men. There were also garages, workshops, a *pulpería* (company store), corrals, and a woolshed for shearing the sheep and storing the clip.

Estancia Güer Aike (☎ 02966-436127 in *Río Gallegos,* ☎/fax 011-4394-3486 in Buenos *Aires, Esmeralda 719, 2nd floor B, 1007 Buenos Aires)* Singles/doubles US$95/115 with breakfast; open Oct-Apr. At the junction of northbound RN 3 and westbound RP 5, about 30km west of Río Gallegos, Güer Aike owns some 18km of river frontage, making its small lodge 'Truchaike' a well-known destination among the trout-fishing elite. The main area can be visited for meals, but call in advance. Lunch or dinner costs US$23.

Hill Station (*Los Pozos,* ☎ 02966-423897, *fax 423970,* **e** *hillstation@carnet.com.ar, Casilla de Correo 74, 9400 Río Gallegos)* US$100 per person full board; open year-round with reservation. Tired of working for the Falkland Island Company on the Malvinas, Scotsman William Halliday and wife Mary McCall immigrated in 1885 to Patagonia to start their own sheep station. The result is Hill Station, which breeds both sheep and Criollo horses. Son Edward Halliday and Silvina Puih, along with their sons, will get you as involved as you want to be in estancia life. This is an excellent choice for equestrians, and spectacular packing trips to penguin colonies can be arranged. Large meals of chops and homegrown veggies,

comfortable period-style rooms and long nights of conversation (in English or Spanish) make Hill Station a fun, casual escape. Take RN 3 35km west then turn at the Yacimiento El Indio turnoff, proceeding another 33km along a potholed road.

Estancia Monte Dinero (☎/fax 02966-426900, **e** *montedinero@southern.com.ar, Casilla de Correo 86, 9400 Río Gallegos)* US$60/140 per person with breakfast/full board plus excursions & demos; open Sept-Apr. Steeped in tradition, Monte Dinero has been run by the same family for five generations. In 1886, the Greenshoes left Ireland with a boatload of possessions, which sunk soon after they arrived. Widowed young, Mrs Greenshoe later married Dr Arthur Fenton, thus establishing the current 26,000-hectare estancia and family. A museum displays an intriguing assortment of goods salvaged from the sunken wreckage, including a working Victrola. Intricate hand-painted doors, well-appointed rooms and billiards all create a comfortable old-worldly environment.

Guests are shown the typical estancia gigs, but can also take trips to the *pingüinera* at **Cabo de Vírgenes**, where some 30,000 Magellanic penguins nest September to the end of March. Travel agents in Río Gallegos arrange tours to the colony, usually making a quick stop at the estancia's *casco* (main house). For nonguests, Día de Campo – dog demos and sheering, plus lunch – costs US$25, or have tea for US$10. The southernmost estancia on the continent, Monte Dinero is 120km south of Río Gallegos on RP 1. Transportation to and from the airport can be arranged for US$35.

Midway between Monte Dinero and Cabo Vírgenes is **Estancia Cóndor**, a beautiful settlement of sparkling white-and-red-roofed houses with picket fences. So storybook in appearance, it's hard to imagine families actually live there. At 190,000 hectares strong, this is the largest estancia, owned and managed by fashion kingpin Benetton. Besides an industry in 'superior' wool, the estancia supports a large oil-drilling operation.

Inland Patagonia (Along RN 40)

Paralleling the awe-inspiring Andean range, north of Bariloche down to almost the Seno Última Esperanza then jigging east to Río Gallegos, the mythic RN 40 (La Ruta Cuarenta) is the uttermost of road trips. Mile upon mile of mostly gravel road give access to Argentina's prized possessions – Los Glaciares and Perito Moreno national parks, rock art at Cueva de las Manos, the desert oasis of Los Antiguos and some of the most renowned fishing lakes in South America.

Traveling the road has its hardships, however: If you're depending on public transportation, buses are limited to a few tourist shuttle services that run only in the summer months, and if you're driving, you will want to invite plenty of preparation and patience to accompany the trip (see the boxed text 'Driving the RN 40').

This section picks up RN 40 at Esquel and its offshoot Trevelin, from where it continues paved until just south of Gobernador Costa. From there on down, it's gravel and washboard most of the way, with certain sections, mainly near higher population centers, paved. There is rumor that the provincial government of Santa Cruz plans to pave a fair chunk of the highway. Should that happen, traveling will certainly be easier for the masses, which will in turn weaken its allure of isolation.

ESQUEL

☎ 02945 • pop 36,000 • elevation 540m

A dusty, sun-beaten town of manicured lawns and white stucco houses, Esquel sits in the western Chubut foothills, primarily attracting visitors with its proximity to Parque Nacional Los Alerces and other Andean recreation areas. It's the southern end of the line for La Trochita, the narrow-gauge steam train that now only runs as far north as El Maitén. Founded at the turn of the century, the town is the area's main commercial and livestock center. It takes its name from a Mapuche term meaning either 'place of the thistles' or 'bog.'

Orientation

On the north shore of the eponymous Arroyo Esquel, the town has a fairly standard grid pattern. RN 259 zigzags through town to a junction with RN 40, which heads north to El Bolsón and Bariloche, and southeast toward Comodoro Rivadavia. South of town, RN 259 leads to the Welsh settlement of Trevelin, with junctions to Parque Nacional Los Alerces and other Andean attractions.

Information

Esquel's tourist office (☎ 451927, e turies quel@teletel.com.ar), at Sarmiento and Alvear, keeps a current price list of accommodations, which includes hotels, casas de familia and campgrounds both in town and in Parque Nacional Los Alerces. There are also details available on travel agencies and tours, transportation and recreation. ACA (☎ 452383) is at 25 de Mayo and Ameghino. The Chilean consulate (☎ 451189) is at Molinari 754.

Banco de la Nación, on Alvear at Roca, changes AmEx traveler's checks only. Banco del Chubut (Alvear 1131) and Bansud (25 de Mayo 737) both have ATMs.

The post office is at Alvear 1192, across Fontana from the bus terminal; the postal code is 9200. The Telefónica in the meridian of Fontana, at Alvear, is a convenient locutorio. Open System (9 de Julio 1041) charges US$3 per hour for Internet service; Data Sur, at the corner of 25 de Mayo and San Martín, charges US$4 an hour, but it's faster.

Laverap, a decent laundry facility, is at Mitre 543. The Hospital Zonal (☎ 452131, 452226) is at 25 de Mayo 150.

Things to See & Do

Most of the area's attractions, notably Parque Nacional Los Alerces, are around Esquel rather than in it. The Museo Indigenista (☎ 451929, Belgrano 330; free; open 9am-1pm & 4pm-9pm weekdays, 4pm-9pm weekends) has a modest collection.

Driving the RN 40

Road tripping up or down RN 40 has become a popular way to discover inland Patagonia. Long stretches of flat isolation punctuated by mountains, quirky towns and hidden lakes draw the intrepid roadsters in. Most gravel stretches on RN 40 are wide and compacted, which makes traveling them much easier. Conditions from December to March are fine, but heavy rains and snow can make some parts inaccessible.

Be Prepared The vehicle should travel with necessary repair equipment. If renting, make sure suspension, brakes and tires are in a good state and that the headlights work. Carry two *neumáticos* (spare tires), also in good condition; Reports say these extras come in handy along the stretch between Perito Moreno and Bajo Caracoles.

Keep an extra gas barrel full, just in case. And always fill up when you've got the chance. Also carry extra water and oil.

Flying rocks and glass are not a welcoming combination, and some potential damages may not be covered under the insurance policies offered by rental agencies; if they aren't, they will have to be paid out of your pocket. Be sure to check with the agency about coverage and deductibles.

Road Rules In Santa Cruz province, it's the law to have headlights on during daylight hours. Abide the speed limits: 70 km/h to 80km/h is a safe maximum speed.

Sheep always get the right of way. While most will scurry out of the way, some will do so in such a haphazard manner that you may wonder if they are actually running toward the car. Slow down, give them distance. *Guardaganados* is the name for the sheep and cattle gates along the roads.

Driving Etiquette Say 'hi' to oncoming drivers either by flashing your headlights or raising an index finger with your hand on the steering wheel. Unwritten rule: Stop to help anyone stranded on the side of the road. Cell phones are useless along some west-east stretches and in the mountains.

Along windy roads, toot the horn before coming around the blind curves.

When another car approaches, slow down and move to the side of the road to avoid stones flying out from under the wheels. If you need to pass a car, flash your headlights and signal the pass. The car in front should slow down to allow passage and get out of the way. If you're being passed, move over and keep the speed down until the cloud of dust has settled. For full security, consider adding a windshield screen for protection from flying rocks. Another recommendation is to tape headlights with transparent, industrial-size tape to minimize the cracking should a stone hit. If you need to stop, don't slam on the brakes, an act that will send the car skidding along the road. Instead, slow down and use the clutch to lower the speeds until you can safely move the car to the side of the road and stop.

Letting Someone Else Deal with It A few agencies run minibuses up the RN 40 to Los Antiguos from El Calafate and El Chaltén (but not from both on the same trip). Service is regular from mid-October to the end of March/early April depending on demand and conditions. Some companies stop at Cueva de las Manos en route.

Chalten Travel (☎ 02902- 492212), Libertador 1177, El Calafate, runs buses on odd-numbered days at 8am from El Calafate to Perito Moreno (US$65) and to Los Antiguos (US$68). Service from El Chaltén is US$11 more. It's possible to hop on and off buses along the route, but space on the next bus is not guaranteed. In El Chaltén, check with Pangea restaurant (☎ 0962-493084), Lago del Desierto & San Martín, and Albergue Patagonia (see the Fitz Roy Area Places to Stay section) for other services.

The Roca train station is now also a **train museum** (no ☎, *Brown & Roggero; free*); even travelers arriving by air or bus should try to witness the arrival or departure of **La Trochita**.

Activities

Esquel's nearby lakes and rivers offer some excellent **fishing**. The season runs from early November to mid-April. Seasonal licenses, valid throughout the Patagonian provinces of Chubut, Santa Cruz, Río Negro and Neuquén, and in national parks, cost US$100. Weekly/monthly licenses are also available for US$30/60; they can be purchased at the Department of Fishing office (☎ 451226, 9 de Julio 1643), or at larger fishing supply shops such as Martín Pescador (☎ 455955, Sarmiento and Alvear).

Mountain biking is also popular. Bikes can be rented for US$15/10 per day/half-day at Tierra (☎ 454366, e epa@ar.inter.net, Rivadavia & Roca). The friendly staff provides trail information or can hook you up with a guide.

Full-day Class II to IV **rafting** trips on the Río Corcovado are arranged by Rafting Adventure (☎ 451891, Miguens 40), north of the train station. Rates (about US$70) include transfers and all equipment, as well as breakfast and lunch. The proprietor of Tierra also owns Expeditiones Patagonia Aventura (mobile ☎ 15-682398), which offers similar rafting trips as well as guided treks and horseback riding.

Organized Tours

Numerous travel agencies, including Esquel Tours (☎ 452704, Av Fontana 754), sell tickets for the Circuito Lacustre boat excursion in Parque Nacional Los Alerces; obtaining a ticket in Esquel assures a place on this often-crowded trip. Full-day excursions including the lake cruise cost US$35 when sailing from Puerto Chucao, US$55 from Puerto Limonao (see the Parque Nacional Los Alerces section, later). This includes transportation to and from the park, but you can also buy the boat excursion separately if you have your own transportation.

There are also full-day trips to Futaleufú in Chile, Cholila/Lago Rivadavia (US$35), El Bolsón/Lago Puelo (US$48), and Corcovado/Carrenleufú. Half-day trips include the La Hoya winter-sports complex; the nearby Welsh settlement of Trevelin and the Futaleufú hydroelectric complex (US$22); and the narrow-gauge railway excursion to Nahuelpan (US$22).

Patagonia Verde (☎ 454396, 9 de Julio 926) deals in less conventional activities like hiking, climbing and horseback riding.

Special Events

February's Semana de Esquel celebrates the 1906 founding of the city. The Fiesta Nacional de Esquí (National Ski Festival) takes place in September.

Places to Stay

Budget Besides the following campgrounds, there's also *Camping Millalén* (☎ 456164, Ameghino 2063), just north of town, which charges US$4.50 per person.

El Hogar del Mochilero (☎ 452166, Roca 1028) Dorm bed US$5, camping US$3 per person. Besides renting dorm beds for an astoundingly low price, this pleasant hostel allows camping in the tree-shaded backyard. It's an excellent deal.

Autocamping La Rural (☎ 0268-428-1429, Ruta 259 Km 1) US$5 per person, plus one-time US$5 charge per car & tent. This shady campground is just south of town on the Trevelin road.

Autocamping La Colina (☎ 454962, Darwin 1400) US$3.50 per person, singles/doubles US$8/15. This campground, two blocks west of Don Bosco, also has hostel accommodations.

Hotel Argentino (☎ 452237, 25 de Mayo 862) Singles/doubles US$12/18 with shared bath, US$18/28 with private bath. This inexpensive and sometimes rowdy hostel-cum-hotel, complete with pool table and bar, also offers cheap floor space for US$3 per person.

Parador Lago Verde (☎ 452251, fax 453901, e lagoverd@hostels.org.ar, Volta 1081) US$15/24 per person in private room with bath. This highly regarded HI affiliate is clean, small, friendly and has a pleasant

ESQUEL

PLACES TO STAY
1 Parador Lago Verde (HI)
8 El Hogar del Mochilero
9 Hotel Argentino
15 Hotel Sol del Sur
28 La Casona de Olgbrun
30 Hostería Angelina
31 Hotel Tehuelche
34 Hotel Maika
35 Hostería La Tour D'Argent
39 Hostería Lihuen
40 Residencial Ski
46 Residencial El Cisne
48 Casa de Familia Rowlands

PLACES TO EAT
13 Don Pipo
20 La Trochita
21 Parrilla La Barra
22 Pizzería Fitzroya
23 De María
24 Vestry
26 Heladería Jauja
27 La Abuela
37 Pizzería Dos-22
44 Empanadería Molinari

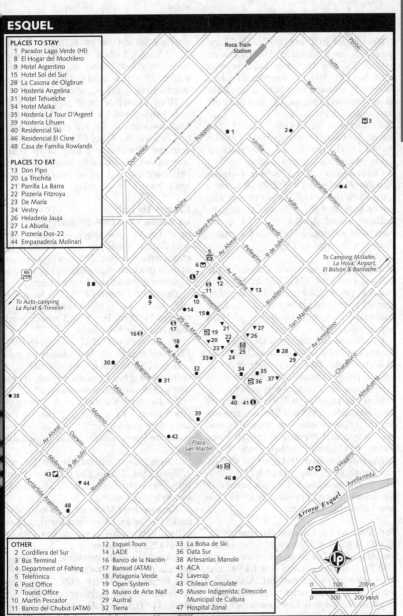

Roca Train Station

To Camping Millalén, La Hoya, Airport, El Bolsón & Bariloche

To Auto-camping La Rural & Trevelin

RN 259

To Camping Millalén, La Hoya, Airport, El Bolsón & Bariloche

Plaza San Martín

Arroyo Esquel

0   100   200 m
0   100   200 yards

OTHER
2 Cordillera del Sur
3 Bus Terminal
4 Department of Fishing
5 Telefónica
6 Post Office
7 Tourist Office
10 Martín Pescador
11 Banco del Chubut (ATM)

12 Esquel Tours
14 LADE
16 Banco de la Nación
17 Bansud (ATM)
18 Patagonia Verde
19 Open System
25 Museo de Arte Naif
29 Austral
32 Tierra

33 La Bolsa de Ski
36 Data Sur
38 Artesanías Manolo
41 ACA
42 Laverap
43 Chilean Consulate
45 Museo Indigenista; Dirección
   Municipal de Cultura
47 Hospital Zonal

backyard. Tours can be organized on-site, and HI members receive a small discount.

Residencial El Cisne (☎ 452256, *Chacabuco 778*) Singles/doubles US$15/25 with bath & TV. The fair price here includes access to a well-equipped communal kitchen, a dining room and a huge parrilla across the street. The rooms are spotless and there are laundry facilities to boot.

Residencial Ski (☎/fax 452254, *San Martín 961*) Singles/doubles US$20/30 with bath & TV. This is a clean, friendly place offering good-value accommodation.

Other cheap options include *Casa de Familia Rowlands* (☎ 452578, *Rivadavia 330*), which charges US$10 per person with shared bath; and the worn and slightly depressing *Hotel Maika* (☎ 452457, *San Martín1042*), charging US$15/28 for singles/doubles with bath and TV.

Mid-Range Singles/doubles, all with bath, will set you back US$25/32 at *Hostería Lihuen* (☎ 452589, *San Martín 822*). Though the rooms are undistinguished, the hostería is in a good location near Plaza San Martín.

Cordillera del Sur (☎ 452813, *Roque Sáenz Peña 1646*) Singles/doubles US$30/40. This small hotel, four blocks north of downtown, is plain but immaculate and, for whatever reason, has an adults-only policy.

Hostería Angelina (☎ 452763, *Alvear 758*) Singles/doubles US$30/40. This hostería has drawn praise for comfort, hospitality and very substantial breakfasts, though some rooms are a bit small for these rates.

Hostería La Tour D'Argent (☎ 454612, *San Martín 1063*) Singles/doubles US$30/46 with breakfast, bath & TV. This is another nondescript place, appealing for its friendliness rather than character.

Top End At *La Casa de Olgbrun* (☎/fax 453813, 450536, **e** *olgbrun@infovia.com.ar, San Martín 1137*) a four-person room costs US$70, a six-person room cost US$90, and off-season rates are half off. Above the artisan shop of the same name, this attractive hostería has only four rooms, each with an iron cooker, a refrigerator and a well-equipped kitchen. They're all tastefully decorated and very comfortable.

Hotel Sol del Sur (☎ 452189, *9 de Julio 1086*) Singles/doubles aboutUS$30/60 with buffet breakfast. The Sol del Sur is a three-star hotel with spacious rooms boasting minibars, refrigerators and comfy beds.

Hotel Tehuelche (☎ 452420, *9 de Julio 831*) Singles/doubles from US$50/60 with breakfast, bath & TV. An enormous hotel for Esquel, the Tehuelche has a friendly young staff with some English speakers. Rooms are comfortable and have large baths, and the best are on the upper levels facing away from the street.

Places to Eat

La Abuela (☎ 451704, *Rivadavia 1109*) Full meal US$6, open lunch & dinner. This friendly mom-and-pop can't be beat for cheap, palatable specials; you get your choice of meat or a sandwich, plus salad, potato and a quarter carafe of cheap house wine.

Parrilla La Barra (☎ 454321, *Sarmiento 638*) Mains US$6, open noon-3:30pm & 8:30pm-11:30pm. For grilled meats, locals insist this is the place to go.

De María (☎ 452503, *Rivadavia 1024*) Full meal US$10. De María has lamb, pork and goat in addition to the usual beef; there's a salad bar and a decent daily special that includes entrée, wine and salad.

La Trochita (☎ 451484, *25 de Mayo 633*) Open noon-3:30pm & 8pm-11pm. La Trochita does decent parrilla, as well as good pasta and sandwiches, all at reasonable prices.

Vestry (no ☎, *Rivadavia 1065*) Open 4:30pm-10pm. This is Esquel's only Welsh teahouse, serving coffee, tea and delicious sweets and pastries.

Empanadería Molinari (☎ 454687, *Molinari 633*) The friendly owner here bakes excellent empanadas, made daily, to go for about US$7 per dozen.

Esquel's several worthwhile pizza houses include *Don Pipo* (☎ 453458, *Fontana 649*) and *Pizzería Dos-22* (☎ 454995, *Ameghino & Sarmiento*). For excellent ice cream head straight to *Heladería Jauja*, at the corner of Rivadavia and Sarmiento.

The Survival of La Trochita

Clearly an anachronism in the jet age, La Trochita, Ferrocarril Roca's narrow-gauge steam train, averages less than 30km/h on its weekly journey between El Maitén and Esquel – if it runs at speed. Despite the precarious economics of its operations, the project has survived even the most concerted efforts to shut it down. In its current incarnation, subsidized by the city of Esquel and the governments of Río Negro and Chubut, La Trochita provides both a tourist attraction and a service for the people of the provinces.

Like many other state projects, completion of the line seemed an interminable process. In 1906, the federal government authorized the southern branch of the Roca line between Puerto San Antonio on the Atlantic coast and Lago Nahuel Huapi. In 1922, Ferrocarriles del Estado began work on the narrow-gauge section; it didn't reach the halfway point of Ñorquinco until 1939. In 1941 the line made it to the workshops at El Maitén, and in 1945 it reached the end of the line at Esquel.

Since then, the line has suffered some of the oddest mishaps in railroad history. Three times within a decade, in the late 1950s and early 1960s, the train was derailed by high winds, and ice has caused other derailments. In 1979 a collision with a cow derailed the train at Km 243 south of El Maitén; the engine driver was the appropriately named Señor Bovino.

In full operation until recently, La Trochita's 402km route between Esquel and Ingeniero Jacobacci was probably the world's longest-remaining steam-train line, with half a dozen stations and another nine *apeaderos* (whistle-stops); the Belgian Baldwin and German Henschel engines refilled their 4000-liter water tanks at strategically placed *parajes* (pumps) every 40km to 45km. Most of the passenger cars, heated by wood stoves, date from 1922, as do the freight cars.

The only regular passenger service aboard La Trochita is the weekly 6½ hour ride between El Maitén and Esquel (see Getting There & Away for El Maitén or Esquel). Another more frequent option is the **Tren Turístico**, La Trochita's twice daily service from Esquel's train station (now a museum) to Nahuel Pan, the first station down the line, 20km east. In summer this three-hour round-trip (US$15) departs twice daily except Thursday; for a small additional charge, you can return with travel agencies by minibus. The rest of the year, service slowly dwindles down to Saturday only.

Entertainment

The *Dirección Municipal de Cultura* (☎ 451929, Belgrano 330) sponsors regular theater and music events. For something a bit more lowbrow, try the bar at *Hotel Argentino* (see Places to Stay), which gets lively on weekends.

Shopping

The tourist office provides a complete listing of Esquel's dozen or so craft shops, but for a start, try the following.

Leather goods, silverwork and all other manners of crafts fill *La Casona de Olgbrun* (☎ 453841, San Martín 1137) from floor to ceiling. In the hostería of the same name, it has loads of beautiful but expensive copperwork, as well as chocolates, smoked salmon and other delicacies. *Artesanías*

Manolo (no ☎, Alsina 483) specializes in woodcraft.

Getting There & Away

Air Esquel's airport is 20km east of town on the RN 40; Esquel Tours runs shuttles from town according to flight schedules.

Austral (☎ 453413, 453614, Fontana 406) flies Monday, Tuesday, Thursday, Friday and Saturday to Buenos Aires (from US$154).

LADE (☎ 452124, Alvear 1085) has flights Monday and Thursday to Bariloche (US$20), Neuquén (US$52) and Viedma (US$75); Monday and Thursday to Comodoro Rivadavia (US$43); Wednesday to El Maitén (US$20), El Bolsón (US$18), Bariloche, San Martín de los Andes (US$31) and Neuquén; and Friday to Puerto Madryn

(US$51), Trelew (US$43) and Comodoro Rivadavia.

Bus Esquel's attractive new bus terminal is at the north end of town, on Av Alvear between Brun and Justo.

Empresa Codao del Sur leaves Monday and Friday at 8am and 5:30pm to Futaleufú, Chile (US$4.50, 2 hours), via RN 259 and the Puente La Balsa border crossing. Andesmar goes daily to Osorno, Chile (US$30) and Santiago (US$49).

There are daily departures to the destinations in the following table.

Destination	Duration in hours	Cost
Bariloche	4½	US$15
Buenos Aires	30	US$90
Córdoba	25	US$84
Comodoro Rivadavia	9	US$30
El Bolsón	2½	US$7
Mendoza	24	US$70
Neuquén	10	US$38
Puerto Madryn	9	US$30
Río Gallegos	19	US$64
Trelew	8½	US$28

Via Bariloche and Transportes Patagonia both go daily to Mar del Plata and La Plata en route to Buenos Aires. Some companies, including Andesmar and TAC, offer service to northwestern Argentine destinations such as Salta, Tucumán and Jujuy, but they require transfers in either Córdoba or Mendoza.

Cadao goes hourly to Trevelin (US$1.50, 30 minutes) and other local and provincial destinations.

Transportes Jacobsen connects Esquel with El Maitén at 6:30am Monday and at 6:30pm Monday, Wednesday, Thursday and Friday, returning Monday, Tuesday, Friday and Saturday at 8am. Jacobsen also goes to Cholila Tuesday and Thursday at 12:30pm, returning at 3pm.

During summer, Transportes Esquel (☎ 453529, 455059) goes through Parque Nacional Los Alerces to Lago Puelo (near El Bolsón) daily at 8am and 2pm, plus a 7:30pm that goes only as far as Lago Verde;

the first service combines with lake excursions. Fares are US$4.50 to the Intendencia and Villa Futalaufquen, US$5 to Bahía Rosales, US$7 to Lago Verde, US$8 to Lago Rivadavia, US$11 to Cholila, US$12.50 to Epuyén, US$15 to El Hoyo and US$18 to Lago Puelo. Winter schedules may differ.

Train The Roca train station (☎ 451403) is at the corner of Brun and Roggero. Its narrow-gauge steam train, La Trochita (also known by the Spanish diminutive El Trencito), has passenger service to El Maitén (US$25, 6½ hours) on Thursday at 11am, and return service from El Maitén on Wednesday at 2pm. It's primarily a recreational tourist train; see the boxed text 'The Survival of La Trochita' for more details.

AROUND ESQUEL
La Hoya
Only 15km north of Esquel, 1350m above sea level, this winter-sports area *(no ☎; full-day lift pass US$18/23 low/high season; half-day US$16/18)* is cheaper and less crowded than Bariloche, but skilled and experienced skiers consider it pretty tame. The season lasts from June to October, with the Fiesta Nacional del Esquí (National Ski Festival) the second week of September.

Equipment can be rented on site or at ski shops in Esquel, including La Bolsa de Ski (☎ 452379, 25 de Mayo 612; skis US$10 per day, snowboard US$20 per day). Buses to La Hoya from Esquel's terminal cost US$5 per person; a taxi or remise costs US$10, a better deal with two or more people and a heck of a lot faster.

Cholila
Bruce Chatwin's literary travel classic *In Patagonia* recounts Butch Cassidy and the Sundance Kid's ranching efforts near this small town at the northeast entrance to Parque Nacional Los Alerces. A few years ago, US author Anne Meadows located their house, just off RP 71 at Km 21 near the conspicuously marked turnoff to the Casa de Piedra teahouse, a short distance north of Cholila.

Transportes Esquel buses from Esquel to Parque Nacional Los Alerces and El Bolsón pass close enough for a fleeting glimpse of the house on the west side of the highway, but visitors with their own vehicle or time to spare can stop for a look at the overlapping log construction, typical of North America but unusual in this region. The occupant of the rapidly deteriorating house, which is reached by the first gate to the right, is Aladín Sepúlveda. Ask permission before looking around or taking photographs.

Follow the signs to the Calderón family's *Casa de Piedra* (☎ 02945-498056, *RP 71 Km 20*), which offers tea, sweets and preserves, as well as information. The wonderfully hospitable Calderóns, of Spanish-Welsh-English-French Basque-Mapuche descent, also provide rooms for US$20 per person with breakfast, from December to the end of March (sometimes longer) and during Semana Santa.

TREVELIN
☎ 02945 • pop 6000 • elevation 1500m
A good day trip from Esquel, historic Trevelin is the only community in interior Chubut that retains any notable Welsh character. It's worth spending a night or two if you want to explore the surrounding countryside – which is all that's left to do after you gorge yourself at Nain Maggie, one of the country's best Welsh teahouses, and check out the tomb of John Evens' horse. Trevelin derives its name from the Welsh words for town *(tre)* and mill *(velin)*, after its first grain mill, now a museum.

Orientation
Just 24km south of Esquel via paved RN 259, Trevelin's urban plan is very unusual for an Argentine city: At the north end of town, eight streets radiate like the spokes of a wheel from Plaza Coronel Fontana. The principal thoroughfare, Av San Martín, is the southward extension of RN 259, toward Corcovado and the Chilean border at Futaleufú.

Information
From December to March, the exceptionally helpful tourist office (☎ 480120), directly on Plaza Coronel Fontana, is open daily 8am to 10:30pm. Winter hours are 8am

to noon and 2pm to 8pm. It has some English-speaking staff and can help arrange guides, mountain bikes and horses. Showers are available here for US$0.50.

Banco del Chubut, at the corner of Av San Martín and Brown, has an ATM.

The post office is on Av San Martín, just off Plaza Coronel Fontana; the postal code is 9203. There's a locutorio south of the plaza at San Martín 386, near Libertad.

Gales al Sur (☎ 480427, Av Patagonia 186) arranges a variety of tours in the area, including horseback riding, trekking, mountain biking and rafting.

The only option for laundry is Laverap (☎ 480682), in the PIPPO service station on the corner of San Martín and John Evans; a load takes 24 hours. Trevelin's hospital (☎ 480132) is on the same intersection.

Things to See & Do
Dating from 1918, the Museo Molino Viejo (☎ *480189, 25 de Mayo & Molino Viejo; admission US$2; open 11am-9pm Nov-Mar, 11am-6:30pm Apr-Oct*) occupies the restored remains of the old grain mill (which was destroyed by fire). The museum is east of the plaza, at the end of 25 de Mayo.

The Welsh chapel of Capilla Bethel (1910) is at the south end of town near Iwan and Laprida. Two blocks northeast of Plaza Coronel Fontana, the monument Tumba de Malacara (☎ *480108, admission US$2*) holds the carcass of a horse whose bravery enabled its Welsh rider, John Evans, to escape a retaliatory raid by Araucanians who had been attacked by the Argentine army during the Conquista del Desierto.

Every Sunday in summer and on alternate Sundays the rest of the year, there's an artisans' market in Plaza Coronel Fontana.

Special Events
On March 19, the Aniversario de Trevelin celebrates the founding of the city. The Eisteddfod, a festival of Welsh choral singing, takes place the second week of October.

Places to Stay
Trevelin has limited, modest, but pleasant accommodations. The tourist office provides

a complete list of lodging, including cabañas and campgrounds outside of town.

Camping Adventure *(☎ 480267)* US$4 per person. Only a block southwest of Plaza Coronel Fontana, off Independencia Argentina, Camping Adventure is the town's most central campground. It's less attractive than some Argentine campgrounds, but facilities include hot showers, electricity, running water and spotless toilets.

La Granja Trevelin *(☎ 480096)* Camping US$5 per person, cabañas US$30 double. This facility is nestled amongst trees, 3km north of Camping Adventure, on RN 259 to Esquel. There are also activities such as horseback riding and yoga.

Residencial Pezzi *(☎ 480146, Sarmiento 353)* US$15 per person with private bath & breakfast. Reservations are a good idea at this pleasant, family-run hotel with a large garden.

Refugio Wilson *(☎ 480427, 15-687419)* US$5 per tent pitch, US$7 per cot. This rustic refugio is west of town on Cerro La Monja, just below the timberline. The owner will provide transport from town if you call and set it up.

Residencial Trevelin *(☎ 480102, Av San Martín 327)* Rooms with shared bath US$15 per person, private bath extra. Breakfast US$2. This is a relatively cheap option to Trevelin's many cabañas.

Cabañas Oregon *(☎ 480408, San Marín & JM Thomas)* 2-person cabaña US$30/45 low/high season with bath, kitchen & TV. These pleasant, rustic log cabins are scattered around an old apple orchard at the southern edge of town.

Küiméy Ruca Cabañas *(☎ 480088, Av Fortín Refugio s/n)* 3-person cabaña US$35. Just off the central plaza, above the pizzeria of the same name, these are comfortable, well-equipped cabins with kitchens.

Places to Eat
Just as visitors to Trelew flock to Gaiman, so visitors to Esquel head to Trevelin for Welsh tea. Cubut cheese is also delicious, and those with a hankering should keep an eye out around town. Trevelin is thin on restaurants, but the following are very good.

Nain Maggie *(☎ 480232, Perito Moreno 179)* This teahouse, the oldest in Trevelin, occupies a modern building but maintains its traditional high standards. Along with a bottomless pot of tea, it offers outstanding sweets made from dulce de leche, chocolate, cream, rhubarb and cheese, as well as traditional Welsh black cake and scones hot from the oven. Tea, with a sample of all the day's treats, costs US$10 and is plenty for two.

Other teahouses include ***Las Mutisias*** *(☎ 480165, Av San Martín 170)* and ***Owen See*** *(☎ 480295, Molino Viejo 361)*.

Pizzería Küiméy Ruca *(☎ 480088, Av Fortín Refugio s/n)* This comfortable pizzeria, across from Plaza Coronel Fontana, serves excellent pizzas and pastas for lunch and dinner.

Ruca Laufquen *(☎ 480181, San Martín & Libertad)* Though slightly pricey, this parrilla, about four blocks south of the Plaza on San Martín, serves delicious meat on tabletop grills so it doesn't get cold. Pastas are also available.

Getting There & Away
The bus terminal is at the corner of Libertad and Roca. There are numerous daily buses to Esquel (US$1.50, 30 minutes). There are three weekly buses to Futaleufú (US$3), just across the Argentine/Chilean border, and five weekly to Carrenleufú, another Chilean border crossing. To travel north, you must first go to Esquel.

AROUND TREVELIN
On RN 259, 17km south of Trevelin, a 7km trail leads to a series of cascades in **Reserva Provincial Nant-y-Fall**, open 9:30am to 5:30pm daily. Trevelin's tourist office arranges excursions but, unfortunately, a landowner dispute has made it impossible to start at the north end and get picked up at the southern end, on RP 17. At Arroyo Baguilt, on RN 259 near the Chilean border, is the provincial **Estación de Salmonicultura** *(salmon hatchery; open 8am-1pm)*.

There are several campgrounds outside of Trevelin. ***Camping El Paso*** *(☎ 44403)*, 32km west of Trevelin on RN 259, charges US$6 per person. ***Camping Puerto Ciprés*** is

5km east of the international border and charges US$5, with a one-time charge of US$5 per vehicle.

Near **Lago Rosario**, 24km southwest of Trevelin via a lateral off RP 17, is a Mapuche Indian reservation. Just to its north, the **Sierra Colorada** offers good hiking.

PARQUE NACIONAL LOS ALERCES

Resembling the giant sequoia of California's Sierra Nevada, the *alerce*, or Patagonian cypress, flourishes in the humid temperate forests of southern Argentina and Chile. Individual specimens of this strikingly beautiful and long-lived tree can measure over 4m in diameter and exceed 60m in height. Like the giant sequoia, it has suffered overexploitation because of its valuable timber. West of Esquel, this 263,000-hectare park protects some of the largest remaining alerce forests.

Geography & Climate

Hugging the eastern slope of the Andes along the Chilean border, the peaks of Parque Nacional Los Alerces do not exceed 2300m, and their receding alpine glaciers are smaller and less impressive than the continental ice fields of Parque Nacional Los Glaciares to the south. They have left, however, a series of nearly pristine lakes and streams that offer attractive vistas, excellent fishing and other outdoor recreation. Many local place names derive from Mapudungun, the Mapuche language, such as Lago Futalaufquen (Big Lake) and Futaleufú (Big River).

Because the Andes are relatively low here, westerly storms drop nearly 3m of rain annually to support the humid Valdivian forest. The eastern part of the park, though, is much drier. Winter temperatures average 2°C, but can be much colder. The summer mean high reaches 24°C, but evenings are usually cool.

Flora

While its wild backcountry supports some wildlife, Los Alerces exists primarily because of its botanical riches. Besides the alerce,

other important coniferous evergreens and deciduous broadleaf trees characterize the dense, humid Valdivian forest, with its almost impenetrable undergrowth of *chusquea*, a solid rather than hollow bamboo. Conifers include another species of cypress and the aromatic Chilean incense cedar.

The genus *Nothofagus* ('false beech,' but commonly known as 'southern beech'), to which most of the larger broadleaf tree species in the park belong, exists only in the Southern Hemisphere. Local species include ñire, coihue, and lenga. Another interesting species is the arrayán, whose foliage and peeling cinnamon-colored bark bear resemblance to the madrone *Arbutus menziesii* of the western US coastal states and British Columbia. More extensive stands can be found at Parque Nacional Los Arrayanes, near Villa La Angostura in Neuquén province.

Information

The Intendencia (park headquarters) is at Villa Futalaufquen ('the Villa'), at the south end of Lago Futalaufquen; for an introduction to the park's natural history, visit the **Museo y Centro del Interpretación** *(free with park entry; open 8am-8pm weekdays, 8am-1pm, 2:30pm-8pm weekends & holidays)*, which includes an aquarium and historical displays and documentation about the park's creation in 1937; rangers can supply park information.

Circuito Lacustre

Traditionally, Los Alerces' most popular excursion sails from Puerto Limonao up Lago Futalaufquen through the narrow channel of the Río Arrayanes to Lago Verde, but low water levels have eliminated part of this segment, making it necessary to hike the short distance between Puerto Mermoud, at the north end of Lago Futalaufquen, and Puerto Chucao on Lago Menéndez.

Launches from Puerto Chucao handle the second segment of the trip to the nature trail to **El Alerzal** (US$35; 1½ hours), the most accessible stand of alerces. From Puerto Limonao, the excursion costs US$55. Scheduled departures are at 10am from

PARQUE NACIONAL LOS ALERCES

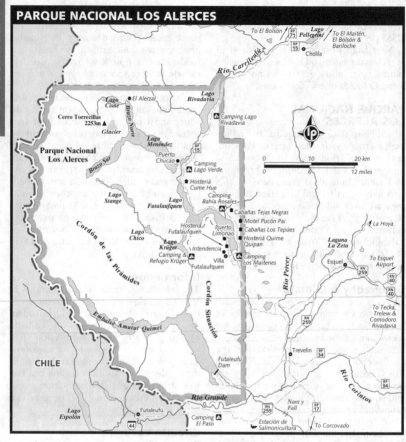

Limonao and noon from Chucao, returning to Chucao at 5pm and to Limonao at 7pm; purchase tickets in Esquel to assure a place on this popular trip.

The launch remains docked over an hour at El Alerzal trailhead, sufficient for a deliberate hike around the loop trail that also passes Lago Cisne and an attractive waterfall to end up at **El Abuelo** (The Grandfather), the finest alerce specimen along the route, which is likely some 4000 years old. Local guides are knowledgeable on forest ecology and conservation, but you may find the group uncom-

fortably large. If so, you may go ahead or lag behind the group, so long as you make it back to the dock in time for the return trip.

Unfortunately, because of fire hazard, authorities do not allow backcountry camping at El Alerzal or in other parts of the park's *zona intangible*, which is open only to scientific researchers. There are several more interpretive trails near Lago Futalaufquen for day hikes, but the only trekking alternative is the trail from Puerto Limonao along the south shore of Futalaufquen to Lago Krüger (see later).

Other Things to See & Do

There are rock-art sites on the **Río Desaguadero**, near Los Maitenes campground near the Intendencia. Park rangers lead guided hikes to **Cerro Alto El Dedal** (US$7, 6 hours) from the trailhead near the Prefectura Naval at Puerto Bustillo, on the eastern shore of Lago Futalaufquen, a few kilometers north of the Intendencia; another nearby alternative, from the same trailhead, is **Cinco Saltos** (2½ hours). Carry water and food.

Since so much of the park is designated as inaccessible zona intangible, the longest possible hike is the 25km trail from Puerto Limonao to Camping & Refugio Krüger (see Places to Stay), along the south shore of Lago Futalaufquen. This is a seven-hour trip (rangers claim the trip takes 12 hours, but are known to exaggerate) that can be broken up by camping at *Playa Blanca*. Boat excursions from Puerto Limonao to Puerto Lago Krüger cost about US$20 per person.

Places to Stay

Camping Los Alerces has several organized campgrounds accessible by road, all of which have hot showers, picnic tables, groceries and restaurants on-site or nearby. Another campground is accessible by foot or boat only. There are free campsites near some of these fee sites.

Camping Los Maitenes (☎ 02945-453328, 471006) Sites US$3 per person plus one-time charge of US$4 per tent and/or vehicle. The campground is 200m from the Intendencia on the Puerto Limonao road.

Camping Bahía Rosales (☎ 02945-471004) Camping US$6 per person, refugios US$40 double, 6-person cabañas US$150. This campground is at the north end of Futalaufquen, 12km from the Intendencia, and also has cabañas and refugios.

Camping Lago Verde (☎ 02945-454421) US$5 per person with one-time charge of US$2 per tent and/or vehicle. On the eastern shore of its namesake lake, this campground is 30km from Villa Futalaufquen. It offers a 30% discount for backpackers who aren't from Chubut.

Camping Lago Rivadavia (☎ 02945-454381) US$5 per person plus one-time charge of US$3 per tent/vehicle. At the south end of Lago Rivadavia, this campground is 42km north of the Villa.

Camping & Refugio Lago Krüger (☎ 454690) Camping US$5 per person; refugio US$15, US$8 with own sleeping bag. Accessible only by the 25km foot trail that leaves from Hotel Futalaufquen, or by launch from Puerto Limonao, this is a relatively isolated campground on Lago Krüger. Its refugio has hot showers and other amenities.

Cabañas & Hosterías With a small- to medium-size group, cabins can be an affordable option.

Hostería Cume Hue (☎ 02945-453639) US$70 per person with private bath and full-pension, US$50 per person breakfast only. This hostería is 25km north of the Villa.

Cabañas Tejas Negras (☎ 02945-471046) 5-person cabins US$160 & 6-person cabins US$180. These nearby cabins are 10km north of the Villa.

Motel Pucón Pai (☎ 02945-471010, 451399) Singles/doubles US$30/48 with private bath & breakfast, US$104/118 with half-pension. Also on Lago Futalaufquen, Pucón Pai is next to the campground of the same name.

Cabañas Los Tepúes (no ☎) Cabins US$80 per day up to 8 persons. These cabins are 8km north of the Villa on the eastern shore of Lago Futalaufquen.

Hostería Quime Quipan (☎ 02945-454134) US$55 per person half-pension with private bath; cabins US$120. Hostería Quime Quipan is at the south end of the lake. It also has cabins suitable for six or seven persons.

Hostería Futalaufquen (☎ 02945-471008, 452704; 011-4394-3808 in Buenos Aires) Doubles US$170 with breakfast. This very dignified, tasteful hostería, 4km north of the Villa on the quieter western shore, is the park's most appealing accommodation, but it comes at a steep price.

Getting There & Away

For details on getting to and from the park, see Esquel's Getting There & Away section.

GOBERNADOR COSTA
☎ 02945 • pop 1700

Along the long stretch between Esquel and Río Mayo, and also on the RP 20 route to Comodoro Rivadavia, cattle town Gobernador Costa has, thankfully, some decent travelers' services. On February 28, the town celebrates its annual festival, the Día del Pueblo. Some 20km west of town, RP 19 leads to Lago General Vintter and several smaller lakes near the Chilean border, all a remote haven for elite anglers, but camping is possible along the shores.

In town, *Camping Municipal* charges US$2 per person for sites with hot water and electricity. *Residencial El Jair* (☎ 491012, San Martín & Sarmiento) and *Mi Refugio* (☎ 491087, Av Roca) both have singles for US$15 with bath.

Several buses a week stop here between Trelew and Esquel, and between Comodoro Rivadavia and Bariloche. To get to Río Mayo, consider skipping this portion of bumpy and slow (and entirely boring) RN 40 by taking RP 20 south instead, paralleling Río Senguer to the RN 40 turnoff towards Río Mayo. Continuing on RP 20 leads to Colonia Sarmiento, with a petrified forest 30km south, then continues to Comodoro Rivadavia. Etap buses also serve Río Mayo via Alto Río Senguer.

RÍO MAYO
☎ 02903 • pop 2700

Only gauchos and soldiers are likely to spend more than a night at this dusty military barrack western crossroads, about 200km from Gobernador Costa, 135km north of Perito Moreno and 274km from Comodoro Rivadavia via paved RN 26 and RP 20. The small Casa de Cultura (☎ 420400, Av Ejército Argentino s/n; open 9am-noon & 3pm-6pm), in an early-20th-century schoolhouse, houses the tourist office and a small museum.

Banco del Chubut has an ATM at the corner of Yrigoyen and Argentina. Río Mayo's postal code is 9030. January's Festival Nacional de la Esquila features sheep-shearing and wool quality competitions, plus the crowning of a National Sheep-Shearing Queen.

Places to Stay & Eat
Lodging ranges from the riverside *Camping Municipal* (☎ 420400, Av E Argentino s/n), US$10 per vehicle, to *Hotel San Martín* (☎ 420066, San Martín 400), US$10 per person with shared bath, to *Hotel Akatá* (☎ 420054, San Martín 640), US$15 per person with private bath or the most upscale *El Viejo Kavadonga* (☎ 420020, San Martín 573). The hotels have reasonable restaurants.

Getting There & Away
LADE (☎ 420060), San Martín 520, flies Friday to Comodoro Rivadavia (US$21).

From the bus terminal (☎ 420264) at Fontana and Irigoyen, Angel Giobbi has daily buses to Comodoro Rivadavia (US$22, 4 hours) at 6am, and goes to Coyhaique, Chile (US$23), at 5:30am Monday and Thursday; the latter services, which start in Comodoro Rivadavia, are often full.

At 10am Monday and at 10pm Thursday, Etap (☎ 420167) covers the 350km to Esquel (US$25, 7 hours) via Río Senguer, San Martín, Gobernador Costa and Tecka. There is no public transportation on the rugged stretch of RN 40 southward toward Perito Moreno and Los Antiguos.

PERITO MORENO
☎ 02963 • pop 3000

This uninspiring agricultural settlement is a brief stopover en route to the Andean oasis of Los Antiguos. Its one appeal is the relatively good selection of transport options to Cueva de las Manos, Cañon del Feo, and to Parque Nacional Perito Moreno. The main drag, San Martín leads north to RP 43 and south to RN 40; it's 128km to Bajo Caracoles and 135km to Río Mayo. Laguna de los Cisnes in the southwest portion of town is little more than a dried-up puddle now and is no longer habitat for black-necked swans.

The town's historic moment of glory came when, in 1898, explorer Perito Moreno challenged Chile's theory of '*divortum aquarum continental*' border definition (basically, that the headwaters of a Pacific-flowing river should be in Chilean territory) by rerouting the Río Fénix, which flows through town, to Atlantic-bound Río Deseado. The river and the area stayed in Argentina, and the town took his name.

Information
The tourist office (☎ 432072, e turismo mpm@tierraaustral.com.ar), San Martín 1065, is open daily 7am to 11:30pm Monday to Friday and 8am to 3pm Saturday and Sunday. Transportation and lodging information is also available at the bus terminal. The post office is on Av JD Perón, near Belgrano; the postal code is 9040. There is an ATM. Talk-Aike is a locutorio at San Martín and Saavedra. CTC, on Perito Moreno before 9 de Julio, has cheap Internet access. The Hospital Distrital (☎ 432040) is at Colón 1237.

Organized Tours
A handful of townspeople are registered guides to Cueva de las Manos; ask around. The company GuanaCondor Tours & Expeditions (☎/fax 432303, e jarinauta@santa cruz.com.ar, Perito Moreno 1087) conducts tours to Arroyo del Feo (see Estancia Telken & Cañadon Arroyo del Feo, later) and Cueva de las Manos, accessing the park from either Estancia Los Toldos (difficult hike) or from Bajo Caracoles. The guide is bilingual and the drive down, in a sturdy, noisy but very reliable 1985 Soviet army van named 'Olga,' is half the fun.

Carlos Matus (☎ 0297-156256143, 1381 San Martín, e carlosmatus@hotmail.com) also runs tours to Cueva de las Manos and a two-day tour to PN Perito Moreno.

Places to Stay & Eat
Camping Municipal (☎ 432072, Laguna de los Cisnes) Sites US$2.50 per person, plus US$1.50 per car or tent, 6-person cabañas US$20. Near the dried-up lagoon and shaded by breezy poplars, this is the cheapest place to stay and has hot showers in heated bathrooms. The cabañas, while private, are very cramped.

Camping Ranch Omar (☎ 4974572, 15-238294, 1.5km from town, Chacra No 33) US$8-10, but negotiable. Owner Jose Luis has all sorts of grandiose plans for his campground, but for now it has tent sites and BBQ pits, cramped A-frame cabins and a cozy mud-brick house for taking *mate*.

Hotel Santa Cruz (☎ 432133, Belgrano 1565) US$20 per room. Boxy rooms are across a gravel driveway and the unkempt bathrooms in a dark corner behind the main house, but locals maintain this is the better choice of the budget places, especially for women. The bar, Patagonically kitsch, is worth a visit to play some pool or enjoy a stiff drink at the Formica counter with the local eccentrics.

Hotel Austral (☎ 432042, San Martín 1381) Dorm beds US$10 per person; meals US$5-10. The place looks like it's falling apart and the management isn't too helpful, but Austral is a decent cheap option.

Posada el Caminante (☎ 432204, fax 432202, Rivadavia 937) Singles/doubles US$30/45. The proprietor will make you feel right at home with her many family photos and knack for a good chat. The three pink frilly rooms, all accessed from the quiet living area, have comfy beds, heat and private bathrooms. Included in the price is an abundant breakfast with lots of seasonal fruit.

Hotel Belgrano (☎ 432019, fax 432235, Av San Martín 1001) Singles/doubles US$25/36. Breakfast US$5, meals US$5-10. The best of the hotels, Belgrano has beds with boxsprings and the bathrooms are clean. The downstairs restaurant serves hearty meals (try the vegetable soup), but service can be unwelcoming.

Hotel Americano (☎ 432074, San Martín 1327) Singles/doubles US$20/30; meals US$7. Small and run by a kind family, this is worth checking out.

Getting There & Away
Taxis are the only transportation between town and the airport and bus station, both at the north end of town near the highway junction.

LADE (☎ 432055), San Martín 1207, flies Monday to Gobernador Gregores (US$27), continuing to El Calafate (US$43), Río Gallegos (US$59), Río Grande (US$83) and Ushuaia (US$95).

Buses leave at 8am and 4:30pm daily to Comodoro Rivadavia (US$17-21, 5 hours), and go through Las Heras (US$9), Pico Truncado (US$14) and Caleta Olivia (US$15-17); and to Los Antiguos (US$4) at 11:15am and 10:15pm daily. In season, backpacker vans, such as that run by Chalten Travel, pick up passengers to go to El Chaltén or El Calafate. See the Fitz Roy Area or El Calafate sections for details.

Plans are in the works to pave RN 40 between Perito Moreno and Tres Lagos. If it's not yet paved, pay close attention along this stretch of windy road.

LOS ANTIGUOS
☎ 02963 • pop 2500

Picturesque rows of Lombardy poplars provide windbreaks for the irrigated chacras of Los Antiguos, a pleasant retreat on the southern shore of Lago Buenos Aires near the Chilean border. Before the arrival of Europeans, Tehuelche Indians and their forerunners frequented this 'banana belt' in their old age – the town's name is a near-literal translation of a Tehuelche name 'I-Keu-khon,' meaning Place of the Elders.

Volcán Hudson's disastrous 1991 eruption covered the town in ash, thus destroying as many as three harvests, but the farms have bounced back successfully: The surrounding fields yield an abundant fruit harvest – raspberries, strawberries, cherries, apples, apricots, pears, peaches and plums – all absurdly cheap. To celebrate its most favored crop, the town hosts the annual three-day Fiesta de la Cereza (Cherry Festival). Held in the second week of January, the festival has become so popular that finding lodging is difficult. In summer, **Lago Buenos Aires** is warm enough for swimming and **Río Jeinemeni** is a favored spot for salmon fishing.

Orientation & Information

Los Antiguos occupies the delta formed by Río Jeinemeni, which constitutes the border with Chile, and Río Los Antiguos. Most services are on or near east-west Av 11 de Julio, which runs the length of town. To the west, the avenue reaches and crosses the border to Chile Chico.

The tourist information office (☎ 491261) at Av 11 de Julio 446, is open 7am to 8pm Monday to Friday, 8am to 8pm Saturday and Sunday from October to March; and 8am to 3pm Monday to Friday the rest of the year.

The post office is at Gobernador Gregores 19; the postal code is 9041. There's a locutorio at Alameda 436. Banco de Santa Cruz is at Av 11 de Julio 531, but doesn't have an ATM.

Places to Stay & Eat

Camping Municipal (☎ 491265, RN 43) US$3 per person, plus US$2.50 per tent, US$5 per vehicle; cabañas US$20. On the lakeshore at the east end of Av 11 de Julio, sites (tables and fire pits) are protected from the wind by forest plantings. Hot showers are available in the evening.

Hotel Argentino (☎ 491132, Av 11 de Julio 850) Singles/doubles US$19/35. Rooms at this recommended place all have private bath and TV, but it's the excellent fixed-price dinners and lunches for US$8, with desserts of local produce and an outstanding breakfast for US$4 that keep the good reviews coming.

Hostería Antigua Patagonia (☎ 491038, fax 491038, e info@antiguapatagonia .com.ar, Ruta 43 s/n) US$95/115. For a bit of lakeside luxury, this place is three-star plush, equipped with sauna, gym, billiards table and bikes. Rooms, each with a lake view, are attractively appointed with rustic furniture and oversized beds. Lunches and dinners show off a fresh bounty of salmon, lamb and produce.

El Disco (☎ 0297-156255690, Pallavicini 134) US$12/25. Basic rooms with private baths are available, but the real draw is the parrilla restaurant.

Getting There & Away

Buses to Perito Moreno (US$4), Caleta Olivia (US$20, 5 hours) and Comodoro Rivadavia (US$26, 6 hours) leave from Patagonia Argentina 428 at 7:30am and 3:30pm daily, and from No 170 at 3pm daily.

Transportes Padilla (☎ 491140), San Martín 44, and Acotrans, Patagonia Argentina 170, cross the border (open 8am to 10pm daily) to Chile Chico (US$3 roundtrip) several times daily.

ESTANCIA TELKEN & CAÑADON ARROYO DEL FEO

Most decidedly one of the best stops along this stretch of RN 40, Estancia Telken is a casual, comfortable and overall welcoming place to rest up and enjoy the countryside. Settlers from New Zealand founded the estancia in 1915, which, despite a growing dependency on tourism, remains a working sheep and horse ranch run by the charming 'Coco' and 'Petti' Nauta. Coco's family hails from Dutch settlers, while Petti descends from a New Zealand clan and has many fascinating stories about yesteryear. Delicious and abundant meals can be served family-style with the couple, who can also provide afternoon tea and sack lunches.

Hiking possibilities are endless, including a worthwhile meander along a creek bed up to the **Meseta de Lago Buenos Aires**. Shallow lagoons favored by flamingos are a short drive away. Or ask Petti to take you to **Cueva de Piedra**, a small cave snuggled in a silent valley of guanacos, eagles and the occasional armadillo. Horseback riding is also available at US$5 to US$10 per hour or US$30 with a guide – opt for the guide.

Estancia Telken (☎ 02963-432079, fax 432303, RN 40, 25km south of Perito Moreno; ☎ 011-4797-7216/1950 Buenos Aires) Mid-Dec-Feb singles US$62-94, doubles US$80-144; early Dec & Mar US$53-78, US$68-120; April-Nov US$39-64, US$56-106; camping US$18 for 2 people with tent & vehicle; cyclists US$6 per person; open year-round. English and Dutch are spoken.

About 25km south of Telken is the turnoff to **Cañadon Arroyo del Feo** a deep red-rock river canyon that narrows into steep ravines. About a 6km walk, which involves fording the swift stream many times, leads to **Cueva Grande del Feo**, also known as Cueva Altamirante, with well-preserved rock art, approximately 7000 years old.

As the story goes, a hermetic descendent of the Tehuelche lived quite peacefully in this cave. Then, in the 1930s, a Spaniard by the last name Quesada, escaping Chilean police, built up two caves, one for himself and another possibly for captured animals, just below the Tehuelche's home. He planted a vegetable garden and protective willow trees. He remained elusive, scurrying to hide at the sound of any approach — even when locals came to tell him he was a free man again. Throughout the years, the two men never exchanged neighborly favors nor talked. The Spaniard disappeared, never to be seen again, and the age-crippled Tehuelche was eventually taken into town, where he quickly passed away soon thereafter.

Harry Nauta, Coco and Petti's son who runs GuanaCondor in Perito Moreno, organizes trips to the arroyo (which is on private land with locked gates), stopping for a quick break at Telken. The trip costs US$40, lunch not included. He may also start organizing overnight stays in a riverside cave. See the Perito Moreno section for details.

CUEVA DE LAS MANOS

RN 40 is very rough but scenic along the Río de las Pinturas, where the rock art of Cueva de las Manos *(Cave of Hands; US$3; open dawn-dusk)* graces the most notable of several archaeological sites. Dating from about 7370 BC, these polychrome rock paintings cover recesses in the near vertical walls with imprints of human hands as well as drawings of guanacos and, from a later period, more-abstract designs.

There are two points of access, one from Bajo Caracoles, 46km away on the south side of the river, and another from Hostería Cueva de las Manos, on the north side, via a footbridge. The cave walls are all fenced off, however. Guides in Perito Moreno organize daylong trips, usually around US$40 per person with a two-person minimum (bring your own food). Guided tours allow visitors to enter the cave to get a better glimpse of the walls, versus straining to see them from the other side of the rail.

There's a small information center and a *confitería* (cold drinks and simple meals) at the southern entrance.

Hostería Cueva de las Manos (☎ 011-4901-0436, fax 011-4903-7161 in Buenos

Aires) Doubles US$55 per person with breakfast, dorm beds US$19 without breakfast; open Nov-Mar & Semana Santa. This hostería, a short distance off RN 40 about 77km south of Perito Moreno, has four carpeted rooms with private bath, restaurant and room service.

Estancia Casa de Piedra (☎ 02963-432-1990) Camping US$2.50 per tent. This estancia, on RN 3 80km south of Perito Moreno, allows camping; showers cost an additional US$2.50.

BAJO CARACOLES

This remote and tiny town has the only reliable gas station located between Perito Moreno (128km) and Tres Lagos (409km). As tourism grows, so may the town. Between Tres Lagos and Bajo Caracoles, the highway has been greatly improved, permitting speeds between 65 and 80km/h.

Bajo Caracoles is also a main stop en route to Cueva de las Manos, and has one place to lodge, *Hotel Bajo Caracoles* (☎ 02963-490100), US$12 per person, run by a chap whose grumpy manner has won him notoriety up and down the highway.

South of Bajo Caracoles RN 40 takes a turn for the worse: It's 100km before reaching **Las Horquetas**, a small blip on the screen where RN 40 and RP 27 intersect. From there it's another 128km to Gobernador Gregores (see later in this chapter).

PARQUE NACIONAL PERITO MORENO

Beneath the Sierra Colorada, a painter's palette of sedimentary peaks, herds of guanacos graze peacefully alongside aquamarine lakes in this gem of the Argentine park system. Honoring the system's founder, this remote but increasingly popular park encompasses 115,000 hectares along the Chilean border, 310km by RN 40 and RP 37 from the town of Perito Moreno.

Besides guanacos, there are also pumas, foxes, wildcats, chinchillas, *huemul* (Andean deer) and many birds, including condors, rheas, flamingos, black-necked swans, upland geese *(cauquén)* and *caranchos* (crested caracaras). Predecessors of the Tehuelche

left evidence of their presence with rock paintings of both human hands and guanaco in caves at Lago Burmeister. Beyond the park boundary, glacier-topped summits such as 3700m Cerro San Lorenzo hover above the landscape.

As precipitation increases toward the west, the Patagonian steppe grasslands of the park's eastern border become sub-Antarctic forests of southern beech, *lenga* and *coihue*. Because the base altitude exceeds 900m, considerably higher than more-accessible southerly parks like Los Glaciares, weather can be severe. Summer visits are usually comfortable, but warm clothing and proper equipment are imperative at any season. Bring all food and supplies, though water is pure and plentiful.

Information

Rangers at the park's information center, on the eastern boundary, require all visitors to register. On hand is a good supply of informative maps and brochures. Rangers offer a variety of guided hikes and visits; they can also be contacted through the national parks office (☎/fax 02962-491477) in Gobernador Gregores.

Things to See & Do

Consult park rangers for guided walks to **Casa de Piedra**, on Lago Burmeister, where there are pictographs, and to **Playa de los Amonites** on Lago Belgrano, where there are fossils. From Estancia La Oriental, it's a 2½-hour hike to the summit of 1434m **Cerro León**, a mostly gentle climb except just above and below the tree line, where it's very steep. Look for Patagonian woodpeckers among the lengas on the lower slopes. From the peak, where troops of guanacos can be found among the climbers, there's a dazzling panorama of the surrounding mountain ranges and the meseta to the east.

Immediately east of the summit, across a low saddle, the volcanic outcrop of **Cerro de los Cóndores** is a nesting site for the Andes' signature bird, and the marshes at its base harbor upland geese, ibis, snipe and many other species. There have also been puma sightings in the area.

There are also several backpacking options ranging from one-day to three-day hikes; ask rangers for the latest details.

Places to Stay

There are free campgrounds at the information center (barren and exposed, no fire allowed); at Lago Burmeister, 16km from the information center, (far more scenic, and well sheltered among dense lenga forest, fire allowed); and at El Rincón, 15km away (no fires). None have showers, but there are pit toilets.

Estancia La Oriental (☎ 02962-452196, fax 02962-452235, Casa de Correo 51, 9310 Puerto San Julián) Camping US$15 per site, doubles US$136, open Nov-Mar. At the foot of Cerro León on the north shore of Lago Belgrano, La Oriental is a great option for those wishing to explore this backcountry more. Colonies of condors and horseback-riding trips, including organized pack trips, add to its Patagonic appeal. Meals are well praised but slightly pricey (lunches US$11, dinners US$22).

Getting There & Away

Public transportation options change often; check with the tourist offices in Perito Moreno, Los Antiguos, El Calafate and El Chaltén for latest details.

Hitchhiking is possible from the highway junction on RN 40, at least in January, but even then the park is so large that getting to trailheads presents difficulties. From April to November, the road becomes impassable at times. If you're driving, equip the car with spare tires and extra gas.

GOBERNADOR GREGORES
☎ 02962 • pop 2200

Gobernador Gregores, 60km east on RP 25, is the nearest town to Parque Nacional Perito Moreno, which is still more than 200km west. Arranging a car and driver here is easier and cheaper than in the town of Perito Moreno, and it's a good place to stock up on supplies. There's a tourist office (☎ 491398, e gregores@uvc.com.ar), at San Martín 409, open 8am to 8pm weekdays. The national parks administration

(☎/fax 491477) maintains an office at San Martín 882.

Seventy kilometers west of town via RP 29, **Lago Cardiel's** saline waters are well loved by anglers for heavyweight salmon and rainbow trout fishing. From the junction to the lake it's another 116km to **Tres Lagos**, where there is a gas station, and another 123km west to El Chaltén and the Fitz Roy area.

Camping Nuestra Señora del Valle (no ☎, Roca & Chile) US$3 per 3-6 person group. Operated in summer, the campground has showers, hot water and barbecue pits. For hotel options, try *Cañadón León* (☎ 491082, Roca 397) with singles/doubles for US$15/35 and the best option for dining, are *Hotel San Francisco* (☎ 491039, San Martín 463) with singles/doubles for US$35/50.

LADE (☎ 491008), Colón 544, flies Wednesday (via El Calafate) and Thursday to Río Gallegos (US$32); on Friday planes go to San Julián (US$20), Puerto Deseado (US$33) and Comodoro Rivadavia (US$39). Transporte Cerro San Lorenzo, at San Martín and Alberdi, has buses that leave Gregores for San Julián (US$17) four times a week at 6pm, while El Pulgarcito, San Martín 704, and El Pegaso, Mariano Pejkovic 520, both go to Río Gallegos.

THE FITZ ROY AREA

The northern end of **Parque Nacional Los Glaciares** takes in the Fitz Roy Range, indisputably one of the most majestic mountain areas of the Andes, and now a famous spot for trekking and mountaineering. **El Chaltén,** a small village at the entrance to the park and tattered from the winds whipping down the Río de las Vueltas floodplain, was slapped together in 1985 to claim the land before Chile could. It's Argentina's youngest town, with a steady winter population of a mere 140 that grows to 400 in the summer, when over 20,000 hikers, mountaineers and climbers from all corners of the world descend on the town to tackle the surrounding mountains. Services catering to peak-baggers continue to develop and improve: The trick will be if the town can retain its quirky frontier feel while adapting to its increasing popularity.

Capilla Toni Egger, a simple chapel in El Chaltén of Austrian design, memorializes the many climbers who lost their lives to the precarious peaks.

Cerro Fitz Roy's Tehuelche name, for which the town is now named, is *el chaltén*, which has been translated as 'peak of fire' or 'smoking mountain,' an apt description of the cloud-enshrouded summit, which the Tehuelche may have considered a volcano. Perito Moreno and Carlos Moyano later named it after the *Beagle*'s Capitan FitzRoy, who navigated Darwin's expedition up the Río Santa Cruz in 1834, coming within 50km of the cordillera.

This section covers the Fitz Roy part of the Parque Nacional Los Glaciares and north of the park's boundary; for information on the southern sector of the park, see that section following El Calafate.

Orientation & Information

Parques Nacionales *guadaparques* (park rangers) (☎ 493004), at the entrance to town just before the bridge over the Río Fitz Roy, do a fabulous job of discussing ecological issues in the park and distribute a small map and town directory that is comprehensive but confusing in scale. Many of the rangers

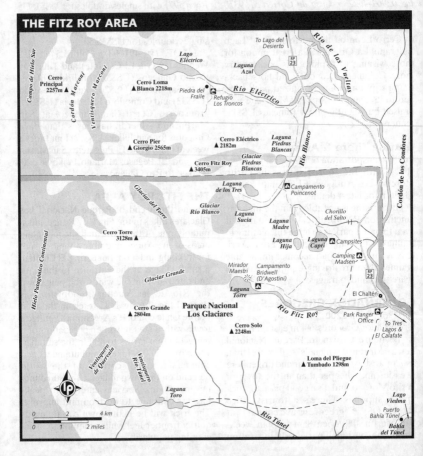

THE FITZ ROY AREA

are bilingual and can answer questions about the area's hikes, and issue climbing permits from 8am to 8pm daily. The several hostels in town are better sources for town information.

Money exchange, ATMs, Internet, cell phones and newspapers have yet to hit El Chaltén, but there is phone service and a gas station. Check out the excellent website www.elchalten.com for town details. Viento Oeste (☎ 493021), at San Martín and Brenner, en route to Camping Madsen, rents some camping equipment (tents US$8-10, bags US$4 per day), as may Rancho Grande, but call to reserve before arriving.

The area code in El Chaltén is ☎ 02962.

Hiking

Laguna Torre If the skies are clear and the weather good (ie, little wind), make this hike (three hours one way) a priority, since the peak of Cerro Torre is the most difficult to see on normal blustery days. The trail can be accessed either from behind the hotel Los Ñires or from the artisans' market in the north of the town. After a gentle initial climb, it's a fairly level walk through tranquil beech forests and along the Río Fitz Roy until a final steep climb up the lateral moraine left by the receding Glaciar del Torre. The Mirador El Torre offers a breathtaking view of the majestic spire of 3128m Cerro Torre rising out of the valley. Look for the 'mushroom' of snow and ice that caps the peak. This precarious formation is the final obstacle for serious climbers, who sometimes spend weeks or months waiting for weather good enough for an ascent.

The trail then meets up with **Madre y Hija**, a moderate, somewhat muddy trail linking to Campamento Poincenot. Another 20 minutes farther is Laguna Torre and some stunning views of the principal southern peaks of the Fitz Roy Range. *Campamento Bridwell* (also known as Campamento D'Agostini), the base camp for climbers of Cerro Torre, is at the lake. Follow the trail along the lake's north side to **Mirador Maestri** (no camping).

Laguna de los Tres This hike to a high alpine tarn, named in honor of the three

A Powerful Blue Berry

Local lore says if you eat the succulent blue berries from the Calafate bush you are sure to return. So, keep your eyes peeled from December to March when the fine bright yellow flowers of this low shrubby boxed-leaf barberry or *Berberis buxifolia* turn into the sweet morsels of desired returns.

Frenchmen who first scaled Fitz Roy, is a bit more strenuous (four hours one-way). The trail starts from the yellow-roofed pack station at *Camping Madsen*. After about an hour, there's a signed lateral to excellent backcountry *campsites* at Laguna Capri. The main trail continues gently through windswept forests and past small lakes, meeting up with the Madre y Hija trail. Carrying on through windworn ñire and along boggy terrain leads to **Río Blanco** and the woodsy *Campamento Poincenot*, named after a French mountaineer who died here in 1952. On the other side of the river, the trail splits at Río Blanco to head to Río Eléctrico. Stay left to reach a climbers' base camp. From here the trail zigzags very steeply up the tarn to the eerily still glacial lake and an extraordinary close view of 3405m Cerro Fitz Roy. Clouds ever huddle in the rocky crevasses, whipping up with a change in wind. Be prepared for high, potentially hazardous winds and allow time for contemplation and recovery. Scurry down 200m to the left of the lookout for an exceptional view of the emerald green **Laguna Sucia**.

Piedra del Fraile At Campamento Poincenot, the trail heads west to Laguna de los Tres (see above) or northeast along Río Blanco to Valle Eléctrico and Piedra del Fraile (eight hours from town; five hours from Río Blanco turnoff). The trail leads to **Glaciar Piedras Blancas**, the last part of which is a scramble over massive granite boulders to a turquoise lake with dozens of floating icebergs and constant avalanches on the glacier's face. Continuing, the trail is very rocky – keep an eye on the trail marks. The trail then passes through pastures and continues along **Río Eléctrico**, enclosed by sheer cliffs, before reaching the privately owned *Refugio Los Troncos* (US$5 camping fee). The campground has excellent services and the owners have information on many well-recommended trails within this private section. Rather than backtrack to Río Blanco and the Laguna de los Tres trail, it is possible to head east, hopping over streams to RP 23, the main road back to El Chaltén. You'll pass **Chorillo del Salto**, about 5km, or one hour, before reaching Camping Madsen.

The bus to Lago del Desierto (see below) drops off hikers at the Río Eléctrico bridge (US$10).

Loma del Pliegue Tumbado Heading south from the park ranger's office, this trail (four to five hours one way) skirts along the eastern face of Loma del Pliegue Tumbado going towards Río Túnel, then cuts west and heads to Laguna Toro. It offers the best views of the Torres and Fitz Roy. In fact, it's the only hike that allows views of both sections at once. The hike is rather gentle, but be prepared for strong winds and carry extra water.

Lago del Desierto Some 30km north of El Chaltén, Argentina appears to be reinforcing its territorial claim against Chile with pretentious plaques, toilet paper and cigarette butts. There is, however, a 500m trail to an overlook with fine views of the lake and surrounding mountains and glaciers, though the weather often intervenes against photography. Chaltén Travel minibus service to Lago del Desierto leaves from Rancho Grande Hostel in El Chaltén at 11am and returns at 4:30pm (US$20-24 roundtrip). Other shuttles leave El Chaltén at 9:30am and return from Estancia El Pilar at 3pm; check around town for latest schedules. Hitchhiking is feasible but not easy.

Ice Trekking
Several companies lead ice treks. Fitzroy Expediciones (☎/fax 493017, **e** fitzroyexpediciones@infovia.com.ar, Lionnel Terray 535)

runs glacier trekking excursions (US$65) from Campamento Bridwell. The trek usually begins at 9:30am, starting with a 1½ hour walk to the glacier, then three hours on the glacier, returning to the campground at 5pm. Some groups head out the same day from El Chaltén, which makes for a very arduous trip; it's recommended to make reservations in town, but to camp at Bridwell the night prior. Bring extra food and water.

They also arrange three- to four-day guided hikes over the **Hielo Patagónico Continental** (Continental Ice Field). This trek, catering to serious trekkers, involves technical climbing, including some strenuous river crossings and use of crampons. Rates range from US$75-150 per day. Alta Montaña (☎ 493108, **e** altamont@infovia.com.ar, Lionnel Terray 501) also arranges trips, often times longer and more strenuous. Also contact the El Chaltén park ranger office for more details and advice.

Horseback Riding
Horses can be used to trot in and around town (US$8 per hour) and to carry equipment with a guide (prices vary), but are not allowed unguided on national park trails. From El Chaltén, guided rides to Laguna Torre cost US$40-45, to Río Blanco US$40-50. A recommended outfitter is Rodolfo Guerra (☎ 493020).

Lake Cruises
Contact Patagonia Discovery (☎ 02902-493017), in El Calafate, about possible tourist launches from Puerto Bahía Túnel on the north shore of Lago Viedma; the trip takes in impressive views of Viedma Glacier, grinding from Cerro Fitz Roy. A five-hour excursion costs US$50. Buses to Puerto Bahía Túnel (US$10) leave from La Senyera del Torre.

Places to Stay
Camping Campgrounds along the trails are very basic, with one pit toilet; bury all human waste at least 30 feet from water sources. Some sites have dead wood with which to create windbreaks. Fires are prohibited. River water is pure; make sure all cleaning is

done down-river from the campground. Pack out all trash.

In town, similar free campsites include a few sites across from the national park information office and **Camping Madsen**, at the end of San Martín along the banks of Río de las Vueltas, with plenty of places to access water and with a few trees. Campgrounds with more amenities and small fees include the rather exposed **Camping El Refugio** (☎ 493007), on San Martín, with sites for US$3, showers for US$2 and sparse firewood available; similarly wind-whipped **El Relincho** for US$5; and bordering the western edge of town, **Ruca Mahuida** (☎ 493018), on Lionnel Terray, with sites for US$6 per person. The latter is an oversized backyard that may get cramped, but the benefits include an adjacent restaurant, hot showers, luggage storage and organized excursions.

Hostels & Hotels **Albergue Patagonia** (☎ 493019, fax 4822-2432, e patagoni@ hostels.org.ar, San Martín 493) US$12 per person plus US$2 for kitchen privileges; US$4 breakfast. It's a great choice to unwind in the cozy living area full of books and old *National Geographic* magazines, cushions and videos. Shared rooms aren't too cramped, but the walls are rather thin. Owners speak Dutch and English.

Rancho Grande Hostel (☎/fax 493005, e bigranch@hostels.org.ar, San Martín s/n) US$10/12 HI members/nonmembers; meals US$3-7. This spacious facility packs in the packers. Four-bed rooms are prepped with plenty of blankets, bathrooms have lots of showers, the kitchen is a tad small, but the common dining area has ample space and lots of light. If you need a break from cooking, the kitchen prepares some superb meals as well as cakes and class-A coffees. Chaltén Travel buses run from here.

Los Ñires (☎ 493009, Lago del Desierto & Hensen) Dorm beds US$10/12 HI/nonmembers, singles/doubles US$45/60, including breakfast; open Oct-Apr. This hostel is a more secluded setting, with small eight-bed rooms and a common kitchen area. The comfortable private rooms all have good bedding

and bathrooms, though some showers are elbow-bumpingly small.

La Base Hospedaje (☎ 493031, Lago del Desierto & Hensen) Doubles/triples US$50/60. Across the street from Los Ñires, La Base is an excellent value with four private rooms, all in an independent bungalow with kitchen facilities and exceptional views. The owners, Eduardo and Marcela, have an impressive collection of art movie videos (in Spanish), to be enjoyed in a loft lounge. They also run a small kiosk with basic essentials.

Posada Poincenot (☎ 493022 or 493005, San Martín 615) Singles/doubles US$35/45. Next door to Rancho Grande, Poincenot is a small serene affair with kind, conscientious owners. The double/triple and quadruple rooms are a good choice for families; all have private bath.

Cabañas Arco Iris (☎ 493079, Halvorsen s/n) Refugio/cabañas US$15/25. Colorful cabins in this small lot all have towels, TV, fridges and private baths. The cheaper refugio cabins, which are shared, are exactly the same, but without the towels or TV. Taqsa buses from Río Gallegos use Arco Iris as their base.

Cabañas Cerro Torre (☎ 421619, fax 493061, Perito Moreno & Halvorsen) Cabins US$20 per person, US$25 with breakfast. On the edge of town, cabins are clustered tightly together away from the town bustle. All have four beds, a fireplace and private bath.

Fitz Roy Inn (☎ 493062, fax 492217, San Martín 520) Singles/doubles US$98/104, including breakfast. Most guests of this inn come as part of a Cal Tur package, including half-pension. Nondescript, with narrow beds and mediocre service, it's merely passable for the non-group tour lot.

Hosterías & Estancias **Hostería El Puma** (☎ 493017, Lionnel Terray 212) Singles/ doubles US$120/145, including buffet breakfast. Quaint and comfortable, El Puma provides the standards of luxury for those that desire it without overt pretensions.

Hostería Estancia Helsingfors (☎/fax 011-4824-3634 or 6623 in Buenos Aires,

0966-420719 *Río Gallegos,* [e] *info@helsing fors.com.ar,* [w] *www.helsingfors.com.ar)* Singles/doubles US$200/360; open Nov-Easter. Helsingfors was established by Finnish pioneers on the south shore of Lago Viedma, 150km from El Calafate and 170km from El Chaltén. Its spectacular setting, personalized service and access to some of the park's gems make it a highly regarded estancia, catering to luxury tourism. Prices represent a one-night, two-day stay, with all meals and an excursion.

Places to Eat

La Senyera del Torre (☎ *493063, Lago del Desierto & Güemes)* is a good option for a light meal followed by an enormous portion of tasty chocolate cake. You might also try *Carrilay Aike* (*San Martín & Lago del Desierto)* for good homemade bread, pizzas and teas (US$4.50-6), or *Josh Aike* (☎ *493008, Lago del Desierto & Hensen)* for slabs of chocolate, hot chocolate and chocolate desserts.

Patagonicus (☎ *493025, Güemes & Madsen)* US$6-13. Tall windows let the light stream over bulky wood tables and through the comfortable bar. Pizza choices run the gamut, all well accompanied by a variety of salads and wine.

Chaltén Art (☎ *493055, Antonio de Viedma)* US$2-7. In the southern block, Art is a simple affair for coffee and pastries, but the main focus is the high-powered telescope.

Ruca Mahuida (☎ *493018, Lionnel Terray)* US$4-12. Kudos to Ruca for creative cuisine in a non-smoking dining room.

La Casita (☎ *493042, San Martín)* US$5-15. Popular for the pastas and an easy meeting spot, La Casita can get crowded and unfortunately too smoky due to poor ventilation.

Los Ñires (☎ *493009, Lago del Desierto & Hensen)* US$3-10. Another good choice is the hostería's airy restaurant, serving espresso coffee, and specializing in pastas, trout and pizzas.

Groceries, especially fruits and veggies, are limited: Bring what you can from El Calafate. For basics, try *Dos de Abril (San Martín & Riquelme)* or closer to the camp-sites *El Gringuito.* Tasty fresh bread can be found at *Elal Panadería*, next-door to Dos de Abril.

Entertainment

Josh Aike (see Places to Eat). Maybe it's the combo of beers and chocolate, or simply the fun, low-key ambience, but this place can stay buzzing into the wee hours.

Zafarrancho (behind Rancho Grande). Dance club, karaoke bar, movie house – this place morphs to meet all diversion needs. Movie language is decided by democratic vote.

La Cervecería (San Martín) US$3-4. Colorful Blanca, the brewmaster, keeps this brewed-on-premises pub hopping till late into the night and sometimes into the morning. Cool, unfiltered dark and lager beer are on offer, as are baskets of peanuts and an oft-times raucous crowd.

Getting There & Away

El Chaltén is 220km from El Calafate via paved RP 11, rugged RN 40, and improved but still very rocky RP 23. It's not uncommon to see minivans with tires blown on the last stretch of road. If you're in a smaller, low-clearance vehicle, take the proper precautions (go *very* slowly), or consider taking a bus. See the El Calafate Getting There & Away section for details on daily buses to El Chaltén.

To get to El Calafate (US$25, 5 hours), Los Glaciares leaves at 5:30pm daily from Av Güemes and Lago del Desierto; Chalten Travel leaves daily in the morning and at 6pm from Rancho Grande; and Cal Tur leaves from Fitz Roy Inn at 5:30pm Monday, Wednesday, Friday and Sunday.

Taqsa leaves from Cabañas Arco Iris to Río Gallegos at 2:00am Monday, Wednesday and Friday (US$50, 10 hours).

EL CALAFATE

☎ 02902 • pop 4000

El Calafate, 320km northwest of Río Gallegos, and 32km west of RP 5's junction with northbound RN 40, is probably one of the ew places that can claim a livelihood from one single tourist attraction – some 80km way.

Taking its fame from the spectacular Moreno Glacier, El Calafate continues to grow as accessibility to the glacier and **Parque Nacional Los Glaciares** improves. At the center of town is the main street, Av del Libertador General San Martín, known as Av Libertado or San Martín, prettily lit, tree-lined and stuffed with souvenir shops, restaurants and pretentious weekend vaca-tioners. But get off the main drag, and the streets, shops and pretensions melt away quickly; horses replace Porsches along muddy roads leading to ad-hoc building de-velopments that show no signs of any city planning. Many backpackers complain of the town's costly services and in-your-face tourism, but it is a gateway to the crashing icebergs of the famed glacier and the trans-port hub to El Chaltén and the Fitz Roy Range in the northern section of Parque Na-cional Los Glaciares.

January and February are the most popular, expensive and crowded months; if possible, plan your visit outside of those months.

Information

Tourist Offices El Calafate's municipal tourist office (Emcatur; ☎ 491090, 492884, ℮ info@elcalafate.net, ⓦ www.calafate.com), at the bus terminal, is open 8am to 10pm No-vember to March, 8am to 8pm the rest of the year. It keeps a list of hotels and prices; has maps, brochures, and a message board; and here's usually an English-speaker on hand.

ACA (☎ 449-1004) is at 1 de Mayo and Av Roca.

The national parks office (☎ 491755, 491005), Av Libertador 1302, is open 7am to 2pm weekdays, and has brochures in-cluding a decent (though not adequate for trekking) map of Parque Nacional Los Gla-ciares.

Asociación Amigos de la Montaña, a re-source for serious climbers, is at El Refugio (☎ 491300, ℮ friendmountain@latinmail com), Gobernador Moyano 839.

Money Banco Santa Cruz, Av Libertador 1285, changes traveler's checks (with 3% commission); it's open 10am to 3pm week-days only, and its ATM is sometimes out of service. Thaler, on the other side of 1 de Mayo, imposes a substantial commission on traveler's checks, but is open Sunday after-noons.

Post & Communications The post office is at Av Libertador 1133; the postal code is 9405. Telefonica's locutorio, called Open Calafate, at Libertad 996, has Internet access. Calafate's Cooperativa Telefónica is at Espora 194; collect calls are not possible, and discounts are available only after 10pm.

Travel Agencies Tiempo Libre (☎ 491265), Libertador 1150, can help with some flights. Most other agents deal exclusively with nearby excursions and are not helpful when dealing with travel beyond the area.

Laundry El Lavadero, Libertador 1118, charges US$8 per load and is open daily, in-cluding Sunday afternoons.

Medical Services Calafate's Hospital Mu-nicipal Dr José Formenti (☎ 491001) is at Av Roca 1487.

Things to See & Do

The **Museo de El Calafate** (*Av Libertador 575; free; open 10am-9pm Mon-Sun*) has humble displays of arrowheads, animals and plants, plus photos of the town's first set-tlers. Alongside the lakeshore, north of town, **Laguna Nimes** has become prime bird habitat.

About 9km east of town, near the shores of Lago Argentino, tourist-trap **Punta Walichu** (*☎ 491059, US$5; open 9am-dusk*), features a tacky display of reproduction rock art followed by some original art, most of which can hardly be seen through the graffiti and birdshit.

Organized Tours

Calafate's numerous travel agencies arrange excursions to the Moreno Glacier and other attractions in the area. Tour prices, which do not include park entrance fees, are similar. Ask the agents and other travelers about added benefits, like extra stops, binoculars, snacks or multilingual guides.

Cal Tur (☎ 491368, fax 492217), Av Libertador 1080, specializes in tours and lodging packages in El Chaltén.

Chalten Travel (☎ 492212), Libertador 1174, runs recommended tours to the glacier, stopping in the park for wildlife viewing; binoculars provided; also specializes in RN 40 trips.

Interlagos Turismo (☎ 491018), Av Libertador 1175, is a large bus company with recommended service.

Patagonia Backpackers (☎ 491243), Los Pioneros 251, operates out of Albergue del Glaciar and organizes recommended trips to the glacier (US$35).

Solo Patagonia (☎ 491298, fax 491790), Av Libertador 963, arranges trips to the glaciers, including a US$110 glacier blitz all-day tour.

Places to Stay

Prices for accommodations can vary seasonally; the peak is usually January and February, but it can extend from early November to late March at some places. Many places close in winter.

Budget *Camping Municipal* (☎ 491829, *José Pantín*) US$4 per person. This woodsy campground, straddling the creek just north of the bridge into town, has separate areas for auto and tent campers, good toilets, hot showers, fire pits (there's wood for sale), and potable water.

Los Dos Pinos (☎ 491271, fax 491632, e losdospinos@cotecal.com.ar, *9 de Julio 218*) US$4 per person. Just one part of the Los Dos Pinos lodging labyrinth, the campground is small and closely packed, but the sites have fire pits and there's hot water, decent showers and an enclosed kitchen.

Hospedaje Jorgito (☎/fax 491323, *Moyano 943*) US$4 per person. In the backyard orchard of a homey hospedaje, sites are adequate; it's the closest camping to the center of town.

Albergue del Glaciar (☎/fax 491243, e info@glaciar.com, *Calle Los Pioneros*

251) Floor US$5, dorm beds US$10/1 HI-members/nonmembers, singles/double US$40/45 with private baths; open Sept mid-Apr. Set away from the main part o town, east of the creek, this sociable, spic and-span hostel is always active wit packers, which may at times strain the energy of the staff. Common rooms are com fortable, the kitchen a tad small, and there' laundry facilities. The multilingual staff pro vides information on the area and organize well-recommended excursions.

Calafate Hostel (☎ 492450, fax 49245* w www.hostelspatagonia.com, *Gobernado Moyano 1226*) Dorm bed US$12/15 without with bathroom, singles/doubles US$40/45 discounts to HI members. Taking up the corner with 25 de Mayo, this log cabin or steroids sets the standard with ample common spaces, a wraparound terrace, grea showers, a well-equipped large kitchen lots of heat on chilly nights and English speaking, considerate staff. Fun trips to the glacier and Fitz Roy are planned.

Albergue Lago Argentino (☎ 491423, fa: 491139, e hostellagoargentino@coteca .com.ar, *Campaña del Desierto 1050*) US$€ per bunk bed. Just a block from the bus ter minal, this place gets crowded with the very budget conscious willing to deal with cell block, thin-walled rooms and an extremely loud dining hall of long, sagging picnic tables. Sheets cost US$2 extra.

Los Dos Pinos (☎ 491271, fax 491632, e losdospinos@cotecal.com.ar, *9 de Julio 358*) Dorm bed US$7 per person, singles US$15/30 shared/private bath. Quieter Los Dos Pinos has dorms (sleeping bag required) with clean bathrooms and kitchen facilities. Rooms with shared bath (clean and easily accessed) are a better deal.

Cayupe Albergue (☎ 491125, *Manzano 355*) US$12 with breakfast. A walk from the center (close to Laguna Nimes), Cayupe is an attractive, modern chalet-style house with shared bunk-bed rooms, spotless bathrooms with great showers and individual storage closets. The friendly owners encourage camaraderie, often around a good guitar jam

Hospedaje Alejandra (☎ 491328, *Espora 60*) US$14 per person with shared

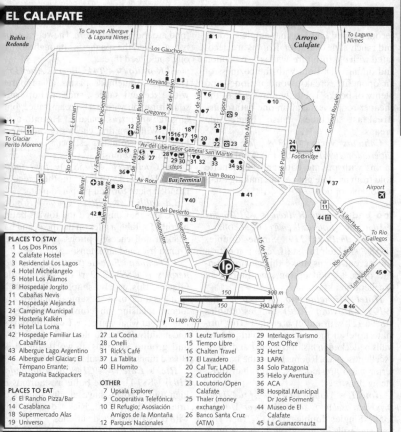

EL CALAFATE

PLACES TO STAY
1 Los Dos Pinos
2 Calafate Hostel
3 Residencial Los Lagos
4 Hotel Michelangelo
5 Hotel Los Álamos
8 Hospedaje Jorgito
11 Cabañas Nevis
21 Hospedaje Alejandra
24 Camping Municipal
39 Hostería Kalkén
41 Hotel La Loma
42 Hospedaje Familiar Las Cabañitas
43 Albergue Lago Argentino
46 Albergue del Glaciar; El Témpano Errante; Patagonia Backpackers

PLACES TO EAT
6 El Rancho Pizza/Bar
14 Casablanca
18 Supermercado Alas
19 Universo
27 La Cocina
28 Onelli
31 Rick's Café
37 La Tablita
40 El Hornito

OTHER
7 Upsala Explorer
9 Cooperativa Telefónica
10 El Refugio; Asosiación Amigos de la Montaña
12 Parques Nacionales
13 Leutz Turismo
15 Tiempo Libre
16 Chalten Travel
17 El Lavadero
20 Cal Tur; LADE
22 Cuatrocición
23 Locutorio/Open Calafate
25 Thaler (money exchange)
26 Banco Santa Cruz (ATM)
29 Interlagos Turismo
30 Post Office
32 Hertz
33 LAPA
34 Solo Patagonia
35 Hielo y Aventura
36 ACA
38 Hospital Municipal Dr José Formenti
44 Museo de El Calafate
45 La Guanaconauta

bath. Run by a sprightly elderly lady, Alejandra offers small but pleasant rooms, all of which have locking closets. There's no breakfast or kitchen use. You will need to ask for hot water.

Hospedaje Jorgito (☎/fax 491323, Moyano 943) US$12 per person. Half house, half camping, Jorgito has practical lodging all surrounded by a colorful bounty of flowers and fruit trees.

Mid-Range Residencial Los Lagos (☎ 491170, fax 491347, 25 de Mayo 220) Singles/doubles US$50/70. While the place is

rather void of atmosphere, the rooms are clean, spacious and have central heating.

Hospedaje Familiar Las Cabañitas (☎ 491118, fax 491118, e lascabanitas@cotecal.com.ar, Valentín Feilberg 218) Singles/doubles US$32/48, 8-bed dorm US$88; open Sept-May. Storybook A-frames with loft beds, gardens overflowing with English lavender and charming owners with an eye for the romantic make this a great option. Breakfast isn't included, but there's tea and coffee service, as well as kitchen use.

Hotel La Loma (☎/fax 491016, e lalomahotel@infovia.com.ar, Av Roca 849) Singles/

doubles US$40/50 to US$50/80, discounts possible. In a quiet upper quarter of town, recommended La Loma has ample gardens and ranch-style character. Rooms are decorated with old furniture, while the reception and dining area brim with the coziness of an open fire, creaky wooden floors and plenty of books. The only drawback of the cheaper rooms is the all-in-one bathrooms. Breakfast includes fresh homemade breads.

Cabañas Nevis (☎ *493180, fax 493193, Libertador 1696)* US$100-130. Mini-alpine cabins with private bath and kitchenette hold from five to eight people, making this a reasonable option.

Top End *Hostería Kalkén* (☎ *491073, fax 491036,* e *hotelkalken@cotecal.com.ar, Valentín Feilberg 119)* Singles/doubles US$80/95. Helpful staff, quiet location and decent rooms make this cheaper top-end place a good option, and there's an excellent breakfast.

Hotel Michelangelo (☎ *491045, fax 491058, Moyano 1020)* Singles/doubles US$96/121 with buffet breakfast. This intimate hotel in the center has solid 'glacial' walls bedecked in historic photos, and offers excellent service. Rooms facing the back interior patio are more peaceful than those facing the street.

Hotel Los Álamos (☎ *491144, fax 491186,* e *posadalosalamos@cotecal.com.ar, Moyano 1355)* Singles/doubles US$177/183. This four-star trills in luxury: plush rooms, puffy sofas, spectacular gardens, putting greens and tennis courts are enough to almost forget about seeing that glacier.

Places to Eat

Universo (☎ *492197, Av Libertador 1108)* US$3-10. Well regarded by locals and tourists alike, the pastas and pizzas are the best fare, dished out in an informal family-style dining room. Vegetarian options (mainly spinach) are available.

Casablanca (☎ *491402, Av Libertador 1202)* US$6-18. There's good music and rather slow service here, plus overpriced coffee drinks and filling burgers.

Onelli (☎ *491184, Libertador 1197)* US$6-10, US$8 tourist menu. Heaping portions of food are the highlight here. The veggie soup is hearty, and the spaghetti, although slightly oily, could feed three.

El Hornito (☎ *491443, Buenos Aires 155)* US$6-12. Homemade pastas, all prepared with excellent sauces, such as butternut squash ravioli with herb cream sauce, plus large crispy pizzas, make El Hornito a favorite. While waiting, check out the bric-a-brac from surrounding estancias or relax to the soulful jazz music.

La Cocina (☎ *491758, Av Libertador 1245)* US$6-13. This is another recommended place for well-prepared pasta.

La Tablita (☎ *491065, Coronel Rosales 28)* US$5-15. Considered the town's better parrilla, La Tablita piles on the meat, and has chicken and cheese options, garlic parsley French fries and an extensive wine list.

El Témpano Errante (☎ *491243, Los Pioneros s/n)* US$3-12. Part of Albergue del Glaciar, this gazebo-shaped, picnic-table spot has some of the best meals in town. The menu, focusing on comfort cooking, is limited but what you get is fresh, full of zest and healthy. The pesto alone, with fresh basil and ground almonds, is worth the trek. Boxed lunches are available for US$7.

Rick's Café (☎ *492148, Av Libertador 1105)* US$9-11. While buffet restaurants in high-tourist towns have all the sounds of dried-out dingy food, Rick's does it right with consistently good varieties.

El Rancho Pizza/Bar (☎ *491644, Gobernador Moyano & 9 de Julio)* US$6-16. Open after 6:30pm. Locals know that *the* place for pizza is El Rancho, in one of the town's oldest houses (1949). The more than 30 varieties of wood-fired pizzas or calzones and mixed salads are well worth the wait.

Supermercado Alas (☎ *491249, 9 de Julio 59)*. To stock up on trekking meals, Alas has the best selections of fresh produce, dried soups and breads, plus a small deli.

Entertainment

La Guanaconauta (☎ *491281, Av Libertador 351)* US$2-6. Lava lamps and candelabras, fireplaces and patio fountains, sitting n swings and sipping at sewing tables, this ightclub aims to appeal to all whims, as do ne generous bar drinks and fruit juices.

Getting There & Away

Air Southern Winds (☎ 491349), 9 de Julio 69, oes to Ushuaia (US$75) twice weekly, to Bariloche (US$109) on Saturday and to Aeroparque (US$189) weekends. Chilean Aerovías DAP flies to Puerto Natales at 10am weekdays (US$50, 30 minutes).

LADE (☎ 491243), Av Libertador 1080, ies Wednesday to Río Gallegos (US$25), Río Grande (US$48) and Ushuaia (US$55). On Monday flights go to Comodoro Rivadavia (US$61) via Gobernador Gregores (US$24) and Perito Moreno (US$43). Prices nd schedules vary. LAPA (☎ 491171), Av Libertador 1015, flies Tuesday and Saturday o Ushuaia (US$97) then to Buenos Aires (US$190).

Bus El Calafate's hilltop bus terminal is on Av Roca, easily reached by a pedestrian taircase from the corner of Av Libertador nd 9 de Julio. For Puerto Natales (US$25, ½ hours) Bus Sur and Zaahj leave daily at ?am except Monday, or Cootra leaves for Río Turbio (US$25, 4½ hours) at 7am daily, rom which there are connections to Puerto Natales. For Río Gallegos (US$25, 4 hours), nterlagos and Taqsa (Quebek Tours) leave t 9am. For El Chaltén (US$25, 5 hours) buses leave at 7:30am, 8am and 6:30pm daily.

From October 15 to the end of March, Chalten Travel (☎ 492212), Av Libertador 174, runs buses on odd-numbered days at 8am along RN 40 to Perito Moreno (US$65) nd to Los Antiguos (US$68). It's possible o hop on and off buses along the route, but pace is not guaranteed. Similar service is lso provided out of El Chaltén.

Getting Around

Aerobus (☎ 491492) and Interlagos provides service to/from the airport for US$5. Cuatrociclón, on Espora near the corner of Av Libertador, rents mountain bikes for US$5/15/20 hour/half day/full day. Hertz representative Annie Millet (☎ 491446), Av

Libertador 1029, rents four-wheel drives. If you're heading to the glacier, note that a one-day rental is cheaper than the daily special with only 50km free mileage.

AROUND EL CALAFATE

Estancia Alice (*☎/fax 491793,* **e** *elgalpon@ estanciaalice.com.ar, Av Libertador 1015, El Calafate; or ☎/fax 011-4774-1069, Av Leandro Alem 822, 3rd floor, Buenos Aires)* Singles/ doubles US$97/124; open Sept-Apr. Also known as El Galpón, Estancia Alice is a working ranch to which many a tour group descends to observe herding and sheep shearing, take birding walks or feast on lamb asado. Tours, organized from El Calafate, cost US$45 including transport or US$75 with dinner. They also offer horseback rides to nearby Cerro Frías (US$50). Alice is 21km west of El Calafate on RP 11, heading towards Glaciar Moreno.

Estancia Alta Vista (*☎ 02902-491247,* **e** *altavista@cotecal.com.ar, Apartado Postal 17, 9405 El Calafate)* Double occupancy US$515 all-inclusive, B&B US$300. Open mid-Oct-mid-Apr. Resplendent Alta Vista is the area's splurge estancia, where society's upper-echelon comes to disconnect. A Relais & Chateau member, Alta Vista treats guests to superior attention, sumptuous meals and exquisite decor. The all-inclusive package includes horseback riding, fishing and bicycling at your whim. Alta Vista, 33km from El Calafate on RP 15, is the casco to Estancia Anita, owned by the Braun family, and where over 15,000 striking agicultural workers were trapped and subsequently killed during the 1921 Patagonia Rebellion.

PARQUE NACIONAL LOS GLACIARES

Parque Nacional Los Glaciares' (US$5) centerpiece is, without a doubt, the breathtaking **Ventisquero Perito Moreno** (Moreno Glacier), one of earth's few advancing glaciers. A low gap in the Andes allows moisture-laden Pacific storms to drop their loads east of the divide, where they accumulate as snow. Over millennia, under tremendous weight, this snow has recrystallized

ARGENTINA

AROUND EL CALAFATE & PARQUE NACIONAL LOS GLACIARES

into ice and flowed slowly eastward. The 1600-sq-km trough of Lago Argentino, the country's largest single body of water, is unmistakable evidence that glaciers were once far more extensive than today.

Fifteen times between 1917 and 1988, as the 60m-high glacier has advanced, it has dammed the Brazo Rico (Rico Arm) of Lago Argentino, causing the water to rise. Several times, the melting ice below has been unable to support the weight of the water behind it and the dam has collapsed in an explosion of ice and water. To be present when this spectacular cataclysm occurs is unforgettable, but the dam hasn't formed since 1988 and it's impossible to predict when it might happen again.

Visiting the Moreno Glacier is no less an auditory than visual experience, as huge icebergs on the glacier's face calve and collapse into the **Canal de los Témpanos** (Iceberg Channel). From a series of catwalks and vantage points on the Península de Magall-

anes visitors can see, hear and photograph the glacier safely as these enormous chunk crash into the water. It is no longer possibl to descend to the shores of the canal.

Hielo y Aventura (☎ 492205, fax 491053 Av Libertador 935) in El Calafate offer **minitrekking** (US$68/53 high/low season plus US$17 for transport) on the glacier, two-hour affair involving a quick boat rid from Puerto Bajo de las Sombras, a wall through lenga forests, a quick chat o glaciology and then a 1½-hour walk on th ice (using crampons). Children under eigh are not allowed; reservations are essentia and bring your own food.

Boat trips allow one to sense the enormit of the glacier walls, even though the boa keep a distance. Hielo y Aventura (se above) runs SafariNautico (US$20, include transport from El Calafate), a one-hour tou of Brazo Rico, Lago Argentino and the sout side of Canal de los Témpanos. Boats leav hourly starting at 11:30am from Puerto Baj e las Sombras; no reservations are necessary. To see the glacier's main north face, **René ernandez Campbell** (☎ *491155*, e *rfcino@ otecal.com.ar; US$10*) runs boats from the unch below the UTVM restaurant near e main lookout every hour on the half hour.

laces to Stay & Eat Camping near the lacier offers the chance to revisit the lacier, to see its changing colors in different egrees of daylight. Just over 72km from El alafate and only 7km from the glacier, *'amping Bahía Escondida* charges US$4 er person for well-maintained and woodsy tes. Those near the store and bathrooms re clustered close together, but there's lenty of room for more space and quiet rther down the small road. There are exellent views, hot water, a small store and re pits. Expect it to be crowded in the ummer. Another choice, although not as ell maintained is *Camping Correntoso,* km east of Bahía Escondida, which may harge a small fee, or try asking the ranger :ation at the glacier if it's possible to camp ere (usually a two-night maximum).

Hostería Los Notros (☎ *499510, fax 99511; reservations ☎ 4814-3934, fax 4815- 5345, Arenales 1457, 7th floor, Buenos Aires,* info@losnotros.com*)* Singles/doubles JS$132/174 off-season, US$280/330 peak :eason. The only formal lodging near the lacier, Los Notros is blessed with a spectacular view, enjoyed from the dining rooms nd outdoor deck and from some of the :ylish rooms, all outfitted in luscious fabrics nd comforts. Prices include a trip to the lacier lookout. Gourmet lunches range om US$35 to US$48.

UTVM Snacks US$3-5; restaurant meals JS$14-18, open year-round. At the lookout, nis snack bar and restaurant offers sandviches, coffee and desserts, and full meals.

ietting There & Away The Moreno jlacier is about 80km from Calafate via vestbound partially paved RP 11, passing nrough the breathtaking scenery of Lago Argentino. Bus tours are frequent and nunerous in summer (off-season transportaon is cut back, but can be arranged); see the

El Calafate section, or simply stroll down Av Libertador. The glacier changes appearance as the day progresses (sun hits the face of the glacier in the morning).

Tours to the glacier leave also from Puerto Natales, Chile, with the option to stay

Glaciology 101

Rivers of ice, creators of contour and subjects of awe: Glaciers are, well, very cool places. And for those who didn't pack the geology textbooks, here's a recap for you to study and impress your friends.

The heart of the glacier, so to speak, is the **accumulation area**, on which snow falls, and as the weight increases, compacts to ice. This extra weight forces the glacier to move. As it pushes along, the melted ice on the bottom mixes with rock and soil, grinding it up and creating a kind of lubricant that helps the glacier keep pushing along. All that movement in turn causes cracks and deformities in the ice, or **crevasses**. At the same time, debris of the crushed rock is pushed to the sides of the glacier, creating **moraines**. Where the glacier melts is called the **ablation area**. When there's more accumulation than melting at the ablation area, the glacier **advances**; but when there's more melting or evaporation, the glacier **recedes**.

What makes a glacier blue? Areas of the glacier that are not compacted have air bubbles into which the long wavelengths of white light are absorbed, thus we see simply white. In the areas where the ice becomes more compact, due to the weight on the top pushing ice particles together, blue light (short wavelengths) is still transmitted. The more compact the ice, the longer the path the light has to travel and the bluer the ice appears. Where the glacier melts and calves into lakes, it dumps with it glacier 'flour' of the ground-up rock, giving the water a milky, gray color. This same sediment remains unsettled in some lakes and diffracts the sun's light, creating the stunning turquoise, pale-mint and azure colors that speckle these glacial regions.

in El Calafate on the way back. This is cheaper than taking regular transportation to El Calafate, spending the night and taking a tour the next day, but it does make for a long day of driving and doesn't allow for the same amount of time at the glacier (US$47 if staying in El Calafate).

GLACIAR UPSALA & ONELLI

Upsala Glacier – 595 sq km huge, 60km long and some 4km wide in parts – is much larger than the Moreno Glacier, but less spectacular. On an extension of the Brazo Norte (North Arm) of Lago Argentino, it is accessible by launch from Puerto Bandera, 45km west of Calafate by RP 11 and RP 8. René Fernández Campbell (see earlier) and Upsala Explorer (☎ 491034, 9 de Julio 69; US$55-110) run **boat tours** to Upsala and more expensive tours to also Onelli and Spegazzini glaciers. If icebergs are cooperating, boats may allow passengers to disembark at Bahía Onelli to walk about a half kilometer to iceberg-choked **Lago Onelli** where the Onelli and Agassiz glaciers merge. Meals are extra and usually expensive; bring your own food.

LAGO ROCA

Mountain forest and lake blend together in the south arm of Lago Argentino to create a serene escape. In this most southerly section of the park are some good hikes and pleasant camping and estancia accommodations. At La Jerónima, **Cerro Cristal** is a rugged but rewarding hike beginning at the education camp (not a campground), found right before reaching the Camping Lago Roca entrance, 55km from El Calafate along RP 15. The hike, crossing variable terrain, takes about 3½ hours. From the summit, Torres del Paine and the Moreno Glacier can be seen. Fishing for rainbow trout and perch are also popular ways to unwind in this part of the park. Leutz Turismo (☎ 492316, 25 de Mayo 43, local 2) runs daylong trips (US$40; meals not included) to Lago Roca, including tours of estancias Nibepo Aike and Anita.

Camping Lago Roca (☎ 02902-499500, La Jerónima) US$6 per person; trailers with beds US$24 a double. A few kilometers past the education camp, this well-sheltered at-

tractive spot offers fishing equipment an horseback riding (US$10 per hour). There a *confitería* with meals for US$12, and hc showers from 7pm to 11pm.

Nibepo Aike (☎ 02966-422626, Perit Moreno 229, 9400 Río Gallegos) US$109/12(Overlooking the southern arm of Lago A gentino, about 5km past the campgrounc Nibepo offers the usual assortment of es tancia highlights, but the real attraction i simply to relax.

RN 40 TO CHILE

From El Calafate, paved RN 40 cuts south east across the infinite vastness of the stepp for 95km, where it jigs south and turns t gravel, while paved RP 5 continues to Rí Gallegos on the coastal RN 3. Staying on R 5 means a long five-hour, 224km bore of trip, but the easiest way to get to coastal des tinations. Halfway down RP 5 is gas-sto town **Esperanza**, where RP 7 can be taken t connect back on to RN 40 to continu heading to Chile. Continuing on RN 4 means more gravel, but access to Parqu Nacional Torres del Paine and Puert Natales.

Estancia Tapi Aike

Estancia Tapi Aike (☎ 02966-420092 in Rí Gallegos; ☎/fax 011-4784-4360 in Bueno Aires) Singles/doubles US$70/120 includin breakfast; open Nov-Apr. At the junction c RN 40 and RP 7 (approximately halfwa between El Calafate and Puerto Natales there's a gas station, a small governmer outpost and this 60,000-hectare estancia founded in the early 1900s by land baro Mauricio Braun, now run by his granc daughter, Victoria Viel, and her husband.

Still a working sheep and cattle station, i mid-December the estancia holds the onl cattle auction in the province. The ground are well maintained – of special note is th *palomare,* once used to house messenge pigeons – and the endless horizon broken i the distance by the massifs of Torres de Paine. In the main house, a comfortabl sitting room is adorned in historic famil photos and brimming with books, while spa cious bedrooms are decorated in full flora regalia. English is spoken, and afternoon tea (US$10) and lunch or dinner (US$22) are available for nonguests as well as guests.

Cancha Carrera

The Chilean border crossing, Cancha Carrera, is 175km from El Calafate. Due to hantavirus scares, agricultural inspections are thorough; fresh meats or produce are not allowed to enter Chile. On the Chilean side is the crossroads town of **Cerro Castillo**, with a couple of small restaurants at which buses heading from Puerto Natales to Torres del Paine stop briefly. It may be possible to hitch rides or hop on buses to the park from here, but be prepared for long waits. If you're planning to drive straight to the park, fill up the tank in Tapi Aike; Cerro Castillo's pump isn't reliable. The road to Puerto Natales is in fine shape, and is a much quicker passage than via Río Turbio.

Río Turbio
☎ 02902 • pop 8000

The other southern border crossing, 30km north of Puerto Natales, is at this coal-mining town. While the town itself is a desolate ruin, the stretch of RN 40 leading to it is a smooth route of gradually greening landscape, rolling pasture lands and picture-perfect Patagonian houses. But, like an ear-shattering crash, the coal town appears – a rusting deposit of factories and conveyor belts.

During WWII energy shortages, local coal deposits (rare in South America) spurred the development of the town; coal was transported by narrow-gauge railway to Río Gallegos (now taken to Punta Loyola north of there), but the depression in the coal market has left Río Turbio with a rather turbulent future. The town offers little of interest, and improved road conditions mean it's possible to skip it altogether when traveling between El Calafate and Puerto Natales.

Chalk up on coal trivia at the **Museo 'Escuela Minera'** (☎ 02902-421250, Paraje Mina 3, open 6am-noon) exhibiting all that is coal inspired, but don't take photos; or talk with the tourist office (☎ 421950), Plazoleta Agustín del Castillo, about visiting a mine.

If you're spending a night, you can shack up with the miners at **Albergue Municipal** (☎ 421191, Mina 1) for US$12 per bed, no meals.

Or try **Hostería Capipe** (☎/fax 482935, fax 482930, RN 40 & Paraje J Dufour) for singles/doubles US$25/45 with private bath and breakfast, 5km east of town.

The RN 40 elbows east at this point, heading for Río Gallegos, 278km east. Buses to Río Gallegos (US$15, 6 hours) leave from Av Jorge Newbery and from the tourist office a few times daily. The border crossing to Chile is at the end of town, near the 'ski resort' (nice gradual hill). Agricultural inspections can be rigid; leave any fresh meat and produce in Argentina. Buses to Puerto Natales (US$4, 1½ hours) are very frequent; catch them from the corner of Mineros and Agustín del Castillo.

Chilean Patagonia

Anyone venturing to Argentina's southern highlights will most likely also make a jaunt into Chile to enjoy the Andes' other side. Chilean Patagonia, a rugged, mountainous area battered by westerly winds, consists of the Aysén and Magallanes regions, separated by the southern continental ice field. This section covers only Punta Arenas, Puerto Natales and the spectacular Parque Nacional Torres del Paine. For more details on Chile, check out Lonely Planet's *Chile & Easter Island* guide.

Most nationals of countries with which Chile has diplomatic relations don't need a visa to enter the country. Upon entering, customs officials give you a tourist card, valid for 90 days and renewable for another 90; authorities take it very seriously, so guard it closely to avoid the hassle of replacing it. If arriving by air, US citizens must pay a US$61 processing fee, Australians US$30 and Canadians US$55. The one-time payment is valid for the life of the passport.

Chile is quite a bit cheaper than Argentina, but US cash is not as easily accepted. At the time of writing the conversion rate was 570 pesos to US$1. There are no health risks in this area of Chile other than possible skin damage from the strong radiation of the sun due to ozone depletion; it's imperative to slather on sunscreen any time of the year, but most importantly in October and November.

PUNTA ARENAS
☎ 61 • pop 113,000

The most convenient base for transportation options around this area, Punta Arenas is an attractive mixture of elaborate mansions dating from the wool boom of the late 19th and early 20th centuries, good traveler's services and a variety of travelers from all corners of the world. Nothing sums it up more than hanging out in the basement bar of the ornate Club de la Unión where Antarctic explorers, geologists, Torres del Paine hikers and cruiseship softies group together, all thrilled to be in such a spectacular corner of the world, faces blushed from the incessant winds and glaring sun. It's a busy place during the week, but shuts down on Sunday.

History

Founded in 1848, Punta Arenas was originally a military garrison and penal settlement that proved to be conveniently situated for ships headed to California during the gold rush. Compared to the initial Chilean settlement at Fuerte Bulnes, 60km south, the town had a better, more protected harbor, and superior access to wood and water. For many years, English maritime charts had called the site 'Sandy Point,' and this became its rough Spanish equivalent.

In Punta Arenas' early years, its economy depended on wild animal products, including sealskins, guanaco hides, and feathers; mineral products, including coal and gold, and guano, firewood and timber. None of these was a truly major industry, and the economy did not take off until the last quarter of the 19th century, after the territorial governor authorized the purchase of 300 purebred sheep from the Falkland Islands. This successful experiment encouraged others to invest in sheep and, by the turn of the century, nearly 2 million animals grazed in the territory.

PLACES TO STAY
2 Hostal Sonia Kuscevic (HI)
4 Hostal Carpa Manzano
7 Hostal de la Patagonia
8 Hostal El Bosque
10 Hospedaje Betty
17 Hospedaje Manuel
18 Backpacker's Paradise
20 Residencial Coirón
22 Hostal de la Avenida
24 Hotel Tierra del Fuego
25 Hotel Finis Terrae
32 Hostal Calafate
37 Hostal del Estrecho
41 Hotel José Nogueira
43 Hostal Calafate II
63 Hotel Cabo de Hornos
68 Hostal del Rey
71 Hotel Plaza
78 Hotel Isla Rey Jorge
80 Hostal O'Higgins
81 Hospedaje Independencia
82 The Blue House
83 Casa de Mena
84 Hospedaje Mireya

PLACES TO EAT
11 Abugoch
14 El Mercado
16 Pachamama; Turismo Aonikenk
19 Rotisería La Mamá
28 Santino Bar e Cucina
29 La Carioca
30 Lomit's
39 Sociedad Empleados Magallanes
64 Quijote
76 Sotito's Bar
79 Cofrima
85 Remezón

OTHER
1 Hospital Regional
3 Museo Regional Salesiano
5 Southern Patagonia Souvenirs & Books
6 Netherlands Consulate
9 GonFish
12 El Madero; Kamikaze

13 Solovidrios
15 Sala Estrella
21 Buses Fernández; Buses Pingüino; Turibús; Queilen Bus
23 Turismo Yamana
26 Central de Transportes de Pasajeros
27 Buses Pacheco
31 Tienda de Letty (Laundry)
33 Spanish Consulate
34 Turismo Pehoé
35 Gabriela Mistral Mural
36 Aerovías DAP
38 Bus Sur
40 Post Office
42 Sara Braun Mansion; Club de la Unión; La Taberna
44 Lubag Rent a Car
45 Hostería Las Torres
46 Turismo Comapa; Navimag
47 Palacio Mauricio Braun
48 Entel
50 Buses Ghisoni; Tecni-Austral
51 LanChile/Ladeco
52 Bus Transfer
53 Budget Rent a Car
54 Adel Rent a Car
55 Automóvil Club de Chile
56 Record (Laundry)
57 Hertz
58 Conaf
59 Disco Morena
60 Mirador La Cruz (Lookout)
61 Sernatur
62 Municipal Information Kiosk
65 Museo Naval y Marítimo
66 British Consulate
67 Turismo Viento Sur
69 La Feria
70 Telefónica/CTC
72 Teatro Cervantes
73 Dynevor Marine Expeditions
74 Turismo Pali Aike
75 Wild Patagonia
77 Olijoe Pub

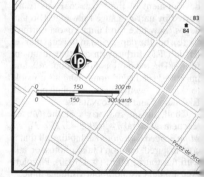

PUNTA ARENAS

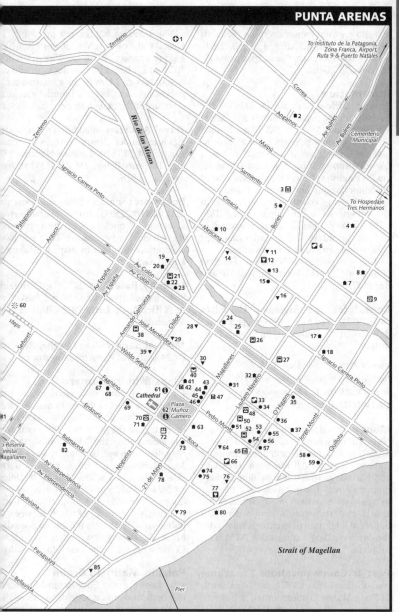

To Instituto de la Patagonia,
Zona Franca, Airport,
Ruta 9 & Puerto Natales

Cementerio
Municipal

To Hospedaje
Tres Hermanos

Strait of Magellan

Pier

The area's speculators (eg, the Menéndez-Brauns) could not have built their commercial and pastoral empires without the labor of immigrants, including English, Irish, Scots, Croats, French, Germans, Spaniards, Italians and others.

Information

Tourist Offices Sernatur (☎ 241330), the national tourist department, has an office at Waldo Seguel 689, just off Plaza Muñoz Gamero. Open weekdays from 8:15am to 6:45pm, until 8pm in summer, it has a friendly and well-informed staff that includes English speakers, it publishes a list of accommodations and transport, and provides a message board for foreign visitors in the summer. The municipal information kiosk (☎ 200610) in the plaza, is open 8am to 7pm weekdays and Saturdays all year 9am to 6pm, and until 8pm in summer.

The Corporación Nacional Forestal (Conaf; ☎ 223841) is located at José Menéndez 1147.

Consulates The Argentine Consulate (☎ 261912), 21 de Mayo 1878, is open weekdays 10am to 3:30pm. Other consulates include:

Italy (☎ 221596), 21 de Mayo 1569
Netherlands (☎ 248100), Magallanes 435
Spain (☎ 243566), José Menéndez 910
UK (☎ 227221), Roca 924

Money Travel agencies along Lautaro Navarro between Errázuriz and Pedro Montt and along Roca change cash and traveler's checks. All are open weekdays and Saturdays, with a few holding Sunday morning hours. Traveler's checks are easier to negotiate here than in Argentina. Many hotels and restaurants also accept US dollars at a fair rate of exchange. Banks dot the city, so finding a compatible ATM is no problem.

Post & Communications The central post office is at Bories 911, one block north of Plaza Muñoz Gamero. Entel, at Navarro 957, stays open until 10pm. Telefónica/CTC

is at Nogueira 1116, on Plaza Muño Gamero. Chile's country code is ☎ 56.

For Internet access, try the lobby c Hostal Calafate II at Magallanes 926, whic has fast connections, or GonFish at Croaci 1028, which has notebook hookups and ex cellent service. Many of the all-in-one back packer hostels also have Internet access, a do many of the main telephone call center

Travel Agencies In addition to the ager cies listed under Organized Tours, try Tecn Austral (☎ 223205), Lautaro Navarro 97 and Turismo Pehoé (☎ 241373), at Jos Menéndez 918.

Bookstores Southern Patagonia Souvenir & Books (☎ 225973), Bories 404, has a grea selection of books about the region, al though most are in Spanish. They also hav a decent assortment of maps and tourist knickknacks.

Laundry Record (☎ 243607), O'Higgin 969, charges about US$5.50 per basket, a does Tienda de Letty (☎ 243075) at Jos Menéndez 832.

Medical Services The Hospital Regiona (☎ 244040) is at Arauco & Angamos.

Plaza Muñoz Gamero

Landscaped with exotic conifers and su rounded by many of the area's most opulen mansions, Plaza Muñoz Gamero is the hear of the city. In the plaza, note the monumen commemorating the 400th anniversary o Magellan's voyage, donated by wool baro José Menéndez in 1920. Facing the nortl side of the plaza is the **Club de la Unió** (☎ 241489, US$2, open 11am-1pm & 4:30pm 8:30pm Tues-Sun), the former Sara Brau mansion, some rooms of which are open t public visits. Just east is the former Socieda Menéndez Behety, now housing the Turism Comapa offices. To the west is the cathedra

Palacio Mauricio Braun

Also known as the Casa Braun-Menéndez this opulent mansion testifies to the wealt and power of pioneer sheep farmers in the

Patagonia's Big Boys: the Story of Menéndez & Braun

How one family, the Menéndez-Braun clan, came to be South America's most influential is a story of swashbucklers, sheep and pure business savvy. It's the stuff of novels, but here's a quick sketch of the incredible story.

In the late 1800s, Punta Arenas had barely a thousand inhabitants, and sea lion hunting was the main industry. After years of working as a deck hand, a young illiterate Portuguese man, José Nogueira, arrived in town. Eager but with no experience, he was taken under the wing of an already established Argentine hunter, Luis Piedrabuena. Soon Nogueira started his own business, but was terrible at bookkeeping. He solicited the help of a young accountant from Lithuania, Mauricio Braun, who, along with his older sister, Sara, managed their father's hotel and bar. Nogueira's business grew; he married his Chilote sweetheart Rosario Peralta, just 15 years old, and built up his fleet of ships. Piedrabuena's business, however, mainly selling guanaco hides and feathers in Chile, didn't fare well after officials discovered he'd been helping Argentina stake territorial claims.

A Buenos Aires bank sent employee José Menéndez to collect on Piedrabuena's debts. Menéndez saw the opportunity of working in the south, bought out Piedrabuena's business instead, and moved to Punta Arenas with his wife, María Behety, and children, Josefina and Alejandro.

Nogueira's businesses flourished; the gold rush brought him more wealth and his shipping company expanded. He became the talk of the town, striking a dashing presence in its social scene. His wife Rosario didn't enjoy this new lifestyle, however, and Nogueira forced her to move to Uruguay, paying her a handsome monthly 'fee' as part of the deal. José Menéndez had a more difficult time setting up his stake in the business world; his office was ransacked and María Behety crippled after a violent revolt in town.

Then came the sheep, the golden fleece, the white gold.

In no time, Nogueira and Menéndez leased large swaths of land. Most of Nogueira's was in Tierra del Fuego, while Menéndez focused on San Gregorio in Chile and purchased the region's first steamship, the *Amadeo*. As profits grew, so did Nogueira's influence within the government, allowing him to renegotiate contracts and increase land holdings to some 500,000 hectares. By 1890, he had on lease a million hectares of land in Tierra del Fuego, much of it unexplored. During all this fanfare, his abandoned wife, Rosario Peralta, died of tuberculosis. A year later Nogueira, possibly also suffering from tuberculosis, married again, this time to Mauricio Braun's sister Sara.

In 1892, with the help of investors, young Mauricio bought 100,000 Santa Cruz hectares. (Around this time Argentina was trying to encourage land use and extended the possibility to purchase, rather than just lease, large chunks of land.) A year later, 48-year-old Nogueira died, leaving Sara as the sole heir to the massive estate and Mauricio as the administrator. A couple of years later, Mauricio fell in love, conveniently enough with Menéndez's daughter, Josefina. Señor Fagnano, who started the Salesian mission to protect the indigenous around Río Grande, married the two socialites in 1895.

A year later Menéndez purchased land originally leased to the gold rush rogue Julius Popper: 'La Primera Argentina' encompassed 60,000 hectares near Río Grande, and 'La Segunda Argentina' became the largest sheep-shearing operation in the world. He continued ordering the massacres of the area's indigenous, the Selk'nam, in order to 'free' the land of them.

By 1906, Mauricio Braun owned 467,000 hectares and leased almost 2 million, the largest landholdings by one person in the south. Sara Braun, in the meantime, managed a few of the estancias and created her own small fortune breeding foxes for pelts.

Menéndez and Braun put rivalries aside in 1908 and joined forces to create Sociedad Anónima Importador y Exportador de la Patagonia, or more simply just 'La Anónima,' the largest business in the south at that time. Josefina and Mauricio's 10 children, along with Menéndez's progeny, became the region's reigning elite for years to come.

late 19th century. One of Mauricio Braun's sons donated the house to the state, although against other family members' wishes. The rooms are divided into one part regional historical museum (booklets with English descriptions are available) and the other half displays the opulent French nouveau original family furnishings, from the intricate wooden inlay floors to the Chinese vases.

The museum (☎ 244216, Magallanes 949; US$1.50; US$2 additional to photograph; open 10:30am-5pm in summer; to 2pm in winter) is most easily accessed from the back of the house from Magallanes.

Museo Regional Salesiano

Especially influential in settling the region, the Salesian order collected outstanding ethnographic artifacts, but their museum (☎ 241096, Av Bulnes 374; US$3; open 10am-12:30pm & 3pm-6pm Tues-Sun) takes a self-serving view of the Christian intervention, portraying missionaries as peacemakers between Indians and settlers. The rotting natural history specimens are nothing to speak of; the best materials are on the mountaineer priest Alberto de Agostini and the various indigenous groups.

Museo Naval y Marítimo

Punta Arenas' naval and maritime museum (☎ 205479; Pedro Montt 981; US$0.75; open 9:30am-12:30pm & 2pm-5pm Tues-Sat) has varied exhibits on model ships, naval history, the unprecedented visit of 27 US warships to Punta Arenas in 1908, and a very fine account of the Chilean mission that rescued British explorer Sir Ernest Shackleton's crew from Antarctica. The most imaginative display is a ship's replica, complete with bridge, maps, charts, and radio room.

Cementerio Municipal

In death as in life, Punta Arenas' first families flaunted their wealth – wool baron José Menéndez's extravagant tomb is, according to Bruce Chatwin, a scale replica of Rome's Vittorio Emanuele monument. But the headstones among the topiary cypresses in the walled municipal cemetery, at Av Bulnes

949, also tell the stories of Anglo, German, Scandinavian, and Yugoslav immigrants who supported the wealthy families with their labor. There is also a monument to the Selk'nam (Onas).

Open daily, the cemetery is about a 15 minute walk from Plaza Muñoz Gamero, but you can also take any taxi colectivo (shared cab with specific route) from the entrance of the Casa Braun-Menéndez on Magallanes.

Instituto de la Patagonia

Part of the Universidad de Magallanes, the Patagonian Institute's Museo del Recuerdo (☎ 207056, Bulnes 01890; US$2; open 8:30am-11:30pm & 2:30pm-6:15pm Mon-Fri, 8:30am-1pm Sat) features a collection of antique farm and industrial machinery imported from Europe, a typical pioneer house and shearing shed (both reconstructed), and a wooden-wheeled trailer that served as shelter for shepherds. The library also has a display of historical maps and a series of historical and scientific publications. Any taxi colectivo to the zona franca (duty-free zone) will drop you across the street.

Reserva Forestal Magallanes

Only 8km from downtown, Mt Fenton has a variety of hiking and mountain-biking trails through thick forests of lenga and coihue. A steady uphill hike goes to the top of Mt Fenton, also known as Cerro Mirador; views are spectacular – if you keep from being blown over by the wind. It is also possible to take the chairlift (US$15/19 weekday/end) to the viewpoint. Other hikes, in the Valle del Río de las Minas section, meander around old coalmines. In winter the slopes provide a rare opportunity to ski while glancing down at an ocean. Club Andino (☎ 241479) runs a quaint restaurant at the chairlift and rents ski equipment; cross-country rental costs US$6 for two hours, downhill rental US$16 per day. Viento Sur (see Organized Tours) runs shuttles in the winter.

Organized Tours

Tours to the pingüinera at Seno Otway cost US$9, plus the US$4 entrance fee, leaving at

4pm. Tours to Fuerte Bulnes and Puerto Hambre cost US$12, plus US$2 entrance fee, leaving at 10am. It is possible to do both tours in one day; however, sharing a rental car for the day and going at opposite times affords a chance to actually see the sites rather than the strings of tour groups – this is especially beneficial at the penguin colony. Just about any lodging can help arrange tours with an agency, if the hotel doesn't run its own operation. Tours to Torres del Paine are abundant from Punta Arenas, but the distance makes for a very long day; best to head to Puerto Natales and organize transportation from there.

Travel agencies include Wild Patagonia (☎ 229399), Lautaro Navarro 1149; Turismo Pali Aike (☎ 223301), Lautaro Navarro 1129; and well-regarded Turismo Aonikenk (☎ 228332), Magallanes 619, with English-, German- and French-speaking guides; and Turismo Viento Sur (☎ 225167), Fagnano 565. All of these agents can also arrange bus tours to Torres del Paine.

Tours to the penguin colonies on Isla Magdalena cost US$30 per person (US$15 for children) on the *Barcaza Melinka,* leaving Tuesday, Thursday and Saturday, December through February. Book tickets through Turismo Comapa (☎ 200200) at Magallanes 990, across from the plaza.

Turismo Yamana (☎ 221130), Colón 568, organizes half- and full-day kayaking trips on the Magellan Strait with Dynevor Marine Expeditions (☎ 225888), Roca 817, Oficina 41.

Places to Stay
Budget Try *Colegio Pierre Fauré* (☎ 226256, Bellavista 697) Singles with/ without breakfast US$7/6, camping US$4 per person. This private school, six blocks south of Plaza Muñoz Gamero, operates as a hostel in January and February. Campers can pitch a tent in the side garden. All bathrooms are shared, but there's plenty of hot water, and it's a good place to hook up with other travelers.

The Blue House (☎ 227006, **e** gar-chef@ yahoo.com, Balmaceda 545) US$6 dorm beds. There's a pretty chaotic family atmos-

phere, but the upstairs rooms are good sized and clean. Extra benefits are a ping-pong table, free pickup from bus terminal, luggage storage, tours and tons of information on how to enjoy the area on the cheap.

Backpacker's Paradise (☎ 240104, Ignacio Carrera Pinto 1022) US$6 dorm beds. Crowded rooms divided only by flimsy curtains. To its advantage are a well-stocked kitchen, Internet access and an oft-times party atmosphere. While the house dog is friendly, many have found it a rambunctious bed hog.

Hospedaje Independencia (☎ 227572, Independencia 374) US$8 with shared bath and breakfast, US$5 for basic dorm beds, no breakfast, US$3 camping. Casual place run by a young couple, Independencia has well-sized dorm rooms, kitchen use and camping in the small somewhat muddy front yard.

Hospedaje Tres Hermanos (☎ 225450, Angamos 1218) US$7. Quiet comfortable rooms in this old converted house come with breakfast included. It's a friendly place and an excellent value.

Hospedaje Betty (☎ 249777, Mejicana 576) US$7. Betty offers a family atmosphere, use of kitchen and breakfast included.

Hospedaje Mireya (☎ 247066, Boliviana 375) US$9 with breakfast. This recommended lodging is in an independent annex with a full kitchen and tiny bathrooms. Rooms don't have heat, but it's still a great deal.

Casa de Mena (☎ 247422, España 1492) US$9 with breakfast. This is another good choice, popular with the Israeli crowd, with central heating and kitchen privileges but no laundry.

Hospedaje Manuel (☎ 245441, fax 220567, O'Higgins 646-648) Singles/doubles US$9/15. All the necessary backpacker amenities are here, plus oversized stuffed toy animals, eccentric owners and plenty of clutter. Dorm rooms upstairs are better quality.

Hostal O'Higgins (☎ 227999, O'Higgins 1205) US$9 per person. In what used to be dormitories for the teams that would play at the adjacent gymnasium, excellently located O'Higgins is spotlessly clean with large, gym-style bathrooms, kitchen privileges, hot showers and parking. Double rooms with private bath cost US$26.

Hostal Sonia Kuscevic (*☎ 248543, Pasaje Darwin 175*) HI members US$14 shared room, singles/doubles US$22/32 private room. Sonia offers cozy but cramped rooms with private bath and breakfast in her home; the ambiance is a bit formal, but she treats her guests very well.

Hostal El Bosque (*☎ 221764, fax 224637, O'Higgins 424*) Singles US$17, shared rooms US$14 with breakfast. Snuggle under heavy goosedown comforters, lined in crisp white cotton and real pillows in this charming old house. Plenty of light streams through the ample kitchen, which is open to guests, as are laundry facilities. It's a small home (only five rooms), which keeps the place intimate and comfortable. The owners have plenty of information about environmental issues in the area.

Residencial Coirón (*☎ 226449, Sanhueza 730*) US$13. Right across from the Fernández bus terminal, Coirón's sunny singles upstairs are the best deal, but all rooms come with breakfast included.

Hostal del Rey (*☎ 223924, e elrey@ enelmundo.com, Fagnano 589*) US$12 dorm bed, 2-/4-person apartments US$21-26/50. Tiny corridors lead to sweet dorms with down-comforter covered beds. The best bets here are the downstairs apartments with full kitchens, hot water and TV.

Hostal Calafate II (*☎/fax 241281, e hostal_calafate@entelchile.net, Magallanes 922*) Singles/doubles US$23/32 shared bath, US$37/45 private bath. In the heart of downtown, Calafate II feels more like a laid-back hotel than hostel, with long hallways, large rooms with TV, breakfast, free parking and friendly youthful staff. The only drawback is the street noise. There's Internet service in the lobby.

Hostal Calafate (*☎ 248415, e calafate@ entelchile.net, Lautaro Navarro 850*) Singles/doubles US$25/38. Staying here feels more like being a guest in somebody's very inviting home. Serve-yourself breakfasts are ample, common spaces comfortable.

Hostal Paredisa (*☎ 224212, Angamos 1073*) Singles/doubles US$14/17 shared bath, US$22/28 private bath. East of the cemetery, Paredisa is another good choice with use of kitchen and central heating.

Mid-Range Prices at more high-end establishments do not reflect the additional 18% IVA charge, which foreigners are not required to pay if paying with credit cards or in US cash. In the off-season, some places drop prices by as much as 40%.

Hostal de la Patagonia (*☎/fax 249970, e ecopatagoina@entelchile.net, Croacia 970*) Singles/doubles US$31/50 with private bath. Rooms are perfectly adequate at this small, quiet and conscientiously run spot. Breakfast is included.

Hostal Carpa Manzano (*☎ 242296, fax 248864, Lautaro Navarro 336*) Singles/doubles US$42/54. Oh so relaxing Carpa Manzano has pleasant rooms, most of which look onto a side path bedecked in flowers. All rooms come with private baths, TV, breakfast and parking. Kitchen privileges are also granted.

Hostal de la Avenida (*☎/fax 247532, Colón 534*) Singles/doubles US$47/56. Near the Fernández bus terminal, Avenida is a simple mid-range option with pleasant, slightly dark rooms and breakfast. Unfortunately they don't recognize the IVA discount.

Hostal del Estrecho (*☎/fax 241011, José Menéndez 1048*) Singles/doubles US$33/40 private bath, US$17/28 shared bath. Whether with a group or on your own, Estrecho's kindly owners will put you up in huge rooms full of bunk beds. Breakfast is included and served in the cozy dining area.

Hotel Plaza (*☎ 241300, fax 248613, Nogueira 1116*) Singles/doubles US$57/68. Staying at the Plaza, located in a converted mansion, brings to light the opulence of the city's history. Cozy rooms with high ceilings, some with great views of the plaza and historic photos make this two-star hotel a worthwhile choice in the heart of the town. Famous Everest climbers have rested their weary feet here many times.

Top End *Hotel Tierra del Fuego* (☎/fax 226200, Av Colón 716) Singles/doubles US$98/109. Rather drab in design and décor, Tierra del Fuego at least has modern amenities, some nice views and an attractive bar that stays pretty active.

Hotel Isla Rey Jorge (☎/fax 222681, e reyjorge@ctcinternet.cl, 21 de Mayo 1243) Singles/doubles US$116/143. Modern and chic, this hotel incorporates maritime details into its attractive rooms and common spaces. Its location close to the port makes it a popular choice for cruise passengers.

Hotel Cabo de Hornos (☎/fax 442134, e rescabo@panamericanahoteles.cl, Plaza Muñoz Gamero 1025) Singles/doubles US$126/149 to US$140/166. The king of the luxury hotels, Cabo de Hornos' solid rooms sport nice views and attractive décor, while the professional staff is quick to help. The bar is cozy but costly.

Hotel José Nogueira (☎ 248840, fax 248832, e noguiera@chileaustral.com, Bories 959) Singles/doubles US$141/198. If Cabo de Hornos is the king, this hotel, in part of the Sara Braun mansion, is surely the queen. The highlight is accessible to even selective backpackers: dining or sipping a cocktail beneath what may be the world's most southerly grape arbor in the posh conservatory/restaurant.

Hotel Finis Terrae (☎ 228200, fax 248124, e finister@ctcreuna.cl, Av Colón 766) Singles/doubles US$140/160. Sunny standard rooms at Finis Terrae are a good deal, with attractive furnishings and courteous staff. The upstairs bar/lounge has spectacular views of town and the Strait.

Places to Eat

Centolla (king crab *season is July to November*, *erizos* (*sea urchins*) are available from November to July. If heading to Torres del Paine, the variety of food supplies and trail mixes are better here than in Natales.

Sociedad Empleados Magallanes (☎ 220153, Chiloé 944) US$3. Along Chiloé are a number of somewhat dicey eateries, but this one stands out for its palatable set-menu lunches.

Quijote (☎ 241225, Lautaro Navarro 1087) Prices US$4-10. Recommended for consistently good meals and service, Quijote fills up at lunchtime with the business folk enjoying US$5 fixed-price lunches. It's also a good bet for a quick espresso and cake.

La Carioca (☎ 224809, José Menéndez 600) US$3-7. Carioca is praised for pizzas, sandwiches and cold lager beer, plus a daily lunch special.

Rotisería La Mamá (☎ 225829, Sanhueza 720) Prices $4-9. Family-run Mamá specializes in homemade pastas, including a hearty bowl of lasagna (the vegetarian option is bland). Read the praises and travelers' reports on the many napkins on the wall. This restaurant is right across from the Fernández bus terminal.

Lomit's (☎ 243399, José Menéndez 722) US$3-5. Despite the slow and sometimes surly service, Lomit's still attracts packs of locals and travelers alike, probably because it's open when other places are closed for the night. The sandwiches that can be made to order are, however, generous and tasty.

El Mercado (☎ 247415, Mejicana 617) US$5-10. Open 24 hours with 10% surcharge between 1am and 8am. A local institution, El Mercado heaps on an assortment of seafood specials, from scallops stewed in garlicky sauce, to baked creamed centolla to mussels a la parmesana.

Santino Bar e Cucina (☎ 220511, Colón 657) US$1.50-9. Hip Santino may be more popular as a bar, but serves tasty pizzas and oversized savory crepes, plus plates of seafood with an assortment of sauces.

Sotito's Bar (☎ 243565, O'Higgins 1138) US$5-24. Sotito's is one of the city's more long-lasting formal affairs and caters heavily to tourists. Salmon with mixed seafood sauce will put you back only US$9, but servings of fresh centolla are dearer.

Remezón (☎ 241029, 21 de Mayo 1469) Appetizers US$4-5, mains US$7-9. Remezón's chef impresses with delicately prepared and supremely delicious dishes, such as oysters and clams au gratin, fresh centolla with lemon, salmon smoked with black tea, or a salad of avocado with marinated beaver.

Equally imaginative are the centolla canellones and baked *sierra*. To add to its appeal the service is unpretentious and welcoming and quick to pour a *pisco* sour to get you going.

Pachamama (*Magallanes 698*) Bulk trailmix munchies can be purchased here, along with organic products.

Abugosh (*Bories 647*) and *Cofrima* (*Navarro & Balmaceda*) are large, wellstocked supermarkets.

Entertainment

Olijoe Pub (☎ 223728, Errázuriz 970) Open 6pm-2am. Faux-historic Olijoe has an upscale feel but relaxing ambiance – a good place for a quiet drink and snack. Try the house special Glaciar, a potent mix of pisco, horchata, curuçao and milk.

La Taberna (☎ 241317, Mansion Sara Braun). In the dark, low-ceiling basement of the mansion, La Taberna is the place to huddle at a booth and swap tales of Antarctic and the Andean adventures. The environment's tops but the mixed drinks could be better.

El Madero (*Bories 655*) El Madero gets packed with the pre-disco crowds saucing up on good strong drinks and bustling about from table to table. Afterwards, head downstairs to *Kamikaze.* US$5 with one free drink, tripped out with tiki torches and South Pacific flares.

Disco Morena (*Menéndez 1173*) Spacious Morena keeps on thumping long after the rest of the city has turned in for the night.

For movies, head to *Teatro Cervantes* (*Plaza Muñoz Gamero*), below the Centro Español, and *Sala Estrella* (*Mejicana 777*), both of which are showing their age.

Shopping

The Zona Franca (*Zofri* or duty-free zone), open daily except Sunday, is a chaotic maze of vendors in which finding anything can get annoying; however, it may prove fruitful if you're looking for camera equipment and film. Taxi colectivos shuttle back and forth from downtown throughout the day. Inexpensive winter parkas can be found at *La Feria* at Fagnano 607 and Chiloé.

Solovidrios (☎ 224835, Mejicana 762) To replace a shattered windshield on a private car – not an unusual occurrence on Patagonia roads – head here. Prices here are a fraction of what they are in Argentina.

Getting There & Away

Sernatur and the municipal tourist kiosk distribute a useful brochure with information on all forms of transportation including those that go to or through Argentina and their schedules to and from Punta Arenas, Puerto Natales and Tierra del Fuego. Note that discount airfares are available from the major airlines between Punta Arenas and mainland Chile but usually involve some restrictions.

Air LanChile (☎ 241100), Lautaro Navarro 999, flies to Santiago (US$170 one way) and Puerto Montt (US$97 one way), and Saturday to the Falkland Islands (US$630 roundtrip).

Aerovías DAP (☎ 223340, fax 221693, **W** www.aeroviasdap.cl), O'Higgins 891, flies to Porvenir (US$22) and back at least twice daily except Sunday; to Puerto Williams on Isla Navarino (US$70) Tuesday, Thursday, and Saturday; to Ushuaia (US$100) on Monday, Wednesday; and in summer to Río Grande (US$79) daily except Sunday. Luggage is limited to 10kg per person. DAP also does three-hour excursion flights over Cabo de Hornos (Cape Horn; US$300) Sundays, possibly also stopping in Puerto Williams en route. DAP also flies monthly to Chile's Teniente Marsh air base in Antarctica (US$2500 includes a one-day tour) to tour Base Frei; the schedule permits one or two nights in Antarctica before returning to Punta Arenas.

Bus Punta Arenas has no central bus terminal, but at the time of writing, plans to make one near the port were underway. Each bus company has its own office from which its buses depart, although most of these are within a block or two of Av Colón. It makes sense to purchase tickets at least a couple hours (if not a day during summer) in advance. Companies include Buses Fernández (☎ 242313), Turíbus, Queilen Bus and

Buses Pingüino all at Armando Sanhueza 745; Bus Transfer at Pedro Montt 966; Central de Transportes de Pasajeros (☎ 245811), Magallanes and Colón; Buses Pacheco, Av Colón 900; Buses Ghisoni, Lautaro Navarro 975; and Bus Sur, Menéndez 565.

To get to Puerto Natales (US$4, 3 hours), Bus Fernández, Bus Sur, Pacheco or Bus Transfer have three to eight departures daily; the first two have the most frequent departures.

To Río Grande Porvenir (US$19, 8 hours), Buses Ghisoni and Pacheco have three to four weekly departures each with some buses going via Porvenir.

To Ushuaia (US$36, 12 hours), Ghisoni buses continue direct, but travelers report Pacheco stops for too long in Río Grande – shuttles to Ushuaia leave throughout the day and may cost slightly less (depends on Chilean currency) than the through ticket. To Río Gallegos (US$12 to US$18, 4 hours), El Pingüino has daily service, while Ghisoni and Pacheco leave three times weekly.

To Coyhaique (US$44, 20 hours), Bus Sur leaves Monday and Thursday at 10:30am. To Puerto Montt and Castro (US$44, 30 hours), Queilen Bus and Buses Pacheco leave twice weekly via Argentina.

Boat From the Tres Puentes ferry terminal north of town (get taxi colectivos from Casa Braun-Menéndez), Transbordadora Austral Broom (☎ 218100) sails to Porvenir, Tierra del Fuego (US$7, 2½-4 hours). Boats depart at 9am Tuesday through Saturday and at 9:30am Sunday, returning at 12:30pm Tuesday, Thursday and Saturday, at 2pm Wednesday and Friday, and at 5pm Sunday and holidays. Make reservations to ferry your vehicle (US$45) by calling the office or visiting Av Bulnes 05075.

A faster way to get to Tierra del Fuego (US$2, 20 minutes) is via the Punta Delgada-Bahía Azul crossing northeast of Punta Arenas. Transbordadora Austral Broom Ferries leave every 1½ hours from 8:30am to 10:15pm. Call ahead for vehicle reservations (US$17).

Broom is also the agent for the ferry *Patagonia*, which sails from Tres Puentes to Puerto Williams, on Isla Navarino, two or three times a month, Wednesday only, returning Fridays, both at 7pm (US$120 to US$150 including meals, 38 hours).

From September through April, Turismo Comapa (☎ 200200) at Magallanes 990, runs weeklong luxury cruises on the 100-passenger *Terra Australis* and on the newer 130-passenger *Mare Australis* from Punta Arenas through the Cordillera de Darwin, the Beagle Channel, and Puerto Williams, Ushuaia (Argentina) and back. Rates start at US$1152 per person double occupancy in low season (September, October and April) and reach US$2971 for a high-season single (mid-December through February). It is possible to do the leg between Punta Arenas and Ushuaia, or vice-versa, separately.

Navimag, which runs ferries from Puerto Natales to Puerto Montt via the spectacular Chilean fjords, is represented by Comapa (☎ 200200) at Magallanes 990, across from the plaza. For schedules and fares, see the Puerto Natales Getting There & Away section.

Getting Around

To/From the Airport The airport is 20km north of town. Bus Transfer has scheduled departures (US$3) throughout the day to coincide with departures and arrivals. Many minibuses also meet flights and offer door-to-door service (US$4). DAP Airlines runs a shuttle service.

Bus & Colectivo Taxi colectivos, with numbered routes, are only slightly more expensive than buses (about US$0.50, a bit more late at night and on Sundays), much more comfortable, and much quicker.

Car Punta Arenas has the most economical rates in the area, and locally owned businesses tend to provide better service. Recommended Adel Rent a Car (☎ 235471), Pedro Montt 968, 2nd floor, provides attentive service, competitive rates and good travel tips for the area. Other choices include

Hertz (☎ 248742), at O'Higgins 987; Budget Rent a Car (☎ 225983, fax 241696), at O'Higgins 964; and Lubag (☎ 242023, fax 214136), at Magallanes 970. The Automóvil Club de Chile (☎ 243-675) is at O'Higgins 931.

AROUND PUNTA ARENAS
Penguin Colonies

There are two substantial Magellanic penguin colonies near Punta Arenas: easier to reach is **Seno Otway** (Otway Sound) with about 6000

When the Edge of the World Just Isn't Far Enough

Falkland Islands/Islas Malvinas
☎ 500 • pop 2826 humans, 700,000 sheep

The sheep boom in Tierra del Fuego and Patagonia owes its origins to a cluster of islands 300 miles (500km) to the east in the South Atlantic Ocean. These islands, the Islas Malvinas (to the Argentines) or Falkland Islands (to the British) were explored, but never fully captured either country's interest. Very little transpired on the islands until the mid-19th century wool boom in Europe, when the Falkland Islands Company (FIC) became the Islands' largest landholder. The population, mostly stranded mariners and gauchos, grew rapidly with the arrival of English and Scottish immigrants. In an unusual exchange, the South American Missionary Society in 1853 began transporting Yahgan Indians from Tierra del Fuego to Keppel Island to catechize them.

Argentina has laid claim to the islands since 1833, but it wasn't until 1982 that Argentine president Leopoldo Galtieri, then drowning in accusations of corruption and economic chaos, decided that reclaiming the islands would unite his country behind him. However, English Prime Minister Margaret Thatcher (who was also suffering in the polls) didn't hesitate for a moment in striking back, thoroughly humiliating Argentina in what became known as the Falkland Islands War. A severe blow to Argentina's nationalist pride, the ill-fated war succeeded in severing all diplomatic ties between the two nations.

On July 14, 1999, a joint statement issued by the British, Falkland Islands and Argentine governments promised closer cooperation on areas of economic mutual interest. In August 2001, British Prime Minister Tony Blair visited Argentina in an effort to further improve ties between the countries.

Besides being an unusually polemic piece of property, what is there about the Falklands that might intrigue the intrepid traveler? Bays, inlets, estuaries and beaches create a tortuous, attractive coastline that is home to abundant wildlife. Striated and crested caracaras, cormorants, oystercatchers, snowy sheathbills, sheldgeese and a plethora of penguins – Magellanic, rockhopper, macaroni, gentoo and king – share top billing with elephant seals, sea lions, fur seals, some five species of dolphins, and killer whales.

Stanley, the Islands' capital, is an assemblage of brightly painted metal-clad houses and a good place to throw down a few pints and listen to island lore. 'Camp' – as the rest of the Islands is known as – is home to settlements that began as company towns (hamlets where coastal shipping could collect wool) and now provide lodging and a chance to experience pristine nature and wildlife.

Planning The best time to visit is from October to March, when migratory birds and mammals return to beaches and headlands. Fun events around which to plan a trip are the sports meetings featuring horse racing, bull riding and sheepdog trials, which take place in Stanley between Christmas and New Year's, and on East and West Falkland in late February. Summer never gets truly hot (maximum high is 24°C or 75°F), but high winds can chill the air.

Information The Jetty Visitors Centre (☎ 22281, fax 22619, e jettycentre@horizon.co.fk), at the public jetty on Ross Rd in Stanley, distributes excellent brochures on things to do in and around Stanley. The 'Visitor Accommodation Guide' lists lodgings and places that allow camping around

breeding pairs, about an hour northwest of the city, while the larger (50,000 breeding pairs) and more interesting **Monumento Natural Los Pingüinos** is accessible only by boat to Isla Magdalena in the Strait of Mag-

ellan (see Organized Tours, earlier). Neither are as impressive as the larger penguin colonies in Argentina or the Falkland Islands. Tours to Seno Otway usually leave in the afternoon; however, coming in the morning

When the Edge of the World Just Isn't Far Enough

the Islands. Another source of information is the Falkland Islands Tourist Board (☎ 22215, fax 22619, **e** manager@tourism.org.fk, **w** www.tourism.org.fk). In the UK there's the Falkland House (☎ 020-7222-2542, fax 020-7222-2375, **e** manager@figo.u-net.com), 14 Broadway, Westminster, London SW1H 0BH.

Visas & Documents Visitors from Britain and Commonwealth countries, the European Union, North America, Mercosur countries and Chile do not need visas. If coming from another country, check with the British Consulate. All nationalities must carry valid passports. Everyone entering is required to have an onward ticket, proof of sufficient funds (credit cards are fine) and pre-arranged accommodations for the first few nights.

Money Pound sterling and US dollars in cash or traveler's checks are readily accepted, but the exchange rate for US currency is low. There's no need to change money to FK£, which are not accepted off the Islands. There is no ATM on the Falklands. In peak season, expect to spend US$70 to US$90 per day, not including airfare, within the islands, less if camping or staying in self-catering cottages.

Getting There & Away From South America, LANChile flies to Mt Pleasant International Airport (near Stanley) every Saturday from Santiago, Chile, via Puerto Montt, Punta Arenas and – one Saturday each month – Río Gallegos, Argentina. Santiago fares are US$410 one-way, US$680 roundtrip. Punta Arenas fares are US$320 one-way, US$490 roundtrip. From RAF Brize Norton, in Oxfordshire, England, there are regular flights to Mt Pleasant (16 hours, plus an hour layover on Ascension Island). The roundtrip fare is UK£2302, but reduced Apex fares cost UK£1414 with 30-day advance purchase. Travelers continuing on to Chile can purchase one-way tickets for half the fare. Contact the Travel Coordinator at Falkland House in London, or in Stanley, the Falkland Islands Company (☎ 27633), on Crozier Place.

Getting Around From Stanley, Figas (☎ 27219) serves outlying destinations in nine-passenger aircraft. Travel within the Falklands costs approximately FK£1 per minute.

Byron Marine Ltd (☎ 22245, fax 22246) carries a few passengers on its freighter MV *Tamar* while delivering wool and other goods to outlying settlements. Berths are limited; day trips cost FK£20, overnights cost FK£25.

Several Stanley operators run day trips to East Falkland settlements, including Tony Smith's Discovery Tours (☎ 21027, fax 22304, **e** discovery@horizon.co.fk), Sharon Halford's Ten Acre Tours (☎ 21155, fax 21950, **e** tenacres@horizon.co.fk) and Dave Eynon's South Atlantic Marine Services (☎ 21145, fax 22674, **e** sams@horizon.co.fk). Neil Rowlands (☎ 21561, **e** nrowlands@horizon.co.fk) conducts fishing and wildlife tours. The agricultural officer (☎ 27355) or Seaview Ltd (☎ 22669, fax 22670) can arrange visits to Kidney Island, with its colonies of rockhopper penguins and sea lions.

Trekking and camping are feasible; however, there are no designated trails on the Islands and getting lost is not unheard of. Permission must be sought before entering private land and details of movements given.

would be better for photography because the birds are mostly backlit in the afternoon.

Since there is no scheduled public transportation to either site, it's necessary to rent a car or take a tour to visit them. For details, see Organized Tours in Punta Arenas. Admission to Seno Otway costs US$4 per person, while admission to Isla Magdalena is included in the price of the ferry trip. There's a small snack bar at the Otway site. Of the two, the trip to Isla Magdalena is more recommended.

Puerto Hambre & Fuerte Bulnes

Founded in 1584 by an overly confident Pedro Sarmiento de Gamboa, 'Ciudad del Rey don Felipe' was one of Spain's most inauspicious (and short-lived) American outposts. Its inhabitants soon failed to conquer the ruthless elements and starved to death at what is now known as Puerto Hambre ('Port Famine').

In 1843, Chilean president Manuel Bulnes ordered army occupation of this southern area, then only sparsely populated by indigenous peoples. Fuerte Bulnes, as the outpost was called, was abandoned a few years after its founding because of its exposed site, lack of potable water, poor, rocky soil, and inferior pasture.

A good gravel road runs 60km south from Punta Arenas to the restored wooden fort, where a fence of sharpened stakes surrounds the blockhouse, barracks, and chapel. There isn't any scheduled public transportation, but several travel agencies make half-day excursions to Fuerte Bulnes and Puerto Hambre; for details, see the Punta Arenas Organized Tours section.

Río Verde

About 50km north of Punta Arenas, a graveled lateral leads northwest toward Seno Skyring (Skyring Sound), passing this former estancia before rejoining Ruta 9 at Villa Tehuelches. Visitors with a car should consider this interesting detour to one of the best-maintained assemblages of Magellanic architecture in the region.

Hostería Río Verde (☎ *311122, fax 311125*) US$30 with private bath. Six kilometers south of Río Verde proper, 90km from Punta Arenas, this hostería is more well-known for its meat-lovers Sunday lunches (US$10) with large portions of lamb, pork or seafood. An enormous fireplace and views over Isla Riesgo make it a welcoming place, and the rooms are plenty comfortable.

Río Rubens

Roughly midway between Villa Tehuelches and Puerto Natales on Ruta 9, Río Rubens is a fine trout-fishing area and a ideal spot to break the journey from Punta Arenas, at least for travelers with their own transport.

Hotel Río Rubens (☎ *09-640-1583Km 183*) US$12 per person with breakfast. This cozy, comfy place is the closest thing to an old country-style inn in the region, and at these rates, it's a bargain. The restaurant serves outstanding meals, including lamb and seafood.

Estancia San Gregorio

Some 125km northeast of Punta Arenas, straddling Ruta 255 to Río Gallegos (Argentina), this once enormous (90,000 hectares) estancia is now more a ghost town of faded yellow corrugated iron, but is still maintained by a few people and the large shearing shed is still used. The skeletal remains of beached ships are a memory of the days the ships transported goods to and from Punta Arenas.

Hotel El Tehuelche (☎ *1983002, at junction to Punta Delgada*) Singles/doubles US$30/49. About 30km northeast of San Gregorio, this is the junction for the road to the ferry that crosses the Strait of Magellan from Punta Delgada to Chilean Tierra del Fuego. Until 1968, the hostería was the casco for Estancia Kimiri Aike, pioneered by the British immigrant family Woods, although they never lived here. High ceilings, fading floral wallpaper, warm yellow bathrooms with clawfoot tubs and antique furnishings plus gas fireplaces in some of the rooms make this a comfortable and entertaining stopover.

Downstairs, the restaurant serves sandwiches and meals either in the main room, or when sunny, in the large sunroom.

Parque Nacional Pali Aike

Along the Argentine border, west of the Monte Aymond border crossing to Río Gallegos, this 5030-hectare park is an area of volcanic steppe where, in the 1930s, Junius Bird's excavations at **Pali Aike Cave** yielded the first Paleo-Indian artifacts associated with extinct New World fauna like the milodón and the native horse *Onohippidium*.

The park has several hiking trails, including a 1700m path through the rugged lava beds of the **Escorial del Diablo** to the impressive **Crater Morada del Diablo**; wear sturdy shoes or your feet could be shredded. There's also a 9km trail from Cueva Pali Aike to **Laguna Ana**, where there's another shorter trail to a site on the main road, 5km from the park entrance.

Cueva Pali Aike itself measures 5m high and 7m wide at the entrance, while it is 17m deep. Bird's excavations in 1936-37 unearthed three cremated human skeletons plus *milodón* and native horse bones some 9000 years old.

Parque Nacional Pali Aike is 196km northeast of Punta Arenas via Ch 9, Ch 255, and a graveled secondary road from Coooperativa Villa O'Higgins, 11km north of Estancia Kimiri Aike. There's also an access road from the Chilean border post at Monte Aymond. There is no public transportation, but Punta Arenas travel agencies can arrange tours.

PUERTO NATALES
☎ 061• pop 18,000

When the Navimag ferry comes in, unloading sea-weary backpackers, the town comes alive. On the shores of Seno Última Esperanza (Last Hope Sound), 250km northwest of Punta Arenas via Ruta 9, Puerto Natales is the southern terminus of the spectacular ferry trip through the Chilean fjords. Once dependent on wool, mutton and fishing, it's now the base for trekkers planning trips to

Parque Nacional Torres del Paine and has convenient transportation options to El Calafate in Argentina.

Information

The municipal tourist office (☎ 411263), at Bulnes 285, in the museum, has attentive staff and up-to-date listings on lodgings in and around town and Torres del Paine. Not as helpful, Sernatur (☎ 412125) is on the Costanera Pedro Montt at the junction with the Philippi diagonal. The national park service, Conaf, has an administrative office (☎ 411-438) at O'Higgins 584. Southern Patagonia Sourvenirs & Books, at Bulnes 688, stocks a decent variety of books (mostly in Spanish) on the area.

Stop Cambios, Baquedano 386, changes cash and traveler's checks, as do many agents along Blanco Encalada. Most banks in town have ATMs. The post office is at Eberhard 429. Telefónica/CTC has a call center at Blanco Encalada 298 and Internet (very slow connections throughout town) at No 169. Entel is at Baquedano 270.

Servilaundry (☎ 412869), Bulnes 513, is the main washhouse in town, but many hostels offer service. Redfarma, at Arturo Prat 158, is the best place to purchase motion sickness pills (Mareamin or Bonamina) before Navimag trips. The hospital (☎ 411533) is at O'Higgins and Ignacio Carrera Pinto.

Travel Agencies Most travel agencies have similar services: Internet access, tours to the park, equipment rental and maps. Path@gone (☎ 413291, **e** pathgone@chile austral.com), at Eberhard 595, is the central point for reserving refugios, campsites and transportation to the park. Recommended Fortaleza Expediciones (☎ 410595), Prat 234, has knowledgeable, English-speaking staff that can steer you in the right direction and rent camping equipment. Also well regarded, Knudsen Tour (☎ 411819), Blanco Encalada 284, has trips to El Calafate, Torres del Paine and also alternative routes along Seno Último Esperanza. Readers have recommended Turismo Yekchal (☎ 413591), Eberhard 564-A, which has details on tours to Puerto Edén and Glaciar Pio XI. In the winter months, Residencial Niko's organizes one- to two-day trips to Torres del Paine (see Places to Stay).

Things to See & Do

The **Museo Histórico** (☎ 411263, Bulnes 285; free; open 8:30am-12:30 & 2:30pm-6pm Tues-Sun) has natural history items (mostly stuffed animals), archaeological artifacts, such as stone and whalebone arrowheads and spear points, plus a Yahgan canoe and Tehuelche bolas, and historical photographs of Puerto Natales' development.

Places to Stay

Budget For a small town, Puerto Natales is chock full of places to stay, keeping prices reasonable. Many places can help arrange transportation and rent equipment, and most include a basic breakfast in the price.

Josmar 2 (☎ 414417, Esmeralda 517) US$3. For those intent on camping, Josmar 2 has organized sites with electricity but crummy toilets, all behind a restaurant.

Backpacker's Magallania (☎ 414950, Rogers 255) US$5. Dorm rooms (bring a sleeping bag) fill up fast at Magallania, run by a friendly fellow who has whimsically

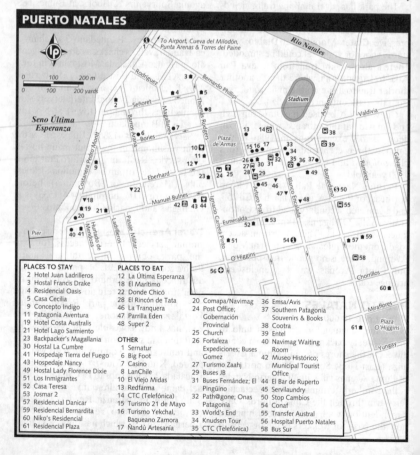

PUERTO NATALES

To Airport, Cueva del Milodón,
Punta Arenas & Torres del Paine

Rio Natales

Seno Última
Esperanza

Plaza
de Armas

Stadium

Seno Última
Esperanza

Pier

PLACES TO STAY	PLACES TO EAT		
2 Hotel Juan Ladrilleros	12 La Última Esperanza	20 Comapa/Navimag	36 Emsa/Avis
3 Hostal Francis Drake	18 El Marítimo	24 Post Office;	37 Southern Patagonia
4 Residencial Oasis	22 Donde Chicó	Gobernación	Souvenirs & Books
5 Casa Cecilia	28 El Rincón de Tata	Provincial	38 Cootra
9 Concepto Indigo	46 La Tranquera	25 Church	39 Entel
11 Patagonia Aventura	47 Parrilla Eden	26 Fortaleza	40 Navimag Waiting
19 Hotel Costa Australis	48 Super 2	Expediciones; Buses	Room
21 Hotel Lago Sarmiento		Gomez	42 Museo Histórico;
23 Backpacker's Magallania	OTHER	27 Turismo Zaahj	Municipal Tourist
30 Hostal La Cumbre	1 Sernatur	29 Buses JB	Office
41 Hospedaje Tierra del Fuego	6 Big Foot	31 Buses Fernández; El	44 El Bar de Ruperto
43 Hospedaje Nancy	7 Casino	Pingüino	45 Servilaundry
49 Hostal Lady Florence Dixie	8 LanChile	32 Path@gone; Onas	50 Stop Cambios
51 Los Inmigrantes	10 El Viejo Midas	Patagonia	54 Conaf
52 Casa Teresa	13 Redfarma	33 World's End	55 Transfer Austral
57 Josmar 2	14 CTC (Teléfonica)	34 Knudsen Tour	56 Hospital Puerto Natales
57 Residencial Danicar	15 Turismo 21 de Mayo	35 CTC (Teléfonica)	58 Bus Sur
59 Residencial Bernardita	16 Turismo Yekchal;		
60 Niko's Residencial	Baqueano Zamora		
61 Residencial Plaza	17 Ñandú Artesanía		

decorated the place. There are kitchen privileges, but no breakfast.

Hospedaje Nancy (☎ *411186, Bulnes 343*) US$7 shared room. Much praised by backpackers, Nancy offers breakfast, comfortable high-ceiling rooms, kitchen access, and has Internet access.

Residencial Bernardita (☎ *411162, O'Higgins 765*) US$9 shared room. Warmly recommended for its quiet rooms, kitchen use and breakfast, Benardita has rooms in the main house and more private ones in the back annex.

Residencial Danicar (☎ *412170, O'Higgins 707*) US$6. Danicar is a strictly non-smoking residence run by a conscientious family that offers good dorm beds.

Los Inmigrantes (☎ *413482, Ignacio Carrera Pinto 480*) US$7 shared room. Part residencial and part equipment rental, this is a good choice for serious hikers who want the inside scoop on the land, which the owner has plenty of. There are kitchen privileges, but no breakfast.

Hospedaje Tierra del Fuego (☎ *412138, Av Bulnes 23*) US$7 shared room. Convenient to the ferry, thin-walled but adequate Tierra del Fuego offers breakfast and is a decent place to crash after a late-night ferry arrival.

Casa Teresa (☎ *410472, Esmeralda 483*) US$7. Basic dorm beds and a good breakfast, plus very kind owners keep Teresa recommended, but there's no kitchen access.

Patagonia Aventura (☎ *411028, Tomás Rogers 179*) US$7 shared room. Well-run by some youthful guys and hiply decorated, Patagonia Adventure has kitchen privileges and can help with all traveling and trekking needs.

Residencial Plaza (☎ *411472, Baquedano 719*) US$8. With large shared rooms, use of the kitchen and pleasant open spaces, La Plaza is a good option; call ahead to be picked up at the bus stop.

Casa Cecilia (☎ *411797, Tomás Rogers 64*) Dorm rooms US$10, singles/doubles US$13/21. Impeccably clean and with excellent bread for morning toast, Cecilia is well loved and often quite full, which doesn't mix well with the thin walls, cramped dorm rooms, small private rooms and even smaller bathrooms. On the plus side, the owners are multilingual and a great help with renting camping equipment.

Residencial Oasis (☎ *411675, Señoret 332*) Singles/doubles US$13/22. Some of the back rooms have outstanding views, and all come with breakfast, making Oasis a very worthwhile consideration.

Hostal La Cumbre (☎ *412422, Eberhard 533*) Singles US$14 with private bath. Comfortable and central with high-ceiling rooms, plush beds and bathtubs, La Cumbre is run by interesting dynamic local women who make sure the place feels like the home it is to them.

Niko's Residencial (☎ *412810, fax 413543,* e *residencialnikos@hotmail.com, Ramirez 669*) US$7/11 shared/private bath with breakfast. Travelers recommend Niko's for the quiet rooms, separate kitchen for travelers and the added bonus of family-style dinner for US$5 more. Bring your own toilet paper and towel.

Concepto Indigo (☎ *413609, fax 410169,* e *indigo@entelchile.net, Ladrilleros 105*) US$14-35. The hip place in town, Concepto Indigo has a range of rooms, some shared and others private, many with five-star views over the harbor. It's a fab place to kick off the shoes and feel right at home, with the advantage of the great bar and restaurant just downstairs.

Mid-Range & Top End Prices at more high-end establishments do not reflect the additional 18% IVA charged, which foreigners are not required to pay if paying with credit cards or in US dollars cash. In the off-season, many places drop prices by as much as 40%.

Hostal Francis Drake (☎ *411553, Phillipi 383*) US$45/50. An attractive spot set apart from the main bustle, Drake has pleasant rooms with plush beds; it's a good choice for couples.

Hotel Lago Sarmiento (☎/*fax 411542 Bulnes 90*) Singles/doubles US$50/70. Family-run Sarmiento is a good mid-range choice, with good bathrooms, lots of light and a great 3rd-floor living room. There's also a poolroom open in the evenings.

Hostal Lady Florence Dixie (☎ *411158, fax 411943,* e *florence@chileanpatagonia .com, Bulnes 659*) Singles/doubles US$60/75. Back rooms at Dixie are motel-style but clean and light, while rooms above the street are polished and an excellent value (but cost US$10 more). It's run by a smart, friendly woman.

Hotel Juan Ladrilleros (☎ *411652, fax 412109,* e *info@aventouraventuras.com, Pedro Montt 161*) Singles/doubles US$93/105. Looking like a 1970s study in angles and bay view windows, Ladrilleros has some great views, but the rooms tend to smell slightly musty.

Hotel Costa Australis (☎ *412000, fax 411881,* e *costaus@ctcreuna.cl, Pedro Montt 262*) Singles/doubles US$130/147 with town view, US$164/181 with harbor view. Australis has all of the amenities expected of luxury lodging, in addition to a pleasant street-level bar/restaurant with plush couches.

Places to Eat

El Rincón de Tata (☎ *413845, Part 236*) US$3-10. Dark and intimate Tata is a popular gathering spot with travelers for some of the better pizza in town, mixed drinks and Internet access. It's a shame that the musical selection tends too much to the '80s and the waiters have to wear those ridiculous outfits.

El Marítimo (☎ *414995, Pedro Montt 214*) US$4-8. An informal eatery near the waterfront, El Marítimo caters heavily to tourists, but does serve consistently good, cheap and heaping platters of fish and seafood.

Concepto Indigo (☎ *410678, Ladrilleros 105*) US$3-7. Sink into a couch, trip out to some Portishead and order a healthy whole-wheat sandwich with fresh veggies, drip coffee and a brownie. Possibly the only thing to keep you from thinking you're back in your favorite café at home is that incredible view out the window.

La Tranquera (☎ *411039, Bulnes 579*) US$3-8. With friendly service and reasonable prices, Tranquera is a worthwhile option for run-of-the-mill meat and fish plates or soups.

La Última Esperanza (☎ *411391, Eberhard 354*) US$3-15. For a splash, this more formal affair, specializing in seafood and fish, is worth the higher prices; main entrees come with side dishes and are exquisitely prepared. Or come for less expensive soups, equally as good, and the powerful pisco sours.

Don Chico (*Eberhard 169*) US$5-8. Full-bellied readers keep praising this all-you-can-eat parrilla. But this place is for full-on meat (lamb) eaters only.

Parrilla Eden (☎ *414120, Blanco Encalada 345*) US$6-10. Meat lovers rejoice! Eden dishes out grilled ribs, beef, lamb, pork and chicken, all of which come with side dishes. To cleanse the palate, try the rhubarb and Calafate mousse.

Super 2 (*Blanco Encalada & Esmeralda*) Of the shops in town, Super 2 has the better selection of hiking snacks and quick meals, plus fresh bread and pastries, ready-made sandwiches and rotisserie chicken.

Entertainment

El Viejo Midas (*no* ☎*; Tomás Rogers 169*) A lively spot across from the plaza, Midas pours mixed drinks and serves some light meals in a ranch-style lounge.

El Bar de Ruperto (☎ *410863, Bulnes & Magallanes*). Ruperto has chess, dominoes and other board games and Internet access, all of which get mighty interesting after a few oversized drinks.

Shopping

Ñandú Artesanía (☎ *414382, Eberhard 586*) Ñandú has shops all over town; all are good places for crafts, post cards and local maps.

World's End (☎ *414725, Blanco Encalada 226-A*) For all the tip-of-the-world souvenirs, this is a good spot and cheaper than the ones in Argentina. It also carries Torres trekking maps.

Getting There & Away

Air Aerovías DAP flies to El Calafate, Argentina (US$50, 30 minutes) at 9am weekdays from the small airfield, a few kilometers north of town on the road to Torres del

Paine. The local LanChile office (☎ 411236), Tomás Rogers 78, can help with flights from Punta Arenas.

Bus Puerto Natales has no central bus terminal, though several companies stop at the junction of Valdivia and Baquedano. Carriers include Buses Fernández (☎ 411111), Eberhard 555; Bus Sur (☎ 411325), Baquedano 534; Transfer Austral, Baquedano 414; Buses JB (☎ 412824), Arturo Prat 258; Turismo Zaahj (☎ 412260), Arturo Prat 236; and Buses Gomez (☎ 410595), at Prat 234. Expect limited service in the off-season.

To Torres del Paine, most companies shuttle back and forth two to three times daily; Buses JB and Gomez are the best bets, leaving at 7:30am and 2:30pm. If you miss the morning bus, you'll have to pay again for the afternoon one. Note that if you're heading to Pehoé in the off-season, you need to take the morning bus to meet the catamaran (US$9 one way, US$16 roundtrip; 2 hours).

To Punta Arenas, Buses Fernández is the best regarded, but also try Bus Transfer and Bus Sur. Book morning departures early the day before (US$7, 3 hours).

To Río Gallegos, Bus Sur leaves Tuesday and Thursday; El Pingüino, at the Fernández terminal, goes at 11 am Wednesday and Sunday (US$12, 4 hours).

To El Calafate, Zaahj and Bus Sur have the most service. Note that taking the very long day-tour to the Moreno Glacier and staying in El Calafate after the tour is slightly cheaper than going by regular bus, spending the night and then paying for the price of a tour the next day (tours from Puerto Natales cost US$47 if staying in El Calafate). If you're returning to Puerto Natales, buy your return ticket in Chile for a cheaper fare (US$23, 5½ hours).

To Río Turbio, Cootra, Baquedano 244, has frequent departures, connecting with buses to both Río Gallegos and El Calafate (US$4, 1 hour).

To Coyhaique, Bus Sur leaves Monday, heading first towards Punta Arenas but transferring to another bus before entering the city (US$48).

Boat A highlight of many people's travels in Patagonia is the four-day, three-night voyage through Chile's spectacular fjords aboard Navimag's car and passenger ferries *Puerto Edén* and the newer *Magallanes* to Puerto Montt.

To find out when the ferries are due to arrive from Puerto Montt, head to Comapa/Navimag (☎ 414300, **W** www.navimag.com), Costanera Pedro Montt 262, a couple of days before and on the estimated arrival date. *Puerto Edén* leaves Tuesday, *Magallanes* leaves on Friday and stops in Puerto Chacabuco. Boats usually arrive in the morning of the same day and depart either later that day or on the following day, but dates and times vary according to weather conditions and tides. Passengers disembarking must stay on board a few hours for cargo to be transported first; those leaving may have to hang out in the tiny passenger lounge until boarding is allowed, or spend the night on board.

High season is December to March, mid-season is September to November and March; and low season is April to August. *Magallanes* has more berths and top-end cabins, which take only two people, but the A cabins don't have views. Prices for the trip include all meals. Per-person fares, which vary according to view and private or shared bath, are as follows:

Class	High Season	Mid Season	Low Season
AAA	US$792	US$738	US$228-315
AA	US$398	US$354	US$166
A	US$345	US$302	US$131
Berths	US$250-297	US$210-256	US$28
*Economic	US$200	US$170	

*(Puerto Edén only)

Getting Around

Car rental is expensive; you'll get better rates in Punta Arenas.

Emsa/Avis (☎/fax 061-410775) is at Bulnes 632. World's End, at Blanco Encalada 226-A, rents bikes.

CUEVA DEL MILODÓN

Just 24km northwest of Puerto Natales, Hermann Eberhard discovered the remains of an enormous ground sloth in the 1890s. Nearly 4m high, the herbivorous *milodón* ate the succulent leaves of small trees and branches, but became extinct in the late Pleistocene. The 30m-high cave contains a tacky plastic life-size replica of the animal. It's a worth a stop, whether to appreciate the cave itself or take an easy walk up to a lookout point.

Conaf charges US$4 admission; camping (no fires) and picnicking are possible. Torres del Paine buses pass the entrance, which is 8km from the cave proper. Tours cost around US$5; alternatively, you can share a taxi (which will cost about US$14 roundtrip with one-hour wait) or hitch.

PARQUE NACIONAL BERNARDO O'HIGGINS

Turismo 21 de Mayo (☎ 411978, Eberhard 554) runs four-hour boat excursions to Glaciar Serrano in the otherwise inaccessible Parque Nacional Bernardo O'Higgins. Leaving at 8am (coffee and cookies provided) the boat passes Glaciar Balmaceda, then goes to the jetty at Puerto Toro. A 20-minute walk along a footpath leads to the base of Glaciar Serrano where visitors can dawdle about for 1½ hours before heading back on the boat to return via the same route to Puerto Natales. En route, passengers will catch glimpses of numerous glaciers and waterfalls, cormorants and occasional Andean condors. Whether the trip justifies the cost of US$52 is debatable; if weather is bad, the boat will turn around and a percentage of the cost will be refunded. Path@gone sells a similar tour on the boat *Galicia*.

Possibly a more interesting alternative and great way to access Torres del Paine is to take the boat to Glaciar Serrano and then hop on a Zodiac, which will take passengers to lunch at Estancia Balmaceda and continue up Río Serrano, arriving at the southern border of the park at 4:30pm. The same tour can be done leaving the park, but may require camping at Río Serrano to catch the Zodiac at 9am. The trip costs US$85 at Turismo 21 de Mayo.

PARQUE NACIONAL TORRES DEL PAINE

Soaring almost vertically more than 2000m above the Patagonian steppe, the Torres del Paine (Towers of Paine) are spectacular granite pillars that dominate the landscape of what may be South America's finest national park (US$11, less for Chilean nationals).

Before its creation in 1959, the park was part of a large sheep estancia, and it's still recovering from nearly a century of overexploitation of its pastures, forests and wildlife. Part of UNESCO'S Biosphere Reserve system since 1978, it shelters large and growing herds of guanacos, flocks of ostrichlike rhea (known locally as the ñandú), Andean condors, flamingos and many other species.

The park's outstanding conservation success has undoubtedly been the guanaco *(Lama guanicoe)*, which grazes the open steppes where its main natural enemy, the puma, cannot approach undetected. After more than a decade of effective protection from poachers, the guanaco barely flinches when humans or vehicles approach.

For hikers and backpackers, this 181,000-hectare park is an unequaled destination, with a well-developed trail network and refugios and campgrounds at strategic spots. The weather is changeable (some say you get four seasons in a day here), with the strong westerlies that typify Patagonia. Good foul-weather gear is essential; a warm synthetic sleeping bag and wind-resistant tent are imperative for those undertaking the Paine circuit and recommended for those doing the extremely popular 'W.'

Guided daytrips from Puerto Natales are possible, but permit only a bus-window glimpse of what the park has to offer. Instead, plan to spend anywhere from three to seven days to enjoy the hiking.

Orientation & Information

Parque Nacional Torres del Paine is 112km north of Puerto Natales via a decent but sometimes bumpy gravel road that passes Villa Cerro Castillo, where there is a seasonal border crossing into Argentina at

Cancha Carrera. The road continues 38km north, where there's a junction to the little-visited Lago Verde sector of the park.

Three kilometers north of this junction the highway forks west along the north shore of Lago Sarmiento to the Portería Sarmiento, the park's main entrance where entrance fees are collected. It's another 37km to the Administración (park headquarters), where the Conaf visitor center features a good exhibit on local ecology, plus videos that provide a good overview of the park.

If you're coming during the high season, plan your trip as far in advance as possible and make reservations for camping and/or refugio stays. Conaf and the concessions in charge of many of the lodgings may regulate the flow of people into the most popular parts of the park.

Climbing Fee Conaf charges a climbing fee of US$100. Before being granted permission, climbers must present a current résumé, emergency contact numbers and authorization from their consulate.

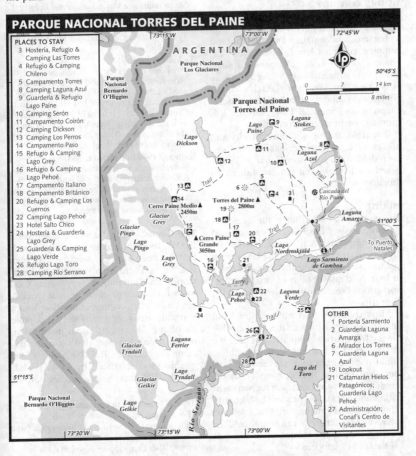

PARQUE NACIONAL TORRES DEL PAINE

PLACES TO STAY
3 Hostería, Refugio & Camping Las Torres
4 Refugio & Camping Chileno
5 Campamento Torres
8 Camping Laguna Azul
9 Guardería & Refugio Lago Paine
10 Camping Serón
11 Campamento Coirón
12 Camping Dickson
13 Camping Los Perros
14 Campamento Paso
15 Refugio & Camping Lago Grey
16 Refugio & Camping Lago Pehoé
17 Campamento Italiano
18 Campamento Británico
20 Refugio & Camping Los Cuernos
22 Camping Lago Pehoé
23 Hotel Salto Chico
24 Hostería & Guardería Lago Grey
25 Guardería & Camping Lago Verde
26 Refugio Lago Toro
28 Camping Rio Serrano

OTHER
1 Portería Sarmiento
2 Guardería Laguna Amarga
6 Mirador Los Torres
7 Guardería Laguna Azul
19 Lookout
21 Catamarán Hielos Patagónicos; Guardería Lago Pehoé
27 Administración; Conaf's Centro de Visitantes

Climbers must also get official permission from the Dirección de Fronteras y Límites (Difrol) in Santiago, which takes 48 hours. Ask for plenty of time on the permission to avoid paying a separate fee each time you enter the park. Avoid delays by arranging the permissions with a consulate before arrival in the country. For more information, contact the Gobernación Provincial (☎ 411423, fax 411954), at Eberhard 417, 2nd floor, on the south side of the Plaza de Armas in Puerto Natales.

Books & Maps

JLM maps, the most up-to-date of the park, are easily found in Puerto Natales.

For more information on trekking and camping, consult Clem Lindenmayer's LP guide *Trekking in the Patagonian Andes*. Bradt Publications' *Backpacking in Chile & Argentina* and William Leitch's *South America's National Parks* both have useful chapters on Torres del Paine, but are less thorough on practical information.

The treks are not without difficulty and hikers have suffered serious injuries and even died; for this reason, Conaf no longer permits solo treks, but it's not difficult to link up with others.

Hiking

To circuit or to 'W,' that is the question. And the answer lies in one's stamina and time. Doing the circuit (basically the 'W' plus the backside of the park) takes from five to seven days, while the 'W' takes three to four. Add another day or two for transportation connections when planning your trip.

Most trekkers start both routes from Laguna Amarga, although it is also possible to hike from park headquarters or take the catamaran to Pehoé and start from there. Conaf does restrict solo trekkers, but how they can regulate it is dubious (if alone, buddy-up with someone when registering at park admissions). It is prudent to hike with others, if only to make sure that someone knows where you are or can help should the weather turn or the vicious winds toss you off the trail (it happens).

The 'W' Most people trek the 'W' right to left, starting at Laguna Amarga, but going the other way provides better views of the Cuernos.

Refugio Las Torres to Mirador Las Torres

Four hours one-way, this relatively easy hike goes up Río Ascencio to a treeless tarn beneath the eastern face of the Torres del Paine proper. The last hour is a knee-popping scramble up boulders. There are camping and refugios at Las Torres and Chileno, with wild camping at Campamento Torres, for a stunning sunrise hike.

Refugio Las Torres to Los Cuernos

Seven hours one-way, hikers should keep to the lower trail (the upper trail, which is not marked on maps, is not recommended – many get lost). There's camping and a refugio. Winds are fierce along this section.

To Valle Frances

Five hours one-way from Cuernos or Pehoé, this hike is considered the most beautiful stretch – in good weather – between 3050m Paine Grande to the west and the lower but still spectacular Cuernos del Paine (Horns of Paine) to the east, with glaciers hugging the trail. There's camping at Italiano, and at Britannico, for those energetic enough to lug everything that far.

Refugio Pehoé to Refugio Lago Grey

Four hours one-way from Pehoé, this hike follows a relatively easy trail with a few bits of challenging downhill scampers. The glacier lookout is another half-hour. Camping and refugios can be found at both ends.

The Circuit Doing the whole loop takes in the 'W,' as described above, plus the backside between Refugio Grey and Refugio Los Torres. There are no refugios along this stretch and camping is very basic. You'll need foul-weather camping and trekking gear, as mud (sometimes knee-deep), snow and wind are inevitable. While the popularity of the 'W' means you'll meet lots of people along the way, that's not the case along the backside. Trekking alone is inadvisable (and restricted by Conaf). Make friends with others before heading out.

Refugio Lago Grey to Campamento Paso

Four hours from Guardas to Paso, about two hours going the opposite way, hikers might want to go west to east, which means ascending the pass rather than slipping downhill.

Campamento Paso to Perros
Approximately four hours, this route has plenty of mud and sometimes snow. What appears to be a campsite right after crossing the pass, isn't. Keep going until you see a shack.

Campamento Perros to Dickson
Around 4½ hours, it is relatively easy but a windy stretch.

Campamento Dickson to Seron
Six hours, as the trail wraps around Lago Paine, winds can get fierce and the trails vague; stay along the trail farthest away from lake. It's possible to break trek at Campamento Coiron.

Campamento Seron to Laguna Amarga
Four to five hours, you can end the trek with a chill-out night and a decent meal at Refugio Los Torres, which comes much recommended.

Other Trails A four-hour hike leading to **Lago Paine**, whose northern shore is accessible only from Laguna Azul, offers considerable solitude and breathtaking scenery. There's a rustic Refugio Lago Paine at the lake in route.

For a shorter day hike, walk from Guardería Lago Pehoé, on the main park highway, to **Salto Grande**, a powerful waterfall between Lago Nordenskjöld and Lago Pehoé. Another easy hour's walk leads to **Mirador Nordenskjöld**, an overlook with superb views of the lake and cordillera.

Glacier Trekking & Kayaking
Big Foot (☎ 414611, 414276, Bories 206) is the only outfitter authorized to lead ice hikes on Glaciar Grey (US$60), which involve a long hike, rappelling on to the glacier, walking on the glacier with crampons and harnesses, chances to view ice caves, and ice climbing before heading back. Three-day kayaking trips along Río Serrano and going to Glaciar Balmaceda cost US$380. A one-day kayak along the Fjord Eberhardt costs US$90.

Horseback Riding
Due to property divisions within the park, horses cannot cross from western sections (Lago Grey, Pehoé, Río Serrano) to the eastern part managed by Hostería Las Torres and vice versa. (Basically, Refugio Los Cuernos is the cut-off.) Baqueano Zamora (☎ 412911, Eberhard 566, Puerto Natales)

has rights to the former areas and charges about US$55 per day, lunch included. Fantástico Sur (contact Hostería Las Torres) controls the eastern area and charges US$70 per day, snack included.

Places to Stay & Eat
Make reservations. Arriving at the park without them, especially in the high season, means you may be without any place to stay, either in the refugios or in the campsites. Most travel agencies can call in reservations, but to make sure, go directly to the main concessions – Path@gone in Puerto Natales and Hostería Los Torres (☎ 226054), at Magallanes 960, in Punta Arenas. The latter manages Torres, Chileno and Los Cuernos refugios and campgrounds; the former manages Pehoé and Grey. Once at a refugio, staff can radio your next destination to confirm the reservation. Also of importance is patience. The staffers at the campsites and refugios do their best to deal with the intense flow of trekkers, but can't meet everyone's expectations.

Camping Campgrounds at the refugios – Las Torres, Chileno, Cuernos, Pehoé and Grey – all charge between US$4 and US$5 for a campsite. Refugios rent equipment: tent US$9 per night, sleeping bag US$4, mat US$1, and stove US$3; but in high season it's prudent to bring your own equipment in case the refugios run out. They also have small stores with expensive pastas, soup packets and butane gas. All other sites (see Hiking, earlier) are administered by Conaf, are free and very basic (rain shelters and pit toilets). Rats and mice have become a problem at many campgrounds; hang food from trees to avoid packs and tents being chewed through. Campsites at Japonés and Británico are used mainly by climbers, but afford spectacular views and welcomed remoteness.

Refugios All of the refugios listed under the hiking descriptions have individual rooms with four to eight bunk beds, kitchen privileges (for lodgers only and during specific hours), hot water and meals. A bed costs US$17 to US$19, sleeping bag rental US$4, meals US$5 to US$11. Should the refugio be full, the staff will provide all necessary camping equipment. Refugios Los Torres, Chileno and Cuernos close at the end of March; Lago Grey closes in mid-April. Refugio Pehoé is the only one that stays open after that. Conaf-controlled Refugio Lago Toro at Administración costs US$5 in one large dorm room with kitchen.

Hotels & Hosterías *Hostería Mirador del Payne* *(Operatur ☎/fax 240513, Av Colón 822, Oficina E, Punta Arenas, or ☎ 228712)* Singles/doubles US$105/128. Formerly Hostería Estancia Lazo, this hostería in the park's Laguna Verde sector comes recommended by readers for spectacular views, serenity and fabulous service. Call to be picked up at the road junction.

Hostería Lago Grey *(☎ 225986, Sector Lago Grey)* Singles/doubles US$173/200. Although at the outlet of iceberg-dotted Lago Grey, rooms are cut off from the views by thick windbreaking trees, but the café overlooks the grandeur. Zodiac boat tours are available on the lake, but not onto the glacier.

Hostería Pehoé *(☎ 244506)* Singles/doubles US$145/160 plus IVA. This hostería is on a small island in the lake of the same name and linked to the mainland by a footbridge. It has panoramic views of the Cuernos del Paine and Paine Grande, but the rooms are small and simple. The restaurant and bar are open to the public, but service can be slow.

Hostería Las Torres *(☎ 226054)* Singles/doubles US$131/149 to US$179/197. Constantly expanding, Las Torres is nestled away 7km from Guardería Laguna Amarga. The wings of the hotel are all connected, separated by spacious living rooms, while

the rooms are attractively decorated and warm. Buffet meals are elaborate, artistic affairs.

Hotel Salto Chico *(☎ 02-206-6060, fax 228-4655 in Santiago,* e *reservexplora@ explora.com)* Singles/doubles US$1347/2080 2 days, 3 nights to US$5388/6738 6 days, 7 nights in suites. Part of the luxury *explora* hotel concept, this is the most extravagant hotel around, at the outlet of Lago Pehoé. Rates include transfers from Punta Arenas, full board and all organized activities with bilingual guides. The building's exterior, although rather unobtrusive, receives scorn, but its interiors gorgeously interweave the landscape colors into the fabrics and intricately simple details. The real strength is the extraordinary view of the entire Paine massif across the lake. Outside of the hotel (beware the winds) is a heated lap pool and outdoor Jacuzzi, which unfortunately doesn't face the massif.

Getting There & Away
For details of transportation to the park, see the Puerto Natales Getting There & Away section. Hitching from Puerto Natales is possible, but competition is heavy.

Getting Around
Buses drop off and pick up passengers at Laguna Amarga, the Hielos Patagónicos catamaran launch at Pudeto and at park headquarters, coordinating with the catamaran schedule, which leaves Pudeto for Pehoé (US$15 per person with one backpack) at 9am, noon and 6pm December to mid-March, noon and 6pm in late March and November and at noon only in October and April. Another tourist boat leaves from Hostería Lago Grey to Refugio Lago Grey, but does not have a regular schedule.

Tierra del Fuego

Ever since the 16th-century voyages of Magellan and the 19th-century explorations of FitzRoy and Darwin on the *Beagle*, and even to the present, this 'uttermost part of the earth' has fascinated travelers. From the barren plains of the north, to virgin lenga forests draped in 'old man's beard,' and glaciers descending nearly to the ocean, the island never ceases to enthrall those who come to explore its mystery. The Yahgan Indians built the fires that inspired Europeans to give this region its name, now famous throughout the world.

The region comprises one large island, Isla Grande de Tierra del Fuego, and many smaller ones, few of them inhabited. The Strait of Magellan separates the archipelago from the South American mainland. This chapter covers both Chilean and Argentine sections of the island, including Chilean Isla Navarino.

If you are searching for what it feels like to be at the end of the world, Tierra del Fuego is it.

History

In 1520, when Magellan passed through the strait that now bears his name, neither he nor any other European explorer had any immediate interest in the land and its people. Seeking a passage to the Spice Islands of Asia, early navigators feared and detested the stiff westerlies, hazardous currents and violent seas that impeded their progress. Consequently, the Selk'nam, Haush, Yahgan and Alacaluf peoples who populated the area faced no immediate competition for their lands and resources.

These groups were mobile hunters and gatherers. The Selk'nam, also known as Ona, and the Haushes subsisted primarily on hunting the guanaco and dressing in its skins, while the Yahgans and Alacalufes, known collectively as 'Canoe Indians,' lived on fish, shellfish and marine mammals. The Yahgans (also known as the Yamaná) consumed the 'Indian bread' fungus that feeds

Highlights

- Río Grande – Buying cheese from Salesian monks at Misión Salesiana de la Candelaria

- Tolhuin – Stopping for the best pastries and breads on the island, and filling up the *mate* thermos

- Lucas Bridges Trail – Trekking through the thick island wilderness from one historic estancia to the other

- Ushuaia – Enjoying the view from Glaciar Martial or visiting the nearby mountains and lakes

- Acatushún Bone Museum – Admiring the impressive collections of sea mammal and bird bones at Estancia Harberton

Chubut

Santa Cruz

ATLANTIC OCEAN

CHILE

Río Grande
page 570

Tierra del Fuego

Ushuaia
page 574

Tierra del Fuego pages 564–565

off the ñire, a species of southern beech. Despite frequently inclement weather they wore little or no clothing, but constant fires (even in their bark canoes) kept them warm.

As Spain's control of its American empire dwindled, the area slowly opened to settlement by other Europeans, ensuring the rapid demise of the indigenous Fuegians, whom Europeans struggled to understand. Darwin, visiting the area in 1834, wrote that the difference between the Fuegians ('among the most abject and miserable creatures I ever saw') and Europeans was greater than that between wild and domestic animals. On an earlier voyage, though, Captain Robert FitzRoy of the *Beagle* had abducted a few Yahgans whom he returned after several years of missionary education in England.

From the 1850s, Europeans attempted to catechize the Fuegians, the earliest such instance ending with the death by starvation of British missionary Allen Gardiner. Gardiner's successors, including missionary GP Despard, working from a base at Keppel Island in the Falklands, were more successful despite the massacre of one party by Fuegians at Isla Navarino. Thomas Bridges, Despard's adopted son, learned to speak the Yahgan language and became one of the first settlers at Ushuaia, in what is now Argentine Tierra del Fuego. His son, Lucas Bridges, born at Ushuaia in 1874, left a fascinating memoir of his experiences among the Yahgans and Onas titled *The Uttermost Part of the Earth* (1950).

Since no other European power had had any interest in settling the region until Britain occupied the Falklands in the 1770s, Spain too paid little attention to Tierra del Fuego, but the successor governments of Argentina and Chile felt differently. The Chilean presence on the Strait of Magellan beginning in 1843, along with increasing British evangelism, spurred Argentina to formalize its authority at Ushuaia in 1884 and install a territorial governor the following year. In 1978 Argentina and Chile nearly went to war over claims to three small disputed islands in the Beagle Channel. International border issues in the area were not resolved until 1984.

Despite minor gold and lumber booms, Ushuaia was for many years primarily a penal settlement for political prisoners and common criminals. Sheep farming brought great wealth to some individuals and families, and is still the island's economic backbone, while the northern area near San Sebastián has substantial petroleum and natural gas reserves.

Geography & Climate

Surrounded by the South Atlantic Ocean, the Strait of Magellan and the easternmost part of the Pacific Ocean, the archipelago of

TIERRA DEL FUEGO

Tierra del Fuego has a land area of roughly 76,000 sq km, about the size of Ireland or South Carolina. The Chilean-Argentine border runs directly south from Cabo Espíritu Santo, at the eastern entrance of the Strait of Magellan, to the Beagle Channel (Canal de Beagle), where it trends eastward to the channel's mouth at Isla Nueva.

The plains of northern Isla Grande are a landscape of almost unrelenting wind, enormous flocks of Corriedales, and oil derricks, while the mountainous southern part offers scenic glaciers, lakes, rivers and seacoast. The maritime climate is surprisingly mild,

even in winter, but its changeability makes warm, dry clothing essential, especially on hikes and at higher elevations. The mountains of the Cordillera Darwin and the Sierra de Beauvoir, reaching up to 2500m in the west, intercept Antarctic storms, leaving the plains around Río Grande much drier than areas nearer the Beagle Channel.

The higher southern rainfall supports dense deciduous and evergreen forests, while the drier north consists of extensive native grasses and low-growing shrubs. Storms batter the bogs and truncated beeches of the remote southern and western zones of the archipelago. Guanaco, rhea and condor can still be seen in the north, but marine mammals and shorebirds are the most common wildlife along the Beagle Channel.

Getting There & Around
Overland, the simplest route to Argentine Tierra del Fuego is via Porvenir, across the Strait of Magellan from Punta Arenas; for details, see the Patagonia chapter. For those with their own vehicle, the roll-on, roll-off ferry *Bahía Azul*, runs from Punta Delgada across the narrows at Primera Angostura to Chilean Tierra del Fuego.

Unlike the rest of Argentina, Tierra del Fuego has no designated provincial highways *(rutas provinciales)*, but has secondary roads known as *rutas complementarias*, modified by a lowercase letter. References to such roads in this chapter will be 'RC-a,' for example.

PORVENIR (CHILE)
☎ 61 • pop 4000
The largest settlement on Chilean Tierra del Fuego, Porvenir is most often visited in a daytrip from Punta Arenas, but this usually means spending only a couple of hours in town and more time than a belly might wish crossing the strait. Spending a night in this quiet village of rusting, metal-clad Victorians and then proceeding to other destinations is a better way to gain a glimpse into Fuegian life.

When gold was discovered nearby in 1879, waves of immigrants, many from Croatia, endured the trip to come here. Whether or not anyone made a fortune is debatable. But when sheep estancias began to spring up, the immigrants found more reliable work. Chilotes (from the Chilean island of Chiloe) came down in droves, for the fishing and estancia work and chance of a better life. Today, most of the population is a Croat-Chilote combo.

The gravel road east, along Bahía Inútil to the Argentine border at San Sebastián, is in excellent condition. Northbound motorists from San Sebastián should take the equally good route from Onaisín to Cerro Sombrero en route to the crossing of the Strait of Magellan at Punta Delgada-Puerto Espora, rather than the heavily traveled and rutted truck route directly north from San Sebastián.

Information
The tourist office (☎ 580098), upstairs at Padre Mario Zavattaro 402, is open 9am to 5pm weekdays, 11am to 5pm weekends. Information is also available at the artisanal shop on the costanera between Phillipi and Schythe.

The post office is at Phillipi 176, on the Plaza de Armas. CTC is at Philippi 277. Porvenir's hospital (☎ 580034) is on Carlos Wood between Señoret and Guerrero.

Things to See & Do
The intriguing **Museo de Tierra del Fuego** *(☎ 580098, Mario Zavattaro 402; US$1; open 9am-5pm weekdays year-round, plus 11am-5pm weekends Jan & Feb)* on the Plaza de Armas, has some unexpected materials, including Selk'nam mummies and skulls, musical instruments used by the mission Indians on Isla Dawson, stuffed animals from the region, and an exhibit on early Chilean cinematography.

Organized Tours
The tourist office can arrange tours of old gold-panning sites, horse riding excursions and other ways to enjoy the area. Explore Patagonia (☎ 580206, **w** www.explore patagonia.cl, Croacia 675) organizes excursions including a 'city tour' and a visit to Peale's dolphins around Bahía Chilote in a traditional Chilote-style fishing boat (US$65, including meals). Its also runs some well-recommended longer camping and horseback-riding trips, one to Río Condor (US$170 per day all-inclusive) and another, more intense six-day adventure in November that involves kayaking, *centolla* (king crab) fishing and riding to Glaciar Marinelli (US$190 per day all-inclusive).

Places to Stay & Eat
Residencial Colón (☎ 581157, Damián Riobó 198) Singles US$7 with shared bath

& breakfast. The rooms are basic and have treacherous heating facilities, but this is the best deal in town. Lunch costs US$4.

Hotel España (☎ 580160, Croacia 698) Singles/doubles US$9/11 with private bath. A dark, wacky hallway leads to rooms with ample beds, large windows and cropped harbor views. Breakfast is US$2 extra.

Hotel Central (☎ 580077, Phillipi & Croacia) Singles/doubles US$19/33 with shared bath, US$24/35 with private bath. The rooms are cozy and small but not all have heat. Prices don't include breakfast, but if you stay longer than a day the owner will add it in for free.

Hotel Rosas (☎ 580088, Philippi 296) Singles/doubles US$22/32 with private bath and breakfast. All the rooms have heat and are clean, the owner Antonio knows heaps about the region, and the restaurant serves up some great seafood dishes. Lunch, with drinks, costs about US$9.

Hostería Los Flamencos (☎ 241321, Teniente Merino) Singles/doubles US$40/50. Overlooking the harbor, Los Flamencos is the fanciest hotel in town, but neglected by its owners. The manager, however, is a charm and does what he can to make your stay more inviting.

El Chispa (☎ 580054, Viel & Señoret) US$5-7, breakfast US$1.50-3. Under tattered green-hued paintings of European garden parties, the staff serves up fresh seafood and large breakfasts. Main meals come with side dishes that are included in the price, making this place a good deal for the money.

Club Croata (☎ 580053, Manuel Señoret 542) US$4-10. A more formal experience, Club Croata serves rich fish dishes. The owner can fill you in on the Croatian influence in town.

Restaurant Puerto Montt (☎ 580207, Croacia 1169) US$3-6. Rough and tumble Puerto Montt is where the fishing crews come to feast on huge portions. This is a great place to capture a bit of Porvenir's personality.

Catef (☎ 580625, Zavattarp 94) US$7. Catef offers creative dishes, all of which are explained on the menu. Try the *pichanga*

caliente, a layer of tomato and avocado topped with meat, then fries and finally cheese.

Getting There & Away

Aerovías DAP (☎ 580089), on Manuel Señoret near Muñoz Gamero, flies to Punta Arenas (US$25) twice daily except Sunday.

To get to Río Grande (US$17, 5½ hours), take either the Pacheco bus, which leaves from the corner of Sampaio and Riobó Tuesday and Thursday at 12:15pm, or the Tecni-Austral bus, which leaves from the corner of Phillipi and Manuel Señoret Wednesday, Friday and Sunday at 12:30pm. Town buses transport workers from in front of the DAP office to Camerón in Timaukel for free, but if the bus is full, you're out of luck (2½ hours). To get to Cerro Sombrero, buses leave from Santos Mardones, near Manuel Señoret.

Transbordadora Broom (☎ 580089) operates the car-passenger ferry *Melinka* to Punta Arenas (2½-4 hours, US$7 per person, US$45 per vehicle) Tuesday through Saturday at 2pm, Sundays and holidays at 5pm.

Getting Around

The bus to the ferry terminal departs from the waterfront kiosk about an hour before the ferry's departure and costs US$1. Taxis cost at least four times as much.

CERRO SOMBRERO (CHILE)

This orderly but half-abandoned town at the north end of Tierra del Fuego, 43km south of the ferry crossing at Primera Angostura, is a company town belonging to Chile's Empresa Nacional de Petróleo (ENAP; National Petroleum Company). North American architects from Tennessee created the town plan in the late 1950s, giving it an awkward suburban style that is unnerving to find in these hinterlands – a pink A-frame church in the middle of a roundabout, surrounded by identical pastel-colored houses and white picket fences. Rumor has it that ENAP may close business on this town, leaving the residents without much of a place to, well, hang their hats.

If you do stop for lunch, try **Club Social** (*O'Higgins s/n*) for a hearty cazuela while enjoying Muzac. Meals go for US$5 to US$7. The only scheduled public transport comes from Porvenir; return buses to Porvenir leave Monday, Wednesday, and Thursday at 8am.

BAHÍA SAN SEBASTIÁN

The entire coastline of northeastern Tierra del Fuego, from Bahía San Sebastián to south of Río Grande, is a migratory bird sanctuary known as **Reserva Provincial Costa Atlántica de Tierra del Fuego**. Here you'll have a good chance of seeing *becasa de mar* and *playera rojizo*; the best months for birdwatching are October to March. Tides change every six hours, and at times there can be as much as 11km difference between high and low tide – a sad trap for the marine mammals that become stranded here as a consequence. Natalie Goodall has collected from this bay many of the skeletons now on view at the Acatushún Bone Museum in Harberton (see Estancia Harberton section).

RÍO GRANDE

☎ 02964 • pop 55,000

The longest that most travelers stay in windswept Río Grande is the short wait before hopping a bus to Ushuaia, 230km southwest. That is, of course, unless they've come to fish: Río Grande is one of the world's top trout-fishing regions. About the only hint of this fame, however, is the monster trout sculpture at the entrance to town. In an attempt to beautify the town, random sculpture gardens of brightly colored piping adorn the main thoroughfares, most of which could pass for a drug-induced jungle gym.

In 1886, the villainous gold-seeker Julius Popper (see boxed text 'Gold at What Cost') stumbled across the mouth of Río Grande, home to Selk'nam (or Ona). As José Menéndez's sheep stations developed, a makeshift service town grew. The Salesian order, under the guidance of Monseñor Fagnano, set up a mission in 1893 in an attempt to 'protect' the Selk'nam from the growing development. (First built at the site of the present-day cemetery, the mission was moved to its current spot in 1897.)

The town continued to grow as a petroleum service center, and its duty-free status, created in an attempt to continue town development, has brought in electronics manufacturing plants and plenty of wholesale appliance stores. The military here played an important role in the Falkland/Malvinas War; the many plaques and memorials pay tribute to the fallen soldiers and testify to the sensitivity of this yet-to-heal national scar.

Information

Most visitor services are along Av San Martín and along Av Manuel Belgrano between San Martín and the waterfront. The tourist kiosk in the plaza has town maps, brochures on nearby estancias and fishing information. Or go to the Instituto Fueguino de Turismo (Infuetur; ☎ 422887, e infuerg@tierradelfuego.org.ar) at Belgrano 319, open 10am to 5pm weekdays.

Scores of banks and ATMs can be found at the intersection of Av San Martín and 9 de Julio, including Banco de la Nación. The post office is on Rivadavia between Moyano and Alberdi; the postal code is 9420. The locutorio at Av San Martín 170 has coin-operated Internet access. Fiesta Travel (☎ 431800, 9 de Julio 663) and Mariani Travel (☎ 426010, Rosales 281) can arrange flights and also act as representatives to some of the area's tourism estancias. El Lavadero is located at Perito Moreno 221. The Hospital Regional (☎ 422088) is at Av Belgrano 350.

Things to See & Do

The **Museo de la Ciudad** (☎ 430647, Alberdi 555; free; open 9am-5pm weekdays, Jan-Feb 9am-8pm weekdays, 3pm-5pm Sat, Mar-Dec), in a restored *galpón* (sheep-shearing shed), has a very impressive display of just about every aspect of town history, from logging to military displays, postal communications to cartography, indigenous artifacts to yet another milodón.

Ten kilometers north of town on RN 3 the 1893 Misión Salesiano de la Candelaria houses a **Museo Salesiano** (☎ 421642, adult

Gold at What Cost

Visions of an El Dorado – a land of endless gold – danced through many an explorer's head during South American expeditions in the 1800s. One such dreamer was a Sorbonne-educated multilingual Romanian named Julius Popper. Upon receiving a degree in mine engineering, Popper traveled through Siberia and Canada, worked as an urban planner in New Orleans and as a journalist in Mexico, then headed south to Brazil, where he heard reports of gold in the Strait of Magellan.

With investment from Buenos Aires, Popper set out to Tierra del Fuego as director of Compañía Anónima Lavaderos de Oro del Sur. His success enticed Croatian, English, Irish, Italian and Scottish men to join him in the bay of San Sebastián, at El Páramo (a bleak, cold place), where Popper and some 35 men produced up to a kilo of gold a day. Popper created his own small army and unscrupulously killed (or made examples of) anyone who interfered in the business.

Calling himself the Fuegian Dictator, Popper began minting his own gold coins of 1 and 5 grams, which became recognized on the island. Official postal stamps followed. His thirst for control was insatiable, and control of the land was his prime directive. He led an all-out assault on the Selk'nam, who lived on the land he then claimed, going so far as to photograph the 'hunt' and pay his army in coin for body parts, a sordid practice that would continue during the establishment – some might say invasion – of the sheep ranches.

The gold rush was short-lived, however, and the government began to notice that a Romanian gone mad was threatening their control. The company was shut down in 1889 and completely stripped of capital. Popper remained on the island, dying alone and penniless in 1893.

child US$2/1; open 10am-12:30pm weekdays, 3pm-7pm daily), containing geological and natural history exhibits and a wealth of ethnographic artifacts, but unfortunately the order does little with them. When the mission's work of protecting the Selk'nam dissolved (basically, there were no more living), the mission was converted into an agrotechnical school, now considered the best in the area; fresh Salesian cheeses and produce may be purchased. Students (female students were not admitted until 1997) conduct informal tours of the greenhouses and dairy farms. Take colectivo Línea B, which runs every hour from Güemes, downtown.

Places to Stay

Since most overnighters at Río Grande are either part of the wholesale business set or high-end anglers, lodging tends to be overpriced, not to mention sparse. A number of places cater to the budget conscious, but many are hard to recommend; those that are fill up fast. High-end places discount 10% for cash payments.

Hotel Argentino (☎ 422365, Av San Martín 64) Dorm beds US$10 per person shared bath. The Argentino offers basic dorm rooms off a main house, but the real draw is the friendly ambience – a mix of locals and travelers kicking back in the common areas. There's hot water, free pick-up, and luggage storage on offer.

Hostería Antares (☎ 425959, Echeverría 49) Shared rooms US$15 per person. In a quiet location, Antares has rooms to share (exception: solo women get a private room), all rather small with tiny dark bathrooms, but clean and well run. There are kitchen privileges, or breakfast is US$2, lunch US$3.50.

Hospedaje Noal (☎ 427516, Rafael Obligado 557) Singles with shared bath US$15, doubles with private bath US$35. Run with a great deal of motherly care and friendly attention, Noal's provides somewhat dark rooms and large shared bathrooms, but no breakfast.

Apart Hotel Keyuk'n (☎ 420367, Colón 630) Singles/doubles US$40/50. Spacious, fully equipped apartments make Keyuk'n

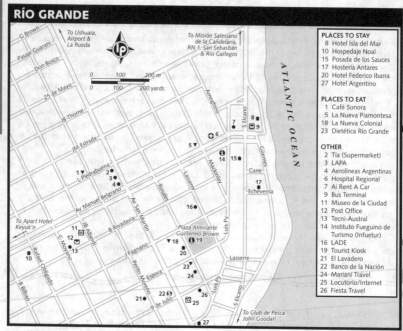

RÍO GRANDE

PLACES TO STAY
8 Hotel Isla del Mar
10 Hospedaje Noal
15 Posada de los Sauces
17 Hostería Antares
20 Hotel Federico Ibarra
27 Hotel Argentino

PLACES TO EAT
1 Café Sonora
5 La Nueva Piamontesa
18 La Nueva Colonial
23 Dietética Río Grande

OTHER
2 Tía (Supermarket)
3 LAPA
4 Aerolíneas Argentinas
6 Hospital Regional
7 Ai Rent A Car
9 Bus Terminal
11 Museo de la Ciudad
12 Post Office
13 Tecni-Austral
14 Instituto Fueguino de Turismo (Infuetur)
16 LADE
19 Tourist Kiosk
21 El Lavadero
22 Banco de la Nación
24 Mariani Travel
25 Locutorio/Internet
26 Fiesta Travel

one of the best deals in town, especially for families or groups of friends. Each two-floor unit has a kitchen, large bathroom, living and dining room, TV, plus comfortable beds with lots of extra bedding.

Hotel Isla del Mar (☎ 422883, fax 427283, Güemes 963) Singles/doubles US$44/55. Around the corner from the bus terminal, facing the bay, Isla del Mar has some decent rooms – ask for one upstairs – with large bathrooms and worn-out furniture. Breakfast is included and the staff quite helpful.

Federico Ibarra Hotel (☎ 430071, fax 430883, Rosales 357) Singles/doubles US$63/75. Attractive rooms with large bathrooms. Rooms with views of the plaza and the bay are pleasant, but can be noisy. Rooms without the view are equally well appointed and much quieter.

Posada de los Sauces (☎ 432895, e posadadelossauces@arnet.com.ar, Elcano 839) Singles/doubles US$78/90 standard,

US$100/125 deluxe. Working almost exclusively with high-end fishing excursions, Los Sauces has the sturdy, woodsy feel of a fancy fishing lodge. Deluxe rooms come with Jacuzzi bath. The upstairs bar, 'Achicoria,' outfitted in forest green and dark wood, is just waiting for cigar smoke and tall tales to fill the air; sensibly priced drinks will certainly speed them along.

Places to Eat

Ibarra Hotel (☎ 430071, Rosales 357) US$1.50-6. The downstairs confitería of this hotel, across from the plaza, is a pleasant sunny spot to enjoy coffee or a light meal.

La Nueva Piamontesa (☎ 421977, Av Belgrano 601) US$2-15. Open 24 hours. Country store gone wild, this fantastic place has anything you could want to eat; and if you can't find it, they'll help you look (within reason, of course). Fun and friendly service, offering parrilla, pizza, pasta and sandwiches for take-away or in-store dining

Café Sonora (☎ *423102, Perito Moreno 705)* US$3-13. Under posters of The Doors and Woodstock, the order here is bready pizza. It's a comfortable, clean place to hang out, watch a soccer match or just have a coffee.

La Rueda (☎ *433982, Islas Malvinas 998)* US$2.50-7. By far the best place to eat in town, La Rueda is an outstanding mix of precise professional service and cheap excellent food. Homemade pasta dishes, large enough to feed two, are served bubbling hot in platters that can be reheated (try the *sorrentinos*). Parrilla and fish entrees are equally filling and come with a self-serve salad bar full of fresh fixings. Wines are equally good value.

La Nueva Colonial (☎ *425353, J Fagnano 669)* Prices US$7-10. Chef Cesar, who has no qualms about sitting down with guests in his sauce-spattered apron while still in a sweat cooks up much-praised pasta and fish dishes. Some find the gruff gregariousness a fun distraction; others consider it an imposition. The front room serves as a pizza parlor, and an open kitchen adds to the relaxed, comfortable ambience.

Tía supermarket is on the corner of Av San Martín and Piedrabuena. *Dietética Río Grande* (*Rosales 293)* sells dry natural foods and vitamins.

Getting There & Around

The airport (☎ 420600) is only a short cab ride from downtown. Aerolíneas Argentinas (☎ 425700, San Martín 607) and LAPA (☎ 432620, Av San Martín 641) fly daily to Río Gallegos and Buenos Aires.

LADE (☎ 422968), Lasserre 425, flies to Ushuaia on Monday and Wednesday, and to Río Gallegos, El Calafate and Gobernador Gregores on Thursday. Schedules and fees vary.

Aerovías DAP (☎ 430249, 9 de Julio 597) flies to Punta Arenas, Chile (US$79) on Monday, Wednesday and Friday at 11am.

Río Grande's bus terminal (☎ 421339) is at the foot of Av Belgrano on the waterfront, or check out Tecni-Austral (☎ 432885, Moyano 516). Buses depart several times daily to Ushuaia (US$15-21, 3 hours) and

may stop in Tolhuin (US$8-10, 1½ hours). A better option is Transportes Montiel (☎ 420997), which runs door-to-door service to Ushuaia and Tolhuin several times daily. Call to reserve a seat; buses can also be picked up at the bus terminal.

The most direct way to Punta Arenas (US$25-30) is via Punta Delgada (buses go via San Sebastián), or take buses to Porvenir (US$20-25), which meet with the slower ferry.

Ai Rent A Car (☎ 430757) is at Ameghino 612, at the corner of Belgrano.

ESTANCIAS AROUND RÍO GRANDE

José Menéndez's first estancia, La Primera Argentina, now known as **Estancia José Menéndez**, 20km southwest of town via RN 3 and RC-b, covered a total landmass of 160,000 hectares, with over 140,000 head of sheep. His second bite into this land, of which he was most proud, was La Segunda Argentina, totaling 150,000 hectares. Later renamed **Estancia María Behety** after his wife, it is still a working ranch and features the world's largest shearing shed, 17km west of town via RC-c. Neither of these estancias is open to public.

Many of the area's smaller estancias have opened to tourism, offering a unique chance to learn of the area's history and enjoy its magic; reserve as far in advance as possible.

Estancia Via Monte (☎ *2964-430861, fax 422008,* e *sgoodall@global.com.ar)* Singles US$80-120, doubles US$150-185, house US$300; discounts for longer stays, 20% discount May-Oct. Open year-round. Thomas Bridges' sons established this estancia in 1902 at the request of the Selk'nam. Meaning 'through the woods,' the estancia is on the northern end of the 40km Lucas Bridges Trail, linking it to Harberton, near Ushuaia. The Selk'nam worked on the estancia, which owned 50,000 hectares and rented another 50,000. The Goodalls, descendents of the Bridges, now run it as a working ranch and a comfortable, unobtrusive place to stay. Horseback riding and fly-fishing are among the activities, as are guided treks on the Lucas Bridges Trail, one

Fish Are Jumpin'

Rivers jump with trout, anglers strain under the pull of the immense beasts, and tales of the one that got away drown out the soccer match on TV: It's fishing season in Tierra del Fuego. Famous the world over, the desolate stretch of the island around Río Grande attracts movie stars, heads of state and former US presidents, all in search of the perfect day of angling. Usually they are in luck.

In 1933, pioneer John Goodall stocked the rivers around Río Grande with brown, rainbow and brook trout. Similar to the success of the sheep stations in the area, the sport-fishing industry took off as the fish populated the rivers. The brown trout, originally from Europe, ventured out to sea, returning to these rivers to spawn. Over the decades they have continued this back-and-forth migration, creating one of the world's best sea-run trout-fishing areas; some specimens from this region weigh in at 11kg. Rainbow trout from the western US are nearly as impressive, with individual fish sometimes reaching 9kg.

Most fishing excursions are organized through outside agents, mostly in the US. 'Public' fishing rivers, on which trips can be organized, include the Fuego, Menéndez, Candelaria, Ewan and MacLennan. Many of the more elite fishing trips are lodged in estancias, which have exclusive use of some of the best rivers.

Season: November 1 to April 15, with throw-back restrictions from April 1 to April 15

Limit: One fish per person per day

Methods: Spinning and fly casting

Flies: Rubber legs and wooly buggers

License 1: Valid for fishing throughout the province, except in the national park
Cost for foreigners: US$100/25 season/day
Contact: Asociación Caza y Pesca (☎ 02901-423168, Maipú 822) and Optica Eduardo's (☎ 02901-433252, San Martín 830), both in Ushuaia, or Club de Pesca John Goodall (☎ 02964-424324, Ricardo Rojas 606) in Río Grande

License 2: Valid for fishing in the national park and in Patagonia areas
Cost for foreigners: US$100/10 season/day
Contact: Administración de Parques Nacionales in Ushuaia (see Porvenir's Information Section)

of the best new trekking options on the island. Via Monte is 45km from Río Grande.

Estancia Las Hijas (☎ 02901-434617, e daniels@netcombbs.com.ar). Enjoying an excellent locale, Las Hijas has plans to open to tourism. If you are planning to hop from one estancia to the other, this would be good choice right before the RC-a junction.

Estancia Tepi (☎ 02901-492161, e tepi@merlins.com.ar, w www.estanciatepi.com.ar, RC-a Km 5) Rooms US$150 full pension. Started by the first rural doctor in Tierra del Fuego, Basque-Provençal-style Tepi Aike offers plenty of things to do, including thermal baths, horseback rides, guided tours and treks. It's open December to March, but may be open other times depending on weather. It's 80km from Río Grande and 150km from Ushuaia.

Estancia Rolito (☎ 02901-492007, 437351 e gonzalez@metcombbs.com, w www.turismocampo.com, RC-a Km 14) Room US$70/90 per person with half-/full pension. In a forest of ñire and lenga, Rolito is a small comfortable and inviting. The owners make sure everyone stays content with meals o heaping plates of Fueguino lamb, homemade bread and garden vegetables. Horseback riding with guide costs US$35/75 half/full day. Nonguests can stop by for meals: Lunch or dinner costs US$25. Rolito is 100km from Río Grande and 120km from Ushuaia.

Hostería San Pablo (☎ 02964-425839 Singles US$93-110 all-inclusive, US$20

...ouse for 4-6 people. A well-known spot in ...ly-fishing circles, Hosteria San Pablo has ...ttractive rooms either in the main house ...vhere service is all-inclusive or in a sepa-...ate house, including breakfast and ...itchen privileges. Lunch or dinner costs ...n additional US$13. It's located about ...20km southeast of Río Grande via RN 3 ...nd RC-a.

TOLHUIN & LAGO FAGNANO

Tolhuin, a quiet town of muddy streets, ...mall plazas and protecting evergreens, ...its on the eastern shore of Lago Fagnano, ...lso known as Lago Kami. Named for the ...elk'nam word meaning 'like a heart,' ...Tolhuin is practically in the heart of Tierra ...lel Fuego – 133km south of Río Grande ...nd 103 northeast of Ushuaia. Most trav-...lers tend to skip right over it, but if you ...re looking for a unique and tranquil spot, ...Tolhuin is worth checking out.

However long your stay, you will likely ...end up in what is undeniably the heart of ...own, **Panadería La Unión** (☎ 02901-492202, ...w www.panaderia-launion.com.ar). All of ...he buses stop here for a quick break, and ...everyone scurries inside to purchase bags of ...excellent pastries and fill up their thermoses ...with hot water. There's also an internal ...garden with peacocks, lots of magazines, ...telephones and Internet access.

Lago Fagnano, a huge glacial trough, is a ...popular spot for boating and fishing.

Places to Stay & Eat

About 10km north of town are two camping ...possibilities, both with bathrooms, hot water ...and fire pits: *Camping Centro de Emplea-*...*dos de Comercio* and *Hain del Lago* ...*Khami* (☎ 02901-1560-3606, e bana@net-...combbs.com.ar), which charges US$3 per ...person for camping or has refugios for ...US$25 for 3 persons or US$50 for 5 persons.

For something more comfortable, check ...out *Albergue Turístico Libertad* (☎ 02901-...1556-6624, Metet 321) Singles/doubles ...US$25/40 shared bath, US$40/50 private ...bath.

Hostería Kaikén (☎ 02964-492208) ...Singles/doubles US$25/30 ground floor,

US$30/35 upper floor, US$60 for 5-person bungalow. With views of the lake, Kaikén shows off its 1965 sense of style with echo-chamber hallways, large stone paneling and lots of drooping potted plants. Downstairs rooms are warmer, but none are enticing. The restaurant serves good, plentiful, but rather costly meals.

Near the panadería in Tolhuin there's *Pizzería La Amistad* and a small asado that looks worth checking out.

Getting There & Away

Buses along RN 3 stop at the panadería; a trip to Ushuaia should cost US$6, to Río Grande US$8-10. Montiel vans (☎ 02964-420997 in Río Grande, ☎ 02901-421366 in Ushuaia) run door-to-door service to Ushuaia and Río Grande for US$8.

USHUAIA

☎ 02901 • pop 36,000

Built between the Beagle Channel and jagged glacial peaks rising from sea level to nearly 1500m, Ushuaia boasts an incredible location that few cities can match. But one is tempted to say Ushuaia boasts a little too much of its 'World's End' status: Yes, it is the southernmost city in the world, but the intense marketing of this superlative runs the risk of overpowering the very desola-tion it aims to promote. Gateway to Antarc-tica, base for sophisticated yachts and coveted destination for many travelers, Ushuaia does cater well to the growing numbers of tourists, offering myriad activi-ties in and around town and enjoying a na-tional park for a neighbor. For those seeking isolation and adventure, excellent hiking and skiing opportunities are just minutes from town.

In 1870, the British-based South Ameri-can Missionary Society made Ushuaia its first permanent outpost in the Fuegian region, but only artifacts, shell mounds, Thomas Bridges' famous dictionary, and memories remain of the Yahgan Indians who once flourished here.

Between 1884 and 1947, Argentina incar-cerated many of its most notorious criminals and political prisoners here and on remote

USHUAIA

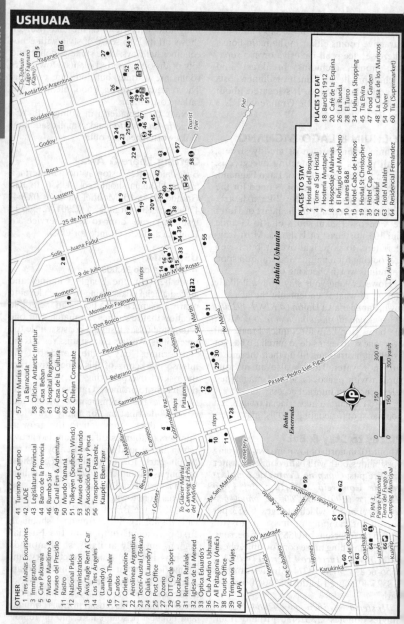

PLACES TO EAT
18 Barcleit 1912
20 Café de la Esquina
26 La Rueda
28 El Turco
34 Ushuaia Shopping
45 Tía Elvira
47 Food Garden
48 La Casa de los Mariscos
54 Volver
60 Tía (Supermarket)

PLACES TO STAY
2 Hostal del Bosque
4 Torre al Sur Hostal
7 Hostería Mustapic
9 Hospedaje Malvinas
8 El Refugio del Mochilero
10 Linares B&B
15 Hotel Cabo de Hornos
19 Hostal St Christopher
35 Hotel Cap Polonio
52 Alakaluf
63 Hotel Maitén
64 Residencial Fernández

OTHER
1 Tres Marías Excursiones
3 Immigration
5 Cine Pakawaia
6 Museo Marítimo &
   Museo del Presidio
11 Rastro
12 National Parks
   Administration
13 Avis/Tagle Rent A Car
14 Los Tres Ángeles
   (Laundry)
16 Cambio Thaler
17 Cardos
21 Orielle Antoine
22 Aerolíneas Argentinas
23 Tecni-Austral (Tolkar)
24 Qialis (Laundry)
25 Post Office
27 Ozono
29 DTT Cycle Sport
30 Localiza
31 Renata Rafalak
32 Iglesia de la Merced
33 Optica Eduardo's
36 Club Andino Ushuaia
37 All Patagonia (AmEx)
38 Tourist Office
39 Témpanos Viajes
40 LAPA
41 Turismo de Campo
42 LADE
43 Legislatura Provincial
44 Banco de la Provincia
46 Rumbo Sur
49 Canal Fun & Adventure
50 Mundo Yamaná
51 Tolkeyen (Southern Winds)
53 Museo Fin del Mundo
55 Asociación Caza y Pesca
56 Transportes Pasarela;
   Kaupén, Eben-Ezer
57 Tres Marías Excursiones;
   La Barracuda
58 Oficina Antarctic Infuetur
59 Casa Beban
61 Hospital Regional
62 Casa de la Cultura
65 ACA
66 Chilean Consulate

Bahía Ushuaia

Bahía Encerrada

To Tolhuin &
Lago Fagnano
(Kami)

Tourist
Pier

Pier

To Airport

Pasaje-Pedro Luis Figue

To Glacier Martial
& Camping La Pista
del Andino

To RN 3,
Parque Nacional
Tierra del Fuego &
Camping Municipal

0   150   300 m
0   150   300 yards

la de los Estados (Staten Island). In 1906, the military prison was moved to Ushuaia and, in 1911, it was combined with the Carcel de Reincidentes, which had incarcerated civilian recidivists in Ushuaia since 1896.

Since 1950, the town has been an important naval base. Industries such as electronics assembly, with higher wages and other such perks, encouraged people to settle here, which in turn resulted in a cacophony of housing developments advancing in the few directions the mad geography allows.

Orientation

Running along the Beagle Channel, Av Maipú becomes Av Malvinas Argentinas west of the cemetery, then turns into RN 3, continuing to Parque Nacional Tierra del Fuego. To the east, public access ends at Yaganes, which heads north to meet RN 3 going north towards Lago Fagnano. Most visitor services are on or within a few blocks of Av San Martín, one block north of Av Maipú.

Information

Tourist Offices The very helpful municipal tourist office (☎/fax 424550, toll-free 0800-333-1476 on the island), San Martín 674, is housed in the 1926 public library. Accommodations listings with current prices, activities and transport listings are available; after closing time they post a list of available lodgings. They have a message board, and English- and French-speaking staff. Hours are 8am to 9pm weekdays, 9am to 8pm weekends and holidays. They also maintain a branch at the airport and at the port for arriving ships.

The Instituto Fueguino de Turismo (Infuetur; ☎ 423340) has an office at the tourist pier. The national parks office (☎ 421315, San Martín 1395) is open 9am to 4pm weekdays. ACA (☎ 421121) is at Malvinas Argentinas and Onachaga.

Immigration & Consulates Immigration (☎ 422334) is at Beauvoir 1536. The Chilean consulate (☎ 430909), at Jainén 50, southwest of town, is open 8:30am to 1:30pm weekdays.

Money Several banks on Maipú and San Martín have ATMs. The best bet for traveler's checks (2% commission) is Banco de la Provincia (San Martín 396). Cambio Thaler (San Martín 877) is open from 9:30am to 1:30pm and 4pm to 8pm weekdays, 10am to 1:30pm and 5:30pm to 8pm Saturday and 5:30pm to 8pm Sunday (3% commission).

Post & Communications The post office is at San Martín and Godoy. The postal code is 9410. Locutorios can be found throughout the city, most with (slow) Internet access.

Laundry Los Tres Ángeles (☎ 422687) is at Juan M de Rosas 139, or you can try Qüalis (☎ 432576, Deloqui 368).

Medical Services The Hospital Regional (☎ 422950, 107 for emergencies) is at Maipú and 12 de Octubre.

Mundo Yamaná

More an experience than museum, Mundo Yamaná (Rivadavia 56, US$3, 1pm-8pm Mon-Sun) attempts to bring the Yamaná culture to life. Some of the expertly detailed dioramas are based on accessible bays and inlets of the national park; coming here before hiking in the park will add a new level of awareness.

Museo Marítimo & Museo del Presidio

When convicts were moved from Staten Island to Ushuaia in 1906 they began building the national prison, which was finished in 1920. The spokelike halls of single cells were designed to house 380 prisoners, but during the prison's most active period it held up to 800 inmates. It closed as a jail in 1947 and now houses the Museo Marítimo & Museo del Presidio (☎ 437481, Yaganes & Gobernador Paz; adult/senior/student/child US$7/5/3/1; open 10am-8pm daily Nov 15-Apr 15; 10am-1pm & 3pm-8pm daily Apr 15-Nov 15). Halls showing the penal life are intriguing, but mainly because of the informative plaques, which are only in Spanish. Some of the more illustrious prisoners included

Masks & Rituals in Tierra del Fuego

As Charles Darwin saw it, the Yamaná (or Yahgan) of the Beagle Channel – naked except for a loincloth and sealskin cape, paddling about in canoes with all their most important possessions, including bows, dogs and even fire – were 'subhuman beings…without spiritual life.'

Perhaps, had old Chuck spent more time on land rather than concocting his theories aboard ship, he might have observed that the Yamaná had a rich system of spiritual beliefs. They believed in a Supreme Being, Watauinewa, and had shamans who talked to spirits who the Yamaná believed controlled the weather and the hunt. Darwin might have seen that during the 'Kina' ceremony, in which boys are initiated to adulthood, the men dressed themselves as gods, painting their bodies with black carbon and the region's white and red clays, holding tall masks and dancing to represent the different spirits: Kina-Miami, the guardian; Tulema-Yaka, the tutor; Hani-Yaka, the energy giver.

North of the island's mountain range, another group held a similar ritual. The Selk'nam (or Ona to the Yamaná and, later, to the Europeans) believed in a Supreme Being, Temankel, and also believed that women once controlled the lands, keeping the men subordinate with clever sorcery. According to the story, the men learned of this ploy and decided the only way to gain control would be to kill all of the women except the youngest, and play the same game of fear. Thus the Hain ceremony was created, held within and around a conical tent that women were not allowed to approach, under penalty of death. Men painted their bodies using the same black carbon and red and white clays mixed with guanaco fat, and they created masks from the bark of trees. Boys went through the initiation process, learning about the different spirits as each zigzagged, striped or dotted body danced, leapt into the air and interpreted its symbolism, all the while instilling fear in the women and small children watching from afar. Spirits included Matan, the magic dancer and spirit of happiness; Kulan, the terrible vixen who descends from the sky, selects her man and then kidnaps him to make love to her; and Koshmenk, Kulan's jealous husband.

Russian anarchist Simón Radowitzky and author Ricardo Rojas.

On the upper floor of one hall is a display on Antarctic exploration. Perhaps the most worthwhile part of the museum is the exhibit containing incredibly detailed scale models of famous ships, spanning 500 years and providing a unique glimpse into the area's history. Informative pamphlets in English about this exhibit are available at reception. In the courtyard are the remains of the narrowest gauge freight train in the world, which transported the prisoners between town and their work stations.

Museo del Fin del Mundo

Built in 1903 for the territorial governor Manuel Fernández Valdés, this building became a branch of the Banco de la Nación up until 1978 when it was transformed into the Museo del Fin del Mundo (☎ 421863, Maipú & Rivadavia; US$5; open 3pm-8pm Mon-Sat, 10am-1pm & 3pm-8pm Mon-Sat in summer). Exhibits on Fuegian natural history, aboriginal life, the early penal colonies, and replicas of an early general store and bank are of moderate interest.

Glaciar Martial

A good hike from downtown leads to Glaciar Martial, from which one can enjoy the views of Ushuaia and the Beagle Channel, in fact, the views are possibly more impressive than the actual glacier. Take San Martín west and keep ascending as it zigzags (there are many hiker shortcuts) to the ski run 7km northwest of town. At this point either take the Aerosilla (US$6; open 10am-7pm) or walk another two hours. The weather is changeable, so take warm, dry clothing and sturdy footwear. Minivans leave from Maipú and

25 de Mayo every half hour from 10am to 6:30pm (US$5 roundtrip).

Historic Buildings

The tourist office distributes a city tour map with information on many of the historic houses around town. **Legislatura Provincial** (Provincial Legislature; 1894) was the governor's official residence at Maipú 465. The century-old **Iglesia de la Merced**, at Av Maipú and Don Bosco, was built with convict labor. **Casa Beban** *(Av Malvinas Argentinas & Pluschow; free; open 10am-8pm Tues-Fri, 4pm-8pm weekends)* was built using parts ordered from Sweden. At the time of its construction, in 1911, it was the most ambitious construction project in town. Today the house hosts local art exhibits.

Activities

Hiking Hiking possibilities should not be limited to the national park; the entire mountain range behind Ushuaia, with its lakes and rivers, is a hiker's high. However, many trails are poorly marked or not marked at all; some hikers who have easily scurried uphill have gotten lost trying to find the trail back down.

The Club Andino Ushuaia (☎ 422335, e cau@tierradelfuego.org.ar, Fadul 50, open 3pm-10pm weekdays) sells a comprehensive trekking, mountaineering and mountain biking guidebook with rough maps and plenty of trail description (in Spanish). The club occasionally organizes hikes and can link parties with hiking guides.

Compañía de Guías de Patagonia is another excellent source of information and organizes treks. Travel agencies Témpanos Viajes and All Patagonia also represent them; see Organized Tours for contact information.

An easy one-day hike to consider accesses Laguna Esmeralda from the Altos del Valle ski resort (Pasarela buses drop off and pick up near the trailhead.) A multi-day trek worth asking about is the Sendero de Lucas Bridges, first created by Lucas Bridges in 1902 to connect the estancias Harberton and Via Monte.

Club Andino strongly encourages unguided trekkers to report with them before heading out. In an emergency situation call the Civil Guard (☎ 103, 22108).

Skiing Ski resorts string the nearby mountains – all accessed from RN 3 – with both downhill and cross-country options. The season runs from June to mid-September, although only early July is really busy.

The largest resort is Cerro Castor (☎ 1560-5595), 27km from Ushuaia, with 15 slopes spanning 400 hectares. Rentals are available for skis, boards, blades and cross-country skis. At the summit is a nice place to chill and have afternoon tea.

Another large area, Altos del Valle (☎/fax 422234, e gatocuruchet@hotmail.com), 19km from Ushuaia, is known for breeding Siberian and Alaskan huskies. In addition to downhill skiing, it has good cross-country and snowshoeing areas, with full rentals. Other well-equipped venues with good cross-country terrain include Tierra Mayor (☎ 437454), 22km from town; Las Cotorras (☎ 499300), 25km from town; also with ice skating, and Haruwen (☎/fax 431099), 37km from town.

For a quick swoosh near town, Club Andino runs cross-country and downhill slopes only 3km and 5km away. Centro de Deportes Invernales Glaciar Martial (☎ 421423, 423340) is 7km northwest of town, with downhill runs well suited for beginners. Rental equipment is available at each site for around US$30 per day.

Ushuaia's biggest ski event is the annual Marcha Blanca, a symbolic re-creation of San Martín's historic August 17 crossing of the Andes; it starts from Las Cotorras and climbs to Paso Garibaldi.

Pasarela and Alvarez buses run shuttles (US$10) from the corner of 25 de Mayo and Maipú to the ski centers along RN 3 three times daily. Each center also provides its own transportation from downtown Ushuaia.

Organized Tours

Ushuaia is so hell-bent on being a tourism capital that it has bent the hell out of every possible activity by adding a big 'organized

The Frozen South

Once the lone continent barely touched by humans, Antarctica is now (for better or for worse) becoming a trendy tourist destination, thanks in large part to Russian research vessels that have turned to tourism. In the summer of 1999-2000, 120 tourist ships voyaged to the frozen south (with 17 vessels reaching the shores), a jump from just 27 tourist ships the previous season. Of those, 75% left from Ushuaia. What this means to anyone suddenly tantalized by the possibility of hopping on board a ship to Antarctica is that such a voyage is not at all out of the question – so long as you've got two or three weeks to spare. Price is another consideration. Tour companies charge anywhere from US$3000 to US$10,000, although some do allow walk-ons, which can cost as little as US$2000.

Some voyages take in Falkland Islands and South Georgia; others go just to the Antarctic Peninsula, while others focus on retracing historic expeditions. The season runs from November to mid-February. The Oficina Antarctica Infuetur (☎ 424431, fax 430694, e antartida@tierradelfuego.ml.org), on Ushuaia's waterfront Muelle Comercial, serves as a clearinghouse for Antarctic tours; it's open 8am to 5pm weekdays; weekends only if there are boats. Tourist agencies All Patagonia, Antartur and Rumbo Sur, all in Ushuaia, handle last-minute bookings for many of the vessels.

Operators arranging Antarctic tours include:

Adventure Associates (☎ 61-2-9389 7466, w www.adventureassociates.com), 197 Oxford Street Mall, Bondi Junction, Sydney NSW 2022, Australia

Adventure Network International (☎ 561-237-2359, 866-395-6664), 4800 N Federal Highway, Suite 307D, Boca Raton, FL 33431, USA

(☎ 44-1494-671-808, w www.adventure-network.com), Canon House, 27 London End, Beaconsfield, Buckinghamshire HP9 2HN, England

(☎ 061-247-735), 935 Arauco, Punta Arenas, Chile

Mountain Travel-Sobek (☎ 510-527-8100 or 888-687-6235, w www.mtsobek.com), 6420 Fairmount Ave, El Cerrito, CA 94530, USA

Quark Expeditions (☎ 203-656-0499, 800-356-5699, w www.adventure-network.com), 980 Post Rd, Darien, CT 06820, USA

(☎ 44-1494-464-080), Crendon St 19A, High Wycombe, Bucks, HP13 6LJ, England

Those who do head to Antarctica should pick up Lonely Planet's *Antarctica* guidebook, which has details on many possible voyages plus tons of background information on the great frozen continent.

---

tour' stamp to each one. These are further categorized as 'conventional' or 'nonconventional' tours, the latter covering trekking, horseback riding, canoeing, mountain biking and backroading. Most of the activities take in Parque Nacional Tierra del Fuego or Lago Fagnano. The key is to line up activities with agencies that know how to have fun. (Those staying in backpacker lodging may want to check out what's on offer there.) Luckily, agents around town are noncompetitive; in other words, they'll refer you to another agency that will better fit your desires. The recommendations below barely skim the surface of what's in town.

Canal Fun & Adventure (☎ 435777, e mail@canalfun.com, Rivadavia 82), run by hip young guys, adds a good level of fun and thrill to their trips. These include trips through the park in inflatable canoes, off-roading to Lago Fagnano (US$80, 8 hours) or kayaking at Lago Roca, going along the Río Lapataia (US$40, 6 hours). All trips include snacks or meals and drinks.

Compañía de Guías de Patagonia (☎ 432642, 1561-8426) organizes full-day treks up Cerro del Medio (excellent views, US$66), to Glaciar Vinciguerra (ice-hiking and climbing, US$66), and two-day high mountain treks to Cerro Alvear (spending the night on a glacier, US$170). They will also guide custom-designed treks. You can get more information on them at All Patagonia (☎ 430725, e allpat@satlink.com, Juana Fadul 26) or Témpanos Viajes (☎ 436020, e tempvia@infovia.com.ar, San Martín 626).

Agents of the more 'conventional' sort, who organize glitzy boat rides and Antarctic expeditions, include Rumbo Sur (☎ 421139, e informes@rumbosur.com.ar, San Martín 342) and All Patagonia (see previous paragraph).

Turismo de Campo (☎ 437451, e info@turismodecampo.com, 25 de Mayo 76) organizes light trekking and sailing trips along the Beagle Channel, and it represents Antarctic-trip leader Quark, whose nine-day expeditions run from US$2500 to US$4000. They also represent Estancia Rolito near Río Grande. Tolkar (☎ 431412, Roca 157) is another helpful agent worth checking out.

Popular boat trips – with destinations such as the sea lion colony at Isla de los Lobos, and Isla de Pájaros, with its extensive cormorant colonies – leave from the Muelle Turístico (tourist jetty) on Maipú between Lasserre and Roca.

Tres Marías Excursiones (☎/fax 421897, Muelle Turístico or Romero 514), charges US$45 for a four-hour morning or afternoon excursion on the Beagle Channel; they are the only outfitter with permission to land on Isla 'H' in Isla Bridges, which has shellmounds, a rock cormorant colony and the occasional king penguin. Or try the historic *Barracuda* (☎ 436453), which chugs to Faro Les Eclaireurs and Isla de los Lobos (US$25, 3 hours).

For weeklong sailboat excursions around Cape Horn or the Cordillera Darwin (about US$1200 per person), contact travel agencies such as All Patagonia or Témpanos Viajes.

Places to Stay

In the summer high season, especially January and February, demand is very high and no one should arrive without reservations. The tourist office posts a list of available accommodations outside after closing time.

Budget The free *Camping Municipal (8km west of town on RN 3)*, en route to Parque Nacional Tierra del Fuego, has minimal facilities but an attractive setting.

La Pista del Andino (☎ 435890, Alem 2873) Sites US$5 per person. Located at the Club Andino's ski area, this place is far more central but still a steep uphill walk, although it offers the first transfer free. It has a bar-restaurant with good atmosphere, but could use more showers and toilets.

Camping Río Tristen Sites US$5 per tent (2 people). This campground, 33km east of Ushuaia at the Haruwen winter-sports center, has a dozen sites, with bathrooms and showers.

Hostal St Christopher (☎ 430062, e hostel_christopher@yahoo.com, Deloqui 636) Dorm beds US$10 per person. Large dorm rooms (with heaters, thin mattresses and bedding) can get noisy, and when filled to capacity, the bathrooms are taxed to the max. But the welcoming and gregarious owners do a fine job of rounding up groups to explore nearby areas. Kitchens are well stocked and tea or coffee always available. Informative brochures are available in several languages.

Torre al Sur Hostel (☎ 430745, e torresur@impsat1.com.ar, Gobernador Paz 1437) Dorm beds US$10/12 HI-/non-HI members. Perched high on a hill, colorful Torre has some fabulous views to go with its caring management. Some travelers, however, caution of cramped and very noisy rooms – don't expect privacy. The crowning glory is the wraparound window tower room, with grand vistas.

El Refugio del Mochilero (☎ 436129, e refmoch@infovia.com.ar, 25 de Mayo 241) Dorm beds US$13 per person. By far the best quality hostel, you'll find good mattresses in cozy but not cramped rooms, plus comfortable kitchen and dining areas, all expertly and artistically lit.

Mid-Range At *Family Basily Sampieri (☎ 423213, e fbasily@quasarlab.com.ar,*

Gobernador Valdez 323) there's only one room, which costs US$20/30 as a single/ double. One of the joys of travel is meeting people who bring out the best in an area, and the Basily Sampieri family does just that. There room's mattress isn't the most comfortable, but for the lucky lodgers, the hospitality is huge (and breakfast is included). English, French and Italian are spoken. In the high season, they also have a 5-person cabin for US$55.

Familia Piatti (☎ 15-613485, **e** jhpiatti@ yahoo.com, Bahía Paraíso 812, Bosque del Faldeo) Singles/doubles US$25/40. Hidden in a wooded neighborhood, this B&B has a couple of rooms plus a great deck on which to relax. Hiking trails nearby lead up the mountains, and the house dog will make sure you don't get lost. The owners speak English and can arrange transport.

Hostería Mustapic (☎ 421718, Piedrabuena 230) Singles/doubles US$30/40 with shared bath, US$35/50 with private bath. Most places try to sell you on the lobby, but in quirky Croat Mustapic, the best part is the top floor – a square fishbowl of a room with views incredible enough to distract from the gaudy 1960s furniture. Rooms with shared bath are light and clean; showers throughout are designed for stick figures. Breakfast costs US$5 and there's no kitchen use.

Alakaluf (☎ 436-705, **e** alakalufes@ arnet.com.ar, San Martín 146) Singles/ doubles US$35/45 with private bath and breakfast. Family-owned and operated Alakaluf sports rooms with harbor and mountain views and allows use of kitchen. It's a good deal, located in the heart of town, and it fills up fast; book early.

Residencial Fernández (☎ 421192, fax 424784, Onachaga 72) Singles/doubles US$35/45, US$15 shared bath. This family-owned place has some charm but sagging beds. Breakfast is an additional US$4.

Linares B&B (☎ 423594, **e** linaresd@ infovia.com.ar, Deloqui 1522) Singles/ doubles US$38/48, suites US$55, with private bath & breakfast. Fragile trinkets and antiques give an air of formality to this B&B, but the rooms are large and comfortable and

some have spectacular views. Taking breakfast while watching the sunrise color the harbor is surely the winning ticket here.

Hotel Maitén (☎ 422733, fax 422745, 12 de Octubre 140) Singles/doubles US$35/50. South of downtown, Maitén is a quiet well-run inn with boxy rooms and a sensible 1970s-style living room. A continental breakfast is included.

Hospedaje Malvinas (☎ 422626, fax 424482, **e** hotelmalvinas@arnet.com.ar, Deloquí 615) Singles/doubles US$50/60. Warmly recommended, Malvinas offers pleasant carpeted rooms, some with great harbor views and all with good bathrooms. Guillermo, the owner and a serious sailor, has incorporated the coziness of a sailboat's galley in the design, especially in the breakfast nook/pub.

Posada Fin del Mundo (☎ 437345, Gobernador Valdez 281) US$55/60. In a grand house, rooms at this posada are mini-studios with kitchenettes. The attractive living room and dining area are comfortable places offering a sense of home.

Aldea Nevada Cabañas (☎/fax 422851, Luis Martial 1430) US$90 for 2-4 persons, US$110 for 6 persons. 3-night minimum. Log cabins line up in a lenga forest 2.5km from town center, each one expertly designed with kitchen, wood stoves, plenty of space and lots of charm.

Top End Singles/doubles cost US$60/70 at *Hotel Cabo de Hornos* (☎ 422187, fax 422313, **e** cabodehornos@arnet.com.ar, Av San Martín at Rosas). A boxy study in beige, the only thing that lightens up this place is the great collection of paper money. Firm mattresses and wooden blinds that block out all light do lend themselves to sound sleep.

Hotel Cap Polonio (☎ 422140, fax 422131, **e** cappolonio@tierradelfuego.org.ar, Av San Martín 476) Singles/doubles US$85/105. In the heart of downtown, Cap Polonio, named after the first German boat to bring in tourists, is geared more for the elite traveler, but is a well-staffed safe choice with posh rooms. A toast-centric buffet breakfast is included.

Hostal del Bosque (☎ 421723, fax 430783, e aparth@iname.com, Magallanes 709) Singles/doubles US$90/110. A good choice, del Bosque has mini-apartments with kitchenettes, tables and sofas, but no fans – smelly food not allowed. Its hillside location offers some good views.

Hotel del Glaciar (☎ 430640, fax 430636, e glaciar@infovia.com.ar, Av Luis Fernando Martial 2355) Singles/doubles US$169/179 with a glacier view, US$179/189 with bay view, US$44 less in low season. Catering more to the convention crowd, with oversized foyers, fireplaces and bars, Glaciar offers tip-top service and cushy rooms with ample windows.

Places to Eat

Tía (12 de Octubre & Karukinka) US$2. This large supermarket contains a cafeteria serving dirt-cheap daily specials or pastas for US$6 per kilo; don't expect excellence, however.

Ushuaia Shopping (☎ 436868, San Martín 788) US$3-10. This shopping arcade eatery is one of the better choices for cheap, good-quality meals. A US$9 menu includes three courses and coffee.

El Turco (☎ 424711, San Martín 1440) US$4.50-13. Fast, attentive service, large portions and a hint of elegance make El Turco a local favorite. Pizzas, minutas, fish and pasta are all available and well prepared. El Turco also runs a cheap take-out joint (US$10 for two pizzas, US$7.50 for a dozen empanadas) at Gobernador Paz & Juan Fadul (☎ 443360).

Food Garden (☎ 424808, San Martín 312) US$3.50-7. A comfortable spot with good informal fare such as sandwiches, draft beer and large breakfasts. Upstairs is a pre-disco bar bordering on glitzy camp.

Barcleit 1912 (☎ 433422, Fadul 148) US$5-10. Rickety and historic, this 1912 gem was home to the early pioneering Fadul family, known for their generous handouts of food to other pioneers and to the Selk'nam. The US$8 menu is the best deal; minutas aren't bad, but they aren't mind-blowing either.

La Rueda (☎ 436540, San Martín 193) US$8-15. Of the parrillas along this strip, this one comes recommended.

La Casa de los Mariscos (☎ 421928, San Martín 232) US$5-13. Open till midnight. Small, simple and decorated with gingham, La Casa prepares some mighty fine fish and shellfish dishes, such as *trucha fuegina*, trout bathed in a creamy sauce with calamari.

Tía Elvira (☎ 424721, Maipú 349) US$11-17. Elvira has a stellar reputation for fish preparations. Before eating, take a gander at the small museum lining the entrance hall.

Volver (☎ 423977, Maipú 37) US$7-15. Perhaps the best choice in town for seafood dishes (especially centolla soup), Volver is also worth a visit for its history. Built by the second chief of the prison (and later police chief), the building housed several prisoners after the Ushuaia prison closed. Later, Rafaela Ishton, the last pure Ona, moved in, remaining until 1985. You can still see the newspapers that were used as insulation or wallpaper, and every nook holds some historic knickknack.

Café de la Esquina (☎ 423676, San Martín 621) US$3.50-9. The best place to scope out the newest flock of tourists in town, de la Esquina is wall-to-wall, floor-to-ceiling windows. The kitchen creates some knockout sandwiches and cakes. It's also a good place for breakfast.

Kaupé (☎/fax 422704, Roca 470) US$8-15. Chef Ernesto Vivian's creations, served in an intimate house, are sublime reminders that haute cuisine reaches even the most southerly global corners. Try parchment-baked seabass with julienned leeks, or chicken Bengali in a buttery curry sauce with mashed potatoes. Or simply come in the evening to enjoy some of Argentina's best wines while taking in a brilliant view.

Chez Manu (☎ 432253, Luis Martial 2135) US$14-22. Chef Emmanuel accents regional cuisine with a French touch. Try salmon *en brioche* with a leek fondue or a mixed plate of cold *fruits de mer*. The three-course lunch (US$18-22) is probably the best deal if you want to splurge. Chez Manu is 2km from the town center heading toward the glacier.

Entertainment

The locals recommend *Orielle Antoine* (☎ *422355, Lasserre & San Martín*) for an evening of drinks and chatter. For late-night dancing, head to *Ozono* (*San Martín 45*).

First-run movies are shown in *Cine Pakawaia* (☎ *436500, Yaganes & Gobernador Paz*), the Presidio's fully restored hangar-style theater. Hidden behind the gymnasium *Casa de la Cultura* (☎ *422417, Av Malvinas Argentinas & 12 de Octubre*) hosts live music shows and art courses.

Shopping

Renata Rafalak (*Piedrabuena 25*) Fragile and impressive Yamaná and Selk'nam ritual masks made of lenga bark are carefully constructed and painted in this small workshop. Arguably the most unique souvenirs in town, they range from key-chain small (US$5) to impressive full-sized masks (US$80 and up).

Getting There & Away

Air The new airport is about 4km southwest of downtown, on the peninsula across from the waterfront. Airport taxes, which are steep, are paid at the airport.

Southern Winds (☎ 437073, Maipú 237), Aerolíneas Argentinas (☎ 421091, Roca 116) and LAPA (☎ 432112, 25 de Mayo 64) all fly to Río Gallegos (US$54-68) and Buenos Aires (US$166-262) daily. LAPA and Aerolíneas Argentinas fly to El Calafate (US$80-100), as does cheaper LADE (☎ 421123, San Martín 542). Routes and schedules always change, so check with the offices.

Chilean airline Aerovías DAP flies Monday and Wednesday to Punta Arenas (US$100), and does a two-hour flyover tour of Cabo de Hornos (US$260).

Aeroclub Ushuaia (☎ 421717, 421892) offers charter tours to Puerto Williams, Chile (US$100) three times a week; the price is for roundtrip only (you could opt not to fly back, but you would still pay for the return). Many travel agents, such as Turismo de Campo or Témpano Viajes, can arrange bookings.

Bus Tecni-Austral buses for Río Grande (US$15, 3½ hours) leave daily from the Tolkar office (☎ 431408, Roca 157) at 7am and 4pm, stopping at Tolhuin (US$6, 2½ hours) en route. The bus to Punta Arenas (US$40, 10-12 hours) departs the same office at 7am Monday to Saturday during high season, three times weekly in low season. Lider buses (☎ 436421) run from Gobernador Paz 921 to Río Grande six times daily Monday to Saturday, four times on Sunday.

Tolkeyen (☎ 437073), at the Southern Winds office at Av Maipú 237, goes to Río Grande at 8am and 7pm.

At the foot of 25 de Mayo at Av Maipú, Transportes Pasarela run shuttles to Lago Esmeralda (US$10), Lago Escondido (US$20) and Lago Fagnano (US$25), leaving at 10am and returning at 3:30pm. If you are planning to stay overnight, ask to pay just one way (more likely if there are many people traveling) and arrange for pick-up. Both Transportes Eben-Ezer and Kaupen offer similar service and leave from the same location.

For transportation to Parque Nacional Tierra del Fuego, see the Getting There & Away entry for the park.

Boat At the time of research, plans for boat transport to Puerto Williams were still stalled. Many charter boats anchor in the harbor of Ushuaia and some will take passengers on board for a fee (usually around US$50) the next time they are heading out. Agencies such as Témpanos Viajes (see Organized Tours) link travelers with yachts but charge extra. Agencia Marítima, next to the LAPA office, tracks maritime transport – possibly useful information for the skilled at persuading captains to let them on board.

Fewer than a dozen private yachts charter trips to Cabo de Hornos, Antarctica and, more seldom, South Georgia Island. These trips must be organized well in advance (see travel agents), and they are pricey – the most popular charter, rounding Cape Horn, costs US$880 to US$1400 for seven days. One recommended charter is the reformed racing yacht *Fernande* (☎/fax 15-561080, **e** pbgrinberg@yahoo.fr), captained by Pascal Grinberg. His 30 years of sailing ensure skill and safety at the helm, while the on-deck ambience is mellow and unpretentious.

The MV *Terra Australis* runs elite three-day sightseeing cruises to Punta Arenas, catering mostly to mature travelers. The cruise stops at some otherwise inaccessible spots, but time alone or hiking opportunities are limited; focus is more on group tours and nature talks. See travel agents for details.

Getting Around
Cab rides from the airport are about US$5, and there's bus service along Av Maipú. DTT Cycles Sport (San Martín 1258) rents bikes.

Including insurance, car rental rates for small vehicles average around US$47 per day plus US$0.30 per km, or US$85 with 150km; for a 4x4, US$100 plus US$0.60 per km or US$170 with free km. The best rates are with Cardos (☎ 436388, San Martín 845) and Rastro (☎ 422021, San Martín 1547). Also check out Avis/Tagle Rent A Car (☎ 433084, San Martín 1195) and Localiza, (☎ 430739, San Martín 1222). Many places don't charge for drop-off in other parts of Argentine Tierra del Fuego – inquire about policies.

PARQUE NACIONAL TIERRA DEL FUEGO
Easily accessed from Ushuaia, Parque Nacional Tierra del Fuego *(12km west of Ushuaia via RN 3; admission US$5; open daily)*, Argentina's first coastal national park, extends 63,000 hectares from the Beagle Channel in the south to beyond Lago Kami/Fagnano in the north. However, only about 2000 hectares in the southern edge of the park is open to the public, with a miniscule system of short, easy trails that are cut out more for day-tripping families than backpacking trekkers. The rest of the park is protected as a *reserva estricta*. Despite this, a few hikes along the bays and rivers, or through dense native forests of evergreen coihue, *canelo* and deciduous lenga, are worthwhile. For truly spectacular color, come in the fall when hillsides of ñire burst out in red.

Plenty of bird life graces the park, especially along the coastal zone. Keep an eye out for condors, albatross, cormorants, gulls, terns, oystercatchers, grebes, kelp geese and the comical, flightless, orange-billed steamer ducks. Other beasts you may spot are the European rabbit and the North American beaver, both of which have wreaked ecological havoc. Come in the early morning or evening to spot the little loggers. Gray and red foxes, enjoying the abundance of rabbits, may also be seen.

Hiking
Just 3km from the entrance gate, the **Senda Pampa Alta** (5km) heads up a hill, passing a beaver dam along the way. Views from the top are impressive. A quick 300m farther leads to a trail paralleling the Río Pipo and some waterfalls. A more popular saunter is along the **Senda Costera** (6.5km), accessed from the end of the Bahía Ensenada road. This trail meanders along the bay, once home to Yamaná. Keep an eye out for shell middens, now covered in grass. The trail ends at the road, which leads 1.2km further to the **Senda Hito XXIV** (5km), a level trail through lenga forest along the northern shore of Lago Roca; this trail terminates at an unimposing Argentine/Chilean border marker. **Senda Cerro Guanaco** (8km) starts at the same trailhead, but climbs up a 970m 'mountain' to reach a great view spot.

After running 3242km from Buenos Aires, RN 3 takes its southern bow at gorgeous Bahía Lapataia. **Mirador Lapataia** (1km), connecting with **Senda Del Turbal** (2km), winds through lenga forest to access this highway terminus. Other walks in this section are the self-guided nature trail **Senda Laguna Negra** (950m), through peat bogs, and the **Senda Castorera** (800m), along which beaver dams and possibly beavers themselves can be spotted in the ponds.

Places to Stay
Campgrounds are the only lodging in the park. Most are free, lack services, and get crowded, which means sites can and do get filthy. *Camping Ensenada* is 16km from the entrance and nearest the Costera trail;

Camping Río Pipo is 6km from the entrance and easily accessed by either the road to Cañadon del Toro or by the Pampa Alta trail. *Camping Las Bandurrias*, *Camping Laguna Verde* and *Camping Los Cauquenes* are on the islands in Río Lapataia.

The only fee-based campground, 9km from the entrance, is *Camping Lago Roca* (US$5 per person). It's also the only one that has hot showers, a confitería and a small (expensive) grocery. However, there's plenty of room in the park to rough it at wild sites. Note that water at Lago Roca is not potable; boil it before using.

Getting There & Away

Buses leave from the corner of Maipú and 25 de Mayo several times daily from 9am to 6pm, returning approximately every two hours from 10am to 7pm. The roundtrip fare is US$10, and you need not return the same day.

The most touristy – and possibly the slowest – way to get to the park is with 'El Tren del Fin de Mundo' (☎ 431600, fax 437696), which leaves from the Estación del Fin de Mundo, 8km west of town.

Hitching to the park is feasible, but many cars will already be packed.

ESTANCIA HARBERTON

Historic Estancia Harberton (☎ 422742, fax 422743; open Oct 15-Apr 15) was founded in 1886 by Thomas Bridges. It was the first estancia in Tierra del Fuego, and it contains the oldest house on the island. Bridges' son Lucas made the location famous in his memoir of life among the Yahgan, *The Uttermost Part of the Earth*. It is now owned and run by the Goodalls, direct descendents of the Bridges.

Harberton is a working station, although only about 1500 sheep remain on 20,000 hectares. The location is splendid and the history alluring, but since most of the estancia is off-limits and other parts ill-kept, the value of spending much time here is a debatable. A **self-guided tour** takes in the family cemetery and a walk through a garden area where foliage names are given in Yahgan, Selknam and Spanish. There's also a replica of a Yahgan dwelling.

Worth the trip is the impressive **Acatushún Bone Museum**, created by Natalie Prosser Goodall, a North American biologist who married into the family. Stressing the region's marine mammals, the museum has more than 2000 mammal and 2000 bird specimens inventoried; among the rarest specimens is a Hector's beaked whale. Much of this vast inventory was found at Bahía San Sebastián, north of Río Grande, where an up to 11km difference between high and low tide leaves animals stranded. The museum is also a private center for biological and historical research and offers work-study programs.

The Goodalls permit *camping* at Río Lasifashaj, Río Varela and Río Cambaceres, free with permission. In the future, they may also offer B&B accommodations in one of the old workers houses.

Harberton is 80km east of Ushuaia via RN 3 and RC-j.

Getting There & Away

Shuttles leave from the base of 25 de Mayo at Av Maipú in Ushuaia at 9am, returning at 3pm (US$30 roundtrip, 1½ hours).

ESTANCIA MOAT

Another 30km east from Estancia Harberton at the end of RC-j is Estancia Moat, owned by descendents of the Anglican Reverend Lawrence, where the blustering winds, twisted trees and endless horizon conjure tip-of-the-world isolation. From here you can see the three small islands of Lennox, Nueva and Picton, which nearly

brought Argentina and Chile to war in 1978; however, papal intervention defused the situation and the islands remain in Chile's possession. There's no public transportation to Estancia Moat, but tours to Harberton may include it in the itinerary.

PUERTO WILLIAMS (CHILE)
☎ 61 • pop 1800

Somewhere along the way, the Chilean town of Puerto Williams got overlooked in all of Ushuaia's 'end of the world' hype. But anyone who visits this outpost will soon know which place can truly lay claim to the title. On Isla Navarino, directly across the Beagle Channel from Argentine Tierra del Fuego, the ramshackle naval settlement isn't much to look at – sterile gray military barracks and makeshift corrugated iron houses, with dogs picking at litter along gravel streets. The center of town is little more than a concrete slab. But above, below and beyond Puerto Williams is some of the most breathtaking scenery around. Within minutes from town you can be deep in lenga forests dripping in old man's beard. Trails lead past beaver dams, bunkers and army trenches as they head deeper into forests and up into the mountains. The townspeople make this one of the most endearing places in Tierra del Fuego.

Missionaries in the mid-19th century and fortune-seekers during the 1890s gold rush established a permanent European presence here. Today it's an official port of entry for yachts en route to Chilean Cape Horn and Antarctica. Near the entrance to the military quarters is the original bow of the *Yelcho*, which rescued Ernest Shackleton's Antarctic expedition from Elephant Island in 1916.

Information
The Centro Comercial near the main roundabout has call centers and the post office. Also in the Centro Comercial, Turismo SIM (☎/fax 621150, e sim@ entelchile.net) offers plentiful information about the island. Money exchange (US cash only) or Visa advances are possible at Banco de Chile; there is no ATM.

Things to See & Do
The **Museo Martín Gusinde** (☎ 621043, US$2, open 10am-1pm & 3pm-6pm weekdays, 3pm-6pm weekends), honoring the German priest and ethnographer who worked among the Yahgans from 1918 to 1923, has mediocre exhibits on natural history and ethnography.

Omora, the most southerly ethnobotanical park in Latin America (and something of a work-in-progress), contains trails showing regional foliage described in Yamaná, Latin nomenclature and Spanish. Take the road to the right of the Virgin altar 4km towards Puerto Navarino. Entrance fees help the foundation further develop the park.

An excellent lookout point, **Cerro Bandera**, can be reached via the beginning of the 'Dientes Circuit.' The trail ascends steeply through the mossy forest to a sparse alpine terrain and great vistas. For details on trekking in the 'Dientes de Navarino' refer to Lonely Planet's *Trekking in Patagonia* guide. Treks to some of the old missionary houses along the western corner of the island are being developed to promote environmentally sound tourism and protect the houses from further destruction. Consult Turismo SIM or Refugio Coirón for details on the treks.

Many of the local lodgings can arrange tours of surrounding areas. For yacht tours to Antarctica and around the Beagle Channel, as well as trekking, climbing and riding expeditions, talk to Turismo SIM.

Places to Stay
In the high season, some families offer rooms; check with SIM on the current status.

Refugio Coirón (☎ 621150, e coiron@ simltda.com, Ricardo Maragano 168) Dorm beds US$13 per person. Catering to a backpacker clientele, Coirón's welcoming atmosphere makes it a top place to swap stories with other hikers. Rooms are shared, as is the one bathroom. Kitchen privileges and a large communal table help promote group meals.

Residencial Onashaga (☎ 621081, Upachun 290) Dorm beds US$16 with breakfast, shared bath. While the bunks are rickety, there are plenty of them. The owners are charming, and they offer tours to their estancia near Bahía Eugenia. A converted ship's exhaust pipe acts as a roaring furnace.

Residencial Pusaki (☎ 621020, fax 621-116, Piloto Pardo 242) Rooms US$12 with shared bath and breakfast. Small, attractive and cozy, owners Tano and Pati offer clean, warm rooms and pleasant family surroundings.

Residencial Temuco (☎ 621113) Rooms US$13/26 shared/private bath with breakfast. The rooms don't have heat, but the beds have electric blankets. Beware the stuffed beaver 'Rambo,' once the family pet. Guests are allowed to use the kitchen and laundry facilities.

Places to Eat

Diente de Navarino (☎ 621074, in the plaza) US$5. A huge 'fisherman's lunch' will fill you up fast at this eatery/bar. Come for food at lunchtime and beers at dinner with the rowdy crowd.

Hostería Camblor (☎ 621033) US$3-8. With great views overlooking the town, Camblor is a good spot for lunch or dinner and serves the best *pan amasado* in Puerto Williams. Thursday nights the place turns into a discotheque.

There are a few supermarkets in town, **Simon & Simon** being the best of the lot, with fresher veggies and great pastries.

Entertainment

Club de Yates Micalvi down at the harbor, serves drinks (US$1.50-8) and crab sandwiches (US$5), but the real reason to go here is to absorb one of the best bar atmospheres in Tierra del Fuego. Sailors and Antarctic expeditioners from around the world hold forth amid souvenirs of former adventurers, vying to outdo one another's stories, which grow louder and grander as the night progresses.

Pingüino Pub (Centro Commercial). Throw down a couple of beers and handfuls of peanuts before heading to **Disco Extasis**, across from Residencial Temuco, on a Friday or Saturday night.

Getting There & Away

Aerovías DAP flies to Punta Arenas Tuesday, Thursday and Saturday (US$67). Seats are limited and advance reservations are essential. DAP flights to Antarctica make a brief stopover here.

The *Crux Australis* ferry leaves Fridays at 7pm for the 38-hour trip to Punta Arenas (US$120 including meals, US$150 for a bunk); be forewarned that passenger berths are small and the reclining Pullman seats not as comfortable as one might wish on a trip this long.

Regular connections between Puerto Williams and Ushuaia, on Argentine Tierra del Fuego, may resume at some point. For the most up-to-date information, ask at the Club de Yates or Turismo SIM.

Uruguay

Uruguay

Tranquil Uruguay is a classic political buffer between the South American megastates of Argentina and Brazil. From Buenos Aires, it's only a short hop across the Río de la Plata to the fascinating old town of Colonia and only a little farther to Montevideo, one of South America's most interesting capitals.

East of Montevideo, the sandy Atlantic beaches attract many Uruguayans and Argentines for summer holidays, but the less-frequented towns up the Río Uruguay, opposite northeastern Argentina, are also clean and attractive. Uruguay's hilly interior is agreeable but rarely visited gaucho country.

Known officially as the República Oriental del Uruguay (Eastern Republic of Uruguay, often abbreviated as ROU), the area was long called the *Banda Oriental,* or 'Eastern Shore,' of the River Plate, and Uruguayans sometimes refer to themselves as Orientales. The name Uruguay is from the Guaraní language; two possible translations of it are 'river of the water snails' and 'river of the wood-quail country.'

For much of the 20th century, foreigners considered Uruguay the 'Switzerland of South America,' but political and economic crises in the 1970s and 1980s undermined this favorable image. Today, as the recession gripping the region has deepened, many hotels have dropped prices in a drastic effort to stay afloat, resulting in some amazing bargains for travelers.

Highlights

- Montevideo – Marveling at the capital's wealth of 19th-century architecture
- Colonia – Wandering shady cobblestone streets in this colonial-era port town
- Punta del Este – Clubbing with the jet set and sunning on some of South America's most chic beaches
- Cabo Polonio – Trekking over massive sand dunes to get a look at the country's second-largest sea lion colony

Facts about Uruguay

HISTORY

Uruguay's aboriginal inhabitants were the Charrúa, a hunting-and-gathering people who also fished extensively. Hostile to outsiders, they discouraged settlement for more than a century by killing Spanish explorer Juan de Solís and most of his party in 1516. In any event, there was little to attract the Spanish who, in the early years of South American exploration, were mostly looking for gold and other quick riches.

In the 17th century, the Charrúa acquired the horse and prospered on wild cattle, eventually trading with the Spanish. Never numerous, they no longer exist as a definable tribal entity, though there remain some mestizo people in the interior along the Brazilian border.

European Colonization

The first Europeans on the Banda Oriental were Jesuit missionaries who settled near present-day Soriano, on the Río Uruguay. In 1680 the Portuguese established a beachhead at Nova Colônia do Sacramento, opposite Buenos Aires on the estuary of the Río de la Plata. As a fortress and contraband center, Colônia posed a direct challenge to Spanish authority, forcing the Spanish to build their own citadel at the sheltered port of Montevideo.

This rivalry between Spain and Portugal led eventually to Uruguayan independence. José Gervasio Artigas, Uruguay's greatest national hero, allied with the United Provinces of the River Plate against Spain, but was unable to prevent Uruguay's takeover by Brazil. Exiled to Paraguay, he inspired the famous '33 Orientales,' Uruguayan patriots under General Juan Lavalleja, who, with Argentine support, launched a campaign to liberate the Banda from Brazilian control. In 1828, after three years' struggle, a British-mediated treaty established Uruguay as a small independent buffer between the emerging continental powers.

Independence & Development

For most of the 19th century, Uruguay's independence was fragile, threatened politically and militarily by Argentina and Brazil, and economically by Britain. Federalist forces, supported by the Argentine dictator Rosas, besieged Montevideo from 1838 to 1851. From this period, Uruguay's two major political parties, the Blancos and the Colorados, can trace their origins as armed gaucho sympathizers of the Federalist and Unitarist causes.

British interest in the Banda, first aroused by that country's occupation of Montevideo in 1807, grew after independence. The UK had long been a market for hides, and in 1840 the British introduced merino sheep

for wool, while the Liebig Meat Extract Company of London (producers of Oxo, a cubed meat extract used as a soup base) opened a plant at Fray Bentos in 1864. In 1868 a British company began construction on the first railway to connect Montevideo with the countryside.

At the turn of the 20th century, Fray Bentos was also the site of the country's first *frigorífico*, an enormous Anglo-Uruguayan slaughterhouse and cold storage plant that is now an industrial museum. This increasing commercialization of one of the country's few abundant resources brought about the demise of the independent gaucho who, as in Argentina, became attached to estancias, whose boundaries soon became fixed by barbed wire. As elsewhere in Latin America, large landholdings *(latifundios)* became a way of life in Uruguay, and these made a major, if reluctant, contribution to the general welfare in the form of taxes.

José Batlle & Modernization

One of the most visionary politicians in Latin American history was Uruguay's José Batlle y Ordóñez, who devised the region's first comprehensive social welfare state. During two terms as president (1903–07 and 1911–15), Batlle (**bah**-zhay) implemented modern pensions, farm credits, unemployment compensation and eight-hour workdays. Despite his own strong, interventionist philosophy, he also sought to overcome the legacy of *caudillismo* (the strong-arm rule of the landowning elite) by constitutional reform. He created a collegial executive on the Swiss model, but this reform was unsuccessful. State economic intervention resulted in the nationalization of many industries, the creation of others and, for a while, unparalleled general prosperity.

To implement and finance his reforms, Batlle relied on the wealth provided by the rural livestock sector; by taxing exports he obtained the revenue to build the state. This worked temporarily, but as exports failed to grow, the welfare state became unsustainable.

Conservative economists have blamed the state for 'killing the goose that laid the

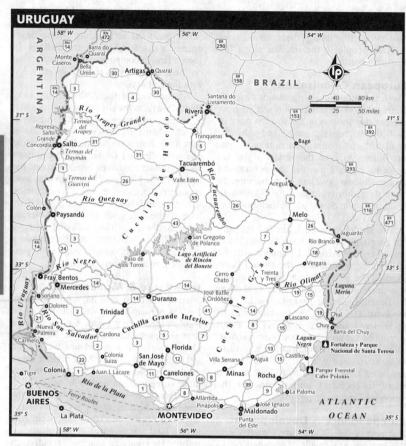

URUGUAY

golden egg' by unsustainably exploiting the pastoral sector for Montevideo's benefit and for political patronage. But it appears that even before the realization of the welfare state, landowners were slow to reinvest their earnings to increase productivity, preferring to squander their wealth in conspicuous consumption.

Economic Decline & Political Breakdown

From the mid-20th century, economic stagnation affected the entire country, but particularly Montevideo, which had become accustomed to middle-class prosperity. Batlle's collegiate presidency, which at one point resulted in a system of nine copresidents, proved calamitous. State-supported enterprise became riddled with patronage and corruption, and the economy was unable to support a pensioner class amounting to over 25% of the total workforce. By the mid-1960s this imbalance had given rise to serious political unrest, when Jorge Pacheco Areco became president.

Under Pacheco, the country slid into dictatorship. He outlawed leftist parties, closed newspapers and invoked state-of-siege measures because of guerrilla activity. The major guerrilla force was the Movimiento de Liberación Nacional (National Liberation Movement), more commonly known as the 'Tupamaros,' a clandestine socialist faction whose members were mostly from the urban middle class.

At first the Tupamaros enjoyed public support, but this eroded quickly as Uruguayans began to blame them for the Pacheco government's excesses, which included the dismissal of a police official who openly disapproved of torture. After the Tupamaros kidnapped and executed suspected CIA agent Dan Mitrione (an incident dramatized in Costa-Gavras' 1973 film *State of Siege*) and then engineered the escape of more than 100 of their comrades from prison, Pacheco placed the military in charge of the counterinsurgency.

In 1971 Pacheco's handpicked successor, Juan M Bordaberry, was elected. He gave control of the country to the army, which virtually eradicated the Tupamaros and went on to depose Bordaberry in 1976. From that time, the military effectively ruled Uruguay through a string of puppet presidents.

Military Dictatorship & Aftermath

The armed forces virtually eliminated free expression, occupying almost every position of importance in the country and ballooning the military budget to bolster 'national security.' Torture or threat of torture became routine; eventually more than 60,000 citizens were detained. The military established a political classification system that determined eligibility for public employment, subjected all political offenses to military courts, actively censored public libraries, and even required prior police approval for large family gatherings.

Attempting to institutionalize their political role, the armed forces drafted a constitution, but the electorate rejected it in a plebiscite in 1980 despite warnings that rejection would delay any return to civilian rule. Four years passed before voters could elect Colorado presidential candidate Julio María Sanguinetti under the Constitution of 1967. Though not a tool of the military, Sanguinetti won only because the military prohibited the candidacy of Blanco leader Wilson Ferreira Aldunate, a vocal and popular opponent of the dictatorship.

Sanguinetti's presidency, while unspectacular, seemed to indicate a return to Uruguay's democratic traditions. He did, however, support a controversial amnesty bill for military human-rights violations that was submitted to a referendum of all Uruguayans in April 1989. Despite serious misgivings, the amnesty passed. Later that year, Blanco presidential candidate Luis Lacalle succeeded Sanguinetti in a peaceful transition of power. Sanguinetti returned to office as the head of a coalition government in the elections of November 1994, and was succeeded in March 2000 by the outspoken Colorado Jorge Batlle Ibáñez, the grandnephew of José Batlle y Ordóñez and son of a former president.

Uruguay Today

Jorge Batlle almost immediately established himself as something of a maverick president. Decrying Uruguay's welfare state as cumbersome, he has begun implementing policies aimed at privatization and free trade. He has also demonstrated a refusal to acquiesce to the military. Upon taking office, he promised to search for the remains of dissidents who disappeared during the 1970s and '80s, a position strongly opposed by the army. In April 2000, he fired the chairman of his joint chiefs of staff, who had implied that a renewal of leftist extremism would necessitate military intervention in the government.

Batlle's presidency has met with significant challenges. A global economic slowdown has resulted in both skyrocketing unemployment and financial troubles. Uruguay's export sector, still dominated by agricultural products, was hit hard by an outbreak of foot-and-mouth disease in April 2001. In May the government announced a vaccination program aimed at eradicating the disease. This policy automatically prohibits the country from exporting its meat as 'vaccine-free' for at least four years, driving prices down and providing an additional shock to the reeling economy.

There seems to be little hope for immediate improvement, as Uruguay's major trading partners, Argentina and Brazil, are also undergoing economic crises. The government hopes that a more disciplined fiscal policy, in combination with repeated interest-rate cuts by the US Federal Reserve, can help pull the country out of debt and restore employment and prosperity.

GEOGRAPHY & CLIMATE

Though one of South America's smallest countries, Uruguay is large by European standards. Its area of 187,000 sq km is greater than England and Wales combined, or about the size of the US state of North Dakota. Lacking energy resources (except for a few hydroelectric sites), minerals, and commercial forests, the country's principal natural asset is agricultural land, which is abundant but less fertile than the Argentine Pampas. For the most part, the country's rolling topography is an extension of southern Brazil, with two main ranges of interior hills, the Cuchilla de Haedo, west of Tacuarembó, and the Cuchilla Grande, south of Melo, neither of which exceeds 500m in height. West of Montevideo, the level terrain resembles the Pampas, while the coastal area east of the capital has impressive beaches, dunes, and headlands. There are some large lagoons near the Atlantic border with Brazil, including the huge Laguna Merín.

The climate is mild, even in winter, and frosts are rare, although wind and rain can combine with cool temperatures to make things very chilly. Along the coast, daytime temperatures average 28°C in January and 15°C in June, while nighttime temperatures average 17°C in January and 7°C in June. Annual rainfall, evenly distributed throughout the year, averages about 1m over the whole country.

FLORA & FAUNA

Consisting mostly of grasslands and trees growing along watercourses, Uruguay's native vegetation does not differ greatly from that of the Argentine Pampas or southern Brazil. Some areas of palm savanna remain in the southeast along the Brazilian border, but only a very small percentage of the land is forested.

Wild animals of any size are uncommon, although the rhea (*ñandú*) can still be found in various areas the country. Uruguay's nature reserves are few and offer little out of the ordinary, although the seal colonies near Punta del Este and at Cabo Polonio make worthwhile visits.

GOVERNMENT & POLITICS

Uruguay's 1967 constitution established three separate branches of government. The president heads the executive branch, while the legislative Asamblea General (General Assembly) consists of a 99-seat Cámara de Diputados (Chamber of Deputies) and a 30-member Senado (Senate). Elections for these seats take place every five years. The Corte Suprema (Supreme Court) is the highest judicial power. Judges are nominated by the president and elected for 10-year terms by the Asamblea General. Administratively, Uruguay consists of 19 departments, which are organized much like the national government.

The electoral system is complex. While the legislature is chosen by proportional representation, each party may offer several presidential candidates. The winner is the candidate with the most votes of the party with the most votes. This means that the winner almost certainly will not win a majority (even within his or her own party) and may not even be the candidate with the most votes overall. In eight elections between 1946 and 1984, no winning candidate obtained more than 31% of the vote.

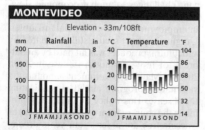

MONTEVIDEO

Elevation - 33m/108ft

The two traditional political parties are the Colorados (Reds), the inheritors of the liberal legacy of 'Batllismo,' and the generally more conservative Blancos (Whites). Sanguinetti, the first postmilitary president (1984-89), was a Colorado candidate, while his successor, Lacalle, who ruled until the 1994 elections, belonged to the Blancos. In March 2000, Jorge Batlle became president at the head of a Colorado-Blanco coalition that captured 54.1% of the vote. Whether the coalition of these traditional opponents will hold together for long remains an open question.

A third party, now the official opposition, is the Encuentro Progresista or Frente Amplio (Broad Front), a center-left coalition that controls the mayorship of Montevideo. Mayor Mariano Arana is one of the country's most powerful individuals outside the national government. Despite continuing links to leftists, the Frente Amplio has made surprising inroads into wealthier barrios such as Carrasco.

The major issues facing the government surround the current economic crisis. Establishing Uruguay's place in the Mercosur common market (see Economy), increasing the value of its exports and reducing unemployment are current key issues. The next elections will take place in late 2004.

ECONOMY

Despite being underpopulated and resource-poor, Uruguay still maintains one of South America's highest standards of living. Historically, the dominant and most productive part of the Uruguayan economy has been the pastoral sector. Cattle and sheep estancias occupy over three-quarters of the land, grazing over nine million cattle and 23 million sheep, but as the agricultural economy has stagnated from the estancieros' unwillingness to invest in improvements, the country has been unable to sustain the progressive social programs established by José Batlle. The low international price for wool, the country's primary export, has been a major factor in recent years, and foot-and-mouth disease has adversely affected meat prices. Only along the southwest littoral

does the country support intensive agriculture, although wet-rice cultivation has increased around Laguna Merín near the Brazilian border. Cropland occupies a relatively small area but makes a disproportionately high contribution to the economy.

Manufacturing is restricted mostly to the area around Montevideo. In part because of Batlle's commitment to encouraging self-sufficiency despite a tiny internal market, many state-supported industries produce inferior products at very high cost, surviving only because of protective tariffs. These industries are threatened by Jorge Batlle's commitment to the free market.

Among the economic activities traditionally controlled by the government are railroads, banking, insurance, telephone service, electricity, water supply, oil refining, fisheries and Montevideo's meat supply. This extensive control makes the country's economy the most state-dominated in Latin America. Social security pensions consume over half of public expenditure.

Tourism plays an increasingly important economic role, as the beaches east of Montevideo attract wealthy Argentines. In many ways, Uruguay is an economic satellite of both Brazil and Argentina, as well as a political buffer between these two major powers. The Mercosur common market, which went into effect in 1995, joined these two countries' economies with those of Paraguay and Uruguay; conceivably, by encouraging investment, this opening could reduce the emigration that has deprived Uruguay of many of its most capable young people, who seek employment in neighboring countries and overseas. Historically, Uruguay has been the most maddeningly bureaucratic of South American states, with a bloated and unmotivated state sector. Jorge Batlle looks to streamline this sector to bolster productivity and international competitiveness.

Hyperinflation has required the introduction of new currencies twice in the past 20 years. Inflation has fallen but is still high by US standards – for the 2000 calendar year, it was roughly 8.5%. Foreign debt is still a major concern, as Uruguay has one of Latin America's largest per capita burdens.

Historically, liberal banking laws have made Uruguay a destination for capital from neighboring countries, but usually only as a stop en route to Switzerland or the USA.

Uruguay's minimum wage is approximately US$95 per month. By March of 2001, unemployment had reached nearly 16%. In 2000, per capita annual income was about US$8600.

POPULATION & PEOPLE

With a population of just over 3.3 million, Uruguay is South America's smallest Spanish-speaking country. It is highly urbanized, with 90% of Uruguayans residing in cities. Nearly half live in Montevideo, leading one political scientist to call Uruguay a 'city-state,' even though, historically, the rural sector has produced most of the country's wealth. The second largest city, Paysandú, has fewer than 100,000 inhabitants.

By world standards, Uruguayans enjoy a high degree of social welfare. Infant mortality rates are low, and the life expectancy of 75 years matches Chile's as South America's highest, only slightly below that of the US and many Western European countries. Yet limited economic opportunity has forced more than half a million Uruguayans to live outside the country. The population growth rate is 0.8%, with a doubling time of about 90 years.

Most Uruguayans are predominantly of Spanish and Italian origin. European immigration has overwhelmed the small but still visible Afro-Uruguayan population of perhaps 100,000, descendants of slaves brought to the country in the 18th and 19th centuries. At one point slaves in Montevideo outnumbered the free populace.

EDUCATION

For more than a century, primary education has been free, secular, and compulsory, with per capita government expenditures among the highest in Latin America. Uruguay's literacy rate is among the foremost in the region, and enrollment in free secondary schools is also very high. Unfortunately, with the economy in a shambles, primary and secondary teachers are not paid a living wage and most make ends meet by working in private institutes. These are increasingly favored over public schools by those who can afford the fees, and educational standards appear to be slipping.

The Universidad de la República in Montevideo is the nation's only public university. For decades, a disproportionate number of students pursued degrees in law, medicine or architecture, resulting in a shortage of professionals in other fields. In recent years, however, computer science has attracted increasing numbers of young scholars.

ARTS

For such a small country, Uruguay has an impressive literary and artistic tradition. Uruguayans consider Montevideo to be as much the birthplace of the tango as Buenos Aires. Conditions in the two cities were similar indeed, both being ports with large immigrant populations (predominantly Italian) augmented by arrivals from the gaucho-dominated countryside.

No one disputes that one of the best-known tangos, 'La Cumparsita,' was composed by an Uruguayan, Gerardo Matos Rodríguez. More controversial is the country's claim to tango singer/god Carlos Gardel as a native son.

One of Uruguay's best-known modern writers is Juan Carlos Onetti, who died in Madrid in 1994. His novels *No Man's Land* (Tierra de nadie), *The Shipyard* (El astillero), *Body Snatcher* (Juntacadáveres), and *A Brief Life* (Una vida breve) are available in English. Poet, essayist, and novelist Mario Benedetti is another luminary.

Uruguay's most famous writer is probably José Enrique Rodó, whose 1900 essay *Ariel*, contrasting North American and Latin American civilizations, is a classic of the country's literature (it's available in a paperback English translation). While none of 19th-century writer Javier de Viana's work has been translated into English, he and his 'gauchesco' novels are the subject of John F Garganigo's biography *Javier de Viana*.

Theater is a popular medium, and playwrights are very prominent. One is Mauricio Rosencof, a Tupamaros founder whose plays have been produced since his release from prison, where he was tortured by the military government in the 1970s.

Uruguayan artists such as Pedro Figari, who painted rural scenes, have earned recognition well beyond the country's borders. Punta Ballena, near Punta del Este, is well known as an artists' colony.

RELIGION

Uruguayans are almost exclusively Roman Catholic, but church and state are officially separate. There is a small Jewish minority, numbering around 25,000, almost all of whom live in Montevideo. Evangelical Protestantism has made some inroads, and Sun Myung Moon's Unification Church owns the afternoon daily, *Últimas Noticias*.

LANGUAGE

Spanish is the official language and is universally understood. Uruguayans fluctuate between use of the *voseo* and *tuteo* (see the boxed text 'El Voseo' in the Language chapter) in everyday speech, and both are readily understood. In the north and east, along the Brazilian border, many people are Spanish-Portuguese bilingual or speak *fronterizo*, an unusual hybrid of the two also called *portuñol*. A uniquely Uruguayan usage is *'ta'*, short for *'está bien'* ('OK'), often in question form. This strangely endearing regionalism sometimes shows up as the plural *'¿tamos?'*, meaning 'are we agreed?' or 'everything's settled, then?' See the Language chapter for more on Latin American Spanish.

Facts for the Visitor

Although Uruguay is a very distinct country, traveling there is similar to traveling in Argentina. Only those facts differing significantly from those for travelers in Argentina are mentioned below.

PLANNING
When to Go

Since Uruguay's major tourist attraction is its beaches, most visitors come in summer and dress accordingly, but the mostly temperate climate requires few special preparations for the rest of the year. Between late April and November strong winds sometimes combine with rain and cool temperatures to make things uncomfortable; a couple of layers of warm clothing and some sort of rain protection are a good idea for visitors at this time.

In ritzy resorts like Punta del Este, people often dress their best when going out for the evening, but even Punta is casual most of the time. Visitors to Montevideo can enjoy its urban attractions in any season. Along the Río Uruguay in summer, temperatures can be smotheringly hot, but the interior hill country is slightly cooler, especially at night.

Maps

Uruguayan road maps are only a partial guide to the highways, but see the Automóvil Club del Uruguay, and Shell and Ancap service stations for the best ones. For more detailed maps, try the Instituto Geográfico Militar (☎ 02-481-6868), at 12 de Octubre and Abreu in Montevideo.

TOURIST OFFICES

As in Argentina, almost every department and municipality has a tourist office, usually on the main plaza or at the bus terminal, often with maps and brochures containing excellent historical information.

A few departments and municipalities maintain offices in Montevideo. The Intendencia Municipal de Maldonado, which includes the key resort of Punta del Este, has an office (☎ 02-903-0272) in the national tourism ministry's building at Colonia 1021. The Intendencia Municipal de Rocha maintains an information office (☎ 02-902-0133) on the 5th floor of the Galería Kambarrere, 18 de Julio 907 at Convención.

The national tourism ministry (see also Information in the Montevideo section) has a Web site at W www.turismo.gub.uy. Larger Uruguayan consulates, such as those in New York and Los Angeles, usually have a tourist representative in their delegation, but they are not especially helpful. See Embassies & Consulates later in this section.

VISAS & DOCUMENTS

Uruguay requires passports of all foreigners, except those from neighboring countries (who need only national identification cards). Nationals of Western Europe, Israel, Japan, the USA, Canada and New Zealand will automatically receive on entry a tourist card, valid for 90 days, renewable for another 90. Other nationals require visas to obtain the card. At the time of research, this included Australians, who need to submit to a 'quick check' at a Uruguayan consulate, but this visa requirement may be dropped soon.

To extend your visa or tourist card, visit the immigration office (☎ 02-916-0471) at Misiones 1513 in Montevideo, or try at the local offices in border towns.

Passports are necessary for many everyday transactions, such as cashing traveler's checks and checking into hotels. See the Getting Around section for information about driving permits.

EMBASSIES & CONSULATES
Uruguayan Embassies & Consulates

Argentina
(☎ 01-4803-6030), Las Heras 1907, Recoleta, Buenos Aires
(☎ 043447-421-999), San Martín 417, Colón
(☎ 0345-421-0380), Pellegrini 709, Concordia
(☎ 03446-426168), Rivadavia 510, Gualeguaychú

Australia
(☎ 02-6273 9100), Suite 2, Level 4, Commerce House, 24 Brisbane Avenue, Barton, ACT 2604
(☎ 02-9251 5544), Level 24, Suite 2403, Westpac Plaza Building, 60 Margaret St, Sydney, NSW 2000

Brazil
(☎ 061-322 4528), SES Av das Naçoes, Lote 14 Quadra 803 Sul, Brasília DF
(☎ 021-553 6030), Praia de Botafogo 242, 6th floor, CEP 22250, Rio de Janeiro
(☎ 011-3085 6492), Rua Estados Unidos 1284, Jardins-CEP 01427-001, São Paulo
(☎ 03-2651151; 0474-2049 from Uruguay), Rua Venezuela 311, Chuí

Canada
(☎ 613-234-2937), 130 Albert St, Suite 1905, Ottawa, Ontario K1P 5G4

Chile
(☎ 02-274 4066), Pedro de Valdivia 711, Santiago

France
(☎ 01 45 00 81 37), 15, rue Le Sueur, 1st floor, 75116 Paris

Germany
(☎ 4930-2291424), Dorotheenstrasse 97, 10117 Berlin

Paraguay
(☎ 021-203864), Av Boggiani 5832, Asunción

UK
(☎ 020-7589 8735), 140 Brompton Rd, 2nd floor, London SW31HY

USA
(☎ 202-331-1313), 2715 M St NW, 3rd floor, Washington, DC 20007
(☎ 312-642-3430), 875 North Michigan Ave, Suite 1422, Chicago IL 60611
(☎ 310-394-5777), 429 Santa Monica Blvd, Suite 400, Santa Monica, CA 90401
(☎ 415-986-5222), 546 Market St, Suite 221, San Francisco, CA 94104

Embassies & Consulates in Uruguay

The following addresses and telephone numbers are all in Montevideo (area code ☎ 02); some are in the outer barrios rather than the downtown area. Contact details for consulates listed as 'also in' can be found in the towns' Information sections later in the chapter.

Argentina
(☎ 902-8623), WF Aldunate 1281
also in Colonia, Fray Bentos, Paysandú, Punta del Este, Salto

Belgium
(☎ 916-2719), Rincón 625

Bolivia
(☎ 708-3563), Prudencio de Pena 2469

Brazil
(☎ 901-2024), 6th floor, Convención 1343
also in Chuy

Canada
(☎ 902-2030). Plaza Independencia 749, Oficina 102

Chile
(☎ 902-6316), 1st floor, Andes 1365

France
(☎ 902-0077), Av Uruguay 853

Germany
(☎ 902-5222), La Cumparsita 1435

Israel
(☎ 400-4164), Bulevar Artigas 1585

Italy
(☎ 708-1245), JB Lamas 2857

Japan
(☎ 418-7645), Bulevar Artigas 953

Netherlands
(☎ 711-2956), Leyenda Patria 2880

Paraguay
(☎ 408-5810), Bulevar Artigas 1191

Peru
(☎ 902-1043), Soriano 1124

Spain
(☎ 708-0048), Libertad 2738

Sweden
(☎ 518-5837), Edificio M1, Local D,
Ruta 8 Km 17.5

Switzerland
(☎ 711-5545), 11th floor, Federico Abadie 2936

United Kingdom
(☎ 622-3630), Marco Bruto 1073

USA
(☎ 203-6061), Lauro Muller 1776

CUSTOMS
Uruguayan customs regulations permit the entry of used personal effects and other items in 'reasonable quantities.'

MONEY
While US dollars are not the currency of convenience that they are in Argentina, they are commonly accepted as payment, especially in the major coastal tourist centers. Even some budget hotels give travelers their prices in US dollars, and better restaurants always accept dollars (or, at present, Argentine pesos). Away from the touristed areas, dollars are less frequently accepted on an everyday basis; it's always a good idea to have an ample supply of pesos.

Currency
The unit of currency is the *peso uruguayo* (Ur$), which replaced the *peso nuevo* (N$) in 1993. Peso uruguayo notes come in denominations of five, 10, 20, 50, 100, 200, 500, and 1000, while there are coins of 50 *centésimos*, and one and two pesos. Older banknotes of N$5000 and N$10,000 are still in circulation but have nearly disappeared (to get current values, deduct three zeros).

Exchange Rates
Because the peso is declining against the dollar, exchange rates are likely to work in your favor. At press time exchange rates were the following:

country	unit		peso
Argentina	Arg$1	=	Ur$13.95
Australia	A$1	=	Ur$7.20
Bolivia	Bol$1	=	Ur$2.13
Brazil	BraR$1	=	Ur$6.24
Canada	C$1	=	Ur$8.87
Chile	Ch$100	=	Ur$2.18
European Union	€1	=	Ur$12.45
Japan	¥100	=	Ur$11.06
New Zealand	NZ$1	=	Ur$5.82
Paraguay	₲1000	=	Ur$3.06
Switzerland	SF1	=	Ur$8.43
United Kingdom	UK£1	=	Ur$20.08
United States	US$1	=	Ur$13.95

Exchanging Money
Money is readily exchanged at casas de cambio in Montevideo, Colonia, and the Atlantic beach resorts, but banks are the rule in the interior. Casas de cambio exchange traveler's checks at slightly lower rates than cash dollars, and sometimes charge commissions, although these tend to be lower than those levied in Argentina. There is no black market for dollars or other foreign currency, which can be purchased without difficulty. Most better hotels, restaurants, and shops accept credit cards, and many Uruguayan ATMs will accept North American and European credit cards but can act up at times. ATM (debit) cards can make the machines even more temperamental, even those with stickers proclaiming they work with your system. The Banco de la República Oriental del Uruguay's ATMs usually tend to be well behaved.

Costs
The inflation rate in 2000 was 8.6%; steady devaluations keep prices from rising substantially in dollar terms. Travelers' costs are generally lower than in Argentina, especially for accommodations. Prices in this book are given in US dollars.

POST & COMMUNICATIONS
Post

Postal rates are reasonable, though service can be slow. As in Argentina, letters and parcels are likely to be opened and the contents appropriated if they appear to be of value. If something is truly important, send it by registered mail or private courier.

For poste restante, address mail to the main post office in Montevideo (which has no postal code). It will hold mail for up to a month, or up to two months with authorization.

Telephone

Uruguay's country code is ☎ 598.

Antel is the state telephone company, with central long-distance offices resembling those in Argentina, but there are private *locutorios* (telephone offices) as well. Some public phones take coins, but more convenient magnetic cards are sold in values of 50, 100, 200 and 300 pesos.

Discount rates (40% off) for international calls are in effect between 9pm and 9am weekdays, and all day Saturday, Sunday and holidays.

Making credit-card or collect calls to the US and other overseas destinations is cheaper than paying locally. When calling other countries from Uruguay, the cheapest option is via prepaid 'virtual cards' from such Web vendors as **w** e-worldphone.com. The 'card' is simply a PIN you enter after dialing a local access number, and costs can be as low as US$0.30 a minute. These cards are most easily purchased from within the US; a credit card is necessary.

The list below gives the numbers of foreign direct operators; some of these numbers can't be dialed from locutorios, but should work with card phones.

Argentina	☎ 000454
Belgium	☎ 0004320
Brazil	☎ 000455
Canada	☎ 000419
Chile	☎ 0004561
France	☎ 000433
Germany	☎ 000449
Italy	☎ 000439
Netherlands	☎ 000431
Paraguay	☎ 0004595
Spain	☎ 000434
Switzerland	☎ 000441
UK	☎ 000444
USA	☎ 000410 AT&T
	☎ 000412 MCI
	☎ 00041877 Sprint

There are a handful of Internet cafés in Montevideo and other cities, and seasonal operations in most resort towns, where you can send email and access the Web for around US$5 an hour, but many towns lack access altogether. Some Internet cafés have the software and headsets for making Web calls, though the usual quality of the connection makes them unsuitable for much more than brief exchanges.

BOOKS

For Uruguayan literature see the Arts section earlier in this chapter.

Compared with neighboring countries, surprisingly little material is available on Uruguay in English. For a discussion of the rise of Uruguay's unusual social-welfare

Internet Resources

The following are some useful URLs for Uruguay:

w www.turismo.gub.uy – the national tourism ministry's site

w www.visit-uruguay.com – a clearinghouse for making hotel reservations in several Uruguayan cities; staff will call the hotel to confirm availability and make reservations, and even negotiate discounts when possible, at no charge to you

w www.montevideo.com.uy – Uruguayan Internet provider offering a good choice of links

w www.uruguay.com – maps, weather, news and more (in Spanish)

policies, see George Pendle's *Uruguay, South America's First Welfare State*, and Milton Vanger's *The Model Country: José Batlle y Ordóñez of Uruguay, 1907-1915*.

The country's agrarian history is covered in RH Brannon's *The Agricultural Development of Uruguay*. William Henry Hudson's novel *The Purple Land* (1916) is a classic portrait of 19th-century Uruguayan life.

For a sympathetic explanation of the rise of the 1960s guerrilla movements, see María Esther Gilio's *The Tupamaro Guerrillas*.

A good starting point for looking at the politics of modern Uruguay is Henry Finch's collection *Contemporary Uruguay: Problems and Prospects* (Institute for Latin American Studies, 1980). See also Martin Weinstein's *Uruguay, Democracy at the Crossroads*, and Luis González's *Political Parties and Redemocratization in Uruguay*. For an account of Uruguay's Dirty War, see Lawrence Weschler's *A Miracle, A Universe: Settling Accounts with Torturers*.

FILMS

Costa-Gavras' famous and engrossing film *State of Siege*, filmed in 1973 in Allende's Chile, deals with the Tupamaro guerrillas' kidnapping and execution of suspected American CIA officer Dan Mitrione in Montevideo.

NEWSPAPERS

Newspapers are very important in Uruguay, which ranks second on the continent (behind Argentina) in per capita circulation. Montevideo has a variety of newspapers, including the morning dailies *El Día* (founded by José Batlle), *La República*, *La Mañana* and *El País*.

Gaceta Comercial is the voice of the business community, as is *El Observador Económico*. Afternoon papers are *El Diario* and *Últimas Noticias*, the latter operated by followers of Reverend Sun Myung Moon. For the most part, newspapers are identified with specific political parties, but the weekly *Búsqueda* takes a more independent stance with respect to political and economic matters.

The *Buenos Aires Herald* and other *porteño* newspapers are readily available in the cities of Montevideo, Punta del Este and Colonia.

RADIO & TV

Radio and television are popular, with 20 television stations (four in Montevideo) and at least 100 radio stations (about 40 in the capital) for Uruguay's three million people. While freedom of speech and the press are generally respected, in 1994 the government revoked the license of a radio station operated by the Tupamaros.

HEALTH

Note that Uruguayan hospitals generally demand cash and refuse to accept insurance coverage; travelers needing hospitalization or other medical services may have to pay first and then ask their insurance companies for reimbursement.

SENIOR TRAVELERS

Elderhostel runs several educational programs to Uruguay, all of which begin with a short orientation stay in Montevideo. Course topics include flora and fauna, and tours of Montevideo and Punta del Este. Two-week tours of the country start at around US$3200. They also offer multicountry trips, which take in parts of Argentina, Brazil and Paraguay, for about the same price. Participants must be at least 55 years of age. For more information or a catalog, contact Elderhostel (☎ 877-426-8056 toll free, **w** www.elderhostel.org), 11 Avenue de Lafayette, Boston, MA 02111-1746.

BUSINESS HOURS & PUBLIC HOLIDAYS

Most shops are open weekdays and Saturday 8:30am to 12:30pm or 1pm, then close until midafternoon and reopen until 7pm or 8pm. Food shops also open on Sunday mornings.

Government office hours vary with the season – in summer, from mid-November to mid-March, offices are open 7:30am to 1:30pm, while the rest of the year their hours are noon to 7pm. Most banks are open weekday afternoons only.

On public holidays, most stores and all public offices are closed. Public transportation does run, but schedules are usually limited. The year's public holidays are as follows:

January 1 – Año Nuevo (New Year's Day)

January 6 – Epifanía (Epiphany)

March/April (dates vary) – Viernes Santo/Pascua (Good Friday/Easter)

April 19 – Desembarco de los 33 (Return of the 33) honors the exiles who returned to Uruguay in 1825 to liberate the country from Brazil with Argentine support.

May 1 – Día del Trabajador (Labor Day)

May 18 – Batalla de Las Piedras (Battle of Las Piedras) commemorates a major battle of the fight for independence.

June 19 – Natalicio de Artigas (Artigas' Birthday)

July 18 – Jura de la Constitución (Constitution Day)

August 25 – Día de la Independencia (Independence Day)

October 12 – Día de la Raza (Columbus Day)

November 2 – Día de los Muertos (All Souls' Day)

December 25 – Navidad (Christmas Day)

Uruguay's Carnaval, which takes place the Monday and Tuesday before Ash Wednesday in April, is a lively affair, at least in Montevideo. In the city's Barrio Sur, much of the black population celebrates with traditional *candombe* (Afro-Uruguayan dance) ceremonies.

Holy Week (Easter) is also La Semana Criolla, during which traditional gaucho activities like *asados* (barbecues) and folk music take place. Most businesses close for the duration.

ACCOMMODATIONS

With the continuing economic recession, many hotels have dropped prices drastically, offering some excellent bargains to travelers, especially those with dollars.

Some tourist offices issue vouchers for discounted stays at budget hotels, usually as part of a system imposed by government-run hotel-oversight associations. These vouchers can place a significant financial burden on the hoteliers, many of whom are struggling to stay afloat. In addition, taxi drivers and touts will try to lead people to certain hotels and then extract commissions from the hotel. You are better off passing up vouchers and finding your lodging on your own; the hoteliers will be happier and you will have room to bargain if you desire.

Uruguay's youth hostel network is a good alternative to standard accommodations, and a youth hostel card may prove worthwhile; at US$24, membership is reasonable. Hostel accommodations range from US$4.50 to US$11 per night. For more information, contact the Asociación de Alberguistas del Uruguay (☎ 02-400-4245, **e** aau@adinet.com.uy), the Uruguay affiliate of Hostelling International, at Pablo de María 1583, Montevideo. It's open weekdays from 11:30am to 7pm; from December to April it's also open Saturdays 9am to 1pm.

Many hotels have odious checkout times, usually 10am, but as early as 9am.

FOOD

Per capita, Uruguayans consume even more beef than Argentines, and the *parrillada* (beef platter) is a standard here. Likewise, the kinds of eating places are very similar – *confiterías*, pizzerias and restaurants closely resemble their Argentine counterparts. There are good international restaurants in Montevideo, Punta del Este and some other beach resorts, but elsewhere the food is fairly uniform. Uruguayan seafood is almost always a good choice, and vegetarians can usually find suitable food, especially in the capital and tourist areas.

The standard of Uruguayan short orders is *chivito*, which is not goat but rather a tasty and filling steak sandwich with a variety of additions – cheese, lettuce, tomato, bacon or other odds and ends. Even more filling is the *chivito al plato*, a cholesterol bomb in which the steak is served topped with a fried egg, and potato salad, green salad and french fries come on the side. Other typical Uruguayan short orders include *olímpicos*, which are club sandwiches, and *húngaros*, which are spicy sausages on a hot-dog roll (probably too spicy for young children, who will prefer the blander *panchos*).

Cubiertos are cover charges added by some restaurants for bread and tablecloth. They range from US$0.25 to US$2 (even higher in some fancy places). You can sometimes (read 'rarely') avoid them by declining a tablecloth. If you don't see *'No cobramos cubierto'* posted outside the restaurant or on the menu, it doesn't hurt to ask *'¿Hay cubierto?'*

Punta del Este, Colonia and other cities with high tourist traffic are the most likely places you'll encounter cubiertos.

DRINKS

Uruguayans consume even more *mate* (Paraguayan tea) than Argentines and Paraguayans. As South America's fourth largest vintner, Uruguay produces some very good and reasonably priced wines. Tannat, a varietal produced only in Uruguay and southwestern France, can be rather flinty when young and is often blended with other grapes for early drinkability. Good vintages to try include Casa Luntro 1997 and Castel Pujol Tannat de Reserva 1997 (Violetas).

Producers of good Cabernet, Merlot, Sauvignon Blanc and other wines include Catamayor, Juanicó and H Stagnari.

Everyone seems to have their own recipe for *clericó*, usually a mixture containing white wine, fruit juice, a liqueur, fruit salad, ice and a carbonated soft drink or cider. A potent variation mixes *caña* (cane liquor) with vermouth. A popular drink in Montevideo is the *medio y medio*, a mixture of sparkling wine and white wine. Uruguayan beer is generally decent.

ENTERTAINMENT

Cinema is extremely popular in Montevideo and throughout the country, although the domestic film industry is very limited. Live theater is also very well patronized, especially in Montevideo.

Tango is nearly as popular here as in Argentina, while Afro-Uruguayan candombe music and dance adds a unique dimension not present in Uruguay's dominating neighbor.

SPECTATOR SPORTS

'Sexo, droga y Peñarol' – Montevideo graffiti

Uruguay has won soccer's World Cup twice, including the very first match, which was played in Uruguay in 1930. The second World Cup win, in 1950, was against the heavily favored Brazilian side in Brazil, after which it is said some disbelieving Brazilian fans committed suicide.

The national team suffered for years until it once again upset Brazil in the 1995 Copa de las Américas. Soccer remains the most popular spectator and participant sport; the most notable teams are Montevideo-based Nacional and Peñarol. If you go to a match between these two, sit on the sidelines, not behind the goal, where the fans tend to get rowdy. This rowdiness can carry over onto the streets afterwards.

The Asociación Uruguayo de Fútbol (☎ 02-400-7101), at Guayabo 1531 in Montevideo, should be able to provide information on matches and venues.

SHOPPING

Most shoppers will be interested in leather clothing and accessories, woolen clothing and fabrics, agates and gems, ceramics, woodcrafts and decorated gourds. One of the most popular places for shoppers is the artisans cooperative Manos del Uruguay, with several locations in Montevideo and elsewhere in the country.

Getting There & Away

The majority of international flights to and from Montevideo's Aeropuerto Carrasco pass through Buenos Aires' Ezeiza Airport on the way in and out, while many others stop at Rio de Janeiro or São Paulo. See the Argentina Getting There & Away chapter for more information.

All river transport and the great majority of land transport also passes through Argentina, though there are several direct land crossings from Brazil.

URUGUAY

AIR

International passengers leaving from Aeropuerto Carrasco pay a departure tax of US$6 if headed to Argentina, and US$12 to other destinations. Addresses and telephone numbers of airline offices appear in the Montevideo Getting There & Away section.

The USA

There are no direct flights to Uruguay from the US; the best connections are probably through São Paulo, Brazil (a route taken by American Airlines among others). Many airlines fly via Buenos Aires' Ezeiza airport. LANChile has flights from Los Angeles, Miami and New York with a change of planes in Santiago. One interesting routing is Lloyd Aéreo Boliviano's to and from Miami, which requires an overnight in Santa Cruz, Bolivia.

Continental Europe

Pluna, an Uruguayan carrier affiliated with Varig, has twice-weekly flights from Madrid. Varig flies to Madrid via Rio de Janeiro or São Paulo. Iberia flies four times weekly to Montevideo via Barcelona, Madrid and Buenos Aires' Ezeiza airport.

South America

There are frequent flights between Carrasco and Buenos Aires' Aeroparque Jorge Newbery, as well as between Aeroparque and Punta del Este. Aerolíneas Argentinas and LAPA offer the most flights. Although it's possible to fly between Carrasco and Ezeiza, it's more expensive and less convenient unless your ticket is valid for an ongoing flight. Aerovip flies between Aeroparque, Colonia and Montevideo (see the Colonia Getting There & Away section).

Pluna flies from Montevideo to Brazilian destinations such as Florianópolis (Sunday only) and São Paulo (two or three times daily). Varig flies daily to Porto Alegre and Rio de Janeiro, and daily to São Paulo continuing on to Rio de Janeiro.

Pluna also flies to Asunción, Paraguay, on Thursday, Saturday and Sunday, and to Santiago, Chile (five times weekly). TAM flies Monday, Wednesday and Friday to Asunción.

Lloyd Aéreo Boliviano flies four times weekly to Santa Cruz de la Sierra and La Paz via Buenos Aires' Ezeiza airport. LANChile flies daily except Wednesday to Santiago, Chile, and has an additional Sunday flight.

Cubana flies weekly between Montevideo, Buenos Aires and Havana.

LAND

Uruguay shares borders with the Argentine province of Entre Ríos and the southern Brazilian state of Rio Grande do Sul. Major highways and bus services are generally good, but there are no rail services.

Border Crossings

Argentina There are direct buses from Montevideo to Buenos Aires via Gualeguaychú, but these are slower and less convenient than the land/river combinations across the Río de la Plata. Farther north, there are bridge crossings over the Río Uruguay from Fray Bentos to Gualeguaychú, Paysandú to Colón and Salto to Concordia. For more information, see the individual city listings in this chapter.

Brazil

Chuy to Chuí & Pelotas
The most frequently used border crossing from Uruguay into Brazil is connected to Montevideo by an excellent paved highway. Chuy and Chuí are twin cities whose parallel main streets are separated only by a median strip, but Uruguayan immigration is about 1km before the actual border and Brazilian immigration 2km beyond it. If continuing any distance into Brazil, complete border formalities on both sides.

Río Branco to Jaguarão
Less frequently used than the crossing at Chuy, this is an alternative route to Pelotas and Porto Alegre via the town of Treinta y Tres, in the department of the same name, or Melo, which is in the department of Cerro Largo. There are buses from Jaguarão to Pelotas.

Rivera to Livramento
The crossing at Rivera and Santana do Livramento is frequented by travelers heading from Colón, Argentina, to Brazil, via Paysandú and the interior city of Tacuarembó. There are

regular buses from Livramento to Porto Alegre. Uruguayan and Brazilian immigration officials share a facility on the Uruguayan side, several blocks from the border, to more easily process those leaving Uruguay and entering Brazil.

Artigas to Quaraí
This route crosses the Puente de la Concordia over the Río Quareim, but the principal highway goes southeast to Livramento.

Bella Unión to Barra do Quaraí
In the extreme northwest corner of Uruguay, this crossing leads to the Brazilian city of Uruguaiana, from which you can cross into the Argentine province of Corrientes and head north to Paraguay or to the Iguazú Falls area. Overland travel to the Iguazú Falls through southern Brazil is slow and difficult.

RIVER & SEA

The most common means of crossing from Montevideo to Argentina is by regular or high-speed ferry, sometimes involving bus combinations to Colonia.

Montevideo to Buenos Aires
High-speed ferries connect the two capitals in about 2½ hours. See the Montevideo Getting There & Away section for more details.

Colonia to Buenos Aires
From Montevideo you can make direct bus connections to Colonia (3 hours), from which several ferries cross daily to Buenos Aires, taking between 45 minutes and 2½ hours. See the Colonia Getting There & Away section for details.

Piriápolis to Buenos Aires
In summer, a three-hour ferry ride connects the resort town of Piriápolis with the Argentine capital at least once a day. Glitzy Punta del Este is less than an hour from Piriápolis by bus.

Carmelo & Nueva Palmira to Tigre
There are launches across the estuary of the Río de la Plata to the Buenos Aires suburb of Tigre. Launches from Carmelo (see that section) take about 2½ hours, while those from Nueva Palmira take slightly longer.

ORGANIZED TOURS

Organized tours to Uruguay are fairly rare. For travelers at least 55 years of age, Elderhostel operates educational tours (see Senior Travelers in the Facts for the Visitor section, earlier).

Getting Around

AIR

Aéromas (☎ 02-604-0011) and Travelair (☎ 02-604-0202), both with offices at Montevideo's airport, offer service to Paysandú, Rivera and Salto. Aeromás also flies to Tacuarembó. Travel times are around an hour and fares between US$50 and US$60. See each city's section for more details.

BUS

Buses are not quite so comfortable as those in Argentina, but the rides are shorter and they are perfectly acceptable; many companies publish accurate timetables. More Uruguayan cities are constructing central bus terminals; in those that lack them the companies are always within easy walking distance of one other, usually around the main plaza.

Buses are frequent to destinations all around the country, so reservations should only be necessary on or near holidays. Fares are very reasonable – for example, the trip from Montevideo to Fray Bentos, a distance of about 300km, costs only about US$14.

In towns with a central bus terminal you can leave your bags (for a fee) either at a luggage-storage room or at the office of one of the bus companies. Where there is no terminal you can usually leave your bags free of charge at the company you're ticketed to leave with later in the day.

TRAIN

Passenger services on Uruguayan trains ceased completely in 1988 when the government decided it could no longer afford to subsidize them. Most of the rolling stock was eventually sold off to ranchers in Brazil and Argentina for use on their private holdings. Service has resumed on the Montevideo to 25 de Agosto line, a distance of about 65km, and has been revived four times on the scenic Tacuarembó to Rivera line (it was not in operation at the time of research). Efforts are being made to resume other services.

CAR

In most parts of the country, Uruguayan drivers are very considerate, even courtly. Montevideo is an exception; many drivers are eager to get ahead, and the lines dividing lanes serve as mere decoration. Even so, it's quite sedate compared to Buenos Aires. Bear in mind that there are plenty of Argentine drivers on the road.

Outside the capital and coastal tourist areas, traffic is minimal and poses few problems. Roads are generally in good shape, but some in the interior roads can be rough. Keep an eye out for livestock and wildlife. Even in Montevideo's busy downtown, horse-drawn carts still operate, hauling trash or freight.

Theoretically, Uruguay requires foreign drivers to carry the Inter-American Driving Permit rather than the International Driving Permit, but neither document is given much attention by police. They are more interested in the driver's home-country license and passport. Arbitrary police stops and searches are less common than in Argentina, but the police are not above soliciting a bribe for minor traffic violations.

Uruguay imports all its oil, and unleaded premium gasoline costs about US$1.30 a liter, making driving more expensive than in Argentina. Rental costs are not astronomical, however; for as little as US$32 a day in the low season, you can rent an economy car, with tax and insurance included. Multi-week rentals of roomier cars can work out even less if you shop around. An annoying practice of some car-rental agencies is to turn the car over to the renter with an empty tank. They say you can return the car the same way, but this is of course very difficult (not to mention nerve-wracking) to do.

Uruguay has no domestic automobile industry and prices are high; if you plan to purchase a car, Argentina is a better bet. Many of the lovingly maintained, truly antique old cars (known as *cachilas*) that were common sights on the streets of Montevideo into the late '90s are gone now, bought by foreign collectors. Happily, you can still see some in the countryside.

The Automóvil Club del Uruguay (☎ 02-902-4792), whose main office is at Avenida Libertador General Lavalleja 1532 in Montevideo, has good maps and information.

LOCAL TRANSPORTATION

Taxis, *remises* (radio-dispatched taxis) and local buses are similar to those in Argentina. Taxis are metered, and drivers calculate fares using meter readings and a photocopied chart. Between 10pm and 6am, and on weekends and holidays, fares are 20% higher. There is a small additional charge for luggage, and riders generally round off the total fare to the next higher peso.

Montevideo

☎ 02 • pop 1.3 million

Uruguay's capital dominates the country's political, economic and cultural life even more than Buenos Aires does Argentina's. Nearly half the country's 3.3 million citizens live here, but there's a logic to this: Montevideo's fine natural port links the country to overseas commerce, and the almost exclusively rural economy hardly requires a competing metropolis for trade and administration.

In many ways, economic stagnation has left modern Montevideo a worn-out city where key public buildings are undistinguished, utilitarian constructions that would not be out of place in Eastern Europe. Still, the municipal administration has spruced up public spaces like Plaza Cagancha and made efforts to restore the Ciudad Vieja (Old City), the colonial core and the city's most appealing feature.

But Montevideo's renaissance is a long way off. The economic crisis gripping South America is devastating Uruguay, and many of Montevideo's museums and public sights are either closed or keeping curtailed hours, while restaurants and hotels struggle to survive. 'For sale' signs are everywhere, and some buildings in the Ciudad Vieja look as though they could give way any moment.

MONTEVIDEO

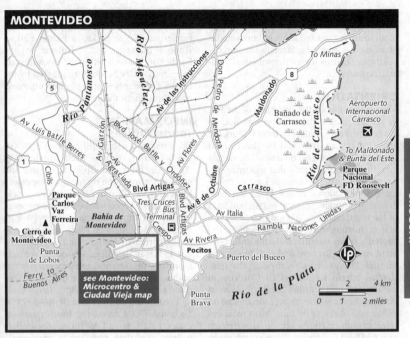

To Minas

Aeropuerto
Internacional
Carrasco

To Maldonado
& Punta del Este

Parque
Nacional
FD Roosevelt

Bañado de
Carrasco

Carrasco

Av Italia

Rambla Naciones Unidas

Puerto del Buceo

Río de la Plata

Pocitos

Punta
Brava

Av Rivera

Crespo

Tres Cruces
Bus
Terminal

Bahía de
Montevideo

Parque
Carlos
Vaz
Ferreira

Cerro de
Montevideo

Punta
de Lobos

Ferry to
Buenos Aires

see Montevideo:
Microcentro &
Ciudad Vieja map

Blvd Artigas

Blvd Artigas

Av 8 de Octubre

Av Flores

Av Agraciada

Av Garzón

Blvd José Batlle y Ordóñez

Av de las Instrucciones

Don Pedro de Mendoza

Maldonado

Río de Carrasco

Río Miguelete

Río Pantanoso

Av Luis Batlle Berres

Cibils

5

1

1

8

0   2   4 km
0   1   2 miles

URUGUAY

HISTORY

Spain's 1726 founding of Montevideo was a response to Portugal's growing influence in the River Plate area; since 1680, the fortress and contraband port of Colonia had been a thorn in Spain's side. Montevideo was in turn a fortress against the Portuguese, as well as the British, French and Danish privateers who came in search of hides in the Banda Oriental. Even more isolated than Buenos Aires, it was modest and unimpressive.

Many of Montevideo's early residents were Canary Islanders. The city's port, superior to Buenos Aires' except for its lack of access to the Humid Pampa, soon made Montevideo a focal point for overseas shipping. An early-19th-century construction boom resulted in a new cathedral, city hall and other neoclassical late-colonial monuments, but after independence authorities demolished many of these buildings and planned a new center east of Ciudad Vieja (Old City) and its port.

From 1843 to 1851 the city endured a siege by the Argentine dictator Rosas, who was determined to create a small client state to Buenos Aires. After Rosas' fall in 1851, normal commerce resumed and, between 1860 and 1911, the British-built railroad network assisted Montevideo's growth. Like Buenos Aires, the city absorbed numerous European immigrants in the early 20th century, mostly from Spain and Italy; by 1908, 30% of Montevideo's population was foreign-born.

Around this time, the country became ever more closely linked to the export trade; construction of the city's first locally financed cold storage plant was followed by two similar foreign-backed enterprises. Growth has continued to stimulate agricultural expansion near Montevideo in response to the demands of the rapidly increasing urban population. Much of this population, consisting mostly of refugees from rural poverty, lives in *conventillos*, large, older houses converted into multifamily slum dwellings. Many of these are in the Ciudad Vieja, but even this population is being displaced as urban redevelopment usurps the picturesque and valuable central area.

ORIENTATION

Montevideo lies on the east bank of the Río de la Plata, almost directly opposite Buenos Aires on the west bank. For most visitors, the most intriguing area will be the Ciudad Vieja, the colonial grid on a small peninsula near the port and harbor that was once surrounded by protective walls. East of this is the city's functional center, Plaza Independencia, with many historic public buildings of the republican era. Avenida 18 de Julio, a major thoroughfare and traditionally the capital's main commercial and entertainment zone, begins here and runs to the east through Plaza Cagancha, dividing the tree-shaded barrio known as El Córdon (in earlier times El Cardal, the birthplace of Artigas). Some streets change their name on either side of Av 18 de Julio. Most inexpensive accommodations are on side streets around Plaza Cagancha, though some are in the Ciudad Vieja.

Avenida Libertador General Lavalleja leads diagonally between Plaza del Entrevero (officially named Plaza Fabini, though no one calls it that) on Av 18 de Julio and the imposing Palacio Legislativo, site of the Uruguay's General Assembly. At the northeastern end of Av 18 de Julio is Parque José Batlle y Ordóñez, a large public park containing the Estadio Centenario, a 75,000-seat stadium built to commemorate the country's centenary in 1930. Running perpendicular to its terminus is Bulevar Artigas, another major artery, while the nearby Av Italia becomes the Interbalnearia, the main highway east to Punta del Este and the rest of the Uruguayan Riviera.

Many points of interest are beyond downtown, a result of Montevideo's sprawl both east and west along the river. Across the harbor to the west, 132m Cerro de Montevideo was a landmark for early navigators and still offers outstanding views of the city. To the east, the Rambla, or waterfront road, leads past attractive residential suburbs with numerous public parks, including Parque Rodó at the south end of Bulevar Artigas. Farther on, but well within the city limits, are numerous sandy beaches frequented by the capital's residents in summer and on weekends throughout the year.

INFORMATION
Tourist Offices

The municipal tourist office's kiosk (☎ 903-0649), in front of the Palacio Municipal at Av 18 de Julio and Ejido, is helpful and usually has someone on hand who speaks a little English. It's open 10am to 7pm weekdays, 11am to 6pm weekends. The national ministry of tourism's main office (☎ 908-9105 interno 130) is on Plaza del Entrevero at the corner of Colonia and Av Libertador General Lavalleja. It's open weekday mornings in summer and weekday afternoons in winter. There is a branch at Carrasco airport open 8am to 8pm daily.

The Oficina de Informes (☎ 409-6399) at Terminal Tres Cruces, the bus terminal at Bulevar Artigas and Av Italia, is open 8am to 9pm weekdays and 9am to 9pm weekends and is well prepared to deal with visitor inquiries. The very useful weekly *Guía del Ocio*, which lists cultural events, cinemas, theaters, and restaurants, comes with the Friday edition of the daily *Últimas Noticias*.

If your Spanish is good, dial ☎ 124 for general information on virtually anything in Montevideo. For entertainment information, call Espectáculos (☎ 0900-2323); the call costs US$0.60 per minute.

Immigration

The immigration office (☎ 916-0471), at Misiones 1513, is open 12:15pm to 5:45pm weekdays.

Money

Terminal Tres Cruces has a bank and good ATMs. Though ATMs abound in the Ciudad Vieja, many of them don't work with foreign cards, and the area is unsafe. Try instead the reliable Banco de la República Oriental

ATM at Av 18 de Julio 996, next to the Museo del Gaucho. There are many exchange houses along the avenue and around Plaza Cagancha as well as Exprinter, Sarandí 700 on Plaza Independencia. American Express (☎ 902-0829), locally represented by Turisport at San José 930, no longer cashes its own traveler's checks, but Cambio Gales at 18 de Julio 1048 will do so, as will Indumex, in the Tres Cruces terminal.

Post & Communications
The main post office is at Misiones 1328 in the Ciudad Vieja, with a branch built into the Palacio Municipal on Ejido between San José and Soriano. Antel has a telephone office at Rincón 501 in the Ciudad Vieja, at San José 1102, and at the Tres Cruces bus terminal.

Cyber Café, with branches at Av 18 de Julio 1772 and 1333, is a noisy videogame parlor but has fast Internet connections at US$1.25 for 15-minute increments. The latter is quieter. Café @, next to the Hotel Solís, charges the same, but in one-minute (US$0.08) increments, and the surroundings are more agreeable.

Travel Agencies
Among many others, Viajes COT (☎ 902-4004), Plaza Cagancha 1126, arranges trips in and out of Montevideo and to neighboring countries. Argentina's nonprofit student travel agency Asatej, an affiliate of STA Travel, has a Montevideo branch (☎ 908-0509, fax 908-4895) at Río Negro 1354, 2nd floor.

Photography Supplies
Kilómetro Cero, 18 de Julio 1180 on Plaza Cagancha, and Laboratorio Central, Yí 1532, offer dependable developing. Tecnifilm, at 18 de Julio 1202, is the place to go for camera repairs.

Bookstores
Montevideo has several fine bookstores. Librería Linardi y Risso (☎ 915-7129), at Juan Carlos Gómez 1435 in the Ciudad Vieja offers outstanding selections in history and literature, including many out-of-print

items. Plazalibros has two locations on 18 de Julio: at 892 and 1185. The latter has a large selection of dictionaries and travel books in English and Spanish.

Cultural Centers
Alianza, the American-Uruguayan cultural center at Paraguay 1217, contains a bookstore, a theater and the Biblioteca Artigas-Washington (☎ 901-7423), a very substantial library with books and newspapers in English. The center also sponsors special programs and lectures.

The Anglo-Uruguayan Cultural Institute (☎ 902-3373), San José 1426, also operates an English-language library. Montevideo has two branches of the Instituto Goethe, at Canelones 1524, and the Alianza Francesa (☎ 408-6012), at 18 de Julio 1772. The Centro Cultural Uruguayo-Brasileiro is at 18 de Julio 994, next to the Museo del Gaucho.

Montevideo's Afro-Uruguayan community has a downtown cultural center, called the Instituto Superior de Formación Afro (commonly known as Mundo Afro, ☎/fax 915-0247) upstairs in the Mercado Central, Ciudadela 1229.

Medical Services
Public medical facilities tend to be grim and clogged with patients. You're better off seeking a recommendation for a private clinic, such as the Asociación Española (☎ 1920) at Av General Rivera 2341, near the stadium.

Dangers & Annoyances
While Montevideo is pretty sedate by most standards, wallet- and purse-snatchings are common in the Ciudad Vieja. These are often perpetrated by boys as young as 12 years old, who will reach into victims' pockets (sometimes after pulling the owner's hand out of same) or grab a wallet while the victim is paying for a taxi ride, then bolt. Less frequent are muggings where a group will surround a victim and extract valuables (including moneybelts kept under clothes).

After dark, avoid the Mercado del Puerto (and other spots deep within the Ciudad Vieja) and Cerro de Montevideo.

URUGUAY

URUGUAY

MONTEVIDEO: MICROCENTRO & CIUDAD VIEJA

Bahía de Montevideo

Ferry to Buenos Aires

Park

Rambla-Franklin-D-Roosevelt

Ferry Terminal

Dársena Fluvial

Naval/Customs Building

Mercado del Puerto

Rambla 25 de Agosto de 1825

Plaza Constitución

Iglesia Matriz

Plaza Zabala

Hospital Maciel

Ciudad Vieja

Sports Field

Escollera Sarandí

Rambla Francia

Río de la Plata

PLACES TO STAY
6   Hotel Arapey
22 Hotel Palacio
27 Radisson Victoria Plaza
33 Hotel Ideal
44 Hotel Aramaya
47 Hotel Ateneo
55 Hotel Alvear
64 Hotel Solís; Café @
77 Hotel Casablanca
83 Balmoral Plaza Hotel; Viajes COT
85 Hotel Lancaster
91 Hotel City
98 London Palace Hotel
104 Hotel Embajador
106 Hotel Windsor
113 Albergue Juvenil
116 Hospedaje del Centro
117 Hotel Lafayette
119 Hotel Kaldi

PLACES TO EAT
5   Club Libanés
17 La Fontana
25 La Vegetariana
31 Oro del Rhin
42 Super Buffet
51 Pizza Bros
58 Confitería de la Corte
60 Confitería La Pasiva
63 La Crêperie
73 Las Brasas
78 La Vegetariana
89 La Vegetariana
97 Micro Macro Supermarket
99 El Fogón
101 Ruffino
102 Euskal Erría
103 Vida Natural
107 La Genovesa
118 Sarao

OTHER
1   Buquebus
2   Immigration Office
3   Casa Mario
4   French Consulate
7   Automóvil Club del Uruguay
8   Laboratorio Central
9   Casa Garibaldi
10 Museo de Arte Decorativo
11 Casa Lavalleja
12 Teatro El Picadero
13 Casa Rivera
14 Museo Romántico
15 Telecentro Antel
16 Linardi y Risso
18 Belgian Consulate
19 Budget Rent A Car
20 Agencia Central; Sabelin; Chadre
21 Museo y Archivo Histórico Municipal; Cabildo
23 Museo Torres García
24 American Airlines
26 Canadian Embassy
28 Localiza Rent A Car
29 Ecuatoriana; TAM
30 Chilean Embassy
32 Lloyd Aéreo Boliviano (LAB)
34 Intendencia Municipal de Rocha
35 Arbiter-Pasqualini
36 Coit
37 Empresa General Artigas
38 Iberia
39 LANChile
40 National Tourist Office
43 Alitalia; Asatej
45 Mercado de los Artesanos
46 TTL
48 Cine Complejo Plaza
49 Teatro Circular
50 Museo Pedagógico José Pedro Varela
52 Plazalibros
53 Multicar
54 Museo del Automóvil; Automóvil Club del Uruguay
56 Alianza Francesa; Cyber Café
57 Main Post Office
59 Banco Santander (ATM)
61 Amatistas Uruguayas
62 Louvre
65 Exprinter (Money Exchange, Travel Agency)
66 Puerta de la Ciudadela
67 Mausoleo del Artigas
68 Palacio Estévez
70 Pluna/Varig
71 Cyber Café
72 Brazilian Consulate; Aerolíneas Argentinas
74 Museo del Gaucho y de la Moneda; Centro Cultural Uruguayo-Brasileiro
75 Sala Zitarrosa
76 Cambio Gales
79 La Calesa
80 Indumex (Money Exchange)

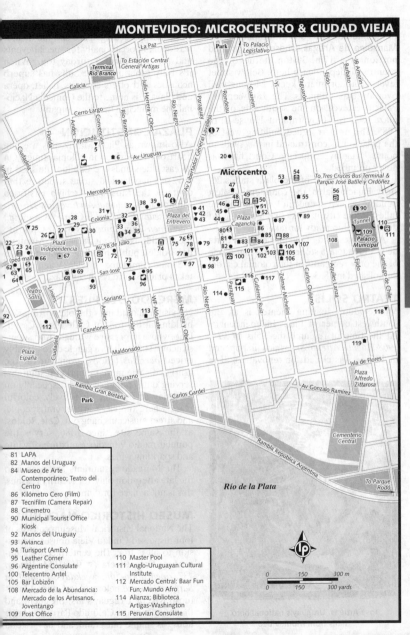

MONTEVIDEO: MICROCENTRO & CIUDAD VIEJA

URUGUAY

81 LAPA
82 Manos del Uruguay
84 Museo de Arte Contemporáneo; Teatro del Centro
86 Kilómetro Cero (Film)
87 Tecnifilm (Camera Repair)
88 Cinemetro
90 Municipal Tourist Office Kiosk
92 Manos del Uruguay
93 Avianca
94 Turisport (AmEx)
95 Leather Corner
96 Argentine Consulate
100 Telecentro Antel
105 Bar Lobizón
108 Mercado de la Abundancia: Mercado de los Artesanos, Joventango
109 Post Office

110 Master Pool
111 Anglo-Uruguayan Cultural Institute
112 Mercado Central: Baar Fun Fun; Mundo Afro
114 Alianza; Biblioteca Artigas-Washington
115 Peruvian Consulate

Río de la Plata

0   150   300 m
0   150   300 yards

PLAZA INDEPENDENCIA

In the middle of this downtown plaza is the **Mausoleo de Artigas**, whose aboveground portion is a 17m, 30-ton statue of the country's independence hero. Below street level an honor guard keeps 24-hour vigil over Artigas' remains. The 18th-century **Palacio Estévez**, on the south side of the plaza, was the Government House until 1985. The modern office building west of the palacio was constructed in the 1980s to house Uruguay's Supreme Court but was never occupied.

On the east side of the plaza stands 26-story **Palacio Salvo**, the continent's tallest building when it opened in 1927 and still the tallest in the city; it looks like a bulging art deco spaceship ready for takeoff.

At the west end of the plaza is the **Puerta de la Ciudadela**, a stone gateway that is one of the only remnants of the colonial citadel demolished in 1833.

TEATRO SOLÍS

Montevideo's leading theater is at the southwest corner of Plaza Independencia. At the time of research the Solís (☎ 915-1968, Buenos Aires 678) – which first opened in 1856 – was closed for renovations. The

José Artigas, Uruguay's national hero, hails from Montevideo

project faced a US$38 million shortfall, but work was proceeding apace and the theater was opening occasionally for special events and the occasional Saturday tour. When it's fully functional, the Solís has superb acoustics and offers concerts, ballet, opera and plays. It is home to the Comedia Nacional, the municipal theater company.

PLAZA CONSTITUCIÓN

Also known as Plaza Matriz, this was the heart of Montevideo in colonial times. On its east side stands the **Cabildo** (finished in 1812), a neoclassical stone structure that contains the **Museo y Archivo Histórico Municipal** (Municipal Archive and Historical Museum; Juan Carlos Gómez & Sarandí; free; open 2pm-6pm Tues-Sun). Opposite the Cabildo is the **Iglesia Matriz**, Montevideo's oldest public building. It was begun in 1784 and completed in 1799. A flea market takes place Saturdays in the plaza.

MERCADO DEL PUERTO

No visitor should miss the old port market building at the foot of Calle Pérez Castellano, whose impressive wrought-iron superstructure still shelters a gaggle of reasonably priced *parrillas* (choose your cut off the grill) and some more upmarket restaurants serving outstanding seafood. Especially on Saturday afternoons, it's a lively, colorful place where the city's artists, craftspeople, and street musicians hang out. **Café Roldós**, at the same site since 1886, serves the popular medio y medio, a mixture of white and sparkling wines.

The Mercado restaurants are open into the late afternoon only; for security reasons, this is not a place for dinner.

MUSEO HISTÓRICO NACIONAL

The National Historical Museum consists of four dispersed Ciudad Vieja houses. Admission to all is free. The centerpiece is 19th-century **Casa Rivera** (☎ 915-1051, Rincón 437, open noon-5pm weekdays, 11am-4pm Sat), which once belonged to General Fructuoso Rivera, Uruguay's first president and the founder of the Colorado Party. The large house is simple but grand, and has a good collection of portraits, paintings, documents, period furniture and indigenous artifacts.

The 18th-century **Museo Romántico** (☎ 915-5361, 25 de Mayo 428, open noon-5pm weekdays, 11am-4pm Sat) is filled with paintings and antique furniture. **Casa Lavalleja** (☎ 915-1028, Zabala 1469, open 11am-4pm Sat) was the home of General Lavalleja from 1830 until his death in 1853. **Casa Garibaldi** (☎ 915-2457, 25 de Mayo 314, open 11am-4pm Sat) contains personal effects of Giuseppe Garibaldi, the tireless soldier who helped bring about Italy's unification. During part of his long military career Garibaldi – fleeing a death sentence in Europe – lived in Montevideo and commanded the Uruguayan navy against Argentina.

MUSEO NACIONAL DE ARTES PLÁSTICOS Y VISUALES

Uruguay's largest collection of paintings is housed in this museum (☎ 711-6124, Av Herrera y Reissig & T Giribaldi; free, open 3pm-7pm Wed-Sun) in Parque Rodó. The large rooms are graced with works by Blanes, Cúneo, Figari and Torres García, as well as sculpture.

OTHER MUSEUMS

Montevideo has many other worthwhile museums; most are downtown and almost all are free. The **Museo del Gaucho y de la Moneda** (☎ 900-8764, Av 18 de Julio 998; free; open 9:30am-noon & 1:30pm-6pm Tues-Fri, 4pm-7pm weekends) is in the amazingly ornate Palacio Heber (worth the visit alone) and features artifacts from Uruguay's gaucho history. On display are horse gear, silver work, weapons and an excellent collection of *mates* and *bombillas* in whimsical designs of silver, horn and other material. A collection of banknotes and coins and changing expositions of paintings unrelated to gaucho life round out the museum.

The **Museo de Arte Decorativo** (25 de Mayo 376; free; open 12:15pm-6pm Thur-Sat, 2pm-6pm Sun) was the residence of a wealthy merchant and his family. The museum's main attractions are the exquisite furnishings, tapestries and other items, many of them original, and the palatial building

itself, constructed in 1810. Free guided tours in Spanish are given at 4:30pm.

The **Museo Pedagógico José Pedro Varela** (☎ 902-0915, Plaza Cagancha 1175; free; open 9am-7pm weekdays, 8am-noon Sat) was named for the man who devised Uruguay's public education system and is located in a functioning school. The first room has interesting photos and a scale model of Montevideo's old fortifications, but the main attraction are the models showing the many forms of punishment inflicted on students in the good old days. Some of them are quite elaborate.

The Automóvil Club del Uruguay's **Museo del Automóvil** (☎ 902-4792 interno 256, 6th floor, Colonia 1251; free; open 5pm-7pm daily) has a superb collection of vintage cars, including a mint 1910 Hupmobile.

Across the harbor from the Ciudad Vieja, the **Museo Militar** (☎ 402-5425, Fortaleza del Cerro; bus No 125 from downtown; admission US$0.80, open 12:30pm-5:30pm Wed-Fri, 10am-5:30pm weekends), in Parque Carlos Vaz Ferreira, has an excellent weapons collection and offers good views of the city. It's not in the best neighborhood; don't visit after dark.

The **Museo Municipal de Artes Juan M Blanes** (☎ 336-2248, Av Millán 4015; free; open 1pm-7pm Tues-Sun), in the suburb of Prado, shows the work of Uruguay's most famous painter, including many historical scenes not just of Uruguay but of the entire River Plate region.

PALACIO LEGISLATIVO

Dating from 1908, the neoclassical legislature is at the north end of Av Libertador General Lavalleja, brilliantly lighted at night; the three-story building is one of the city's most impressive landmarks. Available in English as well as Spanish, guided tours (☎ 200-1334) take place hourly between 8:30am and 6:30pm on weekdays only.

LA RAMBLA

Some visitors find a stroll along this waterfront avenue to be one of the highlights of a visit to Montevideo. You can walk west for several kilometers beyond the foot of Calle

Paraguay, passing rocky beaches and venues for any number of outdoor activities.

SPECIAL EVENTS

Much livelier than its Buenos Aires counterpart, Montevideo's late-summer Carnaval includes candombe dance troupes beating out spirited African-influenced rhythms on large drums.

Semana Criolla festivities during Semana Santa (Holy Week) take place at the Parque Prado, located north of downtown. Because Uruguay is a secular country, official Holy Week celebrations are more nationalistic than religious. The festivities include displays of gaucho skills, *asados* (barbecues) and other such events.

PLACES TO STAY

With the savage economic downturn of recent years, many hotels are teetering on the brink of ruin and have dropped their prices. This has brought some formerly top-end hotels into the mid-range category. If the economy improves, expect costs to rise again.

Budget

Parque Recreativo Punta Espinillo (☎ 312-0667, Camino Basilio Muñoz Km 21) Free. This municipal campground, accessed via Ruta 1 west of town and then the lateral Camino Segundo Sanguinetti, is several kilometers from downtown. It is difficult to reach and has very basic facilities (no hot water), but it's lovely, woodsy and the only campground near the city still in operation.

Albergue Juvenil (☎/fax 908-1324, e almont@adinet.com.uy, Canelones 935) US$9/13 per person with/without HI or ISIC card, breakfast & sheets included. One of the most reasonable and central lodgings for budget travelers is this official Hostelling International facility. It has four-, six- and 12-bed rooms, kitchen and Internet facilities and a lively, spacious central area. 'Smart cards' provide guests 24-hour access.

Hotel Windsor (☎ 901-5080, Zelmar Michelini 1260) Singles/doubles US$8/12 with shared bath, US$11/15 with private bath. The Windsor is cheerless but cheap, with dark rooms.

Hotel City (☎/fax 915-6427, Buenos Aires 462) Singles/doubles/triples US$8/16/19. The amiable Brazilian *dueña* at this recommended hotel speaks a blend of Spanish and Portuguese, and she can lodge guests in two other properties as well. The City is a clean family place with kitchen facilities. All rooms face the spotless sunny patio; some are very dark and musty, but the central location is a strong point.

Hotel Palacio (☎ 916-3612, e fpelaez@internet.com.uy, Bartolomé Mitre 1364) Rooms US$15/25 with shared/private bath. There's lots of brass and wood at this spotless hotel, and rooms have brass beds (some of them sagging), antique furniture, and balconies. Try for one of the two 6th-floor rooms; the water pressure can be erratic, but the views of the Ciudad Vieja from the large balconies are superb.

Hospedaje del Centro (☎ 900-1419, Soriano 1126) Singles/doubles US$8/10 with shared bath, US$12/14.50 with private bath. Once a luxurious single-family residence, it's clean but crumbling a bit, and some rooms are very dark. Only a few of the rooms with shared bath are available, as most are rented by the month.

Hotel Solís (☎ 915-0279, fax 916-4900, e hsolis@adinet.com.uy, Bartolomé Mitre 1314) Singles/doubles with shared bath US$10/18 (US$8/16 with ISIC card), doubles with balcony & private bath US$25. The friendly Solís comes highly recommended and is a very good value. Geared toward the traveler, it offers a cafetería, a large common room with piano and TV, tourist services and limited Internet access (they may be able to steer you to free access elsewhere). Laundry service is available and they also rent a furnished apartment at very reasonable rates for long-term stays.

Hotel Ideal (☎ 901-6389, Colonia 914) Singles/doubles US$12/16 with shared bath, US$17/20 with private bath, fan & cable TV. The Hotel Ideal is clean and friendly, with wooden floors and good bathrooms.

Hotel Ateneo (☎ 901-2630, Colonia 1147) Singles/doubles US$18/20 Sun-Thur, higher Fri & Sat. Some rooms are a bit dark but it's a lovely old building.

Hotel Kaldi (☎ 903-0365, Ejido 1083) Doubles US$25 weekdays, US$30 weekends. This clean, reader-recommended property has rooms with fan, TV, phone and great bathrooms.

Mid-Range

Hotel Arapey (☎ 900-7032, fax 600-2758, e harapey@adinet.com.uy, w www.arapey .com, Av Uruguay 925) Singles/doubles/ triples/quads US$20/25/30/35. Some rooms are dark, others have a funky elegance (cool, not smelly!) elegance, with great wood floors, lots of tile, old brocade curtains and paintings. All have color TV and heat, and the management is very low-key.

Hotel Aramaya (☎ 902-1058, fax 902-9039, e aramaya@adinet.com.uy, Av 18 de Julio 1103) Singles/doubles/triples US$20/30/45 with breakfast. The location is somewhat noisy but the service is good. Rooms are simply furnished; some have double balconies.

Hotel Casablanca (☎/fax 901-0918, San José 1039) US$20 per person with air-con & cable TV. Rooms are modern and tranquil, though most look out on the hall and common areas. Use of a fridge and kitchenette for fixing coffee contribute to the homey feel.

Hotel Lancaster (☎ 902-0029, fax 908-1117, e hotelanc@adinet.com.uy, Plaza Cagancha 1334) Singles/doubles from US$32/48 with buffet breakfast. This central hotel has good service, air-con, TV and some rooms have good views.

Hotel Alvear (☎ 902-0244, fax 902-3728, Yí 1372) Singles/doubles/triples US$48/58/76 with buffet breakfast. Rooms are quiet but getting a bit shabby. The sliding glass shower doors are a welcome sight, and all rooms have central heat, air-con, TV/VCR and minibar.

Top End

Some of Montevideo's top-end hotels lack the luxury of those in Buenos Aires, but as the following listings show, many were offering bargain-basement prices at time of research; all include breakfast in their rates, usually a good buffet spread.

London Palace Hotel (☎ 902-0024, fax 902-1633, e lond@adinet.com.uy, w www .surweb.com/london, Río Negro 1278) Singles/doubles US$50/60/75 with buffet breakfast. Spotless, quiet, comfortable and central, this hotel has a business center with fax, copier and the like. Exterior rooms are US$5 extra.

Balmoral Plaza Hotel (☎ 902-2393, fax 902-2288, e balmoral@netgate.com.uy, w www.balmoral.com.uy, Plaza Cagancha 1126) Singles/doubles/triples US$70/85/101. Rooms at the reader-recommended Balmoral have minibars, safes, big TVs and double-glazed windows to keep out sound and heat. You'll also find a garage, gym, sauna and business center with free Internet access.

Hotel Embajador (☎ 902-0112, fax 902-0009, e hotemb@adinet.com.uy, w www .hotelembajador.com, San José 1212) Singles US$66-88, doubles US$88-118. This four-star hotel offers all you'd expect, plus a pool and sauna, room safes and free Internet access.

Hotel Lafayette (☎ 902-4646, fax 902-1301, e lafayette@montevideo.com.uy, w www.lafayette.com.uy, Soriano 1170) Singles US$94-101, doubles US$110-116. Boasting a pool, gym, sauna and jacuzzi, this ranks among the top Montevideo hotels. Ask for a room with river view.

Radisson Victoria Plaza (☎ 902-0111, fax 902-1628, e radisson@adinet.com.uy, Plaza Independencia 759) Singles/doubles US$170/194. A true five-star hotel, the views from rooms and the 25th-floor restaurant are excellent. A pool, sauna, gym and jogging track contribute to making this Montevideo's most luxurious hotel.

PLACES TO EAT

Montevideo's numerous restaurants are largely unpretentious and offer excellent values.

Meat & Seafood

The *Mercado de la Abundancia* (San José & Aquiles Lanza) and *Mercado Central* (Ciudadela 1229) both have produce stands and a variety of low-priced parrillas. The latter also has a stall serving takeout rotisserie chicken at US$2.25 for a half, US$4 whole. The Mercado del Puerto has a mix of budget parrillas and more upscale establishments, including the following three choices (which, because the area is unsafe at night, are open for lunch only).

La Estancia del Puerto (no ☎, *Mercado del Puerto*) US$1.75-6.50. Grab a counter seat at this no-nonsense parrillada and chow down on meat. They offer half-portions of some cuts and an extensive wine selection as well as sides, salads and *minutas* (short orders).

La Posada de Don Tiburón (☎ 915-4278, *Mercado del Puerto*) US$4.50-12. This very popular indoor/outdoor place features an extensive selection of seafood, meat, crêpes and a good wine list.

El Palenque (☎ 915-4704, *Mercado del Puerto*) US$3.50-12.50. One reader called this indoor/outdoor restaurant the best in Uruguay. Food and service are excellent, and prices can be decent if you choose carefully. It's packed at lunchtime.

Confitería de la Corte (☎ 915-6113, *Ituzaingó 1325*) US$3.25-7. Just off Plaza Constitución, this place has fine, moderately priced lunch specials.

La Genovesa (☎ 900-4411, *San José 1242*) US$4.50-8, open 8pm-4am weekdays, noon-3pm Sun. The Genovesa serves good seafood in abundant portions. A US$1.20 cubierto is added to the bill.

El Fogón (☎ 900-0900, *San José 1080*) US$5-10. White-jacketed waiters serve the usual meat, fish, pasta and salads.

Las Brasas (☎ 900-2285, *San José 909*) US$4-17. Las Brasas is another central, rather upscale parrilla option.

Vegetarian

La Vegetariana (branches: ☎ 900-7661, *Carlos Quijano & 18 de Julio;* ☎ 902-7266, *Rincón 702;* ☎ 901-6418, *Río Negro 1311; other locations*) Lunch US$6, dinner US$4.75. Pay at the front, grab a plate and help yourself from the steam trays – polenta, noodles, ravioli, rice, squash and more. Browse the salad bar, too (bean

sprouts, even!), but watch out, it's soy sauce, not balsamic vinegar. Then hit the desserts. The food is veggie and good at this chain of almost-all-you-can-eat restaurants.

Vida Natural (☎ 908-4157, *San José 1184*) Mains US$3.35, set meals US$2.75-5.25. Tofu! Seitan! Macrobiotic! Upstairs!

Continental

La Crêperie (☎ 915-9511, *Bacacay 1319*) US$4-6. Sweet and savory crêpes, salads, and occasional specials such as *merluza a la plancha* are lovingly presented in intimate, artily decorated but low-key surroundings. Local artists exhibit works and there is sometimes live music.

La Fontana (☎ 916-4462, *JC Gómez 1420*) US$5.25-9.75. Tucked back just off Plaza Constitución. La Fontana offers leafy atrium dining. The menu is haute cuisine, refreshingly short and includes dishes like squash tortellini with Roquefort and mozzarella.

Spanish & Italian

Pizza Bros (☎ 902-8537, *Plaza Cagancha 1364*) US$1.75-8. This small, brick-walled place serves good pizza, calzones and some sandwiches.

Ruffino (☎ 908-3384, *San José 1166*) US$2.75-8.50. For more elaborate dishes in addition to tasty pizzas, visit Ruffino; it even has red-checked tablecloths.

Sarao (☎ 901-1834, *Santiago de Chile 1137*) US$4-10. This Spanish restaurant has flamenco shows on Fridays.

Euskal Erría (☎ 902-3519, *San José 1168*) US$2.50-9.25. The public is welcome in this airy 2nd-floor Basque social club. Choose from a variety of seafood, plus tortillas and paellas (chicken and pork) and eat among the card-players. The excellent *paella de mariscos* (shellfish paella; US$7.50) is easily enough for two.

Middle Eastern & Chinese

Club Libanés (☎ 900-5092, *Paysandú 898*) US$2.75-7; open 9am-11pm weekdays. Here, great Middle Eastern food is served in a decrepit but ornate building.

Super Buffet (☎ 908-5102, *Río Negro 1376*) All-you-can-eat US$6.75. This Chinese *tenedor libre* has a decent variety of veggie dishes among the meaty ones, and a good array of fruits on the dessert table. For US$7.25 a kilo you can take food away.

Breakfast & Sweets
Confitería La Pasiva (☎ 915-8261, *JC Gómez & Sarandí*) US$3.25-8. This confitería (one in a chain), on Plaza Constitución in the Ciudad Vieja, has excellent, reasonably priced minutas and good breakfast specials in a very traditional atmosphere.

Oro del Rhin (☎ 902-2833, *Convención 1403*) Sandwiches US$0.35-3.50. The emphasis here is on sweet stuff, with tons of cakes and pastries, plus fruit or ice-cream *batidos* (shakes).

ENTERTAINMENT
Most of the entertainment venues listed below are in the Ciudad Vieja and the central barrio of El Cordón, but the focus of Montevideo's nightlife is shifting eastward toward Pocitos and Carrasco, where there are plenty of clubs and restaurants, and good beach access. Sections of Av 18 de Julio are closed to motor traffic on Sundays, allowing musical, dance and theater groups to perform.

Music & Dance
The legendary Carlos Gardel spent time in Montevideo, where the tango is no less popular than in Buenos Aires. Other styles of music and dance are popular as well. Some places are strictly for watching, others are for public participation.

Baar Fun Fun (☎ 915-8005, *Ciudadela 1229*) This very informal tango venue is in the Mercado Central. It opens at 11pm or later. Ask prices as you order drinks, and pay for each round when it comes.

La Casa de Becho (☎ 924-4757, *Nueva York 1415*) This place is north of the Tres Cruces bus terminal in the former home of Gerardo Matos Rodríguez, composer of the tango 'La Cumparsita.'

Joventango (☎ 901-5561, *San José & Aquiles Lanza*) Listen to tango singers,

watch the dancing, or join in at this place in the Mercado de la Abundancia.

Sala Zitarrosa (☎ 901-7303, *Av 18 de Julio 1006*) For folkloric music and dance performances, including zarzuela and tango, try this place, opposite Plaza del Entrevero.

Mundo Afro (☎ 915-0247, *Ciudadela 1229*) Afro-Uruguayan candombe shows are the mainstay here, upstairs in the Mercado Central, and you can also take lessons.

Bars
Bar Lobizón (☎ 901-1334, *Zelmar Michelini 1264*) has a good bar atmosphere, with food and entertainment. *Master Pool* (*San José 1410*) is a clean, well-lighted pool hall serving drinks and snacks.

Theaters
Montevideo's theater community has suffered in recent times, with several places closing. Among the survivors are the *Teatro Circular* (☎ 908-1953, *Rondeau 1388*) and *Teatro El Picadero* (☎ 915-2337, *25 de Mayo 390*), in the Ciudad Vieja. Prices are very reasonable, starting at about US$5. Performances are usually in Spanish.

SPECTATOR SPORTS
Soccer, an Uruguayan passion, inspires large and regular crowds. The main stadium, the Estadio Centenario in Parque José Batlle y Ordóñez off Av Italia, opened in 1930 for the first World Cup, in which Uruguay defeated Argentina 4-2 in the title game.

SHOPPING
Central Montevideo's main shopping area is Av 18 de Julio, although the Ciudad Vieja is becoming more attractive as it is redeveloped.

Feria de Tristán Narvaja This Sunday morning outdoor market is a decades-long tradition begun by Italian immigrants. It sprawls from Av 18 de Julio along Calle Tristán Narvaja (seven blocks east of the edge of our map) to Galicia, spilling over onto side streets. In addition to groceries, you can find many interesting trinkets, antiques and souvenirs in its dozens of makeshift stalls.

Mercado de los Artesanos *(Plaza Cagancha)* For attractive handicrafts at reasonable prices in an informal atmosphere, visit this market, which is also a hangout for younger Uruguayans.

Mercado de la Abundancia *(San José & Aquiles Lanza)* There is another artisans market downstairs here, with a bigger selection and nicer atmosphere than at Plaza Cagancha.

Manos del Uruguay *(branches: ☎ 900-4910, San José 1111; ☎ 915-6231, Reconquista 602)* Manos del Uruguay is famous for its quality goods, including woolens.

Casa Mario *(☎ 916-2356, Piedras 641)* Leather is a popular item in Uruguay, and prices are good. This shop in the Ciudad Vieja is worth checking out.

Leather Corner *(☎ 902-8247, San José 950)* This is a branch of Casa Mario.

Arbiter-Pasqualini *(☎ 900-4200, 18 de Julio 943)* For footwear, visit this place, which makes shoes to order.

La Calesa *(☎ 900-7680, Río Negro 1334 bis)* This is a good place to find high-quality Uruguayan woolen goods.

Uruwool *(☎ 401-2868, Tacuarembó 1531)* This is another place to check out excellent Uruguayan woolens.

Louvre *(☎ 916-2686, Sarandí 652)* Louvre has three floors packed with antiques, including gaucho paraphernalia, paintings, furniture and jewelry.

Amatistas Uruguayas *(☎ 916-6456, Sarandí 604)* Uruguay produces some worthwhile gemstones. This place has a wide selection of amethyst, topaz, agate and geodes, as well as products (jewelry, letter-openers and the like) made from them.

GETTING THERE & AWAY
Air
Many more airlines fly to Ezeiza in Buenos Aires than to Montevideo's Carrasco international airport (☎ 604-0272), but many maintain offices in Montevideo. Commuter airlines also provide international services between the two countries. Airlines flying out of Carrasco without stopping in Ezeiza

include Pluna (to Buenos Aires' Aeroparque several Brazilian destinations, Paraguay Chile, and Spain), LAPA (to Aeroparque) TAM (to Paraguay), LANChile (to Santiago), and Varig (to Brazil). Pluna and LAPA offer the cheapest fares to Buenos Aires.

Domestic lines Aeromás and Travelair both offer service to Paysandú, Rivera and Salto. Aeromás also flies to Tacuarembó Travel times are around an hour and fares between US$50 and US$60. See each city's section for more details.

Aerolíneas Argentinas (☎ 901-9466), Convención 1343, 4th floor

Aeromás (☎ 604-0011), Carrasco Airport

Alitalia (☎ 903-1760), Río Negro 1354, 4th floor

American (☎ 916-3929), Sarandí 699 bis

Avianca (☎ 908-4851), Andes 1293, 8th floor

Ecuatoriana (☎ 902-5717), Colonia 820

Iberia (☎ 908-1032), Colonia 873

LANChile (☎ 901-3042), Colonia 993, 4th floor

LAPA (☎ 900-8765), Plaza Cagancha 1339

Lloyd Aéreo Boliviano (LAB; ☎ 902-2656), Colonia 920, 2nd floor

Pluna/Varig (☎ 902-1414), Plaza Independencia 804

Transportes Aéreos del Mercosur (TAM; ☎ 916-6044), Colonia 820

Travelair (☎ 604-0202), Carrasco Airport

United (☎ 902-4630), Plaza Independencia 831, 5th floor

Bus
Montevideo's modern Terminal Tres Cruces (☎ 401-8998), at Bulevar Artigas and Av Italia, is about 3km from the main downtown area. It has tourist information, decent restaurants, clean toilets, a luggage check, public telephones, money exchange, ATM and other services.

Some companies maintain downtown ticket offices; addresses are included below when appropriate. They usually add a small *tasa de embarque* (terminal charge) of around US$0.50 on top of the ticket price.

The following table shows winter fares. All destinations are served daily (except as noted below) and most several times a day. In summer, fares to some destinations may be slightly higher, service more frequent. Travel times are approximate.

Destination	Duration in hours	Cost
Aguas Dulces	4	US$11
Artigas	8	US$20
Asunción (Par)	18	US$70
Barra de Valizas	4½	US$12
Bella Unión	13½	US$25
Buenos Aires	8	US$26
Carmelo	4	US$9.50
Chuy	6	US$13.50
Colonia	3	US$7
Colonia Suiza	2	US$6
Córdoba (Arg)	15½	US$52
Corrientes (Arg)	15	US$48
Curitiba (Bra)	24	US$79
Durazno	3	US$7
Encarnación (Par)	14	US$70
Florianópolis (Bra)	18	US$75
Fray Bentos	4½	US$14
La Paloma	4	US$9.50
Maldonado	2	US$6
Melo	6½	US$16
Mendoza (Arg)	21	US$66
Mercedes	4	US$10
Minas	2	US$5
Nueva Palmira	4½	US$10
Pan de Azúcar	1½	US$4
Paraná (Arg)	10	US$41
Paso de los Toros	3	US$10
Paysandú	4-6	US$15
Pelotas (Bra)	8	US$36
Piriápolis	1½	US$4
Porto Alegre (Bra)	11½	US$49
Posadas (Arg)	13	US$70
Punta del Este	2½	US$7.50
Punta del Diablo	5	US$12
Río Branco	6½	US$17
Rivera	5½-6½	US$20
Rocha	3	US$8.25
Salto	6½-11	US$15-20
San Carlos	2	US$5.50
Santa Fe (Arg)	12	US$45
Santiago de Chile	28	US$113
São Paulo (Bra)	31	US$87
Tacuarembó	6½	US$15
Treinta y Tres	4½	US$11

Among Argentine destinations, Corrientes and Mendoza have at least two departures a week, and Paraná, Santa Fe and Rosario at least four, as does Posadas. There is a minimum of two weekly departures to Santiago, Chile.

Expreso Brújula (☎ 401-9350) goes to Asunción, Paraguay, on Tuesday and Friday, while Coit (☎ 401-5628 at the terminal, 908-6469 at Río Branco 1389) goes Wednesday and Saturday. Both travel via Uruguaiana (Brazil) and Posadas (Argentina), and have reputations for excellent service.

Train

Though sporadic efforts have been made to revive services, the only passenger line in operation in the country is on the Montevideo to 25 de Agosto line, a distance of about 65km. The train makes six stops on the one hour and 50 minute trip (US$2.10), with five runs between 2:40pm and 7:30pm Monday to Friday (returning between 4:50pm and 6:55am), and 1:20pm and 2:20pm departures Saturdays.

Montevideo's Estación Central General Artigas between Río Negro and Paraguay, just north of La Paz is worth a visit in itself, a grand structure in the French style, with imposing statues of James Watt, Alessandro Volta and others out front. It's now a sad relic of better times, where seeing the timetable with its lone destination is enough to break your heart.

Boat

Buquebus has port offices (☎ 916-1910) at the entrance to the Dársena Fluvial on Rambla 25 de Agosto, at the foot of Colón in the Ciudad Vieja, but tickets can also be purchased at the Ferryturismo office (see next paragraph). Buquebus runs up to four high-speed ferries a day across the river to Buenos Aires (2½ hours). Fares are US$58 in *turista*, US$73 in *primera*; children aged three to 10 pay US$38 *turista*, US$53 *primera*; infants up to two pay US$19 in either class.

Ferryturismo, at Río Negro 1400 (☎ 900-6617) and at the Tres Cruces bus terminal (☎ 409-8198), offers bus-boat combinations to Buenos Aires (US$40, 4 hours) via Colonia, with up to four departures a day.

Cacciola (☎ 401-9350), at Terminal Tres Cruces, runs a bus-launch service to Buenos Aires, via the riverside town of Carmelo and the Argentine Delta suburb of Tigre twice a day Monday to Saturday, once Sunday. The eight-hour trip is US$20 one-way, US$37 roundtrip, and prices are higher in summer.

GETTING AROUND
To/From the Airport

Pluna/Varig passengers get free shuttle service between the Plaza Independencia offices and Carrasco. From the Terminal Río Branco at the corner of Rambla 25 de Agosto and Río Branco, any bus with 'Aeropuerto' on its sign will get you there in about an hour for US$1.10. Special red Cutesa and Copsa buses (US$1.20) are much faster. From the airport, any bus with 'Montevideo' on its sign will take you to the Río Branco terminal. They come down Av Uruguay for the last part of their run.

A taxi to the airport from the center costs approximately US$20. From the airport, however, drivers operating cream-colored Mercedes cabs have the monopoly and charge a whopping US$35.

Bus

Montevideo's buses go everywhere for about US$0.75 (more if you travel outside the city proper). Buses 21, 61, 180, 187 and 188 all pass Tres Cruces bus terminal. Any bus from Tres Cruces whose sign reads 'Aduana' or 'Ciudad Vieja' will pass near central Plaza Independencia.

The *Guía de Montevideo Eureka*, available at bookshops or kiosks, lists routes and schedules, as do the yellow pages of the Montevideo phone book. The driver or conductor will sometimes ask your destination. Retain your ticket, which may be inspected at any time. Most routes cease service by 10:30pm or 11pm. For information, contact Cutesa (☎ 200-9021, 200-7527).

Car & Taxi

Before signing a rental contract, verify whether insurance and IVA are included.

Rental agencies include Budget at Mercedes 935 (☎ 902-5353) and the airport (☎ 604-0189); Dollar (☎/fax 412-6427), at JB Amorín 1186; Localiza, at Colonia 813 (☎ 903-3920) and the airport (☎ 604-0380); and Multicar (☎ 902-2555), at Colonia 1227. Multicar tends to have slightly older vehicles but their long-term rates can be quite good.

Montevideo's black-and-yellow taxis are all metered. It costs about US$1.10 to drop the flag and US$0.65 per 600m. Between 10pm and 6am, and on weekends and holidays, fares are 20% higher. There is a small additional charge for luggage, and riders generally round off the total fare to the next higher peso.

Western Uruguay

Lying west of Montevideo, this portion of Uruguay is opposite northeastern Argentina across the Río de la Plata and the Río Uruguay. Like its Argentine counterpart, the region is commonly referred to as *el Litoral* (the littoral, or shore).

One can't-miss attraction here is the 17th-century Portuguese contraband port and fortress of Colonia, directly opposite Buenos Aires. Overland travelers from northeastern Argentina will find the other, slower-paced riverfront towns, with their colonial and 19th-century architecture, pleasant enough to justify a stopover. A stroll along the river is always a treat in these towns, even the larger ones. Several lesser sights make worthwhile day trips from either Colonia or Montevideo.

COLONIA
☎ 052 • pop 29,000

Colonia is an agreeable, slow-paced town whose colonial-era Barrio Histórico is a UNESCO world cultural heritage site. Numerous sycamores offer protection from the summer heat, and the Río de la Plata helps to cool things off while also providing a venue for spectacular sunsets. Though Colonia del Sacramento (the full name is rarely used) attracts relatively few foreign tourists, its proximity to Buenos Aires and its charm draw thousands of Argentine visitors. On weekends, especially in summer, prices rise, and it can be difficult to find a room or enjoy a quiet drink in a restaurant.

Colonia was founded in 1680 by Manoel Lobo, the Portuguese governor of Rio de Janeiro, and occupied a strategic position almost exactly opposite Buenos Aires across the Río de la Plata. The town's major importance was as a source of smuggled trade items, undercutting Spain's jealously defended mercantile monopoly. British goods made their way from Colonia into Buenos Aires and the interior through surreptitious exchange with the Portuguese in the Paraná Delta; for this reason, Spanish forces intermittently besieged Portugal's riverside outpost for decades.

Although the two powers agreed over the cession of Colonia to Spain around 1750, the agreement failed when Jesuit missionaries on the upper Paraná refused to comply with the proposed exchange of territory in their area. Spain finally captured the city in 1762, but failed to hold it until 1777, when authorities created the Viceroyalty of the River Plate. From this time, the city's commercial importance declined as foreign goods proceeded directly to Buenos Aires.

Big changes may be in store for the town; there is a proposal to build a massive bridge linking Uruguay and Argentina. The project is still only in the planning stages and faces a severe shortage of funds. It has drawn criticism on economic, environmental and social grounds, but many residents see it as a source of much-needed employment and a boost to trade.

Orientation

Colonia sits on the east bank of the Río de la Plata, 180km west of Montevideo, but only 50km from Buenos Aires by ferry or hydrofoil. It features an irregular colonial nucleus of narrow cobbled streets, the Barrio Histórico, on a small peninsula jutting into the river. The town's commercial center, around Plaza 25 de Agosto, and the river port are a few blocks east, while the Rambla Costanera (named Rambla de las Américas at the edge of town) leads

north along the river to the Real de San Carlos, another area of interest to visitors. The diagonal Av Roosevelt becomes Ruta 1, the main highway to Montevideo.

Information

The municipal tourist office (☎/fax 26141) is at General Flores 499. Helpful and well informed, the staff has numerous brochures difficult to obtain elsewhere. Hours are roughly 8am to 8pm daily. The national tourism ministry (☎ 24897) maintains a ferry port branch (no ☎).

The Argentine consulate (☎ 22093), at Av General Flores 215, is open weekdays noon to 5pm.

Avoid the bad exchange rates at the port's money exchange – better ones are offered just outside the gate at Cambio Viaggio or downtown at such places as Cambio Dromer (also a Western Union office), at Av General Flores and Intendente Suárez. Red Banc has an ATM at Av General Flores and Rivadavia.

The post office is at Lavalleja 226. Almost next door, at the corner with Rivadavia, Antel has direct fiber-optic lines to the USA (AT&T and MCI) and the UK. Decent Internet access is US$0.80 per half hour at Local 31 inside the (unmarked) Galería América at Rivadavia and Méndez.

Receptivos Colonia (☎ 23388, e recep tivos@usa.net), Av General Flores 508, can arrange air tickets, tours, car rentals, lodging and transportation to the airport.

Walking Tour

The following walk takes in most of the highlights of Colonia's Barrio Histórico, also known as 'la colonia portuguesa' (the Portuguese colony), but you should take time to wander off the itinerary and explore the small streets. Each yields a number of little visual delights. One thing to note: All of Colonia's museums have the same hours and one US$0.80 ticket gives you admission to all. For information call the Casa de la Cultura de Colonia (☎ 23075).

The tour begins at the 1745 **Puerta de Campo** on Calle Manuel de Lobos, the restored entrance to the old city. A thick

COLONIA

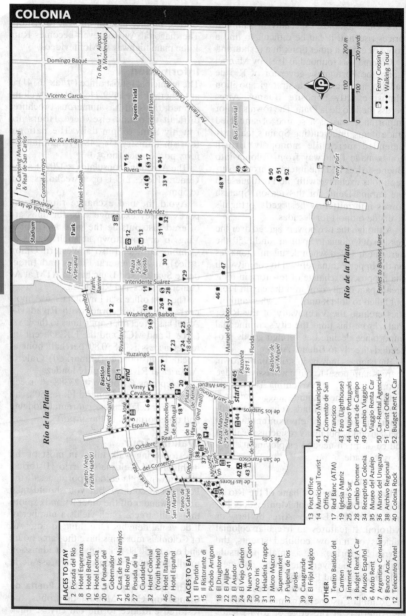

0   100   200 m
0   100   200 yards

Ferry Crossing
Walking Tour

Rio de la Plata

Rio de la Plata

Ferries to Buenos Aires

PLACES TO STAY
2 Posada del Río
8 Hotel Esperanza
10 Hotel Beltrán
16 Hotel Leoncia
20 La Posada del Gobernador
21 Casa de los Naranjos
26 Hotel Royal
27 Posada de la Ciudadela
32 Hotel Colonial (Youth Hostel)
46 Hotel Italiano
47 Hotel Español

PLACES TO EAT
11 El Portón
15 Il Ristorante di Pícholo Arrigoni
18 El Drugstore
22 El Aljibe
23 El Asador
24 El Viejo Galeón
29 Nuevo San Cono
31 Heladería Frappé
31 Micro Macro
37 Pulpería de los Faroles
39 Casagrande
48 El Frijol Mágico

OTHER
1 Teatro Bastión del Carmen
3 Internet Access
4 Budget Rent A Car
5 Museo Español
6 Moto Rent
9 Argentine Consulate
9 Banco Acac
12 Telecentro Antel
13 Post Office
14 Municipal Tourist Office
17 Red Banc (ATM)
19 Iglesia Matríz
25 Cambio Dromer
28 Receptivos Colonia
34 Museo del Azulejo
35 Manos del Uruguay
36 Casa-Rental Agencies
38 Colonia Rock
40 Cambio Viaggio;
    Viaggio Renta Car
41 Museo Municipal
42 Convento de San Francisco
43 Faro (Lighthouse)
44 Museo Portugués
45 Puerta de Campo
49 Cambio Viaggio;
    Viaggio Renta Car
50 Car-Rental Agencies
51 Tourist Office
52 Budget Rent A Car

fortified wall runs south along the Paseo de San Miguel to the river. A short distance west is **Plaza Mayor 25 de Mayo**, off of which the narrow, roughly cobbled **Calle de los Suspiros** (Street of Sighs), lined with tile-and-stucco colonial houses, runs south almost to the water. Just beyond this street, the **Museo Portugués** (*Plaza Mayor 25 de Mayo 180, admission US$0.80; open 11:30am-5pm Tues-Thurs*) has good exhibits on the Portuguese period, including Lusitanian and colonial dress.

Off the southwest corner of the Plaza Mayor are the ruins of the 17th-century **Convento de San Francisco**, within which stands the 19th-century **faro** (*lighthouse; free; open 10:30am-noon weekends*). The lighthouse provides an excellent view of the old town. At the west end of the Plaza Mayor, on Calle del Comercio, is the **Museo Municipal** (*Plaza Mayor 25 de Mayo 77; admission US$0.80; open 11:30am-5pm Tues-Thurs*). On the northwest edge of the plaza, is the **Archivo Regional** (*Calle de las Misiones de los Tapes 115; admission US$0.80; open 11:30am-5pm Tues-Thurs*), which contains a small museum and bookshop.

Head to the west end of Misiones de los Tapes for the dinky **Museo del Azulejo** (*Tile Museum; admission US$0.80; open 11:30am-5pm Tues-Thurs*), a 17th-century house with a sampling of colonial tile work (you can sneak peeks through the windows even if it's closed). From there, the riverfront Paseo de San Gabriel leads north to Plazoleta San Martín. Turn east and you will reach Av General Flores; continue east a block and turn south on Calle Vasconcellos to reach the landmark **Iglesia Matriz** on the shady Plaza de Armas, also known as Plaza Manuel Lobo. The church, begun in 1680, is Uruguay's oldest, though it has been completely rebuilt twice. The plaza holds the foundations of a house dating from Portuguese times.

Heading back north to General Flores then beyond it a block farther north brings you near the **Museo Español** (*San José 164; admission US$0.80; open 11:30am-5pm Tues-Thurs*), which has exhibitions of replica colonial pottery, clothing and maps. At the north end of nearby Calle España is the **Puerto Viejo**, the old port, now the yacht

harbor. One block east, at Calle del Virrey Cevallos and Rivadavia, the **Teatro Bastión del Carmen** (*free admission to exhibitions; open 10am-11pm daily*) is a theater and gallery complex that incorporates part of the city's ancient fortifications. The huge chimney is newer, dating from the 1880s.

Real de San Carlos

At the turn of the 20th century, naturalized Argentine entrepreneur Nicolás Mihanovich spent US$1.5 million to build an immense tourist complex 5km west of Colonia at Real de San Carlos, a spot where Spanish troops once camped before attacking the Portuguese outpost. Among the attractions erected by Mihanovich, a Dalmatian immigrant, were a 10,000-seat bullring (made superfluous after Uruguay outlawed bullfights in 1912), a 3000-seat jai alai frontón, a hotel-casino with its own power plant (the casino failed in 1917 when the Argentine government began to tax every boat crossing the river), and a racecourse.

Only the racecourse functions today, and it may close erelong, but the ruins make an interesting excursion. There is also the **Museo Municipal Real de San Carlos**, which focuses on paleontology, and unfortunately keeps no fixed hours.

Places to Stay

As Colonia has become a more popular destination for Argentine and international travelers, innkeepers have upgraded accommodations, and prices have risen, but there are still reasonable alternatives. The municipal tourist office has lists of real-estate agents who arrange house rentals. Some hotels charge higher rates Friday through Sunday. If you can avoid Colonia on summer weekends, do so. If you can't, it's essential to book ahead.

Budget Really cheap accommodations have nearly disappeared.

Camping Municipal de Colonia (☎ 24444, Rambla Costanera s/n) Sites US$4 per tent. The campground sits in a eucalyptus grove at Real de San Carlos, 5km north of the Barrio Histórico. Close to the Balneario

Municipal, its excellent facilities are open year-round and are easily accessible by public transport. It also has cabañas for US$25-40 double. The pricier ones have private baths and air-con.

Hotel Colonial (☎ 28151, barlocel@ adinet.com.uy, Av General Flores 440) Dorm beds US$10 per person with shared bath. At the time of research, this hotel was being converted into a youth hostel with four-bed rooms, a kitchen and laundry facilities. The name will remain the same.

Hotel Español (cellular ☎ 099-624129, Manuel de Lobos 377) Rooms US$10 per person with shared bath. This place has large but dark rooms facing a pleasant courtyard. It was barely getting by at research time and may close.

Posada de la Ciudadela (☎ 22683, Washington Barbot 164) Rooms US$17 per person with air-con & TV. A small, clean hotel with a touch of charm – most rooms face a quiet courtyard.

Posada del Río (☎/fax 23002, e delrio@ colonianet.com, Washington Barbot 258) Singles/doubles/triples/quads US$20/40/50/60 with breakfast, air-con & cable TV. This serene and friendly place, on a tree-lined street close to a pleasant sandy beach, is probably Colonia's best lodging value.

Mid-Range At *Hotel Royal* (☎ 23139, fax 22169, Av General Flores 340) singles/doubles cost US$20/40 weekdays, US$30/60 weekends with air-con & TV. The Royal has a restaurant and pool, is conveniently central and upper-floor rooms have good views.

Hotel Italiano (☎/fax 22103, Intendente Suárez 105) Doubles US$50 breakfast, air-con & cable TV. The Italiano has a restaurant, heated pool and offstreet parking. Rooms are clean and well maintained; some have balconies.

Hotel Beltrán (☎/fax 22955, e hotel beltran@netgate.com.uy, w www.colonia net.com/hotelbeltran, Av General Flores 311) Doubles with shared/private bath US$30/65 weekdays, US$36/85 weekends, including breakfast. Friendly, quiet and very clean, with rooms facing onto a central patio, this is one of Colonia's oldest hotels.

Hotel Leoncia (☎/fax 22369, e hleoncia@ adinet.com.uy, Rivera 214) Singles/doubles US$45/60 with breakfast, air-con & cable TV. Most of the small but well-appointed rooms look onto a quiet, pleasing courtyard; many have balconies. Favored by businesspeople, it also has a heated pool and a restaurant.

Hotel Esperanza (☎/fax 22922, Av General Flores 237) Singles/doubles US$50/70 with breakfast, air-con, cable TV, minibar & jacuzzi. The Esperanza is near the entrance to the Barrio Histórico; prices go down when demand is low.

Top End The *Casa de los Naranjos* (☎/fax 24630, e naranjos@adinet.com.uy, w www .colonianet.com/naranjos, 18 de Julio 219) rents doubles for US$65-90 (US$85-100 Saturday). A small grassy park with swimming pool and a 200-year-old orange tree highlight this quiet colonial posada in the Barrio Histórico. The US$100 suite is charmingly furnished.

La Posada del Gobernador (☎/fax 22918, e gobernador@colonianet.com, 18 de Julio 205) Doubles US$100 with breakfast minibar, cable TV & phone. Its colonial architecture and location in the Barrio Histórico make this Colonia's most distinctive accommodations. Many of the rooms are furnished with antiques (which include the air-conditioners, unfortunately).

Places to Eat

Colonia's restaurants are just behind Punta del Este in charging cubiertos (see Food in the Facts for the Visitor section of this chapter).

El Asador (☎ 24204, Ituzaingó 168) US$2.50-5. Often jammed with locals, this inexpensive parrilla is an excellent value and has great service. It's the usual cuts of meat but grilled to perfection, and pasta and pizza as well.

Nuevo San Cono (Suárez & 18 de Julio) US$2.50-5. With a well-stocked bar and a very neighborhood feel, this traditional parrilla is a cozy place to pass a chilly evening.

El Portón (☎ 25318, Av General Flores 333) US$2.50-5. El Portón is a more upscale but appealing parrilla.

El Viejo Galeón (18 de Julio & Ituzaingó) US$2.75-8. Renowned for its *chivitos*, the Galeón also serves several pastas in a variety of styles.

El Aljibe (☎ 25342, *Av General Flores & Ituzaingó*) US$3.75-6.50. The higher prices reflect the attractive colonial setting of this parrilla more than the quality of the food. They serve a set meal for US$8 as well.

El Frijol Mágico (☎ 24433, *Manuel de Lobos 449*) US$1.25 per item, BIG salads US$2.25. The menu changes daily at this ovo-lacto vegetarian joint. Savory veggie or cheese tarts are the specialty, but they often serve wheat-gluten dishes; vegans, cross your fingers!

Il Ristorante di Picholo Arrigoni (☎ 25443, *Rivera & Rivadavia*) US$3.25-8. This is a good Italian-flavored choice, with full parrilla and several seafood dishes.

Pulpería de los Faroles (☎ 25399, *del Comercio & Misiones de los Tapes*) US$4-10. With its setting in the Barrio Histórico, this reader-recommended eatery has an upscale ambience but isn't outrageously expensive for a tasty meal.

Casagrande (no ☎, *Misiones de los Tapes 143*) US$5.50-7.50. Two doors away from the Pulpería de los Faroles, in a lovely old building, Casagrande offers innovative dishes, some of which work better than others.

El Drugstore (☎ 25241, *Vasconcellos 179*) Sandwiches & main dishes US$2.50-12. The color scheme is vivid and the decor a pastiche of wildly varying modern-art reproductions. But it works! The food ain't bad, either, especially the *ensalada completa*. El Drugstore is also a bar and venue for live music.

You can scream for ice cream at *Arco Iris* (*Lavalleja 189*) and *Heladería Frappé* (*Av General Flores 442*), or stock up on groceries at the *Micro Macro* (*Rivera 185*) supermarket.

Entertainment

Colonia's most happening nightspot, *El Drugstore* (see Places to Eat, earlier), has a bar, wine list and live music starting at 9pm Friday and Saturday. *Colonia Rock* (no ☎, *Real & Misiones de los Tapes*), in the Barrio Histórico, is Colonia's attempt at a Hard Rock Café. The bar/restaurant occupies a colonial building and has indoor and outdoor courtyard seating. *Barrio Sur* (18 de Julio 267) is a social club that's is open to the public; it has snacks and live music.

Shopping

Many shops sell items of polished agate at reasonable prices. Keep an eye out also for ornate *mate* gourds and Portuguese-style ceramics.

Though it's generally open 10am-7pm or 8pm daily, the hours of Colonia's **handicrafts market** (*Suárez & Fosalba*) vary with the season and volume of business. Colonia's branch of the national handicrafts store *Manos del Uruguay* (☎ 24119, *San Gabriel & Misiones de los Tapes*) is in the Barrio Histórico.

Getting There & Away

Air Aerovip (☎ 28881) flies weekday mornings and evenings between Colonia, Buenos Aires' Aeroparque (US$32, 15 minutes) and Montevideo (US$26, 30 minutes). Saturdays there's an afternoon flight, Sundays an evening.

Bus Colonia's new terminal is at Manuel de Lobos and Av Roosevelt, near the port. Some bus companies have maintained their downtown offices, but all may eventually move them to the terminal. Ruta 1 from Montevideo is divided highway for much of its length; eventually it should be divided the entire distance.

The following table shows winter fares. All destinations are served daily (except as noted below) and most several times a day. Travel times are approximate.

Destination	Duration in hours	Cost
Bella Unión	10	US$22.50
Carmelo	1	US$3
Colonia Suiza	50 min	US$2.50
Mercedes	3	US$7-8
Montevideo	2½-3	US$7-8
Nueva Palmira	1¾	US$4
Paysandú	6	US$13
Salto	8	US$18

Boat From the port at the foot of Rivera, Buquebus (☎ 22975) and Ferrylíneas (☎ 22919) run two slow ferries to Buenos Aires at 4:30am and 6:45pm Monday to Saturday (6:45pm only Sunday). The trip takes three hours and costs US$20 for adults, US$16.25 for children ages three to nine. Their faster boats, taking 45 minutes to an hour and costing US$34, leave three or four times a day between 8am and 9pm. Fares may be higher on selected peak days and in summer.

Immigration for both countries is handled at the port before boarding; be sure to go through the procedures or you will have problems later. At the time of research there was no official luggage storage facility at the port; this may change as more terminals are constructed. In the meantime, the tourist office in town may be willing to keep an eye on your bag.

Getting Around

The airport is 7km from town on Ruta 1. Most Montevideo-bound buses will drop you at the turnoff for the airport (US$1.25), from which it's a 1.3km walk to the terminal. Receptivos Colonia (☎ 23388) can arrange a *remise* for about US$4.

Local buses go to Camping Municipal and Real de San Carlos (US$0.40) from along Av General Flores.

Walking is enjoyable in compact Colonia, but motor scooters and bicycles are popular means of getting around town. Rentals can run as low as US$18 and US$5 a day, respectively. Gas-powered buggies (like large golf carts, holding four to six people) at around US$35 a day have come in handy for readers in casts. Cars start at about US$35 a day. Prices listed are winter promotional rates. Try Moto Rent, on Virrey Cevallos near Av General Flores; Budget Rent A Car (☎ 22939), in the port and at Av General Flores 91; or Viaggio Renta Car (☎ 221504) just outside the port on Rivera.

COLONIA SUIZA

☎ 055 • pop 9600

Colonia Suiza (also known as Nueva Helvecia) is a quiet, pleasant destination with a demonstrably European ambience. It lies 120km west of Montevideo and 60km east of Colonia del Sacramento, along a short lateral off Ruta 1. The town was settled in 1862 by Swiss immigrants attracted by the temperate climate and good land as well as the freedom of worship and opportunity to gain Uruguayan citizenship without renouncing their own. The country's first interior agricultural colony, Colonia Suiza provided wheat for the mills of Montevideo and today produces more than half of Uruguay's cheese.

Be warned that Colonia Suiza is spread out over a large area. The serene hotel zone is not within reasonable walking distance of town.

Information

Colonia Suiza has a formal tourist office at the entrance to town from Ruta 1, but there's also a particularly helpful one at the Artesanos Ciudad Jardín cooperative (☎ 24812) at Colonia Valdense, Ruta 1 Km 120, about 6km from Colonia Suiza.

To change cash, try Banco La Caja Obrera, on the central Plaza de los Fundadores. Antel is at Artigas and Dreyer, across from the landmark OSE water tower. The hospital (☎ 44057) is at 18 de Julio and C Cunier.

Things to See & Do

The center of the town is the Plaza de los Fundadores, with an impressive sculpture, *El Surco*, commemorating the original Swiss pioneers. The **Molino Quemado**, the remains of a flour mill that burned in 1881 under mysterious circumstances, is 4km down a dirt road that takes off from the edge of town. Another interesting building is the historic **Hotel del Prado** today serves double duty as a hotel and youth hostel.

Places to Stay

The Barrio Hoteles (hotel zone) is on the southeastern outskirts of town, which makes for serene isolation. All the hotels here have restaurants.

Hotel del Prado (☎/fax 44169, e *hot prado@adinet.com.uy, Elwin Hoden s/n*) Rooms US$20 per person, hostel beds US$9 with card. Dating from 1896, this 80-room hotel is a magnificent if declining building with huge balconies, a pool and a restaurant serving good meals at reasonable prices. The hostel beds are two and three to a room; each pair of rooms shares a bath. Both hostel and hotel facilities are getting run down, but it's a peaceful and comfortable place.

Granja Hotel Suizo (☎ 44002, fax 44761, e *waltraudstuder@i.com.uy, Av Federico Fischer s/n)* Doubles from US$48 with aircon & buffet breakfast. Dating from 1872, this is the country's oldest tourist hotel and has a renowned restaurant. All rooms have balconies, TV and heating. The ample grounds are tranquil and parklike, and there's a pool and sauna as well.

Hotel Nirvana (☎ 44052, 902-4124 in *Montevideo, fax 44175, e nirvana@adinet .com.uy, Av Batlle y Ordóñez s/n)* Singles/doubles US$94/112 with buffet breakfast; additional nights US$82/98. This luxurious hotel is top of the line. It offers a swimming pool, tennis courts, horseback riding, facilities for children, and 25 hectares of beautifully landscaped grounds. A good restaurant rounds it out, and half-board runs between US$15 and US$21 (US$9 for children).

Places to Eat

Colonia Suiza has several excellent restaurants, including the one at the Hotel Suizo.

Don Juan (☎ 45099, 18 de Julio 1214) US$3-5. Don Juan is a cozy, wood-paneled confitería serving chivitos, pizza and the like.

Pizza y Pico (☎ 46120, Herrera & 25 de *Agosto)* US$2.75-6.50. Readers recommend the chivitos, milanesas and pizza at this very tidy brick building with simple but pleasing decor.

L'Arbalete (☎ 444052, Hotel Nirvana) US$6-12. It's worth a visit just to take in the spacious dining room and the grounds at this resort. The menu has continental and Swiss touches (rösti, of course!), with a full selection of pastas, meat, fish and poultry plus a good wine list.

Heladería Helvecia (Colón 1053) Closed in winter. Try the 'yerba' *(mate)* flavor at this ice-creamery.

Getting There & Away

Don't forget the town is also called Nueva Helvecia, and some bus companies refer to it this way. Bus offices are around the plaza. There's plenty of services to Montevideo (US$6, 2 hours) and Colonia (US$2.50, 50 minutes), as well as buses to area towns.

CARMELO
☎ 0542 • pop 16,000

Carmelo is a laid-back town of cobblestone streets and low old houses, a center for yachting, fishing and exploring the Paraná Delta. It lies opposite the delta just below the point where the Río Uruguay empties into the Río de la Plata, 75km northwest of Colonia del Sacramento and 235km from Montevideo. Launches connect Carmelo to the Buenos Aires suburb of Tigre.

The town dates from 1816, when residents of the village of Las Víboras (The Vipers) petitioned for permission to move to the more hospitable Arroyo de las Vacas (Cow River). The local economy depends on tourism, livestock, and agriculture – local wines have an excellent reputation. In early February the town hosts the Fiesta Nacional de la Uva (National Grape Festival).

Orientation

Carmelo straddles the Arroyo de las Vacas, a stream that widens into a sheltered harbor on the Río de la Plata. North of the arroyo, shady Plaza Independencia is now the commercial center. Most of the town's businesses are along 19 de Abril, which leads to the bridge over the arroyo, across which lies a large park offering open space, camping, swimming and a huge casino. Street numbers rise as you head into town from the arroyo.

Information

The helpful municipal tourist office (☎ 2001) is in the Casa de Cultura on 19 de Abril at Barrios, four blocks north of the bridge over the arroyo. Have a look around; it was built in 1860 and once belonged to Ignacio Barrios, one of San Martín's lieutenants and a signer of Uruguay's declaration of independence.

Banco Hipotecario del Uruguay, across 19 de Abril from the tourist office, changes money from 1pm to 5pm weekdays. The post office is at Uruguay 360, Antel is on Barrios between Uruguay and Zorrilla de San Martín, and the hospital (☎ 2107) is at Uruguay and Artigas.

Things to See & Do
The arroyo, with large, rusty boats moored along it, makes for a great ramble, and just strolling around the town itself is enjoyable. The **Santuario del Carmen**, on Barrios between Varela and del Carmen, dates from 1830. Next door is the **Archivo y Museo Parroquial** (no ☎, Barrios 208, free; opening hours vary), with documents and objects of local historical importance.

Places to Stay
Camping Náutico Carmelo (☎ 2058, Arroyo de las Vacas s/n) US$3 per person. This campground is on the south side of Arroyo de las Vacas and provides camping facilities for yachters as well as walk-ins. Supervision can be lax; at times you may be able to pitch a tent for free. There is a surcharge for electricity.

Hotel Oriental (☎ 2404, 19 de Abril 284) Rooms US$8/4 per adult/child (to age 10). The cheapest in town is this basic place with multibed, mostly windowless rooms.

Hotel La Unión (☎ 2028, Uruguay 368) Singles US$9/12 with shared/private bath, doubles US$20 with private bath. This tidy hotel alongside the post office is not always open.

Hotel Bertoletti (☎ 2030, Uruguay 171) Singles/doubles US$12/25 with shared bath, US$15/30 with private bath. This is a modern and clean if not architecturally pleasing hotel.

Hotel Rambla (☎ 2390, fax 2638, Uruguay 55) Singles/doubles US$16/33 with breakfast. The Rambla is conveniently close to the launch docks. Plusher doubles with TV, fridge and balconies facing the arroyo run US$39.

Hotel Casino Carmelo (☎/fax 2314, Av Rodó s/n) Doubles US$60/86/110 with breakfast/half-board/full board. This hotel and casino is across the arroyo. It's getting a bit worn around the edges, but the views

toward the river are good and it has two pools, and there's a small animal park with peacocks, flamingos and rheas on the grounds.

Places to Eat
Restaurant Simbad (☎ 2247, 19 de Abril & 12 de Febrero) US$2.50-7. This is a good breakfast or lunch spot that's on the town side of the bridge. It serves fish, short orders (including chivitos) and good licuados (blended fruit drinks), and has lots of windows.

The following two listings are across the bridge in the park.

Parrilla Susana (☎ 5327, Av Rodó s/n) US$2-4.50. Open late November to Easter, weekends only March to October. Meat and fished are grilled in this shacklike place in the middle of the Camping Náutico. You can eat in or carry your food to one of the cement tables at water's edge and enjoy the view.

Yacht Club (☎ 2340, Av Rodó s/n) US$3.25-7.25. The club is on a bend in the arroyo and ringed by willow trees. The upscale restaurant serves the usual dishes. Some tables overlook the club's clay tennis courts.

Getting There & Away
All the bus companies are on or near Plaza Independencia. Chadre (☎ 2987), on 18 de Julio just off 19 de Abril, goes to Montevideo (US$9.50, 3½ hours) and north to Fray Bentos (2½ hours), Paysandú (US$9.50, 5½ hours) and Salto (6 hours). Sabelín, at the same address, goes to Nueva Palmira (US$1.25, 30 minutes) six times daily. Turil goes to Colonia (US$3.25, 1 hour), as do Klüver (☎ 23411) and Intertur, both at 19 de Abril and Roosevelt. Klüver also goes to Nueva Palmira and Mercedes (US$4.25, 1¾ hours).

Cacciola (☎ 3042), at Constituyente 219, runs launches to the Buenos Aires suburb of Tigre at 4:30am and 2pm weekdays, 4:30am and 4pm Saturdays, and 4pm Sundays. The three-hour trips costs US$12 one way for adults, US$10.75 for children aged three to nine.

LA ESTANCIA DE NARBONA

Despite the deteriorating condition of its buildings, this 18th-century estancia on the Arroyo Víboras, about 11km west of Carmelo on the road to Nueva Palmira, is deservedly a national historical monument. Its *casco* (main house) and chapel, with a three-story bell tower, sit on the summit of a small hill about 2km from the main road. At the junction and near a hydraulic mill erected to process local wheat, the **Puente Castells**, a brick bridge with six arches, has stood for more than 130 years. Buses bound for Nueva Palmira will drop you at the turnoff.

FRAY BENTOS

☎ 0562 • pop 22,000

Fray Bentos is the southernmost overland crossing point from Argentina, reached by the Libertador General San Martín bridge over the Río Uruguay. This former company town was once dominated by an enormous English-run meat-processing plant, now preserved as a museum. Another museum features excellent works the painter Luis Solari.

Lying on the east bank of the river, opposite the Argentine city of Gualeguaychú, Fray Bentos is capital of Río Negro department, and is about 300km northwest of Montevideo.

Information

The municipal tourist office (☎ 22233) occupies an office in the Museo Solari, on the west side of Plaza Constitución. It has a friendly, helpful, and knowledgeable staff and is open daily 9am to 9pm. The Argentine consulate (☎ 23225) is at 18 de Julio 1225. Banco ACAC is at Treinta y Tres and 18 de Julio. The post office is at Treinta y Tres 3271, and Antel is at Zorrilla 1127. You can access the Internet at the Plaza Hotel (see Places to Stay) for US$4.75 an hour. The Hospital Salúd Pública (☎ 22742) is at Echeverría and Lavalleja.

Things to See & Do

The municipal **Museo Solari** *(☎ 22233, Treinta y Tres s/n; free; open 2pm-8pm daily in winter, 6pm-midnight daily in summer)* is on the west side of Plaza Constitución. It has changing exhibits and features the satirical works of Luis Solari, many of which contain fanciful human figures with the heads of animals. They poke fun at human foibles and are beautifully rendered.

Fray Bentos' most architecturally distinguished landmark, the 400-seat **Teatro Young** bears the name of the Anglo-Uruguayan *estanciero* who sponsored its construction between 1909 and 1912. Now municipal property, it hosts cultural events throughout the year and can be visited upon request; ask at the theater itself or at the tourist office. It's a block north of Plaza Constitución at 25 de Mayo and Zorrilla.

In Parque Roosevelt, on the banks of the river at the foot of 18 de Julio, the open-air **Teatro Municipal de Verano** seats 4000 and has excellent acoustics.

In 1865, the Liebig Extract of Meat Company located its pioneer South American plant, which soon became the most important industrial complex in Uruguay, southwest of downtown Fray Bentos. British-run El Anglo took over operations in the 1920s and by WWII the factory employed a workforce of 4,000, slaughtering cattle at the astronomical rate of 2000 a day. Most of the defunct Frigorífico Anglo del Uruguay has become the **Museo de la Revolución Industrial** *(☎ 23607, Barrio Histórico del Anglo, admission US$1, open Monday to Friday)*, a fascinating maze of corrals, walkways and slaughterhouses. Guided tours, in English and Spanish, are pretty much the only way to see the place; they take place at 10am, 11:30am, 2pm and 3:30pm (more in summer).

Places to Stay

Club Atlético Anglo (☎ 22787, Rambla Cuervo s/n) Sites US$4; open summer only. This club maintains a campground, with hot showers and beach access, about seven blocks south of Plaza Constitución and just across the bridge at the south end of town.

Balneario Las Cañas (☎ 22224) US$4 per tent plus $2 per person. This sprawling municipal facility is 8km south of town.

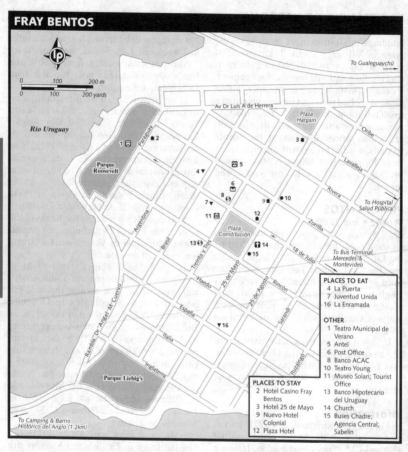

FRAY BENTOS

PLACES TO EAT
4 La Puerta
7 Juventud Unida
16 La Enramada

OTHER
1 Teatro Municipal de Verano
5 Antel
6 Post Office
8 Banco ACAC
10 Teatro Young
11 Museo Solari; Tourist Office
13 Banco Hipotecario del Uruguay
14 Church
15 Buses Chadre; Agencia Central; Sabelin

PLACES TO STAY
2 Hotel Casino Fray Bentos
3 Hotel 25 de Mayo
9 Nuevo Hotel Colonial
12 Plaza Hotel

Nuevo Hotel Colonial (☎ 22260, 25 de Mayo 3293) Singles/doubles/triples US$13/20/25 with shared bath, US$15/25/30 with private bath. This hotel is very clean and friendly, with airy rooms arranged around a sunny interior patio.

Hotel 25 de Mayo (☎ 22586, 25 de Mayo & Lavalleja) Singles/doubles US$13/17, US$21/24 with TV. This is a modernized 19th-century building whose rooms are around a, you guessed it, central courtyard. All have private baths, and some look out on tranquil, leafy Plaza Hargain. Look at a few

rooms until you find the combination of features you like.

Plaza Hotel (☎/fax 22363, 18 de Julio & 25 de Mayo) Singles/doubles/triples/quads US$30/50/60/80 with breakfast and air-con. The price is the same for tiny and large rooms in this modernized building. The big ones are worth it, the small ones probably not. Internet access is US$4.75 an hour.

Hotel Casino Fray Bentos (☎ 22359, Paraguay 23272) The Casino is a modern brick building across from Parque Roosevelt. It was closed for renovations at the time of research, but expect costs to be in the neighborhood of US$45 per person with breakfast.

Places to Eat

La Enramada (☎ 22078, España 1242) US$2.50-4. La Enramada is cheap, very friendly, and basic. It has a small bar and is popular with families.

Juventud Unida (no ☎, 18 de Julio 1124) US$2-4.50. This is another popular place, serving parrilla, sandwiches and pasta.

La Puerta (☎ 23218, Brasil 3275) US$2.50-5. Locals recommend La Puerta highly. It should be pretty safe, as it's also the retired policemen's association.

Getting There & Around

The bus terminal is at 18 de Julio and Varela. Some companies maintain offices on Plaza Constitución, 10 blocks west, but buses don't come into town. ETA has a morning and evening bus to Gualeguaychú (US$5.50, 1¼ hours) Monday to Saturday, evening only Sunday. They also have a midnight departure Monday, Wednesday and Friday for Tacuarembó (US$17, 6 hours) and Rivera (US$21, 7½ hours).

Several buses a day go to Mercedes (US$1.50, 45 minutes) and Montevideo (US$14, 4-7 hours). Buses Chadre has two 'línea litoral' buses daily in each direction between Bella Unión and Montevideo, stopping at Salto, Paysandú, Fray Bentos, Mercedes, Dolores, Nueva Palmira, Carmelo and Colonia. This is a good way to reach the river towns, but it takes nearly seven hours to get to the capital on this route. Plama serves some of the same destinations.

Buses to the campgrounds and the Barrio Histórico (US$0.40) leave from Treinta y Tres and Rincón on the southwest corner of the plaza.

MERCEDES

☎ 053 • pop 40,000

Mercedes, an agreeable city with a fair amount of greenery, is a minor resort on the south bank of the Río Negro, a tributary of the Uruguay. Principal activities are boating, fishing and swimming along the sandy beaches. The city has more frequent connections to Montevideo and other points throughout the country than Fray Bentos does. Mercedes is only 30km from Fray Bentos and 270km from Montevideo. It is a livestock center and capital of the department of Soriano, and buses pass through on the way to many towns in the region.

Information

The municipal tourist office (☎ 22733), on the plaza at Artigas 215, has a friendly, enthusiastic staff and a good city map. It's open 1pm to 7pm weekdays, 9:30am to 12:30pm and 4pm to 7pm weekends.

Cambio Fagalde, on the plaza at Giménez 709, or Cambio España, just off the plaza at Colón 262, will change cash but not traveler's checks. The post office is at Rodó 650, at the corner of 18 de Julio. Antel is at Roosevelt 679, and Virtual Bit, at Ferreira 727, offers Internet access. Hospital Mercedes (☎ 22177) is at Sánchez 204.

Things to See & Do

The imposing **Catedral de Nuestra Señora de las Mercedes**, on the south side of Plaza Independencia, dates from 1788. Head to the opposite side of the plaza for the full view of the cathedral and its facade sporting large statuary. The **Biblioteca Museo Eusebio Giménez** (no ☎, Giménez 560), on Giménez at Sarandí, displays paintings by the local artist.

About 6km west of town is the **Museo Paleontológico Alejandro Berro** (no ☎; free; open 8am-1pm weekdays, 8am-7pm weekends summer; noon to 6pm daily winter), displaying a valuable fossil collection. It is accessible by public transport.

Places to Stay

Camping del Hum (Isla del Puerto) Sites US$0.70 per person plus US$0.90 per tent. Only eight blocks from Plaza Independencia, Mercedes' spacious campground occupies half the Isla del Puerto in the Río Negro, connected to the mainland by a bridge. One of the best campgrounds in the region, it offers excellent swimming, fishing and sanitary facilities. The camping office also rents a small cement house with a 2nd-story balcony offering excellent river views for US$35 a day. It's at the end of the road.

Club Remeros Mercedes (☎ 22534, *de la Ribera 949*) With HI card dorm beds US$6.50/7.25 without/with sheets, without card US$7.25/8.75. There are hostel accommodations at this club near the river.

Hotel Mercedes (☎ 23204, *Giménez 659*) Rooms US$9/12 per person with shared/private bath. Rooms with private bath look onto a tidy courtyard with grapevines and a lemon tree.

Hotel Marín (☎ 22987, *Rodó 668*) Rooms US$9.50 per person. Some of the very basic rooms here are leaky, mildewed and dark, though fairly clean. Back rooms are quiet once the kids have settled down.

Hotel Marín annex (☎ 22115, *Roosevelt 627*) Rooms US$9.50 per person. This annex, between 18 de Julio and Haedo, is brighter and quieter than the main hotel. Some interior rooms are a bit gloomy, but other rooms are around an interior courtyard. Air-con is US$2 extra.

Places to Eat

La Churrasquera (☎ 24036, *Castro y Careaga 790*) US$3-5. You can't miss this place – the parrilla and its firewood are on display in the front window. They serve large portions, and the atmosphere is delightfully old-timey.

Restaurant La Rambla (☎ 27337, *Rambla de la Ribera s/n*) US$3-6.50. The Spanish chef at this restaurant at the foot of 18 de Julio offers some intriguing dishes, including lamb curry, Greek salad with feta cheese, and risotto with chicken and shitake mushrooms. And, to keep everyone happy, parrillada and pastas. Dine inside or under the palapa overlooking the river.

The ***Panadería San Antonio*** (*no ☎, Sarandí & Castro y Careaga*) offers a nice

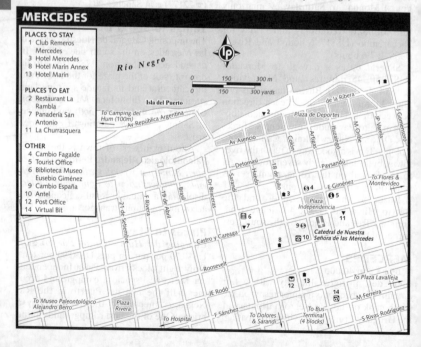

MERCEDES

PLACES TO STAY
1 Club Remeros Mercedes
3 Hotel Mercedes
8 Hotel Marín Annex
13 Hotel Marín

PLACES TO EAT
2 Restaurant La Rambla
7 Panadería San Antonio
11 La Churrasquera

OTHER
4 Cambio Fagalde
5 Tourist Office
6 Biblioteca Museo Eusebio Giménez
9 Cambio España
10 Antel
12 Post Office
14 Virtual Bit

selection of pastries and baked goods, including empanadas.

Getting There & Away

Mercedes' modern terminal is about 10 blocks from the Plaza Independencia, on Don Bosco between Artigas and Colón. It has a shopping center (with a supermarket), a good ATM, luggage storage (US$1 for four hours) and even an emergency medical clinic. No local buses serve the terminal; walking and cabs are the options for getting to the center.

The following table shows winter fares. All destinations are served daily, and many several times a day. Travel times are approximate.

Destination	Duration in hours	Cost
Bella Unión	7	US$15.25
Buenos Aires (Arg)	5	US$19.25
Carmelo	2	US$4
Colonia	3	US$7
Colonia Suiza	4	US$6.50
Durazno	3	US$8
Fray Bentos	45 min	US$1.25
Gualeguaychú	1¾	US$7.50
Montevideo	3½-4½	US$11-14
Nueva Palmira	1½	US$3.50
Paso de los Toros	3½	US$10.75
Paysandú	3	US$4.75
Rivera	13	US$20
Salto	5	US$16
Tacuarembó	5½	US$17

PAYSANDÚ

☎ 072 • pop 86,000

For most travelers, Uruguay's second largest city and industrial center is a stopover en route to or from Argentina. Though a major producer of beer, sugar, textiles, leather and other products, Paysandú is clean and fairly slow-paced, except during its annual beer festival (held during Semana Santa). Traffic lights in the downtown area make wandering it easy and stress-free. The city offers looks at its manufacturing history both in museum exhibits and in current enterprises that use techniques and buildings from an earlier era.

Capital of the department of the same name, Paysandú traces its origins to the mid-18th century, when it was an outpost of cattle herders from the Jesuit mission at Yapeyú, Corrientes. The first *saladero* (slaughterhouse that salts meat and hides) was established in 1840, but construction of its late-19th-century frigorífico was a turning point in Paysandú's industrial history.

Orientation

On the east bank of the Río Uruguay, Paysandú is 370km from Montevideo via Ruta 3 and 110km north of Fray Bentos via Ruta 24. The Puente Internacional General Artigas, 15km north of town, connects it with the Argentine city of Colón.

The city is laid out in a slightly irregular grid; the center of activity is Plaza Constitución, while 18 de Julio, the main commercial street, runs east-west along the south side of the plaza. Except for a small area around the port, directly west of downtown, the entire riverfront remains open parkland due to regular flooding, and provides a welcome refuge from the oppressive summer heat.

Information

The tourist office (☎ 26220 interno 184) is on Plaza Constitución at 18 de Julio 1226. Open 7am to 7:30pm weekdays, 8am to 6pm weekends, it has a good city map and a selection of useful brochures. The Argentine consulate (☎ 22253) is at 1034 Leandro Gómez and is open 1pm to 6pm weekdays.

Banco Santander has an ATM at 18 de Julio 137; Cambio Bacacay, at 18 de Julio 1039, changes traveler's checks for US$3 each. Several banks ranging westward of Bacacay change money.

The post office is at 18 de Julio and Montevideo. For telephones, go to Centel, at Herrera 964, or Antel, Montevideo 875. Bar Centro, on Leandro Gómez at 19 de Abril, offers Internet access, coffee and drinks.

The San Rafael travel agency (☎ 26268) is at Independencia 1059, and the Hospital Escuela del Litoral (☎ 24836) is at Montecaseros 520.

URUGUAY

Things to See & Do

Chunky **Basílica de Nuestra Señora del Rosario** (1860), on Plaza Constitución, has one of the more ornately decorated interiors in Uruguay, with ceiling frescoes, a wooden pulpit and a large pipe organ in the loft. Its Museo Salesiano (Salesian Museum) is closed indefinitely, but portions of the collection are lodged in the Museo de la Tradición (see below). Another downtown landmark is the **Teatro Florencio Sánchez** (1876), at 19 de Abril 926.

There is a small **zoo** (*free; open 8am-6pm daily in winter, 7am-9pm in summer*) in the Parque Municipal, at the south end of Montecaseros, about 10 blocks from the bus terminal. It has a good assortment of birds, specimens of the rare Geoffroy's cat native to the region, and the interesting *mano pelada*, which when standing on its hind legs looks almost like a wallaby. There are also some enormous African lionesses in a cruelly small cage.

The **Museo Histórico** (*no ☎, Zorrilla 874; free; open 8am-4:45pm weekdays, 11:30am-4pm Sat, 7:30am-11:45am Sun*) has an interesting collection of photos and drawings of Paysandú during the war of the Triple Alliance (against Paraguay). Note especially the bullet-riddled, shell-damaged basilica. Old coins, furniture, clothing and weapons round out the exhibits in the 19th-century building.

Far from the center, in the parkland near the riverfront, is the **Museo de la Tradición** (*no ☎, Av de Los Iracundos 5; free; open 9am-noon & 1pm-7pm daily*). Among its features is a small but good selection of anthropological artifacts from the Salesian museum. They're well displayed and their uses are illustrated by photos, many of which are from other parts of the world. The other exhibits consist of gaucho gear and estancia apparatus, and displays of historical and current industrial products and manufacturing processes.

Just inland from the Museo de la Tradición is the massive old **Cympay brewery**, which produces Norteña beer. On its north side are hectares of cordwood waiting to be burned in the brewing process, partially answering the question, 'What do they do with all that eucalyptus?' The brewery can be toured during the Easter Week beer fest.

Places to Stay

The **Balneario Municipal** (*Av de Los Iracundos s/n*) has a free campground near the river's edge, not far from the Museo de la Tradición. It has cold showers.

Another free municipal campground is in the **Parque Municipal**, next to the zoo, at the end of Calle Montecaseros, about 10 blocks south of the bus terminal. It has cold showers and clean bathrooms. Noise from the zoo may be a problem at night.

Hospedaje Victoria (*☎ 24320, 18 de Julio 979*) Rooms US$8/10 per person with shared/private bath. This reader-recommended spot is among the cheapest lodgings in town. It has small, modest rooms and a plant-filled interior courtyard.

Hotel Rafaela (*☎ 24216, 18 de Julio 1181*) Rooms US$12 per person with shared bath, singles/doubles US$18/35 with private bath. All include breakfast, fan & cable TV. The Rafaela is a very good value; its rooms are a bit dark, but they're large, with good baths, and some have their own small patios.

La Posada Hotel (*☎/fax 27879, JP Varela 566*) Singles/doubles/triples/quads US$20/36/48/56 with HI card, US$29/51/68/80 without, all with breakfast, fan, cable TV & heat; air-con costs US$3 extra. The Hostelling International affiliate is four blocks southeast of the bus terminal, in a tranquil, lovely old building with great rooms. It's away from the center, but the grounds are beautifully green, and lunch, dinner and laundry service are available.

Hotel Lobato (*☎/fax 22241, Leandro Gómez 1415*) Singles/doubles/triples/quads US$24/39/51/66 with breakfast, air-con & heat. This is a modern, comfortable option. Rooms are nothing special, but the overall feel is serene and spacious.

Gran Hotel Paysandú (*☎ 23400, fax 27750, 18 de Julio 1103*) Singles/doubles US$36/72 with buffet breakfast & air-con. The inner rooms are nicer at this aging but quiet hotel, the grandest it town in its day. All rooms are large and have big bathtubs.

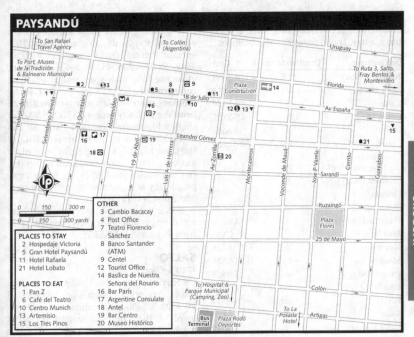

PAYSANDÚ

To San Rafael
Travel Agency

To Colón
(Argentina)

Uruguay

To Port, Museo
de la Tradición
& Balneario Municipal

To Ruta 3, Salto,
Fray Bentos &
Montevideo

Florida

Plaza
Constitución

18 de Julio

Av España

Leandro Gómez

19 de Abril

Av Zorrilla

Montecaseros

Vizconde de Mauá

José P Varela

Cerrito

Guayabos

Sarandí

Ituzaingó

Plaza
Flores

25 de Mayo

To Hospital &
Parque Municipal
(Camping, Zoo)

Colón

Bus
Terminal

Plaza Rodó
Deportes

To La
Posada
Hotel

Artigas

| 0 | 150 | 300 m |
| 0 | 150 | 300 yards |

PLACES TO STAY
2 Hospedaje Victoria
5 Gran Hotel Paysandú
11 Hotel Rafaela
21 Hotel Lobato

PLACES TO EAT
1 Pan Z
6 Café del Teatro
10 Centro Munich
13 Artemisio
15 Los Tres Pinos

OTHER
3 Cambio Bacacay
4 Post Office
7 Teatro Florencio
  Sánchez
8 Banco Santander
  (ATM)
9 Centel
12 Tourist Office
14 Basílica de Nuestra
  Señora del Rosario
16 Bar París
17 Argentine Consulate
18 Antel
19 Bar Centro
20 Museo Histórico

URUGUAY

The hotel has a bar and a restaurant, and offers room and laundry service.

Places to Eat

Centro Munich (no ☎, 18 de Julio 1160) US$1.50-5.75. Pizza, chivitos and milanesas are the featured foods here, about a block off Plaza Constitución.

Pan Z (☎ 29551, 18 de Julio & Pereda) US$1.75-8. 'Panceta' serves good, cheap sandwiches, plus chivitos, pizza, beer, and good coffee, in spiffy surroundings.

Los Tres Pinos (☎ 22302, Av España 1474) US$3.25-8. The well-fed management offer great and pricey pasta and *ñoquis*, as well as meat and chicken.

Artemio (☎ 23826, 18 de Julio 1248) US$3.25-7.25, plus small cover. This recommended place near the tourist office serves fish, meat, pasta and even Norteña beer (just ask).

Café del Teatro (19 de Abril 930) For snacks and coffee, try this historic café.

Entertainment

Bar París (no ☎, Leandro Gómez & 33 Orientales) This is the place to go for lots of old-time local atmosphere.

Zeus Disco (no ☎, Brasil & Manuel Ledesma) In the Zona Industrial near the port, this popular club is open Friday and Saturday nights only. Men pay a US$4.75 cover and a one-drink minimum, while women pay US$1.75 before 1:30am, US$3.25 after.

Getting There & Away

Air Travelair (☎ 02-604-0202 in Montevideo) and Aeromás (☎ 0800-2376 in Montevideo) both fly daily between Montevideo and Paysandú for about US$55. Travelair's fare includes transport from the airport to downtown Paysandú.

Bus Paysandú's bus terminal (☎ 23325) is at Artigas and Zorrilla, directly south of Plaza Constitución. The following table shows winter fares. Except as noted below, destinations are served daily, some several times a day. Travel times are approximate.

Destination	Duration in hours	Cost
Asunción (Par)	15	US$69
Bella Unión	4½	US$11
Carmelo	5	US$9.50
Colón (Arg)	45 min	US$3.25
Colonia	6	US$13
Colonia Suiza	6½	US$13.50
Concepción del Uruguay (Arg)	1½	US$4.25
Córdoba (Arg)	10	US$33
Dolores	3½	US$7
Durazno	3	US$9.50
Encarnación (Par)	9	US$69
Fray Bentos	2	US$4
Mercedes	2½	US$4.75
Montevideo	4-6	US$15
Paraná (Arg)	4½	US$19
Posadas (Arg)	8½	US$69
Rivera	5½	US$14
Salto	2	US$4.75
Santa Fe (Arg)	5	US$20
Tacuarembó	3½	US$10

EGA serves Argentina with Monday and Wednesday departures to Paraná, Santa Fe and Córdoba. Expreso Brújula goes to Asunción, Paraguay, on Tuesday and Friday, while Coit goes Wednesday and Saturday. Both travel via Uruguaiana (Brazil) and Posadas (Argentina). Unfortunately, ticket agents charge the same price whether you're boarding in Montevideo or farther up the line.

The bridge toll for autos and pickups to Argentina is US$4. Bicycles and motorcycles pay US$0.50.

Getting Around
Bus No 104, marked 'Zona Industrial,' runs every half hour heading eastward along Av Soriano (which is one block south of the bus terminal). It serves the sites near the waterfront, including the campgrounds, the museum and the brewery.

TERMAS DE GUAVIYÚ
In a soothing yatay palm savanna 60km north of Paysandú, this sprawling 109-hectare thermal baths complex (☎ 0750-4049, Ruta 3 Km 431.5) has eight pools, including four with spas, and a sprawling *campground* (US$2.25 per person). Fairly spacious *motel-style units* (set well back from the highway) run US$21/28/36/42 for singles/doubles/triples/quads with air-con and kitchenettes, including breakfast. Rates start at US$17 a single for two-night weekday stays. Rooms with fan and fridge (no breakfast) are US$21 for up to three people. If you're not staying in the complex, admission is US$1.50.

Buses between Montevideo and Salto will drop passengers at the Termas; the fare from Paysandú is US$2.75.

SALTO
☎ 073 • pop 83,000
Directly across the Río Uruguay from Concordia, Argentina, 520km from Montevideo via Ruta 3, Salto is the capital of the department of the same name and the most northerly crossing point into Argentina. It is Uruguay's third largest city and boasts a good deal of 19th-century architecture. The enormous Salto Grande hydroelectric project has a recreation area above its dam that attracts some visitors, while the surrounding area is known for citrus, mostly oranges.

Information
The tourist office (☎ 25194, fax 35740) is at Uruguay 1052 and open 8am to 8pm weekdays, 8am to 7pm Saturday, 8am to noon Sunday. The Argentine consulate (☎ 32931) is at General Artigas 1162, on Plaza Artigas.

Banco de Crédito, at Uruguay and Joaquín Suárez, changes money (as do others) and has an ATM. The post office occupies a grand building on Artigas at Treinta y Tres. Antel is at Grito de Asencio 55, and La Telefónica is at Uruguay 885, Local 3. Lavadero Magnolias, at Brasil 774, can make sure you're wearing clean underwear should you need to visit the Hospital Regional Salto (☎ 32155), at 18 de Julio and Varela.

Things to See & Do

Salto's musems are free; for more information call the *intendencia* (☎ 29898) and name the ones you're interested in.

Part of Salto's prime performing arts venue, the **Museo del Teatro Larrañaga** *(Joaquín Suárez 51; free; open 1pm-7pm weekdays)* displays programs, posters, documents, furniture and photos relating to theater. The **Museo de Bellas Artes y Artes Decorativas** *(Uruguay 1057; free; open 3pm-8pm Tues-Sat)* is a fine-arts museum, while the former Mercado Central (Central

Market) has become the **Museo del Hombre y la Tecnología** *(Brasil & Zorrilla; free; open 2pm-7pm Tues-Sat)*, featuring excellent displays on local cultural development and history. The small archaeological section in the basement was closed for renovations at last pass.

Places to Stay

Club Remeros *(☎ 33418, fax 34607, ⓔ cremeros@adinet.com.uy, Gutiérrez s/n)* Dorm beds US$6/7.50 with/without HI card; US$3.25 for sheets. The local HI affiliate has

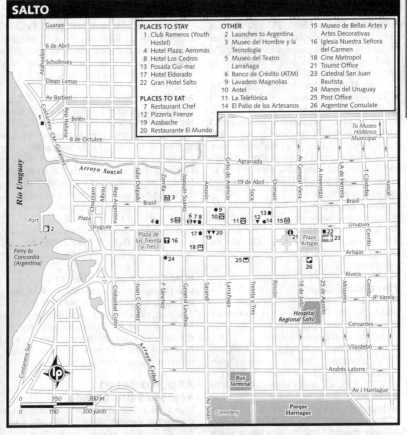

SALTO

PLACES TO STAY
1 Club Remeros (Youth Hostel)
4 Hotel Plaza; Aeromás
8 Hotel Los Cedros
13 Posada Gui-mar
17 Hotel Eldorado
22 Gran Hotel Salto

PLACES TO EAT
7 Restaurant Chef
12 Pizzería Firenze
19 Azabache
20 Restaurante El Mundo

OTHER
2 Launches to Argentina
3 Museo del Hombre y la Tecnología
5 Museo del Teatro Larrañaga
6 Banco de Crédito (ATM)
9 Lavadero Magnolias
10 Antel
11 La Telefónica
14 El Patio de los Artesanos
15 Museo de Bellas Artes y Artes Decorativas
16 Iglesia Nuestra Señora del Carmen
18 Cine Metropol
21 Tourist Office
23 Catedral San Juan Bautista
24 Manos del Uruguay
25 Post Office
26 Argentine Consulate

basic hostel accommodations in a great old brick building at the river's edge. Rooms have two to 18 beds, and some face the water. Three meals are available.

Posada Gui-mar (☎ 32223, Osimani 69) Rooms US$11.25/14.50 per person without/ with breakfast. Gui-mar is simple and friendly. Its big rooms have fans and high ceilings, but most face the noisy street.

Hotel Plaza (☎/fax 33744, e plazatur@ adinet.com.uy, Uruguay 465) Rooms US$15 per person with breakfast & cable TV. The rooms are a bit dark, but they're quiet and a good value.

Hotel Los Cedros (☎ 33984, fax 34235, hlcedros@mundonet.com.uy, Uruguay 657) Singles/doubles/triples US$36/54/72 (less 25% discount for cash) with air-con and buffet breakfast. Big rooms have cable TV, minibars, good baths and doors opening onto small patios, and there's a garage.

Gran Hotel Salto (☎ 34333, fax 33251, e saltotel@adinet.com.uy, 25 de Agosto 5) Singles/doubles/triples US$38/48/72 with air-con & buffet breakfast. Done in grand 1940s-modern style, the Salto is one of the nicest in town. Many of its big rooms have balconies with great views of Plaza Artigas and the city, and some have what appear to be the original phones. There's a restaurant and garage as well.

Hotel Eldorado (☎ 35450, fax 25041, e eldorado@saltoweb.com, Sarandí 20) Singles/doubles/triples/quads US$40/60/72/95 with air-con & breakfast. The Eldorado has clean, quiet smallish rooms, some with their own patios.

Places to Eat
Restaurant Chef (☎ 35328, Uruguay 639) US$3.25-7.25. This is a good downtown choice, with an uptown but inexpensive menu and bright, tasteful decor.

Pizzeria Firenze (Uruguay 945) US$2.25-5. This is one of the many pizzerias in Salto.

Azabache (☎ 32337, Uruguay 702) Mains US$2.75-7.25, set meals US$6-8. Azabache serves good, inexpensive pasta, pizza, meat and sandwiches, ice cream and mixed drinks.

Restaurante El Mundo (Uruguay 714) All-you-can-eat US$5.50 This place serves lunch and dinner. Musicians occasionally perform Saturday evenings here (for an additional charge).

Shopping
Many sidewalk vendors sell knitted caps, leather gloves and hats. *El Patio de los Artesanos (Uruguay 967)* has several handicrafts stalls; you can buy flutes, tattoos and knicknacks too. The local branch of the artisans cooperative *Manos del Uruguay (☎ 29359, Artigas 520)* has a wide selection of crafts to choose from.

Getting There & Away
Air Travelair (☎ 02-604-0202 in Montevideo) and Aeromás (☎ 33744, in Hotel Plaza) together fly at least once daily between Montevideo and Salto for about US$60. Travelair's fare includes transport from the airport to downtown Paysandú.

Bus The bus terminal (☎ 32909) is at Larrañaga and Andrés Latorre. There at least two daily departures to Concordia (US$2.75, 1 hour), with connections to many other Argentine destinations. Good lines among the frequent services to Montevideo (US$20, 6 hours via Ruta 3, 11 hours via litoral) include Chadre and Núñez. Chadre also serves Tacuarembó and Rivera at least twice a week, but you can also take much more frequent service to Paysandú (US$4.75, 2 hours) and change buses. At least two buses a day go to Bella Unión (US$5.50, 2¼ hours).

Boat A ticket booth at the foot of Brasil sells passage on launches that cross the river to Concordia (US$3, 15 minutes) four times a day in winter, five in summer, between 8:45am and 6pm Monday to Saturday (at the time of research, Sunday service had been cancelled, but may resume). There's no extra charge to bring a bicycle over.

AROUND SALTO
Represa Salto Grande
Free guided 1½- to 2-hour visits of the **hydroelectric project** that's at Salto Grande (☎ 26131) take place 7am to 2pm daily

except Sunday. There's no public transport; taxis will do the 14km trip from Salto for US$20, including waiting time.

Termas de Daymán

Only 8km south of Salto, at Km 487.5 of Ruta 3, Termas de Daymán is the largest and most developed of several thermal baths complexes in northwestern Uruguay. Surrounded by a cluster of motels and restaurants, it is a popular destination for Uruguayan and Argentine tourists, offering facilities for a variety of budgets. Visitors roam the town in bathrobes. All the listings here are along the same couple of blocks on the only street in town.

The **Complejo Médico Hidrotermal Daymán** (*☎ 073-69090, open 9am-9pm daily*) provides body wraps, facials, massages and medically oriented physical therapy; other facilities have spa services as well. At the end of the hotel row are the **municipal baths** (*adults/children US$1.80/0.75, open 7am-11pm daily*), which are closest to the source and thus offer the hottest water. **Acuamanía** (*adults/children US$1/0.50*) is a water park with long slides.

Rooms go for US$25/33/41 per person with breakfast/half-board/full board at *La Posta del Daymán* (*☎ 073-69801, fax 073-69618, ⓔ postaday@adinet.com.uy*). This former monastery is nicely done up with big rooms and bathrooms (thermal showers), and a jacuzzi and sauna. It also offers camping for US$3 per person as well as good fixed-price lunches.

A varied menu and reasonable prices (ranging from US$1.50 to US$6.50) are offered at *Parador Municipal Termas de Daymán* (*☎ 073-69992*), next to the municipal baths. *Restaurant San Francisco* (*☎ 073-69690*) is part of a hotel and more stylish than the parador. Dishes go for US$1.75 to US$7.

Between 6:10am and 10pm, hourly buses (US$1.60) leave Salto's port area, head up Brasil and go directly to the baths.

Termas de Arapey

About 90km north and east of Salto on the Río Arapey Grande, Termas de Arapey is another popular hot springs resort.

At *Hotel Municipal* (*☎ 073-34096, fax 073-35740, ⓔ instur@adinet.com.uy*) you'll find singles/doubles/triples for US$55/65/80 with breakfast. Rooms at this complex run by the departmental tourism office have air-con, phone, satellite TV, and hot and cold thermal water. There are also cheaper motel and bungalow accommodations, as well as camping for US$4 per person (four-person minimum).

Daily morning and afternoon buses serve the termas from Salto (US$2.75, 1½ hours).

TACUAREMBÓ
☎ 063 • pop 48,000

Capital of its department, Tacuarembó has sycamore-lined streets and attractive plazas that make it one of the most agreeable towns in Uruguay's interior. The economy relies on livestock, both cattle and sheep, but local producers also grow rice, sunflowers, peanuts, linseed, tobacco, asparagus and strawberries. The late-March gaucho festival merits a detour if you're in the area.

Orientation

In the rolling hill country along the Cuchilla de Haedo, on the banks of the Río Tacuarembó Chico, Tacuarembó is 230km east of Paysandú, 204km northwest of Melo and 390km north of Montevideo. It's a major highway junction for the Uruguayan interior, as Ruta 26 leads west to Argentina and east to Brazil and the Uruguayan coast, while Ruta 5 from Montevideo continues north to Rivera and Brazil.

The town center is Plaza 19 de Abril, but the streets 25 de Mayo and 18 de Julio both lead south past the almost equally important Plaza Colón and Plaza Rivera.

Information

The municipal tourist office (☎ 27144), Joaquín Suárez 215, is open 7am to 7pm weekdays. The friendly, helpful staff offer a simple map and limited brochures. You can change money at the Banco Hipotecario on Suárez, at Plaza 19 de Abril. The post office is at Ituzaingó 262, Antel is at Sarandí 240, and the Hospital Regional (☎ 22955) is at Treinta y Tres and Catalogne.

URUGUAY

Things to See & Do

Tacuarembó's **Museo del Indio y del Gaucho Washington Escobar** (*no ☎, Flores & Artigas; free; open 1pm-7pm weekdays, 8am-noon weekends in winter; longer hours in summer*) pays romantic tribute to Uruguay's nearly forgotten Indians and gauchos and their role in the country's rural history.

Special Events

In the first week of March, the five-day Fiesta de la Patria Gaucha attracts visitors from around the country to exhibitions of traditional gaucho skills, music, and other activities. It takes place in Parque 25 de Agosto, at the north end of town.

Places to Stay

Balneario Municipal Iporá (*☎ 25344, fax 25612*) Buses at 7am, 8am and 10am run length of 18 de Julio and past terminal. Free & US$2 sites. This densely forested campground is alongside a reservoir, 7km north of town. The free sites have clean toilets but lack showers.

Hospedaje Bértiz (*☎ 23324, Ituzaingó 211*) Rooms US$9.75/12 per person with shared/private bath. This place is mellow and quiet place, with very clean baths and some rather large rooms.

Hotel Central (*☎ 22341, fax 22841, Flores 300*) Singles/doubles US$24/27 with air-con. Large, clean rooms have cable TV and heat here.

Hotel Plaza (*☎/fax 27988, 25 de Agosto 247*) Singles/doubles US$20/35 with private bath, air-con & cable TV. The rooms are spacious at this recommended hotel.

Places to Eat

La Rueda (*Beltrán & Flores*) US$2.50-6. You'll get tasty and filling meals at this simple parrilla near the Hotel Central.

La Sombrilla (*☎ 23432, 25 de Mayo & Suárez*) US$2.75-4.75. This is a reasonably priced confitería serving sandwiches, pizza, pizzeta and chivitos.

Getting There & Around

Aeromás (*☎ 28001, 25 de Agosto 237*) flies between Tacuarembó and Montevideo once a day Monday to Friday. They provide airport transport for US$8.

The bus terminal is on the northeastern outskirts of town, at the junction of Ruta 5 and Av Victorino Perera. Turil has direct service to Montevideo (US$18, 4½ hours); other lines charge less but take an hour longer. Infrequent service connects Tacuarembó with Salto; going via Paysandú (US$12, 6 hours) gives many more options. At least two buses per day connect Tacuarembó with Melo (US$8.75, 3½ hours).

VALLE EDÉN

Valle Edén, 24km southwest of Tacuarembó on Ruta 26, is lush with native trees and shrubs rarely seen in such profusion in the rest of the country. The **Cementerio del Indio** is a small granite outcrop, visible from the highway, on whose sides locals have entombed their dead. Despite its name, no Indians are buried here.

Just south of the cemetery is the turnoff to the **Museo Carlos Gardel** (*☎ 0630-8472, Valle Edén, admission US$0.55, open 9am-6pm daily*). Reached via a drive-through creek spanned by a wooden suspension footbridge, the museum is housed in a former *pulpería* (the general store/bar that used to operate on many estancias). It documents the department of Tacuarembó's claim as birthplace of the revered tango singer.

The story (quite plausible) is of an estanciero and army colonel who married three sisters in succession – as one died he would take up with the next. Three years before ailing wife number two passed on, however, the colonel jumped the gun and fathered Carlos out of wedlock of the future number three. The colonel's brother-in-law arranged to have the infant adopted by a French immigrant, Mme Gardes, and the rest is history.

Photos of Gardel's documents, listing Tacuarembó as his place of birth, are among the many on display in the lovely old building. (One biographer states that Gardel falsified these documents when he came from France to avoid being drafted to fight in WWI. This version is more widely accepted in Argentina, which insisted on interring the singer's remains in Buenos Aires, over Uruguay's protests.)

Empresa Calebus leaves the Tacuarembó terminal at 6:30am and 6pm Monday to Saturday (8:30am and 6pm on Sunday). The 20-minute ride is US$1.75. Taxis charge around US$40 for the roundtrip and waiting time.

RIVERA

Wide and smooth Ruta 5 runs 114km north from Tacuarembó through a landscape of granite mesas, buttes and knobs somewhat reminiscent of the American Southwest, though much greener. The highway ends at Rivera, which blends into the Brazilian city of Santana do Livramento.

Rivera's tourist office (☎ 062-31900, ask for Turismo) is in the intendencia. Both Uruguay and Brazil maintain national tourist offices (with very little city information) and immigration desks in a building on Bulevar Presidente Viera at the foot of Sarandí, far from the border. If you're just passing through Rivera on the way to Brazil, you need to ask the bus driver to stop and allow you to get processed.

The post office is at Sarandí 501, Antel is at Artigas 1046, and there are several exchange houses in town. The Brazilian consulate (☎ 062-23278), at Ceballos 1159, is open 9am to 3pm weekdays.

Places to Stay

Camping Municipal (☎ 062-23803, *Agraciada s/n*) Free. This campground, near Calle Presidente Viera, has hot showers.

Hotel Sarandí (☎ 062-23521, *Sarandí 777*) Rooms US$6.50/8 per person with shared/private bath. The rooms are simple, clean and a tad dark at this very friendly hotel. Breakfast is available for an extra US$1.60.

Hotel Nuevo Plaza (☎/fax 062-23039, *Ituzaingó 411*) Rooms US$17/19 per person with shared/private bath, including breakfast. This hotel has arrangements with the Uruguayan hostelling association and gives discounts to HI cardholders. Rooms are spacious and clean, and those on the upper floors have great views of the city. Those with private baths have air-con and minibars.

Places to Eat

Chivito Hut (☎ *062-29311, Sarandí 542*) US$1.75-5. Akbar and Jeff don't work here, but you can stuff your face cheap.

Churrasquería El Rancho (☎ *062-28877, Brasil 1071*) All-you-can-eat US$4. Airy and spacious, this friendly parrilla has an enormous grill and offers whole takeout chickens for US$2.75.

Getting There & Away

Travelair (represented by a realtor at Figueroa 1136; ☎ 062-28600) and Aeromás (☎ 062-25666, Sarandí 335) fly Monday to Friday between Montevideo and Rivera (US$60, 1½ hours). Travelair provides free transport to downtown Rivera; Aeromás charges US$1.50.

The town's bus terminal is on Uruguay and Jacinto Vera, many blocks closer to the border than the immigration desks. At least two buses a day serve Melo (US$13, 5 hours) and Paysandú (US$14, 5½ hours). Many buses serve Tacuarembó (US$4.25, 1¾ hours) and continue to other destinations; see that town's Getting There & Away section.

Eastern Uruguay

East of Montevideo, innumerable beach resorts dot the scenic Uruguayan coast, where vast dunes and dramatic headlands extend all the way to the Brazilian border. The area attracts hordes of summer tourists, but is nearly empty after wealthy Brazilians and Argentines end their holidays in early March. Its showplace is exclusive Punta del Este, where Argentina maintains a summer consulate and the Buenos Aires daily *La Nación* even opens a temporary bureau. Nearby Maldonado offers more reasonably priced accommodations and facilities, but other resorts slightly farther out are just as attractive and more affordable. From the end of the holidays through April prices are lower, the weather stays good and the pace is much more leisurely.

The modern department of Rocha, between Maldonado and the Brazilian border, was subject to a constant tug-of-war between Portugal and Spain in colonial times, and between Brazil and Argentina up to the mid-19th century. This conflict left several valuable historical monuments, such as the fortresses of Santa Teresa and San Miguel, while discouraging rural settlement and sparing from development some of Uruguay's wildest countryside, including Cabo Polonio, with its extensive dunes and a large colony of southern sea lions. The route from Chuy to Lascano passes through a wonderful landscape of palm savannas and marshes rich in bird life. Not often visited by foreigners, the interior departments of Treinta y Tres and Cerro Largo offer several alternatives for crossing into Brazil.

From Montevideo, the Ruta Interbalnearia (coastal highway) heads east and then north toward the Brazilian border; just outside of the capital, it becomes a divided toll highway (US$4, eastbound only). In most of the Uruguayan Riviera (as the coastal area is known), there are abundant accommodations, but prices and availability are highly seasonal. Many places open only between December and April, and nearly all raise prices dramatically between December 15 and March 1, and at Easter Week. From April 1 to December 1, prices are extremely reasonable at the places that remain open.

ATLÁNTIDA

In the department of Canelones, only 50km from Montevideo, Atlántida is the first major resort along the Interbalnearia. It's still on the Río de la Plata, so the water is a mixture of salt and fresh; it's brown but swimmable. There's not much to do besides enjoy the beach, which stretches for kilometers.

The municipal tourist office (☎ 037-226122) is at the intersection of Av 14 (Roger Balet) and Calle 18. COT runs regular buses to Montevideo and on down the coast.

Campsites at *Camping El Ensueño* (☎ 037-23467) cost US$4.75 per person. The campground is on the inland side of the highway, about 10 blocks north of Playa Brava, Atlántida's most popular beach. Fees

include 24-hour hot water and sanitary facilities. Half of the airy, clean comfortable rooms at *Hotel Rex* (☎ 037-22009, *Rambla Costanera & Calle 1*) face the water. Rooms cost US$25 per person with breakfast.

PIRIÁPOLIS
☎ 043 • pop 6000

The westernmost resort in Maldonado department, about 100km from Montevideo, Piriápolis lies on a long stretch of sandy beach. It's less pretentious and more affordable than Punta del Este. Founded in 1893, it was developed as a tourist resort in the 1930s by Argentine entrepreneur Francisco Piria, who built the imposing landmark Argentino Hotel and an eccentric residence known as 'Piria's Castle' (the latter now part of a city park).

The surrounding countryside holds many interesting features, including Cerro Pan de Azúcar, one of Uruguay's highest points, and the hill resort of Minas.

Orientation

Piriápolis is very compact. Almost everything is within reasonable walking distance in an area bounded by the waterfront Rambla de los Argentinos to the south, Calle del Pino (and the Argentino Hotel) in the west, Calle Misiones in the north, and Av Piria on the east. Most residents give directions by noting a site's proximity to the Argentino Hotel.

Information

The city has an information booth in the bus terminal, but the private Asociación de Fomento y Turismo (☎ 22560), at Rambla de los Argentinos 1348, near the Argentino Hotel, has maps, brochures and a listing of current hotel prices. In January and February, it's open 9am to 9pm daily; in March and April, hours are 10am to 8pm. The rest of the year, it's open 10am to 1pm and 3pm to 8pm daily.

Banco de la República, at the east end of Rambla de los Argentinos, has an ATM. At the Argentino Hotel, you can change cash but not traveler's checks. The post office is on Av Piria just before the corner of Tucumán, between Armenia and Manuel Freire. Antel is on Héctor Barrios at Buenos Aires, behind the tall brick apartment building, and there's a locutorio on Rambla de los Argentinos just east of Sanabria. Internet places have been coming and going in town; ask at the friendly tourist office for the webcafé du jour.

Lavadero Familiar, at Piria and Reconquista, is open 9am to 9pm daily.

Things to See & Do
The landmark **Argentino Hotel** is an attraction in itself. For a good view of Piriápolis, climb the **Cerro del Inglés** (also known as Cerro San Antonio) at the east end of town. A chairlift goes to the top, open only on weekends except in summer.

Swimming and **sunbathing** are the most popular activities, and there is good **fishing** off the rocks at the west end of the beach, where Rambla de los Argentinos becomes Rambla de los Ingleses.

Places to Stay
Budget Open mid-December to late April, *Camping Piriápolis FC* (☎ 23275, *Misiones & Niza*) has campsites for US$4 per person and rooms with shared bath for US$7 per person. It's across from the bus terminal and has every necessary facility, including a restaurant, electricity and hot showers.

Albergue Antón Grassi (☎/fax 20394, e *hpiria@adinet.com.uy, Simón del Pino 1106/1136*) Dorm beds US$4.50/6.25 low/high season with HI card, plus US$1.50 sheet-rental fee. Two blocks from the beach (just west of the Argentino), this very well-run hostel is one of South America's largest. There are mostly 4-bed, single-sex rooms, but it has a few doubles for nearly the same price. Smart cards provide 24-hour access, and there are safe-deposit boxes, a TV room, kitchen, weight room and large patio with barbecue. Laundry service is available. The hostel is open year-round but reservations (made through the central office in Montevideo, ☎ 02-400-4245) are essential in January and February.

Hostería Uruguay (☎ 22424, *Uruguay 1026*) Rooms US$12/15 per person off-season/summer. This is one of the cheapest good hotels in town; it closes in winter.

A very few five-person, two-bedroom *apartments* (☎ 22471, *Sanabria 1084*) are on offer for US$50 near Ayacucho, less than three blocks from the beach.

Mid-Range *Hotel San Sebastián* (☎/fax 22546, *Sanabria 942*) Rooms US$12/23 per person off-season/summer, with fan. Tile-floored rooms have agreeable old wooden furniture; breakfast is US$2 extra.

Hotel Danae (☎/fax 22594, *Rambla de los Argentinos 1270*) Rooms US$12/25 per person off-season/summer, with breakfast & fan. This friendly place has simply furnished, tile-floored rooms with cable TV; some face the beach, two share a tiny courtyard, and all have at least a light well to brighten them.

Hotel Colonial (☎/fax 23783, e *rivacol@ adinet.com.uy, Piria 790*) Rooms US$15-20 per person off-season, US$30-40 summer with breakfast. Highly recommended, this hotel is near the verdant Cerro San Antonio on the east side of town. The nicely appointed rooms have fans, minibars and cable TV; some have terraces and some have views the length of the beach. The managers are warm and friendly, contributing to the tranquil atmosphere.

Hotel Centro (☎ 22516, *Sanabria 931*) Rooms US$18/33 per person off-season/summer, with breakfast & fan. The Centro has very tidy, spacious rooms, some with kitchenettes and large baths; a terrace gives views of the hills. Half-board is available for US$40-45 per person.

Top End *Argentino Hotel* (☎ 22791, fax 23107, e *arghotel@adinet.com.uy, Rambla de los Argentinos s/n*) Singles/doubles US$87/112 with half-board, US$105/130 with full board. Even if you don't stay here, you should visit this elegant 350-room European-style spa with two heated river-water pools, a casino, a classic dining room, ice-skating rink and other luxuries.

Places to Eat
There are numerous restaurants on the Rambla and streets coming off it, such as Sanabria and Trápani.

URUGUAY

La Langosta (☎ *23382, Rambla de los Argentinos 1212*) US$4.50-8. La Langosta has fine seafood and *parrillada* at moderate prices.

La Goleta (☎ *22501, Rambla de los Argentinos & Trápani*) US$3.25-8. This is another appealing restaurant along the Rambla.

Parrillada Delta (☎ *22364, Rambla & Atanasio Sierra*) US$4-7; closed off-season. The Delta offers meat and fish dishes.

Devoto (*Piria & Buenos Aires*) is a large supermarket with a snack bar and cafetería.

Getting There & Away

The bus terminal is at Misiones and Niza, about three blocks from the beach. Several buses run daily from Montevideo (US$4, 1½ hours) to Punta del Este (US$2, 50 minutes) and back via Piriápolis. At least five buses daily go to Minas (US$2.75, 1 hour) and to Pan de Azúcar, where there are connections to eastern coastal points.

In summer Buquebus (☎ 23340), at the passenger pier on Rambla de los Ingleses, runs at least one swift ferry a day to Buenos Aires (US$71, 3 hours).

AROUND PIRIÁPOLIS

Ruta 37 leads north out of Piriápolis; about 4km from the edge of town, on the east side of the road, is the **Castillo de Piria** (☎ *043-23268, Ruta 37 Km 4, free; open noon-8pm daily in summer*), Francisco Piria's opulent, outlandish residence. One kilometer north, on the west side of Ruta 37, is the **Reserva de Fauna Autóctona** (*no ☎, Ruta 37 Km 5; free*) with native species such as the capybara, gray fox, and ñandú. The reserve provides access, via a steep path, to the top of Uruguay's third highest point, Cerro Pan de Azúcar (493m).

MINAS

☎ 044 • pop 36,000

Minas is an agreeable hill town in the Cuchilla Grande of the department of Lavalleja, 120km northeast of Montevideo and 60km north of Piriápolis. It draws its name from nearby quarries of granite and other building materials, but its most popular attraction is **Parque Salus**, 10km

west of town, source of Uruguay's best-known mineral water and also site of a brewery. Every April 19, up to 70,000 pilgrims visit the **Cerro y Virgen del Verdún**, 6km west of town.

The municipal tourist office (☎ 29796) is on Batlle y Ordóñez, and the intendencia has a tourist office in the bus terminal. The post office is at Av W Beltrán and 25 de Mayo; Antel is on Rodó just north of Beltrán.

Places to Stay & Eat

In a woodsy area 9km north of town on the road to Polanco (reachable by public transport), *Parque Arequita* (☎ *0440-2503*) has camping for US$2/5 per person, and a limited number of two-bed cabañas for US$10. Sector B has a swimming pool.

Posada Verdún (☎ *24563,* e *posada_verdun@netgate.com.uy, Washington Beltrán 715*) Singles/doubles US$17/26. The posada is three blocks from the bus terminal, just off the corner with Florencio Sánchez. Its clean, quiet, rooms have cable TV, and there's a flowery patio.

Hotel Verdún (☎/*fax 22110,* e *hverdun@adinet.com.uy, 25 de Mayo 444*) Singles/doubles US$45/60, with breakfast & air-con. The Verdún is on central Plaza Libertad. Quiet, spacious rooms have minibars, cable TV and good baths.

Confitería Irisarri (*Plaza Libertad*) is something of a local institution, famous for its alfajores.

Getting There & Away

The bus terminal is on Treinta y Tres, between Sarandí and Williman. There is frequent service to Montevideo (US$5, 2 hours), several daily departures to Maldonado (US$3.50, 1¼ hours), and regular departures for the northeastern destinations Treinta y Tres (US$8, 3 hours) and Melo (US$11.25, 4 hours).

MALDONADO

☎ 042 • pop 39,000

Capital of its namesake department, Maldonado is a popular resort that has retained a semblance of colonial atmosphere despite virtually merging with fashionable Punta del Este. It remains a more economical alternative to Punta del Este, which is easily accessible by public transport.

Maldonado dates from 1755, when Governor JJ de Viana of Montevideo sent the first settlers to establish an outpost to provision ships at the mouth of the Río de la Plata. British forces occupied the town during the siege of Buenos Aires in 1806, and in 1832 Darwin used it as a base during 10 weeks spent collecting natural history specimens.

Orientation

Maldonado is 130km east of Montevideo and only 30km from Piriápolis. Other than the beaches, most points of interest are within a few blocks of its central Plaza San Fernando. The old city center is a standard rectangular grid, but toward Punta del Este it becomes highly irregular. The town sprawls across the mainland just north of Punta and is bordered to the west by the Río de la Plata and to the east the Atlantic coast. Rambla

Claudio Williman and Rambla Lorenzo Batlle Pacheco are coastal thoroughfares that converge from northwest and northeast, respectively. Locations along the ramblas are usually identified by numbered *paradas* (bus stops). There are many attractive beaches along both, but the ocean-facing beaches have rougher surf. For other beach details, see Punta del Este, later in this chapter.

Information

The friendly if somewhat scattered tourist office (no ☎) is on 25 de Mayo on Plaza San Fernando. It's open 8am to 10pm Monday to Saturday in summer, 8am to 9pm in winter. A counter at the bus terminal is sporadically staffed. The immigration office (☎ 237624), on Ventura Alegre between Sarandí and Román Guerra, is open 12:30pm to 6pm weekdays.

Maldonado has many exchanges houses and banks (with ATMs), including a cluster along the northeastern edge of the plaza.

URUGUAY

MALDONADO

PLACES TO STAY
1 Hotel Sancar
6 Hotel Celta
12 Hotel Esteño
14 Hotel Le Petit
17 Hotel Colonial; Heladería Mix

PLACES TO EAT
3 Mundo Natural
4 Pizza Pata
8 Taberna Patxi
9 El Dorado Supermercado
10 Al Paso
18 Pizzería Carlitos
23 Círculo Policial de Maldonado
24 Pizza e Pasta

OTHER
2 Immigration Office
5 Antel
7 Cambio Maldonado
11 Museo Mazzoni
13 Cambio Bacacay; Banco de la República
15 Post Office
16 Buses to Punta del Este
19 Papelería Sienra
20 Museo Nicolás García Uriburu
21 Cuartel de Dragones y de Blandengues; Museo Didáctico Artiguista
22 Tourist Office
25 Lavandería Ferrer
26 Bus Terminal

Cambio Bacacay changes traveler's checks for a commission of US$3 apiece.

The post office is on Ituzaingó between Sarandí and Román Guerra, and Antel is at the corner of Av Joaquín de Viana and Florida. Wash your duds at Lavandería Ferrer (☎ 237208), on Ledesma just east of Sarandí. Hospital Maldonado (☎ 225889) is on Ventura Alegre, about eight blocks west of Plaza San Fernando.

Things to See & Do

The **Catedral de Maldonado** is on Plaza San Fernando; it was completed in 1895 after nearly a century of construction. On Pérez del Puerto, the **Plaza de la Torre del Vigía** features a colonial watchtower built with peepholes for viewing the approach of hostile forces or other suspicious movements.

Another colonial relic, the **Cuartel de Dragones y de Blandengues** is a block of military fortifications with stone walls and iron gates, which was built between 1771 and 1797. It's located along 18 de Julio and Pérez del Puerto. One of its museums is the **Museo Didáctico Artiguista** (☎ 225378; free; open 1pm-7pm Tue-Sun winter, 5pm-11pm Tue-Sun summer), in honor of Uruguay's hero of independence. The block also contains the fine-arts **Museo Nicolás García Uriburu** (☎ 225378, 25 de Mayo s/n; free; open 1pm-7pm Tue-Sun winter, 5pm-11pm summer), which is mostly an impressive collection of sculpture very nicely displayed in two small wings.

The **Museo Mazzoni** (☎ 221107, Ituzaingó 789; free; open 1pm-7pm Tues-Fri winter, 5pm-11pm Tues-Fri summer) is in a house dating from 1782. With all the family's furniture and belongings and the original construction showing, this is a fascinating glimpse at certain aspects of the life of wealthy colonials. The rest of the collection is quite eclectic, and the rear courtyard holds a collection of marine artifacts.

Activities

Sportfishing for corvina, conger eel, bonito, shark and other species is a popular pastime along the coast, at sea, and on Isla Gorriti and Isla de Lobos. The tourist office publishes a brochure with a map of recom-mended fishing spots. Other water sports include surfing, windsurfing and diving; another brochure (when available) recom-mends sites for each of these activities.

Places to Stay

Accommodations in the Maldonado/Punta del Este area are abundant but generally costly. Prices decline considerably after the summer high season, but can vary even within it – the first three weeks of January tend to be very expensive, but prices begin dropping after mid-February. Most places raise prices again during Semana Santa (Easter Week, also called Semana de Turismo). Also note that singles are difficult to find during the high season, and many places close in the off-season.

The prices given here are especially prone to change. Much depends on economic conditions in Argentina: When Argentina's economy and currency are weak (as was the case during research), prices drop in Uruguay.

For lodgings in Punta del Este proper, see the Punta del Este entry, later.

Camping San Rafael (☎ 486715, ☎/fax in Montevideo 02-707-3576, Camino a La Barra s/n) Bus No 5 from downtown Maldonado or micro from Punta del Este. Open Nov 1-Mar 15. Sites US$15 for 2 people, US$17 in Jan, Feb & Easter Week. This campground, on the outskirts of Maldonado near the bridge to La Barra, has well-kept facilities on woodsy grounds, complete with store, restaurant, laundry, 24-hour hot water and other ameni-ties. It's organized almost to the point of reg-imentation, but at least you can expect quiet after midnight. You can pay with Uruguayan pesos, US dollars or almost any credit cards.

Hotel Celta (☎ 230139, Ituzaingó 839) Rooms US$10 per person. This Irish-owned hotel is a popular choice for foreign travel-ers, but the owners may sell it.

Hotel Sancar (☎/fax 223563, Juan Edye 597) Rooms US$10/20 per person winter/summer. The Sancar is well kept and quieter than most hotels in town.

Hotel Le Petit (☎ 223044, fax 444992, Florida & Sarandí) Rooms US$12 per person off-season (no breakfast), doubles

US$40 peak season with breakfast & fan. This 2nd-floor hotel is entered through a little shopping mall on the plaza. It gets some street noise, but has well-kept rooms with cable TV; some overlook the plaza.

Hotel Colonial (☎ 223346, *18 de Julio 841*) Doubles US$60 with breakfast peak season. The Colonial's white rooms are clean and simple, with TVs and tile floors. Some overlook the plaza. It's a bit overpriced, but off-season rates (which don't include breakfast) are approximately 50% less.

Hotel Esteño (☎ 225222, *Sarandí 881*) Doubles US$35 off-season, US$68 peak season, all with breakfast. Exterior rooms have balconies, while quiet interior rooms share tiny patios. Rooms are smallish, with aging carpeting and very small baths.

Places to Eat

Maldonado restaurants are often better values than their pricier and more prestigious counterparts in Punta del Este.

Mundo Natural (☎ 21697, *Román Guerra 918*) Most items US$2. This small, cheerful vegetarian place serves *tartas* made with combinations of spinach, cheese, olives and leeks, as well as soy- and seitan burgers and brown rice.

Pizza Pata (☎ 238932, *Ituzaingó & Román Guerra*) US$2.75-5. Pizza Pata is a modern eatery offering pizza, chivitos and burgers.

Círculo Policial de Maldonado (☎ 222670, *Pérez del Puerto 780*) US$3-5.75. This is a tidy, airy policemen's club with a small but varied menu. The cops are likely to be in back at the bar; challenge them to a game of pool.

Pizzería Carlitos (☎ 221727, *Sarandí 834*) US$2.50-9.75. A good spot for breakfast and lunch specials, Carlitos also serves sandwiches, pizza, parrillada, fish and pasta.

Pizza e Pasta (no ☎, *Treinta y Tres 729*) US$2.25-8. Head here for more elaborate Italian meals in an upscale atmosphere.

Al Paso (☎ 222881, *18 de Julio 889*) US$4-9. Al Paso, a favorite parrilla, is relatively pricey but still a good value.

Taberna Patxi (☎ 238393, *Florida 828*) US$3.25-9. Taberna Patxi serves Basque food, including fish and shellfish.

El Dorado (*18 de Julio between Florida & Ituzaingó*) Though not up to Parisian standards, the croissants *salados* (savory) at this modern supermarket's bakery counter are pretty darn good, and they're cheap. You'll find a good selection of produce and other comestibles here as well.

Heladería Mix (*18 de Julio 839*) This ice-creamery next to the Hotel Colonial and cathedral also serves coffee drinks and breakfasts.

Getting There & Away

For details on air travel to the area, see the Punta del Este section.

The bus terminal (☎ 250490) is at Av Roosevelt and Sarandí, eight blocks south of Plaza San Fernando. A US$0.30 departure tax is added to ticket prices.

Dozens of daily buses ply the route between Maldonado/Punta del Este and Montevideo (US$6, 2 hours); some of them stop in Piriápolis (US$2, 40 minutes), and most stop at Carrasco International Airport outside Montevideo. If you're traveling eastward from Maldonado you'll get many more options by busing 20 minutes to San Carlos, though COT has two morning buses to Chuy (US$8.50, 3 hours) on the Brazilian border, and Tur-Este has one early-morning and one early-evening bus to Rocha (US$3.25, 1¼ hours) and Treinta y Tres (US$9, 3½ hours). Several buses a day go to Minas (US$3.50, 1¼ hours). See the Punta del Este Getting There & Away section for more information.

Getting Around

Bus No 5 ('Manatiales') leaves from behind the bus terminal and stops at Camping San Rafael. Local buses (blue Codesa, 'yellow' Olivera and green Maldonado Turismo) run between Maldonado and Punta del Este (US$0.75) via various routes. Most stop on Av Roosevelt near the terminal, and some stop on Av Joaquín de Viana. In summer they run around the clock, as often as every 15 minutes. Additionally, Codesa's Línea 1 runs between San Carlos, Maldonado and Punta del Este. Olivera's Línea 8 connects Maldonado with Punta Ballena, Portezuelo and the Carlos Curbelo (Laguna del Sauce) airport westbound, while Línea 14 hits the bus terminals in both Maldonado and Punta del Este, the eastern beaches, La Barra and José Ignacio eastbound. See the Punta del Este Getting Around section for other details.

CASA PUEBLO

At Punta Ballena, a scenic headland 10km west of Maldonado, Uruguayan artist Carlos Páez Vilaró built this unconventional, sprawling, multilevel Mediterranean hillside villa and art gallery (☎ 042-578041, admission US$5; open 9am-sunset daily) using no right angles. Visitors can tour five rooms, view a film on the artist's life, including the building's creation, and dine or drink at the bar-cafeteria. Parts of Casa Pueblo are open to member-patrons only, but you can sneak a view from the outside. It's a 2km walk from the junction where Olivera's Línea 8 bus drops you.

PUNTA DEL ESTE

☎ 042 • pop 1200

'Punta' – with its many beaches, elegant seaside homes, yacht harbor, high-rise apartment buildings, and expensive hotels and restaurants – is one of South America's most glamorous resorts. In summer it often fills with so many Argentines that some of them half-jokingly call Uruguay 'one of our provinces.' (Uruguayans, as you might imagine, don't find this amusing.)

Common wisdom holds that this is the place where Argentines come to spend their *plata negra* ('black money,' or unreported income). If this is true, they've been spending a lot less of it in recent years. In late 2000 local authorities, in a desperate effort to attract more tourism, declared topless sunbathing legal.

Prices have dropped as the Argentine recession continues, and Punta has lost some of its luster with the jet set. Budget travelers are still likelier to visit than to lodge here; the selection of reasonable accommodations is small.

Orientation

Punta del Este adjoins Maldonado to the south, and is easily accessible by public transport. Rambla General Artigas circles the peninsula, passing protected Playa Mansa and the yacht harbor on the west side, the exclusive residential zone at the southern tip, and rugged Playa Brava, open to the South Atlantic, in the east.

Punta del Este has two separate grid systems, one on either side of a constricted isthmus just east of the yacht harbor. The newer, high-rise hotel zone is to the north, while the area to the south is almost exclusively residential. Street signs in Punta del Este bear both names and numbers, though locals refer to most streets only by number (many people do not even know the names). This book's map includes both but the addresses in text follow local practice and use the number. An exception is Av Juan Gorlero (Calle 22), the main commercial street, universally referred to as just 'Gorlero' (and not likely to be confused with Comodoro Gorlero, Calle 19).

Information

Tourist Offices The quality of tourist information, maps and literature in Punta is very good. The municipal tourist office (☎ 446510) is at the intersection of Calle 31 and the Rambla; it's open 8am to midnight in summer and 9am to 3pm in winter. Sharing the office is the Liga de Fomento (☎ 440514), a private institution, open 8am to 6pm weekdays, 8am to 3pm weekends.

A private information office (☎ 489468) at the bus terminal is open 24 hours a day in summer. The rest of the year it's open 8am to 6pm Monday and Tuesday, 8am to 9pm Wednesday, 8am to 8pm Thursday and Friday, and 9am to 9pm weekends.

On the western approach to town, at Parada 24 (Las Delicias) on Rambla Williman, there's an excellent tourist office (☎ 230050), which is open 8am to midnight daily in January and February, 8am to 10pm March to mid-April, and 9am to 8pm the rest of the year.

The Centro de Hoteles y Restaurantes (☎ 440512), on Plaza Artigas, distributes a decent map with a list of hotels and restaurants, with up-to-the-minute prices.

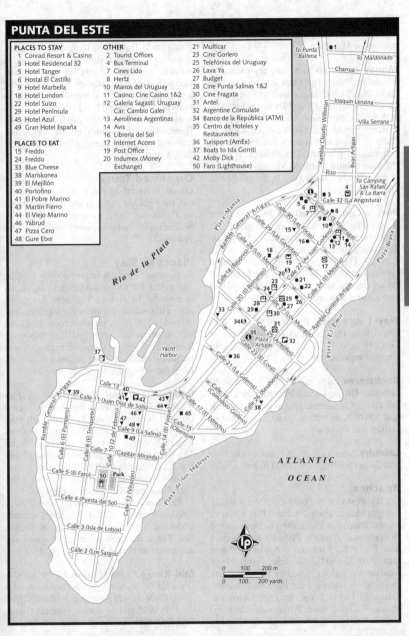

PUNTA DEL ESTE

PLACES TO STAY
1 Conrad Resort & Casino
3 Hotel Residencial 32
5 Hotel Tanger
6 Hostal El Castillo
9 Hotel Marbella
18 Hotel London
22 Hotel Suizo
29 Hotel Península
45 Hotel Azul
49 Gran Hotel España

PLACES TO EAT
15 Freddo
24 Freddo
33 Blue Cheese
36 Mariskonea
39 El Mejillón
40 Portofino
41 El Pobre Marino
43 Martín Fierro
44 El Viejo Marino
46 Yabrud
47 Pizza Cero
48 Gure Etxe

OTHER
2 Tourist Offices
4 Bus Terminal
7 Cines Lido
8 Hertz
10 Manos del Uruguay
11 Casino; Cine Casino 1&2
12 Galería Sagasti; Uruguay Car; Cambio Gales
13 Aerolíneas Argentinas
14 Avis
16 Librería del Sol
17 Internet Access
19 Post Office
20 Indumex (Money Exchange)
21 Multicar
23 Cine Gorlero
25 Telefónica del Uruguay
26 Lava Ya
27 Budget
28 Cine Punta Salinas 1&2
30 Cine Fragata
31 Antel
32 Argentine Consulate
34 Banco de la República (ATM)
35 Centro de Hoteles y Restaurantes
36 Turisport (AmEx)
37 Boats to Isla Gorriti
42 Moby Dick
50 Faro (Lighthouse)

URUGUAY

Consulates The Argentine consulate (☎ 441632) is at Calle 25 544, and open December to March only.

Money Punta has many money exchange offices, including Indumex at Gorlero and Calle 28, which changes cash and traveler's checks, the latter at a slightly lower rate and with a 3% commission. Cambio Gales in the Galería Sagasti, on Gorlero just south of Calle 31, changes traveler's checks for a 1% commission plus US$1 per check. Among the several banks with ATMs along Gorlero is ever-reliable Banco de la República at Calle 25.

Post & Communications The post office is on Calle 29 between Gorlero and Calle 20. Antel is at the corner of Calles 25 and 24; Telefónica del Uruguay is at Gorlero and Calle 27. The snazzy ANCAP gas station at Gorlero and Calle 30 has a locutorio and Internet access. Many other Internet places pop up in season and go bust out of it.

Travel Agencies Turisport (☎ 445500), Local 9 in the Edificio Torre Verona at Gorlero and Calle 21, is the American Express representative.

Bookstores Librería del Sol, on Calle 30 between Gorlero and Calle 20, has a wide selection of books and magazines in English and Spanish, as well as some magazines in Italian and French.

Laundry Lava Ya is on 28 between Gorlero and 24, across from the Hotel Suizo.

Beaches
On the west side of Punta del Este, Rambla Artigas snakes along the calm Playa Mansa on the Río de la Plata, then circles around the peninsula, passing Playa de los Ingleses and Playa El Emir to the wilder Playa Brava on the Atlantic side. From Playa Mansa, west along Rambla Williman, the main beach areas are La Pastora, Marconi, Cantegril, Las Delicias, Pinares, La Gruta at Punta Ballena, and Portezuelo, beyond Punta Ballena. Eastward, along Rambla

Lorenzo Batlle Pacheco, the prime beaches are La Chiverta, San Rafael, La Draga, and Punta de la Barra. All these beaches have *paradores* (small restaurants) with beach service, which are more expensive than bringing your own goodies. Beach-hopping is a popular activity, depending on conditions and the general level of action.

Be warned: They don't call it Playa Brava (Fierce Beach) for nothing; the waves and currents on the Atlantic side claim several lives a year.

Organized Tours
Green Tours (☎ 490570), in the bus terminal, runs guided tours in the day and night to Punta del Este, as well as to nearby beaches and outlying sights such as Cabo Polonio.

Places to Stay
In summer, Punta is jammed with people, and prices for accommodations can be astronomical. In winter it's a ghost town, and places that stay open lower their prices considerably. Wherever possible, high- and low-season prices are given. All the following listings are open year-round; many serve a buffet breakfast in summer and a continental in the off-season.

Budget At *Hostal El Castillo* (mobile ☎ 09-409799, e *reserves@elcastillo.com.uy, Calle 31 between 20 & 18)* dorm beds cost US$8 per person with HI card, doubles US$25. Beds are up to five to a room here. The whole place is a bit musty, some rooms are dark, and the bath facilities are sparse, but it's HI certified and hey, it's Punta del Este. Lockout is from 4pm to 6pm.

Residencial 32 (☎ 491464, Calle 32 640) Singles/doubles US$20/30 low season, US$40/60 high season, with fan & breakfast. The rooms are clean here; some are decorated in an odd but engaging style.

Mid-Range At *Hotel Marbella* (☎ 441814, fax 442039, e *hotel_marbella@starmedia .com, Calle 31 615),* singles/doubles/triples are US$38/45/65 low season, doubles/triples US$80/95 high season; all come with fan and breakfast. The clean, quiet, good-sized and comfortable rooms with minibars are a good value. Most have at least of peek of ocean view.

Hotel Península (☎ *441533, fax 441813,* e *hotel_peninsula@i.com.uy, Gorlero 761)* Singles/doubles US$30/45 in winter, doubles US$98 summer, with fan & breakfast. Rooms have minibars, cable TV and terraces, many overlooking the heated pool. There's a gym as well.

Hotel Suizo (☎ *441517, fax 443985, hotelsuizo01@latinmail.com, Calle 28 590)* Doubles US$45-65 low season, US$70-110 mid-season, US$80-120 high season, with breakfast. There are three classes of rooms here: The cheapest are a bit worn, while the most expensive have air-con and minibars but are nothing special.

Hotel Tanger (☎ *440601, fax 440918, Calle 31 between Calles 18 & 20)* Doubles US$60-70 low season, US$80-95 mid-season, US$95-120 high season, with air-con & breakfast. This recommended hotel has very spacious and comfortable rooms with minibars and safes, and two pools (one on the rooftop, with excellent beach views).

Hotel London (☎ *441911, fax 440503,* e *hotellondon@hotmail.com, Calle 20 877)* Singles/doubles/triples US$30/40/60 low season, US$60/80/120 high season, with air-con & breakfast. The rooms are smallish and the air-con aging, but this hotel is a good value, with great baths, good light and lots of privacy.

Top End At *Hotel Azul* (☎ *441117, fax 442925,* e *hotelazu@adinet.com.uy, Gorlero 540),* you can rent doubles for US$60 low season, US$95 mid-season, US$110 high season, with breakfast and air-con. The Azul is little old but very agreeable. Its big rooms have TV and fridge, good views and heat in winter. There's a restaurant/confitería, and laundry service and parking are available.

Gran Hotel España (☎ *440228, fax 440254,* e *ghespana@adinet.com.uy,* w *www .hotelespana.com, Calle 9 660)* Doubles US$82-89 low season, US$99-115 high season, with breakfast & air-con (singles about US$7 less). Standard rooms are quiet

and comfortable, if a bit small, at this friendly family-run hotel on the low-key southern end of the peninsula. Rooms have minibars, TV, phones and central heat. The owners speak excellent English and offer travel-agency services as well.

Conrad Resort & Casino (☎ *491111, fax 490803,* e *conradpde@conrad.com.uy, Parada 4, Playa Mansa)* Doubles start at US$342/251/205 high/mid-/low season. The high-rise, ultra-modern Conrad is five-star all the way. All rooms have terraces with sea views, and the casino offers entertainment extravaganzas.

Places to Eat

Watch for *cubiertos* (cover charges) in touristy Punta del Este.

Pizza Cero (☎ *445954, Calles 9 & 10)* US$4.25-9. Nosh on Italian food in the courtyard in summer, or tuck yourself away among the many alcoves among the potted plants and hanging ferns inside.

El Pobre Marino (☎ *440207, Calle 11 665)* US$4.50-7.25. Ignore the 'sea-fast-food' sign and chow down on the inexpensive fish and pasta while admiring the nets and glass floats adorning the place.

El Viejo Marino (☎ *443565, Calles 11 & 14)* US$6-12. The nautical decor is subtler here, and the seafood's more expensive, but it's got air-con.

Mariskonea (☎ *440408, Calle 26 650)* US$6.50-24, plus US$5 cubierto; cash only. This is one of the oldest restaurants in Punta, with great views of Playa Brava and Isla de Los Lobos. They raise some of the seafood served here in a pond below the restaurant – aquaculture 1940s style. US$12 lunch and US$20 dinner specials include the cubierto.

Portofino (☎ *440225, Calle 10 & Rambla de la Circunvalación)* US$13-24. Near the yacht harbor, where the Rambla changes names briefly, this upscale restaurant serves seafood, pasta, and meat in leafy surroundings. Full menúes for US$18 and US$24 are offered as well.

Blue Cheese (☎ *440354, Rambla Artigas & Calle 23)* US$9.75-12.75. It's got views of the yacht harbor and Isla Gorriti, but the

US$7.25 salad bar (US$3.25 if accompanying a main dish) is the star attraction here. Steak and fish round out the menu.

Martín Fierro (☎ 4447100, Rambla Artigas & Calle 14) US$7-16. Dine on parrilla, fish and 'international cuisine' on two floors overlooking the yacht harbor.

Yabrud (☎ 446463, Calles 11 & 12) US$4-8. For variety, try this Arab-Armenian eatery, serving shwarma, köfte, döner kebab and more in gleaming white surroundings.

Gure Etxe (☎ 446858, Calles 12 & 9) US$6-20. Here, seafood with a Basque accent is served in old-time surroundings, for a refreshing change from modern Punta ambience.

El Mejillón (☎ 44589, Rambla Artigas & Calle 11) US$7.25-16. Unmatchable views across the water to Isla Gorriti and Playa Mansa are a big draw here. 'The Mussel' serves seafood, steaks, and reasonably priced sandwiches and breakfasts.

Freddo (branches: Calles 30 & 20; Gorlero & Calle 27) is an Argentine ice-creamery said by some to be the best.

Entertainment

Punta's dynamic social scene kicks off with drinks at *Moby Dick (☎ 441240, Rambla de la Circunvalación between Calles 12 & 10)*, a pub near the yacht harbor. Later, clubbers head north along Rambla Batlle Pacheco to such fashionable *boliches* as *Punta News (Parada 10)*, owned by actor Christopher Lambert, *Space (Parada 31)* and *La Morocha (☎ 094-417383, Ruta 10 s/n)*, just across the bridge in La Barra, where the Rambla changes to Ruta 10. The names change frequently, but the general area remains the same. Bear in mind that it's social suicide to turn up at a nightclub before 2am here.

Shopping

Manos del Uruguay (☎ 441953, Gorlero between Calles 30 & 31) The artisans cooperative has a leather outlet here.

Getting There & Away

Air There are flights to Maldonado/Punta del Este from Argentina year-round, but many more in summer, when there are also services to Brazil and sometimes Paraguay and Chile. Aeropuerto Carlos Curbelo (☎ 042-578386), also known as Aeropuerto Laguna del Sauce, is at Laguna del Sauce west of Maldonado. At present, the airport cannot handle aircraft larger than 737s, but there are plans to expand it to international standards.

Pluna (☎ 490101), at Parada 8½ on Rambla Batlle Pacheco near Roosevelt, has 29 weekly flights to Buenos Aires' Aeroparque (US$94, 40 minutes). In summer it has flights to São Paulo and other Brazilian destinations, sometimes via Montevideo.

Aerolíneas Argentinas (☎ 444343), in the Edificio Santos Dumont on Gorlero between Calles 30 & 31, flies to Aeroparque up to seven times daily in season, and once a day on Friday, Saturday and Sunday off-season. LAPA (☎ 490840), in the Edificio Punta del Este at Av Roosevelt Parada 14½, flies to Aeroparque Friday and Sunday.

Bus The bus terminal (☎ 489467) is at Calle 32 and Bulevar Artigas. Most bus services to Punta del Este are an extension of those to Maldonado; see that Getting There & Away section for information on domestic buses. Many services require a transfer at San Carlos.

Brazilian destinations include Porto Alegre (US$49, 10½ hours), Florianópolis (US$75, 17 hours) and São Paulo (US$114, 29 hours). Most Argentine cities require connections in Montevideo.

Getting Around

To/From the Airport COT runs buses to the airport (US$4), leaving 1½ hours before each flight. Alternatively, you can catch a US$2 Piriápolis-bound COPSA bus for the half-hour trip, but these drop you on the highway, from which it's about a four-block walk to the terminal.

Bus See the Maldonado Getting Around section for details of the frequent transport between Maldonado and Punta. Micros leave every 15 minutes in summer from Bay

1 at Punta's bus terminal and serve the eastern beaches and nightspots on Rambla Batlle Pacheco on their way to La Barra (US$1.60, 20 minutes); from Parada 39, just before the superb rollercoaster bridge to La Barra, it's a 1km walk west to Camping San Rafael. Others run to points west, including Punta Ballena and Piriápolis. Línea 14 (by Codesa) hits the bus terminal in both Maldonado and Punta del Este, the eastern beaches, La Barra and José Ignacio (US$1.85, 45 minutes) eastbound.

Car Budget (☎ 446363) has offices on Calle 27 near Gorlero; Avis (☎ 442020) is on Calle 31, between Gorlero and Calle 24; and Hertz (☎ 489775) on Calle 31, between Gorlero and Calle 20. Local agencies include Multicar (☎ 443143), at Gorlero 860, and Uruguay Car (☎ 441036), in the Galería Sagasti on Gorlero.

AROUND PUNTA DEL ESTE
Isla Gorriti
Boats leave every half hour or so (daily in season, weekends in off-season) from the yacht harbor for this nearby island, which has excellent sandy beaches and ruins of the **Baterías de Santa Ana**, an 18th-century fortification. It also has two restaurants, Parador Puerto Jardín and Playa Honda. The boat trip costs US$5.75 for adults, US$1.75 for children.

Isla de Lobos
About 10km offshore, the nature reserve of Isla de Lobos hosts a population of some 200,000 southern sea lions. During the invasion of 1806, British forces stranded numerous prisoners here without food or water, and many perished while attempting to swim to Maldonado. To arrange trips to the reserve, contact the Unión de Lanchas (☎ 442594) in Punta del Este.

ROCHA
Picturesque Rocha is capital of its namesake department and merits at least an afternoon visit for those staying on the beach at La Paloma. In the narrow alleyways off Plaza Independencia are a number of interesting houses from late colonial and early independence times.

Virtually everything of interest, as well as hotels and transport, is on or near Plaza Independencia. There's a departmental tourist office (☎ 047-28202) on the highway at the turnoff to La Paloma. The post office is at 18 de Julio 131. Antel is at General Artigas and Rodó. Banco la Caja Obrera on the plaza exchanges money.

Places to Stay
Accommodations are very reasonable, perhaps enough so to justify staying here rather than in La Paloma.

Hotel Municipal Rocha (☎ 047-2404, 19 de Abril 87) Singles/doubles US$20/27 with breakfast. This tidy hotel a block southwest of the plaza has clean simple rooms with fans.

Hotel Trocadero (☎/fax 047-2267, 25 de Agosto & 18 de Julio) Singles/doubles/triples US$35/55/66, with buffet breakfast. Spacious rooms here have parquet floors, cable TV, writing desks and 1950s-vintage bathrooms.

Getting There & Away
Rocha is a hub for bus travel between Montevideo and the Brazilian border. Rutas del Sol (☎ 3541), at Ramírez and 25 de Agosto, runs 10 buses daily to Montevideo (US$8.25, 3 hours); eight daily to Chuy (US$6.50, 2 hours); five to La Paloma (US$1.25, 30 minutes), three of which continue to La Pedrera and Barra de Valizas (US$3.50, 1½ hours). Cynsa has several to La Paloma. COT (☎ 047-2119), half a block east of the plaza at 25 de Agosto 112, serves several of the above destinations as well as Maldonado (US$3.25, 1¼ hours) and Punta del Este (US$4, 1½ hours).

LA PALOMA
☎ 0479 • pop 5000
Some 28km south of Rocha and 250km from Montevideo, placid La Paloma is less developed, less expensive, and much less crowded than Punta del Este, but still has almost every important comfort and amenity except for Punta's hyperactive

nightlife. As elsewhere on the coast, there are attractive sandy beaches in town and beyond – those to the east are less protected from ocean swells.

Orientation & Information

La Paloma occupies a small peninsula at the south end of Ruta 15. Its center, flanking Av Nicolás Solari, is small and compact. Although the streets are named, the buildings, including the hotels and restaurants, lack numbers and are more easily located by their relationship to prominent intersections and other landmarks.

The Liga de Fomento has a desk in the bus terminal (☎ 9764), intermittently staffed. Its main office (☎ 6008) is on the traffic circle at the east end of Av Nicolás Solari. In summer, it's open 9am to 11pm daily; the rest of the year hours are 1:30pm to 6:30pm Monday to Saturday.

Banco de la República is at the corner of Av Nicolás Solari and Titania; it has an ATM and changes money but doesn't cash traveler's checks. The post office and Antel are on Av Nicolás Solari. Internet access is US$0.08 a minute in the upstairs place next door to Restaurant Arrecife on Av Solari.

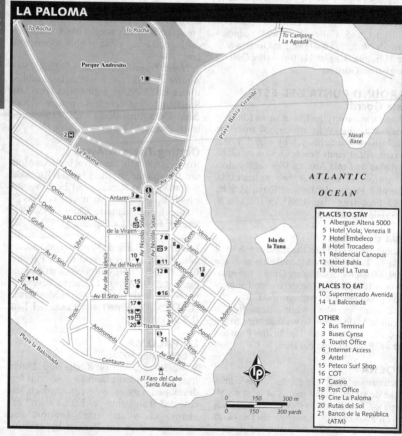

LA PALOMA

To Rocha
To Rocha
To Camping La Aguada

Parque Andresito

Playa Bahía Grande

Naval Base

La Paloma

Antares

ATLANTIC

OCEAN

Orion
Antares
Delfin
BALCONADA
de la Virgen
Grulla
Libra
Av El Sirio
Lira
Perseo
Leo

Av del Puerto
Alicia
Ceres
Venus
Juno
Uranio
Mercurio
Neptuno
Júpiter
Saturno
Apolo
Eros
Adonis

Isla de la Tuna

Av Nicolás Solari
Av del Navio
Av de la iglesia
Canopus
Picos
Andromeda
Centauro
Titania
Av del Sol
Av El Sirio

Playa la Balconada

El Faro del Cabo Santa María

0   150   300 m
0   150   300 yards

PLACES TO STAY
1 Albergue Altena 5000
5 Hotel Viola; Venezia II
7 Hotel Embeleco
8 Hotel Trocadero
11 Residencial Canopus
12 Hotel Bahía
13 Hotel La Tuna

PLACES TO EAT
10 Supermercado Avenida
14 La Balconada

OTHER
2 Bus Terminal
3 Buses Cynsa
4 Tourist Office
6 Internet Access
9 Antel
15 Peteco Surf Shop
16 COT
17 Casino
18 Post Office
19 Cine La Paloma
20 Rutas del Sol
21 Banco de la República (ATM)

Things to See & Do

The 1874 completion of **El Faro del Cabo Santa María** *(free; open 4:30pm-7:30pm daily in summer; weekends only rest of year)*, the local lighthouse, marked the beginning of La Paloma's growth as a summer beach resort. The unfinished first attempt collapsed in a violent storm, killing 17 French and Italian workers.

Uruguay isn't widely known for its **surfing**, but the Peteco Surf Shop, on Av Solari between Sirio and Navío, can offer suggestions for the best local spots, and rents boards for US$10 a day. The shop next door rents bicycles for US$6 per day.

Laguna de Rocha, 10km west of La Paloma, is an ecological reserve with populations of black-necked swans, storks, and waterfowl.

Places to Stay

As elsewhere on the coast, rates are highest in January and February, and may drop by 50% in other months.

Camping La Aguada (☎ 6239, fax 6485, Ruta 5 Km 2.5) Sites US$12 for 2 people, US$1.50 each additional person; cabañas US$64; 50% less off-season. This campground, at the eastern entrance to town, has amenities such as hot showers, a market (seasonal), a restaurant and electricity, and there's also excellent beach access. The cabañas are a steal, accommodating up to six people and equipped with fridge, stove and private bath. Buses from Rocha will stop in front on request, and micros from town pass regularly.

Albergue Altena 5000 (☎ 6396, Parque Andresito) US$4.50/6 HI members low/high season, US$6/10 nonmembers. Open year-round. The hostel is in the shady park on the edge of town. The male dorm room holds 16 beds on two levels; the female section has two 11-bed rooms. There's a small common room and, for member use only, a kitchen with microwave.

Residencial Canopus (☎ 6068, Av Nicolás Solari) Doubles US$30 high season. The bright rooms at this hotel are one of the best values in town. Rates drop in the off-season.

Hotel La Tuna (☎/fax 6083, Neptuno) Rooms US$10 per person low season, singles/

doubles/triples US$25/40-50/55 high season, with breakfast. Management is cranky, and the baths are tiny; better rooms have minibar and TV. You can't get much closer to the water without a boat, though, and there are some good views, including a panoramic one from the 3rd-floor dining room.

Hotel Trocadero (☎/fax 6007, e trocade@ adinet.com.uy, Juno) Doubles US$26-30 low season, US$50-60 high season, with breakfast. This older hotel has flagstone corridors, a shady inner patio with ping-pong table, and spacious rooms and baths. A good value.

Hotel Viola (☎ 6020, fax 9528, Av Nicolás Solari) Singles/doubles US$20/35 low season, doubles US$55-60 high season, with breakfast & fan. The Viola is a simple, clean and friendly place with ample, breezy rooms. Some of the upstairs rooms have balconies, and there's a good restaurant.

Hotel Embeleco (☎ 6108, Av El Sol & de la Virgen) Singles/doubles/triples US$20/30/45 low season, doubles/triples US$65/85 high season, with breakfast & fan. All of the good-sized rooms at this well-run establishment have balconies, minibars and TV.

Hotel Bahía (☎/fax 6029, Av El Navío & Av El Sol) Singles/doubles/triples US$22/36/46 low season, doubles/triples US$74/100 high season, with breakfast & fan. The Bahía's large, quiet and very comfortable rooms have TVs and minibars; some have terraces.

Places to Eat

Venezia II (Av Nicolás Solari) US$2.75-7. Pizza is the specialty here, but seafood is on the menu too, all served in a warm Mediterranean ambience. The restaurant is part of Hotel Viola.

Hotel Embeleco (see Places to Stay) US$2-5. Marine paraphernalia and swords adorn the walls, and the ceiling is covered in pinecones. The usual array of dishes are accompanied by a reasonable wine list (with photos).

Hotel Bahía (see Places to Stay) US$6.25-10, plus US$2 cubierto. Portions are on the small side, but presentation is good at this well-lit place, and there's a non-smoking section.

La Balconada (☎ 6197, *La Balconada*) US$8-11.25, plus US$2.50 cubierto. This is probably the best restaurant in town; it's relatively expensive, but worth it. A tasting menu for two is US$28.

Getting There & Around

All buses use the new terminal near Aries and La Paloma, but some companies still have offices in town for the moment. You'll find a wider variety of bus schedules from Rocha (US$1, 30 minutes); buses go there frequently. At least seven daily buses serve Montevideo (US$10, 3½-4 hours). Rutas del Sol (☎ 6019), at Av Solari and Titania, goes twice daily (once in winter, at 10:45am) to Chuy (US$6.25, 2½ hours) via Barra de Valizas (US$2.50, 1 hour), along coastal Ruta 10. It also runs four summer and two winter buses from Montevideo through La Paloma, ending at Barra de Valizas.

Spiffy micros (US$1) run from the terminal, up and down Av Solari, then head out Av del Puerto and past Camping La Aguda regularly year-round (at least half-hourly in summer).

CABO POLONIO

East of La Paloma on Ruta 10, at Km 264.5, visitors can hike 9km over dunes in one of Uruguay's wildest areas to visit the country's second biggest sea lion colony, near a tiny fishing village. At the beginning of the access road to the dunes, many people advertise 4WD rides to the reserve (US$5.25 roundtrip), which otherwise is a strenuous walk of about two hours (bring water). The sea lions (as well as a group of penguins) have colonized an island close offshore; some days they gather onshore, some days they don't.

Buses between La Paloma and Barra de Valizas stop at the turnoff for Cabo Polonio. You can also arrange tours from La Paloma, Barra de Valizas, and other towns in the area.

BARRA DE VALIZAS

This tiny beach town 4km off Ruta 10 has thus far managed largely to escape the development creeping eastward from Punta del Este. Valizas has the slow-paced feel of an artists' colony, with friendly dogs and the occasional inquisitive horse wandering the streets, and dunes stretching toward Cabo Polonio. A few modest dwellings are sometimes available for rent (expect cabañas to pop up soon). The youth hostel *Albergue Artigas* (☎ 0470-5273, *reserve through the hostelling association in Montevideo*, ☎ 02-400-4245) charges US$7/10 per bed with/without card and is open from December 10 to April 16 only. It has kitchen facilities and hot showers. See La Paloma Getting There & Around section for transit details.

PARQUE NACIONAL SANTA TERESA

This coastal park, 35km south of Chuy, incorporates the hilltop **Fortaleza de Santa Teresa** (*admission US$0.80, open 9am-5pm daily*), which was begun by the Portuguese in 1762 and finished by the Spaniards after its capture in 1793. Across Ruta 9, the enormous Laguna Negra and the marshes of the Bañado de Santa Teresa support abundant bird life, as well as some highly venomous snakes.

Santa Teresa is administered by the army and attracts many Uruguayan and Brazilian visitors to its relatively uncrowded beaches. The park does, however, get crowded in summer and during Carnaval. It offers dispersed camping in eucalyptus and pine groves, a very small zoo and a plant conservatory. Camping costs US$8 per site in summer, US$6 in winter, for up to six people, and includes basic facilities such as hot showers. There are also various grades of cabañas for rent for US$15 to US$50.

You must register and pay at the *Capatacía* (park headquarters), which has a phone, post office, market, bakery and other facilities. Some buses (including almost all Rutas del Sol services) plying Ruta 9 between Chuy and Rocha enter the park and stop at the Capatacía (US$1.75, 40 minutes from Chuy). Others will stop at the entrance.

If you're driving and just want to see the fortress, don't use the park's main entrance; it costs US$2 per car to enter. The fortress turnoff is 4km northeast and signed with a campground symbol.

BARRA DEL CHUY

The beach stretches as far as the eye can see at this town near the mouth of Arroyo San Miguel, at the end of a lateral that branches off from Ruta 9 10km south of Chuy.

There are some small restaurants in town, as well as a few cabañas for rent. On the edge of town, about 1km in from the beach, are two campgrounds. Set in a pine grove, deluxe *Camping Chuy* (*☎/fax 0474-900-6122,* e *turchuy@adinet.com.uy*) has US$10 sites, a heated pool and other amenities. Tiny four-person A-frames rent for US$28, and even more luxurious lodging is available. *Camping de la Barra* (*☎ 0474-9206*), closed in winter, costs US$3.75 per person. It's more down-home, and has hot showers, clothes-washing facilities, a restaurant and store, and a soccer field where locals play on Sundays.

Some buses traveling between Montevideo and Chuy (US$1.25, 30 minutes) service Barra, including four to six by Rutas del Sol. Local buses from Chuy run every two hours.

CHUY
☎ 0474 • pop 9500

Chuy is an energetic Uruguayan-Brazilian border town at the end of Ruta 9, 340km from Montevideo. Pedestrians and vehicles cross freely between the Uruguayan and Brazilian sides, which are separated only by a median strip along the main avenue (on the Uruguayan side, it's Av Brasil; on the Brazilian side, it's Av Uruguaí). Duty-free shops line both sides of the street.

Orientation & Information

General Artigas is the main drag into town from Ruta 9; Crossing the border it becomes Av Argentina. A block east of Argentina is Venezuela, a block west is Colombia (Olivera back on the Uruguayan side). If proceeding beyond Chuy into Brazil, complete Uruguayan emigration formalities at the customs post on Ruta 9, 1km south of town, where there is also a national tourist office (☎ 2554).

The Brazilian consulate (☎ 2049; 2651011 from Brazil), at Fernández 147, is open 10am to 3:30pm weekdays. On the Brazilian side, there's an Uruguayan consulate (☎ 2651151; 2690 from Uruguay) at Rua Venezuela 311, open 8am to 2pm weekdays. Visas cost US$28 for those who need them.

Uruguayan currency is worthless any distance into Brazil. There are several exchange houses along the border street.

Places to Stay & Eat

Hotel Internacional (*☎/fax 2055, Río San Luis 121*) Singles US$6.50-10.50, doubles US$12-24. This place has old and new sections with a variety of rooms and prices, and a gated parking lot. Some of the cheapies are dark, but rooms are generally good.

Nuevo Hotel Plaza (*☎/fax 2309, Av Artigas 553*) Singles/doubles from US$29/45, with discounts for cash. Quiet, clean, simple and comfortable rooms have cable TV and tidy baths.

Rivero Hotel (*☎ 651271, Colombia 163*) Rooms US$6.50 per person. On the Brazilian side, the Rivero has plain white rooms with cable TV and fan.

Parrillada Javier (*☎ 3033, Av General Artigas 125*) US$2.75-6. This friendly parrilla has an inexpensive salad bar and some great taxidermy, including a capybara head. Some nights there's live music too.

Getting There & Away

COT, Cotec and Rutas del Sol are all in a row on Calle Olivera; Cynsa/Núñez is just around the corner at Brasil 587. Several buses connect Chuy with Montevideo (US$13.50, 6 hours). Cotec serves Treinta y Tres (US$6.25, 3 hours) morning and evening via the very scenic route through Lascano and José Pedro Varela.

The Brazilian *rodoviária* (terminal) is on Venezuela, three blocks north of the border. Two buses daily serve Rio Grande (US$5.75, 4 hours) and Pelotas (US$6, 4 hours), where travelers can connect for Rio de Janeiro and other destinations. To Porto Alegre (US$12.25 regular, US$14.50 semidirect, 6½ to 7½ hours), there are five buses daily.

FUERTE SAN MIGUEL & AROUND

This pink-granite fortress *(no ☎, Ruta 19 Km 9; admission US$1; open 9am-5pm daily)*, 9km west of Chuy, was built in 1734 during hostilities between Spain and Portugal. Its entrance, guarded by a moat, overlooks the border from a high, isolated point. When it's closed you can still glimpse the interior and visit the nearby Museo Criollo/Museo Indígena, with indoor and outdoor displays relating to gaucho, Indian and pioneer life, and an impressive array of carts and machinery.

Ruta 19 continues northwest through some of the most interesting countryside in Uruguay. The wide-open, marshy land holds range animals grazing among scattered palms, sometimes up to their chests in water. The abundant bird life here includes egrets, hawks, jaunty kingfishers, the enormous, storklike jabirú and flocks of the small green parrots so often heard but not seen in other parts of the country. You may spot turtles basking in the sun and the occasional ñandú. The pasturelands are broken up by large fields of rice. The stretch of highway just before the junction with Ruta 15 (which leads to the enormous Laguna Merín, shared between Uruguay and Brazil) is well-graded dirt. Outside of Lascano, where Ruta 14 heads north toward Varela, Ruta 8 and Treinta y Tres, the landscape reverts to the typically Uruguayan rolling hills and grassland.

TREINTA Y TRES
☎ 045 • pop 30,000

Little-visited Treinta y Tres is a gaucho town in the scenic hill country of the Cuchilla Grande, on the Río Olimar. Founded in 1853 on the interior route to Brazil, via Río Branco or Melo, it is also the department capital. The town is 290km northeast of Montevideo via Ruta 8 and 150km northwest from Chuy via Rutas 19, 14 and 8. Aside from strolling by the river there's not a lot to do in town.

The tourist office (☎ 22911), on Ruta 8 at Araújo, the main street into town, is open 6:30am to 7pm weekdays, till 3pm weekends. As with many Uruguayan towns,

hotels, restaurants, bus agencies and money-changers are on or near the main plaza. The town has a dual numbering system; this book uses the low numbers.

Places to Stay & Eat
Hotel Olimar (☎ 22115, Lavalleja 564) Singles US$14.50/23 with cable TV. This simple but clean and friendly hotel is on the plaza.

Hotel 33 (☎ 22325, e hotel33@adinet .com.uy, Lavalleja 688) Singles US$29-35, doubles US$38-44 with buffet breakfast. This remodeled hotel has good-sized private rooms with cable TV, as well as a sauna, heated pool, a small gym and a luxurious noon checkout time.

Parrillada Tahiti (☎ 25556, JA Lavalleja & Meléndez) US$2.75-5.50. One block north of the plaza, this simple and very cheap place serves good salads, licuados and meat. Try the excellent *costillas de cerdo a la plancha*, a lean and meaty cut of pork rib.

Getting There & Away
In addition to running its own buses, Tur-Este (☎ 23516, Zufriátegui 209) does ticketing for some other lines that pass through town.

Some 16 buses run daily between Treinta y Tres and Montevideo (US$11.50, 4½ hours), by Cota (☎ 20278, Manuel Freire 632), Rutas del Plata (☎ 22680, Zufriátegui 1069), Expreso Minuano (☎ 25364, Araújo 242) and Núñez (☎ 23073, Freire & M Lavalleja). Most of these are via Minas (US$7, 2½ hours). Maldonado (US$9, 3½ hours) is served daily by Tur-Este and Olivera Hermanos (Freire 615), as is San Carlos. Tur-Este has tickets for Río Branco on the border with Brazil (US$5.25, 2 hours, 10 buses), Chuy (US$6.25, 3 hours, one early-morning and one afternoon bus), and Rocha (US$7, 4 hours). Melo (US$4.50, 1½ hours) is served about seven times a day by Núñez and Cota.

MELO
☎ 064 • pop 46,000

Founded in 1795, the capital of Cerro Largo department is 110km north of Treinta y Tres via Ruta 8. Featuring a few late-colonial buildings, Melo is a transport hub for

Uruguay's interior, with bus connections to Río Branco, Aceguá and Rivera, all of which have border crossings to Brazil.

The main Plaza Independencia is at Colón and Muñiz, five blocks southwest of the bus terminal. The post office is at Herrera 671, Antel at 18 de Julio and Herrera.

Parque Rivera has a free public *campground* across the river about 2km west of the center, on Ruta 26. Two blocks southeast of the plaza, *Hotel Centro* (☎ 22084, Saravia 711) has spacious, clean rooms for US$10/12 per person with shared/private bath, with air-con & cable TV; it's a good value. Rooms with shared bath and no air-con or TV are US$8.75.

Forno's (☎ 25439, Saravia & Batlle Ordóñez) is a first-rate and popular parrilla serves pizza as well. Meals cost US$2.50 to US$5.50. *Pizzería Aroztegui* (☎ 2570, Saravia 588) is another option for meals.

At least five buses serve Montevideo (US$16, 6½ hours) daily, while Treinta y Tres (US$4.50, 1½ hours) has about seven. Two buses per day (morning and mid-afternoon) serve Tacuarembó (US$8.75, 3½ hours) and Rivera (US$13, 5 hours). Of the other Brazilian border towns Río Branco (US$3.50, 1½ hours) gets four or five buses Monday to Saturday, and Aceguá (US$2.25, 1 hour) gets two; each has at least one Sunday bus.

Paraguay

Paraguay

Depending where you're arriving from, Paraguay for the first time can be something of a shock, culturally, psychologically and physically. But by keeping your eyes, ears and mind open, you may find that the place starts to grow on you, and until near the end of your stay you begin to wax nostalgic for this fascinating country before even leaving it.

Isolated geographically and politically for much of its history, and poorly known even to its neighbors, Paraguay now welcomes foreign visitors. Among its offerings are ruined Jesuit missions in the south, slow-paced river towns with grand old buildings in the northeast, several national parks, and the riverside capital of Asunción. The Gran Chaco to the north is a paradise for bird-watchers and other nature-oriented travelers, and home to the Mennonite colonies, industriously scratched out of an inhospitable environment. Possibly the country's most compelling aspect, however, is the unique interweaving of the bloodlines and languages of its conquerors and conquered, augmented by hefty threads from later waves of immigrants, to form a cultural tapestry unlike any other in South America.

Facts about Paraguay

HISTORY

Paraguay's pre-Columbian cultural patterns were more complex than either Argentina's or Uruguay's. Upon European contact, Guaraní-speaking people inhabited most of what is now southern Paraguay, except for enclaves of dense tropical and subtropical forests, near the borders of present-day Brazil, occupied by hunter-gatherers such as the Aché (Guayakí). West of the Río Paraguay a multitude of Indian groups (known collectively as 'Guaycurú,' a term used by the majority Guaraní people) inhabited overlapping territories in the Chaco. Among these groups were the Tobas, Matacos, Mbayás, Abipones and many others, some of whom are now extinct.

Highlights

- Trinidad and Jesús - Visiting well-preserved, relatively untouristed Jesuit mission ruins
- The Chaco – Spotting wildlife in one of South America's last great wildernesses
- The Río Paraguay – Roughing it aboard a cargo boat on the way to your own personal heart of darkness
- Asunción – Sipping drinks while overlooking the presidential palace

BOLIVIA

BRAZIL

Southern Paraguay
page 695

Downtown Asuncion
pages 682-683

Ciudad del Este
page 706

Encarnación
page 702

ARGENTINA

URUGUAY

OTHER MAPS
Paraguay page 661

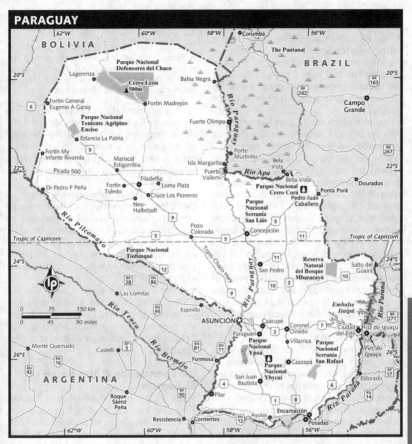

PARAGUAY

The Guaraní were semisedentary cultivators, while the Chaco were mostly hunter-gatherers who also fished along the Río Pilcomayo and other watercourses. Although predominantly a peaceful people, the Guaraní sometimes ventured into Guaycurú territory and battled with them. They even raided the foothills of the Andes, obtaining gold and silver objects that later aroused the Spaniards' interest. The Guaycurú did not hesitate to fight back, and later Spanish-Guaraní expeditions into the Chaco were frequently violent. Well into the 20th century, Indian hostility deterred settlement of many parts of the region.

European Exploration & Settlement

Europeans first entered the upper Paraná in 1524 when Alejo García, a survivor of Juan de Solís' ill-fated expedition to the Banda Oriental, walked across southern Brazil and Paraguay to the foothills of Bolivia with Guaraní guides. García found silver in the Andes, but he died on the return journey. His discoveries resulted in the renaming of the Río de Solís as the Río de la Plata (Silver River).

Sebastián Cabot sailed up the Río Paraguay in 1527, but Pedro de Mendoza's expedition made the major advance: After

Querandí attacks foiled their plans to establish a permanent settlement at Buenos Aires, Mendoza's men founded a fortress called Nuestra Señora de la Asunción on the east bank of the Río Paraguay. At Asunción, the Guaraní were far more tolerant of the Spanish presence and made a military alliance with them against the hostile Chaco peoples.

Relations between Indians and Spaniards took an unusual course here. The Guaraní attempted to absorb 350 Spanish men (and a few other Europeans) into their social system by pairing them up with local women; since women bore the major responsibility for Guaraní agriculture, this assured the men would have food. The Spaniards adopted Guaraní food, customs, and even language, but cultural assimilation was a two-way process. Gradually there emerged a hybrid, Spanish-Guaraní society in which the Spaniards were politically dominant. The mestizo children of the Spaniards and Indians adopted Spanish cultural values, and at the same time used the Guaraní language and followed other local customs.

Jesuit Missions

In the colonial period, Paraguay comprised a much larger area than it does now and included large parts of present-day Brazil and Argentina. In this area, on both sides of the upper Paraná, Jesuit missionaries conducted a remarkable experiment, creating a series of highly organized settlements in which the Guaraní learned many aspects of European high culture as well as new crafts, crops, and methods of cultivation. For more than a century and a half (until the expulsion of the Jesuits in 1767 because of local jealousies and Madrid's concern that the order's power had become too great), Jesuit organization deterred Portuguese intervention and protected the interests of the Spanish crown. (See the boxed text 'Jesuit Missions' in the Northeast Argentina chapter for more information on the missions.)

Jesuit influence was less effective among the non-Guaraní peoples of the Chaco, whose resistance to the Spaniards discouraged any proselytizing. Martin Dobrizhoffer,

an Austrian Jesuit who spent nearly 20 years in the region, wrote about these people:

The savage Guaycurus, Lenguas, Mocobios, Tobas, Abipones, and Mbayas, wretchedly wasted the province with massacres and pillage, without leaving the miserable inhabitants a place to breathe in, or the means of resistance.

Having acquired the horse, groups like the Abipones and Tobas were mobile and flexible in their opposition, while the Payaguá used canoes to attack riverboats, looting cargoes and slaughtering the crews. They would also launch raids on settlements from the rivers.

Several Jesuit missionaries, some of them, like Dobrizhoffer, excellent amateur ethnographers and naturalists, managed to live among the Chaco tribes from the mid-17th century, but much of the area remained an Indian refuge even into the mid-20th century. If recent reports are correct, parts of it may still be.

After secular Spaniards realized that the Chaco route promised neither gold nor silver, they abandoned the area entirely, and the most important political and economic developments occurred east of the Río Paraguay.

Independence & the Reign of El Supremo

When Paraguayans deposed their Spanish governor and declared independence in 1811, the Spanish crown declined to contest the action, since the colony was so isolated and economically insignificant. Within a few years, Dr José Gaspar Rodríguez de Francia, a former theologian who had studied at the University of Córdoba (in what is now Argentina), emerged as the strongest member of the governing junta. From 1814 to 1840, the autocratic Francia ruled the country as El Supremo Dictador.

Recognizing Paraguay's inability to compete with its neighbors, Francia made a virtue of necessity by sealing off the country's borders to commerce and promoting self-sufficiency – subsistence on a countrywide scale. As a member of the junta he had adroitly derailed Argentine efforts to absorb

Paraguay, and later as supreme dictator he steered the country clear of trouble with Brazil.

Francia was deeply influenced by events in France at the end of the 18th century and saw himself as the leader of a revolution. He broke the backs of the criollo elite by expropriating properties of landholders, merchants, and the Church (outlawing monastic orders and closing the seminary at which he had once taught), establishing the state as the dominant economic as well as political power. Much of the seized land was leased to poor farmers and families.

Like his successors almost to the present day, Francia ruled by fear, operating a large secret police force and confining his opponents under horrendous conditions, chained in dark cells without room to lie down, and forbidden to speak. Many were tortured in Francia's most notorious dungeon, the 'Chamber of Truth.'

Francia himself was not immune to the climate of terror. After escaping an assassination attempt in 1820, El Supremo so feared assassination that his food and drink were consistently checked for poison, no one could approach him closer than six paces, the streets were cleared for his carriage, and he slept in a different place every night. In 1840 he died a natural death and was replaced by Carlos Antonio López in 1841. In 1870, political opponents who knew how to hold a grudge disinterred Francia's remains and threw them into the Río Paraguay. Today his likeness is on the 10,000-guaraní note (worth about US$2.50).

López 'Dynasty' & the War of the Triple Alliance

With the income from state enterprises, Carlos Antonio López ended Paraguay's extreme isolation, building railways, schools, a telegraph, an iron foundry, and a shipyard. López was no less autocratic than Francia, but where the latter had led an ascetic life, eschewing luxury and even returning a portion of his income to state coffers, López used his power to accumulate a tremendous personal fortune. Asunción's Senate building was originally his private mansion.

López also lacked Francia's circumspection in regional politics, declaring war in 1845 on Argentine leader Juan Manuel de Rosas, who was occupied with other matters at the time (and in any case was overthrown in 1852, largely by internal forces). By the time of his death in 1862, López had amassed a standing army of 28,000 men and another 40,000 reserves (Argentina, at the time, had only 6000 men in uniform). His rather grotesque image, which looks like the caricature of a man but is said to be accurate, graces the 5000-guaraní note today.

Carlos Antonio was succeeded by his megalomaniacal son, Francisco Solano López. Appointed *mariscal* (field marshal, the title by which he is most often known) at the age of 19 by his father, Francisco fancied himself the Napoleon of South America. He perhaps picked up this notion while on a visit to France, where he also acquired an Irish mistress, Eliza Lynch, who accompanied him back to Paraguay and bore him several sons out of wedlock. Known as 'Madame Lynch,' she wielded enormous influence in the country; streets and plazas bear her name.

When Brazil attacked the federalist Blanco faction in Uruguay in 1864, Solano López rallied to their defense. Argentina refused his troops permission to cross its territory on their way to Brazil, and López declared war on that country as well. A subjugated Uruguay joined in against Paraguay, and in 1865 the catastrophic War of the Triple Alliance was under way.

Within four years Triple Alliance forces captured Asunción, and an increasingly unstable, paranoid and bloody-minded Solano López had begun ordering the execution of thousands of Paraguayans he perceived as having turned against him. These included military officers, foreign diplomats and even two of his own brothers. He is said to have had his 70-year-old mother publicly whipped for speaking against him.

After Asunción's fall, López retreated into the bush with his hugely outnumbered forces, which by now had conscripted almost all able-bodied males in the country, including the aged and boys as young as 10. Many of these, lacking adequate weapons, fought using clubs, machetes and farm implements. In 1870 at Cerro Corá, near present-day Pedro Juan Caballero, López met his end. The official version says he was killed by a Brazilian soldier, but it is whispered that he succumbed to dysentery.

Paraguay lost 150,000 sq km of territory, but even worse, much of its population through combat, famine, and disease – it was often said that only women, children, and burros remained. By some contemporary accounts, women outnumbered men three to one at the end of the war; others said that the country lost more than half its population. This was a blow from which the country never completely recovered. The episode of the child soldiers is held up as a glorious example of patriotic sacrifice, and many Paraguayan history books portray López as a beleaguered hero fighting to save his country. Mariscal Francisco Solano López's portrait appears on the 1000-guaraní note.

Reconstruction & the Chaco War

After 1870, despite a new constitution, Paraguay underwent a decades-long period of political instability. As borders opened, a trickle of European and Argentine immigrants arrived and slowly resuscitated the agricultural economy. The Colorado (Red) party, formed in 1887, helped reestablish the country as a sovereign state, encouraged agricultural development and brought about reforms in public education. The other major party, the Liberales, took power after the turn of the century.

About this time, tension began to arise between Paraguay and Bolivia over the ill-defined borders of the Chaco, which neither country effectively occupied. As early as 1907, both began to build fortifications in anticipation of war, but full-scale hostilities did not erupt until 1932. After a 1935 ceasefire that left no clear victor, a peace treaty awarded Paraguay three-quarters of the territory in dispute, or around 52,000 sq km. The country paid dearly, however, both financially and in the loss of another sizable portion of its population. Approximately

40,000 Paraguayan and 60,000 Bolivian soldiers died in the conflict.

The reasons underlying the war remain unclear. The Paraguayans, by encouraging Mennonite immigrants to settle in the Chaco, certainly provoked the Bolivian government, which, having earlier lost its Pacific coast to Chile, was concerned about Atlantic access via the Río Paraguay. The possibility of large oil deposits in the Chaco spurred both countries' interest, and Paraguay accused Standard Oil of financing Bolivia's military buildup in exchange for oil-exploration rights in the region. Shell Oil was in turn accused of backing Paraguay. In any event, no oil was discovered, and the region remains a thinly populated backwater.

Stroessner Dictatorship & Backlash

Following the Chaco War, Paraguay endured more than a decade of disorder until the end of a brief civil war, which returned the Colorados to power in 1949. A military coup in 1954 removed the constitutional president and brought to power General Alfredo Stroessner, who through bogus elections ('guided democracy'), an extensive network of informers, nearly annual declaration of martial law, and other brutally repressive tactics, went on to rule the country for decades.

Dominating Paraguay's post-WWII history, Stroessner implemented one of the Western Hemisphere's most odious and long-lasting dictatorships. Extremely corrupt electoral politics were controlled by a government that allowed only token opposition. Lack of any limitation to presidential or congressional terms helped solidify the Stroessner dictatorship (now referred to as the *stronato*) for 35 years.

Both the Liberales and the Febreristas, a moderate labor-oriented party, operated within the stringent bounds of acceptable public dialogue under the Stroessner regime, but others, including Liberal and Colorado factions, boycotted the farcical elections.

In early 1989, General Andrés Rodríguez overthrew Stroessner in a palace coup. Not long after deposing the dictator,

Rodríguez won the presidency, unopposed, via an election in which the entire spectrum of opposition parties obtained a larger percentage of congressional seats than ever before. Since Stroessner's overthrow, the government has made a concerted effort to eradicate the thousands of monuments to him and his relatives, even renaming the city of Puerto Presidente Stroessner as Ciudad del Este, but reminders of his brutal regime linger.

In the 1990s some Paraguayans expressed a certain nostalgia for the elderly Stroessner (suffering poor health in Brazilian exile), who publicly sought permission to return to Asunción. An amicable return seems unlikely, though, as of June 2001 a Paraguayan judge requested the extradition of Stroessner to stand trial for his crimes.

Transition to Democracy

Leading up to the 1991 elections, political activity and dialogue flourished on a scale unprecedented in recent Paraguayan history. In December 1991, in what was probably the fairest election held in Paraguay up to that point, General Rodríguez's Colorados won a legislative majority. One of the great ironies of Stroessner's overthrow was Rodríguez's triumphant appearance on Paraguayan television with his daughter and grandchildren – also Stroessner's grandchildren, since Rodríguez's daughter was married to Stroessner's son.

In 1993, Juan Carlos Wasmosy became Paraguay's first elected civilian president in eons. Though nominated by the ruling Colorados as a figurehead, he soon came into conflict with the still-powerful military, most notably coup-monger General Lino Oviedo.

After threatening a coup in 1996, the populist Oviedo drew a 10-year prison sentence from the military, rendering him ineligible for the 1998 presidential election, but his vice-presidential candidate, Raúl Cubas, took over the ticket. After handily defeating Alianza Democrática candidate Domingo Laíno, whose campaign focused on Colorado corruption, Cubas almost immediately pardoned Oviedo. This act enraged even some ardent Colorados, including Vice President Luis María Argaña, who called for

Cubas' impeachment. In March 1999, Argaña was assassinated in Asuncíon, and Cubas resigned amid accusations that he masterminded the killing.

Cubas joined Stroessner in Brazilian exile, while Oviedo fled to Argentina, whose president, Carlos Menem, despite vigorous criticism, granted him political asylum. With the opposition Alianza's taking power in Argentina's 1999 presidential elections, Oviedo became a fugitive. Reportedly hiding out in Paraguay, he was instead discovered in Brazil in 2000. In June 2001, Brazil rejected his appeal for asylum and prepared to extradite him to Paraguay.

Paraguay Today

Upon Cubas' resignation, Senate president Luis Ángel González Macchi became the country's president. Enjoying the support of the army, the Colorado leader was hailed by cheering crowds as he was sworn in. Almost immediately, though, the new president and his party were dogged by charges of continuing corruption. In August 2000, the Liberales won their first major victory as their vice-presidential candidate, Julio César Franco, narrowly defeated Argaña's son.

Responding to the dim international view of his government, González launched a comprehensive anticorruption policy, Paraguay's first, in December 2000. However, in the spring of 2001 he was forced to accept the resignation of the head of Paraguay's central bank, which had been charged with embezzling millions of dollars. Just weeks earlier, it was revealed that the deluxe BMW González drove was a stolen vehicle arriving from Brazil.

Political troubles continue to brew. In May 2001 an attempted coup by supporters of General Oviedo was suppressed. The summer of that year saw discontent growing among Paraguay's agricultural workers and increased international censure for black-market activities, as well as mounting anger over a series of bank frauds and outright robberies, some involving government officials or their relatives. Meanwhile, the economy is in decline, with overall GDP shrinking despite rapid population growth.

Paraguay's challenges for the upcoming years include protecting its fledgling democracy, pulling out of economic recession and increasing its citizens' standard of living.

GEOGRAPHY & CLIMATE

Landlocked and isolated in the South American heartland, surrounded by gigantic Brazil, Argentina, and Bolivia, Paraguay appears much smaller than it really is. Its area of 407,000 sq km makes the country slightly larger than Germany and almost exactly the size of California. More than half of it is forested, but most of the timber has little commercial value.

The Río Paraguay (which connects the capital of Asunción with the Río Paraná, the rest of the Río de la Plata drainage, and the Atlantic Ocean) divides the country into two unequal halves. Small ranges of mountains and hills, such as the Serranía San Rafael and the Cordillera Ybytyruzú keep the topography interesting in the smaller southeastern sector, which comprises about 40% of the country's territory and contains the great majority of the population. A well-watered, elevated plateau of rolling grasslands and patches of subtropical forest here separate the valley of the Río Paraguay from the upper Paraná.

These rivers and the Río Pilcomayo form much of Paraguay's borders with Brazil and Argentina. The Paraná is an enormous source of hydroelectric power, with the potential to produce even more. Mineral resources, including petroleum, are almost nonexistent.

Southern Paraguay's climate is humid, with rainfall distributed fairly evenly throughout the year. In the east, near the Brazilian border, it averages an abundant 2000mm a year, declining to about 1500mm near Asunción. Since elevations do not exceed 600m, temperatures are almost uniformly hot in summer – the average high in December, January, and February is 35°C (95°F), with daily temperatures ranging between 25°C and 43°C (77°F to 109°F). Winter temperatures are more variable and can reach freezing or hover at 6°C (42°F), though the average high in July, the coldest month, is 22°C (71°F).

Paraguay is vulnerable to cold fronts known as *pamperos*, which work their way north from temperate Argentina in the spring and fall, causing temperatures to drop dramatically – as much as 20°C in only a few hours.

Paraguay's northwestern sector is an extensive plain, known as the Gran Chaco, rising gradually toward the Bolivian border and broken up by occasional peaks such as the 500m Cerro León. Only about 4% of all Paraguayans live in the Chaco, whose principal economic activities are cattle ranching on very large *estancias* and dairy production, an industry typically associated with German Mennonite settlers. Temperatures are even higher than in eastern Paraguay, often exceeding 40°C (104°F), and rainfall is erratic; precipitation does not exceed 1000mm. This, combined with high evaporation rates, makes rain-fed agriculture undependable. Nonetheless the Mennonite colonies have successfully raised cotton, sorghum, and other commercial crops in the region.

FLORA & FAUNA

Paraguay's vegetation correlates strongly with rainfall and diminishes from east to west, but nearly the entire country has abundant greenery of one form or another. Its humid subtropical forest is densest in the moist valleys of eastern Paraguay, near the Brazilian frontier, and sparser on the thinner upland soils. The most important tree species are *lapacho, quebracho colorado, trébol, peroba,* and *guatambú.* Between this forest and the Río Paraguay, the dominant vegetation is savanna with occasional gallery forests along watercourses, while west of the

ASUNCIÓN

Elevation - 53m/175ft

Río Paraguay, caranday palm savanna gradually gives way to scrub and thorn forest, including the valuable quebracho, a source of natural tannin. Throughout the country, there is a particular abundance of aroid plants (such as philodendrons) and orchids.

Paraguayan wildlife is equally diverse, but the dense human population of rural southern Paraguay has put great pressure on the local fauna. Mammals in danger of extinction include the giant anteater, giant armadillo, maned wolf, river otter, Brazilian tapir, jaguar, pampas deer and marsh deer. One modest but notable wildlife success has been the rediscovery in the mid-1970s of the Chacoan peccary, which was thought to be extinct for at least half a century, and its nurture by a joint effort of Paraguayan and international conservationists.

Bird life is abundant, especially in the Chaco, and Paraguay has 365 bird species, including 21 species of parrots and parakeets, jabirú and wood storks, plumed ibis and waterfowl, among many others.

In the riverine lowlands, the numerous reptiles include anacondas, boa constrictors and two species of caiman. Short-term visitors are unlikely to see the truly rare species, but they have a good chance of seeing many reptiles they have never seen before.

NATIONAL PARKS & RESERVES

Paraguay has several national parks and lesser reserves protecting an impressive diversity of habitats throughout the country, but only a few are easily accessible to travelers. The three largest are in the Chaco, while the smaller and more biologically diverse units are in eastern Paraguay.

Unfortunately, because of corruption, economic pressure, and a traditionally weak political commitment, some of Paraguay's parks have experienced serious disruption. Despite these difficulties, some environmental organizations like the Fundación Bertoni have accomplished a great deal by publicizing environmental issues both locally and abroad. See Useful Organizations in the Facts for the Visitor section later in this chapter for contact information on Paraguayan parks and reserves.

Some of the more interesting parks and reserves are listed below.

Reserva Natural del Bosque Mbaracuyú – Managed in conjunction with the Nature Conservancy and the Fundación Moisés Bertoni, this 64,000-hectare unit in Canindeyú department upstream from the Itaipú Dam holds the largest remaining extents of Alto Paraná rain forest. Contact the Fundación Bertoni about guided trips.

Parque Nacional Serranía San Rafael – In hilly terrain in the southwestern departments of Itaipúa and Caazapá, San Rafael includes forests and wetlands, as well as historical sites and indigenous communities on 78,000 hectares.

Parque Nacional Tinfunqué – On the Río Pilcomayo, 300km northwest of Asunción, this 280,000-hectare unit of savanna and marshland is the country's second-largest park. Consisting entirely of private estancias, it is effectively a paper park, with neither a management plan nor direct protective activities, but landowners do not object to visitors. Wildlife includes capybara, swamp deer, caiman and a great variety of bird life.

Parque Nacional Teniente Agripino Enciso – In semiarid upper Chaco, 665km from Asunción on the Ruta Trans-Chaco, 40,000-hectare Teniente Enciso features low, dense thorn forest and wildlife (similar to that of the larger and less accessible Defensores del Chaco) and also preserves Chaco War battle sites. Managed jointly by the Ministry of Defense and Ministry of Agriculture and Livestock, it has resident rangers and some visitor facilities.

Parque Nacional Defensores del Chaco – In semiarid northwest Chaco, 830km from Asunción, this 780,000-hectare park is by far the country's largest, although direct protective activities are minimal over most of the area. Its dominant vegetation is thorn forest of quebracho, *algarrobo*, and *palo santo*; and large mammals include jaguar, puma, tapir, peccary, and monkeys. Access is difficult but not impossible (see the relevant section later in this chapter).

Parque Nacional Cerro Corá – In the department of Amambay, 500km from Asunción, 22,000-hectare Cerro Corá is probably the most scenic of Paraguay's parks, with transitional humid subtropical forest among isolated peaks up to 450m high. It also features numerous cave sites and was the scene of Francisco Solano López's death, which marked the end of the War of the Triple Alliance. The park has a visitor center, camping area, and several *cabañas* (cabins) for lodging (see the relevant section later in this chapter).

Parque Nacional Ybycuí – In the department of Paraguarí, only 150km from Asunción, 5000-hectare Ybycuí, with its humid subtropical forest, is the most accessible and probably best managed of Paraguay's parks, despite the presence of agricultural colonists and problems with timber poachers. There are several self-guided nature trails, a longer backpack trail, a visitor center, and a campground plus the ruins of Paraguay's first iron foundry. A small restaurant serves meals on weekends (see the Parque Nacional Ybycuí section later in this chapter).

Parque Nacional Serranía San Luis – In the department of Concepción, 670km north of Asunción, 10,000-hectare San Luis is an area of rugged subtropical forest near the Brazilian border. It has limited visitor infrastructure, but contains much wildlife.

GOVERNMENT & POLITICS

Paraguay is a republic with a 1992 constitution that establishes a strong president, popularly elected for a five-year term, who in turn appoints a seven-member cabinet to assist in governing. Congress consists of a lower Cámara de Diputados (Chamber of Deputies) and an upper Senado (Senate), elected concurrently with the president by popular vote. The Corte Suprema (Supreme Court) is the highest judicial authority. Administratively, the country comprises 17 departments.

The hegemony of the business-as-usual, authoritarian Colorado party has been eroded by relatively free elections. Most dominant in opposition are the center-left Liberales; the major third party is the right-of-center Encuentro Nacional (National Encounter).

Paraguay's 45 senators are now chosen by proportional representation in nationwide elections, while the 80 deputies are chosen geographically, by department. Thanks to political decentralization, the various departments choose their own civilian governors.

The elections held in 1998 saw the Colorados with 25 seats in the Senate and 45 in the Chamber of Deputies. The Liberales ended up with 13 senators and 26 deputies, while the Encuentro Nacional took seven senate seats and nine deputy positions. Fourteen of 17 departmental governorships are under Colorado control. The next elections are scheduled for 2003.

ECONOMY

Already one of South America's poorest countries, Paraguay has been hit hard by the regional economic decline. Inflation in 2000 doubled to 9% from the low rate of 1999. Per-capita GDP is US$3700. The official minimum wage is about US$240 per month, but the Ministry of Justice and Labor is unable to enforce regulations, and probably three-quarters of Paraguayan workers earn less than this level. A large proportion of the rural populace cultivates subsistence crops on small landholdings, selling any surplus at local markets and laboring on large estancias and plantations to supplement the household income.

Historically, Paraguay's economy depended on agriculture and livestock. Its principal exports have been beef, maize, sugarcane, soybeans, lumber and cotton. High transportation costs, due primarily to Paraguay's landlocked isolation, have driven up the cost of its exports. The country's major source of income is its 'informal economy' – primarily contraband, including electronics and agricultural produce, most of which passes through Ciudad del Este to or from Brazil. Stolen cars, firearms and illegal drugs are other goods that pass into or through Paraguay, and the country is a major producer of cannabis. In 2001 Paraguay was 'certified' by the US as cooperating in counternarcotics operations, thus avoiding sanctions, but it remains on the US's list of major drug-producing or transit countries.

The gradual reduction of tariffs in Mercosur (see Economy in Facts about Argentina), of which Paraguay is a charter member, may reduce the prevalence of smuggling by making imported goods cheaper in the neighboring member countries of Argentina, Brazil, and Uruguay. However, the region's economic woes have sharply reduced trade with these nations, and Paraguay's legitimate exports have stagnated.

Paraguay lacks mineral energy resources, but enormous multinational dam projects have developed its hydroelectric potential.

Brazil takes most of the electricity from Itaipú, on the upper Paraná above Ciudad del Este, while the output of corruption-plagued Yacyretá, on the border with the Argentine province of Corrientes, goes in large part to Argentina. Already burdened with substantial foreign debt, Paraguay faces grave consequences should it prove unable to repay its share of capital costs and maintenance.

Privatization has not been fully implemented in Paraguay, and much of the economy remains open to state corruption and political influence.

POPULATION & PEOPLE

Paraguay's population of about 5.6 million is less than one-sixth that of the US state of California, which has roughly the same area. With more than 600,000 residents, Asunción is by far the largest city. Only half of Paraguayans live in urban areas, compared with about 90% in Argentina and Uruguay. Many Paraguayans are peasant cultivators who produce a small surplus for sale.

By global and even South American welfare standards, Paraguayans rank comparatively low. Infant mortality rates are relatively high, though significantly lower than in Bolivia, Brazil, Ecuador, Guyana, Suriname and Peru, but life expectancy has increased to a respectable 74 years. Population growth is 2.6% per annum, with a doubling time of only 28 years.

Mestizos – those of mixed Spanish and indigenous blood – make up more than 85% of the population. Descendants of European immigrants in Paraguay include about 100,000 of German ancestry. Japanese immigrants have settled in parts of southern Paraguay, and Asunción has seen a substantial influx of Koreans. Recently, tens of thousands of Brazilians have moved to Paraguay in response to Brazil's poor economy, prompting both economic growth and nationalist resentment among some Paraguayans.

In the Chaco and in scattered areas of southern Paraguay, there are small but significant populations of indigenous people, some of whom, until very recently, relied on hunting and gathering for their livelihood. The largest groups are the Nivaclé and Lengua, both of whom number around 10,000. Many of them have become dependent labor for the region's agricultural colonists. In total, Indians comprise about 3% of the population. The Stroessner dictatorship conducted an active campaign of genocide against the Aché (Guayakí) Indians of southern Paraguay in the 1970s.

EDUCATION

Education is compulsory only to the age of 12. In the country as a whole, literacy is 90%, the lowest of the Río de la Plata republics but higher than all the Andean countries. Higher education is largely the responsibility of the Universidad Nacional and the Universidad Católica in Asunción, but both have branches throughout the country.

ARTS

In general, very little Paraguayan literature is available to English-speaking readers, but novelist and poet Augusto Roa Bastos put Paraguay on the international literary map by winning the Spanish government's Cervantes Prize in 1990. Despite having spent much of his adult life in exile from the Stroessner dictatorship, Roa Bastos focuses on Paraguayan themes and history in the larger context of politics and repressive government. He returned to Paraguay in 1996.

Some of Roa Bastos' best work is available in English. *Son of Man*, originally published in 1961, is a novel tying together several episodes in Paraguayan history, including the Francia dictatorship and the Chaco War. *I the Supreme* is a historical novel about the paranoid dictator Francia.

Works by other important Paraguayan writers, such as novelist Gabriel Casaccia and poet Elvio Romero, are not readily available in English. Josefina Pla's historical and critical works on Guaraní-Baroque art and the British in Paraguay have been translated, but her poetry has not. For books on history and other aspects of Paraguay, see Books & Film in the Facts for the Visitor section.

As in Buenos Aires and Montevideo, theater is a popular medium, with occasional offerings in Guaraní as well as Spanish. In 1933, during the Chaco War, theatergoers in

Asunción swarmed to see the Guaraní dramatist Julie Correa's *Guerra Ayaa*. The visual arts are very important and popular; Asunción has numerous galleries, most notably the Museo del Barro, which emphasizes modern, sometimes very unconventional, works.

Both classical and folk music are performed at venues in Asunción. Much of Paraguayan music is entirely European in origin. The most popular instruments are the guitar and harp, while traditional dances include the lively *polcas galopadas* and the *danza de la botella*, in which dancers balance bottles on their heads.

Paraguay's most famous traditional craft is the production of multicolored *ñandutí* (spider-web lace) in the Asunción suburb of Itauguá. Paraguayan harps and guitars, as well as filigree gold and silver jewelry and leather goods, are made in the village of Luque, while other high-caliber artisanal goods come from the Indian communities of the Chaco. While production for sale rather than for use may have debased the quality of certain items, such as spears and knives, woodcarvings are truly appealing (the eastern Paraguayan village of Tobatí is well known for this).

SOCIETY & CONDUCT

English-speaking visitors will find Paraguay in some ways more 'exotic' than either Argentina or Uruguay due to the country's unique racial and cultural mix; however, Paraguayans in general are eager to meet and speak with foreign visitors. Take advantage of any invitation to drink *mate*, often in the form of ice-cold *tereré*, which can be a good introduction to Paraguay and its people.

Many Paraguayans are willing to discuss politics openly, though some can become uncomfortable at the sight of a notebook or even being asked their name. This is a legacy of the stronato, during which, some say, seven out of 10 Paraguayans acted as informants of one sort or another.

In the Mennonite colonies of the Chaco, an ability to speak German helps dissolve barriers to this culturally insular community. It's more difficult, though, to make contact with the region's indigenous people, and it's undiplomatic to probe too quickly into the relations between the two, which are a controversial subject. From contact with the Mennonites, some Chaco Indians speak German rather than Spanish as a second language.

RELIGION

Roman Catholicism is Paraguay's official religion, but folk variants are important, and the Church is weaker and less influential than in most other Latin American countries. Traditionally, Paraguay's isolation and the state's indifference to religion have resulted in a wide variety of irregular religious practices – according to one anthropologist, rural Paraguayans view priests more as healers or magicians than spiritual advisers. Women typically express greater religious devotion than men.

Protestant sects have made fewer inroads in Catholic Paraguay than in some other Latin American countries, although fundamentalist Mennonites have proselytized among Chaco Indians since the 1930s, and the Unification Church (Moonies) recently purchased 360,000 hectares in the Chaco, including the entire town of Puerto Casado. Other evangelical groups, including the controversial New Tribes Mission, used to operate with the collusion and, some say, active support of the Stroessner dictatorship. This regime was no friend to the country's indigenous people, who, of course, have their own religious beliefs, many of which they have retained or only slightly modified, despite nominal allegiance to Catholicism or evangelical Protestantism.

LANGUAGE

Paraguay is officially bilingual in Spanish and Guaraní, a legacy of colonial times when vastly outnumbered Spaniards had no alternative but to interact with the indigenous population. Though undoubtedly influenced by Spanish, Guaraní has also modified the European language in its vocabulary and pattern of speech. The most noticeable example of this is the pronunciation of the letter 'r' commonly heard in Paraguay, sounding almost like the speaker is imitating an American's bad Spanish pronunciation. During the Chaco War of the 1930s, Guaraní enjoyed resurgent popularity when, for security purposes, field commanders prohib-

Guaraní Words & Phrases

The following is a small sample of Guaraní words and phrases that travelers may find useful, if only to break the ice. Those given are not so consistently phonetic as Spanish but are still fairly easy to pronounce. A few have obviously been adapted from Spanish.

I	*che*
you	*nde*
we	*ñande*
this	*péva*
that	*amóa*
no	*nahániri*
all	*entéro*
many	*hetá*
big	*guazú*
small	*mishí*
one	*peteí*
two	*mokoi*
eat	*okarú*
drink	*hoiú*
water	*y*
meat	*soó*
hot	*hakú*
cold	*roí*
woman	*kuñá*
man	*kuimbaé*
person	*hente*
road	*tapé*
rain	*amá*
cloud	*araí*
mountain	*sero*
new	*piahú*
good	*porá*
name	*héra*
How are you?	*Mba'eichapa?*
Fine, and you?	*Iporãiterei, ha nde?*
I'm fine, too.	*Iporãiterei avei.*
Where are you from?	*Moõguápa nde?*
I'm from Australia.	*Che Australia gua.*
Where do you live?	*Moõpa reiko?*
I live in California.	*Che aiko California.*

ited Spanish on the battlefield. Listeners tuned to Paraguayan radio will hear otherwise familiar soft-drink jingles in Guaraní rather than Spanish, and the yellow pages of telephone directories have Guaraní sections.

Several other Indian languages are spoken in the Chaco and isolated parts of southern Paraguay, including Lengua, Nivaclé, and Aché.

Facts for the Visitor

Travelers will find Paraguay similar to Argentina and Uruguay in some respects but very different in others. Only facts that differ significantly from the other Río de la Plata republics are mentioned in this chapter.

PLANNING
When to Go

Because of Paraguay's intense summer heat, visitors from midlatitudes may prefer the winter months from, say, May to August or September. The weather can vary in these months, as chilly days alternate with warm ones. Nights can be very cool, and frosts are not unusual.

Maps

For about US$7.50, the *Guía Shell*, contains the most useful road map of the country, plus a good general country map at a scale of 1:2,000,000, and a map of Asunción, with a street index, at 1:25,000. Its tourist information is limited, making the price a bit high. The Servicio Geografico Militar (☎ 021-206344), Artigas 920, has topographical maps at 1:50,000, and some city and town maps as well.

The tourist office in Asunción gives out a decent country map, with schematics of each region, as well as a very good city map that includes a blowup of the *microcentro* (downtown). In Filadelfia, it's possible to purchase an excellent, detailed map of the Mennonite colonies.

What to Bring

During the summer heat, Paraguayans dress very informally. Light cotton clothing suffices for almost all conditions except in winter

(when you'll want some layers of clothing), but a sweater or light jacket is advisable for changeable spring weather. If you're spending any time outdoors in the brutal subtropical sun, do not neglect a wide-brimmed hat or baseball cap, a lightweight long-sleeved shirt and sunblock. Mosquito repellent is imperative in the Chaco and many other places.

TOURIST OFFICES

Paraguayan tourist offices are fewer than in Argentina or Uruguay and less well organized. They can be found in Asunción, Encarnación, Ciudad del Este and a handful of other places.

The larger Paraguayan consulates, such as in New York and Los Angeles (see Embassies & Consulates, later), usually have a tourist representative in their delegation.

VISAS & DOCUMENTS

All foreigners need a valid passport, except visitors from bordering countries (who need national ID cards). Americans, Canadians, Australians and New Zealanders need to obtain visas in advance from a Paraguayan consulate. These are free and good for 90 days, but require filling out a form and the following: two photos, a photocopy of your return or onward tickets and proof of sufficient funds (cash, traveler's checks, a credit card or ATM card). Depending on the volume of paperwork they're facing, consulates can often process your application the same day. Readers have reported being solicited at some consulates for 'fees' to speed the process and avoid long delays. A calm but firm insistence may get you past this should it arise; threatening to contact your own embassy is another possible tactic.

Be sure to get your passport stamped on entering and leaving the country; the fine for lacking an entrance stamp is US$85, and some officials are only too eager to collect. Passports are necessary for many everyday transactions, such as cashing traveler's checks, checking in at hotels, and passing the various military and police checkpoints in the Chaco and elsewhere. Paraguay officially requires that foreign drivers possess the International Driving Permit, but passports, vehicle registration and rental contracts are usually the only documents requested at traffic stops.

EMBASSIES & CONSULATES
Paraguayan Embassies & Consulates

Paraguay has no diplomatic representation in Australia or New Zealand, but maintains missions in the following countries:

Argentina
(☎ 011-4814-4803), Viamonte 1851, Buenos Aires
(☎ 03718-421988), José F Cancio 1393, Clorinda
(☎ 03783-426576), Córdoba 969, 2nd floor, Corrientes
(☎ 03752-423858), San Lorenzo 179, Posadas

Bolivia
(☎ 02-443-416), Edificio Illimani II, 1st floor, Av 6 de Agosto, La Paz

Brazil
(☎ 045-523-2898), Bartolomeu de Gusmão 738, Foz do Iguaçu
(☎ 067-431-6312), Av Presidentes Vargas 120, Ponta Porã
(☎ 067-724-4934), Praia de Botafogo 242, Rio de Janeiro
(☎ 38492793), Rua Bandeira Paulista 600, São Paulo

Canada
(☎ 613-567-1283), 151 Slater St, Suite 501, Ottawa, Ontario K1P 5H3

Chile
(☎ 639-4640), Huérfanos 886, Santiago

France
(☎ 1 42 22 85 05), 1, rue St Dominique, Paris

Germany
(☎ 228-356727), Uhlandstrasse 32 53173, Bonn 2

UK
(☎ 0207-937-1253), Braemar Lodge, Cornwall Gardens, London SW7 4AQ

Uruguay
(☎ 02-408-5810), Bulevar Artigas 1191, Montevideo

USA
(☎ 202-483-6960, fax 234-4508), 2400 Massachusetts Ave NW, Washington, DC 20008
(☎ 310-820-5451), 2301 Wilshire Blvd, Suite 205, Los Angeles, CA 90007
(☎ 305-374-9090, fax 374-5522), 2800 Biscayne Blvd, Suite 9078A, Miami, FL
(☎ 212-682-9441), 675 3rd Ave, Suite 1604, New York, NY 10017

The light of dawn over Lago Nahuel Huapi, Argentina

Punta Arenas, in the Chilean Patagonia, attracts Antarctic explorers and tip-of-the-continent travelers.

AARON MCCOY

In Chilean Patagonia, Parque Nacional Torres del Paine embraces open meadows...

BRENT WINEBRENNER

...and vertical peaks over 1000m high and beautiful lakes.

Embassies & Consulates in Paraguay

Australians must rely upon their consulate in Buenos Aires or the British Consulate. The following addresses are all in or near Asunción; contact details for consulates listed as 'also in' can be found in the towns' Information sections later in the chapter.

Argentina
(☎ 021-442151), Palma 319, 1st floor

Belgium
(☎ 028-33326), Km 17.5 Ruta 2, Capiatá

Bolivia
(☎ 021-203656), América 200

Brazil
(☎ 021-444088), General Díaz 521, 3rd floor

Canada
(☎ 021-227207), Profesor Ramírez & Juan de Salazar

Chile
(☎ 021-662756), Capitán Neudelmann 351

France
(☎ 021-212439), Av España 893

Germany
(☎ 021-214009), Av Venezuela 241

Israel
(☎ 021-495097), Yegros 437, 8th floor

Italy
(☎ 021-225918), Teniente Morales 680

Japan
(☎ 021-604616), Av Mariscal López 2364

Netherlands
(☎ 021-492137), Chile 668

Peru
(☎ 021-607431), Agustín Barrios 852

Spain
(☎ 021-490686), Yegros 437, 6th floor

Switzerland
(☎ 021-490848), Juan O'Leary 409, 4th floor

UK
(☎021-612611), Av Boggiani 5848

Uruguay
(☎ 021-203864), Av Boggiani 5832

USA
(☎ 021-213715), Av Mariscal López 1776

CUSTOMS

Paraguayan customs officially admit into the country 'reasonable quantities' of personal effects, alcohol and tobacco; since contraband is the national sport, though,

officials at overland crossings wink at anything that's not flagrantly illegal.

Nevertheless, foreign motorists may run into corrupt customs officials who claim that their vehicles may not enter the country without posting a bond of half the vehicle's local value – which is much higher than it is overseas. Anyone encountering such a problem should politely but firmly remind them that Mercosur regulations, which establish a common external tariff between Brazil, Argentina, Uruguay and Paraguay, do not require this. Keep photocopies of vehicle documentation from neighboring countries for proof and reference when crossing borders.

MONEY

The unit of currency is the *guaraní* (plural *guaraníes*), indicated by a ₲. Banknote values are 500 (rare), 1000, 5000, 10,000, 50,000 and 100,000 guaraníes; there are coins for 50, 100 and 500 guaraníes.

Annual inflation has risen to about 14%; prices in general are slightly lower than in Uruguay. *Casas de cambio* (exchange houses, sometimes shortened to *cambios*) in Asunción and at border towns change both cash and traveler's checks, but banks are the rule in the interior. Street changers give slightly lower rates than cambios, but they can be helpful on weekends or in the evening, when cambios are closed.

Better hotels, restaurants and shops in Asunción accept credit cards, but their use is less common outside the capital. ATMs are becoming more widespread, and many of them recognize foreign credit and debit cards.

Exchange Rates

Cambios accept traveler's checks at slightly lower rates than cash, and sometimes charge small commissions. German marks are more welcome in Asunción than in other South American capitals, although prices are given in US dollars, still the most popular foreign currency. There is no black market. Many exchange houses will not cash traveler's checks without the bill of sale, and all want to see a passport.

At press time exchange rates were as follows:

country	unit		guaraníes
Argentina	Arg$1	=	G4867
Australia	A$1	=	G2538
Bolivia	Bol$1	=	G744
Brazil	BraR$1	=	G1994
Canada	C$1	=	G3093
Chile	Ch$1	=	G7.34
European Union	€1	=	G4360
Japan	¥1	=	G39
New Zealand	NZ$1	=	G2028
UK	UK£1	=	G6930
Uruguay	Ur$1	=	G352
USA	US$1	=	G4863

POST & COMMUNICATIONS

Postal rates are cheaper in Paraguay than in Argentina or Uruguay, but as elsewhere in Latin America, truly essential mail should be registered. Paraguayan post offices charge about US$0.25 per item for general delivery (poste restante) services.

For local calls, public phone boxes are few and far between and take *fichas* (cards) rather than coins; unfortunately they are often the only way to connect to the toll-free local numbers used with international credit and calling cards.

Antelco, the corruption-riddled state telephone company, has central long-distance offices resembling those of Uruguay's Antel; it was slated to undergo privatization by the end of 2001. In the meantime, private *locutorios* (phone offices) have sprung up in many places, often with Internet service as well.

Credit card or collect calls to the US and other overseas destinations are expensive, but cheaper than paying locally; the cheapest option is via prepaid 'virtual cards' from such Web vendors as **w** http://e-worldphone.com. The 'card' is simply a PIN you enter after dialing a local access number, and costs can be as low as US$0.30 a minute. These cards are most easily purchased from within the US with a credit card.

For an international operator, dial ☎ 0010; for Discado Directo Internacional (DDI),

dial ☎ 002. The country code is ☎ 595; when calling Paraguay from another country, drop the '0' in the area code.

Internet cafés offering inexpensive Web and email access can usually be found in any town of over 10,000. Many have the software and headsets for making Web phone calls, though the usual quality of the connection makes them unsuitable for much more than brief exchanges.

INTERNET RESOURCES

To read news stories on Paraguay, try **w** www.paraguay.com; **w** www.yagua.com is a good search engine on the country. The national tourist office's site, **w** www.senatur.gov.py, has links to information on the Itaipú hydroelectric project and more.

BOOKS & FILMS

Despite a slightly misleading title, J Richard Gorham's edited collection *Paraguay: Ecological Essays* (Academy of the Arts and Sciences of the Americas, 1973) contains excellent material on pre-Columbian and colonial Paraguayan history and geography.

Harris Gaylord Warren's *Rebirth of the Paraguayan Republic* tells the story of Paraguay's incomplete recovery, under the direction of the Colorado Party, from the disastrous War of the Triple Alliance.

Anthropologist Pierre Clastres recorded his experiences of the 1960s with the Aché in *Chronicle of the Guayaki Indians* (1998) translated by Paul Astor. Richard Arens' edited collection *Genocide in Paraguay* is an account of the Paraguayan government's role in the attempted extermination of the Aché Indians. 'The General' *(Granta No 31*, Spring 1990) is a short piece by Isabel Hilton detailing her research into, and eventual interview with, Stroessner following his overthrow. Carlos Miranda's *The Stroessner Era* is a thoughtful, nonpolemical analysis of the general's rise and consolidation of power, plus a short political obituary.

Birders may want to acquire Floyd E Hayes' *Status, Distribution and Biogeography of the Birds of Paraguay* (American Birding Association, Monographs in Field Ornithology No 1, 1995).

Roland Joffe's 1986 epic film *The Mission,* starring Robert DeNiro as a conquistador turned Jesuit priest, is worth watching for its footage of Iguazú Falls and (rather idealized) look at life on the *reducciones.* Gregory Peck portrays the evil Dr. Mengele hanging out in Paraguay in Franklin Schaffner's 1978 implausible but gripping thriller *The Boys from Brazil.*

NEWSPAPERS & RADIO

The Stroessner dictatorship severely punished press criticism, closed opposition papers, jailed and tortured editors and reporters, and monitored foreign press agencies. Asunción's daily *ABC Color* (w www.abc.com.py) made its reputation as nearly the sole opposition to Stroessner, despite being subjected to severe restrictions. The editorially bold newspaper *Última Hora* (w www.ultimahora.com) is very independent; it also has an excellent cultural section. *Patria,* the official Colorado Party newspaper, is controlled by Stroessner relatives.

Asunción's German-speaking community publishes a twice-monthly newspaper, *Neues für Alle,* which is widely distributed throughout the country, and the weekly *Rundschau.* The *Buenos Aires Herald* and other Argentine newspapers are available in Asunción, at a kiosk on the corner of Chile and Palma, but they are hard to find elsewhere.

PHOTOGRAPHY

Asunción is a good place to buy film. Fuji Sensia II 100 slide film can be found for around US$5.50 for 36 exposures. This is suitable for Paraguay's tropical light conditions and verdant greens, but in the dense subtropical rain forests of eastern Paraguay high-speed film is better. Inexpensive fast print film is readily available, but high-speed slide film is harder to find and best brought from elsewhere.

TIME

Paraguay is three hours behind GMT; from around April 1 to September 30 daylight-saving time puts it four hours behind. The exact dates are supposed to be set each year by government edict, but in some years the announcement is slow in coming or isn't issued at all, and clocks are untouched.

HEALTH

Paraguay presents relatively few health problems for travelers. Tap water, even in some cities, often comes from wells rather a than central source. In the Chaco it can be undrinkably salty. You're probably best off drinking bottled water, which is readily available. In summer, sunscreen and a hat are good ideas, and you should avoid becoming overheated or dehydrated.

Mosquito-Borne Illnesses

Malaria is not a major health hazard in Paraguay, but the Itaipú hydroelectric project on the Brazilian border has created a new habitat for mosquitoes. The US Centers for Disease Control in Atlanta recommend chloroquine for malaria prophylaxis.

Dengue fever has struck hard in Paraguay in recent years, with more than 500,000 cases reported since 1998. Asunción's suburbs have been hardest hit. Efforts are being made to eradicate the mosquito that transmits the disease.

Symptoms include the fast onset of high fever, severe frontal headache and pain in muscles and joints; there may be nausea and vomiting, and a skin rash may develop about three to five days after the first symptoms, spreading from the torso to arms, legs and face. The disease is usually self-limiting, but dengue hemorrhagic fever (DHF) is serious and potentially fatal.

Risk of contraction, though low for the average traveler, is highest during the summer (December to February), several hours after daybreak and before dusk, and on overcast days. Dengue is much more common in urban areas. No medicines exist to combat or prevent the four different viruses.

Mosquitoes seem to be attracted more to dark colors than to light, so in mosquito-infested areas wear light-colored long trousers, socks, a long-sleeved shirt and a hat. Clothing should be loose fitting, as mosquitoes can drill right through the weave of a

PARAGUAY

tight T-shirt. Mosquitoes also seem to be attracted by scents such as those in perfume, cologne, lotions, hair spray, etc, so avoid using these cosmetics if possible. Sleep in screened rooms or beneath mosquito netting after you have disposed of any little suckers that have gotten in.

Use insect repellent that has at least a 20% but no more than a 30% concentration of DEET (N, N-diethyl-metatoluamide) on clothing and exposed skin. Repellents with higher concentrations of DEET work longer, but are also more likely to cause allergic reactions, as are mosquito coils. Many hotels in mosquito-infested areas routinely spray rooms, or will spray on request.

Other Illnesses

Other causes for concern, but not hysteria, are Chagas' disease, tuberculosis, typhoid, hepatitis, and hookworm *(susto)* – avoid going barefoot. Cutaneous leishmaniasis *(ura)*, a malady transmitted by sandflies that bite and resulting in open sores, is very unpleasant and can be dangerous if untreated. Though leprosy is endemic, the odds of contracting it are near nil. Yellow fever is uncommon.

WOMEN TRAVELERS

Paraguay is generally safe for women travelers, but modest dress is important in deterring unwanted attention: no halter tops, short-shorts or miniskirts. Women should, in general, avoid eye contact with unfamiliar males, especially in the countryside, and women traveling alone should also avoid even 'friendly' conversation with men on buses, as local men may misinterpret this as a sign of sexual interest.

USEFUL ORGANIZATIONS

For visitors interested in natural history and conservation, the Fundación Moisés Bertoni (☎ 021-608740, ✉ mbertoni@pla.net.py), Prócer Carlos Argüello 208, Asunción, is an indispensable organization. Named for a 19th-century Swiss-Paraguayan naturalist, it sponsors projects that encourage biological diversity and restoration of degraded ecosystems, cooperates with the state in

strengthening national parks and other reserves, promotes environmental education and research, and tries to involve Paraguayan citizens and private enterprise in conservation. Many if not most of the staff speak English.

The government organization in charge of Paraguay's national parks, working in concert with the Fundación Bertoni, the US Peace Corps and other groups, is the Dirección General de Protección y Conservación de la Biodiversidad (☎ 021-615812), at Av Madame Lynch 3500 in Asunción. It is under the newly formed Secretaría del Ambiente (Office of the Environment) and sorely underfunded.

DESDEL (☎ 0918-2191, fax 2235, ✉ fdschaco@telesurf.com.py), in Loma Plata, is an organization that works with the Secretariat of the Environment to strengthen and guide local governments in sustainable development of the Chaco region; it is a good source of information on conditions in Parque Nacional Defensores del Chaco.

For motorists, the Touring y Automóvil Club Paraguayo is a useful resource, providing information, road services, and good maps and guidebooks for its members and those of overseas affiliates. The Asunción office (☎ 021-210550) is on Calle Brasil, between Cerro Corá and 25 de Mayo.

DANGERS & ANNOYANCES

Though crimes against travelers have been few in the past, the deteriorating economic situation has fostered a rise in such incidents. It is inadvisable to walk around on your own late at night in Asunción and border towns. There have been reports of armed robbery on buses traveling at night and of carjackings. Many Paraguayans carry handguns, even in the cities. Police and military operate with less impunity than they used to, but try not to aggravate them and always carry your passport.

There are very few police vehicles on the roads. When stopped at Chaco highway checkpoints, be polite and show your papers, and you are unlikely to be seriously inconvenienced.

In the Chaco especially, watch for poisonous snakes. They are less active in the cooler months (April through September), and many will slither away given the chance, but some are very aggressive and can be deadly.

BUSINESS HOURS & PUBLIC HOLIDAYS

Most shops are open Monday to Saturday from 7am to noon, closed for siesta until 2:30pm or 3pm, then open again until 7pm or 8pm. Banks are usually open 7:30am to noon weekdays, but cambios keep longer hours.

A recently passed law ordering government offices to stay open a continuous eight hours has met with resistance; some offices operate from 7am to 3pm, others 8am to 4pm, and some still take siestas or close early. From mid-November to mid-March, many open as early as 6:30am. The following is a list of national holidays on which government offices and businesses are closed.

January 1 – Año Nuevo (New Year's Day)

February 3 – Día de San Blas (Patron Saint of Paraguay)

February (date varies) – Carnaval, a popular Latin American festival, is liveliest in Asunción, Encarnación, Ciudad del Este, Caacupé and Villarrica.

March 1 – Cerro Corá (Death of Mariscal Francisco Solano López) commemorates the War of the Triple Alliance in the 1860s.

March/April (dates vary) – Viernes Santo/Pascua (Good Friday/Easter)

May 1 – Día de los Trabajadores (Labor Day)

May 15 – Independencia Patria (Independence Day)

June 12 – Paz del Chaco (End of Chaco War)

August 15 – Fundación de Asunción (Founding of Asunción)

September 29 – Victoria de Boquerón (Battle of Boquerón) commemorates the Chaco War of the 1930s.

December 8 – Día de la Virgen (Immaculate Conception) is recognized at the important religious center of Caacupé.

December 25 – Navidad (Christmas Day)

ACCOMMODATIONS

Paraguay's variety of accommodations is the same as Argentina's (see the Argentina Facts for the Visitor chapter). Camping facilities are rarer in Paraguay, but in most remote areas you can camp just about anywhere. In the Chaco, accommodations are sparse outside the few towns, but estancias or *campesinos* (countryfolk) may offer a bed with a mosquito net.

As in Uruguay, many places are struggling to survive in the harsh economic climate, and have lowered prices. Quite a few establishments, even some top-end places, will give discounts on their rates, especially if you're paying in cash and don't require a receipt. If you're staying more than one night, or business looks slow, or you and the owner speak German, try asking for a *promoción* (deal). Note, however, that rates in Mennonite-run hotels tend to be less negotiable. Always ask if tax (IVA) is included in the rate you are quoted.

Taxi-drivers and touts in Paraguay will sometimes try to lead travelers to hotels and then extract commissions from the hotel, or even the traveler. It's best to arrive at the front desk unaccompanied.

FOOD

The Paraguayan diet resembles that of Argentina and Uruguay in many aspects, but differs greatly in others. Meat consumption is much lower than in either of the other Río de la Plata republics, although *parrillada* (grilled meat) is still a restaurant standard. Tropical and subtropical foodstuffs, originating in the country's Guaraní heritage, play a greater role in the Paraguayan diet. Grains, particularly maize, and tubers such as *mandioca* (manioc or cassava) are part of almost every meal.

Chipas, made with manioc flour or cornmeal, plus eggs and cheese, are sold almost everywhere, as are Paraguay's cheap and filling version of *empanadas,* (with the usual fillings). Variants include *chipa guazú,* a sort of cheese cornmeal soufflé, and *chipa de almidón,* similar to guazú, but in which manioc flour dominates instead of cornmeal.

Sopa paraguaya is a cornbread with cheese and onion. *Mbaipy so-ó* is a hot maize pudding with chunks of meat, while *bori-bori* is a chicken soup with cornmeal balls. *Locro* is a maize stew resembling its

PARAGUAY

Argentine namesake, while *mazamorra* is a corn mush. *Sooyo sopy* is a thick soup of ground meat, accompanied by rice or noodles. *Mbaipy heé* is a dessert of corn, milk and molasses.

Mbeyú, also known as *torta de almidón,* is a plain grilled manioc pancake that resembles the Mexican tortilla. During Holy Week, the addition of eggs, cheese and spices transforms ordinary food into a holiday treat.

Paraguay is one of the best places in South America to sample a variety of Asian food, prepared by Chinese, Korean and Japanese immigrants who have arrived over the past several years.

DRINKS

Like Argentines and Uruguayans, Paraguayans consume enormous amounts of *mate,* but more commonly in the form of *tereré,* served refreshingly ice cold in the withering summer heat and often augmented with *yuyos* (medicinal herbs).

Throughout southern Paraguay, roadside stands offer *mosto* – sugarcane juice. Local beers include *Baviera,* an attempt at pilsner that gives some people an immediate headache, and *Pilsen Dorada* and *Pilsen Blanca,* decent lagers often served nearly frozen. *Ouro Fino* and other Brazilian brands, when available, are better and often cheaper. Fiery *caña* (cane alcohol), is the most common liquor.

ENTERTAINMENT

Cinema and live theater are popular in Asunción, and many bars feature live music ranging from flamenco to jazz. In even the most isolated towns there is usually a disco or two that blasts out the popular tropical beat known as *cachaca* and inexplicably features a procession of catwalk models at some stage during the night.

SPECTATOR SPORTS

Paraguayans in general are very sports-minded and, like the rest of South America, are soccer-mad. The most popular teams, Olimpia and Cerro Porteño, have beaten the best Argentine sides. Tennis, basketball and

volleyball are also popular spectator sports, while the elite indulge in golf and squash.

SHOPPING

Paraguay's most well-known handicraft is ñandutí lace, ranging in size from doilies to bedspreads. The women of Itauguá, a village east of Asunción, are the best-known weavers. In the town of Luque, artisans produce stunningly beautiful handmade musical instruments, particularly guitars and harps, for surprisingly reasonable prices.

Paraguayan leather goods are excellent, and bargains are more readily available than in either Argentina or Uruguay. Chaco Indians produce replicas of spears and other weapons, carvings of animals from the aromatic wood of the palo santo, and traditional string bags *(yiscas).*

Getting There & Away

Asunción is convenient for Southern Cone air transport and has good overland connections to and from Brazil and Argentina. Access to Bolivia via the Chaco is tenuous, but feasible, at most times of the year.

AIR

Few if any flights from North America and Europe go directly to Asunción; it is most common to connect via Buenos Aires or São Paulo. Paraguay collects a departure tax of US$18 for international flights, but travelers spending less than 24 hours in the country are exempt. The main airport is Asunción's Aeropuerto Internacional Silvio Pettirossi.

The USA

American Airlines has daily flights between Asunción and Miami, New York and Dallas, all via São Paulo. Paraguay's Transportes Aéreos del Mercosur (TAM) flies twice daily from Miami, also via São Paulo. Lloyd Aéreo Boliviano (LAB) has Tuesday and Friday flights to Miami via Santa Cruz, Bolivia, but the Friday layover is 10½ hours (hotel and meals are included in the ticket price).

Continental Europe

TAM flies twice daily from Paris via São Paulo. Iberia flies daily from Madrid via Buenos Aires (TAM connects Ezeiza and Asunción).

South America

TAM flies from Asunción twice daily to Buenos Aires; daily to Santiago, Chile, and a number of Brazilian destinations via São Paulo; and to Santa Cruz and Cochabamba (Bolivia). TAM also flies three times a week to Montevideo and Punta del Este (Uruguay).

At the time of research, Aerolíneas Argentinas had suspended its three weekly services to Buenos Aires' Ezeiza. Lloyd Aéreo Boliviano flies Tuesday and Friday to Santa Cruz, with onward connections to La Paz. Varig flies daily to São Paulo and Rio de Janeiro. LanChile flies four times weekly to Santiago and three times to Iquique.

See the Asunción Getting There & Away section for a listing of airline offices.

LAND & RIVER

Paraguay's relatively few overland crossings underscore the country's geographical isolation. There are only three legal border crossings from Argentina, two from Brazil, and one from Bolivia.

Border Crossings

Argentina There are two direct border crossings between Paraguay and Argentina, plus one that requires a brief detour through Brazil (all involve river bridges). Frequent bus service links each of the three pairs of cities. Efforts to open a regular crossing from Ayolas to Ituzaingó via the Yacyretá hydroelectric project on the Río Paraná have been stymied by red tape and fears of sabotage.

Clorinda to Puerto Falcón

Clorinda is in the Argentine province of Formosa; this crossing is renowned for ferocious customs checks. Local Sunday bus service connecting Clorinda, Falcón and Asunción is very limited, so either avoid crossing Sunday or take a bus that goes all the way through.

Posadas to Encarnación

Posadas is in the Argentine province of Misiones. The short trip can take over an hour if the bridge is busy. Launches across the river are quicker but are basically for locals only, as there are no immigration facilities for foreigners at the docks.

Puerto Iguazú to Ciudad del Este

Puerto Iguazú is in the Argentine province of Misiones, Ciudad del Este appears on older maps as Puerto Presidente Stroessner. This route is via the Brazilian city of Foz do Iguaçu but requires no Brazilian paperwork if you're only passing through.

Bolivia Regularly scheduled buses run from Asunción north up the Ruta Trans-Chaco, turning west on Picada 500, a dirt road that leads to Fortín Infante Rivola on the Bolivian border, and continuing to the Bolivian towns of Boyuibe and Santa Cruz de la Sierra. The dirt road is subject to days-long delays in the event of heavy rains. In optimal conditions it takes 30 hours to Santa Cruz.

You must get a Paraguayan exit stamp either in Asunción before boarding the bus, or at Pozo Colorado, 274km northwest of the capital; without the stamp you will be turned back at the border. There is talk of moving the immigration facility farther north. Bus drivers on the route are notoriously indifferent to travelers' paperwork needs; try to determine beforehand from the immigration office in Asunción (☎ 02-446673) whether the checkpoint has moved.

Brazil There are a couple bus routes and a (long) river ride between Brazil and Paraguay.

Ciudad del Este to Foz do Iguaçu

This is the most frequently used overland border crossing between the two countries. Vehicles and pedestrian traffic move freely across the Puente de la Amistad (Friendship Bridge) that connects the two cities across the Paraná. If you plan to spend more than a day in Brazil, be sure to complete immigration procedures, and always do so when entering Paraguay.

Pedro Juan Caballero to Ponta Porã

Pedro Juan Caballero is a growing contraband center on the Paraguayan-Brazilian border, while Ponta Porã is its Brazilian counterpart. Each town has a consulate of the neighboring country. There are regular bus services from Asunción to Pedro Juan Caballero. From the Brazilian city of Campo Grande, there are several buses daily.

Río Paraguay

There are no regularly scheduled international boat services, but it's still occasionally possible to catch vessels heading upriver toward Brazil. See the boxed text 'Up the Lazy River,' later in this chapter, for further information.

ORGANIZED TOURS

Intertours (☎ 021-211747), Perú 436, Asunción, is Paraguay's largest and most experienced tour operator, offering brief or extended excursions to Asunción and its surroundings, the Jesuit mission area around Encarnación, and the Iguazú Falls of Brazil and Argentina.

Getting Around

Public transport in Paraguay is generally cheap and efficient, if not always as comfortable as in Argentina or Uruguay.

AIR

Arpa connects Asunción with Ciudad del Este, Concepción, Vallemí, Fuerte Olimpo and Puerto Casado. A one-way ticket from Asunción to Ciudad del Este costs around US$68. For further details, see the appropriate geographical entries. Note that the Mercosur Pass is good only for flying into Asunción; no domestic flights can be made with it.

BUS

The quality of bus services varies considerably, depending on whether you take *servicio removido*, which makes flag stops, or *servicio directo*, which stops only at fixed locations in each city or town. Other common terms are *regular* (buses that stop at every shady spot along the highway), *común* (a basic bus that stops in only a limited number of places), and *ejecutivo* (a faster, deluxe bus with toilets, tea and coffee service and other facilities). Some directo bus drivers give común service, and trip durations cited by bus companies are sometimes more optimistic than realistic.

Larger Paraguayan cities have central bus terminals, but in those cities that do not, bus companies are within easy walking distance of one another, usually around the plaza.

Buses run very frequently to destinations all around the country, and only on or near holidays should reservations be necessary. Fares are very reasonable – for example, Asunción to Filadelfia, a distance of about 450km, costs only about US$10.

TRAIN

Paraguay's antique, woodburning trains are used only for cargo these days. Plans to revive the Asunción to Areguá run, a pleasant day trip, are put forth from time to time. Try inquiring at the Estación Ferrocarril Central (☎ 021-447316) on Plaza Uruguaya in Asunción.

CAR

Unfortunately, Paraguayans appear to be taking driving lessons from their Argentine neighbors, with all the hazards that implies – like high-speed tailgating and passing on blind curves. Driving in Paraguay also presents some problems that are less common to Argentina and Uruguay, most notably the presence of high-wheeled wooden oxcarts and livestock on the road. For the most part, carts stick to tracks that parallel the highway, but on occasion they must cross. Everywhere in the country, but especially in the Chaco, watch for cattle and wildlife on the road. Such hazards make driving at night inadvisable.

Paraguay formally requires the International Driving Permit, as well as a state or national driver's license, but cars with foreign license plates are rarely stopped except at military checkpoints in the Chaco. Car theft is common, and many stolen vehicles are imported illegally from Argentina and Brazil, with authorities turning a blind eye. If your vehicle is conspicuous, be especially certain it is secure.

Operating a car in Paraguay is more economical than in either Argentina or Uruguay because of the lower price of super-grade gasoline, around US$0.65 per liter. The country also offers an abundance of cheap spares; if you need to purchase tires, Asunción is the place to do so. If you need repairs, competent Paraguayan mechanics are much cheaper than those in Argentina.

The Touring y Automóvil Club Paraguayo (☎ 021-215011), in Asunción on Brasil between Cerro Corá and 25 de Mayo, has a few offices throughout the country and honors foreign auto club cards.

Renting a car can be expensive if you drive over the allowed number of daily kilometers; some agencies charge US$0.29 to US$0.50 per kilometer. Daily rates are otherwise reasonable. It's best to shop around by phone to avoid lengthy negotiations in the agencies; one company offering straightforward service and very good long-term rates is Hertz/Diesa; see the Asunción Getting Around section for more details.

BOAT

Boats ply the Río Paraguay between Asunción and Bahía Negra, in the extreme north near the borders with Brazil and Bolivia. See the boxed text 'Up the Lazy River,' later in this chapter, for details.

LOCAL TRANSPORTATION

Asunción and other sizable towns have extensive public transport systems, but late-night buses are infrequent. Retain your ticket, since an inspector may check it. The usual fare is about US$0.30.

Cabs operate on the basis of direct meter readings. Fares are slightly cheaper than in Argentina and Uruguay. Drivers legally levy a 30% *recargo* (surcharge) after 10pm, on Sunday and on holidays, and will often add a small luggage surcharge as well.

Asunción

☎ 021 • pop 1.2 million

From its central location on the Río Paraguay, Asunción has always been landlocked Paraguay's link to the outside world and the pivot of its political, economic, and cultural life. About 20% of the country's population live in the capital and its suburbs, and most of the remainder live within 150km of here. Past minor construction booms have given the city a scattering of high-rise offices and some modern hotels, but it retains some lovely 19th-century buildings and shady plazas. While there is some industry on the outskirts of the city, mostly the processing of agricultural materials, Asunción's economy is largely commercial.

In spite of certain unpleasant aspects, Asunción offers some good museums, interesting architecture and a variety of world cuisines, and makes a good introduction to quirky Paraguay.

HISTORY

Founded in 1537 by Juan de Salazar, an officer from Pedro de Mendoza's failed colony at Buenos Aires, Asunción enjoyed abundant food supplies and a hospitable Guaraní population. By 1541, its European residents numbered about 600 and, until the refounding of Buenos Aires in 1580, it was the Río de la Plata region's most important settlement. The Spanish initially expected Asunción to be the gateway to Perú, but the hot, dry Chaco, with its hostile Indians, proved too great a barrier to travel and was superseded by the route from Buenos Aires to Córdoba, Tucumán, Salta and up the eastern side of the Andes.

By European standards, colonial Asunción was a stagnant backwater. Austrian Jesuit missionary Martin Dobrizhoffer, who visited in the mid-18th century, was unimpressed with the city and its society: After independence in 1811, the despotic José Rodríguez de Francia ordered dilapidated buildings replaced and streets straightened to square up the city plan. Unfortunately Francia's sweeping plans were rather arbitrary and many sound and handsome buildings from the colonial period were destroyed in carrying them out.

With Francia's death in 1840, Asunción's isolation ended, as Carlos Antonio López opened the country to foreign influence. López and his son, Francisco Solano López, built many major public edifices that still stand in Asunción – destroying in the process most of the colonial structures that had escaped Rodríguez de Francia. But Francisco Solano López effectively ended this brief era of material progress by foolishly plunging Paraguay into the War of the Triple Alliance.

PARAGUAY

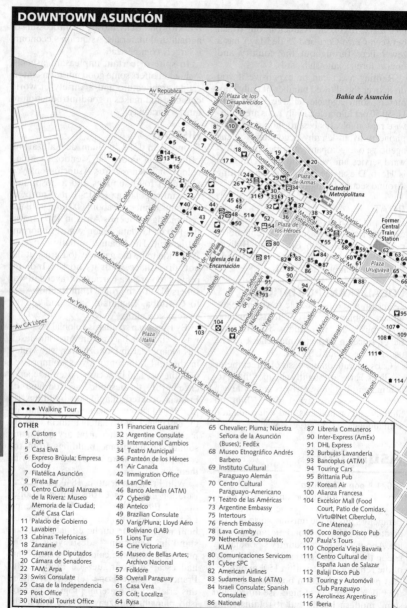

DOWNTOWN ASUNCIÓN

Av República

Plaza de los Desaparecidos

Bahía de Asunción

Av República

Presidente Franco

Palma

Plaza de Armas

Estrella

Catedral Metropolitana

General Díaz

Oliva

Former Central Train Station

Plaza de los Héroes

Iglesia de la Encarnación

Plaza Uruguaya

Manduvira

Jejuí

Av Ygatymi

Av CA López

Plaza Italia

Manuel Domínguez

Teniente Farina

Av Doctor R de Francia

República de Colombia

Bolívar

••• Walking Tour

OTHER
1 Customs
3 Port
5 Casa Elva
6 Expreso Brújula; Empresa Godoy
7 Filatélica Asunción
9 Pirata Bar
10 Centro Cultural Manzana de la Rivera: Museo Memoria de la Ciudad; Café Casa Clari
11 Palacio de Gobierno
12 Lavabien
13 Cabinas Telefónicas
18 Zanzanie
19 Cámara de Diputados
20 Cámara de Senadores
22 TAM; Arpa
23 Swiss Consulate
25 Casa de la Independencia
29 Post Office
30 National Tourist Office

31 Financiera Guaraní
32 Argentine Consulate
33 Internacional Cambios
34 Teatro Municipal
36 Panteón de los Héroes
41 Air Canada
42 Immigration Office
44 LanChile
46 Banco Alemán (ATM)
47 Cyberi@
48 Antelco
49 Brazilian Consulate
50 Varig/Pluna; Lloyd Aéro Boliviano (LAB)
51 Lions Tur
54 Cine Victoria
56 Museo de Bellas Artes; Archivo Nacional
57 Folklore
61 Casa Vera
63 Coit; Localiza
64 Rysa

65 Chevalier; Pluma; Nuestra Señora de la Asunción (Buses); FedEx
68 Museo Etnográfico Andrés Barbero
69 Instituto Cultural Paraguayo Alemán
70 Centro Cultural Paraguayo-Americano
71 Teatro de las Américas
73 Argentine Embassy
75 Intertours
76 French Embassy
78 Lava Gramby
79 Netherlands Consulate; KLM
80 Comunicaciones Servicom
81 Cyber SPC
82 American Airlines
83 Sudameris Bank (ATM)
86 Israeli Consulate; Spanish Consulate
86 National

87 Librería Comuneros
90 Inter-Express (AmEx)
91 DHL Express
92 Burbujas Lavandería
93 Bancoplus (ATM)
94 Touring Cars
95 Brittania Pub
97 Korean Air
100 Alianza Francesa
104 Excelsior Mall (Food Court, Patio de Comidas, Virtu@lNet Ciberclub, Cine Atenea)
105 Coco Bongo Disco Pub
107 Paula's Tours
110 Chopperia Vieja Bavaria
111 Centro Cultural de España Juan de Salazar
112 Balaji Disco Pub
113 Touring y Automóvil Club Paraguayo
115 Aerolíneas Argentinas
116 Iberia

PARAGUAY

DOWNTOWN ASUNCIÓN

PLACES TO STAY		PLACES TO EAT		
2	Residencial	37 Rivera Apart Hotel	8 Anahí; Michael Bock	60 El Café Literario
	Ambassador	45 Granados Park Hotel	26 Rodizio Churrasquería	66 Bar San Roque
4	Hotel Continental	59 Chaco Hotel	27 Pacholo	67 La Flor de la Canela
14	Hotel Asunción	62 Plaza Hotel	35 Lido Bar	72 Confitería El Molino
	Palace	77 Hotel España	38 Heladería Amandau	74 Formosa
15	Hotel Zaphir	85 Hotel Hispania	39 Munich	89 Restaurant Oliver's
16	Hotel Sahara	88 Hotel Miami	40 Taberna El Antojo	96 Talleyrand
17	Hotel Sagaró	99 Hotel Cecilia	43 Fa Hua Hsuan	98 La Preferida
21	Hotel Internacional	103 Manduvirá Plaza Hotel	52 Confitería Bolsi	101 Il Capo
24	Ñandutí Hotel	106 Hotel Amalfi	53 San Marcos	102 La Pérgola Jardín
28	Hotel Embajador	108 Hotel Azara	55 Tío Lucas	109 Restaurant Latino
		114 Residencial Itapúa		117 Han II

To Jardín Botánico
Gardens & Camping
Municipal

Parque
Caballero

Fortín
Toledo

Manuel Gondra

Av Artigas

Av España

Teniente Ruiz

Juan de Salazar

Manuel Perez

Fortín Toledo

Boquerón

Morales

Washington

Padre Cardozo

68

70

72

71

69

José Berges

Av Perú

73

76

74

75

Rosa Peña

San José

De la Residenta

Pucheu

Río Paraguay

Juan de
Mena

Av Mariscal López

Eligio Ayala

96

97

100

99

98

Av Estados Unidos

Mariscal Estigarribia

25 de Mayo

110

112

113

Boquerón

101

102

Escobar

Ríos

Rep Francesa

Río de Janeiro

José Berges

General Santos

To Hospital
Privado Francés,
Museo del Barro
& Airport

Azara

Brasil

Constitución

Cerro Corá

Luis Irrazábal

República Francesa

Fleitas

115

116

Decoud

Melgarejo

Curupayty

Gral Peña

Luis A Herrera

Av Perú

Río de Janeiro

Asunción

Plaza

Buguey

Bullo

22 de Setiembre

Av Pettirossi

Hermínio Giménez

Speratti

Mercado Cuatro

Teodoro S.
Mongelos

Ecuador

117

José Asunción Flores

9 de Marzo

Eusebio Ayala

To Bus Terminal

0   150   300 m
0   150   300 yards

PARAGUAY

As European immigrants trickled in, the city gradually improved its appearance and eventually developed exclusive residential suburbs to the east. Yet, well into the 20th century, many of central Asunción's streets were unpaved.

The city has sprawled to encompass ever more distant areas, such as the university center of San Lorenzo. At the same time, the influx of people from the impoverished countryside has resulted in enormous shantytowns along the riverfront, the railway, or anywhere else there happens to be a vacant lot.

ORIENTATION

Asunción sits on a bluff above the east bank of the Río Paraguay. Like most colonial cities, it features a conventional grid pattern, refashioned by the irregularities of a riverside location, a slightly hilly topography, and some modern developments. Like Buenos Aires and Montevideo, the city consists of numerous barrios, but most key sights, as well as inexpensive hotels and restaurants, lie within about eight blocks of Plaza de los Héroes, the city center. Bordering the plaza to the east is Independencia Nacional, either side of which east-west streets change names.

It's worth noting that the Plaza de Armas and Plaza de los Héroes are divided into subplazas and the former is sometimes referred to as Plaza Constitución. Blocks tend to be very short running east-west. Commercial and financial institutions are concentrated along Palma and its eastward extension, Mariscal Estigarribia, which leads to Plaza Uruguaya, the shadiest and most agreeable in the center.

Asunción's most prestigious residential areas are east of downtown, out Avs España and Mariscal López toward Aeropuerto Silvio Pettirossi. Most of the capital's embassies, discos and chic restaurants are here, in barrios such as Recoleta and Villa Morra. Northeast of downtown, at the end of Av Artigas, the Jardín Botánico (Botanical Gardens) was once the López family estate and is now the city's largest open space, a popular site for weekend outings.

INFORMATION
Tourist Offices

The sometimes friendly national tourist office (☎ 441530, 441620, ⒠ senatur1@pla.net.py, ⓦ www.senatur.gov.py), at Palma 468 between Alberdi and 14 de Mayo, distributes an excellent city map, a decent map of Paraguay and several regional brochures. It also has loose-leaf notebooks full of tourist information. It's open 7am to 7pm weekdays and 8am to 1pm Saturday.

The Touring y Automóvil Club Paraguayo (☎ 215011) is located on Brasil, between Cerro Corá and 25 de Mayo. It sells the *Guía Shell* and its accompanying maps at a discount to members of its organization and those of affiliated overseas clubs. The staff is happy to provide other member services as well.

For more detailed maps, visit the Dirección del Servicio Geográfico Militar (☎ 206344), Av Artigas 920 near Perú.

Tiempo Libre, a weekly calendar of entertainment and cultural events, is widely distributed throughout the city.

Immigration

The Immigration Office (☎ 446673) is at the corner of Juan O'Leary and General Díaz, on the 1st floor, open 7am to 1pm weekdays.

Money

Financiera Guaraní (which charges about US$0.80 per traveler's check changed) is at Palma 449. Several other exchange houses on Palma and nearby side streets include Internacional Cambios (which charges about US$2.50 for cashing traveler's checks), at Palma 364, and Banco Alemán at Estrella and 14 de Mayo. There are also moneychangers with name tags near ticket offices on the 2nd floor of the bus terminal. It doesn't hurt to shop around.

Post & Communications

The main post office, on Alberdi just off Paraguayo Independiente, is open 7:30am to 7pm weekdays, 7am to noon Saturday. It also has a patio garden, a museum (worthwhile if you're already in the building or nearby), and good rooftop views of downtown Asunción.

Antelco, at 14 de Mayo and Oliva, has card phones outside useful for making collect or credit-card calls that require dialing toll-free numbers. There is another office at the bus terminal. Numerous locutorios around the city include the centrally located Comunicaciones Servicom, at Oliva 243.

Of the many Internet places, some that stand out for their combination of equipment, price and connection quality are Cyberi@, on Oliva between 15 de Agosto and 14 de Mayo, Cyber SPC, at Chile 677, and Cabinas Telefónicas, at Colón 445. All charge a little over US$1 an hour.

For private international mail service, try DHL Express, at Haedo 105. Fedex has a branch at Mariscal Estigarribia and Antequera.

Cultural Centers

Asunción's several international cultural centers offer artistic and photographic exhibitions, as well as films, at little or no cost. These include the Centro Cultural de España Juan de Salazar (☎ 449221), at Herrera 834; the Alianza Francesa (☎ 210382), at Estigarribia 1039; and the Instituto Cultural Paraguayo Alemán (☎ 226242), at Juan de Salazar 310 just off Av Artigas. The Centro Cultural Paraguayo-Americano (☎ 224831), Av España 352, has American books, magazines, videos and a small café.

Travel Agencies

Asunción has a multitude of downtown travel agencies, including Inter-Express (☎ 490111), the AmEx representative, at Yegros 690. Paula's Tours (☎ 446021), Cerro Corá 886, is a full-service agency that can arrange transportation and tours (including guided bird-watching tours) to the Chaco and other areas.

Bookstores

Librería Comuneros, Cerro Corá 289, offers a good selection of historical and contemporary books on Paraguay. A selection of English books and magazines can be found at Books SRL at Mariscal López 3971. Plaza Uruguaya holds two book 'greenhouses' and a semi-open-air bookstall.

Laundry

Lavabien is a drop-off and self-service laundry downtown at Hernandarias 636. Try also friendly Lava Gramby, on Humaitá just west of 15 de Agosto, or Burbujas Lavandería, Independencia Nacional 738.

Medical Services

Private clinics, such as the Hospital Privado Francés (☎ 295250), on Av Brasilia 1194, offer better services than public facilities.

Dangers & Annoyances

Asunción's kamikaze bus drivers are even more frightening than their Buenos Aires counterparts, barreling down narrow streets in poorly maintained machines. The soot spewed out by the buses is awful, settling on everything and everyone. When inversion layers suspend this soot and the city's various other outpourings in a hanging veil of pollution, the air is as bad as it gets anywhere.

In the evening much of the downtown area becomes a red-light district.

WALKING TOUR

Asunción's compact downtown has a handful of colonial buildings and a number of respectable museums.

Begun in 1860 but not completed until 1892, the **Palacio de Gobierno** (presidential palace), on El Paraguay Independiente between Ayolas and O'Leary, was intended as a residence for Francisco Solano López, who died in the War of the Triple Alliance without ever occupying it (compare its size to that of other government buildings). A flag ceremony takes place daily at sunset.

Across the street and entered from Ayolas is the **Centro Cultural Manzana de la Rivera** (☎ 442448, Ayolas & El Paraguay Independiente; free; open 8am-10:30pm), a complex of eight beautifully restored houses dating from 1750 to the early 20th century. The oldest is Casa Viola, which houses the **Museo Memoria de la Ciudad**, a good historical museum chronicling Asunción's urban development with engravings and photos of the old city. Other houses have very well-displayed art exhibitions, and there are two small theaters as well as the Café Casa Clari (see Bars & Clubs later in this chapter), whose terrace provides excellent views across to the Palacio de Gobierno.

Two blocks east, at 14 de Mayo, the **Cámara de Diputados** is a remnant of late Jesuit times, where Paraguay's congress meets. Northeast across the Plaza de Armas and above the river is the **Cámara de Senadores**, once Carlos Antonio López's residence and now housing the Senate. It was begun in 1844 and completed in 1857.

At the east end of the plaza is the neoclassical **Catedral Metropolitana** (1845), which has the **Museo del Tesoro de la Catedral** (no ☎, free; open 8am-11am Mon-Sat). On Alberdi between El Paraguayo Independiente and Benjamín Constant, the early-20th-century **Edificio de Correos** is the central post office and also the site of the **Museo Postal Telegráfico**. At Alberdi and Presidente Franco is the **Teatro Municipal** (1893, undergoing renovation at the time of research). One block west, at Presidente Franco and 14 de Mayo, Paraguayans declared independence in 1811 at the **Casa de la Independencia** (1772). This house holds a good museum (☎ 493918; free; open 7:30am-6:30pm Mon-Fri, 8am-12:30pm Sat) filled with period pieces of furniture, paintings and Jesuit mission relics. The volunteer guides here are happy to discuss their country's history.

On the Plaza de los Héroes, at Chile and Palma, a somber honor guard at the **Panteón de los Héroes** protects the remains of Carlos Antonio López, his son Francisco Solano López, Bernardino Caballero, José Félix Estigarribia, and other key figures (it's difficult to call most of them heroes) of Paraguay's catastrophic wars. Work commenced on the Panteón, originally intended as a religious shrine, during the rule of Francisco Solano López in 1863, but it was not finished until after the end of the Chaco War in 1936.

The very modest **Museo de Bellas Artes** (☎ 447716, Iturbe & Mariscal Estigarribia; free; open 7am-7pm Tues-Fri, 7am-noon Sat) features a badly lit Courbet; the modern exhibitions are better displayed. Next door, the borgesian **Archivo Nacional** has some nice dark woodwork and an interesting spiral staircase.

On the north side of Plaza Uruguaya, the British-built former **Estación Ferrocarril Central** dates from 1856 and now serves mostly as a parking garage. One antique steam locomotive can be seen within; go to the northeast side and ask the attendant if you can take a closer look.

MUSEO ETNOGRÁFICO ANDRÉS BARBERO

Founded by and named for the former president of the Sociedad Científica del Paraguay, this anthropological and archaeological museum (☎ 441696, Av España 217; free; undergoing renovation at the time of research), one of Asunción's best, displays Paraguayan Indian tools, ceramics, weavings, and a superb collection of photographs, with good maps to indicate where everything comes from.

MERCADO CUATRO

This is a lively market area occupying the wedge formed by the intersection of Avs Dr Francia and Pettirossi and stretching several blocks west toward Brasil. It deserves a visit, but don't make the mistake of trying to drive through it or, even worse, attempting to park.

JARDÍN BOTÁNICO

Once the López family estate, Asunción's botanical gardens (no ☎, entrance at Av Artigas & Av Primer Presidente; admission US$0.50 covers all attractions; open 7am-nightfall daily) are no longer really what the name implies, but they are the city's largest open space and a popular area for weekend outings. The park contains a zoo (home to exotic rather than Paraguayan species), the municipal campground and the **Museo de Historia Natural** (☎ 291255; open 8am-4pm Mon-Fri, 8am-1pm Sat & Sun). This vintage building houses an impressive collection of specimens. Though the exhibits are poorly labeled and displayed, with no attempt to place them in any ecological context, it's worth seeing for the spectacular display of insects – one butterfly has a wingspan of 274mm.

Uruguayan independence hero José Artigas spent his later years in exile in the house near the gardens' entrance.

From downtown, good buses to the Jardín are the No 44B ('Artigas') from Oliva and 15 de Agosto, the No 23 or No 35.

MUSEO DEL BARRO

Asunción's foremost art museum (☎ 607996, *Grabadores del Cabichui s/n; admission US$0.50; open 3:30pm-8pm Wed-Sun*), in the newly developed area of Isla de Francia, is a don't-miss spot displaying a bit of everything, including modern paintings, indigenous art and masks, pre-Columbian sculpture and ceramics from several countries, and political caricatures of prominent Paraguayans. You can buy handicrafts here as well.

To get there, take any No 30 bus out Av Aviadores del Chaco and ask the driver to drop you at Av Molas López; the museum is to the south off of Callejón Cañada in a contemporary building.

MUSEO BOGGIANI

From 1887 to the turn of the century, Italian ethnographer Guido Boggiani conducted fieldwork among the Chamacoco Indians of the upper Río Paraguay. After he declined to marry a Chamacoco woman, the group, fearing that he would live with another faction of their tribe or with their traditional enemies (the Caduveo), killed him.

Part of Boggiani's impressive collection of feather art remains on exhibit in this well-organized museum (☎ 584717, *Coronel Bogado 888; free; open 3pm-6pm Tues-Fri, 9am-noon & 3pm-6pm Sat*) in the suburb of San Lorenzo, which also has a noteworthy Gothic-style cathedral. The museum is well worth the 45-minute bus ride from downtown out Av Mariscal López on Línea 27. Handicrafts are sold here as well.

'Eye-zhess' Mania

Only a short distance from Asunción, across the Puente Remanso over the Río Paraguay, lies Villa Hayes. It is an undistinguished city that takes its name from one of the most obscure and undistinguished of US presidents, who, oddly, is a hero in the hearts and minds of Paraguayans. Many consider him an honorary Paraguayan.

Rutherford Birchard Hayes (pronounced 'eye-zhess' in Paraguay's River Plate accent) occupied the White House from 1877 to 1881, leaving office without seeking a second term. Even in his hometown of Delaware, Ohio, the only monument to his memory is a modest plaque on the site of his birthplace – now a gasoline station. In Paraguay, by contrast, he is commemorated by the Club Presidente Hayes, which sponsors the local soccer team, an Escuela Rutherford B Hayes, and a separate monument outside the school. In 1928 and 1978, the town held major festivities to honor Hayes.

Why this homage to a man almost forgotten in his own country, who never even set foot in Paraguay, 7400km to the south? At the end of the War of the Triple Alliance, Argentina claimed the entire Chaco, but after delicate negotiations, both countries agreed to submit claims over a smaller area, between the Río Verde and the Río Pilcomayo, to arbitration. In 1878, Argentine and Paraguayan diplomats traveled to Washington to present their cases to Hayes, who decided in Paraguay's favor; in gratitude, the Congreso in Asunción immortalized the American president by renaming the territory's largest town, Villa Occidental, in his honor.

To attend the Hayes sesquicentennial in 2028, take bus No 46 from Estados Unidos or Av España in downtown Asunción. It leaves every half-hour between 5:30am and noon, and every 45 minutes from noon to 9pm.

PARAGUAY

ART GALLERIES

In addition to the cultural centers and museums listed above, Asunción's arts community displays its work in several private galleries, among them **Artesanos** (☎ 227853, *Cerro Corá 2192*); and **Pequeña Galería** (☎ 603177, *Local 39-40, Shopping Center de Villa Morra, Mariscal López & De Gaulle*). See the weekly handout *Tiempo Libre* for current gallery offerings and the latest openings.

ORGANIZED TOURS

For city tours, day or night, as well as excursions to outlying areas such as San Bernardino, the Iguazú Falls (Cataratas del Iguazú) and the Jesuit missions, contact Lions Tur (☎ 490591), Alberdi 456. Some travelers consider its seven-hour *circuito central* tour overpriced (starting at US$40 per person on a double basis).

Intertours (☎ 021-211747), Perú 436, offers brief or extended excursions to Asunción and its surroundings, the Jesuit mission area around Encarnación and Iguazú Falls.

PLACES TO STAY

Asunción has an abundance of budget lodging, much of it owned by Korean immigrants. Most of these hotels are clean and plain, but several have air-conditioning, a welcome feature in steamy Asunción. Mid-range hotels are often very good values, and the best top-end places are superior to those in Montevideo but not quite equal to those in Buenos Aires.

Budget

Camping Municipal (no ☎, entrance at Avs Artigas & Primer Presidente) US$1 per person plus US$1.50 per vehicle or tent, plus US$0.50 per person admission to gardens. Asunción's campground is in the shady Jardín Botánico, about 7km from downtown. It is generally quiet and secure, and the staff is friendly, but the animals in the nearby zoo may keep you awake. There are lukewarm showers and adequate toilet facilities, but take care not to pitch your tent over an ant colony – their bites are painful. Bring mosquito repellent. From downtown,

the most direct bus is the No 44B ('Artigas') from the corner of Oliva and 15 de Agosto. You can also take No 23 or No 35.

Residencial Ambassador (☎ 445901, Montevideo & El Paraguay Independiente) US$4.50/5 per person with shared/private bath. This place, just a stone's throw from the Palacio de Gobierno, is probably the cheapest passable lodging. It's plain and a bit musty, and not in the best neighborhood, but it's friendly and quiet, and has ceiling fans in most rooms.

Hotel Familiar Yasy (☎ 551623, fax 557095, Fernando de la Mora 2390) Singles US$5.50-18, doubles US$8-18, triples US$16-24. If catching an early bus, you may prefer a place across from the terminal; try this friendly and quiet option with a wide variety of rooms.

Hotel Azara (☎ 449754, Azara 850) Singles/doubles US$6.50/12 with private bath, air-con. Rooms have fridges; some look over an overgrown patio and pool. It is not so clean or friendly, but it is very quiet.

Hotel Hispania (☎ 444018, Cerro Corá 265) Singles/doubles US$6.50/12 with shared bath, US$8/13 with private bath; air-con US$2.50 extra. This has been a popular budget alternative for years, with clean but rather gloomy downstairs rooms. Laundry service and short-order food items are available.

Residencial Itapúa (☎ 445121, Moreno 943) Singles/doubles US$6.50/13 with shared bath, US$8/18 with private bath; all with breakfast. On a quiet but still central block, this residencial occupies an unlikely neocolonial brick building with spacious, comfortable common spaces.

Hotel 2000 (mobile ☎ 0981-124702, Fernando de la Mora 2332) Singles/doubles US$8/13 with breakfast and aging air-con. Also across from the bus terminal, the 2000 has decent, simple rooms and a patio in back.

Hotel Sahara (☎ 494935, fax 493247, Oliva 920) US$10 per person with fan; singles/doubles/triples US$15/25/35 with air-con; all include breakfast. The latest Peace Corps hangout at the time of research, the Sahara is bursting with an eclectic accumulation of objects and animals. A hostel section is in the works, offstreet parking is available and there is a large courtyard with a garden and swimming pool at this recommended hotel.

Hotel Miami (☎ 444950, *México 449*) Singles/doubles/triples US$13/18/24 with private bath, breakfast & air-con. Ask for a room away from the busy front door so this friendly, recommended hotel, and admire the unique John Wayne tapestry.

Hotel Embajador (☎/fax 493393, *Presidente Franco 514*) Singles/doubles/triples US$14/22/30 with fan, US$17/28/36 with air-con. This hotel is clean and spacious, with high ceilings; the rooms without TV are cheaper, but still a bit expensive for what you get. Internet access is available.

Ñandutí Hotel (☎ 440483, *Presidente Franco 551*) Singles/doubles US$14/24 with private bath and breakfast. This congenial hotel is a good value.

Mid-Range
All hotels in this category have air-con, *frígobar* (minibar) and cable TV.

Hotel Sagaró (☎ 440377, fax 442912, e *hsagaro@telesur.com.py*, *Presidente Franco 657*) Singles/doubles/triples US$25/30/40 with breakfast. This newish, central hotel with a rooftop pool and bar has good rooms (but bad shower placement).

Hotel Amalfi (☎ 494154, fax 441162, e *amalfi@mmail.com.py*, *Caballero 877*) Singles/doubles/triples US$27/34/42 with breakfast. Large, comfortable and quiet rooms with good air-con and baths make this one of the best values in the category.

Rivera Apart Hotel (☎/fax 497311, *Presidente Franco 261*) Singles/doubles/triples US$30/35/40. These are very modern and spacious units with fridges, microwave kitchenettes, and great baths. There are no windows to speak of, but it's very quiet and central and a real steal at these prices.

Hotel Continental (☎ 493760, fax 496176, e *hconti@rieder.net.py*, *Av Colón 350*) Singles/doubles US$35/45 with breakfast and parking. The very well maintained and decorated Continental features a pool, restaurant and good-sized doubles with large TVs.

Hotel Asunción Palace (☎ 492151, fax 492153, *Av Colón 415*) Singles/doubles/triples US$38/52/66 with breakfast. Built in 1840, the Palace has been nicely remodeled. It has spacious rooms; some facing the (noisy) street have good-sized balconies. There's parking, and the hotel offers cash discounts.

Hotel Zaphir (☎ 490025, e *zaphir@pla.net.py*, *Estrella 955*) Singles/doubles US$45/56 with buffet breakfast. Comfortable rooms, some with balconies and views of the bay.

Manduvirá Plaza Hotel (☎ 447533, fax 491562, e *macisa@conexion.com.py*, w *www.manduvira.com.py*, *Manduvirá 345*) Singles/doubles US$45/55 with breakfast. Rooms in this high-rise have good baths. Many have balconies; try for an 11th-floor room for the best views.

Hotel España (☎ 443192, fax 445893, *Haedo 667*) Singles/doubles/triples US$55/65/75 with breakfast. The España has a Spanish restaurant, parking, a pool, and nice, big rooms. You may be able to get a 20% discount via a brochure at the front desk.

Top End
All hotels in this category have air-con; most have cable TV and frígobars as well.

Hotel Cecilia (☎ 210365, fax 497111, e *cecilhotel@uninet.com.py*, *Estados Unidos 341*) Singles/doubles US$66/88 (cash) with breakfast. Rooms are sizeable here, some on the upper floors have river views. There's a rooftop pool, a gym, laundry and airport services, and Restaurant La Preferida is attached (see Places to Eat).

Chaco Hotel (☎ 492066, fax 444223, e *chacotel@conexion.com.py*, *Caballero & Mariscal Estigarribia*) Singles/doubles US$83/95 with breakfast. It's no great shakes from the outside, but inside the Chaco is very comfortable. There's parking, and the 11th-floor pool offers great views of the city and river.

Hotel Internacional (☎ 494113, fax 494383, e *reservas@hotelinternacional.com.py*, w *www.hotelinternacional.com.py*, *Ayolas 520*) Singles/doubles US$90/120 with buffet breakfast. Ample rooms have free Internet jacks, and there's a pool, sauna, gym and restaurant here. Some floors are decorated to appeal to Japanese visitors.

Granados Park Hotel (☎ *497921, fax 445324,* e *reservas@granadospark.com.py,* w *www.granadaspark.com.py, Estrella & 15 de Agosto)* Singles/doubles US$154/170 with buffet breakfast. Very large rooms (junior suites), a gym and a rooftop pool with bay views are among the features making this five-star hotel stand out from the others.

PLACES TO EAT

From modest snack bars to formal international restaurants, Asunción has a surprising variety of quality food. Many downtown eateries are closed Sunday, particularly in the evening.

Budget

San Marcos (☎ *447302, Alberdi & Oliva)* US$1.25-2.50. This confitería/bar/café offers good food and coffee.

Tío Lucas (☎ *44714, 25 de Mayo & Yegros)* US$1.25-3.25. This is a no-nonsense eatery serving excellent Uruguayan-style chivitos, cheap *menúes,* (set-course meals) and pizza, sandwiches and pasta.

Confitería El Molino (☎ *210671, Av España 382)* US$1.25-3.75. El Molino serves *minutas* (short orders), salads, soups, sandwiches, pizza and excellent banana *licuados* (blended fruit drinks).

Confitería Bolsi (☎ *491841, Estrella 399)* US$1.50-2.25. It's a restaurant! It's a bar! It serves everything from sandwiches and short orders to escargots, curried rabbit and garlic pizza! Readers recommend the *surubí casa nostra,* the pasta and the soothing air-con.

Anahi (☎ *495846, Presidente Franco & Ayolas)* US$1-5. This is an outstanding *confitería,* with good food, coffee drinks and ice cream at moderate prices; it's open for breakfast and Sunday dinner as well.

Han Il (☎ *226796, Av Perú 1090)* US$2.75-5.50. Han Il is between Rodríguez de Francia and República de Colombia, on Peru's west side. The sign bears only Korean characters; look for the smoked glass door and windows. The menu's in Korean, but Paulina will help

you order *kim chi chiggae, bi bim bap* and *bulgogi* (delicious marinated meat grilled at your table; ask for garlic).

Lido Bar (☎ *447232, Chile & Palma)* US$3-6. Grab a stool and belly up to the granite counter to enjoy a variety of tasty, reasonably priced Paraguayan specialties. It's good for meals or snacks at any hour (including Sunday night), and has the best paper napkins in the country.

Rodizio Churrasquería (☎ *451281, Palma 591)* The tasty self-service food sold by the kilo here includes a bountiful salad bar and several hot vegetarian choices along with the array of meat. Lofty ceilings and granite tabletops make for an elegant dining experience.

Café Literario (☎ *491640, Mariscal Estigarribia 456)* This bookstore-café just west of Plaza Uruguaya is a good place to read or write while sipping a coffee or specialty tea.

Pacholo (☎ *600408, Palma 547; also at Brasilia 1493, Excelsior Mall, Mariscal López & Salaskin)* This is a food court with stands serving beer, hot dogs, burgers and delicious pizza (US$1.25 for a one-person pie; US$5 family size).

Excelsior Mall *(Chile near Manduvirá)* The upstairs food court at this mall offers fast-food versions of various ethnic cuisines: **Don Vito** (empanadas), **Sabor Brasil, Cervecería Austria, Taberna Española,** and **Apolo** (Chinese). Don Vito has another branch at José Berges 595.

Michael Bock *(820 Presidente Franco)* Next door to the Anahi restaurant, this is an excellent German bakery.

Heladería Amandau *(Eligio Ayala & Independencia Nacional)* Ice cream!

Mid-Range

La Preferida (☎ *210641, 25 de Mayo 1005)* US$3-8. This German restaurant is connected to the Hotel Cecilia and has good US$6.50 *menúes.* There's a bakery/cheese shop on the ground floor.

Bar San Roque (☎ *446015, Tacuary & Ayala)* US$3.25-6.75. Waiters in bow ties, a classic, air-conditioned old building, good food, great presentation, inexpensive specials: What are you waiting for? Try the *capelletti de pollo* or the pig's knuckles with sauerkraut and potatoes.

La Flor de la Canela (☎ *498928, Tacuary 167*) US$3-11. La Flor has excellent Peruvian food – try the *surubí al ajo* (garlic catfish). It also has Chinese food and is open for Sunday lunch.

Restaurant Latino (☎ *494616, Cerro Corá 948*) US$3.50-7. Equally good but more reasonably priced Peruvian fare is served here, including tasty *pisco* sours and plenty of seafood.

Restaurant Oliver's (☎ *494931, Azara & Independencia*) US$3.75-7.50. When times are good, a hot and cold buffet with dessert runs US$7.50. Otherwise a salad bar (with bean sprouts!) and a hot dish will set you back US$5.25, or order one of the menúes at this upscale place.

Fa Hua Hsuan (☎ *446270, Haedo 638*) US$4.50 per kilo. Pink-garbed, kindly staff assist you at this Taiwanese vegetarian buffet and takeout. Some dishes are mock-meat and the juices (including carrot) are made to order.

Formosa (☎ *211075, Av España 780*) US$4-9. This is another Chinese option, serving large dishes amid old-style, fairly nice Chinese decor.

Taberna El Antojo (☎ *441743, Ayolas 631*) Fixed-price meal US$8, mains US$4.50-8. This Spanish restaurant serves tapas, paellas, fish and other dishes. The interior is plastered with proverbs, shells, bottles, and hanging bells, making for great ambience. In winter there's sometimes live music and dance.

Munich (☎ *447604, Eligio Ayala 163*) US$4.50-9. The recommended Munich serves German dishes, of course, as well as pasta, fish, and *shaslik* (kabobs). Dine in the courtyard or air-con salon.

Top End

Il Capo (☎ *213022, Perú 291*) US$4.50-20. Il Capo has Italian food and a soothing ambience.

La Pérgola Jardín (☎ *210219, Perú 240*) US$6.50-12; open daily. Haute cuisine served here includes duck, oyster and scallop dishes. They also have excellent breakfasts and a big lunch buffet.

Talleyrand (☎ *441163, Estigarribia 932*) US$8.50-11. This highly regarded French-international restaurant's menu includes Greek salads, salmon and snow crab dishes.

ENTERTAINMENT

The weekly *Tiempo Libre*, a calendar of entertainment and cultural events, is widely distributed throughout the city.

Bars & Clubs

The downtown area has a variety of venues ranging from sedate to raucous.

Café Casa Clari (☎ *223266, Ayolas 129*) In Centro Cultural Manzana de la Rivera. The Clari serves reasonably priced (considering the location) drinks and snacks in a mellow, young atmosphere. The balcony has an unequalled view of the presidential palace across the street. It's usually open till midnight or 'whenever,' and serves lunch on weekdays.

Britannia Pub (☎ *443990, Cerro Corá 851*) This rowdy expat hangout serves Guinness in cans and is popular on Sunday nights when it has live music.

Choppería Vieja Bavaria (*mobile* ☎ *0981-506704, Estados Unidos 422*) This classic bar has draft beer and serves short orders. It's a hangout for German visitors, but everyone is welcome.

Balaji Disco Pub (*no* ☎*, Estados Unidos & Cerro Corá*) Near the Britannia, Balaji features karaoke, all-you-can-eat pizza (US$2.50) and a dance floor from 9pm on.

Coco Bongo Disco Pub (*no* ☎*, Independencia Nacional 958*) The name says it all. Well, OK, sometimes local radio personalities DJ here.

Zanzanie (☎ *449018, Presidente Franco & 15 de Agosto*) This African-themed pub/restaurant/disco in the heart of the downtown has live music and dancing Friday and Saturday nights.

Pirata Bar (*Benjamín Constant & Ayolas*) is a popular, pirate-themed club (look for the Jolly Roger flag).

The greatest concentration of clubs is on Av Brasilia north of España, several blocks north and east of downtown. They're bigger, louder, fancier and open later than downtown nightspots. Two of the most popular are *Mouse Cantina* (☎ 228794, *Patria & Brasilia*), a huge, MTV-esque place drawing a young, wealthy crowd (don't dress down), and *Tequila Rock (Brasilia 872)* also with a young crowd. Other popular clubs among the many others in the area are *Tequila Cancún (Brasilia 808)* and *Habitacion 330 (Brasilia 330)*, where the crowd dances to techno and alternative music. *Faces Pub (Brasilia 786)* has a slightly older and less affluent clientele.

Theater

Asunción has several venues for live theater and music; the season generally runs March to October. Possibilities include the *Centro Cultural Manzana de la Rivera* (☎ 442448, *Ayolas & El Paraguayo Independiente)*; the *Teatro Arlequín* (☎ 605107, *De Gaulle & Quesada)* in Villa Morra; and the *Teatro de las Américas* (☎ 224831, *José Berges 297)*, which often has plays in English.

SHOPPING

Most shops are open 8am to noon and 3pm to 7pm weekdays, mornings only on Saturday. Some keep slightly longer hours.

Casa Elva (☎ 492364, *Estrella 990)* Leather, ñandutí lace, *ao po'i, mate* sets and lots of other *artesanías* are sold here.

Casa Vera (☎ 445868, *Estigarribia 470)* This is a *talabartería* (saddlery) and then some, selling cowboy gear from saddles, tack, boots and hats to *mate* sets and leather bags. There's enough here to costume a movie cast, and the prices are very reasonable.

Overall Paraguay (☎ 448657, *Caballero & Estigarribia)* There's a good selection of ñandutí and leather goods here.

Folklore (☎ 450148, *Estigarribia near Iturbe)* Open Sunday and holidays. A good place to buy CDs, cassettes, and souvenir handicrafts.

Filatélica Asunción (☎ 446218, *Presidente Franco 845)* Stamp collectors take note!

The open-air *market* in the southeast corner of Plaza de los Héroes is a good place for crafts, but remember that items made with feathers are probably subject to endangered-species regulations overseas.

Maká Indian women sitting on the sidewalk along the north side of the plaza sell brightly colored woven bags and other items.

GETTING THERE & AWAY
Air

Aeropuerto Internacional Silvio Pettirossi (☎ 672855) is in the suburb of Luque, east of Asunción, but is easily reached by buses out Av Aviadores del Chaco.

Airlines with representatives in Asunción, though some have their connections through neighboring countries, include the following:

Aerolíneas Argentinas (☎ 450577, 491012), Av Mariscal López 706

Air Canada (☎ 448917), Juan O'Leary 690

Alitalia (☎ 660435), General Genes 490

American Airlines (☎ 443330), Independencia Nacional 557

Arpa (☎ 495265), Oliva 761

Iberia (☎ 214246), Av Mariscal López 995

KLM (☎ 449393), Chile 668

Korean Air (☎ 495059), Estados Unidos 348

LanChile (☎ 490782), 15 de Agosto & General Díaz

Lloyd Aéreo Boliviano (LAB; ☎ 441586), 14 de Mayo 563

TAM (Transportes Aéreos del Mercosur; ☎ 491039), Oliva 761

Varig/Pluna (☎ 448777), General Díaz and 14 de Mayo

Arpa (Aerolíneas Paraguayas), in the same offices as TAM, flies 14-seat planes between Asunción and Ciudad del Este (US$68, 1¼ hours) three to five times a day (once Sunday). TAM has one bigger plane daily (US$100, 45 minutes). Arpa also serves Concepción, Vallemí, Fuerte Olimpo and Puerto Casado.

Bus

Asunción's bus station (☎ 551728, 551740) is at Av Fernando de la Mora and República Argentina in the Barrio Terminal; some companies continue to operate ticket offices near the port or on Plaza Uruguaya, enabling you to avoid an unnecessary trip to the terminal. Asunción has excellent and frequent international as well as national connections; fares vary depending on the quality of the service.

See the Paraguay Getting There & Away section, earlier, for a quick rundown of border crossings, and consult the table, later, for trip durations and costs. Telephone numbers beginning with 55 are at the terminal.

International Destinations Several companies serve Buenos Aires, including Expreso Brújula and Empresa Godoy, which share an office (☎ 491720) at Presidente Franco 985. They also have multiple daily services to Formosa and Resistencia, and run to Rosario and Santa Fe, and on Thursday and Sunday to Córdoba. NSA (Nuestra Señora de la Asunción; ☎ 492274, 551667) shares an office at Estigarribia and Antequera with Chevalier and Pluma (☎ 445024, 551758). Together they serve Corrientes, Buenos Aires and other Argentine points.

Stel Turismo (☎ 551647) and Yacyretá (☎ 551725) now operate three to four services weekly to the Bolivian destinations of Boyuibe and Santa Cruz, where there are connections to La Paz. Meals are included, but you should carry extra water and food on this hot, dusty trip. Santa Cruz is 30 hours away in ideal conditions, but if it rains the trip can take days.

You must get your Paraguayan exit stamp either in Asunción or Pozo Colorado, on the way north; see Bolivia Border Crossings in the Paraguay Getting There & Away section.

Pluma and NSA (among others) frequently connect Asunción with Foz do Iguaçu. Pluma also serves São Paulo, Paranaguá, Río de Janeiro, Curitiba and Florianópolis. Rysa (Rápido Yguazú; ☎ 442244, 551601), at Antequera and Ayala, also goes to Foz, São Paulo and Rio de Janeiro (every other Friday). Expreso Brújula serves São Paulo five times weekly and Porto Alegre twice.

Montevideo is served by Expreso Brújula Tuesday and Friday at 1:30pm, and by Coit (☎ 492473, 551738), Eligio Ayala 693, 11am Thursday and Sunday. Both travel via Encarnación, Posadas and Paso de los Libres (Argentina), Uruguiana (Brazil) and the Uruguayan cities of Bella Unión, Salto, Paysandú, Young and San José. Both have reputations for excellent service.

Expreso Pullman del Sur (☎ 551553) goes to Santiago 9pm Tuesday and Friday.

Domestic Destinations There are countless buses to Ciudad del Este and Encarnación; Rysa & NSA are two options with downtown offices.

Multiple lines offer frequent service to Pedro Juan Caballero and Concepción.

Long-distance Chaco carriers are Nasa (Nueva Asunción; ☎ 551731) and Stel Turismo (☎ 551647), with services to Pozo Colorado, Concepción, Neuland and Mariscal Estigarribia, where the paved portion of the Ruta Trans-Chaco currently ends. Nasa is the only company to travel this part of this route in daylight.

Destinations near Asunción, such as San Bernardino and Caacupé, have such frequent services that it would be awkward to list them all here; see the Getting There & Away section for the destination for details.

The following table shows winter fares. Most destinations are served daily, and many several times a day. Travel times are approximate.

Destination	Duration in hours	Cost
Bella Unión (Uru)	12	US$57
Boyuibe (Bol)	24	US$42
Buenos Aires	18-20	US$27-52
Ciudad del Este	5	US$5.25
Clorinda (Arg)	2	US$3
Concepción	5½-8	US$6.75
Córdoba (Arg)	18	US$42
Curitibá (Bra)	14-16	US$26-30
Encarnación	5-6	US$7-9.25
Filadelfia	6½	US$10.50
Florianópolis (Bra)	20	US$35
Foz do Iguaçu (Bra)	5½	US$12-16
Loma Plata	7	US$8.50
Montevideo	18	US$57-70
Neuland	8-9	US$9
Paranaguá (Bra)	16-18	US$29
Pedro Juan Caballero	7-8	US$8-12
Posadas (Arg)	6½	US$13

Destination	Duration in hours	Cost
Pozo Colorado	3½	US$5.25
Puerto Falcón	1½	US$2
Resistencia (Arg)	6	US$12
Rio de Janeiro (Bra)	22-27	US$50
Rosario (Arg)	14-18	US$21-29
Santa Cruz (Bol)	32	US$42
Santiago (Chi)	28	US$78
São Paulo (Bra)	18-20	US$37-42
Villarrica	2½-4	US$2.75-5
Ybycuí	3	US$2

Boat

It's possible to travel by boat from Asunción to Vallemí and sometimes as far as Bahía Negra in the extreme north (and to continue into Brazil from various points). The river is much more scenic beyond Concepción, which makes a better departure point. See the boxed text 'Up the Lazy River' for further details on boat travel.

GETTING AROUND
To/From the Airport

Bus No 30A (with a blue sign) runs from downtown to Aeropuerto Silvio Pettirossi (US$0.30, 50-60 minutes). Vip's Tour (☎ 441199) provides airport transfers for US$5 per person (minimum US$10). Taxis cost about US$15.

To/From the Bus Terminal

From the terminal, walk out to the stops on Av de la Mora and look at the route signs. Buses Nos 8, 25, 31, 38 and 42 run between the terminal and downtown. Most pass through Mercado Cuatro; at rush hours (early morning, noonish, and about 6pm) and on Saturday, leave yourself extra time to get through the congestion there, or avoid it altogether.

Bus

Asunción city buses go almost everywhere for around US$0.30, but Paraguayans are less night people than Argentines or Uruguayans, and buses are few after about 10pm or 11pm. Plan your late-night trip well or else take a cab. On the other hand, buses start running very early in the morning, since

Paraguayans start work around 6:30am or 7am. Around noon, buses are jammed with people going home for an extended lunch, so avoid travel into outlying barrios or suburbs at this hour.

Car & Taxi

Asunción has several car rental agencies. Hertz/Diesa (☎ 605708), at Camilo Recalde and Cerafina Dávalos just north of Eusebio Ayala at Km 4.5 or at Aeropuerto Silvio Pettirossi (☎ 645600), is highly recommended for good rates and service. National (☎ 491379, e national@infonet.com.py) is at Yegros and Cerro Corá; Localiza (☎ 446233) is at Eligio Ayala and Antequera; and Touring Cars (☎ 447945) is at Iturbe 682. Daily rates start around US$40 with tax, insurance and 100km included.

Cabs are metered and reasonable, but tack on a surcharge late at night. A cab from downtown to the bus terminal costs US$4 to US$5 with a 30% *recargo* (surcharge) after 10pm and on Sunday and holidays.

Southern Paraguay

East of the Río Paraguay and beyond Asunción is the nucleus of historical Paraguay, the homeland of the Guaraní people among whom the Spaniards began to settle in the 16th century. Many of Paraguay's finest cultural, historical, and natural attractions are within a short distance of Asunción, on the Circuito Central, a convenient and popular excursion route from the capital. These include the weaving center of Itauguá, the lakeside resorts of San Bernardino and Areguá, the celebrated shrine of Caacupé, colonial villages like Piribebuy and Yaguarón, and, a bit farther, Parque Nacional Ybycuí. On and near the highway between Asunción and Encarnación lie Jesuit ruins in equal or better repair than those in Argentine Misiones. The contraband center of Ciudad del Este is Paraguay's gateway to the Iguazú Falls, and the gigantic Itaipú hydroelectric project is itself a tourist attraction of sorts.

This section proceeds counterclockwise around the region after describing the

Circuito Central, a roughly 200km roundtrip from Asunción that can be broken up into day trips, weekend excursions, or longer outings from the capital. Some tourist literature refers to it as the Circuito de Oro.

AREGUÁ

This modest resort on Paraguay's largest lake, Lago Ypacaraí, is a popular artist's retreat renowned for its ceramics, 28km from Asunción. Swimming in the polluted lake is not recommended, but there's a pleasant sandy beach and you can rent rowboats for US$3 per hour. The cathedral on the hill offers good views of the lake, and the surrounding wooded landscape is good hiking country; try the one-hour trek to the summit of Cerro Koi (take any bus out of town and ask to be dropped off at the base of the hill).

On the main avenue from the old train station to the lake, *Hospedaje Ozli* (☎ 0291-2380, Av del Lago 860) has rooms with fans and detached baths for US$12 per person,

and doubles with air-con and private bath for US$24. All rates include breakfast, and reasonable lunches and dinners are available. Most buses from Asunción stop a short distance up the street.

Ña Eustaquia (*Mariscal Estigarribia & Candelaria*) serves excellent pizza, while popular *La Casona* (*Yegros near 25 de Diciembre*) is a cheaper lunch alternative.

Frequent buses on Línea 110 and 111 leave from Av Perú and Av Díaz in Asunción's Mercado Cuatro (US$0.30).

ITAUGUÁ

Though it doesn't look like much from the highway, getting a few blocks into Itauguá reveals picturesque houses, tilting colonnades and fragrant citrus trees – a pleasant setting for the production of Paraguay's famous ñandutí.

Townswomen learn to tat the multicolored, spiderweb lace as children and practice the skill well into old age. On both

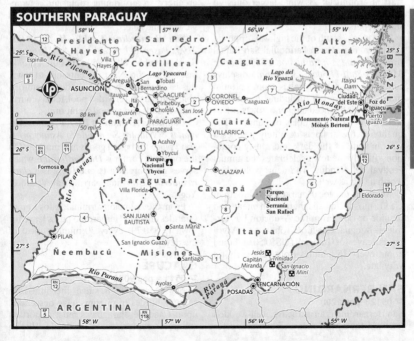

sides of Ruta 2, the main highway to Ciudad del Este, weavers display their merchandise, ranging in size from doilies to bedspreads. It's possible to visit the artisans' houses, where you can see the women working on their latest projects. Itauguá is 30km from Asunción, and is the cradle and center of the ñandutí industry.

At the cooperative *Mutuales Tejedoras* (☎ 0294-20525, Km 28.5; open 7am-6pm Mon-Sat, 7am-1pm Sun), you can see the lace being made before you buy. Next door is *Salón Flora* (☎ 0294-21059; open 7am-7pm Mon-Sun), another ñandutí outlet. Farther east on the highway, *Casa Miryam* (☎ 0294-20372) is a good place for anyone in search of a US$1500 wedding dress, hand sewn for nine months by four women; they can arrange for you to visit lacemakers' homes here as well.

The lace comes in two grades, *fino* and *grueso* (fine and thick). Smaller grueso pieces can be had for about a dollar; fino pieces start at around US$3, while larger ones go for US$50 and up. You can bargain with shopkeepers.

Two blocks south of the highway, opposite the plaza, the **Museo Parroquial San Rafael** (no ☎, Cálvarez s/n; admission US$0.25; open Mon-Fri 8am-11:30am, 3pm-6pm) displays religious and secular relics from colonial times to the present, including Jesuit- and Franciscan-influenced indigenous artwork as well as very early samples of ñandutí. The quality of the artifacts definitely justifies a visit, in spite of the dark and musty conditions. In July the town celebrates the annual **Festival del Ñandutí**. The nearby church is worth a visit as well.

Meals in the local market cost less than US$1, mostly for spaghetti with meat and manioc or rice. From the Asunción bus terminal, Itauguá, Caacupé, Tobatí, and Atyrá buses leave for Itauguá (US$0.50, 1 hour) about every 15 minutes from very early till very late.

SAN BERNARDINO
☎ 0512 • pop 1200

San Bernardino is an attractive, well-wooded lakeside town with many restaurants, cafés and hotels, 48km east of Asunción on Lago Ypacaraí's eastern shore. German colonists settled here in 1881, and the town soon became a recreational refuge from the capital. It's still a weekend resort for Asunción's elite, but there are a few reasonable budget alternatives, and the lake is cleaner here than at Areguá. A pleasure boat takes passengers for short cruises on the lake (US$1.40). Artisans in the nearby village of Altos create exceptional woodcarvings, particularly animal masks.

Hotel Balneario (☎ 2252, Nuestra Señora de la Asunción & Yegros) US$11-13 per person with breakfast. The cheapest place in town serves lunch and dinner as well.

Hotel del Lago (☎/fax 2201, 021-214098 in Asunción, CA López & Teniente Weiler) US$12.50 per person with fan and breakfast. The grandeur is slightly faded but still present in this 1888 hotel. Rooms have tile floors and antique furniture, frígobars and cable TV. There's a swimming pool, lots of greenery, an airy dining room and a wraparound 2nd-floor balcony that provides views of the lake.

San Bernardino Pueblo Hotel (☎/fax 2195, Paseo del Pueblo & Av Mbocayá) Singles/doubles US$45/50 with buffet breakfast and air-con. Near the entrance to town, this is a very nicely done, modern, comfortable four-star hotel with a pool, tennis courts, lush grounds and a good restaurant.

Confitería Alemán (☎ 2227, Colonos Alemanes & Nuestra Señora de la Asunción) A good place for baked goods and minutas. On the opposite corner is *Die Kaffestube*, which serves good breakfasts, and there is a *churrasquería* (Brazilian parrilla) at Vaché & Yegros.

From the Asunción terminal, Altos Lomas Grandes and San Bernardino buses leave for town (US$0.70) every 30 minutes most of the day.

CAACUPÉ
☎ 0511 • pop 9000

Every December 8 since the mid-18th century, hordes of pilgrims have descended upon Caacupé, Paraguay's most important religious center, for **Día de la Virgen**

(Immaculate Conception). It draws the faithful throughout the year as well, including military conscripts from the region. After ending their tour of duty in the Chaco, many walk the length of the Ruta Trans-Chaco and the last 54km across Asunción and its suburbs to the imposing **Basílica de Nuestra Señora de Los Milagros**.

The rather charmless basilica, whose construction began in the 1970s and was finished in 1981, dominates the townscape, presiding over a huge cobblestone plaza that easily accommodates the up to 300,000 pilgrims who gather here. Pope John Paul II blessed it on a visit in 1988; the event is commemorated in stained glass. Carved wooden panels above the front doors depict pilgrims arriving by truck, bus and 4WD.

Hospedaje Uruguayo (☎ 2977, *Eligio Ayala & Asunción*) Doubles US$8-21. The Uruguayo, two blocks from the basilica, has comfortable rooms and ample foliage. Price variations are dependent on a combination of private or shared bath and fan or air-con. The fan rooms are a bit musty.

Katy María (☎ 2860, *Dr Pino & Eligio Ayala*) Singles/doubles US$16/21 with breakfast and air-con. The rooms in this modern, clean and friendly hotel across from the basilica have cable TV and frígobars. Some have balconies.

In addition to the *restaurants* at both hotels listed, there are several others in the blocks alongside the plaza and basilica. Also by the plaza is the *Nuevo Super* market (*Solís & Eligio Ayala*), with a variety of hot prepared food to take out.

Transporte La Caacupeña and Transporte Villa Serrana (both Línea 119) run buses from Asunción (US$0.70, 1¼ hour) almost every 10 minutes between 5am and 10pm.

PIRIBEBUY
☎ 0515 • pop 5000

The road heading south to Piribebuy from Ruta 2 passes through citrus groves; in season many little roadside stands have strings of oranges hung out for sale. The town itself is a good place to get a glimpse of rural Paraguay without getting too far from the

Caacupé's famed basilica

PARAGUAY

capital. Peasants grow maize, beans, and manioc at the north end of town; a skilled wainwright fashions traditional wooden-wheeled oxcarts of *lapacho* wood at the south end (ask for Ledo Correa). The town's mid-18th-century church, set in a grassy central plaza, is in excellent repair, and retains some of its original woodwork and sculpture.

Only 74km from Asunción, on a southern branch of Ruta 2, Piribebuy was founded in 1640. During the War of the Triple Alliance, it saw serious combat and briefly served as the national capital. The **Museo Histórico Comandante Pablo Juan Caballero** *(no ☎, Mariscal Estigarribia & Yegros; admission US$0.30; open 7:30am-11:30am, 1pm-6pm Tue-Fri)*, one block west of the plaza, has valuable but deteriorating artifacts on local history and the Chaco War.

Hotel Restaurant Viejo Rincón *(☎ 2251, Teniente Horacio Giní & Maestro Fermín)* Doubles/triples US$11/13 with fan and breakfast. A block east of the church, the rooms are fairly musty, with small baths, but the restaurant and central location are convenient.

Hotel Los Carlos *(☎ 2223, Mariscal Estigarribia 688)* US$6.50/10.50 per person with fan/air-con; all with breakfast. Los Carlos is a few blocks west of the plaza, and has decent rooms around a secure internal courtyard.

Empresa Piribebuy (Línea 197) has buses from Asunción (US$0.80, 1½ hours) every half hour between 5am and 9pm.

AROUND PIRIBEBUY

South of Piribebuy the road narrows and becomes bumpier, leading through cane-brakes, palm groves and lush greenery to **Chololó**, less a village than a series of river-side *balnearios* (bathing resorts) with camp-grounds in a verdant, relatively undeveloped area. There's a branch road to the modest **Saltos de Pirareta**, a waterfall with nearby camping areas. Continuing south, the road descends through dense forests, offering the occasional impressive glimpse of hills, rock formations and the valley below. At the town of **Paraguarí** the road connects with Ruta 1, and you can stay on the Circuito by heading back toward Asunción or take Ruta 1 south

toward Encarnación. Scenic Paraguarí is worth a walk around.

Hospedaje El Triángulo, on Ruta 1 at the south end of town, is a 'short-stay' hotel but you might coax a room for the night out of them.

Transporte Ciudad de Paraguarí (Línea 193) has buses to Asunción (US$0.75, 1½ hours) about every 15 minutes between 5am and 8pm. Buses from Ciudad del Este pass through town en route to Piribebuy at 6am, 7am and 8am, and buses for Chololó run from 7am until 5:30pm.

About 21km south of Paraguarí on Ruta 1, the village of **Carapeguá** is noted for its cotton hammocks, known by the Guaraní term *poyvi*. The **Festival del Poyvi** takes place in November. **Ñande Hotel** *(☎ 0971-233-696, Ruta 1 Km 83)* has air-con singles/doubles for US$8/16. It's a motel by the Esso station at the turnoff for Ybycuí.

YAGUARÓN & ITÁ

These are the last two towns of any note on the return leg of the Circuito Central. Yaguarón's pride is its landmark 18th-century Franciscan church *(open 7:30am-11:30am & 1:30pm-5pm Tue-Sat, open during mass only Sun)*, a barnlike wooden structure 70m long and 30m wide, with an excellent gilt baroque altar, a splendid carved wooden pulpit held atop his head by San Son, other fine carvings and a painted ceiling. The church was restored between 1985 and 1991 with the help of the German, Spanish and French governments.

Yaguarón is also home to the **Museo del Dr Francia** *(no ☎, Dr Francia & General Bernardino Caballero; free; open 7am-11:30am Tue-Sun; ask for key at Caballero 440)*, 2 1/2 blocks from the church in a well-preserved colonial house where Francia was appointed colonial administrator. Its collection of colonial and early independence portraiture includes a likeness of El Supremo holding his *mate* and looking a bit mad.

Across Ruta 1 from the church is **Hotel Ani Rehasa Rei** *(☎ 0533-210)*, which charges US$2.75 per person for rooms with fans, mosquito nets and private baths. Three meals are available. Transporte Ciudad Paraguarí

(Línea 193) runs buses every 15 minutes (5am to 8:15pm) to Asunción (US$0.65, 1½ hours), 48km north.

Eleven kilometers closer to Asunción is **Itá**, founded in 1539 and known for its black-clay pottery, especially the *gallinitas* (small chicken figures), though nowadays pieces come in different colors and include bright-yellow Pokémons. *Centro Artesano Capici San Blas (General Díaz Y Cerro Corá)* is a ceramicists' cooperative at the north end of town. Five bus lines serve the capital (US$0.65), 37km away.

PARQUE NACIONAL YBYCUÍ

Ybycuí is the most accessible unit in the national parks system. Its 5000 hectares preserve one of southern Paraguay's last remaining stands of Brazilian subtropical rain forest. Steep hills dominate here, reaching up to 400m and dissected by creeks that form a series of attractive waterfalls and pools. You can take hikes of up to 14km on dirt roads in the park.

The dense forest makes it difficult to see animals, which often hide rather than run. The exception is a remarkable assemblage of stunningly colorful butterflies. They and the abundant poisonous snakes keep a lower profile in the cooler months. The park's campground is mobbed at New Year's and Easter Week; it's best to avoid the place completely at these times.

Things to See & Do

Ybycuí is tranquil and undeveloped, although the influx of weekenders from Asunción can disrupt its peacefulness; in this event, take refuge on the extensive hiking trails. Be sure to sign in at the *administración* (a little under 2km from the entrance) on arrival and ask about conditions. Rangers here distribute a brochure for a self-guided nature trail. The campground is a short distance up the road.

Near the campground is the **Salto Guaraní**. Below this waterfall a bridge leads to a pleasant creekside trail, along which, if the gods are smiling, you will see a wealth of butterflies, including the large metallic blue morpho. Watch for poisonous snakes, but

bear in mind that the rattler and coral snake are not normally aggressive, and the very aggressive yarará is largely nocturnal. The rangers say no park visitor has been bitten.

The trail continues 2km west to the park entrance and **La Rosada**, the first iron foundry of its kind in South America. It was destroyed by Brazilian forces during the War of the Triple Alliance, but not before turning out the ironwork used in some of Asunción's fine buildings, including the Palacio de López. The old waterwheel has been restored, and there's a **museum** *(free; open 8am-4pm daily)*.

Much of Ybycuí's forest is second growth, having recovered from overexploitation during the years when the foundry operated on wood charcoal, 2 tons of which were required to produce a single ton of iron. Engineers dammed Arroyo Mina to provide water and power for the bellows, and oxcarts hauled ore from several different sites more than 25km away.

Places to Stay & Eat

The park has no hotels, so your only alternative is to *camp* at Arroyo Mina, which has adequate sanitary facilities, cold showers, and a confitería serving meals on weekends. Level sites are scarce. Fortunately, mosquitoes are also few, but swarming moths and flealike insects are a nighttime nuisance, even though they do not bite.

Hotel Pytu'u Renda (☎ 0534-364, Av Quyquyho s/n) US$9 per person with shared bath, doubles US$21-26 with private bath and air-con; all with breakfast. This hotel is at the nearby cotton-mill village of Ybycuí and has a restaurant. Rooms are clean and decent but nothing special.

Getting There & Away

Parque Nacional Ybycuí is 151km southeast of Asunción. Ruta 1, the paved highway to Encarnación, leads 84km south to Carapeguá, where there is a turnoff to the park, which is a another 67km via the villages of Acahay and Ybycuí.

Empresa Salto Cristal has buses roughly hourly from Asunción to Ybycuí village (US$2, 3 hours) between 4am and 6pm.

PARAGUAY

From there buses to the park entrance leave 10am Monday, Wednesday and Saturday. At least two buses, at 11am and noon Monday to Saturday, enter the park and will stop at the administración. Six buses make the return trip to the village between 7am and 3:30pm (ask rangers for the schedule). Salto Cristal runs one Sunday bus from Asunción all the way in; it leaves the park at 3:30pm.

VILLA FLORIDA

Villa Florida is a popular balneario and fishing and camping spot on the banks of the Río Tebicuary, 161km southeast of Asunción. It has long stretches of sandy river beach.

Camping Paraíso (no ☎) US$2.50 per site plus US$0.50 per person; open summer only. This riverside campground has basic showers and toilets and serves simple meals. It's 2km out a dirt road that begins across the highway from the Hotel Misionero.

Hotel Nacional de Turismo (☎ 083207, *Ruta 1 Km 160*) Singles/doubles/triples US$13/26/34 with breakfast and air-con. Ample rooms with big beds and tile floors, a large pool and a restaurant are among this hotel's selling points.

SAN IGNACIO GUAZÚ

About 140km northwest of Encarnación on Ruta 1, San Ignacio was the first Jesuit reducción in the region. Its church was demolished in 1920, but one wing of the 18th-century mission remains, and is now the **Museo Diocesano** (☎ 082-2223, *Calle Iturbe s/n; admission US$0.75, paid at the parish office next door; open 8am-11:30am & 2pm-5:30pm daily*). It has a collection of exquisite Guaraní Indian carvings (both wood and stone) from the period. The various saints and demons are being repainted and restored by an Italian expert.

Down the street is the **Museo Histórico Semblanza de Héroes** (no ☎, *Calle Iturbe s/n; free; open 7:30am-11:30am & 2pm-5:30pm Mon-Sat*).

Hotel Arapyzandú (☎/fax 082-2213) Singles/doubles US$11/13 with air-con, US$6.50/11 with fan; all with breakfast. This hotel is on Ruta 1, behind the LP gas station

at the north end of town. Some of the beds are a bit saggy, but the air-con is good and there's a passable restaurant.

There are more than 30 buses daily to Asunción (US$4-4.50, 3-4½ hours), 20 to Encarnación (US$3.75, 1½ hours *directo*), and many to the departmental capital of San Juan Bautista, and the Río Paraná port of Ayolas. Five or six a day serve the Jesuit village of Santa María.

SANTA MARÍA

Twelve kilometers north and east from San Ignacio off Ruta 1, Santa María is another former Jesuit reducción, with dirt roads and a shady plaza. Its **Museo Jesuítico** (*admission US$0.50; open 8am-11:30am & 1pm-6pm*) has a superb collection of Jesuit statuary.

From San Ignacio Guazú about five buses a day ply the 10km of cobblestone road between Ruta 1 and Santa María. The 6:30am and 10:30am buses give you a good amount of time to see the museum. Taxis charge about US$11 for the roundtrip, including waiting time.

SANTIAGO

Santiago, 40km southeast of San Ignacio via Ruta 1 and a paved spur, is yet another former mission with a good collection of Jesuit relics. It also hosts, on the third weekend in January, the **Fiesta de la Tradición Misionera**, one of the largest folklore events in Paraguay, drawing more than 10,000 each year to the pueblo of 3000. It includes three days of music and dancing from Paraguay, Brazil and Argentina, a procession of riders from local estancias, floats featuring Paraguayan traditions (making chipa, harvesting manioc, etc), and a wide selection of typical dishes to sample. The festival culminates with the **Día del Campo**, which features a rodeo demonstrating the daily work of the *vaqueros* with cows and horses, and a non-lethal bullfight.

More information on the festival and accommodations in the area (including B&B estancias) can be obtained from Santiago González (☎/fax 0782-20286). He is the governor of Misiones province and runs

Emitur, a tourism agency promoting estancia stays and eco-tourism in Paraguay.

ENCARNACIÓN
☎ 071 • pop 50,000

Paraguay's southern gateway is a good base for visiting the Jesuit mission ruins at Trinidad and Jesús as well as other, lesser ruins and Parque Nacional Serranía San Rafael (see the earlier National Parks section). Encarnación sits on the north bank of the Río Paraná, upstream from the massive Yacyretá hydroelectric project, directly opposite the much larger city of Posadas, Argentina. The modernly handsome Puente Internacional Beato Roque González, built by Argentina at Paraguay's insistence as part of the Yacyretá agreement, links the two cities.

Since the completion of the dam, Encarnación comprises two very different parts: an older, colonial-style quarter along the flood-prone riverfront and a newer section on the bluff overlooking the river.

Information

The staff speak English at the tourist office (☎ 203508), Tomás Romero Pereira 125, open 7am to 1pm weekdays. The Touring y Automóvil Club Paraguayo (☎ 202203) is in the Shell station on Av Caballero between Mallorquín and Av Estigarribia. Both the Argentine consulate (☎ 201066, Carlos Antonio López 690) and the Brazilian vice-consulate (☎ 203950, Memmel 452) are open 8 am to noon weekdays. The Japanese consulate (☎ 202288) is at the corner of CA López and 14 de Mayo, and the German consulate (☎ 204041) is at Memmel 631.

Financiera Guaraní is a cambio at Av Estigarribia 1405. Banco Continental, across Estigarribia and south, has an ATM on the Cirrus and Plus systems, as do a few other banks on and around the avenue. Moneychangers jam the bus terminal on weekends and during off-hours.

The post office is at Capellán Molas 337, in the old city. Antelco is at PJ Caballero and Carlos Antonio López. There are Internet facilities upstairs at Phono Uno on the corner of Estigarribia and 14 de Mayo (US$2.50 an hour for decent connections), and phones downstairs.

El Dorado Turismo (☎ 202558) is at Av Estigarribia 964. Also try Aruba Tour (☎ 205158) at Tomás Romero Pereira 347.

Serpylcolor, on the corner of Av Estigarribia and Curupayty, has inexpensive print and slide film (Agfa 100 only); travelers in Posadas may want to cross the border to load up before continuing to Iguazú or Buenos Aires.

Lavamatic is on Carlos Antonio López almost at Curupayty. Laverap is at 25 de Mayo 485, and the Hospital Regional (☎ 202272) is at Independencia and General Bruguez.

Things to See & Do

Radiating out a few blocks outward from the intersection of Carlos Antonio López and General Gamarra, the **Feria Municipal** (municipal market) is a warren of stalls selling cheap imported trinkets, including digital watches, personal cassette players and the like. It's also a good, inexpensive place to eat. In better economic times, Argentines throng the market.

At the corner of Tomás Romero Pereira and Carlos Antonio López, opposite Plaza Artigas, the **Iglesia Ucraniana** reflects the presence of Eastern Orthodox immigrants in southern Paraguay. At the west end of Romero Pereira, the **train station** is a bit of a working museum, where woodburning locomotives pull freight cars.

Places to Stay

Camping El Paraíso, 5km out of town on Ruta 6 (take any bus from downtown marked 'Santa Maria-Arroyo Porá'), charges US$3.50 a site.

Hotel Germano (☎/fax 203346, Cabañas near Carlos Antonio López) Singles/doubles US$4/6.50 with shared bath, US$5.25/9 with private bath; all have fans; air-con adds US$2.75. The excellent Germano is directly across from the bus terminal. It's clean, comfortable, traveler-oriented and very helpful (Spanish, German and Japanese spoken), and there's secure parking.

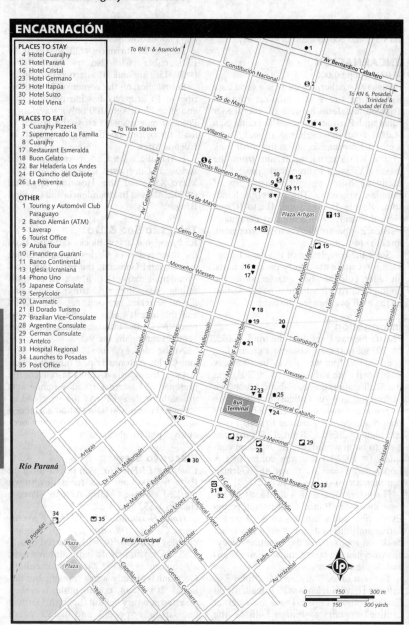

ENCARNACIÓN

PLACES TO STAY
4 Hotel Cuarajhy
12 Hotel Paraná
16 Hotel Cristal
23 Hotel Germano
25 Hotel Itapúa
30 Hotel Suizo
32 Hotel Viena

PLACES TO EAT
3 Cuarajhy Pizzería
7 Supermercado La Familia
8 Cuarajhy
17 Restaurant Esmeralda
18 Buon Gelato
22 Bar Heladería Los Andes
24 El Quincho del Quijote
26 La Provenza

OTHER
1 Touring y Automóvil Club
    Paraguayo
2 Banco Alemán (ATM)
5 Laverap
6 Tourist Office
9 Aruba Tour
10 Financiera Guaraní
11 Banco Continental
13 Iglesia Ucraniana
14 Phono Uno
15 Japanese Consulate
19 Serpylcolor
20 Lavamatic
21 El Dorado Turismo
27 Brazilian Vice-Consulate
28 Argentine Consulate
29 German Consulate
31 Antelco
33 Hospital Regional
34 Launches to Posadas
35 Post Office

Hotel Suizo (☎ 203692, Av Estigarribia 562) Singles/doubles/triples US$5.25/9/12. The rooms here are around a leafy patio.

Hotel Itapúa (☎/fax 205045, Carlos Antonio López 814) US$2.75 per person with shared bath, US$4 per person with private bath and fan, US$9 for a double with private bath and air-con. Stick with the top-floor, air-con rooms at this hotel near the bus terminal; the cheaper rooms are shabby and the shared baths grotty.

Hotel Viena (☎ 203486, PJ Caballero 568) Singles/doubles US$6/10 with fan, US$15/25 with air-con. Rooms at this clean, simple and fairly quiet hotel are a decent value – German speakers may get a small discount and special attention.

Hotel Cuarajhy (☎ 202155, fax 202740, 25 de Mayo 415) Singles/doubles/triples US$10/20/25 with breakfast and air-con. Baths are a bit ragged and streetside rooms are noisy, but all in all it's a good value.

Hotel Paraná (☎ 204440, fax 202252, Av Estigarribia 1414) Singles/doubles US$18/25 with breakfast. Very large rooms with frígobars, good air-con and baths make this one of the nicest places in town.

Hotel Cristal (☎ 202371, fax 202372, e hcristal@telesurf.com.py, Av Estigarribia 1157) Singles/doubles/triples US$10/16/23 with fan, US$15/22/30 with air-con, TV and phone; all with breakfast. A large pool tips the balance to make this hotel the best in town in summertime.

Places to Eat

The inexpensive stalls around the *Feria Municipal* (Carlos Antonio López & General Gamarra) are but one place to fill up.

Cuarajhy (☎ 204249, Av Estigarribia & Tomás Romero Pereira) US$2-7; open 24 hours. Packed with both locals and Argentines, Cuarajhy, on Plaza Artigas, is a good, moderately priced confitería/parrilla. The same owners run a pizzeria at Av Estigarribia and 25 de Mayo (☎ 203639).

El Quincho del Quijote (no ☎, Carlos Antonio López & General Cabañas) US$2-5. This place opposite the bus terminal is a good value for its decent food and great service.

Bar Heladería Los Andes (no ☎, General Cabañas near CA López) US$1.50-3. This restaurant next to the Hotel Germano serves Japanese dishes and ice cream.

Restaurant Esmeralda (☎ 202371, Av Estigarribia 1152) US$3.25-5.25. The Esmeralda is part of the Hotel Cristal and serves meat, fish, sandwiches and pizza.

La Provenza (☎ 204618, Mallorquín & Pedro Juan Caballero) US$3.50-5.25. La Provenza has a wide selection of Italian dishes and a full bar; it's a bit more upscale than most places in town.

Buon Gelato (Av Estigarribia 1044) Come here for decent ice cream and empanadas.

Supermercado La Familia (Mallorquín & Tomás Romero Pereira) This very well-stocked, modern supermarket has prices that are amazingly low if you've been shopping in Argentina, even for Argentine products, and produce is dirt cheap.

Getting There & Away

Air Arpa may begin flights to and from Asunción from Encarnación's nearby airport (☎ 203940). Nearby Posadas has air service to Buenos Aires; see its Getting There & Away section in the Northeast Argentina chapter.

Bus The chaotic bus terminal (☎ 202412) is at Av Estigarribia and Cabañas. Touts for the various lines shout out destinations and try to hustle passengers aboard; don't let yourself be rushed onto any buses without first determining details at the agency. For information on buses to Posadas, see Getting Around.

Several companies offer comfortable daily service to Buenos Aires (US$42, 18 hours). Many more buses depart from Posadas, where prices are slightly lower.

Domestic services are frequent, but most buses are not in good shape. Yacyretá is one line to avoid if you can help it; NSE (Nuestra Señora de la Encarnación) is preferable. Numerous buses serve Asunción (US$7-9.25, 5-6 hours) and Ciudad del Este (US$4.50-5.25, 4½-6 hours). There are also connections to Ayolas, San Cosme y Damián, Villarrica, and many lesser destinations.

Boat Though launches cross to Posadas from the dock at the foot of Av Estigarribia every half hour between 7am and 5pm (US$1.20, 30 minutes), this service is basically for locals. There are no immigration facilities for foreigners at either end; procedures must be handled at the offices on the bridge, requiring a walk of several kilometers. Remember, being caught in Paraguay without the proper stamps can result in a hefty fine.

Getting Around

Encarnación has a good local bus system, but for all practical purposes, your feet should get you around town. Most buses to the old town use Carlos Antonio López and return by General Artigas.

Between 6am and 11pm, frequent buses cross the bridge to Posadas for US$1.50 *regular*, US$2 *servicio diferencial* (the latter are air-conditioned and pass more quickly through customs at busy morning hours). These begin at Av Bernardino Caballero and travel down Mallorquín, passing the bus terminal and the port. Under optimal conditions the trip takes about 50 minutes, including stops for customs and immigration on each side of the bridge. Buses from Posadas come into town via Molas, then up Av Estigarribia. These local buses going in either direction do not wait at customs/immigration; you must get off with your luggage on both sides of the bridge to get your passport stamped. Hold on to your ticket and catch the next bus.

TRINIDAD & JESÚS

These lovely former Jesuit missions are the best-preserved ruins of their kind in Paraguay, rivaling those across the river in Argentine Mesopotamia and easily reached from Encarnación. Both occupy grassy, hilltop sites with distant views, in marked contrast to the more jungly settings of the Argentine ruins.

Trinidad *(no ☎; admission US$0.50; open daily 7am-5:30pm winter, to 7pm summer)* is 28km northeast of Encarnación via Ruta 6. Founded only in 1706, it was one of the later Jesuit establishments, but by 1728 boasted a Guaraní population of more than 4000. As elsewhere, the Jesuits introduced European crafts and industry, and Trinidad became famous for the manufacture of bells, organs, harps, and statuary. It also operated three cattle estancias, two large *yerba mate* plantations, and a sugar plantation and mill.

The main church and some living quarters and workshops still stand. Highlights of the church include the baptismal font, an elaborately constructed stone pulpit, some statuary, and carved reliefs of angels playing musical instruments. All are in good shape despite exposure to the elements.

The ride from Ruta 6 is interesting in itself, leading through lush countryside and areas farmed by descendants of German immigrants, who grow manioc, bananas, citrus, *mate*, maize and other crops.

The Jesús mission *(no ☎; admission US$0.50; open daily 7am-5:30pm winter, to 7pm summer)*, whose full name is Jesús de Tavarangüé, has fewer outlying structures than Trinidad, but even more commanding vistas. The church was unfinished by the time the Jesuits abandoned the area and never got a roof. It is impressive for its size and clean lines; there is little ornamentation beyond some carved cornices in the interior and a frieze above the entrance, below which is a carved bishop's hat with crossed swords, indicating the sometimes-militant nature of the Jesuit order.

Stairs on the right side of the church lead to the roof, which yields good views of the interior and the surrounding area; on a clear day you can see the Trinidad site.

Camping is possible just outside the ruins of Trinidad. Another option is the German-run *Hotel León* (☎ 0985-777341), where doubles with breakfast are US$11. Directly in front of the ruins, it has three spacious rooms with good baths, and a restaurant.

Hotel Tirol (☎ 075555, Ruta 6 Km 21) Singles/doubles from US$45/63. This hotel is on Ruta 6, 21km from Encarnación, between Capitán Miranda and Trinidad. The excellent facilities include tennis courts and a pool.

From the bus terminal at Encarnación, most of the frequent buses headed toward Ciudad del Este will drop you at the turnoff to either site for about US$0.50. Trinidad is

Baking in the sun at fashionable Punta del Este, Uruguay

Once the continent's tallest building, Palacio Salvo still dominates the skyline of Montevideo, Uruguay.

On the count of three, let's moon 'em!

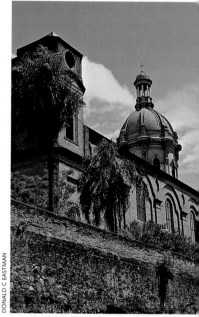

A colonial church in Asunción, Paraguay

A statue guards the entrance to Asunción's pink Palacio de Gobierno, Paraguay.

about a 1km walk from the bus stop on Ruta 6. The turnoff for Jesús is a short distance past Trinidad's, on the opposite (north) side of the highway. The site itself is 11km north by a generally good dirt road. A small bus makes the trip about once an hour for US$0.65, or you can take one of the shareable taxis that are sometimes waiting (US$0.85 per person or US$3 for the whole cab). Neither is an option when the road is muddy; at such times, owners of 4WDs wait near the Encarnación terminal to offer their services.

CIUDAD DEL ESTE
☎ 061 • pop 104,000

Grubby, chaotic Ciudad del Este is a key border crossing, a transportation hub, and one of the gateways to the world-famous Iguazú Falls. It also has the unfortunate reputation as one of South America's most corrupt cities, frequented by smugglers and money launderers, and is one of Latin America's biggest shopping centers. During the day the streets can be a heaving, frantic mass of Brazilian and Argentine shoppers in search of cheap electronic goods, cigarettes and liquor, but by 5pm all business is cleared away and the city has a deserted and sinister feel. Economic depression and new Brazilian customs laws have hit Ciudad del Este hard, and business (although still booming by most standards) is not what it used to be.

Much of the merchandise has been smuggled into the country, avoiding import duties. Many of the items for sale, from brand-name cell phone batteries to sportswear and designer clothing and accessories, are counterfeit, while some are 'near-name' brands (such as 'Panasuonic'). Pirated copies of videos, software and music CDs and cassettes abound, and are of varying degrees of quality.

Not far from the city are the gargantuan Itaipú hydroelectric project, an interesting natural preserve, and Paraguay's highest waterfall, Salto Monday. There's little other reason to stop.

Orientation
Ciudad del Este (still appearing on some maps as Puerto Presidente Stroessner) sits on the west bank of the Río Paraná, linked to the Brazilian city of Foz do Iguaçu by the Puente de la Amistad (Bridge of Friendship). The center, though a bit complex and very disorderly, is compact and easily manageable on foot.

Information
The tourist office (no ☎) at the immigration border post on the bridge may look intimidating (and closed) with its blacked-out windows, but inside the staff is friendly and armed with an extensive supply of brochures. The Touring y Automóvil Club Paraguayo (☎ 512340) is on Av San Blas, at the Shell station about 1km west of Plaza Madame Lynch, on Ruta 7 to Asunción. The Brazilian consulate (☎ 500984), at Pampliega 205, is open 8am to noon weekdays.

Moneychangers are everywhere, especially at the border, but they give poorer rates than banks or cambios. Various banks have good ATMs, including Banco Sudameris on Av Monseñor Rodríguez at Curupayty, which changes traveler's checks for a 1% commission.

The post office is at Av de los Pioneros and Oscar Rivas Ortellado, across from the bus terminal. Compacom, at the corner of Av de los Pioneros and Adrián Jara, has telephones and Internet access, though better 'net connections and equipment can be had at Cíber Café, on Pampliega south of Jara, which charges about US$1.50 an hour.

Exchange Tour (☎ 500766) is a full-service travel agency in the Edificio SABA on Nanawa, just off Monseñor Rodríguez. Laverap (☎ 561511), on Pampliega between Adrián Jara and Paí Pérez, will handle your laundry needs.

Drivers speed through town on the through road to the bridge, often ignoring red lights. The downtown area in this border city is best avoided at night, and if you have a vehicle, try to keep it in a secure location.

Places to Stay
Hotel Tía Nancy (☎ 502974, Garcete & Cruz del Chaco) Singles US$8-13, doubles US$10-15. This is a very friendly place opposite the bus terminal. Spotless rooms have white tile

CIUDAD DEL ESTE

PLACES TO STAY
1 Hotel Munich
2 Hotel Austria
6 Convair Hotel
11 Hotel Mi Abuela
20 Nuevo Hotel Cosmopolitán;
   Coffee Pub Cosmopolitán

PLACES TO EAT
4 Arco Iris (Supermarket)
12 New Tokyo
15 Restaurant Oriental
16 Lebanon
17 Taiwan
18 Kokorelia

OTHER
3 Immigration & Customs;
   Tourist Office
5 Compacom (Internet &
   Telephone)
7 Banco Amambay
8 Banco Sudameris
9 Exchange Tour
10 Banco de Asunción (ATM)
13 Ciber Café
14 Citibank (ATM)
19 Laverap
21 Brazilian Consulate

floors and fans; air-con is optional. Laundry service and three meals are available as well, and Nancy will generally mother you.

Hotel Mi Abuela (☎ 500347, Adrián Jara near Av de los Pioneros) Singles/doubles/triples US$8/13/20 with breakfast and air-con. This cozy place has an attractive garden courtyard and is popular with travelers. The air-con is rather decrepit.

Hotel Munich (☎ 500347, Emiliano Fernández & Capitán Miranda) Singles/doubles/triples/quads US$13/16/20/23 with breakfast and air-con. The German-run Munich is a good value. Placid rooms have frígobars, TVs and good views of green hills, and there's parking.

Hotel Austria (☎ 504213, fax 500883, Emiliano Fernández 165) Singles/doubles US$14/19 with breakfast and air-con. This popular and recommended hotel serves a tasty breakfast and has pleasing views from its balcony. Lunch and dinner are available as well.

Convair Hotel (☎ 500342, fax 500857, e convairhotel@compacom.com.py, Adrián Jara near Av de los Pioneros) Singles/doubles/triples US$30/40/50 with breakfast and air-con. This hotel has big rooms with big beds and big TVs, phones, and other amenities.

Nuevo Hotel Cosmopolitan (☎ 511030, fax 511090, Pai Pérez & Pampliega) Singles/doubles US$32/48 with breakfast and air-con. These are actually apartments, very spacious and quiet, each with a kitchen, living room, balcony and cable TV. Two-bedroom units are available as well.

Places to Eat

The pleasant surprise in Ciudad del Este is the variety of Asian food – Japanese, Chinese, and Korean – at reasonable prices.

Restaurant Oriental (no ☎, Adrián Jara s/n) US$1.75-6. The Oriental has Japanese and Chinese food, with a good *agropicante* (hot-and-sour) soup.

PARAGUAY

Taiwan (☎ *510635, Boquerón s/n*) US$1.50-5.25. This clean and friendly restaurant serves Chinese food, of course. It's popular with locals.

New Tokyo (☎ *514379, Pampliega s/n*) US$3.75-12. Relax in the air-con while enjoying the sounds of mahjongg and the tastes of a variety of Japanese dishes here.

Kokorelia (☎ *540649, Av Boquerón 169*) US$4-15. Hankerin' for kim chi, grilled meat or *ramyun* (noodles)? This is the place for such Korean delicacies.

Lebanon (*Adrián Jara & Boquerón*) International and Middle Eastern dishes are served here.

Coffee Pub Cosmopolitan (☎ *511424, Pai Pérez & Pampliega*) US$2.25-5.25. For snacks and sandwiches, try this snazzy place below the New Hotel Cosmopolitan.

Arco Iris (*Av Pioneros del Este at foot of Adrián Jara*) This supermarket is worth a visit even if you're not buying anything. The variety of foodstuffs and household goods, from nori and umeboshi plums to 20 brands of toothbrushes, is staggering.

Getting There & Away

Air Ciudad del Este's Aeropuerto Internacional Guaraní is 30km west of town on Ruta 7.

Arpa (☎ 506030), at Curupayty and Ayala, flies three or four 14-seaters a day to Asunción (US$68-90, 70 minutes) with onward international connections; TAM, in the same office, has one daily flight in a larger plane (US$100, 45 minutes).

There are also major airports at Foz do Iguaçu in Brazil and Puerto Iguazú in Argentina. See those sections in the Northeast Argentina chapter for details of service to Brazil and Buenos Aires.

Bus For information on getting to Foz do Iguaçu and Puerto Iguazú, see Getting Around, below. Numerous buses serve Asunción (almost all stop in Coronel Oviedo on the way) and Encarnación daily. From Foz do Iguaçu there is more Brazilian service (see that section in the Northeast Argentina chapter). The following table shows winter fares. All destinations are served daily, and many several times a day. Travel times are approximate.

Destination	Duration in hours	Cost
Asunción	5	US$5.25
Buenos Aires (Arg)	15-17	US$29-40
Caaguazú	2½	US$2.75
Curitiba (Bra)	10	US$17
Encarnación	4½-6	US$4.50-5.25
Florianópolis (Bra)	14	US$26
Pedro Juan Caballero	8	US$9
Rio de Janeiro (Bra)	23	US$39
São Paulo (Bra)	17	US$29-42
Villarrica	4	US$4

Getting Around

Ciudad del Este's long-distance bus terminal is Cruz del Chaco and Arturo Garcete, 2km south of downtown; take bus No 4 (US$0.40) from Mariscal Estigarribia at the west end of Av Adrián Jara, or a cab for about US$3.

Catch buses for Foz do Iguaçu (US$0.75, 40 minutes) – which leave every 10 minutes Monday to Saturday, and every half hour Sunday and holidays – from the entrance to the bridge over the Paraná after going through Paraguayan immigration. On the other side, unless you're just crossing for the day, you *must* get off to go through Brazilian immigration. Hold on to your ticket, and most following buses will take you to Foz. Direct buses to Puerto Iguazú (US$1.50, 1½ hours), in Argentina, are almost as frequent (and don't require getting processed at Brazilian immigration). Several of the Foz do Iguaçu and Puerto Iguazú buses pass Ciudad del Este's bus terminal via Arturo Garcete before heading to the bridge, but you will still have to get off at Paraguayan immigration.

Combis (vans) line up on Ruta 7 just before immigration and head over the bridge when full. They charge from US$1 to US$5, depending on your destination in Foz (and bargaining skills), and will often drop you at your hotel. The motorcycle taxis that locals use to thread through busy bridge traffic are dangerous and *not* a recommended mode of transport.

AROUND CIUDAD DEL ESTE
Itaipú Dam
With an installed capacity of 12.6 million kilowatts, the binational Itaipú Dam is the world's largest hydroelectric project (at least until China's Three Gorges Dam project is completed). It's also an extraordinary illustration of the ways in which massive development projects have plunged countries like Brazil many billions of dollars into debt without hope of repayment. Paraguay, though, has benefited economically from Itaipú because of the construction boom, its own low domestic demand (in 1997, Itaipú's record 89,237,001 Mwh production was 18 times Paraguay's total domestic consumption), and Brazil's need to purchase the Paraguayan surplus.

Project propaganda omits any reference to the costs of the US$25-billion project, and environmental concerns figured not at all into the Itaipú equation. The dam created a 220m-deep reservoir covering 1350 sq km, which drowned the falls at Sete Quedas, a larger and even more impressive natural feature than Iguazú. Research indicates that the reservoir's stagnant waters have provided new habitat for anopheles mosquitoes, posing an increased malaria risk in an area where the disease had nearly been eradicated.

On both sides of the border, well-rehearsed guides lead tours that stop long enough for visitors to take photographs. On the Paraguayan side, these leave from the Centro de Recepción de Visitas, north of Ciudad del Este near the town of Hernandarias. Hours are 8:30am, 10:30am, 2:30pm and 3:30pm Monday to Saturday; passports are required. There is a documentary film, also available in English-language video format, a half-hour before the tour departs. Most visitors are disappointed, as you're not allowed off the bus and only get to see the low, back side of the dam (granted, it's a lot of concrete). Only engineers on special tours can look at the turbines.

From Ciudad del Este, take any Hernandarias Transtur or Tacurú Pucú bus from the roundabout at the intersection of Av San Blas and Av de los Pioneros. These leave every 10 to 15 minutes throughout the day – ask to be dropped at the entrance to the conspicuous project.

Salto Monday & Monumento Natural Moisés Bertoni
Pity Salto Monday: In most parts of the world, this 80m-high waterfall would be quite a sight, but here, so close to the Iguazú Falls, it seems puny. Still, it's Paraguay's largest since the Sete Quedas were submerged, and the surrounding park (admission US$0.50; open 7am-4pm daily) is green and little visited.

It's just outside the town of Puerto Presidente Franco, 10km from Ciudad del Este, but there is no scheduled public transport directly to the park. Taxis will take you from Ciudad del Este, or you can bus from to Puerto Presidente Franco and walk.

If you're staying in Foz do Iguaçu, you can take an inexpensive tour of the waterfall by land or by boat up the Río Monday. See the Foz Organized Tours section in the Northeast Argentina chapter.

Some of the same tours also go to the Monumento Natural Moisés Bertoni, 25km south of Ciudad del Este. This is a small (200-hectare) unit of rain forest on the Río Paraná preserving the home and library of the Swiss immigrant who situated himself here at the end of the 19th century. Bertoni was a naturalist who conducted decades of meteorological and agricultural studies, the results of which are still used by Paraguayan farmers, who refer to him as 'el sabio Bertoni.'

In the already lush jungle surroundings he planted many kinds of trees from around the world that still flourish. While the jackfruit, yellow mangosteen, avocado, guava, teak and vanilla don't look out of place, the pines, cypress, eucalyptus and huge cactus in the humid *monte* seem very anomalous. The walk in is an adventure, with birds calling, butterflies swirling (including enormous blue morphos), and fruit littering the path. A tiny cemetery holds the remains of the Bertoni family. Tours offered by the Hotel del Rey in Foz do Iguaçu (see Foz do Iguaçu's Organized Tours section in the Northeast Argentina chapter) can include visits to a nearby

Indian village, and an hacienda (with swimming pool), for lunch.

CORONEL OVIEDO

Just north of Ruta 2 midway between Asunción and Ciudad del Este, Coronel Oviedo is a major crossroads in eastern Paraguay; long-distance buses pass through at least every 15 minutes all day. Ruta 3 goes north toward Pedro Juan Caballero (with branches to Salto del Guairá and Concepción), while Ruta 8 heads south to Villarrica, center of an area of German colonization on the Asunción-Encarnación railway. There's no reason to stop here unless you're between buses or badly in need of a rest.

There are a few places to stay on either side of the junction, and many shacks selling food. The best lodging value is tidy *Hotel Yguazú* (☎ 0521-202442, *Av Mariscal Estigarribia & Cruce Internacional*), whose singles/doubles/triples run US$9/13/16 with breakfast and air-con. It's on the highway to Pedro Juan Caballero, just steps north of the junction with Ruta 2.

VILLARRICA

☎ 0541 • pop 44,000

Villarrica is a quiet provincial town, where a person entering a business is likely to shake hands with all present. It is known as one of Paraguay's cultural capitals, due in part to the impressive Franciscan church that dates from colonial times, and in part to the town's three universities, which keep things from getting *too* quiet and infuse the town with a youthful atmosphere. The Cordillera Ybytyruzú is a small mountain range to the east providing some scenic vistas, and several plazas and parks in town (including one with a spring-fed lake and a tethered capybara) make wonderful places to relax.

The nearby village of Yataity is renowned for artisans who produce ao po'i or *lienzo* (loose-weave cotton) garments. The **Fiesta del Ao po'i** takes place there in November.

Villarrica is about 40km south of Coronel Oviedo via paved Ruta 8, which becomes Av Thompson past the plaza, then Av Carlos Antonio López at Bulevar Ayolas.

Hotel Guairá (☎ 42369, *Talavera & Av Mariscal Estigarribia*) Singles/doubles US$6.75/9.25 with fan. Not far from the bus terminal, the modest Guairá is clean and roomy, with decent light and a restaurant.

Hotel Ybytyruzú (☎ 42390, *fax 40844, Carlos Antonio López & Dr Bottrell*) Singles/doubles US$12/18 with fan, US$14/21 with air-con; all include breakfast. This hotel has clean, spacious rooms, but some ground-floor rooms are musty. It tends to book up on weekends. The restaurant serves lunch and dinner.

El Refugio (☎ 43492, *General Díaz 538*) There's no menu but the lasagna, tallarines and other dishes are reasonably priced.

Casa Vieja Among the three or four dance clubs in town, this spot at the north entrance to town is the most likely to have live music.

Frequent buses connect Villarrica with Asunción (US$2.75-5, 2½-4 hours) and Ciudad del Este (US$5, 4 hours); most stop at the Coronel Oviedo junction.

Northern Paraguay

This section covers the country north of Asunción, starting with the river town of Concepción and continuing east to the Brazilian border. This area contains two worthwhile parks and varied landscapes with some impressive geological formations. It also includes a stretch of the Río Paraguay that leads through frontier towns and the wildlife-rich Paraguayan pantanal, even providing a back door into Brazil for the truly adventurous.

The text then shifts west to describe the bulk of northern Paraguay, comprising 60% of the country's territory: the Gran Chaco, where great distances separate tiny settlements. Though much of the Chaco's native vegetation is thorny, the region is green and rich in animal life, with a huge variety of birds in addition to lesser-seen mammals such as anteaters, a peccary species once thought extinct, pumas and the elusive jaguar.

The area also holds the Mennonite colonies, communities carved out of an unforgiving wilderness by settlers seeking religious freedom. There are perhaps 15,000 Mennonites. Among themselves, Mennonites prefer to speak *Plattdeutsch* (Low German) dialect, but most readily speak and understand *Hochdeutsch* (High German), the language of instruction in the schools. Most adults now speak Spanish and a number speak passable English. Local Indians are as likely to speak German as Spanish, although most prefer their native language.

Historically, the Chaco has been the last refuge of indigenous peoples such as the Ayoreo and Nivaclé, who managed an independent subsistence until very recently by hunting, gathering and fishing. Later industries included cattle ranching and extraction of the tannin-rich quebracho. It was the Mennonite colonists, first arriving in 1927, who proved that parts of the Chaco were suitable for more intensive agriculture and permanent settlement.

A glance at the map reveals an inordinate number of Chaco place names that begin with the word 'Fortín'; these were the numerous fortifications and trenches, many of which remain nearly unaltered, from the Chaco War (1932-35) with Bolivia. Most of these sites are abandoned, but small settlements have grown up near a few. The Paraguayan military still retains a visible presence throughout the region.

A network of war-era dirt roads has largely deteriorated since hostilities ended. The Mennonite communities, however, have done an outstanding job of maintaining those roads within their autonomous jurisdiction. Most others are impassable except to 4WD vehicles. Travel in the Chaco can be rough, and accommodations are scarce outside the few main towns; it is possible to camp almost anywhere, but beware of snakes. In a pinch, the estancias or the campesinos along the Trans-Chaco will put you up in a bed with a mosquito net if they have one. Otherwise, you're on your own.

CONCEPCIÓN
☎ 031 • pop 50,000

Concepción is an easygoing city with an abundance of late-19th-century architecture, 300km up the Rio Paraguay from Asunción. Horse-drawn carts haul watermelons and other goods across town from the busy port, and locals gather upriver on the sandy beaches in the late afternoon to swim and play guitars. Although it is connected to the rest of the country by road, the city still looks toward the river, its trade conduit with Brazil. Concepción offers opportunities for sport fishing and is a good jumping-off point for boat travel to Bahía Negra and beyond, into Brazil. It's also a good base for visiting Parque Nacional Serranía San Luis, about 55km to the northeast and home to much wildlife.

The Brazilian vice-consulate (☎ 42655) is at Presidente Franco 972 and is open 8am to 1pm weekdays. The Banco Nacional de Fomento, at the corner of Presidente Franco and Cerro Corá, has an ATM, and Cybercom Internet, on Presidente Franco just west of Nuestra Señora de la Concepción, has good connections for US$2.50 an hour.

The **Museo del Cuartel de la Villa Real** *(no ☎, Carlos Antonio López & Cerro Cordillera; free; open 7am-noon Mon-Fri)* is the restored barracks from which Paraguayan forces marched to launch the War of the Triple Alliance. The bulk of the exhibits consist of Chaco War paraphernalia, and there are some great photos as well as displays about Indian culture. The unrestored section of the barracks to the south is impressive too.

Places to Stay & Eat

Pensión Estrella del Norte (☎ 42400, opposite the port) Singles/doubles with shared bath US$3.25/5.25. It's very basic and the mosquitoes are ferocious, but some rooms have good river views.

Hotel Victoria (☎ 42556, fax 42826, Presidente Franco & Juan Pedro Caballero) US$9.25 per person with fan, US$13.25 per person with air-con & TV; all include breakfast. The Victoria is an aged two-story building with somewhat worn rooms and beds.

Hotel Francés (☎ 42383, fax 425750, Presidente Franco & Carlos Antonio López) Singles/doubles/triples US$25/36/44 with breakfast and air-con. Rooms at this popular and recommended hotel have frígobars and cable TV, and there's secure parking as well as an excellent restaurant. Try the *brocheta de lomito* (beef brochette, US$3.75); it's worth the wait.

El Quincho del Victoria (no ☎, *Presidente Franco & Caballero*) US$1.50-4. This is a lively parrillada with pleasant courtyard seating.

Pollería El Bigote (no ☎, *Presidente Franco & Garay*) US$1. Excellent chicken roasted over wood fires is served here. *Pollería Bulldog*, virtually next door, is as good or better.

Heladería Amistad (*Presidente Franco & Concepción*) is the place for good ice cream and snacks, as well as information on local fishing.

Getting There & Around

Arpa (☎ 42259), with offices at Presidente Franco 973, flies daily to Asunción (US$44), and Vallemí (US$33), and Monday and Friday to Fuerte Olimpo (US$44) and Puerto Casado (US$33), both farther upriver. The airline provides shuttle service to the airport for US$2.75.

Several buses go to the Chaco crossroads of Pozo Colorado (US$4, 1½ hours) and on to Asunción (US$6.75-8, 5½-6½ hours). Ten buses daily serve Pedro Juan Caballero (US$3.75, 4 hours); some continue to Campo Grande, Brazil. Nasa/Golondrina goes to Filadelfia at 7:30am (US$9, 5-6 hours).

The bus terminal is on Garay, eight blocks north of central Presidente Franco. Taxis between the bus station and the center (worth it if you have luggage) cost a little over US$2. The town's lone bus line (US$0.20) describes a circuitous route through town, along Franco at one point, and past the terminal.

PEDRO JUAN CABALLERO
☎ 036 • pop 38,000

This border town is the best place from which to visit Parque Nacional Cerro Corá. Pedro Juan Caballero is capital of the department of Amambay, 214km northeast of Concepción by Ruta 5 and 397km northeast of Coronel Oviedo via Rutas 3 and 5. It blends in to the Brazilian town of Ponta

Porã, the border delimited by a street named Av Internacional on the Brazilian side and Dr Francia on the Paraguayan.

You can cross freely from one side to the other, but before continuing any distance into either country, visit the immigration offices of both in the Aduana building at Naciones Unidas and Dr Francia. Paraguay's facility (☎ 72195) is open 7am to 6pm weekdays, till 3pm Saturday. A sign indicates where to go at other times. The Brazilian office (no ☎) is open 7:30 to 11:30am and 1pm to 5pm weekdays; at other times go to the Federal Police station in Ponta Porã, at Av Presidentes Vargas 70.

The Brazilian consulate is on Mariscal Estigarribia between Mariscal López and CA López, and the Paraguayan consulate in Ponta Porã (☎ 067-724-4934) is at Av Presidentes Vargas 120, open from 8am to noon weekdays.

Exchange houses are numerous, especially around the intersection of Mariscal López and Curupayty, where there is also a Banco del Paraná with ATM. Shopping China, at Julia Estigarribia and Mariscal López, has good Internet connections for a flat US$1.30 an hour (no increments). It's an amazing shopping center packed to the gills with imported food, clothing, alcohol, jewelry and other merchandise; have a look.

Drug traffickers and growers operate with relative impunity on both sides of the border, and their squabbles sometimes erupt into violence that catches innocents in the crossfire. Watch your step and don't piss off anyone.

Places to Stay & Eat

Hotel Guavirá (☎ 72743, *Mariscal López 1325*) Singles US$4 with breakfast. This once-recommended place is being renovated by the new owner; prices may rise.

Hotel La Siesta/Arauá (☎ 73021, *fax 73022, Alberdi & Dr Francia*) US$9-18 per person with breakfast and air-con. This large, clean hotel serves a big breakfast and rents in 24-hour increments; the clock starts when you check in. It is a good value.

Hotel Eiruzú (☎ 72604, *fax 72435, Av Mariscal JF Estigarribia 48*) Singles/doubles/

triples US$21/30/42 with buffet breakfast and air-con. Rooms are large and comfy, with creaking air-con (make sure yours works), frígobars and cable TV. There's a pool, a bar and restaurant (not recom- mended, though the breakfast is good), and private parking.

Hotel Casino Amambay (☎/*fax 72963*, **e** *hcasino@uol.com.br, Rodríguez de Fran- cia 1*) Singles/doubles/triples US$21/30/49

Up the Lazy River

Though conditions are rugged and creature comforts lacking, it's possible to travel the Río Para- guay from Asunción all the way to Bahía Negra in the extreme north of Paraguay, where the river turns northwest into Brazil. These upper reaches abound in wildlife-watching opportunities, and offer an aspect of Paraguay that few outsiders glimpse. Though not officially allowed, it's some- times possible to continue upriver into the Brazilian pantanal.

Between Asunción and Concepción river commerce is lively and the boats witness frequent comings and goings. Above Concepción the pace slackens and you begin to see a lot more wildlife. The farther north you go, the nicer the river gets, and the more chances you will have to see caimans, capybaras, monkeys, and birds galore: jabirú, herons, egrets, spoonbills, even macaws. A pair of binoculars can come in handy, as a lot of the time you are far from either riverbank.

Vallemí, about 150km north of Concepción, is the beginning of the pantanal and Chamacoco Indian territory, and the end of the line for some passenger boats from Asunción, though other boats run between Concepción and Bahía Negra, another 175km or so upriver. It's also a good turn- around point if you need to get back south in a hurry, being a five-hour bus ride to Concepción (in dry weather). Anywhere farther north you will be dependent on catching a boat headed downriver.

A short way upriver from Vallemí is Isla Margarita (called Puerto Esperanza on most maps), where you can disembark and catch a skiff to Porto Murtinho, Brazil, which has bus connections to Corumbá.

Fuerte Olimpo, roughly halfway between Isla Margarita and Bahía Negra, is the only place north of Concepción that you can get a Paraguayan exit stamp in your passport. It's also a nice place to spend a day or three exploring, birdwatching or lazing. The water is much cleaner up this way, and there are some lovely white-sand beaches.

Practical Details At least two boats carry passengers up the Río Paraguay from Asunción to Concepción (US$8, 30 hours) and beyond to Vallemí (US$12, 2½ days). The *Cacique II* leaves Asunción Wednesday morning while the *Guaraní* leaves every other Friday morning. A *camarote* (cabin) sleeping two costs an additional US$6; most passengers sleep either on deck, or in ham- mocks (rentable for US$1 a night) below deck, crammed into hot spaces with an unbelievable as- sortment of cargo ranging from chickens to motorbikes. Two very basic meals are served on board for a small charge, and some snacks are available, but bring your own drinking water (lots) and toilet paper (lots). Departure days can vary; check a day or two before in Asunción at the port, just east of the Aduana (Customs) building at the end of Calle Montevideo.

Unless you're nuts about long boat rides, you'll get more bang for your buck reaching Concep- ción by bus and *then* heading upriver. Boats from Concepción include the *Guaraní* (every other Monday), *Aquidabán* (late Tuesday morning), *Carmenleticia* (Friday morning), and the *Cacique II* (Saturday morning).

The approximate fare from Concepción to Vallemí is US$8, to Fuerte Olimpo US$11, and to Bahía Negra (2½ days) US$15. Camarotes run an additional US$6 per night. For information and tickets for the *Guaraní* and *Carmenleticia* call ☎ 031-4243, or the *Cacique II*, try ☎ 031-42621 (both numbers in Concepción).

with buffet breakfast and air-con. This is the nicest place in town and the best deal. Good rooms have balconies, and there's a huge pool amid private, lush landscaping.

Banana Azul *(☎ 74210, Mariscal López between Julia Estig & José de Martínez)* US$1-1.75. The Banana serves good sandwiches, chicken salad, burgers and fruit drinks with and without alcohol. It's very popular with the young set and faces a lagoon.

Casa Verde *(no ☎, Av Internacional 2564)* On the Brazilian side of the border street, this place dishes up good, healthy vegetarian food by the kilo.

Several **lanchonetes** (small stands) along the border street serve good, cheap food, and the **market** on the southeast side of town offers many Paraguayan dishes.

Getting There & Around

Ten buses daily connect Pedro Juan Caballero with Asunción (US$8-12, 7-8 hours) via Coronel Oviedo (US$6.50-9, 5-6 hours).

There are also 10 buses daily to Concepción (US$3.75, 4 hours), from which it's conceivable to travel downriver to Asunción, and two per day to Ciudad del Este (US$10.75, 8½ hours). Nasa goes daily to Campo Grande, Brazil (US$3.75, 5 hours) and São Paulo (US$31, 16 hours), but there are more bus services to points Brazilian from across the border in Ponta Porã.

Taxis are a good way to get around town; they charge a minimum of US$2.50 and will travel 10km for US$4.

PARQUE NACIONAL CERRO CORÁ

Visitors passing through the area should not skip 22,000-hectare Parque Nacional Cerro Corá, only 40km southwest of Pedro Juan Caballero, which protects an area of dry tropical forest and savanna grasslands in a landscape of steep, isolated hills rising above the central plateau. Besides a representative sample of Paraguayan flora and fauna, the park also has cultural and historical landmarks, including pre-Columbian caves and petroglyphs, and was the site of Francisco Solano López's death at the end of the War of the Triple Alliance. A *sendero histórico*

(historical trail) has busts of figures from the war ending at the creek by which López died, and where Eliza Lynch, according to the story, dug his grave with her hands.

The park *(☎ 036-72069, vehicle entrance open 8am-5pm)* has nature trails, a **camping area** (bring insect repellent, and watch out for the bats in the bathrooms). There is also a small visitor center/museum with a very curious monkey, where visitors who phone ahead can bunk for free.

Buses running between Concepción and Pedro Juan Caballero (50 minutes; US$0.80) will stop at the park entrance; walk just under 1km to the visitor center. The helpful staff can tell you the bus schedule for your return trip.

POZO COLORADO

Pozo Colorado is 270km northwest of Asunción and 144km east of Concepción. It has nothing of interest, but is the only major crossroads in the entire Chaco, and an important immigration post. Ruta 9, usually known as the Ruta Trans-Chaco, passes through on its way north from Asunción to the Bolivian border, and Ruta 5 runs east to Concepción and beyond to the Brazilian border at Pedro Juan Caballero.

There's a military checkpoint here and Pozo is currently the only place besides Asunción for Bolivia-bound travelers to get the vitally important exit stamps in their passports. The immigration post may (and, by all logic, should) move northward, perhaps to just south of Mariscal Estigarribia, but don't rely on your bus driver to inform you. Many a traveler has been turned back at the border for lack of a stamp, so inquire here or at the immigration office in Asunción.

Parador Pozo Colorado *(☎ 093516, Ruta Trans-Chaco Km 270)* US$5.25 per bed with fan. This place at the 24-hour Shell station has two modest rooms and plans to expand. It serves meals and is a good source of information on buses and immigration procedures.

Buses from Concepción to Asunción pass through Pozo Colorado regularly throughout the day until at least 3pm, as do buses to the Mennonite settlement of Filadelfia; some serve the other settlements of Loma Plata and Neu-Halbstadt.

PARAGUAY

CRUCE LOS PIONEROS

A traditional stopping place on the Trans-Chaco, also known as Cruce Loma Plata, this tiny town 19km south of the turnoff for Filadelfia has a rural supermarket and a *parador* (state-run hotel), as well as a good hotel.

Hotel Cruce de los Pioneros (☎ 091-2170, *Trans-Chaco Km 415*) Singles/doubles with breakfast US$20/23 with private bath and air-con; US$6.50 per person with fan and shared bath; all with breakfast. The hotel has very good accommodations and a restaurant, and the owner will organize trips into the Chaco interior.

FILADELFIA
☎ 091

Filadelfia is the administrative and service center for the Mennonite farmers of Fernheim colony. It is the most visited of the three colonies, and has the most reasonable accommodations and outgoing people. In some ways it resembles the cattle towns of the Australian outback or the American West, but dairy products and cotton are the primary products rather than beef. Just as Aboriginal people work Australia's cattle stations, so Nivaclé, Lengua, Ayoreo, and other indigenous people work the Mennonite farms. The controversial New Tribes Mission, an evangelical group not related to the Mennonites, maintains an office in town.

Filadelfia is still a religious community and shuts down almost completely on Sunday. On weekday mornings, you will see Mennonite farmers drive to town in their pickup trucks in search of Indians for day labor, returning with them in the afternoon. Most businesses in town close at 11:30am, as Mennonites have adopted the custom of the siesta in this hot land.

The Mennonite Colonies

Mennonites are Anabaptists, believing in adult rather than infant baptism. This might sound harmless enough today, but in 16th-century Holland and Switzerland it caused serious trouble with both Catholics and other Protestants. As pacifists, the Mennonites also believed in separation of church and state and rejected compulsory military service, making their situation even worse and leading them to flee to Germany, Russia and Canada. By the early 20th century, political upheaval once again caused them to seek new homes, this time in Latin America. Their primary destinations were Mexico and Paraguay.

For Mennonites, Paraguay's attractions were large extents of nearly uninhabited land, where they could follow their traditional agricultural way of life, and the government's willingness to grant them political autonomy under a Privilegium: They were responsible for their own schools (with German-language instruction) and community law enforcement, and enjoyed separate economic organization, freedom from taxation, religious liberty and exemption from military service. The first group to arrive in Paraguay, in 1927, were the Sommerfelder (Summerfield) Mennonites from the Canadian prairies, who left after Canadian authorities failed to live up to their promise of exemption from military service. These Sommerfelder formed Menno colony, the first of three distinct but territorially overlapping Mennonite groups. Centered around the town of Loma Plata, it is still the most conservative and traditional of the colonies.

Only a few years after the founding of Menno colony, refugees from the Soviet Union established Fernheim (Distant Home), with its 'capital' at Filadelfia. Neuland (New Land) was founded in 1947 by Ukrainian-German Mennonites, many of whom had served unwillingly in the German army in WWII and had managed to stay in the west after being released from prisoner-of-war camps. Its largest settlement is Neu-Halbstadt.

In 1932, Paraguayan and Bolivian tensions erupted into open warfare, with Mennonite settlements the scene of ground fighting and even Bolivian air attacks. During the war, nomadic Indians,

Orientation

Filadelfia is some 450km northwest of Asunción via the Trans-Chaco. The town itself lies about 20km north of the highway, on a spur whose pavement ends roughly 1km south of town.

Filadelfia's dusty, unpaved streets form an orderly grid. The *Hauptstrasse* (main street) is north-south Hindenburg, named for the German general and president whose government helped the Fernheim refugees escape the Soviet Union. The other main street, on the north side of town, is Trébol. It leads east to Loma Plata, the center of Menno colony, and west to the Trans-Chaco and Fortín Toledo. Nearly every important public service is on or near Hindenburg.

Information

Filadelfia has no formal tourist office, but the Hotel Florida shows a video on the Mennonite colonies. Change cash or traveler's checks, at good rates with no commission and no receipt required, at the Financiera Cooperativa, near the corner of Unruh and Hindenburg. Antelco is next door, and the post office next to it, on the corner. Expensive (US$0.10 a minute) and often slow Internet access is offered at Automax Internet Café on Av Trébol 110E, just east of Hindenburg. Filadelfia's modern hospital (☎ 2851) is at Hindenburg and Trébol.

Museo Unger

This well-arranged museum *(Hindenburg & Unruh; free; open 7am-11:30am Mon-Sat)* tells the story of Fernheim colony from its foundation in 1930 to the present, and contains ethnographic materials on the Chaco Indians. Hartmut Wohlgemuth, manager of the Florida, provides guided tours in Spanish or German when his schedule

The Mennonite Colonies

who felt allegiance to neither country, were targets for both the Bolivians and Paraguayans. Some found refuge with the Mennonites, but others so strongly resented the Mennonite intrusion that they resisted violently. As late as the 1940s, Ayoreo hunter-gatherers attacked and killed members of a Mennonite family in the northwestern Chaco, although it is not clear who was at fault.

Such extreme cases were unusual, but more than a few Indians thought the Mennonites invaders and did not hesitate to let their cattle graze on Mennonite crops. From motives that were both religious and expedient, Mennonites encouraged the Indians to become settled cultivators, following their own example. But the Mennonites also distanced themselves from the Indians; those who adopted the Mennonite religion were encouraged to form their own church and to integrate more closely into Paraguayan rather than Mennonite society. Over time, many Lengua and Nivaclé (Chulupí) Indians became seasonal laborers on Mennonite farms. This opportunistic exploitation and some Mennonites' patronizing attitude alienated many Indians whose cultural system was more egalitarian and reciprocal. There is no doubting the sincerity of the Mennonites' Christian convictions and their pacifism, but as one member of the community said, 'Not all of us live up to our ideals.'

As more Paraguayans settle in the Chaco, the Mennonite communities have come under pressure from authorities, and there is concern that the government may abrogate the Privilegium. Few Mennonites are reinvesting their earnings in Paraguay, and some are openly looking for alternatives elsewhere. On the other hand, the election of a Mennonite governor of the department of Boquerón, whose capital is Filadelfia, perhaps indicates a desire to participate more directly in a wider Paraguayan context.

Some Mennonites are disgruntled, however, with developments in Filadelfia, where material prosperity has contributed to a generation more interested in motorbikes and videos than traditional Mennonite values. Beer and tobacco, once absolutely *verboten* in Mennonite settlements, are now sold openly, although only non-Mennonites would normally consume them in public.

PARAGUAY

permits, and may lend you the key outside of regular hours.

Places to Stay & Eat

Camping is free at shady *Parque Trébol*, 5km east of Filadelfia, but there is no water and you may have to share the single pit toilet with highly venomous (but timid) coral snakes.

Hotel Florida (*☎/fax 2151, Hindenburg between Unruh & Trébol*) Singles/doubles/ triples from US$6.50/11/16 with shared bath and fan to US$30/40/50 with private bath, breakfast and air-con. The grounds are well-planted, with a large swimming pool and a very decent *restaurant*, and there's laundry service available. Motel-style double rooms have air-con. Try for the small building outside, which has comfortable beds, cold showers and fans (breakfast for annexers is an extra US$2.75).

Hotel Safari (*☎/fax 2218, Av Industrial 149-E*) Singles/doubles US$24/32 with air-con. This hotel has large, pleasant rooms with TVs, a small pool and a friendly manager who speaks Spanish, German and English.

Several *shops* along Hindenburg offer snacks and homemade ice cream. For meals, try the *parrillada* at *La Estrella* (*no ☎, Unruh 126-E*), just east of Hindenburg; it has a shady outdoor dining area.

Churrasquería Girasol (*☎ 2078, Unruh 126-E*) US$4.50 lunch, US$5 dinner. Across the street from La Estrella, Girasol has gone the Brazilian all-you-can-eat route, with plenty of meat and a salad bar to boot.

The modern *Cooperativa Mennonita* supermarket stocks excellent local peanut butter and dairy products, and a homemade Mennonite variation of kim chi (pickled white cabbage with garlic, spices and hot red peppers), as well as a huge variety of imported groceries and other products.

Shopping

Librería El Mensajero (*☎ 2354, Hindenburg between Unruh & Trébol*) This evangelical bookstore, next door to the Hotel Florida, also offers a selection of Chaco Indian crafts.

Getting There & Around

Nasa and Golondrina, on Chaco Boreal near the corner of Miller, have three to four services a day to and from Asunción (US$10, 5-6 hours) weekdays, and at least one each Saturday and Sunday. They also run a bus at 10:30am to Concepción (US$9- 5-6 hours) Monday to Saturday.

Stel Turismo, on the east side of Hindenburg two doors north of Av Industrial, also connects Filadelfia with Asunción. Note that although their buses to Bolivia stop in Filadelfia, at the time of research you could not get the required passport stamp to leave Paraguay anywhere but Asunción or Pozo Colorado, making it useless to try to make the trip from Filadelfia across the border.

A local bus connects Filadelfia with Loma Plata (25km) 7:30am and 10pm daily (timed to meet arriving buses from Asunción).

Hitching or asking for a lift is worth a try if you plan to go anywhere else, like Fortín Toledo or Loma Plata, at odd hours.

DIPAR (*☎ 2450*), on Chaco Boreal between Hindenburg and Miller, rents air-conditioned cars for US$55 per day with 100km included, but they may be used only within the Mennonite colonies. For travel to outlying areas, such as the Iguazú Falls and Parque Nacional Defensores del Chaco, they can sometimes arrange chauffeured vehicles.

FORTÍN TOLEDO

About 40km west of Filadelfia, Fortín Toledo saw extended trench warfare during the Chaco conflict. It is now home to the **Proyecto Taguá**, a small reserve nurturing a population of the Chaco, or Wagner's, peccary, thought for nearly half a century to be extinct, until its rediscovery in a remote area in 1975. The current project manager is Juan Campos – he welcome visits if his schedule permits.

The peccaries are confined within a large fenced and forested area with a large pond, which attracts many Chaco birds. Nearby you can visit the fortifications of Fortín Toledo, some of which are still in excellent repair, and a Paraguayan military cemetery. Try to imagine yourself in the dusty or muddy trenches, awaiting the charge of the Bolivians.

To get to Fortín Toledo from Filadelfia, hitch or take a bus (such as the Nasa bus to Mariscal Estigarribia) out Trébol to the intersection with the Trans-Chaco. From there, cross the highway and continue about 3km to an enormous tire on which are painted the words 'pasar prohibido.' Continue on the main road another 7km, passing several buildings of an old estancia, before taking a sharp right that leads to a sign reading 'Proyecto Taguá' (if walking, avoid the midday heat). You may be able to hitch this segment as well.

LOMA PLATA

Loma Plata, 25km east of Filadelfia, is the administrative and service center of Menno colony, the oldest and most traditional of the Mennonite settlements. It has an excellent **museum** *(free; open 7am-11:30am & 2pm-6pm Mon-Fri, 7am-11:30am Sat)* with an outdoor exhibit of early farming equipment and a typical pioneer house plus an outstanding photographic exhibit on the colony's history. Ask for the key at the small tourist office (☎ 0918-2301) next door, where Sr Wiebe Wiebe can also arrange free tours of the Mennonite cooperative's palo santo oil-extraction plant and other facilities when possible.

Hotel El Algarrobo (☎ 0918-2353, Loma Plata) Singles/doubles/triples US$15/20/31 with breakfast and air-con. This newish hotel is 1km east of town. The owners are friendly but their Spanish and German are limited. They can direct you to other lodging if they're full up.

Restaurants include *Amambay* (a popular local hangout) and *Chaco's*, an excellent Brazilian *churrascaria* (think parrilla).

Very few buses from Asunción serve Loma Plata directly. See Filadelfia Getting There & Around details on the local bus.

NEU-HALBSTADT

Founded in 1947 by Ukrainian-German Mennonites, 33km south of Filadelfia, the service center of Neuland colony is named Neu-Halbstadt, but most people (and road signs) simply refer to it as Neuland.

There's a *campground* north of Fortín Toledo. *Hotel Boquerón (☎ 0951-311, Av Neu-Halbstadt s/n)* Singles/doubles US$13/21 with breakfast and air-con. The air-con is good, but mattresses are overstuffed. It has a decent *restaurant* with main courses from US$1.75-4.

Fortín Boquerón, 15km to the south, preserves a sample of Chaco War trenches. South of Neuland are the largest Indian reserves, where many Lengua and Nivaclé have settled with the assistance of the Asociación del Servicio de Cooperación Indígena Menonita (ASCIM) to become farmers. Neu-Halbstadt is a good place to obtain Indian handicrafts, including bags and hammocks, and woven goods, including belts and blankets colored with natural dyes.

Several buses that run from Asunción to Filadelfia continue to Neuland, while others come directly from Asunción.

MARISCAL ESTIGARRIBIA

This is where the pavement ends; the last sizeable settlement on the Trans-Chaco before the Bolivian border. Mariscal Estigarribia is 540km from Asunción and has a military base, a hotel, stores, a gas station and places to eat; motorists should bear in mind that there is no dependable source of gasoline beyond here, so be sure to fill up and carry extra gas, food and water. Buses for Bolivia used to pass through here regularly, and may once again if plans to pave the last stretch of the Trans-Chaco ever pan out. Now they only come if the new route is in worse shape than the old, or to wait out really bad conditions. The new route, Picada 500, takes off to the west at a customs checkpoint about 17km south of town and makes a beeline for the border.

Hotel Francés (☎ 0952-358) Singles/ doubles US$4/6. There is also a restaurant at this hotel just around the highway bend at the north side of town, not far from the base.

Nasa runs daily buses to Asunción at 10am and 8pm weekdays, 10am on Saturday and at 6pm on Sunday (US$11, 11 hours).

PARQUE NACIONAL DEFENSORES DEL CHACO

The High Chaco park of Defensores del Chaco is Paraguay's largest (780,000 hectares) and most remote unit. Once the exclusive province of nomadic Ayoreo foragers, it is mostly a forested alluvial plain about 100m in elevation, but the isolated 500m peak of Cerro León is the park's greatest landmark.

Quebracho, algarrobo, palo santo, and cactus are the dominant species in the dense thorn forest, which harbors populations of important animal species despite illicit hunting, which has proved difficult to control over such a large, thinly populated area. This is the likeliest place in Paraguay to view large cats such as jaguar, puma, ocelot, and Geoffroy's cat, plus other unique species, although, as everywhere, such species are only rarely seen.

Defensores del Chaco is 830km from Asunción over roads that are impassable to most ordinary vehicles, especially after rain. Park headquarters are reached by a road north from Filadelfia to Fortín Teniente Martínez and then to Fortín Madrejón, another 213km north. Further facilities are at Aguas Dulces, 84km beyond Madrejón.

As there is no regular public transportation to Defensores del Chaco, access is difficult, but not impossible. Ecoturismo Boquerón in Loma Plata does tours of the northern Chaco and Defensores; see also the DIPAR entry in Filadelfia's Getting There & Around section, and the Useful Organizations section earlier in this chapter. The Dirección General de Protección y Conservación de la Biodiversidad (☎ 021-615812) in Asunción may be able to put you in contact with rangers who must occasionally travel to Asunción. They will sometimes, if space is available, take passengers on the return trip. Getting away may present some difficulty, but have patience – you are unlikely to be stranded forever.

Language

In addition to flamboyance, an Italian-accented Spanish pronunciation and other language quirks readily identify an Argentine elsewhere in Latin America or abroad. The most prominent particularities are the usage of the pronoun *vos* in place of *tú* for 'you,' and the trait of pronouncing the letters 'll' and 'y' as 'zh' (as in 'azure') rather than 'y' (like English 'you') as in the rest of the Americas. Note that in American Spanish, the plural of the familiar 'tú' or 'vos' is *ustedes*, not *vosotros*, as in Spain.

There are many vocabulary differences between European and American Spanish, and among Spanish-speaking countries in the Americas. The speech of Buenos Aires, in particular, abounds with words and phrases from the colorful slang known as *lunfardo*. Although you shouldn't use lunfardo words unless you are supremely confident that you know their *every* implication (especially in formal situations), you should be aware of some of the more common everyday usages (see Lunfardo in the Buenos Aires chapter). Argentines normally refer to the Spanish language as *castellano* rather than *español*.

Every visitor should make an effort to speak Spanish, whose basic elements are easily acquired. If possible, take a brief night course at your local university or community college before departure. Even if you can't speak very well, Argentines are gracious folk and will encourage your use of Spanish, so there is no need to feel self-conscious about vocabulary or pronunciation. There are many common cognates, so if you're stuck, try Hispanicizing an English word – it is unlikely you'll make a truly embarrassing error. Do not, however, admit to being *embarazada* unless you are in fact pregnant. (See Cognates & Condoms for other usages to avoid.)

Phrasebooks & Dictionaries

Lonely Planet's *Latin American Spanish phrasebook* is not only amusing but can also get you by in many adventurous situations. Another exceptionally useful language resource is the *University of Chicago Spanish-English, English-Spanish Dictionary*. Its small size, light weight and thorough entries make it perfect for travel.

Pronunciation

Spanish pronunciation is, in general, consistently phonetic. Until you become confident of your ability, speak slowly to avoid getting tongue-tied.

Vowels Vowels are very consistent and have easy English equivalents; see also Dipthongs, later.

a is like 'a' in 'father'
e is like 'ai' in 'sail'
i is like 'ee' in 'feet'
o is like 'o' in 'for'
u is like 'oo' in 'food'; it is silent after 'q' and in the groups 'gue' and 'gui,' unless modified by a diaresis, as in *Güemes*, when it is pronounced 'w'
y is a consonant except when it stands alone or appears at the end of a word, in which case its pronunciation is identical to the Spanish 'i'

Consonants Spanish consonants resemble their English equivalents, with some major exceptions. Pronunciation of the letters **f, k, l, m, n, p, q, s** and **t** is virtually identical to English.

Although **y** is identical in most Latin American countries when used as a consonant, most Argentines say 'zh' for it and for **ll**, which is a separate letter.

Ch and **ñ** are also separate letters, with separate dictionary entries.

b resembles its English equivalent but is almost undistinguishable from 'v'. For clarity, refer to the former as 'b larga', the latter as 'v corta' (the word for either letter itself is pronounced like English 'bay').

Rolling Rs – A Practice

Speaking Argentine *castellano* involves rolling your tongue in a way many foreigners, even those who have learned to speak Spanish fluently, can't do. Try this neat little phrase to get the train steaming along. Have a helpful *porteño* standing nearby who can guide you.

> R con R guitarra
> R con R carril
> Miran que rápido ruedan las ruedas cargadas de azúcar del ferrocarril.

c is like the 's' in 'see' before 'e' and 'i,' otherwise like English 'k'

d closely resembles 'th' in 'feather'

g is like a guttural English 'h' before Spanish 'e' and 'i,' otherwise like 'g' in 'go'

h is invariably silent. If your name begins with this letter, listen carefully when immigration officials summon you to pick up your passport

j most closely resembles the English 'h' but is slightly more guttural

ñ is like 'ni' in 'onion'

r is nearly identical to English except at the beginning of a word, when it is often rolled

rr is very strongly rolled

v resembles English, but see 'b,' earlier

x is like 'x' in 'taxi' except for very few words for which it follows Spanish or Mexican usage as 'j'

z is like 's' in 'sun'

Diphthongs Diphthongs are vowel combinations forming a single syllable. In Spanish, the formation of a diphthong depends on combinations of 'weak' vowels ('i' and 'u') or strong ones ('a,' 'e,' and 'o'). Two weak vowels or a strong and a weak vowel make a diphthong, but two strong ones are pronounced as separate syllables.

A good example of two weak vowels forming a diphthong is the word *diurno* (during the day). The final syllable of *obligatorio* (obligatory) is a combination of weak and strong vowels.

Stress Stress, often indicated by visible accents, is very important, since it can change the meaning of words. In general, words ending in vowels or the letters **n** or **s** have stress on the next-to-last syllable, while those with other endings have stress on the last syllable. Thus *vaca* (cow) and *caballos* (horses) both have accents on their next-to-last syllables.

Written accents will almost always appear in words that do not follow the above rules, such as *sótano* (basement), *América* and *porción* (portion). When a word appears in capitals, the written accent is generally omitted but still pronounced.

Greetings & Civilities

In their public behavior, Argentines may be very conscious of civilities, sometimes to the point of ceremoniousness. Never, for example, approach a stranger for information without extending a greeting like *buenos días* or *buenas tardes*.

Yes.	*Sí.*
No.	*No.*
Please.	*Por favor.*
Thank you.	*Gracias.*
You're welcome.	*De nada.*
Hello.	*¡Hola!*
Good morning.	*Buenos días.*
Good afternoon.	*Buenas tardes.*
Good evening.	*Buenas noches.*
Good night.	*Buenas noches.*
Goodbye.	*Chau* (informal)/*Adios.*

I understand.	*Entiendo.*
I don't understand.	*No entiendo.*

I don't speak much Spanish.
  Hablo poco castellano.

Excuse me	Con permiso
I'm sorry	Perdón

Useful Words & Phrases

and	*y*
to/at	*a*
for	*por, para*

of/from	*de, desde*	Do you speak English?	
in/inside	*en/adentro*	*¿Habla Usted inglés?*	
with/without	*con/sin*		
before/after	*antes/después*	Speak slowly, please.	*Despacio, por favor.*
now/later	*ahora/más tarde*		
soon	*pronto*	**Getting Around**	
already	*ya*	airplane	*avión*
right away	*en seguida*	train	*tren*
here/there	*aquí/allí*	bus	*colectivo, micro,*
large/small	*grande/chico*		*omnibus*
good/bad	*bueno/malo*	ship	*barco, buque*
Where?	*¿Dónde?*	ferry	*barca de pasaje*
Where is/are … ?	*¿Dónde está/están …?*	hydrofoil	*aliscafo*
When?	*¿Cuándo?*	car	*auto*
How?	*¿Cómo?*	taxi	*taxi*
		truck	*camión*
I would like …	*Me gustaría …*	pick-up	*camioneta*
coffee	*café*	bicycle	*bicicleta*
tea	*té*	motorcycle	*motocicleta*
beer	*cerveza*	hitchhike	*hacer dedo*
wine	*vino*		

I would like a ticket to …
    Quiero un boleto/pasaje a …

How much?	*¿Cuánto?*
How many?	*¿Cuántos?*
Is/Are there … ?	*¿Hay … ?*

What's the fare to … ?
    ¿Cuanto cuesta el pasaje a … ?

Cognates & Condoms

False cognates are words that appear to be very similar but have different meanings in different languages. In some instances, these differences can lead to serious misunderstandings. The following is a list of some of these words in English with their Spanish cousins and their meaning in Spanish. Note that this list deals primarily with the Río de la Plata region, and usages may differ elsewhere in South America. Also, be careful with some words from Spain, like *'coger,'* which in Mexico and South America doesn't mean 'to get or catch' but 'to fuck.' It will take only one instance of being laughed at for claiming you need to fuck the bus before you quickly learn what to really say.

English	Spanish	Meaning in Spanish
actual	*actual*	current (at present)
carpet	*carpeta*	looseleaf notebook
embarrassed	*embarazada*	pregnant
fabric	*fábrica*	factory
to introduce	*introducir*	to introduce (as an innovation)
notorious	*notorio*	well known, evident
to present	*presentar*	to introduce (a person)
precise	*preciso*	necessary
preservative	*preservativo*	condom
sensible	*sensible*	sensitive
violation	*violación*	rape

When does the next bus leave for … ?
¿Cuando sale el próximo omnibus para …?
Is there a student/university discount?
¿Hay descuento estudiantil/universitario?
Do you accept credit cards?
¿Trabajan con tarjetas de crédito?

first/last/next
primero/último/próximo
first/second class
primera/segunda clase

single/roundtrip	*ida/ida y vuelta*
sleeper	*camarote*

luggage storage
guardería de equipaje

Accommodations

Below you will find English phrases with useful Spanish equivalents for Argentina.

hotel	*hotel, pensión, residencial, hospedaje*
single room	*habitación para una persona*
double room	*habitación doble, matrimonial*

How much does it cost?
¿Cuanto cuesta?

May I see it?	*¿Puedo verla?*
I don't like it.	*No me gusta.*
per night	*por noche*
full board	*pensión completa*
shared bath	*baño compartido*
private bath	*baño privado*
too expensive	*demasiado caro*
discount	*descuento*
cheaper	*mas económico*
the bill	*la cuenta*

Around Town

tourist information	*oficina de turismo*
airport	*aeropuerto*
train station	*estación de ferrocarril*
bus terminal	*terminal de ómnibus*
bathing resort	*balneario*
post office	*correo*
telephone office	*locutorio*
letter	*carta*

parcel	*paquete*
postcard	*postal*
airmail	*correo aéreo*
registered mail	*certificado*
express mail	*puerta a puerta*
stamps	*estampillas*
person to person	*persona a persona*
collect call	*cobro revertido*

Toilets

The most common word for toilet is *baño*, but *servicios sanitarios* (services) is a frequent alternative. Men's toilets usually bear a descriptive term like *hombres*, *caballeros* or *varones*. Women's restrooms have a *señoras* or *damas* sign.

Countries

The list below contains only countries whose spelling differs significantly in English and Spanish.

Denmark	*Dinamarca*
England	*Inglaterra*
Germany	*Alemania*
Great Britain	*Gran Bretaña*
Ireland	*Irlanda*
Japan	*Japón*
Netherlands	*Holanda*
New Zealand	*Nueva Zelandia*
Scotland	*Escocia*
Spain	*España*
Sweden	*Suecia*
Switzerland	*Suiza*
United States	*Estados Unidos*
Wales	*Gales*

Numbers

Should hyperinflation return, you may have to learn to count in very large numbers.

0	*cero*
1	*uno*
2	*dos*
3	*tres*
4	*cuatro*
5	*cinco*
6	*seis*
7	*siete*
8	*ocho*
9	*nueve*

El Voseo

Spanish in the Río de la Plata region differs from that of Spain and the rest of the Americas, most notably in the familiar form of the second person singular pronoun. Instead of the *tuteo* used everywhere else, Argentines, Uruguayans and Paraguayans commonly use the *voseo*, a relict 16th-century form requiring slightly different endings. Regular and most irregular verbs differ from *tú* forms; regular verbs change their stress and add an accent, while irregular verbs do not change internal consonants, but add a terminal accent. This is true for -ar, -er and -ir verbs, examples of which are given below, with the *tú* forms included for contrast. Imperative forms also differ, but negative imperatives are identical in both the tuteo and the voseo.

In the list below, the first verb of each ending is regular, while the second is irregular; the pronoun is included for clarity, though most Spanish-speakers normally omit it.

Verb	Tuteo/Imperative	Voseo/Imperative
hablar (to speak)	*tú hablas/habla*	*vos hablás/hablá*
soñar (to dream)	*tú sueñas/sueña*	*vos soñás/soñá*
comer (to eat)	*tú comes/come*	*vos comés/comé*
poner (to put)	*tú pones/pon*	*vos ponés/poné*
admitir (to admit)	*tú admites/admite*	*vos admitís/admití*
venir (to come)	*tú vienes/ven*	*vos venís/vení*

Note that some of the most common verbs, like *ir* (to go), *estar* (to be) and *ser* (to be) are identically irregular in both the tuteo and the voseo, and that Argentines continue to use the possessive article *tu* (*Vos tenés tu lápiz?*) and the reflexive or conjunctive object pronoun *te* (*Vos te das cuenta?*).

An Argentine inviting a foreigner to address him or her informally will say *Me podés tutear* (you can call me *tú*) rather than *Me podés vosear* (you can call me *vos*), even though the expectation is that both will use *vos* forms in subsequent conversation.

10	*diez*	90	*noventa*
11	*once*	100	*cien*
12	*doce*	101	*ciento uno*
13	*trece*	110	*ciento diez*
14	*catorce*	120	*ciento veinte*
15	*quince*	200	*doscientos*
16	*dieciséis*	300	*trescientos*
17	*diecisiete*	400	*cuatrocientos*
18	*dieciocho*	500	*quinientos*
19	*diecinueve*	600	*seiscientos*
20	*veinte*	700	*setecientos*
21	*veintiuno*	800	*ochocientos*
22	*veintidós*	900	*novecientos*
30	*treinta*	1000	*mil*
31	*treinta y uno*	1100	*mil cien*
32	*treinta y dos*	2000	*dos mil*
40	*cuarenta*	5000	*cinco mil*
50	*cincuenta*	10,000	*diez mil*
60	*sesenta*	50,000	*cincuenta mil*
70	*setenta*	100,000	*cien mil*
80	*ochenta*	1,000,000	*un millón*

Days of the Week

Monday   *lunes*
Tuesday   *martes*
Wednesday   *miércoles*
Thursday   *jueves*
Friday   *viernes*
Saturday   *sábado*
Sunday   *domingo*

Months of the Year

January   *enero*
February   *febrero*
March   *marzo*
April   *abril*
May   *mayo*
June   *junio*
July   *julio*
August   *agosto*
September   *se(p)tiembre*
October   *octubre*
November   *noviembre*
December   *diciembre*

Time

Telling time is fairly straightforward. Eight o'clock is *las ocho*, while 8:30 is *las ocho y treinta* (literally, eight and thirty) or *las ocho y media* (eight and a half). However, 7:45 is *las ocho menos quince* (literally, eight minus fifteen) or *las ocho menos cuarto* (eight minus one quarter). Times are modified by *de la mañana* (morning) or *de la tarde* (afternoon) instead of am or pm. Noon is *mediodía*; midnight is *medianoche*. Transportation schedules commonly use the 24-hour clock.

Glossary

ACA – Automóvil Club Argentino, which provides maps, road service, insurance and other services, and operates hotels and campgrounds throughout the country; a valuable resource even for travelers without motor vehicles

acequia – irrigation canal, primarily seen in the Mendoza area

aerosilla – chairlift

alameda – tree-lined street

albergue juvenil – youth hostel

albergue transitorio – not to be mistaken for an *albergue juvenil*, this is a love hotel; the Uruguayan euphemism is *hotel de alta rotatividad*

alerce – large coniferous tree, resembling a California redwood, from which Argentina's Parque Nacional Los Alerces takes its name

alfajor – a sweet snack made with two flat, soft cookies often filled with *dulce de leche* and covered in chocolate or meringue

alíscafo – hydrofoil from Buenos Aires across the Río de la Plata to Colonia, Uruguay

altiplano – high Andean plain, often above 4000m, in the northwestern Argentine provinces of Jujuy, Salta, La Rioja and Catamarca

ananá – pineapple

apunamiento – altitude sickness

argentinidad – a concept of Argentine national identity, may be associated with extreme nationalistic feelings

arrayán – tree of the myrtle family, from which Argentina's Parque Nacional Los Arrayanes takes its name

arroyo – creek, stream

asado – the famous Argentine barbecue, often a family gathering in summer

autopista – freeway or motorway

bache – pothole in a road or highway

balneario – any swimming or bathing area, including beach resorts, river beaches and swimming holes

balsa – a launch or raft

bandoneón – an accordion-like instrument used in tango music

bañado – marsh or other seasonally flooded zone on the rivers of northern Argentina; they are good habitat for migratory birds, but are also often used for temporary cultivation.

bárbaro – slang term meaning 'wonderful' or 'great'

barras bravas – violent soccer fans; the Argentine equivalent of Britain's 'football hooligans'

barrio – neighborhood or borough

bencina – white gas, used for camp stoves; also known as *nafta blanca*

bicho – any small creature, from insect to mammal

biota – the fauna and flora of a region

boga – tasty river fish common in Argentina

boleadoras – weighted, leather-covered balls attached to a length of thin rope, historically used as a hunting weapon by gauchos and some of Argentina's indigenous peoples; thrown at a guanaco or rhea's legs, they entangle the animal and bring it down; also called *bolas*

boliche – nightclub

bombachas – a gaucho's baggy pants; can also mean women's underwear

bronca – anger, frustration; a very *porteño* term

cabalgatas – organized horseback rides

cabildo – colonial town council; also, the building that housed the council

cachila – in Uruguay, an antique automobile, often beautifully maintained

cacique – Indian chief

cajero automático – an automated teller machine (ATM)

caldén – a tree characteristic of the Dry Pampa

cambio – money-exchange office, also a *casa de cambio*

campo – the countryside; alternately, a field or paddock

candombe – In Uruguay, Afro-Uruguayan dance and music

caña – strong, usually cheap, liquor made from sugar cane

caracoles – winding roads, usually in a mountainous area

característica – telephone area code

carne – though this is the general word for meat, in Argentina it is used specifically for beef; chicken, pork and the like may be called *carne blanca* (white meat)

carpincho – capybara, a large (but cute) aquatic rodent that inhabits the Paraná and other subtropical rivers

cartelera – an office selling discount tickets

casa de cambio – money-exchange office, often shortened to *cambio*

casa de familia – modest family accommodations, usually in tourist centers

casa de gobierno – literally 'government house,' a building now often converted to a museum, offices, etc

casco – 'big house' of a livestock *estancia*

castellano – the term used in much of South America for the Spanish language spoken throughout Latin America; literally refers to Castilian Spanish

catarata – waterfall

caudillo – in 19th-century Argentine politics, a provincial strongman whose power rested more on personal loyalty than political ideals or party affiliation

cerro – hill, mountain

chachacoma – Andean shrub whose leaves produce an herbal tea that relieves symptoms of altitude sickness

chacra – small, independent farm

charlar – word meaning 'to chat'

chimichurri – a spicy marinade for meat, usually made of parsley, garlic, spices and olive oil

chivito – in Uruguay, a steak sandwich

chocho/a – to be happily satisfied, as in 'Estoy chocho/a'

chopp – draft or lager beer

chopería – an establishment serving *chopp* and food

chupar – to drink, usually alcohol

churro – long, fried doughnut-type snack, often filled with dulce de leche or chocolate

chusquea – solid bamboo of the Valdivian rain forest in Patagonia

coima – a bribe; one who solicits a bribe is a *coimero*

colectivo – local bus

combi – long-distance bus

comedor – basic cafeteria or a dining room in a house or hotel

completo/solo – with/without *medialunas* (when ordering coffee for breakfast)

CONAF – Corporación Nacional Forestal, Chilean state agency in charge of forestry and conservation, including management of national parks like Torres del Paine

confitería – café that serves coffee, tea, desserts and simple dishes; confiterías can be important social centers in Argentina and Uruguay

conjunto – a musical band

Conquista del Desierto – Conquest of the Desert, a euphemism for General Julio Argentino Roca's late-19th-century war of extermination against the Mapuche of northern Patagonia

conventillo – tenements that housed immigrants in older neighborhoods of Buenos Aires and Montevideo; these survive on a reduced scale in the Buenos Aires barrio of San Telmo and the Ciudad Vieja of Montevideo

cordobazo – the 1969 uprising against the Argentine military government in the city of Córdoba, which paved the way for the return of Juan Perón from exile

correo – post office

cortado – a small coffee with a touch of milk

cospel – token used in public telephones

costanera – seaside, riverside or lakeside road or walkway

criollo – in colonial period, an American-born Spaniard, but the term is now used for any Latin American of European descent; the term also describes the feral cattle of the Pampas

cuadra – a city block; see also *manzana*

cubierto – in restaurants, the cover charge you pay for utensil use and bread

curanto – Chilean seafood stew; also, an unrelated Argentine Andes dish made of red or white meat, or vegetables

DDI – Discado Directo Internacional (International Direct Dialing), which provides direct access to home-country operators for long-distance collect and credit-card calls; a much cheaper alternative to the rates of the Argentine companies Telecom and Telefónica

démedos – literally, 'give me two,' a pejorative nickname for Argentines who travel to Miami, where everything is so cheap that they buy two of everything

(los) desaparecidos – the disappeared; the victims (estimated at up to 30,000) of Argentina's Dirty War who were never found

despelote – a mess, a fiasco; often used when describing the current government

dique – a dam; the resultant reservoir is often used for recreational purposes. In some cases, dique refers to a drydock

Dirty War – see *Guerra Sucia*

dorado – large river fish in the Paraná drainage, known among fishing enthusiasts as the 'Tiger of the Paraná' for its fighting spirit

dulce de leche – Argentina's national sweet; a creamy, spreadable caramel eaten on bread or found in many desserts, snacks and pastries

edificio – a building

efectivo – cash

encomienda – colonial labor system, under which Indian communities were required to provide laborers for Spaniards *(encomenderos)*, and the Spaniards were to provide religious and language instruction; in practice, the system benefited Spaniards far more than native peoples

epa – an explanation meaning 'Hey! Wow! Look out!'

ERP – Ejército Revolucionario del Pueblo, a revolutionary leftist group in the sugar-growing areas of Tucumán province in 1970s that modeled itself after the Cuban revolution; it was wiped out by the Argentine army during the Guerra Sucia

esquí alpino – downhill skiing

esquí de fondo – Nordic or cross-country skiing

esquina – street corner

estancia – extensive ranch for cattle or sheep, with an owner or manager *(estanciero)* and dependent resident labor force. Many are now open to tourists for recreational activities such as riding, tennis and swimming, either for weekend escapes or extended stays

facón – a knife used by gauchos that is traditionally worn in the small of the back behind the belt

facturas – pastries, but also the term for a receipt

forro – slang term for condom or, when used to describe a person, a 'scumbag'; to be avoided in polite conversation

frígobar – minibar in a hotel room

frigorífico – a cold-storage plant, usually with attached slaughterhouse

fronterizo – hybrid Spanish-Portuguese dialect spoken along the border between Uruguay and Brazil

gardeliano – fan of the late tango singer Carlos Gardel

gas-oil – diesel fuel

gasolero – motor vehicle that uses diesel fuel, which is much cheaper than ordinary gasoline in Argentina

genial – a word meaning 'wonderful, great, fine'

guarango – coarse, rude, crude; also, a person with these characteristics; this term is used throughout Spanish-speaking South America, but note that many Paraguayans are offended by it, thinking it a slur on Guaraní speakers

guardaganado – cattle guard (on a road or highway)

Guerra Sucia – the Dirty War of the 1970s, of the Argentine military against left-wing revolutionaries and anyone suspected of sympathizing with them

gurí – the Guaraní word for child, which has been adopted into regional speech in Northeast Argentina and Paraguay

hacer dedo – to hitchhike; literally 'to make thumb'

hinchapelota – a crude term for someone who bothers you a lot; literally, 'swelled balls'

humita – stuffed corn dough, resembling Mexican tamales

ichu – bunchgrass of the Andean altiplano

ida y vuelta – roundtrip

ida – one-way

iglesia – church

interno – extension off a central telephone number or switchboard
IVA – value-added tax; often added to restaurant or hotel bills in Argentina and Uruguay

jabalí – wild European boar, a popular game dish in Argentine Patagonia
jineteada – any horseback riding competition, as in a rodeo
joder – pull someone's leg, bother someone (crude, but not as bad as in Spain)

licuado – blended fruit drink cut with either water or milk
literatura gauchesca – literature *about* idealized gauchos and their values, usually written by urban and rural elite, as opposed to literature *by* gauchos, whose traditions were oral rather than written
locro – a spicy stew of corn, beans, beef, pork and sausage
locutorio – private long-distance telephone office; usually offers fax and Internet services as well
lomito – a thin steak sandwich
lunfardo – street slang of Buenos Aires

manta – a shawl or bedspread
manzana – literally, 'apple'; also used to define one square block of a city
mara – Patagonian hare
mate – see *yerba mate*
mazamorra – thickish maize soup, typical of the Northwest Andean region
mazorca – political police of 19th-century Argentine dictator Juan Manuel de Rosas
medialuna – croissant
mediero – sharecropper, a tenant who farms another's land in exchange for a percentage of the crop
menú – a set meal, often with multiple courses
merienda – light afternoon teatime meal
meseta – interior steppe of eastern Patagonia
mestizo – a person of mixed Indian and Spanish descent
miga – Argentina's most basic sandwich, always on white bread, usually crustless, and almost always with ham and/or cheese

milanesa – breaded steak filet
milonga – in tango, refers to a song, a dance or the dance salon itself
minuta – in a restaurant or confitería, a short order such as spaghetti or *milanesa*
mirador – scenic viewpoint, usually on a hill but often in a building
monte – scrub forest; the term is often applied to any densely vegetated area
Montoneros – left-wing faction of the Peronist party that became an underground urban guerrilla movement in 1970s
municipalidad – city hall

nafta – gasoline or petrol
novela – television soap opera
ñandú – rhea; there are two Argentine species of this large, flightless bird, which resembles the ostrich
ñoqui – a public employee whose primary interest is collecting a monthly paycheck, so-called because inexpensive *ñoquis* (potato pasta, from the Italian *gnocchi)* are traditionally served in financially strapped Argentine households on the 29th of each month, the implication being that the employee shows up to work around that time

paisanos – countryfolk
palmitos – the edible heart of a palm tree, a tasty white asparagus-like cylinder that's great in salads
pampero – South Atlantic cold front that brings dramatic temperature changes to Uruguay, Paraguay and the interior of northern Argentina
parada – a bus stop
parapente – paragliding
parrilla – a restaurant that specializes in *parrillada*
parrillada – a mixed grill of steak and other beef cuts
paseaperros – professional dog-walker in Buenos Aires
paseo – an outing, such as a walk in the park or downtown
pato – duck; but also a gaucho sport where players on horseback wrestle for a ball encased in a leather harness with handles
pavada – an elaborate lie

peatonal – pedestrian mall, usually in the downtown area of major Argentine cities

pehuén – araucaria, or 'monkey puzzle' tree of southern Patagonia

peña – club that hosts informal folk-music gatherings

picada – in rural areas, a trail, especially through dense woods or mountains; in the context of food, hors d'oeuvres

pingüinera – penguin colony

piropo – a sexist remark directed at a woman, ranging from complimentary and relatively innocuous, to rude and offensive

piso – floor

pollo – chicken, as in the food

porquería – a mess, a fiasco; often used when describing the local government (see *despelote*)

porteño/a – inhabitant of Buenos Aires, a 'resident of the port'

precioso/a – word used to describe something as dear or cute; a very porteño term

precordillera – foothills of the Andes

primera – 1st class on a train

Proceso – short for El Proceso de Reorganización Nacional, a military euphemism for its brutal attempt to remake Argentina's political and economic culture between 1976 and 1983

propina – a tip, for example, in a restaurant or cinema

pucará – in the Andean Northwest, a pre-Columbian fortification, generally on high ground commanding an unobstructed view in several directions

puchero – soup combining vegetables and meats, served with rice

puesto – 'outside house' on a cattle or sheep estancia

pulpería – a country store or tavern

puna – Andean highlands, usually above 3000m

puntano – a native or resident of Argentina's San Luis province

quebracho – literally, 'axe-breaker'; tree common to the Chaco that is a natural source of tannin for the leather industry

quebrada – a canyon

quincho – thatch-roof hut, often used to refer to any thatch-roof building

quinoa – a native Andean grain, the dietary equivalent of rice during pre-Columbian times

rambla – avenue or shopping mall

rancho – a rural house, generally of adobe, with a thatched roof

recargo – additional charge, usually 10%, that many Argentine businesses add to credit-card transactions

reducción – an Indian settlement created by Spanish missionaries during the colonial period; the most famous are the Jesuit missions in the triple-border area of Argentina, Paraguay and Brazil

refugio – a usually rustic shelter in a national park or remote area

remise – a taxi with a radio connection to a dispatcher; also *remís*

RN – Ruta Nacional; in Argentina, a national highway

RP – Ruta Provincial; in Argentina, a provincial highway

ruta – highway

s/n – *sin número,* indicating a street address without a number

sábalo – popular river fish in the Paraná drainage

saladero – a slaughterhouse that salts meat and hides

salar – salt lake or salt pan, usually in the high Andes or Argentine Patagonia

sendero – a trail in the woods

SIDA – AIDS

siesta – lengthy afternoon break for lunch and, occasionally, a nap

sobremesa – after-dinner conversation

soroche – altitude sickness

sorrentinos – large raviolis

stronato – the period of Stroessner dictatorship (1954-89)

Subte – the Buenos Aires subway system

sucursale – a branch office

sudestada – southeasterly storm out of the South Atlantic that often combines high tides and heavy runoff to flood low-lying Buenos Aires barrios such as La Boca

surubí – popular river fish frequently served in restaurants

'ta – heard in Uruguay and parts of Northeast Argentina, this is short for '¿*Está bien?*'; also used in plural, as '¿*Tamos?*' – 'OK? Are we in agreement? Everything cool?'

taguá – Wagner's peccary, a species of wild pig thought extinct but recently rediscovered in the Paraguayan Chaco

tapir – large hoofed mammal of subtropical forests in northern Argentina and Paraguay, a distant relative of the horse

tarjeta telefónica – magnetic telephone card

teleférico – gondola cable-car

tenedor libre – all-you-can-eat restaurant; also called *diente libre*

tercera edad – literally 'third age'; a euphemism equivalent to 'senior citizen'

tereré – cold *yerba mate* drink, as consumed by Paraguayans

terminal de omnibus – bus terminal

todo terreno – mountain bike

tola – high-altitude shrubs in the altiplano of northwestern Argentina

tragamonedas – slot machine, literally 'coin-swallower'

trapiche – antique sugar mill

trasnochador – one who stays up very late or all night, as do many Argentines

trucho – bogus; a term widely used by Argentines to describe things that are not what they appear to be

turco – Turk, an often derogatory term for any Argentine of Middle Eastern descent

turista – 2nd class on a train, usually not very comfortable

tuteo – use of the informal pronoun *tú* in Spanish and its corresponding verb forms

vicuña – wild relative of domestic llama and alpaca, found in Argentina's Andean Northwest only at high altitudes

villas miserias – shantytowns on the outskirts of Buenos Aires and other Argentine cities

viviendas temporarias – riverfront shantytowns of Asunción, Paraguay

vizcacha – wild relative of the domestic chinchilla

voseo – the use of the informal pronoun *vos* and its corresponding verb forms, used commonly in Argentina, Uruguay and Paraguay

vuelos de cabotaje – domestic flights

yacaré – South American alligator, found in humid, subtropical areas

YCF – Yacimientos Fiscales Carboníferos, Argentina's state coal company

yerba mate – Paraguayan tea, consumed by Argentines in large quantities as an important everyday social ritual; many Paraguayans, Uruguayans, and Brazilians also drink it regularly

yisca – bag made of vegetable fiber, traditional among the Toba Indians of the Chaco

YPF – Yacimientos Fiscales Petrolíferos, Argentina's former state oil company

yungas – in northwestern Argentina, transitional subtropical lowland forest

yuyos – aromatic herbs, which in northern Argentina are mixed with *yerba mate*

zona franca – duty-free zone

zonda – in the central Andean provinces, a powerful, dry north wind like the European foehn or North American chinook

Thanks

Many readers wrote with helpful information and suggestions, including:

Hugo Achugar, Jadwiga Adamczuk, Hayley Adams, Doug and Pat Adamson, Tim Alcott, Erik Alcron, Daniel and Dai Alford, Rune Alkstrand, Bill Allen, Mariam Allen, Spencer Allman, Mercedes Anchezar, Daniel Anderbring, Debbie Anderson, Matt Anderson, EB Andersson, Belinda Andrews, Miguel Angel Alonso, Claudia Ardison, Gilles Arie, Wayne Arizmendi, Dudley Arnold, Robert Aronoff, Chris Ashton, Tessa Atkins, Elinor Awkin, Michael Ayling, Marfarida Azevedo, John Backiel, Christine Badre, Bernard Badzioch, Juan Baiocchi, Joze Balas, David Ballantyne, Philipp and Claudia Balscheit, Carolyn Barnato, Norris Barr, Craig Barrack, Richard and Kathy Barragan, Nick Barraud, Tim Barrett, Dom Barry, Alice Barton, Mick Bauer, Christoph Baumgarten, John Beaven, Frans Beems, Daphne Bell, Anne-Trine Benjaminsen, Cindy Benner, Max and Miranda Berends, BJ Bernstein, Goran Berntsson, Mariano Besio, John Beston, Roberta Bianchi, Loretta Biasutti, Ueli Bischof, Simon Bishop, Gordon Bissar, Paul and Frances Black, Ray Black, Ray E Black, Colleen Blake, Andre Boessenkool, Cristian Bolero Sutter, Olivier Bongard, Justin Boocock, Clelia Booman, Chris Booth, Savannah Borsellino, Mireille Bos, Eric Boschmann, Anthony Boult, Eddie Bowden, Patrick Bowes, Gert-jan Bremer, Catherine Brew, Fran Brew, Marianne Brito, Linda Broschofsky, Berne Broudy, Dawson Brown, Sabine Brueschweiler, Peter Bugarski, Ian Bunton, Paige Burgess, Rollo Burgess, Matthew Burke, Agi and Shanf Burra, Carlos Alberto Fortuno Burset, Stephen Busack, Helen Butler, Pedro Butler, Rev RCB Butler, Jasper F Buxton, Charles and Valerie Calderbank, Joshua D Callahan, Emma Callow, Julie Cameron, Kerry Cameron, Nadia Candolt, Stuart Candy, Laura Cangas, Eric Carlson, Caroline Carlsson, Laura Carrizo, Jens Cartsen Jackwerth, Jordi Carvallo, Debora Casarin, Mike Cavendish, Julio Cesar Lovece, Jukie and Antoine Chambaz, MM Chan, Brandyn Chapman, Ginni Chave, Helene Clappaz, Peter Clark, Alex Cloutier, Karen and Andrew Cockburn, Kevin and Dale Coghlan, Helen Cole, Pablo Collavino, Peter Collins, Simona Colombo, David Connor, Filippa Connor, Ravindra Conway, Kit Cooper, Edward Corbett, Aaron Corcoran, Arnaud Corin, Juan Costa Diez, Bryce Coulter, Laura Creasey, Brian Cuff, Andreas Dorr, Phillip A Dale, Leonne and Alan Damson, Elisabethe Dank, Jane Davey, Kimberly de Berzunza, Hans de Bont, Annie de Elia, Julianne de Lange, Lydia de Visser, Jodie Deignan, Uta Dempwolff, Sebastian Detomaso, Millie Dobson, Paul Doyle, Jason Drautz, Jorg Droste, Laurent and Catherine Ducrest, Phil Dunnington, Julio Duran, Alain and Margaret Duval, Denis Duysens, Chris Dziadul, Yasmin Ebrahim, Sandy Edelsward, Peter Eliason, Dana Ellerbrock, Klaus Elskamp, Philippa Eng, Mannie English, Donald C Erbe, Maren Erchinger, Marie Eugelstad, William Evelyn, Sze Fairman, Michael Feder, Judy Fennessy, Gazda Ferenc, Anotnia Fernandez, Alexis Ferrand, Marcelo Ferrante, Andreas Fertin, Suki Finney, Kent Foster, Jonathan Freeman, Marjolein Friele, Richard Fromer, Lesly Furness, C Gabriel Alperovich, Tomasz and Anna Galka, Carlos Galvalizi, Cristian Gamarra, Odile Garaffa, Andres Garcia, Ben Garrett, George Gayoso, Melanie Geppert, Vital Gil, Monti Godfrey, Albert D Goldson, Nick Goldwater, Maria Gomez, Lori Goodfellow, Luca Graf, Robert Grant, Charles Green, Charles Greenwood, Maura Griffin, David P Grill, Michael K Gschwind, Tora and Anders Gudmundsson, Flavio Guidotti, Wade Guthrie, Daniel Gutsell, Matthias Gutzeit, Erich Haas, Patrick Hagans, Sonja Hagen, Robert Harding, Lynda Harpley, Deanna Harris, Anthony Harvey, Rhonda Hawkins, Susan Hayre, Michelle Hecht, Darlene Hector, Darlene R Hector, Mike and Linda Hehir, Cyndi Heller, Katrine Helsing Andersen, Neil and Christine Hepburn, Peter Hertrampf, Dawn Hewitt, Michele Heymann, Paula Hill, M Hinten, Trude Holmen, Andrew Holmes, Leo Horochowski, Koosje van der Horst, Richard Howitt, Stephanie Hughes, David Hulsenbek, Jason Humphreys, David L Huntzinger, Carsten Hviid, Marco Ibarra, Peter Irvine, Chloe Jacob, Gygax Jacqueline, Margarete Jager, Karmen Jehovcan, Dorothea Jensen, Ken Jewkes, Bill Johnson, Horst Jung, Manfred Jung, Dale Kabat, Harry Kangassalo, C Karp, George Kechagiouglou, Elisa Kelly, Dr Vera Kempe, Ton Kersbergen,

Nazruddin Khan, Rolando Kienitz, Josef Klimek, Helke Knuetter, Gabi Koch, Steven Koenig, Jim Koppensteiner, Michiel Kraak, Gitta and Rainer Krukenberg, Andreas D KSch, Lars Kuipers, Jessica Kullander, Peter Kunkel, Kerstin Labatzke, Peter Lambert, Chris Larkin, Lise Larsen, TB Laursen, Dominique and Siobhan Le Meur, Marcel Lensvelt, Manfred Lenzen, Vallann Lester, Milton Lever, Tim Lewis, Frederico Lifsichtz, Bill Lira, Joachim Loeblein, Antoine and Agnes Lorgnier, Jorge Romero and Inge Lozano, Andrew Ludasi, A Lukosky, Walt Lukflcs, Francesco Lulli, PD Lynam, Gregor Macek, Ron Machado, Mary Mackenzie, Kimberly Mahony, Richard Manasseh, Fabian and Nadine Mannequin, Will Markle, Milena Marmora, Peter Marson, Trajan Martin, David Martinez, George Martinez, Daniel Masse, Fatimah Mateen, Mario Mathieu, Maria Maxfield, Marilyn McDonald, Gary McKenzie, Mark McNulty, Arnout Meester, Bjoern Mehlhorn, B Meijer, Martie Meijer, Hans Meister, Ulla Melchiorsen, Gordon Merrick, David Meurer, Hamid Mezaib, Pete Minor, David Mitchell, Wilfred E Mole, Angel Daniel Molina, Daniel Molina, Janie Moore, Amalia Moran, Jose Maria Moreno, Catherine Moroz, Doug Morrison, Fernando Moser, Maria Cristina Mossa, Fabiono Mouro Viera, Patrick Moyroud, Franklin Murillo, Marco Murillo, Lori Murphy, Nikki Murphy, Shannon Murphy, Eleanor Nauman, David Neidermeier, Michelle Nelder, Marcia and Bruce Nesbitt, Linn Nichels, Jan Nielsen, Gustavo Nisivoccia, Alejandra Novillo, Petra Nowak, Michael Ny, Clare O'Brien, Betty Odell, Carlos Omar Campora, Dave Orton, Alice Owen, Claudia and Joe Pace, Luciana Volcato Panzarini, Victorio Panzica, Spiras and Julie Pappas, Nisim and Alexa Parliyan, Michael Partington, Douglas Peacocke, Vito Perillo, Steve Perry, Beate Pesch, Ginger and Jim Peterson, Jim and Ginger Peterson, Patricio Phelan, Julie Pike, Andreas Poethen, Tom Polk, Sergio Gustavo Pollastri, Elisabeth Post-Madden, Daniel Pozzi, Jean-Luc Praz, Reinhard Prenzel, Ian Prior, Julie Wood Prosperi, Tatiana Prowell, Mike Quick, Ramon Rabinovitch, Christa Randzio-Plath, Chris and Peggy Raphael, Malcolm Reid, Vincent Reidy, Mary Richards, Veronique Rigaud, Mike Robinson, Vanessa Rodd, Alfredo Rodriguez, Gonzalo Rodriguez, Albert Van de Rooy, Joachim Rose, Adriana Rossini, Hans R Roth, Harald Roy, Andrew Ruben, Michael Ruppert, Rania Salameh, Claudio Sanchez, Larissa Sanio, Jorge Santamaria, Anderson Santos, Carolina Sanz, April Schauer, Renate Schepen, Iris Schick, Bernd Schmidt, Marion Schosser, Toralf Schrinner, Andreas Schafer, Marianne Scott, JEO Screen, Jonathan Sear, Javier Segurotti, Joel Selanikio, Jerome Sgard, Amy Shatzkin, Craig Shaw, David Shotlander, Bogdan Siewierski, Daniel Simons, Jean Sinclair, Harold Smith, Sally and CB Smith Smith, Steven Smith, TJ Snow, Charlotte Snowden, P Sobczuk, Erica Sonneveld, Maurizio Spadari, Carlo Spagnolo, Uh Stamm, Richard Stanaway, Lilian Starobinas, Paul Steng, Janig Stephens, Patrick Sterckx, Peter Sterni, Kristin Stokeng, Bill and Ann Stoughton, Adrian Stuerm, Alexander Sturm, Kathie and Mark Sund, Carl Swanson, Wilbert Sybesma, Pete Syms, Marc Szaleniec, Andreas Tolke, Celeste Tarricone, Alexandra Tayler, Alison Teeman, Angelika and Kurt Teuschl, Sabine Thielicke, Michel Thomas, Jacques and Beatriz Thuery, Aranea Tigelaar, Sally Tillett, Jos Tilmans, Carl Tiska, A Toelle, Mari Tomine Lunden, Elizabeth Tompkin, Paul Toms, Natalie Tornatore, Heidi Tschanz, David Twine, Tom Tyler, Stefan Uhl, Lorena Uriarte, Marcelo Vallejos, Zoltan Vamosi, Reijco Van De Pol, Maurits van den Boorn, Hans van der Veen, Hans van Dommele, Regina Van Horne, Stan Van Loon, Christophe Van Overloop, Ingrid Van Wentlann, Steven Vanderhilst, Robert Varga, Fernando Velazquez, Ann Vercouture, Sebastian Villarreal, Thomas Villette, Karina VM, Peer Voss, Rory Walsh, Jeanie Wantz, JP Watney, Robert Watson, Michael Watt, Carrie Wayne, Alex West, Harry and Deborah Whitehill, Peter and Museum of Paleontology Wilf, Hanna Wilhelm, Tia and Spencer Williams, Russell Willis, Sylvia Wilson, Godofredo Wimmer, Norbert Winkler, Andrew Wolton, Heather Wright, John M Wright, Lisa Wright, Mary Lee Wu, Prescottr Wurlitzer, Darrin Yoder, Dasa Zabric, Martina Zavoico, Dieter Zeiml, Paula Zimbrean, Vamosi Zoltan and Georg Schulze Zumkley

Index

Bold indicates maps.

733

Bold indicates maps.

Bold indicates maps.

Boxed Text

Bold indicates maps.

MAP LEGEND

ROUTES

City | **Regional**

============= Freeway	Pedestrian Mall
....Toll Freeway	Steps
Primary Road	Tunnel
Secondary Road	Trail
Tertiary Road	•••••••• Walking Tour
Dirt Road	Path

ROUTE SHIELDS

ARGENTINA
- [RN 40] Ruta Nacional
- [RP 21] Ruta Provincial
- [RC a] Ruta Complementaria

BOLIVIA
- [5] Red Fundamental
- [601] Red Complementaria

CHILE
- [5] Ruta Nacional

BRAZIL
- [BR 040] National Highway Fundamental
- [SP 300] State Highway

PARAGUAY
- [2] National Highway

URUGUAY
- [5] Ruta Nacional
- [13] Ruta Secundaria

TRANSPORTATION

Train	Bus Route
Metro	Ferry

BOUNDARIES

International	County
Provincial	Disputed

HYDROGRAPHY

- River; Creek
- Canal
- Lake
- Water
- Spring; Rapids
- Waterfalls
- Dry; Salt Lake
- Glacier

AREAS

- Beach
- Building
- Cemetery
- Forest
- Garden; Zoo
- Park
- Plaza
- Sports Field
- Swamp; Mangrove

POPULATION SYMBOLS

◎ NATIONAL CAPITAL ...... National Capital	● **Large City** ....Large City	● Small City ....Small City
◉ PROVINCIAL CAPITAL ....Provincial Capital	● **Medium City** ......Medium City	● Town; Village ....Town; Village

MAP SYMBOLS

■ ....Place to Stay	▼ ....Place to Eat	● ....Point of Interest

Airfield	Church	Museum
Airport	Cinema	Observatory
Archeological Site; Ruin	Dive Site	Park
Bank	Embassy; Consulate	Parking Area
Baseball Diamond	Footbridge	Pass
Battlefield	Gas Station	Picnic Area
Bike Trail	Hospital	Police Station
Border Crossing	Information	Pool
Buddhist Temple	Internet Access	Post Office
Bus Station; Terminal	Lighthouse	Pub; Bar
Cable Car; Chairlift	Lookout	RV Park
Campground	Mine	Shelter
Castle	Mission	Shipwreck
Cathedral	Monument	Shopping Mall
Cave	Mountain	Skiing - Cross Country

Skiing - Downhill	
Stately Home	
Surfing	
Synagogue	
Tao Temple	
Taxi	
Telephone	
Theater	
Toilet - Public	
Tomb	
Trailhead	
Tram Stop	
Transportation	
Volcano	
Winery	

Note: Not all symbols displayed above appear in this book.

LONELY PLANET OFFICES

Australia
Locked Bag 1, Footscray, Victoria 3011
☎ 03 8379 8000 fax 03 8379 8111
email talk2us@lonelyplanet.com.au

USA
150 Linden Street, Oakland, California 94607
☎ 510 893 8555, TOLL FREE 800 275 8555
fax 510 893 8572
email info@lonelyplanet.com

UK
10a Spring Place, London NW5 3BH
☎ 020 7428 4800 fax 020 7428 4828
email go@lonelyplanet.co.uk

France
1 rue du Dahomey, 75011 Paris
☎ 01 55 25 33 00 fax 01 55 25 33 01
email bip@lonelyplanet.fr
www.lonelyplanet.fr

World Wide Web: www.lonelyplanet.com *or* AOL keyword: lp
Lonely Planet Images: lpi@lonelyplanet.com.au